The EBONY HANDBOOK

The
EBONY
HANDBOOK

by the Editors of EBONY

JOHNSON PUBLISHING COMPANY, INC.   CHICAGO, 1974

First printing, 1974

Library of Congress Cataloging in Publication

Data Main entry under title:

The Ebony Handbook, ed. by Ebony Editors

and Doris E. Saunders.

Earlier ed., compiled by the editors of Ebony,

published in 1966 under title: The Negro

Handbook. 1. Negroes—Handbook. II. Title

E185.S25 1974   917.3'06'96073   *July 24, 1974* 73-16179

ISBN: 0-87485-064-9

$20.00

Printed in the United States of America.

Publisher
John H. Johnson

Editor
Doris E. Saunders

Designer
Norman L. Hunter

Production Coordinator
Paula R. Materre

Production Assistants
Janice E. Bek
Gail S. Langholz
Julie A. Scanlan

PUBLISHER'S FOREWARD

The philosophy of reference books in general has been to let facts speak for themselves. In compiling *The Ebony Handbook,* the editors have not felt it possible, or desirable, to abandon this principle. However, the pattern of events and statistics supplies its own emphasis; historically there has had to be considerable coverage of events in legislation, education, employment, and legal decisions.

Every effort has been made to check the information at original sources and, where possible, to correct and update materials up to press time (September, 1973). However, error is inevitable, and the editors accept responsibility for any misstatements or mistakes that have eluded their best efforts.

Acknowledgement of the help given by government agencies, their publications, departments, and officials is gratefully made. Private individuals, institutions, and associations, too numerous to list, have cooperated generously to make publication possible, and we thank them, individually and collectively.

It is our hope that *The Ebony Handbook* will succeed in documenting the present-day status of the black American, and will be a useful reference for schools, colleges and universities, libraries and individuals.

John H. Johnson
Publisher

TABLE OF CONTENTS

INDEX TO TABLES

The EBONY HANDBOOK

Section I

POPULATION

THE USE OF "BLACK" AS IDENTIFICATION

The 1966 edition of *The Negro Handbook* contained a definition of the word "Negro" as used by the U.S. Census Department. The controversy over the proper designation for identifiable Americans of African descent has gone on since the beginning of slavery in the United States. Many argued for the use of the word "Afro–American" as a historically accurate designation for this segment of the population. To many the word "Negro" connotes the master-slave relationship and mind-set. Lerone Bennett, Jr. in an article, "What's in a Name" in *Ebony*, November, 1967, delineated the rationals for the various nomenclatures. He explained the use of the word "black" to identify Americans of African descent as having multiple purposes. Black has been used historically as a term of denigration and opprobrium and by 1967 the realization had come that blacks must define themselves. As Bennett says, "Names are of the essence of the game of power and control, and . . . a change in name will shortcircuit the stereotyped thinking patterns that undergird the system of racism in America." *Ebony* subsequently conducted a poll of its readers in terms of the ethnic identification that they wished to have used in describing them. In the response, the results were weighed between "Afro-American" and "Black." *Ebony* editors voted in favor of the use of the word "black" and in that same spirit, this Handbook has used "black," instead of any other identification, where it is not a part of quoted material or out of context with the original source material.

BLACK AMERICA IN THE SEVENTIES
A Socio-Economic Profile

The position of the Black American in the United States in relation to the size of population and its location and density, together with age, education, mobility, labor force status, and other vital statistics, is broadly sketched in the following profile. The conclusions are based on the 1970 Census of Population and on subsequent social and economic reports.

Population and Migration

From 1960-1970 the black population of the United States increased by 3.7 million persons to 22.6 million persons, 11.1 percent of the total population. The white population of the United States increased by 18.8 million persons and other races by 1.3 million persons (PHC (2)-1). The greatest increase in the black population occurred in metropolitan areas. The black population of non-metropolitan areas declined in the decade by more than one quarter of one million persons.

The metropolitan rate of increase for black and other races was 22 percent, twice that of the white population. Their net immigration rate was five times as great.

Where growth has taken place in the nation's central cities it was due almost entirely to black population increases. While this segment of the population increased by 3 million, and the population of other races by more than one half million, the white population of central cities declined over the decade by 600,000. The number of blacks in the suburbs grew at about the same rate as the number of whites (by 29.2 percent, compared to the white rate of 27.5 percent), but their numerical increase was much lower—only 800,000, or about 5 percent of the total population increase there. As a result of these changes, blacks increased considerably as a proportion of the nation's total central city population, from 16 percent in 1960 to 21 percent in 1970. In the suburbs, their position did not change at all; in 1970 as in 1960, black residents comprised just under 5 percent of all suburban residents.

The effect of these growth patterns on the distribution of the two racial groups by area of residence has also been substantial. In 1960, 53 percent of the black population lived in cities; in 1970, 58 percent of the black population were urban dwellers. In 1960, one third (33.3 percent) of the white population lived in central cities; by 1970, this had declined to 28 percent, a loss of approximately 5 percent. The black population in 1970 comprised a larger proportion of the population in the northern and western regions of the United States and a lower percentage of the population of the South.

Long-term migration patterns were reflected in the fact that about 45 percent of the blacks in the West and 34 percent of those in the North were born in the South. In each of the last three decades, the South lost about 1.5 million blacks through net out-migration.

In the northeastern and north central states, significant proportions of the overall population increases during the 1960-1970 decade were black: 30 percent of the population growth in the northeastern states and 23 percent of the growth in the north central states were produced by shifts in black population. Nonetheless, the South still contains more than one-half of the nation's total black population. The growth rate of the black population for the South was 7 percent of the total population increase (753,000 out of 7.8 million). In the West the growth rate was 609,000 out of 6.8 million total population.

With the exception of the South, the black population of every region is more metropolitan than the white population. More than 94 percent of all blacks in the North and the West are concentrated in metropolitan areas, contrasted with two-thirds to four-fifths of the white population of these regions. In the South the proportions are equal: 56 percent of each racial group, both black and white, are metropolitan. Within the metropolitan areas of every region, including the South, whites are found in the largest numbers in the suburbs, while blacks are concentrated in the central cities.

In every area of the United States the black population is younger. Nationally, the median age for blacks is 23 years, compared to 30.5 years for whites. In 1970, in both the metropolitan and non-metropolitan areas of the northeast, approximately 34 percent of the blacks were under 15 years old, while 6 percent were 65 years and over. By contrast, only 22 percent of the white population was under 15 years of age, but 14 percent was 65 and over.

There was a sharp decline in the fertility rate of black women during the decade between 1960 and 1970, but the median rate of 3.13 children per black woman in 1968 remained substantially higher than that of 2.37 children per white woman. Between 1960 and 1971, the average number of children born declined, particularly in the group of black women 20 to 24 years old. Fertility of women 35 to 44 years of age seems closely related to education and economic status. Working women of all races with higher educational levels seem less likely to have large numbers of children.

The infant mortality rate for black infants (31.4 per 11,000 live births) was much higher than that for whites (17.4) in 1970. The maternal mortality rate for all mothers was below 1.0 per 1,000 live births.

Income

In early 1972 there were 5.2 million black families, comprising 10 percent of all families.

The 1971 median family income for all families was $10,290, about 4 percent higher than the 1970 median of $9,870. In terms of constant dollars it was about the same. The median income in 1971 was about $6,400 for black families and about $10,670 for white families, providing a black to white median income ratio of 60 percent. In 1971, the relative position of black to white family income was the same as in 1970. The 1971 ratio represented a significant improvement over the ratio of 54 percent in 1964, which was the first year for which corresponding survey data on blacks were available.

Among the 5.1 million black families with civilian heads, approximately 49 percent were headed by year-round full-time workers. The median income of these families was $9,130.00.

The proportion of black families and other minority races in the $10,000-and-over-income category increased during the 1960's. By 1970, approximately 28 percent were at this income level, compared to the 11 percent in 1960, taking into account higher living costs. The proportion with relatively high incomes was still far below that of white families. About half of the white families had incomes of $10,000 or more in 1970. A very small segment of black families have made significant gains in achieving income parity with whites.

For the most part, these were young husband-wife families residing in the North and West in which both the husband and wife worked. Among these families the ratio of black to white income was about 104 percent in 1970 compared with 85 percent in 1959. In the South, for the comparable group of black families, the median income was 75 percent of the median income of whites, an increase over the 56 percent in 1959. The working wife was an important factor in explaining the narrowing of the income differential between young black and white families. Where only the husband worked, the income differential in the North and West remained at about 75 percent in 1970, whereas in the South the ratio of 63 percent was up from 52 percent in 1959.

Among the young husband-wife families, black wives were more likely than white wives to have participated in the employed labor force and as year-round workers in 1970. Nationally, about 68 percent of the young black wives contributed to the family income by working, compared to 56 percent for young white wives. In the North and West, a larger percentage of the young black wives worked year round. These black wives earned approximately 30 percent more and also made a larger contribution to the family income than did their white counterparts. For the North and West, the ratio of young wives earnings to the family income was 35 percent for blacks and 27 percent for whites.

There were 7.4 million blacks below the poverty or low-income level in 1971. The low-income threshold for a non-farm family of four was $4,137 in 1971. This comprised about 32 percent of the black population in the nation. In 1959, the proportion of blacks who were below the low-income level was much higher—55 percent (2,973,000). From 1959 to 1971, the proportion of whites below the low-income level declined from 18 percent to about 10 percent. Although blacks made up about 11 percent of all persons, they comprised

approximately three-tenths of all people below the low-income level.

The majority of black men who were heads of low-income families worked some time during 1970. About one-fourth of the black men who were heads of low-income families had a full-time job the year round.

Black families below the low-income level were more likely than the comparable group of white families to have received public assistance income, but less likely to have received Social Security benefits.

Family heads with low educational attainment are more likely to be below the low-income level. This was found to be true regardless of race or sex of the family head.

Labor Force

The civilian labor force grew during the 1960s from 60 million to 83 million for the total population; employment from 66 million to 79 million. Almost half of the total employed in 1970 were in the white-collar category. Black and minority white-collar workers in 1960 comprised 16.1 percent of the total employed. By 1971, there were over 9 million black and other minority races in the civilian labor force, 8 million of whom were employed. In 1970, they comprised 27.9 percent of the total employed, or an increase of 11.8 percent over the decade.

In the area of blue-collar employment (construction workers, mechanics, etc.) the increased participation in the labor force was much smaller, from 40.1 to 42.2 percent of the total labor force. In the construction industry, specifically, the increase was from 1.6 percent to 1.8 percent participation over a ten-year period, less than one-half of a percentage point. This occurred in a period when the construction industry was a particular target of various equal employment and affirmative action programs, at federal and local levels.

In specific areas where participation by black persons had been traditional, there were substantial declines in the percentage of employment. These are in the service industries and among farm workers. Here, private household workers declined from 1960 to 1970 by 6.5 percent; from 14.2 percent in 1960 to 7.7 percent in 1970. Waiters, cooks, and bartenders declined from 3.6 percent in 1960 to 3.4 percent in 1970. Farm workers in the labor force declined from 12.1 percent in 1960 to 3.9 percent in 1970—a pronounced decline of 8.2 percent.

So, while there was an increase in black and minority participation in the white-collar (11.8), and to a much more limited degree in the blue-collar (2.1) employment areas, there was an equal decline in participation in the service (5.7) and farm labor (8.2) categories; up 13.9 percentage points at the top of the scale, and down 13.9 percentage points at the bottom of the economic scale. There were 671,000 (9.9 percent) black and other minority people unemployed in 1971 as compared with 6.4 percent in 1969 and 4.5 percent in 1953. In 1960, teenaged (16-19 year olds) unemployment among black and other minorities was 24.4 percent, while in 1971 it was 31.7 percent of the total.

In the total civilian labor force of 30 million, there were 4,130,000 black and other minority women; 1,506,000 black females headed families, with 783,000 black female family heads in the labor force; 725,000 with children under 18 years of age; 2,449,452 black women were wives with husbands at the head of the family; and 1,880,000 were families in which both partners worked.

Housing

In 1970, two of every five housing units occupied by blacks were owned by the occupant, compared with about two in every three occupied by whites.

Between 1960 and 1970, the proportion of blacks living in homes they owned increased from 38 percent to 42 percent. In 1970 the rate of owner occupancy was highest for black households in the South, 47 percent. The North Central Region was next highest in black-owner occupancy. Home ownership rates in 1970 were higher outside the central cities than in the central cities of metropolitan areas.

Crowding sometimes measured by the index of "persons per room" was much greater in black-occupied housing units than in white-occupied housing units. In 1970, 20 percent of black households lived in units with 1.01 or more persons per room compared to 7 percent of white households. Renter-occupied housing was more crowded than owner-occupied units for both black and white households.

The proportion of black households lacking some or all plumbing facilities was 17 percent of the 1970 total of black households, more than three times the rate for white households. The greatest disparity was in the South. In the West, where the lack of plumbing facilities was least prevalent, the same proportion of black and white households had incomplete plumbing. Approximately 95 percent of black households in central cities had complete plumbing facilities.

Automobiles and Household Items

In 1970, 57 percent of black families owned at least one car, and 13 percent owned two or more automobiles. Ninety-two percent own television sets, 17.4 percent own color T.V., 12 percent have clothes dryers, and 3 percent have dishwashers.

Voting and Elections

Approximately 60 percent of blacks were registered to vote in 1970—about the same proportion as in 1966; about 44 percent reported that they had actually voted. These figures compare with about 70 percent of whites who registered and 56 percent who reported voting in 1970.

Notable gains have been made in the number of blacks holding public office since the civil rights legislation of 1964 and the Voting Rights Act of 1965. Between 1962 and 1972, the number of blacks elected to the United States Congress had increased from 4 congressmen to 16 congressmen, and one senator, and the number elected to state legislatures has increased from 52 to 238.

In 1972, of the 2,600 black elected officials, 238 were state legislators—more than double the 94 blacks in these offices in 1964. The increase had been greatest in the South, and, consequently, a greater share of all black state legislators were holding office in the South in 1972.

Marked increases also have been noted in the number of black mayors. In 1972, there were 83 mayors compared to 29 in 1968 (the earliest year for which data were available). In 1968, about 58 percent of all black mayors were located in the South; by 1972 the proportion declined to about 51 percent.

Projections of the voting-age population indicate that blacks will represent 14 million, or about 10 percent of the 139 million persons of voting age in November, 1972. In the District of Columbia, almost 70 percent of the voting-age population will be black. Blacks will represent from 22 to 30 percent of the total electorate in five Southern states—South Carolina, Georgia, Alabama, Mississippi, and Louisiana.

Education

Blacks have made significant advances in education during the five-year period, 1967 to 1972.

About one-half million, or 18 percent of all blacks 18 to 24 years old, were enrolled in college in 1972—a substantial gain over the 1967 figures. The 1972 proportion of whites 18 to 24 years old remained at about the same level as it was in 1967. Overall, there were 727,000 blacks enrolled in college in 1972, about double the 1967 level.

The dropout rate for blacks declined between 1967 and 1972—from 22.8 to 17.5 (for those 14 to 24 years old). However, blacks were still more likely than white to be high school dropouts.

About 90 percent of the black 16- and 17-year-olds were enrolled in school in 1972

compared to 84 percent in 1967; and for the first time in 1972, the enrollment rates for black and white 16- and 17-year-olds were at the same level.

The rising educational attainment of young black men and women in this country is further evidenced by the recent gains in the proportions who were high school or college graduates. The proportion of 20- to 29-year-olds who were high school graduates rose from 54 percent in 1967 to 65 percent in 1972. During the same period, the proportion of those 25 to 34 years old with four years of college or more increased from 5 to 8 percent. Despite these gains, the proportion of blacks completing high school or college is below that of whites.

Family

In 1973, about three-fifths of all black families were husband-wife families. About 35 percent of black families were headed by a woman; this is an increase over the comparable proportion five years earlier. Within the last year, the proportion of black families headed by women increased from 32 to 35 percent.

Blacks were less likely than whites to have their first marriage intact, and more likely to have been widowed or divorced in 1970.

The proportion of men who were married and living with their spouses was closely related to their income and educational levels. Black men 25 to 54 years old with incomes of $10,000 or more in 1969, were more likely than men with lower incomes—under $3,000—to have a wife living with them. Likewise, those black men who had completed high school were more likely than those without a high school education to have their first wife living with them.

Between 1967 and 1972, the proportion of own black children living with both parents decreased from 68 to 61 percent. Among whites, 89 percent of own children lived with both parents in 1972; it was 92 percent in 1967.

In 1970, among women who have almost completed their child-bearing years (35 to

44 years old), the fertility level (children ever born) of blacks surpasses that of whites at all educational levels below college. On the other hand, black women with college training had a lower fertility rate than white women in the same educational group.

In 1969, for most occupations, the earnings of black women 25 to 54 years, who worked year round, were closer to that of the comparable group of white women than black men to white men. However, the average earning level of the young black men 25 to 34 years old who worked year round was about equal (ratios of 0.90 or more) to that of white men for a few specific occupations—engineers, teachers, except college and university, engineering and science technicians, bus drivers, taxicab drivers and chauffeurs, protective workers, and policemen and detectives. The average earning level of both the younger and older black women who worked year round was equal (ratio of 1.00 or more) to that of white women for these specific occupations —secretaries, stenographers, typists, dressmakers and seamstresses, and workers in health services.

Health
For both black and other races and whites, major cardiovascular diseases and malignant neoplasms were the two leading causes of death in 1969. However, the death rate for both diseases was higher for blacks than for whites.

The next three major causes of death among blacks and other races in rank order were—accidents (including motor vehicle), influenza and pneumonia, and homicide.

Although significant reductions have been made in the infant mortality rate for black and other races during the last three decades, both neonatal mortality (under 28 days) and post-neonatal mortality (28 days to 11 months) were much higher for black and other races children than for white children in 1971. In 1968 (latest year data available), the maternal mortality rate for mothers of black and other races and white mothers was very low—below 1.0 per 1,000 live births.

In 1970, three out of five persons of black and other races under 65 years of age compared to four out of five whites in this age category had hospital insurance. With the introduction of Medicare, almost all persons 65 years old and over have health insurance coverage.[1] The proportion of blacks and whites with hospital insurance coverage varied according to family income level and region of residence. Lowest rates were observed for persons in the under $5,000 income level and for persons who lived in the South.

[1]U.S. Department of Health, Education, and Welfare, National Center for Health Statistics, *Monthly Vital Statistics Report*, Volume 21, No. 9, Supplement 2, 12/18/72.

THE BLACK POPULATION UNDERCOUNT
According to a 1973 report compiled by two demographers at the Office of Population Research at Princeton University, there has been an undercount of the nation's black population in every U.S. census from 1880 to 1970. The report, "A Statistical Reconstruction of the Black Population of the United States, 1880 to 1970: Estimates of True Numbers by Age and Sex, Birthrates, and Total Fertility," states that the overall omission of blacks ranged from a high of approximaely 15 percent in 1920 to a low of some 8 percent in 1970—each undercount varying with age and sex. The undercounts of children under five and of females over 50 were as great as 20 percent in the censuses from 1880 to 1910. In the 1960 and 1970 censuses, approximately the same proportion of males 20 to 40 years of age were undercounted. The first part of the report mathematically reconstructs the population through international migration. The second part of the report compares black and white fertility trends since the early 19th century. Average lifetime numbers of children born per woman in 1880 was about 7.5 for blacks, compared to only 4.3 whites. The fertility of the black population then declined sharply, so that in recent years the differences are much less than in the past. Since about 1920, black fertility has fluctuated in much the same manner as white fertility.

HIGHLIGHTS OF STATISTICS RELATING TO SOCIAL AND ECONOMIC STATUS OF BLACKS IN THE UNITED STATES, 1972

POPULATION/INCOME   1972 (April) black population, 23.4 million
1970 (April) black population, 22.6 million

- 1970
  - —28 percent black and other races families with income above $10,000
  - —about 50 percent of white families with incomes above $10,000
- 1971
  - —30 percent black and other races families with incomes above $10,000
  - —about 54 percent of white families with incomes above $10,000
  - —7.4 million blacks below the poverty or low-income level; 32 percent of the black population
  - —10 percent of the white population below the low-income level
  - —one-fourth of black families received public assistance income; of these about
    61 percent were below the low-income level. Five percent of white families had income
    from public assistance; of those receiving it, 45 percent were below the low-income level
- 1972
  - —median income of black families was about $6,900, up from $6,400 in 1971
  - —median income for white families was about $11,500, up from $10,670 in 1971
  - —black to white median income ratio of 59 percent, down one point from the 60 percent
    ratio of 1971
  - —7.7 million blacks below the poverty or low-income level; 32.9 percent of the black population
  - —8.7 percent of the white population below the low-income level
  - ⋅—about two-thirds of low-income black families headed by women
  - —about one-half of low-income population were children under 18 years of age

EMPLOYMENT AND LABOR FORCE PARTICIPATION

- 1971
  - —black and other minority race workers more likely than whites to experience long-term
    employment (15 weeks or more) and multiple periods of unemployment
  - —black and other minority race workers were more prevalent among discouraged workers—
    those not in the labor force who were not looking for employment because of black
    job prospects
  - —blacks and other minority races 25 to 54 years of age who had achieved higher levels
    of schooling were more likely to be in the labor force
  - —at all educational levels, women of black and other races were more likely than white
    women to be in the labor force
  - —blacks and other minority races still under-represented in higher paying jobs
- 1972
  - —8.6 million black and other minority persons were employed, up about 2 percent
    from 1971 level
  - —white employment increased by 3 percent
  - —jobless rate for black and other minorities remained at 1969 level of 10 percent
  - —decline in white jobless rate from 5.4 to 5.0 percent. The ratio of black and other
    minority joblessness to whites rose to 20.1 in 1972.

HOUSING

- 1970
  - —annual housing cost was at least one-fourth of the income for 30 percent of black
    home-owning households, compared to 18 percent for a comparable white group in 1970
- 1972
  - —black renters paid a larger proportion of their income for rent than did whites—
    about 43 percent of black households and 35 percent of white households expended
    at lease one-fourth of their income for gross rent

VOTING

- 1972
  - —voter participation rate for blacks of voting age in the 1972 presidential election was
    about 6 percentage points lower than in the two preceeding presidential elections—
    52 percent in 1972; 58 percent in 1964 and 1968

Source: Series P-23, No. 46-Special Studies.

BLACK COMMUNITY ATTITUDINAL STUDY: 1973

In order to determine the social-political views and attitudes of the national black community and the lifestyle values of black Americans, a survey of the metropolitan, literate black population, 18 years and over, was taken in 1972. This population group is estimated to be over 40 percent of the total black population in the United States, roughly 9 million persons. The survey sample, which was designed according to accepted probability methods and projectable to the specified population, was based on over 1,000 personal interviews. For purposes of comparison with the general population, other recent studies dealing with similar or related subjects and value measurements were used.

The survey covered key questions such as the extent to which frustration, alienation, and radicalization now prevail in the black community; the role and importance of black identification and how all of these things relate to and are reflected in the day-to-day responses and aspirations of black people, and the extent to which the present mood and thinking of the black community is similar or different in its views and attitudes from the rest of the country.

SUMMARY OF FINDINGS

• The black community is composed of many different views and attitudes.

• The community sharply divides on such critical questions as integration, the viability of the social system, the need for radical change, use of violence, and integration versus separatism.

• The basic division splitting the black community squarely down the middle is between hope and hopelessness.

• One out of every two blacks continue to have at least moderate faith in the American system and believes that it is possible to effect change within it. They believe in integration and reject violence.

• The other 50 percent of the black community is more despairing. Among this group, the majority express little hope in the present system, but are not quite sure how to resolve present problems. They tend to favor separatism and/or violence—but are not really committed to either one.

• There are few real radicals in the black community. Only 7 percent strongly support the need for radical change and are ready to back it up with whatever means are required—including violence. It is primarily the radicals who support black separatism.

• These differences in viewpoint are creating sharp cleavages among the black community. At the same time, there is evidence of a shared sense of black pride and identification—and a prevailing set of personal lifestyle values.

• The values of the black community are characterized by a strong commitment to the basic "Protestant Ethic" with black men and women attaching the same importance as other Americans to family, economic self-sufficiency, integrity, and order.

• The striving of the black community is indicated by the heightened importance black men and women attach to such values as personal fulfillment, self-expression, and quality of life.

• On marketplace issues, blacks are somewhat different than other consumers. They share the same concern as others with declining product quality, but generally are less brand loyal and more prone to buying tangibles rather than intangibles.

FINDINGS IN DETAIL

Four major currents dominate black life and thinking: black pride and identification; mounting frustration with the inequities of the American system; a readiness for radical change, but a simultaneous rejection of violence; and a new kind of integration based on equality first, and integration second.

Black Identification. The single strongest current in the black community is the singular emphasis placed on black identification.

Black men and women neither think of themselves as, nor aspire to be, "just Americans." Instead, the emphasis is at least equally on the word "Black" and pride in being black.

Only a handful of the people (12%) think of themselves first as Americans. Instead, the vast majority (62%) regard themselves as "equally black and American." And a sizable group (24%) go considerably beyond even this view and say forthrightly that they are first blacks and then Americans.

This sense of black pride and identification is undoubtedly a factor influencing black thinking, orientation, outlook, and day-to-day lifestyle.

Frustration, Impatience, Radicalization. The second major current is the deep despair, frustration, and impatience about the inequities of American society which has led to a considerable degree of radicalization within the black community.

Black men and women share the same uneasy feelings of most Americans that things are not going well in this country. Where they differ from white society, including college youth, is in their estimate of our social system and the opportunities for change within it. Today, four out of ten blacks hold the view that the American system is no longer viable and that radical alternatives are necessary. This same view is held by only 27 percent of all college youth.

Rejection of Violence. Radical change is one thing; support of violence as a philosophy is something else. Most black men and women (62%) reject inalterably the concept of violence. Another 30 percent believe that violence is only justified when all else has failed. Only 8 percent believe that violent means are often necessary.

Only 56 percent of the college youth has the same strong antipathy to violence as the black community. Indeed, college students as a whole are far more willing than blacks to justify the use of such protest tactics as sit-ins, resisting police, blockading buildings, or destroying or mutilating property.

Another measure of the black community's attitudes toward violence is indicated by the measure of support and admiration accorded to various black leaders. Those who are the most admired include black men and women who have rejected violence and sought to correct problems within the system.

Rev. Martin Luther King, Congresswoman Shirley Chisholm, Mayor Charles Evers, Rev. Ralph Abernathy, Georgia Representative Julian Bond, Whitney Young, and Rev. Jesse Jackson head the list. On the other hand, when it comes to more radical black leaders, such as Black Panther Huey Newton, Bobby Seale, Eldridge Cleaver, or Stokely Carmichael, there are almost as many black people who do not admire these people as there are admirers.

A Different Formula for Integration. The black community divides on the subject of integration. Less than half (47%) support the traditional concept that integration is the best method for overcoming racial inequities. The majority hold differing views. One small sector (16%) stands squarely behind separatism as the solution to black problems. A much larger group (36%) favors what might be called a modified formula for integration. Their solution calls for first ending present inequities by giving black community equal rights in housing and education, and then encouraging integration among equals.

These four currents cut across every segment of black society—young, old, employed, unemployed, educated, and uneducated. They help define and explain the major groupings within the black community.

Four major groupings were identified, ranging all the way from the small group of really satisfied blacks to the even smaller group of radical revolutionaries. For most blacks, however, the choice is between moderate hope and moderate pessimism concerning the future. Here are the four major social groups in black society as indicated by this study:

The Satisfieds. About ten percent of black society are members of this group. These are the men and women who are firmly committed to the American way of life. They strongly favor integration and are firmly opposed to violence. In a very real sense, this group could be considered the traditionalists, for it includes primarily older, less well educated, and low-income black men and women.

The Optimistic Moderates. Four out of ten blacks are in this group. The optimistic moderates are as concerned as other blacks about the inequities of present society but they still view the American system as basically sound and able to resolve these problems. Based on this premise, the moderates hope for change within the system; support integration; and are opposed to violence. Optimism is based in part on current educational and income advantages. There are also more women than men in this group.

The Troubled and Unhopeful. This is the single largest sector in the black community with a membership of 43 percent. These are the men and women who are beginning to despair with the system, but have not yet come to any firm conclusions about how to change the situation or resolve the problems. Essentially they are tolerant of, but still unsure about, violence and black separatism. The group includes many young men and women. Thirty-seven percent are under 30 years old, and half of them have less than a high school education.

The Radicals. This is the smallest group with a membership of only 7 percent. It is also the most militant and extremist. Members of the group are almost totally dissatisfied with the American system. They see violence and/or separatism as viable means of resolving the problems of the black community. Like many radical groups, this one tends to be fairly elitist in character. Fifty-two percent are under 30 years of age; 28 percent have attended college; and 30 percent are earning over $10,000. As a result of its composition, the radical group probably has more influence and impact than its size would ordinarily warrant.

This then is the social-political picture of the black community—teetering between optimism and pessimism, hope and no hope, faith and no faith. On one point, however, almost all agree—black identity is most important.

• Examination of black personality/life style values reveals a quite different picture from the social-political environment, for there is far less ambivalence and far more support for basic values of the white society.

• Support for traditional "Protestant Ethic" values runs deep within the black community. Black men and women share the same commitment as other Americans to belief in familism, economic self-sufficiency, the importance of planning, and personal integrity. Blacks tend to be even more conformist than other people, and lag behind only in their stress on achievement and advancement. Their values in this instance, undoubtedly reflect black perception of society's realities.

• On other more personal values, black men and women indicate an even stronger sense of commitment than other people. These include such personal-fulfillment values as the importance of sophistication and cultivation, physical attractiveness, and self-improvement. These, too, are part of black pride, identity, and future aspirations.

• Similarly black people express even greater concern than other Americans about the importance of self-expression and an enriched quality of life.

THE END RESULTS:

• 73% of black men and women hold creativity as an important value compared to 53% for other people.

• 67% of blacks stress the importance of individuality compared to 47% for other people.

• 75% consider gracious surroundings as extremely important, a view shared by only 62% of the rest of the population.

The black marketplace, in spite of the similarity in values, is somewhat different from the general market. For one thing, black values cannot be viewed in a vacuum. The widespread sense of black pride, black identity, and black uniqueness is an integral part of the social climate in the black community. For another, black consumers react somewhat differently from other consumers. They are less likely to spend their money on intangibles than on tangibles; even more important, black consumers feel strongly about not being taken for granted. They are considered less brand-loyal than other consumers, but share others' present concern about declining quality standards.

*Source: An Insight into the Black Community; a study prepared for Ebony Magazine by Daniel Yankelovich, Inc. N. Y., 1973.

Standard Metropolitan Statistical Areas, Cities, and Places with Black Population of 100,000 or more

	Number of Blacks	% of Total Population
Atlanta, Ga.	310,619	22.3
Baltimore, Md.	490,224	23.7
Birmingham, Ala.	217,884	29.5
Boston, Mass.	127,035	4.6
Buffalo, N.Y.	108,784	8.1
Chicago, Ill.	1,230,919	17.6
Cincinnati, Ohio	152,333	11.0
Cleveland, Ohio	332,614	16.1
Columbus, Ohio	106,401	11.6
Dallas, Tex.	248,666	15.9
Detroit, Mich.	757,083	18.0
Gary, Ind.	112,174	17.7
Greensboro, N.C.	118,398	19.6
Houston, Tex.	383,807	19.3
Indianapolis, Ind.,	137,335	12.4
Jacksonville, Fla.	118,140	22.3
Kansas City, Mo., Kan.	151,127	12.1
Los Angeles, Cal.	762,844	10.8
Louisville, Ky.	101,255	12.3
Memphis, Tenn.	288,916	37.5
Miami, Fla.	189,763	15.0
Milwaukee, Wis.	106,532	7.6
Mobile, Ala.	112,959	30.0
New York, N.Y.	1,883,292	16.3
Newark, N.J.	348,342	18.8
New Orleans, La.	323,940	31.0
Norfolk, Va.	167,970	24.7
Philadelphia, Pa.	844,300	17.5
Pittsburgh, Pa.	169,884	7.1
Richmond, Va.	130,246	25.1
San Francisco, Cal.	330,107	10.6
St. Louis, Mo.	378,816	16.0
Tampa, Fla.	109,422	10.8
Washington, D.C.	703,745	24.6

*1970 Census of Population
  U.S. Summary—Final Report PHC (2)—1
  General Demographic Trends for Metropolitan Areas, 1960-1970; October, 1971
  Standard Metropolitan Statistical Areas by Race, 1970

Standard Metropolitan Statistical Areas, Cities, and Places with Black Population of 50,000 or more

	Number of Blacks	% of Total Population
Akron, Ohio	54,299	8.0
Augusta, Ga.	70,339	27.8
Baton Rouge, La.	81,415	28.5
Beaumont, Tex.	67,584	21.4
Charleston, S.C.	94,775	31.2
Charlotte, N.C.	94,624	23.1
Columbia, S.C.	84,474	26.2
Columbus, Ga.	67,980	28.5
Dayton, Ohio	93,676	11.0
Denver, Colo.	50,164	4.1
Durham, N.C.	53,414	28.1
Fayetteville, N.C.	50,602	23.9
Flint, Mich.	60,677	12.2
Fort Worth, Tex.	83,282	10.9
Ft. Lauderdale, Fla.	77,382	12.5
Hartford, Conn.	50,518	7.6
Jackson, Miss.	96,418	37.2
Jersey City, N.J.	61,095	10.0
Little Rock, Ark.	61,352	19.0
Macon, Ga.	59,514	28.8
Montgomery, Ala.	70,203	34.9
Nashville, Tenn.	96,401	17.8
Newport News, Va.	74,630	25.5
Oklahoma City, Okla.	54,465	8.5
Orlando, Fla.	62,510	14.6
Paterson, N.J.	75,114	5.5
Raleigh, N.C.	50,576	22.1
Rochester, N.Y.	57,688	6.5
San Antonio, Tex.	59,887	6.9
San Bernadino, Cal.	50,474	4.4
San Diego, Cal.	62,028	4.6
Savannah, Ga.	63,522	33.8
Shreveport, La.	96,554	32.8
Toledo, Ohio	57,125	8.2
West Palm Beach, Fla.	61,015	17.5
Wilmington, Del.	60,896	12.2
Youngstown, Ohio	50,621	9.4

*1970 Census of Population
  U.S. Summary—Final Report PHC (2)—1
  General Demographic Trends for Metropolitan Areas, 1960-1970; October, 1971
  Standard Metropolitan Statistical Areas by Race, 1970

Standard Metropolitan Statistical Areas, Cities, and Places with Black Population of 20,000 or more

	Number of Blacks	% of Total Population
Albany, Ga.	30,642	34.2
Albany, N.Y.	23,652	3.3
Atlantic City, N.J.	30,403	17.4
Austin, Tex.	32,859	11.1
Biloxi, Miss.	22,743	16.9
Bridgeport, Conn.	28,913	7.4
Canton, Ohio	21,558	5.8
Chattanooga, Tenn.	49,927	16.4
Fresno, Cal.	20,370	4.9
Gainesville, Fla.	21,563	20.6
Galveston, Tex.	33,315	19.6
Grand Rapids, Mich.	23,429	4.3
Greenville, S.C.	45,366	15.1
Harrisburg, Pa.	28,103	6.8
Huntsville, Ala.	35,875	15.7
Knoxville, Tenn.	28,691	7.2
Lafayette, Ind.	24,179	22.0
Lake Charles, La.	31,927	22.0
Las Vegas, Nev.	24,760	9.1
Lexington, Ky.	21,784	12.5
Lynchburg, Va.	25,024	20.3
Monroe, La.	31,765	27.5
New Haven, Conn.	41,300	11.6
Omaha, Neb.	36,807	6.8
Pensacola, Fla.	42,541	17.5
Petersburg, Va.	41,030	31.9
Phoenix, Ariz.	32,872	3.4
Pine Bluff, Ark.	34,927	40.9
Portland, Ore.	23,284	2.3
Providence, R.I.	21,083	2.3
Roanoke, Va.	20,912	11.5
Sacramento, Cal.	37,911	4.7
Saginaw, Mich.	26,856	12.2
Seattle, Wash.	41,609	2.9
Springfield, Mass.	24,153	4.6
Syracuse, N.Y.	23,398	3.7
Tallahassee, Fla.	26,021	25.3
Texarkana, Tex.	22,716	22.4
Trenton, N.J.	49,802	16.4
Tulsa, Okla.	39,328	8.2
Tuscaloosa, Ala.	28,964	25.0
Tyler, Tex.	23,975	24.7
Waco, Tex.	23,789	16.1
Wichita, Kan.	28,017	7.2
Wilmington, N.C.	25,897	24.2

*1970 Census of Population
  U.S. Summary—Final Report PHC (2)—1

Standard Metropolitan Statistical Areas, Cities, and Places with Black Population of 1,000—20,000—Continued

	Number of Blacks	% of Total Population
Abilene, Tex.	6,313	5.5
Albuquerque, N. Mex.	6,689	2.1
Allentown–Bethlehem–Easton, Pa.–N.J.	6,441	1.2
Amarillo, Tex.	6,972	4.8
Anaheim–Santa Ana–Garden Grove, Calif.	10,179	0.7
Anderson, Ind.	8,026	5.8
Ann Arbor, Mich.	17,822	7.6
Asheville, N.C.	15,285	10.5
Bakersfield, Calif.	18,637	5.7
Binghamton, N.Y.–Pa.	2,606	0.9
Bloomington–Normal, Ill.	2,053	2.0
Brockton, Mass.	3,260	1.7
Brownsville–Harlingen–San Benito, Tex.	1,395	0.1
Bryan–College Station, Tex.	9,689	16.7
Cedar Rapids, Iowa	1,807	1.1
Champaign–Urbana, Ill.	10,677	6.5
Charleston, W. Va.	14,347	6.3
Colorado Springs, Col.	12,226	5.2
Columbia, Mo.	4,299	5.3
Corpus Christi, Tex.	12,241	4.3
Danbury, Conn.	2,850	3.6
Davenport–Rock Island–Moline, Iowa–Ill.	12,147	3.3
Decatur, Ill.	9,879	7.9
Des Moines, Iowa	11,916	4.2
Duluth–Superior, Minn.–Wis.	1,089	0.4
El Paso, Texas	11,079	2.8
Erie, Pa.	8,951	3.4
Evansville, Ind.–Ky.	13,555	5.8
Fitchburg–Leominster, Mass.	1,003	1.0
Fort Smith, Ark.–Okla.	7,330	4.6
Fort Wayne, Ind.	19,298	6.9
Gadsden, Ala.	13,382	14.2
Great Falls, Mont.	1,067	1.3
Hamilton–Middletown, Ohio	11,171	4.9
Honolulu, Hawaii	7,388	1.2
Huntington–Ashland, W. Va.–Ky.–Ohio	7,584	3.0
Jackson, Mich.	8,492	5.9
Johnstown, Pa.	3,566	1.4
Kalamazoo, Mich.	9,579	4.8
Kenosha, Wis.	1,930	1.6
Lafayette–West Lafayette, Ind.	1,035	0.9
Lancaster, Pa.	5,365	1.7
Lansing, Mich.	14,699	3.9
Laredo, Tex.	1,257	1.7
Lawrence–Haverhill, Mass.–N.H.	1,328	0.6
Lawton, Okla.	11,373	10.5
Lima, Ohio	9,352	5.5
Lincoln, Nebr.	2,432	1.4
Lorain–Elyria, Ohio	16,388	6.4

Standard Metropolitan Statistical Areas, Cities, and Places with Black Population of 1,000—20,000

Lowell, Mass.	1,114	0.5
Lubbock, Tex.	13,626	7.6
Madison, Wis.	3,124	1.1
Mansfield, Ohio	8,669	6.7
Meriden, Conn.	1,477	2.6
McAllen–Pharr–Edinburg, Tex.	1,416	0.9
Midland, Tex.	6,475	9.9
Minneapolis–St. Paul, Minn.	32,118	1.8
Modesto, Calif.	1,938	1.0
Muncie, Ind.	6,959	5.4
Muskegon–Muskegon Heights, Mich.	16,722	10.6
New Bedford, Mass.	3,894	2.6
New Britain, Conn.	3,953	2.7
New London–Groton–Norwich, Conn.	7,156	3.4
Norwalk, Conn.	9,610	8.0
Ogden, Utah	2,073	1.6
Odessa, Tex.	4,749	5.2
Owensboro, Ky.	3,449	4.3
Oxnard–Ventura, Calif.	6,354	1.7
Peoria, Ill.	14,977	4.4
Pittsfield, Mass.	1,222	1.5
Pueblo, Colo.	2,161	1.8
Racine, Wis.	10,572	6.2
Reading, Pa.	6,614	2.2
Reno, Nev.	1,987	**1.6**
Rockford, Ill.	16,040	5.9
Salinas–Monterey, Calif.	12,148	4.9
Salt Lake City, Utah	4,196	0.8
San Angelo, Tex.	3,175	4.5
San Jose, Calif.	18,090	1.7
Santa Barbara, Calif.	6,426	2.4
Santa Rosa, Calif.	2,108	1.0
Sherman–Denison, Tex.	6,865	8.2
Sioux City, Iowa	1,052	0.9
South Bend, Ind.	18,652	6.7
Spokane, Wash.	2,989	1.0
Springfield, Ill.	7,847	4.9
Springfield, Mo.	2,421	1.6
St. Joseph, Mo.	2,511	2.9
Springfield, Ohio	13,236	8.4
Stamford, Conn.	15,079	7.3
Steubenville–Weirton, Ohio–W. Va.	6,919	4.2
Stockton, Calif.	15,783	5.4
Tacoma, Wash.	18,501	4.5
Terre Haute, Ind.	5,555	3.2
Topeka, Kans.	11,196	7.2
Tucson, Ariz.	10,322	2.9
Utica–Rome, N.Y.	7,681	2.3
Vallejo–Napa, Calif.	17,172	6.9
Vineland–Millville–Bridgeton, N.J.	16,566	13.6

Waterbury, Conn.	11,554	5.5
Waterloo, Iowa	6,644	5.0
Wheeling, W. Va.–Ohio	3,934	2.2
Wichita Falls, Tex.	9,769	7.6
Wilkes-Barre–Hazelton, Pa.	1,856	0.5
Worcester, Mass.	3,665	1.1
York, Pa.	7,799	2.4

*1970 Census of Population
  U.S. Summary—Final Report PHC (2)—1
  General Demographic Trends for Metropolitan Areas, 1960-1970; October, 1971
*Standard Metropolitan Statistical Areas by Race, 1970

SOCIAL CHARACTERISTICS OF THE BLACK POPULATION, FOR SELECTED AREAS: 1970

	Alabama			Arizona			Arkansas		
	TOTAL	Urban Total	Rural Total	TOTAL	Urban Total	Rural Total	TOTAL	Urban Total	Rural Total
BLACK POPULATION—									
Male, All ages	**423,083**	**258,874**	**164,209**	**26,969**	**23,695**	**3,274**	**167,019**	**89,692**	**77,327**
Under 5 years	47,546	28,172	19,374	2,974	2,750	224	19,005	10,335	8,670
5 to 9 years	55,581	33,125	22,456	3,628	3,363	265	22,136	11,674	10,462
10 to 14 years	60,530	36,265	24,265	3,580	3,241	339	23,861	12,148	11,713
15 to 19 years	52,636	31,509	21,127	3,062	2,582	480	20,877	10,742	10,135
20 to 24 years	29,333	18,781	10,552	2,546	2,029	517	10,473	6,231	4,242
25 to 29 years	19,343	12,052	7,291	1,456	1,262	194	6,702	3,923	2,779
30 to 34 years	17,114	10,657	6,457	1,394	1,233	161	5,642	3,198	2,444
35 to 39 years	16,744	10,765	5,979	1,452	1,236	216	5,552	3,179	2,373
40 to 44 years	17,616	11,571	6,045	1,162	998	164	5,946	3,316	2,630
45 to 49 years	18,215	12,003	6,212	1,099	965	134	6,188	3,466	2,722
50 to 54 years	17,599	11,467	6,132	1,028	902	126	6,664	3,600	3,064
55 to 59 years	18,183	11,559	6,624	957	820	137	7,073	3,813	3,260
60 to 64 years	16,408	10,007	6,401	849	730	119	7,051	3,679	3,372
65 to 69 years	14,464	8,705	5,759	755	649	106	6,975	3,583	3,392
70 to 74 years	9,505	5,570	3,935	448	406	42	5,197	2,764	2,433
75 to 79 years	5,996	3,298	2,698	299	274	25	3,797	2,038	1,759
80 to 84 years	3,485	1,886	1,599	170	154	16	2,130	1,090	1,040
85 years and over	2,785	1,482	1,303	110	101	9	1,750	913	837
Under 18 years	198,018	117,914	80,104	12,059	10,965	1,094	78,773	41,050	37,723
62 years and over	45,851	26,708	19,143	2,266	2,000	266	24,075	12,627	11,448
65 years and over	36,235	20,941	15,294	1,782	1,584	198	19,849	10,388	9,461
Median age	19.5	20.1	18.8	20.5	19.8	23.2	19.4	20.0	18.9
Female, All ages	**480,384**	**304,567**	**175,817**	**26,375**	**24,301**	**2,074**	**185,426**	**104,433**	**80,993**
Under 5 years	47,194	27,888	19,306	3,003	2,775	228	19,064	10,355	8,709
5 to 9 years	55,016	32,667	22,349	3,505	3,220	285	22,043	11,721	10,322
10 to 14 years	60,165	36,504	23,661	3,577	3,282	295	23,726	12,241	11,485
15 to 19 years	54,885	34,188	20,697	2,743	2,483	260	20,905	11,328	9,577
20 to 24 years	34,519	23,197	11,322	1,914	1,748	166	12,004	7,642	4,362
25 to 29 years	23,481	15,392	8,089	1,571	1,485	86	8,057	4,979	3,078
30 to 34 years	21,997	14,617	7,380	1,525	1,426	99	7,375	4,436	2,939
35 to 39 years	22,415	15,023	7,392	1,375	1,262	113	7,373	4,323	3,050
40 to 44 years	24,362	16,647	7,715	1,303	1,189	114	8,197	4,761	3,436
45 to 49 years	22,972	15,629	7,343	1,209	1,109	100	8,225	4,757	3,468
50 to 54 years	22,057	14,606	7,451	1,081	991	90	8,267	4,766	3,501
55 to 59 years	21,929	14,516	7,413	1,004	927	77	8,538	4,819	3,719
60 to 64 years	19,984	12,879	7,105	815	757	58	8,386	4,816	3,570
65 to 69 years	19,303	12,254	7,049	675	631	44	8,511	4,985	3,526
70 to 74 years	12,430	7,935	4,495	483	451	32	5,975	3,437	2,538
75 to 79 years	8,217	5,002	3,215	292	278	14	4,198	2,425	1,773
80 to 84 years	5,018	3,004	2,014	151	141	10	2,480	1,413	1,067
85 years and over	4,440	2,619	1,821	149	146	3	2,102	1,229	873
Under 18 years	197,123	118,100	79,023	11,771	10,801	970	78,150	41,114	37,036
62 years and over	61,205	38,336	22,869	2,210	2,077	133	28,324	16,378	11,946
65 years and over	49,408	30,814	18,594	1,750	1,647	103	23,266	13,489	9,777
Median age	23.3	24.5	20.8	20.9	21.1	19.4	22.9	24.3	20.5

RELATIONSHIP TO HEAD OF HOUSEHOLD

All persons	903,467	563,441	340,026	53,344	47,996	5,348	352,445	194,125	158,320
In households	882,847	549,781	333,066	50,392	46,409	3,983	344,083	188,348	155,735
Head	229,525	151,923	77,602	14,503	13,321	1,182	93,429	54,635	38,794
14 to 24 years	11,440	8,005	3,435	1,257	1,175	82	5,080	3,530	1,550
25 to 34 years	32,509	22,091	10,418	2,937	2,784	153	11,668	7,303	4,365
35 to 44 years	39,553	27,273	12,280	2,961	2,723	238	13,470	8,134	5,336
45 to 64 years	89,974	60,099	29,875	4,932	4,435	497	34,239	19,547	14,692
65 years and over	56,049	34,455	21,594	2,416	2,204	212	28,972	16,121	12,851
Primary individual: Male	16,563	11,350	5,213	1,968	1,684	284	8,956	5,299	3,657
Female	28,382	21,174	7,208	1,710	1,606	104	13,558	9,171	4,387
Family head: Male	133,700	83,767	49,933	8,069	7,384	685	53,632	28,710	24,922
Female	50,880	35,632	15,248	2,756	2,647	109	17,283	11,455	5,828
Wife of head	124,347	77,999	46,348	7,330	6,725	605	49,906	26,740	23,166
Child of head	402,277	244,070	158,207	24,060	22,234	1,826	157,453	82,890	74,563
Other relative of head	113,165	65,852	47,313	3,417	3,166	251	37,701	20,152	17,549
Not related to head	13,533	9,937	3,596	1,082	963	119	5,594	3,931	1,663
In group quarters	20,620	13,660	6,960	2,952	1,587	1,365	8,362	5,777	2,585
Inmate of institution	8,958	4,009	4,949	1,030	441	589	3,928	2,080	1,848
Other	11,662	9,651	2,011	1,922	1,146	776	4,434	3,697	737
Persons per household	3.85	3.62	4.29	3.47	3.48	3.37	3.68	3.45	4.01
Persons per family	4.47	4.25	4.86	4.22	4.20	4.38	4.46	4.23	4.75
Persons, under 18 years old	395,141	236,014	159,127	23,830	21,766	2,064	156,923	82,164	74,759
Head or wife of head	1,198	718	480	88	78	10	501	298	203
Own child of head	316,922	192,291	124,631	20,945	19,348	1,597	128,879	67,690	61,189
In husband-wife households	218,832	125,459	93,373	13,675	12,424	1,251	90,705	43,345	47,360
Percent of total persons under 18 years	55.4	53.2	58.7	57.4	57.1	60.6	57.8	52.8	63.4
In household with female head	88,586	61,185	27,401	6,760	6,474	286	33,729	22,084	11,645
Other relative of head	72,216	40,015	32,201	2,225	2,044	181	25,073	12,884	12,189
Not related to head	2,406	1,461	945	199	178	21	1,043	618	425
In group quarters	2,399	1,529	870	373	118	255	1,427	674	753
Persons, 65 years old and over	85,643	51,755	33,888	3,532	3,231	301	43,115	23,877	19,238
Head of family: Male	24,918	14,076	10,842	954	867	87	13,254	6,600	6,654
Female	10,351	6,281	4,070	231	223	8	3,692	2,186	1,506
Wife of head	12,762	6,866	5,896	487	445	42	7,039	3,471	3,568
Other family member	12,928	8,061	4,867	345	322	23	4,710	2,582	2,128
Not related to head	2,044	1,426	618	121	110	11	1,026	692	334
Primary individual: Male	6,039	3,746	2,293	571	487	84	4,053	2,229	1,824
Female	14,741	10,352	4,389	660	627	33	7,973	5,106	2,867
Inmate of institution	1,569	746	823	141	130	11	1,260	922	338
Other, in group quarters	291	201	90	22	20	2	108	89	19

(continued overleaf)

SOCIAL CHARACTERISTICS OF THE BLACK POPULATION, FOR SELECTED AREAS: 1970

Alabama, Arizona, Arkansas—continued

	ALABAMA			ARIZONA			ARKANSAS		
	TOTAL	Urban Total	Rural Total	TOTAL	Urban Total	Rural Total	TOTAL	Urban Total	Rural Total
FAMILIES BY PRESENCE AND NUMBER OF OWN CHILDREN UNDER 18 YEARS									
All families	184,580	119,399	65,181	10,825	10,031	794	70,915	40,165	30,750
With own children under 18 years	104,944	67,754	37,190	7,015	6,505	510	39,153	22,223	16,930
Number of own children under 18 years	316,922	192,291	124,631	20,945	19,348	1,597	128,879	67,690	61,189
Number of own children under 6 years	86,250	51,595	34,655	6,249	5,802	447	36,103	19,651	16,452
Number of own children 6 to 17 years	230,672	140,696	89,976	14,696	13,546	1,150	92,776	48,039	44,737
With own children under 6 years only	17,457	11,663	5,794	1,502	1,388	114	6,817	4,412	2,405
With own children under 6 and 6 to 17 years	33,869	20,493	13,376	2,311	2,164	147	13,495	7,190	6,305
Husband-wife families	124,261	77,967	46,294	7,664	7,012	652	49,861	26,725	23,136
With own children under 18 years	71,969	44,499	27,470	4,725	4,318	407	27,178	14,315	12,863
Number of own children under 18 years	218,832	125,459	93,373	13,675	12,424	1,251	90,705	43,345	47,360
Number of own children under 6 years	63,518	36,060	27,458	4,266	3,884	382	26,580	13,275	13,305
Number of own children 6 to 17 years	155,314	89,399	65,915	9,409	8,540	869	64,125	30,070	34,055
With own children under 6 years only	13,953	9,093	4,860	1,130	1,027	103	5,298	3,270	2,028
With own children under 6 and 6 to 17 years	23,733	13,535	10,198	1,563	1,443	120	9,504	4,591	4,913
Families with female head	50,880	35,632	15,248	2,756	2,647	109	17,283	11,455	5,828
With own children under 18 years	29,286	20,967	8,319	2,084	2,002	82	10,331	7,045	3,286
Number of own children under 18 years	88,586	61,185	27,401	6,760	6,474	286	33,729	22,084	11,645
Number of own children under 6 years	20,581	14,283	6,298	1,887	1,833	54	8,390	5,770	2,620
Number of own children 6 to 17 years	68,005	46,902	21,103	4,873	4,641	232	25,339	16,314	9,025
With own children under 6 years only	3,006	2,252	754	336	329	7	1,258	268	990
With own children under 6 and 6 to 17	9,300	6,461	2,839	717	695	22	3,593	2,387	1,206
MARITAL STATUS									
Male, 14 years old and over	271,880	168,781	103,099	17,432	14,921	2,511	106,944	57,941	49,003
Single	101,844	61,160	40,684	6,348	5,142	1,206	37,925	19,937	17,988
Married, except separated	137,042	85,563	51,479	8,536	7,614	922	54,126	29,162	24,964
14 to 19 years	1,457	912	545	98	87	11	538	327	211
20 to 24 years	9,798	6,359	3,439	852	739	113	3,649	2,296	1,353
25 to 34 years	24,608	15,480	9,128	2,017	1,828	189	8,540	4,910	3,630
35 to 44 years	25,304	16,391	8,913	1,934	1,705	229	8,568	4,728	3,840
45 to 64 years	52,193	33,080	19,113	2,677	2,379	298	19,997	10,450	9,547
65 years and over	23,682	13,341	10,341	958	876	82	12,834	6,451	6,383
Separated	12,341	8,301	4,040	829	686	143	4,624	2,757	1,867
Widowed	14,318	8,904	5,414	828	731	97	7,269	4,066	3,203
Divorced	6,335	4,853	1,482	891	748	143	3,000	2,019	981
Female, 14 years old and over	330,268	214,945	115,323	16,986	15,659	1,327	125,286	72,486	52,800
Single	98,903	62,507	36,396	4,309	3,888	421	34,631	19,401	15,230
Married, except separated	138,514	87,018	51,496	7,965	7,291	674	54,411	29,439	24,972
14 to 19 years	5,018	3,067	1,951	332	299	33	1,924	1,156	768
20 to 24 years	14,390	9,358	5,032	980	904	76	5,277	3,208	2,069
25 to 34 years	27,647	17,685	9,962	2,050	1,917	133	9,785	5,677	4,108
35 to 44 years	29,194	19,039	10,155	1,764	1,587	177	10,030	5,375	4,655
45 to 64 years	48,468	30,400	18,068	2,314	2,102	212	19,935	10,317	9,618
65 years and over	13,797	7,469	6,328	525	482	43	7,460	3,706	3,754
Separated	23,320	17,119	6,201	1,258	1,206	52	7,748	5,279	2,469
Widowed	58,215	39,060	19,155	2,151	2,021	130	23,757	14,793	8,964
Divorced	11,316	9,241	2,075	1,303	1,253	50	4,739	3,574	1,165

BLACK POPULATION—

	California			Colorado			Connecticut		
Male, All ages	**683,026**	**660,603**	**22,423**	**34,047**	**33,286**	**761**	**85,649**	**82,147**	**3,502**
Under 5 years	75,233	74,007	1,226	3,560	3,501	59	11,248	11,010	238
5 to 9 years	86,601	84,973	1,628	4,141	4,053	88	12,275	11,968	307
10 to 14 years	83,354	81,187	2,167	4,043	3,968	75	10,883	10,513	370
15 to 19 years	70,073	66,795	3,278	3,414	3,313	101	8,202	7,809	393
20 to 24 years	59,054	55,324	3,730	4,840	4,720	120	6,939	6,555	384
25 to 29 years	49,527	47,748	1,779	2,508	2,443	65	6,610	6,315	295
30 to 34 years	45,906	44,519	1,387	2,146	2,086	60	5,670	5,378	292
35 to 39 years	40,399	39,131	1,268	2,111	2,063	48	4,763	4,499	264
40 to 44 years	37,263	36,050	1,213	1,760	1,727	33	4,613	4,373	240
45 to 49 years	35,462	34,438	1,024	1,488	1,453	35	4,120	3,903	217
50 to 54 years	29,444	28,575	869	1,190	1,168	22	3,130	2,980	150
55 to 59 years	23,760	22,871	889	863	848	15	2,450	2,338	112
60 to 64 years	17,732	17,070	662	702	688	14	1,726	1,629	97
65 to 69 years	12,839	12,282	557	475	467	8	1,300	1,244	56
70 to 74 years	7,764	7,419	345	319	313	6	854	825	29
75 to 79 years	4,431	4,214	217	236	233	3	414	392	22
80 to 84 years	2,306	2,197	109	124	121	3	259	236	23
85 years and over	1,878	1,803	75	127	121	6	193	180	13
Under 18 years	288,292	281,524	6,768	13,726	13,450	276	39,629	38,494	1,135
62 years and over	38,986	37,312	1,674	1,687	1,653	34	3,993	3,795	198
65 years and over	29,218	27,915	1,303	1,281	1,255	26	3,020	2,877	143
Median age	22.2	22.1	23.9	21.9	21.9	22.4	20.2	19.9	26.0
Female, All ages	**717,117**	**703,998**	**13,119**	**32,364**	**31,871**	**493**	**95,528**	**92,608**	**2,920**
Under 5 years	74,306	73,061	1,245	3,420	3,362	58	11,633	11,417	216
5 to 9 years	85,664	84,123	1,541	4,104	4,040	64	12,229	11,934	295
10 to 14 years	83,728	81,975	1,753	3,950	3,889	61	10,642	10,321	321
15 to 19 years	68,102	66,715	1,387	3,158	3,126	32	9,094	8,915	179
20 to 24 years	62,954	62,139	815	2,824	2,789	35	8,130	7,953	177
25 to 29 years	54,201	53,536	665	2,424	2,386	38	6,829	6,587	242
30 to 34 years	47,901	47,185	716	2,215	2,162	53	5,663	5,451	212
35 to 39 years	42,902	42,228	674	2,034	1,998	36	5,157	4,956	201
40 to 44 years	40,317	39,602	715	1,802	1,780	22	4,608	4,406	202
45 to 49 years	38,084	37,440	644	1,555	1,538	17	3,613	3,464	149
50 to 54 years	32,168	31,489	679	1,211	1,195	16	2,832	2,679	153
55 to 59 years	26,575	25,943	632	1,010	994	16	2,182	2,064	118
60 to 64 years	20,663	20,104	559	755	746	9	1,777	1,696	81
65 to 69 years	16,170	15,732	438	676	661	15	1,122	1,070	52
70 to 74 years	10,375	10,075	300	529	520	9	623	600	23
75 to 79 years	6,353	6,178	175	315	312	3	440	421	19
80 to 84 years	3,616	3,509	107	198	194	4	328	308	20
85 years and over	3,038	2,964	74	184	179	5	280	260	20
Under 18 years	285,860	280,410	5,450	13,401	13,197	204	39,725	38,712	1,013
62 years and over	51,177	49,777	1,400	2,322	2,281	41	5,535	5,273	262
65 years and over	39,552	38,458	1,094	1,902	1,866	36	4,290	4,095	195
Median age	23.7	23.7	23.9	22.7	22.7	24.5	22.5	22.4	30.2

(continued overleaf)

SOCIAL CHARACTERISTICS OF THE BLACK POPULATION, FOR SELECTED AREAS: 1970

California, Colorado, Connecticut—continued

	CALIFORNIA			COLORADO			CONNECTICUT		
	TOTAL	Urban Total	Rural Total	TOTAL	Urban Total	Rural Total	TOTAL	Urban Total	Rural Total
RELATIONSHIP TO HEAD OF HOUSEHOLD									
All persons	1,400,143	1,364,601	35,542	66,411	65,157	1,254	181,177	174,755	6,422
In households	1,352,386	1,327,405	24,981	61,384	60,346	1,038	175,832	170,856	4,976
Head	425,235	417,993	7,242	18,780	18,484	296	50,108	48,874	1,234
14 to 24 years	41,647	41,231	416	2,081	2,061	20	5,699	5,660	39
25 to 34 years	107,028	105,871	1,157	4,798	4,708	90	14,311	14,064	247
35 to 44 years	95,076	93,710	1,366	4,539	4,469	70	11,407	11,062	345
45 to 64 years	138,223	135,394	2,829	5,370	5,291	79	14,544	14,061	483
65 years and over	43,261	41,787	1,474	1,992	1,955	37	4,147	4,027	120
Primary individual: Male	57,550	56,563	987	2,179	2,142	37	4,820	4,719	101
Female	55,570	54,866	704	2,212	2,189	23	5,492	5,412	80
Family head: Male	224,327	219,696	4,631	10,891	10,669	222	27,694	26,731	963
Female	87,788	86,868	920	3,498	3,484	14	12,102	12,012	90
Wife of head	205,072	200,839	4,233	9,755	9,546	209	25,735	24,852	883
Child of head	594,531	583,408	11,123	27,549	27,093	456	82,959	80,952	2,007
Other relative of head	90,646	89,058	1,588	3,649	3,609	40	11,397	11,084	313
Not related to head	36,902	36,107	795	1,651	1,614	37	5,633	5,094	539
In group quarters	47,757	37,196	10,561	5,027	4,811	216	5,345	3,899	1,446
Inmate of institution	22,512	15,465	7,047	1,095	950	145	3,079	1,850	1,229
Other	25,245	21,731	3,514	3,932	3,861	71	2,266	2,049	217
Persons per household	3.18	3.18	3.45	3.27	3.26	3.51	3.51	3.50	4.03
Persons per family	3.85	3.85	4.05	3.85	3.84	3.99	4.02	4.02	4.04
Persons, under 18 years old	574,152	561,934	12,218	27,127	26,647	480	79,354	77,206	2,148
Head or wife of head	1,660	1,619	41	97	96	1	185	185	—
Own child of head	511,536	501,877	9,659	24,289	23,889	400	71,885	70,197	1,688
In husband-wife households	322,168	314,849	7,319	16,409	16,046	363	44,534	43,068	1,466
Percent of total persons under 18 years	56.1	56.0	59.9	60.5	60.2	75.6	56.1	55.8	68.2
In household with female head	177,436	175,343	2,093	7,457	7,428	29	25,808	25,626	182
Other relative of head	47,801	46,788	1,013	2,065	2,043	22	5,358	5,190	168
Not related to head	6,871	6,645	226	356	345	11	1,052	984	68
In group quarters	6,284	5,005	1,279	320	274	46	874	650	224
Persons, 65 years old and over	68,770	66,373	2,397	3,183	3,121	62	7,310	6,972	338
Head of family: Male	16,752	16,023	729	756	744	12	1,699	1,633	66
Female	4,897	4,787	110	234	232	2	595	584	11
Wife of head	9,340	8,907	433	434	426	8	949	907	42
Other family member	10,544	10,350	194	470	458	12	1,299	1,246	53
Not related to head	2,692	2,607	85	127	126	1	399	345	54
Primary individual: Male	7,197	6,890	307	308	303	5	606	589	17
Female	14,415	14,087	328	694	676	18	1,247	1,221	26
Inmate of institution	2,460	2,276	184	125	122	3	454	390	64
Other, in group quarters	473	446	27	35	34	1	62	57	5

FAMILIES BY PRESENCE AND NUMBER OF OWN CHILDREN UNDER 18 YEARS

All families	312,115	306,564	5,551	14,389	14,153	236	39,796	38,743	1,053
With own children under 18 years	201,305	198,040	3,265	9,620	9,463	157	27,218	26,559	659
Number of own children under 18 years	511,536	501,877	9,659	24,289	23,889	400	71,885	70,197	1,688
Number of own children under 6 years	158,915	156,369	2,546	7,548	7,419	129	25,238	24,782	456
Number of own children 6 to 17 years	352,621	345,508	7,113	16,741	16,470	271	46,647	45,415	1,232
With own children under 6 years only	50,086	49,469	617	2,371	2,330	41	7,311	7,204	107
With own children under 6 and 6 to 17 years	56,094	55,089	1,005	2,681	2,631	50	8,380	8,172	208
Husband-wife families	211,743	207,286	4,457	10,432	10,214	218	26,067	25,146	921
With own children under 18 years	128,901	126,391	2,510	6,652	6,508	144	17,154	16,569	585
Number of own children under 18 years	322,168	314,849	7,319	16,409	16,046	363	44,534	43,068	1,466
Number of own children under 6 years	105,374	103,369	2,005	5,381	5,260	121	16,056	15,651	405
Number of own children 6 to 17 years	216,794	211,480	5,314	11,028	10,786	242	28,478	27,417	1,061
With own children under 6 years only	34,996	34,474	522	1,781	1,742	39	4,915	4,816	99
With own children under 6 and 6 to 17 years	36,541	35,769	772	1,862	1,815	47	5,212	5,027	185
Families with female head	87,788	85,858	920	3,498	3,484	14	12,102	12,012	90
With own children under 18 years	66,832	66,169	663	2,748	2,738	10	9,421	9,364	57
Number of own children under 18 years	177,436	175,343	2,093	7,457	7,428	29	25,808	25,626	182
Number of own children under 6 years	50,718	50,230	488	2,058	2,052	6	8,787	8,753	34
Number of own children 6 to 17 years	126,718	125,113	1,605	5,399	5,376	23	17,021	16,873	148
With own children under 6 years only	14,055	13,971	84	547	545	2	2,267	2,265	2
With own children under 6 and 6 to 17 years	18,605	18,396	209	781	780	1	3,037	3,018	19

MARITAL STATUS

Male, 14 years old and over	453,752	435,860	17,892	23,054	22,496	558	53,323	50,655	2,668
Single	156,423	147,756	8,667	8,466	8,221	245	19,009	17,888	1,121
Married, except separated	228,978	222,376	6,602	11,940	11,679	261	28,336	27,078	1,258
14 to 19 years	2,331	2,199	132	153	148	5	247	238	9
20 to 24 years	20,596	19,553	843	1,627	1,593	34	2,784	2,705	79
25 to 34 years	62,000	60,507	1,493	3,298	3,214	84	8,574	8,253	321
35 to 44 years	54,293	52,922	1,371	2,997	2,931	66	6,907	6,551	356
45 to 64 years	73,055	71,070	1,985	3,091	3,032	59	8,130	7,710	420
65 years and over	16,903	16,125	778	774	761	13	1,694	1,621	73
Separated	26,037	25,018	1,019	898	877	21	2,872	2,716	156
Widowed	13,608	13,054	554	577	570	7	1,583	1,521	62
Divorced	28,706	27,656	1,050	1,173	1,149	24	1,523	1,452	71
Female, 14 years old and over	489,299	480,356	8,913	21,628	21,310	318	63,061	60,899	2,162
Single	123,447	121,173	2,274	5,250	5,195	55	18,815	18,132	683
Married, except separated	219,025	214,358	4,667	10,671	10,459	212	27,893	26,847	1,046
14 to 19 years	7,040	6,914	126	443	442	1	759	754	5
20 to 24 years	28,347	27,954	393	1,457	1,428	29	4,031	3,977	54
25 to 34 years	61,193	60,203	990	3,102	3,025	77	8,613	8,335	278
35 to 44 years	50,138	49,120	1,018	2,587	2,534	53	6,473	6,177	296
45 to 64 years	62,052	60,381	1,671	2,593	2,549	44	6,913	6,557	356
65 years and over	10,255	9,786	469	489	481	8	1,104	1,047	57
Separated	47,372	46,818	554	1,405	1,398	7	7,240	7,116	124
Widowed	48,843	47,865	978	2,139	2,108	31	5,691	5,488	203
Divorced	50,612	50,142	470	2,163	2,150	13	3,422	3,316	106

SOCIAL CHARACTERISTICS OF THE BLACK POPULATION, FOR SELECTED AREAS: 1970

	Delaware			District of Columbia			Florida		
	TOTAL	Urban Total	Rural Total	TOTAL	Urban Total	Rural Total	TOTAL	Urban Total	Rural Total
BLACK POPULATION—									
Male, All ages	37,646	26,422	11,224	252,602	252,602	—	498,695	407,890	90,805
Under 5 years	4,404	2,981	1,423	26,041	26,041	—	58,300	48,193	10,107
5 to 9 years	5,105	3,574	1,531	28,582	28,582	—	66,287	54,365	11,922
10 to 14 years	5,013	3,393	1,620	28,678	28,678	—	68,646	55,761	12,885
15 to 19 years	3,985	2,846	1,139	24,218	24,218	—	54,995	44,186	10,809
20 to 24 years	2,781	2,111	670	22,124	22,124	—	36,110	29,377	6,733
25 to 29 years	2,247	1,598	649	20,332	20,332	—	28,402	23,525	4,877
30 to 34 years	2,004	1,471	533	16,484	16,484	—	27,388	23,064	4,324
35 to 39 years	1,974	1,409	565	14,726	14,726	—	25,396	21,268	4,128
40 to 44 years	1,903	1,340	563	14,737	14,737	—	24,770	20,650	4,120
45 to 49 years	1,850	1,294	556	14,089	14,089	—	22,407	18,654	3,753
50 to 54 years	1,635	1,140	495	12,103	12,103	—	21,285	17,518	3,767
55 to 59 years	1,440	1,011	429	10,538	10,538	—	19,055	15,372	3,683
60 to 64 years	1,143	781	362	7,829	7,829	—	16,086	12,818	3,268
65 to 69 years	872	591	281	5,281	5,281	—	13,228	10,551	2,677
70 to 74 years	600	404	196	3,324	3,324	—	7,789	6,092	1,697
75 to 79 years	358	247	111	1,856	1,856	—	4,169	3,191	978
80 to 84 years	165	117	48	897	897	—	2,306	1,729	577
85 years and over	167	114	53	763	763	—	2,076	1,576	500
Under 18 years	17,025	11,690	5,335	98,375	98,375	—	228,489	186,540	41,949
62 years and over	2,826	1,930	896	16,487	16,487	—	38,849	30,574	8,275
65 years and over	2,162	1,473	689	12,121	12,121	—	29,568	23,139	6,429
Median age	20.6	21.0	19.6	24.2	24.2	—	20.2	20.5	19.9
Female, All ages	40,630	28,760	11,870	285,110	285,110	—	542,956	451,880	91,076
Under 5 years	4,436	3,028	1,408	25,822	25,822	—	57,918	47,993	9,925
5 to 9 years	5,161	3,509	1,652	28,538	28,538	—	66,303	54,401	11,902
10 to 14 years	4,967	3,437	1,530	28,459	28,459	—	69,152	56,561	12,591
15 to 19 years	4,112	2,864	1,248	26,833	26,833	—	56,190	45,962	10,228
20 to 24 years	3,435	2,548	887	29,951	29,951	—	42,071	36,010	6,061
25 to 29 years	2,628	1,927	701	23,401	23,401	—	33,650	28,881	4,769
30 to 34 years	2,321	1,714	607	18,047	18,047	—	32,018	27,464	4,554
35 to 39 years	2,240	1,654	586	17,000	17,000	—	29,677	25,399	4,278
40 to 44 years	2,153	1,497	656	16,843	16,843	—	29,252	24,881	4,371
45 to 49 years	2,072	1,483	589	16,571	16,571	—	25,632	21,588	4,044
50 to 54 years	1,712	1,207	505	14,501	14,501	—	23,849	19,908	3,941
55 to 59 years	1,516	1,097	419	12,174	12,174	—	21,566	17,853	3,713
60 to 64 years	1,231	916	315	9,333	9,333	—	18,203	14,876	3,327
65 to 69 years	1,028	750	278	7,083	7,083	—	15,874	13,037	2,837
70 to 74 years	715	481	234	4,682	4,682	—	9,562	7,629	1,933
75 to 79 years	445	324	121	2,796	2,796	—	5,720	4,511	1,209
80 to 84 years	265	180	85	1,622	1,622	—	3,381	2,642	739
85 years and over	193	144	49	1,454	1,454	—	2,938	2,284	654
Under 18 years	17,077	11,677	5,400	98,604	98,604	—	228,869	187,723	41,146
62 years and over	3,348	2,419	929	23,002	23,002	—	47,975	38,648	9,327
65 years and over	2,646	1,879	767	17,637	17,637	—	37,475	30,103	7,372
Median age	22.4	23.0	20.5	25.6	25.6	—	22.6	22.9	20.7

RELATIONSHIP TO HEAD OF HOUSEHOLD

All persons	78,276	55,182	23,094	537,712	537,712	—	1,041,651	859,770	181,881
In households	75,152	52,641	22,511	525,021	525,021	—	1,010,249	836,725	173,524
Head	20,570	14,778	5,792	164,040	164,040	—	276,517	231,939	44,578
14 to 24 years	1,716	1,291	425	16,922	16,922	—	20,278	17,770	2,508
25 to 34 years	4,427	3,313	1,114	40,380	40,380	—	56,244	49,051	7,193
35 to 44 years	4,438	3,226	1,212	34,833	34,833	—	58,200	49,960	8,240
45 to 64 years	7,218	5,111	2,107	55,745	55,745	—	98,232	81,154	17,078
65 years and over	2,771	1,837	934	16,160	16,160	—	43,563	34,004	9,559
Primary individual: Male	2,227	1,532	695	20,607	20,607	—	28,204	23,101	5,103
Female	2,269	1,725	544	23,755	23,755	—	32,779	28,074	4,705
Family head: Male	11,561	8,068	3,493	85,329	85,329	—	153,870	127,556	26,314
Female	4,513	3,453	1,060	34,349	34,349	—	61,664	53,208	8,456
Wife of head	10,633	7,407	3,226	78,421	78,421	—	143,619	119,109	24,510
Child of head	33,911	23,642	10,269	209,340	209,340	—	455,911	375,068	80,843
Other relative of head	7,074	4,682	2,392	49,992	49,992	—	104,552	84,274	20,278
Not related to head	2,964	2,132	832	23,228	23,228	—	29,650	26,335	3,315
In group quarters	3,124	2,541	583	12,691	12,691	—	31,402	23,045	8,357
Inmate of institution	1,263	960	303	4,987	4,987	—	15,062	9,121	5,941
Other	1,861	1,581	280	7,704	7,704	—	16,340	13,924	2,416
Persons per household	3.65	3.56	3.89	3.20	3.20	—	3.65	3.61	3.89
Persons per family	4.21	4.10	4.49	3.82	3.82	—	4.27	4.20	4.61
Persons, under 18 years old	34,102	23,367	10,735	196,979	196,979	—	457,358	374,263	83,095
Head or wife of head	76	51	25	459	459	—	1,835	1,480	355
Own child of head	28,536	19,950	8,586	169,460	169,460	—	380,509	314,175	66,334
In husband-wife households	18,654	12,614	6,040	109,300	109,300	—	253,632	205,080	48,552
Percent of total persons under 18 years	54.7	54.0	56.3	55.5	55.5	—	55.5	54.8	58.4
In household with female head	9,006	6,784	2,222	55,203	55,203	—	115,660	99,999	15,661
Other relative of head	4,171	2,591	1,580	22,655	22,655	—	65,355	50,949	14,406
Not related to head	675	411	264	2,625	2,625	—	4,331	3,645	686
In group quarters	644	364	280	1,780	1,780	—	5,328	4,014	1,314
Persons, 65 years old and over	4,808	3,352	1,456	29,758	29,758	—	67,043	53,242	13,801
Head of family: Male	1,145	741	404	6,813	6,813	—	17,510	13,385	4,125
Female	446	308	138	2,798	2,798	—	7,582	5,956	1,626
Wife of head	630	417	213	3,501	3,501	—	8,551	6,527	2,024
Other family member	775	570	205	6,346	6,346	—	9,378	7,844	1,534
Not related to head	311	243	68	2,169	2,169	—	3,078	2,695	383
Primary individual: Male	457	292	165	2,073	2,073	—	6,468	4,954	1,514
Female	723	496	227	4,476	4,476	—	12,003	9,709	2,294
Inmate of institution	283	249	34	1,105	1,105	—	1,964	1,717	247
Other, in group quarters	38	36	2	477	477	—	509	455	54

(continued overleaf)

SOCIAL CHARACTERISTICS OF THE BLACK POPULATION, FOR SELECTED AREAS: 1970

Delaware, District of Columbia, Florida—continued

	DELAWARE			DISTRICT OF COLUMBIA			FLORIDA		
	TOTAL	Urban Total	Rural Total	TOTAL	Urban Total	Rural Total	TOTAL	Urban Total	Rural Total
FAMILIES BY PRESENCE AND NUMBER OF OWN CHILDREN UNDER 18 YEARS									
All families	16,074	11,521	4,553	119,678	119,678	—	215,534	180,764	34,770
With own children under 18 years	10,072	7,269	2,803	70,539	70,539	—	133,669	112,646	21,023
Number of own children under 18 years	28,536	19,950	8,586	169,460	169,460	—	380,509	314,175	66,334
Number of own children under 6 years	8,688	6,070	2,618	51,854	51,854	—	113,193	94,505	18,688
Number of own children 6 to 17 years	19,848	13,880	5,968	117,606	117,606	—	267,316	219,670	47,646
With own children under 6 years only	2,229	1,635	594	17,402	17,402	—	27,133	23,457	3,676
With own children under 6 and 6 to 17 years	3,077	2,189	888	17,846	17,846	—	42,054	34,946	7,108
Husband-wife families	10,673	7,455	3,218	78,919	78,919	—	143,533	119,053	24,480
With own children under 18 years	6,540	4,577	1,963	46,022	46,022	—	88,450	73,342	15,108
Number of own children under 18 years	18,654	12,614	6,040	109,300	109,300	—	253,632	205,080	48,552
Number of own children under 6 years	5,734	3,882	1,852	36,190	36,190	—	79,879	65,615	14,264
Number of own children 6 to 17 years	12,920	8,732	4,188	73,110	73,110	—	173,753	139,465	34,288
With own children under 6 years only	1,520	1,105	415	12,813	12,813	—	20,256	17,354	2,902
With own children under 6 and 6 to 17 years	2,031	1,393	638	11,815	11,815	—	28,539	23,259	5,280
Families with female head	4,513	3,453	1,060	34,349	34,349	—	61,664	53,208	8,456
With own children under 18 years	3,132	2,428	704	22,092	22,092	—	40,589	35,523	5,066
Number of own children under 18 years	9,006	6,784	2,222	55,203	55,203	—	115,660	99,999	15,661
Number of own children under 6 years	2,690	2,031	659	14,531	14,531	—	30,510	26,629	3,881
Number of own children 6 to 17 years	6,316	4,753	1,563	40,672	40,672	—	85,150	73,370	11,780
With own children under 6 years only	612	472	140	4,109	4,109	—	6,041	5,417	624
With own children 6 to 17	972	746	226	5,677	5,677	—	12,542	10,895	1,647
MARITAL STATUS									
Male, 14 years old and over	24,076	17,105	6,971	174,837	174,837	—	318,610	260,155	58,455
Single	8,888	6,305	2,583	61,235	61,235	—	111,306	89,295	22,011
Married, except separated	11,816	8,306	3,510	86,677	86,677	—	159,600	131,623	27,977
14 to 19 years	90	66	24	720	720	—	1,890	1,541	349
20 to 24 years	1,047	775	272	7,727	7,727	—	13,136	11,088	2,048
25 to 34 years	2,908	2,100	808	22,428	22,428	—	38,378	32,517	5,861
35 to 44 years	2,655	1,855	800	19,347	19,347	—	35,989	30,149	5,840
45 to 64 years	3,991	2,764	1,227	29,490	29,490	—	53,187	43,229	9,958
65 years and over	1,125	746	379	6,965	6,965	—	17,020	13,099	3,921
Separated	1,621	1,191	430	14,283	14,283	—	22,183	18,551	3,632
Widowed	1,054	722	332	6,471	6,471	—	15,240	12,187	3,053
Divorced	697	581	116	6,171	6,171	—	10,281	8,499	1,782
Female, 14 years old and over	27,007	19,445	7,562	207,943	207,943	—	363,149	304,013	59,136
Single	8,414	6,043	2,371	63,389	63,389	—	98,770	81,942	16,828
Married, except separated	11,673	8,120	3,553	85,987	85,987	—	159,251	132,190	27,061
14 to 19 years	361	242	119	2,291	2,291	—	6,451	5,264	1,187
20 to 24 years	1,494	1,059	435	11,654	11,654	—	19,556	16,749	2,807
25 to 34 years	2,970	2,126	844	22,620	22,620	—	41,157	34,924	6,233
35 to 44 years	2,663	1,836	827	19,176	19,176	—	36,103	30,276	5,827
45 to 64 years	3,467	2,372	1,095	26,224	26,224	—	46,428	37,591	8,837
65 years and over	718	485	233	4,022	4,022	—	9,556	7,386	2,170
Separated	2,546	1,975	571	23,121	23,121	—	36,685	32,145	4,540
Widowed	3,235	2,354	881	24,193	24,193	—	50,821	41,774	9,047
Divorced	1,139	953	186	11,253	11,253	—	17,622	15,962	1,660

	Georgia			Illinois			Indiana		
	TOTAL	Urban Total	Rural Total	TOTAL	Urban Total	Rural Total	TOTAL	Urban Total	Rural Total
BLACK POPULATION—									
Male, All ages	558,207	362,890	195,317	673,097	659,089	14,008	171,942	166,230	5,712
Under 5 years	65,607	42,089	23,518	78,414	77,663	751	19,088	18,883	205
5 to 9 years	73,842	46,619	27,223	90,387	89,457	930	21,907	21,672	235
10 to 14 years	75,816	47,494	28,322	90,421	89,113	1,308	23,229	22,879	350
15 to 19 years	65,898	40,882	25,016	70,142	68,130	2,012	19,990	17,973	2,017
20 to 24 years	46,198	31,390	14,808	47,776	46,137	1,639	12,531	11,700	831
25 to 29 years	33,551	23,269	10,282	44,432	43,199	1,233	10,390	9,840	550
30 to 34 years	27,534	18,929	8,605	39,604	38,634	970	8,889	8,610	279
35 to 39 years	25,084	17,534	7,550	38,322	37,435	887	8,674	8,487	187
40 to 44 years	24,221	16,662	7,559	36,926	36,163	763	9,306	9,114	192
45 to 49 years	23,195	15,745	7,450	33,472	32,830	642	8,833	8,688	145
50 to 54 years	22,908	15,159	7,749	27,523	27,000	523	7,175	7,028	147
55 to 59 years	21,570	14,068	7,502	22,605	22,049	556	6,445	6,325	120
60 to 64 years	17,886	11,422	6,464	18,341	17,869	472	5,157	5,043	114
65 to 69 years	14,546	9,111	5,435	15,105	14,613	492	4,092	3,977	115
70 to 74 years	9,133	5,657	3,476	9,734	9,396	338	2,942	2,860	82
75 to 79 years	5,477	3,397	2,080	5,309	5,032	277	1,739	1,676	63
80 to 84 years	3,168	1,880	1,288	2,575	2,455	120	860	817	43
85 years and over	2,573	1,583	990	2,009	1,914	95	695	658	37
Under 18 years	257,013	161,589	95,424	304,651	300,328	4,323	77,117	75,002	2,115
62 years and over	44,974	27,995	16,979	45,061	43,466	1,595	13,192	12,794	398
65 years and over	34,897	21,628	13,269	34,732	33,410	1,322	10,328	9,988	340
Median age	19.8	20.7	18.7	20.8	20.7	26.5	20.7	20.7	20.3
Female, All ages	628,942	423,794	205,148	752,577	743,542	9,035	185,522	183,199	2,323
Under 5 years	65,110	41,961	23,149	79,245	78,528	717	19,151	18,970	181
5 to 9 years	73,802	47,203	26,599	89,767	88,881	886	22,196	21,978	218
10 to 14 years	75,223	47,311	27,912	91,625	90,505	1,120	23,185	22,913	272
15 to 19 years	68,151	44,036	24,115	74,064	73,136	928	17,750	17,509	241
20 to 24 years	52,188	37,223	14,965	62,768	62,327	441	14,858	14,692	166
25 to 29 years	38,373	27,485	10,888	54,759	54,415	344	11,834	11,729	105
30 to 34 years	33,039	23,582	9,457	49,676	49,303	373	10,446	10,322	124
35 to 39 years	31,169	22,309	8,860	45,982	45,587	395	10,549	10,447	102
40 to 44 years	31,359	22,109	9,250	43,257	42,798	459	10,713	10,568	145
45 to 49 years	28,897	20,075	8,822	37,660	37,157	503	9,639	9,511	128
50 to 54 years	28,353	19,621	8,732	31,221	30,732	489	7,980	7,849	131
55 to 59 years	26,521	18,224	8,297	25,664	25,135	529	6,905	6,803	102
60 to 64 years	23,012	15,903	7,109	22,138	21,605	533	5,777	5,661	116
65 to 69 years	21,081	14,589	6,492	18,218	17,737	481	4,930	4,828	102
70 to 74 years	13,801	9,506	4,295	12,005	11,637	368	3,285	3,201	84
75 to 79 years	8,614	5,785	2,829	7,113	6,916	197	2,154	2,110	44
80 to 84 years	5,610	3,700	1,910	4,010	3,864	146	1,237	1,209	28
85 years and over	4,639	3,172	1,467	3,405	3,279	126	933	899	34
Under 18 years	256,555	162,860	93,695	307,184	303,852	3,332	76,878	76,054	824
62 years and over	67,010	45,894	21,116	57,442	55,805	1,637	15,891	15,535	356
65 years and over	53,745	36,752	16,993	44,751	43,443	1,318	12,539	12,247	292
Median age	23.1	24.2	20.3	23.3	23.3	31.1	22.9	22.8	29.0

(continued overleaf)

SOCIAL CHARACTERISTICS OF THE BLACK POPULATION, FOR SELECTED AREAS: 1970

Georgia, Illinois, Indiana—continued

	GEORGIA			ILLINOIS			INDIANA		
	TOTAL	Urban Total	Rural Total	TOTAL	Urban Total	Rural Total	TOTAL	Urban Total	Rural Total
RELATIONSHIP TO HEAD OF HOUSEHOLD									
All persons	1,187,149	785,684	400,465	1,425,674	1,402,631	23,043	357,464	349,429	8,035
In households	1,155,233	762,858	392,375	1,394,777	1,379,853	14,924	346,517	342,277	4,240
Head	302,150	213,147	89,003	396,558	392,197	4,361	96,851	95,592	1,259
14 to 24 years	22,692	17,422	5,180	33,702	33,494	208	8,026	7,946	80
25 to 34 years	56,541	42,137	14,404	96,000	95,534	466	20,144	19,975	169
35 to 44 years	55,348	40,949	15,399	92,735	92,107	628	21,114	20,889	215
45 to 64 years	110,063	75,501	34,562	128,066	126,384	1,682	33,725	33,257	468
65 years and over	56,596	37,138	19,458	46,055	44,678	1,377	13,842	13,515	327
Primary individual: Male	21,609	15,732	5,877	41,272	40,753	519	9,342	9,183	159
Female	36,060	28,768	7,292	47,537	46,926	611	10,540	10,418	122
Family head: Male	174,205	115,193	59,012	219,146	216,579	2,567	57,945	57,071	874
Female	70,276	53,454	16,822	88,603	87,939	664	19,024	18,920	104
Wife of head	162,502	107,543	54,959	204,432	202,028	2,404	54,287	53,446	841
Child of head	523,805	334,043	189,762	644,432	637,828	6,604	159,128	157,419	1,709
Other relative of head	143,389	89,289	54,100	109,910	108,706	1,204	27,955	27,676	279
Not related to head	23,387	18,836	4,551	39,445	39,094	351	8,296	8,144	152
In group quarters	31,916	23,826	8,090	30,897	22,778	8,119	10,947	7,152	3,795
Inmate of institution	15,416	9,653	5,763	17,654	10,099	7,555	5,798	3,670	2,128
Other	16,500	14,173	2,327	13,243	12,679	564	5,149	3,482	1,667
Persons per household	3.82	3.58	4.41	3.52	3.52	3.42	3.58	3.58	3.37
Persons per family	4.39	4.15	4.94	4.12	4.11	4.16	4.14	4.14	3.89
Persons, under 18 years old	513,568	324,449	189,119	611,835	604,180	7,655	153,995	151,056	2,939
Head or wife of head	1,927	1,303	624	1,542	1,509	33	398	393	5
Own child of head	417,460	267,888	149,572	546,766	541,213	5,553	133,837	132,453	1,384
In husband-wife households	286,096	170,911	115,185	335,521	331,504	4,017	91,964	90,746	1,218
Percent of total persons under 18 years	55.7	52.7	60.9	54.8	54.9	52.5	59.7	60.1	41.4
In household with female head	119,846	90,117	29,729	197,416	196,051	1,365	38,538	38,404	134
Other relative of head	86,464	50,166	36,298	52,737	51,990	747	15,468	15,318	150
Not related to head	3,758	2,608	1,150	5,192	5,095	97	1,790	1,753	37
In group quarters	3,959	2,484	1,475	5,598	4,373	1,225	2,504	1,139	1,363
Persons, 65 years old and over	88,642	58,380	30,262	79,483	76,843	2,640	22,857	22,235	632
Head of family: Male	22,781	13,404	9,377	20,076	19,397	679	6,431	6,253	178
Female	11,746	7,866	3,880	5,683	5,550	133	1,769	1,738	31
Wife of head	11,716	6,831	4,885	10,393	10,038	355	3,368	3,263	105
Other family member	15,321	10,316	5,005	14,483	14,289	194	3,583	3,517	66
Not related to head	2,386	1,810	576	5,148	5,082	66	1,002	980	22
Primary individual: Male	6,065	3,940	2,125	6,919	6,684	235	1,929	1,879	50
Female	16,004	11,928	4,076	13,377	13,047	330	3,713	3,645	68
Inmate of institution	2,227	1,939	288	2,805	2,184	621	947	839	108
Other, in group quarters	396	346	50	559	572	27	125	121	4

FAMILIES BY PRESENCE AND NUMBER OF OWN CHILDREN UNDER 18 YEARS

All families	244,481	168,647	75,834	307,749	304,518	3,231	76,969	75,991	978
With own children under 18 years	144,775	99,234	45,541	196,732	195,032	1,700	48,163	47,671	492
Number of own children under 18 years	417,460	267,888	149,572	546,766	541,213	5,553	133,837	132,453	1,384
Number of own children under 6 years	123,655	81,265	42,390	165,374	163,889	1,485	38,765	38,388	377
Number of own children 6 to 17 years	293,805	186,623	107,182	381,392	377,324	4,068	95,072	94,065	1,007
With own children under 6 years only	29,741	21,886	7,855	43,616	43,333	283	10,465	10,375	90
With own children under 6 and 6 to 17 years	45,804	29,697	16,107	59,619	59,058	561	14,096	13,960	136
Husband-wife families	162,492	107,575	54,917	205,596	203,193	2,403	54,657	53,822	835
With own children under 18 years	98,121	63,677	34,444	125,321	123,996	1,235	33,267	32,833	434
Number of own children under 18 years	286,096	170,911	115,185	335,521	331,504	4,017	91,964	90,746	1,218
Number of own children under 6 years	90,803	56,150	34,653	106,282	105,194	1,088	28,190	27,844	346
Number of own children 6 to 17 years	195,293	114,761	80,532	229,239	226,310	2,929	63,774	62,902	872
With own children under 6 years only	23,242	16,513	6,729	31,370	31,147	223	8,053	7,970	83
With own children under 6 and 6 to 17 years	31,779	19,232	12,547	36,677	36,277	400	9,865	9,740	125
Families with female head	70,276	53,454	16,822	88,603	87,939	664	19,024	18,920	104
With own children under 18 years	42,103	32,676	9,427	65,943	65,543	400	13,527	13,483	44
Number of own children under 18 years	119,846	90,117	29,729	197,416	196,051	1,365	38,538	38,404	134
Number of own children under 6 years	30,108	23,477	6,631	55,691	55,340	351	9,826	9,826	25
Number of own children 6 to 17 years	89,738	66,640	23,098	141,725	140,711	1,014	28,687	28,578	109
With own children under 6 years only	5,756	4,884	872	11,299	11,253	46	2,189	2,185	4
With own children under 6 and 6 to 17 years	13,024	9,870	3,154	21,702	21,558	144	3,980	3,970	10

MARITAL STATUS

Male, 14 years old and over	358,173	236,285	121,888	431,218	419,871	11,347	112,314	107,284	5,030
Single	131,819	84,168	47,651	147,374	141,726	5,648	38,587	35,306	3,281
Married, except separated	182,334	120,513	61,871	221,982	217,952	4,030	58,652	57,346	1,306
14 to 19 years	2,508	1,702	806	2,121	2,706	45	565	554	11
20 to 24 years	17,597	12,191	5,406	18,233	17,850	383	4,825	4,667	148
25 to 34 years	41,841	28,922	12,919	56,655	55,769	886	13,515	12,848	367
35 to 44 years	36,201	24,641	11,560	54,003	53,243	760	13,419	13,185	234
45 to 64 years	62,415	39,986	22,429	70,974	69,754	1,220	20,362	20,007	355
65 years and over	19,474	13,071	8,751	19,996	19,260	736	6,266	6,075	191
Separated		14,225	5,249	26,103	25,448	655	4,500	4,358	142
Widowed	16,975	11,321	5,624	17,906	17,421	485	4,566	4,456	110
Divorced	7,521	6,058	1,463	17,853	17,324	529	6,009	5,818	191
Female, 14 years old and over	429,835	296,758	133,077	509,532	502,981	6,551	125,395	123,697	1,698
Single	123,196	81,686	41,510	138,752	137,009	1,743	33,943	33,500	443
Married, except separated	181,946	120,963	60,983	220,387	217,577	2,810	57,931	57,020	911
14 to 19 years	7,743	5,209	2,534	7,067	6,990	77	1,950	1,930	20
20 to 24 years	23,648	16,620	7,028	27,964	27,766	198	6,979	6,889	80
25 to 34 years	43,180	30,013	13,167	60,728	60,322	406	13,847	13,682	165
35 to 44 years	37,989	25,575	12,414	52,934	52,401	533	13,792	13,596	196
45 to 64 years	56,428	35,856	20,572	60,038	58,892	1,146	17,693	17,366	327
65 years and over	12,958	7,690	5,268	11,656	11,206	450	3,670	3,547	123
Separated	39,182	30,752	8,430	56,171	55,618	553	8,322	8,281	41
Widowed	71,614	51,437	20,177	59,709	58,564	1,145	14,717	14,488	229
Divorced	13,897	11,920	1,977	34,513	34,213	300	10,482	10,408	74

SOCIAL CHARACTERISTICS OF THE BLACK POPULATION, FOR SELECTED AREAS: 1970

BLACK POPULATION—	Iowa			Kansas			Louisiana		
	TOTAL	Urban Total	Rural Total	TOTAL	Urban Total	Rural Total	TOTAL	Urban Total	Rural Total
Male, All ages	15,958	15,516	442	52,932	49,503	3,429	515,231	343,861	171,370
Under 5 years	1,961	1,921	40	5,556	5,358	198	62,511	41,588	20,923
5 to 9 years	2,136	2,104	32	6,643	6,360	283	68,946	45,467	23,479
10 to 14 years	1,974	1,923	51	6,683	6,366	317	72,709	47,390	25,319
15 to 19 years	1,824	1,766	58	5,463	5,143	320	62,842	41,293	21,549
20 to 24 years	1,424	1,378	46	6,003	5,663	340	38,054	26,814	11,240
25 to 29 years	924	904	20	3,214	2,997	217	27,147	18,608	8,539
30 to 34 years	829	800	29	2,501	2,291	210	22,946	15,520	7,426
35 to 39 years	756	742	14	2,549	2,306	243	21,423	14,662	6,761
40 to 44 years	758	735	23	2,379	2,136	243	22,123	15,518	6,605
45 to 49 years	714	703	11	2,238	2,068	170	21,270	15,188	6,082
50 to 54 years	601	592	9	2,038	1,870	168	19,923	13,513	6,410
55 to 59 years	544	520	24	1,895	1,751	144	19,133	12,753	6,380
60 to 64 years	450	420	30	1,612	1,482	130	17,433	11,454	5,979
65 to 69 years	374	354	20	1,406	1,273	133	15,453	9,980	5,473
70 to 74 years	312	297	15	1,144	1,034	110	10,331	6,463	3,868
75 to 79 years	191	185	6	808	716	92	6,447	3,871	2,576
80 to 84 years	110	104	6	482	411	71	3,634	2,082	1,552
85 years and over	76	68	8	318	278	40	2,906	1,697	1,209
Under 18 years	7,113	6,960	153	22,198	21,209	989	244,246	160,103	84,143
62 years and over	1,312	1,240	72	5,107	4,576	531	48,929	30,760	18,169
65 years and over	1,063	1,008	55	4,158	3,712	446	38,771	24,093	14,678
Median age	20.3	20.2	24.3	21.8	21.3	30.9	19.3	19.5	18.7
Female, All ages	16,638	16,224	414	54,045	51,648	2,397	571,601	393,555	178,046
Under 5 years	1,801	1,752	49	5,752	5,535	217	61,985	41,385	20,600
5 to 9 years	2,081	2,045	36	6,542	6,285	257	68,910	45,490	23,420
10 to 14 years	2,016	1,983	33	6,573	6,279	294	70,931	46,655	24,276
15 to 19 years	1,876	1,833	43	5,374	5,158	216	64,293	43,030	21,263
20 to 24 years	1,478	1,445	33	4,382	4,236	146	45,017	33,049	11,968
25 to 29 years	984	959	25	3,222	3,113	109	32,535	23,451	9,084
30 to 34 years	938	915	23	2,817	2,697	120	28,745	20,637	8,108
35 to 39 years	870	847	23	2,782	2,639	143	27,531	19,871	7,660
40 to 44 years	805	789	16	2,689	2,573	116	28,138	20,439	7,699
45 to 49 years	772	754	18	2,504	2,389	115	25,943	18,743	7,200
50 to 54 years	660	642	18	2,223	2,129	94	24,052	16,970	7,082
55 to 59 years	589	567	22	2,100	1,986	114	22,225	15,354	6,871
60 to 64 years	506	490	16	1,897	1,780	117	20,761	14,537	6,224
65 to 69 years	396	379	17	1,753	1,657	96	19,572	13,479	6,093
70 to 74 years	361	340	21	1,409	1,328	81	12,868	8,658	4,210
75 to 79 years	249	238	11	896	827	69	8,498	5,536	2,962
80 to 84 years	135	130	5	650	601	49	5,066	3,305	1,761
85 years and over	121	116	5	480	436	44	4,531	2,966	1,565
Under 18 years	6,950	6,805	145	22,156	21,255	901	242,161	159,654	82,507
62 years and over	1,560	1,490	70	6,304	5,897	407	62,596	42,352	20,244
65 years and over	1,262	1,203	59	5,188	4,849	339	50,535	33,944	16,591
Median age	21.8	21.7	27.6	23.2	23.0	28.1	22.2	23.1	19.9

RELATIONSHIP TO HEAD OF HOUSEHOLD

All persons	32,596	31,740	856	106,977	101,151	5,826	1,086,832	737,416	349,415
In households	30,820	30,147	673	100,468	96,000	4,468	1,061,006	719,560	341,445
Head	8,911	8,736	175	30,054	28,646	1,408	276,580	196,590	79,990
14 to 24 years	1,029	1,017	12	2,993	2,927	66	18,566	14,535	4,031
25 to 34 years	1,938	1,905	33	5,739	5,526	213	47,892	35,567	12,225
35 to 44 years	1,798	1,768	30	5,611	5,371	240	50,605	37,269	13,336
45 to 64 years	2,778	2,716	62	9,580	9,132	448	99,414	70,095	29,319
65 years and over	1,368	1,330	38	6,131	5,690	441	60,103	39,024	21,079
Primary individual: Male	1,083	1,065	18	3,082	2,897	185	21,882	15,886	5,996
Female	982	971	11	4,102	3,951	151	33,344	25,748	7,596
Family head: Male	4,866	4,732	134	16,640	15,780	860	160,204	107,733	52,471
Female	1,980	1,968	12	6,230	6,018	212	61,150	47,223	13,927
Wife of head	4,433	4,286	147	15,472	14,683	789	149,566	100,684	48,882
Child of head	14,343	14,067	276	46,177	44,230	1,947	504,524	334,672	169,852
Other relative of head	2,219	2,174	45	6,522	6,265	257	114,543	75,273	39,270
Not related to head	914	884	30	2,243	2,176	67	15,793	12,341	3,452
In group quarters	1,776	1,593	183	6,509	5,151	1,358	25,826	17,856	7,970
Inmate of institution	720	598	122	2,314	1,349	965	11,076	4,495	6,581
Other	1,056	995	61	4,195	3,802	393	14,750	13,361	1,389
Persons per household	3.46	3.45	3.85	3.34	3.35	3.17	3.84	3.66	4.27
Persons per family	4.07	4.06	4.21	3.98	3.99	3.79	4.47	4.30	4.89
Persons, under 18 years old	14,063	13,765	298	44,354	42,464	1,890	485,407	319,757	166,650
Head or wife of head	52	50	2	153	149	4	1,673	1,176	497
Own child of head	12,351	12,128	223	39,381	37,703	1,678	405,963	269,520	136,443
In husband-wife households	7,413	7,212	201	24,710	23,623	1,087	280,103	173,938	106,165
Percent of total persons under 18 years	52.7	52.4	67.4	55.7	55.6	57.5	57.6	54.4	63.7
In household with female head	4,694	4,674	20	13,901	13,354	547	114,459	88,629	25,830
Other relative of head	1,261	1,242	19	3,854	3,715	139	71,332	44,458	26,874
Not related to head	202	185	17	470	446	24	3,449	2,312	1,137
In group quarters	197	160	37	496	451	45	3,990	2,291	1,699
Persons, 65 years old and over	2,325	2,211	114	9,346	8,561	785	89,306	58,037	31,269
Head of family: Male	609	580	29	2,590	2,370	220	25,440	15,109	10,331
Female	157	155	2	674	653	21	10,552	7,178	3,374
Wife of head	365	335	30	1,500	1,368	132	13,097	7,590	5,507
Other family member	334	322	12	990	935	55	12,181	8,534	3,647
Not related to head	98	93	5	307	294	13	2,022	1,559	463
Primary individual: Male	215	213	2	904	809	95	7,673	5,003	2,670
Female	387	382	5	1,963	1,858	105	16,438	11,734	4,704
Inmate of institution	146	117	29	383	242	141	1,552	1,031	521
Other, in group quarters	14	14	—	35	32	3	351	299	52

(continued overleaf)

SOCIAL CHARACTERISTICS OF THE BLACK POPULATION, FOR SELECTED AREAS: 1970

Iowa, Kansas, Louisiana—continued

	IOWA			KANSAS			LOUISIANA		
	TOTAL	Urban Total	Rural Total	TOTAL	Urban Total	Rural Total	TOTAL	Urban Total	Rural Total
FAMILIES BY PRESENCE AND NUMBER OF OWN CHILDREN UNDER 18 YEARS									
All families	**6,846**	**6,700**	**146**	**22,870**	**21,798**	**1,072**	**221,354**	**154,956**	**66,398**
With own children under 18 years	4,390	4,321	69	13,912	13,354	558	134,143	93,951	40,192
Number of own children under 18 years	12,351	12,128	223	39,381	37,703	1,678	405,963	269,520	136,443
Number of own children under 6 years	3,912	3,825	87	12,059	11,601	458	121,100	81,619	39,481
Number of own children 6 to 17 years	8,439	8,303	136	27,322	26,102	1,220	284,863	187,901	96,962
With own children under 6 years only	1,056	1,042	14	3,272	3,160	112	27,648	20,452	7,196
With own children under 6 and 6 to 17 years	1,348	1,323	25	4,366	4,198	168	42,641	28,668	13,973
Husband-wife families	**4,592**	**4,461**	**131**	**15,849**	**15,038**	**811**	**149,537**	**100,680**	**48,857**
With own children under 18 years	2,739	2,675	64	9,033	8,640	393	91,812	61,155	30,657
Number of own children under 18 years	7,413	7,212	201	24,710	23,623	1,087	280,103	173,938	106,165
Number of own children under 6 years	2,479	2,395	84	7,734	7,424	310	87,814	55,822	31,992
Number of own children 6 to 17 years	4,934	4,817	117	16,976	16,199	777	192,289	118,116	74,173
With own children under 6 years only	738	724	14	2,307	2,212	95	21,414	15,402	6,012
With own children under 6 and 6 to 17 years	796	772	24	2,774	2,673	101	29,617	18,641	10,976
Families with female head	**1,980**	**1,968**	**12**	**6,230**	**6,018**	**212**	**61,150**	**47,223**	**13,927**
With own children under 18 years	1,540	1,536	4	4,556	4,404	152	37,905	29,943	7,962
Number of own children under 18 years	4,694	4,674	20	13,901	13,354	547	114,459	88,629	25,830
Number of own children under 6 years	1,379	1,376	3	4,144	4,010	134	30,416	24,069	6,347
Number of own children 6 to 17 years	3,315	3,298	17	9,757	9,344	413	84,043	64,560	19,483
With own children under 6 years only	294	294	—	911	897	14	5,464	4,542	922
With own children under 6 and 6 to 17 years	536	535	1	1,521	1,458	63	12,033	9,435	2,598
MARITAL STATUS									
Male, 14 years old and over	**10,253**	**9,922**	**331**	**35,375**	**32,689**	**2,685**	**325,758**	**218,930**	**106,828**
Single	3,797	3,647	150	12,681	11,711	970	121,928	79,919	42,009
Married, except separated	5,013	4,864	149	17,947	16,723	1,224	165,270	111,158	54,112
14 to 19 years	67	67	—	201	196	5	2,303	1,740	563
20 to 24 years	466	454	12	2,135	2,047	88	14,336	10,483	3,853
25 to 34 years	1,152	1,120	32	3,869	3,642	227	34,645	23,830	10,815
35 to 44 years	1,094	1,071	23	3,653	3,350	303	32,619	22,513	10,106
45 to 64 years	1,620	1,571	49	5,556	5,184	372	57,328	38,257	19,071
65 years and over	614	581	33	2,533	2,304	229	24,039	14,335	9,704
Separated	444	441	3	1,237	1,128	109	15,295	11,505	3,790
Widowed	419	406	13	1,545	1,403	142	15,521	10,318	5,203
Divorced	580	564	16	1,965	1,724	241	7,744	6,030	1,714
Female, 14 years old and over	**11,123**	**10,819**	**304**	**36,389**	**34,699**	**1,690**	**383,884**	**269,201**	**114,683**
Single	3,192	3,105	87	9,178	8,786	392	114,981	78,674	36,307
Married, except separated	4,789	4,619	170	16,584	15,655	929	166,314	112,598	53,716
14 to 19 years	187	181	6	646	627	19	6,978	4,960	2,018
20 to 24 years	624	608	16	2,007	1,925	82	20,249	14,652	5,597
25 to 34 years	1,099	1,064	35	3,778	3,602	176	37,614	25,978	11,636
35 to 44 years	1,011	985	26	3,455	3,249	206	34,987	24,196	10,791
45 to 64 years	1,461	1,405	56	5,117	4,808	309	52,293	34,475	17,818
65 years and over	407	376	31	1,581	1,444	137	14,193	8,337	5,856
Separated	731	726	5	2,238	2,188	50	30,199	24,234	5,965
Widowed	1,297	1,270	27	5,046	4,810	236	56,631	40,442	16,189
Divorced	1,114	1,099	15	3,343	3,260	83	15,759	13,253	2,506

BLACK POPULATION—	Maryland			Massachusetts			Michigan		
Male, All ages	**336,950**	**274,268**	**62,682**	**82,573**	**78,931**	**3,642**	**479,144**	**461,623**	**17,521**
Under 5 years	36,931	31,063	5,868	10,711	10,429	282	55,625	54,422	1,203
5 to 9 years	43,792	36,003	7,789	11,401	11,035	366	56,752	55,286	1,466
10 to 14 years	43,624	35,336	8,288	9,998	9,550	448	60,429	58,595	1,834
15 to 19 years	35,339	27,484	7,855	8,244	7,822	422	51,326	49,058	2,268
20 to 24 years	26,130	21,271	4,859	7,326	7,028	298	39,115	37,157	1,958
25 to 29 years	22,303	18,729	3,574	6,293	6,012	281	31,630	30,360	1,270
30 to 34 years	19,456	16,243	3,213	4,976	4,762	214	23,966	22,957	1,009
35 to 39 years	18,686	15,623	3,063	4,538	4,314	224	24,548	23,651	397
40 to 44 years	18,649	15,418	3,231	4,185	3,934	251	27,287	26,322	965
45 to 49 years	17,318	14,275	3,043	3,943	3,724	219	26,784	25,890	394
50 to 54 years	14,875	12,083	2,792	3,247	3,073	174	22,631	21,880	751
55 to 59 years	12,449	9,880	2,569	2,233	2,115	118	19,010	18,270	740
60 to 64 years	9,674	7,561	2,113	1,637	1,550	87	14,360	13,757	503
65 to 69 years	7,549	5,834	1,715	1,358	1,287	71	11,285	10,641	544
70 to 74 years	4,925	3,699	1,226	1,068	989	79	6,789	6,789	486
75 to 79 years	2,768	2,007	761	693	639	54	3,853	3,581	272
80 to 84 years	1,425	993	432	423	387	36	1,869	1,714	155
85 years and over	1,057	766	291	299	281	18	1,399	1,293	106
Under 18 years	146,971	119,984	26,987	37,078	35,694	1,384	205,273	199,399	5,874
62 years and over	23,213	17,558	5,655	4,738	4,431	307	33,700	31,688	2,012
65 years and over	17,724	13,299	4,425	3,841	3,583	258	25,681	24,018	1,663
Median age	21.7	21.7	21.6	20.6	20.4	25.1	22.0	21.8	25.1
Female, All ages	**362,529**	**302,516**	**60,013**	**93,244**	**90,425**	**2,819**	**511,922**	**498,480**	**13,442**
Under 5 years	36,642	30,542	6,100	10,761	10,539	222	55,261	54,092	1,169
5 to 9 years	43,351	35,846	7,505	11,468	11,136	332	56,669	55,203	1,466
10 to 14 years	43,609	35,547	8,062	10,198	9,854	344	59,860	58,267	1,593
15 to 19 years	36,918	30,073	6,845	8,798	8,498	300	53,361	51,939	1,422
20 to 24 years	31,197	27,111	4,086	9,062	8,894	168	45,513	45,513	830
25 to 29 years	25,834	22,499	3,335	9,062	8,894	149	34,842	34,204	638
30 to 34 years	22,602	19,516	3,086	7,767	7,618	170	29,024	28,397	627
35 to 39 years	21,422	18,281	3,141	6,079	5,909	179	29,270	28,635	635
40 to 44 years	20,540	17,318	3,222	5,335	5,156	179	30,585	29,873	712
45 to 49 years	19,082	16,003	3,079	5,028	4,849	169	28,206	27,498	708
50 to 54 years	15,896	13,209	2,687	4,517	4,348	136	23,814	23,149	665
55 to 59 years	13,259	10,913	2,346	3,583	3,447	125	19,241	18,563	678
60 to 64 years	10,424	8,396	2,028	2,827	2,702	97	15,291	14,626	665
65 to 69 years	8,837	7,119	1,718	2,246	2,149	88	12,251	11,628	623
70 to 74 years	5,719	4,555	1,164	1,907	1,819	73	8,230	7,754	476
75 to 79 years	3,446	2,702	744	1,491	1,418	40	4,819	4,560	259
80 to 84 years	2,089	1,587	502	1,009	969	26	2,684	2,535	149
85 years and over	1,662	1,299	363	634	612	22	2,171	2,044	127
Under 18 years	146,395	120,317	26,078	508	508	26	204,569	199,387	5,182
62 years and over	27,724	22,076	5,648	37,364	36,278	1,086	38,777	36,762	2,015
65 years and over	21,753	17,262	4,491	6,846	6,535	311	30,155	28,521	1,634
Median age	23.3	23.6	21.8	5,575	5,326	249	23.3	23.3	26.9

(continued overleaf)

SOCIAL CHARACTERISTICS OF THE BLACK POPULATION, FOR SELECTED AREAS: 1970

Maryland, Massachusetts, Michigan—continued

	MARYLAND			MASSACHUSETTS			MICHIGAN		
	TOTAL	Urban Total	Rural Total	TOTAL	Urban Total	Rural Total	TOTAL	Urban Total	Rural Total
RELATIONSHIP TO HEAD OF HOUSEHOLD									
All persons	699,479	576,784	122,695	175,817	169,356	6,461	991,066	960,103	30,963
In households	676,966	564,641	112,325	168,147	162,653	5,494	968,764	944,676	24,088
Head	182,325	155,323	27,002	51,494	49,923	1,571	277,425	270,446	6,979
14 to 24 years	14,251	13,241	1,010	6,120	6,053	67	27,175	26,863	312
25 to 34 years	41,460	37,041	4,419	13,821	13,557	264	59,076	58,164	912
35 to 44 years	41,593	35,958	5,635	11,263	10,873	390	60,629	59,496	1,133
45 to 64 years	63,024	52,232	10,792	14,631	14,057	574	98,067	95,366	2,701
65 years and over	21,997	16,851	5,146	5,659	5,383	276	32,478	30,557	1,921
Primary individual: Male	17,282	14,722	2,560	5,916	5,764	152	30,325	29,576	749
Female	18,167	16,196	1,971	7,050	6,924	126	28,694	27,943	751
Family head: Male	107,254	89,187	18,067	25,320	24,182	1,138	162,280	157,621	4,659
Female	39,622	35,218	4,404	13,208	13,053	155	56,126	55,306	820
Wife of head	99,695	82,994	16,701	22,930	21,934	996	150,684	146,311	4,373
Child of head	301,282	250,245	51,037	78,073	75,643	2,430	432,381	422,339	10,042
Other relative of head	69,375	55,173	14,202	10,529	10,268	261	79,462	77,459	2,003
Not related to head	24,289	20,906	3,383	5,121	4,885	236	28,812	28,121	691
In group quarters	22,513	12,143	10,370	7,670	6,703	967	22,302	15,427	6,875
Inmate of institution	13,258	5,173	8,085	2,806	1,983	823	14,354	8,003	6,321
Other	9,255	6,970	2,285	4,864	4,720	144	7,948	7,394	554
Persons per household	3.71	3.64	4.16	3.27	3.26	3.50	3.49	3.49	3.45
Persons per family	4.20	4.12	4.65	3.89	3.90	3.85	4.03	4.03	4.00
Persons, under 18 years old	293,366	240,301	53,065	74,442	71,972	2,470	409,842	398,786	11,056
Head or wife of head	628	520	108	190	188	2	1,300	1,279	21
Own child of head	245,103	204,995	40,108	67,965	65,924	2,041	361,256	352,733	8,523
In husband-wife households	165,090	133,740	31,350	39,073	37,320	1,753	237,879	231,070	6,809
Percent of total persons under 18 years	56.3	55.7	59.1	52.5	51.9	71.0	58.0	57.9	61.6
In household with female head	73,683	66,260	7,423	27,546	27,285	261	114,301	112,845	1,456
Other relative of head	38,146	28,954	9,192	4,628	4,505	123	39,604	38,463	1,141
Not related to head	4,754	3,716	1,038	845	769	76	4,270	4,059	211
In group quarters	4,735	2,116	2,619	814	586	228	3,412	2,252	1,160
Persons, 65 years old and over	39,477	30,561	8,916	9,416	8,909	507	55,836	52,539	3,297
Head of family: Male	9,882	7,302	2,580	2,022	1,879	143	15,617	14,564	1,053
Female	3,820	2,923	897	766	741	25	3,821	3,656	165
Wife of head	5,112	3,707	1,405	1,162	1,081	81	7,884	7,267	617
Other family member	7,696	6,337	1,359	1,373	1,300	73	9,677	9,314	363
Not related to head	2,641	2,252	389	397	375	22	3,143	3,019	124
Primary individual: Male	3,174	2,358	816	902	853	49	4,788	4,489	299
Female	5,121	4,268	853	1,969	1,910	59	8,252	7,848	404
Inmate of institution	1,683	1,146	537	717	663	54	2,338	2,077	261
Other, in group quarters	348	268	80	108	107	1	316	305	11

FAMILIES BY PRESENCE AND NUMBER OF OWN CHILDREN UNDER 18 YEARS

All families	146,876	124,405	22,471	38,528	1,293	218,406	212,927
With own children under 18 years	91,572	78,616	12,956	25,916	783	135,694	132,812
Number of own children under 18 years	245,103	204,995	40,108	67,965	2,041	361,256	352,733
Number of own children under 6 years	71,844	61,411	10,433	23,953	567	112,904	110,550
Number of own children 6 to 17 years	173,259	143,584	29,675	44,012	1,474	248,352	242,183
With own children under 6 years only	19,871	17,904	1,967	7,159	141	33,259	32,720
With own children under 6 and 6 to 17 years	27,003	22,783	4,220	7,803	210	38,607	37,743
Husband-wife families	100,061	83,353	16,708	23,816	1,101	152,241	147,799
With own children under 18 years	62,069	52,087	9,982	15,110	673	90,385	88,087
Number of own children under 18 years	165,090	133,740	31,350	39,073	1,753	237,879	231,070
Number of own children under 6 years	51,037	42,737	8,300	14,028	490	77,145	75,217
Number of own children 6 to 17 years	114,053	91,003	23,050	25,045	1,263	160,734	155,853
With own children under 6 years only	14,890	13,296	1,594	4,410	124	24,138	23,683
With own children under 6 and 6 to 17 years	18,564	15,230	3,334	4,574	185	25,708	24,995
Families with female head	39,622	35,218	4,404	13,208	155	56,126	55,306
With own children under 18 years	26,676	24,223	2,453	10,225	95	41,447	40,954
Number of own children under 18 years	73,683	66,260	7,423	27,546	261	114,301	112,845
Number of own children under 6 years	19,171	17,397	1,774	9,558	71	33,621	33,256
Number of own children 6 to 17 years	54,512	48,863	5,649	17,988	190	80,680	79,589
With own children under 6 years only	4,377	4,091	286	2,634	15	8,408	8,338
With own children under 6 and 6 to 17 years	7,910	7,143	767	3,108	23	12,185	12,057

MARITAL STATUS

Male, 14 years old and over	220,796	178,313	42,483	52,287	2,647	318,508	305,064
Single	79,212	60,800	18,412	19,675	1,050	107,675	101,683
Married, except separated	110,260	90,924	19,336	25,963	1,307	164,873	159,351
14 to 19 years	922	778	144	237	9	1,910	1,866
20 to 24 years	8,964	7,900	1,064	2,462	58	15,217	14,797
25 to 34 years	27,633	23,668	3,965	6,208	280	36,187	35,214
35 to 44 years	26,447	22,039	4,408	7,545	358	36,858	35,837
45 to 64 years	36,598	29,323	7,275	7,498	447	59,124	57,166
65 years and over	9,696	7,216	2,480	2,013	155	15,577	14,471
Separated	16,728	14,575	2,153	2,837	99	19,076	18,316
Widowed	8,689	6,850	1,839	1,743	84	11,755	11,236
Divorced	5,907	5,164	743	2,069	107	15,129	14,478
Female, 14 years old and over	247,192	207,256	39,936	62,696	1,990	352,053	342,494
Single	74,808	61,014	13,794	19,683	576	94,176	91,659
Married, except separated	109,681	90,942	18,739	25,069	1,091	162,384	157,575
14 to 19 years	3,047	2,630	417	720	13	6,037	5,931
20 to 24 years	13,372	11,782	1,590	3,408	72	21,405	21,070
25 to 34 years	29,274	25,088	4,186	7,464	259	37,710	36,858
35 to 44 years	26,035	21,561	4,474	5,730	289	38,017	37,047
45 to 64 years	32,109	25,625	6,484	6,417	366	50,457	48,591
65 years and over	5,844	4,256	1,588	1,330	92	8,758	8,078
Separated	26,195	24,017	2,178	7,181	61	32,725	32,267
Widowed	27,193	22,779	4,414	6,455	185	37,915	36,576
Divorced	9,315	8,504	811	4,308	77	24,853	24,417

SOCIAL CHARACTERISTICS OF THE BLACK POPULATION, FOR SELECTED AREAS: 1970

	Minnesota			Mississippi			Missouri		
	TOTAL	Urban Total	Rural Total	TOTAL	Urban Total	Rural Total	TOTAL	Urban Total	Rural Total
BLACK POPULATION—									
Male, All ages	17,641	17,105	536	386,580	152,191	234,389	226,296	214,795	11,501
Under 5 years	2,219	2,171	48	48,280	19,078	29,202	24,977	23,718	1,259
5 to 9 years	2,152	2,099	53	53,979	20,816	33,163	29,242	27,710	1,532
10 to 14 years	2,085	2,051	34	58,113	21,593	36,520	30,578	28,861	1,717
15 to 19 years	1,869	1,815	54	49,848	18,477	31,371	24,698	23,234	1,464
20 to 24 years	1,568	1,510	58	25,120	10,627	14,493	16,461	15,857	604
25 to 29 years	1,304	1,254	50	16,306	7,280	9,026	13,218	12,810	408
30 to 34 years	1,107	1,056	51	14,018	6,133	7,885	11,251	10,867	384
35 to 39 years	940	891	49	13,004	5,742	7,262	10,718	10,362	356
40 to 44 years	928	899	29	13,575	5,893	7,682	11,104	10,701	403
45 to 49 years	872	850	22	13,553	5,752	7,801	10,638	10,223	415
50 to 54 years	655	641	14	14,714	5,932	8,782	9,225	8,768	457
55 to 59 years	563	546	17	15,275	6,010	9,265	8,839	8,333	506
60 to 64 years	434	422	12	14,957	5,703	9,254	7,688	7,204	484
65 to 69 years	328	314	14	13,934	5,165	8,769	6,732	6,209	523
70 to 74 years	266	248	18	9,298	3,370	5,928	4,890	4,479	411
75 to 79 years	159	156	3	6,301	2,415	3,886	2,966	2,695	271
80 to 84 years	104	99	5	3,467	1,226	2,241	1,728	1,566	162
85 years and over	88	83	5	2,838	979	1,859	1,343	1,198	145
Under 18 years	7,534	7,379	155	192,777	73,246	119,531	100,631	95,113	5,518
62 years and over	1,165	1,112	53	44,704	16,552	28,152	22,046	20,234	1,812
65 years and over	945	900	45	35,838	13,155	22,683	17,659	16,147	1,512
Median age	21.6	21.4	27.1	18.3	19.0	17.9	21.1	21.2	19.2
Female, All ages	17,227	16,884	343	429,190	179,670	249,520	253,876	242,298	11,578
Under 5 years	2,108	2,054	54	48,771	19,541	29,230	25,113	23,873	1,240
5 to 9 years	2,216	2,169	47	53,825	21,119	32,706	28,764	27,277	1,487
10 to 14 years	1,946	1,916	30	56,694	21,576	35,118	30,891	29,241	1,650
15 to 19 years	1,760	1,722	38	50,177	19,405	30,772	25,367	24,016	1,351
20 to 24 years	1,634	1,613	21	29,952	13,524	16,428	20,022	19,433	589
25 to 29 years	1,263	1,251	12	20,114	9,412	10,702	15,824	15,369	455
30 to 34 years	1,000	980	20	18,477	8,612	9,865	14,033	13,561	472
35 to 39 years	926	911	15	17,568	8,123	9,445	14,004	13,535	469
40 to 44 years	864	853	11	18,909	8,592	10,317	13,845	13,332	513
45 to 49 years	823	809	14	18,067	7,918	10,149	12,951	12,455	496
50 to 54 years	615	595	20	18,078	7,922	10,156	11,245	10,740	505
55 to 59 years	551	541	10	17,820	7,762	10,058	10,476	9,968	508
60 to 64 years	435	427	8	17,368	7,601	9,767	9,269	8,777	492
65 to 69 years	394	376	18	16,994	7,285	9,709	8,511	8,016	495
70 to 74 years	288	277	11	10,984	4,765	6,219	5,838	5,493	345
75 to 79 years	196	187	9	7,151	3,053	4,098	3,777	3,551	226
80 to 84 years	111	106	5	4,361	1,850	2,511	2,218	2,047	171
85 years and over	97	97	—	3,880	1,610	2,270	1,728	1,614	114
Under 18 years	7,272	7,119	153	191,376	74,338	117,038	100,635	95,345	5,290
62 years and over	1,330	1,284	46	53,663	23,062	30,601	27,281	25,655	1,626
65 years and over	1,086	1,043	43	43,370	18,563	24,807	22,072	20,721	1,351
Median age	21.8	21.8	20.6	20.9	23.0	19.5	24.2	24.3	20.5

RELATIONSHIP TO HEAD OF HOUSEHOLD

All persons	34,868	33,989	879	815,770	331,851	483,909	480,172	457,093	23,079
In households	33,042	32,419	623	800,925	325,537	475,388	466,311	444,132	22,179
Head	10,365	10,207	158	196,264	88,658	107,606	136,487	130,566	5,921
14 to 24 years	1,303	1,297	6	10,724	5,548	5,176	10,259	9,976	283
25 to 34 years	2,575	2,546	29	27,971	14,029	13,942	26,726	26,052	674
35 to 44 years	2,180	2,147	33	31,072	14,889	16,183	27,233	26,399	834
45 to 64 years	3,049	3,003	46	74,407	32,731	41,676	47,185	45,030	2,155
65 years and over	1,258	1,214	44	52,090	21,461	30,629	25,084	23,109	1,975
Primary individual: Male	1,623	1,604	19	15,291	7,170	8,121	14,735	13,915	820
Female	1,238	1,225	13	23,599	13,769	9,830	19,501	18,845	656
Family head: Male	5,368	5,251	117	116,945	46,618	70,327	72,798	69,351	3,447
Female	2,136	2,127	9	40,429	21,101	19,328	29,453	28,455	3,197
Wife of head	4,436	4,327	109	108,443	43,272	65,171	67,618	64,421	
Child of head	15,120	14,833	287	381,174	147,835	233,339	210,385	199,824	10,561
Other relative of head	1,828	1,800	28	102,601	38,824	63,777	40,570	38,471	2,099
Not related to head	1,293	1,252	41	12,443	6,948	5,495	11,251	10,850	401
In group quarters	1,826	1,570	256	14,845	6,324	8,521	13,851	12,961	900
Inmate of institution	885	735	150	5,469	1,426	4,043	6,709	6,044	665
Other	941	835	106	9,376	4,898	4,478	7,152	6,917	235
Persons per household	3.19	3.18	3.94	4.08	3.67	4.42	3.42	3.40	3.75
Persons per family	3.85	3.84	4.37	4.76	4.40	5.04	4.12	4.10	4.57
Persons, under 18 years old	14,806	14,498	308	384,153	147,584	236,569	201,266	190,458	10,808
Head or wife of head	27	27	—	1,367	576	791	674	626	48
Own child of head	13,311	13,053	258	308,542	120,262	188,280	174,431	165,516	8,915
In husband-wife households	7,870	7,627	243	217,465	75,507	141,958	105,776	99,697	6,079
Percent of total persons under 18 years	53.2	52.6	78.9	56.6	51.2	60.0	52.6	52.3	56.2
In household with female head	5,156	5,146	10	80,609	41,033	39,576	63,809	61,320	2,489
Other relative of head	922	908	14	69,101	24,693	44,408	22,157	20,683	1,474
Not related to head	306	280	26	2,879	1,204	1,675	1,638	1,510	128
In group quarters	240	230	10	2,264	849	1,415	2,366	2,123	243
Persons, 65 years old and over	2,031	1,943	88	79,208	31,718	47,490	39,731	36,868	2,853
Head of family: Male	523	499	24	24,775	8,507	16,268	10,384	9,432	952
Female	112	108	4	8,363	3,707	4,656	3,059	2,849	210
Wife of head	274	258	16	12,911	4,292	8,619	5,548	5,038	510
Other family member	261	247	14	11,093	4,463	6,630	5,809	5,569	240
Not related to head	84	82	2	1,936	983	953	1,790	1,723	67
Primary individual: Male	241	232	9	6,258	2,610	3,648	4,057	3,643	414
Female	382	375	7	12,694	6,637	6,057	7,584	7,185	399
Inmate of institution	143	131	12	957	391	566	1,209	1,149	60
Other, in group quarters	11	11	—	221	128	93	291	280	11

(continued overleaf)

SOCIAL CHARACTERISTICS OF THE BLACK POPULATION, FOR SELECTED AREAS: 1970

Minnesota, Mississippi, Missouri—continued

	MINNESOTA			MISSISSIPPI			MISSOURI		
	TOTAL	Urban Total	Rural Total	TOTAL	Urban Total	Rural Total	TOTAL	Urban Total	Rural Total
FAMILIES BY PRESENCE AND NUMBER OF OWN CHILDREN UNDER 18 YEARS									
All families	7,504	7,378	126	157,374	67,719	89,655	102,251	97,806	4,445
With own children under 18 years	4,943	4,876	67	91,616	39,417	52,199	61,035	58,620	2,415
Number of own children under 18 years	13,311	13,053	258	308,542	120,262	188,280	174,431	165,516	8,915
Number of own children under 6 years	4,594	4,495	99	88,723	35,784	52,939	50,906	48,461	2,445
Number of own children 6 to 17 years	8,717	8,558	159	219,819	84,478	135,341	123,525	117,055	6,470
With own children under 6 years only	1,369	1,356	13	15,858	7,612	8,246	12,826	12,471	355
With own children under 6 and 6 to 17 years	1,407	1,392	15	32,904	13,218	19,686	18,903	17,968	935
Husband-wife families	5,075	4,965	110	108,322	43,231	65,091	68,001	64,820	3,181
With own children under 18 years	3,058	2,995	63	63,684	24,948	38,736	38,366	36,726	1,640
Number of own children under 18 years	7,870	7,627	243	217,465	75,507	141,958	105,776	99,697	6,079
Number of own children under 6 years	2,777	2,680	97	66,033	24,179	41,854	32,984	31,290	1,694
Number of own children 6 to 17 years	5,093	4,947	146	151,432	51,328	100,104	72,792	68,407	4,385
With own children under 6 years only	896	883	13	12,664	5,771	6,893	9,487	9,220	267
With own children under 6 and 6 to 17 years	871	857	14	23,293	8,321	14,972	11,481	10,848	633
Families with female head	2,136	2,127	9	40,429	21,101	19,328	29,453	28,455	998
With own children under 18 years	1,753	1,750	3	24,136	12,993	11,143	20,668	20,013	655
Number of own children under 18 years	5,156	5,146	10	80,609	41,033	39,576	63,809	61,320	2,489
Number of own children under 6 years	1,746	1,746	—	20,233	10,706	9,527	16,699	16,027	672
Number of own children 6 to 17 years	3,410	3,400	10	60,376	30,327	30,049	47,110	45,293	1,817
With own children under 6 years only	445	445	—	2,645	1,617	1,028	2,947	2,875	72
With own children under 6 and 6 to 17 years	513	513	—	8,714	4,568	4,146	7,014	6,742	272
MARITAL STATUS									
Male, 14 years old and over	11,596	11,187	409	237,943	94,937	143,006	147,410	140,045	7,365
Single	4,343	4,160	183	90,856	34,472	56,384	49,909	47,117	2,792
Married, except separated	5,499	5,330	169	118,876	47,540	71,336	74,174	70,722	3,452
14 to 19 years	68	67	1	1,515	617	898	934	902	32
20 to 24 years	491	481	10	8,740	3,921	4,819	6,141	5,953	188
25 to 34 years	1,462	1,417	45	21,073	9,423	11,650	16,327	15,832	495
35 to 44 years	1,256	1,210	46	19,981	8,528	11,453	15,376	14,829	547
45 to 64 years	1,676	1,634	42	44,127	16,933	27,194	25,233	23,944	1,289
65 years and over	546	521	25	23,440	8,118	15,322	10,163	9,262	901
Separated	546	525	21	10,667	5,219	5,448	8,985	8,663	322
Widowed	385	376	9	13,609	5,537	8,072	7,689	7,127	562
Divorced	823	796	27	3,935	2,169	1,766	6,653	6,416	237
Female, 14 years old and over	11,311	11,095	216	281,521	121,723	159,798	175,079	167,543	7,536
Single	3,467	3,399	68	86,257	34,717	51,540	47,119	44,880	2,239
Married, except separated	4,695	4,576	119	120,090	48,333	71,757	73,323	69,883	3,440
14 to 19 years	123	120	3	4,925	2,036	2,889	2,570	2,456	114
20 to 24 years	601	592	9	12,690	5,785	6,905	8,689	8,435	254
25 to 34 years	1,269	1,243	26	23,853	10,567	13,286	17,060	16,494	566
35 to 44 years	1,044	1,025	19	23,118	9,662	13,456	16,012	15,337	675
45 to 64 years	1,355	1,311	44	41,692	15,640	26,052	22,938	21,643	1,295
65 years and over	303	285	18	13,812	4,643	9,169	6,054	5,518	536
Separated	846	842	4	19,808	10,862	8,946	16,447	16,037	410
Widowed	1,141	1,121	20	47,446	22,719	24,727	25,284	24,065	1,219
Divorced	1,162	1,157	5	7,920	5,092	2,828	12,906	12,678	228

BLACK POPULATION—

	Nebraska			Nevada			New Jersey		
Male, All ages	19,291	18,855	436	13,940	13,401	539	363,756	342,600	21,155
Under 5 years	2,184	2,171	13	1,943	1,903	40	44,653	42,747	1,906
5 to 9 years	2,723	2,712	11	1,921	1,873	48	48,727	46,308	2,419
10 to 14 years	2,623	2,589	34	1,667	1,608	59	46,014	43,195	2,819
15 to 19 years	2,291	2,125	166	1,298	1,222	76	36,251	33,515	2,736
20 to 24 years	1,703	1,590	113	1,257	1,168	89	27,592	25,878	1,714
25 to 29 years	1,125	1,111	14	1,186	1,157	29	24,744	23,612	1,132
30 to 34 years	1,078	1,065	13	944	906	38	22,340	21,343	997
35 to 39 years	1,052	1,045	7	781	747	34	21,351	20,318	1,033
40 to 44 years	944	935	9	713	677	36	20,533	19,362	1,171
45 to 49 years	803	795	8	547	526	21	18,329	17,239	1,090
50 to 54 years	618	615	3	546	526	20	14,832	13,847	985
55 to 59 years	564	557	7	381	361	20	11,754	10,885	869
60 to 64 years	501	496	5	338	325	13	9,413	8,679	734
65 to 69 years	411	402	9	204	197	7	7,435	6,811	624
70 to 74 years	290	283	7	119	115	4	4,654	4,226	428
75 to 79 years	181	174	7	57	54	3	2,669	2,404	265
80 to 84 years	117	114	3	15	15	—	1,389	1,245	144
85 years and over	83	76	7	23	21	2	1,076	986	90
Under 18 years	8,935	8,783	152	6,401	6,203	198	162,393	153,443	8,950
62 years and over	1,375	1,340	35	594	572	22	22,570	20,599	1,971
65 years and over	1,082	1,049	33	418	402	16	17,223	15,672	1,551
Median age	19.6	19.6	19.8	20.6	20.4	22.6	21.1	21.1	22.0
Female, All ages	20,620	20,373	247	13,822	13,442	380	406,536	386,453	20,083
Under 5 years	2,342	2,327	15	1,840	1,793	47	44,449	42,469	1,980
5 to 9 years	2,713	2,703	10	1,993	1,941	52	47,962	45,621	2,341
10 to 14 years	2,652	2,633	19	1,746	1,697	49	45,705	43,056	2,649
15 to 19 years	2,146	2,101	45	1,227	1,181	46	37,567	35,507	2,060
20 to 24 years	1,790	1,750	40	1,260	1,234	26	34,051	32,848	1,203
25 to 29 years	1,370	1,349	21	1,144	1,127	17	31,494	30,435	1,059
30 to 34 years	1,258	1,251	7	945	917	28	28,321	27,183	1,138
35 to 39 years	1,176	1,170	6	844	815	29	25,957	24,799	1,158
40 to 44 years	1,085	1,069	16	696	680	16	23,837	22,645	1,192
45 to 49 years	865	858	7	553	533	20	20,949	19,906	1,043
50 to 54 years	709	704	5	478	453	25	16,996	15,933	1,063
55 to 59 years	632	621	11	403	384	19	14,166	13,276	890
60 to 64 years	545	540	5	247	245	2	11,583	10,833	750
65 to 69 years	479	472	7	239	237	2	9,591	8,981	610
70 to 74 years	376	369	7	97	96	1	6,347	5,942	405
75 to 79 years	211	202	9	55	55	—	3,648	3,367	281
80 to 84 years	128	120	8	33	32	1	2,189	2,059	130
85 years and over	143	134	9	22	22	—	1,724	1,593	131
Under 18 years	9,012	8,949	63	6,380	6,200	180	161,333	152,999	8,334
62 years and over	1,647	1,603	44	588	582	6	30,065	28,075	1,990
65 years and over	1,337	1,297	40	446	442	4	23,499	21,942	1,557
Median age	21.3	21.2	24.3	20.4	20.4	19.6	24.1	24.0	24.2

(continued overleaf)

SOCIAL CHARACTERISTICS OF THE BLACK POPULATION, FOR SELECTED AREAS: 1970

Nebraska, Nevada, New Jersey—continued

	NEBRASKA			NEVADA			NEW JERSEY		
	TOTAL	Urban Total	Rural Total	TOTAL	Urban Total	Rural Total	TOTAL	Urban Total	Rural Total
RELATIONSHIP TO HEAD OF HOUSEHOLD									
All persons	**39,911**	**39,228**	**683**	**27,762**	**26,843**	**919**	**770,292**	**729,053**	**41,239**
In households	**38,076**	**37,856**	**220**	**26,955**	**26,193**	**762**	**748,334**	**710,981**	**37,353**
Head	11,051	10,991	60	7,392	7,176	216	215,802	205,975	9,827
14 to 24 years	1,356	1,351	5	768	746	22	18,340	17,941	399
25 to 34 years	2,578	2,564	14	2,214	2,167	47	53,563	51,971	1,592
35 to 44 years	2,453	2,441	12	1,708	1,653	55	51,332	49,183	2,149
45 to 64 years	3,155	3,140	15	2,124	2,049	75	68,677	64,726	3,951
65 years and over	1,509	1,495	14	578	561	17	23,890	22,154	1,736
Primary individual: Male	1,271	1,262	9	986	952	34	20,129	19,197	932
Female	1,270	1,263	7	649	640	9	25,164	24,249	915
Family head: Male	5,918	5,875	43	4,396	4,237	159	118,734	112,178	6,556
Female	2,592	2,591	1	1,361	1,347	14	51,775	50,351	1,424
Wife of head	5,463	5,400	63	4,042	3,899	143	110,004	103,963	6,041
Child of head	18,422	18,347	75	12,897	12,563	334	341,549	324,613	16,936
Other relative of head	2,255	2,241	14	1,845	1,807	38	58,102	54,774	3,328
Not related to head	885	887	8	779	748	31	22,877	21,656	1,221
In group quarters	**1,835**	**1,372**	**463**	**807**	**650**	**157**	**21,958**	**18,072**	**3,886**
Inmate of institution	824	550	274	267	227	40	10,858	7,888	2,970
Other	1,011	822	189	540	423	117	11,100	10,184	916
Persons per household	3.45	3.44	3.67	3.65	3.65	3.53	3.47	3.45	3.80
Persons per family	4.07	4.07	4.45	4.26	4.27	3.98	3.99	3.97	4.30
Persons, under 18 years old	**17,947**	**17,732**	**215**	**12,781**	**12,403**	**378**	**323,726**	**306,442**	**17,284**
Head or wife of head	71	71	—	49	49	—	707	679	28
Own child of head	16,085	16,021	64	11,419	11,115	304	287,806	273,874	13,932
In husband-wife households	9,290	9,228	62	7,617	7,348	269	179,542	168,819	10,723
Percent of total persons under 18 years	51.8	52.0	28.8	59.6	59.2	71.2	55.5	55.1	62.0
In household with female head	6,463	6,461	2	3,482	3,456	26	101,270	98,514	2,756
Other relative of head	1,270	1,266	4	1,055	1,022	33	27,797	25,859	1,938
Not related to head	133	128	5	162	157	5	3,816	3,423	393
In group quarters	388	246	142	96	60	36	3,600	2,607	993
Persons, 65 years old and over	**2,419**	**2,346**	**73**	**864**	**844**	**20**	**40,722**	**37,614**	**3,108**
Head of family: Male	583	576	7	212	208	4	10,040	9,132	908
Female	173	173	—	51	49	2	3,636	3,422	214
Wife of head	328	320	8	105	104	1	5,287	4,845	442
Other family member	301	298	3	110	108	2	7,321	6,911	410
Not related to head	113	112	1	49	49	—	2,319	2,169	150
Primary individual: Male	282	278	4	124	114	10	3,393	3,120	273
Female	471	468	3	191	190	1	6,821	6,480	341
Inmate of institution	161	114	47	15	15	—	1,566	1,217	349
Other, in group quarters	7	7	—	7	7	—	339	318	21

FAMILIES BY PRESENCE AND NUMBER OF OWN CHILDREN UNDER 18 YEARS

All families	8,510	8,466	44	5,757	5,584	173	170,509	162,529	7,980
With own children under 18 years	5,696	5,669	27	3,999	3,880	119	110,365	105,632	4,733
Number of own children under 18 years	16,085	16,021	64	11,419	11,115	304	287,806	273,874	13,932
Number of own children under 6 years	4,960	4,936	24	4,124	4,036	88	94,437	90,651	3,786
Number of own children 6 to 17 years	11,125	11,085	40	7,295	7,079	216	193,369	183,223	10,146
With own children under 6 years only	1,391	1,383	8	1,087	1,058	29	25,656	24,871	785
With own children under 6 and 6 to 17 years	1,729	1,720	9	1,343	1,311	32	33,060	31,537	1,523
Husband-wife families	5,584	5,542	42	4,149	3,996	153	111,202	105,039	6,163
With own children under 18 years	3,462	3,436	26	2,749	2,644	105	69,472	65,799	3,673
Number of own children under 18 years	9,290	9,228	62	7,617	7,348	269	179,542	168,819	10,723
Number of own children under 6 years	2,907	2,884	23	2,903	2,821	82	60,656	57,702	2,954
Number of own children 6 to 17 years	6,383	6,344	39	4,714	4,527	187	118,886	111,117	7,769
With own children under 6 years only	926	919	7	835	807	28	17,469	16,816	653
With own children under 6 and 6 to 17 years	982	973	9	907	878	29	20,986	19,806	1,180
Families with female head	2,592	2,591	1	1,361	1,347	14	51,775	50,351	1,424
With own children under 18 years	2,084	2,083	1	1,111	1,100	11	37,797	36,899	898
Number of own children under 18 years	6,463	6,461	2	3,482	3,456	26	101,270	98,514	2,756
Number of own children under 6 years	1,977	1,976	1	1,142	1,137	5	31,937	31,229	708
Number of own children 6 to 17 years	4,486	4,485	1	2,340	2,319	21	69,333	67,285	2,048
With own children under 6 years only	438	437	1	226	225	1	7,601	7,493	108
With own children under 6 and 6 to 17 years	720	720	—	404	402	2	11,479	11,185	294

MARITAL STATUS

Male, 14 years old and over	12,294	11,903	391	8,731	8,319	412	233,049	218,436	14,513
Single	4,538	4,242	296	3,083	2,904	179	81,563	75,767	5,796
Married, except separated	6,066	6,002	64	4,569	4,383	186	121,151	114,035	7,116
14 to 19 years	93	88	5	26	23	3	1,017	956	61
20 to 24 years	656	643	13	472	444	28	9,761	9,274	487
25 to 34 years	1,544	1,532	12	1,523	1,480	43	31,949	30,611	1,338
35 to 44 years	1,476	1,464	12	1,146	1,092	54	30,344	28,698	1,646
45 to 64 years	1,730	1,718	12	1,190	1,136	54	38,167	35,493	2,674
65 years and over	567	557	10	212	208	4	9,913	9,003	910
Separated	511	501	10	411	398	13	16,454	15,628	826
Widowed	509	498	11	229	219	10	8,638	8,026	612
Divorced	670	660	10	439	415	24	5,243	4,980	263
Female, 14 years old and over	13,379	13,169	210	8,619	8,374	245	276,997	263,352	13,645
Single	3,643	3,548	95	2,173	2,112	61	79,234	75,386	3,848
Married, except separated	5,866	5,793	73	4,355	4,204	151	119,433	112,708	6,725
14 to 19 years	235	233	2	168	160	8	3,220	3,057	163
20 to 24 years	796	788	8	736	716	20	14,303	13,782	521
25 to 34 years	1,577	1,562	15	1,371	1,333	38	34,161	32,699	1,462
35 to 44 years	1,388	1,370	18	991	956	35	29,183	27,491	1,692
45 to 64 years	1,515	1,494	21	954	905	49	32,590	30,201	2,389
65 years and over	355	346	9	115	114	1	5,976	5,478	498
Separated	1,078	1,071	7	701	697	4	36,408	35,318	1,090
Widowed	1,484	1,458	26	635	623	12	31,447	29,791	1,656
Divorced	1,308	1,299	9	755	738	17	10,475	10,149	326

SOCIAL CHARACTERISTICS OF THE BLACK POPULATION, FOR SELECTED AREAS: 1970

BLACK POPULATION—	New Mexico			New York			North Carolina		
	TOTAL	Urban Total	Rural Total	TOTAL	Urban Total	Rural Total	TOTAL	Urban Total	Rural Total
Male, All ages	9,833	9,115	718	1,001,996	980,203	21,793	540,718	257,163	283,555
Under 5 years	1,117	1,075	42	116,661	115,104	1,557	58,365	27,749	30,616
5 to 9 years	1,379	1,308	71	128,399	126,476	1,923	67,259	30,322	36,937
10 to 14 years	1,267	1,181	86	118,810	116,234	2,576	72,999	31,576	41,423
15 to 19 years	1,117	1,029	88	97,347	94,281	3,066	69,930	31,576	38,354
20 to 24 years	1,048	972	76	74,090	71,789	2,301	47,112	27,015	20,097
25 to 29 years	593	543	50	74,864	73,117	1,747	30,074	15,565	14,509
30 to 34 years	540	501	39	68,058	66,480	1,578	24,519	12,235	12,284
35 to 39 years	608	558	50	62,671	61,249	1,422	23,381	11,344	12,037
40 to 44 years	477	422	55	59,299	58,015	1,284	25,197	12,030	13,167
45 to 49 years	379	349	30	54,255	53,177	1,078	25,274	11,989	13,285
50 to 54 years	337	302	35	42,636	41,780	856	23,981	11,484	12,497
55 to 59 years	273	251	22	33,518	32,755	763	21,707	10,280	11,427
60 to 64 years	238	208	30	26,265	25,707	558	17,190	8,212	8,978
65 to 69 years	192	179	13	20,211	19,739	472	14,172	6,829	7,343
70 to 74 years	127	116	11	12,565	12,285	280	9,046	4,285	4,761
75 to 79 years	83	75	8	6,674	6,492	182	5,382	2,393	2,989
80 to 84 years	34	27	7	3,259	3,168	91	2,892	1,289	1,603
85 years and over	24	19	5	2,414	2,355	59	2,238	990	1,248
Under 18 years	4,451	4,186	265	425,554	417,585	7,969	241,470	107,513	134,227
62 years and over	601	540	61	59,715	58,303	1,412	43,384	20,338	23,046
65 years and over	460	416	44	45,123	44,039	1,084	33,730	15,786	17,944
Median age	20.2	19.8	24.7	22.7	22.6	23.9	20.2	21.4	19.3
Female, All ages	9,722	9,182	540	1,166,953	1,150,969	15,984	585,760	289,659	296,101
Under 5 years	1,141	1,095	46	115,424	113,424	1,577	57,860	27,503	30,357
5 to 9 years	1,326	1,253	73	126,185	124,203	1,982	66,601	30,536	36,065
10 to 14 years	1,307	1,225	82	118,201	116,074	2,127	72,682	32,103	40,579
15 to 19 years	1,099	1,053	46	101,464	99,826	1,638	69,621	32,249	37,372
20 to 24 years	839	793	46	97,539	98,419	1,120	48,786	26,976	21,810
25 to 29 years	584	557	27	97,497	96,529	968	32,259	17,321	14,938
30 to 34 years	581	557	24	86,682	85,696	986	28,605	14,809	13,796
35 to 39 years	583	552	31	78,591	77,616	975	28,912	14,843	14,069
40 to 44 years	517	482	35	74,210	73,274	936	31,252	15,736	15,516
45 to 49 years	377	351	26	65,855	65,033	822	29,704	15,034	14,670
50 to 54 years	321	297	24	54,962	54,279	683	27,526	14,011	13,515
55 to 59 years	340	316	24	44,682	44,079	603	25,011	13,235	11,776
60 to 64 years	234	215	19	36,064	35,533	531	21,157	11,199	9,958
65 to 69 years	190	178	12	28,491	28,052	439	18,587	10,029	8,558
70 to 74 years	113	104	9	18,164	17,906	258	11,887	6,349	5,538
75 to 79 years	82	74	8	10,389	10,227	162	7,298	3,679	3,619
80 to 84 years	51	46	5	5,878	5,780	98	4,400	2,207	2,193
85 years and over	37	34	3	4,675	4,596	79	3,612	1,840	1,772
Under 18 years	4,422	4,191	231	421,679	414,958	6,721	240,227	108,491	131,736
62 years and over	604	555	49	87,734	86,410	1,324	57,979	30,586	27,393
65 years and over	473	436	37	67,597	66,561	1,036	45,784	24,104	21,680
Median age	19.9	19.8	22.5	26.2	26.2	23.0	22.7	24.2	20.8

RELATIONSHIP TO HEAD OF HOUSEHOLD

All persons	19,555	18,297	1,258	2,168,949	2,131,172	37,777	1,126,478	546,822	579,656
In households	18,197	17,164	1,033	2,106,708	2,079,363	27,345	1,084,768	517,321	567,447
Head	5,175	4,871	304	655,890	648,611	7,279	277,237	147,503	129,734
14 to 24 years	580	553	27	51,454	51,038	416	18,668	11,616	7,052
25 to 34 years	1,184	1,138	46	165,683	164,165	1,518	47,826	27,347	20,479
35 to 44 years	1,236	1,163	73	156,319	154,527	1,792	53,052	27,873	25,179
45 to 64 years	1,534	1,423	111	215,706	213,082	2,624	108,173	55,451	52,722
65 years and over	641	594	47	66,728	65,799	929	49,518	25,216	24,302
Primary individual: Male	571	525	46	69,962	69,105	857	20,100	11,866	8,234
Female	498	466	32	96,006	95,441	565	26,952	18,831	8,121
Family head: Male	3,109	2,909	200	332,860	327,971	4,889	170,600	81,041	89,559
Female	997	971	26	157,062	156,094	968	59,585	35,765	23,820
Wife of head	2,794	2,621	173	308,829	304,362	4,467	159,349	75,702	83,647
Child of head	8,938	8,452	486	902,179	890,065	12,114	492,576	221,856	270,720
Other relative of head	943	899	44	162,620	160,490	2,130	135,180	58,956	76,224
Not related to head	347	321	26	77,190	75,835	1,355	20,426	13,304	7,122
In group quarters	1,358	1,133	225	62,241	51,809	10,432	41,710	29,501	12,209
Inmate of institution	268	68	200	40,863	31,928	8,935	14,547	5,899	8,648
Other	1,090	1,065	25	21,378	19,881	1,497	27,163	23,602	3,561
Persons per household	3.52	3.52	3.40	3.21	3.21	3.76	3.91	3.51	4.37
Persons per family	4.09	4.09	4.11	3.80	3.80	4.19	4.42	4.05	4.80
Persons, under 18 years old	8,873	8,377	496	847,233	832,543	14,690	481,967	216,004	265,963
Head or wife of head	48	47	1	2,084	2,060	24	1,555	771	784
Own child of head	8,005	7,575	430	753,431	743,024	10,407	385,868	176,598	209,270
In husband-wife households	5,311	4,927	384	456,700	448,566	8,134	279,864	114,575	165,289
Percent of total persons under 18 years	59.9	58.8	77.4	53.9	53.9	55.4	58.1	53.0	62.1
In household with female head	2,551	2,510	41	278,702	276,745	1,957	95,943	57,654	38,289
Other relative of head	607	582	25	68,762	67,486	1,276	84,906	34,515	50,391
Not related to head	87	83	4	11,330	10,884	446	4,168	2,027	2,141
In group quarters	126	90	36	11,626	9,089	2,537	5,470	2,093	3,377
Persons, 65 years old and over	933	852	81	112,720	110,600	2,120	79,514	39,890	39,624
Head of family: Male	276	255	21	25,525	25,015	510	22,599	9,920	12,679
Female	63	60	3	9,682	9,583	99	10,726	5,448	5,278
Wife of head	150	136	14	13,067	12,783	284	11,820	5,185	6,635
Other family member	91	84	7	20,154	19,909	245	13,672	6,709	6,963
Not related to head	18	16	2	6,309	6,181	128	2,234	1,442	792
Primary individual: Male	130	116	14	9,708	9,567	141	5,106	2,702	2,404
Female	172	163	9	21,813	21,634	179	11,087	7,146	3,941
Inmate of institution	23	13	10	5,276	4,782	494		1,131	816
Other, in group quarters	10	9	1	1,186	1,146	40	323	207	116

(continued overleaf)

SOCIAL CHARACTERISTICS OF THE BLACK POPULATION, FOR SELECTED AREAS: 1970

New Mexico, New York, North Carolina—continued

	NEW MEXICO			NEW YORK			NORTH CAROLINA		
	TOTAL	Urban Total	Rural Total	TOTAL	Urban Total	Rural Total	TOTAL	Urban Total	Rural Total
FAMILIES BY PRESENCE AND NUMBER OF OWN CHILDREN UNDER 18 YEARS									
All families	4,106	3,880	226	489,922	484,065	5,857	230,185	116,806	113,379
With own children under 18 years	2,826	2,686	140	309,182	305,497	3,685	135,772	67,396	68,376
Number of own children under 18 years	8,005	7,575	430	753,431	743,024	10,407	385,868	176,598	209,270
Number of own children under 6 years	2,535	2,431	104	247,663	244,472	3,191	106,328	52,102	54,226
Number of own children 6 to 17 years	5,470	5,144	326	505,768	498,552	7,216	279,540	124,496	155,044
With own children under 6 years only	693	662	31	75,203	74,432	771	26,020	14,755	11,265
With own children 6 and 6 to 17 years	904	871	33	86,205	84,996	1,209	39,593	18,421	21,172
Husband-wife families	2,981	2,791	190	310,957	306,330	4,627	159,321	75,768	83,553
With own children under 18 years	1,945	1,826	119	190,387	187,483	2,904	97,647	44,379	53,268
Number of own children under 18 years	5,311	4,927	384	456,700	448,566	8,134	279,864	114,575	165,289
Number of own children under 6 years	1,754	1,658	96	156,278	153,712	2,566	82,596	37,392	45,204
Number of own children 6 to 17 years	3,557	3,269	288	300,422	294,854	5,568	197,268	77,183	120,085
With own children under 6 years only	529	500	29	50,903	50,264	639	21,350	11,559	9,791
With own children under 6 and 6 to 17 years	616	586	30	52,964	52,002	962	29,252	12,273	16,979
Families with female head	997	971	26	157,062	156,094	968	59,585	35,765	23,820
With own children under 18 years	811	794	17	110,323	109,659	664	33,954	21,090	12,864
Number of own children under 18 years	2,551	2,510	41	278,702	276,745	1,957	95,943	57,654	38,289
Number of own children under 6 years	757	751	6	86,643	86,092	551	21,629	13,814	7,815
Number of own children 6 to 17 years	1,794	1,759	35	192,059	190,653	1,406	74,314	43,840	30,474
With own children under 6 years only	157	156	1	22,656	22,550	106	4,108	2,928	1,180
With own children under 6 and 6 to 17 years	276	274	2	31,684	31,456	228	9,516	5,800	3,716
MARITAL STATUS									
Male, 14 years old and over	6,293	5,756	537	660,476	644,171	16,305	357,326	173,863	183,463
Single	2,265	2,062	203	234,878	226,995	7,883	141,375	67,231	74,144
Married, except separated	3,304	3,050	254	341,634	335,179	6,455	178,108	85,279	92,829
14 to 19 years	41	41	—	2,717	2,663	54	2,331	1,241	1,090
20 to 24 years	370	339	31	24,656	24,128	528	16,668	9,404	7,264
25 to 34 years	863	810	53	94,060	92,357	1,703	37,321	19,225	18,096
35 to 44 years	874	813	61	86,350	84,717	1,633	35,425	16,557	18,868
45 to 64 years	889	803	86	108,174	106,207	1,967	64,877	29,265	35,612
65 years and over	267	244	23	25,677	25,107	570	21,486	9,587	11,899
Separated	201	187	14	45,453	44,308	1,145	16,329	9,593	6,736
Widowed	216	190	26	23,551	23,054	497	15,742	8,131	7,611
Divorced	307	267	40	14,960	14,635	325	5,772	3,629	2,143
Female, 14 years old and over	6,206	5,842	364	829,890	819,160	10,730	403,518	205,977	197,541
Single	1,709	1,596	113	246,795	243,349	3,446	129,135	63,398	65,737
Married, except separated	3,078	2,889	189	341,413	336,338	5,075	178,392	84,721	93,671
14 to 19 years	129	126	3	8,181	7,071	110	6,750	3,300	3,450
20 to 24 years	399	384	15	39,527	39,050	477	21,906	11,488	10,418
25 to 34 years	834	797	37	101,481	100,195	1,286	38,748	19,459	19,289
35 to 44 years	801	744	57	84,483	83,185	1,298	38,831	17,862	20,969
45 to 64 years	757	696	61	92,448	90,897	1,551	59,116	26,826	32,290
65 years and over	158	142	16	15,293	14,940	353	13,041	5,786	7,255
Separated	338	324	14	112,805	111,958	847	28,602	19,084	9,518
Widowed	578	546	32	95,315	94,191	1,116	58,030	32,253	25,777
Divorced	503	487	16	33,562	33,316	246	9,359	6,521	2,838

	Ohio			Oklahoma			Oregon		
BLACK POPULATION—									
Male, All ages	**461,274**	**445,632**	**15,642**	**81,299**	**66,534**	**14,765**	**13,188**	**12,375**	**813**
Under 5 years	49,073	48,224	849	9.045	7,764	1,281	1,478	1,424	54
5 to 9 years	55,474	54,332	1,142	10,724	9,091	1,633	1,521	1,458	63
10 to 14 years	60,104	58,412	1,692	11,044	8,975	2,069	1,541	1,470	71
15 to 19 years	50,206	47,781	2,425	9,430	7,249	2,181	1,572	1,374	198
20 to 24 years	33,132	31,468	1,664	6,848	5,893	955	1,234	1,103	131
25 to 29 years	26,864	25,907	957	4,133	3,640	493	874	831	43
30 to 34 years	24,189	23,350	839	3,356	2,918	438	704	666	38
35 to 39 years	24,983	24,098	885	3,265	2,851	414	621	589	32
40 to 44 years	27,121	26,146	975	3,269	2,816	453	638	600	38
45 to 49 years	25,963	25,076	887	3,303	2,772	531	687	651	36
50 to 54 years	21,694	20,914	780	3,038	2,442	596	638	606	32
55 to 59 years	18,361	17,722	639	3,079	2,359	720	561	534	27
60 to 64 years	14,529	13,973	556	2,869	2,148	721	439	426	13
65 to 69 years	12,074	11,583	491	2,824	2,070	754	301	283	18
70 to 74 years	8,397	8,022	375	2,089	1,481	608	173	164	9
75 to 79 years	4,878	4,638	240	1,396	977	419	97	90	7
80 to 84 years	2,403	2,253	150	891	624	267	65	65	—
85 years and over	1,829	1,733	96	696	464	232	44	41	3
Under 18 years	197,238	192,110	5,128	36,707	30,382	6,325	5,482	5,166	316
62 years and over	37,789	36,102	1,687	9,593	6,877	2,716	911	866	45
65 years and over	29,581	28,229	1,352	7,896	5,616	2,280	680	643	37
Median age	22.4	22.2	25.3	20.3	20.2	21.1	22.0	22.1	20.8
Female, All ages	**509,203**	**496,080**	**13,123**	**90,593**	**75,222**	**15,371**	**13,120**	**12,264**	**856**
Under 5 years	48,439	47,559	880	8,997	7,731	1,266	1,323	1,282	41
5 to 9 years	56,069	54,929	1,140	10,720	9,048	1,672	1,526	1,461	65
10 to 14 years	60,971	59,415	1,556	10,844	8,945	1,899	1,555	1,512	43
15 to 19 years	51,965	49,970	1,995	9,701	7,923	1,778	1,745	1,339	406
20 to 24 years	42,116	40,762	1,354	6,878	5,971	907	1,225	1,138	117
25 to 29 years	32,346	31,785	561	4,871	4,325	546	788	769	19
30 to 34 years	30,105	29,487	618	4,412	3,889	513	704	679	25
35 to 39 years	30,570	29,921	649	4,419	3,816	603	600	580	20
40 to 44 years	31,790	31,082	708	4,266	3,634	632	664	636	28
45 to 49 years	28,863	28,087	776	4,114	3,454	660	731	711	20
50 to 54 years	23,803	23,143	660	3,788	3,091	697	617	597	20
55 to 59 years	20,153	19,580	573	3,931	3,085	846	513	500	13
60 to 64 years	16,285	15,785	500	3,757	2,935	822	413	400	13
65 to 69 years	13,926	13,534	392	3,554	2,656	898	271	266	5
70 to 74 years	9,790	9,473	317	2,579	1,937	642	167	160	7
75 to 79 years	6,034	5,837	197	1,701	1,259	442	109	102	7
80 to 84 years	3,304	3,184	120	1,042	755	287	65	62	3
85 years and over	2,674	2,547	127	1,019	758	261	74	70	4
Under 18 years	197,811	193,161	4,650	36,490	30,522	5,968	5,343	5,012	331
62 years and over	44,974	43,550	1,424	12,150	9,122	3,028	920	884	36
65 years and over	35,728	34,575	1,153	9,895	7,365	2,530	686	660	26
Median age	24.4	24.4	23.7	23.7	23.3	26.5	21.6	22.4	18.4

(continued overleaf)

SOCIAL CHARACTERISTICS OF THE BLACK POPULATION, FOR SELECTED AREAS: 1970

Ohio, Oklahoma, Oregon—continued

	OHIO			OKLAHOMA			OREGON		
	TOTAL	Urban Total	Rural Total	TOTAL	Urban Total	Rural Total	TOTAL	Urban Total	Rural Total
RELATIONSHIP TO HEAD OF HOUSEHOLD									
All persons	970,477	941,712	28,765	171,892	141,756	30,136	26,308	24,639	1,669
In households	944,582	923,429	21,153	163,480	135,160	28,320	24,367	23,519	848
Head	282,455	276,487	5,968	49,575	41,017	8,558	7,601	7,347	254
14 to 24 years	23,641	23,450	191	4,077	3,768	309	945	926	19
25 to 34 years	56,563	55,865	698	8,380	7,609	771	1,650	1,600	50
35 to 44 years	62,574	61,432	1,142	8,400	7,415	985	1,419	1,363	56
45 to 64 years	100,105	97,570	2,535	16,400	13,342	3,058	2,733	2,640	93
65 years and over	39,572	38,170	1,402	12,318	8,883	3,435	854	818	36
Primary individual: Male	29,409	28,828	581	5,073	4,065	1,008	1,210	1,152	58
Female	35,559	35,063	496	7,550	6,206	1,344	854	836	18
Family head: Male	158,613	154,303	4,310	25,278	20,634	4,644	4,091	3,921	170
Female	58,874	58,293	581	11,674	10,112	1,562	1,446	1,438	8
Wife of head	148,299	144,252	4,047	23,779	19,468	4,311	3,615	3,477	138
Child of head	419,341	410,214	9,127	74,662	62,383	12,279	10,690	10,305	385
Other relative of head	69,879	68,336	1,543	12,985	10,107	2,878	1,504	1,472	32
Not related to head	24,608	24,140	468	2,479	2,185	294	957	918	39
In group quarters	25,895	18,283	7,612	8,412	6,596	1,816	1,941	1,120	821
Inmate of institution	16,403	11,277	5,126	3,314	2,466	848	678	560	118
Other	9,492	7,006	2,486	5,098	4,130	968	1,263	560	703
Persons per household	3.34	3.34	3.54	3.30	3.30	3.31	3.21	3.20	3.34
Persons per family	3.93	3.93	4.01	4.02	3.99	4.14	3.86	3.85	4.12
Persons, under 18 years old	395,049	385,271	9,778	73,197	60,904	12,293	10,825	10,178	647
Head or wife of head	1,052	1,031	21	259	214	45	34	33	1
Own child of head	349,314	341,989	7,325	63,360	53,581	9,779	9,182	8,835	347
In husband-wife households	227,138	220,832	6,306	36,726	30,089	6,637	5,871	5,565	306
Percent of total persons under 18 years	57.5	57.3	64.5	50.2	49.4	54.0	54.2	54.7	47.3
In household with female head	114,828	113,969	859	25,310	22,454	2,856	3,127	3,095	32
Other relative of head	35,910	34,994	916	8,187	6,194	1,993	874	859	15
Not related to head	4,207	4,062	145	415	343	72	213	208	5
In group quarters	4,566	3,195	1,371	976	572	404	522	243	279
Persons, 65 years old and over	65,309	62,804	2,505	17,791	12,981	4,810	1,366	1,303	63
Head of family: Male	17,349	16,555	794	4,938	3,347	1,591	380	362	18
Female	4,770	4,637	133	1,501	1,084	417	87	86	1
Wife of head	9,166	8,740	426	2,728	1,830	898	195	185	10
Other family member	10,094	9,869	225	1,470	1,143	327	170	167	3
Not related to head	3,238	3,159	79	388	331	57	62	59	3
Primary individual: Male	6,192	5,954	238	1,918	1,416	502	174	162	12
Female	11,261	11,024	237	3,961	3,036	925	213	208	5
Inmate of institution	2,832	2,467	365	818	732	86	65	54	11
Other, in group quarters	407	399	8	69	62	7	20	20	—

FAMILIES BY PRESENCE AND NUMBER OF OWN CHILDREN UNDER 18 YEARS

All families	217,487	212,596	4,891	36,952	30,746	5,537	5,359	178
With own children under 18 years	133,857	131,166	2,691	22,008	18,997	3,475	3,364	111
Number of own children under 18 years	349,314	341,989	7,325	63,360	53,581	9,182	8,835	347
Number of own children under 6 years	101,038	99,299	1,739	18,683	16,223	2,861	2,756	105
Number of own children 6 to 17 years	248,276	242,690	5,586	44,677	37,358	6,321	6,079	242
With own children under 6 years only	29,978	29,598	380	4,769	4,352	898	874	24
With own children under 6 and 6 to 17 years	36,089	35,385	704	6,771	5,759	948	913	35
Husband-wife families	150,089	145,982	4,107	23,937	19,617	3,858	3,709	159
With own children under 18 years	88,031	85,717	2,314	13,153	11,132	2,255	2,157	98
Number of own children under 18 years	227,138	220,832	6,306	36,726	30,089	5,871	5,565	306
Number of own children under 6 years	66,174	66,174	1,549	11,180	9,493	1,885	1,790	95
Number of own children 6 to 17 years	159,415	154,658	4,757	25,546	20,596	3,986	3,775	211
With own children under 6 years only	21,193	20,848	345	3,166	2,872	615	592	23
With own children under 6 and 6 to 17 years	23,917	23,294	623	2,897	3,216	635	602	33
Families with female head	58,874	58,293	581	11,674	10,112	1,446	1,438	8
With own children under 18 years	42,562	42,247	315	8,326	7,443	1,128	1,120	8
Number of own children under 18 years	114,828	113,969	859	25,310	22,454	3,127	3,095	32
Number of own children under 6 years	31,743	31,590	153	7,219	6,495	938	928	10
Number of own children 6 to 17 years	83,085	82,379	706	18,091	15,959	2,189	2,167	22
With own children under 6 years only	8,263	8,236	27	1,528	1,413	272	271	1
With own children under 6 and 6 to 17 years	11,625	11,555	70	2,762	2,455	299	297	2

MARITAL STATUS

Male, 14 years old and over	308,441	296,134	12,307	52,606	42,361	10,245	8,277	644
Single	102,805	97,141	5,664	18,848	14,695	4,153	2,907	373
Married, except separated	160,512	155,393	5,119	26,173	21,490	4,683	4,001	208
14 to 19 years	1,519	1,476	43	289	267	22	59	2
20 to 24 years	12,409	12,133	276	2,477	2,254	223	371	19
25 to 34 years	34,174	33,318	856	5,110	4,557	553	903	51
35 to 44 years	37,847	36,676	1,171	4,790	4,193	597	828	52
45 to 64 years	57,555	55,574	1,981	8,682	6,914	1,768	1,483	66
65 years and over	17,008	16,216	792	4,825	3,305	1,520	357	18
Separated	15,119	14,734	385	1,810	1,538	272	387	13
Widowed	13,348	12,839	509	2,989	2,255	734	328	13
Divorced	16,657	16,027	630	2,786	2,383	403	654	37
Female, 14 years old and over	355,613	345,751	9,862	62,089	51,172	10,917	8,278	715
Single	96,724	92,914	3,810	16,443	13,328	3,115	2,291	495
Married, except separated	158,423	154,010	4,413	25,957	21,265	4,692	3,711	159
14 to 19 years	4,701	4,609	92	1,015	884	131	121	9
20 to 24 years	18,193	17,904	289	3,067	2,758	309	468	12
25 to 34 years	36,827	36,044	783	5,373	4,751	622	849	37
35 to 44 years	38,922	37,877	1,045	5,040	4,295	745	753	39
45 to 64 years	49,757	48,016	1,741	8,526	6,577	1,949	1,310	52
65 years and over	10,023	9,560	463	2,936	2,000	936	210	10
Separated	27,929	27,664	265	3,821	3,406	415	629	21
Widowed	42,698	41,690	1,008	10,298	8,118	2,180	799	24
Divorced	29,839	29,473	366	5,570	5,055	515	848	16

SOCIAL CHARACTERISTICS OF THE BLACK POPULATION, FOR SELECTED AREAS: 1970

	Pennsylvania			Texas			Utah		
	TOTAL	Urban Total	Rural Total	TOTAL	Urban Total	Rural Total	TOTAL	Urban Total	Rural Total
BLACK POPULATION—									
Male, All ages	476,666	457,236	19,430	672,901	557,956	114,945	3,987	3,550	437
Under 5 years	51,072	49,851	1,221	76,205	65,279	10,926	272	243	29
5 to 9 years	57,729	56,228	1,501	84,869	71,898	12,971	355	325	30
10 to 14 years	59,087	57,002	2,085	86,124	70,878	15,246	333	303	30
15 to 19 years	49,108	46,146	2,962	75,043	59,238	15,805	1,235	1,140	95
20 to 24 years	33,601	31,391	2,210	54,408	46,893	7,515	507	395	112
25 to 29 years	28,092	26,657	1,435	40,814	35,695	5,119	182	147	35
30 to 34 years	24,528	23,384	1,144	33,903	29,595	4,308	161	129	32
35 to 39 years	25,199	24,051	1,148	33,045	28,760	4,285	136	109	27
40 to 44 years	27,438	26,323	1,115	32,866	28,356	4,510	155	138	17
45 to 49 years	27,814	26,791	1,023	30,267	25,917	4,350	177	169	8
50 to 54 years	23,365	22,546	819	26,943	22,282	4,661	138	129	9
55 to 59 years	19,665	19,015	650	25,335	20,208	5,127	116	111	5
60 to 64 years	16,267	15,678	589	22,680	17,316	5,364	77	77	—
65 to 69 years	13,954	13,407	547	19,600	14,386	5,214	68	65	3
70 to 74 years	9,893	9,439	454	13,728	9,807	3,921	27	27	—
75 to 79 years	5,402	5,119	283	8,741	5,969	2,772	25	23	2
80 to 84 years	2,541	2,406	135	4,582	3,093	1,489	12	10	2
85 years and over	1,911	1,802	109	3,748	2,566	1,182	11	10	1
Under 18 years	199,741	193,194	6,547	293,735	244,103	49,632	1,716	1,575	141
62 years and over	42,972	41,080	1,892	63,633	45,858	17,775	184	176	8
65 years and over	33,701	32,173	1,528	50,399	35,821	14,578	143	135	8
Median age	23.2	23.1	24.4	21.3	21.2	21.7	19.2	19.0	21.5
Female, All ages	539,848	524,714	15,134	726,104	611,638	114,466	2,630	2,487	143
Under 5 years	50,556	49,402	1,154	75,395	64,507	10,888	309	285	24
5 to 9 years	57,455	55,928	1,527	85,054	71,988	13,066	311	292	19
10 to 14 years	59,812	58,020	1,792	85,019	70,658	14,361	318	303	15
15 to 19 years	51,565	49,190	2,375	74,766	62,047	12,719	238	231	7
20 to 24 years	42,852	41,521	1,331	60,107	53,670	6,437	247	232	15
25 to 29 years	34,961	34,272	689	45,384	40,646	4,738	154	138	16
30 to 34 years	31,549	30,848	701	39,963	35,392	4,571	137	120	17
35 to 39 years	32,226	31,478	748	39,043	34,201	4,842	132	122	10
40 to 44 years	33,664	32,863	801	38,865	33,747	5,118	147	142	5
45 to 49 years	32,075	31,287	788	34,823	29,596	5,227	154	149	5
50 to 54 years	27,651	26,957	694	30,648	25,266	5,382	128	125	3
55 to 59 years	23,595	22,972	623	28,979	23,062	5,917	93	91	2
60 to 64 years	19,475	18,945	530	26,185	20,480	5,705	81	81	—
65 to 69 years	17,197	16,679	518	23,770	18,305	5,465	67	64	3
70 to 74 years	11,615	11,245	370	16,191	12,128	4,063	43	42	1
75 to 79 years	6,790	6,574	216	10,466	7,637	2,829	37	36	1
80 to 84 years	3,772	3,629	143	6,162	4,437	1,725	20	20	—
85 years and over	3,038	2,904	134	5,284	3,871	1,413	14	14	—
Under 18 years	199,510	193,752	5,758	291,203	244,363	46,840	1,087	1,023	64
62 years and over	53,510	51,819	1,691	77,251	58,328	18,923	233	228	5
65 years and over	42,412	41,031	1,381	61,873	46,378	15,495	181	176	5
Median age	26.1	26.2	22.7	23.6	23.4	24.8	22.8	22.9	22.2

RELATIONSHIP TO HEAD OF HOUSEHOLD

	(1)	(2)	(3)	(4)	(5)	(6)	(7)	(8)	(9)
All persons	**1,016,514**	**981,950**	**34,564**	**1,399,005**	**1,169,594**	**229,411**	**6,617**	**6,037**	**580**
In households	**988,302**	**963,244**	**25,058**	**1,354,772**	**1,136,581**	**218,191**	**5,192**	**4,848**	**344**
Head	297,809	290,854	6,955	388,546	328,175	60,371	1,680	1,575	105
14 to 24 years	21,336	21,057	279	30,276	28,248	2,028	212	200	12
25 to 34 years	56,811	55,895	916	74,495	68,224	6,271	341	300	41
35 to 44 years	63,698	62,356	1,342	76,311	67,780	8,531	325	298	27
45 to 64 years	110,174	107,434	2,740	132,470	109,518	22,952	600	583	17
65 years and over	45,790	44,112	1,678	74,994	54,405	20,589	202	194	8
Primary individual: Male	32,513	31,728	785	36,294	30,163	6,131	263	254	9
Female	41,033	40,362	671	47,982	40,682	7,300	184	179	5
Family head: Male	154,035	149,455	4,580	231,010	193,220	37,790	967	878	89
Female	70,228	69,309	919	73,260	64,110	9,150	266	264	2
Wife of head	142,209	137,997	4,212	217,489	182,078	35,411	834	768	66
Child of head	424,951	413,998	10,953	597,653	502,301	95,352	2,240	2,080	160
Other relative of head	88,180	85,931	2,249	125,975	101,362	24,613	299	291	8
Not related to head	35,153	34,464	689	25,109	22,665	2,444	139	134	5
In group quarters	**28,212**	**18,706**	**9,506**	**44,233**	**33,013**	**11,220**	**1,425**	**1,189**	**236**
Inmate of institution	17,070	9,746	7,324	18,506	10,807	7,699	112	64	48
Other	11,142	8,960	2,182	25,727	22,206	3,521	1,313	1,125	188
Persons per household	3.32	3.31	3.60	3.46	3.46	3.61	3.09	3.08	3.28
Persons per family	3.92	3.92	4.17	4.09	4.05	4.31	3.74	3.75	3.57
Persons, under 18 years old	**399,251**	**385,946**	**12,305**	**584,938**	**488,466**	**96,472**	**2,803**	**2,598**	**205**
Head or wife of head	981	958	23	2,504	2,187	317	17	16	1
Own child of head	342,503	333,781	8,722	497,111	421,116	75,995	1,968	1,823	145
In husband-wife households	205,904	199,131	6,773	352,078	292,948	59,130	1,416	1,276	140
Percent of total persons under 18 years	51.6	51.5	55.0	60.2	60.0	61.3	50.5	49.1	68.3
In household with female head	127,960	126,241	1,719	132,645	118,275	14,370	518	514	4
Other relative of head	44,508	43,066	1,442	75,709	59,619	16,540	176	168	8
Not related to head	5,554	5,356	198	3,841	3,255	586	26	25	1
In group quarters	5,705	3,785	1,920	5,773	2,739	3,034	616	566	50
Persons, 65 years old and over	**76,113**	**73,204**	**2,909**	**112,272**	**82,199**	**30,073**	**324**	**311**	**13**
Head of family: Male	19,350	18,502	848	32,577	22,451	10,126	87	83	4
Female	6,775	6,602	173	10,678	7,952	2,726	24	24	—
Wife of head	10,028	9,624	404	17,538	11,779	5,759	50	47	3
Other family member	12,347	12,097	250	13,637	10,699	2,938	42	41	1
Not related to head	4,710	4,590	120	2,586	2,156	430	7	7	—
Primary individual: Male	7,140	6,824	316	10,606	7,535	3,053	30	28	2
Female	12,525	12,184	341	21,133	16,449	4,684	61	59	2
Inmate of institution	2,588	2,152	406	3,190	2,874	316	22	21	1
Other, in group quarters	680	629	51	327	286	41	1	1	—

(continued overleaf)

SOCIAL CHARACTERISTICS OF THE BLACK POPULATION, FOR SELECTED AREAS: 1970

Pennsylvania, Texas, Utah—continued

	PENNSYLVANIA			TEXAS			UTAH		
	TOTAL	Urban Total	Rural Total	TOTAL	Urban Total	Rural Total	TOTAL	Urban Total	Rural Total
FAMILIES BY PRESENCE AND NUMBER OF OWN CHILDREN UNDER 18 YEARS									
All families	224,263	218,764	5,499	304,270	257,330	46,940	1,233	1,142	91
With own children under 18 years	132,546	129,422	3,124	179,488	155,695	23,793	797	728	69
Number of own children under 18 years	342,503	333,781	8,722	497,111	421,116	75,995	1,968	1,823	145
Number of own children under 6 years	102,087	99,882	2,205	151,231	130,999	20,232	623	563	60
Number of own children 6 to 17 years	240,416	233,899	6,517	345,880	290,117	55,763	1,345	1,260	85
With own children under 6 years only	28,131	27,630	501	40,136	36,428	3,708	222	200	22
With own children under 6 and 6 to 17 years	37,055	36,180	875	53,458	45,819	7,639	210	186	24
Husband-wife families	143,157	138,855	4,292	217,976	182,632	35,344	926	838	88
With own children under 18 years	81,103	78,621	2,482	127,450	109,177	18,273	574	508	66
Number of own children under 18 years	205,904	199,131	6,773	352,078	292,948	59,130	1,416	1,276	140
Number of own children under 6 years	63,942	62,192	1,750	113,289	96,959	16,330	454	397	57
Number of own children 6 to 17 years	141,962	136,939	5,032	238,789	195,989	42,800	962	879	83
With own children under 6 years only	18,999	18,572	427	32,037	28,944	3,093	168	147	21
With own children under 6 and 6 to 17 years	22,662	21,961	701	38,190	32,219	5,971	151	129	22
Families with female head	70,228	69,309	919	73,260	64,110	9,150	266	264	2
With own children under 18 years	47,529	46,985	544	46,817	42,264	4,553	207	205	2
Number of own children under 18 years	127,960	126,241	1,719	132,645	118,275	14,370	518	514	4
Number of own children under 6 years	36,136	35,719	417	34,983	31,657	3,326	159	156	3
Number of own children 6 to 17 years	91,824	90,522	1,302	97,662	86,618	11,044	359	358	1
With own children under 6 years only	8,459	8,400	59	7,204	6,730	474	49	48	1
With own children under 6 and 6 to 17 years	13,719	13,552	167	14,218	12,775	1,443	57	56	1
MARITAL STATUS									
Male, 14 years old and over	320,190	305,065	15,125	442,508	363,523	78,985	3,094	2,738	356
Single	111,338	103,980	7,358	145,304	115,990	29,314	1,807	1,585	222
Married, except separated	156,792	150,891	5,901	237,524	198,194	39,330	1,030	915	115
14 to 19 years	1,455	1,408	47	3,216	2,822	394	18	16	2
20 to 24 years	11,548	11,124	424	21,692	19,497	2,195	122	108	14
25 to 34 years	32,643	31,412	1,231	53,445	47,667	5,778	242	193	49
35 to 44 years	34,853	33,489	1,364	49,809	43,407	6,402	206	174	32
45 to 64 years	57,531	55,523	2,008	77,825	62,931	14,894	352	338	14
65 years and over	18,762	17,935	827	31,537	21,370	9,667	90	86	4
Separated	26,866	26,037	829	19,237	16,633	2,604	84	75	9
Widowed	15,790	15,113	677	20,448	15,500	4,948	48	44	4
Divorced	9,404	9,044	360	19,995	17,206	2,789	125	119	6
Female, 14 years old and over	383,684	372,635	11,049	497,439	418,267	79,172	1,753	1,666	87
Single	110,003	105,634	4,369	124,447	103,351	21,096	403	391	12
Married, except separated	155,059	150,482	4,577	236,331	197,977	38,354	895	825	70
14 to 19 years	4,346	4,257	89	9,827	8,639	1,188	22	21	1
20 to 24 years	16,425	16,112	313	30,029	27,131	2,898	136	124	12
25 to 34 years	35,149	34,270	879	56,428	50,201	6,227	199	168	31
35 to 44 years	36,510	35,410	1,100	51,414	44,362	7,052	190	175	15
45 to 64 years	51,513	49,770	1,743	69,774	54,803	14,971	294	286	8
65 years and over	11,116	10,663	453	18,859	12,841	6,018	54	51	3
Separated	49,960	49,425	535	30,977	28,021	2,956	106	105	1
Widowed	52,396	51,085	1,311	69,539	55,786	13,753	189	187	2
Divorced	16,266	16,009	257	36,145	33,132	3,013	160	158	2

	Virginia		Washington		Wisconsin	
BLACK POPULATION—						
Male, All ages	419,248	171,792	37,837	2,087	62,116	1,213
Under 5 years	42,302	17,008	3,905	126	8,676	70
5 to 9 years	50,188	20,927	4,164	146	8,964	61
10 to 14 years	53,783	23,024	4,158	165	8,729	123
15 to 19 years	48,250	20,932	4,065	423	7,079	358
20 to 24 years	34,238	12,474	5,015	306	5,279	168
25 to 29 years	24,245	9,464	2,870	180	4,070	68
30 to 34 years	20,783	8,211	2,180	149	3,517	61
35 to 39 years	20,516	8,124	2,015	113	3,294	38
40 to 44 years	21,545	8,500	2,083	122	3,261	61
45 to 49 years	21,516	8,657	2,006	84	2,688	42
50 to 54 years	20,615	8,062	1,745	82	1,934	25
55 to 59 years	18,151	7,580	1,331	65	1,571	35
60 to 64 years	13,906	5,857	918	50	1,099	31
65 to 69 years	11,185	4,948	610	26	816	20
70 to 74 years	7,679	3,464	348	28	552	20
75 to 79 years	4,851	2,394	195	9	292	16
80 to 84 years	2,641	1,281	111	7	139	9
85 years and over	1,854	885	109	6	156	7
Under 18 years	176,566	74,408	14,440	694	30,888	535
62 years and over	35,927	16,285	1,872	106	2,551	91
65 years and over	28,210	12,972	1,382	76	1,955	72
Median age	22.2	21.6	22.6	23.0	18.3	19.9
Female, All ages	442,120	270,552	33,471	990	66,108	719
Under 5 years	41,923	25,179	3,866	129	8,638	64
5 to 9 years	50,278	29,335	4,167	130	8,994	67
10 to 14 years	53,672	31,012	4,269	141	8,668	90
15 to 19 years	47,844	27,747	3,384	123	7,151	132
20 to 24 years	34,677	22,483	3,237	54	6,329	58
25 to 29 years	25,690	16,696	2,257	44	4,849	33
30 to 34 years	23,425	14,900	1,935	64	4,344	44
35 to 39 years	23,713	15,050	1,717	53	4,019	26
40 to 44 years	24,634	15,700	1,900	45	3,505	37
45 to 49 years	24,182	15,660	1,930	56	2,597	27
50 to 54 years	21,641	13,819	1,438	36	1,988	19
55 to 59 years	18,920	11,932	1,109	30	1,572	25
60 to 64 years	15,212	9,488	796	36	1,220	29
65 to 69 years	13,851	8,505	544	22	929	23
70 to 74 years	9,658	5,692	394	16	602	17
75 to 79 years	6,269	3,598	240	4	303	11
80 to 84 years	3,685	2,133	151	2	212	11
85 years and over	2,846	1,623	133	5	188	9
Under 18 years	175,807	102,528	14,390	485	30,731	333
62 years and over	45,094	27,089	1,913	64	2,920	83
65 years and over	36,309	21,551	1,466	49	2,234	68
Median age	23.9	24.9	21.6	18.9	19.7	20.6

(continued overleaf)

SOCIAL CHARACTERISTICS OF THE BLACK POPULATION, FOR SELECTED AREAS: 1970

Virginia, Washington, Wisconsin—continued

	VIRGINIA			WASHINGTON			WISCONSIN		
	TOTAL	Urban Total	Rural Total	TOTAL	Urban Total	Rural Total	TOTAL	Urban Total	Rural Total
RELATIONSHIP TO HEAD OF HOUSEHOLD									
All persons	861,368	518,008	343,360	71,308	68,231	3,077	128,224	126,292	1,932
In households	826,817	495,631	331,186	65,487	63,463	2,024	124,082	123,148	934
Head	219,029	139,756	79,273	20,900	20,337	563	32,863	32,609	254
14 to 24 years	13,704	10,341	3,363	2,678	2,639	39	4,593	4,581	12
25 to 34 years	38,840	26,758	12,082	4,890	4,779	111	9,009	8,974	35
35 to 44 years	43,432	28,329	15,103	4,436	4,311	125	8,070	8,032	38
45 to 64 years	84,672	52,971	31,701	7,072	6,856	216	8,873	8,775	98
65 years and over	38,381	21,357	17,024	1,824	1,752	72	2,318	2,247	71
Primary individual: Male	17,891	11,585	6,306	3,292	3,182	110	3,324	3,277	47
Female	21,185	15,779	5,406	2,248	2,203	45	3,135	3,105	30
Family head: Male	137,218	81,990	55,228	11,816	11,453	363	18,268	18,109	159
Female	42,735	30,402	12,333	3,544	3,499	45	8,136	8,118	18
Wife of head	127,835	76,735	51,100	9,906	9,591	315	16,843	16,692	151
Child of head	361,834	212,234	149,600	29,085	28,141	944	62,986	62,603	383
Other relative of head	95,285	50,666	44,619	3,449	3,332	117	7,985	7,888	97
Not related to head	22,834	16,240	6,594	2,147	2,062	85	3,405	3,356	49
In group quarters	34,551	22,377	12,174	5,821	4,768	1,053	4,142	3,144	998
Inmate of institution	15,294	7,653	7,641	1,484	776	708	2,477	1,636	841
Other	19,257	14,724	4,533	4,337	3,992	345	1,665	1,508	157
Persons per household	3.77	3.55	4.18	3.13	3.12	3.60	3.78	3.78	3.68
Persons per family	4.25	4.02	4.63	3.76	3.75	4.37	4.33	4.32	4.56
Persons, under 18 years old	352,373	204,686	147,687	28,830	27,651	1,179	61,619	60,751	868
Head or wife of head	915	579	336	112	111	1	232	232	—
Own child of head	287,014	171,659	115,355	25,661	24,816	845	55,610	55,291	319
In husband-wife households	211,577	116,702	94,875	17,153	16,436	717	34,619	34,362	257
Percent of total persons under 18 years	60.0	57.0	64.2	59.5	59.4	60.8	56.2	56.6	29.6
In household with female head	68,131	51,087	17,044	7,929	7,814	115	19,732	19,680	52
Other relative of head	55,202	27,201	28,001	2,013	1,932	81	4,103	4,032	71
Not related to head	4,821	2,631	2,190	561	524	37	763	743	20
In group quarters	4,421	2,616	1,805	483	268	215	911	453	458
Persons, 65 years old and over	64,519	36,789	27,730	2,848	2,723	125	4,189	4,049	140
Head of family: Male	17,422	8,878	8,544	654	624	30	1,010	978	32
Female	7,690	4,214	3,476	143	142	1	278	277	1
Wife of head	9,214	4,710	4,504	363	345	18	539	513	26
Other family member	11,247	6,749	4,498	358	348	10	815	806	9
Not related to head	2,809	1,988	821	141	137	4	197	195	2
Primary individual: Male	4,702	2,561	2,141	448	420	28	400	384	16
Female	8,567	5,704	2,863	579	566	13	630	608	22
Inmate of institution	2,480	1,730	750	109	88	21	276	245	31
Other, in group quarters	388	255	133	53	53	—	44	43	1

FAMILIES BY PRESENCE AND NUMBER OF OWN CHILDREN UNDER 18 YEARS

	(1)	(2)	(3)	(4)	(5)	(6)	(7)	(8)	(9)
All families	179,953	112,392	67,561	15,360	14,952	408	26,404	26,227	177
With own children under 18 years	104,263	65,546	38,717	10,145	9,882	263	19,027	18,934	93
Number of own children under 18 years	287,014	171,659	115,355	25,661	24,816	845	55,610	55,291	319
Number of own children under 6 years	79,949	49,799	30,150	8,360	8,105	255	18,491	18,383	108
Number of own children 6 to 17 years	207,065	121,860	85,205	17,301	16,711	590	37,119	36,908	211
With own children under 6 years only	20,254	13,956	6,298	2,872	2,813	59	4,999	4,979	20
With own children under 6 and 6 to 17 years	30,357	18,313	12,044	2,583	2,508	75	6,135	6,108	27
Husband-wife families	127,994	76,933	51,061	11,245	10,902	343	17,218	17,064	154
With own children under 18 years	76,628	45,144	31,484	7,005	6,785	220	11,848	11,771	77
Number of own children under 18 years	211,577	116,702	94,875	17,153	16,436	717	34,619	34,362	257
Number of own children under 6 years	61,118	35,305	25,813	5,657	5,429	228	11,883	11,792	91
Number of own children 6 to 17 years	150,459	81,397	69,062	11,496	11,007	489	22,736	22,570	166
With own children under 6 years only	16,260	10,727	5,533	2,066	2,013	53	3,325	3,308	17
With own children under 6 and 6 to 17 years	22,644	12,526	10,118	1,802	1,738	64	3,875	3,852	23
Families with female head	42,735	30,402	12,333	3,544	3,499	45	8,136	8,118	18
With own children under 18 years	24,597	18,699	5,898	2,857	2,819	38	6,696	6,682	14
Number of own children under 18 years	68,131	51,087	17,044	7,929	7,814	115	19,732	19,680	52
Number of own children under 6 years	17,305	13,705	3,600	2,562	2,540	22	6,320	6,308	12
Number of own children 6 to 17 years	50,826	37,382	13,444	5,367	5,274	93	13,412	13,372	40
With own children under 6 years only	3,554	2,972	582	737	732	5	1,591	1,589	2
With own children under 6 and 6 to 17 years	7,144	5,495	1,649	752	742	10	2,149	2,145	4

MARITAL STATUS

	(1)	(2)	(3)	(4)	(5)	(6)	(7)	(8)	(9)
Male, 14 years old and over	283,669	168,215	115,454	26,413	24,723	1,690	37,388	36,388	1,000
Single	105,901	60,152	45,749	9,992	9,125	867	14,297	13,639	658
Married, except separated	145,307	86,869	58,438	12,873	12,305	568	18,485	18,242	243
14 to 19 years	1,556	1,000	556	190	178	12	283	279	4
20 to 24 years	12,105	8,040	4,065	1,645	1,580	65	2,061	2,036	25
25 to 34 years	30,891	19,206	11,685	3,356	3,191	165	5,307	5,260	47
35 to 44 years	30,867	18,550	12,317	2,958	2,822	136	4,734	4,681	53
45 to 64 years	53,242	31,360	21,882	4,059	3,898	161	5,054	4,978	76
65 years and over	16,646	8,713	7,933	665	636	29	1,046	1,008	38
Separated	12,946	8,753	4,193	1,121	1,034	87	1,697	1,665	32
Widowed	12,634	7,519	5,115	652	614	38	1,007	985	22
Divorced	6,881	4,922	1,959	1,775	1,645	130	1,902	1,857	45
Female, 14 years old and over	307,037	191,224	115,813	21,975	21,350	625	41,474	40,951	523
Single	89,880	53,879	36,001	5,840	5,653	187	13,135	12,894	241
Married, except separated	143,620	85,809	57,811	10,738	10,390	348	18,003	17,824	179
14 to 19 years	4,740	2,873	1,867	356	348	8	744	742	2
20 to 24 years	16,300	10,423	5,877	1,531	1,495	36	2,845	2,831	14
25 to 34 years	32,380	19,862	12,518	2,518	2,739	92	5,364	5,331	33
35 to 44 years	32,557	19,436	13,121	2,517	2,432	85	4,518	4,480	38
45 to 64 years	47,392	27,889	19,503	3,105	2,997	108	3,929	3,866	63
65 years and over	10,251	5,326	4,925	398	379	19	603	574	29
Separated	21,602	16,660	4,942	1,453	1,440	13	3,761	3,727	34
Widowed	41,601	26,548	15,053	1,780	1,726	54	3,195	3,115	44
Divorced	10,334	8,328	2,006	2,164	2,141	23	3,416	3,391	25

SOCIAL CHARACTERISTICS OF THE BLACK POPULATION, FOR SELECTED AREAS
AGE BY RACE, SEX, AND HOUSEHOLD RELATIONSHIP: 1970

	Male	Female	Relationship to Head of Household	
ATLANTA, GEORGIA			**1970 Black Population**	
All ages..................	117,736	137,315	Black, all persons...............	255,051
			In households.......................	248,609
Under 5 years......................	13,447	13,353	Head..............................	71,169
5 to 9 years........................	14,536	14,713	14 to 24 years......................	7,372
10 to 14 years.....................	14,346	14,509	25 to 34 years......................	17,400
15 to 19 years.....................	12,326	13,922	35 to 44 years......................	14,451
20 to 24 years.....................	10,582	13,943	45 to 64 years......................	22,580
25 to 29 years.....................	9,307	10,685	65 years and over...................	9,366
			Primary individual: Male............	5,418
30 to 34 years.....................	7,595	8,947	Female............	8,742
35 to 39 years.....................	6,532	7,750	Family head: Male...................	39,627
40 to 44 years.....................	5,808	7,237	Female.................	17,382
45 to 49 years.....................	5,109	6,221	Wife of head........................	36,991
50 to 54 years.....................	4,693	6,121	Child of head.......................	106,352
55 to 59 years.....................	4,279	5,436	Other relative of head..............	26,366
			Not related to head................	7,731
60 to 64 years.....................	3,338	4,636	In group quarters..................	6,442
65 to 69 years.....................	2,502	4,056	Inmate of institution...............	2,490
70 to 74 years.....................	1,661	2,600	Other...............................	3,952
75 to 79 years.....................	831	1,509	Persons per household...............	3.49
80 to 84 years.....................	482	852	Black, all families................	57,009
85 years and over..................	362	825	With own children under 18 years...........	34,389
			With own children under 6 years............	18,330
Under 18 years.....................	49,799	50,464	Black, husband-wife families.....	37,004
62 years and over..................	7,702	12,463	With own children under 18 years...........	22,327
65 years and over..................	5,838	9,842	With own children under 6 years............	12,899
Median age.........................	22.0	24.4	Black, families with female head..	17,382
			With own children under 18 years...........	11,165
			With own children under 6 years............	5,084

	Male	Female	Relationship to Head of Household	
BALTIMORE, MARYLAND			**1970 Black Population**	
All ages..................	197,925	222,285	Black, all persons...............	420,210
			In households.......................	413,413
Under 5 years......................	21,785	21,392	Head..............................	114,095
5 to 9 years........................	25,782	25,776	14 to 24 years......................	9,398
10 to 14 years.....................	26,025	26,503	25 to 34 years......................	24,066
15 to 19 years.....................	20,741	22,984	35 to 44 years......................	25,688
20 to 24 years.....................	14,808	19,454	45 to 64 years......................	41,581
25 to 29 years.....................	12,140	14,811	65 years and over...................	13,362
			Primary individual: Male............	11,772
30 to 34 years.....................	10,341	13,160	Female............	12,996
35 to 39 years.....................	10,389	13,084	Family head: Male...................	60,558
40 to 44 years.....................	11,179	13,068	Female.................	28,769
45 to 49 years.....................	11,033	12,529	Wife of head........................	55,817
50 to 54 years.....................	9,491	10,558	Child of head.......................	183,457
55 to 59 years.....................	7,797	8,739	Other relative of head..............	43,327
			Not related to head................	16,717
60 to 64 years.....................	6,034	6,665	In group quarters..................	6,797
65 to 69 years.....................	4,662	5,709	Inmate of institution...............	3,409
70 to 74 years.....................	2,905	3,554	Other...............................	3,388
75 to 79 years.....................	1,551	2,102	Persons per household...............	3.62
80 to 84 years.....................	739	1,213	Black, all families................	89,327
85 years and over..................	550	984	With own children under 18 years...........	54,871
			With own children under 6 years............	27,333
Under 18 years.....................	86,835	87,752	Black, husband-wife families.....	55,930
62 years and over..................	13,767	17,363	With own children under 18 years...........	33,219
65 years and over..................	10,407	13,562	With own children under 6 years............	17,249
Median age.........................	21.6	23.7	Black, families with female head..	28,769
			With own children under 18 years...........	19,866
			With own children under 6 years............	9,368

SOCIAL CHARACTERISTICS OF THE BLACK POPULATION, FOR SELECTED AREAS
AGE BY RACE, SEX, AND HOUSEHOLD RELATIONSHIP: 1970

	1970 Black Population		
	Male	Female	Relationship to Head of Household

BIRMINGHAM, ALABAMA

	Male	Female		
All ages..................	57,921	68,467	Black, all persons................	126,388
			In households........................	124,912
Under 5 years......................	5,647	5,651	Head......................................	36,258
5 to 9 years.........................	6,905	6,776	14 to 24 years............................	1,888
10 to 14 years......................	7,788	7,953	25 to 34 years............................	5,003
15 to 19 years......................	6,591	7,281	35 to 44 years............................	6,322
20 to 24 years......................	4,005	5,097	45 to 64 years............................	14,527
25 to 29 years......................	2,750	3,553	65 years and over....................	8,518
			Primary individual: Male.............	2,802
30 to 34 years......................	2,405	3,270	Female.............	5,280
35 to 39 years......................	2,448	3,501	Family head: Male......................	20,369
40 to 44 years......................	2,804	3,966	Female......................	7,807
45 to 49 years......................	2,856	3,754	Wife of head..............................	19,034
50 to 54 years......................	2,799	3,501	Child of head..............................	53,048
55 to 59 years......................	2,912	3,467	Other relative of head....................	14,081
			Not related to head......................	2,491
60 to 64 years......................	2,592	3,225	In group quarters...................	1,476
65 to 69 years......................	2,249	3,011	Inmate of institution....................	591
70 to 74 years......................	1,529	2,057	Other......................................	885
75 to 79 years......................	853	1,189	Persons per household....................	3.45
80 to 84 years......................	444	663	Black, all families................	28,176
85 years and over..................	344	552	With own children under 18 years............	15,503
			With own children under 6 years............	6,957
Under 18 years....................	24,726	25,020	Black, husband-wife families.....	19,024
62 years and over..................	6,928	9,335	With own children under 18 years............	10,439
65 years and over..................	5,419	7,472	With own children under 6 years............	5,068
Median age.........................	22.5	27.1	Black, families with female head..	7,807
			With own children under 18 years............	4,589
			With own children under 6 years............	1,753

	1970 Black Population		
	Male	Female	Relationship to Head of Household

BOSTON, MASSACHUSETTS

	Male	Female		
All ages..................	47,654	57,053	Black, all persons................	104,707
			In households........................	102,035
Under 5 years......................	6,716	6,870	Head......................................	31,854
5 to 9 years.........................	7,162	7,119	14 to 24 years............................	4,163
10 to 14 years......................	5,796	6,070	25 to 34 years............................	8,964
15 to 19 years......................	4,532	5,252	35 to 44 years............................	6,777
20 to 24 years......................	3,814	5,887	45 to 64 years............................	8,764
25 to 29 years......................	3,748	5,108	65 years and over....................	3,186
			Primary individual: Male.............	3,897
30 to 34 years......................	2,832	3,698	Female.............	4,760
35 to 39 years......................	2,494	3,193	Family head: Male......................	13,907
40 to 44 years......................	2,292	2,988	Female......................	9,290
45 to 49 years......................	2,249	2,704	Wife of head..............................	12,690
50 to 54 years......................	1,822	2,079	Child of head..............................	47,694
55 to 59 years......................	1,260	1,638	Other relative of head....................	6,815
			Not related to head......................	2,982
60 to 64 years......................	899	1,303	In group quarters...................	2,672
65 to 69 years......................	779	1,095	Inmate of institution....................	987
70 to 74 years......................	599	868	Other......................................	1,685
75 to 79 years......................	348	545	Persons per household....................	3.20
80 to 84 years......................	189	344	Black, all families................	23,197
85 years and over..................	123	292	With own children under 18 years............	15,826
			With own children under 6 years............	9,396
Under 18 years....................	22,508	23,002	Black, husband-wife families.....	12,946
62 years and over..................	2,534	3,859	With own children under 18 years............	8,108
65 years and over..................	2,038	3,144	With own children under 6 years............	4,992
Median age.........................	19.6	22.7	Black, families with female head..	9,290
			With own children under 18 years............	7,339
			With own children under 6 years............	4,248

SOCIAL CHARACTERISTICS OF THE BLACK POPULATION, FOR SELECTED AREAS
AGE BY RACE, SEX, AND HOUSEHOLD RELATIONSHIP: 1970

	Male	Female	1970 Black Population Relationship to Head of Household	

CHICAGO, ILLINOIS

	Male	Female	Relationship to Head of Household	
All ages..................	515,929	586,691	**Black, all persons**...............	**1,102,620**
			In households........................	**1,090,981**
Under 5 years......................	59,635	60,601	Head...................................	314,640
5 to 9 years........................	69,768	69,350	14 to 24 years......................	26,135
10 to 14 years.....................	69,774	70,894	25 to 34 years......................	78,048
15 to 19 years.....................	51,176	56,472	35 to 44 years......................	75,210
20 to 24 years.....................	35,382	48,944	45 to 64 years......................	100,925
25 to 29 years.....................	34,619	44,294	65 years and over..................	34,322
			Primary individual: Male...............	34,417
30 to 34 years.....................	31,220	39,998	Female...............	38,444
35 to 39 years.....................	30,288	36,993	Family head: Male......................	170,069
40 to 44 years.....................	29,073	34,390	Female.....................	71,710
45 to 49 years.....................	26,431	29,718	Wife of head..........................	158,444
50 to 54 years.....................	21,486	24,431	Child of head..........................	499,667
55 to 59 years.....................	17,375	19,757	Other relative of head.....................	86,768
			Not related to head......................	31,462
60 to 65 years.....................	13,989	16,976	**In group quarters**...................	**11,639**
65 to 69 years.....................	11,485	13,961	Inmate of institution...................	5,877
70 to 74 years.....................	7,228	9,139	Other...........................	5,762
75 to 79 years.....................	3,853	5,359	Persons per household......................	**3.47**
80 to 84 years.....................	1,778	2,980	**Black, all families**.................	**241,777**
85 years and over..................	1,369	2,434	With own children under 18 years.............	153,680
			With own children under 6 years.............	79,485
Under 18 years.....................	233,000	236,854	**Black, husband-wife families**.....	**159,126**
62 years and over..................	33,620	43,591	With own children under 18 years.............	95,842
65 years and over..................	25,713	33,873	With own children under 6 years.............	51,373
Median age.......................	21.1	23.7	**Black, families with female head**..	**71,710**
			With own children under 18 years.............	53,484
			With own children under 6 years.............	26,450

	Male	Female	1970 Black Population Relationship to Head of Household	

CLEVELAND, OHIO

	Male	Female	Relationship to Head of Household	
All ages..................	134,633	153,208	**Black, all persons**...............	**287,841**
			In households........................	**284,740**
Under 5 years......................	13,979	13,819	Head...................................	86,474
5 to 9 years........................	16,037	16,633	14 to 24 years......................	6,902
10 to 14 years.....................	17,833	18,286	25 to 34 years......................	17,263
15 to 19 years.....................	14,302	15,218	35 to 44 years......................	20,026
20 to 24 years.....................	8,920	12,366	45 to 64 years......................	31,228
25 to 29 years.....................	7,329	9,787	65 years and over..................	11,055
			Primary individual: Male...............	9,100
30 to 34 years.....................	6,999	9,318	Female...............	11,015
35 to 39 years.....................	7,516	9,742	Family head: Male......................	46,571
40 to 44 years.....................	8,494	10,153	Female.....................	19,788
45 to 49 years.....................	8,247	9,164	Wife of head..........................	43,458
50 to 54 years.....................	6,773	7,296	Child of head..........................	124,801
55 to 59 years.....................	5,629	6,085	Other relative of head.....................	21,834
			Not related to head......................	8,173
60 to 64 years.....................	4,256	4,841	**In group quarters**...................	**3,101**
65 to 69 years.....................	3,433	4,140	Inmate of institution...................	1,452
70 to 74 years.....................	2,430	2,906	Other...........................	1,649
75 to 79 years.....................	1,396	1,728	Persons per household......................	**3.29**
80 to 84 years.....................	618	939	**Black, all families**.................	**66,359**
85 years and over..................	442	787	With own children under 18 years.............	40,212
			With own children under 6 years.............	19,213
Under 18 years.....................	57,231	58,244	**Black, husband-wife families**.....	**43,779**
62 years and over..................	10,712	13,242	With own children under 18 years.............	24,742
65 years and over..................	8,319	10,500	With own children under 6 years.............	12,176
Median age.......................	22.9	25.1	**Black, families with female head**..	**19,788**
			With own children under 18 years.............	14,506
			With own children under 6 years.............	6,752

SOCIAL CHARACTERISTICS OF THE BLACK POPULATION, FOR SELECTED AREAS
AGE BY RACE, SEX, AND HOUSEHOLD RELATIONSHIP: 1970

		1970 Black Population	
	Male	Female	Relationship to Head of Household

COMPTON, CALIFORNIA

	Male	Female		
All ages	26,899	28,882	Black, all persons	55,781
			In households	55,415
Under 5 years	3,270	3,244	Head	13,394
5 to 9 years	4,448	4,185	14 to 24 years	1,198
10 to 14 years	4,333	4,370	25 to 34 years	3,785
15 to 19 years	3,050	3,355	35 to 44 years	4,043
20 to 24 years	1,656	2,282	45 to 64 years	3,851
25 to 29 years	1,610	2,044	65 years and over	517
			Primary individual: Male	903
30 to 34 years	1,643	2,045	Female	702
35 to 39 years	1,727	2,009	Family head: Male	9,166
40 to 44 years	1,586	1,685	Female	2,623
45 to 49 years	1,356	1,334	Wife of head	8,692
50 to 54 years	971	852	Child of head	29,245
55 to 59 years	533	523	Other relative of head	3,271
			Not related to head	813
60 to 64 years	331	316	In group quarters	366
65 to 69 years	185	270	Inmate of institution	129
70 to 74 years	85	161	Other	237
75 to 79 years	47	97	Persons per household	4.14
80 to 84 years	36	53	Black, all families	11,789
85 years and over	32	57	With own children under 18 years	9,122
			With own children under 6 years	4,709
Under 18 years	14,147	14,001	Black, husband-wife families	8,805
62 years and over	551	809	With own children under 18 years	6,707
65 years and over	385	638	With own children under 6 years	3,640
Median age	17.3	18.9	Black, families with female head	2,623
			With own children under 18 years	2,219
			With own children under 6 years	1,009

		1970 Black Population	
	Male	Female	Relationship to Head of Household

DENVER, COLORADO

	Male	Female		
All ages	22,588	24,423	Black, all persons	49,369
			In households	48,112
Under 5 years	2,592	2,422	Head	14,909
5 to 9 years	3,043	3,050	14 to 24 years	1,434
10 to 14 years	2,994	2,962	25 to 34 years	3,719
15 to 19 years	2,269	2,289	35 to 44 years	3,609
20 to 24 years	1,590	1,997	45 to 64 years	4,511
25 to 29 years	1,525	1,814	65 years and over	1,636
			Primary individual: Male	1,758
30 to 34 years	1,471	1,631	Female	1,881
35 to 39 years	1,446	1,544	Family head: Male	8,271
40 to 44 years	1,314	1,452	Female	2,999
45 to 49 years	1,146	1,294	Wife of head	7,457
50 to 54 years	951	1,014	Child of head	21,504
55 to 59 years	669	824	Other relative of head	3,049
			Not related to head	1,193
60 to 64 years	585	622	In group quarters	1,257
65 to 69 years	386	555	Inmate of institution	508
70 to 74 years	256	415	Other	749
75 to 79 years	168	251	Persons per household	3.23
80 to 84 years	96	146	Black, all families	11,270
85 years and over	87	141	With own children under 18 years	7,433
			With own children under 6 years	3,770
Under 18 years	10,109	9,916	Black, husband-wife families	7,893
62 years and over	1,335	1,851	With own children under 18 years	4,934
65 years and over	993	1,508	With own children under 6 years	2,578
Median age	21.2	23.7	Black, families with female head	2,999
			With own children under 18 years	2,325
			With own children under 6 years	1,128

SOCIAL CHARACTERISTICS OF THE BLACK POPULATION, FOR SELECTED AREAS
AGE BY RACE, SEX, AND HOUSEHOLD RELATIONSHIP: 1970

	1970 Black Population		
	Male	Female	Relationship to Head of Household

DETROIT, MICHIGAN

	Male	Female	Relationship to Head of Household	
All ages..................	316,170	344,258	Black, all persons................	660,428
			In households.......................	653,728
Under 5 years......................	36,348	35,751	Head..........	192,902
5 to 9 years........................	36,134	36,336	14 to 24 years....................	17,782
10 to 14 years.....................	38,948	38,859	25 to 34 years....................	39,883
15 to 19 years.....................	32,344	34,723	35 to 44 years....................	41,695
20 to 24 years.....................	24,603	30,887	45 to 64 years....................	70,819
25 to 29 years.....................	20,816	23,600	65 years and over.................	22,723
			Primary individual: Male........	22,306
30 to 34 years.....................	15,550	19,433	Female...........	21,035
35 to 39 years.....................	16,133	20,029	Family head: Male...............	110,713
40 to 44 years.....................	18,544	21,327	Female.............	38,848
45 to 49 years.....................	18,951	20,321	Wife of head......................	102,744
50 to 54 years.....................	16,198	17,249	Child of head.....................	282,967
55 to 59 years.....................	13,522	13,799	Other relative of head............	55,431
			Not related to head...............	19,684
60 to 65 years.....................	10,205	10,857	In group quarters..............	6,700
65 to 69 years.....................	7,996	8,618	Inmate of institution.............	3,643
70 to 74 years.....................	5,092	5,817	Other.............................	3,057
75 to 79 years.....................	2,657	3,399	Persons per household.............	3.39
80 to 84 years.....................	1,242	1,824	Black, all families.............	149,561
85 years and over..................	887	1,429	With own children under 18 years..........	89,967
			With own children under 6 years..........	46,936
Under 18 years.....................	132,340	132,499	Black, husband-wife families.....	103,531
62 years and over..................	23,551	27,186	With own children under 18 years..........	69,238
65 years and over..................	17,874	21,087	With own children under 6 years..........	32,399
Median age.........................	22.9	24.3	Black, families with female head..	38,848
			With own children under 18 years............	28,102
			With own children under 6 years............	13,583

	1970 Black Population		
	Male	Female	Relationship to Head of Household

GARY, INDIANA

	Male	Female	Relationship to Head of Household	
All ages..................	44,095	48,600	Black, all persons................	92,695
			In households.......................	92,211
Under 5 years......................	4,749	5,022	Head..........	24,861
5 to 9 years........................	5,669	5,719	14 to 24 years....................	1,911
10 to 14 years.....................	6,361	6,441	25 to 34 years....................	5,296
15 to 19 years.....................	5,089	5,509	35 to 44 years....................	5,948
20 to 24 years.....................	2,931	3,801	45 to 64 years....................	8,771
25 to 29 years.....................	2,560	3,207	65 years and over.................	2,935
			Primary individual: Male........	2,348
30 to 34 years.....................	2,236	2,779	Female...........	2,119
35 to 39 years.....................	2,360	2,915	Family head: Male...............	15,696
40 to 44 years.....................	2,636	3,086	Female.............	4,698
45 to 49 years.....................	2,468	2,525	Wife of head......................	14,774
50 to 54 years.....................	1,925	2,091	Child of head.....................	43,381
55 to 59 years.....................	1,632	1,603	Other relative of head............	7,236
			Not related to head...............	1,959
60 to 64 years.....................	1,241	1,331	In group quarters..............	484
65 to 69 years.....................	949	1,094	Inmate of institution.............	229
70 to 74 years.....................	651	679	Other.............................	255
75 to 79 years.....................	340	395	Persons per household.............	3.71
80 to 84 years.....................	167	241	Black, all families.............	20,394
85 years and over..................	131	162	With own children under 18 years..........	13,227
			With own children under 6 years..........	6,380
Under 18 years.....................	20,099	20,768	Black, husband-wife families.....	14,818
62 years and over..................	2,937	3,374	With own children under 18 years..........	9,412
65 years and over..................	2,238	2,571	With own children under 6 years..........	4,786
Median age.........................	20.3	22.1	Black, families with female head..	4,698
			With own children under 18 years............	3,476
			With own children under 6 years............	1,481

SOCIAL CHARACTERISTICS OF THE BLACK POPULATION, FOR SELECTED AREAS
AGE BY RACE, SEX, AND HOUSEHOLD RELATIONSHIP: 1970

	1970 Black Population		
	Male	Female	Relationship to Head of Household
HOUSTON, TEXAS			
All ages..................	150,927	165,624	Black, all persons................ 342,775
			In households........................ 339,271
Under 5 years......................	18,221	18,012	Head.. 96,623
5 to 9 years.......................	20,078	20,041	14 to 24 years........................... 9,059
10 to 14 years.....................	18,866	19,153	25 to 34 years........................... 23,127
15 to 19 years.....................	14,806	16,268	35 to 44 years........................... 21,962
20 to 24 years.....................	11,940	15,811	45 to 64 years........................... 30,804
25 to 29 years.....................	10,977	12,656	65 years and over...................... 11,671
			Primary individual: Male............... 9,358
30 to 34 years.....................	9,251	10,867	Female............. 10,296
35 to 39 years.....................	8,616	9,980	Family head: Male..................... 59,411
40 to 44 years.....................	8,394	9,471	Female................... 17,558
45 to 49 years.....................	7,376	7,905	Wife of head.............................. 56,062
50 to 54 years.....................	5,921	6,223	Child of head............................. 151,303
55 to 59 years.....................	5,014	5,400	Other relative of head................ 28,313
			Not related to head..................... 6,970
60 to 64 years.....................	4,114	4,623	In group quarters................. 3,504
65 to 69 years.....................	3,227	3,836	Inmate of institution..................... 1,177
70 to 74 years.....................	1,965	2,391	Other.. 2,327
75 to 79 years.....................	1,104	1,388	Persons per household................... 3.51
80 to 84 years.....................	573	823	Black, all families................. 76,969
85 years and over..................	484	776	With own children under 18 years........... 48,439
			With own children under 6 years............ 25,962
Under 18 years.....................	66,382	66,924	Black, husband-wife families..... 56,142
62 years and over..................	9,716	11,908	With own children under 18 years........... 35,233
65 years and over..................	7,353	9,214	With own children under 6 years............ 20,014
Median age.........................	21.5	23.0	Black, families with female head.. 17,558
			With own children under 18 years........... 11,877
			With own children under 6 years............ 5,434

	1970 Black Population		
	Male	Female	Relationship to Head of Household
INDIANAPOLIS, INDIANA			
All ages..................	63,208	71,112	Black, all persons................ 134,320
			In households........................ 131,930
Under 5 years......................	7,115	6,970	Head.. 38,177
5 to 9 years.......................	8,354	8,444	14 to 24 years........................... 2,977
10 to 14 years.....................	8,535	8,529	25 to 34 years........................... 7,865
15 to 19 years.....................	6,299	6,963	35 to 44 years........................... 8,258
20 to 24 years.....................	4,157	5,527	45 to 64 years........................... 13,537
25 to 29 years.....................	3,736	4,527	65 years and over...................... 5,540
			Primary individual: Male............... 3,668
30 to 34 years.....................	3,357	4,140	Female............. 4,738
35 to 39 years.....................	3,286	4,130	Family head: Male..................... 22,057
40 to 44 years.....................	3,472	4,190	Female................... 7,714
45 to 49 years.....................	3,419	3,893	Wife of head.............................. 20,659
50 to 54 years.....................	2,749	3,194	Child of head............................. 58,536
55 to 59 years.....................	2,575	2,934	Other relative of head................ 11,192
			Not related to head..................... 3,366
60 to 64 years.....................	2,040	2,364	In group quarters................. 2,390
65 to 69 years.....................	1,583	2,039	Inmate of institution..................... 1,553
70 to 74 years.....................	1,190	1,405	Other.. 837
75 to 79 years.....................	721	928	Persons per household................... 3.46
80 to 84 years.....................	353	530	Black, all families................. 29,771
85 years and over..................	267	405	With own children under 18 years........... 18,046
			With own children under 6 years............ 9,230
Under 18 years.....................	28,227	28,343	Black, husband-wife families..... 20,791
62 years and over..................	5,254	6,662	With own children under 18 years........... 12,200
65 years and over..................	4,114	5,307	With own children under 6 years............ 6,608
Median age.........................	21.6	24.2	Black, families with female head.. 7,714
			With own children under 18 years........... 5,331
			With own children under 6 years............ 2,453

SOCIAL CHARACTERISTICS OF THE BLACK POPULATION, FOR SELECTED AREAS
AGE BY RACE, SEX, AND HOUSEHOLD RELATIONSHIP: 1970

	1970 Black Population		
	Male	Female	Relationship to Head of Household
JACKSON, MISSISSIPPI			
All ages...................	28,198	32,865	Black, all persons................ 61,063
			In households...................... 58,874
Under 5 years.......................	3,639	3,516	Head.. 15,398
5 to 9 years........................	3,898	3,885	14 to 24 years............................ 1,387
10 to 14 years......................	3,823	3,900	25 to 34 years............................ 3,162
15 to 19 years......................	3,307	3,806	35 to 44 years............................ 3,041
20 to 24 years......................	2,537	3,352	45 to 64 years............................ 5,335
25 to 29 years......................	1,640	2,076	65 years and over....................... 2,473
			Primary individual: Male............... 1,050
30 to 34 years......................	1,311	1,843	Female............. 1,857
35 to 39 years......................	1,171	1,628	Family head: Male...................... 8,829
40 to 44 years......................	1,176	1,623	Female.................... 3,662
45 to 49 years......................	1,072	1,413	Wife of head............................... 8,269
50 to 54 years......................	1,020	1,314	Child of head.............................. 27,559
55 to 59 years......................	968	1,157	Other relative of head.................... 6,043
			Not related to head....................... 1,605
60 to 64 years......................	890	1,077	In group quarters................... 2,189
65 to 69 years......................	725	1,000	Inmate of institution...................... 201
70 to 74 years......................	427	567	Other....................................... 1,988
75 to 79 years......................	322	321	Persons per household.................... 3.82
80 to 84 years......................	143	193	Black, all families.................. 12,491
85 years and over..................	129	194	With own children under 18 years....... 7,737
			With own children under 6 years........ 4,276
Under 18 years.....................	13,267	13,304	Black, husband-wife families..... 8,257
62 years and over.................	2,257	2,905	With own children under 18 years....... 5,120
65 years and over.................	1,746	2,275	With own children under 6 years....... 3,048
Median age........................	19.1	22.0	Black, families with female head.. 3,662
			With own children under 18 years.......... 2,357
			With own children under 6 years............ 1,122

	1970 Black Population		
	Male	Female	Relationship to Head of Household
LITTLE ROCK, ARKANSAS			
All ages...................	15,151	17,923	Black, all persons................ 33,074
			In households...................... 32,308
Under 5 years.......................	1,761	1,777	Head.. 9,254
5 to 9 years........................	1,942	2,017	14 to 24 years............................ 921
10 to 14 years......................	2,052	1,998	25 to 34 years............................ 1,721
15 to 19 years......................	1,639	1,854	35 to 44 years............................ 1,531
20 to 24 years......................	1,224	1,681	45 to 64 years............................ 3,050
25 to 29 years......................	938	1,104	65 years and over....................... 2,031
			Primary individual: Male............... 799
30 to 34 years......................	640	935	Female............. 1,354
35 to 39 years......................	637	837	Family head: Male...................... 5,095
40 to 44 years......................	627	844	Female.................... 2,006
45 to 49 years......................	617	835	Wife of head............................... 4,774
50 to 54 years......................	650	771	Child of head.............................. 14,321
55 to 59 years......................	586	751	Other relative of head.................... 3,029
			Not related to head....................... 930
60 to 64 years......................	510	697	In group quarters................... 766
65 to 69 years......................	489	688	Inmate of institution...................... 414
70 to 74 years......................	365	472	Other....................................... 352
75 to 79 years......................	242	313	Persons per household.................... 3.49
80 to 84 years......................	135	183	Black, all families.................. 7,101
85 years and over..................	97	166	With own children under 18 years....... 4,147
			With own children under 6 years........ 2,250
Under 18 years.....................	6,795	6,858	Black, husband-wife families..... 4,775
62 years and over.................	1,632	2,252	With own children under 18 years....... 2,710
65 years and over.................	1,328	1,822	With own children under 6 years....... 1,514
Median age........................	20.7	23.9	Black, families with female head.. 2,006
			With own children under 18 years.......... 1,312
			With own children under 6 years............ 666

SOCIAL CHARACTERISTICS OF THE BLACK POPULATION, FOR SELECTED AREAS
AGE BY RACE, SEX, AND HOUSEHOLD RELATIONSHIP: 1970

	1970 Black Population		
	Male	Female	Relationship to Head of Household
LONG BEACH, CALIFORNIA			
All ages..................	9,483	9,508	Black, all persons............... 18,991
			In households........................ 17,926
Under 5 years.......................	1,262	1,313	Head................................... 5,738
5 to 9 years........................	1,252	1,264	14 to 24 years....................... 910
10 to 14 years......................	1,023	1,055	25 to 34 years....................... 1,848
15 to 19 years......................	862	869	35 to 44 years....................... 1,182
20 to 24 years......................	1,144	1,014	45 to 64 years....................... 1,449
25 to 29 years......................	847	873	65 years and over.................... 349
			Primary individual: Male............... 901
30 to 34 years......................	797	683	Female............... 669
35 to 39 years......................	558	478	Family head: Male.................... 2,945
40 to 44 years......................	441	471	Female.................... 1,223
45 to 49 years......................	366	367	Wife of head......................... 2,635
50 to 54 years......................	301	329	Child of head........................ 8,245
55 to 59 years......................	204	287	Other relative of head............... 930
			Not related to head.................. 378
60 to 64 years......................	182	198	In group quarters.................. 1,065
65 to 69 years......................	106	143	Inmate of institution................ 192
70 to 74 years......................	71	78	Other................................. 873
75 to 79 years......................	29	44	Persons per household................ 3.12
80 to 84 years......................	21	22	Black, all families............... 4,168
85 years and over..................	17	20	With own children under 18 years........... 2,927
			With own children under 6 years............ 1,831
Under 18 years.....................	3,991	4,099	Black, husband-wife families.... 2,762
62 years and over..................	340	411	With own children under 18 years........... 1,814
65 years and over..................	244	307	With own children under 6 years............ 1,186
Median age.........................	21.5	21.2	Black, families with female head.. 1,223
			With own children under 18 years........... 1,025
			With own children under 6 years............ 606

	1970 Black Population		
	Male	Female	Relationship to Head of Household
LOS ANGELES, CALIFORNIA			
All ages..................	236,769	266,837	Black, all persons............... 503,606
			In households........................ 494,652
Under 5 years.......................	27,112	27,096	Head................................... 170,684
5 to 9 years........................	28,927	29,013	14 to 24 years....................... 16,482
10 to 14 years......................	26,767	27,601	25 to 34 years....................... 42,464
15 to 19 years......................	21,359	23,023	35 to 44 years....................... 36,736
20 to 24 years......................	18,408	24,153	45 to 64 years....................... 56,075
25 to 29 years......................	18,367	21,085	65 years and over.................... 18,927
			Primary individual: Male............... 26,437
30 to 34 years......................	16,589	17,762	Female............... 27,833
35 to 39 years......................	14,601	15,858	Family head: Male.................... 78,894
40 to 44 years......................	13,356	15,351	Female.................... 37,520
45 to 49 years......................	12,920	14,696	Wife of head......................... 71,829
50 to 54 years......................	10,821	12,963	Child of head........................ 201,973
55 to 59 years......................	9,138	11,277	Other relative of head............... 35,840
			Not related to head.................. 14,326
60 to 64 years......................	7,015	9,038	In group quarters.................. 8,954
65 to 69 years......................	4,919	7,247	Inmate of institution................ 4,494
70 to 74 years......................	3,070	4,676	Other................................. 4,460
75 to 79 years......................	1,795	2,914	Persons per household................ 2.90
80 to 84 years......................	887	1,694	Black, all families............... 116,414
85 years and over..................	718	1,390	With own children under 18 years........... 70,945
			With own children under 6 years............ 37,769
Under 18 years.....................	96,338	97,686	Black, husband-wife families..... 73,521
62 years and over..................	15,247	23,020	With own children under 18 years........... 41,365
65 years and over..................	11,389	17,921	With own children under 6 years............ 23,578
Median age.........................	23.9	25.6	Black, families with female head.. 37,520
			With own children under 18 years........... 27,423
			With own children under 6 years............ 13,425

SOCIAL CHARACTERISTICS OF THE BLACK POPULATION, FOR SELECTED AREAS
AGE BY RACE, SEX, AND HOUSEHOLD RELATIONSHIP: 1970

	1970 Black Population		
	Male	Female	Relationship to Head of Household
LOUISVILLE, KENTUCKY			
All ages..................	39,779	46,261	Black, all persons...............	86,040
			In households.......................	85,073
Under 5 years.......................	4,291	4,191	Head....................................	26,238
5 to 9 years.......................	4,992	4,861	14 to 24 years.......................	2,093
10 to 14 years.......................	5,353	5,373	25 to 34 years.......................	4,377
15 to 19 years.......................	4,238	4,661	35 to 44 years.......................	4,942
20 to 24 years.......................	2,582	3,510	45 to 64 years.......................	9,861
25 to 29 years.......................	1,976	2,577	65 years and over....................	4,965
			Primary individual: Male.............	2,835
30 to 34 years.......................	1,728	2,373	Female....	3,913
35 to 39 years.......................	1,815	2,419	Family head: Male....	13,243
40 to 44 years.......................	1,983	2,629	Female....	6,247
45 to 49 years.......................	2,173	2,594	Wife of head..........................	12,286
50 to 54 years.......................	1,930	2,446	Child of head.........................	36,685
55 to 59 years.......................	1,792	2,124	Other relative of head................	7,676
			Not related to head...................	2,188
60 to 64 years.......................	1,602	1,979	In group quarters..................	967
65 to 69 years.......................	1,362	1,737	Inmate of institution.................	549
70 to 74 years.......................	921	1,228	Other..................................	418
75 to 79 years.......................	584	761	Persons per household.................	3.24
80 to 84 years.......................	265	420	Black, all families...............	19,490
85 years and over...................	192	378	With own children under 18 years...........	10,890
			With own children under 6 years............	5,296
Under 18 years.......................	17,362	17,392	Black, husband-wife families.....	12,348
62 years and over...................	4,219	5,705	With own children under 18 years...........	6,292
65 years and over...................	3,324	4,524	With own children under 6 years............	3,173
Median age.........................	22.0	26.0	Black, families with female head..	6,247
			With own children under 18 years...........	4,261
			With own children under 6 years............	1,992

	1970 Black Population		
	Male	Female	Relationship to Head of Household
MEMPHIS, TENNESSEE			
All ages..................	112,489	130,024	Black, all persons...............	242,513
			In households.......................	240,380
Under 5 years.......................	13,292	13,325	Head....................................	63,207
5 to 9 years.......................	15,253	15,422	14 to 24 years.......................	4,334
10 to 14 years.......................	15,886	16,163	25 to 34 years.......................	12,176
15 to 19 years.......................	12,910	13,906	35 to 44 years.......................	12,419
20 to 24 years.......................	7,819	10,394	45 to 64 years.......................	22,452
25 to 29 years.......................	6,359	7,904	65 years and over....................	11,826
			Primary individual: Male.............	4,866
30 to 34 years.......................	5,061	7,115	Female....	7,532
35 to 39 years.......................	4,805	6,717	Family head: Male....	36,072
40 to 44 years.......................	5,112	6,688	Female....	14,737
45 to 49 years.......................	4,770	6,043	Wife of head..........................	33,525
50 to 54 years.......................	4,509	5,419	Child of head.........................	110,303
55 to 59 years.......................	4,290	5,241	Other relative of head................	27,990
			Not related to head...................	5,355
60 to 64 years.......................	3,958	4,790	In group quarters..................	2,133
65 to 69 years.......................	3,328	4,310	Inmate of institution.................	772
70 to 74 years.......................	2,361	2,878	Other..................................	1,361
75 to 79 years.......................	1,414	1,762	Persons per household.................	3.80
80 to 84 years.......................	786	1,056	Black, all families...............	50,809
85 years and over...................	576	891	With own children under 18 years...........	30,347
			With own children under 6 years............	15,361
Under 18 years.......................	52,907	53,799	Black, husband-wife families.....	33,535
62 years and over...................	10,701	13,678	With own children under 18 years...........	19,751
65 years and over...................	8,465	10,897	With own children under 6 years............	10,727
Median age.........................	19.6	23.0	Black, families with female head..	14,737
			With own children under 18 years...........	9,629
			With own children under 6 years............	4,288

SOCIAL CHARACTERISTICS OF THE BLACK POPULATION, FOR SELECTED AREAS
AGE BY RACE, SEX, AND HOUSEHOLD RELATIONSHIP: 1970

	1970 Black Population		
	Male	Female	Relationship to Head of Household

MILWAUKEE, WISCONSIN

	Male	Female		
All ages..................	50,006	55,082	Black, all persons...............	105,088
			In households........................	104,120
Under 5 years.......................	7,263	7,274	Head.......................................	27,540
5 to 9 years.........................	7,503	7,574	14 to 24 years........................	3,791
10 to 14 years.......................	7,217	7,319	25 to 34 years........................	7,492
15 to 19 years.......................	5,372	5,774	35 to 44 years........................	6,846
20 to 24 years.......................	3,840	5,102	45 to 64 years........................	7,496
25 to 29 years.......................	3,099	4,057	65 years and over..................	1,915
			Primary individual: Male...............	2,662
30 to 34 years.......................	2,786	3,659	Female...............	2,669
35 to 39 years.......................	2,658	3,391	Family head: Male.................	15,121
40 to 44 years.......................	2,692	2,964	Female...............	7,088
45 to 49 years.......................	2,214	2,227	Wife of head..........................	13,938
50 to 54 years.......................	1,597	1,659	Child of head.........................	53,234
55 to 59 years.......................	1,287	1,284	Other relative of head...............	6,746
			Not related to head....................	2,662
60 to 64 years.......................	895	1,014	In group quarters..................	968
65 to 69 years.......................	675	777	Inmate of institution..................	433
70 to 74 years.......................	451	478	Other.................................	535
75 to 79 years.......................	226	223	Persons per household...............	3.78
80 to 84 years.......................	106	162	Black, all families...............	22,209
85 years and over..................	125	144	With own children under 18 years...........	16,082
			With own children under 6 years...........	9,377
Under 18 years......................	25,506	25,818	Black, husband-wife families.....	14,236
62 years and over..................	2,060	2,372	With own children under 18 years...........	9,846
65 years and over..................	1,583	1,784	With own children under 6 years...........	5,962
Median age.........................	17.8	19.7	Black, families with female head..	7,088
			With own children under 18 years...........	5,829
			With own children under 6 years...........	3,252

	1970 Black Population		
	Male	Female	Relationship to Head of Household

MINNEAPOLIS, MINNESOTA

	Male	Female		
All ages..................	9,345	9,660	Black, all persons...............	19,005
			In households........................	18,659
Under 5 years.......................	1,237	1,182	Head.......................................	5,915
5 to 9 years.........................	1,215	1,270	14 to 24 years........................	750
10 to 14 years.......................	1,184	1,106	25 to 34 years........................	1,534
15 to 19 years.......................	865	927	35 to 44 years........................	1,262
20 to 24 years.......................	768	904	45 to 64 years........................	1,747
25 to 29 years.......................	689	749	65 years and over..................	622
			Primary individual: Male...............	926
30 to 34 years.......................	588	595	Female...............	730
35 to 39 years.......................	500	528	Family head: Male.................	2,914
40 to 44 years.......................	504	504	Female...............	1,345
45 to 49 years.......................	485	470	Wife of head..........................	2,347
50 to 54 years.......................	356	341	Child of head.........................	8,614
55 to 59 years.......................	304	299	Other relative of head...............	1,064
			Not related to head....................	719
60 to 64 years.......................	228	225	In group quarters..................	346
65 to 69 years.......................	144	217	Inmate of institution..................	125
70 to 74 years.......................	115	144	Other.................................	221
75 to 79 years.......................	85	103	Persons per household...............	3.15
80 to 84 years.......................	43	56	Black, all families...............	4,259
85 years and over..................	35	40	With own children under 18 years...........	2,856
			With own children under 6 years...........	1,636
Under 18 years......................	4,192	4,111	Black, husband-wife families.....	2,751
62 years and over..................	542	689	With own children under 18 years...........	1,674
65 years and over..................	422	560	With own children under 6 years...........	989
Median age.........................	21.1	21.9	Black, families with female head..	1,345
			With own children under 18 years...........	1,108
			With own children under 6 years...........	618

SOCIAL CHARACTERISTICS OF THE BLACK POPULATION, FOR SELECTED AREAS
AGE BY RACE, SEX, AND HOUSEHOLD RELATIONSHIP: 1970

	Male	Female	1970 Black Population — Relationship to Head of Household	
NASHVILLE, TENNESSEE				
All ages.................	41,249	46,602	Black, all persons...............	87,851
			In households........................	81,806
Under 5 years......................	3,890	3,815	Head....................................	24,213
5 to 9 years........................	4,683	4,728	14 to 24 years........................	2,022
10 to 14 years.....................	5,007	5,059	25 to 34 years........................	4,433
15 to 19 years.....................	4,661	5,164	35 to 44 years........................	4,659
20 to 24 years.....................	4,137	4,610	45 to 64 years........................	8,687
25 to 29 years.....................	2,615	2,768	65 years and over....................	4,412
			Primary individual: Male.............	2,337
30 to 34 years.....................	2,071	2,425	Female..............	3,307
35 to 39 years.....................	1,994	2,547	Family head: Male...................	13,418
40 to 44 years.....................	2,058	2,458	Female..................	5,151
45 to 49 years.....................	1,986	2,379	Wife of head.........................	12,499
50 to 54 years.....................	1,858	2,232	Child of head........................	33,668
55 to 59 years.....................	1,715	2,114	Other relative of head...............	8,768
			Not related to head..................	2,658
60 to 64 years.....................	1,473	1,918	**In group quarters.................**	**6,045**
65 to 69 years.....................	1,261	1,725	Inmate of institution................	2,567
70 to 74 years.....................	857	1,152	Other.................................	3,478
75 to 79 years.....................	525	708	Persons per household................	3.38
80 to 84 years.....................	269	393	**Black, all families.................**	**18,569**
85 years and over..................	189	407	With own children under 18 years...........	10,233
			With own children under 6 years............	5,007
Under 18 years.....................	16,261	16,318	**Black, husband-wife families.....**	**12,509**
62 years and over..................	3,974	5,500	With own children under 18 years...........	6,898
65 years and over..................	3,101	4,385	With own children under 6 years............	3,597
Median age.........................	22.9	24.9	**Black, families with female head..**	**5,151**
			With own children under 18 years...........	3,035
			With own children under 6 years............	1,308

	Male	Female	1970 Black Population — Relationship to Head of Household	
NEWARK, NEW JERSEY				
All ages.................	96,349	111,109	Black, all persons...............	207,458
			In households........................	205,194
Under 5 years......................	13,510	13,450	Head....................................	60,446
5 to 9 years........................	13,945	13,766	14 to 24 years........................	6,281
10 to 14 years.....................	12,762	12,528	25 to 34 years........................	16,619
15 to 19 years.....................	9,284	10,228	35 to 44 years........................	14,858
20 to 24 years.....................	6,981	9,920	45 to 64 years........................	17,549
25 to 29 years.....................	6,731	9,382	65 years and over....................	5,139
			Primary individual: Male.............	6,577
30 to 34 years.....................	6,015	8,129	Female..............	7,485
35 to 39 years.....................	5,769	7,380	Family head: Male...................	29,359
40 to 44 years.....................	5,032	6,321	Female..................	17,025
45 to 49 years.....................	4,484	5,404	Wife of head.........................	27,045
50 to 54 years.....................	3,541	3,985	Child of head........................	97,237
55 to 59 years.....................	2,685	3,324	Other relative of head...............	15,262
			Not related to head..................	5,204
60 to 64 years.....................	2,128	2,572	**In group quarters.................**	**2,264**
65 to 69 years.....................	1,558	2,021	Inmate of institution................	1,018
70 to 74 years.....................	915	1,337	Other.................................	1,246
75 to 79 years.....................	569	645	Persons per household................	3.39
80 to 84 years.....................	232	416	**Black, all families.................**	**46,384**
85 years and over..................	208	301	With own children under 18 years...........	31,470
			With own children under 6 years............	17,438
Under 18 years.....................	46,282	46,049	**Black, husband-wife families.....**	**27,115**
62 years and over..................	4,714	6,187	With own children under 18 years...........	17,416
65 years and over..................	3,482	4,720	With own children under 6 years............	10,055
Median age.........................	19.3	22.8	**Black, families with female head..**	**17,025**
			With own children under 18 years...........	13,149
			With own children under 6 years............	7,041

SOCIAL CHARACTERISTICS OF THE BLACK POPULATION, FOR SELECTED AREAS
AGE BY RACE, SEX, AND HOUSEHOLD RELATIONSHIP: 1970

	1970 Black Population		
	Male	Female	Relationship to Head of Household
NEW YORK, NEW YORK			
All ages..................	761,933	906,182	Black, all persons............... 1,668,115
			In households...................... 1,639,231
Under 5 years......................	88,433	87,151	Head............................... 524,534
5 to 9 years.......................	96,750	94,971	14 to 24 years................... 39,826
10 to 14 years....................	88,641	88,628	25 to 34 years................... 133,413
15 to 19 years....................	72,905	77,174	35 to 44 years................... 124,385
20 to 24 years....................	55,953	77,862	45 to 64 years................... 173,291
25 to 29 years....................	58,288	77,742	65 years and over.............. 53,619
			Primary individual: Male............... 56,809
30 to 34 years....................	52,921	68,703	Female............ 80,566
35 to 39 years....................	47,924	61,806	Family head: Male.............. 259,934
40 to 44 years....................	45,450	58,608	Female.............. 127,225
45 to 49 years....................	41,864	52,561	Wife of head...................... 241,281
50 to 54 years....................	32,819	43,422	Child of head..................... 691,538
55 to 59 years....................	25,621	35,331	Other relative of head............. 126,866
			Not related to head.............. 55,012
60 to 64 years....................	20,021	28,653	In group quarters................. 28,884
65 to 69 years....................	15,311	22,679	Inmate of institution............. 16,939
70 to 74 years....................	9,655	14,381	Other.............................. 11,945
75 to 79 years....................	5,142	8,216	Persons per household............. 3.13
80 to 84 years....................	2,427	4,630	Black, all families.............. 387,159
85 years and over................	1,808	3,664	With own children under 18 years........... 241,039
			With own children under 6 years........... 124,338
Under 18 years....................	319,965	317,701	Black, husband-wife families..... 242,285
62 years and over................	45,439	69,631	With own children under 18 years........... 146,295
65 years and over................	34,343	53,570	With own children under 6 years........... 79,368
Median age........................	23.1	26.8	Black, families with female head.. 127,225
			With own children under 18 years........... 88,117
			With own children under 6 years........... 42,499

	1970 Black Population		
	Male	Female	Relationship to Head of Household
NORFOLK, VIRGINIA			
All ages..................	42,336	44,925	Black, all persons............... 87,261
			In households...................... 82,887
Under 5 years......................	4,309	4,378	Head............................... 23,903
5 to 9 years.......................	5,165	5,179	14 to 24 years................... 2,100
10 to 14 years....................	5,099	5,286	25 to 34 years................... 4,376
15 to 19 years....................	4,838	4,519	35 to 44 years................... 4,627
20 to 24 years....................	4,567	3,659	45 to 64 years................... 9,195
25 to 29 years....................	2,327	2,616	65 years and over.............. 3,605
			Primary individual: Male............... 2,294
30 to 34 years....................	2,008	2,302	Female............ 2,998
35 to 39 years....................	1,882	2,388	Family head: Male.............. 12,781
40 to 44 years....................	2,095	2,514	Female.............. 5,830
45 to 49 years....................	2,257	2,644	Wife of head...................... 11,766
50 to 54 years....................	2,197	2,327	Child of head..................... 36,483
55 to 59 years....................	1,702	1,991	Other relative of head............. 7,976
			Not related to head.............. 2,759
60 to 64 years....................	1,336	1,646	In group quarters................. 4,374
65 to 69 years....................	1,042	1,449	Inmate of institution............. 505
70 to 74 years....................	708	912	Other.............................. 3,869
75 to 79 years....................	414	537	Persons per household............. 3.47
80 to 84 years....................	211	314	Black, all families.............. 10,611
85 years and over................	179	264	With own children under 18 years........... 10,992
			With own children under 6 years........... 5,671
Under 18 years....................	17,325	17,625	Black, husband-wife families..... 11,784
62 years and over................	3,263	4,457	With own children under 18 years........... 6,761
65 years and over................	2,554	3,476	With own children under 6 years........... 3,562
Median age........................	21.9	24.2	Black, families with female head.. 5,830
			With own children under 18 years........... 3,895
			With own children under 6 years........... 1,992

SOCIAL CHARACTERISTICS OF THE BLACK POPULATION, FOR SELECTED AREAS
AGE BY RACE, SEX, AND HOUSEHOLD RELATIONSHIP: 1970

	Male	Female	1970 Black Population — Relationship to Head of Household	

OAKLAND, CALIFORNIA

	Male	Female		
All ages..................	59,934	64,776	Black, all persons...............	124,710
			In households.......................	123,500
Under 5 years.....................	6,159	6,004	Head.....................................	39,645
5 to 9 years......................	7,300	7,324	14 to 24 years......................	3,878
10 to 14 years....................	7,266	7,396	25 to 34 years......................	8,871
15 to 19 years....................	6,271	6,484	35 to 44 years......................	8,132
20 to 24 years....................	4,992	6,018	45 to 64 years......................	14,420
25 to 29 years....................	4,052	4,683	65 years and over...................	4,344
			Primary individual: Male............	5,745
30 to 34 years....................	3,415	3,835	Female............	5,127
35 to 39 years....................	2,939	3,593	Family head: Male................	20,560
40 to 44 years....................	3,325	3,787	Female...............	8,213
45 to 49 years....................	3,616	4,027	Wife of head.........................	19,013
50 to 54 years....................	3,130	3,369	Child of head........................	52,965
55 to 59 years....................	2,568	2,644	Other relative of head...............	8,740
			Not related to head..................	3,137
60 to 64 years....................	1,875	1,963	In group quarters...................	1,210
65 to 69 years....................	1,379	1,569	Inmate of institution................	425
70 to 74 years....................	847	931	Other................................	785
75 to 79 years....................	412	571	Persons per household................	3.12
80 to 84 years....................	225	322	Black, all families................	28,773
85 years and over.................	163	256	With own children under 18 years............	17,724
			With own children under 6 years.............	8,731
Under 18 years....................	24,691	24,805	Black, husband-wife families.....	19,349
62 years and over.................	4,049	4,774	With own children under 18 years............	10,950
65 years and over.................	3,026	3,649	With own children under 6 years.............	5,648
Median age........................	23.0	24.3	Black, families with female head..	8,213
			With own children under 18 years............	6,234
			With own children under 6 years.............	2,895

	Male	Female	1970 Black Population — Relationship to Head of Household	

OKLAHOMA CITY, OKLAHOMA

	Male	Female		
All ages..................	23,156	26,947	Black, all persons...............	50,103
			In households.......................	49,445
Under 5 years.....................	2,896	2,866	Head.....................................	14,451
5 to 9 years......................	3,401	3,461	14 to 24 years......................	1,470
10 to 14 years....................	3,301	3,379	25 to 34 years......................	3,160
15 to 19 years....................	2,351	2,649	35 to 44 years......................	2,868
20 to 24 years....................	1,550	2,278	45 to 64 years......................	4,687
25 to 29 years....................	1,399	1,708	65 years and over...................	2,266
			Primary individual: Male............	1,331
30 to 34 years....................	1,130	1,601	Female............	1,867
35 to 39 years....................	1,072	1,398	Family head: Male................	7,722
40 to 44 years....................	1,100	1,421	Female...............	3,531
45 to 49 years....................	1,086	1,282	Wife of head.........................	7,314
50 to 54 years....................	909	1,074	Child of head........................	23,359
55 to 59 years....................	797	996	Other relative of head...............	3,545
			Not related to head..................	776
60 to 64 years....................	698	894	In group quarters...................	658
65 to 69 years....................	575	720	Inmate of institution................	377
70 to 74 years....................	400	532	Other................................	281
75 to 79 years....................	216	303	Persons per household................	3.42
80 to 84 years....................	158	195	Black, all families................	11,253
85 years and over.................	117	190	With own children under 18 years............	7,285
			With own children under 6 years.............	3,866
Under 18 years....................	11,222	11,377	Black, husband-wife families.....	7,348
62 years and over.................	1,856	2,467	With own children under 18 years............	4,410
65 years and over.................	1,466	1,940	With own children under 6 years.............	2,412
Median age........................	19.2	22.5	Black, families with female head..	3,531
			With own children under 18 years............	2,704
			With own children under 6 years.............	1,390

SOCIAL CHARACTERISTICS OF THE BLACK POPULATION, FOR SELECTED AREAS
AGE BY RACE, SEX, AND HOUSEHOLD RELATIONSHIP: 1970

	1970 Black Population		
	Male	Female	Relationship to Head of Household
PHILADELPHIA, PENNSYLVANIA			
All ages..................	302,989	350,802	Black, all persons............... 653,791
			In households........................ 643,483
Under 5 years......................	32,986	32,988	Head...................................... 194,955
5 to 9 years.......................	37,332	36,991	14 to 24 years...................... 14,101
10 to 14 years.....................	37,607	38,542	25 to 34 years...................... 38,967
15 to 19 years.....................	29,559	31,873	35 to 44 years...................... 43,185
20 to 24 years.....................	20,960	28,008	45 to 64 years...................... 71,897
25 to 29 years.....................	18,660	23,867	65 years and over.................. 26,805
			Primary individual: Male............... 21,480
30 to 34 years.....................	16,354	21,414	Female............... 27,614
35 to 39 years.....................	16,715	21,881	Family head: Male................. 98,307
40 to 44 years.....................	18,033	22,274	Female................. 47,554
45 to 49 years.....................	18,261	21,176	Wife of head...................... 90,866
50 to 54 years.....................	15,117	18,077	Child of head..................... 273,969
55 to 59 years.....................	12,271	15,218	Other relative of head.................... 59,490
			Not related to head..................... 24,203
60 to 64 years.....................	9,865	12,357	In group quarters.................... 10,308
65 to 69 years.....................	8,148	10,741	Inmate of institution.................... 5,705
70 to 74 years.....................	5,618	7,153	Other........................... 4,603
75 to 79 years.....................	2,957	4,081	Persons per household................. 3.30
80 to 84 years.....................	1,421	2,321	Black, all families............... 145,861
85 years and over..................	1,125	1,840	With own children under 18 years........... 86,509
			With own children under 6 years............ 42,492
Under 18 years.....................	127,498	128,334	Black, husband-wife families..... 91,107
62 years and over.................	24,789	33,078	With own children under 18 years........... 52,105
65 years and over.................	19,269	26,136	With own children under 6 years............ 26,989
Median age........................	23.3	26.5	Black, families with female head.. 47,554
			With own children under 18 years........... 31,868
			With own children under 6 years............ 14,656

	1970 Black Population		
	Male	Female	Relationship to Head of Household
PHOENIX, ARIZONA			
All ages..................	13,387	14,509	Black, all persons............... 27,896
			In households........................ 27,431
Under 5 years......................	1,642	1,652	Head...................................... 7,852
5 to 9 years.......................	1,984	1,921	14 to 24 years...................... 664
10 to 14 years.....................	1,944	1,933	25 to 34 years...................... 1,645
15 to 19 years.....................	1,455	1,442	35 to 44 years...................... 1,564
20 to 24 years.....................	826	1,064	45 to 64 years...................... 2,685
25 to 29 years.....................	711	913	65 years and over.................. 1,294
			Primary individual: Male............... 970
30 to 34 years.....................	653	849	Female............... 998
35 to 39 years.....................	662	731	Family head: Male................. 4,173
40 to 44 years.....................	559	712	Female................. 1,711
45 to 49 years.....................	577	681	Wife of head...................... 3,866
50 to 54 years.....................	527	599	Child of head..................... 13,265
55 to 59 years.....................	496	571	Other relative of head.................... 1,921
			Not related to head..................... 527
60 to 64 years.....................	429	455	In group quarters.................... 465
65 to 69 years.....................	368	364	Inmate of institution.................... 324
70 to 74 years.....................	235	269	Other........................... 141
75 to 79 years.....................	158	162	Persons per household................. 3.49
80 to 84 years.....................	94	93	Black, all families............... 5,864
85 years and over..................	67	98	With own children under 18 years........... 3,810
			With own children under 6 years............ 2,065
Under 18 years.....................	6,542	6,388	Black, husband-wife families..... 3,942
62 years and over.................	1,171	1,245	With own children under 18 years........... 2,398
65 years and over.................	922	986	With own children under 6 years............ 1,372
Median age........................	18.9	21.4	Black, families with female head.. 1,711
			With own children under 18 years........... 1,298
			With own children under 6 years............ 661

SOCIAL CHARACTERISTICS OF THE BLACK POPULATION, FOR SELECTED AREAS
AGE BY RACE, SEX, AND HOUSEHOLD RELATIONSHIP: 1970

	1970 Black Population		
	Male	Female	Relationship to Head of Household
PITTSBURGH, PENNSYLVANIA			
All ages....................	48,788	56,116	Black, all persons............... 104,904
			In households....................... 103,275
Under 5 years......................	4,981	4,813	Head............................. 33,712
5 to 9 years.......................	5,773	5,895	14 to 24 years.................... 2,317
10 to 14 years.....................	5,827	5,932	25 to 34 years.................... 5,387
15 to 19 years.....................	4,996	5,217	35 to 44 years.................... 6,463
20 to 24 years.....................	3,056	4,189	45 to 64 years.................... 12,702
25 to 29 years.....................	2,320	3,275	65 years and over................. 6,843
			Primary individual: Male.. 4,267
30 to 34 years.....................	2,120	2,918	Female........... 5,492
35 to 39 years.....................	2,227	3,139	Family head: Male.................. 15,884
40 to 44 years.....................	2,720	3,592	Female................. 8,069
45 to 49 years.....................	2,850	3,398	Wife of head...................... 14,660
50 to 54 years.....................	2,509	3,111	Child of head..................... 43,226
55 to 59 years.....................	2,377	2,743	Other relative of head............ 7,975
			Not related to head.............. 3,702
60 to 65 years.....................	2,076	2,351	In group quarters................. 1,629
65 to 69 years.....................	2,020	2,209	Inmate of institution............. 809
70 to 74 years.....................	1,528	1,625	Other............................. 820
75 to 79 years.....................	840	940	Persons per household............. 3.06
80 to 84 years.....................	339	422	Black, all families............... 23,953
85 years and over..................	229	347	With own children under 18 years........... 13,467
			With own children under 6 years........... 6,527
Under 18 years.....................	19,831	19,837	Black, husband-wife families..... 14,810
62 years and over..................	6,196	6,909	With own children under 18 years........... 7,438
65 years and over..................	4,956	5,543	With own children under 6 years........... 3,653
Median age.........................	24.6	28.1	Black, families with female head.. 8,069
			With own children under 18 years........... 5,654
			With own children under 6 years............ 2,761

	1970 Black Population		
	Male	Female	Relationship to Head of Household
PORTLAND, OREGON			
All ages....................	10,584	10,988	Black, all persons............... 21,572
			In households....................... 21,059
Under 5 years......................	1,241	1,133	Head............................. 6,541
5 to 9 years.......................	1,311	1,322	14 to 24 years.................... 757
10 to 14 years.....................	1,314	1,360	25 to 34 years.................... 1,397
15 to 19 years.....................	1,166	1,153	35 to 44 years.................... 1,207
20 to 24 years.....................	795	973	45 to 64 years.................... 2,426
25 to 29 years.....................	663	687	65 years and over................. 754
			Primary individual: Male.. 944
30 to 34 years.....................	546	610	Female........... 757
35 to 39 years.....................	487	521	Family head: Male.................. 3,484
40 to 44 years.....................	500	589	Female................. 1,356
45 to 49 years.....................	571	656	Wife of head...................... 3,110
50 to 54 years.....................	547	544	Child of head..................... 9,347
55 to 59 years.....................	491	465	Other relative of head............ 1,331
			Not related to head.............. 730
60 to 64 years.....................	379	371	In group quarters................. 513
65 to 69 years.....................	257	250	Inmate of institution............. 180
70 to 74 years.....................	145	146	Other............................. 333
75 to 79 years.....................	80	93	Persons per household............. 3.22
80 to 84 years.....................	52	53	Black, all families............... 4,840
85 years and over..................	39	62	With own children under 18 years........... 3,040
			With own children under 6 years........... 1,593
Under 18 years.....................	4,601	4,497	Black, husband-wife families..... 3,290
62 years and over..................	768	810	With own children under 18 years........... 1,904
65 years and over..................	573	604	With own children under 6 years........... 1,026
Median age.........................	21.6	22.7	Black, families with female head.. 1,356
			With own children under 18 years........... 1,059
			With own children under 6 years............ 542

SOCIAL CHARACTERISTICS OF THE BLACK POPULATION, FOR SELECTED AREAS
AGE BY RACE, SEX, AND HOUSEHOLD RELATIONSHIP: 1970

	Male	Female	1970 Black Population — Relationship to Head of Household	
SACRAMENTO, CALIFORNIA				
All ages.................	13,119	14,125	Black, all persons...............	27,244
			In households.......................	27,131
Under 5 years.......................	1,533	1,526	Head...........................	7,938
5 to 9 years........................	1,858	1,916	14 to 24 years.......................	749
10 to 14 years......................	1,926	1,988	25 to 34 years.......................	1,729
15 to 19 years......................	1,475	1,460	35 to 44 years.......................	1,948
20 to 24 years......................	795	1,016	45 to 64 years.......................	2,705
25 to 29 years......................	677	889	65 years and over....................	807
			Primary individual: Male...............	1,098
30 to 34 years......................	689	864	Female..............	866
35 to 39 years......................	707	919	Family head: Male..................	4,249
40 to 44 years......................	772	822	Female...................	1,725
45 to 49 years......................	729	731	Wife of head........................	3,852
50 to 54 years......................	602	558	Child of head.......................	13,105
55 to 59 years......................	458	447	Other relative of head..............	1,589
			Not related to head.................	647
60 to 64 years......................	330	347	In group quarters..................	113
65 to 69 years......................	262	269	Inmate of institution..............	4
70 to 74 years......................	157	177	Other............................	109
75 to 79 years......................	87	100	Persons per household..............	3.42
80 to 84 years......................	35	45	**Black, all families**...............	5,974
85 years and over..................	27	51	With own children under 18 years....	4,103
			With own children under 6 years.....	2,115
Under 18 years.....................	6,292	6,360	**Black, husband-wife families**.....	4,021
62 years and over..................	754	835	With own children under 18 years....	2,584
65 years and over..................	568	642	With own children under 6 years....	1,374
Median age........................	19.2	20.8	**Black, families with female head**..	1,725
			With own children under 18 years....	1,404
			With own children under 6 years.....	706

	Male	Female	1970 Black Population — Relationship to Head of Household	
SAN BERNARDINO, CALIFORNIA				
All ages.................	6,977	7,609	Black, all persons...............	14,586
			In households.......................	14,198
Under 5 years.......................	818	839	Head...........................	3,861
5 to 9 years........................	1,110	1,050	14 to 24 years.......................	389
10 to 14 years......................	1,103	1,062	25 to 34 years.......................	952
15 to 19 years......................	753	794	35 to 44 years.......................	928
20 to 24 years......................	430	603	45 to 64 years.......................	1,181
25 to 29 years......................	403	480	65 years and over....................	411
			Primary individual: Male...............	354
30 to 34 years......................	409	502	Female..............	355
35 to 39 years......................	369	479	Family head: Male..................	2,228
40 to 44 years......................	354	409	Female...................	924
45 to 49 years......................	332	362	Wife of head........................	2,006
50 to 54 years......................	263	267	Child of head.......................	7,205
55 to 59 years......................	188	211	Other relative of head..............	871
			Not related to head.................	255
60 to 64 years......................	168	177	In group quarters..................	388
65 to 69 years......................	117	143	Inmate of institution..............	324
70 to 74 years......................	69	101	Other............................	64
75 to 79 years......................	47	60	Persons per household..............	3.68
80 to 84 years......................	23	42	**Black, all families**...............	3,152
85 years and over..................	21	28	With own children under 18 years....	2,225
			With own children under 6 years.....	1,190
Under 18 years.....................	3,492	3,461	**Black, husband-wife families**.....	2,111
62 years and over..................	361	479	With own children under 18 years....	1,406
65 years and over..................	277	374	With own children under 6 years....	788
Median age........................	18.0	20.5	**Black, families with female head**..	924
			With own children under 18 years....	753
			With own children under 6 years.....	376

SOCIAL CHARACTERISTICS OF THE BLACK POPULATION, FOR SELECTED AREAS

AGE BY RACE, SEX, AND HOUSEHOLD RELATIONSHIP: 1970

	1970 Black Population		
	Male	Female	Relationship to Head of Household

SAN DIEGO, CALIFORNIA

	Male	Female		
All ages..................	26,792	26,169	**Black, all persons**...............	**52,961**
			In households........................	49,547
Under 5 years......................	2,940	2,976	Head...............................	14,736
5 to 9 years.......................	3,574	3,636	14 to 24 years.....................	1,632
10 to 14 years.....................	3,244	3,283	25 to 34 years.....................	4,061
15 to 19 years.....................	3,342	2,497	35 to 44 years.....................	3,394
20 to 24 years.....................	3,089	2,231	45 to 64 years.....................	4,320
25 to 29 years.....................	1,742	1,917	65 years and over..................	1,329
			Primary individual: Male..............	1,844
30 to 34 years.....................	1,935	1,887	Female..............	1,653
35 to 39 years.....................	1,409	1,523	Family head: Male.................	8,299
40 to 44 years.....................	1,371	1,415	Female..............	2,940
45 to 49 years.....................	1,188	1,223	Wife of head.......................	7,571
50 to 54 years.....................	926	1,014	Child of head......................	23,010
55 to 59 years.....................	659	811	Other relative of head.............	3,001
			Not related to head................	1,229
60 to 64 years.....................	502	622	**In group quarters**..................	**3,414**
65 to 69 years.....................	343	475	Inmate of institution..............	351
70 to 74 years.....................	255	294	Other..............................	3,063
75 to 79 years.....................	140	174	Persons per household..............	3.36
80 to 84 years.....................	61	103	**Black, all families**.............	**11,239**
85 years and over..................	72	88	With own children under 18 years............	7,653
			With own children under 6 years.............	4,242
Under 18 years.....................	11,404	11,418	**Black, husband-wife families**....	**7,938**
62 years and over.................	1,136	1,456	With own children under 18 years............	5,104
65 years and over.................	871	1,134	With own children under 6 years.............	2,940
Median age........................	20.5	21.6	**Black, families with female head**..	**2,940**
			With own children under 18 years............	2,367
			With own children under 6 years.............	1,229

	1970 Black Population		
	Male	Female	Relationship to Head of Household

SAN FRANCISCO, CALIFORNIA

	Male	Female		
All ages..................	46,767	49,311	**Black, all persons**...............	**96,078**
			In households........................	93,965
Under 5 years......................	4,773	4,702	Head...............................	32,500
5 to 9 years.......................	5,302	5,158	14 to 24 years.....................	3,490
10 to 14 years.....................	5,156	5,186	25 to 34 years.....................	8,102
15 to 19 years.....................	4,421	4,498	35 to 44 years.....................	6,817
20 to 24 years.....................	4,172	4,899	45 to 64 years.....................	11,287
25 to 29 years.....................	3,746	3,925	65 years and over..................	2,804
			Primary individual: Male..............	5,930
30 to 34 years.....................	3,249	3,125	Female..............	4,744
35 to 39 years.....................	2,703	2,774	Family head: Male.................	15,058
40 to 44 years.....................	2,744	2,988	Female..............	6,768
45 to 49 years.....................	2,838	3,100	Wife of head.......................	13,593
50 to 54 years.....................	2,375	2,655	Child of head......................	37,639
55 to 59 years.....................	1,924	2,145	Other relative of head.............	6,400
			Not related to head................	3,833
60 to 64 years.....................	1,410	1,591	**In group quarters**..................	**2,113**
65 to 69 years.....................	999	1,141	Inmate of institution..............	664
70 to 74 years.....................	497	651	Other..............................	1,449
75 to 79 years.....................	238	397	Persons per household..............	2.89
80 to 84 years.....................	106	203	**Black, all families**.............	**21,826**
85 years and over..................	114	173	With own children under 18 years............	13,305
			With own children under 6 years.............	6,824
Under 18 years.....................	17,979	17,753	**Black, husband-wife families**.....	**14,162**
62 years and over.................	2,730	3,438	With own children under 18 years............	7,697
65 years and over.................	1,954	2,565	With own children under 6 years.............	4,059
Median age........................	24.5	25.3	**Black, families with female head**..	**6,768**
			With own children under 18 years............	5,264
			With own children under 6 years.............	2,637

SOCIAL CHARACTERISTICS OF THE BLACK POPULATION, FOR SELECTED AREAS
AGE BY RACE, SEX, AND HOUSEHOLD RELATIONSHIP: 1970

	Male	Female	Relationship to Head of Household	
SAN JOSE, CALIFORNIA			**1970 Black Population**	
All ages..................	5,462	5,493	Black, all persons...............	10,955
			In households........................	10,575
Under 5 years......................	710	656	Head.......................................	2,930
5 to 9 years......................	823	831	14 to 24 years...........................	399
10 to 14 years.....................	661	666	25 to 34 years...........................	1,107
15 to 19 years.....................	506	562	35 to 44 years...........................	687
20 to 24 years.....................	518	591	45 to 64 years...........................	605
25 to 29 years.....................	558	564	65 years and over.......................	132
			Primary individual: Male...............	373
30 to 34 years.....................	470	422	Female............	265
35 to 39 years.....................	324	314	Family head: Male.......................	1,872
40 to 44 years.....................	287	232	Female....................	420
45 to 49 years.....................	198	184	Wife of head............................	1,655
50 to 54 years.....................	135	129	Child of head...........................	4,976
55 to 59 years.....................	101	107	Other relative of head.................	605
			Not related to head....................	409
60 to 64 years.....................	66	78	**In group quarters..................**	**380**
65 to 69 years.....................	44	61	Inmate of institution..................	173
70 to 74 years.....................	28	42	Other..................................	207
75 to 79 years.....................	7	30	Persons per household..................	3.61
80 to 84 years.....................	12	14	**Black, all families...............**	**2,292**
85 years and over..................	14	10	With own children under 18 years...........	1,695
			With own children under 6 years............	1,065
Under 18 years.....................	2,514	2,446	**Black, husband-wife families.....**	**1,787**
62 years and over..................	141	198	With own children under 18 years...........	1,316
65 years and over..................	105	157	With own children under 6 years............	860
Median age.........................	20.3	20.3	**Black, families with female head..**	**420**
			With own children under 18 years...........	337
			With own children under 6 years............	187

	Male	Female	Relationship to Head of Household	
SEATTLE, WASHINGTON			**1970 Black Population**	
All ages..................	18,806	19,062	Black, all persons...............	37,858
			In households........................	37,128
Under 5 years......................	2,157	2,079	Head.......................................	12,511
5 to 9 years......................	2,162	2,200	14 to 24 years...........................	1,653
10 to 14 years.....................	2,177	2,219	25 to 34 years...........................	2,795
15 to 19 years.....................	1,703	1,853	35 to 44 years...........................	2,443
20 to 24 years.....................	1,619	1,964	45 to 64 years...........................	4,464
25 to 29 years.....................	1,421	1,310	65 years and over.......................	1,156
			Primary individual: Male...............	2,178
30 to 34 years.....................	1,088	1,061	Female............	1,516
35 to 39 years.....................	965	932	Family head: Male.......................	6,426
40 to 44 years.....................	1,083	1,125	Female....................	2,391
45 to 49 years.....................	1,149	1,230	Wife of head............................	5,492
50 to 54 years.....................	1,043	943	Child of head...........................	15,585
55 to 59 years.....................	829	709	Other relative of head.................	2,210
			Not related to head....................	1,330
60 to 64 years.....................	559	516	**In group quarters..................**	**740**
65 to 69 years.....................	373	354	Inmate of institution..................	180
70 to 74 years.....................	215	241	Other..................................	560
75 to 79 years.....................	133	158	Persons per household..................	2.97
80 to 84 years.....................	59	89	**Black, all families...............**	**8,817**
85 years and over..................	71	79	With own children under 18 years...........	5,592
			With own children under 6 years............	2,971
Under 18 years.....................	7,526	7,634	**Black, husband-wife families.....**	**6,049**
62 years and over..................	1,149	1,209	With own children under 18 years...........	3,515
65 years and over..................	851	921	With own children under 6 years............	1,913
Median age.........................	23.7	23.0	**Black, families with female head..**	**2,391**
			With own children under 18 years...........	1,890
			With own children under 6 years............	995

SOCIAL CHARACTERISTICS OF THE BLACK POPULATION, FOR SELECTED AREAS
AGE BY RACE, SEX, AND HOUSEHOLD RELATIONSHIP: 1970

	1970 Black Population		
	Male	Female	Relationship to Head of Household
ST. LOUIS, MISSOURI			
All ages................	117,401	136,790	Black, all persons............... 254,191
			In households....................... 250,369
Under 5 years......................	13,250	13,269	Head.... 73,230
5 to 9 years........................	14,836	14,854	14 to 24 years...................... 5,553
10 to 14 years.....................	16,133	16,413	25 to 34 years...................... 13,816
15 to 19 years.....................	12,846	13,667	35 to 44 years...................... 14,696
20 to 24 years.....................	8,192	11,050	45 to 64 years...................... 26,231
25 to 29 years.....................	6,659	8,313	65 years and over................... 12,934
			Primary individual: Male................ 7,611
30 to 34 years.....................	5,455	7,346	Female............. 10,941
35 to 39 years.....................	5,406	7,661	Family head: Male.............. 37,035
40 to 44 years.....................	5,872	7,670	Female................ 17,643
45 to 49 years.....................	5,614	7,287	Wife of head............. 34,135
50 to 54 years.....................	5,026	6,265	Child of head............. 112,732
55 to 59 years.....................	4,806	5,984	Other relative of head............ 23,731
			Not related to head................ 6,541
60 to 64 years.....................	4,204	5,271	In group quarters................... 3,822
65 to 69 years.....................	3,722	4,784	Inmate of institution................. 2,142
70 to 74 years.....................	2,547	3,089	Other.................... 1,680
75 to 79 years.....................	1,426	1,920	Persons per household............. 3.42
80 to 84 years.....................	818	1,104	Black, all families............... 54,678
85 years and over..................	589	843	With own children under 18 years......... 32,201
			With own children under 6 years......... 16,439
Under 18 years.....................	52,661	53,124	Black, husband-wife families..... 34,314
62 years and over..................	11,514	14,681	With own children under 18 years....... 18,826
65 years and over..................	9,102	11,740	With own children under 6 years....... 10,125
Median age........................	21.0	24.6	Black, families with female head.. 17,643
			With own children under 18 years........... 12,272
			With own children under 6 years........... 5,860

	1970 Black Population		
	Male	Female	Relationship to Head of Household
ST. PAUL, MINNESOTA			
All ages................	5,376	5,554	Black, all persons............... 10,930
			In households....................... 10,638
Under 5 years......................	651	633	Head.... 3,402
5 to 9 years........................	673	690	14 to 24 years...................... 411
10 to 14 years.....................	669	635	25 to 34 years...................... 736
15 to 19 years.....................	597	596	35 to 44 years...................... 661
20 to 24 years.....................	376	513	45 to 64 years...................... 1,062
25 to 29 years.....................	333	364	65 years and over................... 532
			Primary individual: Male................ 555
30 to 34 years.....................	305	281	Female............. 417
35 to 39 years.....................	236	277	Family head: Male.............. 1,700
40 to 44 years.....................	269	283	Female................ 730
45 to 49 years.....................	272	262	Wife of head............. 1,441
50 to 54 years.....................	227	208	Child of head............. 4,846
55 to 59 years.....................	208	216	Other relative of head............ 617
			Not related to head................ 332
60 to 64 years.....................	153	180	In group quarters................... 292
65 to 69 years.....................	147	137	Inmate of institution................. 102
70 to 74 years.....................	117	113	Other.................... 190
75 to 79 years.....................	54	74	Persons per household............. 3.13
80 to 84 years.....................	45	44	Black, all families............... 2,430
85 years and over..................	44	48	With own children under 18 years......... 1,542
			With own children under 6 years......... 827
Under 18 years.....................	2,352	2,305	Black, husband-wife families..... 1,596
62 years and over..................	478	514	With own children under 18 years....... 903
65 years and over..................	407	416	With own children under 6 years....... 494
Median age........................	21.3	22.2	Black, families with female head.. 730
			With own children under 18 years........... 593
			With own children under 6 years........... 317

SOCIAL CHARACTERISTICS OF THE BLACK POPULATION, FOR SELECTED AREAS
AGE BY RACE, SEX, AND HOUSEHOLD RELATIONSHIP: 1970

TACOMA, WASHINGTON

	Male	Female	Relationship to Head of Household	1970 Black Population
All ages.................	5,124	5,312	Black, all persons...............	10,436
			In households.......................	10,311
Under 5 years......................	583	623	Head...........	3,056
5 to 9 years.......................	740	737	14 to 24 years........................	336
10 to 14 years.....................	749	810	25 to 34 years........................	689
15 to 19 years.....................	554	554	35 to 44 years........................	790
20 to 24 years.....................	355	416	45 to 64 years........................	1,029
25 to 29 years.....................	302	318	65 years and over....................	212
			Primary individual: Male...............	380
30 to 34 years.....................	258	291	Female..............	322
35 to 39 years.....................	277	316	Family head: Male...................	1,778
40 to 44 years.....................	333	326	Female...................	576
45 to 49 years.....................	326	297	Wife of head.............................	1,432
50 to 54 years.....................	244	189	Child of head...........................	5,142
55 to 59 years.....................	157	142	Other relative of head....................	427
			Not related to head......................	254
60 to 64 years.....................	108	85	In group quarters...................	125
65 to 69 years.....................	67	77	Inmate of institution......................	75
70 to 74 years.....................	32	54	Other...............................	50
75 to 79 years.....................	10	27	Persons per household.....................	3.37
80 to 84 years.....................	14	26	Black, all families...............	2,354
85 years and over..................	15	24	With own children under 18 years...........	1,665
			With own children under 6 years............	855
Under 18 years.....................	2,459	2,551	Black, husband-wife families.....	1,701
62 years and over..................	191	258	With own children under 18 years...........	1,136
65 years and over..................	138	208	With own children under 6 years............	587
Median age........................	19.4	19.4	Black, families with female head..	576
			With own children under 18 years...........	490
			With own children under 6 years............	254

TULSA, OKLAHOMA

	Male	Female	Relationship to Head of Household	1970 Black Population
All ages..................	16,283	18,994	Black, all persons...............	35,277
			In households.......................	34,777
Under 5 years......................	2,172	2,048	Head...........	10,610
5 to 9 years.......................	2,367	2,200	14 to 24 years........................	992
10 to 14 years.....................	2,204	2,228	25 to 34 years........................	2,102
15 to 19 years.....................	1,655	1,780	35 to 44 years........................	1,939
20 to 24 years.....................	1,054	1,503	45 to 64 years........................	3,492
25 to 29 years.....................	883	1,204	65 years and over....................	2,085
			Primary individual: Male...............	992
30 to 34 years.....................	734	1,043	Female..............	1,541
35 to 39 years.....................	675	1,041	Family head: Male...................	5,351
40 to 44 years.....................	721	957	Female...................	2,726
45 to 49 years.....................	709	910	Wife of head.............................	5,098
50 to 54 years.....................	584	813	Child of head...........................	16,028
55 to 59 years.....................	635	837	Other relative of head....................	2,463
			Not related to head......................	578
60 to 64 years.....................	536	727	In group quarters...................	500
65 to 69 years.....................	570	682	Inmate of institution......................	284
70 to 74 years.....................	362	439	Other...............................	216
75 to 79 years.....................	229	289	Persons per household.....................	3.28
80 to 84 years.....................	122	140	Black, all families...............	8,077
85 years and over..................	71	153	With own children under 18 years...........	5,035
			With own children under 6 years............	2,719
Under 18 years.....................	7,848	7,606	Black, husband-wife families.....	5,119
62 years and over..................	1,681	2,142	With own children under 18 years...........	2,895
65 years and over..................	1,354	1,703	With own children under 6 years............	1,605
Median age........................	19.2	24.1	Black, families with female head..	2,726
			With own children under 18 years...........	2,054
			With own children under 6 years............	1,086

SOCIAL CHARACTERISTICS OF THE BLACK POPULATION, FOR SELECTED AREAS
AGE BY RACE, SEX, AND HOUSEHOLD RELATIONSHIP: 1970

	Male	Female	1970 Black Population Relationship to Head of Household	

TUCSON, ARIZONA

	Male	Female	Relationship to Head of Household	
All ages.................	4,470	4,709	Black, all persons...............	9,179
			In households.......................	9,005
Under 5 years......................	489	472	Head............................	2,695
5 to 9 years........................	615	554	14 to 24 years...................	219
10 to 14 years.....................	627	620	25 to 34 years...................	541
15 to 19 years.....................	453	505	35 to 44 years...................	579
20 to 24 years.....................	317	326	45 to 64 years...................	877
25 to 29 years.....................	259	257	65 years and over...............	479
			Primary individual: Male..............	322
30 to 34 years.....................	239	302	Female..............	350
35 to 39 years.....................	246	264	Family head: Male..................	1,547
40 to 44 years.....................	228	219	Female..................	476
45 to 49 years.....................	180	229	Wife of head........................	1,392
50 to 54 years.....................	193	207	Child of head.......................	4,112
55 to 59 years.....................	156	181	Other relative of head...............	579
			Not related to head.................	227
60 to 64 years.....................	131	180	In group quarters................	174
65 to 69 years.....................	148	164	Inmate of institution................	66
70 to 74 years.....................	88	104	Other............................	108
75 to 79 years.....................	61	67	Persons per household...............	3.34
80 to 84 years.....................	23	28	Black, all families...............	2,023
85 years and over..................	17	30	With own children under 18 years............	1,261
			With own children under 6 years............	662
Under 18 years.....................	2,012	1,981	Black, husband-wife families.....	1,480
62 years and over..................	409	489	With own children under 18 years............	876
65 years and over..................	337	393	With own children under 6 years............	490
Median age........................	20.8	23.1	Black, families with female head..	476
			With own children under 18 years............	352
			With own children under 6 years.............	163

	Male	Female	1970 Black Population Relationship to Head of Household	

WASHINGTON, D.C.

	Male	Female	Relationship to Head of Household	
All ages.................	252,602	285,110	Black, all persons...............	537,712
			In households.......................	525,021
Under 5 years......................	26,041	25,822	Head............................	164,040
5 to 9 years........................	28,582	28,538	14 to 24 years...................	16,922
10 to 14 years.....................	28,678	28,459	25 to 34 years...................	40,380
15 to 19 years.....................	24,218	26,833	35 to 44 years...................	34,833
20 to 24 years.....................	22,124	29,951	45 to 64 years...................	55,745
25 to 29 years.....................	20,332	23,401	65 years and over...............	16,160
			Primary individual: Male..............	20,607
30 to 34 years.....................	16,484	18,047	Female..............	23,755
35 to 39 years.....................	14,726	17,000	Family head: Male..................	85,329
40 to 44 years.....................	14,737	16,843	Female..................	34,349
45 to 49 years.....................	14,089	16,571	Wife of head........................	78,421
50 to 54 years.....................	12,103	14,501	Child of head.......................	209,340
55 to 59 years.....................	10,538	12,174	Other relative of head...............	49,992
			Not related to head.................	23,228
60 to 64 years.....................	7,829	9,333	In group quarters................	12,691
65 to 69 years.....................	5,281	7,083	Inmate of institution................	4,987
70 to 74 years.....................	3,324	4,682	Other............................	7,704
75 to 79 years.....................	1,856	2,796	Persons per household...............	3.20
80 to 84 years.....................	897	1,622	Black, all families...............	119,678
85 years and over..................	763	1,454	With own children under 18 years............	70,539
			With own children under 6 years............	35,248
Under 18 years.....................	98,375	98,604	Black, husband-wife families.....	78,919
62 years and over..................	16,487	23,002	With own children under 18 years............	46,022
65 years and over..................	12,121	17,637	With own children under 6 years............	24,628
Median age........................	24.2	25.6	Black, families with female head..	34,349
			With own children under 18 years............	22,092
			With own children under 6 years.............	9,786

Section II

VITAL STATISTICS

Health and Welfare: 1970

Tables

VITAL STATISTICS HEALTH AND WELFARE

Generations of malnutrition can produce an insidious effect on health, intellect, productivity and prospects for longevity.

Black Americans, according to the 1968 Report of the National Advisory Commission Civil Disorders, are significantly less healthy than most other Americans. They suffer from higher mortality rates, higher incidence of major diseases, and lower availability and utilization of medical services. They also experience higher admission rates to mental hospitals.

From the standpoint of health, poverty means deficient diets, lack of medical care, inadequate shelter and clothing, and a general lack of awareness of potential health needs. As a result, almost 30 percent of all persons with family incomes under the poverty level suffer from chronic health conditions that adversely affect their ability to earn a living.

Poor families have the greatest need for financial assistance in meeting medical expenses, and yet only about 34 percent of families with incomes under the poverty level use health insurance benefits, as compared to nearly 90 percent of those with incomes over the $7,000 level. Those factors are aggravated for blacks, when compared to whites, because the proportion of persons in the United States who are poor is higher among blacks than among whites.

The fact that the life expectancy of a black infant male at birth was, in 1971, seven years less than a white male infant, or that a black female baby could anticipate living five years less than a white female infant, indicates that there is still a long way to go in remediation of the decades of abuse suffered by the black child born in America in the past three hundred years.

In the first year of life, 31.4 black babies died out of every 1,000 born in 1970, while 17.4 white infants under one year of age failed to survive out of every 1,000 born.

Black families spend less on medical services and visit medical specialists less often than white families, even in the same income range. Since the lowest income group contains a larger proportion of nonwhite families than white, the overall discrepancy in medical care spending between these two groups is significant.

Blacks spend less on medical care for several reasons. Black households are generally larger, requiring greater non-medical expenses for each household and leaving less money for meeting medical expenses. Blacks also generally pay more for their basic necessities, such as food and consumer durables. In addition

fewer doctors, dentists, and medical facilities are conveniently available to blacks than are available to most whites—a result both of geographic concentration of doctors in higher income areas in large cities and of discrimination against blacks by doctors and hospitals. A survey in Cleveland indicated that there were 0.45 physicians per 1,000 people in poor neighborhoods, compared to 1.13 per 1,000 in nonpoverty areas. In many inner cities, private hospitals have closed or moved to the suburbs leaving the community without hospital care or medical and emergency service. The result is fewer visits to physicians and dentists. Widespread use of health insurance has led many hospitals to adopt nondiscriminatory policies, yet some private hospitals still refuse to admit black patients or to accept black physicians on their staff. As a result, blacks are more likely to be treated in hospital clinics than whites, and are less likely to receive personalized service.

Grave concern was aroused in the black community in 1972 with the revelation of a U.S. Public Health Service syphilis study involving 600 Alabama black men. In the study, conducted in Tuskegee, Alabama, and undertaken in 1932, four hundred of the group had syphilis and deliberately received no treatment for it. The other two hundred did not have the disease and were also not given any specific therapy. Ten years after the study was begun, and penicillin was discovered to be a cure, the four hundred in the group were still left untreated. The NAACP Legal Defense fund filed a $1.8 billion damage suit against the federal government and the state of Alabama, charging that state and federal agencies had conspired to lure the men into an experiment by telling them that they were joining a health program, and leaving them uninformed and unaware of the true nature of their illness.

Cases of involuntary sterilization of poor blacks aroused charges of state-directed genocide against welfare agencies which had approved sterilization of young black females in South Carolina, Texas and North Carolina. In New Bern, North Carolina, in 1973 the American Civil Liberties Union sought a declaratory judgement that the North Carolina sterilization statute be declared unconstitutional. Charging that race is a determining factor in the North Carolina sterilization case, the A.C.L.U. attorney revealed statistics which showed that 65 percent of the people sterilized in 1968 were black. Suits have been filed on behalf of victims against the Office of Economic Opportunity, HEW, and the Food and

Drug Administration.

Meanwhile the federal government made an initial commitment to a program of education, screening and treatment of sickle cell anemia, a blood disease that primarily affects young blacks. The program is under the National Institute of Health's direction.

Environmental factors in disadvantaged black neighborhoods further complicate the health situation with regard to the black community. High population density, poor housing, sanitation, lack of proper storage facilities for food, and inadequate garbage collection and disposal all add to the problems inherent in the conditions affecting the health and welfare of the black American in the 1970s.

SELECTED LIFE TABLE VALUES: 1939 TO 1969

Prior to 1959, excludes Alaska, and 1960, Hawaii.

AGE AND SEX	WHITE					BLACK AND OTHER				
	1939-1941	1949-1951	1959-1961	1968	1969	1939-1941	1949-1951	1959-1961	1968	1969
Annual Rate of Mortality per 1,000 Living at Specified Age										
At birth: Male	48.1	30.7	25.9	21.9	21.3	83.0	50.9	47.0	37.8	35.2
Female	37.9	23.6	19.6	16.4	16.1	66.8	40.9	38.3	31.1	28.6
Age 20: Male	2.1	1.6	1.6	1.9	2.0	(NA)	3.1	2.4	3.1	3.4
Female	1.5	0.7	0.6	0.6	0.7	(NA)	2.3	1.2	1.2	1.2
Age 40: Male	5.1	3.9	3.3	3.4	3.5	13.6	8.8	7.5	9.3	9.5
Female	3.7	2.4	1.9	2.0	2.0	11.8	7.7	5.6	5.6	5.3
Age 50: Male	11.6	10.1	9.6	9.3	9.0	25.4	19.1	15.7	17.3	17.3
Female	7.6	5.6	4.7	4.8	4.7	21.9	16.0	11.7	10.5	10.2
Age 65: Male	36.9	34.5	33.9	34.5	33.8	(NA)	45.8	43.7	49.7	46.5
Female	26.4	20.6	17.4	16.4	15.9	(NA)	37.0	30.7	36.5	34.2
Average Expectation of Life in Years										
At birth: Male	62.8	66.3	67.6	67.5	67.8	52.3	58.9	61.5	60.1	60.5
Female	67.3	72.0	74.2	74.9	75.1	55.5	62.7	66.5	67.5	68.4
Age 20: Male	47.8	49.5	50.3	49.9	50.1	39.7	43.7	45.8	43.6	43.9
Female	51.4	54.6	56.3	56.7	56.9	42.1	46.8	50.1	50.5	51.2
Age 40: Male	30.0	31.2	31.7	31.6	31.8	25.2	27.3	28.7	27.4	27.8
Female	33.3	35.6	37.1	37.6	37.8	27.3	29.8	32.2	32.7	33.3
Age 50: Male	22.0	22.8	23.2	23.0	23.3	19.2	20.3	21.3	20.3	20.8
Female	24.7	26.8	28.1	28.6	28.8	21.0	22.7	24.3	24.8	25.4
Age 65: Male	12.1	12.8	13.0	12.8	13.0	12.2	12.8	12.8	12.1	12.6
Female	13.6	15.0	15.9	16.4	16.6	14.0	14.5	15.1	15.1	15.7
Number Surviving to Specified Age per 1,000 Born Live										
Age 20: Male	923	951	959	963	963	868	919	931	939	942
Female	940	965	971	975	975	885	935	947	956	958
Age 40: Male	869	912	924	925	924	728	828	857	842	842
Female	898	941	953	957	957	759	861	897	905	909
Age 65: Male	583	635	658	654	659	359	452	514	475	481
Female	687	768	807	811	815	407	524	608	632	645

NA   Not available.

Source: U.S. Public Health Service; "U.S. Life Tables and Actuarial Tables, 1939-41, Vital Statistics"—Special Reports, vols. 41 and 52, and "Vital Statistics of the United States," annual.

EXPECTATION OF LIFE AND MORTALITY RATES, BY AGE, RACE, AND SEX: 1969

AGE (years)	EXPECTATION OF LIFE IN YEARS					MORTALITY RATE PER 1,000 LIVING AT SPECIFIED AGE				
	Total	White		Black and other		Total	White		Black and other	
		Male	Female	Male	Female		Male	Female	Male	Female
Under 1	70.4	67.8	75.1	60.5	68.4	21.08	21.33	16.08	35.18	28.58
1	71.0	68.2	75.3	61.7	69.4	1.30	1.18	1.07	2.32	1.88
2	70.1	67.3	74.4	60.8	68.5	0.85	0.81	0.66	1.54	1.22
3	69.1	66.4	73.5	59.9	67.6	0.68	0.70	0.55	0.94	0.88
4	68.2	65.4	72.5	59.0	66.6	0.58	0.58	0.49	0.87	0.67
5	67.2	64.4	71.5	58.0	65.7	0.63	0.80	0.41	1.15	0.59
6	66.2	63.5	70.6	57.1	64.7	0.51	0.59	0.37	0.80	0.51
7	65.3	62.5	69.6	56.1	63.8	0.40	0.43	0.33	0.56	0.45
8	64.3	61.6	68.6	55.2	62.8	0.32	0.31	0.29	0.41	0.39
9	63.3	60.6	67.6	54.2	61.8	0.27	0.25	0.26	0.35	0.35
10	62.3	59.6	66.7	53.2	60.8	0.26	0.24	0.24	0.38	0.33
11	61.4	58.6	65.7	52.2	59.9	0.29	0.30	0.24	0.49	9.34
12	60.4	57.6	64.7	51.2	58.9	0.37	0.42	0.27	0.68	0.38
13	59.4	56.6	63.7	50.3	57.9	0.50	0.60	0.32	0.94	0.47
14	58.4	55.7	62.7	49.3	56.9	0.66	0.84	0.39	1.25	0.58
15	57.5	54.7	61.8	48.4	56.0	0.85	1.11	0.48	1.61	0.72
16	56.5	53.8	60.8	47.5	55.0	1.04	1.37	0.56	2.00	0.86
17	55.6	52.9	59.8	46.6	54.0	1.19	1.60	0.62	2.38	0.98
18	54.6	51.9	58.9	45.7	53.1	1.30	1.75	0.64	2.73	1.06
19	53.7	51.0	57.9	44.8	52.2	1.36	1.86	0.65	3.07	1.12
20	52.8	50.1	56.9	43.9	51.2	1.41	1.96	0.65	3.43	1.19
21	51.8	49.2	56.0	43.1	50.3	1.47	2.05	0.65	3.78	1.27
22	50.9	48.3	55.0	42.2	49.3	1.50	2.09	0.66	4.05	1.35
23	50.0	47.4	54.0	41.4	48.4	1.50	2.05	0.66	4.19	1.44
24	49.1	46.5	53.1	40.6	47.5	1.48	1.96	0.66	4.26	1.54
25	48.1	45.6	52.1	39.8	46.5	1.45	1.85	0.67	4.29	1.64
26	47.2	44.7	51.1	38.9	45.6	1.42	1.76	0.68	4.35	1.75
27	46.3	43.8	50.2	38.1	44.7	1.42	1.69	0.70	4.47	1.89
28	45.3	42.8	49.2	37.3	43.8	1.44	1.66	0.73	4.67	2.06
29	44.4	41.9	48.2	36.4	42.9	1.50	1.67	0.78	4.95	2.25
30	43.5	41.0	47.3	35.6	42.0	1.56	1.70	0.84	5.24	2.47
31	42.5	40.1	46.3	34.8	41.1	1.64	1.74	0.90	5.55	2.69
32	41.6	39.1	45.4	34.0	40.2	1.73	1.81	0.98	5.87	2.92
33	40.7	38.2	44.4	33.2	39.3	1.85	1.91	1.06	6.20	3.18
34	39.8	37.3	43.5	32.4	38.4	1.99	2.05	1.16	6.56	3.44
35	38.8	36.3	42.5	31.6	37.5	2.15	2.21	1.26	6.94	3.73
36	37.9	35.4	41.6	30.8	36.7	2.32	2.40	1.38	7.35	4.03
37	37.0	34.5	40.6	30.0	35.8	2.52	2.62	1.51	7.81	4.34
38	36.1	33.6	39.7	29.3	35.0	2.74	2.87	1.66	8.33	4.66
39	35.2	32.7	38.7	28.5	34.1	2.97	3.15	1.82	8.90	4.99
40	34.3	31.8	37.8	27.8	33.3	2.24	3.47	2.00	9.53	5.34
41	33.4	30.9	36.9	27.0	32.5	3.52	3.82	2.20	10.18	5.71
42	32.5	30.0	36.0	26.3	31.7	3.83	4.21	2.40	10.81	6.10
43	31.7	29.1	35.1	25.6	30.9	4.15	4.63	2.61	11.39	6.51
44	30.8	28.3	34.1	24.9	30.1	4.50	5.08	2.83	11.96	6.95
45	29.9	27.4	33.2	24.2	29.3	4.88	5.59	3.07	12.54	7.42
46	29.1	26.6	32.3	23.5	28.5	5.29	6.14	3.34	13.19	7.92
47	28.2	35.7	31.4	22.8	27.7	5.75	6.76	3.62	13.98	8.44
48	27.4	24.9	30.6	22.1	26.9	6.26	7.45	3.94	14.94	8.98
49	26.5	24.1	29.7	21.4	26.2	6.83	8.21	4.28	16.06	9.55
50	25.7	23.3	28.8	20.8	25.4	7.44	9.04	4.65	17.27	10.17
51	24.9	22.5	27.9	20.1	24.7	8.10	9.93	5.05	18.52	10.84
52	24.1	21.7	27.1	19.5	23.9	8.82	10.93	5.47	19.84	11.59
53	23.3	20.9	26.2	18.9	23.2	9.62	12.04	5.92	21.22	12.44
54	22.5	20.2	25.4	18.3	22.5	10.48	13.26	6.40	22.66	13.37
55	21.8	19.5	24.5	17.7	21.8	11.42	14.55	6.93	24.21	14.42
56	21.0	18.7	23.7	17.1	21.1	12.41	15.94	7.51	25.86	15.55
57	20.3	18.0	22.9	16.5	20.4	13.49	17.47	8.13	27.57	16.76
58	19.5	17.3	22.1	16.0	19.8	14.66	19.18	8.78	29.33	18.04
59	18.8	16.7	21.3	15.5	19.1	15.91	21.04	9.48	31.17	19.42
60	18.1	16.0	20.5	14.9	18.5	17.26	23.06	10.26	33.11	20.77
61	17.4	15.4	19.7	14.4	17.9	18.71	25.18	11.13	35.22	22.29
62	16.8	14.8	18.9	13.9	17.3	20.26	27.33	12.12	37.59	24.34
63	16.1	14.2	18.1	13.5	16.7	21.92	29.46	13.25	40.32	27.12
64	15.4	13.6	17.3	13.0	16.2	23.72	31.61	14.54	43.40	30.47
65	14.8	13.0	16.6	12.6	15.7	25.60	33.80	15.92	46.52	34.17
66	14.2	12.5	15.8	12.2	15.2	27.61	36.19	17.45	49.82	37.85
67	13.6	11.9	15.1	11.8	14.8	29.91	39.00	19.23	53.84	41.27
68	13.0	11.4	14.4	11.4	14.4	32.56	42.41	21.34	58.88	44.15
69	12.4	10.8	13.7	11.1	14.0	35.53	46.36	23.74	64.79	46.52

Source: U.S. Public Health Service, "Vital Statistics of the United States," annual.

LIVE BIRTHS—TOTAL AND RATE, 1960 TO 1970, AND BY RACE, 1968: STATES

By place of residence, except as noted. Represents registered births.

STATE	NUMBER (1,000)							RATE PER 1,000 POPULATION[2]				
			1968									
	1960	1965	Total	White	Black and other	1969[1] (prel.)	1970[1] (prel.)	1960	1965	1968	1969[1] (prel.)	1970[1] (prel.)
United States....	4,258	3,760	3,502	2,912	589	3,571	3,718	23.7	19.4	17.5	17.7	18.2
New England.........	237	213	193	182	11	202	200	22.5	19.1	16.9	17.6	16.9
Maine...............	23	20	17	17	0	18	18	24.0	19.9	17.4	17.9	17.6
New Hampshire.......	14	13	12	12	0	12	13	22.8	19.5	17.7	17.3	17.3
Vermont.............	9	8	8	8	0	8	8	24.1	20.5	18.0	17.8	18.2
Massachusetts........	115	101	92	87	5	100	96	22.4	18.8	16.8	18.2	16.9
Rhode Island.........	18	17	15	14	1	16	16	21.4	19.4	16.7	17.4	17.1
Connecticut..........	57	54	49	44	5	49	50	22.4	19.2	16.6	16.4	16.4
Middle Atlantic........	733	665	603	508	95	613	628	21.5	18.3	16.3	16.4	16.9
New York.............	359	336	302	250	53	312	319	21.4	18.6	16.7	17.1	17.5
New Jersey...........	132	125	114	95	20	114	116	21.8	18.5	16.1	16.0	16.2
Pennsylvania.........	241	205	186	164	23	186	193	21.3	17.8	15.9	15.8	16.4
East North Central.....	877	751	706	610	96	706	750	24.2	19.7	17.8	17.7	18.6
Ohio................	231	195	186	164	22	184	203	23.8	19.1	17.5	17.2	19.0
Indiana..............	113	98	92	83	8	92	97	24.2	20.0	18.1	17.9	18.7
Illinois..............	239	208	194	156	38	192	203	23.7	19.6	17.6	17.4	18.3
Michigan............	195	167	160	136	24	164	170	25.0	20.1	18.3	18.7	19.1
Wisconsin............	100	83	74	70	4	74	77	25.2	20.0	17.6	17.4	17.5
West North Central....	369	297	268	248	20	278	288	24.0	18.7	16.7	17.2	17.6
Minnesota...........	88	71	65	63	2	66	69	25.7	19.9	17.7	17.8	18.0
Iowa................	64	51	47	46	1	48	49	23.3	18.5	16.8	17.2	17.4
Missouri.............	98	81	74	63	11	82	84	22.7	18.1	16.1	17.5	18.0
North Dakota........	17	13	11	10	1	11	12	26.3	20.2	16.9	18.4	18.7
South Dakota........	18	14	11	10	1	11	12	25.9	19.7	17.4	17.3	17.4
Nebraska............	34	28	24	23	1	24	26	24.3	18.8	16.9	16.8	17.7
Kansas..............	51	39	36	33	3	36	36	23.3	17.6	25.5	15.4	16.1
South Atlantic........	629	575	535	383	152	549	566	24.2	20.0	17.8	18.0	18.5
Delaware............	12	11	10	8	2	10	10	25.9	21.2	18.4	19.3	18.7
Maryland............	77	74	68	53	15	61	61	24.9	21.0	18.1	16.1	15.5
Dist. of Columbia......	20	18	15	2	13	27	25	26.0	22.5	18.5	34.3	32.8
Virginia..............	96	89	82	63	19	79	82	24.1	20.0	17.8	16.8	17.5
West Virginia........	39	32	29	28	1	29	29	21.2	17.7	16.3	16.2	16.9
North Carolina.......	110	98	93	65	28	94	99	24.1	19.9	18.1	18.1	19.4
South Carolina.......	60	53	49	30	19	50	51	25.1	20.8	18.4	18.7	19.6
Georgia..............	100	94	87	59	29	91	96	25.3	21.7	19.1	19.6	20.9
Florida..............	116	107	102	76	26	108	114	23.3	18.4	16.6	17.0	16.8
East South Central.....	294	258	233	169	64	242	252	24.4	20.1	17.8	18.5	19.6
Kentucky............	72	62	56	51	5	58	61	23.8	19.4	17.5	17.9	19.0
Tennessee...........	82	73	67	53	14	74	76	23.0	19.0	16.9	18.5	19.3
Alabama.............	81	71	64	42	22	63	67	24.7	20.4	17.9	17.8	19.5
Mississippi..........	59	52	46	23	23	47	48	27.2	22.5	19.5	20.0	21.5
West South Central....	431	375	360	284	76	369	378	25.4	20.2	18.8	18.9	19.5
Arkansas............	41	37	33	24	9	33	35	22.7	18.7	16.7	16.7	18.0
Louisiana............	90	80	74	46	29	75	72	27.7	22.5	19.9	19.9	19.9
Oklahoma............	51	43	41	34	7	42	43	21.9	17.3	16.3	16.2	17.0
Texas...............	249	216	212	180	32	220	227	26.0	20.4	19.3	19.6	20.3
Mountain.............	187	160	153	139	14	160	171	27.3	20.6	19.3	19.9	20.6
Montana.............	17	14	12	11	1	12	12	25.9	19.3	17.3	16.8	17.9
Idaho...............	17	13	13	13	0	13	14	25.7	19.3	18.7	18.1	19.5
Wyoming.............	9	7	6	5	0	6	6	25.8	19.3	18.3	18.5	19.1
Colorado............	43	37	37	35	2	40	43	24.5	18.7	18.1	19.0	19.4
New Mexico..........	31	24	20	17	3	21	22	32.3	23.6	20.2	21.6	21.5
Arizona..............	37	34	33	27	6	34	37	28.2	21.1	19.7	20.1	21.0
Utah................	26	22	23	23	1	25	27	29.5	22.5	22.4	23.6	25.9
Nevada..............	7	9	9	8	1	9	9	25.5	21.5	19.3	19.5	18.5
Pacific..............	501	465	450	389	61	459	485	23.6	19.0	17.6	17.7	18.3
Washington...........	65	53	57	53	4	57	61	22.9	17.7	17.5	16.7	17.9
Oregon..............	38	33	32	31	1	34	36	21.7	17.4	16.0	17.0	17.3
California............	372	356	340	296	44	345	364	23.7	19.1	17.6	17.8	18.2
Alaska..............	8	7	6	5	2	7	7	33.4	27.9	23.5	24.2	24.5
Hawaii..............	17	16	15	4	10	16	17	27.2	23.0	18.6	19.8	21.5

[1] By place of occurrence. Details by race not yet available.
[2] Based on population (excluding Armed Forces abroad) enumerated as of Apr. 1 for 1960 and 1970, and estimated as of July 1 for other years.

Source: U.S. Public Health Service, "Vital Statistics of the United States," annual, and "Monthly Vital Statistics Report."

LIVE BIRTH RATES, BY RACE AND AGE OF MOTHER: 1940 TO 1968

Births per 1,000 women in each specified group. Prior to 1960, excludes Alaska and Hawaii. Data for 1940-1955 are adjusted for underregistration; thereafter, registered births only.

YEAR	15–44 YEARS[1]			AGE OF MOTHER							
	Total	White	Black and other	10–14 years	15–19 years	20–24 years	25–29 years	30–34 years	35–39 years	40–44 years	45–49 years[2]
1940........	79.9	77.1	102.4	0.7	54.1	135.6	122.8	83.4	46.3	15.6	1.9
1945........	85.9	83.4	106.0	0.8	51.1	138.9	132.2	100.2	56.9	16.6	1.6
1950........	106.2	102.3	137.3	1.0	81.6	196.6	166.1	103.7	52.9	15.1	1.2
1955........	118.5	113.8	155.3	0.9	90.5	242.0	190.5	116.2	58.7	16.1	1.0
1960........	118.0	113.2	153.6	0.8	89.1	258.1	197.4	112.7	56.2	15.5	0.9
1965........	96.6	91.4	133.9	0.8	70.4	196.8	162.5	95.0	46.4	12.8	0.8
1966........	91.3	86.4	125.9	0.9	70.6	185.9	149.4	85.9	42.2	11.7	0.7
1967........	87.6	83.1	119.8	0.9	67.9	174.0	142.6	79.3	38.5	10.6	0.7
1968........	[3]85.7	81.5	114.9	1.0	66.1	167.4	140.3	74.9	35.6	9.6	0.6

[1]Rates computed by relating total births, regardless of age of mother, to women aged 15–44 years.
[2]Through 1960, rates computed by relating births to mothers aged 45 years and over to women aged 45–49 years.
[3]Live birth rates for 1969 and 1970 were 85.8 and 87.6, respectively. Detailed data not available.

ATTENDED LIVE BIRTHS AND BIRTH WEIGHT, BY RACE: 1940 TO 1968

Prior to 1960, excludes Alaska and Hawaii. Represents registered births.

YEAR	BIRTHS ATTENDED (1,000)			MEDIAN BIRTH WEIGHT[2]		
	By physician		By midwife, other, and not specified	Total	White	Black and Other
	In hospital[1]	Not in hospital				
1940.................	1,317	825	218	(NA)	(NA)	(NA)
1945.................	2,156	403	177	(NA)	(NA)	(NA)
1950.................	3,126	252	177	7 lb.–5 oz.	7 lb.–5 oz.	7 lb.–3 oz.
1955.................	3,819	101	128	7 lb.–5 oz.	7 lb.–5 oz.	7 lb.–1 oz.
1960.................	4,114	49	94	7 lb.–5 oz.	7 lb.–6 oz.	6 lb.–15 oz.
1965.................	3,661	33	66	7 lb.–4 oz.	7 lb.–5 oz.	6 lb.–14 oz.
1966.................	3,535	17	55	7 lb.–4 oz.	7 lb.–5 oz.	6 lb.–14 oz.
1967.................	3,460	14	47	7 lb.–4 oz.	7 lb.–5 oz.	6 lb.–14 oz.
1968.................	3,449	13	39	7 lb.–4 oz.	7 lb.–5 oz.	6 lb.–14 oz.

NA Not available.   [1]Includes all births in hospitals or institutions and in clinics.

BIRTHS AND BIRTH RATES: 1950 TO 1970

In thousands, except as indicated. Prior to 1960, excludes Alaska and Hawaii. For 1950 and 1955, births adjusted for underregistration; thereafter, regsitered births.

ITEM	1950	1955	1960	1965	1966	1967	1968	1969 (prel.)	1970 (prel.)
Live births.............................	3,632	4,104	4,258	3,760	3,606	3,521	3,502	3,571	3,718
Percent urban[1].........................	60.6	61.0	62.3	54.5	54.6	54.6	54.0	(NA)	(NA)
White..	3,108	3,488	3,601	3,124	2,993	2,923	2,912	2,939	3,078
Black and other...........................	524	617	657	636	613	598	589	632	640
Percent of total...........................	14.4	15.0	15.4	16.9	17.0	17.0	16.8	17.7	17.2
Male..	1,863	2,103	2,180	1,927	1,846	1,803	1,796	1,829	1,907
Female......................................	1,768	2,001	2,078	1,833	1,760	1,718	1,705	1,742	1,811
Males per 100 females...................	105.4	105.1	104.9	105.1	104.9	105.0	105.3	105.0	105.3
Birth rate per 1,000 population..........	24.1	25.0	23.7	19.4	18.4	17.8	17.5	17.7	18.2
White..	23.0	23.8	22.7	18.3	17.4	16.8	16.6	16.6	15.5
Black and other...........................	33.3	34.7	32.1	27.6	26.1	25.0	24.2	25.4	25.2
Male..	24.9	25.8	24.7	20.3	19.2	18.7	18.4	18.6	19.1
Female......................................	23.3	23.9	22.8	18.6	17.6	17.0	16.7	16.8	17.3
Plural births per 1,000 live births........	20.9	21.1	20.4	20.1	19.8	19.7	20.1	(NA)	(NA)

NA Not available.   [1]Based on registered births.
Source: U.S. Public Health Service, "Vital Statistics of the United States," annual.

EXPECTATION OF LIFE AT BIRTH: 1920 TO 1970

In years. Prior to 1960, excludes Alaska and Hawaii. Data prior to 1930 for death-registration States only.

YEAR	TOTAL			WHITE			BLACK and other		
	Total	Male	Female	Total	Male	Female	Total	Male	Female
1920	54.1	53.6	54.6	54.9	54.4	55.6	45.3	45.5	45.2
1930	59.7	58.1	61.6	61.4	59.7	63.5	48.1	47.3	49.2
1940	62.9	60.8	65.2	64.2	62.1	66.6	53.1	51.5	54.9
1950	68.2	65.6	71.1	69.1	66.5	72.2	60.8	59.1	62.9
1955	69.6	66.7	72.8	70.5	67.4	73.7	63.7	61.4	66.1
1960	69.7	66.6	73.1	70.6	67.4	74.1	63.6	61.1	66.3
1965	70.2	66.8	73.7	71.0	67.6	74.7	64.1	61.1	67.4
1968	70.2	66.6	74.0	71.1	67.5	74.9	63.7	60.1	67.5
1969	70.4	66.8	74.3	71.3	67.8	75.1	64.3	60.5	68.4
1970 (prel.)	70.8	67.1	74.6	71.7	68.1	75.4	64.6	60.5	68.9

Source: U.S. Public Health Service, "Vital Statistics of the United States," annual.

CHILDREN EVER BORN TO WOMEN EVER MARRIED, BY SELECTED CHARACTERISTICS OF WOMEN: 1960 AND 1969

Refers to total population as of April 1960, based on 5-percent sample from 1960 census; and to noninstitutional population as of January 1969, based on Current Population Survey.

CHARACTERISTIC	WOMEN 15-44 YEARS OLD				WOMEN 45-59 YEARS OLD		
	Num-ber of women, 1969 (1,000)	Children ever born per 1,000 women[1]			Num-ber of women, 1969 (1,000)	Children ever born per 1,000 women	
		1960	1969	Percent change, 1960-69		1960[2]	1969
Women ever married	28,742	2,292	2,466	7.6	16,061	2,712	2,604
Residence:							
Nonfarm	27,634	2,252	2,445	8.6	15,060	2,636	2,549
Farm	1,107	2,898	2,919	0.7	1,001	3,615	3,522
Standard metropolitan statistical areas[3]	18,848	2,156	2,394	11.0	10,476	2,408	2,410
Nonmetropolitan areas	9,893	2,550	2,608	2.3	5,585	3,220	2,967
Race:							
White	25,413	2,229	2,390	7.2	14,454	2,672	2,551
Black and other	3,329	2,787	3,046	9.3	1,607	3,109	3,079
Black	3,016	2,807	3,118	11.1	1,482	3,046	3,080
Years of school completed:							
Elementary: Less than 8 years	1,550	3,091	3,398	9.9	2,042	3,602	3,523
8 years	1,656	2,637	3,206	21.6	2,225	2,820	2,827
High school: 1–3 years	6,007	2,470	2,944	19.2	3,143	2,393	2,754
4 years	13,636	2,074	2,286	10.2	6,239	1,989	2,298
College: 1–3 years	3,446	1,965	2,116	7.7	1,383	1,896	2,378
4 years or more	2,448	1,704	1,790	5.0	1,029	1,646	1,996
Labor force status:							
In labor force	12,878	1,788	2,123	18.7	8,136	[4]2,178	2,416
Not in labor force	15,864	2,559	2,737	7.0	7,925	[4]2,937	2,796

[1]Standardized for age based on distribution of women ever married, by age, in the United States in 1950.
[2]For women 45 years old and over.   [3]See text, p. 2.   [4]Partly estimated.
Source: U.S. Bureau of the Census, "Current Population Reports," series P–20.

PLURAL BIRTH RATIOS, BY RACE AND AGE OF MOTHER: 1968

Ratios are all plural live births per 1,000 total live births in specified groups

RACE	AGE OF MOTHER (in years)								
	Total	Under 15	15–19	20–24	25–29	30–34	35–39	40–44	45–49
Total	20.1	8.2	12.7	18.0	22.6	26.6	30.4	23.2	13.2
White	19.4	9.0	11.9	17.1	21.6	25.4	29.0	23.4	11.2
Black and other	23.8	7.8	20.8	23.3	29.2	33.3	37.7	22.2	20.9

Source: U.S. Public Health Service, "Vital Statistics of the United States," annual.

DEATHS AND DEATH RATES: 1920 TO 1970

Prior to 1960, excludes Alaska and Hawaii. Excludes fetal deaths. Population enumerated as of April 1 for 1940, 1950, 1960, and 1970, and estimated as of July 1 for all other years.

ITEM	1920	1930	1940	1950	1960	1965	1967	1968	1969[1]	1970[1]
DEATHS										
Total......1,000....	1,118	1,327	1,417	1,452	1,712	1,828	1,851	1,930	1,916	1,921
Percent urban[2]........	(NA)	(NA)	(NA)	64.6	65.9	56.4	56.4	56.3	(NA)	(NA)
White...........1,000....	991	1,137	1,231	1,276	1,505	1,605	1,627	1,690	1,678	1,681
Black and other....1,000....	127	190	186	176	207	223	224	241	237	240
Male...........1,000....	586	727	791	828	976	1,035	1,046	1,087	1,075	1,079
Female...........1,000....	532	601	626	625	736	793	805	843	841	842
DEATH RATES[3]										
Total..............	13.0	11.3	10.8	9.6	9.5	9.4	9.4	9.7	9.5	9.4
White..................	12.6	10.8	10.4	9.5	9.5	9.4	9.4	9.6	9.5	9.4
Black and other...........	17.7	16.3	13.8	11.2	10.1	9.6	9.4	9.9	9.5	9.5
Male..................	13.4	12.3	12.0	11.1	11.0	10.9	10.8	11.1	10.9	10.8
Female.................	12.6	10.4	9.5	8.2	8.1	8.0	8.0	8.2	8.1	8.0
Age:[4]										
Under 1 year.............	92.3	69.0	54.9	33.0	27.0	24.1	22.3	22.3	21.2	20.4
1–4 years................	9.9	5.6	2.9	1.4	1.1	0.9	0.9	0.9	0.8	0.8
5–14 years...............	2.6	1.7	1.0	0.6	0.5	0.4	0.4	0.4	0.4	0.4
15–24 years..............	4.9	3.3	2.0	1.3	1.1	1.1	1.2	1.2	1.3	1.3
25–34 years.............	6.8	4.7	3.1	1.8	1.5	1.5	1.5	1.6	1.6	1.6
35–44 years.............	8.1	6.8	5.2	3.6	3.0	3.1	3.1	3.2	3.2	3.1
45–54 years.............	12.2	12.2	10.6	8.5	7.6	7.4	7.3	7.5	7.3	7.2
55–64 years.............	23.6	24.0	[5]22.2	[5]19.0	17.4	16.9	16.7	17.2	16.8	16.6
65–74 years.............	52.5	51.4	[5]48.4	[5]41.0	38.2	37.9	37.5	38.5	37.2	36.7
75–84 years.............	118.9	112.7	112.0	93.3	87.5	81.9	79.0	80.8	79.1	77.7
85 years and over........	248.3	228.0	235.7	202.0	198.6	202.0	194.2	196.1	188.5	178.7

NA Not available.   [1]Preliminary. Based on a 10-percent sample of deaths.
[3] Per 1,000 population of specified groups.
[4] Includes deaths for which age was not stated, and not distributed among age groups.
[5] Based on enumerated population adjusted for age bias in population other than white at ages 55–69 years.

Source: U.S. Public Health Service, "Vital Statistics of the United States," annual, and unpublished data.

INFANT, MATERNAL, FETAL, AND NEONATAL DEATH RATES, BY RACE: 1940 TO 1970

Deaths per 1,000 live births, except as noted. Prior to 1960, excludes Alaska and Hawaii.

ITEM	1940	1950	1955	1960	1965	1966	1967	1968	1969 (prel.)	1970 (prel.)
Infant deaths[1].............	47.0	29.2	26.4	26.0	24.7	23.7	22.4	21.8	20.7	19.8
White..................	43.2	26.8	23.6	22.9	21.5	20.6	19.7	19.2	(NA)	(NA)
Black and other..........	73.8	44.5	42.8	43.2	40.3	38.8	35.9	34.5	(NA)	(NA)
Maternal deaths[2]..........	376.0	83.3	47.0	37.1	31.6	29.1	28.0	24.5	27.4	24.7
White....................	319.8	61.1	32.8	26.0	21.0	20.2	19.5	16.6	(NA)	(NA)
Black and other..........	773.5	221.6	130.3	97.9	83.7	72.4	69.5	63.6	(NA)	(NA)
Fetal deaths[3]..............	(NA)	19.2	17.1	16.1	16.2	15.7	15.6	15.8	(NA)	(NA)
White....................	(NA)	17.1	15.2	14.1	13.9	13.6	13.5	13.8	(NA)	(NA)
Black and other..........	(NA)	32.5	28.4	26.8	27.2	26.1	25.8	25.6	(NA)	(NA)
Neonatal deaths[4]..........	28.8	20.5	19.1	18.7	17.7	17.2	16.5	16.1	15.4	14.9
White....................	27.2	19.4	17.7	17.2	16.1	15.6	15.0	14.7	(NA)	(NA)
Black and other..........	39.7	27.5	27.2	26.9	25.4	24.8	23.8	23.0	(NA)	(NA)

NA Not available.   [1] Represents deaths of infants under 1 year old, exclusive of fetal deaths.
[2] Per 100,000 live births from deliveries and complications of pregnancy, childbirth, and the puerperium. For 1960–1967, deaths are classified according to seventh revision of "International Lists of Diseases and Causes of Death"; thereafter, according to the eighth revision.
[3] Includes only fetal deaths (stillbirths) for which period of gestation was 20 weeks (or 5 months) or more, or was not stated.   [4] Represents deaths of infants under 28 days old, exclusive of fetal deaths.

Source: U.S. Public Health Service, "Vital Statistics of the United States," annual.

DEATHS FROM SELECTED CAUSES, BY SPECIFIED RACE AND SEX: 1969

Cause of Death	TOTAL			BLACK		
	Both sexes	Male	Female	Both sexes	Male	Female
All Causes	1,921,990	1,080,926	841,064	225,537	127,145	98,392
1. Infective and Parasitic Diseases............	16,791	9,901	6,890	4,164	2,489	1,675
2. Neoplasms..............................	327,769	178,306	149,463	32,231	18,084	14,147
3. Endocrine, Nutritional & Metabolic Diseases..	46,543	19,333	27,210	6,712	2,436	4,276
4. Diseases of the Blood and Blood-Forming Organs.................................	4,921	2,342	2,579	857	415	442
5. Mental Disorders........................	6,722	4,758	1,964	1,604	1,195	409
6. Diseases of the Nervous System and Sense Organs.................................	16,921	9,376	7,545	2,232	1,352	880
7. Diseases of the Circulatory System...........	1,029,363	558,342	471,021	100,315	51,968	48,347
8. Diseases of the Respiratory System..........	116,457	73,957	42,500	14,233	8,838	5,395
9. Diseases of the Digestive System............	73,926	43,044	30,882	8,897	5,200	3,697
10. Diseases of the Genitourinary System........	29,280	16,476	12,804	5,429	2,951	2,478
11. Complications of Pregnancy, Childbirth & the Puerperium............................	801	...	801	323	...	323
12. Diseases of the Skin and Subcutaneous Tissue.................................	1,876	805	1,071	354	154	200
13. Diseases of the Musculoskeletal System and Connective Tissue	4,908	1,649	3,259	618	186	432
14. Congenital Anomalies......................	17,008	9,147	7,861	2,425	1,272	1,153
15. Certain Causes of Mortality in Early Infancy...	43,171	25,369	17,802	10,341	5,874	4,467
16. Symptoms and Ill-Defined Conditions........	26,160	15,755	10,405	8,394	4,792	3,602
17. Accidents, Poisonings and Violence..........	159,373	112,366	47,007	26,408	19,939	6,469

Source: U.S. Department of Health, Education and Welfare Health Services and Mental Health Administration, National Center for Health Statistics—DVS-SRS.

Section III

HISTORICAL RECORD:

Chronology of Contemporary Events, 1954–1973

THE HISTORICAL RECORD:
A CHRONOLOGY OF CONTEMPORARY EVENTS, 1954–1973

1954

MAY

17   Supreme Court ruled that racial segregation in public schools was unconstitutional.

JULY

11   First White Citizens Council unit organized in Indianola, Miss.

SEPTEMBER

7-8   School integration began in Washington, D.C. and Baltimore, Md., public schools.

OCTOBER

30   Defense Department announced complete abolition of black units in armed forces.

1955

MAY

31   Supreme Court ordered school integration "with all deliberate speed."

AUGUST

28   Emmett Till, 14, kidnapped and lynched in Money, Miss.

NOVEMBER

7   Supreme Court in Baltimore case banned segregation in public recreational facilities.

25   Interstate Commerce Commission banned segregation in busses, in waiting rooms and in travel coaches involved in interstate travel.

DECEMBER

5   Bus boycott began in Montgomery, Alabama.

1956

FEBRUARY

29   Autherine J. Lucy admitted to University of Alabama, February 3. She was suspended February 7 after a riot at the university, and expelled February 29.

MARCH

11-12 Manifesto denouncing Supreme Court ruling on segregation in public schools issued by 100 Southern senators and representatives.

APRIL

23   Supreme Court refused to review lower court decision which banned segregation in intrastate bus travel

MAY

30   Bus boycott began in Tallahassee, Florida.

JUNE

5   Federal court ruled that racial segregation on Montgomery city busses violated the Constitution.

SEPTEMBER

10   Louisville, Kentucky public schools integrated.

17   Black students entered Clay, Kentucky elementary school under National Guard protection, September 12. They were barred from school, September 17.

NOVEMBER

13   Supreme Court upheld lower court decision which banned segregation on city busses in Montgomery, Alabama.

DECEMBER

20   Federal injunctions prohibiting segregation on the busses were served on city, state, and bus company officials.

21   At two mass meetings, Montgomery blacks called off year-long bus boycott. Busses were integrated on December 21.

DECEMBER

27   Federal Judge Dozier Devane granted temporary injunction restraining city officials from interfering with integration of Tallahassee, Florida, city busses, said "every segregation act of every state or city is as dead as a doornail."

1957

FEBRUARY

14   Southern Christian Leadership Conference organized at meeting in New Orleans, with Martin Luther King, Jr., as president.

MAY

17   Prayer Pilgrimage, biggest civil rights demonstration ever staged by U. S. blacks, held in Washington.

JUNE

Tuskegee boycott began, June. Blacks boycotted city stores in protest against act of state legislature which deprived them of municipal votes by placing their homes outside city limits.

AUGUST

29   Congress passed Civil Rights Act of 1957, August 29. This was first federal civil rights legislation since 1875.

SEPTEMBER

24   President Eisenhower ordered federal troops to Little Rock, Ark., to prevent interference with school integration at Central High School.

DECEMBER

5   New York City became first to legislate against racial or religious discrimination in housing market with adoption of Fair Housing Practice Law.

1958

MAY

27 Ernest Green graduated from Little Rock's Central High School with 600 white classmates.

JUNE

30 Supreme Court reversed decision of lower court which had confirmed $100,-000 contempt fine imposed by Alabama on NAACP for refusing to divulge membership.

AUGUST

19 Members of NAACP Youth Council began series of sit-ins at Oklahoma City lunch counters.

SEPTEMBER

20 Martin Luther King, Jr. stabbed in chest by crazed black woman while he was autographing books in a Harlem department store. Woman was placed under mental observation.

1959

APRIL

25 Mack Parker lynched, Poplarville, Mississippi.

MAY

22 Brig. Gen. B. O. Davis, Jr., promoted to major general.

JUNE

26 Prince Edward County, Va., Board of Supervisors, abandoned public school system in attempt to prevent school integration.

DECEMBER

21 Citizens of Deerfield, Ill. authorized plan which blocked building of interracial housing development.

1960

U.S. population: 179,323,175; Black population: (10.5%): (Decennial Census year): 18,871,831.

FEBRUARY

1 Four students from North Carolina A. and T. College started sit-in movement at Greensboro, N.C. five-and-dime store.

10 Movement had spread to fifteen Southern cities in five states.

MARCH

16 San Antonio, Texas became first large Southern city to integrate lunch counters.

APRIL

25 Consent judgment in Memphis, Tennessee, federal court ended restrictions against black voting in Fayette County, Tenn., first voting case under Civil Rights Act.

MAY

6 President Eisenhower signed Civil Rights Act of 1960.

OCTOBER

17 Four national chain stores announced on October 17 that counters in about 150 stores in 112 cities in North Carolina, Virginia, West Virginia, Kentucky, Texas, Tennessee, Missouri, Maryland, Florida, and Oklahoma had been integrated.

DECEMBER

30 Two U.S. courts issued temporary injunctions to prevent about 700 black sharecroppers from being evicted from farms in Haywood and Fayette counties, Tenn., reportedly for registering to vote.

1961

JANUARY

3 Adam Clayton Powell became chairman of Education and Labor Committee of House of Representatives.

FEBRUARY

15 U.S. and African nationalists disrupted UN session on Congo with demonstration for slain Congo Premier Patrice Lumumba.

FEBRUARY

11 Robert Weaver sworn in as Administrator of the Housing and Home Finance Agency, highest federal post ever held by an American black.

MARCH

7 Atlanta Chamber of Commerce announced that black and white leaders had agreed on plan for desegregation of lunchroom and other facilities.

MARCH

9 Clifton R. Wharton sworn in as ambassador to Norway.

MARCH

25 Meeting place of National Civil War Centennial Commission shifted from Charleston to Charleston Naval Station after nation-wide controversy over segregated hotels in Charleston.

MAY

4 Thirteen "Freedom Riders," including national director of CORE, set out for bus trip through South.

SEPTEMBER

18 Federal Court was asked to order school integration in Chicago in suit filed by citizens. Suit was later dismissed.

21 Southern Regional Council announced September 21, that the sit-in movement had affected 20 states and more than 100 cities in Southern and border states in period from February, 1960, to September, 1961. At least 70,000 blacks

and whites had participated in the movement, the report said. The council estimated that 3,600 had been arrested and that at least 141 students and 58 faculty members had been expelled by college authorities. SRC said one or more establishments in 108 Southern and border state cities had been desegregated as a result of sit-ins.

1962

JANUARY

18-28 Southern University closed because of series of demonstrations protesting expulsion of sit-in demonstrations.

31 Lt. Commander Samuel L. Gravely assumed command of destroyer escort, USS "Falgout." Navy said he was first black to command U.S. warship.

FEBRUARY

5 Suit seeking to bar Englewood, N.J., from maintaining "racially segregated" elementary school filed in U.S. District

MAY Court.

10 Southern School News reported that 246,988 or 7.6% of the black pupils in public schools in 17 Southern and border states and the District of Columbia attended integrated classes in 1962.

MAY

28 Suit alleging de facto school segregation filed in Rochester, N.Y. by NAACP.

OCTOBER

James H. Meredith, escorted by federal marshals, registered at the University of Mississippi.

NOVEMBER

20 President Kennedy issued Executive Order barring racial and religious discrimination in federally-financed housing.

1963

MARCH

1 Emancipation centennial protests began with massive voter registration campaign in Greenwood, Mississippi.

'JNE

1 Two black students, escorted by federalized National Guard troops and federal officials, enrolled at University of Alabama despite oppositon of Governor George C. Wallace.

JUNE

12 Medgar W. Evers, 37, NAACP field secretary in Mississippi, assassinated in front of his Jackson home by segregationists.

27 W.E.B. DuBois, scholar, Pan-Africanist, N.A.A.C.P. founder and long-time *Crisis* editor, died in Accra, Ghana.

AUGUST

28 More than 250,000 persons participated in March on Washington demonstration.

SEPTEMBER

15 Four black girls killed in bombing of 16th Street Baptist Church in Birmingham, Alabama.

OCTOBER

22 Some 225,000 students boycotted Chicago public schools in Freedom Day protest of de facto segregation.

NOVEMBER

22 John Fitzgerald Kennedy, 46, 35th President of the United States, assassinated in Dallas, Texas.

1964

APRIL

13 Sidney Poitier became first black man to win "Oscar" as best actor of year.

JULY

2 U.S. Senate imposed cloture for first time on civil rights measure, ending Southern filibuster by a vote of 71-29, June 10. Civil rights bill, with public accommodation and fair employment sections, was signed by President Lyndon B. Johnson.

AUGUST

4 Bodies of three civil rights workers discovered on farm near Philadelphia, Mississippi August 4. Three young men, two white and one black, had been missing since June 21. FBI said they were murdered on night of their disappearance by white segregationists.

SEPTEMBER

15 Rev. K.L. Buford and Dr. Stanley Smith were elected to Tuskegee City Council and became first blacks elected to public office in Alabama in Twentieth Century.

DECEMBER

3 J. Raymond Jones elected leader of New York Democratic organization (Tammany Hall).

10 Dr. Martin Luther King, Jr. awarded Nobel Prize at ceremonies in Oslo.

1965

FEBRUARY

21 Malcolm X assassinated before rally of his followers at Audubon Ballroom, New York.

MARCH

9 Three white Unitarian ministers, including the Rev. James J. Reeb, attacked on streets of Selma, Alabama. Reeb, who was participating in civil rights demonstrations, died later in Birmingham hospital.

21 Thousands of marchers, led by the Rev. Martin Luther King, Jr., completed first leg of five-day Selma-to-Montgomery march.

APRIL

16 Maj. Gen. B. O. Davis, Jr., assistant deputy chief of staff of Air Force, named lieutenant general, highest rank attained by a black in the armed services.

AUGUST

4 President signed voting rights bill which authorized the suspension of literacy tests and the sending of federal examiners into South.

11 U.S. Senate confirmed nomination of Thurgood Marshall as U.S. Solicitor General.

Jonathan M. Daniels, white Episcopal seminary student from Massachusetts, killed and Richard F. Morrisroe, white Roman Catholic priest from Chicago, seriously wounded by shotgun blasts fired by white special deputy sheriff in Hayneville, Alabama. Two men were participating in civil rights demonstrations in Lowndes County.

DECEMBER

25 Congress of Racial Equality announced that its national director James Farmer would resign on March 1.

1966

JANUARY

3 Floyd B. McKissick, North Carolina attorney, named to succeed James Farmer as national director of Congress of Racial Equality.

JANUARY

6 Harold R. Perry became second American black to become Roman Catholic bishop with his consecration in New Orleans.

10 Julian Bond, communications director of Student Nonviolent Coordinating Committee, denied seat in Georgia House of Representatives, purportedly because of his opposition to Vietnamese War.

18 Robert Weaver took oath as Secretary of Department of Housing and Urban Development and became first black cabinet member.

APRIL

21 Milton Olive, Jr. awarded Congressional Medal of Honor for gallantry in action in Vietnam War.

JUNE

1-2 More than 2,400 persons attended White House Conference on Civil Rights.

6 James Meredith wounded by white assassin as he walked along U.S. Highway 51

near Hernando, Mississippi, on second day of 220-mile voter registration march from Memphis to Jackson.

7 March was continued by Martin Luther King, Jr. Floyd McKissick, Stokely Carmichael and other civil rights workers. It ended with rally of some 30,000 at Mississippi state capitol.

NOVEMBER

8 Edward W. Brooke (Republican, Massachusetts) elected U.S. Senator, the first black senator since the Reconstruction.

1967

JANUARY

9 Rep. Adam Clayton Powell, Jr. ousted as chairman of House Education and Welfare Committee on charge of wrongfully appropriating congressional funds. Powell denied the charges and accused his critics of racism.

16 Lucius D. Amerson, first black sheriff in the South in the twentieth century, sworn in at Tuskegee (Macon County) Ala.

MARCH

1 U.S. House of Representatives ousted Rep. Adam Clayton Powell. Civil Rights leaders charged that Powell was ousted because of his race.

APRIL

8 Riot, Nashville, Tennessee.

28 World Boxing Association and New York State Athletic Commission withdrew recognition of Muhammad Ali as world heavyweight champion because of his refusal to serve in U.S. Armed Forces.

29 Mrs. Robert W. Claytor elected president of YWCA. She was first black president of the organization.

MAY

12 H. Rap Brown replaced Stokely Carmichael as chairman of Student Nonviolent Coordinating Committee.

JUNE

12 Supreme Court struck down Virginia law banning marriage between blacks and whites.

13 Thurgood Marshall, U.S. solicitor general, nominated as associate justice of Supreme Court. He was confirmed by Senate on August 30.

20 Muhammad Ali, world heavyweight champion, convicted in Houston, Tex., federal court of violating Selective Service fined $10,000.00, sentenced to five years in prison, and released on $5,000.00 bond, pending appeal. Ali, an opponent of the Vietnam War, had refused to report for service on grounds

that he was a Muslim minister.

JULY

20-23 More than one thousand persons attended Black Power Conference, Newark, N.J.

SEPTEMBER

6   President Lyndon B. Johnson named Walter E. Washington Commissioner and "unofficial" mayor of Washington, D.C. Washington was first black man to head government of major American city.

NOVEMBER

7   Carl B. Stokes elected mayor of Cleveland, Ohio, and Richard G. Hatcher elected mayor of Gary, Indiana. They were first black men elected mayors of major American cities.

1968

FEBRUARY

15   Henry Lewis, 36, was named director of the New Jersey Symphony to succeed Kenneth Schermerhorn. Lewis is the first black to head a symphony orchestra in the U.S.

MARCH

4   Martin Luther King, Jr. announced that he would lead Poor People's Campaign in Washington in April.

11   The U.S. Supreme Court unanimously ruled, upholding a 1966 Federal District Court decision, that Alabama must desegregate its prisons within a year. The court rejected Alabama's contention that segregation was necessary to maintain order.

APRIL

4   Martin Luther King, Jr. assassinated by sniper in Memphis, Tennessee. Assassination precipitated national crisis and rioting in more than one hundred cities. Forty-six persons were killed in major rebellions in Washington, Chicago, and other cities. More than twenty thousand federal troops and 34,000 National Guardsmen were mobilized to quell disturbances. Memorial marches and rallies were held throughout the country, many public school systems closed and the opening of the baseball season was postponed. President Lyndon B. Johnson declared Sunday, April 6, a national day of mourning and ordered all U.S. flags on government buildings in all U.S. territories and possessions to fly at half-mast until King interment.

9   Ralph David Abernathy elected to succeed King as president of Southern Christian Leadership Conference.

10   U.S. Congress passed civil rights bill banning (in three stages) racial discrimination in the sale or rental of approximately 80 per cent of the nation's housing.

11   President Johnson signed bill. Bill also made it a crime to interfere with civil rights workers and to cross state lines to incite a riot.

APRIL

29-30 Poor People's Campaign began with Ralph Abernathy, SCLC president, leading delegation of leaders representing poor whites, blacks, Indians and Spanish-Americans to Capitol Hill for conferences with cabinet members and congressional leaders.

MAY

16   Paul Freeman, 33, was named associate conductor of the Dallas (Texas) Symphony Orchestra.

JUNE

24   Resurrection City closed. More than one hundred residents were arrested when they refused to leave site. Other residents, including Rev. Abernathy, were arrested during demonstration at Capitol. National Guard was mobilized later in the day to quell disturbances that erupted in the city after closing of camp.

JULY

10   Lincoln Alexander, 44, was elected the first black member of the Canadian Parliament, as a conservative member from the West Hamilton, Ontario district.

18   The 4th Assembly of the World Council of Churches meeting in Uppsala, Sweden, elected three black Americans to the Central Committee, the policy-making body of the assembly.

AUGUST

5   Senator Edward Brooke named temporary chairman of Republican National Convention, Miami, Florida.

25   Lt. Arthur Ashe, 25, became the first American since 1955 to win the U.S. amateur singles title when he defeated Bob Lutz, 20—4-6, 6-3, 8-10, 6-0, 6-4, at the Longwood Cricket Club in Brookline, Mass.

28   Rev. Channing E. Phillips of Washington, D.C., became first black man nominated for president by a major national party. Phillips was nominated as favorite son candidate by District of Columbia delegation at Democratic convention in Chicago, and received 67½ votes on first ballot.

31   Harry Edwards, leader of a group of

athletes who had threatened a boycott of the Mexico City Olympics, cancelled a threatened boycott, following the barring of South Africa from the games and the refusal of all 26 participating black athletes to support the boycott.

SEPTEMBER

9   Arthur Ashe became the first winner of the new U.S. Open Championship when he defeated Tom Okker of the Netherlands—14-12, 5-7, 6-3, 3-6, 6-3—at the Forest Hills Stadium in New York.

OCTOBER

16   Sprinters Tommy Smith and John Carlos, (Smith set a world record in the 19.8 time, a gold medalist, and Carlos, a 3rd place bronze medalist) gave the black power salute with bowed heads at the Olympics in Mexico City following their victory in the 200 meter dash. Two days later, the U.S. Olympic Committee suspended them for the act.

NOVEMBER

5   A record number of black Congressmen, all Democrats, were elected in the House of Representatives. The previous high was 7 during the Reconstruction years, 1873-74. Six were incumbents: William L. Dawson, Illinois; Adam Clayton Powell (N.Y.), who had been refused his seat in 1967; Charles C. Diggs, Michigan; Robert N.C. Nix. Pa.; Augustus Hawkins, California; and John Conyers, Jr., Michigan. The three newcomers are the first black woman, Mrs. Shirley Chisholm (N.Y.) of Brooklyn, who defeated civil rights activist, James Farmer; Louis Stokes (Ohio) of Cleveland, brother of Cleveland Mayor, Carl Stokes; and William L. Clay (Mo.) of St. Louis.

NOVEMBER

19   President Lyndon B. Johnson, speaking at National Urban League Equal Opportunity Awards dinner at New York City, reviewed the record of his administration in the Civil Rights area, and recounted the following achievements: The Civil Rights Act of 1964; the Voting Rights Act of 1965; the Fair Housing Act of 1968. He said, "We are nowhere in sight of where we must be before we can rest." He cited 4 requirements to raise black income from its current level of 60% of white income . . . to change the conditions of the one American family in three currently below the poverty line; to find jobs for the one teenager in 4 who is now unemployed; to cut the nonwhite infant mortality rate, currently three times of the white population.

DECEMBER

6   President Lyndon B. Johnson, accepting the first Achievement Award of the United Negro College Fund, stated that he hoped the new (Nixon) administration would "recognize our (the nation's) shortcomings and inadequacies" in the field of civil rights. UNCF president, Dr. Stephen Wright, characterized Mr. Johnson as, The "Civil Rights President" and as the "Education President."

28   The U.S. Tennis team consisting of Arthur Ashe, Clark Graebner, and Donald Dell, won the Davis cup competition in Adelaide, Australia.

1969

JANUARY

3   Bobby Seale, Panther leader, charged that efforts were being made to prevent the use of the organization by "provocateur agents, kooks and avaricious fools" seeking a base for crime. Seale said that a number of criminal suspects had been expelled by the Panthers under the group's rule against stealing "even a needle or a piece of thread."

13   Attorney General Ramsey Clark, reporting on 1968 civil rights activities of the Justice Department warned that progress could not be halted because "nothing could be better calculated to irreconcilably divide the country than the failure to enforce the civil rights of all our citizens." Clark noted that the Justice Department undertook 125 school desegregation actions in 1968. This included 39 suits or interventions and 86 supplemental proceedings. The department emphasized nationwide enforcement while still fighting to integrate Southern schools.

17   Two members of the Black Panther Party were shot to death during a student meeting called at the University of California at Los Angeles (UCLA) to discuss the choice of a director for a proposed Afro-American Studies Center. The victims, both considered major contenders for the center leadership, were John Jerome Huggins, 23, area captain of the Panthers, and Alprentice (Bunchy) Carter, 26, a Panther deputy minister of defense.

30   Judges John Godbold, Harold Cox and Dan Russell, Jr., sitting on a three-judge federal court in Jackson, Miss., ruled that a five-year-old Mississippi program

of tuition grants to private school pupils was unconstitutional because it "fostered the creation of private segregated schools." The suit had been filed against Mississippi and its State Educational Finance Commission, which administered the program.

FEBRUARY

1   Mrs. Martin Luther King was the top choice of blacks surveyed in an Annual Gallup Poll list of women most admired by Americans. Mrs. King was fourth in the list of most admired by all Americans. Mrs. Robert F. Kennedy was first. Gov. Mills E. Godwin, Jr. names Hilary H. Jones, Jr., 45, a black lawyer and Norfolk school board member, and Thomas C. Boushall, 74, a white Richmond banker, to fill two vacancies on the Virginia State Board of Education.

12 James Farmer, 49, ex-national director of the Congress of Racial Equality, was named assistant secretary of Health, Education and Welfare (HEW) for administration and to serve as liaison with militant black youths. Farmer had been defeated in a bid for Congress by Rep. Shirley Chisholm (D., N.Y.).

27 A report, entitled "One Year Later," issued by the Urban Coalition on Urban America, Inc. recalled the March 1, 1968 findings of the President's National Advisory (Kerner) Commission on Civil Disorders that America was "Moving toward two societies, one black, one white—separate and unequal." The new report charged that the nation was "a year closer to two societies—black and white, increasingly separate and scarcely less unequal." Two former members of the Kerner Commission, N.Y. Mayor John V. Lindsay and Sen. Fred R. Harris (D., Okla.), and the commission's staff director, Washington lawyer David Ginsburg, served on the review board for the new study, a joint effort of the Urban Coalition and Urban America, Inc. Lindsay and Harris had led an unsuccessful effort to reconvene the Kerner Commission; they had argued that without follow-up, the Kerner report would have little effect. Donald Canty, director of Urban America's information center, headed the staff that made the three-month study and wrote the 90-page report. John W. Gardner, ex-secretary of Health, Education and Welfare and chairman of the Urban Coalition, released the study and emphasized that the report "makes it clear that the nation's response to the crisis of the cities has been perilously inadequate." A major finding of "One Year Later" was that the "most recent trend" in population movement had not diminished the "physical distance" between black and white Americans. The report said that the trend showed a "virtual stoppage" of black immigration from the South and a "sharp increase" in the rate of white departure from central city areas. The study found that while city ghettos were increasing in area and declining in population density, there were also indications of growth in suburban ghettos. The study further noted an increased division between blacks and whites in the "perceptions and experiences of American society." The deepening concern of some white Americans over ghetto problems, which had grown with the publication of the Kerner report and the death of Martin Luther King, Jr., had been counterbalanced—perhaps overbalanced—by a deepening of aversion and "outright resistance to slum-ghetto needs and demands," the report cited an increasing concern for law and order that followed the assassination of Sen. Robert F. Kennedy and was highlighted during the Presidential campaign. The report warned that the mood of Negroes, standing somewhere "in the spectrum between militancy and submission," was "not moving in the direction of patience." The report noted that Kerner Commission predictions about the consequences of U.S. policies dealing with the urban crisis had proved accurate: there was some change in ghetto conditions but not enough and an increase in number but a decline in intensity of civil disorders "due primarily to more sophisticated response by police and the military." If the Kerner Commission proved to be "equally correct about the long run," the report warned, "the nation in its neglect may be sowing the seeds of unprecedented future disorders and division."

MARCH

5   An executive order establishing an Office of Minority Business Enterprise was signed by President Nixon. The new office was to be established in the Commerce Department, and Commerce Secretary Maurice H. Stans said it would deal mainly with administration and coordination of federal and private efforts to promote business ownership by

minority groups. The signing ceremony was attended by 36 black, Mexican-American, Puerto Rican, and American Indian leaders.

27   The Black Academy of Arts and Letters, whose purpose would be to give recognition to those making "notable" contributions to black culture, was organized in Boston, Mass. The organization was founded by 50 prominent black scholars, artists and performers with the aid of the 20th-Century Fund, which would fund the academy for three years. Dr. C. Eric Lincoln, author and professor of religion and sociology at the Union Theological Seminary in New York was elected president of the academy. Headquarters wil be in New York City.

MAY

1   The U.S. Civil Rights Commission charged that the U.S. government had subsidized racial discrimination in employment by cooperating with private firms that defied the 1964 Civil Rights law prohibiting job bias. The charge was included in the commission's release of a Brookings Institute report calling on the government to take disciplinary action against firms whose employment practices reflected racial discrimination.

6   Mrs. Elizabeth Cofield, dean of women at Shaw University was elected to the Raleigh, N.C. school board. She led a field of eight in an election for four seats on the board.

15   Federal district judge Julius J. Hoffman issued a permanent injunction banning racial discrimination in School District 151 (South Holland, Ill.), a suburban area south of Chicago. Ruling in the first Justice Department desegregation suit against a northern school district, Judge Hoffman ordered a plan putting all pupils in the sixth through eighth grades into two formerly all-black schools and all pupils in kindergarten through fifth grade into four schools that formerly were nearly all-white. Hoffman's order followed a temporary injunction issued July 8, 1968 and upheld by the U.S. Court of Appeals Dec. 17, 1968.

21-23   Trouble which began at the all-black Dudley High School and spilled over onto the 4,100-student A&T campus, in Greensboro, N.C., ended with one black student dead and five police injured when police and national guardsmen fired on alleged snipers among the student body.

22   Eight Black Panthers were arrested in

New Haven, Conn., on murder and conspiracy charges after the body of a black man identified as Alex Rackley, 24, was discovered in the Coginchaug River in Middlefield, Conn. Rackley, a member of the New York Panther Party, allegedly had been tried and tortured in a Kangaroo court by Black Panthers, reportedly because he was suspected of being a double agent and informer for the F.B.I. Those arrested included six women and two men.

JUNE

19   The U.S. Civil Service Commission said it had found some evidence of racial discrimination in the Government Printing Office. They reported a lack of minority group members in higher level supervisory and administrative positions. The report said that the GPO had a favorable minority employment record if compared with the private printing industry and other federal agencies.

JULY

4   Stokely Carmichael, prime minister of the Black Panther Party, announced his resignation from the party in a letter calling the organization "dogmatic" and condemning its tactics as "dishonest and vicious." He criticized the organization's alliance with white radicals, claiming it would only lead to the whites through control of the black organization."

17   Presidents of 31 black colleges ended a three-day meeting in Mobile, Ala. by passing a resolution that criticized the federal government's lack of understanding of the role of the 113 predominantly black colleges in the U.S. An HEW Office of Education official, sponsors of the conference, said the meeting had been called to reassure black college presidents that their applications for special funds would find sympathy in Washington.

31   Five Chicago policemen were wounded in a gun battle with Black Panther party members at the offices of the Illinois chapter of the militant organization. Both sides accused the other of firing the initial shot. Agents of the FBI had raided the same offices June 4, allegedly in search of a Black Panther fugitive.

AUGUST

16   The Southern Christian Leadership Conference (SCLC) officially ended the long period of mourning for the Rev. Martin Luther King. Jr. and re-elected the Rev. Ralph David Abernathy as president at the SCLC's 12th annual convention in

Charleston, S.C. Abernathy had been elected president after Dr. King was assassinated in April, 1968.

19   Bobby Seale, national chairman of the Black Panther Party, was arrested by FBI agents in San Francisco on a murder charge in the May, 1969 torture-slaying of a former party member, Alex Rackley in New Haven, Conn.

SEPTEMBER

12   Robert F. Williams, black expatriate who had called for an armed insurrection in the U.S. in radio broadcasts from Hanoi, Havana and Peking, returned to the U.S. after eight years in self-imposed exile. He faced a charge of kidnapping a white couple in Monroe, N.C. in 1961.

OCTOBER

17   Dr. Clifton Reginald Wharton, Jr., 43, an economist and vice president of the Agricultural Development Council in New York, was elected president of Michigan State University (400,000 students), thus becoming the first black to head a major, predominantly white U.S. University.

NOVEMBER

1   Black community leaders in East St. Louis, Ill. acceded to the demands of the U.S. Department of Labor that a $1.9 million job training program be established following the Labor Department's threats to withdraw $10 million in federal aid to the city. Black civil rights groups had protested the plan because of the department's failure to consult the black community when drawing up the program. The government said the job-training program would prepare laborers for major housing programs in East St. Louis.

13   Dr. Lewis C. Dowdy, president of North Carolina A & T State University, was elected the first black chairman of the Council of Presidents at the convention of the National Association of State Universities and Land Grant Colleges.

17   The Philadelphia Orchestra hired its first black musician, violinist Renard Edwards, 25, of the Symphony of the New World.

29   The Southern Regional Council charged that the U.S. Department of Agriculture was the federal government's "worst offender in discriminating against blacks," The council, a private research agency, said that unless the Agriculture Department takes forceful action to end patterns of dominance "by Southern white supremacists, black Southern

farmers will be denied equal protection under the law." The report cited patterns of racial discrimination within the Extension Service, Soil Conservation Service and Agricultural Stabilization and Conservation Service of the federal agency.

DECEMBER

4   State's Attorney's police staged a pre-dawn raid on an apartment near the headquarters of the Black Panther party on Chicago's West Side and killed Fred Hampton, Illinois party chairman, and Mark Clark, Peoria, Ill. leader. Four others, two of them women, were wounded in the ambush.

8   Los Angeles police, armed with tear gas rifles, fought a four-hour battle with members of the Black Panther party, following a raid on the party's headquarters. Three policemen and three Panthers were wounded.

12   The Justice Department announced that it had instructed its civil rights division to conduct a preliminary investigation into the Dec. 4 slaying of two Black Panther party officials by police in Chicago, Ill. A spokesman for the department said the investigation would seek to determine whether Chicago police had committed a federal crime or violated civil rights laws.

13   Bobby Seale, the national chairman of the Black Panther party, denounced recent police raids against the party as part of a national plan "to commit genocide against the Black Panther party." Seale, in a San Francisco jail, was waiting to be extradited to Connecticut, where he faced charges of conspiring to kidnap and murder.

15   Former U.S. Supreme Court Justice Arthur J. Goldberg and NAACP leader Roy Wilkins announced that 25 private citizens representing civil rights, law, politics, and business had joined them in sponsoring "searching inquiry" into recent clashes between the police and members of the Black Panther party.

19   Attorney General John N. Mitchell sent a seven-man team of Justice Department lawyers to Chicago to investigate the fatal shooting of Fred Hampton and Mark Clark of the Black Panther party Dec. 4. Mitchell said the investigation, headed by Jerris Leonard, assistant attorney general for the Justice Department's Civil Rights Division, would also be joined by a specially designated federal grand jury.

28 The American Civil Liberties Union (ACLU), in a report of a documented survey of nine metropolitan centers, concluded that law enforcement agencies across the country were "having a drive against the Black Panther party resulting in serious civil liberties violations."

29 Edgar Labat and Clifton A. Poret, two convicted rapists who spent 14 years awaiting execution in a New Orleans, La. prison, were freed after they pleaded guilty to a charge of attempted aggravated rape. District Court Judge Edward A. Haggerty Jr. accepted their pleas and announced that the district attorney's office was prepared to accept a sentence equal to the time that Labat and Poret had served. Labat and Poret, both black, had been sentenced to death in March 1953 after being convicted of raping a white woman in New Orleans in 1950. In 1966 the two were granted a new trial after a decision by the U.S. Court of Appeals for the Fifth Circuit in August 1966. The defendants maintained that blacks had been systematically excluded from their trial jury.

1970

JANUARY

8 The 2.8 million-member Church of Jesus Christ of Latter-Day Saints (Mormon) reaffirmed church policy barring black members (about 200) from the priesthood.

9 The Census Bureau, in a report of a survey on poverty in the U.S. from 1959 to 1968 said that the number of persons officially classified as poor dropped from 39.5 million to 25.4 million during the eight-year period, but that one of every eight Americans was still classified as poor in 1968. The report said the number of whites below the poverty line fell from 28.5 million in 1959 to 17.4 million in 1968 while the number of poor blacks declined from 11 million to 8 million.

15 Blacks and whites across the nation celebrated the 41st anniversary of the birth of Dr. Martin Luther King Jr., the slain civil rights leader. Several governors, including Nelson A. Rockefeller of New York, Frank Licht of Rhode Island, and Kenneth M. Curtis of Maine, declared Martin Luther King day in their states.

In some cities, including Baltimore, New York, Harrisburg, Pa., Philadelphia, Kansas City, Mo. and Poughkeepsie, N.Y., public schools were closed. In Illinois the state legislature designated a "commemorative holiday," and although Illinois schools remained open, part of the school day was devoted to the study of King's work. The same classroom routine was set up in San Francisco.

Memorial church services were held across the country.

In Atlanta, 400 persons heard Atlanta Mayor Sam Massell eulogize King. Following the service Mrs. Coretta Scott King, King's widow, dedicated Atlanta's new Martin Luther King Jr. Memorial Center, which included King's home, the Ebenezer Baptist Church and the crypt where King was buried.

17 Right Rev. John M. Burgess was installed as the 12th bishop of the Massachusetts Episcopal Diocese and the first black man to head an Episcopal diocese in the U.S. The installation service was in St. Paul's Cathedral, Boston.

17 Cleveland Mayor Carl B. Stokes named Lt. Gen. Benjamin Oliver Davis Jr., 57, deputy commander of the U.S. Strike Command and the highest-ranking black in the U.S. military to become Cleveland's public safety director. Davis was the son of the first black to attain the rank of general in the armed forces.

19 The U.S. Supreme Court refused to strike down jury selection laws in Alabama and Georgia on appeals by blacks that the laws had been used to exclude blacks from jury lists. Justice Potter Stewart, who wrote the court's opinion in both cases, said the court had found proof that the laws had been used to discriminate against blacks, but he argued that other states had similar laws requiring the selection of "upright" and "intelligent" jurors. He said the laws should not be voided if they were "capable" of unbiased enforcement.

Justice William Douglas dissented in the Alabama case, arguing that the governor of Alabama should be ordered to appoint blacks to the Greene County jury commission in proportion to their percentage of the population. In the Georgia case, the court found the jury selection laws in Taliaferro County "not inherently unfair" but said discrimination had been proved. The case was sent back to a lower court for further hearings.

22 In his first State of the Union Message,

delivered before a joint session of Congress, President Richard Nixon called for attention to domestic issues, stressing reform of the welfare system, reform of federal, state and local government, and reform to "expand the range of opportunities for all Americans"—equal voting rights, equal employment opportunity and new opportunities for ownership and property rights. Priority also was to be given to a redoubled anti-crime effort by strengthening law enforcement and to a continued fight against inflation.

27 Confirmation hearings on G. Harrold Carswell's nomination to the Supreme Court opened before the Senate Judiciary Committee. Senators questioned the judge on a "white supremacy" speech that Carswell admitted he made during a 1948 political campaign in Georgia. In response to questions by Democratic members of the committee, Carswell said that "the force of 22 years of history" had changed him as well as the South and that he was "aghast" that he had supported white supremacy in 1948. "Those notions are obnoxious to me," "I am not a racist. I have no notions, secretive or otherwise, of racial superiority," he said.

28 Arthur Ashe, black American tennis star, was refused a visa by the South African government to compete in the South African open tennis championships in March. Frank W. Waring, minister of sport, said the decision to bar Ashe was based on Ashe's views of South Africa's policy of apartheid, or racial separation. Waring said, as a member of the U.S. Davis cup team, Ashe would be permitted to enter the country if the U.S. was scheduled to play in South Africa.

30 The seven black Panthers who had been indicted for their alleged role in a December 1969 shootout with Chicago policemen during a raid in which two Panther officials were slain, were freed and all criminal charges against them dropped.

FEBRUARY

2   Leroy O. Clark, formerly NAACP Legal Defense and Educational Fund Inc. lawyer, described how he had briefed inexperienced lawyers who were about to appear before Harrold Carswell, nominee of our U.S. Supreme Court: "I usually spent the evening before, having them go over their arguments, while I harassed them."

13 Joseph L. Searles, III, 30, former direc-

tor of local business development for New York, became the first black man to become a member of the New York Stock Exchange. He began training as a floor partner for the firm Newburger, Loeb & Co.

16 Joe Frazier succeeded Muhammad Ali as the sole world heavyweight champion when he scored a two round knockout over Jimmy Ellis of New York.

24 Muhammad Ali was denied his plea that the Fifth Circuit Court of Appeals meet to consider his appeal of a conviction for refusing to be inducted into the U.S. Army.

24 The U.S. Supreme Court upheld a lower court ruling that invalidated a New York State law requiring newly arrived welfare applicants to give "clear and convincing proof" that they did not come to the state merely to take advantage of high relief payments. In a brief order, the justices cited a 1969 decision that struck down state residency laws for welfare benefits on the basis that the laws restricted poor people's freedom to travel.

24 A confrontation between Rep. Charles C. Diggs, Jr. (D. Mich.) and Georgia Governor Lester Maddox began when Maddox passed out ax handles to several people in the House restaurant. The handles were frequently distributed by Maddox as a souvenir of the days when he wielded one to bar black persons from entering his restaurant in Atlanta. When Diggs saw the handles being passed out he threatened to have Maddox ousted from the premises. Maddox told Diggs that he was acting "more like an ass and baboon than a member of Congress." A policeman intervened and broke off the confrontation. After the lunch recess, Rep. John Conyers, Jr. (D. Mich.) one of the nine black members of the House, denounced Maddox's conduct as "totally disgraceful."

25 Three former Detroit policemen and a private security guard were acquitted of conspiring to violate the civil rights of 10 black occupants of Detroit's Algiers Motel during the Detroit riots of 1967.

27 The U.S. Supreme Court refused to consider an appeal by seven Ku Klux Klan members convicted on Federal conspiracy charges arising from the 1964 murder of three civil rights workers, Michael Schwerner, Andrew Goodman and James Earl Chaney.

28 Daniel P. Moynihan, domestic adviser

to President Nixon, proposed in a private memorandum to the White House that "the time may have come when the issue of race could benefit from a period of 'benign neglect'." The 1,650-word "Memorandum for the President" was leaked to the press and later confirmed by Moynihan at the White House.

MARCH

4   Curt Flood, the former St. Louis Cardinals' star outfielder who filed a violation of anti-trust laws lost the initial round of his battle when a federal judge in New York denied his bid for a temporary injunction that would have authorized him to negotiate his contract for the 1970 season as a free agent.

5   Twenty-one civil rights leaders, including authors, leading black educators and a U.S. congressman, charged that Moynihan's memorandum was "symptomatic of a calculated, aggressive and systematic" effort by the Nixon Administration to "wipe out" nearly two decades of civil rights gains.

6   The concern of civil rights staffers in the Department of Health, Education and Welfare (HEW) over civil rights continued as 2,000 HEW employees signed a petition calling on HEW Secretary Robert H. Finch to explain the department's position on civil rights enforcement.

6   Thirty-seven top black officials in the Nixon Administration met with President Nixon and urged him to clarify his position on school desegregation and to take more action in the field of civil rights. The officials who met with Nixon at the White House said they were feeling heavy pressure from the black community and that only stronger action from him would relieve it.

     According to reports, the President asked the officials to put their views and recommendations in writing and resubmit them. James Farmer, assistant secretary of Health, Education and Welfare (HEW), urged the President to "clarify his posture on school desegregation." The meeting marked the first time the President had met with all black appointees at one session.

9   The Supreme Court ruled 7-0 that the Memphis school system end racial segregation immediately. The court said the U.S. Court of Appeals for the Sixth Circuit and the district court judge had erred in declaring that Memphis had already achieved a unitary school system

and in not ordering prompt integration action. The Memphis school system served 74,000 black students and 60,000 whites. The lower courts had already ordered faculty integration but had refused to move beyond a "freedom of choice" plan for pupil integration.

9   The Leadership Conference on Civil Rights, an umbrella organization of civic, religious, labor and civil rights groups, opened an intensive lobbying campaign to block the Carswell nomination. A spokesman for the group said 30 senators had been visited in an effort to line up enough votes to block confirmation.

9   In a concurring opinion, Chief Justice Warren E. Burger said the court would resolve unanswered questions on constitutional requirements for school integration soon after a justice was confirmed to fill the current court vacancy. Justice Thurgood Marshall, who was general council of the NAACP Legal Defense and Educational Fund, Inc. when it had filed the initial Memphis case in 1960, did not take part in the ruling.

21   Dr. Andrew F. Brimmer, member of the Board of Governors of the Federal Reserve System said that although blacks as a group had made significant economic progress during the last decade, the gains were so unevenly distributed that there was a "deepening schism in the black community." He said the gap was "widening between the able and the less able, between the well prepared and those with few skills." Brimmer, said that in his judgment "this deepening schism within the black community should interest us as much as the real progress that has been made by blacks as a group."

30   A black citizens group in Atlanta announced that it had successfully negotiated agreements with 22 of the city's 28 TV and radio stations calling for increased black involvement in programming and employment. Details of the agreements varied with the size of the 22 stations.

30   A nationwide survey by two private organizations released indicated that nearly 1,500 blacks held elective public office in the U.S. The survey was conducted jointly by the Metropolitan Applied Research Center, Inc. of New York and Washington, D.C. and the Voter Education Project of the Southern Regional Council in Atlanta.

APRIL

8   President Nixon suffered a major defeat when the Senate, by a 51-45 vote, rejected his nominee to the Supreme Court Judge G. Harrold Carswell.

9   Jerome H. Holland, the first U.S. ambassador to Sweden in 14 months was greeted on his arrival in Stockholm by placard-carrying demonstrators shouting anti-war slogans.

14   Holland, a black American and former President of Hampton Institute delivered his credentials to King Gustaf VI Adolf at the royal palace where protestors shouted "Nigger! Nigger!" at the new envoy. The Swedish government announced that it would apologize for the incident.

Demonstrators protesting U.S. military involvement in Vietnam threw eggs at Ambassador Holland during the opening of a U.S. cultural center. A U.S. State Department spokesman called the incident "insulting and uncalled for." The Swedish government termed the protestors "scoundrels."

27   The U.S. Supreme Court, over the dissents of Justices Thurgood Marshall, William J. Brennan, Jr., and William O. Douglas, dismissed the appeal of Arthur Lee Hester, a Chicago black youth, who was sentenced to 55 years in prison for a murder committed at the age of 14. Two majority justices had indicated that Hester's lawyer had failed to point out a legal basis for reversal.

27   James E. Allen, Jr., U.S. Commissioner of education, said in a statement that he intended to continue his work to end school segregation whether it was de-facto or de jure.

27-28 Police dressed in riot gear and carrying fixed bayonets patrolled the streets of River Rouge, Michigan, a predominantly black industrial suburb of Detroit, April 29, after two nights of firebombings and lootings. Police from 14 neighboring communities were called in to stop the disorders which threatened to overflow into downtown Detroit.

MAY

8   The Illinois state attorney disclosed that the seven Black Panthers who had been indicted January 30 for their alleged role in a December 1969 shootout with Chicago policemen during a raid in which two Panther officials were slain had been freed and all criminals charges against them dropped.

12   Six black men were shot and killed and 20 other persons wounded during a night of racial violence in Augusta, Ga., marked by looting, burning and sniper fire. According to witnesses at the scene, at least three of the six dead blacks were unarmed bystanders who were not involved in the rioting. According to the witnesses, the police did not fire in self defense. They said none of the six slain men were carrying firearms.

14   Two black youths were shot and killed by police and national guardsmen during a night of violence outside a women's dormitory on the campus of Jackson State College in Jackson, Miss.

18   Attorney General John Mitchell conferred with police and authorities in Jackson. Also present at the closed conference was Jackson Mayor Russell C. Davis and Leonard Garment, special assistant to President Nixon. They said the meeting had been "useful."

19   Rev. Ralph D. Abernathy, President SCLS, announced that he would lead a 100-mile mass march through Georgia to combat the "growing repression" of blacks and students in Georgia and the rest of the nation. The march would begin in Perry, Ga., May 19, and end May 23 in Atlanta.

19   U.S. Office of Education official said that he agreed with recent findings that Census Bureau statistics seriously underestimated the problem of functional illiteracy in the U.S. Commenting on an article by David Harman, an Israeli adult education expert currently at Harvard University, Paul Delker, director of adult education programs, said he agreed with the "problem of definition" pointed out in Harman's study. Harman, in an article printed in the Harvard Educational Review, challenged the Census Bureau estimate that 8.3% of the U.S. population over age 25 was functionally illiterate. Harman said, "In fact, over half that group may be functionally illiterate." He pointed out that the Census Bureau defined as functionally illiterate any individual that completed the fourth or fifth grade.

20   Fifty-one persons were arrested in Rahway, N.J. May 21, following a racial clash May 20 in the Rahway high school that precipitated fighting in the streets.

22   The New York Times reported that a citizens' panel which had been formed in 1969 by former Supreme Court Justice Arthur J. Goldberg to conduct an inquiry into the slaying of two Black

Panther leaders by Chicago Police during a December, 1969 police raid, had remained inactive since that time as a result of a plea by a chief Nixon Administration official.

22   A plane chartered by Sen. Edmund S. Muskie flew the Maine Democrat and a planeload of U.S. congressmen and civil rights partisans to Jackson, Miss. for the funeral of James Earl Green, one of the two victims slain by Mississippi highway patrolmen at Jackson State College, May 14.

26   A federal district court judge in Newark, N.J. approved an out-of-court settlement to compensate 66 blacks whose homes were searched by New Jersey state police in a mass hunt for weapons during the Plainfield riot of 1967. The New Jersey branch of the American Civil Liberties Union had filed suit on behalf of the plaintiffs for $1 million in damages. The out-of-court settlement called for compensation totaling $19,000.

JUNE

1   The Supreme Court postponed an important ruling on capital punishment when it sent back to trial court the case of William L. Maxwell, a Hot Springs, Ark., black man sentenced to death in 1962 for the rape of a white woman, without considering the principal arguments by lawyers seeking the abolition of the death penalty. Maxwell's lawyers had argued that the fate of 505 of the 510 persons awaiting execution across the country depended on the outcome of the case. However, the court apparently decided it needed a ninth justice to resolve the capital punishment issues, and the court's newest appointees, Judge Harry A. Blackmun, would be disqualified from ruling on Maxwell's case since he had ruled against Maxwell in a lower court decision.

1   The Supreme Court ruled 6-2 that a suit for damages brought under an 1871 antidiscrimination law must show that racial bias had legal sanction and was not simply discrimination based on an individual's private views.

5   Earl Caldwell, a black reporter for the New York Times, was found guilty of civil contempt by a federal district court judge in San Francisco for refusing to testify before a grand jury investigating the activities of black militant organizations.

9   In Virginia municipal elections, blacks won city council seats for the first time

since Reconstruction in Roanoke, Charlottesville, Lynchburg and Emporia.

14   Cheryl Adrenne Browne, a 19-year-old sophomore at Luther College in Decorah, Iowa, was chosen Miss Iowa. She became the first black woman to compete in the Miss America beauty pageant in Atlantic City, New Jersey.

16   Kenneth A. Gibson was elected mayor of Newark, N.J. to become the first black mayor of a major Eastern city.

17   The House, by a 272-132 vote, approved a measure to lower the voting age to 18 and to extend the Voting Rights Act of 1965 five more years.

22   President Nixon signed the Voting Rights Act but called for an immediate court test of the constitutionality of lowering the voting age by statute instead of by amendment to the Constitution.

29   The chairman of the board of directors of the National Association for the Advancement of Colored People (NAACP) labeled the Nixon Administration antiblack and accused it of a "calculated policy to work against the needs and aspirations of the largest minority of its citizens."

30   Two members of the ultraconservative John Birch Society were elected to Congress in special elections in California. Former Rep. John H. Rousselot (R), 42, won a 24th Congressional District vote over Mrs. Myrlie B. Evers (D), 37, by a 68%-32% margin. Mrs. Evers is the widow of NAACP leader Medgar Evers who was slain in Mississippi in 1963.

JULY

3   The National Committee of Black Churchmen, a group of 41 black U.S. church and civil rights leaders, published a "Black Declaration of Independence" as a full-page advertisement in The New York Times. The declaration contained a pledge by the black leaders to "renounce all allegiance" to the U.S., unless black people received "full redress and relief" from "the injustice, exploitative control, institutionalized violence and racism of white America . . ." The Committee also charged that black Americans had been taxed without protection of their constitutional rights. The committee listed as sponsors the Ministerial Interfaith Association of New York, the IFCO Black Caucus of New York and the Black Economic Development Conference.

15   James H. McGee, a 51-year-old lawyer, was sworn in July 15 as Dayton, Ohio's first black mayor.

15   Missouri State Rep. Leon M. Jordan
      was shot to death July 15 in Kansas City,
      Mo. Two men who were arrested July 17
      in connection with the murder, were
      released July 28 for lack of evidence.
16   Delegates to the national convention of
      the Benevolent and Protective Order of
      Elks in San Francisco voted to retain
      the fraternal society's whites-only mem-
      bership rule in its charter, which re-
      quired that members be white, older
      than 20, believers in God and U.S. citi-
      zens.
22   The U.S. Court of Appeals for the
      Fourth Circuit upheld as constitutional
      July 22 South Carolina's riot statute.
      In its ruling, the court struck down a
      challenge by the Rev. Ralph D. Aber-
      nathy, president of the Southern Chris-
      tian Leadership Conference (SCLC),
      that the law violated the freedom of
      speech clause of the First Amendment.
22   The Republican party was urged to end
      its so-called "Southern strategy" to woo
      the deep South by conservative stances
      and seek instead the vote of the "peri-
      pheral South" by pursuing a moderate
      policy of social progress.
31   U.S. District Court Judge Harold Cox
      of Mississippi ordered the Hinds County
      Circuit Court clerk's office July 31 to
      issue marriage licenses to interracial
      couples, overturning a Mississippi mis-
      cegenation law. The ruling was sought
      by Roger Mills, 24, a white law clerk,
      and Berta Linson, 21, his black fiancée,
      a Jackson State College student. The
      couple was married August 2.

AUGUST

7   Superior Court Judge Harold J. Haley,
      65, and two San Quentin convicts were
      killed in a gun battle following an at-
      tempted escape and kidnapping at the
      San Rafael, Calif. courthouse.
12   The President's Commission on Campus
      Unrest held three days of hearings Aug.
      11-13 in Jackson, Miss. to gather testi-
      mony on the May 14 shooting at Jackson
      State College, which resulted in the
      death of two students. Commission
      Chairman William W. Scranton said
      Aug. 11 that the panel would not try
      to identify persons who fired weapons
      or fix blame, which he said were grand
      jury functions.
      Jackson Police Lt. Warren M. Magee,
      who had led city and state police in-
      volved in the shooting, refused to tes-
      tify on certain details of the police action
      because he said it would violate state

law to reveal testimony he had already
delivered before a state grand jury.
He did say, however, that firing on the
students was contrary to his orders.
Highway Patrol Inspector Lloyd Jones
testified that the patrolmen had no orders
to fire, but he said there had not been
enough time to issue such orders. Charles
Snodgrass, state patrol personnel officer,
said that he and two other officials had
investigated the actions of patrolmen involved and had concluded that they had
acted properly.

19   Whitney M. Young Jr., executive direc-
      tor of the National Urban League,
      charged that the Nixon Administration's
      racial policies were "marked by great
      unevenness, by a sort of indecisiveness,
      flabbiness."
      "The record is consistent for its incon-
      sistency." Young queried "The issue is
      how soon will . . . the decent, enlightened
      Americans take over, take charge? When
      will we decide that this issue is too
      crucial for everybody to be left to the
      kooks and the crackpots, whatever color
      they may be?"
      He denied his availability for any Nixon
      administration past. "I am not available
      for any position with the Administration,
      either temporary or permanent," he said.
29   Army Spec. 4 Pondexteur E. Williams,
      a black serviceman killed in Vietnam
      during a mortar barrage, was buried in
      a formerly all-white cemetery in Fort
      Pierce, Fla. The cemetery had refused
      to bury the soldier since August 20, but
      a U.S. district court judge ordered the
      cemetery's supervisors to accept Wil-
      liams' body for burial. A white woman
      had donated a gravesite at Hillcrest to
      the Williams family for interment of
      their son's body. The cemetery had re-
      fused to bury Williams.

SEPTEMBER

3-7   More than 2,500 blacks from four con-
      tinents convened in Atlanta to hold the
      first Congress of African People. Dele-
      gations from 27 African countries, the
      Caribbean nations, four South American
      countries, Australia and the U.S., assem-
      bled on the campus of Atlanta Univer-
      sity to hear the conference's leadership
      delineate the concepts of "nation build-
      ing" and "Pan Africanism."
      Organized and convened by Hayward
      Henry, a 27-year-old black studies lec-
      turer the conference theme called for
      black unity, the building of black insti-
      tutions and functioning alliances with

nonwhites. A second leader, poet-playwright LeRoi Jones, urged the delegates to create a World African party. Jones proposed to the delegates that local community organizing be the base for creating and developing "an international Pan-Africanist party" capable of dealing with problems on both the international scale and also on "the smallest level."

OCTOBER

2 Whitney M. Young Jr., 49, executive director of the National Urban League, became the second black to be named to the board of trustees of the Massachusetts Institute of Technology. The first, Dr. Jerome H. Holland, ambassador to Sweden, was elected in 1969.

12 The U.S. Commission on Civil Rights reported that there had been a "major breakdown" in the enforcement of the nation's legal mandates forbidding racial discrimination.

12 The U.S. Commission on Civil Rights reported that there had been a "major breakdown" in the enforcement of the nation's legal mandates forbidding racial discrimination.

The commission urged President Nixon to exercise "courageous moral leadership" and to establish, within the White House machinery, committees to oversee enforcement of court decrees, executive orders, and legislation relating to civil rights.

These findings were announced by the Rev. Theodore M. Hesburgh, the panel's chairman and president of the University of Notre Dame. Hesburgh said the report based on a six-month study of the executive departments and agencies charged with enforcing the nation's civil rights laws, showed that "the credibility of the government's total civil rights effort has been seriously undermined." He added that "unless we get serious about this, the country is on a collision course."

NOVEMBER

In a state race, Richard Austin, a black Democrat who ran unsuccessfully for mayor of Detroit in 1969, was easily elected secretary of state over Emil Lockwood, a Republican state senator.

3 Twelve Blacks, all Democrats, were elected to Congress. Seven were incumbents: Mrs. Shirley Chisholm (N.Y.), William Clay (Mo.), John Conyers (Mich.), Charles C. Diggs, Jr. (Mich.), Augustus F. Hawkins (Calif.), Robert N.C. Nix (Pa.) and Louis Stokes (Ohio).

3 In a surprising upset, Max Rafferty, a champion of many ultraconservative causes, was defeated by Wilson Riles, a black, for the nonpartisan office of state superintendent of public instruction.

16 Ossie Davis, Dick Gregory, and a group of U.S. blacks and Puerto Ricans, asked the United Nations to censure the U.S. for what the group termed a policy of genocide against minority groups. The delegation met with officials of the Human Rights Commission who promised to place the matter on its agenda in February, 1971.

DECEMBER

3 The Justice Department filed a suit asking the federal district court in Birmingham, Ala. to invalidate provisions of Alabama's Constitution and statutory laws making it a crime for blacks and whites to marry. It was the first time the government had taken such an action.

3 The government's suit asked the court to order Alabama authorities to grant a marriage license to Sgt. Louis Voyer, a white soldier based at Fort McClellan, Ala., so that he could marry Phyllis Bett, a black woman from Anniston. The complaint said that the couple had applied for a marriage license Nov. 10 but were denied it by a state judge on the grounds that approval of a permit would violate the state's constitutional and statutory laws.

The judge who denied the license, Probate Judge C. Clyde Britain, and the State of Alabama were named as defendants.

The federal government's complaint said Britain's action denied Voyer and Miss Bett their constitutional rights against improper state action and imposed an undue burden on the rights of Sgt. Voyer as a member of the armed forces.

10 In response to a question at his first news conference in four months, President Nixon said that he believed "forced integration in the suburbs is not in the national interest." He said the government would act only to the extent that the law required. He said his Administration would see "as a result of acts passed by Congress, that the federal government not provide aid to housing or to urban renewal where a community has a policy of discrimination and has taken no steps to remove it," but that his Administration would not use the power of the federal government "in ways not

required by the law" for forced integration of suburban communities.

11 A U.S. judge discharged a federal grand jury in Jackson, Miss. after it failed to return any indictments in the shooting deaths of two black students by Mississippi lawmen on the campus of Jackson State College May 14. The absence of any indictments apparently ended the possibility that any of the 40 state highway patrolmen or 26 Jackson City policemen involved in the shooting would be prosecuted.

1971

JANUARY

1 James Floyd becomes the first black mayor of the predominantly white community of Princeton, New Jersey.

The Ninety-second Congress convenes with twelve black congressmen, the largest number since Reconstruction.

Dr. Melvin H. Evans, a native Virgin Islander, is inaugurated as the first elected governor of the Virgin Islands. Evans, a Republican, is the last appointed governor of the Islands, having been named by President Nixon in 1969.

Milton B. Allen is sworn in a chief prosecutor of Baltimore, Maryland, becoming the first black to hold that office in the nation.

Walter E. Fauntroy, thirty-seven, a Baptist minister, wins the Democratic nomination for nonvoting delegate to the House of Representatives from Washington, D.C., in a primary election.

George E. Johnson, president of Johnson Products Company, is named to the governing board of the U.S. Postal Service.

Six black elected officials are installed in Greene County, Alabama, where blacks hold all but two of the county's elective offices. Greene County has been center of campaigns by SCLC, NAACP, SNCC and the National Democratic Party of Alabama.

Leon H. Sullivan, founder of Opportunities Industrialization Centers of America, Inc. (OIC), is elected to the board of directors of the General Motors Corporation, and becomes the first black director of a U.S. auto company.

6 Illinois State Senator Cecil A. Partee is elected president pro-tem of the state senate.

The Dance Theatre of Harlem, the first all-black classical ballet company in the U.S., makes its debut at the Guggenheim Museum of Art in New York City. The company was founded by Arthur Mitchell, a soloist with the New York City Ballet.

6 U.S. Supreme Court, in a 6-3 ruling, upholds the right of state and local welfare officials to enter the homes of recipients and to cut off funds from persons who refuse such entry. The court overturns a federal district court ruling in New York that welfare caseworkers without search warrants could not force their way into the homes of persons on public assistance. Dissenting are Justices Marshall, Brennan and Douglas.

6 The U.S. Circuit Court of Appeals rules that Shaw, Mississippi, has to provide public services—street lights, drainage facilities, paved streets and traffic signals—to all residents, equally. Decision is viewed as a major breakthrough in cases dealing with inadequate public services.

22 Black Congressmen boycott State of the Union message because of President Nixon's "consistent refusal" to hear pleas and concerns of black Americans.

25 The U.S. Supreme Court rules that companies cannot deny employment to women with preschool children unless the same criteria pertain to men. In its first sex discrimination ruling on the equal hiring provisions of the 1964 Civil Rights Act, the court says the law forbids "one hiring policy for women and another for men."

FEBRUARY

Brooks Robinson is named winner of the twenty-first annual Hickok Professional Athlete of the Year Award. He led the Baltimore Orioles to a five-game win in the 1970 World Series:

The Navy announces that it will name a destroyer escort in honor of Ensign Jesse Leroy Brown, America's first black naval aviator and the first black naval officer killed in the Korean War.

9 Leroy ("Satchel") Paige is elected to the Hall of Fame in a "special" category established for members of the old Negro League.

10 Elliot L. Richardson, secretary of HEW, and J. Stanley Pottinger, head of the Civil Rights section of HEW, inform the Senate that eleven school districts have received notices that their grants will be terminated for failure to comply with federal requirements for biracial advisory school committees and nondis-

criminatory treatment of faculty and students.

11 HEW Secretary Elliot L. Richardson announces that he will seek $800,000 to pay for fifty-five federal inspectors to make spot checks in the homes of welfare recipients.

11 The Building and Constructions Trades Department of the AFL-CIO announces opposition to proposed quota rules issued by the Labor Department. Under the Labor Department rules, unions with federally registered trainee programs would be required to adopt affirmative action plans to bring more nonwhites into the programs.

13 Cornelius McNeil Cooper Jr. wins an honorable discharge from the U.S. armed forces as a conscientious objector. He is the first West Point graduate to receive such action on a discharge petition. Cooper stated in his application for discharge that he believed "service in the armed forces is an immoral action. As a black man, I am caused to be more than usually sensitive to the fact of violence in life and the effect of violence on men's lives."

17 Sheriff Lucius D. Amerson of Macon County, Alabama, the first black sheriff in Alabama since Reconstruction, is arrested in Montgomery on a federal indictment accusing him of beating a black prisoner. He was later acquitted by a jury.

18 California Governor Ronald Reagan vetoes, for the third time, federal funds for California anti-poverty projects. The latest veto was of a $1.6 million grant to the Oakland Economic Development Council, Inc., on the grounds that the staff had engaged in politics.

18 President Nixon tells news conference that "this administration will enforce the law of the land which provides for open housing, but will not go beyond the law or in violation of the law by going beyond it by using federal coercion or federal money to force economic integration of neighborhoods."

22 The U.S. Supreme Court refuses an emergency plea by Rev. Jesse L. Jackson, who wanted the court to order Illinois to place his name on the ballot for the February 23 mayoral primary in Chicago.

24 The U.S. Supreme Court, in a 5-4 ruling, limits the scope of the 1966 Miranda decision, which held that incriminating statements taken by policemen before a prisoner had been fully warned of his rights were inadmissible. The new ruling states that defendant can testify or refuse to testify, but the privilege cannot be construed to include the right to commit perjury, and, therefore, evidence heretofore held as inadmissible can be used by the prosecutor to contradict a suspect's testimony if he testifies in his own defense. Justices Marshall, Brennan and Douglas dissented. Marshall stated that "this goes far toward undoing much of the progress in conforming police methods to the Constitution."

25 Frank Carlucci, acting Director of the Office of Economic Opportunity, overrules Mississippi Governor J.B. Williams veto of a $200 grant for a Jackson legal services project.

26 Huey P. Newton and Eldridge Cleaver, Black Panther party leaders, hold a transatlantic telephone debate that is broadcast by an San Francisco television station.

MARCH

2 Justice Department files suit in Jackson, Mississippi, U.S. District Court, charging that Governor J.B. Williams and other Mississippi officials have "unreasonably interfered" with a federally funded program to supply health services to the poor, through the Tri Country Community Center in Jackson.

U.S. Supreme Court rules unanimously that persons cannot be jailed solely because of economic inability to pay fines.

3 U.S. Census Bureau announces that 1970 statistics indicate that the rate of black migration from the South to the North has remained steady over the last two decades. The figures indicated that the migration level during the sixties was nearly the same as the high level of the forties and fifties. More than 75 percent of the 1.4 million blacks who left the South during the decade settled in five large industrial states: New York, California, New Jersey, Michigan and Illinois, with the largest population influx into the New York metropolitan area. According to the 1970 figures, the black population in the South declined from 77 percent in 1940 to 53 percent in 1970.

The U.S. Supreme Court rules that employers cannot use job tests that have the effect of screening out other minorities, if the tests are not related to ability to do the work.

8 Joe Frazier wins fifteen-round decision in New York's Madison Square Garden

against challenger Muhammad Ali. It was the richest single sports event in history.

23 Walter E. Fauntroy becomes the first nonvoting congressional delegate from the District of Columbia since the Reconstruction.

23 Flip Wilson, television star and comedian, receives the International Broadcasting Award's "Man of the Year" citation.

25 President Nixon meets with members of the Congressional Black Caucus and appoints a White House staff panel to study a list of recommendations made by the group. The group recommendations were presented in a thirty-two page report which said that the Nixon administration is preceived in the black community as "having retreated from the national commitment to make Americans of all races and cultures equal in the eyes of their government." The recommendations encompassed a whole range of problems, and the caucus indicated that the demands will be taken to the people if no action has been taken on them by May 17.

APRIL

6 Two black lawyers, D'Army Bailey, twenty-nine, and Ira T. Simmons, twenty-eight, win election to the Berkeley, California City Council.

7 Joe Frazier, a native of South Carolina, becomes the first black man since Reconstruction to speak before the South Carolina legislature.

11 Adam Clayton Powell, former Congressman from Harlem announces his resignation as pastor of the Abyssinian Baptist Church, a post he has held since his father resigned in 1937. He said he will move his permanent residence to Bimini in the Bahamas. The former congressman was defeated for the Congressional post he had held since 1945 by Charles B. Rangel in November, 1970.

19 George Braithwaite, thirty-four, member of the U.S. table tennis team, says he received more applause than other members of the team when they played in Shanghai during a tour of Red China. Braithwaite told newsmen that "one of the teachings of Mao Tse-tung is that black people are being oppressed." Other team members confirmed the observation that Braithwaite had been singled out for extra applause and attention.

20 The U.S. Supreme Court rules 9-0 that busing is a constitutionally acceptable method of destroying the dual school systems.

23 The Philadelphia Plan, a project devised to increase the employment of blacks in the building trades, is upheld by the U.S. Court of Appeals for the Third Circuit. The plan was attacked by the Contractors Association of Eastern Pennsylvania, which said it violated the 1964 Civil Rights Act because it required racial 'quotas.' The Court said that the plan did not violate the 1964 Civil Rights Act because the contractors were not required to hire "a definite percentage" of a minority group.

26 The U.S. Supreme Court upholds a California law that allows a community to block, by a referendum, federal construction of low-cost housing.

28 Samuel Lee Gravely Jr. is promoted to admiral, thus becoming the first black admiral in the history of the U.S. Navy. He was commander of the guided missile frigate USS Jouett at the time the promotion was announced.

28 The National Academy of Sciences rejects a recommendation of one its committees that it sponsor federal studies of possible racial factors in intelligence. The academy also rejected a recommendation of the National Science Foundation that it consult with other U.S. agencies on "educational implications of human behavioral genetics." Dr. William Shockey, a Nobel Prize winner and a member of the academy, had urged a major study into the effects of genetic factors in human performance.

JUNE

14 The U.S. Supreme Court rules 5–4 that local communities have the right to close public recreation facilities as an alternative to desegregation.

15 Vernon E. Jordan, Jr., former executive director of the United Negro College Fund, is appointed executive director of the National Urban League. He succeeds the late Whitney M. Young, Jr.

28 The U.S. Supreme Court unanimously reverses the conviction of Muhammad Ali for draft evasion, citing the fact that he had been improperly drafted. Ali claimed exemption as a Muslim minister.

29 President Nixon vetoes a bill calling for an accelerated public works program to eliminate unemployment in urban areas.

30 The Twenty-sixth Amendment to the U.S. Constitution permitting eighteen-year-olds to vote is ratified.

JULY

6 Dr. Andrew F. Brimmer, the only black on the Board of Governors of the Federal Reserve System, tells the NAACP's sixty-second annual meeting that the job outlook for black Americans is so dismal that some have "given up and no longer attempt to enter the labor force."

7 The NAACP bestows the Spingarn Medal upon "Dr. Leon Sullivan, clergyman, activist and prophet in admiration of the singular steadfastness with which he had melded religious leadership and social vision for the advancement of black folk."

7 William H. Hastie, recently retired as the chief judge of the Third U.S. Circuit Court of Appeals, tells NAACP convention that the trend of outward racial separatism can only lead to an "even more inferior status than black Americans now experience." He expresses concern at the "alarming number of Negroes" who have accepted and encouraged racial separatism as a "desirable and potentially rewarding" way of life.

10 Fannie Lou Hamer, Mississippi civil rights leader and political activist, is among the two hundred women meeting in Washington, D.C., to mobilize the Women's Rights movement and to organize the National Women's Political Caucus which has as its goal the equal representation of women with men at all levels of the political system. Other black women on the twenty-one member ruling council are Congresswoman Shirley Chisholm (D., N.Y.), Myrlie Evers, Dorothy Height, and Vivian Carter Mason.

AUGUST

2 Mrs. Whitney M. Young, Jr. announces the creation of the Whitney M. Young Memorial Foundation to honor the memory of the late executive secretary of the National Urban League. The foundation will provide financial assistance to young black leaders in the field of social relations.

7 The National Bar Association denounces the "repressive grand jury system" which led to the indictment of Angela Davis. The Association agreed to contribute $2,500 to the Davis Defense Fund and also sought legal solutions for dealing with racism in the administration of justice.

7 George W. Crockett Jr. of Detroit is elected head of the Judicial Council, the first formal organization of black judges in the United States. Meeting in Atlanta during the forty-sixth annual convention of the National Bar Association, a predominant black organization of lawyers, judges, and law professors, the judges indicate that they intend to operate as an independent and autonomous unit in studying judicial problems as they relate to the black and poor.

21 Althea Gibson Darden, former winner of the U.S. and Wimbledon championships, is among four persons elected to the National Lawn Tennis Hall of Fame in Newport, Rhode Island.

27 George Jackson, one of three convicts known as the Soledad Brothers, is killed in an alleged escape attempt from the California Prison at San Quentin. Jackson, twenty-eight, was the best known of the trio because of the publication of his prison letters under the title, Soledad Brother. In an abortive attempt to free the Soledad Brothers, a courtroom shootout took place, leading to the death of Jackson's younger brother, and the charging of Angela Davis with murder.

31 U.S. Supreme Court Chief Justice Warren Burger announces in a memorandum to lower courts that racially balanced public schools are not required in all cases. He expresses concern that many "unwarranted" decisions requiring busing are being handed down by lower courts.

SEPTEMBER

9 Inmates stage rebellion at Attica Prison in New York. On September 15, some one thousand New York state troopers and police stormed the Attica State Correctional Facility where 1,200 inmates held guards hostage. The inmates issued a list of fifteen demands that included coverage by state minimum wage laws, an end to censorship of reading materials, better food, and no reprisals for the revolt. After four days of negotiating with the prisoners, Russell G. Oswald, New York State Commissioner of Corrections, ordered an air and ground assault to put down the revolt. It ended with the deaths of thirty-two prisoners and ten guards. Investigation following the deaths indicates that nine of the ten guards had been killed by the law enforcement officers who stormed the prison yard.

A revised autopsy report shows that George Jackson died as the result of a

shot in the back, not through the top
of the head as was originally reported.
Jackson, killed August 21 in an alleged
escape attempt, according to the second
autopsy, was shot in the lower back
and ankle, with the bullet traveling up
through the body and exiting through
the skull. The new autopsy cast doubt
on statements that he was shot from
above by a prison guard as he ran
through the prison yard.

26 Shirley Chisholm (D., N.Y.) announces
that she will seek the Democratic presidential nomination. She says she will
seek the support of a coalition of poor
whites, Spanish-speaking Americans,
blacks and other minority groups. The
first and only black woman in Congress,
Rep. Chisholm says she will enter the
1972 presidential primary races in Florida, Wisconsin, California and North
Carolina.

27 A federal court judge in Detroit finds
the Detroit public school system guilty
of planned segregation.

OCTOBER

9 The Ford Foundation announces that it
will give $100 million to private black
colleges over a six-year period to help
them improve their academic and fiscal
condition.

NOVEMBER

2 Mayor Richard G. Hatcher of Gary,
Indiana, wins reelection to a second
term. Black mayors are elected in Englewood, New Jersey, Kalamazoo, Michigan and Benton Harbor, Michigan.
Charles Evers, mayor of Fayette, Mississippi, loses his bid for the governor-
ship of Mississippi. Arnold R. Pinkey
is also defeated in his race for mayor of
Cleveland.

2 Congressional Black Caucus and black
political leaders, meeting in Washington,
issue a call for a national black political
convention. The goal of the convention,
according to the call, is to insure proportionate representation for blacks at the
major party nominating conventions and
to persuade the major parties to develop
programs to meet the needs of blacks.

DECEMBER

1 Arthur A. Fletcher, former assistant secretary of labor and United Nations delegate, is named executive director, United
Negro College Fund, filling the post
vacated by Vernon Jordan, Jr., the new
director of the National Urban League.

3 The Newark Board of Education is enjoined by the New Jersey Superior Court

from carrying out a resolution to hang
the black liberation flag in all schools
and classrooms with a majority of black
enrollment.

11 Rev. Jesse L. Jackson resigns his position
as national director of SCLC's Operation
Breadbasket, the economic arm of the
Southern Christian Leadership Conference, following a dispute over the establishment of a foundation and the dis-
position of funds from Black Expo., a
business trade fair. He later announced
the formation of Operation PUSH
(People United to Save Humanity), a
national political and economic development organization.

17 Congressman Charles C. Diggs Jr. (D.,
Mich.) resigns from the U.S. delegation
to the United Nations to protest the
"stifling hypocrisy" of the Nixon administration's African policies. He is the
first member of an American delegation
to resign in protest against U.S. policies.

1972

JANUARY

3 New York City Steamfitters Union, Local 638, is ordered by a federal judge
to upgrade 169 black and Puerto Rican
apprentices to journeyman status.

3 A three-judge federal court in Montgomery, Alabama, orders the adoption
of a new reapportionment plan that
would divide the Alabama legislature
into single member districts. The present
legislature includes only two blacks, and
the new plan could conceivably put as
many as twenty or more blacks into the
legislature.

10 Federal District Court Judge Robert R.
Merhige Jr. orders the merger of the
predominantly black public schools of
Richmond, Virginia, with the predominantly white schools of suburban Hen-
rico and Chesterfield counties.

10 A black rally in Baton Rouge, Louisiana,
ends in a gun battle with police, leaving
thirty-one persons injured and two white
deputy sheriffs and two young black
men dead. No weapons were traced to
blacks, although police charge that they
opened fire when a young black pulled
a pistol from his pocket.

11 A three-judge federal court takes away
the special tax status and concomitant
tax benefits granted to fraternal organizations that exclude nonwhites from
membership. The ruling bars federal income tax exemptions to fraternal orders
and denies individual members the right

to claim tax deductions for charitable contributions to the lodges. The ruling came in a suit brought against Treasury Secretary John B. Connally and other government officials by C.V. McGlotten, who was denied membership in the Benevolent and Protective Order of the Elks in Portland, Oregon, allegedly because he was black.

12 The Department of Health, Education and Welfare reports that integration in the South has led to a smaller proportion of black students attending totally segregated schools in the South than in the North and West.

17 The Justice Department is charged by a House Judiciary subcommittee report with having failed to adequately enforce provisions of the 1965 Voting Rights Act.

17 The U.S. Supreme Court agrees to hear the appeal of a group of parents (Mexican-American and black), seeking to get a busing order for the desegregation of the Denver school system. The Denver case presented the court with the issue of whether a large urban city with all-black schools resulting from de facto segregation must desegregate if it is shown that segregation in some schools is encouraged by acts of public officials.

20 The president calls upon Congress in his State of the Union Address to act upon his Family Assistance Plan. He again reiterates his opposition to "unnecessary busing" for the "sole" purpose of achieving racial balance.

21 Eleven Congressmen, including Ralph Metcalfe, criticize President Nixon's State of the Union message in a national television appearance.

24 The U.S. Supreme Court unanimously turns down appeal by black Mississippi voters who wanted to invalidate the 1971 legislative elections on the grounds that the state was guilty of malapportionment and racial discrimination.

24 A panel of experts, commissioned by the College Entrance Examination Board, recommends a series of reforms of financial aid programs for needy students. The panel recommends loans rather than grants in cases where the family prospects for repayment are reasonable. The panel also suggests that low-income families should receive direct supplementary aid, in addition to student aid, and asks that grants be made according to family needs.

25 Representative Shirley Chisholm (D., N.Y.) announces that she will seek the Democratic presidential nomination. She is the first black woman to become a serious candidate for president of the United States.

26 The U.S. Senate grants the Equal Employment Opportunity Commission the right to order companies and unions to cease racial, religious and sexual discrimination.

27 Lucius Theus, forty-nine, director of management and analysis at U.S. Air Force headquarters in Washington, is promoted to brigadier general.

30 Wilt Chamberlain of the Los Angeles Lakers becomes the NBA's all-time rebound champion by snaring his 21,772 rebound in a game against Portland. The previous holder of the record was the Boston Celtics' Bill Russell with 21,721 rebounds.

30 Huey P. Newton, cofounder of the Black Panther party, announces that the party has abandoned the "pick up the gun" approach in favor of community work and voter registration.

FEBRUARY

1 Vice President Agnew becomes involved in a dispute regarding the propriety of the OEO's Legal Services Program representing clients in lawsuits against governmental bodies. The case that touched off the controversy occurred in Camden, New Jersey, where low-income groups charged that the urban renewal program failed to provide substitute housing for displaced families as required by federal law.

1 A survey by the Associated Press reports that there are only twenty-seven blacks among five-thousand state policemen in eight Southern states.

5 Bob Douglas, the eighty-seven-year-old owner-coach of the Harlem Renaissance Five, is elected to the Naismith Basketball Hall of Fame in Springfield, Massachusetts. Over a twenty-two year period, the "Rens" won 2,318 games. In 1933, they won eighty-eight consecutive games. The team was named to the Hall of Fame in 1964.

7 In response to a suit brought by the NAACP, U.S. District Court Judge Frank M. Johnson Jr. orders the Alabama Department of Public Safety to hire an equal number of whites and blacks until 25 percent of the personnel are black, roughly the proportion of blacks in the state population.

8 The Fourth U.S. Circuit Court of Appeals, grants the Virginia State Board

of Education a stay in implementing a court-ordered desegregation plan that would consolidate Richmond's public schools with those of two adjoining suburban and mainly white districts.

8   The Congressional Black Caucus elects Congressman Louis Stokes (D. Ohio) chairman. Stokes succeeds Congressman Charles C. Diggs, Jr. (D., Mich.), who has been the leader of the group since it came together informally in 1969 as a study group.

10   In an informal news conference, President Nixon continues his attack on school busing for the purpose of racial integration. The president indicates that he has ordered a study to determine whether a constitutional amendment or legislation is needed to make the federal courts desist from issuing further busing orders.

10   Donald L. Miller, assistant secretary of defense for equal opportunity, announces that Defense Department personnel in the civil rights area will now be judged by performance. Failure to adhere to and promote the Defense Department's civil rights program could lead to expulsion, according to Miller.

11   Members of the Congress of Racial Equality (CORE) meet in the offices of Congressman Augustus Hawkins (D., Cal.) to demand that black opposing busing be given a voice in the national educational conference of the Congressional Black Caucus. CORE spokesman Victor A. Solomon says CORE is concerned about "community control and separate but really equal schools."

14   Florida Governor Reubin Askew announces that he will ask voters to reject an anti-busing proposal that has been placed on the Florida primary ballot for referendum on March 14. The governor, who has supported busing as one method for achieving racial balance, says amendments passed by the legislature "may begin the destruction of what is one of the greatest documents (the U.S. Constitution) ever conceived."

15   The AFL-CIO Executive Council, meeting at Bal Harbour, Florida, adopts a statement backing the busing of children when it improves educational opportunity.

15   Roy Wilkins, executive director of the NAACP, notes that President Nixon's proposed moves against school busing "would return segregation to this country, return "Jim Crowism" to the schools

and nullify the Civil Rights Act of 1964." He charges that Nixon has ignored "22 million people who have millions of children in the schools."

18   The California State Supreme Court holds that the death penalty is cruel and unusual punishment and is in violation of the state constitution.

23   Angela Davis is released from jail where she has been held since arrest on $102,-500. bail. She still faces charges of murder, kidnap, and conspiracy. She was released following a ruling which ended the death penalty in California, thus eliminating capital crimes.

28   The Angela Davis trial opens at the courthouse in San Jose, California, with jury selection and pre-trial hearings.

MARCH

6   A three-judge panel, including U.S. Court of Appeals Judge William Hastie, overturns a Pennsylvania law reimbursing parents for tuition payments at private schools. The court holds that such a law would "subsidize parents in providing a religious education for their children."

7   A three-judge federal panel rules that the Illinois law requiring a voter to wait twenty-three months before switching parties is unconstitutional.

7   Kerry Pourciau is elected the first black student body president at Louisiana State University.

8   Congressional Black Caucus, following two days of hearings, during which blacks in communications media charged employment bias and insensitivity to black problems by white-owned and edited media, calls upon President Nixon to nominate a black man to the next vacancy on the Federal Communications Commission. The Caucus also indicates that it will establish a national task force to fight discrimination in the employment of blacks and the coverage of black activities and events in the major news media.

9   John A. Morsell, assistant executive director of the NAACP, announces that the preamble to the proposed political agenda of the National Black Assembly is unacceptable "because of its separatist implications."

10   The first National Black Political Convention opens in Gary, Indiana, and a preliminary political agenda with a preamble calling for an independent black political movement is adopted. Some three-thousand delegates and five-thou-

sand observers attended the two-day meeting which was hosted by Mayor Richard Hatcher of Gary.

13   The Institute of Criminal Law at the Georgetown University Law Center and the Vera Institute of Justice of New York, in a coordinated study of the Washington pretrial jailing law (preventive detention), say the government has not proved conclusively that preventive detention is essential to controlling crime. Preventive detention gives law enforcement officers the power to imprison before trial a suspect they consider potentially dangerous.

15   Mayor Richard G. Hatcher of Gary, Indiana, reports that the National Black Political Convention, after passing a widely publicized resolution against busing passed a supplementary resolution supporting busing "in cases where it serves the end of providing quality education for black people."

15   The Congressional Black Caucus issues a statement saying "we strongly reaffirm our support of busing as one of the many ways to implement the constitutional requirement of equal opportunities in education." The Caucus criticizes "those who would exploit the issue for personal, political or monetary gain."

16   Two memorandums, prepared by Associate Supreme Court Justice William H. Rehnquist when he was assistant attorney general in the Justice Department, are revealed by the New York Times. The memorandums, dated March 3 and March 5, 1970, suggested a constitutional amendment prohibiting the busing of school children for purposes of racial integration.

17   President Nixon sends a message to Congress proposing legislation to deny courts the power to order busing of elementary school-children to achieve racial balance. He asks for a moratorium on all new busing orders, a congressional mandate on acceptable desegregation methods, and a program to concentrate federal aid to education in economically deprived school districts.

17   A Commission of Inquiry, cochaired by former Attorney General Ramsey Clark and NAACP Executive Director Roy Wilkins, into the 1969 Black Panther raid in which Illinois Chairman Fred Hampton and Mark Clark were killed, reveals in a draft report that neither the federal government nor the state sought to establish the truth about the raid by the Cook County (Chicago) states attorney's police. According to the Commission report, the Panthers fired only one shot during the raid.

20   The Council of Black Appointees of the Nixon Administration announces that it is studying ways to amend Nixon's legislative proposals "to safeguard the rights of black Americans." The Council says bills proposed by the administration pose "grave constitutional questions" which "unintentionally may adversely affect" blacks.

21   All claims are rejected by an all-white jury in a damage suit brought by relatives of the victims of the 1970 shooting at Jackson State (Miss.) College, where two black students were killed and twelve were wounded by police gunfire.

21   Associate Supreme Court Justice Thurgood Marshall, writing the opinion for the majority of the court which struck down (6-1) lengthy residency requirements as a prerequisite for voting in state and local elections, says that "thirty days appears to be an ample period of time" for states to register new arrivals to vote. Marshall asserts that residency requirements burden the constitutional right of citizens to travel from state to state and that the laws could not be upheld unless they were "necessary to uphold a compelling state interest." Chief Justice Warren Burger files a dissent.

21   A bill authorizing $105 million for a three-year program to fight sickle cell anemia, a blood disease that primarily affects blacks, is passed by the House. The Senate passed a similar bill in December, 1971, and appropriated $14 million for the program. There is no known cure for the disease, which afflicts one in every five-hundred black Americans.

23   The Justice Department files a petition seeking to intervene in the Detroit metropolitan school desegregation plans.

23   The United Church of Christ adopts a new program for the Council of Christian Social Action and announces that the Church will no longer take a leading role in national social action programs.

24   A three-judge federal court strikes down a Louisiana law prohibiting biracial adoptions. The Court, ruling on suits filed by a mixed couple and a white couple, declares the state statute "arbitrary, invidious racial discrimination."

25   Some thirty thousand adults and children march in a Washington rally to the White House and the Washington Monu-

ment in protest against President Nixon's welfare, education and child care policies. The rally was sponsored by the National Welfare Rights Organization and the marchers were overwhelmingly black.

27   The Angela Davis trial begins in San Jose, California, with a predominantly white jury.

27   The U.S. Justice Department files suit to bar 1972 elections for the Georgia House of Representatives, and requests the court to order the state to propose a plan in conformity with the one-man, one-vote decisions and the fourteenth and fifteenth Amendments.

27   The two surviving Soledad Brothers, Fleeta Drumgo, twenty-six, and John Cluchette, twenty-eight, are freed after a three month trial by an all-white jury. The third Soledad Brother, George Jackson, was killed in August, 1971. They were charged with the slaying of a white guard in 1970 at Soledad Prison.

28   Clarence Mitchell, director of the Washington Office, NAACP, announces that the National Association for the Advancement of Colored People will challenge anti-busing legislation in the courts "before the ink is dry." He calls the bills offered by the president in opposition to busing "the most blatant products of racism that I have seen in the federal government."

28   U.S. District Court Judge Stephen J. Roth rules that "relief of segregation in the public schools of the city of Detroit cannot be accomplished within the corporate geographical limits of the city." He rejects three integration plans which limits integration to the city of Detroit, and rules that school district lines are arbitrary, and can not be used to deny constitutional rights. He also says that he considers it his duty, under the 1954 Brown Decision of the U.S. Supreme Court, to "look beyond the limits of the Detroit school district for a solution."

28   The Chicago Law Enforcement Study Group, in a report on police behavior in major American cities, says that Chicago police killed citizens at a dramatically higher rate than police in other large cities.

29   Rev. Theodore M. Hesburgh, U.S. Civil Rights Commission chairman criticizes Nixon's anti-busing proposal as a step backward in the cause of equal rights for Americans.

APRIL
10   A bill authorizing nonvoting delegates in the House of Representatives for the territories of Guam and the Virgin Islands is signed by President Nixon.

11   Stephen Horn, U.S. Civil Rights Commission vice-chairman testifying against the Nixon anti-busing proposals, says that a study of school busing costs by the Department of Transportation showed that only $2 million was spent nationally on additional busing for desegregation in 1971.

11   Benjamin L. Hooks, a forty-seven-year-old black Memphis lawyer and Baptist minister, is named by President Nixon to the seven-man Federal Communications Commission for a term of seven years. Hooks is a board member of SCLC and a member of NAACP.

12   A three-judge federal court orders into effect a New Jersey congressional district plan that will add one seat for the state's growing suburbs and create a predominantly black district with Newark as its central political focus.

12   Harvard University President Derek C. Bok and thirty-four members of the law school faculty send a letter to the House and Senate Judiciary Committees indicating that Nixon's proposals to limit court-ordered busing would "sacrifice the functions of the judiciary under a rule of law."

17   Rev. A. I. Dunlap, head of the Chicago Coalition for United Community Action, warns that minority groups may resume demonstrations in order to obtain more construction industry jobs.

19   The Department of Health, Education and Welfare cuts off federal aid to Ferndale, Michigan, school district because of violation of desegregation laws. The department charges that the district, encompassing several surburban municipalities near Detroit, built a school in a black area to draw pupils away from an integrated school. It is the first district in the North to lose funds because of racial violations.

19   Major General Frederick E. Davidson, the highest ranking black officer in the U.S. Army, is assigned to command the Eighth Infantry Division in Europe and becomes the first black officer to lead an army division.

24   Robert Wedgeworth, thirty-four, is named executive director of the American Library Association. He is the first black to head the 30,000 member nation-

al library group.

24 The Congressional Black Caucus demands that the House of Representatives vote on the expulsion of convicted Rep. John Dowdy (D., Tex.). The Caucus says "Congressman Dowdy has been convicted of bribery, while Congressman Adam C. Powell was never convicted of any major criminal offense. It had been recommended that Congressman Dowdy be suspended—which is minimal action —when Powell received the maximum penalty the House could impose. This is sufficient documentation that a double standard is indeed operating in the U.S. House."

24 Rep. Ralph H. Metcalfe (D., Ill.) leads a delegation of "concerned" citizens into the office of Chicago Police Supt. James B. Conlisk Jr. to protest what Metcalfe termed "police misconduct towards decent black people."

24 The U.S. Supreme Court reverses an earlier court action and decides against a reconsideration of the 1966 Miranda ruling, which holds that confessions may not be used against a suspect who had not been advised of his right to remain silent and to have an attorney present.

24 Vernon Jordan, executive Director of the National Urban League, tells the American Bankers Association that the extension of basic civil rights to black people may be coming to an end, as it did in 1877 when the first Reconstruction period ended.

24 James M. Rogers of Durham, North Carolina, is named Teacher of the Year in White House ceremonies.

25 A letter, signed by 95 of the 148 lawyers in the Justice Department's Civil Rights Division and sent to congressional leaders and committees, opposes any legislation which "would limit the power of federal courts to remedy, through busing, the unconstitutional segregation of public school children." The ninety-five signatories say such legislation is of doubtful constitutionality and inconsistent "with our national commitment to racial equality."

Ten black lawyers in the Justice Department issue a separate statement, charging that "much of the progress made in desegregation area in recent years would be undone" if the Nixon policies are implemented.

27 Radical groups announce their endorsement of Rep. Shirley Chisholm's bid for the presidency of the United States.

MAY

3 Republic of New Africa leader Hekima Ana is convicted in Jackson, Mississippi, of murdering a white policeman in the 1971 police raid on the RNA headquarters in Jackson. Ana did not deny firing the gun that killed the police officer, but maintained that he fired after hearing what he thought were shots upon being awakened by police and Federal Bureau of Investigation agents entering the building. The defense charged that the "overreaction of the police to the black nationalist group had created a hostile environment." The police denied they shot first as they entered to serve four warrants. Ana, first of the eleven persons to be tried, was given a life sentence.

6 Texas State Senator Barbara Jordan wins Democratic primary election in Houston district. She defeated three male opponents.

11 The Equal Employment Opportunity Commission files suit in U.S. District Court in Jacksonville, Florida, against the Container Corporation of America and four international unions and six union locals, charging job discrimination against women and blacks.

14 Bobby Seale, chairman of the Black Panther party, announces in Oakland, California, that he will be a candidate for mayor of Oakland in the 1973 election on a platform of community control of police and rent ceilings.

16 Federal Judge John T. Curtin rules in Buffalo, New York, that state correction officials cannot bar reporters from interviewing willing prisoners unless the security of the penal institution is clearly endangered. Judge Curtin agrees with the contention of newsmen that a state ban on prison interviews violates the First Amendment's guarantee of freedom of the press.

19 The fifty-eight page Black Agenda of the National Black Political Convention is released. The group modified provisions on school busing and on Israel but the NAACP says it is withdrawing from the convention.

23 Black P Stone Nation leader Jeff Fort, twenty-five, and four other members of the organization are sentenced to prison for their roles in defrauding a $1 million federal job training program in Chicago's Woodlawn district.

29 The Department of Labor releases a report of evaluation of the Job Opportunities in the Business Section (JOBS) pro-

gram, which characterizes the program as "ineffective and wasteful." The report states that businesses have been paid for "excessive costs in those cases where an enrollee only required placement assistance."

29   Lester Jackson, father of the slain brothers, Jonathan and George Jackson, refuses to testify in the Angela Davis trial in San Jose, California, telling the judge: "Because of the deaths of my sons, I would hope you would understand my position. I buried two sons. I just don't want to take part in this proceeding for the sake of my mental health." Judge Richard E. Arnason imposes a fine of $100 on Jackson.

31   The Union Theological Seminary's board in New York City votes to require that all students, faculty, staff and directors be one-third female and nonwhite.

JUNE

2   H. Rap Brown, who has been in custody in New York since October, 1971, is resentenced in New Orleans to five years in prison and fined $2,000 for a 1968 conviction on a federal weapons charge. Brown was convicted for carrying a rifle in Baton Rouge while under indictment in another state.

2   In the first noncompliance action against a major Northern school system, the Department of Health, Education and Welfare cites Boston public schools for a hearing on alleged racial discrimination against black and Spanish-speaking children.

4   Angela Davis is acquitted of murder, kidnapping and criminal conspiracy by an all-white jury. The charges grew out of a 1970 shootout in which four persons were killed.

6   The Fourth U.S. Circuit Court of Appeals in Richmond, Virginia, overturns the ruling of U.S. District Court Judge Robert R. Merhige who had ordered the merger of Richmond and two suburban school districts to achieve desegregation. The court says that Merhige interpreted the fourteenth Amendment in an "excessive" manner.

7   Five black colonels are promoted to general, along with fifty-seven whites. There are four other black army generals.

8   Richard G. Kleindienst is approved as attorney general by the Senate on a vote of 64-19. He was opposed by many blacks and civil rights groups on the basis of his position on preventive detention, wire-tapping, and civil rights.

10   Black Republicans meet in Washington conference to devise strategy to obtain a goal of 25 percent of the black vote for the reelection of President Nixon. Stanley S. Scott, assistant director of communications at the White House, indicates that many of those attending are the recipients of "government contracts and should show the Administration they care about where their money comes from."

12   Lake County (Fla.) Sheriff Willis McCall is charged with second-degree murder in the April 23 death of Tommy J. Vickers, a black prisoner who was jailed on a traffic violation because of inability to post cash bond. He died of injuries received while in custody. Florida Governor Reubin Askew suspended McCall from duty.

12   The U.S. Supreme Court rules 6-3 that a policeman may search a suspect for a weapon, even if the suspicion is based on informer's tip rather than his own observation. The decision extends the 1968 "stop and frisk" ruling of the court.

14   U.S. District Court Judge Stephen J. Roth orders the integration of 780,000 Detroit and fifty-three suburban school districts. It is the most extensive desegregation order issued by a federal court and entails the busing of over 310,000 students.

14   Jerome H. Holland resigns as ambassador to Sweden and joins the board of the New York Exchange.

17   Frank Willis, an alert black security guard, summons police to the Washington, D.C., Watergate complex where five men were arrested for breaking into the offices of the Democratic National Committee. The men were carrying cameras and electronic surveillance equipment.

20   The American Medical Association proposes that tax incentives be used to motivate doctors to practice in rural areas and the inner city where the shortages of medical service is most acute.

22   The U.S. Supreme Court, in its first non-unanimous decision in the area of school desegregation, rules in a 5-4 decision that the town of Emporia, Virginia, cannot, within the framework of the Constitution, remove its schools from the Greensville County school system, which has a large proportion of black students.

22   Potter Stewart, in his decision for the majority, says, "A new school district may not be created where its effect

would be to impede desegregation."

24   The Democratic National Convention Rules Committee approves the nomination of California Assemblywoman Yvonne Brathwaite Burke as cochairman of the convention.

25   Patricia Roberts Harris, former ambassador to Luxembourg, is named the permanent chairman of the credentials committee of the Democratic National Convention.

26   The U.S. Senate confirms the appointment of W. Beverly Carter, Jr. as ambassador to the Republic of Tanzania.

27   The Equal Employment Opportunity Commission files suit in U.S. District Court in St. Louis against General Motors Corporation, charging discrimination against women and discriminatory promotion practices.

29   The U.S. Supreme Court rules (5-4) that the death penalty is a violation of the cruel and unusual provision of the eighth Amendment of the Constitution. It was estimated that six-hundred men and women were awaiting execution at the time of the ruling, including three-hundred and twenty-nine blacks, one-hundred and fifty-four Mexicans, Puerto Ricans or American Indians, and two-hundred and fifty-seven whites. Justices Thurgood Marshall and William J. Brennan said in their opinions that any form of capital punishment must be considered cruel and unusual punishment under current moral standards. Justice William O. Douglas said the disproportionate number of minority or lower-class individuals sentenced to death are victims of unconstitutional discrimination.

29   The NAACP annual report says that more school desegregation occurred in 1971 than in any year since the 1954 Supreme Court ruling. The same report says that the employment situation of "urban blacks in 1971 was worse than at any time since the great depression of the thirties." One third of the nation's black youths are unemployed, according to the report.

29   The Anti-Defamation League of B'Nai B'rith and the American Jewish Congress criticize the use of preferential quotas for admission and employment of minority group members by educational institutions in an effort to redress previous discrimination.

29   The U.S. Supreme Court in a 5-4 decision rules that journalists do not have the constitutional right to refuse to testify before grand juries about information they have obtained in confidence. The ruling was made in three cases, one of which was the civil contempt conviction of New York Times reporter Earl Caldwell, who refused to enter, in 1970, a grand jury room where the Black Panther party was being investigated. In the second case, Paul Pappas, a New Bedford, Massachusetts, television newsman refused to reveal to a grand jury what had transpired at the Black Panther headquarters he had visited.

30   The Justice Department is sued by the Lawyers Committee for Civil Rights for failing to oppose changes in the Canton, Mississippi, election procedures that discriminate against blacks. Federal law requires the Justice Department to screen proposed voting rule changes for bias.

JULY

1   Elliot C. Roberts becomes Commissioner of Hospitals in Detroit. He resigned as the executive director of Harlem Hospital, where he was the first black administrator.

3   HUD Secretary George Romney announces that Floyd McKissick's new town, Soul City, North Carolina, will have $14 million in land development bonds guaranteed by HUD, Soul City will be the first federally guaranteed plan with a black sponsor and the first outside a metropolitan region. Soul City is to be located in Warren County, N.C.

4   The NAACP adopts an emergency resolution condemning President Nixon for his stand on school busing and charges him with "leading the mob in its assault upon the 14th Amendment's equal protection clause."

5   Louisiana repeals holdover segregation laws, which have been superseded by congressional and court actions, and the measure is signed by Governor Edwin Edwards. The outlawed bans cover interracial marriage, and segregation in housing and public accommodations.

5   Rev. Jesse L. Jackson, national president of PUSH, speaking at the NAACP convention in Detroit, urges a summit meeting of black leaders to unify the demands and strategies of black people.

6   James E. Baker, a black career foreign service officer, is named economic and commercial officer at the U.S. Embassy at Pretoria, South Africa. He is the first black American diplomat to be named to South Africa on a permanent basis.

9   In order to avoid loss of $13 million in federal research contracts, the City University of New York agrees to supply the Office of Civil Rights of the Department of Health, Education and Welfare a master list of the race and sex of all employees.

9   Rep. Ronald V. Dellums (D., Calif.), a Shirley Chisholm supporter, joines the McGovern forces at the Democratic National Convention, following Chisholm's plea to the caucus of black delegates for their support through the first ballot. Dellums indicates that he abandoned Chisholm because of her stand on the California credentials issue, where she sided with the "stop McGovern" forces of Hubert Humphrey, Muskie and Jackson.

10   Sen. Hubert H. Humphrey (D., Minn.), candidate for the Democratic nomination for president, in a last-minute attempt to "stop McGovern," releases his ninety-three black delegates and ninety-seven black alternates so they can cast their first ballots for Rep. Shirley Chisholm, the black woman candidate for a presidential nomination.

10   The trial of Illinois State's Attorney Edward V. Hanrahan, an assistant, and twelve Chicago police assigned to the state's attorney's office, begins in Chicago. They are charged with conspiring to obstruct justice in connection with the 1969 killing of Fred Hampton and Mark Clark in a raid on the Black Panther Chicago headquarters.

10   The Democratic National Convention opens in Miami Beach, Florida, under reformed rules. New proportional representation includes a relatively large number of blacks (fifteen percent), woman, Spanish-Americans and young people. The convention nominated Senator George McGovern for the presidency.

11   The Federal Power Commission rules that it does not have the power under federal law of the "public interest" concept to enforce fair employment practices by utilities. Twelve civil rights groups, including the NAACP, indicate that the ruling will be appealed in federal court.

14   Dr. Samuel DeWitt Proctor, professor of theology at Rutgers University and former president of Virginia Union College, is elected to succeed the late Adam Clayton Powell Jr. as pastor of the Abyssinian Baptist Church in New York City.

17   The median income of all U.S. families is $10,275., according to the Census Bureau. The 1971 median for white families was $10,670., and for black families $6,440. Forty-two percent of the elderly were classified as poor and 15 percent of all of those under eighteen years of age. Female-headed households accounted for 40 percent of all poor families. The official poverty level for an urban family of four was $4,137.

25   Government officials admit that blacks were used as guinea pigs in syphilis experiments at Tuskegee Institute and that physicians permitted four-hundred victims to go untreated for forty-years. No medical treatment was given the four-hundred participants in this experiment, even though penicillin, which gives relief and often cure, had been available to the medical profession since the latter 1940s. The study was organized to determine from autopsies what untreated syphilis did to the human body.

31   Daniel (Chappie) James Jr. is promoted to major general, thus becoming the highest ranking officer in the air force.

AUGUST

1   Five air hijackers with three children take over a Delta Airlines jet, forcing officials to give them $1 million in ransom. After freeing the passengers, the hijackers made the captain fly them to Algeria, where they joined the expatriate Black Panthers colony. Although the money was demanded by Black Panther leader Eldridge Cleaver for "liberation," it was returned by the Algerian government to the airline officials.

3   The Federal Communications Commission upholds the right of a candidate to broadcast paid political appeals that are racist in content if there is no danger of violence or incitement to violence.

4   Samuel J. Simmons resigns as assistant secretary of Housing and Urban Development to become the president of the National Center for Housing Management. Simmons was the highest ranking black in the Nixon administration at the time of his resignation.

7   The Justice Department files civil suits against local government agencies in Montgomery, Alabama, charging them with giving black workers lower-paying job classifications even though they perform the same work as whites, who are paid at higher wage levels. A second suit is filed against the Los Angeles (Calif.)

Fire Department for "pursuing policies and practices that discriminate against black, Mexican-American and Oriental applicants for jobs."

7 Buck Leonard and Josh Gibson, stars of the old Negro League are inducted into the Baseball Hall of Fame at Cooperstown, New York.

8 Selma, Alabama, elects five blacks to the ten member city council.

14 Dr. James C. Bond, vice president of the Bowling Green State University in Ohio, is named president of California State University (Sacramento) and becomes the first black to head a major western institution of higher education.

14 Edward C. Sylvester Jr. is named national campaign coordinator for Democratic presidential candidate George McGovern. Sylvester formerly served in the Democratic administration of Lyndon B. Johnson as an assistant secretary of Health, Education and Welfare.

16 Rev. Philip A. Potter, a black Methodist from the West Indian island of Dominica, is named general secretary of the World Council of Churches, succeeding Dr. Eugene Carson Blake. Rev. Potter had been director of the council's Commission on World Mission and Evangelism. The group also agreed to sever connections with banks that "maintain direct banking operations in Rhodesia, South Africa, Mozambique and Portuguese Guinea.

17 The Justice Department files a civil suit against the National Committee for Impeachment, charging it with election law violations. The suit grew out of an ad which featured a reprint of a House resolution introduced (May 10) by Congressman John J. Conyers Jr. (D., Mich.), and endorsed by seven other Democrats.

21 The Republican National Convention open in Miami Beach, Florida. There were fifty-six black delegates—4.2 percent (up from 1.9 percent in 1968). There were four hundred fifty-two black delegates at the Democratic convention. The convention nominated President Richard Nixon.

22 Boycott threats by black athletes lead to expulsion of the Rhodesian athletic contingent from the Olympic Games in Munich, Germany.

24 An indefinite stay is granted Detroit schools which were under court order to begin a massive busing program to integrate Detroit area schools.

27 The Miss Black America pagent in Los Angeles is full of surprises. The winner, Diane Jackson, 22, refuses the title because she has been offered an opportunity to sing professionally. The first runner-up, Linda Barney, nineteen, is the new queen. Joyce Warner, Miss Black America 1971 refuses to crown her successor or to attend the pageant, because she claims the promoters exploited her unfairly.

SEPTEMBER

2 Three blacks become the first black patrolmen in Mississippi.

3 President Nixon, in a Labor Day speech, characterizes quotas as "a dangerous detour away from the traditional value of measuring a person on the basis of ability."

3 The Labor Department and Arthur A. Fletcher, former assistant secretary of Labor, indicate that the Philadelphia Plan, which was designed to increase minority employees on federal construction projects, is undergoing review in light of President Nixon's statement opposing job quotas for minority groups and will probably be dropped.

4 The second person convicted in the Republic of New Africa trial in Jackson, Mississippi, is Offago Quaddus (Wayne M. James) of New Jersey.

13 A.J. Cooper unseats the incumbent mayor of Pritchard, Alabama, in a runoff election. He is the first black mayor of Alabama's seventh largest city. Pritchard has a population of 45,000, 52 percent of which is black. A graduate of Notre Dame University and the New York University Law School, Cooper is a veteran of the NAACP Legal Defense Fund campaigns.

13 John Ford, a black businessman, is elected mayor of Tuskeegee, Alabama, a town with a population of 11,000 and an 80 percent black population.

15 Labor Secretary James D. Hodgson sends memo to heads of federal agencies stating that the Office of Federal Contract Compliance does not require "quotas or proportional representation" of minorities, although "the goals required of government contractors may have been misinterpreted or misapplied. The goals are targets and failure to reach them is not to be regarded as, per se, a violation."

17 Three American prisoners of war are released by Hanoi, among them Navy Lieutenant Norris A. Charles, who was

shot down and captured December 30, 1971. The men were turned over to anti-war activist.

18   Art Williams becomes the first black umpire in the National League and officiates in the Los Angeles Dodgers-San Diego Padres game in San Diego. Emmet Ashford, the first black umpire in major league baseball, watched from the stands.

20   President Nixon signs a $4.75 billion bill extending the Office of Economic Opportunity for three years.

27   Rev. Jesse Jackson, national president of PUSH, announces the signing of a $4 million pact with Joseph A. Schlitz Brewing Company of Milwaukee, which guarantees jobs and other economic benefits for the black community. A similar pact with the General Foods Corporation of White Plains, New York, was also negotiated.

27   The Justice Department drops charges against Bobby Seale, Black Panther leader, who was sentenced for contempt of court in the Chicago 7 conspiracy trial.

27   Push Expo 72, the black and minorities business and cultural trade exhibition, opens at the International Amphitheater in Chicago.

28   Secretary of the Army Robert F. Froehike orders the clearing of military records of the 167 "Brownsville Raid" soldiers who were dishonorably discharged in 1906 by President Theodore Roosevelt. The soldiers, all members of the First Battalion, Twenty-fifth Infantry, an all-black unit, angered the president by refusing to testify or to name any of their group who had been involved in an alleged "shooting spree" in Brownsville, Texas. Froehike's order does not grant compensation for families of men involved in "the only documented case of mass punishment in history."

29   The international division of the Black Panther party announces in Algiers the appointment of William R. Holder as its new leader. He succeeds Eldridge Cleaver.

29   The Labor Department Office of Federal Contract Compliance enters the American Telephone and Telegraph case, "assuming jurisdiction" over contract agreement between the AT&T and the General Services Administration in response to criticism from the NAACP, women, and Mexican-American rights groups, who claim the contract violated federal law in failing to provide for back pay to victims of past discrimination, unfair testing, and transfer policies for women and minorities.

OCTOBER

4   U.S. District Court Judge Frank M. Johnson Jr. orders Alabama to "immediately improve its prison medical services for inmates." He says "the present services in Alabama's prisons constitute a willful and intentional violation of the right of prisoners guaranteed under the Eighth and Fourteenth Amendments."

11   Inmates at the District of Columbia Jail in Washington, overpower guards and seize ten hostages, whom they later released upon the immediate hearings on their problems by U.S. District Court Judge Albert C. Bryant. Bryant orders the city to provide every inmate involved in the rebellion with an attorney and orders a psychiatrist made available to inmates. No reprisals are orders against the inmates involved.

15   U.S. Census Bureau summary findings of 1970 census indicates that the employment of black women increased from 37.1 percent in 1950 to 44.4 percent in 1970; and that the number of black women domestics declined from nine-hundred-thousand to five-hundred-thousand between 1960 and 1970. The report says about one-third of all blacks have incomes below the poverty level, but only 13.3 percent of all Americans are in this category. According to census data, black family income nearly doubled between 1960 and 1970. In 1970, 17.6 percent of black families were on welfare, compared with 4 percent of white families. In education, the median school years attained by those over twenty-four was 12.1 in 1970; the median years of education was 9.7 for black men and 10.2 for black women. The female head of the black household continued to prevail—1.33 million of 4.8 million black families had a female head of the house. Blacks constituted 11.1 percent of the population of central cities. Nine large cities had black populations of over 40 percent, and four over 50 percent.

21   The National Black Assembly meets in Chicago to establish a permanent organizational structure, as mandated by the National Black Political Convention in Gary (March, 1972). Rep. Charles

C. Diggs, Jr. (D., Mich.) is chosen president, and Mayor Richard G. Hatcher of Gary is voted chairman of the fifty-four member National Political Council. Imamu Amiri Baraka is elected secretary-general of the assembly and the council.

25 Cook County (Ill.) Court Judge Philip J. Romiti acquits state's attorney Edward V. Hanrahan and thirteen codefendants of charges of conspiring to obstruct justice in the shootout slayings of Black Panthers Fred Hampton and Mark Clark.

27 Thirty-one black and Puerto Rican students from a housing project in an overcrowded area of Canarsie, New York, are bused to a neighboring junior high school in a district attended mostly by children of working-class whites. The Canarsie parent-teacher association recommended a boycott on October 28, which lasted until November 9 when school board commissioner H.B. Scribner offered to devise a new zoning plan to "equalize integration" among the district schools.

30 All U.S. generals and admirals will attend race relations seminars beginning January, 1973, according to the Defense Race Relations Institute.

NOVEMBER

7 Barbara Jordan (D., Tex.) is elected to the House of Representatives from Texas's Eighteenth District and Andrew Young (D., Ga.) is elected from Georgia's Fifth District. They are the first two blacks to the House of Representatives from the South since the turn of the century. The election of Yvonne Brathwaite Burke (D., Calif.) brings the total number of blacks to sixteen in the House of Representatives. Republican Senator Edward Brooke (R., Mass.) is overwhelmingly approved for a second term of six years. He is the only black in the Senate. President Richard Nixon is reelected.

8 The U.S. Navy delays the trial of nineteen black sailors aboard the aircraft carrier U.S.S. *Kitty Hawk,* charged with assault and rioting on the request of Roy Wilkins, executive director of the NAACP. Wilkins sought the time to provide civilian counsel for the seamen.

10 Navy Secretary John W. Warner and Chief of Naval Operations Admiral Elmo R. Zumwalt charge more than one hundred Navy admirals and Marine Corps generals with failing to make every effort to eliminate racial discrimination in their services. According to the Navy, in June, 1972, 5.8 percent of the enlisted men and .07 percent of the officers were black.

14 Army Private Billy Dean Smith, the first U.S. serviceman to be tried for "fragging" in this country, is acquitted by a military jury at Fort Ord (Calif.) of charges of killing two officers with a booby-trapped grenade at an airbase in Vietnam. Smith is judged guilty of assaulting a military policeman who arrested him, and is given a bad conduct discharge.

16 Rev. Theodore M. Hesburgh, president of Notre Dame University and chairman of the Commission on Civil Rights, resigns his post as commission chairman, on request from the president.

16 Two Southern University students are killed in Baton Rouge, Louisiana, following a demonstration for better food and housing and a bigger voice in university decisions. The shootings occurred after East Baton Rouge Parish sheriff's deputies and state police ordered students to leave the administration building and its environs, and began to fire tear gas into the crowd. Louisiana Governor Edwin Edwards declared a state of emergency and sent the National Guard to seal off the campus.

19 Baton Rouge Sheriff Al Amiss says that buckshot from rifles handled by some of his deputies might have killed the Southern University students. Dismissal notices were received by Dr. Joseph Johnson and George W. Baker, Jr., from the president, G. Leon Netterville, who said the professors had served as advisers to dissident students, contributing to the disruptions. The American Association of University Professors Committee on College and University Governance protested the dismissals, citing the fact that Southern had been on the association's censure list for improper faculty dismissals since 1968.

29 D'Army Bailey, Berkeley, California, city councilman and chairman of the Black People's Committee of Inquiry in the Southern University situation, announces that the committee found that students had not been occupying the administration building as charged, that they had been negotiating in good faith on their demands, and that police had been undisciplined in their action against the students. Other members of the com-

mittee are Haywood Burns, president of the National Conference of Black Lawyers, Georgia State Representative Julian Bond, and Owusa Saduki, president of Malcolm X University in Greensboro, N.C.

30   Defense Secretary Melvin R. Laird releases a Pentagon study group report that cites intentional and systematic discrimination against blacks in the armed forces. The panel, biracial in makeup, called for long-term reform at any cost. The report states that blacks in the military have been subjected to bias in pretrial confinement and administrative punishment.

DECEMBER

1   A biracial Louisiana state commission reports that the fatal shooting of two Southern University students at Baton Rouge (Nov. 16) was triggered by an unidentified policeman who threw a teargas canister at the students. The commission also reports that the buckshot pellets that killed the two black youths came from a shotgun.

1   Theodore Berry, a black lawyer and city councilman, becomes the first black mayor of Cincinnati.

2   Robert J. Brown, a special assistant to President Nixon and the highest ranking black on the White House staff, resigns his post to return to private industry.

7   The Supreme Court rules in an unanimous decision that tenants in racially segregated housing projects can sue landlords over discrimination. At issue was a suit filed by a black tenant and a white tenant against the Metropolitan Life Insurance housing development in San Francisco.

7   Upon advice of NAACP counsel, the twenty-one black U.S.S. *Kitty Hawk* sailors facing disciplinary action in connection with fights between black and white crewmen on the aircraft carrier refuse to testify before a House Armed Services subcommittee. According to some of the sailors, a breakdown in communication occurred when there was a command disagreement over the way to stop the fighting between the Marines and the sailors. According to the sailors, there was open disagreement between Captain Marland W. Townsend Jr., white, and his chief executive officer, Benjamin Cloud, black, over the order Cloud issued directing blacks to one end of the ship and Marine guards to the other end in an effort to cool the

fighting. Townsend countermanded the order and the Marines went on a "club swinging" spree.

8   Mrs. Jewel Lafontant, Chicago lawyer and member of the U.S. delegation to the United Nations, is designated deputy solicitor general.

9   Basil Paterson is retained by Robert Strauss, new chairman of the Democratic National Committee, in his post as vice-chairman of the committee.

11   The Supreme Court rules unanimously that fraternal groups which admit guests to their clubs can not discriminate against such guests on racial grounds.

11   The Chicago chapter of the Southern Christian Leadership Conference closes after internal leadership controversy.

12   Former President Lyndon Baines Johnson urges that massive compensatory programs be developed to enable blacks and other minorities to "overcome unequal opportunity." He spoke at a two-day symposium sponsored by the Lyndon Baines Johnson Library, which made available to the public the civil rights papers of the Johnson years.

13   The White House announces that William H. Brown will be retained as chairman of the Equal Employment Opportunities Commission.

14   The White House announces the resignation of Mrs. Elizabeth D. Koontz, director of the Women's Bureau of the Labor Department.

1973

JANUARY

4   Attorney General Richard G. Kleindienst said that the Administration intended to request a law imposing a federal death penalty for certain crimes, probably including kidnapping, assassination, bombing of a public building, airplane hijacking and killing a prison guard. Kleindienst also reported that the department's Civil Rights Division would have to conduct a "very careful examination" of a report by the Federal Bureau of Investigation on the killing of two students at Southern University in Baton Rouge, La. before deciding

27   The Supreme Court ruled that a suburban Maryland swimming club could not deny admission to blacks when the sole criteria for admission is that one live within a specified distance of the club.

The Wheaton-Haven Recreation Association, a non-profit organization, operated a swimming club in the Washington suburb of Wheaton, Md. Anyone living within a three-quarter mile radius of the pool enjoyed preference in becoming a member.

In 1968 the club denied membership to a black radiologist who met requirements, and it also denied admittance to blacks who were guests of white members.

In the 9-0 ruling, which reversed the lower courts, the court cited the civil rights law of 1866 that insured to all citizens the right to buy, sell, or rent property. Justice Harry A. Blackmun, in writing the opinion, said "the right to acquire a home in the area is abridged and diluted" by the policy.

MARCH

29   H. Rap Brown and three co-defendants were convicted in New York of the October 16, 1971 robbery of a Manhattan bar and of assault with a deadly weapon. The jury was unable to agree on charges of attempted murder.

APRIL

2   At the American Cancer Society's annual science writers' seminar, Drs. Ingegerd and Karl Erik Hellstrom, a husband and wife team from the University of Washington at Seattle told the seminar they had isolated a factor in the blood of a high percentage of American blacks that apparently improved the body's defense against cancer of the pigment cells of the skin. They said this factor was operative only for this form of cancer which primarily attacked whites.

3   The murder-kidnap trial of Ruchell Magee in San Francisco ended in a mistrial after jurors, who had deliberated for eight days, reported they were hopelessly deadlocked. The vote was 11–1 for acquittal on the murder charge and 11–1 for conviction on the kidnapping charge.

MAY

7   The Supreme Court ruled 6–3 that the Justice Department could require prior approval of a Southern State's legislative reapportionment plan, when the plan threatened to dilute the power of black voters.

The decision, upholding broad interpretation of the 1965 and 1970 Voting Rights Acts, reversed a lower court ruling invalidating 1972 Justice Department reapportionment guidelines. The U.S. Attorny general had said he was unable to conclude that a 1971 Georgia redistricting plan would not have a discriminatory racial effect on voting.

Justice Potter Stewart wrote for the majority, "The question is not whether the redistricting of the Georgia House . . . in fact had a discriminatory purpose or effect. The question . . . is whether such changes have the potential for diluting the values of the Negro vote."

Dissenting were Justices Lewis F. Powell, Jr., William H. Rehnquist, and Byron R. White.

JUNE

18   The Supreme Court declared deviations of less than 10% from its one-man one-vote ideal were too minor for court attention. This formula was arrived at in an effort to limit the number of state reapportionment plans coming before the court.

At the same time it was made clear that Congressional redistricting plans were subject to close scrutiny by the courts. By a 6–3 vote, the court reinstated a redistricting plan for Connecticut that mandated state legislative districts with maximum population deviations of 7.8%.

While affirming unanimously the unconstitutionality of a Texas Congressional plan that allowed a maximum population deviation of 4%, it restored in a 6–3 vote a state legislative redistricting plan with a maximum variation of 9.9%. However, the court upheld unanimously the invalidation of multimember district in Texas on the grounds they submerged the voting power of blacks in Dallas and Mexican-Americans in San Antonio.

Justice Byron R. White wrote for the majority favoring flexibility in districting: "It is time to recognize that minor deviations from mathematical equality among state legislative districts are insufficient to make out a prima facie case for invidious discrimination under the 14th Amendment so as to require justification by the state."

AUGUST

24   Louis B. Russell, 48, who on August 24, 1968 received the 34th heart transplant, is today the longest-surviving heart transplant patient in the world.

Section IV
EDUCATION

The Status of Education

Career Guide

United Negro College Fund

National Scholarship Service and Fund for Negro Students (NSSFNS)

Tables

THE STATUS OF EDUCATION

Desegregation

The U.S. Commission on Civil Rights in a 1971 report on *Understanding School Desegregation*, stated that "sixteen years after the Supreme Court of the United States ruled that school segregation compelled or sanctioned by law was unconstitutional, there is still no widespread understanding of the nature and scope of the issues, and public discussion has been more heated than enlightening."

The Supreme Court decision on May 17, 1954, in the landmark case of Brown v. Board of Education of Topeka, ordered that public schools be desegregated with "all deliberate speed." In the two decades since that decision desegregation in the 17 Southern states most immediately affected has taken place in varying degrees.

In 1971 HEW statistics revealed that only 76 of 2,700 school districts remained segregated, and according to the Southern Regional Council more schools were desegregated than not. The SRC charged that the statistics were misleading because the measurement device had been changed from determining the percentage of black students attending desegregated schools to one of determining the number of units desegregated. Under the unitary system of measuring the level of desegregation, a school system can be counted as desegregated, while containing within the unit schools which are still all black or white.

Black students in predominantly white schools had increased from 18.4 to 39.1 percent between 1968-69 and 1970-71, while all black schools dropped from 68 percent to 14.1 percent, overall.

Racial Isolation

In the North and West where state laws did not require segregation, but in actual practice quasi-systems of segregation existed, increasing numbers of black students have been isolated in predominantly black schools.

In examining the extent of segregation in large school districts, the Senate Select Committee[1] learned that about half the nation's black students, 3.4 million, are in our 100 largest school districts. These districts are, by far, the most segregated in the nation. They include all of the nation's major cities. Collectively their school population in the Fall of 1971 was 34 percent black. In 73.4 percent of these districts, black students were in 80-100 percent minority schools and 59 percent were in 95-100 percent minority schools. Even more significant, schools in large districts are well above the rest of the nation in terms of minority-group isolation.

Large city school district black student populations range from 95.2 percent in Washington, D.C. and 72.1 percent in Atlanta, Georgia, to 2.6 percent in Albuquerque, N. Mex. The schools of the District of Columbia are, by definition, minority-group isolated schools. No significant decrease in school isolation is possible within such a district. On the other hand, in a city such as Fresno, Calif.—where 9.3 percent of the students are black and 51 percent of such students are in 90-100 percent minority schools—it is apparent that racial isolation exists in a school district where it is mathematically feasible to eliminate.

[1]*Toward Equal Educational Opportunity*: The Report of the Select Committee on Equal Educational Opportunity, U.S. Senate, Dec. 31, 1972.

No assessment of racial isolation in schools or school districts can fail to take account of the relationship between the percentage of minority-group students in the district as a whole and the percentage attending schools at any particular level of isolation.

Surveys of large school districts were conducted in 1965, 1968, 1970, and 1971.[2] Not all such districts were surveyed in each of those years. Statistics were gathered for different levels of school isolation in different years. Therefore, the statistics contain only such figures as are available for the years indicated.

In Northern cities increased isolation of black students accounted for a decline in the percentage of black students in predominantly white schools, although in the "Alexander" decision of 1969, the Supreme Court had arrived at a decision which was a mandate to school districts and municipalities to eliminate dual school systems wherever they happened to be.

Busing

The "Alexander" decision in October, 1969, which terminated dual school systems throughout the South and gave immediate deadlines to areas where "all deliberate speed" had been the accepted time-frame, was followed shortly by the April, 1971, decision of the U.S. Supreme Court in Swann V. Charlotte-Mecklenburg (N.C.) Board of Education. The court held unanimously that busing is a proper method by which to achieve school desegregation in so long as neither "the time nor the distance is so great as to risk either the health of the children or significantly impinge on the educational process."

New court tests of "busing" were soon being sought by opponents of integration and of busing. A new political issue had been found and was successfully used by President Richard Nixon in the 1972 election campaigns. He stated in 1971 and repeated often thereafter: "I have consistently opposed the busing of our nation's school children to achieve a racial balance, and I am opposed to the busing of our children simply for the sake

of busing." Opponents of busing for integration were encouraged and on June 23, 1972, President Richard Nixon signed a bill which would delay the implementation of busing orders from lower courts until all appeals have been exhausted, or January 1, 1974. "Busing" was a major issue in the political campaigns for all offices and among both parties in 1972.

Educators—Victims of Desegregation

In May, 1972, a joint report from six civil rights groups (the American Friends Service Committee, the Delta Ministry of the National Council of Churches, the Lawyers Committee for Civil Rights under Law, the Constitutional Defense Committee, the Washington Research Committee and the NAACP Legal Defense and Educational Fund) stated that at least 384 black schools had been closed within three years, while at least a dozen major school systems in the urban South were operating under inadequate and outmoded desegregative planning. Segregation, even in desegregated schools, remained in classrooms, extra curricular activities, and transportation facilities. Further, desegregation as it has been implemented in the South and Southwest, particularly, has resulted in massive dismissals, demotions, and reassignment of black personnel, teachers, principals, counselors, athletic directors, and specialists.

The National Education Association reported in 1971 that 1,072 black educators had lost their jobs in six Southern states over a two year period. In the same six states (Alabama, Georgia, Louisiana, Florida, Mississippi, and Texas), 5,575 white educators were hired during the same time span.

In the brief filed as an "amicus curia" in the Fifth Circuit Court of Appeals in New Orleans, the NEA sought extensive changes in the controversial "Singleton decree" in an attempt to protect black educators from being phased out.

[2] Dept. of HEW Surveys of Elementary and Secondary Schools, various dates.
[3] Containing 94 percent of the nation's black students.

BLACK STUDENT ISOLATION IN LARGE SCHOOL DISTRICTS (1970)
(Figures are Percentages)

Area	%	Percent Minority Schools				
		50-100	80-100	90-100	95-100	100
Black student isolation:						
100 largest school districts	32.3	83.9	71.8	65.7	59.0	21.0
Continental United States	14.9	66.9	49.4	43.3	38.2	14.0
21 States & District of Columbia[3]	18.5	68.3	50.5	44.5	41.8	14.8

According to the Singleton decree, issued by the court in 1969, school systems must apply "reasonable, objective, and non-discriminatory standards" when faced with staff reductions caused by school desegregation.

In its brief, the NEA presented statistics based on data from the U.S. Department of Health, Education, and Welfare (HEW) to show that the Singleton decree has not halted elimination of blacks from the teaching profession in the South. Over half the districts reported complete data for the three school years (1968-71) with another quarter of the districts reporting for two of the three years.

The NEA action was significant in that it sought a circuitwide strengthening of the rules to remedy the black teacher displacement problem.

The figures represent the first use before the court of data collected by HEW as reported by the individual school districts.

In every state but Florida, black teachers suffered losses in positions. White teachers enjoyed increases in every state but Mississippi, the NEA brief states. The Mississippi decrease coincides with a drop in white students' enrollment because of the growth of white, private academies.

The NEA brief states HEW figures disclose that Georgia has surpassed all other states in the Fifth Circuit in displacing black educators.

One of the primary causes of discrimination against black educators, the NEA brief stresses, is the insufficiency of the Singleton decree. The NEA brief charges that the decree is inadequate because it places too great a burden on black educators to litigate discriminatory practices by school districts and does not: provide workable safeguards against racial discrimination in terminations and demotions other than reductions in force; protect black educators against racial discrimination in hiring and promotion procedures; require school districts to actively recruit black teachers and administrators.

"In our view, Singleton leaves to the school districts too much discretion in terminating and demoting teachers pursuant to reduction in force," the brief states.

The brief urges that the court make seniority the standard in such cases. It also suggests that the court require school districts to replace educators terminated or demoted for other reasons with a person of the same race.

In addition, the brief urges extension of the Singleton decree to cover hiring, promotion, demotion, and all decisions regarding employment and dismissal of faculty.

The NEA also calls for the court to place the burden on the school district to prove that it did not discriminate where the racial ratio in hiring or promoting black educators fails to approximate that of 1965-66.

Further, the brief asks the court to require school districts to adopt reviewable standards and procedures for evaluating applicants, to actively recruit black educators, and to file reports with courts.

Resegregation

This study, based on a survey of 43 Southern cities, also indicated that resegregation in urban centers was occuring, at an accelerated pace, with the assistance of the Federal government. It found that there was a disproportionate percentage of black pupils under disciplinary action, and an increased use of police in schools where they were not needed. It found that the increased use of police and security guards in schools, "does not seem to have eliminated or significantly decreased the number of disciplinary problems. Indeed, there are some districts in which their use has escalated tensions and resentment in the black community."

These findings were reinforced on a national level by the Report of the Select Committee on Equal Educational Opportunity of the United States Senate, published December 31, 1972. The findings in both reports served only to reiterate the results of the Kerner Commission Report (Report of the National Advisory Commission on Civil Disorders, March 1968) which found that the nation was rapidly becoming two separate and unequal entities.

It was the finding of the independent study that the power structure in many Southern cities had operated to maintain black neighborhoods with one-race schools. "The Federal Housing Administration, local planning commissions and housing authorities, urban renewal, school boards, and even transit companies received credit for contributing consciously to racial impaction. In city after city, federally sponsored housing projects have almost always been built in segregated or transitional neighborhoods, the effect being to drive out the remaining whites, leaving the neighborhood schools all black. School authorities have generally cooperated by building schools in the impacted areas. Escape for minority groups is impossible, thanks to real estate and finance policies of private business."

Financing Public Education

Nonetheless, with increasing pressure for integration in public schools, private and parochial educational institutions have been increasingly powerful in their lobbying efforts to break down the separation of church and state through various proposals to achieve public funding and tax support for private education since black and other minorities are the principal consumers of public education. About half of the money spent on U.S. education has gone traditionally to support public elementary and secondary schools. Approximately half of that money has come from local property taxes. The property tax has, since the 1954 school integration decision, come increasingly under attack as a method of supporting public education. Among the reasons given is that poor school districts raise less income from property taxes than they need to support their schools, and as a result wealthy districts provide better schools and better programs than their counterparts in less affluent areas. For example, the suburbs of New York, Chicago, Detroit and other major cities spend at least twice as much per pupil as the central city spends per pupil.

In 1971, the California Supreme Court ruled in the case of Serrano v. Priest that the use of the property tax was unconstitutional. The court declared that such a system of financing schools discriminated against children in poor school districts. It held that the system therefore violated the equal protection guarantee of the U.S. Constitution. Other states' courts, including Minnesota and Texas, later handed down similar decisions. In 1972, the U.S. Supreme Court agreed to hear an appeal of the Texas decision in the case of Rodriguez v. San Antonio Independent School District. The court's decision could affect the quality of schools and the system of taxation in every state except Hawaii.

About five percent of the amount spent yearly on U.S. education goes to support private elementary and secondary schools. Most of these are Roman Catholic parochial schools. Parochial schools have traditionally raised almost all of their funding from private sources, such as tuition fees and church donations. The First Amendment to the Constitution prohibits a state religion in the United States. In a number of school cases, the Supreme Court has interpreted the First Amendment to mean that public tax money may not be used for support of parochial schools. Many state constitutions also restrict aid to parochial schools.

Rising costs, reduced revenues and increased pupil loads forced hundreds of parochial schools to close in the early 1970's. In the 1960's and early 1970's, several states had adopted laws that provided financial aid to parochial schools. In 1971, the Supreme Court declared that parochial school aid laws in Pennsylvania and Rhode Island were unconstitutional. The laws provided funds to help pay the salaries of parochial school teachers of nonreligious subjects. Several states proposed making financial grants to the parents of parochial school pupils instead of to the schools themselves. The parents were to use the grants themselves to pay school tuitions. However, federal courts in 1972 ruled such laws in Ohio and Pennsylvania to be unconstitutional.

The voucher system of financing public and private education has been suggested as an alternative by a number of economists and educators who see it as fulfilling many of the criteria of an open educational system. A certificate or voucher would be issued by a governmental body to the parents of school-aged children, who would in turn give it to a school of their choice in return for their children's education. The school would then present the voucher back to the issuing body in return for cash. The arguments for use of such a system are that black and other minorities as well as white families would end up with equal opportunity and access to educational facilities. It would also enable community groups and others dissatisfied with the "status quo" to promote creative and educational programs.

Who Shall Be Educated?

At the same time that the adequate funding for public education is becoming increasingly difficult to guarantee, another long accepted principle of American education is being reexamined. For generations educators and the general public have held that *ALL* children should attend school for a certain number of years, resulting in mandatory requirements for students to be in school. In recent years a concerted effort had been made to promote the theory that today's school attendance laws are too strict, and that many high school students would profit more from vocational or on-the-job training than they would from high school studies. They believe such students should be free to leave school at an earlier age than most states now permit.

Relevancy and Accountability

While black and the other minority groups have not been in the forefront of movements to relax compulsory education laws, they have been increasingly vocal on the subjects of relevancy, accountability, and community control of educational curriculum and institutions. Education, it is felt, must respond to the students' needs and the curriculum should relate to the personal and social experiences of the student body. These views were reflected in the demands black and other students made on educational authorities in the late 1960's and early 1970's. Their demands included the opportunity to participate in decision-making policies that affected them and the development of curriculum more related to the world in which they live. High on the list of priorities were courses in Black Studies. At many colleges and universities black student groups called for departments that would award degrees in Black Studies and that would be controlled by black faculty members.

At the elementary and secondary level, control of the decision-making apparatus became a focal point in many community controversies. Efforts to achieve greater participation took place in New York City, Chicago, Detroit, and other large cities. Black and other minority groups demanded that control of the public schools be transferred from citywide boards of education to elected neighborhood councils of parents. In 1969, New York City established 31 local school boards. School systems in many cities established school-community boards designed to help meet the perceived educational needs of the entire community. In some areas schools which provided both general and vocational education for adults as well as children were established. Many of these schools were run jointly by professional administrators and community specialists. Many of these programs have met with opposition from organized teacher groups opposed to non-professionals being given recognized status in the academic hierarchy.

While black and other minority parents are complaining that their children are not being educated to cope with an increasingly computerized society, a group of educational studies issued in the past several years have raised new questions of who should be educated and for what purpose.

Can Education Change Things?

These reports have suggested that based on substantial evidence the inequality of student performance in terms of educational attainment, academic achievement, and the other data points that are the benchmarks of a successful formal education are more directly related to the family background, socioeconomic status, and home environment than to the kind of school or teachers that the pupil attends. These reports, when taken in the aggregate, suggest that schools have little or no effect independent of the child's background.

The first of these studies, the Coleman Report, *Equality of Educational Opportunity*, stated that:

• "schools bring little influence to bear on a child's achievement that is independent of his background and general social context; and . . . this very lack of independent effect means that the inequalities imposed on children by their home, neighborhood, and peer environment are carried along to become the inequalities with which they confront adult life at the end of school."

The Report found that:

• "Variations in academic achievement in school are determined primarily by family background, home environment and the social class of the students. The differences in schools' physical facilities, formal curricula and the school staff characteristics account for relatively little of the differences in achievement among students.

• As currently organized, schools are predominantly culturally homogenous and racially segregated. This cultural and racial homogeneity maintains and reinforces the differences that are imposed by family backgrounds and social origins."

• "What differences there are in school factors such as facilities, curriculum, teachers, etc., have a stronger effect—up or down—on the recorded achievement of minority pupils than on non-minority students.

• Of all the possible in-school variations, the strongest factor is the quality of the teacher, particularly the teacher's verbal ability.

• One pupil attitude factor—the extent to which the child feels he can control his own destiny—is more strongly related to achievement than other in-school factors. Minority pupils, except for Orientals, show far less belief than non-minorities that they can control their own futures and environments but, when they do have that conviction, their achievement levels tend to be higher than non-minorities who do not hold that conviction."

Using the Coleman Report as the basis for a re-examination, Dr. Daniel Moynihan and Frederick Mosteller state: "The (Coleman) findings constitute the most powerful empirical critique of the Myths (the unquestioned basic assumptions, the socially perceived beliefs) of American education ever produced. It is the most important source of data in the sociology of American education yet to appear. It was the most complex analysis ever made of educational data in such quantity. And, again, it is more than that. Flowing from the very provisions of the Civil Rights Act of 1964, it is a document of profound significance for the future of racial and ethnic relations in America."

Following Coleman, Moynihan, and Mosteller, came Dr. Arthur R. Jensen of the University of California at Berkeley, who, in 1969, asserted in a Harvard Educational Review paper that intelligence was largely determined by heredity and could not be substantially changed by improving the environment or educational programs designed to increase the intelligence of disadvantaged children by enhancing their cultural surroundings.

The most recent in this group of evaluators is Professor Christopher S. Jencks,[4] who again, reanalyzed the Coleman data, with a Harvard University-Carnegie Foundation sponsored team of researchers, to state that the gap in achievement test scores between black and white children, rich and poor children, would only be reduced ten to twenty (10-20) percent with racial, socioeconomic integration, and that the kind of facilities or programs have little bearing on the final outcome insofar as changing from a disadvantaged to an advantaged position.

Taking the opposite position, in the 1969 Urban Coalition Study, Schools and Inequality, Professors Guthrie, Kleindorfer, Levin and Stout reviewed the results of 17 studies dealing with the relationship between school services and student achievement, and presented their own findings in the State of Michigan. On the basis of these studies they concluded:

"It is evident there is a substantial degree of consistency in the studies' findings. The strongest findings by far are those which relate to the number and quality of professional staff, particularly teachers . . . Teacher characteristics, such as verbal ability, amount of experience, salary level, amount and type of academic preparation, degree level, and employment status (tenured or non-tenured) (are) significantly associated with one or more measures of pupil performance."

In addition they found that student performance was related to the frequency of contact and proximity of students to professional staff in terms of student-staff ratios, classroom size, school size, and the length of the school year.

They state that a number of studies, including their own, suggest that the age of school buildings and the adequacy and amount of physical facilities are also "significantly linked to increments in scales of pupil performance." Finally, because all of these school factors cost money, the authors found that expenditures per pupil and teacher salary levels "are correlated significantly with pupil achievement levels."

The Urban Coalition held that:

"A relationship exists between the quality of school services provided to a pupil and his academic achievement, and that relationship is such that higher quality school services are associated with higher levels of achievement. There can be little doubt that schools have an effect that is independent of the child's social environment. In other words, schools do make a difference."

The Senate Select Committee did not completely subscribe to the evidence furnished by Coleman, et al, but rather noted that "Our survey of the evidence that is available demonstrates a definite positive relationship between racial-socioeconomic integration and academic achievement of educationally disadvantaged children. This relationship is strongest when integration begins in the first years of schooling and is strengthened by special efforts to improve school curricula and teaching methods.

We find that if racial-socioeconomic integration is combined with major efforts to strengthen curricula, improve teaching methods, better train teachers, substantially reduce class size, and encourage the meaningful involvement of parents and community members, school integration can be the basis for impressive improvement in the educational achievement of minority-group and low-income students . . ."

They further quoted the 1971 report of the National Advisory Committee on the Education of Disadvantaged Children, which found that "desegregation is the best form of compensatory education," and a memorandum from the then Secretary of HEW, Elliot Richardson, in support of the "Equal Educational Opportunities Act" which stated: "We know that children learn less effectively when there is a great degree of economic or social isolation."

[4]*Inequality: A Reassessment of the Effect of Family and Schooling in America,* Christopher Jencks, et al, (Basic Books, New York, 1972).

Early Childhood Education

One of the main threads running through the numerous studies that have been made of disadvantaged children is the necessity for positive influences in the early childhood years. The home environment has been singled out as most crucial in those formative years from birth to six years of age.

The 1971 Report of the Education Commission of the States urged that developmental programs be designed for children younger than age six. It urged that the inadequate day care situation to which many children are exposed be improved. It urged that parents be assisted in their efforts to do a better job in parenting and it asked that steps be taken to detect and correct the problems facing those youngsters who had mental or physical handicaps or other learning disabilities.

The 1970 White House Conference on Children voted as their first priority the provision of "Comprehensive family-oriented child development programs, including health services, day-care, and early childhood education."

There are 3.2 million pre-school children in the U.S., 515 thousand of whom are black youngsters under 6 years of age. Forty-nine and one-half percent of these live in homes where the income is under $5,000 per year; 26% under $3,000.

Programs for the pre-school child which were subsidized by federal funding faced elimination in 1973.

Federal day-care programs enrolling a total of several hundred thousand children were administered in 1971 by no fewer than five federal agencies and subagencies. One source of federal day-care funds is the 1967 amended Social Security Act, which provides for two programs administered by the Social and Rehabilitation Service (under the Department of Health, Education, and Welfare) and the Department of Labor: the Work Incentive Program and Aid to Families With Dependent Children. Day-care programs provided for under the Economic Opportunity Act of 1964 are Head Start and its adjunct, Parent and Child Centers, both administered by the Office of Child Development; the Concentrated Employment Program day care, administered by the Department of Labor; and migrant children day care, administered by the Office of Economic Opportunity. A 1967 amendment to the Economic Opportunity Act ordered the coordination of day-care programs at the federal, state and local levels, and in 1968 an interagency Federal Panel on Early Childhood was created; the panel's offshoot was the Community Coordinated Child Care program, which attempts to provide maximum use within the community of funds, facilities & staffing.

The proposed Comprehensive Child Development Act of 1971, a major social innovation that would have provided, for the first time in the U.S. universal child-care services, was vetoed in December 1971 by President Richard M. Nixon.

The existing programs have been severely crippled or eliminated by the directives of the President and the budget cuts.

Higher Education

Many of the barriers which had discouraged maximum participation in higher education by black students, were lowered during the period of the late sixties and early seventies. Active recruitment of minority students, open admissions policies, educational assistance, and remediation programs for students with inadequate secondary school preparation, increased student aid and loan programs where some of the techniques utilized in the move to bring affirmative action to the college campuses. Black students constituted a high of 9.1 percent by 1970, of total enrollment in all institutions.

Since then, cutbacks in funding, work-study, scholarship, and loan sources have been in part responsible for the figure dropping to 6.3 percent in 1971. The future prospects of most federally funded student aid programs and the drying up of foundation resources holds little promise for dramatic future growth for participation, black, and other minority, in higher education.

In the fall of 1971, according to published estimates of the American Council on Education, Office of Research, blacks constituted 6.3 percent of the total enrollment of all institutions. In absolute numbers, the enrollment of black students in colleges increased from 234,000 in 1964 to 492,000 in 1969.

Black and other minority groups still represent a fractional degree of participation in higher education, particularly at the post-baccalaureate level. A Ford Foundation publication, "Graduate Education and Black Americans" reported a survey of 105 predominantly white U.S. graduate schools of arts and sciences, related to black enrollments and Ph. D.'s awarded to black scholars. The institutions represented a cross-section of one-third of the U.S. doctoral-granting universities in the nation. The findings indicate that the proportion of black students in the total enrollment of U.S graduate schools is 1.72 percent and the number of Ph. D.'s awarded to black scholars between 1964 and 1968 is 0.78 percent. It was estimated that between 160 and 175 black Americans were awarded the Ph. D. in 1969.

In June, 1972, there were a total of 22,302 black graduate and professional students enrolled in post-baccalaureate medical, legal, and other graduate programs. Of that number, 1,845 were black non-undergraduate medical students; 597 were non-undergraduate dental students; and 2,552 were non-undergraduate law students.

Vocational Education

Many urban school systems have instituted programs to encourage drop-outs to return to school, if not the conventional classroom, to participate in some of the programs which permit a student to earn a high school equivalency diploma. Most of these programs have been federally funded and as with other adult education programs will be hard-pressed to function with the withdrawal of federal funding and no allocations yet proposed for sharing in the general revenue. Other programs hard hit by federal budget cuts will be those affecting vocational and para-professional educational programs.

On the one hand there is a vast untrained and uneducated pool of human resources and on the other are unmet demands for trained and skilled mechanics and repairmen, hospital attendants, draftsmen, painters, electricians, plumbers, bakers, welders, practical nurses, health service technicians, and other workers who could be taken from this resource pool.

Drop-Outs

Finally, among the most seriously deprived children are those who, only get an inferior education, but worse, do not complete enough school years to qualify for even marginal employment. There are an estimated seven million children ages 3-17, who are not enrolled in any kind of school or educational program. Fifteen percent of that group, or 1,131,000 black children can be counted as out of the educational marketplace.

Because there is a strong relationship between the amount of schooling an adult citizen has received and his occupational status and income, the loss of potential earning for this large segment of the black population is noteworthy.

REPORT OF THE NATIONAL ASSOCIATION OF SECONDARY SCHOOL PRINCIPALS OF JUNE 10, 1971

Regardless of what is being done:—The ranks of the black principal in the South are being depleted; and those remaining are generally in all black schools.

Virginia
1965—29% of secondary principals were black
1970—6½% of secondary principals were black

North Carolina*
1963—227 black high school principals
1970— 8 black high school principals
* Figures disputed by white leadership personnel

Alabama
1967—250 black principals
1970— 50 black principals

Georgia
In 30 North Georgia school systems:
1963—White principals, 284; Black principals, 54
1968—White principals, 308; Black principals, 24 (22 in all black schools)

Kentucky
1954—Black principals, 350
1969-70—Black principals, 36; with 22 of them in Louisville and
        only 2 black high school principals in the entire state.

Maryland
1954— 44 Black high school principals
       167 White high school principals
1968— 31 Black high school principals
       280 White high school principals

CAREER GUIDE

(This selected list contains information concerning a variety of employment opportunities. Some listings, such as police and fire department positions, have been omitted, since information concerning them can best be obtained from local government offices.)

ACCOUNTANTS
(tax and cost accountant, controller, commercial loan officer, budget manager, area commercial manager, buyer)
> Bachelor's degree with major in accounting, business administration, or related field is asset and may be required. Master's degree is desirable. Outlook indicates that accounting occupancies are expected to expand very rapidly during the 1970s.

Write to:

American Bankers Association
(commercial loan officer)
Personnel Administration and
Manpower Development Committee
1120 Connecticut Avenue, NW
Washington, DC 20036

The American Management Association
(budget manager, area commercial manager)
135 W. 50th Street
New York, NY 10020

American Marketing Association
(buyer)
230 North Michigan Ave.
Chicago, IL 60601

Financial Executives Institute
(tax accountant, cost accountant, controller)
50 W. 44th Street
New York, NY 10036

The Institute of Internal Auditors, Inc.
(tax accountant, cost accountant, controller)
170 Broadway
New York, NY 10038

National Association of Accountants
(tax accountant, cost accountant, controller)
505 Park Avenue
New York, NY 10022

National Association of Bank Women, Inc.
(commercial loan officer)
National Office
111 E. Wacker Drive
Chicago, IL 60601

National Bankers Association
(commercial loan officer)
4310 Georgia Avenue, NW
Washington, DC 20011

National Society of Public Accountants
(tax accountant, cost accountant, controller)
1717 Pennsylvania Avenue, NW
Washington, DC 20006

Society for Advancement of Management
(budget manager, area commercial manager)
1412 Broadway
New York, NY 10036

AIRLINES
Commercial Pilot
> Requires FAA license following at least 200 hours of flight experience. For instrument rating and airline transport license additional hours are required. Advancement from co-pilot to captain often takes many years.
> Rapid rise in airline pilot employment expected through 1970s.

Write to:

Air Line Pilots Association
1329 E. Street, NW
Washington, DC 20004

Executive Pilot:
> Training received through military service or a private flying school.
> Outlook excellent.

Write to:

Air Line Pilot's Association, International
1329 E. Street, NW
Washington, DC 20004

Ground Support Director
(responsible for buying, distribution and maintenance of all such equipment for the airline)
> Degree in business administration or management required. Degree in engineering is desirable.
> Outlook indicates a moderate increase in the need for aerospace engineers.

Write to:

American Institute of Aeronautics and Astronautics, Inc.
1290 Avenue of the Americas
New York, NY 10019

Reservations Supervisor
> Strict hiring standards with respect to appearance, personality, and education. High school education required and college training desirable.
> Positions for traffic personnel will increase rapidly over the next several years.

Write to:

Air Line Employees Association
5600 So. Central Avenue
Chicago, IL 60638

Sales Representative
College degree in marketing, business administration, finance, or a related field is required for managerial position.
Outlook in sales is excellent.

Write to:

American Marketing Association
230 North Michigan Avenue
Chicago, IL 60601

The American Management Association
135 W. 50th Street
New York, NY 10020

Travel Marketing
Degree in business administration, marketing, economics, or other related field required. Good knowledge of statistical analysis methods useful.
Demand for specialists likely to continue throughout the 1970s.

Write to:

American Marketing Association
230 North Michigan Avenue
Chicago, IL 60601

Sales and Marketing Executives International
Student Education Division
630 Third Avenue
New York, NY 10017

CHEMISTS
(analytical, polymer, research)
College graduates holding bachelor's degree in chemistry begin careers in industry or government working in applied research. Graduate (doctorate) degree required for those interested in research or college teaching.
Outlook expected to continue at favorable level through the 1970s.

Write to:

American Chemical Society
1155 16th Street, NW
Washington, DC 20036

Manufacturing Chemists' Association
1825 Connecticut Avenue, NW
Washington, DC 20009

COMPUTER ANALYSTS
AND PROGRAMMERS
Preparation for work in systems analysis varies from bachelor's degree and experience in mathematics, science, engineering, accounting, or business, to graduate degree, to experience in programming, which can be learned on the job, through courses at the firm, or at outside schools. Outlook indicates excellent opportunities through the 1970s.

Write to:

American Federation of Information Processing Societies
210 Summit Avenue
Montvale, NJ 07645

Data Processing Management Association
505 Busse Highway
Park Ridge, IL 60068

DENTAL
Dental Assistant
(prepares for examination and treatment, sterilizes instruments, helps dentist, mixes fillings, helps in taking X-rays, answers phone, makes appointments, etc.)
Training involves one- or sometimes two-year courses, depending on training school. Some dentists train assistants on the job. (Two years training leads to certification.)

Write to:

American Dental Assistants Association
211 E. Chicago Avenue
Chicago, IL 60611

Division of Dental Health
Public Health Service
Department of Health, Education & Welfare
Washington, DC 20201

Dental Hygienist
(cleans and polishes teeth, locates possible disease area for diagnosis by dentist, may take and develop x-rays, and generally assists dentist)
2 years training usually required (there are some longer courses) plus state license.

Dental Laboratory Technicians

Write to:

American Dental Association
Council on Dental Education
211 E. Chicago Avenue
Chicago, IL 60611

National Association of Certified Dental Laboratories, Inc.
3801 Mt. Vernon Avenue
Alexandria, Va. 22305

DIETARY MANAGEMENT
Bachelor's degree with major in foods and nutrition or institution management required. Knowledge of government standards also required.
Opportunities for qualified dietitians expected to be very good during the 1970s.

Write to:

The American Dietetic Association
620 North Michigan Avenue
Chicago, IL 60611

DRAFTSMEN

Necessary training can be acquired from technical institutes, junior and community colleges, extension divisions of universities, vocational and technical high schools, correspondence schools, or on-the-job training programs, combined with part-time schooling or three- or four-year apprenticeship programs.
Employment opportunities for draftsmen are expected to be favorable.

Write to:

American Institute for Design and Drafting
P.O. Box 2955
Tulsa, OH 74101

American Federation of Technical Engineers
1126 16th Street, N.W.
Washington, DC 20036

ENGINEERS
Electrical

Bachelor's degree in engineering required. Electrical engineers usually specialize in major area of work.
Opportunities expected to increase very rapidly through the 1970s.

Write to:

Institute of Electrical and Electronic Engineers
345 E. 47th Street
New York, NY 10017

Chemical

Bachelor's degree required.
Outlook indicates moderate growth in opportunities.

Write to:

American Institute of Chemical Engineers
345 E. 47th Street
New York, NY 10017

Design

Bachelor's degree in engineering required.
Outlook favorable.

Write to:

Engineers' Council for Professional Development
345 E. 47th Street
New York, NY 10017

Engineering Manpower Commission
Engineers Joint Council
345 E. 47th Street
New York, NY 10017

National Society of Professional Engineers
2029 K Street, NW
Washington, DC 20006

Industrial Sales

Degree in mechanical engineering preferred. Prospects best for those with mechanical specialty.

Write to:

American Society of Mechanical Engineers
345 E. 47th Street
New York, NY 10017

Research Management

Bachelor's degree required with advancement depending on experience and additional study in the field.
Outlook favorable through the 1970s.

Write to:

Engineering Manpower Commission
Engineers Joint Council
345 E. 47th Street
New York, NY 10017

National Society of Professional Engineers
2029 K Street, NW
Washington, DC 20006

Technician

Necessary training obtainable from a great variety of educational institutions or on-the-job training. Specialized training preferred for more responsible jobs.
Outlook very good through the 1970s.

Write to:

Engineers' Council for Professional Development
345 E. 47th Street
New York, NY 10017

National Council of Technical Schools
1835 K Street, NW
Washington, DC 20006

American Society for Engineering Education
Suite 400
1 Dupont Circle
Washington, DC 20036

LAW
Corporate

(corporate law subdivides into many areas, among them labor law, tax, trade, and contract)

Four years of college and three years of accredited law school required. Seminars, conferences, and courses advantageous to keep up to date.
Opportunities best in large metropolitan areas.

Write to:

Information Service
American Bar Association
1155 E. 60th Street
Chicago, IL 60637

Association of American Law Schools
1 Dupont Circle, NW, Suite 370
Washington, DC 20036

Courtroom
Minimum of three years law study beyond bachelor's degree required. Highly competitive. Lawyer required to pass bar examination in state where he wishes to practice. Outlook for private practice best in small and suburban communities.

Write to:

See: Corporate Law

Labor Relations
(subdivision of corporate law)
College degree in a social science, management, or business is best preparation.
Outlook indicates an expanding demand for those with labor law and labor relations training.

Write to:

The American Management Association
135 W. 50th Street
New York, NY 10020

Society for Advancement of Management
1412 Broadway
New York, NY 10036

Patent
Four years of college and three years of accredited law school required.
Outlook indicates salaried employment limited mainly to metropolitan areas.

Write to:

See: Corporate Law

Tax
(subdivision of corporate law)
Four years of college and three years of law school required.
Opportunities best in large metropolitan areas.

Write to:

See: Corporate Law

Trade and Contract
(subdivision of corporate law)
Four years of college and three years of law school required.
Opportunities best in large metropolitan areas.

Write to:

See: Corporate Law

LIBRARY SPECIALIST
One-year master's degree program in library science required to qualify as professional librarian. PH.D. advantageous for teaching career in library schools or top administrative posts.
Employment outlook for trained librarians expected to be good through the 1970s. Best chances in school, college and university libraries.

Write to:

American Library Association
50 E. Huron Street
Chicago, IL 60611

Special Libraries Association
235 Park Avenue, South
New York, NY 10003

American Society for Information Science
1140 Constitution Avenue, NW
Washington, DC 20203

MEDICAL
Assistants
(helps prepare patients for examinations, sterilizes instruments, takes temperatures, measures weight and height, etc. May perform routine laboratory tests.)
Twelve months to two years special training at junior college or other school required.

Write to:

American Association of Medical Assistants
200 E. Ohio Street
Chicago, IL 60611

American Medical Association
Council on Medical Education
535 N. Dearborn Street
Chicago, IL 60610

Engineering Technicians
(assembles, adapts, and maintains new devices and instruments.)
Four years training but new specialty courses may require less.

Illustrators
(uses drawings, painting, sculpture, photography for illustrating books, hospital charts, etc.)
At least two years training, including pre-medical studies as well as graphic technology.

Laboratory technicians
(assists scientists by setting up equipment, performing routine chemical and physical tests, recording experimental results)

Usually two years of junior college or other technical school is required with supervised clinical experience in approved laboratory.

Microbiologist
College training required—bachelor's degree for beginning positions in laboratories, etc.; master's degree or doctorate for research positions or college or university teaching positions.
Employment expected to increase rapidly throughout the 1970s. Keen competition anticipated for more desirable positions.

Write to:

American Institute of Biological Sciences
3900 Wisconsin Avenue, NW
Washington, DC 20016

Physician's Associates
(very new field)
Training through special programs established at university schools of medicine. Usually two years of classroom and clinic training required.
Outlook very good throughout the 1970s. Demand expected to rise rapidly.
Contact the state employment office for information on programs offered through the Manpower Development Training Act. Or write to:

American Association of Medical Assistants
200 East Ohio Street
Chicago, IL 60611

Physicians
Training usually consists of eight years beyond secondary school. Licensing exam required in all states and one-year hospital internship in 33 of the states. Most medical schools require three years of college.
Outlook indicates excellent opportunities for physicians throughout the 1970s.

Write to:

Council on Medical Education
American Medical Association
535 No. Dearborn Street
Chicago, IL 60610

Association of American Medical Colleges
1 Dupont Circle, NW
Washington, DC 20036

Records Administrators
Graduation from approved school in medical record science required. Upon passing the national registration examination given by the American Medical Record Association, graduates receive professional recognition as Registered Record Librarians.
Outlook indicates excellent employment opportunities throughout the 1970s.

Write to:

The American Medical Record Association
875 North Michigan Avenue
Suite 1850
Chicago, IL 60611

Records Librarians
(in charge of all classification material in hospital; indexes catalogues of all information; controls traffic of case records; prepares reports on request)
Minimum of three years study (one year in hospital plus two years at college) or four-year program in an accredited college giving degrees in medical records administration.

Senior Animal Laboratory Technician
(helps in feeding, care, breeding of animals in research)
Three years on the job or two years study at Animal Technology Laboratory School, plus one year's experience lead to certification.

Technologists
(performs chemical, microscopic, bacteriological and other tests in laboratory under supervision of experienced physician or pathologist in hospital or clinical laboratory)
Three years of college training, with emphasis on sciences, plus one year in hospital school of medical technology leading to certification.

NEWSPAPER EDITOR
Position usually achieved by journalists after years of experience. College education with degree in journalism or liberal arts usually required.
Outlook indicates favorable employment opportunities throughout the 1970s for well-qualified beginners with exceptional writing talent.

Write to:

American Newspaper Publishers Association
750 Third Avenue
New York, NY 10017

The Newspaper Fund, Inc.
Box 300
Princeton, NJ 08540

American Council on Education for Journalism
School of Journalism
University of Missouri
Columbia, MO 65201

NURSING
Practical (care of the sick)
Training takes 12 to 18 months—high school (some courses are part of high school curriculum) or 10th grade.

Write to:

ANA-NLN Committee on Nursing Careers
American Nurses' Association
10 Columbus Circle
New York, NY. 10019

National Federation of Licensed Practical
Nurses, Inc.
250 W. 57th Street
New York, NY 10019

Professional
(has overall responsibility for patient's nursing
needs under direction of physician, with assistance of nurse's aides, practical nurses, etc.
Usually begins as general duty nurse in hospital or clinic; can serve in doctor's office,
private homes, as well as a public health
nurse, etc. For men and women)
   License required in all states and District of
Columbia. A nurse must have graduated
from a school approved by the state board
of nursing and must pass a board examination to obtain license. Three types of programs offer the basic education required for
registered nursing.
   1. Diploma—offered at hospitals and in-
      dependent schools of nursing and gen-
      erally requires three years of attend-
      ance.
   2. Baccalaureate—obtained from colleges
      and universities and requires four (or
      sometimes five) years of training.
   3. Associate—offered at junior and com-
      munity colleges after two years of
      study.
Employment opportunities for registered
nurses are expected to be very good for
near future.

Write to:

ANA-NLN Committee on Nursing Careers
American Nurses' Association
10 Columbus Circle
New York, NY 10019

For information on employment in the Vet-
erans Administration write to:
Department of Medicine and Surgery
Veterans Administration
Washington, DC 20420

OCCUPATIONAL THERAPY ASSISTANTS
(works with occupational therapist, assisting
in rehabilitating patients in hospitals or other
health care facilities. Instructs patients in man-
ual and creative arts, prepares materials and
supplies, helps in maintaining tools and equipment.)
   Usually one year training, conducted by
hospitals or other health agencies leading to
certification exam.

Write to:

The American Occupational Therapy Association
251 Park Avenue
New York, NY 10010

OPTOMETRIC ASSISTANTS
Write to:

American Optometric Association
7000 Chippewa Street
St. Louis, MO 63119

PHARMACY ASSISTANTS
(under professional supervision, compounds
routine pharmaceuticals, unpacks and sorts
supplies, keeps stock, pre-packages weekly dos-
ages.)
   On-the-job training.

PHOTOGRAPHIC LABORATORY
OCCUPATIONS
Write to:

Master Photo Dealers' and Finishers' Association
603 Lansing Avenue
Jackson, MI 49202

Professional Photographers of America, Inc.
1090 Executive Way
Des Plaines, Illinois 60018

PHYSICIST
Bachelor's degree with major in physics is
minimum requirement. Graduate training,
often to doctorate level, needed for employment involving research and development responsibility.
Employment outlooks favorable throughout
1970s, but graduate training is increasingly
requisite.

Write to:

American Institute of Physics
335 E. 45th Street
New York, NY 10017

Interagency Board
U.S. Civil Service Examiner
1900 E Street, N.W.
Washington, DC 20415

RADIO/TV OCCUPATIONS
For information on television and radio service technicians write to:

National Alliance of Television Associations
5908 S. Troy Street
Chicago, IL 60629

Television stations manager
   Managers generally promoted from the

ranks of experienced personnel. Those who eventually rise to station manager responsibility were, in some cases, program managers, news or promotion directors. Training for positions at entry-level may be through degree programs offered at an increasing number of colleges, universities, and communications schools. Management training is also an excellent entry-level background.

Stiff competition throughout the 1970s, however, opportunities for blacks should be somewhat better because of new hiring guidelines. For information on the managerial aspects of television write to:

The American Management Association
135 W. 50th Street
New York, NY 10020

Society for the Advancement of Management
1412 Broadway
New York, NY 10036

SOCIAL SCIENTISTS

Economists
Thorough background in economic theory and methods of economic analysis needed. Bachelor's degree with major in economics and minor in mathematics and/or statistics is excellent. Advanced degrees required for teaching positions and private industry research positions of high responsibility.
Outlook indicates a rapid increase in employment opportunities throughout the 1970s.

Write to:

American Economic Association
1313 21st Avenue, South
Nashville, TN 37212

THE INTERNATIONAL DEVELOPER
(ECONOMIST)
Professional Talent Search
Office of Personnel and Manpower
Agency for International Development
Washington, DC 20523

Demographic Specialist
(Demographics is a social science dealing with characteristics of populations.)
Strong sociology and economics background required. Master's degree is minimum requirement. Doctorate is essential for teaching positions in most colleges or universities and is commonly required for the heads of major research projects, important administrative positions or consultants.
Employment opportunities for sociologists with doctorates are expected to be good during the 1970s. Those having only a master's degree are likely to face considerable competition.

Write to:

The American Sociological Association
1001 Connecticut Avenue, NW
Washington, DC 20036

Associate Professor of Sociology
Master's degree required for most beginning positions in colleges and universities. All requirements for the doctorate except the dissertation may be required. For teaching, specialization in some field is necessary. College teaching opportunities expected to be good for those having completed the Ph.D. or all the requirements thereof except the dissertation. Opportunities will be best in junior colleges for those having only a master's degree.

Write to:

American Association of University Professors
One Dupont Circle, NW
Washington, DC 20036

American Council on Education
One Dupont Circle, NW
Washington, DC 20036

American Federation of Teachers
1012 14th Street, NW
Washington, DC 20005

National Education Association
1201. 16th Street, NW
Washington, DC 20036

TEACHING

College
Master's degree required for beginning positions. Specialization in some field necessary. Outlook good for those having completed the Ph.D. or all the requirements thereof except the dissertation. Opportunities will be best in junior colleges for those having only a master's degree.

Write to:

American Association of University Professors
One Dupont Circle, NW
Washington, DC 20036

American Council on Education
One Dupont Circle, NW
Washington, DC 20036

American Federation of Teachers
1012 14th Street, NW
Washington, DC 20005

National Education Association
1201 16th Street, NW
Washington, DC 20036

VETERINARIANS

Write to:

TWO-YEAR PROGRAMS
  Animal Science Technology Department
  Agricultural and Technical College
  State University of New York
  Delhi, NY 13753

  Biological Technology Department
  Laboratory Animal Technology Emphasis
  Agricultural and Technical College
  State University of New York
  Farmingdale, NY 11735

  Veterinary Medical Technology Department
  Central Carolina Technical Institute
  Sanford, NC 27330

  Laboratory Animal Technology Program
  College of Agriculture
  Pennsylvania State University
  University Park, PA 16802

FOUR-YEAR PROGRAM
  Veterinary Technology Program

Department of Animal Diseases
College of Agriculture
University of Connecticut
Storrs, CT 06268

Laboratory Animal Science Major
Department of Animal Science
Institute of Food and Agricultural Sciences
University of Florida
Gainesville, FL 32601

Laboratory Animal Science Program
College of Health Related Professions
State University of New York
Downstate Medical Center
450 Clarkson Avenue
Brooklyn, NY 11203

Biomedical Science Program
Department of Veterinary Public Health
College of Veterinary Medicine
Texas A & M University
College Station, TX 77843

Source: *Ebony Success Library,* vol. 3.,
Johnson Publishing Company, Chicago, 1973.

UNITED NEGRO COLLEGE FUND

In 1943, F. D. Patterson, the then President of Tuskegee Institute, wrote an article for the *Pittsburgh Courier* on the financial plight of the black colleges.

"Private colleges for Negroes have carried the brunt of our educational effort for the better part of this experience. They yet educate, to the extent of their means, nearly 50 percent of those who receive college training .... These Negro institutions may well take a cue from the general program of organization which seems to involve most charitable efforts today. Various and sundry drives (financial) are being unified with a reduction in overhead for publicity and in behalf of a more purposeful and pointed approach to the giving public."

As a result of this article and a series of conferences with Presidents of other black colleges, two foundations—The Julius Rosenwald Fund and The General Education Board—agreed to help underwrite the organization of such a joint fund-raising effort.

On April 15, 1944, The United Negro College Fund was chartered in the state of New York. William J. Trent, Jr. was its first Executive Director. This was the first time in the history of American education that private educational institutions of higher learning had joined in co-operative fund raising. This is one of the significant contributions of the United Negro College Fund to the financing of higher education. Since 1944, some forty joint educational fund-raising organizations have been started.

Twenty-seven black colleges were charter members. Membership in the Fund was restricted to privately supported black colleges most of which were church related. The colleges delegated their responsibility for raising funds for current purposes to the United Negro College Fund. The colleges were still responsible for finding money for building and could, of course, appeal to alumni. The money raised by the Fund was to be used for scholarships, teacher salaries, library books, laboratory supplies and equipment, etc.

ANNUAL CAMPAIGNS

The first campaign of the United Negro College Fund was launched in the spring of 1944. A strong Fund supporter from the very beginning was John D. Rockefeller, Jr. The Rockefeller family has been a long-time contributor for the education of blacks. Campaigns were organized in some twenty communities and appeals were made to individuals, foundations, alumni, and corporations. A total of $765,000 was raised the first year. This was approximately three times the amount the colleges raised through their individual efforts the previous year. As a result of this first campaign, three questions were answered.

1. Individuals would support a group of colleges. This destroyed the myth that people would only support an individual college whereby they could get certain public acclaim.

2. Alumni, while still loyal to their alma mater would work for and support higher education for blacks.

3. American business would contribute to the support of higher education. This was a significant breakthrough in the financing of colleges and universities in America. The United Negro College Fund was responsible for opening up this source of support.

From 1944 to 1972, the membership of the Fund grew from twenty-seven to forty colleges. In the 1972 campaign the Fund raised $11,166,000 for current support of its membership. From its beginning through 1972, the Fund raised $130,000,000 in twenty-eight annual campaigns. Currently, it receives support from both the black and white populations, and significant support from corporations and foundations.

CAPITAL FUNDS CAMPAIGNS

When the United Negro College Fund was organized it accepted as its primary responsibility the raising of funds for current operations. The member colleges still were responsible for raising building and endowment funds. By 1950, it became apparent that the private black colleges were having very little success in raising capital funds individually. As a result, the United Negro College Fund was asked to organize a campaign for building money. Mr. John D. Rockefeller, Jr. gave leadership to this effort. Associated with him were some of America's outstanding businessmen. By 1954, 18 million dollars had been raised.

In 1963, the member colleges of the Fund again requested that the United Negro College Fund organize another drive for funds to finance plant expansion. The goal was set at 50 million dollars—30 million to be raised jointly by the Fund and 10 million to be raised through the individual efforts of member colleges. The need for strengthening the private members was discussed with the late President John F. Kennedy who had had a longtime interest in the Fund. He gave it his strong support and asked leading businessmen to help. He persuaded Mr. Charles Mortimer of the General Foods Corporation to lead the campaign. A significant challenge gift of 15 million dollars was made by the Ford Foundation and by the middle of 1964 the first 30 million dollars had been raised. Member colleges have subsequently raised approximately 10 million dollars. The United Negro College Fund has raised 48 million dollars in two capital fund campaigns.

INSTITUTIONAL SERVICES

In recognition of the fact that history and the dynamics of social change have thrust upon private black colleges an important role of academic leadership, the United Negro College Fund created a new Division of Institutional Services in September 1970. Incorporating and building upon the College Fund's experience wtih educational services and research services, the United Negro College Fund's institutional services are designed to strengthen and maximize the Fund's capacity to serve the forty-one member institutions through a variety of services. These include Technical Assistance, Educational Services, Research and Publications, Consulting, Counseling, and Information Services as well as Academic, Administrative, and Instructional Services.

Some specific objectives of the United Negro College Fund in the field of institutional services include: 1) strengthening individual colleges in areas common to all; 2) sharing among the colleges of experience, research, innovations, and personnel by which all may benefit; 3) developing and extending educational services to colleges as well as to consortia or convenient college clusters; 4) extending to other educational institutions reasonable access to information and other benefits derived from cooperative efforts; 5) serving as a strong articulate voice from the United Negro College Fund at the federal level in Washington, D. C.; and 6) maintaining an Information Center on higher education with reference to needs, problems, and issues affecting black people.

RESEARCH

In support of its role of leadership and spokesmanship on behalf of the forty-one member colleges in relation to corporations, foundations, governmental officials, agencies, and representatives, the Fund has developed research, consulting, and counseling services.

The Fund has prepared from time to time background studies and position papers. These have included a series of papers on "The Financial Problems of Private Colleges," "A Directory of Black Colleges and Universities," and "A Survey of Voluntary Support of UNCF Institutions."

EDUCATION SERVICES

The following four services form a part of the Fund's program to help improve the quality of the educational programs at the private black colleges.

1. *Student Recruitment Sessions.* Through special grants the Fund has been able to conduct a joint information and admissions counseling program, called a Rap Session, sponsored in behalf of the undergraduate member institutions of the United Negro College Fund.

2. *Faculty Fellowship Program.* The Fund has secured special grants to finance further graduate study by faculty members of UNCF institutions. This program is responsible for a significant increase in the number of blacks earning doctoral degrees.

3. *Florina Lasker Scholarship Progam.* A dedicated friend of the Fund has made several grants to finance graduate work for several women graduates of UNCF institutions each year.

4. *Creative Writing Contest.* Through the courtesy of the *Reader's Digest* money is made available to sponsor a creative writing competition on the campuses of the member colleges.

Since 1944, for all purposes the United Negro College Fund has raised approximately 110 million dollars for its member colleges. It has helped strengthen the colleges through educational services. Through these means it has helped move these institutions into the mainstream of American education where they are beginning to service students without regard to race, creed, or color.

NATIONAL SCHOLARSHIP SERVICE AND FUND FOR NEGRO STUDENTS (NSSFNS)

Founded in 1947, with offices in New York City and Atlanta, Georgia, its president is Hugh W. Lane, Executive Director, David B. Kent, Board Chairman, John H. Mortimer, and SE Regional Director, Samuel H. Johnson.

NSSFNS is a non-profit college advisory and referral service which was established to assist black high school students obtain access to higher education. Using a computerized system with a data bank of nearly 3,000 post-secondary institutions, it refers applicants to those schools which are most likely to offer admission and financial aid. A supplementary scholarship fund provides limited financial assistance to extremely needy students who have been counseled by the agency.

NSSFNS also conducts an annual series of Student-College Interview Sessions in urban areas to introduce students to a variety of college representatives. Its counselors regularly visit colleges, high schools and community agencies, and attend professional meetings to keep abreast of changes in education and guidance.

All of the agency's services are available free of charge to all black high school juniors and seniors who are interested in furthering their education.

With a special grant from the Office of Education, the basic counseling service is also extended to all students enrolled in Talent Search and Upward Bound programs.

In 1972, NSSFNS published *A National*

Profile of Black Youth: The Class of 1971. This research report on the educational aspirations of more than 5,400 college-bound students in 7,000 high schools is considered the most comprehensive study of its nature. A second segment entitled *Characteristics Related to Geographical Distribution* was also issued.

NSSFNS is supported by contributions from corporations, foundations, and individuals.

A student who has been counseled by the NSSFNS college advisory and referral service is eligible to apply for a supplementary scholarship if the following criteria are met: 1) the student has been admitted to a 2 or 4 year college; 2) the student has received, from the college or another source, a scholarship of $200 or more (loans do not fill this requirement); and 3) after all other sources of aid have been exhausted (family contribution, loan, part-time employment and summer employment), the student still has insufficient funds to meet the total yearly college costs.

Scholarships range from $200–$600 a year and are renewable through the junior year in college. The number of scholarships awarded in any given year is, of course, dependent on the resources available.

The NSSFNS Supplementary Scholarship Fund was established to help fill the gap between students' total resources and college costs. Resources are provided by gifts from corporations, corporate foundations, foundations, organizations and individuals.

EDUCATIONAL CHARACTERISTICS OF THE BLACK POPULATION FOR CITIES WITH 100,000 OR MORE BLACKS: 1970

SELECTED CITIES	Number of Black children enrolled in grades 1-12 (thousands)	Percent Black of children in public elementary school	Black persons 25 years old and over		
			Percent functional illiterates[1]	Percent high school graduates	Percent college graduates
New York, N.Y.........	414	37	7	41	4
Chicago, Ill.............	316	56	8	39	4
Detroit, Mich...........	174	64	8	37	4
Philadelphia, Pa........	173	61	9	32	3
Washington, D.C........	134	93	7	44	8
Los Angeles, Calif......	126	25	6	50	6
Baltimore, Md...........	121	67	11	28	4
Houston, Texas.........	86	32	11	35	6
Cleveland, Ohio........	81	57	8	35	3
New Orleans, La.......	78	68	15	26	4
Atlanta, Ga.............	66	65	15	34	7
St. Louis, Mo...........	72	65	11	31	4
Memphis, Tenn.........	73	51	16	24	4
Dallas, Texas..........	58	34	10	37	5
Newark, N.J............	58	72	9	33	2
Indianapolis, Ind.......	37	23	8	36	4
Birmingham, Ala........	35	53	18	29	4
Cincinnati, Ohio........	34	46	12	29	3
Oakland, Calif..........	36	57	8	43	4
Jacksonville, Fla........	34	28	17	29	5
Kansas City, Mo........	32	32	8	40	5
Milwaukee, Wis.........	33	28	8	34	3
Pittsburgh, Pa..........	28	42	9	35	3
Richmond, Va..........	29	57	14	26	4
Boston, Mass...........	27	32	5	45	4
Columbus, Ohio........	28	26	7	41	5

[1]Less than 5 years of school completed.
Source: U.S. Department of Commerce, Social and Economic Statistics Administration, Bureau of the Census.

YEARS OF SCHOOL COMPLETED, BY RACE: 1940 TO 1971

Persons 25 years old and over as of March of year indicated. Based on Current Population Survey; includes inmates of institutions and members of the Armed Forces living off post or with their families on post, but excludes all other members of the Armed Forces; see text, p. 1

AGE AND YEAR	ALL RACES				BLACK			
	Years completed (percent)			Median school years com- pleted[2]	Years completed (percent)			Median school years com- pleted[2]
	Elemen- tary school, less than 5 years[1]	High school, 4 years or more	College, 4 years or more		Elemen- tary school, less than 5 years[1]	High school, 4 years or more	College, 4 years or more	
25 YEARS AND OVER								
1940.........................	13.7	24.5	4.6	8.6	42.0	7.3	1.3	5.7
1950.........................	11.1	34.3	6.2	9.3	32.9	12.9	2.1	6.8
1960.........................	8.3	41.1	7.7	10.5	23.8	20.1	3.1	8.0
1970.........................	5.3	55.2	11.0	12.2	15.1	33.7	4.5	9.9
1971.........................	5.0	56.4	11.4	12.2	13.5	34.7	4.5	10.1
25-29 YEARS								
1940.........................	5.9	38.1	5.9	10.3	27.7	11.6	1.6	7.0
1950.........................	4.7	52.8	7.7	12.1	16.8	22.2	2.7	8.6
1960.........................	2.8	60.7	11.1	12.3	[3]7.2	[3]38.6	[3]5.4	[3]10.8
1970.........................	1.1	75.4	16.4	12.6	2.5	56.2	7.3	12.2
1971.........................	1.1	77.2	16.9	12.6	1.8	57.5	6.4	12.2

[1]Includes persons reporting no school years completed.
[2]For definition of median, see preface.   [3]Includes other minority races.
Source: U.S. Bureau of the Census, "Current Population Reports," series P-20.

YEARS OF SCHOOL COMPLETED, BY RACE AND SEX: 1960 AND 1970

Persons 25 years old and over. 1960 data as of April 1, based on 25-percent sample; 1970 data as of March, based on Current Population Survey; see text, p. 1. For definition of median, see preface

| YEAR, RACE, AND SEX | Persons 25 years old and over (1,000) | PERCENT OF POPULATION COMPLETING— | | | | | | | Median school years completed |
| | | Elementary school | | | High school | | College | | |
		0–4 years	5–7 years	8 years	1–3 years	4 years	1–3 years	4 years or more	
1960, all races	99,438	8.3	13.8	17.5	19.2	24.6	8.8	7.7	10.6
White	89,581	6.7	12.8	18.1	19.3	25.8	9.3	8.1	10.9
Male	43,259	7.4	13.7	18.4	18.9	22.2	9.1	10.3	10.7
Female	46,322	6.0	11.9	17.8	19.6	29.2	9.5	6.0	11.2
Black	9,054	23.8	24.2	12.9	19.0	12.9	4.1	3.1	8.2
Male	4,240	28.3	23.9	12.3	17.3	11.3	4.1	2.8	7.7
Female	4,814	19.8	24.5	13.4	20.5	14.3	4.1	3.3	8.6
1970, all races	109,310	5.3	9.1	13.4	17.1	34.0	10.2	11.0	12.2
White	98,112	4.2	8.3	13.6	16.5	35.2	10.7	11.6	12.2
Male	46,606	4.5	8.8	13.9	15.6	30.9	11.3	15.0	12.2
Female	51,506	3.9	7.8	13.4	17.3	39.0	10.1	8.6	12.2
Black	10,089	15.1	16.7	11.2	23.3	23.4	5.9	4.5	9.9
Male	4,619	18.6	16.0	11.1	21.9	22.2	5.7	4.6	9.6
Female	5,470	12.1	17.3	11.3	24.5	24.4	6.0	4.4	10.2

YEARS OF SCHOOL COMPLETED, BY RACE, SEX, AND AGE: 1971

Persons 25 years old and over as of March 1971.

| RACE, SEX, AND AGE | Popula-tion (1,000) | PERCENT OF POPULATION COMPLETING— | | | | | | | Median school years completed[1] |
| | | Elementary school | | | High school | | College | | |
		0–4 years	5–7 years	8 years	1–3 years	4 years	1–3 years	4 years or more	
All races	110,627	5.0	8.7	13.0	16.8	34.4	10.6	11.4	12.2
Male	52,357	5.6	8.9	13.4	15.8	30.6	11.1	14.6	12.2
Female	58,270	4.5	8.4	12.7	17.7	37.8	10.3	8.5	12.2
25–29 years	13,914	1.1	2.8	4.1	14.8	43.6	16.7	16.9	12.6
30–34 years	11,631	1.4	3.8	5.3	16.6	44.4	12.9	15.6	12.5
35–44 years	22,794	2.6	5.9	7.4	18.0	41.2	11.6	13.3	12.4
45–54 years	23,500	3.6	7.8	11.6	18.3	38.0	10.4	10.3	12.2
55 years and over	38,787	9.8	14.5	22.7	16.0	21.8	7.4	7.7	9.5
Black	10,250	13.5	17.4	10.8	23.5	24.2	6.0	4.5	10.1
25–29 years	1,495	1.8	5.8	6.7	28.2	40.2	11.0	6.4	12.2
30–34 years	1,236	2.3	8.0	5.3	30.4	38.9	8.7	6.2	12.1
35–44 years	2,335	5.4	14.2	8.8	30.3	29.3	6.9	5.1	11.1
45–54 years	2,146	11.8	21.0	15.0	23.2	19.6	5.9	3.7	9.3
55 years and over	3,037	31.2	27.0	13.7	13.5	9.6	2.0	2.8	7.1

[1]For definition of median, see preface.

Source of tables 168 and 169: U.S. Bureau of the Census, "U.S. Census of Population: 1960," vol. I and "Current Population Reports," series P–20.

PERCENT ENROLLED IN SCHOOL, BY AGE AND RACE: 1955 TO 1971

As of October.

AGE (in years)	1955 White	1955 Black and other	1960 White	1960 Black and other	1965 White	1965 Black and other	1970 White	1970 Black and other	1971 White	1971 Black and other
Total, 5–34.......	50.8	50.7	56.4	55.9	59.6	60.0	58.6	60.6	58.0	61.7
5 and 6...............	79.2	71.1	82.0	73.3	85.3	79.3	89.2	83.6	91.0	88.9
7–9...................	99.3	98.2	99.7	99.3	99.4	99.0	99.3	99.4	99.1	99.0
10–13................			99.5	99.0	99.4	99.3	99.1	99.4	99.2	98.9
14 and 15...........	87.5	82.8	98.1	95.9	99.0	98.2	98.2	97.6	98.7	98.2
16 and 17...........			83.3	76.9	87.8	84.6	90.6	86.2	90.5	88.8
18 and 19...........	32.1	27.6	38.9	34.6	47.1	40.1	48.7	41.9	49.4	48.1
20–24................	11.6	7.2	13.9	7.5	20.2	10.2	22.5	15.2	22.4	19.0
25–34................	2.8	3.3	3.8	1.9	4.9	3.1	6.1	5.2	6.6	6.4

Source: U.S. Bureau of the Census, "Current Population Reports," series P–20, and unpublished data.

SCHOOL ENROLLMENT, BY RACE, LEVEL OF SCHOOL, AND AGE: 1960, 1970, AND 1971

In thousands, except percent. As of October.

YEAR AND AGE	WHITE Total enrolled	WHITE Elemen- tary[1]	WHITE High school[1]	WHITE College[1]	BLACK AND OTHER Total enrolled	BLACK AND OTHER Elemen- tary[1]	BLACK AND OTHER High school[1]	BLACK AND OTHER College[1]
1960, total........	40,348	27,884	9,122	3,342	5,910	4,556	1,127	227
5–13 years..............	27,723	27,149	574	0	4,336	4,285	51	0
14–17 years.............	9,028	731	8,084	214	1,213	268	937	8
18–24 years.............	2,854	4	431	2,420	312	2	132	178
25–34 years.............	743	1	33	709	49	1	7	41
1970, total........	50,464	30,980	12,723	6,759	8,337	5,689	1,992	654
5–13 years..............	30,390	30,063	327	0	5,459	5,392	67	0
14–17 years.............	12,769	898	11,639	230	2,027	295	1,703	30
18–24 years.............	5,979	14	661	5,304	701	5	196	499
25–34 years.............	1,326	5	95	1,224	150	0	24	125
1971, total........	50,812	30,540	12,998	7,273	8,740	5,743	2,185	814
5–13 years..............	30,022	29,642	380	0	5,541	5,467	74	0
14–17 years.............	13,023	882	11,889	249	2,121	265	1,824	32
18–24 years.............	6,278	8	675	5,596	885	5	263	617
25–34 years.............	1,489	8	52	1,428	193	3	26	165
Percent change:								
1960–1970..............	25.9	9.5	42.5	117.4	47.9	26.1	93.9	258.6
1970–1971..............	0.7	—1.4	2.2	7.6	4.8	0.9	9.7	24.5

[1]Elementary includes kindergarten; high school, grades 9–12; college includes professional schools.
Source of tables 161 and 162: U.S. Bureau of the Census, "Current Population Reports," series P–20, and unpublished data.

SCHOOL ENROLLMENT OF PERSONS 5 TO 17 YEARS OLD, BY RACE AND RESIDENCE: 1960 TO 1971

Enrollment in thousands. As of October.

RESIDENCE	WHITE 1960	WHITE 1965	WHITE 1970[1]	WHITE 1971[1]	WHITE Percent change, 1960-71	BLACK AND OTHER 1960	BLACK AND OTHER 1965	BLACK AND OTHER 1970[1]	BLACK AND OTHER 1971[1]	BLACK AND OTHER Percent change, 1960-71
Total	36,750	40,928	43,232	43,105	17.3	5,549	6,554	7,508	7,680	38.4
Metropolitan...............	22,279	26,309	26,807	26,509	19.0	3,378	4,344	5,174	5,448	61.3
In central cities...........	9,645	9,806	9,238	8,844	—8.3	2,615	3,433	3,930	4,070	55.6
Outside central cities......	12,634	16,503	17,568	17,664	39.8	763	911	1,243	1,377	80.5
Nonmetropolitan...........	14,471	14,619	16,425	16,596	14.7	2,171	2,210	2,333	2,232	2.8

[1]Includes nursery school enrollment.
Source: U.S. Bureau of the Census, "Current Population Reports," series P–20, and unpublished data.

PREPRIMARY SCHOOL ENROLLMENT OF CHILDREN 3 TO 5 YEARS OLD, BY SELECTED CHARACTERISTICS: 1965, 1970, AND 1971

In thousands, except percent. As of October. Relates to civilian noninstitutional population. Includes both public and nonpublic pre-kindergarten and kindergarten programs; excludes 5-year-olds enrolled in programs above kindergarten and 6-year-olds enrolled in preprimary programs.

CHARACTERISTIC	1965			1970			1971		
	Population	Enrolled		Population	Enrolled		Population	Enrolled	
		Number	Percent		Number	Percent		Number	Percent
Total, 3-5 years of age[1]....	12,549	3,407	27.1	10,949	4,104	37.5	10,610	4,148	39.1
White........................	10,608	2,957	27.9	9,098	3,443	37.8	8,799	3,469	39.4
Negro and other...............	1,941	451	23.3	1,851	661	35.7	1,811	679	37.5
Family income:									
Less than $3,000.............	1,719	247	14.4	916	224	24.4	908	298	32.8
$3,000-$4,999...............	2,503	525	21.0	1,312	392	29.9	1,286	412	32.0
$5,000-$7,499...............	3,821	1,004	26.3	2,277	737	32.4	1,918	611	31.9
$7,500-$9,999...............	3,744	1,402	37.4	2,321	856	36.9	2,124	785	37.0
$10,000 and over.............				3,320	1,577	47.5	3,656	1,794	49.1
Occupation of family head:									
White-collar.................	4,177	1,516	36.3	3,807	1,791	47.0	3,665	1,731	47.2
Manual or service...........	6,264	1,453	23.2	5,231	1,678	32.1	4,877	1,711	35.1
Farm........................	659	63	9.6	346	82	23.6	331	81	24.5
Unemployed or not in labor force.....................	1,006	244	24.3	1,213	415	34.2	1,318	476	36.1
Residence:									
Metropolitan areas:[2]									
Central cities.............	3,500	1,048	29.9	3,088	1,218	39.4	2,788	1,219	43.7
Outside central cities.......	4,619	1,500	32.5	3,949	1,705	43.2	3,907	1,728	44.2
Nonmetropolitan areas........	4,430	861	19.4	3,913	1,181	30.2	3,915	1,201	30.7
Education of household head:									
Elementary, 0-8 years.........	(NA)	(NA)	(NA)	1,686	397	23.6	1,646	475	28.9
High School:									
1-3 years..................	(NA)	(NA)	(NA)	2,103	734	34.9	1,903	610	32.1
4 years....................	(NA)	(NA)	(NA)	3,831	1,381	36.0	3,720	1,416	38.1
College, 1 year or more.......	(NA)	(NA)	(NA)	2,977	1,452	48.8	2,922	1,499	51.3

NA   Not available.   [1]Includes children with family income, occupation of family head, and education of household heads not reported, not shown separately below.
[2] For definition of standard metropolitan statistical areas, see text, p. 2.
Source: U.S. Office of Education, "Preprimary Enrollment," annual.

BLACK-STUDENT ISOLATION IN LARGE CITY SCHOOL DISTRICTS, RANKED BY PERCENTAGE OF BLACK STUDENTS IN THE DISTRICT

	Present black	50 to 100 percent				80 to 100 percent			90 to 100 percent			100 percent		
		1965	1968	1970	1971	1968	1970	1971	1965	1968	1970	1968	1970	1971
Washington, D.C., 1971	95.2	99.3	99.1	98.8	99.7	96.5	97.0	97.6	90.4	94.2	95.0	27.8	33.5	35.2
Compton, Calif., 1971	85.0			100.0	100.0		92.7	97.8			90.5		15.8	7.4
Atlanta, Ga., 1971	72.1	98.8	94.6	93.4	92.0	91.8	87.0	85.9	97.4	90.0	77.9	78.1	33.6	21.6
Newark, N.J., 1971	72.0	90.3	97.9	97.1	97.4	88.4	91.2	91.3	51.3	85.6	86.4	19.3	19.8	22.5
Orleans Parish, La., 1971	71.4		91.2	92.2	93.4	83.3	81.9	80.8		81.2	78.6	62.3	48.5	47.2
Richmond, Va., 1971	69.1	98.5	93.6	88.3	93.9	88.6	56.8	36.5	98.5	84.6	44.7	78.0	9.6	.1
Baltimore City, Md., 1971	68.2	92.3	92.0	90.6	90.8	83.8	81.0	84.1	84.2	78.6	79.2	43.5	42.9	42.6
St. Louis, Mo., 1971	67.7	93.7	92.3	97.5	90.9	89.0	87.9	89.8	84.9	87.6	82.7	49.9	49.8	47.5
Gary, Ind., 1971	67.5	94.8	96.9	96.5	96.2	90.7	91.7	95.7	89.9	85.0	85.7	32.4	39.1	17.4
Detroit, Mich. 1971	65.0	91.5	91.0	92.6	93.7	79.1	79.3	78.6	72.3	69.0	73.0	10.6	13.7	12.1
Philadelphia, Pa. 1970	60.5	90.2	90.4	92.6		76.9	80.2		72.0	67.1	70.0	4.3	5.1	
Oakland, Calif., 1971	58.1	83.2	94.5	93.5	93.7	90.8	75.2	73.1	48.7	63.4	58.6	4.7	2.6	1.6
Cleveland, Ohio, 1971	57.3	94.6	95.2	95.8	95.4	92.7	90.9	91.3	82.3	86.0	89.2	24.7	34.8	35.4
Birmingham, Ala., 1971	56.4		92.8	84.2	86.1	90.8	73.5	74.7		91.6	69.7	84.6	33.5	34.6
Chicago, Ill., 1971	55.8	96.9	96.8	97.0	97.8	90.3	91.8	91.6	89.2	86.6	89.7	47.4	45.4	46.1
Memphis, Tenn., 1971	53.7	98.8	97.4	93.5	92.9	95.4	90.1	89.2	95.1	92.7	89.5	73.3	49.8	41.5
Kansas City, Mo., 1971	52.2	85.5	86.0	90.7	90.3	78.1	83.4	86.4	69.1	69.8	74.8	14.6	14.9	24.9
Caddo Parish, La., 1971	49.6		97.5	74.3	74.5	97.4	68.0	66.6		97.4	65.1	94.0	44.5	30.3
Louisville, Ky., 1971	48.8	84.5	86.5	88.3	87.3	64.9	77.4	82.3	69.5	52.7	68.4	77.1	4.3	15.6
Chatham County, Ga., 1971	48.2		90.7	80.5	40.6	86.5	67.1	7.6		86.5	48.5	84.2	15.6	0
Charleston County, S.C., 1971	48.0		87.2	69.2	71.3	84.2	59.9	62.4		84.2	53.7	49.6	13.6	24.9
Norfork, Va., 1971	47.9		88.5	67.1	49.6	82.3	55.9	1.2		79.6	46.3	16.9	26.1	0
Cincinnati, Ohio, 1971	46.1	88.0	78.1	83.1	86.3	50.9	54.0	54.9	49.4	43.9	39.5	59.9	15.7	10.6
Mobile County, Ala., 1971	45.9	99.9	89.1	81.8	64.2	87.5	54.4	44.2	99.9	87.5	47.1	22.2	10.1	15.3
Dayton, Ohio, 1971	42.7		89.1	87.0	84.4	82.7	77.8	78.1		82.7	73.4	9.8	9.5	14.6
Pittsburgh, Pa., 1971	41.1	82.8	78.7	76.7	76.6	60.0	57.5	61.6	49.5	52.5	56.2	0	13.2	9.5
Flint, Mich. 1971	40.9	85.9	75.8	81.0	79.6	42.4	38.2	46.6	67.9	37.3	30.4	5.6	2.1	1.9
Buffalo, N.Y., 1971	39.5	88.7	73.0	73.2	72.6	65.1	59.7	59.0	77.0	62.6	56.1	80.0	6.6	14.0
Baton Rouge Parish, La., 1971	39.0		94.4	78.0	77.1	94.2	71.9	72.0		91.0	68.7	64.5	29.1	21.0
Houston, Tex., 1971	37.8	97.6	94.7	91.6	91.3	90.9	85.4	86.0	93.0	88.0	73.7	10.8	8.8	8.7
Indianapolis, Ind., 1971	37.7	84.2	77.6	79.5	76.5	62.5	60.3	60.1	70.5	57.6	55.6	32.1	8.7	12.7
Dallas, Tex., 1971	36.3	90.3	97.9	97.3	85.0	93.0	94.1	83.4	82.6	87.6	91.4	0	23.2	10.5
Rochester, N.Y. 1971	35.7		54.4	59.1	51.0	34.4	44.2	33.7		12.1	24.2	10.2	0	0
New York, N.Y. 1971	34.3	55.5	80.3	83.7	83.9	60.5	65.7	69.2	20.7	52.2	57.9	70.0	11.9	6.0
Muscogee County, Ga., 1971	32.5		92.9	88.0	4.0	87.5	85.8	1.5		87.5	80.9	39.0	61.9	1.6
Charlotte-Mecklenburg County, N.C., 1971	31.8		72.3	9.3	2.1	68.1	4.1			58.9	1.8	76.7	0	0
Boston, Mass., 1971	31.7	79.5	76.7	82.0	85.1	54.5	65.1	63.2	35.4	43.1	52.0	.4	11.0	1.3
Duval County, Fla. 1971	31.3		87.4	74.4	64.0	87.4	57.5	38.2		87.4	54.9		37.0	23.0
San Francisco, Calif., 1971	30.4	72.3	84.5	85.8	90.6	46.6	55.5	22.3	21.1	34.3	31.7		1.1	1.3

City														
Winston-Salem-Forsyth County, N.C., 1971	29.4		84.7	63.0	4.3	84.7	57.4	2.7		84.4	57.0	70.9	43.8	0
Palm Beach County, Fla., 1971	28.6		81.4	74.9	37.1	79.5	40.6	10.8		76.2	29.4	72.3	0	0
Escambia County, Fla., 1971	28.4		77.5	58.7	57.6	71.3	16.6	15.2		70.0	29.9	70.0	48.4	20.4
Forth Worth, Tex., 1971	28.3	82.9	90.3	90.2	78.6	85.4	80.0	67.0	39.2	85.4	75.3	60.7	3.0	2.9
Richmond, Calif., 1971	28.2	80.8	6.16	49.7	51.2	43.4	33.2	30.8	34.3	34.8	45.2	5.1	3.0	1.7
Columbus, Ohio, 1971	28.0	86.8	71.2	74.1	71.9	56.9	53.0	53.9	72.4	40.7	62.4	3.1		5.6
Milwaukee, Wis., 1971	27.8		87.6	87.6	85.2	75.9	76.2	78.8		63.2	23.8	15.5	21.1	2.9
Akron, Ohio, 1971	27.2		62.3	63.5	66.3	39.4	49.3	40.2		23.7	62.4	3.9	3.5	
Nashville-Davidson County, Ky., 1971	27.2	87.5	83.2	75.9	17.5	69.4	67.0	0	39.5	61.3	48.5	51.8	47.8	2.6
Toledo, Ohio, 1971	26.7	96.8	77.4	80.7	77.5	64.1	59.3	59.4	90.5	52.4	77.6	9.8	12.3	30.0
Jefferson County, Ala., 1971	25.7		97.0	78.3	60.6	96.7	78.4	56.7		96.7	41.9	96.7	8.7	12.9
Dade County, Fla., 1971	24.9	81.1	87.6	94.1	77.0	82.0	53.1	53.2	47.7	80.7	83.3	48.6	22.8	7.6
Los Angeles, Calif., 1971	23.6		95.3	87.5	93.2	88.2	87.1	86.6		83.0	75.1	12.3	15.8	32.1
Oklahoma City, 1971	23.3	75.2	87.5	47.9	78.1	83.3	75.1	68.3	29.4	83.3	39.2	5.7	2.3	2.3
Broward County, Fla., 1971	22.4	82.9	88.5	59.2	71.3	79.7	41.1	8.0	60.8	79.7	20.2	68.9		1.5
Prince Georges County Md., 1971	22.2	77.2	43.9	1.5	61.3	25.6	35.0	39.8	65.9	20.7	11.4	13.9	19.5	0
Greenville, County, S.C., 1971	22.2	89.1	85.2	27.5	.9	83.3	.6	11.7	63.5	83.3	31.7	74.3	11.3	0
Polk County, Fla., 1971	20.7	86.1	67.3	51.3	20.1	66.7	12.1	.6	86.1	66.7	49.4	66.7	16.6	12.6
Jefferson Parish, La., 1971	19.5	98.7	79.5	76.6	6.1	79.5	36.3	.6	90.7	79.5	33.3	79.5		8.6
Hillsborough County, Fla., 1971	18.4		81.7	59.3	2.2	77.4	62.8	28.3		73.3	48.0	64.3	4.8	10.1
Orange County, Fla., 1971	18.0	00.4	79.9	73.3	47.1	77.1	52.0	61.6	9.9	77.1	3.3	77.1		
Omaha, Nebr., 1971	16.3		79.5	34.2	70.7	55.0	64.3	6.7		39.1	20.5	0	11.1	4.9
Sacramento, Calif., 1971	16.3	73.3	29.7	54.5	36.0	5.3	3.8	36.5	13.9	3.5	37.5	25.9	4.0	0
Pinellas County, Fla., 1971	15.7		78.3	55.4	5.2	73.2	20.9	36.1		72.1	20.5	0	14.7	0
Denver County, Colo., 1971	15.6	59.2	80.0	70.4	54.7	65.9	44.5	71.2	46.5	56.1	37.5	52.7	17.7	12.6
Fort Wayne, Ind., 1971	15.5	39.2	73.1	90.7	48.8	57.1	49.2	58.1	0	32.2	40.6	0		8.6
San Antonio, Tex., 1971	15.5		89.4	35.6	91.7	85.6	67.1	51.2		85.3	60.1	22.2	5.4	10.1
Wichita, Kans., 1971	14.7		54.5	84.0	63.9	53.4	31.5	3.1		47.4	31.5	45.7	0	
Austin, Tex., 1971	14.1		58.9	72.5	59.7	86.0	68.7	18.7		84.6	78.5	0	0	3.7
Tulsa, Okla., 1971	12.9		84.4	21.3	21.1	77.0	3.5			77.0	68.7	0	0	
Anne Arundel County, Md., 1971	12.9		19.7	37.7	32.4	2.5	30.0	8.3		0	2.4	30.2	0	
Clark County, Nev., 1971	12.8		51.9	59.4	44.3	51.9	25.1	55.6		51.9	30.0	29.2	.3	0
Seattle, Wash., 1970	12.8		55.2	44.1	64.8	24.4	7.8	10.5		8.1	3.1	0	.9	0
Rockford, Ill., 1971	12.8	00.4	41.5	67.9	10.5	64.3	56.3			54.7	7.8	0	0	0
San Diego, Calif., 1971	11.1		74.9	11.2	0	30.2	11.2	8.3		30.2	46.4	30.2	.5	0
Brevard County, Fla., 1971	10.2		30.2	12.6	65.5	37.8	12.6	55.6		37.8	11.2	29.2	0	.3
Virginia Beach, Va., 1971	10.1		37.8	65.0	47.6	12.4	21.3	10.5		20.5	12.6	0	3.2	0
Long Beach, Calif., 1971	9.8	73.3	63.4	37.9	35.2	24.9	67.0	0	13.9	76.6	17.4	25.6	0	0
Portland, Oreg., 1971	9.7		42.6	42.4	71.0	0	.6	21.2		0	51.2	0	.9	0
Minneapolis, Minn., 1971	9.3	59.2	29.2	75.6	42.8	76.6	67.0	6.7	46.5	47.0	14.7	4.3	0	0
Fresno, Calif., 1971	8.4	39.2	43.0	41.5	29.7	11.3	0	64.0	0	0	10.7	6.7		.3
Des Moines, Iowa, 1971	7.2		55.4	29.5	31.6	47.0	.6	8.0		47.0	54.0	0		0
De Kalb County, Ga., 1971	7.0		12.4	35.4	12.6	12.4	14.7	22.2		12.4	18.5	25.6		0
St. Paul, Minn., 1971	6.6		18.1	13.8	94.5	0	10.7	9.6		0	19.0	0	.5	.6
Kanawha County, W. Va., 1971	5.7		98.3	97.3	69.7	78.5	84.0	80.0		77.6	54.0	4.3	0	0
Corpus Christi, Tex., 1971	5.3		81.1	73.0	14.2	34.5	34.6	35.4		23.7	18.5	6.7	3.2	0
Tucson, Ariz., 1971	3.8		26.4	19.0	29.1	26.4	19.0	14.2		26.4	19.0	0		0
Jefferson County, Ky., 1971	3.0		38.2	42.2		24.1	20.3	18.5		25.9	18.5			0
El Paso, Tex., 1971	2.9			0	0	6.7				31.4	27.1	0		
Cobb County, Ga., 1971	2.6		72.4	63.8	65.6	51.2	38.0	46.9						
Albuquerque, N. Mex., 1971														

[1]*Toward Equal Educational Opportunity: The Report of the Select Committee on Equal Educational Opportunity, U.S. Senate, Dec. 31, 1972.

SEGREGATION OF BLACK STUDENTS IN PUBLIC SCHOOLS: 1968

For public elementary and secondary schools. Enrollment in thousands. As of fall. Excludes Hawaii.

STATE	Black students enrollment		Percent of Black enrollment in schools with total minority group enrollment of—			
	Total	Percent of total enrolled	Under 50 percent	50–100 percent	95–100 percent	100 percent
U.S.........	6,282	14.5	23.4	76.6	61.0	39.7
Ala..............	269	34.9	8.3	91.7	90.9	85.6
Alaska..........	2	3.0	100.0	0	0	0
Ariz.............	16	4.3	33.4	66.6	27.6	5.0
Ark.............	107	25.6	22.6	77.4	74.1	71.1
Calif............	388	8.7	22.5	77.5	47.8	7.2
Colo............	18	3.4	30.5	69.5	45.0	0
Conn...........	53	8.3	43.3	56.7	18.3	0.6
Del.............	24	19.4	54.2	45.8	21.6	0
D.C.............	139	93.5	0.9	99.1	89.2	27.8
Fla..............	312	23.2	23.2	76.8	72.1	59.1
Ga..............	315	31.5	14.0	86.0	83.4	76.4
Idaho...........	(Z)	0.2	100.0	0	0	0
Ill..............	406	18.0	13.6	86.4	72.4	38.6
Ind.............	106	8.8	30.0	70.0	43.5	12.8
Iowa............	10	1.5	73.1	26.9	3.6	0
Kans............	31	5.9	53.4	46.6	31.8	7.5
Ky..............	64	9.2	53.7	46.3	26.6	5.2
La..............	317	38.8	8.9	91.1	88.1	81.9
Maine..........	1	0.6	27.2	72.8	0	0
Md.............	201	23.4	31.1	68.9	52.6	31.2
Mass...........	47	4.3	51.2	48.8	18.3	0.2
Mich...........	276	13.3	20.6	79.4	46.4	9.0
Minn...........	9	1.1	79.0	21.0	4.0	0
Miss...........	224	49.0	6.7	93.3	92.7	88.2
Mo.............	138	14.5	24.6	75.4	66.0	33.4
Mont...........	(Z)	0.1	100.0	0	0	0
Nebr...........	12	4.6	27.3	72.7	35.0	0
Nev............	9	7.7	53.1	46.9	39.5	0
N.H.............	1	0.4	100.0	0	0	0
N.J.............	209	14.9	33.9	66.1	32.8	7.3
N. Mex.........	6	2.1	47.9	52.1	15.9	7.0
N.Y.............	473	14.1	32.3	67.7	35.8	7.5
N.C.............	352	29.4	28.3	71.7	65.1	59.0
N. Dak..........	1	0.4	100.0	0	0	0
Ohio...........	287	12.0	27.7	72.3	42.8	13.2
Okla...........	49	9.0	37.8	62.2	48.3	17.3
Oreg............	7	1.6	63.3	36.7	0	0
Pa..............	269	11.7	27.5	72.5	44.1	4.4
R.I.............	8	4.7	89.4	10.6	0	0
S.C.............	238	39.4	14.2	85.8	84.1	79.3
S. Dak..........	(Z)	0.3	93.7	6.3	3.1	0
Tenn...........	185	20.8	21.2	78.8	71.6	58.7
Tex.............	380	15.1	25.3	74.7	63.1	43.5
Utah............	2	0.5	73.9	26.1	0	0
Vt..............	(Z)	0.1	100.0	0	0	0
Va..............	245	23.5	26.9	73.1	68.2	58.0
Wash...........	19	2.4	64.2	35.8	0	0
W. Va..........	20	5.0	82.0	18.0	5.7	4.1
Wis.............	37	4.0	22.5	77.5	39.6	12.9
Wyo............	1	0.8	72.5	27.5	0	0

Z Less than 500.

Source: Dept. of Health, Education, and Welfare; Office of the Secretary.

ILLITERACY—AGE, SEX, AND RACE: 1959 AND 1969

In thousands of persons 14 years old and over, except percent. As of March 1959 and November 1969. 1959 excludes Alaska and Hawaii. Relates to civilian noninstitutional population. Based on Current Population Survey; see text, p. 1. Persons unable to both read and write in any language classified as illiterate. Information on illiteracy was obtained only for persons completing less than 6 years of school. See also "Historical Statistics, Colonial Times to 1957," series H 407–411]

AGE AND SEX	1959					1969				
	Population		Percent illiterate			Population		Percent illiterate		
	Total	Illiterate	Total	White	Black	Total	Illiterate	Total	White	Black
Total, 14 and over.....	121,373	2,619	2.2	1.6	7.5	143,137	1,433	1.0	0.7	3.6
14–24 years...............	25,118	144	0.6	0.5	1.2	36,853	97	0.3	0.2	0.5
25–44 years...............	46,143	575	1.2	0.8	5.1	46,501	237	0.5	0.4	1.3
45–64 years...............	35,205	929	2.6	1.8	11.3	40,985	449	1.1	0.7	5.5
65 years and over..........	14,907	971	6.5	5.1	25.5	18,798	650	3.5	2.3	16.7
Male, 14 and over.......	58,378	1,480	2.5	1.7	9.8	67,306	708	1.1	0.7	4.3
14–24 years...............	12,063	100	0.8	0.7	1.7	17,484	61	0.3	0.3	0.6
25–44 years...............	22,486	363	1.6	1.0	7.1	22,272	118	0.5	0.4	2.1
45–64 years...............	17,059	548	3.2	2.0	15.6	19,513	257	1.3	0.8	7.4
65 years and over..........	6,770	469	6.9	5.3	28.3	8,037	272	3.4	2.1	17.2
Female, 14 and over.....	62,995	1,139	1.8	1.4	5.4	75,831	727	1.0	0.7	2.9
14–24 years...............	13,055	44	0.3	0.3	0.7	19,369	37	0.2	0.2	0.3
25–44 years...............	23,657	212	0.9	0.6	3.4	24,229	121	0.5	0.5	0.6
45–64 years...............	18,146	381	2.1	1.6	7.3	21,472	191	0.9	0.6	4.0
65 years and over..........	8,137	502	6.2	5.0	23.0	10,761	378	3.5	2.4	16.2

Source: U.S. Bureau of the Census, Current Population Reports, series P–20, Nos. 99 and 217.

HIGH SCHOOL GRADUATES AND SCHOOL DROPOUTS, 16 TO 21 YEARS OLD— EMPLOYMENT STATUS, BY SEX AND RACE: 1965 TO 1971

In thousands, except percent. As of October. Data for high school graduates relate to those not enrolled in college and include those who attended college prior to survey date; data for dropouts relate to persons not in regular school and not high school graduates. Based on samples and subject to sampling variability.

EMPLOYMENT STATUS, SEX, AND RACE	GRADUATES				DROPOUTS			
	1965	1969	1970	1971	1965	1969	1970	1971
Civilian noninstitutional population.......	4,898	5,339	5,823	5,973	2,986	2,683	2,757	2,812
Not in labor force.............................	1,129	1,115	1,257	1,257	1,123	1,096	1,146	1,097
In labor force...................................	3,769	4,223	4,566	4,716	1,863	1,588	1,611	1,715
Percent of population.......................	76.9	79.1	78.4	79.0	62.4	59.2	58.4	61.0
Male...	1,617	1,650	1,966	2,105	1,265	977	1,024	1,111
Female..	2,152	2,573	2,600	2,566	598	611	587	604
White..	3,375	3,742	4,065	4,233	1,469	1,223	1,243	1,355
Black and other..............................	394	481	501	483	394	365	368	360
Employed.......................................	3,451	3,897	4,038	4,182	1,585	1,358	1,264	1,355
Percent of labor force.....................	91.6	92.3	88.4	88.7	85.1	85.5	78.5	79.0
Male...	1,512	1,540	1,730	1,901	1,105	868	805	894
Female..	1,939	2,357	2,308	2,281	480	490	459	461
White..	3,116	3,490	3,636	3,804	1,266	1,058	1,011	1,091
Black and other..............................	335	406	402	378	319	301	253	264
Unemployed.....................................	318	326	528	534	278	230	347	360
Percent of labor force.....................	8.4	7.7	11.6	11.3	14.9	14.5	21.5	21.0
Male...	105	110	236	249	160	109	219	217
Female..	213	216	292	285	118	121	128	143
White..	259	250	429	429	203	165	232	264
Black and other..............................	59	76	99	105	75	65	115	96

Source: U.S. Bureau of Labor Statistics, "Special Labor Force Report," Nos. 66, 121, and forthcoming report.

PERCENT WITH 4 YEARS OF HIGH SCHOOL OR MORE
IN THE CIVILIAN LABOR FORCE, AGES 25-34, 1970 AND 1980

	Black and other	White
1970	59	78
1980[1]	74	84

[1]Projection
Source: Johnston, Dennis, "Education of Adult Workers," Special Labor Force Report No. 122, and William Deutermann, "Educationa
Attainment of Workers, March 1969 and 1970," Special Labor Force Report No. 125.

PERCENT OF BLACK MEN WITH
4 YEARS OF HIGH SCHOOL OR MORE,
1970, BY REGION

Region	Younger men Ages 25-44	Older men Ages 45-64
West	72.4	45.6
North	50.0	29.5
South	36.0	17.3

Source: U.S. Department of Commerce, Bureau of the Census, "Current Population Reports," Series P-20, No. 207.

PERCENT OF POPULATION AGES 25-29
WITH 4 YEARS OF HIGH SCHOOL OR MORE,
AND 4 YEARS OF COLLEGE OR MORE

Year	4 years high school or more Black	White	4 years college or more Black	White
1960	38.6[1]	63.7	5.4[1]	11.8
1964	45.1	72.1	5.6	13.6
1968	55.9	75.2	5.4	15.6
1970	56.1	77.8	7.3	17.2

[1]Black and other races.
Source: U.S. Department of Commerce, Bureau of Census, "Current Population Reports," Series P-20, Numbers 138, 182, 194, and 207.

COURSES AND ENROLLMENTS IN ETHNIC STUDIES

FIELD OF STUDY	Insts. Offering Minimum of One Course*	Courses, Fall 1972	Combined Enrollments, Fall 1972	Insts. Offering Specialization, 1972-73 Major	Minor	Graduates with Specialization, July '71-June '72 Major	Minor
American Indian....	344	593	17,329	3	4	3	16
Asian-American....	272	866	15,891	19	13	21	95
Black..............	1,272	5,611	142,934	182	96	335	141
Spanish-speaking...	394	1,883	53,294	98	58	205	24
White Ethnic........	135	315	6,074	25	4	53	0
Other Ethnic........	110	242	4,127	6	4	49	18
Multiethnic.........	339	690	31,135	25	7	392	0
Total.............	1,584**	10,200	270,784	***	***	1,058	294

*Institutions represent a 20-per-cent weighted sample of the eligible population of 2,578.
**Column does not add because some institutions offer courses in more than one ethnic-studies area.
***Totals not applicable.
Source: American Council on Education.

MAJOR OCCUPATION GROUP OF EMPLOYED PERSONS, BY SEX, RACE, AND YEARS OF SCHOOL COMPLETED: 1959 AND 1971

Relates to civilian noninstitutional population 18 years old and over as of March of years indicated. Based on Current Population Survey.

YEAR, SEX, AND OCCUPATION GROUP	WHITE			BLACK AND OTHER		
	Total	Less than 4 years of high school	4 years of high school or more	Total	Less than 4 years of high school	4 years of high school or more
1959						
Male, number..................1,000..	37,766	18,740	19,026	3,745	2,928	816
Percent, by occupation:						
White collar...................................	39.7	20.3	58.8	12.6	5.3	38.8
Blue collar...................................	45.5	58.9	32.3	59.3	65.4	37.3
Service, incl. private household workers...........	5.6	7.2	4.0	14.3	12.6	20.2
Farm...	9.2	13.7	·4.9	13.9	16.7	3.7
Female, number..................1,000..	17,776	6,994	10,782	2,484	1,725	759
Percent, by occupation:						
White collar...................................	61.1	31.5	80.3	17.6	5.8	44.5
Blue collar...................................	17.2	31.4	8.0	14.7	15.7	12.4
Service, incl. private household workers...........	18.5	31.6	10.0	64.3	73.8	42.6
Farm...	3.2	5.5	1.6	3.4	4.7	0.5
1971						
Male, number..................1,000..	42,159	13,737	28,422	4,575	2,503	2,072
Percent, by occupation:						
White collar...................................	44.6	18.5	57.2	22.1	8.2	38.8
Blue collar...................................	43.7	63.3	34.2	57.9	66.9	47.1
Service, incl. private household workers...........	7.0	9.7	5.7	15.2	17.3	12.7
Farm...	4.8	8.5	3.0	4.8	7.7	1.3
Female, number..................1,000..	24,998	6,616	18,382	3,527	1,549	1,978
Percent, by occupation:						
White collar...................................	64.9	29.9	77.4	37.8	11.6	58.3
Blue collar...................................	15.3	34.4	8.4	17.2	20.7	14.4
Service, incl. private household workers...........	18.6	33.2	13.4	44.3	66.4	27.0
Farm...	1.2	2.6	0.8	0.7	1.3	0.3

Source: U.S. Bureau of Labor Statistics, "Special Labor Force Report."

WORK AND SCHOOL STATUS OF BLACK TEENAGERS: OCTOBER 1971

SUBJECT	Number (thousands)	Percent
Total....................	1,912	(X)
Enrolled in school...........	1,320	100
Employed......................	191	14
Unemployed....................	113	9
Looking for full-time work.....	14	1
Looking for part-time work.....	99	7
Not in labor force..............	1,016	77
Not enrolled in school.......	592	100
Employed......................	262	44
Unemployed....................	104	18
Looking for full-time work.....	96	16
Looking for part-time work.....	8	1
Not in labor force..............	226	38

X   Not applicable.

Source: U.S. Department of Commerce, Social and Economic Statistics Administration, Bureau of the Census.

ESTIMATE OF INCOMES FORGONE BY FAILURE TO INVEST IN A MINIMUM OF HIGH SCHOOL COMPLETION FOR ALL MALES 25 TO 34 YEARS OLD

	Gross income forgone (billions)	After 25 percent ability adjustment
White:		
High school completion...................	$178	$133.5
College................................	90	67.5
Total whites...........................	268	201.0
Nonwhite:		
High school completion...................	32	24.0
College................................	16	12.0
Total nonwhites.......................	48	36.0
Total all males 25 to 34 years old.........	316	237.0

ESTIMATED COST OF WELFARE EXPENDITURES FROM INADEQUATE EDUCATION IN 1970

	Millions
Aid to families with dependent children....................	$4,082
Medical assistance......................................	1,199
General assistance......................................	640
Public assistance total...............................	5,921
Unemployment compensation.............................	4,322
Upper estimate:	
Public assistance total X 50 percent....................	2,961
Unemployment compensation X 25 percent..............	1,081
Upper estimate total..............................	4,042
Lower estimate:	
Public assistance total X 25 perecnt...................	1,480
Unemployment compensation X15 percent..............	648
Lower estimate total..............................	2,128

Source: AFDC. General Assistance and Medical Assistance Expenditures—Sources of Funds Expended for Public Assistance Payments, table 1, 25 percent of medical assistance payments were approximated as AFDC share. The 1968 share was 27.9 percent. See U.S. Department of Health, Education, and Welfare. Social and Rehabilitation Service. Medicaid, Selected Statistics 1951–69. Unemployment compensation payments are taken from U.S. Department of Health, Education, and Welfare, Social Security Bulletin (April 1971), table M1.

WORK AND TRAINING PROGRAMS—SELECTED CHARACTERISTICS OF ENROLLEES: 1970 AND 1971

For years ending June 30. Covers work and training programs administered by the U.S. Department of Labor

YEAR AND PROGRAM	Total enrollees (1,000)	PERCENT							
		Male	Black and other races (excl. white)	Age in years			Education, by grade		
				Under 22	22–44	45 and over	Less than 9th	9th–11th	12th and over
1970									
Manpower Development and training Program:									
Institutional	130	59	41	37	54	9	15	38	47
Jobs optional program/On-the-job training	91	66	33	35	54	11	17	37	46
Neighborhood Youth Corps:									
In school (enrolled Sept.–May)	74	50	46	100	–	–	17	82	1
Out of school (enrolled Sept.–Aug.)	46	48	50	98	2	–	32	66	2
Summer (enrolled June–Aug.)	362	54	56	100	–	–	21	78	1
Operation Mainstream	13	71	38	4	46	51	52	28	20
Public Service Careers[2]	4	23	68	21	72	7	13	42	45
Concentrated Employment Program	110	59	74	41	51	8	20	45	35
JOBS Program[3]	87	69	78	47	49	4	15	50	35
Work Incentive Program	93	29	48	23	71	6	24	44	32
Job Corps	43	74	74	100	–	–	37	56	7
1971									
Manpower Development and Training Program:									
Institutional	156	58	44	40	52	8	13	36	51
Jobs optional program/On-the-job training	72	74	31	35	55	10	15	33	52
Neighborhood Youth Corps:									
In school[4]	687	55	62	100	–	–	20	76	4
Out of school (enrolled Sept.–Aug.)	53	51	47	94	6	–	29	69	3
Operation Mainstream	22	73	36	5	55	40	45	30	25
Concentrated Employment Program	94	60	69	46	48	6	16	44	40
JOBS Program[3]	93	66	64	45	50	5	18	44	38
Work Incentive Program	112	38	44	27	60	5	20	43	37
Job Corps	50	74	73	100	–	–	32	59	9

– Represents zero.   [1]See footnote 4, table 219.   [2]Includes new careers programs.
[3]Job opportunities in the business sector.   [4]Includes enrollees in summer programs.
Source of tables 219 and 220: U.S. Manpower Administration, "Manpower Report of the President," 1972.

ADULT EDUCATION—PARTICIPATION, BY SEX, RACE, AGE, AND SOURCE OF INSTRUCTION: AS OF MAY 1969

SOURCE OF INSTRUCTION	Total	SEX		RACE			AGE	
		Male	Female	White	Black	Other	Under 35	35 and over
Total participants.....................1,000....	13,150	6,898	6,253	12,036	981	133	6,852	6,298
Percent:[1]								
Public or private schools	27.7	22.6	33.3	27.1	33.8	36.8	27.2	28.2
College or university, part-time	25.2	26.9	23.3	25.5	21.9	21.8	30.4	19.5
Job training	27.5	37.1	16.9	27.4	28.7	21.8	28.3	26.6
Correspondence courses	8.0	10.7	5.0	8.3	4.6	4.5	9.3	6.6
Community organizations	13.4	8.3	19.1	13.6	11.4	15.8	9.4	17.8
Tutor or private instructor	5.8	3.9	7.9	5.9	3.3	10.5	4.6	7.1
Other	10.3	10.2	10.4	10.3	9.4	12.8	9.5	11.1

[1]Percentages total more than 100, since some adults received instruction from more than one source.
Source: U.S. Office of Education, "Participation in Adult Education, 1969: Initial Report." Also in "Digest of Educational Statistics, 1970."

BLACK ORIENTED INSTITUTIONS OF HIGHER EDUCATION

	President	Control	Enrollment	Faculty
ALABAMA				
Alabama A&M University, Normal (1875)	Richard D. Morrison	Pub.	3,009	156
Alabama State, Montgomery (1874)	Levi Watkins	Pub.	2,704	115
Miles College, Birmingham (1905)	W. C. Williams	Pr.	1,270	78
Oakwood College, Huntsville (1896)	Calvin B. Rock	Pr.	684	45
Stillman College, Tuscaloosa (1876)	Harold N. Stinson	Pr.	660	45
Talladega College, Talladega (1867)	Herman H. Long	Pr.	520	57
Tuskegee Institute, Tuskegee (1881)	Luther H. Foster	Pr.	3,073	246
ARKANSAS				
Arkansas Baptist College, Little Rock (1884)	J. C. Oliver	Pr.	430	39
Philander Smith College, Little Rock (1877)	Walter Hazzard	Pr.	670	45
University of Arkansas—Pine Bluff (1873)	Lawrence A. Davis	Pub.	2,936	167
DELAWARE				
Delaware State College, Dover (1891)	Luna I. Mishoe	Pub.	1,921	105
DISTRICT OF COLUMBIA				
District of Columbia Teachers College (1851)	Paul P. Cooke	Pub.	2,878	155
Federal City College (1966)	Elgy S. Johnson	Pub.	7,184	300
Howard University (1867)	James E. Cheek	Pr.	10,152	1,400
FLORIDA				
Bethune-Cookman College, Daytona Beach (1872)	Richard V. Moore	Pr.	1,219	61
Edward Waters College, Jacksonville (1866)	William B. Stewart	Pr.	803	50
Florida A&M University, Tallahassee (1887)	Benjamin L. Perry, Jr.	Pub.	4,944	295
Florida Memorial College, Miami (1879)	Royal W. Puryear	Pr.	821	50
GEORGIA				
Albany State College, Albany (1903)	Charles L. Hayes	Pub.	1,926	133
Atlanta University, Atlanta (1865)	Thomas D. Jarrett	Pr.	1,048	N.A.
Clark College, Atlanta (1869)	Vivian W. Henderson	Pr.	1,182	107
Ft. Valley State College, Ft. Valley (1939)	Waldo W. E. Blanchet	Pub.	2,373	114
Interdenominational Theological Center, Atlanta, (1958)	Oswald P. Bronson	Pr.	164	
Morehouse College, Atlanta (1867)	Hugh M. Gloster	Pr.	1,227	84
Morris Brown College, Atlanta (1881)	John A. Middleton	Pr.	1,524	92
Paine College, Augusta (1882)	Lucius H. Pitts	Pr.	737	61
Savannah State College, Savannah (1776)	Prince A. Jackson, Jr.	Pub.	2,728	105
Spelman College, Atlanta (1881)	Albert E. Manley	Pr.	1,118	90
KENTUCKY				
Kentucky State, Frankfort (1886)	Carl M. Hill	Pub.	1,970	145
LOUISIANA				
Dillard University, New Orleans (1869)	Broadus N. Butler	Pr.	982	112
Grambling College, Grambling (1901)	Ralph W. E. Jones	Pub.	3,193	203
Southern University, Baton Rouge (1880)	G. Leon Netterville, Jr.	Pub.	8,414	534
Southern University, New Orleans (1956)	Emmett W. Bashful	Pub.	2,134	N.A.
Xavier University, New Orleans (1925)	Norman C. Francis	Pr.	1,554	131
MARYLAND				
Bowie State College, Bowie (1865)	Samuel L. Myers	Pub.	2,353	137
Coppin State College, Baltimore (1900)	Calvin W. Burnett	Pub.	2,488	83
Morgan State College, Baltimore (1867)	King V. Cheek, Jr.	Pub.	5,743	279
University of Maryland, Eastern Shore (1970)	Archie L. Buffkins	Pub.	771	60
MISSISSIPPI				
Alcorn A&M College, Lorman (1871)	Walter Washington	Pub.	2,677	116
Jackson State, Jackson (1877)	John A. Peoples, Jr.	Pub.	5,058	300
Mississippi Industrial College, Holly Springs (1905)	Edgar E. Rankin, Jr.	Pr.	285	N.A.
Mississippi Valley State College, Itta Bena (1946)	Ernest A. Boykins	Pub.	2,410	132
Rust College, Holly Springs (1866)	William A. McMillan	Pr.	747	42
Tougaloo College, Tougaloo (1869)	George A. Owens	Pr.	750	65
MISSOURI				
Lincoln University, Jefferson City (1866)	Walter C. Daniel	Pub.	2,620	147

NORTH CAROLINA

Barber-Scotia College, Concord (1867)	Jerome L. Gresham	Pr.	550	44
Bennett College, Greensboro (1873)	Isaac H. Miller, Jr.	Pr.	582	71
Elizabeth City State University, Elizabeth City (1891)	Marion D. Thorpe	Pub.	1,084	82
Fayetteville State University, Fayetteville (1877)	Charles A. Lyons, Jr.	Pub.	1,490	96
Johnson C. Smith University, Charlotte (1867)	Wilbert Greenfield	Pr.	1,036	73
Livingstone College, Salisbury (1879)	F. George Shipman	Pr.	754	82
North Carolina A&T State University, Greensboro (1891)	Lewis C. Dowdy	Pub.	4,445	274
North Carolina Central University, Durham (1910)	Albert N. Whiting	Pub.	3,723	269
St. Augustine's College, Raleigh (1867)	Prezell R. Robinson	P.	1,284	73
Shaw University, Raleigh (1865)	James A. Hargraves	Pr.	1,061	84
Winston-Salem State University, Winston-Salem (1892)	Kenneth R. Williams	Pub.	1,623	109

OHIO

Central State University, Wilberforce (1887)	Lionel H. Newsome	Pub.	2,525	158
Wilberforce University, Wilberforce (1856)	Rembert E. Stokes	Pr.	1,328	46

OKLAHOMA

Langston University, Langston (1897)	William E. Sims	Pub.	1,236	79

PENNSYLVANIA

Cheyney State College, Cheyney (1837)	Wade Wilson	Pub.	2,362	210
Lincoln University, Lincoln (1854)	Herman R. Branson	Pub.	1,067	98

SOUTH CAROLINA

Allen University, Columbia (1870)	J. W. Hairston	Pr.	456	66
Benedict College, Columbia (1870)	Luns Richardson (Act.)	Pr.	1,487	88
Claflin College, Orangeburg (1869)	Hubert V. Manning	Pr.	795	55
Morris College, Sumter (1908)	Henry E. Hardin	Pr.	520	N.A.
South Carolina State, Orangeburg (1896)	M. Maceo Nance, Jr.	Pub.	2,383	145
Voorhees College, Denmark (1897)	Harry P. Graham	Pub.	736	46

TENNESSEE

Fisk University, Nashville (1865)	James R. Lawson	Pr.	1,413	120
Knoxville College, Knoxville (1875)	Edward J. Brantley	Pr.	1,039	100
Lane College, Jackson (1882)	Herman Stone, Jr.	Pr.	921	58
Le Moyne-Owen College, Memphis (1870)	Odell Horton	Pr.	712	56
Meharry Medical College, Nashville (1876)	Lloyd C. Elam	Pr.	571	239
Morristown Normal & Ind. College, Morristown (1881)	Raymon E. White	Pr.	150	14
Tennessee State University, Nashville (1912)	Andrew P. Torrence	Pub.	4,576	276

TEXAS

Bishop College, Dallas (1881)	Milton K. Curry, Jr.	Pr.	1,561	142
Huston-Tillotson College, Austin (1876)	John T. King	Pr.	717	58
Jarvis Christian College, Hawkins (1912)	John Paul Jones	Pr.	645	51
Paul Quinn College, Waco (1872)	Stanley E. Rutland	Pr.	457	45
Prairie View A&M, Prairie View (1876)	Alvin I. Thomas	Pub.	4,115	N.A.
St. Phillips College, San Antonio (1898)	John B. Murphy	Pub.	3,122	N.A.
Texas College, Tyler (1894)	Allen C. Hancock	Pr.	511	39
Texas Southern University, Houston (1947)	Granville M. Sawyer	Pub.	6,174	260
Wiley College, Marshall (1873)	Robert E. Hayes	Pr.	510	41

VIRGINIA

Hampton Institute, Hampton (1868)	Roy D. Hudson	Pr.	2,587	208
Norfolk State College, Norfolk (1935)	Lyman B. Brooks	Pub.	5,678	300
St. Paul's College, Lawrenceville (1888)	James A. Russell, Jr.	Pub.	512	43
Virginia College, Lynchburg (1888)	M. C. Southerland	Pr.	91	N.A.
Virginia State College, Petersburg (1882)	Wendell P. Russell	Pub.	3,684	216
Virginia Union University, Richmond (1865)	Allix B. James	Pr.	1,107	81

WEST VIRGINIA

Bluefield State College, Bluefield (1895)	Wendell G. Hardway	Pub.	1,177	83
West Virginia State College, Institute (1891)	William J. L. Wallace	Pub.	3,590	154

ENROLLMENT IN INSTITUTIONS OF HIGHER EDUCATION—TOTAL AND BLACK BY GEOGRAPHIC DIVISION: 1968 AND 1970

Enrollment in thousands. As of fall. Excludes Alaska and Hawaii. Covers full-time undergraduate students taking credits equal to at least 75 percent of a normal load. Excludes federally controlled institutions.

Geographic Division	Number of institutions	Total enrollment	BLACK ENROLLMENT	
			Number	Percent
1968, total..............	2,054	4,820	287	6.0
1970, total..............	[1]2,054	5,187	357	6.9
New England.................	182	342	10	2.8
Middle Atlantic...............	309	798	46	5.7
East North Central............	315	1,017	58	5.7
West North Central...........	256	484	13	2.6
South Atlantic................	354	671	93	13.9
East South Central............	153	302	45	15.0
West South Central...........	172	505	50	9.9
Mountain....................	86	294	4	1.5
Pacific......................	227	774	37	4.8

[1]1968 data latest available.

Source: U.S. Office for Civil Rights, "Undergraduate Enrollment by Ethnic Group in Federally Funded Institutions of Higher Education, Fall 1968" and "Fall 1970."

INSTITUTIONS OF HIGHER EDUCATION ATTENDED PREDOMINANTLY BY BLACKS—NUMBER, FACULTY, AND ENROLLMENT, BY TYPE: 1950 TO 1970

YEAR	Number of institutions	FACULTY			ENROLLMENT (1,000)			
		Male	Female	Total	Public		Private	
					2-year	4-year	2-year	4-year
1950[1]..............	105	4,151	2,782	76.6	(NA)	(NA)	(NA)	(NA)
1960[1]..............	106	(NA)	(NA)	88.9	(NA)	(NA)	(NA)	(NA)
1964[1]..............	107	6,209	3,759	105.5	4.3	60.7	1.9	38.6
1968..............	(NA)	(NA)	(NA)	162.5	2.6	99.0	6.3	54.6
1969..............	(NA)	(NA)	(NA)	170.5	2.8	105.5	9.2	53.0
1970..............	(NA)	(NA)	(NA)	179.2	2.8	113.2	8.3	54.9

NA Not available.   [1]Enrollment ⅞ resident degree-credit students, regular session, only.

Source: U.S. Office of Education, "Biennial Survey of Education in the United States"; "Faculty and Other Professional Staff in Institutions of Higher Education;" "Total Enrollment in Institutions of Higher Education, First Term, 1959–60;" "Resident and Extension Enrollment in Institutions of Higher Education, Fall 1963;" and "Report on Higher Education."

COLLEGE FACULTY MEMBERS—BY SEX: 1969

Percent distribution. As of Spring. Covers all universities, 4-year colleges, and 2-year colleges, both publicly and privately controlled. Based on a sample survey.

CHARACTERISTIC	Total	Male	Female
Total..............	100.0	100.0	100.0
Race:			
White..............	96.3	96.6	94.7
Black..............	2.2	1.8	3.9
Other..............	1.6	1.6	1.4

Source: U.S. Office of Education, "Digest of Educational Statistics, 1971."

AVAILABLE SCHOLARSHIPS, FELLOWSHIPS, AND LOANS

GENERAL AID

ALPHA PHI ALPHA EDUCATIONAL FOUNDATION, INC.
4778 Lakewood Rd.
Ravenna, Ohio 44266
Scholarship awards of $300 to $500 available to H.S. seniors. Awards are renewable for four years.

AMERICAN LEADERS FOUNDATION
c/o Northwestern Pennsylvania
Bank and Trust Co.
P.O. Box 037
Scranton, Pa. 18501
Amounts vary according to individual need. Student must have at least one year of college and not be over 28.

CATHOLIC SCHOLARSHIPS FOR NEGROES, INC.
Mrs. Roger L. Putnam, President
254 Union Street
Springfield, Mass. 01105
For H.S. seniors (not limited to Catholics). Applications must be made in the fall for consideration for the following school year.

COCA-COLA CO.
P.O. Drawer 1743
Atlanta, Ga. 30310

COOPERATIVE PROGRAM, EDUCATIONAL OPPORTUNITY
17 Hill House Avenue
New Haven, Conn. 06520
For H.S. seniors. Major part of the program focuses on blacks. Students admitted to program receive necessary amount of financial aid.

COUNCIL ON LEGAL EDUCATION OPPORTUNITY
863 Fair St., S. W., Atlanta, Ga. 30314

DIRECTOR OF INDIAN EDUCATION
Centennial Building
St. Paul, Minn. 55101
Minnesota students of at least one-fourth Indian ancestry attending advanced or specialized education in accredited or approved college, business, technical or vocational schools are eligible for tuition, incidental fees, and room and board not to exceed $800 per academic year for four years.

ELKS NATIONAL FOUNDATION SCHOLARSHIPS
Mr. John F. Malley
40 Court Street, Boston, Mass. 02108
Grants student awards annually from $800 to $1,500. H.S. seniors and college undergraduates are eligible.

FORD FOUNDATION DOCTORAL FELLOWSHIPS FOR BLACK STUDENTS
320 East 43rd Street
New York, N.Y. 10017
Doctoral fellowships for black students.

GENERAL MOTORS CORPORATION
8163 G. M. Building
Detroit, Mich. 48202
Any H.S. senior is eligible to apply for GM scholarships. The awards range from $200 to $2,000 (depending on need) and are renewable.

HATTIE M. STRONG FOUNDATION
409 Cafritz Bldg.
1625 1 St. N.W.
Washington, D.C. 20006

HERBERT L. LEHMAN EDUCATION FUND
10 Columbus Circle, Suite 2030
New York, N.Y. 10019

MANHATTAN COLLEGE SCHOLARSHIP
Financial Aid Office Manhattan College
Bronx, N.Y. 10471
For black students at Manhattan College. Amounts up to tuition costs each year.

THE MARTIN LUTHER KING, JR. FELLOWSHIP
Woodrow Wilson Fellowship Foundation
32 Nassau St.
Princeton, N.J. 08540

MARTIN LUTHER KING MEMORIAL SCHOLARSHIP
Financial Aid Department
University of Southern California
Los Angeles, Calif. 90024
For black students. Tuition, plus several hundred dollars for miscellaneous expenses.

MARTIN LUTHER KING, JR. SCHOLARSHIP FUND
Office of Admission and Financial Aid
New York University
13 University Place
New York, N.Y. 10003
For graduate and undergraduate minority students —awarded according to financial need.

MINORITY GROUPS SCHOLARSHIP PROGRAM
Write to:
Antioch College, Yellow Springs, Ohio 45387
Carleton College, Northfield, Minn. 55057
Grinnell College, Grinnell, Iowa 50112
Oberlin College, Oberlin, Ohio 44074
Reed College, Portland, Oreg. 97202
Occidental College, Los Angeles, Calif. 90041
Swarthmore College, Swarthmore, Pa. 19081
Available through the Rockefeller Foundation, these scholarships are open to any H.S. student applying to one of the above colleges.

N.A.A.C.P. "INC. FUND"
10 Columbus Circle, Suite 2030
New York, N.Y. 10019

NATIONAL ACHIEVEMENT AND SCHOLARSHIP PROGRAM FOR OUTSTANDING NEGRO STUDENTS
900 Grove Street
Evanston, Ill. 60201
H.S. seniors, apply through your H.S. principal or guidance counselor ($1,000-$6,000 scholarships for four years). Candidates must take the National Merit Scholarship Qualifying Test.

THE NATIONAL MERIT SCHOLARSHIP CORPORATION
990 Grove Street
Evanston, Ill. 60201
For eng., lib. arts, bus. adm., education, pharmacy, and nursing.

NATIONAL MERIT SCHOLARSHIP CORPORATION
990 Grove Street
Evanston, Ill. 60201
For biomedical eng., science eng., industrial relations, dramatic arts, music, etc. Students must qualify on the basis of the NMSQT and the SAT. These tests are administered at the students' respective high schools. Winners are given up to $1,500 per year respective high schools. Winners are given up to $1,500 per year (according to need) and may attend the colleges of their choice.

NATIONAL SCHOLARSHIP SERVICE AND FUND FOR NEGRO STUDENTS
1776 Broadway
New York, N.Y. 10019
Applicant must receive some counseling from NSSFNS

OPPORTUNITY FELLOWSHIP PROGRAM
John Hay Whitney Foundation
111 W. 50th St.
New York, N.Y.

RADIO CORPORATION OF AMERICA
These awards are administered through individual educational institutions and are offered in a number of fields. Each award is $800 (renewable). Additional information is available through college admissions offices.

ROCKEFELLER FOUNDATION
Write to:
  Duke University, Durham, N.C.
  Emory University, Atlanta, Ga.
  Tulane University, New Orleans, La.
  Vanderbilt University, Nashville, Tenn.
Scholarship aid primarily, but not exclusively, for disadvantages students—graduates of Southern high schools.

UNITED NEGRO COLLEGE FUND
55 E. 52nd Street
New York, N.Y. 10022
Available to H.S. seniors and college undergraduates for use at any of the forty member-colleges of the fund. Application may be made through the admissions officer of the respective college, or to the above address.

JOHN HAY WHITNEY FOUNDATION
111 West 50th Street
New York, N.Y. 10020
Primarily for students deprived because of racial discrimination. Must be a college senior about to begin graduate work. $3,000 yearly maximum.

GOVERNMENT AID PROGRAMS

(In this category are listed a limited number of scholarships and fellowships offered through governmental agencies.)

HIGHER EDUCATION PERSONNEL FELLOWSHIPS
Write to:
  Division of University Programs
  Bureau of Higher Education
  U.S. Department of Health, Education
  and Welfare
  Washington, D.C. 20202
Grants are made to colleges and universities to assist them in training teachers, administrators or education specialists. Priority is extended to programs to prepare personnel for junior colleges and for work with the disadvantaged at colleges and universities.

THE NATIONAL DEFENSE STUDENT LOAN PROGRAM
Each year, this program provides loans totaling close to $100 million to full-time students in colleges or universities (two- to four-year institutions) who need help and are eligible. Loans are repayable within ten years after graduation; 50 percent is forgiven if the graduate goes into teaching. Students should apply directly to the college they intend to enter, not to the federal government. Maximum of $1,000 per year; $5,000 total loans.

NATIONAL RESEARCH COUNCIL
Write to:
  National Research Council
  National Academy of Sciences
  2101 Constitution Avenue
  Washington, D.C. 20418
The Fellowship Office of the Office of Scientific Personnel at the National Research Council annually prepares a list of major fellowship opportunities and aids to advanced education for U.S. citizens and a selected list of the same for foreign nationals. Copies are available upon request.

NATIONAL WILDLIFE FEDERATION
Write to:
  The Executive Director
  National Wildlife Federation
  1412 16th Street, N. W.
  Washington, D.C. 20036
The federation and its state affiliates award a limited number of graduate fellowships of $2,000 to $4,000 for study in conservation fields at an accredited institution.

PUBLIC LAW 91-230, PART D
Write to:
Director, Division of Training Programs
Bureau of Education for the Handicapped
U.S. Office of Education
Washington, D.C. 20202
Grants to institutions of higher education for the training of personnel to work with handicapped children. College juniors, seniors, and graduates are eligible. Tuition and fees are paid for all except the junior-level awards. The stipends are offered as follows: junior year, $300; senior year, $800; master's level, $2,200; post-master's, $3,200. An allowance of $600 is offered for each dependent of a graduate fellow.

REHABILITATION SERVICES ADMINISTRATION
Write to:
Division of Manpower Training
Rehabilitation Services Administration
U.S. Department of Health, Education
and Welfare
Washington, D.C. 20201
Teaching and trainee grants to institutions for graduate students in rehabilitation careers. These careers include physical medicine and rehabilitation, dentistry, physical therapy, occupational therapy, speech pathology and audiology, rehabilitation nursing, rehabilitation social work, prosthetics and orthotics, rehabilitation psychology, rehabilitation counseling, recreation for the ill and handicapped, work evaluation and rehabilitation workshop administration, and other specialized fields such as rehabilitation of the blind, deaf and mentally retarded.

SOCIAL AND REHABILITATION SERVICE
The U.S. Department of Health, Education, and Welfare offers traineeships to institutions for social work education at the master's and doctoral levels. Students should apply directly to the graduate school of social work where they are currently enrolled, or when applying for admission.

SOCIAL SECURITY ACT—TITLE II
The act extends support to unmarried sons and daughters of a deceased, disabled or retired parent who continue their education full-time at accredited schools. Information is available at your local Social Security Administration Office.

VOCATIONAL REHABILITATION PROGRAMS
Write to:
National Rehabilitation Counseling Service
1522 K Street
Washington, D.C. 20005
Assistance is extended to disabled persons. Includes counseling and guidance, medical examinations and needed restorative services, training and other services.

STATE AID

ALABAMA

ALABAMA DEPARTMENT OF EDUCATION
Write to:
Alabama Department of Education
Montgomery, Ala. 36104
Grants are made to needy resident students attending Florence State College, Jacksonville State University, Livingston University and Troy State University who agree to teach at least three years in Alabama elementary schools. The 250 scholarships are divided equally among the schools and do not exceed $100 annually.

TUSKEGEE INSTITUTE SCHOOL OF NURSING
Write to:
Tuskegee Institute
Tuskegee, Ala. 36088
Scholarships of $600 are available to resident black men or women accepted at Tuskegee Institute of Nursing. The student must agree to practice nursing for at least two years in Alabama.

BOARD OF MEDICAL (OR DENTAL) SCHOLARSHIP AWARDS
Write to:
Board of Medical Scholarship Awards
University Station
1600 8th Avenue, South
Birmingham, Ala. 35294
or

Board of Dental Scholarship Awards
1919 7th Avenue, South
Birmingham, Ala. 35233
For information on guaranteed loans, write to: Director of Higher Education, Office of Education, Region IV, 50 Seventh St, NE, Atlanta, Ga. 30323

Awards up to $8,000 for four years are available to any Alabama resident of good character who has been accepted for study at the Medical College of Alabama, the University of Alabama School of Dentistry, or at comparable institutions.

ALASKA

UNIVERSITY OF ALASKA
Write to:
Financial Aid Officer
University of Alaska, College, Alaska 99701
The highest-ranking senior in each Alaska high school is eligible for scholarships covering room-and-board costs for two years.

COMMISSIONER OF EDUCATION
Write to:
Commissioner of Education
State Department of Education, Pouch F
Alaska Office Building, Juneau, Alaska 99801
A scholarship whose amount is determined by the

Commissioner is available to students attending any institution of higher education in Alaska. Grant is to be applied to tuition, fees, books, or room and board. Students must have been Alaska residents for at least two years.

COMMISSIONER OF PUBLIC SAFETY
Write to:
   Commissioner of Public Safety
   State Capitol, Pouch N, Juneau, Alaska 99801
For information on guaranteed loans, write to: United Student Aid Funds, Inc., 845 Third Avenue, New York, NY, 10022
The department offers a grant or loan of $1,500 per year up to two years to a resident enrolled in a program leading to an associate or baccalaureate degree in the field of law enforcement, law probation and parole, or penology.

ARIZONA

For information on guaranteed loans, write to: Director of Higher Education, Office of Education, Region IX, 760 Market Street, San Francisco, Calif. 94102

Waiver of tuition and, in some cases, funds to meet expenses are offered to Arizona residents recommendd by high schools to state universities or junior colleges. Make application through H. S. or school of choice.

ARKANSAS

For information on guaranteed loans, write to: Student Loan Guarantee Foundation of Arkansas, 1515 W. Seventh Street, Suite 615, Little Rock, Ark. 72202

CALIFORNIA

STATE SCHOLARSHIP AND LOAN COMMISSION
Write to:
   State Scholarship and Loan Commission
   714 P Street, Sacramento, Cal. 95814
For information on guaranteed loans, write to: Director of Higher Education, Office of Educatino, Region IX, 50 Fulton Street, San Francisco, Calif. 94102

More than 9,000 competitive scholarships—tuition and fees—are offered to resident students under thirty (in financial need) at any school in the state accredited by the Western Association of Schools and Colleges. Funds are also applicable to students classified as disadvantaged whose potential for college success is not necessarily identified by conventional means (e.g., Scholastic Aptitude Tests, etc.). Grants are to be initiated primarily at public community colleges.

COLORADO

COLORADO DENTAL COMMITTEE
Write to:
   Colorado Dental Committee
   University of Colorado Medical Center
   4200 E. 9th Avenue, Denver, Colo. 80220
Grants approximating the difference between resident and non-resident tuition at the student's chosen school, plus a modest travel allowance, are available. These are for the use of Colorado residents at any accredited dental school in the United States.

Applications for the following should be made through the financial aids officer at the institution the student wishes to attend.

MINORITY TEACHER INCENTIVE GRANT

A maximum grant of $1,000 (based on need) for a year and a summer session is available to resident students of racial and ethnic minority groups who agree to teach in Colorado for two years following completion of education. Funds are renewable.

COLORADO WORK-STUDY
Funds are available to provide institutional jobs for resident undergraduate students. Amount is determined by need.

COLORADO STUDENT GRANT
Amounts to be determined by institution are available to assist students enrolled at state institutions.

For information on guaranteed loans, write to: Director of Higher Education, Office of Education, Region VIII, 9017 Federal Office Building, 19th and Stout Streets, Denver, Colo. 80202

CONNECTICUT

Yearly awards of $300 (maximum) are to be used by students at Connecticut state colleges who are preparing to teach. Apply directly to the state college.

STATE BOARD OF EXAMINERS FOR NURSING
Write to:
   State Board of Examiners for Nursing
   79 Elm Street, Hartford, Conn. 06115
Awards (amount to be determined by board) are extended to students in any accredited school of nursing in Connecticut. Also, financial aid may be granted for graduate study in nursing at recognized schools in or out of the state.

COMMISSIONER FOR HIGHER EDUCATION
Write to:
   Commissioner for Higher Education
   P. O. Box 1320, Hartford, Conn. 06115
Scholarships of $100 to $1,000 for full-time use at any school accredited by the Commissioner of

Higher Education are available for resident high school seniors in upper half of their classes.

A legal resident of Connecticut whose educational achievement is restricted by economic, environmental or social disadvantages, and who is enrolled in full-time study at an approved college or university in Connecticut, may apply directly to the financial aid officer at the institution.

For information on guaranteed loans, write to: Connecticut Student Loan Foundation, 251 Asylum Street, Hartford, Conn. 06103

DELAWARE

UNIVERSITY OF DELAWARE
Write to:
Office of the Director of Financial Aid
University of Delaware, Newark, Del. 19711
Delaware residents attending the university are eligible for renewable awards of varying amounts, depending on financial need.

SCHOLARSHIP ADVISORY COUNCIL
Write to:
Scholarship Advisory Council
c/o State Board of Education, Dover, Del. 19901
Delaware resident students pursuing courses not available in Delaware state institutions may receive renewable funds of up to $800 per year, depending on need and academic qualifications.

For information on guaranteed loans, write to: Delaware Higher Education Loan Program, 200 W. Ninth Street, Wilmington, Del. 19801

DISTRICT OF COLUMBIA

For information on guaranteed loans, write to: Program-Coordinating Unit, 1329 E Street NW, Washington D.C. 20004

FLORIDA

Two-year residents of Florida with an adjusted family income of less than $15,000 may apply to the office of financial aid at a college or university in Florida. Schools offer 4 percent loans for tuition, room and board, and books and supplies. Write directly to school.

DEPARTMENT OF EDUCATION
Write to:
Scholarships and Loans Section
Department of Education, Tallahassee, Fla. 32304
Grants from $200 to $1,200 are awarded to two-year residents of Florida with demonstrated exceptional financial need.

DIVISION OF MENTAL HEALTH
Write to:
Manpower Division of Mental Health
200 E. Gaines Street, Tallahassee, Fla. 32304
Florida residents accepted in graduate training programs in the field of psychiatry, clinical psychology, clinical social work or psychiatric nursing may receive $240 per month. (Psychology interns are eligible for $300, and rates for psychiatric residents depend on year level.) Persons must work in approved agencies for one month for each month of grant, or repay with 5 percent interest. Applications may also be made through school's clinical training program director.

OSTEOPATHIC TRAINING OFFICE MEDICAL SCHOLARSHIPS
Write to:
Osteopathic Training Office Medical
Scholarships
Florida State Board of Health
P. O. Box 210, Jacksonville, Fla. 32201
Five-year residents accepted for admission by an approved college of osteopathic medicine, and in need of assistance, may apply for renewable $1,000 awards. Recipient must agree to practice osteopathic medicine for five years in a Florida community in need of a physician.

For information on guaranteed loans, write to: Director of Higher Education, Office of Education, Region IV, 50 Seventh Street NE, Atlanta, Ga. 30323

GEORGIA

STATE MEDICAL EDUCATION BOARD
Write to:
State Medical Education Board
244 Washington Street, S. W., Room 468
Atlanta, Ga. 30334
Georgia residents who have been accepted at accredited medical colleges, and have financial need, are eligible for a maximum of $10,000 for four years.

Regents' scholarships are available to Georgia residents attending institutions in the state system. Applications are made through the director of student aid at the institution selected.

STATE SCHOLARSHIP COMMISSION
Write to:
State Scholarship Commission
P. O. Box 38005
Capitol Hill Station, Atlanta, Ga. 30334
Georgia residents attending accredited institutions preparing for careers in paramedical, professional, or educational fields such as nursing, dentistry, pharmacy, dental hygiene, etc., and who are needy, may apply for amounts to be determined by the commission.

Georgia citizens attending approved Georgia colleges or universities not in the system may apply to the respective institution for $400 per academic year. Funds are limied to freshmen, sophomores, and juniors during 1973–74. Extended to undergraduate students in the following 1973–74 academic year, except where study leads to a degree in theology, divinity, or religious education.

For information on guaranteed loans, write to: Georgia Higher Education Assistance Corporation, P.O. Box 38005, Atlanta, Ga. 30334

HAWAII

High school senior residents of five years wishing to attend one of six community colleges or a four-year college on the island of Hawaii, Hilo College and in Honolulu (Manoa Campus) for undergraduate study may apply to the financial aids at school selected. Amount to be determined by school.

For information on guaranteed loans, write to: Director of Higher Education, Office of Education, Region X, 50 Fulton St., San Francisco, Calif. 94102

IDAHO

IDAHO STATE UNIVERSITY
Write to:
    Idaho State University, Pocatello, Idaho 83201
Write to the above address for information on Idaho State University Club Scholarships which are available to graduating seniors who demonstrate good scholarship and outstanding performance in extra-curricular activities. Awards are $185 each.

Under the same Idaho State University provisions, the State Board of Education may waive a limited number of non-resident tuition fees for disadvantaged and deserving students.

The university awards $180 per student for use by state residents at Idaho State University. A freshman honorary scholarship is offered to each high school in Idaho. Selection is to be made by the high school principal and is awarded to a top academic student with regard to need, special skills, or outstanding interest and ability in academic areas.

UNIVERSITY OF IDAHO
Write to:
    Director of School of Music
    University of Idaho, Moscow, Idaho 83843
Scholarships of $300 for University of Idaho students for musical activities in band, orchestra and choir. Available to in- and out-of-state students.

UNIVERSITY OF IDAHO
Write to:
    Student Financial Aid Service
    University of Idaho, Moscow, Idaho
The university offers out-of-state tuition scholarships for non-resident entering freshmen or transfer students who plan to enroll in the College of Mines to study geological engineering, geology, engineering, or metallurgical engineering.

Idaho Mining Association Scholarships are offered ($500) for the freshman year. Also included is guaranteed full-time summer employment in the mining industry during college career including the summer prior to freshman enrollment provided a 2.5 average is maintained.

Idaho Mining Memorial Scholarships of $400 to $500 are offered for use in freshman year to entering freshmen only (in- and out-of-state) with good scholastic records who plan to enroll in the College of Mines to study geography, geological engineering, geology, mining engineering or metallurgical engineering.

For information on guaranteed loans, write to: Director of Higher Education, Office of Education, Region X, 1321 Second Avenue, Seattle, Wash. 98101

ILLINOIS

MILITARY SERVICE SCHOLARSHIPS
Tuition and fee funds are available for veterans at an Illinois state-supported college or university or a Class 1 junior college.

GENERAL ASSEMBLY AWARDS
To determine eligibility for awards (tuition and fees), the student may write directly to the local member of the General Assembly. Recipient must be a resident of the district and selected by a state legislator. Student must also intend to enroll at an Illinois state-supported college or university.

ILLINOIS STATE SCHOLARSHIP COMMISSION
Write to:
    Illinois State Scholarship Commission
    102 Wilmot Road, Deerfield, Ill. 60015
The commission selects recipients for the Illinois Monetary Award. (Amount of award varies.) Illinois residents are selected on the basis of need and class rank and must attend an approved college or university.

GOVERNMENT AID PROGRAMS
Write to:
    Division of Vocational Rehabilitation
    623 E. Adams, Springfield, Ill. 62706

DEPARTMENT OF CHILDREN AND FAMILY SERVICES
Write to:
    524 S. 2nd Street, Springfield, Ill. 62706
The department offers college tuition waiver and maintenance fees to children of needy families.

DEPARTMENT OF SCHOLARSHIP SERVICES
Write to:
    Department of Scholarship Services
    212 E. Monroe, Springfield, Ill. 62705
A special education grant of $500 per year plus

tuition is offered to college juniors and seniors attending approved colleges and universities. Recipient must work in field six months for every year of grant.

Apply through the H.S. principal for Special Education Teacher awards of tuition and some fees. Recipient must be in upper half of class, intend to teach special education, and enroll in an Illinois state-supported college or university.

ILLINOIS STATE SCHOLARSHIP COMMISSION
Write to:
Illinois State Scholarship Commission
102 Wilmont Road, Deerfield, Ill. 60015
Commission offers special bilingual education grants in varying amounts.

For information about guaranteed loans, write to: Illinois Guaranteed Loan Program, 102 Wilmont Road, P.O. Box 33, Deerfield, Ill. 60015

INDIANA

All of the following awards are availabile through financial aids officers at Indiana state-supported institutions of higher learning.

Tuition is offered to full-time students who are children of regular paid law enforcement officers and firemen who have been killed in the line of duty. Must attend a state-supported college, university, or technical school.

A partial remission of fees is offered to resident students at state supported colleges and universities through State and Merit Scholarships. Basis of award determined by institution.

Merit scholarships for remission of non-resident tuition charges are available for non-resident students at state-supported universities.

STATE SCHOLARSHIP PROGRAM
Write to:
State Scholarship Commission of Indiana
514 State Office Building
100 N. Senate Avenue, Indianapolis, Ind. 46204
State scholarships of $100 to $1,400 for tuition and fees are set aside for Indiana residents with superior academic merit and potential, and with financial need. Awards are applicable at eligible institutions within Indiana.

EDUCATIONAL GRANT PROGRAMS
Write to above address for information on the grants, which are offered to neediest students. Academic requirement is fulfilled by acceptance for admission into college.

For information about guaranteed loans, write to: Director of Higher, Education, Office of Education, Region V, 226 W. Jackson Boulevard, Chicago, Ill. 60606

IOWA

DIVISION OF SPECIAL EDUCATION
Write to:
Division of Special Education
State Department of Public Instruction
Grimes State Office Building
Des Moines, Iowa 50319
Funds are for the use of persons preparing professionally for education of the handicapped. Assistance is in the form of summer traineeships at the graduate level in approved special education programs.

IOWA STATE UNIVERSITY
Write to:
Coordinator of Student Financial Aids
Iowa State University, Ames, Iowa 50010
Student residents of Iowa entering Iowa State University are eligible for general scholarships and student aid scholarships (renewable in amounts to be determined by institution). Application should be made by March 1. Parents' Confidential Statement is required.

UNIVERSITY OF NORTHERN IOWA
Write to:
Director of Financial Aid
University of Northern Iowa
Cedar Falls, Iowa 50613
U.S. citizens with Iowa residence entering the University of Northern Iowa may apply for aid of $530 renewable for four years.

STATE OF IOWA SCHOLARSHIP PROGRAM
Write to:
State of Iowa Scholarship Program
Higher Education Facilities Commission
201 Jewett Building
Ninth and Grand, Des Moines, Iowa 50309
Funds from $100 to $600 assist high school graduates who are U.S. citizens and Iowa residents planning to attend an approved Iowa college or university, Area Community School or school of professional nursing.

Applicants should take the ACT on any test date between October of junior year and October of senior year of high school. Students identified as State of Iowa Scholars on the basis of ACT scores and class rank will be invited to compete for award by filing a Parents' Confidential Statement with the College Scholarship Service by January 18 of year prior to award.

UNIVERSITY OF IOWA
Write to:
Director of Financial Aid
University of Iowa, Iowa City, Iowa 52240
Students entering the University of Iowa should apply for freshman scholarships. Awards based on need and academic record. Must be in upper 10 percent of class or have an ACT score (composite) of 28 or higher. Amounts determined by university.

REHABILITATION SERVICES
Write to:
  Branch Rehabilitation Education & Services
  801 Bankers Trust Building
  Des Moines, Iowa 50309
Tuition, fees and other assistance offered to disabled students at Iowa State University, University of Iowa, University of Northern Iowa and other training facilities.

HIGHER EDUCATION FACILITIES COMMISSION
Write to:
  Higher Education Facilities Commission
  201 Jewett Building
  Ninth and Grand, Des Moines, Iowa 50309
Grants from the commission vary from $50 to $1,000, depending on need, but may not exceed tuition and fees minus the average amount the student would pay at a state university. Students enrolled at Iowa private colleges are eligible and must file a Parents' Confidential Statement. Apply no later than January 1 prior to award.

For information about guaranteed loans, write to:
  Director of Higher Education, Office of Education, Region VII, 601 E. 12th Street, Kansas City, Mo. 64106

KANSAS

TUITION GRANT PROGRAM
Write to:
  Tuition Grant Program
  State Education Commission
  700 Kansas Avenue, Topeka, Kans. 66612
A maximum of $1,000 is offered to Kansas students to attend a fully accredited Kansas independent college. Monies are to be applied to tuition and required fees.

STATE SCHOLARSHIPS PROGRAM
Write to:
  State Scholarship Programs
  State Department of Education
  120 E. 10th Street, Topeka, Kans. 66612
Resident Kansas students may apply for $500 freshmen awards which are renewable for sophomore year. These are for use at any accredited Kansas college or university.

For information about guaranteed loans, write to:
Director of Higher Education, Office of Education, Region VII, 601 E. 12th Street, Kansas City, Mo. 64106

KENTUCKY

BUREAU OF REHABILITATION
Write to:
  Bureau of Rehabilitation
  State Department of Education
  State Office Building, Frankfort, Ky. 40601
Resident students who are disabled and can demonstrate financial need, academic aptitude, good

citizenship and character are eligible for a partial to full payment of tuition, books, and other fees with renewable privileges.

HIGHER EDUCATION ASSISTANCE AUTHORITY
Write to:
  Kentucky Higher Education Assistance Authority
  319 Ann Street, Frankfort, Ky. 40601
Based on need and the availability of funds, grants are made to resident students accepted as full-time students in an approved Kentucky nonprofit college or university who are not enrolled in a course of study leading to a degree in theology, divinity or religious education, and who have no more than seven semesters (or the equivalent) of completed education.

KENTUCKY DENTAL ASSOCIATION
Write to:
  Kentucky Dental Association
  1940 Princeton Drive, Louisville, Ky. 40205
College graduates of five years residence are eligible for $1,500 (per year for four years) when accepted for enrollment in an accredited dental school. Must agree to practice one year in an assigned locality for each $1,500 received.

Honor scholarships based on need are available for Kentucky residents. Information is offered through the college of student's choice.

KENTUCKY MEDICAL ASSOCIATION
Write to:
  Rural Kentucky Medical Scholarship Fund
  Kentucky Medical Association
  3532 Ephraim McDowell Drive
  Louisville, Ky. 40205
Residents of Kentucky who have been admitted to an accredited medical school may request loans of up to $2,500 per year. Recipients must agree to practice in rural Kentucky for one year for each loan received. Persons may also practice with the Kentucky Public Health Service in an approved area.

For information about guaranteed loans, write to:
Director of Higher Education, Office of Education, Region IV, 50 Seventh Street NE, Atlanta, Ga. 30323

LOUISIANA

STATE SUPERINTENDENT OF EDUCATION
Write to:
  State Superintendent of Education
  Baton Rouge La. 70804
Academic scholarships of $600 are awarded on the basis of achievement, testing, interviews and recommendations of high school teachers and principals.

T. H. HARRIS SCHOLARSHIPS
Write to above address for information on these funds for use at state-supported colleges and uni-

versities except Airline, Delgado and St. Bernard. Number and amount of scholarship varies. Maximum is $300.

LOUISIANA STONEWALL JACKSON MEMORIAL BOARD SCHOLARSHIP

Write to State Superintendent of Education (listed above) for information on grants to H.S. students entering essay competitions. Students must attend a Louisiana institution of higher learning.

FEE EXEMPTIONS

The State Superintendent of Education offers fee exemption scholarships for the following: Board of Supervisors, band and orchestra, ministerial, 4H Club, Future Farmers of America and Pelican State.

Through H.S. principals scholarships are available (amount to be determined by the State Board of Education) awarded annually to a graduate in the upper one-third of each graduating class of twenty-five or less. More scholarships are available in larger schools.

Outstanding freshman students are considered for renewable Louisiana State University Centennial Honor Awards of $100 to $750 per year. Information is obtained from Committee of Student Employment and Scholarships at college where student is admitted as a freshman.

DEPARTMENT OF HOSPITALS

Write to:
    Training Officer
    Department of Hospitals
    655 No. 5th Street, Baton Rouge, La. 70804
This aid is for students desiring further education for improved training as special educators, nurse anesthetists, occupational therapists, medical students, interns, resident physicians medical records librarians, medical technologists physical therapists, speech therapists, X-ray technicians and other professional trainees for the purposes of enhancing their employment possibilities with state owned and operated hospitals, and in schools and day-care centers for the mentally retarded.

NURSE TRAINING PROGRAMS

Write to Department of Hospitals at the address listed above.

The Department of Hospitals assists students with stipends (of varying amounts) to complete nursing training if the students agree to be employed at one of the state hospitals for time equivalent to that for which the stipend was received.

Details of $100 per month in the Diploma Nurse Training programs are available from the admission officer of school selected within the state.

For information about guaranteed loans, write to: (in-state students) Louisiana Higher Education Assistance Commission, P.O. Box 44095, Capitol Station, Baton Rouge, La. 70802; (out-of-state students) United Student Aid Funds, Inc., 5259 N. Tacoma Avenue, Indianapolis, Ind. 46220

MAINE

UNIVERSITY OF MAINE

Write to:
    Student Aid Office
    University of Maine, Orono, Maine 04473
Awards in values up to full tuition are available to students in attendance at the University of Maine.

Write to student aid offices at the college of student's choice for further facts on the following: Students accepted or enrolled at any of the campuses of the University of Maine system are eligible for awards in varying amounts according to need. Parents' Confidential Statement is required.

Room, board, tuition and required fees for North American Indians, (one-year residents of Maine) who are included on a tribal census, or whose parents or grandparents were so included, and who have been accepted at one of the campuses of the University of Maine system.

For information about guaranteed loans, write to: United Student Aid Funds, Inc., 5259 North Tacoma Avenue, Indianapolis, Ind. 46220

MARYLAND

STATE SCHOLARSHIP BOARD

Write to:
    State Scholarship Board, Baltimore, Md. 21218
General State Scholarships are for resident high school seniors or previous graduates accepted as full-time students. Awards of $200 to $1,500 are offered at Maryland degree-granting institutions including junior and community colleges.

Write to the above address for details on assistance (reimbursement of tuition upon completion of course of study) to regular paid and volunteer firemen engaged in the profession in the state for study programs in fire service technology.

The State Scholarship Board also offers facts on state senators' nominations from respective districts. Selection for the $250 to $1,500 scholarships is made from a competitive examination listing.

Likewise, each member of the House of Delegates may appoint two students from the respective district for free tuition at the University of Maryland, College Park. Appointees are selected on no special basis. Contact the State Scholarship Board through the address listed above.

Ten medical scholarships of $1,500 per year are awarded annually to students who have been residents of Maryland at least five years and have received the bachelor's degree from an accredited college. Recipients agree to practice three years in an area of medical need in Maryland. Apply before April 1 to State Scholarship Board address given above.

Write to:
    University of Maryland
    Fellowship Office, Graduate School
    College Park, Md. 20470
Twelve fellowships ($2,500 maximum for three years) are awarded to graduates of an accredited four-year college for post-graduate work in the graduate school of the University of Maryland at College Park. Recipients agree to teach in a public institution of higher learning in Maryland.

PROFESSIONAL SCHOOL SCHOLARSHIPS
Money ($200 to $1,000, based on need) is available for students who are three-year residents of Maryland prior to award for use in professional schools of medicine, dentisty, law, nursing and pharmacy. Details and application obtainable through financial aid director of school selected by student.

STATE SCHOLARSHIP BOARD
Write to:
    State Scholarship Board
    2100 Guilford Avenue, Baltimore, Md. 21218
Recommended senior undergraduates or candidates for a master's degree in education of the deaf may receive aid equal to tuition at the selected training center. Awards are based on financial need.

FIREMAN ASSOCIATION
Write to:
    Fireman Association
    Route 1, Box 523, Frostberg, Md. 21532
Persons sixteen to twenty-three with a parent killed in line of duty as a volunteer fireman in Maryland are eligible for a maximum of $500 to be applied toward tuition, matriculation fees, room, board, books and supplies.

For information about guaranteed loans, write to: Maryland Higher Education Loan Corporation, 2100 Guilford Avenue, Baltimore, Md. 21218

MASSACHUSETTS

DEPARTMENT OF EDUCATION
Write to:
    Department of Education
    Commonwealth of Massachusetts
    182 Tremont Street, Boston, Mass. 02111
Four Commonwealth scholarships (free tuition for four years at the University of Massachusetts, a state college or state technological institute) in each senatorial district are awarded to resident students who achieve the four highest marks in a competitive examination.

The department can also be contacted for details on the following programs:

Partial or full scholarships for needy and worthy students with minimum residence of four consecutive years prior to application can be applied to study in medical and dental schools and recognized schools of nursing.

Scholarships exist for Massachusetts H. S. graduates whose parent is a deceased member of paid fire or police departments where injuries were received in the performances of duty. Funds cover tuition at an institution operated by the Commonwealth. Aid applies also to Metropolitan District Commission or the Capitol Police.

Special education scholarships are offered to undergraduates who plan to become certified teachers of the mentally retarded. Applicants must be needy and academically worthy full-time students domiciled in Massachusetts in order to qualify for funds (not to exceed $500 per year for three years).

Needy and worthy full-time undergraduates (Commonwealth residents) may apply for $200 in public-supported institutions and $700 in private institutions at any regionally-accredited institution in the U.S. In Massachusetts, awards must be used at institutions approved for degree authority by the Board of Higher Education.

For information on guaranteed loans, write to: Massachusetts Higher Education Assistance Corporation, 511 Statler Building, Boston, Mass. 02116

FITCHBURG STATE COLLEGE
Write to:
    President
    State College, Fitchburg, Mass. 01420
Special education scholarships—upon recommendation of the college president—are obtainable for high school graduates of the Commonwealth who enter the State College at Fitchburg for training as teachers of the mentally retarded. Awards are for $300 for not more than four years.

UNIVERSITY OF MASSACHUSETTS, AMHERST
UNIVERSITY OF MASSACHUSETTS, BOSTON
Write to:
    Director of Financial Aid
    University of Massachusetts
    Amherst, Mass. 01002
or
    Director of Financial Aid
    University of Massachusetts
    Boston, Mass. 02116
Scholarships (amounts determined by state appropriation) and grants are available for members of each of the four undergraduate classes who have a financial need and who have attained the scholarship requirements of the University Committee on Financial Aid.

MICHIGAN

DEPARTMENT OF EDUCATION
Write to:
    Department of Education
    Division of Student Financial Aids
    P. O. Box 420, Lansing, Mich. 48902
A Michigan Competitive Scholarship or Tuition

Grant is awarded to students of good moral character who have been residents of Michigan for eighteen months, who are H. S. graduates, and who plan to attend college full-time. Scholarship applicants may attend any approved college or university in Michigan. (Limited to tuition and fees.) Tuition grant applicants may attend an eligible private, non-profit college or univeristy in Michigan.

For information about guaranteed loans, write to: Michigan Higher Education Assistance Authority, 700 Prudential Building, Box 420, Lansing, Mich. 48902

MINNESOTA

MINNESOTA BOARD OF NURSING
Write to:
   Minnesota Board of Nursing
   393 No. Dunlap Street, St. Paul, Minn. 55104
Resident students of ability and financial need accepted by approved schools preparing students for registered or practical nursing are eligible for funds ($2,000 maximum for registered nurse programs and $300 for practical nurse programs). Recipients must practice one year in Minnesota following graduation.

MINNESOTA HIGHER EDUCATION COORDINATING COMMISSION
Write to:
   Minnesota Higher Education Coordinating Commission
   Suite 400, Capitol Square
   550 Cedar Street, St. Paul, Minn. 55101
Renewable state scholarships determined by financial need are extended to Minnesota residents ranked in upper quartile of H. S. class. Recipient must enter a Minnesota approved college, university or vocational school.

Contact the above address for details about the State Grant-in-Aid extended to Minnesota residents, regardless of class rank. Applicants for the maximum of $1,000 annually must be needy and must plan to enter a Minnesota approved college, university of vocational school.

STATE DEPARTMENT OF PUBLIC WELFARE
Write to:
   Personnel Director
   State Department of Public Welfare
   Centennial Building, St. Paul, Minn. 55101
Assistance is available for graduate training in social work. The maximum award for a single person is $2,250; married, $2,700; married, plus one child, $3,150 married plus two or more children $3,600. Additional allowances up to $1,200 per school year for tuition expenses is attached. Eligibility is determined only by admission to an approved graduate school of social work in the U.S. or Canada.

Write to the same address for information on aid for advanced training in psychiatric nursing. Applicants for amounts specified above for social work must be registered nurses and must be accepted at an approved school of psychiatric nursing.

The State Department of Public Welfare also offers grants of comparable amounts to juniors and seniors who have been accepted at schools offering approved courses leading toward certification in occupational therapy.

Acceptance in a graduate school offering approved courses leading to a master's degree in hospital recreation or recreational therapy is the only eligibility requirement for State Department of Public Welfare funds covering tuition and stipend. Write to the address listed.

Baccalaureate, diploma and licenses practical nursing programs also come under the State Department of Public Welfare. Contact the department for information on these programs at schools approved by the Minnesota Board of Nursing. Monthly award for a single person is $250; married, $300; married, one child, $350; married, two or more children, $400.

For information about guaranteed loans write to: Director of Higher Education, Office of Education, Region V, 226 W. Jackson Boulevard, Chicago, Ill. 60606

MISSISSIPPI

PROFESSIONAL AND GRADUATE EDUCATION PROGRAM
Write to:
   Professional and Graduate Education Program
   P. O. Box 2336
   Jackson, Miss. 39205
Scholarship aid is extended for pursuit of graduate or professional work in out-of-state institutions. Applicant must have been a legal resident of Mississippi for one year prior to date of application and must qualify for graduate or professional courses not available in regularly supported Mississippi institutions of higher education.

BOARD OF TRUSTEES
Write to:
   Board of Trustees
   Institutions of Higher Learning
   P. O. Box 2336, Jackson, Miss. 39205
College Scholarships are available for children of law officers and full-time firemen fatally injured or totally disabled from injuries which occurred in the performance of their official duties.

For information about guaranteed loans, write to: Director of Higher Education, Office of Education, Region IV, 50 Seventh Street NE, Atlanta, Ga. 30323

MISSOURI

Residents of Missouri who score high on the Ohio Psychological Test (administered on a statewide basis) are eligible for scholarships to apply toward tuition and incidental fees. Those interested should apply through the registrars of state colleges at Warrensburg, Maryville, Kirksville, Cape Girardeau or Springfield, or the University of Missouri.

For information about guaranteed loans, write to: United Student Aid Funds, Inc., 5259 N. Tacoma Avenue, Indianapolis, Ind. 46220

MONTANA

Apply through the institution of the student's choice for the following aid:

ADVANCED HONOR SCHOLARSHIP
A waiver of fees (approximately $225 per year) is awarded to a qualified student at the conclusion of the freshman year of college.

Non-resident fee may be waived in the case of an out-of-state student. Waiver based on scholarship, promise, and character.

Fee waivers are granted to Indians (Montana residents) of at least one-fourth Indian ancestry.

Information is available through the high school principal for High School Honor Scholarships. Grant waives fees for freshman year only.

For information about guaranteed loans, write to: Director of Higher Education, Office of Education, Region VIII, 9017 Federal Office Building, 19th and Stout Streets, Denver, Colo. 80202

NEBRASKA

High school principals or counselors have information on approximately three hundred Regents Scholarships awarded annually at the University of Nebraska to resident students in the upper one-fourth of their graduating class. Based on competitive examination.

DEPARTMENT OF AGRICULTURE
Write to:
    Department of Agriculture
    P. O. Box 4844
    State Control, Lincoln Nebr. 68509
Nebraska farm or ranch youths who need financial assistance to pursue education beyond high school may receive low-interest loans up to $1,500 per year. Residents must enroll in an institution owned or controlled by the state or a government subdivision thereof.

For information about guaranteed loans, write to: Director of Higher Education, Office of Education, Region VII, 601 E. 12th Street, Kansas City, Mo. 64108

NEVADA

Resident students are not charged tuition at state-supported universities. After six months' residence in Nevada, military personnel are eligible for resident fees. Children of military personnel are not charged nonresident fees if the parent has lived in the state six months. For further details, write to the director of admissions at college selected.

For information about guaranteed loans, write to: United Student Aid Funds, Inc., 5259 N. Tacoma Avenue, Indianapolis, Ind. 46220

NEW HAMPSHIRE

KEENE STATE COLLEGE
PLYMOUTH STATE COLLEGE
Write to:
    Director of Student Personnel
    Keene State College, Keene, N.H. 03431
or
    Director of Student Personnel
    Plymouth State College, Plymouth, N.H. 03264
Students of state colleges with teaching majors, good scholastic standing, leadership ability, and financial need who agree to teach in New Hampshire one year or every year assisted are eligible for aid of $200 a year maximum (renewable).

BOARD OF NURSING EDUCATION
Write to:
    New Hampshire State Board of Nursing
    Education and Nurse Registration
    105 Loudon Road, Concord, N.H. 03301
Qualifications for up to $1,200 for three years (of which not more than $400 may be awarded for any one year) include financial need and New Hampshire residence. In addition, applicant must be accepted in a New Hampshire approved school of nursing and must agree to practice in the state for one year following graduation and licensure.

For information about guaranteed loans, write to: New Hampshire Higher Education Assistance Foundation, 3 Capitol Street, Concord, N.H. 03301

NEW JERSEY

DEPARTMENT OF HIGHER EDUCATION
Write to:
    Department of Higher Education
    Office of Student Financial Aid
    225 W. State Street, Trenton, N.J. 08625
Satisfactory scholarship record, financial need, demonstrated moral character, good citizenship, and dedication to American ideals qualify New Jersey residents for State Competitive Scholarships. Applicants for the $500 a year grants (or amount charged for tuition, whichever is smaller) must have graduated, or will graduate, within one year of application.

Apply to the above address for Incentive Scholarships. Basic awards to meet the cost of tuition and fees in amounts of $100 to $500 are slated for students attending New Jersey schools. For further eligibility requirements, apply to the Department of Higher Education.

New Jersey residents with demonstrated need, and who are graduates of New Jersey county colleges, with plans to attend four-year institutions fulltime, are eligible for $500 (or tuition, whichever is less. Renewable). Write to Department of Higher Education at address listed above.

Tuition aid grants of $200 to $1,000 are earmarked for New Jersey residents enrolled at a New Jersey college or university. Aid granted on the basis of need where tuition exceeds $450. Apply to Department of Higher Education at address listed above.

For information about guaranteed loans, write to: New Jersey Higher Education Assistance Authority, 225 W. State Street, Trenton, N.J. 08625

NEW MEXICO

New Mexico universities and colleges have discretionary power to award and grant scholarships (matriculation fees or tuition, or both) to students who have state residence, high moral character and scholastic standing. Contact state colleges and universities.

For information about guaranteed loans, write to: Director of Higher Education, Office of Education, Region VI, 1114 Commerce Street, Dallas, Tex. 75202

NEW YORK

REGENTS EXAMINATION AND
SCHOLARSHIP CENTER
Write to:
Regents Examination and Scholarship Center
State Education Department
Albany, N.Y. 12224
Resident students of New York seeking full-time study in approved schools of nursing in the state are eligible for $200 to $500 depending on need (four years maximum).

Write to the above address for details on $100 to $1,000 (depending on need; four of five years maximum) offered to resident students who will attend Cornell University (including the New York State College at Cornell University).

Scholar incentive awards ($100 to $600 yearly) are available for legal residents enrolled in a fulltime program of study leading to a degree at a college or hospital school of nursing, trade or technical school, or in a two-year program in a registered private business school in the state which has tuition in excess of $200.

Accredited schools grant scholarships to children of state and local corrections officers, civilian employees of a correctional facility, as well as law enforcement personnel throughout the state who died in the line of duty. Must attend accredited school of higher education in New York State and must apply through respective financial aid offices.

REGENTS EXAMINATION AND
SCHOLARSHIP CENTER
Write to:
Regents Examination and Scholarship Center
State Education Department
Albany, N.Y. 12224
New York residents studying medicine or dentistry in an approved medical or dental school in New York State, or in an approved school of osteopathy in the United States, may receive up to $1,000 per year depending on need.

STATE UNIVERSITY OF NEW YORK
Write to:
State University of New York
8 Thurlow Terrace, Albany, N.Y. 12201
State University Scholarships are awarded to students who are legal residents and who have enormous learning deficiency because of color, income level, family and/or neighborhood background. Intent of the program is to fill the gap between the formal high school curriculum and the entering level at a two- or four-year college program. Funds are available at state university campuses including thirty-three community colleges.

For information about guaranteed loans, write to: New York Higher Education Assistance Corporation, 50 Wolfe Road, Albany, N.Y. 12205

NORTH CAROLINA

MEDICAL CARE COMMISSION
Write to:
The North Carolina Medical Care Commission
P. O. Box 25459
437 No. Harrington Street, Raleigh, N.C. 27611
Students of one-year residence immediately preceding full-time enrollment in dentistry, medicine pharmacy, nursing, nurse anesthesia, medical technology, optometry, physical therapy, medical records library science, occupational therapy, dietetics, medical social work, clinical psychology, medical sociology, sociology of health, osteopathy medical recreation or public health (physicians only) may receive grants from commission. (Contact the commission for amounts.) Students must agree to practice in North Carolina a full calendar year or fraction thereof for which a loan is received. Otherwise, payment is due upon demand at 7 percent interest per year.

PROSPECTIVE TEACHERS SCHOLARSHIP
LOAN FUND
Write to:
Prospective Teachers Scholarship Loan Fund
State Department of Public Instruction
Raleigh, N.C. 27602
Resident students interested in a career in teaching may receive $600 annually (renewable).

For those currently teaching in North Carolina with less than an a certificate, summer school scholarships of $75 each are available. Write to above address.

SCHOLARSHIPS FOR TEACHERS OF THE MENTALLY RETARDED
Write to:
Scholarships for Teachers of the Mentally Retarded
State Department of Public Instruction
Raleigh, N.C. 27602
Renewable scholarships of $900 are extended to full-time enrollees planning to teach the mentally retarded.

For information about guaranteed loans, write to: State Education Assistance Authority, 1307 Glenwood Avenue, Raleigh, N.C. 27605

NORTH DAKOTA

NURSING SCHOLARSHIP LOAN COMMITTEE
Write to:
North Dakota Nursing Scholarship Loan Committee
219 No. 7th Street, Bismark, N. Dak. 58501
Residents of North Dakota who agree to practice in the state one year or repay amount of loan plus interest are eligible for $300 (for practical nursing programs).

Residents of North Dakota who agree to practice two years in the state or repay amount of loan plus interest are eligible for $1,000 (for two-year, three-year or four-year nursing programs). Write to above address.

Acceptance of two years of employment entitles North Dakota residents to $1,800 for a graduate nursing program. Write to above address.

UNIVERSITY OF NORTH DAKOTA
Write to:
Dean, School of Medicine
University of North Dakota
Grand Forks, N. Dak. 58201
Medical students in third year and fourth year of schooling are eligible for a maximum grant of $2,500 per year. Five years of practice in a small town in North Dakota cancels debt.

STATE HIGHWAY DEPARTMENT
Write to:
Commissioner,
North Dakota State Highway Department
Bismark, N. Dak. 58501
A student who has completed one year of college in civil engineering or in civil engineering technology, and who agrees to accept employment or repayment of loan, may receive $600 per year for three years at either the University of North Dakota or North Dakota State University.

Resident students who demonstrate academic apti-

tude, need, good citizenship and good character may receive funds for school fees. Apply to North Dakota state institution of choice.

For information about guaranteed loans, write to: Director of Higher Education, Office of Education, Region VIII, Federal Office Building, Room 9017, 19th and Stout Streets, Denver, Colo. 90202

OHIO

The Ohio Instructional Grants Program is aid extended to assist resident students having exceptional financial need as undergraduates in an eligible Ohio institution of higher education. Information can be obtained from high schools or from the college or university the student wishes to attend.

For information about guaranteed loans write to: Ohio Student Loan Association, Wyandotte Building, 21 W. Broad Street, Columbus, Ohio 43215

OKLAHOMA

Schools of the Oklahoma state system are authorized to waive enrollment fees as a scholarship benefit. Interested students should contact the high school counselor or the admissions officer of respctive colleges.

For information about guaranteed loans, write to: Oklahoma State Regents for Higher Education, State Capitol, State Capitol Station, Box 533893, Oklahoma City, Okla. 73105.

OREGON

Contact the high school principal or counselor for information on the following aid opportunities:

Four-year state cash awards are available to Oregon residents at two-year and four-year public and private accredited degree-granting institutions in Oregon. Renewable is dependent on student's academic standing and continud financial need.

Community College Awards of $300 or the amount of tuition and all fees (whichever is less) are available (on the basis of financial need) to Oregon residents at two-year community colleges located in Oregon.

Need Grant Programs (not to exceed 50 percent of student's computed financial need) are extended to Oregon residents at any two-year or four-year non-profit, generally accredited institution in the state. Also, grants are applicable at any hospital school of nursing located in Oregon and accredited by the National League of Nursing. Applicant must meet institution's entrance requirements and must demonstrate financial need.

For information about guaranteed loans, write to: State of Oregon Scholarship Commission, Box 3175, Eugene, Oreg. 97401

PENNSYLVANIA

Each state senator may award partial tuition scholarships to students entering state schools. Awards are renewable where grades meet standards above minimum passing requirements. Students must be resident and must attend full-time. Requests should be addressed to state senators.

HIGHER EDUCATION ASSISTANCE AGENCY
Write to:
  Pennsylvania Higher Education Assistance Agency, Towne House, Harrisburg, Pa. 17102
Depending on appropriation of funds, needy secondary school graduates may receive aid to attend the college of their choice. Applicants must be enrolled full-time in an approved institution, must be of satisfactory character, must be a U. S. citizen or taking steps to become a citizen, and must have been a state resident for at least one year prior to application. Applications may be made by current H. S. graduates, upper-classmen attending approved institutions, and students who have had a year or more lapse between secondary school graduation and college enrollment.

For information about guaranteed loans, write to:
Pennsylvania Higher Education Assistance Agency, Towne House, 660 Boas Street, Harrisburg, Pa. 17102

PUERTO RICO

For information about guaranteed loans, write to: Director of Higher Education, Office of Education, Region IV, 50 Seventh Street NE, Atlanta, Ga. 30323

RHODE ISLAND

DEPUTY COMMISSIONER OF EDUCATION
Write to:
  Deputy Commissioner of Education
  State Department of Education
  Roger Williams Building
  Hayes Street, Providence, R.I. 02908
Rhode Island State Scholarships are available to 5 percent of graduating classes of public and private secondary schools based on scholastic records and financial need.

Undergraduate study in nursing education is subsidized for qualified high school graduates. Make application through college, hospital, or State Department of Education at address listed above.

DEPUTY COMMISSIONER OF EDUCATION
Write to:
  Deputy Commissioner of Education
  State Department of Education
  Roger Williams Building
  Hayes Street, Providence, R.I. 02908
The Deputy Commissioner offers aid of varying

amounts to those seeking post graduate study in registered nursing.

DIVISION OF VOCATIONAL REHABILITATION
Write to:
  Division of Vocational Rehabilitation
  Fountain Street, Providence, R.I. 02919
Anyone physically or emotionally handicapped may be assisted (with aid determined by the division) through academic, vocational, or on-the-job training in attaining a vocational objective within his or her physical and mental capacity.

BRYANT COLLEGE
Write to:
  Registrar
  Bryant College, Smithfield, R.I. 02917
Two years' residence and agreement to each business in Rhode Island for two years after completion of study qualifies students for full-tuition awards. Make application before February 1.

For information about guaranteed loans, write to: Rhode Island Higher Education Assistance Corporation, 139 Mathewson Street, Room 404, Providence, R.I. 02901

SOUTH CAROLINA

Students may apply to the financial aid director of the college of their choice for details of available scholarships and grants.

AMERICAN LEGION
Write to:
  Department Headquarters
  American Legion
  132 Pickens Street
  P. O. Box 11355, Columbia, S.C. 29205
Veterans should apply to the American Legion for full information on veterans benefits.

For information about guaranteed loans, write to: United Student Aid Funds, Inc., 5259 N. Tacoma Avenue, Indianapolis, Ind. 46220

SOUTH DAKOTA

Contact the college of student's choice for details on the following:

Resident students who served honorably in the armed forces in any war (including Red Cross service) may receive full-tuition (unless federal educational aid is being given) for use at a state institution under control and management of the South Dakota Board of Regents.

Blind students attending state educational institutions may receive full tuition and fee scholarships. (Degree of sight loss must be established by an ophthalmologist recognized by Social Service Board.)

For information about guaranteed loans, write to: Director of Higher Education, Office of Education, Region VIII, Room 9017, Federal Office building, 19th and Stout Streets, Denver, Colo. 80202

TENNESSEE

Contact chairman of scholarship committee at state college or university selected by the student for information on academic scholarships (amount .to be determined by school for high school graduates attending state colleges and universities.

For information on guaranteed loans, write to: Tennessee Education Loan Corporation, State Department of Education, 313 Capitol Towers, Nashville, Tenn. 37219

TEXAS

The high school guidance counselor or financial aid officer of selected institutions has facts and applications for the following Texas programs:

Exemption from payment of tuition and fees for blind students.

Payment of tuition and fees for high school graduates boarded at state orphanages.

Tuition fees for two semesters paid for the highest-ranking graduate of accredited high schools.

Payment of tuition fees (one year) for certain students from other nations in the Americas.

Resident student tuition fees offered to members of the armed forces stationed in Texas.

Resident tuition fees extended to teachers, professors, and/or other employees of the state institutions of higher learning, their husbands or wives (as the case may be) and their children.

The Connally-Carrillo Act exempting tuition fees for persons with family incomes of not more than $4,800.

Exemption of tuition and fees for dependent children of Texas military personnel listed as missing in action or as prisoners-of-war.

Exemption of certain students from payment of part of tuition where hardship was created as a result of tuition increases passed by the 1957 legislature.

Payment of tuition and lab fees amounting to approximately $110 for a nine-month session waived for children of certain firemen, peace officers, employees of Texas Department of Corrections and game wardens.

Scholarships determined by institution (extended to needy resident and non-resident students), and based on financial need, character and scholastic record.

Provision, by the coordinating board, Texas College and University System, or equalization grants to Texas residents enrolled as full-time students in approved private Texas colleges or universities. (Awarded on a financial-need basis.)

For information about Direct State loans, write to: Director of Student Financial Aid, Texas College and University System, Sam Houston State Office Building, 201 E. 14th Street, Austin Tex. 78701; guaranteed loans, write to: Director of Higher Education, Office of Education, Region VI, 1114 Commerce Street, Dallas, Tex. 75202

UTAH

SCHOLARSHIPS AWARD COMMITTEE
Write to:
  Scholarships Award Committee
  University of Utah, Salt Lake City, Utah 84100
Resident students at the University of Utah are granted tuition funds based on grades, talent, leadership, and need.

For information about guaranteed loans, write to: Director of Higher Education, Office of Education, Region VIII, Federal Office Building, Room 9017, 19th and Stout Streets, Denver Colo. 80202

VERMONT

Resident students attending Bennington, Castleton State, Goddard, Johnson State, Lydon State, Marlboro, Middlebury, Trinity, St. Michael's, or Windham Colleges, or a Vermont school of nursing, the University of Vermont or Norwich University, may contact the county senator or director of admissions at appropriate schools for details on partial tuition payments (renewable).

For information about guaranteed loans, write to: Vermont Student Assistance Corporation, 109 S. Winowski Avenue, Burlington, Vt. 05401

VIRGINIA

VIRGINIA COMMONWEALTH UNIVERSITY
Write to:
  Dean, School of Dentistry
  Virginia Commonwealth University
  Richmond, Va. 23219
Resident dental students at Virginia Commonwealth University School of Dentistry who agree to practice with the State Health Department for one year for each year assisted are eligible for annual awards of $1,500.

DIVISION OF DENTAL HEALTH
Write to:
  Division of Dental Health
  109 Governor Street, Richmond, Va. 23219
Dental hygienists at Virginia Commonwealth University or at Old Dominion University who agree to practice dental hygiene in Virginia for each

year assisted may receive an annual award of $500.

STATE HEALTH DEPARTMENT
Write to:
State Health Department
Director, Bureau of Public Nursing
109 Governor Street, Richmond, Va. 23219
Resident student nurses attending an approved Virginia school of nursing who agree to practice for a period of time related to amount and number of scholarships received are eligible for $250 to $1,000.

Write to the same address for details on assistance ($500 to $2,000 annually) for registered professional nurses (those seeking a B.S. or higher degrees) who agree to practice in Virginia in positions related to type of preparation for period of time determined by amount and number of scholarships.

VIRGINIA COMMONWEALTH UNIVERSITY
Write to:
Associate Dean, School of Medicine
Virginia Commonwealth University
Richmond, Va. 23219
Resident medical students at Virginia Commonwealth University Medical College who agree to engage continuously in the practice of family medicine in an area of need in Virginia for a period of time equal to number of years assisted, or as determined by the State Health Commissioner, are offered $2,500 annually.

For information about guaranteed loans write to: (in-state students) Virginia State Education Assistance Authority, 1116 United Virginia Bank Building, Richmond Va. 23216; (out-of-state students) Director of Higher Education, Office of Education Region, III, 401 N. Broad Street, Philadelphia, Pa. 19108

VIRGIN ISLANDS

For information about guaranteed loans, write to: United Student Aid Funds, Inc., 5259 N. Tacoma Avenue, Indianapolis, Ind. 46220

WASHINGTON

STATE BOARD OF EDUCATION
Write to:
State Board of Education
Olympia, Wash. 98504
Legally blind students admitted to an institution of higher education, and who are in need of assistance, are eligible for tuition and lab fee aid not to exceed $200 per quarter.

For information about guaranteed loans, write to: Director of Higher Education, Office of Education, Region X, 1319 2nd Avenue, Seattle, Wash. 98101

WEST VIRGINIA

COMMISSION OF HIGHER EDUCATION
Write to:
West Virginia Commission of Higher Education
1316 Charleston National Plaza
Charleston, W. Va. 25301
Applicants for $100 to $900 must be high school graduates or must have the equivalent of a high school diploma and must demonstrate need for financial assistance to attend the college of his or her choice. Applicant must be enrolled full-time at a college or university in the state, must be a citizen of the United States, must be a resident of West Virginia prior to application, must meet the admissions requirements of the selected institution, and must be an undergraduate student of good moral character.

For information about guaranteed loans, write to: Director of Higher Education, Office of Education, Region III, 401 N. Broad Street, Philadelphia, Pa. 19108

WISCONSIN

TUITION GRANT PROGRAM
Write to:
Wisconsin Tuition Grant Program
Higher Education Aids Board
115 West Wilson Street, Madison, Wis. 53703
Undergraduate tuition grants are available to residents in good academic standing at Wisconsin private institutions. Awards (based on difference between public and private tuition charges) are granted according to need.

WISCONSIN HONOR SCHOLARSHIP PROGRAM
Write to:
Wisconsin Honor Scholarship Program
Higher Educational Aids Boards
115 West Wilson Street, Madison, Wis. 53703
Honor scholarships are available to graduating high school seniors. Awards are based on academic achievement in high school as shown by rank in the top 10 percent of the graduating class. Students must be Wisconsin residents and must attend a Wisconsin public or private institution. The program (providing up to $800) is for freshman year only.

Address inquiries about Tuition Reimbursement Program to the above address. Grants of up to $500 per year are open to residents enrolled at private institutions in Wisconsin and at public or private institutions outside Wisconsin in courses leading to a first professional degree in programs not offered in Wisconsin public institutions.

Non-resident members of the armed forces (and their dependents) stationed in the state should contact the registrar at school of student's choice for facts on exemption from tuition and fees.

The State Board of Nursing may grant scholarships to qualified nurses who desire to become nursing school instructors or administrative personnel in accredited schools of professional and practical nursing in Wisconsin. Apply to Wisconsin State Board of Nursing.

DIVISION OF FAMILY SERVICES (or whichever of the following is applicable):
Division of Mental Hygiene, Division of Corrections, Division of Vocational Rehabilitation
Write to:
   State Department of Health and Social Services
   1 West Wilson Street, Madison, Wis. 53702
The State Department of Health and Social Services (through the above named divisions) grants stipends to qualified applicants who desire to become graduate social workers or rehabilitative counselors in public agencies in Wisconsin. Applicants must have a B.A. degree and must meet entrance requirements of accredited graduate schools. Address inquiry to the appropriate division.

For information about guaranteed loans, write to: Wisconsin Higher Education Corporation, State Office Building, 115 W. Wilson Street, Madison, Wis. 53702

WYOMING

Students selected on the basis of need, character, extra-curricular activities and scholastic ability are eligible for County Commissioner Scholarships of $150.75 per semester. Contact commissioner in county of residence.

Wyoming high school honor student scholarships in the amount of $111 (for eight semesters) are available for use at the University of Wyoming. High school principal should be contacted for details.

For information about guaranteed loans, write to: Director, Higher Education, Office of Education, Region VIII, Federal Office Building Room 9017, 19th and Stout Streets, Denver, Colo. 80202

PRIVATE AND LIMITED ELIGIBILITY FUNDS

Many students with interest in a professional area are eligible for aid established to promote entrance into that field. Industry and private organizations often make a commitment to higher education by offering scholarships and loans to worthy students, while some agencies act as consultants which students may write or call for information about sources often overlooked. We can provide information about only a few of the numerous financial aid sources. It is hoped that the student will be motivated to seek additional information from his or her high school counselor and/or principal and from the admissions officers of the colleges selected. The public library is also an excellent repository for such information. Below are listed several more sources of financial aid. Some are listed according to profession. Elig-

ibility requirements are given in cases where information was available.

CONSULTANT AGENCY

NATIONAL SCHOLARSHIP SERVICE AND FUND FOR NEGRO STUDENTS
Write to:
   National Scholarship Service and Fund for Negro Students
   1776 Broadway, New York, N.Y. 10019
The Fund is primarily a college advisory and referral service (provided at no charge) for black H. S. students. Funds disbursed through NSSFNS are sometimes restricted by the contributor to certain major fields of study, sex, or geographical location, and are available only to students counseled by NSSFNS.

ARCHITECTURE AND ENGINEERING

THE AMERICAN INSTITUTE OF ARCHITECTS
Write to:
   American Institute of Architects
   110 Pearl Street, Buffalo, N.Y. 14202
The Institute offers one scholarship (amount determined by the institute) to a student interested in architecture as a career.

THE COOPER UNION FOR THE ADVANCEMENT OF SCIENCE AND ART
Write to:
   The Cooper Union, New York, N.Y. 10003
Scholarships valued at $1,500 to $2,000 are awarded on the basis of standing in competition. Funds offered in art, architecture, engineering and science.

ANTIOCH-NIAGARA FRONTIER COUNCIL
Write to:
   Antioch-Niagara Frontier Council
   116 Hartwell Road, Buffalo, N.Y. 14216
Two scholarships, from $400 to $800, are offered for studies in engineering.

POLYTECHNIC INSTITUTE OF BROOKLYN
Write to:
   Director
   Polytechnic Institute of Brooklyn
   Brooklyn N.Y. 11201
Students wishing to graduate in electrical engineering are eligible. Special consideration given those from black high schools in the South. Grant includes tuition and all maintenance costs.

UNION CARBIDE EDUCATION FUND
Write to:
   Union Carbide Education Fund
   270 Park Avenue, New York, N.Y. 10017
The fund extends awards of varying amounts administered through thirty-five engineering colleges and universities.

LOCKHEED LEADERSHIP FUND
The Lockheed Company offers ten awards in en-

gineering and five in other fields. Scholarships cover tuition fees and have a $500 stipped. Write to admissions director of selected college.

AMERICAN INSTITUTE OF STEEL CONSTRUCTION, INC.
Write to:
American Institute of Steel Construction, Inc.
101 Park Avenue, New York, N.Y. 10017
Non-renewable awards of $3,000 are awarded to senior graduate civil or architectural engineering students.

ALLEGHENY-LUDLUM INDUSTRIES, INC.
Write to:
Allegheny-Ludlum Industries, Inc.
2000 Oliver Building, Pittsburgh, Pa. 15222
While some of the company's scholarships are limited to sons and daughters of employees, A-L also makes awards to engineering students entering their sophomore year ($700; renewable).

THE U. S. SURGEON GENERAL
Write to:
U.S. Surgeon General
U.S. Public Health Service
Washington, D.C. 20203
ATTN: Office of Personnel
For juniors and seniors in health-related fields, and for students in programs of engineering and science. Funds in amounts to be determined by U.S. Surgeon General are available.

JOURNALISM, COMMUNICATIONS AND DRAMA

THE NEWSPAPER FUND
Write to:
The Newspaper Fund
P.O. Box 300, Princeton, N.J. 08540
Any college junior interested in journalism in general and in newspaper work in particular is eligible. Recipient must work as reporter or copy editor on a U.S. newspaper. Internship is served between junior and senior years (summer), and scholarship is awarded in September following internship.

WILLIAM RANDOLPH HEARST FOUNDATION
Write to:
William Randolph Hearst Foundation
3rd and Market Street
San Francisco, Calif. 94103
Grants for study to undergraduate journalism students range from $75 to $100 per month.

GEORGE ABBOTT EDUCATIONAL FOUNDATION, INC.
Write to:
George Abbott Educational Foundation, Inc.
630 Fifth Avenue, New York, N.Y. 10020
Established for students with talent in dramatic playwriting to attend the University of Rochester (N.Y.). Contact foundation for amounts.

AMERICAN NEWSPAPER PUBLISHERS ASSOCIATION FOUNDATION
Write to:
American Newspaper Publishers Association Foundation
750 Third Avenue, New York, N.Y. 10017
The foundation offers awards of varying amounts to black college studying journalism.

HAROLD E. FELLOWS MEMORIAL SCHOLARSHIP
Write to:
National Association of Broadcasters
1771 N Street, N.W., Washington, D.C. 20036
$1,100 awarded to juniors in college.

LAW

INFORMATION SERVICES:

AMERICAN BAR ASSOCIATION
1155 E. 60th Street, Chicago, Ill. 60637

NAACP LEGAL DEFENSE AND EDUCATIONAL FUND
10 Columbus Circle, New York, N.Y. 10019

SCHOLARSHIP INFORMATION CENTER
YMCA-YWCA, University of North Carolina
Chapel Hill, N.C. 27514

EXECUTIVE DIRECTOR COUNCIL ON LEGAL EDUCATIONAL OPPORTUNITY
Box 105, Morehouse College
Atlanta, Ga. 30314

MARTIN LUTHER KING, JR. FELLOWSHIP PROGRAM WOODROW WILSON NATIONAL FELLOWSHIP FOUNDATION
Box 642, Princeton, N.J. 08540

MEDICAL AND ALLIED PROFESSIONS

AMERICAN FUND FOR DENTAL EDUCATION
Write to:
American Fund for Dental Education
211 E. Chicago Avenue, Chicago, Ill. 60611
Pre-dental undergraduates in junior year are eligible for $2,500 for final year of undergraduate study and $2,500 for each year of regular dental school.

NATIONAL INSTITUTES OF HEALTH
Write to:
U.S. Department of Health, Education & Welfare
National Institutes of Health
Student Loan and Scholarship Branch
9000 Raskille Parkway, Bethesda, Md. 20014
The NIH provides up to $1,500 renewable per academic year to nursing students.

AMERICAN MEDICAL ASSOCIATION
Write to:
American Medical Association
Education and Research Foundation
535 No. Dearborn Street, Chicago, Ill. 60610
The AMA offers loans (of varying amounts) to students admitted to approved medical schools.

BETA CHI, INC.
Write to:
Beta Chi, Inc.
1211 Leeds Street, Utica, N.Y. 13501
The group extends one scholarship of $500 for a girl to attend any accredited hospital school of nursing.

BUREAU OF STATE SERVICES
Write to:
Bureau of State Services (Community Health)
U.S. Department of Health, Education & Welfare
Washington, D.C. 20201
Persons enrolled or accepted full-time in an accredited school of nursing having a loan fund under the Community Health Act may borrow up to $1,000 per academic year.

The Community Health Act also establishes student loan funds for those pursuing degrees in medicine, dentistry, optometry or osteopathy. Students may obtain up to $2,000 per year.

Write to the addresses listed above.

SURGEON GENERAL
Write to:
U.S. Surgeon General
U.S. Public Health Service
Washington, D.C. 20203
ATTN: Office of Personnel
Funds in varying amounts are available for juniors and seniors in health-related fields and students in programs of engineering and science.

NATIONAL LEAGUE FOR NURSING
Write to:
National League for Nursing
10 Columbus Circle, New York, N.Y. 10019
The League offers funds in varying amounts for persons interested in nursing.

LEVER BROTHERS
Write to:
Lever Brothers
390 Park Avenue, New York N.Y. 10022
The company provides fifty-one (one in each state and the District of Columbia) renewable $500 scholarships for pharmaceutical studies.

ADDITIONAL SOURCES

COOPERATIVE ADMISSION AND AID PROGRAM
Write to:
Association of College Admissions Counselors
610 Church Street, Evanston, Ill. 60201
Awards are given to culturally disadvantaged

youths upon recommendation of counselor.

ELEANOR ROOSEVELT SCHOLARSHIP PROGRAM
Write to:
Congress of Racial Equality
150 Nassau Street, Room 1312
New York, N.Y. 10038
Up to $1,500 per year is awarded to undergraduates actively involved in the civil rights movement.

ELKS OF THE WORLD
Write to:
Elks of the World
Imperial Lodge No. 127
160 W. 129th Street, New York, N.Y. 10027
The organization awards scholarships of varying amounts to black H. S. graduates.

HERBERT LEHMAN FUND
Write to:
Herbert Lehman Educational Fund
10 Columbus Circle, Suite 2030
New York, N.Y. 10019
The fund offers aid in varying amounts to black undergraduate students.

NATIONAL HONOR SOCIETY SCHOLARSHIP PROGRAM

High school members of the National Honor Society should indicate desire for candidacy on the Preliminary Scholastic Aptitude Test (PSAT).

GENERAL MOTORS SCHOLARSHIP PLAN
Write to:
General Motors Scholarship Plan
General Motors Building, Detroit, Mich. 48202
The GM Corporation offers scholarships ranging from $200 to $2,000 per year for high school seniors.

S & H FOUNDATION INC. NATIONAL SCHOLARSHIP PROGRAM

Interested high school seniors should check item 10 on the Scholastic Aptitude Test (SAT), Code No. 0329. Award is $1,000 annually.

WESTINGHOUSE SCIENCE TALENT SEARCH
Write to:
Science Clubs of America
1719 N Street, N.W., Washington, D.C. 20530
The fund is established for students interested in science careers. A high school science teacher should inquire.

JOHN MCKEE SCHOLARSHIP COMMITTEE
Write to:
John McKee Scholarship Committee
643 Lawson Avenue, Haverton, Pa. 19183
Orphan boys in the Philadelphia area who are H.S. graduates not over eighteen years of age are eligible for these awards.

NATIONAL ASSOCIATION OF SECONDARY SCHOOL PRINCIPALS

Write to:

National Association of Secondary School
Principals
1201 16th Street, N.W., Washington, D.C. 20036

The association makes awards of $1,000 to senior members of the National Honor Society in respective high schools.

PULITZER SCHOLARSHIPS

Seniors in public high schools in New York City must be nominated by their high school principals for these awards. Contact the principal

or

Write to:

Pulitzer Scholarship, 202 Hamilton Hall
Columbia University, New York, N.Y. 10027

GENERAL MILLS, INC.

Write to:

General Mills, Inc.
9200 Wayzata Boulevard
Minneapolis, Minn. 55440

The company offers awards in varying amounts to H. S. senior girls only.

NATIONAL 4-H SERVICES COMMITTEE, INC.

Write to:

National 4-H Services Committee Inc.
59 E. Van Buren Street, Chicago, Ill. 60654

Currently enrolled and past members are eligible for grants up to $1,600. Not renewable.

ARMCO STEEL CORPORATION COMMUNITY SCHOLARSHIPS

Write to:

Armco Steel Corporation Community
Scholarships
703 Curtis Street, Middleton, Ohio 45042

Students who rank in the top one-third of class and perform well on SAT are in line for renewable awards of $750. Student must live in a designated community in California, Kentucky, Maryland, Ohio, Missouri, Kansas, Oklahoma, Pennsylvania, Texas, or West Virginia.

RALPH E. SMITH FREEDOM SCHOLARSHIPS

Write to:

Macalester College, St. Paul Minn. 55105

Funds are valid for use at Macalester College. High school seniors may apply.

FINANCIAL AID: LOANS

AMERICAN MEDICAL ASSOCIATION EDUCATION AND RESEARCH FOUNDATION

Write to:

American Medical Association Education
535 North Dearborn Street, Chicago, Ill. 60610

Applicant must have completed first term of medical school. Apply through medical school financial aid officer. Up to $1500 per year.

STATE OF ALABAMA BOARD OF MEDICAL SCHOLARSHIP AWARDS

Write to:

State of Alabama Board of Medical
Scholarship Awards
Scholarship Awards
1919 Seventh Avenue, South
Birmingham, Ala. 35233

Maximum $2,000 per year, $8,000 over a four-year period. Restricted to residents of Alabama who have been accepted for matriculation by the Medical College of Alabama, or a comparable institution.

AMERICAN MEDICAL WOMEN'S ASSOCIATION, INC.

Write to:

American Medical Women's Association Inc.
1750 Broadway, New York, N.Y. 10019

Maximum $1,000 per year. Available to women who are U.S. citizens enrolled in a U.S. medical school.

BERGEN FOUNDATION

Write to:

Bergen Foundation, 6536 Sunset Boulevard
Hollywood, Calif. 90028

Nursing loans. Usually covers tuition costs for H.S. graduates or girls who are in nursing school.

EDDY STUDENT LOAN FUND

Write to:

Eddy Student Loan Fund
c/o Thomas and Thomas
504 Broadway
Suite 1016, Gary, Ind. 64602

Up to $1 500 a year for college juniors and seniors, or a student who just completed two years of work at an accredited college.

EDUCATIONAL AND SCIENTIFIC TRUST OF THE PENNSYLVANIA MEDICAL SOCIETY

Write to:

Educational and Scientific Trust of the
Pennsylvania Medical Society
Taylor Bypass and Erford Road
Lemoyne, Pa. 17043

Available to Pennsylvania residents attending medical schools in the United States.

EDUCATIONAL FUND, INC.

Write to:

Educational Fund, Inc.
10 Dorance Street, Providence R.I. 02901

From $700 to $14,000 over a four-year period H.S. students and college students.

ENTRENOUS CLUB OF DETROIT

Write to:

Entrenous Club of Detroit
Student Loan Fund
Office of Scholarship and Financial Aid
Wayne State University, Detroit, Mich. 48202

Maximum $200 per quarter. Student must be matriculated at Wayne State U. Preference is given to black students.

FELLOWS MEMORIAL FUND
Write to:
  Fellows Memorial Fund
  c/o President, Pensacola Junior College
  1000 College Boulevard, Pensacola, Fla. 32504
Generous loans provided for medical, nursing, or
theological students who are bona fide residents
of one of the four counties of northwestern Florida and who intend to practice in that region.

FRIENDS EDUCATION FUND
Write to:
  Friends Education Fund
  F.E.F.F.N.
  1004 State Office Building, Indianapolis, Ind.
For black students. Must be used at Indiana col-
leges and universities.

FUNDS FOR EDUCATION, INC.
Write to:
  Funds for Education, Inc.
  319 Lincoln Street, Manchester, N.H. 01201
Loans from $350 to $2,500 for use at any school,
college or university.

THE HEALTH PROFESSIONS LOAN
PROGRAM
Write to:
  The Health Professions Loan Program
  Bureau of Health Manpower
  U.S. Public Health Service
  National Institutes of Health—Bldg. 31
  9000 Rockville Pike, Bethesda, Md. 20014
Careers in medicine, dentistry, osteopathy, opto-
metry, pharmacy, and podiatry.

W. K. KELLOGG FOUNDATION
Write to:
  W. K. Kellogg Foundation
  Hospital Administration Loan Fund
  Office of Student Financial Aid
  George Washington University
  Washington, D.C. 20006
Available for full-time graduate students in hospi-
tal administration at George Washington Uni-
versity.

NATIONAL ASSOCIATION OF COLORED
WOMEN
Write to:
  National Association of Colored Women
  1601 R Street, N.W.
  Washington, D.C. 20009
Amounts vary.

NEW YORK HIGHER EDUCATION
Write to:
  New York Higher Education
  Assistance Corporation
  159 Delaware Avenue, Delmar, N.Y. 12054
Full-time students may borrow up to $1,000 for
the freshman year, $1,000 for the sophomore
year, $1,250 the thrid year and $1,500 the fourth
and subsequent years of school. Maximum
amount for any one student is $7,500. Students
may borrow from any lending institution in the
State of New York which participates in the Student Loan Program.

HENRY WARREN ROTH EDUCATION FUND
Write to:
  Henry Warren Roth Education Fund
  Financial Aid Office
  Theil College, Greenville, Pa. 16125
May be applied for by all undergraduate students.

HATTIE M. STRONG LOAN FOUNDATION
Write to:
  Hattie M. Strong Loan Foundation
  409 Cafritz Building
  1625 I Street, N.W., Washington, D.C. 20006
From $800 to $1,500 available for graduating
H.S. seniors.

THE TUITION PLAN
Write to:
  The Tuition Plan
  410 North Michigan Avenue, Chicago, Ill. 60611
Loans regardless of location of school.

UNITED STUDENT AID FUND
Write to:
  United Student Aid Fund
  845 3rd Avenue, New York, N.Y. 10022
Loans up to $1,000 for graduates and undergrad-
uates of any of the 700 participating schools.

Section V

LIBRARIES

LIBRARIES IN THE BLACK COMMUNITY

It is impossible to extricate libraries and library service from the educational whole, and many of the problems affecting education for blacks also affect library services to blacks.

During the period preceding the civil rights revolution (50s and 60s), blacks were systematically denied access to libraries throughout the South, and required to use "libraries for Negroes." If there was one available, its resources were apt to be less than adequate. In other areas of the country, where segregated facilities were not a part of the legal structure, the problem of access was determined by the placement of library facilities.

When there are no major library facilities within walking distance of a large segment of a community, when there are no regular bookmobile stops or deposit services within easy range of children, then that community can effectively be listed as having either no library service or sub-standard library service. In the opening years of the decade of the seventies, many black communities in the U.S. are still without effective or adequate library resources.

Pressure was brought by citizens and library groups in 1956 to assist communities in providing better library services to all. The Library Services Act (1956), and later the Library Services and Construction Act (1964-66-70) sought to provide necessary financial aid to urban and rural communities to expand library service. Funds provided by the Act have gone to aid in library construction, as well as to the purchase of materials.

The 1960s saw more attention given to the development of inner city library service. Storefront libraries and other techniques were utilized to get books to black readers.

The picture which was getting better suddenly grew bleak. The 1973 Nixon Administration cut-back on federal funding to specific programs, such as the Library Services and Construction program deleted direct grants to states and local municipalities for library-oriented programs on a matching basis. These cuts eliminated upwards of 50 million dollars a year from programs designed to provide more adequate library service to a wide variety of users.

The emphasis then shifted from library service per se, to the issue of who was to construct the libraries and provide the service.

A Caucus on Black Librarians, under the leadership of E. J. Josey and others, was formed to address themselves specifically to the problems of professional training, recruitment, wage and salary bias, and whether or not southern library integration was not, in fact, black librarian elimination. Through greater and more active participation in professional associations, such as the American Library Association, Special Libraries Association, and Association of College and University Libraries, the black professional sought to make the entire profession acutely aware of the problem. A notable issue was raised when the Black Caucus and the black employees of the Library of Congress charged the Library of Congress with discrimination against blacks. The District of Columbia Public Library was included in the attack, and Milton Byam, a black professional librarian and administrator has since been named head of the D.C. Public Library.

In several major cities, including Pittsburgh and Chicago, construction on library buildings within black communities has been halted until participation by black contractors or sub-contractors on the project has been assured, as a result of black protest groups such as Operation PUSH and SCLC's work with black builders.

Finally, as more and more blacks are being named to library boards, as directors or as trustees, they are moving into the realm of decision-making authority, and substantive changes in the quality of library service to minority groups can be expected.

LIBRARY SERVICE AND THE BLACK LIBRARIAN

Robert Wedgeworth*

Like many other cultural institutions, libraries have recently been anxiously seeking to increase their minority group employee representation. The two most obvious reasons for these efforts are institutional survival and the need to comply with governmental policies against discriminatory practices.

Many libraries have pursued objectives which were somewhat irrelevant to the information needs and uses of blacks in their user communities. While few would argue that this situation stems in part from rapid shifts in the racial composition of our population centers, nevertheless such institutions may well face extinction if they are unable or unwilling to re-orient their objectives toward their current immediate constituents.

In considering the importance of improving library service to blacks, perhaps it is significant to begin by noting that a majority of the more than 23 million blacks in the United tates live in the complex environment of our central cities. Add to this that blacks tend to gain less education, be unemployed more often, make less money when employed, and be more often under-represented by elected officials than their white counterparts, and a picture emerges of a group at a disadvantage socially, politically and economically in a highly competitive, information-oriented setting. While it is true that knowledge or information is power, in order to assist individuals to understand and perhaps influence the forces that shape their lives, they must be either already in possession of the appropriate information or be aware of where it is readily accessible.

Although the range of the information needs and uses within black communities is similar to that within other communities, the need has been shown to be much more acute. Certainly housing improvement assistance services are most important to those with the least housing improvement opportunities. Employment information is a priority to those who are frequently unemployed. It is partly to assist in the redirection of library services toward these ends that more blacks are being encouraged to pursue library careers.

The need to comply with governmental policies against discriminatory practices has been offered as the second motivating factor for recruiting more blacks to librarianship. In recent years, a number of university and public libraries have implemented affirmative action plans to increase their minority group employee representation. The American Library Association's (ALA) Committee on Equal Employment Opportunity is completing a recommended policy statement which will commit the Association, "through its organized resources and membership support, to a policy of equality of opportunity for all library employees or applicants for employment, regardless of race, color, creed, sex, individual life style or national origin. This policy of employment equality logically begins with recruitment to the occupation of librarianship." Currently existing federal policies include:

Statutes

(a) Title VII of the Civil Rights Acts of 1964 as amended by the Equal Employment Opportunity Act of 1972.
(b) Fair Labor Standards Act of 1938 as amended, particularly by the Equal Act of 1963 and the Education Amendments of 1972.

Executive Orders

(a) 11246 (September 24, 1965) as amended by EO 11375 (October 13, 1967) and EO 11478 (August 8, 1969).

Federal Court Cases

(a) Griggs v. Duke Power Company, 401 U.S. 424, 91 S. CT. 849, 28 L. Ed. 2d 158 (1971).
(b) Gregory v. Litton System, Inc. 316 F. Supp. 401 (D.C. Cal. 1970).

Although blacks are under-represented in librarianship in proportion to their numbers in the population at large, the occupational outlook remains good for black librarians. According to the U.S. Department of Labor, there are approximately 18,000 male librarians in the United States 6%, or 1,080, are black, while there are approximately 96,000 female librarians, 7%, or 6,720, are black.

A 1972 study published in *Library Journal* (June 15, 1973) provides information on 6,079 graduates of accredited graduate library programs. Of the total, 285 were not in library positions, 3,751 were known library placements, and 1,801 were of undetermined status.

Although the salary figures reported do not account for variations in vacation allowances, length of work week, sick leave or other fringe benefits, the average annual salary for the group was $9,248.00.

The National Registry of Librarians operated by the U.S. Department of Labor handles a librarian placement service at the ALA Annual Conference each summer. Their statistics on the job market for librarians over the past four years reveals the following:

	1970	1971	1972	1973
Applicants	923	1,133	1,416	1,193
Employers	757	320	530	288
Vacancies	892	521	572	525

Although there has been some deterioration of the job market from applicants' point of view there was still roughly one available position for every two applicants in 1973.

For the black librarian, librarianship offers the opportunity to assume a leadership role in re-directing a tradition-oriented profession toward a more dynamic future. Moreover, as black librarian E. J. Josey puts it:

Libraries and information centers preserve the vast heritage of mankind in general, and Black people in particular. Only recently have these reservoirs of knowledge begun to collect on a wide scale the heritage of Black people. In order to ensure the preservation of the Black experience in America and throughout the world, it is imperative that more Black young people enter the field of librarianship.

Notwithstanding the stereotype of the librarian as elderly, shy, and female, librarianship has begun to attract larger numbers of best entrants to the job market. The wide variety of employment settings—from public library community outreach programs to university libraries, business and industrial libraries and school media centers—offer exciting opportunities to work with the young or old, blind and physically handicapped—or perhaps in areas of computer technology or cable television.

It is important to remember that libraries as institutions have done more than just survive the onslaught of technological society. It remains the one institution stable enough to provide for community based information needs which transcend political jurisdictions by cooperative agreements, and flexible enough to adjust to many different individual requirements and capabilities.

For further information on library careers, write to the American Library Association. Office of Library Personnel Resources, 50 East Huron Street, Chicago, Illinois 60611.

*Robert Wedgeworth is the Executive Director of the American Library Association.

BLACK CAUCUS OF LIBRARIANS

Ninety-eight percent of the black librarians in attendance at the Mid-Winter meeting of the A. L. A. in Chicago, January 21, 1970, convened in a black caucus for the expressed purpose of addressing themselves to many of the pressing problems and issues facing this country in general, and the A. L. A., in particular.

They expressed concern about the effects of institutional racism, poverty, the continued lack of educational, employment and promotional opportunities upon blacks and other minorities. They pointed out that although the social-economic ills have been condemned by the Kerner Commission, the Commission on violence, and many other studies, the library profession has been slow in response to these problems. They presented the following resolution:

Whereas, the United States Supreme Court of this land has called for the desegregation of public schools by February 1, 1970, and,

Whereas, public academic and school libraries in areas where desegregation has been ordered are in some cases lending and in other cases planning to lend materials to racist institutions conceived for the purpose of circumventing the law of the land and,

Whereas, such school administrations and many civil leaders in such areas have in fact asked for active support from libraries because funding for their schools and institutions is inadequate to provide for libraries and text books and,

Whereas, the A. L. A. is cognizant of the social responsibilities of libraries serving the people of the United States and is on record as being opposed to racism in any or all of its forms.

Therefore, be it resolved that the libraries and/or librarians who do in fact, through either services or materials, support any such racist institutions, be censured by the A. L. A.

OFFICERS

ALA BLACK CAUCUS

Founding Chairman (1970–72) . . . . . . Mr. E. J. Josey, Chief, Bureau of Academic and Research Libraries, Division of Library Development, N. Y. State, Department of Education

Chairman (1972–73) . . . . Mr. William Cunningham, University of Maryland

Chairman (1973–74) . . . . Mr. James Wright, Rochester Public Library

Secretary-Treasurer . . . . Ms. Louise Giles

PROGRAM COMMITTEE

Program Chairman . . . . Mr. James E. Crayton, Pasadena City College

Co-Chairman . . . . Ms. Louise Moses, L. A. County Public Library

Chairman, Host and Hostess Committee . . . . Ms. E. M. Fisher, UC San Diego

LIBRARIES AND "SOCIAL REALITIES"

Robert Wedgeworth, the executive director of the American Library Association, speaking to The National Commission on Libraries and Information Science, in Chicago, in late 1972, urged libraries to meet social realities head on. Libraries, he said, must devise new patterns of service to mesh with the new types of education that have emerged: "schools without walls," independent study programs, and continuing education. They must also respond to growing pressures for change coming from minority groups, women, youth, and the poor, and provide services for the aged and the handicapped. It is crucial, he said, to redress the imbalance of financial resources between the cities, which operate major libraries and information services, and the suburbs, which now make the greatest use of them.

Libraries, said Wedgeworth, are stuck at the "general store" stage when it's the era of the supermarket. He called for "experiments in library economics:" among them, "training laboratories" to improve the skills of practicing librarians and "library renewal centers" to serve as labs where librarians, merchandisers, designers, programmers, administrators, educators, public relations people and other special-

ists could hammer out new patterns in services and procedures, judging them according to "test marketing" criteria. He also suggested combining the collections of public libraries and junior colleges and stressed the need for a new vocabulary—comprehensible to both professionals and the lay public—which could pinpoint "social and economic indicators" to evaluate and predict the present and future needs of libraries.

Wedgeworth asked for a review of library legislation, particularly where it applies to tax support for library services. While noting that revenue sharing legislation has elevated library service to the status of a "national priority," he stressed that legal problems "which constrain the development of library networks" on a nationwide basis must not be overlooked. He urged NCLIS to participate on a more regular basis in the meetings of library associations, using them as a sounding board for the airing of library problems and possible solutions to them.

Source: Excerpted from *Library Journal*, Dec. 15, 1972 National Library Commission meeting in Chicago, by Noël Savage

SPECIAL COLLECTIONS

Atlanta University Center

The Atlanta University Center contains the libraries of six institutions—Morris Brown, Spelman, Clark, Morehouse. The Interdenominational Theological Center and Atlanta University. The Trevor Arnett Library at Atlanta University serves as the central library for the students and faculty of the various institutions. The total holdings number more than 305,000 cataloged volumes, with Atlanta University having 280,034. Outstanding collections in the group are the Henry P. Slaughter Collection of black materials and the Countee Cullen Memorial Collection, established by Harold Jackman. The Cullen Collection is strong in the manuscripts and working papers of contemporary black authors and poets including James Baldwin. The John Brown Letters are a part of the Slaughter collection and an outstanding collection of Lincolniana in the Southern states if found here. The Slaughter Collection is also known for its extensive pamphlet and print collection. Mrs. Gaynelle W. Barksdale is librarian.

W. E. B. DuBois Collection

The University of Massachusetts at Amherst acquired the manuscripts, correspondence and papers in the collection of the late William E. Burghardt DuBois in 1973 from DuBois' widow, Mrs. Shirley Graham DuBois. The DuBois papers include eight four-drawer filing cabinets of correspondence, and about 75,000 letters that treat every significant political and ideological question of the years from 1890 to 1960. There are reputedly between a hundred and a hundred and fifty thousand pieces of material. Randolph W. Bromery, chancellor of the University of Massachusetts, said two-thirds of the collection had been appraised at $250,000.

It will not be available for use by scholars until at least 1976.

Fisk University Special Collections

The Fisk University Library and Media Center houses 55 collections of materials in its Special Collections. Among the most widely used collections are: the Charles W. Chesnutt Collection consisting of correspondence with publishers, personal correspondence, published and unpublished books, articles, speeches, plays and poems; the Jean Toomer Collection, containing correspondence with Sherwood Anderson, Waldo Frank, Forham Munson and others, autobiographical materials, novels, short stories, plays, poems and lectures; the Jubilee Singers Archives, consisting of materials of the original Singers such as autograph diaries, clippings, programs, photographs, scrapbooks, and souvenirs collected by the Singers on their tours; John W. Work Collection, containing general and personal correspondence, music (published and unpublished), compositions in manuscript (choruses, piano solos, orchestrals) and autographed copies of music by black composers, and the Charles S. Johnson Collection, containing correspondence, addresses, interviews, studies and other materials accumulated while he was head of the Social Science Department and President of Fisk University.

Other important collections include those of W.E.B. DuBois, Langston Hughes, Thomas Elsa Jones, James Weldon Johnson, Julius Rowenwald Fund, George Edmund Haynes, James Napier, Winifred Holtby, John Mercer Langston, Scott Joplin and others.

A complete list of the Special Collections may be obtained by writing to Mrs. Ann A. Shockley, Associate Librarian and Head of Special Collections.

Fisk University's Black Oral History Program

The Fisk University Library's Black Oral History program is geared to conduct planned taped interviews with persons from all walks of life who have contributed to, or can give, information germane to the black experience in America. The program engages a relatively new technique in historical research and attempts to bridge gaps in black history and culture, to disclose different and fresh information, and to supplement other primary and secondary sources. The collection and preservation of this assemblage of unwritten history is significant for scholarly research, for support to Black Studies programs of colleges and universities, and for its value to the existing rich resources of the Library's archival collection.

Interviews are conducted by faculty and staff members, students, and others who have specialized knowledge or interest in a particular subject, person, or event. The interviews are topical, biographical, and autobiographical. Currently, there are over three hundred tapes in the collection and all tapes are indexed and transcribed.

Such persons as Mrs. Jean Toomer, Mrs. Shirley Graham DuBois, Mrs. Countee Cullen, Hank Aaron, Benjamin Mays, Arna W. Bontemps, Don L. Lee, Margaret Walker

Alexander, Angela Davis, C. Eric Lincoln, Shirley Chisolm, Aaron Douglas, Fannie Lou Hamer, Julian Bond, and Harold Cruse have been taped. Topics in the collection include the Attica Prison Riot (1971), Vietnam War veterans and prisoners of war, life histories of local and national centenarians, outstanding contributions made by physicists, and the Civil Rights Movement.

An annotated bibliography of the collection to date is now in process.

Hampton Institute

The collection of the Huntington Memorial Library is particularly strong in biography, history, social sciences, music, and education. There are 152,963 cataloged items including books, prints, manuscripts, and pamphlets. Outstanding special collections include the collection of early photographs of Hampton Institute, the Carnegie Collection of Classical Art, the Archives of Hampton Institute, and the George Foster Peabody Collection of materials by and about the black man. The Peabody Collection consists of '17,000 cataloged items, including books, scrapbooks of clippings, pamphlets on slavery, recordings and microfilm. Jason C. Grant, III is Director of the library.

The Vivian G. Harsh Collection

The Vivian G. Harsh Collection on Afro-American History and Literature is located in the George Cleveland Hall Branch of the Chicago Public Library, 4801 South Michigan Avenue, Chicago, 60615. The collection, which covers every phase of Afro-Americana and Africana, includes the following items: (1) over 15,500 books and periodicals in print and on microfilm; (2) 310 Afro-American newspapers on microfilm from 1827 to the present; (3) approximately 9,500 pamphlets, including "The Negro in Illinois: the Illinois Writers Project File;" (4) 1300 recordings; (5) the 100 poster Frank London Brown Historical Exhibit; and (6) original manuscripts by Richard Wright and Langston Hughes. Material in the collection is for room use only.

James Weldon Johnson Memorial Collection of Negro Arts and Letters

This collection, founded by Carl Van Vechten in 1941 and added to by Mrs. Johnson, Langston Hughes, Dr. W.E.B. Du Bois, Walter White and Mrs. (Poppy Cannon) White, Miss Dorothy and Dr. Sidney Peterson, Chester Himes and others, is administered as part of the Yale Collection of American Literature. Although writings by and about blacks

all over the world are represented, the collection is centered on the contribution of the American black in the late nineteenth and twentieth centuries to the arts in the United States. It includes manuscripts and correspondence of Langston Hughes, James Weldon Johnson, Claude McKay, and Walter White, with books from their libraries, as well as manuscripts and letters of many other black writers of the twentieth century and programs and clippings documenting the careers of blacks in the theater, in music, and in most other fields. Besides manuscripts and books, the collection contains prints and Kodachrome slides of Mr. Van Vechten's photographs of blacks, as well as other photographs, and a large collection of recordings. The James Weldon Johnson Memorial Fund, established by the James Weldon Johnson Memorial Committee and added to annually by Mr. and Mrs. Van Vechten and other friends, provides funds for the purchase of material.

Martin Luther King, Jr. Center for Social Change

The Martin Luther King, Jr. Center for Social Change, Library-Documentation Project, at 671 Beckwith St. SW, Atlanta, Georgia is designed as a core of resources for the activities of the Center and a Research Center for the people. The Project includes an Archives and Oral History Collection with papers, tapes, photographs, and memorabilia from individuals and organizations active in the Civil Rights Movement; "From Montgomery To Memphis," 1954-68, focussing on the life of Dr. Martin Luther King, Jr.; and a library encompassing published materials to augment the archival collection. Other special collections included for Outreach Programs of the Center are: A Permanent Exhibit of Portraits of Dr. M.L. King, Jr. donated by artists to Mrs. Coretta Scott King; photo prints of activities in the 1954 Civil Rights Movement; sculptures and other art work; Postage Stamp Collection honoring Dr. King and other memorabilia; Multilingual Collection of Books by and about Dr. Martin Luther King, Jr.; Story Hour Collection of books and non-book materials about the life of black people designed for the Story Hour Project; and The Coretta Scott King Award Committee Book Collection. Requests for a list of the Special Collections and other distributive resources may be sent to the Center librarian, Mrs. Minnie Clayton.

The Library of Congress

In both its general and special collections, the Library of Congress houses a wealth of materials valuable for the study of the black Americans and of black history in the United States. A sampling of works in the Library's general collections is revealed in the selective bibliography published in 1970 entitled *The Negro in the United States,* edited by Dorothy B. Porter. This guide lists over 1,800 titles, mostly recent monographs in the Library's collections, on a wide range of topics relating to various aspects of black life. In her introduction to the bibliography, Mrs. Porter also reviews earlier Library guides to black materials.

The Library's special collections are found in several different divisions. Major Manuscript Division collections include the noncurrent records of the National Association for the Advancement of Colored People, and the official papers of the National Urban League (including its Southern Regional Office), the American Colonization Society, and the Brotherhood of Sleeping Car Porters. The papers of Booker T. Washington, acquired in 1943, and those of Frederick Douglass, transferred from the National Park Service in 1972, are but two distinct collections of the papers of prominent blacks. Many other manuscript holdings, including the papers of most United States Presidents and of 19th- and 20th-century literary figures, contain materials important to the study of the black in the United States.

Other special collections are found throughout the Library. The Rare Book Division houses the Slave Narrative Collection of the Federal Writers Project, while the Recorded Sound Section and the Archive of Folk Song, both part of the Music Division, contain published recordings by black writers and unpublished recordings of native black music. The Prints and Photographs Division includes several relevant collections, including photographs from the files of the American Colonization Society. A final source of background materials of interest to the student of black history and culture is the Library's African Section, formed just over 10 years ago. The section concentrates on the acquisition of items from sub-Saharan Africa.

A recent development is the appointment in 1973 of a new Library of Congress Manuscript Historian and Specialist in Afro-American History and Culture, Dr. Sylvia Lyons Render, who will assist researchers in the use of the Library's Afro-American manuscripts.

The Schomburg Collection

The Schomburg Collection, a reference and research library, is one of the most important centers in the world for the study of black people.

International in scope, it covers every phase of black activity wherever black people have lived in significant numbers. Its materials range from early rarities to contemporary publications from Benin to Watts.

The nucleus of this collection is the distinguished private library assembled by Arthur A. Schomburg, a Puerto Rican of African descent. In 1926, the Carnegie Corporation of New York purchased the Collection from Mr. Schomburg and presented it to The New York Public Library. Today, its holdings, multiplied and broadened, serve as a major resource to those seeking documentation of the black experience throughout the world.

Located in Harlem, The Schomburg Collection provides books of black authorship and literary and historical works in which accounts of black life and history appear. The collection is greatly strengthened by its numerous magazines, pamphlets, manuscripts, personal papers, photographs, prints, newspaper clippings, playbills, programs, broadsides and music. Also included are several thousand phonograph and tape recordings, both music and spoken word, of works by black people.

The Schomburg Collection is distinguished by its large holdings in West Indian history, social conditions, poetry, fiction and folklore. The accumulation of Haitian literature and history is unique in its comprehensiveness and has recently been enriched by the addition of the Kurt Fisher Haitian Collection.

Other items indicative of the collection's holdings are: The 81 manuscript volumes of field notes and memoranda used by Gunnar Myrdal in writing *An American Dilemma;* The Archives of the National Negro Congress and the Civil Rights Congress; manuscripts of Claude McKay and Richard Wright; The Harry A. Williamson Library on the Negro in Masonry; Records of African folk music, thoroughly indexed by tribe, type of song and instruments, and of Afro-American jazz and rhythm and blues; microfilm files of some 400 black newspapers.

The file of black newspapers on microfilm offers a reflection of contemporary and historical black thought and life. African newspapers, such as the *West African Pilot, East African Standard, Evening News* (Ghana) and *Central African Post,* are now available on microfilm. The Afro-American newspaper collection includes long, complete runs of newspapers dating from 1827 through the First World War, such as the *California Eagle, Cleveland Gazette* and *Savannah Tribune.* Current issue of black newspapers giving national coverage are microfilmed at the end of each year.

On display in the Schomburg Collection are art objects of ivory, metal and wood, including the Eric de Kolb Collection of African Arms.

Traveling exhibits on the history of the Afro-American and on contemporary Africa are available for loan to organizations other than schools.

Because material from the Schomburg Collection cannot be borrowed, but must be used within the building, it has the advantage of being always available. Materials may be photocopied on the premises, or arrangements may be made for quality photo-reproduction by the Photographic Service of The New York Public Library. Though the best use of the collection can be made by working in the building, telephone and mail inquiries are answered by the staff of reference librarians.

The Moorland Spingarn Research Center

The Moorland Spingarn Research Center at Howard University in Washington, D.C. is a separate and autonomous research library which also includes the Howard University Archives. It is a center for much of the research in the social studies and black history that is conducted at Howard University. A rapidly growing collection with new acquisitions weekly, it has over 180,342 cataloged items, including books, pamphlets, manuscripts, records and microfilm. Among the valuable original materials in this collection are papers of the following historically important persons: Frederick Douglass, Blanche Kelso Bruce, James T. Rapier, Oliver Otis Howard, Pinckney B. Pinchback, Archibald and Francis Grimke, Henry McNeil Turner, Daniel Hale Williams, Louis T. Wright, Alain Locke, E. Franklin Frazier, the Leigh Whipper Papers and the Rose McLendon Collections of Photographs by Carl Van Vechten. Also included are papers of Joel E. and Arthur B. Spingarn, and four volumes of inventors'

patents, collected by Henry E. Baker.

A projected "Union List" of the holdings of all major black collections will make the combined resources of these libraries available for scholars having an active public interest in these holdings. There is also a National Black History Museum planned which will be a part of the Moorland Spingarn Research Center. Mr. Michael R. Winston is director of the Center.

The Tuskegee Institute Washington Collection and Archives

The Special Collection at Tuskegee Institute consists of the Washington Collection and the Tuskegee Archives. The Washington Collection, named for Booker T. Washington, founder of Tuskegee, contains more than 15,000 books and materials by and about blacks. It is particularly strong in holdings on African history.

Among the collections in the Archives are papers of Booker T. Washington; the George Washington Carver papers, dating from 1896 to 1943; the Thomas C. Campbell papers (first U.S. Department of Agriculture Black Extension agent), and historical Tuskegee Institute Agriculture Extension files, dating from 1885 to 1935; papers of R. R. Moton and F. D. Patterson, second and third presidents of Tuskegee Institute; the lynching records, dating from 1882, from which the Monroe Work annual lynching reports were prepared; files of the *Southern Courier Newspaper*; files of the Southern Conference for Human Welfare and many other collections of correspondence, addresses, memoranda and personal papers of persons connected with the early history of Tuskegee Institute, as well as outstanding leaders in the black struggle dating from the Civil War.

The Washington Collection and Archives are a part of the Tuskegee Institute Library. Daniel T. Williams serves as archivist. Annie G. King is librarian.

A LIST OF SIGNIFICANT BOOKS

Achebe, Chinua. *No Longer at Ease.* Fawcett World, 1970.

Achebe, Chinua. *Things Fall Apart.* Fawcett World, 1969.

Alhamsi, Ahmed and Wangara, Harun K., eds. *Black Arts: An Anthology of Black Creations.* Broadside, 1969.

Amini, Johari. *Let's Go Somewhere.* Third World, 1970.

Anthony, Earl. *Picking Up the Gun: A Report on the Black Panthers.* Dial, 1970.

Baker, Houston A. *Black Literature in America.* McGraw-Hill, 1971.

Baraka, Imamu Amiri. *In Our Terribleness.* Bobbs-Merrill, 1971.

Bennett, Lerone, Jr. *Before the Mayflower: A History of Black America.* 2d rev. ed. Johnson Pub. Co., 1969.

———. *Black Power U.S.A., 1867–1877: The Human Side of Reconstruction.* Johnson Pub. Co., 1967.

———. *Challenge of Blackness.* Johnson Pub. Co., 1973.

———. *Pioneers in Protest.* Johnson Pub. Co., 1969.

———. *What Manner of Man.* Johnson Pub. Co., 1968.

Boulware, Marcus H. *Oratory of Negro Leaders: 1900–1968.* Negro Uni Press, 1969.

Braizer, Arthur. *Black Self Determination: The Story of the Woodlawn Organization.* Eerdmans, 1969.

Brooks, Gwendolyn. *Riot.* Broadside, 1970.

———. *World of Gwendolyn Brooks.* Harper & Row, 1971.

Brown, Cecil. *Life & Loves of Mister Jiveass Nigger.* Farrar, Straus & Giroux, 1970.

Brown, Patricia, Lee, Don L., and Ward, Francis, eds. *To Gwen With Love.* Johnson Pub. Co., 1970.

Cartey, Wilfred. *Black Images.* Teacher's College, 1970.

Cartey, Wilfred. *Whispers from a Continent.* Random, 1969.

Casey, Bernie. *Look at the People.* Doubleday, 1969.

Chevault, John. *Blue Blackness.* Seven Hills Press, 1970.

Chisholm, Shirley. *Unbought & Unbossed.* HM, 1970.

Chuks-Onji, Oganna. *Names From Africa.* Johnson Pub. Co., 1972.

Clark, John Henrik, ed. *Malcolm X: The Man and His Times.* Unipub., 1969.

———. *Harlem, Voices from the Soul of Black America.* 1971.

Cleage, Albert B. *The Black Messiah.* Sheed, 1968.

Clifton, Lucille. *Good Times.* Random House, 1970.

Colter, Cyrus. *Beach Umbrella.* U. of Iowa Press, 1970.

Cone, James H. *Black Theology & Black Power.* Seabury, 1969.

Cornish, Sam & Dixon, Lucian W., eds. *Chicory: Young Voices from the Black Ghetto.* Association Press, 1970.

Cornish, Sam. *Generations.* Beacon Press, 1971.

———. *Your Hand In Mine.* Harcourt, Brace & World, 1970.

DeKnight, Freda. *The Ebony Cookbook.* 2d rev. ed. Johnson Pub. Co., 1973.

Dent, Tom and Schechner, Richard. *Free Southern Theater.* Bobbs-Merrill Co., 1969.

Duerden, Dennis and Pieterse, Cosmo, eds. *African Writers Talking.* Africana, 1972.

Ebony, Editors of. *The Black Revolution.* John and Book of Life. Johnson Pub. Co., 1970.

Ebony, Editors of. *Pictorial History of Black America.* 4 Vols. Johnson Pub. Co., 1971–73.

Ebony, Editors of. *Martin Luther King, Jr.,* An Ebony Picture Biography. Johnson Pub. Co., 1968.

Emanuel, James A. *Panther Man.* Broadside, 1970.

Evans, Mari. *I Am a Black Woman.* Morrow, 1970.

Fannon, Franz. *Colonialism and Alienation in the Work of Franz Fannon.* François Maspero, 1971.

Foner, Philip, ed. *W. E. B. Du Bois Speaks 1890–1919* Vol. 1. New York: Pathfinder Press, Inc., 1970; Vol. 2, *1920–1963.*

Ford, Nick Aaron, Dr. *Black Insights: Significant Literature by Afro-Americans, 1760 to the Present.* Ginn-Blaisdell, 1970.

Gayle, Addison, Jr., ed. *Black Aesthetic.* Doubleday, 1972.

Gayle, Addison, Jr. *Black Situation.* Dell, 1972.

Gilbert, Herman C. *The Uncertain Sound.* Pathfinder Press, 1970.

Giovanni, Nikki. *Black Feeling, Black Talk, Black Judgment.* William Morrow & Co., 1970.

———. *Gemini: An Extended Autobiographical Statement on My First Twenty-Five of Being a Black Poet.* Bobbs, 1972.

———. *Re: Creation.* Broadside, 1971.

Graves, Wallace. *Trixie.* Knopf, 1969.

Grier, William and Cobbs, Price. *The Jesus Bag.* Bantam, 1972.

Grimes, Nikki. *Poems by Nikki*. Celebrated Blackness, 1971.

Guy, Rosa. *Children of Longing*. Holt Rinehart, 1972.

Hayden, Robert, ed. *Afro-American Literature: An Introduction*. Harcourt, Brace & World, 1972.

Himes, Chester. *Blind Man With A Pistol*. Dell, 1972.

———. *Quality of Hurt: The Autobiography of Chester Himes*. Doubleday, 1972.

Jackson, George. *Soledad Brothers: The Prison Letters of George Jackson*. Coward, 1971.

James, C. L. *History of Pan-African Revolt*. Drum and Spear, 1971.

Jordan, Norman. *Destination: Ashes*. Third World, 1972.

Josey, E. J., ed. and intro. *Black Librarian in America*. Scarecrow, 1970.

Kemp, Arnold. *Eat of Me, I Am the Savior*. Morrow, 1972.

Killens, John O. *The Cotillion*. Trident 1971.

King, Coretta Scott. *My Life With Martin Luther King*. Holt, Rinehart, Winston, 1969.

King, Woodie, Jr. & Milner, Ron, eds. *Black Drama Anthology*. Columbia University Press, 1972.

Kiswahili, Kusema. *Speaking Swahili*. Drum and Spear, 1971.

Knight, Etheridge. *Black Voices from Prison*. Pathfinder Press, Inc., 1970.

Lacy, Leslie Alexander. *The Rise and Fall of a Proper Negro* PB, 1971.

Lester, Julius. *Revolutionary Notes*. Grove, 1970.

Lewis, David L. King. *A Critical Biography*. Penguin, 1970.

London, Frank. *The Myth Maker*. Path Press, 1970.

Long, Doughtry. *Song for Nia*. Broadside Press, 1972.

McKissick, Floyd. *Three-Fifths of a Man*. Macmillan, 1969.

Mahadi, M. A. *Third World Poets Speak the Truth*. Third World Publications, 1971.

Mahone, Barbara. *Sugarfields*. Broadside, 1970.

Marshall, Paule. *Chosen Place, the Timeless People*. Harcourt, Brace & World, 1969.

Matthews, Marcia M. *Henry Ossawa Tanner, American Artist*. U. of Chicago Press, 1970.

Mayfield, Julian. *Which Way Does the Blood Red River Run?* Random House, 1970.

Meriwether, Louise. *Daddy Was a Number Runner*. P - H, 1970.

Miller, Adam David, ed. *Dices or Black Bones: Black Voices of the Seventies*. HM, 1970.

Miller, Ruth. *Blackamerican Literature: 1760 to the Present*. Glencoe, 1971.

Morrison, Toni. *The Bluest Eye*. Holt, Rinehart, Winston, 1971.

Murray, Albert. *The Omni-Americans*. Outerbridge, 1970.

Nkrumah, Kwame. *Handbook of Revolutionary Warfare, A Guide to the Armed Phase of the African Revolution*. International Publishers, 1970.

Ofari, Earl. *Myth of Black Capitalism*. Monthly Review, 1970.

Peters, Margaret. *The Ebony Book of Black Achievement*. Johnson Pub. Co., 1970.

Plumpp, Sterling D. *Portable Soul*. Third World, 1970.

Poinsett, Alex. *Black Power: Gary Style—The Making of Mayor Richard G. Hatcher*. Johnson Pub. Co., 1970.

Quarles, Benjamin. *Black Abolitionists*. Oxford U. Pr., 1969.

Randall, James. *Don't Ask Me Who I Am*. Broadside, 1971.

Reed, Ishmael. *Mumbo Jumbo*. Doubleday, 1972.

Rodgers, Carolyn M., ed. *For Love of Our Brothers*. Third World Press, 1970.

Sanchez, Sonia. *Homecoming*. Broadside, 1968.

Scobie, Edward. *Black Britannia: A History of Blacks in Britain*. Johnson Pub. Co., 1972.

Scott-Heron, Gil. *The Vulture*. Belmont-Tower, 1971.

Seale, Bobby. *Seize the Time: The Story of the Black Panther Party and Huey P. Newton*. Random, 1970.

Slater, Philip E. *Pursuit of Loneliness: American Culture at the Breaking Point*. Beacon Press, 1971.

South, Wesley and Drotning, Phillip T. *Up From the Ghetto*. WSP, 1971.

Thompson, Julius Eric. *Hopes Tied Up In Promises*. Dorrance, 1969.

Turner, Darwin T., ed. *Afro-American Writers*. Appleton, 1970.

Turner, Darwin T. *In a Minor Chord: Three Afro-American Writers and Their Search for Identity*. Southern Illinois U. Press, 1971.

———. *The Naked Soul of Iceberg Slim*. Holloway House, 1972.

Vance, Samuel. *Courageous and the Proud*. Norton, 1970.

Van Dyke, Henry. *Dead Piano*. Farrar, Strauss and Giroux, 1971.

Yerby, Frank. *The Dahomean*. Dell, 1972.

———. *The Dahomean*. Dial, 1971.

———. *Speak Now*. Dial, 1969.

Yette, Samuel F. *The Choice: The Issue of Black Survival in America.* Berkley Pub., 1972 Putnam, 1971

Young, Doc. *Black Love Black Hope.* Broadside, 1971.

BLACK CULTURE SERIES FOR YOUNG READERS*

FAR LANDS & PEOPLE—Nonfiction

Archer, Jules
  AFRICAN FIREBRAND: Kenyatta of Kenya
Bernheim, Marc
  FROM BUSH TO CITY: A Look at the New Africa
Bernheim, Marc
  A WEEK IN AYA'S WORLD: The Ivory Coast
Bishop, Claire H.
  MARTIN DE PORRES, HERO
Bond, Jean C.
  A IS FOR AFRICA
Buckley, Peter
  OKOLO OF NIGERIA
Chu, Daniel
  THE BLACK A B C'S
Chu, Daniel
  A GLORIOUS AGE IN AFRICA
Dobler, Lavinia
  GREAT RULERS OF THE AFRICAN PAST
Donna, Natalie
  BOY OF THE MASAI
Kaula, Edna M.
  THE LAND AND PEOPLE OF KENYA
Legum, Colin
  THE BITTER CHOICE: Eight South Africans' Resistance to Tyranny
MacGregor-Hastie, Roy
  AFRICA: BACKGROUND FOR TODAY
McKown, Robin
  THE CONGO: River of Mystery
Scherman, Katherine
  SLAVE WHO FREED HAITI: The Story of Toussaint Louverture
Sherlock, Philip M.
  LAND AND PEOPLE OF THE WEST INDIES
Spencer, William
  THE LAND AND PEOPLE OF ALGERIA

FOLKLORE

Aardema, Verna
  TALES FROM THE STORY HAT: African Folk Tales
Arkhurst, Joyce C.
  THE ADVENTURES OF SPIDER

*Books selected by The Chicago Public Library and available in branches and the main library's section for young readers.

Arnott, Kathleen
  AFRICAN MYTHS AND LEGENDS
Bertol, Roland
  SUNDIATA, THE EPIC OF THE LION
Carpenter, Frances
  AFRICAN WONDER TALES
Courlander, Harold
  TERRAPIN'S POT OF SENSE
Davis, Russell and Ashabranner, Brent
  THE LION'S WHISKERS: Tales of High Africa
Elkin, Benjamin
  SUCH IS THE WAY OF THE WORLD
Green, Lila
  FOLKTALES AND FAIRY TALES OF AFRICA
Guirma, Frederic
  PRINCESS OF THE FULL MOON
Haley, Gail E.
  A STORY, A STORY
Harman, Humphrey
  TALES TOLD NEAR A CROCODILE
Harris, Joel C.
  COMPLETE TALES OF UNCLE REMUS
Heady, Eleanor B.
  WHEN THE STONES WERE SOFT: East African Fireside Tales
Holladay, Virginia
  BANTU TALES
Kaula, Edna M.
  AFRICAN VILLAGE FOLKTALES
Keats, Ezra J.
  JOHN HENRY, AN AMERICAN LEGEND
Kirn, Ann
  BEESWAX CATCHES A THIEF: From a Congo Folktale
Kirn, Ann
  TALES OF A CROCODILE
Nunn, Jessie A.
  AFRICAN FOLKTALES
Rockwell, Anne
  WHEN THE DRUM SANG

HISTORY & BIOGRAPHY

Adams, Russell L.
  GREAT NEGROES, PAST AND PRESENT
Adoff, Arnold
  MALCOLM X
Aliki
  A WEED IS A FLOWER: Life of George Washington Carver

Bertol, Roland
CHARLES DREW
Bontemps, Arna W.
FAMOUS NEGRO ATHLETES
Bontemps, Arna W.
FREDERICK DOUGLASS, SLAVE FIGHTER, FREE-MAN
Boone-Jones, Margaret
MARTIN LUTHER KING, JR.
Bowen, David
THE STRUGGLE WITHIN: Race Relations in the United States
Buckmaster, Henrietta
FLIGHT TO FREEDOM
Carruth, Ella Kaiser
SHE WANTED TO READ: The Story of Mary McLeod Bethune
Cohen, Robert
THE COLOR OF MAN
Dahl, Mary B.
FREE SOULS
Dobler, Lavinia G.
PIONEERS AND PATRIOTS
Douglass, Frederick
MIND AND HEART OF FREDERICK DOUGLASS: Adapted by Barbara Ritchie
Douty, Esther
FORTEN THE SAILMAKER
Drotning, Phillip T.
UP FROM THE GHETTO
Durham, Phillip
THE NEGRO COWBOYS
Epstein, Sam
HARRIET TUBMAN: Guide to Freedom
Fenderson, Lewis H.
THURGOOD MARSHALL, FIGHTER FOR JUSTICE
Gould, Jean
THAT DUNBAR BOY: The Story of America's Famous Black Poet
Graham, Shirley
DR. GEORGE WASHINGTON CARVER, SCIENTIST
Graham, Shirley
JEAN BAPTISTE POINTE DE SABLE, FOUNDER OF CHICAGO
Haber, Louis
BLACK PIONEERS OF SCIENCE AND INVENTION
Harris, Janet
THE LONG FREEDOM ROAD: The Civil Rights Story
Heard, J. Norman
BLACK FRONTIERSMEN: Adventures of Negroes Among American Indians, 1528–1918
Henri, Florette
BITTER VICTORY: A History of Black Soldiers in World War I

Hirshberg, Al
HENRY AARON: Quiet Superstar
Hopkins, Lee Bennett
IMPORTANT DATES IN AFRO-AMERICAN HISTORY
Hughes, Langston
BLACK MISERY
Hughes, Langston
A PICTORIAL HISTORY OF THE NEGRO IN AMERICA
Ingraham, Leonard W.
THE FIRST BOOK OF SLAVERY IN THE UNITED STATES
Jackson, Florence
THE BLACK MAN IN AMERICA
Krementz, Jill
SWEET PEA, A BLACK GIRL GROWING UP IN THE RURAL SOUTH
Kugelmass, J. Alvin
RALPH J. BUNCHE, FIGHTER FOR PEACE
Lacey, Leslie A.
CHEER THE LONESOME TRAVELER: Life of W. E. B. DuBois
Latham, Frank B.
DRED SCOTT DECISION, MARCH 6, 1857
Lee, Irvin H.
NEGRO MEDAL OF HONOR MEN
Lincoln, C. Eric
MARTIN L. KING: A Profile
Lindemeyer, Otto
BLACK AND BRAVE: Black Soldier in America
Meltzer, Milton
IN THEIR OWN WORDS: A History of the American Negro, Vol. 1 1619–1865
Meltzer, Milton
TIME OF TRIAL, TIME OF HOPE: The Negro in America, 1919–1941
Petry, Ann L.
TITUBA OF SALEM VILLAGE
Place, Marian T.
RIFLES AND WAR BONNETS
Ripley, Sheldon N.
MATTHEW HENSON, ARCTIC HERO
Ritchie, Barbara
RIOT REPORT
Robinson, Jackie and Duckett, Alfred
BREAKTHROUGH TO THE BIG LEAGUES
Robinson, Louis
ARTHUR ASHE, TENNIS CHAMPION
Rollins, Charlemae
BLACK TROUBADOUR: Langston Hughes
Rollins, Charlemae
THEY SHOWED THE WAY
Sterling, Dorothy
CAPTAIN OF THE PLANTER

Sterling, Dorothy
FOREVER FREE: The Story of the Emancipation Proclamation
Sterling, Dorothy
LIFT EVERY VOICE
Swift, Hildegarde H.
NORTH STAR SHINING
Washington, Booker T.
UP FROM SLAVERY
Yates, Elizabeth
AMOS FORTUNE, FREE MAN

POETRY, MUSIC & ART

Adoff, Arnold, ed.
BLACK OUT LOUD
Adoff, Arnold, ed.
I AM THE DARKER BROTHER
Bontemps, Arna, ed.
HOLD FAST TO DREAMS
Brooks, Gwendolyn
BRONZEVILLE BOYS AND GIRLS
Burroughs, Margaret Taylor, ed.
DID YOU FEED MY COW?
Clifton, Lucille
SOME OF THE DAYS OF EVERETT ANDERSON
Cullen, Countee
THE LOST ZOO
D'Amato, Janet
AFRICAN CRAFTS FOR YOU TO MAKE
Dunbar, Paul L.
LITTLE BROWN BABY
Glubok, Shirley
ART OF AFRICA
Graham, Lorenz
EVERY MAN HEART LAY DOWN
Grossman, Barney
BLACK MEANS . . . .
Hopkins, Lee, ed.
I THINK I SAW A SNAIL
Hughes, Langston
THE DREAM KEEPER AND OTHER POEMS
Hughes, Langston
THE FIRST BOOK OF JAZZ
Johns, Altona T.
PLAY SONGS OF THE DEEP SOUTH
Johnson, James Weldon
GOD'S TROMBONES
Johnson, James Weldon
LIFT EVERY VOICE AND SING
Jordan, June, ed.
SOULSCRIPT: Afro-American Poetry
Jordan, June
WHO LOOK AT ME
Landeck, Beatrice
ECHOES OF AFRICA IN FOLK SONGS OF THE AMERICAS

Mendoza, George
AND I MUST HURRY FOR THE SEA IS COMING IN . . . .
Richardson, Willis, ed.
NEGRO HISTORY IN THIRTEEN PLAYS
Rollins, Charlemae, ed.
CHRISTMAS GIF'
Rollins, Charlemae
FAMOUS AMERICAN NEGRO POETS
Rollins, Charlemae
FAMOUS NEGRO ENTERTAINERS OF STAGE, SCREEN, AND TV
Sutherland, Efua
PLAYTIME IN AFRICA
Zeitlin, Patty
CASTLE IN MY CITY

TALES OF THEN & NOW

Adoff, Arnold
BROTHERS AND SISTERS
Agle, Nan
MAPLE STREET
Armstrong, William
SOUNDER
Blanton, Catherine
HOLD FAST TO YOUR DREAMS
Blue, Rose
A QUIET PLACE
Bonham, Frank
DURANGO STREET
Bonham, Frank
HONOR BOUND
Bonham, Frank
MYSTERY OF THE FAT CAT
Bontemps, Arna W.
CHARIOT IN THE SKY
Bourne, Miriam
RACCOONS ARE FOR LOVING
Burchard, Peter
BIMBY
Burchardt, Nellie
JOEY'S CAT
Butters, Dorothy G.
MASQUERADE
Carlson, Natalie Savage
ANN AURELIA AND DOROTHY
Carlson, Natalie Savage
THE EMPTY SCHOOLHOUSE
Carlson, Natalie Savage
MARCHERS FOR THE DREAM
Caudill, Rebecca
A CERTAIN SMALL SHEPHERD
Clymer, Eleanor
THE BIG PILE OF DIRT
Colman, Hila
CLASSMATES BY REQUEST
Coolidge, Olivia
COME BY HERE

Section VI

ARMED FORCES

The Armed Forces, 1940-1973
Black Participation in U.S. Wars
Black Generals on Active Duty in the Armed Services
Congressional Medal of Honor
The Service Academies
Military Chronology, 1969-73

Tables

THE ARMED FORCES, 1940–1973

In the years since 1940, the armed services have moved from a policy of deliberate segregation to a policy of deliberate integration, even as far as off-base recreational and housing facilities are concerned. In a statement made by the War Department on October 9, 1940, it was stated that the strength of the black personnel in the army would be maintained on the general basis of the proportion of the black population, and that "the policy of the War Department is not to intermingle colored and white personnel in the same regimental organizations. This policy has been proven satisfactory over a long period of years, and to make changes would produce situations destructive to morale and detrimental to the preparations for national defense."

Word War II, Korea, and Viet Nam have followed, and in the years since this policy was formulated, many studies and many reports have been issued contradicting the theory of military efficiency based on racial separation. The Gillem Report, while not going as far in its recommendations as the black community desired, did place a major responsibility for the shortcomings of black units on the lack of adequate staff preparation and planning. Toward the end of World War II (December 26, 1944), an order was issued by Lieutenant General John C. H. Lee permitting black enlisted men in service units within his command to volunteer for duty as infantrymen. All such volunteers had to sacrifice any ratings they held. About twenty-five hundred took advantage of this dubious privilege and served in combat. They were placed in eleven different divisions.

The proportion of blacks in the armed forces at the close of the war in Europe ranged from 8 to 10 percent. The War Department announced at that time that the post-war occupation forces in Germany would include 10 percent black troops, and the blacks would also be represented in the occupation forces in Japan and other areas of the Pacific. In May, 1946, the Army announced that blacks would form 10 percent of the country's peacetime forces.

The first black to reach the rank of general in the United States was Benjamin O. Davis, Sr., who was promoted to the rank of brigadier general in 1940, having joined the army in 1896 and risen from the ranks. He reached retirement age shortly after his promotion to general, but was retained in the service and was attached to the Inspector General's office in Washington. Prior to World War II, only four blacks apart from Davis had served as colonel or lieutenant colonel in the army. They were Colonel Charles Young, third black graduate of West Point, Colonel Franklin Dennison, Lieutenant Colonel John E. Green, Lieutenant Colonel Otis B. Duncan, and Colonel Lew Carter, a chaplain. During the war, approximately thirty-four blacks reached the rank of either colonel or lieutenant colonel.

The highest rank held by a black in the Navy up to 1966 was commander, but in that year Chaplain David T. Parham was promoted to captain, making him the highest-ranking black naval officer. In general, however, the Navy was approaching integration by a different route. Blacks had been enlisted in the Navy for general service from the earliest period in United States history until the end of World War I, and black sailors had served throughout the naval establishment. It was after the war that enlistment of blacks ceased, and when it was resumed in 1932, recruits were sought only for the messman's branch. Ten years later, in April, 1942, the Navy announced that blacks would be enlisted for general service, as well as for mess attendants, both male and female, but blacks thus accepted for general service were trained in segregated camps and schools, assigned to segregated units which were limited to shore installations and harbor craft.

In 1943, the Coast Guard commissioned two black officers, and two fighting ships were manned by predominantly black crews. After much discussion, in August, 1944, black sailors were assigned to 25 auxiliary ships of the fleet. Not more than 10 percent of the enlisted personnel aboard any ship were black, but those there were integrated with the white crews. In April, 1945, it was announced that black personnel would be eligible for service in all auxiliary fleet vessels, though a 10 percent quota would still be observed. By July, 1945, there were no segregated navy schools or camps left, and segregation, according to the Navy Department's Dennis R. Nelson, was abolished entirely in February, 1946.

Following the Gillem Report in 1947, many specific changes were made, or, at least directives issued, regarding greater equalization of opportunity, and broader use of black manpower in the army. The Fahy Committee*, three years later, found that the broad objectives stated in the Gillem Report had not been achieved. The Fahy report observed that segregation, even in modified form, was conducive to inefficiency in two ways: "By requiring skilled blacks to serve in racial units, the army lost skills which would find no place in black organizations. On the other hand, by concentrating large numbers of unskilled blacks in combat units it multiplied inefficiency."

The Fahy Committee investigation led to a revision of Army policy. In January, 1950, Special Regulations Nos. 600–629–1 were issued, removing the color bar from all army jobs and schools, abolishing all racial quotas, including the 10 percent limit, and allowing the assignment of blacks to any unit in the Army as merited by individual qualifications and indicated by military considerations.

On June 16, 1951, an article by H. H. Martin on the performance of black troops in Korea appeared in the *Saturday Evening Post.* At that time, some 25 percent of the black infantry replacements in the Korean theatre were assigned as individuals scattered through the Command and not to all-black units. At the same time the all-black 24th Infantry Regiment and other segregated units were in the line.** Integration was less half-hearted than in World War II, and officers commanding integrated units reported that black soldiers fought as bravely as whites and some proved to be outstanding combat leaders. "No disciplinary or morale problems have arisen by reason of the integration of black soldiers into white units, and there has been no friction between the troops that could be traced to differences in color." In the Korean conflict, as elsewhere in the army in both war and peace, segregation fomented complaints and dissipated energy in interecine hostilities.

In 1966, only 8.2 percent of the 2.7 million in the armed forces were black. In 1962, President Kennedy's Committee on Equal Opportunity in the Armed Forces reported that blacks comprised only one-fifth of 1 percent of the officers in the navy and marine corps, and 3.2 and 1.2 percent, respectively, in the army and air force.

The primary task then was for the Defense Department to achieve off-base integration. A December, 1964 report of the President's Committee on Equal Opportunity in the Armed Forces indicated that "immediate and, if necessary, drastic action" should be taken to end off-base discrimination experiences by U.S. black troops serving abroad. Bias, according to the report, has been shown by owners of foreign housing and recreational facilities in response to pressure from some white American troops. The committee suggested the use of Title VI of the 1964 Civil Rights Act to end discrimination in National Guard units in the United States if voluntary means failed.

In a February 12, 1965 directive, Deputy Defense Secretary Cyrus R. Vance warned that beginning in the 1966–67 school year, the Defense Department would withdraw Reserve Officers Training Corps (ROTC) units from any school or college that practiced racial segregation. The directive added: "No ROTC unit . . . will be established at an educational institution which discriminates with respect to admission or subsequent treatment of students on the basis of race, color or national origin."

From 1967 to 1973, conditions for black soldiers improved, but all of the areas of tension have not disappeared. Blacks presently account for 18.6 percent of the Army's enlisted ranks and with the end of the draft and the improved salary schedule and benefit program, blacks have been enlisting in record numbers. In March, April, May and June, 1973, blacks accounted for more than 25 percent of the 32,000 men to enlist in the Army. These figures were not expected to decline because the re-enlistment rate of black soldiers was also increasing. In fiscal year 1971, 51.8 percent of all blacks eligible for re-enlistment did so, in comparison with 32.5 percent of the whites eligible for re-enlistment.

While the ratio of blacks in the enlisted ranks is sharply increasing, the percentage of black officers is not increasing as rapidly. Before 1964, about 3.4 percent of the Army officer strength was black. Now the figure is 3.9 percent.

In 1964, black enlisted men made up 13.4 percent of the ranks. In 1968, it was 12.6; 1973, 18.6 percent.

Much of the improvement in the morale of the black serviceman has come from the assignment of black senior officers in command of large units. One, particularly, was the appointment of General Frederick Ellis Davison, to command the Eighth Infantry Division at Bad Freuznach Germany, the first black officer to command a division of the U.S. Army. Further, the army has initiated sensitivity sessions and seminars for officers, noncoms and black soldiers. Equal opportunities staff officers are available to examine complaints of discrimination and a military magistrate reviews cases of soldiers who are being charged with rule infractions that would result in courts-martial proceedings. The official policy of the army is to end racial discrimination toward black American soldiers.

*The Fahy Committee bore the name of the chairman of President Truman's first President's Committee on Equality of Treatment and Opportunity in the Armed Services.

**The first United States victory in Korea was won on July 20, 1950 by the 24th Infantry Regiment, who regained Yech'on, a strategic railhead position, from the North Korean forces.

BLACK PARTICIPATION IN U.S. WARS

THE AMERICAN REVOLUTION, 1775–83

Blacks, slave and free, fought for the American forces at the majority of decisive battles including Lexington, Bunker Hill, Charleston, and Valley Forge. Further, 10,000–12,000 black slaves served the British cause with Lord Dunmore's Ethiopian Regiment being the most renowned unit.

Crispus Attucks
A fugitive mulatto slave was the first American to die in the American Revolution during a Boston protest on March 5, 1770.

Prince Easterbrooks
A Lexington, Mass. slave enlisted in Captain John Parker's company. Reported to be one of first to get into the fight at Lexington and Concord on April 19, 1775. Served in several major campaigns of the war.

William Flora
A black freeman from Portsmouth, Va. at the Battle of Great Bridge, near Norfolk, was "the last sentinel that came into the breastwork and . . . did not leave his post until he had fired several times." Thirty years later, in 1806, his former commander, Captain Thomas Nash, testified that Flora had served "in the Continental line until the siege of York . . . and was held in high esteem as a soldier." For his services, the Commonwealth of Virginia granted William Flora 100 acres in gratitude.

Jordan Freeman
Launched spear that killed British commander, Major W. Montgomery at the battle of Groton Heights and was himself killed in the same battle.

Barzillai Lew
A veteran of the French and Indian Wars, was 32 years old when he enlisted in Captain John Ford's company of the 27th Massachusetts Regiment. He marched at Ticonderoga and at Bunker Hill. He served for seven years in the service as a soldier, fifer and drummer.

Peter Salem
Credited by numerous historians with turning the tide at the battle of Bunker Hill when he killed Major Pitcairn, commander of the British forces.

Jack Sisson
During the successful kidnapping of British General Prescott, Sisson broke down two doors, disarmed the General and held him helpless on his bed.

STATISTICS

Black Population	Black Servicemen	Black Percentage of Army
3,500,000	5,000–7,000	2%

Note: Severe restrictions were placed on the black, especially in the South, who wished to serve. In numerous southern states, blacks not allowed to serve the American Cause fought for the Crown.

THE WAR OF 1812, 1812–15

Three black Americans—William Ware, Daniel Martin, John Strachan—were numbered among four seamen forcibly taken from the American frigate Chesapeake by the British frigate Leopold. The British had claimed the men were deserters and had demanded their surrender by the United States government. The government refused, claiming the men were free Americans. The consequent British action is considered by numerous historians as the first overt act of hostility. Black participation in the war was extensive although few reliable statistics were recorded. It is known, for example, that approximately 9 percent of General Jackson's famous Army, and some 25 percent of Commodore Perry's Navy were black.

Primarily notable at the Battle of Lake Erie and the Battle of New Orleans, black heroism appeared to be collective rather than individual.

SEMINOLE WARS, 1814–18, 1835–42

Perhaps the most fascinating role of blacks during this period was not their role as a part of the U.S. military, but rather their being found on the side of the Indians during the famous Seminole Wars of 1814–18 and 1835–42. The black-Seminole combination came as a result of the fusion of the two groups by the acceptance of escaped slaves into the Seminole nation and, to a lesser degree, from the purchasing and capture of slaves. Many historians have cited the cause of the 2nd Seminole War as the kidnapping (for purposes of slavery) of Che-cho-ter, wife of the Seminole chief Osceola. Osceola's revenge was marked by the massacre of Major F. L. Dade and some 100 men on December 28, 1835—beginning the hostilities. Che-cho-ter and Osceola are believed to be of black-Indian parentage.

Osceola was the most famous of the black-Seminole heroes.

THE AMERICAN CIVIL WAR 1861–65

The Massachusetts 54th Regiment
July 18th, 1863, the black 54th under command of Robert Gould Shaw led the assault

on Fort Wagner against great odds, storming and entering the objective. They were later repulsed, leaving behind more dead and wounded than any other regiment. Sgt. William H. Carney, the standard bearer of the 54th, although wounded, dragged himself to safety, still "holding the colors high."

William Tillman
A steward aboard the *S.J. Waring* when that ship was captured July 7, 1861, by the Confederate privateer, the Jeff Davis. On July 16, Tillman killed three of the occupational crew of five—the captain, first mate and second mate—became captain and returned the ship to the Union, a national hero.

The Louisiana 9th and 11th Regiments
The Mississippi 1st Regiment
Comprising approximately eight-tenths of the Union forces, these brave black soldiers repulsed Confederate forces, braving nearly 3 to 1 odds, in the Battle of Milliken's Bend.

The 1st, 2nd, and 3rd Phalanx Regiments
The 1st Engineer Regiment
In the unsuccessful siege of Port Hudson, these black Union soldiers were the heroes of the day, displaying more courage, many eye-witness accounts report, than either allies or enemy.

South Carolina 1st Regiment
The first Union soldiers in the South Carolina campaign. Won acclaim for routing the enemy and capturing Township Landing, allowing Union forces to break through and gain the valuable South Carolina timberland.

The 8th United States Regiment
The 1st North Carolina Regiment
The 54th Massachusetts
In the Battle of Olustee, Florida, a Union defeat, these black Regiments displayed valor which was acclaimed not only by their comrades but, following the war, by the commander of the southern forces.

The United States 28th, 29th, and 30th Regiments
Credited with the capture of Fort Harrison after white regiments had been repulsed. This victory was the principal cause of the later fall of Richmond.

D.B. Birney's Negro Division, 10th Army
Cited for exceptional courage in the Battle of Fort Gilmer. Although the Union charge was repulsed, the bravery of the black troops was the basis for a moving plea made ten years later for black civil rights by General B.F. Butler before the United States Congress.

Note: History records that the decisive battles of the Civil War were fought where black Union soldiers won their greatest victories and

honor. Those who have written unprejudiced accounts of the Civil War credit the black with contributing more than his share to the Virginia Campaign.

The United States 6th Heavy Artillery
After aiding the courageous defense of Fort Pillow, this regiment of 262 men was completely erased by the Confederate forces. Those who lived through the assault were murdered along with their women and children by Confederate forces led by Nathan Bedford Forrest. The massacre of Fort Pillow, after it had surrendered, not only disgraced the South, but the cry of "Remember Fort Pillow" became the battle cry of black troops in the Virginia campaign and throughout the war. A Congressional investigation followed this notorious incident.

Battery B, Second Light Artillery, 9th Army
1st Infantry Regiment, 9th Army
10th Infantry Regiment, 9th Army
When, with superior numbers, famed Confederate cavalry leader Fitz-Hugh Lee stormed Fort Powhatan, Virginia, the Confederate forces were routed by the black troopers.

Hinck's Negro Division Brigade
The United States 4th, 5th, 6th, and 7th Regiments
Hinck's brigade led the original successful charge against Fort Clinton, Virginia, after which the capture of the position has been generally attributed to the bravery of the black troops involved.

Duncan's Negro Brigade
Hinck's Negro Division Brigade
The United States 4th, 5th, and 22nd Regiments
The Massachusetts 5th Colored Cavalry
In the siege of Petersburg, these black soldiers are credited with an outstanding victory at the Battle of Baylor's Farm. Major-General W.F. Smith, in command of the Union forces, lauded the blacks for capturing what he described as the most formidable enemy earthworks of the Virginia campaign.

Chaffin's Hill Farm, Battle of
Thirteen black regiments fought at Chaffin's Hill Farm in Virginia, September 29-30, 1864 and 14 black soldiers earned Congressional Medals of Honor as a result of that engagement. Among the hardest hit were the 7th U.S. Colored Troops, the 5th U.S. Colored Troops, and General Paines' Negro Third Division.

The United States 14th Infantry
Assisted in the repulsion of a Confederate force attacking the Union garrison at Dalton, Georgia. After the battle had been won, white

Union soldiers, most of whom had been born in border states and were fairly prejudiced, openly cheered the black regiment.

The United States 12th, 13th, 14th, 16th, 17th, 18th, 44th, and 100th Infantry Regiments
Organized into the Department of the Cumberland Corp., these black servicemen captured Overton Hill, causing the rout of Hood's Confederate troops at the Battle of Nashville. In this great Union victory, black troops bore a conspicuous part—one-fourth of all Union losses were sustained by the blacks.

STATISTICS

	Total	Black	Black Percentage
Union Army	2,213,363	278,312	12
Battle Deaths	140,414	36,847	14

THE INDIAN WARS, 1865–98
"The Buffalo Soldiers"
Of the fourteen U.S. cavalry regiments serving on the frontier during the Indian Wars, four were composed of black troopers. The most renowed of the units were the 9th and 10th. Organized in 1866, the 9th Cavalry served with distinction in Texas (1867–75), New Mexico (1875–81), Kansas and Indian Territory (1881–85), and Nebraska and Utah (1885–95). The 10th Cavalry, created in 1866, honored its colors in Kansas (1867–68), Texas and Oklahoma (1868–75), Texas, New Mexico and Arizona (1875–82), and Texas and Arizona (1882–91). In total, the four black cavalry regiments comprised 40 percent of the cavalry personnel (4,388 black soldiers) and 17.5 percent of the entire U.S. forces engaged. Although in the Indian campaigns the black soldier represented a greater percentage of the Army than in any other U.S. war, the least coverage has been given to black participation. Commenting on the quality of the black troopers, S.E. Whitman stated in his book, *The Troopers*, that not only were they the peers of the white troops in fighting ability, but they had higher morale and a lower court-martial and desertion record.

THE SPANISH-AMERICAN WAR, 1898
In this, the least of United States wars in terms of time and casualties, blacks were extremely important.

Elijah B. Tunnell
A cabin cook on the *U.S.S. Winslow* on May 11, 1898, when that ship was under fire in

Cardenas Harbor, Cuba. Safe below decks, Tunnell chose to join in the fight and was killed by a bursting shell. He was the first American to die for the United States in the Spanish–American War.

The United States 10th Cavalry
En route to Santiago, the first battle of the Spanish–American War was fought on June 24, 1898, against a Spanish Fort. It was the 10th Cavalry which, manning a Hotchkiss gun, blasted down the defenses, led the charge, and overran the objective.

The United States 25th Infantry
This regiment charged and captured the blockhouse at the Battle of El Caney, considered the 2nd most important battle of the war.

The United States 9th and 10th Cavalry Regiments
Credited with saving the Rough Riders from annihilation at the Battle of San Juan Hill, these regiments participated fully in the winning charge.

MEXICAN CAMPAIGN, 1916
A punitive force under Brigadier-General John J. Pershing ("Black Jack")* crossed the Mexican border in pursuit of Pancho Villa March 16th, 1916. Three black regiments, the 10th Cavalry and the 24th and 25th Infantry, were part of the American force. Villa had raided and burned the border town of Columbus, New Mexico. Pershing's long pursuit broke Villa's power and caused the band to break up and go into hiding.

A black detachment of about 80 men from the 10th Cavalry, commanded by Captain Charles T. Boyd and Captain Lewis Morey, was sent by Pershing to the Mexican town of Villa Ahumada, and met opposition at Carrizal, where Villa, the Mexican commander, halted his troops, took cover and, without warning, opened fire with machine guns and rifles. Captain Boyd led a charge against the machine gun position, in which he was killed. Captain Morey held an adobe hut for hours against Mexican attack until, seriously wounded and with a few survivors, he escaped. After a few days in hiding he sent his men with a report to his commander. Reinforcements reached him in time to save his life.

*According to rumor and legend the nickname stemmed from the time he commanded the 10th Cavalry in the Santiago campaign in the Spanish-American War.

THE SEMINOLE NEGRO INDIAN SCOUTS
A group of fifty black Indians known as the "Seminole Negro Indian Scouts" were skilled descendants of slave runaways who had fled

the southern states and settled among the Seminole tribes in Florida before the Civil War (*See* Seminole Wars). The Seminole Indians were moved westward under President Andrew Jackson's Indian removal policy, and the policy continued even after the Civil War.

Settled at Fort Clark and Fort Duncan, Texas for a time, they remained in the United States, but migrated to Mexico when again faced with attempts to reenslave them and their children. In 1870 General Zenas R. Bliss of the U.S. Army, desperate for scouts in the mounting campaigns against the Plains Indian tribes, traveled to Mexico and, accepting as sincere promises of land and food, the men agreed to serve as U.S. Army scouts. On July 4, 1870, the first group of scouts and their families arrived at Fort Duncan, Texas.

After two years under the command of their own chief, John Kibbett, the scouting unit was placed under the command of Lt. John Bullis.

During the nine years under Bullis' command the outfit, often assigned to various cavalry and infantry units, black and white, rolled up a record unequaled in the military annals of the day. In twelve major engagements they never lost a man in battle or had one seriously wounded.

The Seminole Negro Indian scouts learned that the government promises of land and food would not be kept. Rations to families had been drastically reduced and government agencies denied responsibility for the original agreement that had brought the two-hundred men, women and children to Texas. Repeatedly, leaders of the group protested their treatment through petitions. Generals Augur, Bliss, and Sheridan, and Lieutenant Bullis supported their pleas, but to no avail.

Their stay was made even more untenable by the hostility of white towns people. Following several skirmishes which involved local people, the black Indian Scouts and their families were put off the reservations and treated so inhospitably in the towns that the group disintegrated and finally disbanded in 1912. The cemetery at Fort Clarke contains the graves of many of the Seminole scouts.

WORLD WAR I, 1914–18

Under the original Selective Service draft, enacted May 18, 1917, 8,848,882 whites were registered and 711,213 (24.75%) were certified, 737,626 blacks were registered and 75,697 (36.23%) were certified. Thus, in America's first Selective Service draft, 36 out of every 100 blacks, as against 25 out of every 100 whites, were accepted. For the entire war,

comprising approximately 9.4 percent of the population, black registrants made up approximately 9.6 percent of the registered total.

The 366th Infantry Regiment
Cited for bravery by both American and French officers. Nine individuals in the unit were awarded the Distinguished Service Cross.

The 367th Infantry Regiment
For bravery at the Battle of Metz, the final engagement of the war, the entire First Battalion was awarded the French Croix de Guerre.

The 369th United States Infantry
Transferred to French command, this regiment was actually under fire longer than any other United States unit. Displaying exceptional bravery at Bois d'Hauze, Minancourt and Maison-en-Champagne, the entire regiment was awarded the Croix de Guerre, while 171 individual officers and enlisted men were additionally honored with the Legion of Honor medal.

The 370th United States Infantry
The pride of Chicago, the 8th Illinois National Guard Regiment won distinctive honor as the 370th Infantry. It was the first United States unit to enter the French Fortress of Leon and fought the last battle of the war, capturing a German wagon train one-half hour after the Armistice. Twenty-one American Distinguished Service Crosses, sixty-eight French Croix de Guerre and one Distinguished Service Medal were awarded the heroes of the 370th.

The 371st United States Infantry
Exhibiting exceptional courage during the Champagne offensive, the regiment was awarded the Army Citation by the French government. In addition, the French Legion of Honor was awarded to one officer; the Croix de Guerre to 89 enlisted men and 34 officers; and the American Distinguished Service Cross to 12 enlisted men and 10 officers. The 371st is reportedly the first American draft regiment to enter the trenches in the war.

The 372nd United States Infantry
Another black fighting unit collectively awarded the French Croix de Guerre, the 372nd fought as part (along with the 371st) of the famous French 157th Division ("Red Hand"). Paying a lasting tribute to the men of the 372nd, the officers of the French 157th accepted a trust of over 10,500 francs, donated by their men, to erect a monument in their honor.

Private Henry Johnson
Private Needham Roberts
The first American soldiers to win the Croix de Guerre, Johnson and Roberts completely

routed a German raiding party of twelve. Four Germans were killed and several wounded in hand-to-hand combat in which Johnson was wounded 3 times and Roberts twice.

STATISTICS

	Total	Blacks	Black Percentage
American Army	4,744,000	400,000	9.5
Battle Deaths	292,000	700	4.5
Wounded	204,000	4,000	19.4

WORLD WAR II, 1941–45

From December, 1941 through the end of hostilities, approximately 920,000 black service men were in the United States Armed Forces with some 850 officers and 200,000 enlisted men in the American expeditionary forces. There were 130 individual decorations of high honor awarded black servicemen, excluding unrecorded thousands of Purple Hearts.

The 99th Fighter Squadron
First unit of blacks in Air Force (blacks had been forbidden to fly until a training school was established at Tuskegee in 1941), the 99th flew 500 combat missions and in excess of 3,725 sorties during one year of combat before uniting with the 332nd fighter group.

The 332nd Fighter Squadrons
A group consisting of 3 squadrons, the 332nd established an outstanding record in the Italian sector. Flying a total of 15,553 missions and 10,730 sorties, the 332nd destroyed 433 units of enemy property including 261 aircraft, 57 locomotives, and a destroyer. The unit was awarded the Distinguished Unit Citation.

Note: Eighty individual pilots of the 99th and 332nd were awarded the Distinguished Flying Cross.

The 969th Field Artillery Battalion
Awarded a Presidential Distinguished Unit Citation for bravery in the Normandy and northern France campaigns.

The 614th Tank Destroyer Battalion
Awarded the Distinguished Unit Citation for exceptional combat records in the European Theater.

Collectively, the number of America's high honors for courage to be won by blacks included, in addition to the aforementioned eighty Distinguished Flying Crosses, the following individual awards.

DISTINGUISHED SERVICE CROSS
  Vernon J. Baker, Cheyenne, Wyo.

Edward A. Carter, Jr., Los Angeles, Calif.
Jack Thomas, Albany, Ga.
George Watson, Birmingham, Ala.*
*Awarded posthumously.
NAVY CROSS
  Eli Benjamin, Norfolk, Va.
  Leonard Roy Harmon, Cuero, Tex.*
  Dorie Miller, Waco, Texas*
  William Pinckney, Beaufort, S.C.
*Awarded posthumously.

FOREIGN HONORS
A number of black servicemen were honored by foreign nations. Among them were:
  Macon H. Johnson, Charlestown, S.C.—
    The Order of the Soviet Union
  Arthur Jackson, Jr., Detroit, Michigan—
    The French Croix de Guerre
  William W. Green, Staunton, Va.—
    The Yugoslav Partisan Medal for Heroism
  Norman Day, Danville, Ill.—
    The British Distinguished Service Medal

STATISTICS

Peak Strength U.S. Forces:	12,300,000
Peak Strength Black U.S. Forces:*	920,000
U.S. Forces White % Total Population:	9.5%**
Black Forces % Black Population:	9.2%**

*Blacks were not allowed to serve beyond population percentage.
**Figures tabulated from average of 1940-1950 population.

THE KOREAN WAR

In spite of military and civil rulings that restricted black participation, blacks made courageous contributions. Perhaps the most meaningful incident was the integration of fighting units for the first time in United States history (officially)—an experience which led to the integration of the armed forces following the war.

The 24th Infantry
Captured the city of Yechon, winning the first United States victory. As a unit, the 24th won 126 individual Silver Stars, 282 Bronze Stars and 7 Distinguished Service Crosses.

Lieut. Thomas J. Hudner (white), Fall River, Mass.

Awarded the Congressional Medal of Honor for risking his life in a vain attempt to save the life of a squadron mate, Ensign Jesse Leroy Brown, Hattiesburg, Mississippi. Brown was the first black American naval officer to lose his life in combat and the Navy's first black aviator.

THE VIETNAM CONFLICT

The United States involvement in the Vietnam conflict accounted for a continuously increasing deployment of troops, both black and white. Steady escalation in numbers of military personnel involved and in bombing missions occurred. Since the murder of Ngo Din Diem in 1963, forces in Vietnam were integrated, although separate components within larger units were not unusual.

STATISTICS

As of December 31, 1972 there had been 274,-900 blacks involved in the Vietnam conflict; between January, 1961 and June, 1973, 3,905 black enlisted men and 93 officers had been killed in action.

There were 18 black prisoners of war, with 16 returning and two dying in captivity. As of June 12, 1973, there were 54 black MIAs (missing in action).

From 1961 to 1968, black soldiers represented 10.6 of the military serving in Southeast Asia and accounted for 13.5 of the battle deaths.

Percent of Enlisted Men—Blacks, Whites and Other Races—Who Entered Training Under Veterans Administration Programs (of Men Separated from the Armed Forces June-Dec. 1968)

Training	Black	Other races including white
Percent who entered training.........	18	24
Type of training: all types............	100	100
College..........................	57	68
Below college schooling..........	35	23
On-the-job training..............	8	10

Source: U.S. Department of Labor, Bureau of Labor Statistics, 1971.

Status of Selective Service Draftees Examined for Military Service, 1950 to 1971, and by Race, 1971

Number in thousands. Includes Puerto Rico, Guam, Mariana Islands, and Virgin Islands. Based on results of preinduction examinations.

STATUS	1950-1971[1]		1970		1971					
					Number			Percent		
	Number	Percent	Number	Percent	Total	White	Black and other	Total	White	Black and other
Examined..............	15,841	100.0	1,017	100.0	596	528	68	100.0	100.0	100.0
Found acceptable............	9,347	59.0	549	54.0	301	271	30	50.5	51.4	43.2
Disqualified.................	6,494	41.0	468	46.0	295	257	38	49.5	48.6	56.8
Medically disqualified only...	3,740	1.2	380	37.4	242	227	15	40.4	42.9	22.5
Failed mental requirements only....................	2,190	13.8	63	6.2	31	15	16	5.4	2.9	24.0
Failed mental test only[2].....	1,725	10.9	54	5.3	25	12	13	4.3	2.3	19.6
Trainability limited[3]......	465	2.9	9	0.9	6	3	3	1.1	0.6	4.4
Failed mental test and medically disqualified..........	379	2.4	15	1.4	13	8	5	2.2	1.4	7.9
Administratively disqualified..	185	23.6	10	1.0	9	7	2	1.5	1.4	2.4

[1] 1950 data are for July through December only.   [2] Examinees who failed minimum requirement (10 percentile on Armed Forces Qualification Test (AFQT) or minimum requirement (below raw score of 60) on its equivalent (ECFA) administered to Spanish-speaking examinees in Puerto Rico.
[3] Examinees classified as mental group IV on basis of AFQT but who failed to meet additional aptitude area requirements effective in August 1958 and called Army Classification Battery (ACB) tests until mid-September 1961 and Army Qualification Battery (AQB) since then. The AQB requirements were raised in May 1963 and lowered in November 1965, April 1966, October 1966, and December 1966.

Source: U.S. Dept. of the Army, Office of the Surgeon General, unpublished data.

Black Officers and Enlisted Men in the Armed Forces, 1969 and 1970 (in Thousands)

Rank and area	Total		Black		Percent Black	
	1969	1970	1969	1970	1969	1970
Total........................	3,439	3,074	323	293	9	10
Officers......................	419	366	9	8	2	2
Outside Southeast Asia........	354	NA	7	NA	2	NA
In Southeast Asia.............	65	NA	2	NA	3	NA
Enlisted men..................	3,020	2,708	314	284	10	11
Outside Southeast Asia........	2,447	NA	249	NA	10	NA
In Southeast Asia.............	573	NA	65	NA	11	NA

NA   Not Available.

BLACK GENERALS ON ACTIVE DUTY IN THE ARMED SERVICES

BECTON, COL. JULIUS WESLEY, JR.

Military officer, United States Army, is Chief, Armor Branch, Officer Personnel Directorate, Personnel Operations, United States Army. Born June 29, 1926 in Bryn Mawr, Pennsylvania, he received a B.S. Degree in Mathematics from Prairie View A&M College, Prairie View, Texas, and an M.A. in Economics from University of Maryland; Infantry School, Basic and Advanced Courses, United States Army Command and General Staff College, Armed Forces Staff College, and the National War College. He has served in Europe and Vietnam, having completed over 26 years of active service and has received nine medals and awards.

BROOKS, BRIG. GEN. HARRY W., JR.

Military officer, is a brigadier general and Assistant Division Commander, 2nd Infantry Division of the U.S. Army. His work involves the planning, organizing, and supervision of division activities. Promoted to brigadier general in Aug. 1972, General Brooks was director of Equal Opportunity Programs in Washington before assuming his present duties in January, 1973. He was born May 17, 1928 in Indianapolis, Ind. He attended four military schools and is a graduate of the University of Omaha (B.A., 1962; M.A., 1973). With twenty-five years of service in the army, he has won the Legion of Merit Award, the Bronze Star, and the Army Commendation Medal. He recently completed a fact-finding mission on race relations on army installations in Europe, South Korea, Okinawa, and Hawaii.

CARTWRIGHT, BRIG. GEN. ROSCOE C.

Military officer, is assistant division commander of U.S. Military Headquarters USAREUR and 7th Army, 3rd Infantry Division. Born May 27, 1919 in Kansas City, Mo., he has degrees from San Francisco State College (A.B.) and the University of Missouri (M.B.A.). He has been in service since 1941 and has received specialized military training from the Command and General Staff College and the Industrial College of the Armed Forces. His assignment in 1972 as assistant division commander made General Cartwright the second black man in military history to serve in that capacity. He is responsible for assisting in the training, administration, and housing of 14,000 officers and men into combat ready forces. During his military tenure, he served tours in World War II, Korea, and Vietnam.

Included in his numerous military citations and decorations are World War II Victory, Meritorious Service, Armed Forces Honor, United Nations, Korea Service, and Vietnam Campaign Medals.

DAVISON, MAJ. GEN. FREDERIC

Deputy Chief of Staff, Personnel, at U.S. Army Headquarters in Europe and the Seventh Army here. Born September 28, 1917 in Washington, D.C., he was commissioned after he completed the ROTC course at Howard University, where he graduated cum laude in 1938 with a B.S. degree. He earned a graduate degree as Master of Arts in International Affairs at George Washington University. He has served in Vietnam as Commander of the 199th Brigade. Davison is the first black general to command an Army division in U.S. history, the 8th Infantry Division.

DILLARD, BRIG. GEN. OLIVER W.

Military officer, is deputy director of the U.S. Army's Civil Operations and Rural Development Support at headquarters of the Military Assistance Command in Vietnam. He has been in the military service for 27 years and was the fifth black to achieve the rank of brigadier general of the army. He was the first black to attend the National War College (1964). Born September 28, 1926 in Margaret, Ala., he attended Tuskegee Institute and is a graduate of Omaha University (bachelor of general education, 1959) and George Washington University (M.S., international affairs, 1965). He was inducted into the Army in 1945, was commissioned as a second lieutenant in 1947, and was promoted to his present rank in 1972. He has served in Europe, Africa, and the Far East. He has received numerous citations and medals of honor—including the Purple Heart, the Silver Star, and the Bronze Star—during his military career.

GRAVELY, REAR ADMIRAL SAMUEL L., JR.

Military officer (U.S. Navy) the Navy's only black flag officer, is commander of a cruiser-destroyer flotilla of approximately 30 ships—the first time a black has commanded a naval flotilla. Formerly Gravely served as director of Naval Communications and commander of the Naval Communications Command, Office of the Chief of Naval Operations, in Washington, D.C. Born June 4, 1922 in Richmond, Va., he is a graduate of Virginia Union University (A.B., 1948). He enlisted in the U.S. Naval Reserve (1942) and completed mid-shipment school at Columbia University (1944), becoming the first black man to be commissioned as an ensign in World War II. He was assigned to the submarine chaser PC 1264, on which he served successively as communications officer, electronics officer, and personnel officer. Released from active duty in 1946, he completed college in 1948. In August, 1949, the Navy recalled him to active duty, and he saw both sea and shore duty during the Korean War. He transferred from the Navy Reserve to the regular Navy in 1955. In February, 1961, as temporary skipper of the destroyer USS *Chandler*, he became the first black man ever to command a Navy ship. Rising to lieutenant commander, he was given his own ship, the radar picket destroyer, USS *Falgout*. Two other ship commands followed. He was promoted to captain in 1967, to read admiral and director of Naval Communications in 1971, and to flotilla commander in July, 1973.

GREER, BRIG. GEN. EDWARD

Military officer, is deputy commanding general of the U.S. Army Training Center Engineer and Fort Leonard Wood (Fort Leonard Wood, Missouri). Born March 8, 1924 in Gary, W. Va., he is a graduate of West Virginia State College (B.S., biological sciences, 1948) and George Washington University (M.S., international affairs, 1967). He has served since 1947 in the military and has received special military training at Ground General School, Strategic Intelligence School, Command and General Staff College and National War College. Named to this post in 1972, he is one of two blacks to be assigned as deputy commanding general of the six Army training centers in the world. He assists in the command, direction, and control of the 28,000 officers and men at the military site. He is affiliated with Kappa Alpha Psi fraternity, Association of the United States Army, and the Reserve Officers Association. He was awarded the Silver Star, the Legion of Merit with Oak Leaf Cluster, and the Bronze Star Medal with Oak Leaf Cluster.

GREGG, BRIG. GEN. ARTHUR J.

General officer, is deputy director of supply and maintenance with the United States Army. Born May 11, 1928 in Florence, S.C. he has a B.S. degree from St. Benedict College in Atchison, Kan., where he graduated summa cum laude. He also attended graduate-level military schools, the Command and General Staff College at Fort Leavenworth, Kan. and the Army

War College. In October of 1972, he was promoted to brigadier general. He feels that he can provide inspiration, guidance and assistance to young men, and also can exercise considerable influence on Army policy and operations as a result of his new appointment.

HAMLET, MAJOR GENERAL JAMES FRANK

Military officer, U.S. Army, is commanding general, 4th Infantry Division (Mechanized), Fort Carson, Colorado. Born December 13, 1921 in Alliance, Ohio, he has a B.S. degree in Business Administration from St. Benedict's College, Atchison, Kansas. He also attended the Infantry School (Basic and Advanced Courses) the United States Army Command and General Staff College and the United States Army War College. He served in Vietnam for 3 years, his last assignment there being Commanding General, 3d Brigade, 1st Cavalry Division. He has served in the United States Army for over 29 years and has received 10 medals and awards.

JAMES, MAJ. GEN. DANIEL, JR. ("CHAPPIE")

Military officer (U.S. Air Force), is assistant secretary of defense. Born February 11, 1920 in Pensacola, Fla., he is a graduate of Tuskegee Institute (B.P.E.). While at Tuskegee, he took flying lessons and became a licensed pilot and flight instructor of Army Air Corps cadets until January, 1943 when he entered the aviation cadet program himself. Commissioned in July, 1943, he entered fighter overseas combat training at Selfridge Field, Mich. He was assigned to Korea as a flight leader in July, 1950, where he became known as the "Black Panther," flying F-51s and F-80s. He flew 101 combat missions before his assignment to Otis Air Force Base in Massachusetts in July, 1951, as an all-weather jet pilot. After assignments as operations officer and commander of various squadrons, he attended the Air Command and Staff School, Maxwell AFB in Alabama in September, 1956. In July, 1957, he became an air staff officer in the Office of the Deputy Chief of Staff for Operations, Air Defense Division at Headquarters, U.S. Air Force, in Washington, D.C. After duties in England and Arizona, he became director of operations for the 8th Tactical Fighter Wing in Thailand. He led a total of 78 missions over North Vietnam. Among his 14 decorations are the Distinguished Flying Cross (with oak leaf cluster), the Air Medal (with seven oak leaf clusters), and the Presidential Unit Citation.

ROBINSON, COL. ROSCOE, JR.
Military officer, United States Army, is Commanding Officer, 2nd Brigade, 82nd Airborne Division, Fort Bragg, N.C. Born October 11, 1928 in St. Louis, Mo., he received his B.S. degree in Military Engineering from the United States Military Academy, and an M.P.I.A. Degree-International Affairs, University of Pittsburgh; he also attended the U.S. Army Command and General Staff College, the Infantry School, and the National War College. During his 21 years of active service, he has served in the Pacific and Vietnam, and received 18 medals and awards.

ROBERS, COL. CHARLES CALVIN
Military officer, United States Army, is Commanding Officer, 42nd Field Artillery Group, Europe. Born September 6, 1929 in Claremont, West Virginia, he received his B.S. degree in General Mathematics from West Virginia State College and an M.S. in Vocational/Educational Guidance from Shippensburg State College; the Field Artillery School, United States Army Artillery and Missile School, U.S. Army Command and General Staff College and the U.S. Army War College. He has served in Europe and Vietnam, with over 21 years of active service, and has received 18 medals and awards—the most prestigious being the Congressional Medal of Honor.

SHEFFEY, COL. FRED CLIFTON
Military officer, United States Army, is Chief, Financial Resources Division, Supply and Material Directorate Office, Deputy Chief of Staff for Logistics, Washington, D.C. Born August 27, 1928, he received a B.S. Degree (Economics and Business) from Wilberforce University, an M.B.A. (Business Administration) from Ohio State University, and an M.S. (International Affairs) from George Washing-

ton University. He attended the Quartermaster School, United States Army Command and General Staff College, and the National War College. With over 22 years of active service, he has received 5 medals and awards for his service in the Pacific and Vietnam.

SHUFFER, COL. GEORGE MACON, JR.
Military officer, United States Army, is Deputy Chief of Staff for Personnel in Washington, D.C. Born September 27, 1923 in Palestine, Texas, he received a B.S. in Military Science and an M.A. in European History from the University of Maryland. He also attended Infantry School, Advanced Course, United States Army Command and General Staff College and U.S. Army War College. He has served in China, Vietnam, and the Canal Zone, during his more than 31 years of active service, and has received 11 medals and awards.

THEUS, BRIG. GEN. LUCIUS
Military officer, is special assistant for social actions in the U.S. Air Force. Among his duties in this capacity is supervision of the Air Force Social Actions Program, which includes guidelines for equal opportunity and treatment; race relations education; drug and alcohol abuse control; and domestic actions. Gen. Theus was born Oct. 11, 1922 in Madison County, Tenn. He is a graduate of the University of Maryland (B.S., 1956) and George Washington University (M.B.A., 1957). On Jan. 27, 1972, he became the third black officer in Air Force history to be promoted to the rank of brigadier general. He believes that "opportunities were never greater in the Air Force for blacks and other minorities." Gen. Theus also holds the Legion of Merit medal awarded him at the same time that he received his general's star.

THE BLACK VETERAN

The black veteran in 1973 may have served in three or more armed conflicts over the past half-century. World War I, II, Korea and Viet Nam account for the majority of surviving veterans, with the greatest number being veterans of the Viet Nam era.

Questions relating to benefits, educational, employment and loan opportunities, counseling and supportive services, medical benefits and facilities, drug detoxification and rehabilitation and discharges other than honorables may be answered by applying to one or more of the following agencies:

National Urban League

National Association for the Advancement of Colored People

Veterans Employment State Employment Service

Veterans Administration, V.A. Information Service, Washington, D.C. 20420

American Red Cross

CONGRESSIONAL MEDAL OF HONOR
1869-1973

YEAR	PLACE	RECIPIENT	UNIT	DATE ISSUED
		ARMY		
1863	Ft. Wagner	Sgt. William Harvey Carney	Co. C 54th Mass.	May 23, 1900
1864	New Market	Maj. Christian A. Fleetwood	4th U.S.C.T.	April 6, 1865
1864	Chapin's Farm	Sgt. Alfred B. Hilton	Co. H 4th U.S.C.T.	April 6, 1865
1864	Chapin's Farm	Cpt. Charles Veal	Co. D 4th U.S.C.T.	April 6, 1865
1864	Chapin's Farm	Sgt. Milton M. Holland	Co. C 5th U.S.C.T.	April 6, 1865
1864	Chapin's Farm	1st Sgt. James E. Bronson	Co. D 5th U.S.C.T.	April 6, 1865
1864	Chapin's Farm	1st Sgt. Powhatan Beatty	Co. G 5th U.S.C.T.	April 6, 1865
1864	Chapin's Farm	1st Sgt. Robert A. Pinn	Co. I 5th U.S.C.T.	April 6, 1865
1864	Chapin's Farm	Sgt. Alexander Kelly	Co. F 6th U.S.C.T.	April 6, 1865
1864	Chapin's Farm	Cpl. Miles James	Co. B 36th U.S.C.T.	April 6, 1865
1864	Chapin's Farm	Pvt. James Gardiner	Co. I 36th U.S.C.T.	April 6, 1865
1864	Chapin's Farm	1st Sgt. Edward Radcliffe	Co. C 38th U.S.C.T.	April 6, 1865
1864	Chapin's Farm	Sgt. James H. Harris	Co. B 38th U.S.C.T.	April 6, 1865
1864	Chapin's Farm	Pvt. William H. Barnes	Co. C 38th U.S.C.T.	April 6, 1865
1864	Deep Bottom	Sgt. Maj. Thomas R. Hawkins	6th U.S.C.T.	Feb. 8, 1870
1864	Petersburg	Sgt. Decatur Dorsey	Co. B 39th U.S.C.T.	Nov. 8, 1865
1870	Kickapoo Spr., Texas	Sgt. Emanuel Stance	Troop F 9th U.S. Cav.	June 28, 1870
1877	Fla. Mountain, N.M.	Cpl. Clinton Greaves	Troop C 9th U.S. Cav.	June 26, 1879
1879	New Mexico	Sgt. Thomas Boyne	Troop C 9th U.S. Cav.	Jan. 6, 1882
1879	Las Animas Canyon, Mexico	Sgt. John Denny	Troop 9th U.S. Cav.	Nov. 27, 1894
1879	Milk River, Colorado	Sgt. Henry Johnson	Troop D 9th U.S. Cav.	Oct. 25, 1879
1880	Ft. Tulersu, & Carrizo Canyon, N.M.	Sgt. George Jordan	Troop K 9th U.S. Cav.	Aug. 12, 1881
1881	Carrizo Canyon, N.M.	Sgt. Thomas Shaw	Troop K 9th U.S. Cav.	Dec. 1890
1881	Cuchillo Negro Mountains, N.M.	1st Sgt. Moses Williams	Troop I 9th U.S. Cav.	Nov. 12, 1896
1881	New Mexico	Sgt. Brent Woods	Troop B 9th U.S. Cav.	July 12, 1894
1881	Cuchillo Negro Mountains, N.M.	Pvt. Augustus Walley	Troop I 9th U.S. Cav.	Oct. 1, 1890
1889	Arizona	Sgt. Benjamin Brown	Co. C 24th Inf. Reg.	Feb. 19, 1890
1889	Arizona	Cpl. Isaiah Mays	Co. B 24th Inf. Reg.	Feb. 19, 1889
1890	Sioux campaign	Cpl. William O. Wilson	Troop I 9th U.S. Cav.	Sept. 17, 1891
1890	Arizona	Sgt. William McBryar	Troop K 10th U.S. Cav.	May 15, 1890
1898	Tayabacoa, Cuba	Pvt. Dennis Bell	Troop H 10th U.S. Cav.	June 23, 1899
1898	Tayabacoa, Cuba	Pvt. William H. Thompkins	Troop G 10th U.S. Cav.	June 23, 1899
1898	Tayabacoa, Cuba	Pvt. Fitz Lee	Troop M 10th U.S. Cav.	June 23, 1899
1898	Tayabacoa, Cuba	Pvt. George H. Wanton	Troop M 10th U.S. Cav.	June 23, 1899
1898	Santiago, Cuba	Sgt. Edward L. Baker	Troop M 10th U.S. Cav.	June 23, 1899
1951	Korea	Pfc. William Thompson*	Co. M 24th Inf.	June, 1951
1952	Korea	Sgt. Cornelius H. Charlton*	Co. C 24th Inf.	Feb. 12, 1952
1966	Viet Nam	Pvt. Milton L. Olive III*	Co. B 503rd Inf.	April 12, 1966
1967	Viet Nam	Sp-6 Lawrence Joel	1st Bn. 503rd Inf. U.S.A.	Nov. 8, 1965
1968	Viet Nam	Sgt. Donald R. Long	Troop C 1st Sqd. U.S.A.	June 30, 1966
1968	Viet Nam	Sp-5 Dwight H. Johnson	Co. B 1st Bn. U.S.A.	Jan. 15, 1968
1968	Viet Nam	Cpt. Riley L. Pitts	Co. C 2nd Bn. U.S.A.	Oct. 31, 1967
1968	Viet Nam	Plt. Sgt. Matthew Leonard	Co. B 1st Bn. U.S.A.	Feb. 28, 1967
1969	Viet Nam	Sp-5 Clarence E. Sasser	3rd Bn. 60th Inf. U.S.A.	Jan. 10, 1968
1969	Viet Nam	1st Lt. Ruppert L. Sargent	3rd Bn. 60th Inf. U.S.A.	March 15, 1967
1969	Viet Nam	Sfc. Webster Anderson	Battery A 2nd Bn. U.S.A.	Oct. 15, 1967
1969	Viet Nam	Sfc. Eugene Ashley, Jr.	Co. C 5th Spec. For. Group U.S.A.	Feb. 6, 1968
1969	Viet Nam	Sgt. Clifford C. Sims	Co. D 2nd Bn. U.S.A.	Dec. 21, 1969
1970	Viet Nam	Pfc. Garfield M. Langhorn	Troop C 7th Squadron U.S.A.	Jan. 15, 1969
1970	Viet Nam	Ltc. Charles C. Rogers	1st Bn. 5th Artillery U.S.A.	Nov. 1, 1968
1970	Viet Nam	1st Lt. John E. Warren, Jr.	Co. C 2nd Bn. U.S.A.	Jan. 14, 1969
1971	Viet Nam	Sfc. William M. Bryant	U. S. A.	March 24, 1969
		NAVY		
1863	Stono River	Robert Blake	Contraband USS Marblehead	April 16, 1864
1864		Joachim Pease	Seaman U.S.S. Kearsarge	Dec. 31, 1864
1864	Battle of Mobile Bay	John H. Lawson	Landsman, U.S.S. Hartford	Dec. 31, 1864
1864	Battle of Mobile Bay	James Mifflin	Landsman, U.S.S. Brooklyn	Dec. 31, 1864
1864		Clement Dees†	Seaman U.S.S. Pontoosuc	
1865	Mattox Creek	Aaron Anderson	Landsman U.S.S. Wyandank	June 22, 1865
1872		Joseph B. Noil	Seaman U.S.S. Powhatan	May 20, 1898
1898		Daniel Atkins	Ship's Cook U.S.S. Cushing	May 20, 1898
1898	Santiago, Cuba	Robert Penn	Fireman U.S.S. Iowa	Dec. 14, 1898
		MARINES		
1968	Viet Nam	Pfc. James Anderson, Jr.	Co. F 2nd Battalion U.S.M.C.	Aug. 21, 1968
1969	Viet Nam	Sgt. Rodney M. Davis	U.S.M.C.	March 26, 1973
1970	Viet Nam	Pfc. Oscar P. Auston	Co. E 2nd Battalion U.S.M.C.	April 20, 1970
1970	Viet Nam	Pfc. Ralph H. Johnson	Co. A 1st Reconnaissance U.S.M.C.	April 20, 1970

*Awarded posthumously.
†Dees, a slave,
was recommended for
a Medal of Honor, but
ran away in search of
his freedom before he
actually received it.

THE SERVICE ACADEMIES

Three young black men graduated from the United States Military Academy at West Point, New York, between 1870 and 1935. They were Henry O. Flipper, 1877; John H. Alexander, 1887; and Charles Young, 1889. Flipper, the first to graduate, though the fourth to be admitted, was assigned to the all-black 10th Cavalry. The 9th and 10th Cavalry were considered black units but the commissioned officers were white. The fact lends credence to the theory that Flipper was "railroaded" out of the Army when he was accused of mishandling company funds and court-martialed. Flipper was found not guilty of the charges, but nonetheless, was dismissed from the service for "conduct unbecoming to an officer and a gentleman." Using his West Point training and his Army experiences (he had surveyed Fort Sill, Oklahoma and laid it out so that the swamp land could be drained and utilized), Flipper became a mining engineer in Mexico, and worked there for many years before returning to the United States where, for a time, he worked in the Department of the Interior under Secretary Albert Fall. Flipper worked for the rest of his life seeking an Act of Congress which would reinstate him in the service and restore his rank and pay. He was unsuccessful and died on May 3, 1940, in Atlanta, Georgia.

John H. Alexander, who graduated in 1887, was assigned as a military officer to Wilberforce University. He died of tuberculosis on March 26, 1894, while still serving at that post.

Charles Young was admitted June 15, 1885. He graduated in 1889. In his senior year he was discovered to be "deficient" in mathematics, but he elected to make up the deficiency and, even though the one subject cost him an extra year at West Point, he stayed on and graduated. This perseverance and determination characterized his entire career. Upon graduation he was assigned to duty with the 9th Cavalry in Nebraska and Utah. Following Alexander's death he became military officer at Wilberforce University. During the Spanish–American War, Young commanded the 9th Ohio Battalion and received many commendations. He served continuously in the Philippines, in Liberia, and on the punitive Mexican Expedition with General John Pershing. At the outbreak of World War I, Lieutenant Colonel Young was in line to command the 92nd Infantry Combat Division, an all-black unit, but he was disqualified and retired from active duty. His disqualification was based on a medical examination indicating that he had high blood pressure. To disprove this finding, Young rode horseback from Wilberforce, Ohio to Washington, D.C., ending up in front of the War Department. The trip took 16 days and covered a distance of 497 miles. Special Orders No. 175, dated July 30, 1917, from the U.S. Army contains paragraphs 51, which retired Lieutenant Colonel Young from active service with the rank of Colonel, and 52, which placed him on active military duty. Later he was ordered to Camp Grant in Rockford, Illinois, where he was assigned to troop training details. After World War I, he was sent back to Liberia as a military attaché to the Liberian government. He died in Lagos, Nigeria on January 8, 1922, and his body was returned to the United States for burial with full military honors at Arlington Cemetery.

Between 1889—when Charles Young graduated—and 1936, when Benjamin O. Davis Jr. finished, there was a period of 47 years when no black man was commissioned from West Point. Between 1886 and 1918 there were no blacks admitted to West Point. John Alexander of Ohio was admitted in June of 1918 and dismissed in December 1918. Another decade elapsed before Alonzo Parham of Illinois was admitted in July, 1929. He lasted until January, 1930. Benjamin O. Davis Jr., also of Illinois, was admitted in July, 1932 and graduated on schedule in June, 1936. It is significant that these dates coincide with the period in which black civil rights were at their lowest point. Parham's appointment coincided with the election of the first black Congressman from the North and the first to serve in the U.S. Congress since Reconstruction, Oscar DePriest of Illinois. From 1870 to 1966, 63 percent of those admitted have graduated, the national average for that period being 69 percent.

The United States Naval Academy at Annapolis admitted its first black midshipman in 1872. He was John Henry Conyers from South Carolina, and he lasted two months. Alonzo C. McLellan, also from South Carolina, was admitted in 1873, and Henry E. Baker, Jr. of Mississippi was admitted in 1874. McLellan lasted six months and Baker was dismissed after he had been there for over a year. Sixty-two years passed before another black was admitted to the Naval Academy. James Lee Johnson of Illinois attended from June, 1936 to February, 1937. His resignation was protested by the black community and by Congressman Arthur Mitchell (R., Ill.,), who had appointed Johnson. It was held that Johnson had been discriminated against both in terms of grades and in the kind of treatment he had been given at the hands of his fellow students. He reported that he had suffered cruel hazing which affected both his conduct and his grades.

Wesley A. Brown of New York City was admitted in June, 1945 as an appointee of Congressman Adam Clayton Powell, Jr. He graduated in the class of 1949 and became the first black commissioned officer in the United States Navy to be graduated from the Naval Academy.

The United States Naval Academy at Annapolis, Md. accepted 52 black students from 1872 to 1966, with the first graduate in 1949. From 1967 to 1973 there have been 24 black officers commissioned in the United States Navy following graduation from Annapolis. Seventeen black cadets have been commissioned officers in the United States Marine Corps since 1968 when Charles F. Bolden Jr. graduated.

The first black to be graduated from the Coast Guard Academy was Merle James Smith, Jr., who was commissioned an ensign in the United States Coast Guard Academy in 1966.

The first black cadets at the Air Force Academy at Colorado Springs, which opened in July, 1955, were Roger Sims, Isaac S. Payne, IV, and Charles V. Bush. All were graduated with the class of 1963. From 1963, when the first three black students graduated, until 1973, 69 black men have graduated and 67 of them have been commissioned as U.S.A.F. officers. Weldon K. Groves (1968) graduated but was not commissioned, and Leon G. White (1971) died, but had completed requirements for graduation prior to his death.

UNITED STATES MILITARY ACADEMY

Flipper, Henry O. 1877 Infantry*
Alexander, John H. 1887 Infantry*
Young, Charles D. 1889 Cavalry*
Davis, Benjamin O., Jr. 1936 USAF
Fowler, James D. 1941 Infantry
Tresville, Robert B., Jr. 1943 USAF*
Davenport, Clarence M. 1943 Artillery
Francis, Henry M. 1944 Artillery****
Davis, Ernest J., Jr. 1945 USAF
Rivers, Mark E., Jr. 1945 USAF****
McCoy, Andrew A., Jr. 1946 USAF*
Howard, Edward B. 1949 Signal Corps
Smith, Charles L. 1949 Signal Corps
Carlisle, David K. 1950 Corps of Engineers**
Green, Robert W. 1950 Corps of Engineers**
Brown, Norman J. 1951 Armor*
Wainer, Douglas F. 1951 Signal Corps
Robinson, Roscoe, Jr. 1951 Infantry
Woodson, William B. 1951 Artillery**
Young, James R., Jr. 1951 USAF
Corprew, Gerald 1953 Signal Corps
Hughes, Bernard C. 1953 Corps of Engineers
Worthy, Clifford 1953 Artillery
Lee, Ronald B. 1954 Signal Corps

Turner, Leroy 1954 Signal Corps**
Robinson, Hugh G. 1954 Corps of Engineers
Hamilton, John M., Jr. 1955 Infantry
Olive, Lewis C., Jr. 1955 USAF
Cassells, Cyrus 1955 USAF
Batchman, G.R. 1955 Infantry
Brown, John 1955 Infantry
Blunt, Roger 1956 Corps of Engineers
Bradley, Martin G. 1957 USAF
McCollum, Cornell, Jr. 1957 USAF
Brunner, Ronald S. 1958 Artillery
Baugh, Raymond C. 1959 Signal Corps
Kelley, Welbourne A., III 1959
    Corps of Engineers
Dorsey, Ira 1960 Artillery
Brown, Reginald J. 1961 Infantry
Quinn, Kenneth L. 1961 Signal Corps
Gorden, Fred A. 1962 Artillery
Handcox, Robert C. 1963 Infantry
Banks, Edgar 1963 Artillery
Ivy, William L. 1963 USAF
Jackson, David S. 1963 Artillery
Miller, Warren F., Jr. 1964 Artillery
Ramsay, David L. 1964 USAF

Anderson, Joseph B. 1965 Infantry
Conley, James S. 1965 Artillery
Hester, Arthur C. 1965 Armor
Jenkins, Harold A., Jr. 1965 Infantry
Cox, Hobart R. 1966 Armor
Davis, Thomas B., III 1966 Infantry
Ramsay, Robert B. 1966 Air Force
Fowler, James D., Jr. 1967 Field Artillery
Hackett, Jerome R. 1969 Signal Corps
Minor, James A., Jr. 1969 Infantry
Steele, Michael F. 1969 Infantry
Tabela, Francis E., Jr. 1969 Infantry
Williams, Michael M. 1969 Infantry
Cousar, Robert J., Jr., 1970 Signal Corps
Mason, Robert E. 1970 Air Def. Artillery
Morgan, Roderick H. 1970 Infantry
Price, Willie J. 1970 Infantry
Reid, Trevor A. 1970 Infantry
Robinson, Bruce E. 1970 Infantry
Thomas, Kenneth L. 1970 Air Force
Steele, Gary R. 1970 Infantry
Freeman, Robert E. 1971 Infantry
James, Kevin T. 1971 Infantry
Plummer, William W. 1971 Military Police
Anderson, Edgar 1972 Infantry
Brice, David L. 1972 Infantry
Dedmond, Tony L. 1972 Armor

Edwards, Joe E. 1972 Military Police
Mension, Danny L. 1972 Infantry
Squires, Percy 1972 Infantry
Burns, Cornelius 1972 Infantry
Adams, Jesse B. 1973 Field Artillery
Bell, Richard, Jr. 1973 Infantry
Bivens, Courtland C., III 1973 Armor
Bonner, Garland C. 1973 Signal Corps
Christopher, Clyde J. 1973 Signal Corps
Coats, Charles S., Jr. 1973 Infantry
Coleman, Frederick D. 1973
    Adjutant General Corps
Crisp, William Ira 1973 Armor
Edwards, Lawrence D. 1973 Field Artillery
Ferguson, Mercer E. 1973 Infantry
Fountain, Foster F., III 1973 Infantry
Gaines, Michael B. 1973 Finance
Jenkins, Gil S. 1973 Military Intelligence
Johnson, Edward C., Jr. 1973 Infantry
Lewis, Brett H. 1973 Infantry
Martin, Edwin L. 1973 Infantry
Moore, William L. 1973 Infantry
Perry, William H. 1973 Signal Corps
Robinson, Lenwood, Jr. 1973 Infantry
Rowe, Dennis W. 1973 Military Intelligence
Sayles, Andre H. 1973 Corps of Engineers
Sutton, Lloyd L. 1973 Air Def. Artillery

*Deceased
**Resigned
***Graduated but not commissioned
****Retired

UNITED STATES NAVAL ACADEMY

Brown, Wesley A. 1949 USN ****
Chambers, Lawrence 1952 USN
Taylor, Reeves 1953 USN
Raiford, John 1954***
Gregg, Lucius P., Jr. 1955 USAF**
Sechrest, Edward 1956 USN
Bauduit, Harold S. 1956 USAF
Jamison, Vencin 1957 USN
Slaughter, Kent W. 1957 USAF*
Fennell, George M. 1958 USN*
Bruce, Malvin D. 1959 USN
Bush, William S., III 1959 USN
Clark, Maurice E. 1959 USN
Powell, William E., Jr. 1959 USN

Byrd, Willie C. 1961 USN
Johnson, Mack, Jr. 1961 USN
Shelton, John A. 1961 USN
Jackson, John T. 1962 USAF
McCray, Donald 1962 USN
Newton, Robert C. 1963 USN
Jones, W. C. 1964 USMC
McDonald, James E. 1964 USMC
Prout, Patrick M. 1964 USMC
Thomas, Benjamin F. 1964 USN
Carter, Stanley J., Jr. 1965 USN Air
Grayson, Floyd F., Jr. 1965 USN
Reason, Joseph Paul 1965 USN
Huey, Calvin W. 1967 USN

Tzomes, Chancellor A. 1967 USN
Bolden, Charles F., Jr. 1968 USMC
Clark, William S., Jr. 1968 USN
Lucas, Robert G. 1968 USN
Simmons, David F. 1968 USN
Carr, Emerson F. 1969 USN
Jones, Frederick E. 1969 USN
Williams, Leo V. 1970 USMC
Freeman, Joseph B. 1970 USMC
Greene, Everett L. 1970 USMC
Henry, Bruce A. 1970 USMC
Roberts, Michael C. 1970 USN
Watson, Anthony J. 1970 USN
Collier, Charles M. 1971 USN
Porter, John F. 1971 USN
Shaw, Hank (NMI) 1971 USN
Burnette, Edwin A. 1972 USMC
Coleman, Alfred B. 1972 USN
Crump, Walter L., Jr. 1972 USMC
Jones, Nelson M. 1972 USMC

Keaser, Lloyd W. 1972 USMC
Lovely, Eugene (NMI) 1972 USN
Mason, Matthew T. 1972 USMC
McMillan, Julius A. 1972 USMC
Rucks, Charles H. 1972 USMC
Smith, Earl M. 1972 USN
Staton, Ronald B. 1972 USN
Tindall, Julius S. 1972 USMC
Young, Ernest C. 1973 USN
Calhoun, Larry W. 1973 USMC
Caliman, Kerry H. 1973 USN
Campbell, James H. 1973 USMC
Evans, William G. 1973 USN
Faust, Homer L. 1973 USN
Jackson, James E. 1973 USMC
Jones, Larry W. 1973 USMC
Kennard, Wayne M. 1973 USN
Samuels, Richard G. 1973 USN
Shockley, Rodney L. 1973 USN
Watts, Robert D. 1973 USN

UNITED STATES AIR FORCE ACADEMY

Bush, Charles Vernon 1963 USAF
Payne, Isaac S., IV 1963 USAF
Sims, Roger 1963 USAF
Gregory, Frederick 1964 USAF
Beamon, Arthur 1965 USAF
Thomas, Charles 1965 USAF
Plummer, Bentley V. 1965 USAF
Wiley, Fletcher H. 1965 USAF
Cunningham, Thomas L. 1967 USAF
Ecung, Maurice A. 1968 USAF
Gibson, Samuel B. 1968 USAF
Groves, Weldon K. 1968***
Marshall, Marion A. 1968 USAF
Moore, Francis M. 1968 USAF
Thompson, James E. 1968 USAF
Hopper, John D., Jr. 1969 USAF
Howland, Walter T. 1969 USAF
Little, Kenneth H. 1969 USAF
Love, James E. 1969 USAF
Spooner, Richard E. 1969 USAF
Stevenson, Kenneth E. 1969 USAF
Arnold, Harry (NMI) 1970 USAF
Battles, Dorsey B. 1970 USAF
Bowie, Harold V., Jr. 1970 USAF
Bryant, Robert S. 1970 USAF
Elliot, Norman L. 1970 USAF
Jones, Reuben D., Jr. 1970 USAF
Keys, George R., Jr. 1970 USAF
Mohr, Dean B., Jr. 1970 USAF
Banks, Reginald I. 1971 USAF
Edmondson, William E. 1971 USAF
Jennings, Ernest R. 1971 USAF
Martin, Curtis J. 1971 USAF
Rogers, Robert P. 1971 USAF

Sprott, Robert E. 1971 USAF
Watson, Orrin S. 1971 USAF
White, Leon G. 1971*
Wimberly, Bruce P. 1971 USAF
Bassa, Paul, Jr. (NMI) 1972 USAF
Brown, Ralph B., Jr. 1972 USAF
Harrison, Booker (NMI) 1972 USAF
Henderson, Clyde R. 1972 USAF
Jones, Raymond J. 1972 USAF
McDonald, Michael (NMI) 1972 USAF
Meredith, Keith S. 1972 USAF
Nelson, Michael V. 1972 USAF
Parks, Reginald D. 1972 USAF
Rhamey, Mahlon C., Jr. 1972 USAF
Ross, Joseph D., Jr. 1972 USAF
Rucker, Raymond I. 1972 USAF
Slade, John B., Jr. 1972 USAF
Abraham, Robert E. 1973 USAF
Baker, Richard A. 1973 USAF
Bolton, Robert M. 1973 USAF
Butler, Ernest E., Jr. 1973 USAF
Childress, Charlie, Jr. (NMI) 1973 USAF
Dunn, Arthur L., Jr. 1973 USAF
Gilbert, Robert L. 1973 USAF
Harrison, Herbert A. 1973 USAF
Hodges, Rudnaldo (NMI) 1973 USAF
Lewis, Gerald E. 1973 USAF
Mitchell, David L. 1973 USAF
Mitchell, Joseph R., Jr. 1973 USAF
Mitchell, Arderia F. 1973 USAF
Richardson, Donald L. 1973 USAF
Stallworth, Charles E. 1973 USAF
Thompson, William L. 1973 USAF
Way, Spencer, Jr. (NMI) 1973 USAF

MILITARY CHRONOLOGY, 1969-73

1969

Jan. 3—Pentagon figures showed that although there were more than 300,000 blacks, or 8.9% of the total personnel on active duty in the Army, Navy, Marine Corps and Air Force, only 8,335 officers, or 2.1% of the total, were black. The Army revealed that 27 blacks were among the 1,053 lieutenant colonels listed Nov. 6, 1968 for promotion to full colonel.

Jan. 7—Pentagon officials said that the Johnson Administration would begin a drive to increase the number of blacks in National Guard units across the country. A goal of about 12% black membership in Army and Air Force Guard units in each state was set for recruitment efforts over the next five years. An official estimated that black representation in the Guard had grown by about 1.5% during 1968. At the end of 1967 blacks accounted for 1.24% of the Army Guard and 0.73% of the Air Guard.

Mar. 23—The Defense Department released a study indicating that the percentage of blacks in the National Guard had increased only slightly in 1968. Despite efforts by the federal government to increase black representation in the Guard, the percentage of blacks had risen from 1.24% in 1967 to 1.26% in 1968, while the number of black Guardsmen had declined from 5,184 to 4,944. Total strength of the Guard had fallen from 418,037 in 1967 to 390,874 in 1968. Overall, the participation of blacks in the Guard had decreased in 25 states, including 12 Midwest and Northern states.

The imbalance between black percentage of population and representation in the Guard was highest in the South. In Mississippi, for example, where blacks comprised 42% of the population, there was only one black in a Guard force of 10,365 men. In New York, 1.8% of the Guard's personnel was black, but blacks comprised an estimated 8.4% of the state's population.

The percentage of blacks in the Air National Guard also rose only slightly in 1968, from 0.73% in 1967 to 0.77%. But the number of blacks decreased from 623 to 597 of the total of 77,100 Air Guardsmen.

The Defense Department reportedly did not plan a crash program to increase black participation in the Guard. Rather, it planned to reach a 12% black force, the national percentage of blacks among military-age men over the next five years. Until passage of the 1964 Civil Rights Act, several Southern states had barred blacks from the Guard.

June 9—In a 5-3 decision, the U.S. Supreme Court refused to hear the case of Cleveland L. Sellers Jr.., who claimed that blacks had the right to refuse induction on orders given by white or virtually all-white draft boards. Justices Douglas and Thurgood Marshall and Chief Justice Earl Warren dissented and said that the issue should

be heard by the court. Justice Douglas commented: "The system of using an all-white board may well result in black registrants being sent to Vietnam to do service for white registrants. Whether that is true or not is not shown by the present record as there was no hearing." Sellers, 24, was sentenced to five years in jail in 1967 for refusing induction.

Sept. 3—Gen. Leonard F. Chapman Jr., commandant of the Marine Corps, issued an order relaxing some of the corps' traditional rules in an attempt to end racial violence and eliminate discrimination against blacks. Chapman's announcement came in the wake of racial incidents at Camp Lejeune, S.C., and other Marine garrisons in recent weeks.

Chapman said the "Afro" or "natural" haircut would be permitted if it conformed with Marine regulations. He added that the corps would not bar the "black power" clenched-fist salute, as long as it was not used "in a manner suggesting direct defiance of duly constituted authority."

Chapman also outlined steps to eliminate discrimination against blacks in the Marine Corps. In the 1,000-word message, the commandant deplored the recent racial disorders and ordered acts of discrimination in promotions and assignments to be eliminated immediately. Chapman ordered all senior officers to review the corps' directive against discrimination and to instruct their subordinates about the rules. He also warned that no officer should deny a Marine's right to see the local commanding officer about any instance of alleged discrimination.

Dec. 29—The Air Force nominated Col. Daniel James Jr., 49, of Pensacola, Fla. to be the fourth black general in U.S. history. Brig. Gen. Frederic Ellis Davison is an Army general, and Lt. Gen. Benjamin O. Davis Jr., due to retire Feb. 1, 1970, is an Air Force general. Davis' father, Brig. Gen. Benjamin O. Davis, retired, was the first black general in U.S. military history.

1970

Jan. 24—Army investigators found that "all indications point toward an increase in racial tension" on bases throughout the world, according to an official summary of a survey released to newsmen in Saigon. The report of the investigation, ordered by Gen. William C. Westmoreland, Army chief of staff, had been presented to the Joint Chiefs of Staff in Washington Sept. 18, 1969 and had been sent to congressmen and to military commanders in the U.S. and abroad.

The report said that "Negro soldiers seem to have lost faith in the Army system," and the investigators predicted increased racial problems unless "aggressive command action, firm but impartial discipline and good leadership can prevent physical confrontation of racial groups." The survey indicated that tensions were more serious on overseas bases than in the U.S., and that in

Vietnam "polarization of the races" was "more obvious in those areas where groups were not in direct contact with an armed enemy."

Although the study said the Army "has a race problem because our country has a race problem," the investigators cited conditions within the Army that could contribute to unrest among black GIs. According to the report, the number of black junior officers had been decreasing although there were more black noncommissioned officers of lower rank. The survey found that on bases in Europe, where one of every eight soldiers was black, one of every four nonjudicial punishments (minor penalties fixed without trial) was imposed on a black GI.

On the Black Panther party, the report stated: "It does not appear that this organization had been able to gain a foothold in the Army nor does it pose a serious threat at this time."

The study said there was no immediate solution to the problems of racial tension in the Army, but commanders were warned not "to take an ostrichlike approach to racial fear, hostility and misunderstanding." "Our principal problem," the report said, "is that people simply don't communicate on this matter."

Jan. 26—The Defense Department said that Project 100,000, a three-year-old program for incorporating men into the armed forces who previously would have been declared unfit because of physical or mental reasons, was a "tentative success." The report studied performance records of 246,000 men who had been admitted to the services under "new standards" set up by Project 100,000 from October 1966 through September 1969.

Data on men admitted under the program showed that 53% had volunteered for military service but could not qualify under regular standards: 41.2% were nonwhite, compared with 9.1% who had entered the services through regular channels; and 49.3% were from the South. The average Project 100,000 man was described as a 20-year-old white with sixth-grade reading and arithmetic ability and without a high school diploma.

The study compared "new standards" men to a control group admitted under regular screening procedures and found: 94.6% of Project 100,000 servicemen graduated from basic training compared with 97.5% of the control group; 10% of project men in skilled training courses flunked or dropped out compared with 4% in the control group; and 37% of the "new standards" group were assigned to direct combat positions compared with 23% of the control group. Project 100,000 men were shown to have a higher court-martial conviction rate—3% as compared with 1.4%. Blacks within the project finished their tours of duty at a higher rate than white participants: the black attrition rate was 9.4% compared to 14.1% for whites.

Feb. 3—Defense Secretary Melvin Laird, ordered the creation of an Interservice Task Force on Education in Race Relations to develop a pro-

gram to promote racial harmony throughout the armed forces. Despite recent progress in race relations in the military, Laird said, "it is a fact that the armed forces have a race problem because our nation has a race problem." Laird asked each branch of the armed forces to "examine in depth its own communications" and develop ways to promote better understanding between races.

Feb. 3—Col. Daniel (Chappie) James Jr., 49, commander of Wheelus Air Force Base in Libya, was named by Secretary of Defense Melvin R. Laird to become deputy assistant secretary of defense for public affairs. James would be the first military man named to the post; upon Senate confirmation of his promotion in December 1969 to brigadier general, James would be the second black general in the history of the Air Force.

Feb. 26—A National Guard survey showed that efforts to increase black enlistments had proved largely unsuccessful. Black membership in the Air and Army National Guard was reported at 5,487 at the end of 1969 of a total enlistment of 478,860 men, representing 1.15% of the force. Blacks constituted 1.18% of the force at the end of 1968. Congress had refused a request for $6.5 million to recruit blacks into the Guard in 1969, and the Defense Department had not included the item in requests for fiscal 1971 funds.

Aug. 1—The Defense Department reported that the percentage of black servicemen killed in Vietnam combat had declined substantially the first three months in 1970. The Pentagon said that for the first time, the percentage of black soldiers killed in action in Southeast Asia had fallen below the percentage of blacks among U.S. forces there.

The Pentagon data showed that as of March 31, blacks serving in Indochina represented about 10% of the total American military presence in the area. During the same months, black battle fatalities accounted for 8.5% of the combat deaths in Southeast Asia. In 1969, blacks represented 9.7% of the total American force in the area and accounted for 10.8% of the combat facilities. From 1961 to 1968, blacks represented 10.6% of the GIs serving in Southeast Asia and accounted for 13.5% of the battle deaths. Defense officials said there had been no specific effort to decrease the casualty rates among black servicemen in Indochina.

Defense Department figures showed that blacks accounted for about 3.2% of Army officers, 1.7% of Air Force officers, 1.2% of Marine officers and .7% of Navy officers.

Dec. 16—Virginia Gov. Linwood Holton named Ernest D. Fears Jr., a 38-year-old assistant professor at Norfolk State College, as director of the state's Selective Service System. Fears' appointment marked the first time a black person had been selected to head a statewide draft apparatus.

Dec. 17—A Pentagon task force reported that it had found "frustration and anger" among black troops in West Germany during a fact-finding tour of U.S. bases in Europe. Shortly after the 15-man mission submitted its report, the Defense Department issued new and more far-reaching directives to deal with racial discrimination in the armed forces.

Under the new directive, an officer could be removed from his command for his failure to deal with racial discrimination. The order also gave base commanders in the U.S. the power to declare housing off limits if landlords practiced racial discrimination.

The task force's report was presented by Frank W. Render II, deputy assistant secretary for equal opportunity. It was based on the results of a three-and-a-half week survey of six Army bases in Germany, Naval installations in Spain and Italy, and Air Force bases in Great Britain and Germany.

Commenting on the report Mr. Render said that "a dramatic turnabout of behavior and attitudes in the area of race and human relations is imperative in the military services if we are to maintain highly effective combat and support-oriented units." He said, however, that he did not believe racial tensions had lowered the combat readiness of American soldiers stationed in West Germany. He told newsmen that he felt the visit by the task force had served to calm the anger of some black GIs in West Germany and head off "violent action."

The task force said it had found that many black soldiers expressed anger and frustration in being in what they said was a white man's army to fight a white man's battles. According to the mission, many black GIs said "their place was back in the States . . . where they could fight to liberate and free their black sisters and brothers" from racial oppression, bigotry and discrimination.

Render said the study group turned up no evidence to indicate that the Black Panthers were active among the troops.

The Defense Department's directives were issued by Assistant Secretary for Manpower Roger T. Kelley. Kelley said that the new powers given to base commanders regarding housing applied only to the U.S. and that base commanders overseas would still have to consult with superiors before taking punitive action.

Dec. 18—Adm. Elmo R. Zumwalt Jr., chief of Naval operations, said that he and Secretary of the Navy John H. Chafee had ordered an investigation to study reports that people in the Navy "are tacitly contributing to discrimination in housing" against black sailors.

Zumwalt said he was "particularly distressed by the numerous examples of discrimination black families still experience in attempting to locate housing for their families." He also indicated that some Navy personnel were not doing all they could on behalf of black sailors who had encountered difficulty in locating housing for their families.

1971

Feb. 13—The American Civil Liberties Union

announced that favorable action on the discharge application of Cornelius McNeil Cooper Jr. had been taken and marked the first time a graduate of West Point had been released as a CO.

In his application for discharge filed in October 1970, Cooper said he believed "service in the armed forces is an immoral action." He said he opposed violence and killing and that as a black man, "I am caused to be more than usually sensitive to the fact of violence in life and the effect of violence on men's lives."

Cooper said he had first looked favorably on military service but had become a conscientious objector while at West Point. Cooper's father was a lieutenant in World War II and his uncle was a lieutenant colonel and chaplain.

Mar. 5—Secretary of Defense Melvin R. Laird announced a pioneering program March 5 to improve race relations between blacks and whites serving throughout America's armed forces. The keystone of the new directive was an educational program requiring every U.S. soldier to attend classes in race relations.

Laird said the compulsory instruction would be given as the men entered the military. Six-hour refresher courses would be given each year thereafter.

The basic purpose of the new program, Laird said, "is to achieve a more harmonious relationship among all military personnel so that organizational efficiency and combat readiness will not be impaired by racial unrest, tension or conflict."

To implement the new program, the Defense Deparment said it would establish a Defense Race Relations Institute to join the already-formed Defense Race Relations Education Board. The institute would train 1,400 instructors within a year, who would then set up the race relations classes.

The institute was to be staffed by 44 military and civilian volunteers and headed by one white and one black officer—Army Col. Edward F. Krise, 46, director, and Air Force Col. Claude M. Dixon, 49, deputy director.

Mar. 13—Pentagon officials returned Captain Curtis R. Smothers to the U.S. from West Germany. Smothers, a black Army judge, was to report on his efforts to have the Army investigate alleged racial bias against black GIs in West Germany.

Capt. Smothers was one of seven black officers and enlisted men who had asked for a court of inquiry to look into reports of housing discrimination against black servicemen.

Smothers, 28, was a military circuit judge who traveled throughout the American section of Germany, sitting primarily on courts-martial.

He was summoned to Washington in what was considered to be an effort by the government to have him withdraw the application for a court of inquiry. Smothers and the six other black servicemen had petitioned the secretary of the Army, Stanley R. Resor, for the inquiry in December, 1970. The seven black soldiers complained of widespread housing discrimination in West Germany and said that such "discrimination is due solely to petitioners' race." They charged that the bias was going unchallenged because the U.S. government failed to press the West Germans to enforce the laws against discrimination.

The petition said that "only an open court of inquiry convened by the secretary of the Army could adequately determine the facts, assess the feasibility of alternative solutions and inquire into factors motivating the long-standing noncompliance with applicable laws and regulations."

A court of inquiry was usually convened when the issues involved were so complex that normal military proceedings would not go far enough into them, or when charges were leveled against high-ranking officers.

Joining Smothers in the request for an inquiry were Major Washington C. Hill, 1st Lt. Edwin Dorn, Sgt. Willie Payne and three specialists 4th class,· Gregory Jones, Bobby Metcalf and James Wilder.

Mar. 19—The U.S. Army announced major policy changes designed to end housing discrimination against black U.S. servicemen stationed anywhere in the world and insure that all American soldiers—black and white—receive equal treatment under military law.

The new policy directives, announced by Secretary of the Army Stanley R. Resor, came one week after Pentagon officials disclosed that they were meeting with a black Army judge to discuss race problems encountered by black GIs in West Germany.

After learning of the changes, the judge, Capt. Curtis Smothers, said they would "require strict monitoring and the imposition of sanctions" if they were to succeed.

The Army announced eight policy revisions, most designed to remedy complaints from black soldiers that European landlords, especially in West Germany, often refused to rent apartments to them. Resor said all Army personnel wanting to live off base in the future would have to "process through a housing referral office" that would insure that housing "should be open to all soldiers or it should be open to none." Resor said Army commanders were given authority to put off-base housing units off-limits to all Army personnel if a landlord discriminated against any soldiers under their command.

Under the second set of new orders, which Resor called a "major change in the administration of military justice," the Army required that every soldier facing any type of disciplinary action be permitted to consult with a lawyer. He said base commanders would be required to post the results of nonjudicial punishment conspicuously on bulletin boards. This, the Army said, would make it more difficult for a commander to impose harsher punishments on black soldiers than on whites for the same offense.

On March 21, 1971, West German Chancellor Willy Brandt, in a Bonn radio speech broadcast, criticized Germans who discriminated against black U.S. servicemen.

Mar. 31—Adm. Elmo R. Zumwalt Jr., chief of naval operations, announced the formation of a six-man team—including three admirals—to oversee a five-year program to recruit for the Navy more black officers and enlisted men. The aim of the recruiting drive was to bring the number of black personnel up to the level of their 12% representation in the U.S. population.

Zumwalt also announced plans for changes within the Navy to make it more attractive to minorities.

As part of the campaign, black recruiters were being added to the staffs of 37 recruiting stations across the nation. Twenty were already selected. Another step included opening new Navy Reserve Officer Training Corps units at Savannah State in Georgia and Southern University in Baton Rouge, La., which were scheduled to supplement the sole existing black Navy ROTC unit at Prairie View A&M in Prairie View, Tex. The Navy also said it would increase the number of black midshipmen at the Naval Academy at Annapolis, Md.

According to Navy officials, the prime object of the drive was to raise the number of black enlisted men from the present level of 13,200, or 5.5% of the 567,000-man enlisted force. The 540 black officers made up 0.67% of the 77,600-officer staff.

The internal reforms were intended to create better relations between black sailors and the white majority. Included was assignment of men of all ranks to the Defense Department's new Institute of Race Relations, re-examination of base facilities to insure that the needs and tastes of nonwhites were answered, guaranteeing equal social opportunity by a new, close examination of service clubs and of housing used by minority dependents, and a review of the General Classification Test which was used to assign Navy men to categories of duty.

Apr. 28—Capt. Samuel L. Gravely Jr., the black commander of a guided missile frigate, was named for promotion to the rank of rear admiral by the Navy.

Gravely, 48, was captain of the guided missile ship U.S.S. Jouett, based at Pearl Harbor, and he saw duty in World War II and the Korean conflict. Gravely would be the first black admiral in the history of the U.S. Navy.

May 10—The U.S. Commission on Civil Rights reported the Army, among other departments, had set up a program to establish goals for minority employment in its own offices.

May 13—The Army announced that it had nominated for promotion three black colonels to the rank of brigadier general. The three officers were approved by President Nixon for promotion to one-star rank.

The three black officers promoted were Col. Oliver W. Dillard, 44, Col. James F. Hamlet, 49, and Col. Roscoe C. Cartwright, 49.

Their nominations would bring the number of black generals in the Army to four.

May 19—Figures released by the Defense Department showed that the combat death rate for black servicemen in 1970 was 8.8% of the total number of fatalities. This represented a drop from the 16% recorded for the 1962–66 period. The black death rate for the subsequent three years had been 12.7%, 12.9% and 10.8%.

The year 1970 was the first year the percentage of black dead was lower than the percentage of blacks in uniform, 9.8%. Twelve-and-one-half percent, or 5,521 men of all those killed during 1961–70, were black.

May 24—Black and white servicemen battled for four hours at the Travis Air Force Base near Marysville, Calif. Military police and local lawmen succeeded in quelling the disorders which left one fireman dead and 10 airmen injured. Ninety-seven servicemen were arrested.

The fireman died of a heart attack suffered while fighting a blaze that damaged officers' quarters on the base. California authorities were investigating the fire to determine if it was intentionally set.

The trouble at the 10,000-man base erupted when 200 blacks marched on the Travis stockade to protest the detention of three blacks who were being held after an alleged fight with whites. The black airmen found the stockade ringed by military police. Returning to the barracks area, fighting erupted between some of the protesters and white airmen.

July 10—Nathaniel Jones, the NAACP's general counsel, announced that the NAACP would soon charter its first branch in West Germany in response to appeals by black U.S. servicemen stationed there.

July 27—Frank W. Render II, deputy assistant secretary of defense, said at the National Urban League Convention that nearly a dozen military officers had been relieved of command, transferred to new assignments, or reprimanded for failure to adequately enforce the Defense Department's guidelines for racial equality in the armed services. He declined to identify the officers beyond saying they ranged from general down to company grade.

Aug. 26—The Pentagon confirmed that Frank W. Render II, the Defense Department's highest ranking black, had resigned his post.

Render, 35, had been the deputy assistant secretary of defense for equal opportunity since July 20, 1970.

Roger T. Kelley, assistant secretary of defense for manpower and reserve affairs, said he had asked for Render's resignation, but declined to discuss what led to his request.

Sept. 1—Lt. Gen. George B. Simler was reported to have begun a new "quiet" program to eliminate racial irritations.

Simler said a "quiet approach will have greater effect over the long range." He added, "there is no solution in a violent, one-time effort."

Simler's program was disclosed after a 15-man human relations team of Air Force personnel sharply rebuked the manner in which the leadership at many Air Force bases was dealing with racial problems.

He said the group's report confirmed similar reports from other Air Force commands and other branches of the armed forces.

The team's charge that there was a lack of leadership or "supervisory effort" at the middle levels of his command particularly surprised him, Simler said. The Air Training Command, of which Simler was the commanding officer, included basic, technical and flight training in the Air Force.

Oct. 22—Gen. Michael S. Davison dismissed all charges against 29 black soldiers and rescinded non-judicial punishment of 17 others stemming from a racial melee in Darmstadt, West Germany. Lawyers for the men said they would file suit to prevent the "illegal and punitive" transfer of the men to other bases.

The charges resulted from a mess hall fight between white and black troops July 19, a subsequent alleged attempt by the accused to prevent an arrest, and a demonstration against the arrest. The blacks said the fight had been brought on by a pattern of discrimination and a failure to suppress white racism, and charged lack of fairness in pre-trial investigations.

Lawyers for the defendants included representatives of the National Association for the Advancement of Colored People and the American Civil Liberties Union (ACLU).

Oct. 27—The Pentagon announced moves designated to recruit more blacks for the nation's National Guard.

The black recruiting drive was aimed at doubling the number of blacks in the National Guard to 11,964, or about 4.6%. Presently, the proportion of blacks in reserve units was 1.7%.

The recruiting effort was described by the Pentagon as the first step in a major program to make reserve forces reflect the ethnic and religious makeup of the communities from which the units draw recruits.

Under the new policy, reserve unit commanders would not have to draw recruits from the waiting lists which had been compiled in their own community. Commanders were free to step up recruiting drives in their communities, bypassing the waiting lists.

In some areas, waiting lists reached the thousands as draft-eligible men signed up in hopes of escaping the draft. Under the new policy, those young men would have the slimmest chance of being called to fill the reserve vacancies.

Nov. 15-18—Members of the Congressional Black Caucus held hearings at various military installations in the U.S. and in Washington to investigate charges of racism in the armed forces. The hearings were dominated by reports that blacks were unfairly treated by the military justice system, that racial tensions had become "explosive" at some bases in the U.S. and abroad, and that the Defense Department limited the number of black servicemen stationed in some foreign countries at the request of the countries involved.

Rep. Ronald V. Dellums (D., Calif.), who co-chaired the hearings with Rep. Shirley Chisholm (D., N.Y.), said at the conclusion of the hearings that the Caucus would seek legislation giving federal courts jurisdiction over military defendants, and would press for more black command officers.

The inquiry had been announced November 3, by Reps. Chisholm and Dellums, who pointed to a Justice Department report that blacks formed a heavily disproportionate percentage of servicemen in confinement, ranging from 16.2% in the Navy to 53.4% in the Air Force, as possible evidence of discrimination.

Secret Navy and State Department memoranda were quoted by Dellums at the hearings documenting charges that the armed forces had carefully limited the number of blacks stationed in Iceland. According to the documents, the Iceland government in 1961 modified its former refusal to admit any black servicemen, but informal agreements sharply limiting the number of black personnel were still in effect as late as September 9, 1970.

The Iceland U.N. mission in New York denied that such agreements had been made. Previously Rear Adm. John Beling, Iceland military chief, said that 40 of 3,000 American troops in his country were black, about twice as many as in 1970.

U.S. Defense Secretary Melvin Laird said that no discriminatory accords were currently in effect. White House Press Secretary Ronald Ziegler the same day reported President Nixon's opinion that such accords, if they existed, would be improper.

Dellums also charged that the governments of West Germany, Greece, and Turkey demanded restrictive assignment for blacks, but he was unable to provide documentation.

The conviction among black soldiers of unfair treatment by the military justice system was found to be common. At a Ft. Meade, Md. hearing conducted by Rep. Parren J. Mitchell (D., Md.), Army attorney Arthur Stein said authorities frequently imprisoned soldiers who had psychological problems, and unfairly issued less than honorable discharges. Victims of both practices were disproportionately black. But several black commissioned and noncommissioned officers at the base denied the allegations, and praised the Army's efforts to counteract racism.

Nathaniel Jones, general counsel for the National Association for the Advancement of Colored People (NAACP), who had led an NAACP probe of bases in West Germany, called judicial practices "the most intense problem" he uncovered. Black troops mistrust the system, he said, partly because of "the near total absence of black judges and total absence of black military lawyers."

Other witnesses commented on a growing danger of violence at European bases. Samuel Berry, a former sergeant at any Army installation in Heidelberg, West Germany and founder of a group called the Unsatisfied Black Soldier, claimed that organized groups of disaffected black and white soldiers were proliferating, and were "poised and ready to raise the level of the struggle to a defensive, violent stand," in cooperation with radical German groups.

A similarly "explosive" situation was reported at some bases in the U.S., including the Great Lakes Naval Training Station in Illinois, which Rep. Ralph H. Metcalfe (D., Ill.) had visited, and Ft. Hood, Tex., investigated by Rep. Louis Stokes (D., Ohio).

Nov. 19—Defense Secretary Melvin R. Laird named Donald L. Miller 39, a black New York shipbuilding executive and former Army major, to be the Pentagon's new Assistant Secretary of Defense for equal opportunity.

Miller succeeded Frank W. Render II, who was forced to resign in August.

The Pentagon rights post was charged with the responsibility of trying to end racial discrimination in the armed forces.

1972

Jan. 27—The Air Force named Col. Lucius Theus, 49, director of management and analysis at Air Force headquarters in Washington to be elevated to general. He is the third black to attain the rank.

Feb. 10—Donald L. Miller, Assistant Secretary of Defense for equal opportunity, said that the performance by Defense Department personnel in the civil rights area would now be a major consideration in determining their efficiency and competence.

"Failure to adhere to and promote the Defense Department's civil rights program could lead to expulsion," Miller said and he pledged that his administration would not be one that redefined long-known problems but rather "will be one of action."

Apr. 19—Maj. Gen. Frederic E. Davidson, 54, the highest ranking black officer in the U.S. Army, was assigned to command the 8th Infantry Division in Europe—the first black officer to lead an Army division.

July 31—The highest-ranking black officer in the Air Force, Daniel (Chappie) James Jr., 52, was promoted to major general in a Pentagon ceremony.

Sept. 28—Secretary of the Army Robert F. Froehlke ordered cleared the military records of 167 black soldiers who were dishonorably discharged in 1906 in connection with an alleged "shooting" spree in Brownsville, Texas. In announcing Froehlke's order, the Army said the action against the black soldiers was the only documented case of mass punishment in its history. The 167 soldiers were members of the 1st Battalion, 25th Infantry, an all-black unit.

The soldiers had been punished on orders by President Theodore Roosevelt after they refused to inform against their fellow soldiers in connection with the shooting charges. There were no charges, no courts-martial, and no trial in the summary dismissals of the group. *The Brownsville Raid* by a white man, John Weaver (Norton, 1970), had brought the case to public attention.

Oct. 22—Forty-six black and white crewmen were injured Oct. 12–13 in racial brawls involving more than 100 men aboard the aircraft carrier *Kitty Hawk* off North Vietnam. Some 5,000 men were aboard the ship at the time of the fighting.

The Navy said Oct. 17 that the clash began as a fight between black and white crewmen in the ship's mess deck and then spread to other parts of the *Kitty Hawk*. A Navy spokesman said three men seriously injured in the fighting had been evacuated to a base hospital in the Philippines.

The Navy announced that 25 black crewmen aboard the ship had been charged with assault and rioting. The men were to face courts-martial on the *Kitty Hawk*.

Oct. 30—The Defense Race Relations Institute (DRRI) said that all 1,114 U.S. generals and 317 admirals would attend race relations seminars beginning in January 1973. The officers would attend two days of seminars a year. The institute, located at Patrick Air Force Base in Florida, had already trained 574 field instructors, and was planning to have 1,400 instructors in the field by mid-1973 to conduct seminars for all service personnel.

Nov. 8—The Navy agreed to delay trials for 19 of 25 blacks charged with assault and rioting aboard the aircraft carrier *Kitty Hawk* until the ship returned to San Diego about Dec. 1, when civilian lawyers could be provided. Roy Wilkins, executive secretary of the National Association for the Advancement of Colored People (NAACP), had asked Navy Secretary John W. Warner for the delay, after the 19 sailors had requested to be defended by the NAACP.

Nov. 10—More than 100 Navy admirals and Marine Corps generals were rebuked by Navy Secretary John W. Warner and Chief of Naval Operations Adm. Elmo R. Zumwalt Jr. for failing to act sufficiently against racial discrimination in their services.

Warner said recent clashes, such as those on the carriers *Constellation* and *Kitty Hawk*, had all demonstrated a "lack of communications." Zumwalt charged that the problem stemmed from "the failure of commands to implement" equal opportunity programs "with a full heart," because of allegiance to "hallowed routine."

The officers were warned that "every effort" would be made "to seek out and take appropriate action, either punitive or administrative, against those persons who are engaged in or condoning discriminatory practices, or who have violated either the spirit or the letter of our equal opportunity policy."

On the other hand, Warner said the Navy was "not going to tolerate such things as sit-down strikes" by seamen even when provoked by genuine grievances.

Warner said a top-level Human Relations Council was being established to apply "downward pressure" through the ranks. Zumwalt said he was instituting a system of rewards and punishments for effectiveness in equal opportunity, and would give race relations the same priority as professional performance.

Blacks, in June 1972, comprised 5.8% of Navy enlisted men and .7% officers.

Nov. 14—The Navy reassigned 123 crewmen of the aircraft carrier *Constellation* after the seamen, most of them black, refused to reboard the ship before resolution of grievances over discrimination in assignments, ratings and discharges.

The men, along with 14 others, had been put on shore leave at the North Island Naval Air Station near San Diego Nov. 4 by the ship's skipper, Capt. J. D. Ward, after they refused to report for scheduled duty during a sit-down demonstration. About a dozen of the men were whites.

The *Constellation* returned to port Nov. 7. Ward met Nov. 9 with the men and with Navy minority affairs officers and attorneys for the dissidents. Although apparently conceding that some of the complaints might have been justified, Ward ordered the men back on ship, promising to give their complaints priority. A few of the men had reboarded ship the previous day, but the remainder refused Ward's order. Some of the men were reported to say that the tense racial situation on board before the incident made them "fear for their lives" unless the dispute was settled on shore.

The 123 men were then reassigned to three installations in the San Diego area. It was reported that the transfer order had come directly from the Bureau of Navy Personnel. The Navy announced Nov. 11 that "full dress" individual grievance hearings would be held at the new installations. The Black Servicemen's Caucus protested the procedure, which they said would "scatter" the men.

Captain's mast disciplinary hearings on unauthorized absence were begun Nov. 10 by North Island commander Capt. Robert T. McKenzie. The first five men tried were ordered to forfeit part of their pay.

Ward said Nov. 14 that he had received a petition of support from the ship's 5,000-man crew. Ward said of the protesters that "a cadre of men" had been "trying very hard" to start "physical violence."

Ward also charged that incidents of possible sabotage of equipment had occurred while the ship was in the western Pacific war zone. He said the incidents were apparently not connected with the refusal of eight antiwar seamen to sail with the ship when it was deployed in 1971.

The dissidents had charged that six blacks had recently been given unfair administrative discharges, that blacks had been given unfair low quarterly marks, had suffered discrimination at captain's mast proceedings and had been assigned to relatively unskilled positions. They claimed that Ward had refused to hear their grievances as a group.

Nov. 18—The Navy announced that six of the 123 dissident Constellation crewmen had been discharged "under honorable conditions." Two of the six were given honorable discharges and the other four general discharges. The Navy did not identify the crewmen.

The announcement followed the last of the captain's mast hearings for the 123 sailors, mostly blacks.

In addition to the six discharged Nov. 18, 23 other crewmen were reported Nov. 25 to receive administrative discharges for inability to adjust to Navy life or because of "personality problems." Most of the other protesters were punished in the form of fines and loss of pay, extra work duties and reduction in rank.

Nov. 28—Sailors from the Kitty Hawk defied orders by discussing racial disorders at sea with newsmen when the warship returned to San Diego.

Capt. M. W. Townsend Jr., captain of the Kitty Hawk, had ordered the ship's crew not to talk with reporters because "it's not healthy to deal in rumors."

Some of the sailors said the fighting was so intense that even the Kitty Hawk's executive officer was attacked. But other crewmen said the trouble was a one-night incident that had been improperly called a race riot.

Both black and white sailors agreed there was severe fighting. A black sailor said Benjamin Cloud, the ship's executive officer, had been beaten. Another black said Marines, called out to quell the disorders, "started beating" every black they saw. Some white sailors confirmed that observation.

Nov. 20—A special House Armed Services subcommittee opened an investigation into the racial disorders aboard the Navy aircraft carriers Constellation and Kitty Hawk.

After five days of testimony about the racial trouble on the Constellation, Congressional investigators recessed the inquiry until early December, when they would look into the problems aboard the Kitty Hawk.

Chief of Naval Operations Adm. Elmo R. Zumwalt was the leadoff witness behind closed doors in Washington. Zumwalt discounted some claims by Navy officials and others that a breakdown in discipline had led to the disorders. He denied that there was "permissiveness" in the Navy, and said the Navy "will maintain order and discipline."

Zumwalt's remarks followed an opening statement by subcommittee chairman Floyd V. Hicks (D., Wash.) that the panel "cannot overlook the possibility that there may exist at this time an environment of—for lack of a better word—'permissiveness,' where all that is needed is a catalyst. Perhaps perceptions of racial relations in these cases provided that spark."

Nov. 21—In San Diego Nov. 21, the armed services sub-committee panel heard Capt. J. D. Ward, commanding officer of the Constellation, relate how he called off maneuvers at sea and put 137 crewmen off ship to avoid open racial warfare aboard the carrier. Ward's testimony was heard in secret session at the North Island Naval Air Station in San Diego Bay.

Ward was reported to have testified that the disorders on the Constellation, as well as those on the Kitty Hawk, were symptomatic of a national social problem. He was said to have testified that the racial problems could be traced to a comparatively small group of "hard core dissidents determined to create trouble."

The Constellation's executive officer, Cmdr. John Schaub, described for the panel Nov. 22 what he called the Navy's "poorly conceived and totally unfair" system of minority recruitment. Schaub was one of several officers who testified that the racial problems could be tied to the Navy's recruiting of educationally disadvantaged black youths.

Speaking to newsmen, Schaub said he believed the Navy's program of recruiting such men was "totally unfair" because it placed them in competition with other recruits "more fortunate."

Twelve sailors from the Constellation, 12 blacks and a white, were called before the subcommittee Nov. 24. All the black seamen painted the same picture: Ward, the ship's captain, had refused for three weeks to hear their grievances while racial tensions were mounting. According to the blacks, Ward had refused to hear a delegation of dissidents wanting to discuss with him problems on the ship. He was also said to have ordered Marines with bayonets to surround a group of blacks during a sitdown protest on the ship's main mess deck. One black sailor, Howard Smith, told newsmen after his appearance before the subcommittee that all Ward had to do to head off trouble was to "show us he was concerned about our problems."

Smith and the other 11 sailors who appeared were drawn from the 137 men "beached" at North Island before the Constellation put to sea. The panel recessed its probe after hearing further testimony from Ward and Capt. Robert McKenzie, commander of the North Island Naval Air Station. McKenzie had been conducting disciplinary hearings for 123 of the Constellation's crew.

Nov. 25-26—Two new clashes between black and white seamen were reported by the Navy. One clash involved 130 sailors Nov. 25 at the naval station on Midway Island in the Pacific. The other was at the Navy Correctional Center in Norfolk, Va. on Nov. 26.

Four white sailors and a black sustained minor injuries in the Midway disorder. The incident was reported to have begun with a dispute between blacks and whites at a recreation area.

Navy officials said 33 sailors, 32 blacks and one white, remained confined at the Norfolk Correctional Center as the result of the fighting there. According to the Navy, the 23 black sailors burned mattresses, smashed a door and defied Marine guards trying to confine four demonstrators.

Nov. 30—The Navy continued its own inquiry into the racial disorders as *Kitty Hawk* crewmen reportedly told Navy officials about a command disagreement over the way to stop the fighting. According to the sailors, there was an open disagreement between Capt. Marland W. Townsend Jr. and his chief executive officer, Cmdr. Benjamin Cloud, over an order to separate those involved in the fighting. Cloud, a black, had issued an order directing the blacks to one end of the *Kitty Hawk* and the Marine guards to the other end in an effort to cool tempers. Minutes later, however, Townsend countermanded that order. Townsend then reportedly said that Cloud was "misinformed" in issuing that order.

Defense Secretary Melvin R. Laird released a report by a Pentagon study group that found intentional and systematic discrimination against blacks in the armed forces. The panel, biracial in makeup, called for long-term reform at any cost.

Laird called the report a landmark move toward military equality, "the very essence of an ordered, free society."

The report said blacks in the military had been subjected to bias in pretrial confinement and administrative punishment when penalties were given on the prerogative of the commanding officer alone. Blacks, more often than whites, were not permitted to remain free pending trials, and they received stiffer punishments for minor infractions of command orders, the report stated.

Dec. 12—A House Armed Services subcommittee probing the racial disorders aboard Navy ships ended the investigative stage of its inquiry in San Diego.

Rep. Floyd V. Hicks (D., Wash.), chairman of the subcommittee, said the panel would submit an official report to the full committee.

1973

Jan. 23—A House subcommittee concluded that rioting aboard the Navy aircraft carrier *Kitty Hawk* on Oct. 12-13, 1972 was not provoked by racial discrimination.

Subcommittee chairman Floyd V. Hicks (D., Wash), in summarizing the report, stated: "The riot on the *Kitty Hawk* consisted of unprovoked assaults by a very few men, most of whom were of below-average mental capacity and had been aboard for less than one year, and all of whom were black."

According to Hicks, the subcommittee found that "blacks, armed with chains, wrenches, bars, broomsticks and perhaps other instruments, went marauding through sections of the ship, seeking out white personnel for senseless beatings with their fists and with those instruments they had seized upon as weapons."

The result, Hicks said, "was extremely serious injury to three men and lesser injury requiring

medical treatment of many more, including some blacks."

Hicks attributed the rioting to a climate of "permissiveness" and a possible breakdown in discipline. He said the "generally smart appearance" of Navy personnel had deteriorated and that there had been a "failure in the middle management area to utilize the command authority."

Commenting on the Nov. 3-4, 1972 sit-in aboard the aircraft carrier *Constellation,* Hicks said 20–25 blacks encouraged the idea among the ship's blacks that racism pervaded the Navy. He referred to the sit-in as the "result of a carefully orchestrated demonstration of passive resistance." Hicks was critical of the Navy decision to negotiate with the dissidents.

Feb. 2—The Navy confirmed that it had discharged nearly 3,000 enlisted men whom it considered a "burden to the command." Adm. Elmo R. Zumwalt Jr., chief of naval operations, had issued the order Dec. 26, 1972. The directive provided for voluntary-for-mutual-benefit-discharges for sailors with at least one year of service "whose records reflect marginal performance or substandard conduct." Of the number discharged, about 14% were black.

At the same time the Navy said it was tightening its standards of recruitment, with a new emphasis on education and character qualifications. According to reports, one of every four enlistees was at level 4 of the Armed Forces Qualifications Test during 1972, indicating a sixth grade reading level. The 1971 figure was 14%. One of every six 1972 recruits had a police record.

The Navy said the discharges would be mostly under honorable conditions, with not stigma attached. The report said, however, that the discharges would carry code numbers, which knowledgeable employers could understand to mean "undesirable" or "unsuitable for reenlistment."

A Navy spokesman said: "There are too many recruits—not only blacks but members of other minorities and underprivileged whites, as well —who cannot cope with the technical training in the skills needed to operate our sophisticated weapons and navigational systems. As a result they are forced into menial jobs, in the laundries, in mess galleys and in deck crews. Their work performance is poor and their opportunities for advancement are very limited. This frequently produces festering resentment which may erupt violently. The blame is not the Navy's, it goes deeper into the American social system."

Feb. 12—The only white sailor to go on trial in connection with the *Kitty Hawk* riot was acquitted of the charge of assault. Fifteen black crewmen had been tried in connection with the Oct. 12–13 riot. Nine of those were convicted.

Feb. 20—The Army released a survey that concluded that both black and white soldiers felt favoritism was extended to soldiers of the other color. The Human Resources Research Organization of Alexandria, Va. collected 86,297 responses from basic trainees at Ft. Ord, Calif. and Ft. Jackson, S.C. in 1971. The study questioned soldiers during their first, eighth, and sixteenth weeks of training about how they thought the Army treated minorities.

Of the blacks questioned during the first week, 15% said whites received better treatment. This rose to 38% in the final survey.

In the final survey, 23% of the whites said blacks got favored treatment, which compared with a 5% response the first week.

Feb. 26—Rep. Ronald V. Dellums (D., Calif.), the first black member of the House Armed Services Committee, called for the reopening of the investigation of the racial incidents that took place aboard Navy aircraft carriers in 1972.

Dellums said, "There was a notable failure to

receive testimony from black sailors and/or their counsel who could have given the version of the incidents as the blacks involved perceived it."

Rep. Floyd V. Hicks, (D., Wash.), who headed the investigation, conceded after the news conference that his investigators had failed to talk to the black sailors, but he claimed the blacks refused to be interviewed.

Feb. 26—A suit asking the courts to order Secretary of the Navy John W. Warner to make a "complete and impartial investigation of the Oct. 12 and 13, 1972 incidents on the carrier *Kitty Hawk*" was filed in federal district court in San Diego on behalf of 17 sailors charged in the disturbances. The 40-page complaint accused a Navy witness of lying in his testimony before a court martial board and accused the prosecutor of racial prejudice.

The suit was filed by San Diego lawyer Milton Silverman and the National Association for the Advancement of Colored People (NAACP).

Mar. 11—The Navy had embarked upon a program to recruit more blacks at all levels, from neighborhood recruiting offices to the Naval Academy in Annapolis, Md.

However, the Navy admitted at the same time that its standards had been raised. It had taken many poorly educated blacks during recruiting drives in recent years. A Navy directive said only blacks with high school diplomas or those who passed the high school equivalency test could be signed. A Navy spokesman said, with regard to the Naval Academy, "We're looking for the blue chip kids."

The recruiting effort was reflected in the numbers of blacks attending the academy: the class of 1974 had 11 blacks, the class of 1975 had 34, the class of 1976 had 66, and the class of 1977 was projected to have 150 blacks.

In 1971, 518 blacks were officers in the Navy, of a total of 76,486 officers.

April 9—The last of the courts-martial of the sailors involved in the racial disturbances October 12–13, 1972, aboard the aircraft carrier *Kitty Hawk* ended in San Diego. Result: four black sailors were found guilty of rioting, two by guilty pleas in return for reduced sentences; 14 were found guilty on all counts; and five had charges dropped against them. Of those found guilty, seven were sentenced to the brig, and most were fined and reduced in rank.

Black Men in the Armed Forces: 1965 to 1971

In thousands, except percent. As of December 31

YEAR AND ITEM	Total	Officers[1]	Enlisted men	PARTICIPATION IN VIETNAM					Vietnam battle deaths since 1961
				Total	Army	Navy[2]	Marine Corps	Air Force	
1965, Armed Forces	2,843	338	2,505	184	117	8	38	21	2
Black	269	6	263	22	17	(Z)	4	1	(Z)
Percent of total	9.5	1.9	10.5	12.0	14.5	5.1	10.5	4.8	14.6
1966, Armed Forces	3,322	362	2,960	385	239	24	69	53	7
Black	303	7	296	41	30	1	5	5	1
Percent of total	9.1	1.9	10.0	10.6	12.6	5.4	8.0	10.3	16.0
1967, Armed Forces	3,384	402	2,982	486	320	32	78	56	16
Black	303	8	295	48	35	1	6	6	2
Percent of total	8.9	2.1	9.9	9.8	11.1	4.7	8.2	10.5	14.1
1968, Armed Forces	3,395	418	2,977	536	360	37	81	58	31
Black	313	9	304	59	44	1	8	6	4
Percent of total	9.2	2.1	10.2	10.9	11.7	4.0	10.7	10.0	13.5
1969, Armed Forces	3,285	408	2,877	475	331	30	55	58	40
Black	286	9	277	46	33	· 1	6	6	5
Percent of total	8.7	2.1	9.6	9.7	10.0	4.1	10.9	10.5	12.9
1970, Armed Forces	2,861	389	2,472	335	250	17	25	43	44
Black	279	8	271	37	29	1	3	5	6
Percent of total	9.8	2.2	11.0	11.1	11.4	3.5	11.3	12.0	12.5
1971, Armed Forces	2,505	359	2,146	171	135	8	(Z)	28	45
Black	267	8	259	22	18	(Z)	(Z)	4	6
Percent of total	10.7	2.2	12.1	13.0	13.4	4.3	8.0	13.4	13.3

Z Less than 500.   [1] Includes warrant officers.   [2] Includes Coast Guard.

PAY SCALE FOR THE ARMED FORCES (January, 1973)*

COMMISSIONED OFFICERS

Pay Grade	Army or Air Force Rank	Navy Rank	2 or less	Over 2	Over 3	Over 4	Over 6	Over 8	Over 10	Over 12	Over 14	Over 16	Over 18	Over 20	Over 22	Over 26	Over 30
O-6	Colonel	Captain	$1,194.00	$1,312.20	$1,397.70	$1,397.70	$1,397.70	$1,397.70	$1,397.70	$1,397.70	$1,445.10	$1,673.70	$1,759.20	$1,797.30	$1,902.00	$2,062.50	$2,062.50
O-5	Lt. Colonel	Commander	954.90	1,121.70	1,198.80	1,198.80	1,198.80	1,198.80	1,235.70	1,301.40	1,388.40	1,492.50	1,578.30	1,625.70	1,683.00	1,683.00	1,683.00
O-4	Major	Lieutenant Commander	805.20	979.80	1,046.10	1,046.10	1,064.70	1,112.10	1,187.70	1,254.90	1,312.20	1,369.20	1,407.30	1,407.30	1,407.30	1,407.30	1,407.30
O-3²	Captain	Lieutenant	748.20	836.40	893.70	989.40	1,036.50	1,073.70	1,131.30	1,187.70	1,216.80	1,216.80	1,216.80	1,216.80	1,216.80	1,216.80	1,216.80
O-2²	First Lt.	Lieutenant (Junior Grade)	652.20	712.50	855.90	884.40	903.00	903.00	903.00	903.00	903.00	903.00	903.00	903.00	903.00	903.00	903.00
O-1²	Second Lt.	Ensign	566.10	589.50	712.50	712.50	712.50	712.50	712.50	712.50	712.50	712.50	712.50	712.50	712.50	712.50	712.50

Commissioned officers with over 4 years service as enlisted members.

Pay Grade	Army or Air Force Rank	Navy Rank	2 or less	Over 2	Over 3	Over 4	Over 6	Over 8	Over 10	Over 12	Over 14	Over 16	Over 18	Over 20	Over 22	Over 26	Over 30
O-3	Captain	Lieutenant				989.40	1,036.50	1,073.70	1,131.30	1,187.70	1,235.70	1,235.70	1,235.70	1,235.70	1,235.70	1,235.70	1,235.70
O-2	First Lt.	Lieutenant (Junior Grade)				884.40	903.00	931.50	979.80	1,017.90	1,046.10	1,046.10	1,046.10	1,046.10	1,046.10	1,046.10	1,046.10
O-1	Second Lt.	Ensign				712.50	760.80	789.30	817.50	846.50	884.40	884.40	884.40	884.40	884.40	884.40	884.40

WARRANT OFFICERS

Pay Grade	Army or Air Force Rank	Navy Rank	2 or less	Over 2	Over 3	Over 4	Over 6	Over 8	Over 10	Over 12	Over 14	Over 16	Over 18	Over 20	Over 22	Over 26	Over 30
W-4	Chief Warrant	Commissioned Warrant	762.00	817.50	817.50	836.40	874.50	912.90	950.70	1,017.90	1,064.70	1,102.50	1,131.30	1,169.10	1,207.80	1,301.40	1,301.40
W-3	Chief Warrant	Commissioned Warrant	693.00	751.50	751.50	760.80	770.10	826.50	874.50	903.00	931.50	959.70	989.40	1,027.20	1,064.70	1,102.50	1,102.50
W-2	Chief Warrant	Commissioned Warrant	606.00	656.10	656.10	675.30	712.50	751.50	780.00	802.20	836.40	865.50	893.70	922.20	959.70	959.70	959.70
W-1	Warrant Officer	Warrant Officer	505.50	579.90	579.90	627.90	656.10	684.60	712.50	741.60	770.10	789.60	826.50	855.90	855.90	855.90	855.90

²Does not apply to commissioned officers who have been credited with over 4 years active service as enlisted members.

ENLISTED MEMBERS

Pay Grade	Army or Air Force Rank	Navy Rank	2 or less	Over 2	Over 3	Over 4	Over 6	Over 8	Over 10	Over 12	Over 14	Over 16	Over 18	Over 20	Over 22	Over 26	Over 30
E-9¹	Sergeant Major	Master Chief Petty Officer	$ 0	$ 0	$ 0	$ 0	$ 0	$ 0	865.80	885.60	905.70	926.40	946.80	965.40	1,016.40	1,115.10	1,115.10
E-8	Master Sergeant	Senior Chief Petty Officer	0	0	0	0	0	726.60	746.70	765.50	786.60	807.00	826.20	846.60	896.10	996.00	996.00
E-7	Sgt. 1st class	Chief Petty Officer	507.30	547.20	567.60	587.40	607.20	627.00	646.80	667.20	697.50	717.00	736.80	746.70	796.60	896.10	896.10
E-6	Staff Sergeant	Petty Officer 1st class	438.00	477.90	497.70	518.10	537.90	557.70	577.80	607.80	627.00	646.80	657.00	657.00	657.00	657.00	657.00
E-5	Sergeant	Petty Officer 2nd class	388.60	418.80	438.90	458.10	488.10	507.90	528.00	547.20	557.70	557.70	557.70	557.70	557.70	557.70	557.70
E-4	Corporal	Petty Officer 3rd class	369.80	390.60	413.10	445.50	463.20	463.20	463.20	463.20	463.20	463.20	463.20	463.20	463.20	463.20	463.20
E-3	Private 1st class	Seaman	355.80	375.30	390.30	405.60	405.60	405.60	405.60	405.60	405.60	405.60	405.60	405.60	405.60	405.60	405.60
E-2	Private	Seaman Apprentice	342.30	342.30	342.30	342.30	342.30	342.30	342.30	342.30	342.30	342.30	342.30	342.30	342.30	342.30	342.30
E-1	Private	Seaman Recruit	307.20	307.20	307.20	307.20	307.20	307.20	307.20	307.20	307.20	307.20	307.20	307.20	307.20	307.20	307.20

¹While serving as Sergeant Major of the Army, Master Chief Petty Officer of the Navy, Chief Master Sergeant of the Air Force, or Sergeant Major of the Marine Corps, basic pay for the grade is $1,355.40 regardless of cumulative years of service computed under section 205 of this title.

*Effective Oct. 1, 1973, all Armed Forces personnel received a 6.16 percent pay increase, in compliance with the cost of living increase passed by Congress for all federal employees, both civilian and non-civilian.

HAZARDOUS DUTY
Flying Duty (crew member) and Submarine Duty
Additional Monthly Pay, 1972

	Under 2 Yrs.	Over 2 Yrs.	Maximum Over-Amt.
O-6	$200	$200	18 yrs.-245
O-5	190	190	18 yrs.-245
O-4	170	170	18 yrs.-240
O-3	145	145	14 yrs.-205
O-2	115	125	14 yrs.-185
O-1	100	105	14 yrs.-170
W-4	115	*	18 yrs.-165
W-3	110	115	14 yrs.-140
W-2	105	110	14 yrs.-135
W-1	100	105	12 yrs.-130
E-9	105	105	105
E-8	105	105	105
E-7	80	85	12 yrs.-105
E-6	70	75	14 yrs.-100
E-5	60	70	12 yrs.- 95
E-4	55	65	8 yrs.- 80
E-3	55	60	2 yrs.- 60
E-2	50	60	2 yrs.- 60
E-1	50	55	2 yrs.- 55

Aviation Cadet under 2 years $50.
*W-4 Under 6 years receives $115.

INCENTIVE PAY, 1972

Officers and Warrant officers............$110.00
Enlisted men........................ 55.00
Types of duties for which these flat rates are payable are as follows: (1) Frequent and regular aerial flights not as a crew member. (2) Parachute jumping as an essential part of military duty. (3) Duty involving intimate contact with leprosy. (4) Duty involving demolition of explosives. (5) Army and Navy enlisted men, $65 to 110 dependent upon rating or job (billet); Marine Corps enlisted men $65; All Air Force $65; scuba divers. (6) Deep sea diving duty (including helium-oxygen diving). (7) Human acceleration or deceleration duty. (8) High or low-pressure chamber duty. (9) Thermal stress duty. (10) Training or assignment to submarines of advanced design or for positions of increased responsibility aboard a submarine. Rates payable for this catagory are the same as those paid flying crew members listed under Hazardous Duty. (11) Flight deck duty.

SEA AND FOREIGN DUTY, 1972
Defense Secretary designates places where special duty pay may be awarded
(See Pay Guides listed above)

E-9	$22.50	E-4	$13.00
E-8	22.50	E-3	9.00
E-7	22.50	E-2	8.00
E-6	20.00	E-1	8.00
E-5	16.00		

BASIC ALLOWANCES FOR SUBSISTENCE, 1972

This allowance, the quarters allowance, and any other allowance are not subject to income tax.
Officers-Subsistence (food) is paid to all officers regardless of rank...........$47.88 per month.
Enlisted members:
When rations in kind are not available....................$2.57 per day
When permission is granted to mess off the base..............$1.46 per day
When assigned to duty under emergency conditions where no government messing facilities are available.................$3.42 per day
(maximum rate)

FAMILY SEPARATION ALLOWANCE, 1972

Under certain conditions of family separation of more than 30 days, members in Pay Grades E-4 (with over 4 years' service) and above will be allowed $30 a month in addition to any other allowances to which he is entitled. When separated from family and required to maintain a home for his family and one for himself, the member is entitled to an additional monthly basic allowance for quarters at the "without dependents" rate for his grade.

UNIFORM ALLOWANCE, 1972

Enlisted personnel receive an initial uniform allowance valued at $164 to $285, with variations between Services. After 6 months and up to the 36th month, a monthly maintenance allowance of $4.20 is paid. After 36 months the monthly allowance varies between $6.30 and $9.00. An officer is entitled to an initial allowance of not more than $200 as reimbursement for purchase of required uniforms or equipment.

REENLISTMENT BONUS, 1972

A person who enlists in or extends his initial period of active duty in a combat element of an armed force to a total of at least 3 years may be paid a cumulative bonus of not more than $3,000. Reenlistment bonuses are paid in amounts up to $10,000, depending upon length or reenlistment period.

SPECIAL PAY, 1972

Members of the uniformed services entitled to receive basic pay shall, in addition thereto, be entitled to receive incentive pay for the performance of hazardous duty required by competent orders. The President may, in time of war, suspend the payment of incentive pay for the performance of any or all hazardous duty. Officers receive no additional pay for overseas or sea duty.

DUTY SUBJECT TO HOSTILE FIRE, 1972

Except in time of war declared by the Congress, a special pay of $65 a month is allotted to any member of the Uniformed Services during any month in which he was subject to hostile fire.

MEDICAL AND DENTAL CORPS, 1972

Commissioned officers in the Medical and Dental Corps of the Army, Navy and Air Force and commissioned medical, dental, and veterinary officers of the Regular Corps of the Public Health Service receive special pay based on cumulative years of service as follows: 0-2 years, $100; 2 to 6 years, $150; 6 to 10 years, $250; over 10 years $350. These rates are in addition to basic pay and allowance. Optometrists and Veterinary Corps Officers receive $100 per month extra.

Source: United States Department of Defense

In addition to the pay figures listed on the preceding page, military personnel also receive a subsistence allowance and a quarters allowance according to the following schedules:

SUBSISTENCE ALLOWANCE:

Officers. . . . . $47.88 a month
Enlisted members when rations in kind are not available. . . . . $25.65 a day
Enlisted members when assigned to duty under emergency conditions where no messing facilities of the United States are available. Not more than $3.42 a day

QUARTERS ALLOWANCE:

Pay Grade	Without dependents	With dependents
0-6.	$211.80	$258.30
0-5.	198.30	238.80
0-4.	178.80	215.40
0-3.	158.40	195.60
0-2.	138.60	175.80
0-1.	108.90	141.60
W-4.	172.50	207.90
W-3.	155.40	191.70
W-2.	137.10	173.70
W-1.	123.90	160.80
E-9.	130.80	184.20
E-8.	122.10	172.20
E-7.	104.70	161.40
E-6.	95.70	150.00
E-5.	92.70	138.60
E-4 (over 4 years' service).	81.60	121.50
E-4 (four years' or less service).	81.60	121.50
E-3	72.30	105.00
E-2.	63.90	105.00
E-1.	60.00	105.00

Source: "Pay and Allowances of the Uniformed Services," prepared for the Committee on Armed Services U.S. House of Representatives.

Section VII

CRIME, LAW ENFORCEMENT AND CRIMINAL JUSTICE

Tables

CRIME, LAW ENFORCEMENT AND CRIMINAL JUSTICE

In spite of the growing awareness of the prevalence of "white collar" crime, the mass of white Americans over the past decade have been subjected to a campaign for "law and order" and "safe streets" that equates "welfare chiselers" with "armed robbery." In the use of phrases which are synonomous with code words for "black crime, black rapists, black muggers and black hoodlum gangs," the American public has become polarized into two worlds, which the white public perceives as, one, black and criminal, and the other, white and law-abiding.

The physical and economic interdependence of each upon the other seems forgotten as the suburbs and the exurbs receive wave after wave of fleeing whites, and the cities, which contain the majority of jobs to which the suburban commuter must travel daily, become real or imagined places of fear after dark.

There is, according to the statistical evidence, valid reason for fear. Violent crime has increased dramatically over the past ten years. Four presidential commissions have made investigations and each of them has reported virtually the same findings and made the same recommendations for the control and eradication of this violent criminal activity. Yet, as the National Commission on the Causes and Prevention of Violence pointed out in 1969, "lacking effective action in curbing social ills," cities would be reduced to "high-rise residential compounds and ghetto neighborhoods, which would be 'places of terror'."

In 1969, police protection outlays by all governments amounted to $4.4 billion. The "Safe Streets Act," which provided funds for communities to beef up police departments and stockpile riot control materials, became law. The Justice Department prepared recommendations in the District of Columbia Crime Bill to permit the imprisonment of a person for up to 60 days, without bail, if there was a probability that the defendant was guilty of a criminal act. This included narcotics addicts, who had been charged with a crime of violence, and any defendants charged with crimes defined as dangerous, due process and the danger of imprisonment of innocent persons notwithstanding. The so-called "D.C. crime bill" also permitted life sentences for felons convicted three times, allowed police with warrants to search premises without notice ("no-knock"), and raised the penalties for narcotics convictions. At the same time in 1969, 6 million firearms were produced or imported for private sale (in 1968, the number was 5.25 million). The bills to prevent the acquisition and sale of firearms have been routinely defeated by the strong gun-lobby and the American Rifle Association.

Gun control would go a long way toward reducing violent crime. Dr. Milton Eisenhower, in 1969, said that there were "thirty million" handguns loose in America. There are probably five times that number today. The powerful gun-lobby in Washington makes certain that legislation is not passed to control the sale and manufacture of these weapons.

Criminal justice, according to the Eisenhower Commission, "does not deter, does not detect, does not convict and does not correct." Crime is not diminishing. In any million crimes committed, the rates of arrest are 12 percent; conviction, 6 percent; and jail sentence, 1.5 percent. Yet—for blacks—the system of criminal justice results in more black arrests, more black convictions and more black jail sentences, although there is no scientific, or other evidence, to show that blacks commit crimes because they are black, and not because they are victims of the even greater crime of institutional racism.

The findings and recommendations of the Kerner, Eisenhower and Scranton Commissions, related to the causes of crime and violence, have largely been ignored by the chief executives who commissioned them—Presidents Johnson and Nixon; and the undergirding causes of crime that have been festering in the social body of the nation remain untreated, the victim of "benign neglect" and outright abuse.

Crime

In the report, "Violent Crime—Homicide, Assault, Rape and Robbery," statistics based on 10,000 arrests in 17 major cities—Boston, New York, Philadelphia, Washington, Atlanta, Miami, New Orleans, Dallas, Cleveland, Chicago, Detroit, Minneapolis, St. Louis, Denver, Seattle, Los Angeles and San Francisco, showed that 45% of the major violent crimes committed in the U.S., were reported in those cities which contained only 17% of the nation's total population (500,000). Most of the violent crimes were commited by youths between 15 and 20 years of age. Between 1958 and 1967, arrest rates of the 10–14 age group for assault and robbery had increased 200–300%.

Black community leaders complain that a black youth, uninvolved in gang activity or other misdeeds, may be prey to violence from either the police or from gangs who cannot permit "outsiders" to survive on the "turf" they control. In the next decade, the number of young blacks aged 14 to 24 will increase rapidly, particularly in central cities. This group will be held responsible for a disproportionately high share of crimes in all parts of the nation. Over half of the offenders under 20 years of age who were arrested in 1971 were repeat offenders. For all index crimes together, the arrest rate for blacks is about four times higher than that for whites. The number of young blacks aged 14 to 24 in central cities will rise about 63 percent in the decade from 1966 to 1975, as compared to only 32 percent for the total black population of central cities.

Violent crime in cities, according to the report, are committed "primarily by individuals at the lower end of the occupational scale." Urban arrest rates were, accordingly, disproportionately high for urban blacks, as a result of conditions of life in the ghetto slums. Victim-offender studies show that assaultive violence, as opposed to robbery "is primarily the result of action between white offenders and white victims and black offenders and black victims."

The cities connected to the suburbs by "sanitized corridors" of expressways are viewed as areas of "intensified hatred and deepening division" while the residents of the ghettos become the victims of widespread crime, "perhaps entirely out of police control during nighttime hours."

White residents in prime locations in the cities would live in "fortified cells for upper middle- and high-income populations while suburban communities would be protected from the central city by distance and economic homogeneity." The report predicted that "ownership of guns will be almost universal in the suburbs" and "armed citizens in cars" would patrol neighborhoods closer to the city. The probability that the radical right as well as the left would have "tremendous armories of weapons which could be brought into play with or without provocation" was examined.

The Uniform Crime Reports for 1971, issued August 1972, indicate that the committee

prognosis was all too realistic.

In general, crime rates in large cities are much higher than in other areas of the nation. Within such cities, crime rates are higher in disadvantaged black areas than anywhere else.

The most widely used measure of crime is the number of "index crimes" (homicide, forcible rape, aggravated assault, robbery, burglary, grand larceny and auto theft), in relation to population. In 1971, 5,995 such crimes were reported to police for every 100,000 Americans, up 83% over 1966. Large core cities were up 2 percent in volume, while the rural areas registered a 6 percent upswing.

Within larger cities, personal and property insecurity has consistently been highest in the older neighborhoods encircling the downtown business district. In most cities, crime rates for many decades have been higher in these inner areas than anywhere, except in downtown areas themselves, where they are inflated by the small number of residents.

High crime rates have persisted in these inner areas even though the ethnic character of their residents continually changed. Poor immigrants used these areas as "entry ports," then usually moved on to more desirable neighborhoods as soon as they acquired enough resources. Many "entry port" areas have now become racial ghettos.

The difference between crime rates in these disadvantaged neighborhoods and in other parts of the city is usually startling, as a comparison of crime rates in five police districts in Chicago for 1965 illustrates. These five include one high-income, all-white district at the periphery of the city, two very low-income, virtually all-black districts near the city core with numerous public housing projects, and two predominantly white districts, one with mainly lower middle-income families, the other containing a mixture of very high-income and relatively low-income households. The table shows crime rates against persons and against property in these five districts, plus the number of patrolmen assigned to them per 100,000 residents, as follows:

Incidence of Index Crimes and Patrolmen Assignments per 100,000 Residents in 5 Chicago Police Districts, 1965

Number	High-income white district	Low middle-income white district	Mixed high- and low-income white district	Very low income black district No. 1	Very low income black district No. 2
Index crimes against persons	80	440	338	1,615	2,820
Index crimes against property	1,038	1,750	2,080	2,508	2,630
Patrolmen assigned	93	133	115	243	291

These data indicate that:

—Variations in the crime rate against persons within the city are extremely large. One very low income black district had 35 times as many serious crimes against persons per 100,000 residents as did the high-income white district.

—The lower the income in an area, the higher the crime rate there. Yet low-income black areas have significantly higher · crime rates than low-income white areas. This reflects the high degree of social disorganization in black areas, as well as the fact that poor blacks as a group have lower incomes than poor whites as a group.

—The presence of more police patrolmen per 100,000 residents does not necessarily offset high crime in certain parts of the city. Although the Chicago Police Department had assigned over three times as many patrolmen per 100,000 residents to the highest crime areas shown as to the lowest, crime rates in the highest crime area for offenses against both persons and property combined were 4.9 times as high as in the lowest crime area.

There is little comprehension of the sense of insecurity that characterizes the ghetto resident to the non-ghetto dweller. Moreover, official statistics normally greatly understate actual crime rates because the vast majority of crimes are not reported to the police. For example, studies conducted for the President's Crime Commission in Washington, D.C., Boston and Chicago showed that three to six times as many crimes were actually committed against persons and homes as were reported to the police.

Citizens who do not believe that the police want to prevent them from becoming victims do not seek their protection. Black on black crime has become almost epidemic in urban communities across the nation. Much of this is due to the rampant rise of narcotics (not including marijuana) use in the country. In the first 8 months of the year (1971), there were 946 narcotic deaths in New York City alone, an increase of 63 from the same period the previous year. There has also been an increase in deaths related to methadone maintenance. In 1970, there were 45 and in 1971, 330. Drug addicts who must steal to support their habits will also mug and murder in the tensed-up drive to get their need fulfilled.

Statistics reveal that proportionately more blacks get arrested, jailed, convicted and given severer sentences than whites. Police are charged by black civic leaders with brutality and indifference and the courts are notorious for giving stiff sentences to black offenders

when the victim is white, and being more permissive and lenient when the victim is black.

A small minority of blacks commit most of the crimes in the black ghettos of the nation, but the principal victims of their crimes are other blacks. Throughout the United States the great majority of crimes committed by blacks involve other blacks as victims. A special tabulation made by the Chicago Police Department for the President's Crime Commission indicated that over 85 percent of the crimes committed against persons by blacks between September, 1965, and March, 1966, involved black victims.

As a result, the majority of law-abiding citizens who live in disadvantaged black areas face much higher probabilities of being victimized than residents of most higher income areas, including almost all suburbs. For nonwhites, the probability of suffering from any index crime, except larceny, is 78 percent higher than for whites. The probability of being raped is 3.7 times higher among nonwhite women, and the probability of being robbed is 3.5 times higher for nonwhites, in general.

The problems associated with high-crime rates generate widespread hostility toward the police in these neighborhoods. Thus, crime not only creates an atmosphere of insecurity and fear throughout black neighborhoods but also causes continuing attrition of the relationship between black residents and police. This bears a direct relationship to civil disorder.

Law Enforcement and Police

Police departments and correctional institutions, two of the most important elements in public safety, are among those areas of public employment which make the poorest showing in minority group relations. There is no question of the deep hostility between the police and ghetto communities. In nearly every city that has experienced racial disruption since the summer of 1964, abrasive relationships between police, blacks, and other minority groups, such as Puerto Rican or Spanish speaking, have been a major source of grievance, tension and ultimately, disorder. According to the Commission on Nonviolence, "the policeman in the ghetto symbolizes the entire system of law enforcement and criminal justice. He is the tangible target for grievances against shortcomings throughout the system; against assembly-line justice in teeming lower courts, against wide disparities in sentences, against antiquated correctional facilities and against the basic inequities imposed by the system on the poor, to whom the option of bail means, generally, only jail."

"Blacks feel that they are being leaned upon and that the police are the agents of repression, tending toward defiance, of what they regard as order, maintained at the expense of justice. To many blacks, police have come to symbolize white power, white racism and white repression."

The fact is that many police do reflect and express these white attitudes. The atmosphere of hostility and cynicism is reinforced by widespread perception among blacks of the existence of police brutality and corruption and of a double standard of justice and protection—one for blacks and one for whites. Such racist attitudes and an accompanying "lack of dedication" among police officers leads to less law enforcement in the areas that need it most.

Police officials admit there are white policemen who are more reluctant to take risks in apprehending criminals when the victims are black. Many white officers also have a tendency to "diminish the importance of crimes committed against black people by other blacks." These are categorized as "neighborhood feuds" or "family trouble."

It is attitudes such as these among police officers that lead to subpar law enforcement that criminals take advantage of, and also to resentment among black citizens that make it difficult for even the most dedicated police officers to enforce the law. Black citizens, for instance, have found that even when they are the victims of crime, they are abused by police officers unless they prove immediately that they have a job, can protect themselves in court, and are otherwise upstanding citizens. Blacks feel that they are too often left to fend for themselves by police who are less diligent in protecting them and their property than they are whites. They are also convinced that the rest of the justice system discriminates against them. These conditions and attitudes have therefore fostered an unhealthy cynicism regarding the law and justice and explains the apathy police encounter when they try to get black citizens to help them apprehend criminals. Many blacks also feel they would be subjecting another black to brutality and inhuman treatment if they were to turn a black suspect over to the police. They also fear that the criminal may not be held and that they would then be subject to reprisals for having cooperated with the police.

The Crime Commission Police Task Force found that for police in a black community to be predominantly white can serve as a dangerous irritant; a feeling may develop that the community is not being policed to maintain civil peace, but to maintain the status quo. It

further found that contact with black officers can help to avoid stereotypes and prejudices in the minds of white officers. Black officers also can increase departmental insight into ghetto problems and provide information necessary for early anticipation of the tension and grievances that can lead to disorders.

There is evidence that trusted black officers also can be particularly effective in controlling any disorders that break out. The need for increased participation of blacks in police departments as correctional officers is equally acute, but most state and local governments have historically had a substantial underrepresentation of black police or correctional officers among their personnel.

Despite this obvious need and some recent efforts to hire more black police, the proportion of blacks on police forces still falls far below the proportion of blacks in the total population. Of 28 departments which reported information of this kind in a commission survey of police departments, the percentage of black sworn personnel ranged from less than 1 percent to 21 percent. The median figure for black sworn personnel on the force was 6 percent; the median figures for the black population was approximately 24 percent. In no case was the proportion of blacks in the police department equal to the proportion in the population. There are even more marked disproportions of black supervisory personnel. The survey showed the following ratios: One in every 26 blacks is a sergeant; the white ratio is one in 12. One in every 114 blacks is a lieutenant; the white ratio is 26. One in every 235 blacks is a captain or above; the white ratio is one in 53.

Public Safety Director Patrick V. Murphy of the District of Columbia testifying before the Commission, said, "I think one of the serious problems facing the police in the nation today is the lack of adequate representation of blacks in police departments. I think the police have not recruited enough blacks in the past and are not recruiting enough of them today. I think we would be less than honest if we didn't admit that blacks have been kept out of police departments in the past for reasons of racial discrimination."

The National Advisory Commission on Civil Disorders defined five problem areas which needed attention if further disorders were to be minimized:

—The need for change in police operation in the ghetto to insure proper conduct by individual officers and to eliminate abrasive practices.

—The need for more adequate police protection of ghetto residents, to eliminate the present high sense of insecurity to person and property.

—The need for effective mechanisms for resolving citizen grievances against the police.

—The need for policy guidelines to assist police in areas where police conduct can create tension.

—The need to develop community support for law enforcement.

The National Commission on the Causes and Prevention of Violence recommended:

—Increased use of interracial police foot patrols.

—Improved police-community relations.

—A controlled drug program for narcotics addicts.

—Restrictive licensing of handguns.

Criminal Justice

The system of criminal justice in the United States, according to the evidence contained in numerous studies and reports, is such that justice is weighted against the black, the poor and those who belong to other nonwhite minority groups.

Statistics show that blacks are generally treated more severely in courts than whites, particularly if the victim of the crime is white. Courts, in general, have lost the confidence of the poor and the minority group defendant. According to the reports issued by the President's Commission on Law Enforcement and the Administration of Justice, *The Challenge of Crime in a Free Society,* and The Task Force on the Administration of Justice, *The Courts* (1967), "The belief is pervasive among ghetto residents that lower courts in our urban communities dispense 'assembly-line justice'; that from arrest to sentencing, the poor and uneducated are denied equal justice with the affluent, and that procedures such as bail and fines have been perverted to perpetuate class inequities."

"No program of crime prevention will be effective without a massive overhaul of the lower criminal courts," states the Commission on Law Enforcement, and they recommend the following broad court reforms:

● Increasing judicial manpower and reforming the selection and tenure of judges.

● Providing more prosecutors, defense counsel and probation officers and training them adequately.

● Modernizing the physical facilities and administration of the courts.

● Creating unified state court systems.

● Coordinating statewide operations of local prosecutors.

● Improving the informational bases for pretrial screening and negotiated pleas.

● Revising the bail system and setting up systems for station-house summonses and release of persons accused of certain offenses.

● Revising sentencing laws and policies toward a more just structure.

● Admitting recognized community leaders to all processing and detention centers (particularly in case of mass arrests) to avoid allegations of abuse or fraud and to reassure the community about the treatment of the arrested persons.

The black community, overall, is more adversely affected by the practices of law-enforcement officers and the courts than the white community. Black Americans over 18 years of age, for example, are about five times more likely to have been arrested than whites. Blacks and other minorities are also more likely to be arrested without probable cause. The fact that the majority of male residents, estimated between 50 and 90 percent, of urban slum areas have some sort of arrest record indicates the gravity of the problem. In neighborhoods and areas having a high proportion of disadvantaged people and characterized by gang activities, it is frequently the practice of the police to "bring in" for questioning individuals or groups. A child of ten or twelve can have a "record" for curfew violation which, if followed by being brought in on a charge of pilfering or other minor offense, still makes him a repeat offender. A record of these arrests will often mitigate against employment and other benefits. A careful distinction should be made by prospective employers between arrests for questioning, arrests followed by acquittal, and convictions for breaking the law. The practice of investigating potential job holders for possible police records frequently serves to automatically disqualify an applicant with an arrest record. Juvenile offenses are rarely ignored by prospective employers.

The Congressional Black Caucus April 6, 1971, in a report on criminal justice, reinforced the previous reports by charging that "the whole system of criminal justice is looked upon by increasing numbers of black people as being terminally diseased with racism. Many blacks increasingly view the police as the ultimate racist arbiter, or an occupying force within the community."

The CBC report stated that the courts were "the second stage of the criminal justice tragedy. American courts usually dispense discount justice to the poor and black, sometimes appearing openly contemptuous of the fundamental legal notions of fairness. . . . Reforms intent on bringing a measure of 'justice' into the criminal justice system have bureaucratically destroyed their initial premise."

"Pleas bargaining is a cruel joke often played upon the unwittingly poor at their expense. Jury duty remains largely a white-skin privilege. The archaic bail system constitutes a de facto system of prevention detention of the poor. Segregation within the prison system remains, especially in regards to certain preferred prison assignments and programs. Library, educational and rehabilitative services are inadequate. Inmate discipline is unjust and capricious. Health and mental care units are ineffective and substandard . . . like its dual educational systems, American society has practiced a dual system of justice—one for the rich and white, another for the black and poor. Law and justice are mutually exclusive concepts for blacks within this legal system."

ARRESTS—NUMBER, BY RACE: 1970

In thousands. Represents arrests reported by 5,208 agencies with a total 1970 population of 142,474,000 as estimated by FBI. For method of counting arrests, see headnote, table 241.

OFFENSE CHARGED	Total	White	Black	Other	OFFENSE CHARGED	Total	White	Black	Other
Total.................	6,257.1	4,373.2	1,688.4	195.6	All other—Con.				
					Embezzlement, fraud....	82.8	61.9	20.3	0.6
Serious crimes........	1,199.1	739.3	436.6	23.2	Stolen property²..........	49.0	30.1	18.3	0.6
Murder and nonneg-					Weapons (carrying,				
ligent manslaughter...	11.8	4.5	7.1	0.2	etc.).................	96.1	46.0	48.4	1.7
Manslaughter by					Prostitution and				
negligence..........	2.9	2.2	0.6	0.1	commercialized vice...	42.3.	14.6	27.2	0.3
Forcible rape..........	14.4	7.3	6.9	0.3	Sex offenses³..........	46.7	35.7	10.1	0.9
					Narcotic drug laws......	291.6	226.8	61.2	3.6
Robbery..............	74.5	24.8	48.3	1.4	Gambling..............	70.2	20.5	46.6	3.1
Aggravated assault.....	114.2	59.6	52.3	2.3					
Burglary¹.............	270.5	174.5	91.3	4.7	Offenses against fam-				
Larceny—theft........	590.7	392.8	186.7	11.2	ily and children......	55.9	38.9	16.4	0.6
Auto theft............	120.1	73.7	43.3	3.1	Driving, intoxicated....	415.0	334.0	60.3	11.8
					Liquor laws............	218.1	190.0	22.8	5.0
All other:					Drunkenness...........	1,496.4	1,101.6	298.8	96.0
Other assaults........	269.7	162.1	103.0	4.7	Disorderly conduct......	572.2	364.0	191.3	16.9
Forgery and coun-					Vagrancy..............	66.7	47.9	16.6	2.1
terfeiting...........	40.1	27.4	12.3	0.4	Other, except traffic.....	1,245.1	932.3	289.2	23.6

¹ See footnote 1, table 241.   ² See footnote 2, table 241.   ³ See footnote 3, table 241.

Source: U.S. Federal Bureau of Investigation, "Uniform Crime Reports for the United States," 1970.

PRISONERS EXECUTED UNDER CIVIL AUTHORITY: 1930 TO 1971

Includes 3 Federal executions in Alaska, 1 each in 1939, 1948, and 1950. Excludes executions by military authorities. The Army (including the Air Force) carried out 160 (148 between 1942 and 1950, 3 each in 1954, 1955, and 1957, and 1 each in 1958, 1959, and 1961). Of the total, 106 were executed for murder (including 21 involving rape), 53 for rape, and 1 for desertion. The Navy carried out no executions during the period.

TYPE OF OFFENSE AND RACE	All years	1930-1939	1940-1949	1950-1959	1960-1964	1965	1966	1967	1968-1971
Total..............	3,859	1,667	1,284	717	181	7	1	2	—
White.............	1,751	827	490	336	90	6	1	1	—
Black.............	2,066	816	781	376	91	1	—	1	—
Other.............	42	24	13	5	—	—	—	—	—
Murder..............	3,334	1,514	1,064	601	145	7	1	2	—
White¹.............	1,664	803	458	316	79	6	1	1	—
Black¹.............	1,630	687	595	280	66	1	—	1	—
Other.............	40	24	11	5	—	—	—	—	—
Rape................	455	125	200	102	28	—	—	—	—
White.............	48	10	19	13	6	—	—	—	—
Black.............	405	115	179	89	22	—	—	—	—
Other.............	2	—	2	—	—	—	—	—	—
Other offenses²......	70	28	20	14	8	—	—	—	—
White³.............	39	14	13	7	5	—	—	—	—
Black.............	31	14	7	7	3	—	—	—	—

— Represents zero.
¹ White includes 18 females; black, 12 females.
² 25 armed robbery, 20 kidnaping, 11 burglary, 8 espionage (6 in 1942 and 2 in 1953), and 6 aggravated assault.
³ Includes 2 females, both executed in 1953, 1 for kidnaping and 1 for espionage.

VICTIMS OF CRIME: 1965

Number per 100,000 population. Based on a nationwide sample survey of 10,000 households conducted by the National Opinion Research center of the University of Chicago.

CHARACTERISTICS OF VICTIMS	Total	Forcible rape	Robbery	Aggravated assault	Burglary	Larceny—$50 and over	Motor vehicle theft
Total...............................	2,117	43	94	218	949	607	206
White...............................	1,860	22	58	186	822	608	164
Black and other races...................	2,592	82	204	347	1,306	367	286
Male, all ages.........................	3,091	(X)	112	287	1,583	841	268
10–19 years........................	951	(X)	61	399	123	337	31
20–29 years........................	5,924	(X)	257	824	2,782	1,546	515
30–39 years........................	6,231	(X)	112	337	3,649	1,628	505
40–49 years........................	5,150	(X)	210	263	2,365	1,839	473
50–59 years........................	4,231	(X)	181	181	2,297	967	605
60 years and over...................	3,465	(X)	98	146	2,343	683	195
Female, all ages.......................	1,059	83	77	118	314	337	130
10–19 years........................	334	91	—	91	30	122	—
20–29 years........................	2,424	238	238	333	665	570	380
30–39 years........................	1,514	104	157	52	574	470	157
40–49 years........................	1,908	48	96	286	524	620	334
50–59 years........................	1,132	—	60	119	298	536	119
60 years and over...................	1,052	—	81	40	445	405	81
Income:							
Under $3,000........................	2,369	76	172	229	1,319	420	153
$3,000–$5,999......................	2,331	49	121	316	1,020	619	206
$6,000–$9,999......................	1,820	10	48	144	867	549	202
$10,000 and over....................	2,237	17	34	252	790	925	219

— Represents zero.   X Not applicable.
Source: Executive Office of the President, The President's Commission on Law Enforcement and Administration of Justice, "The Challenge of Crime in a Free Society," 1967.

Murder Victims by Age, Sex, and Race, 1971

Age	Number	Percent	Sex		Race					
			Male	Female	White	Black	Indian	Chinese	Japanese	All others
Total...............	16,183	—	12,730	3,453	7,103	8,830	84	50	5	111
Percent.............	—	[1]100.0	78.7	21.3	43.9	54.6	0.5	0.3	—	0.7
Infant (under 1)........	100	.6	48	52	60	39	—	—	—	1
1–4....................	320	2.0	171	149	186	125	1	2	—	6
5–9....................	129	.8	78	51	80	48	—	1	—	—
10–14..................	220	1.4	136	84	113	107	—	—	—	—
15–19..................	1,422	8.8	1,131	291	542	863	4	4	—	9
20–24..................	2,616	16.2	2,137	479	990	1,579	15	9	1	22
25–29..................	2,360	14.6	1,933	427	908	1,419	14	6	—	13
30–34..................	1,768	10.9	1,410	358	701	1,038	12	7	—	10
35–39..................	1,616	10.0	1,289	327	616	973	13	5	2	7
40–44..................	1,396	8.6	1,112	284	609	771	7	5	—	4
45–49..................	1,164	7.2	931	233	519	632	6	1	2	4
50–54..................	913	5.6	740	173	470	435	3	3	—	2
55–59..................	622	3.8	495	127	352	261	6	—	—	3
60–64..................	487	3.0	376	111	298	184	—	3	—	2
65–69..................	331	2.0	259	72	217	107	1	2	—	4
70–74..................	217	1.3	149	68	140	73	1	1	—	2
75 and over............	266	1.6	150	116	206	59	1	—	—	—
Unknown...............	236	1.5	185	51	96	117	—	1	—	22

[1]Because of rounding the percentages may not add to total.
Source: U.S. Federal Bureau of Investigation, "Uniform Crime Reports for the United States," 1971.

GRIEVANCES IN CITIES WHERE CIVIL DISORDERS OCCURRED: 1967

Based on surveys made in 20 cities where civil disorders occurred. Grievances evaluated as to significance in each city and rank and points assigned to the 4 most serious, as follows: 4 points for 1st place, 3 for 2d, 2 for 3d, and 1 for 4th. Total points for each grievance category represents number of cities in which it was ranked among the top 4 multiplied by the number of points. Thus, a 4-point grievance assigned to 2 cities amounted to 8 points. Judgments of severity based on frequency of mention of a particular grievance, relative intensity with which it was discussed, references to incidents exemplifying it, and estimates of severity.

GRIEVANCE CATEGORY	Cities[1]	Points	GRIEVANCE CATEGORY	Cities[1]	Points
Police practices.....................	14	45.5	Disrespectful white attitudes..........	4	6.5
Unemployment, underemployment.....	17	42.0	Discriminatory admin. of justice.......	3	4.5
Inadequate housing..................	14	36.0	Inadequate Federal programs.........	1	2.5
Inadequate education................	9	21.0			
Poor recreational facilities...........	8	21.0	Inadequate municipal services..........	1	2.0
Ineffective political structure and			Discriminatory consumer and credit		
grievance mechanisms..............	5	14.0	practices.........................	2	2.0

[1] Where grievances were mentioned as significant.

Source: The National Advisory Commission on Civil Disorders, "Report," March 1968.

CIVIL DISTURBANCES AND RELATED DEATHS: 1967 TO 1972

PERIOD OR REGION	DISTURBANCES Total	DISTURBANCES Major[1]	DISTURBANCES Other[2]	Related deaths	PERIOD OR REGION	DISTURBANCES Total	DISTURBANCES Major[1]	DISTURBANCES Other[2]	Related deaths
1967, June-Oct......	52	12	40	87	1970................	76	18	58	33
					Jan–Mar...........	26	8	18	10
1968................	80	26	54	83	Apr–June..........	24	7	17	11
Jan–Mar...........	6	2	4	9	July–Sept.........	20	3	17	6
Apr–June..........	46	19	27	52	Oct–Dec..........	6	—	6	6
July–Sept.........	25	5	20	21					
Oct–Dec..........	3	—	3	1	North.............	11	4	7	2
					South.............	12	5	7	9
North.............	17	6	11	21	Midwest..........	44	8	36	11
South.............	29	9	20	16	West.............	9	1	8	11
Midwest..........	21	9	12	37					
West.............	13	2	11	9	1971................	39	10	29	10
					Jan–Mar...........	12	4	8	6
1969................	57	8	49	19	Apr–June..........	21	5	16	4
Jan–Mar...........	5	—	5	—	July–Sept.........	5	—	5	—
Apr–June..........	27	5	22	8	Oct–Dec..........	1	1	—	—
July–Sept.........	19	3	16	9					
Oct–Dec..........	6	—	6	2	North.............	4	—	4	—
					South.............	14	6	8	5
North.............	18	3	15	5	Midwest..........	10	2	8	1
South.............	13	2	11	3	West.............	11	2	9	4
Midwest..........	8	1	7	3					
West.............	18	2	16	8	1972, Jan–Mar.......	3	—	3	5

— Represents zero. [1] Characterized by all of the following: (a) vandalism; (b) arson; (c) looting or gunfire; (d) outside police forces or troops used; (e) more than 300 persons involved, excluding police; (f) twelve hours or longer duration. [2] Characterized by: Any three elements (a)-(d) described in footnote 1; duration of at least three hours; and more than 150 persons involved, exclusive of police.

Source: U.S. Dept. of Justice, Internal Security Division, unpublished data.

Percentage Repeaters by Race and Sex: Persons Arrested in 1971

Sex	Total	Race White	Race Black	Race Other
Total:				
Number of persons arrested.........	68,914	40,380	27,727	807
Percent repeaters.................	68.5	66.6	71.6	55.1
Male:				
Number of persons arrested	60,487	35,997	23,782	708
Percent repeaters	70.6	68.7	73.9	58.8
Female:				
Number of persons arrested.........	8,427	4,383	3,945	99
Percent repeaters.................	53.0	49.1	58.0	29.3

Source: U.S. Federal Bureau of Investigation, "Uniform Crime Reports for the United States," 1971.

Percent of Blacks in the Population and in Police and Fire Departments in Central Cities Surveyed, 1967

| Central city | Population 1965 (est.) | Blacks as a percent of— | | | | | |
| | | Police department | | | Fire department | | |
		Total	Civilian staff	Uniformed force	Total	Civilian staff	Uniformed force
San Francisco	12.0	4.9	12.7	3.9	0.1	2.2	0.1
Oakland	34.0	5.2	10.7	3.2	4.3	12.0	4.0
Philadelphia	31.0	24.0	63.0	20.4	7.8	25.3	7.3
Detroit	34.0	10.1	42.7	4.6	3.8	35.1	2.1
Atlanta	44.0	10.4	19.7	9.1	12.1	16.7	11.9
Houston	23.0	4.2	6.0	3.5	3.4	2.8	3.5
Memphis	40.0	13.8	29.2	5.5	2.1	25.0	1.3
Baton Rouge	32.0	3.2	0	3.8	2.7	14.3	2.4

Source: "For All the People . . . By All the People," A report of the United States Commission on Civil Rights. 1969.

Percent of Blacks in Central County Employment by Occupation and by Function for SMSA's Surveyed, 1967

OCCUPATIONS	Alameda San Francisco-Oakland	Wayne Detroit	Shelby Memphis	Harris Houston	Fulton Atlanta
All occupations	20.2	27.0	26.9	6.6	16.6
Uniformed police	8.1	25.2	10.0	2.9	5.3
Uniformed firemen	0	**	**	10.0	**
Custodial	52.4	87.7	7.5	9.1	100.0
Nonuniformed public safety	14.8	46.8	3.3	2.1	4.1
Other service workers	63.4	57.7	88.9	16.9	93.3
FUNCTIONS					
All functions	20.2	27.0	26.9	6.6	16.6
Public welfare	13.0	37.6	0	18.1	35.7
Public safety	15.7	41.9	8.9	5.0	5.4
Police	7.7	28.7	9.5	3.1	5.1
Fire	0	**	**	5.9	**
Correction	21.0	77.2	7.2	7.2	5.9

**No function.

NOTE.—The city of Baton Rouge and East Baton Rouge Parish though separate geographic entities, also have consolidated governments. In both San Francisco and Philadelphia the city and the county are coterminous and have consolidated governments.
Figures are for full-time noneducational employees.
Source: "For All the People . . . By All the People," A report of the United States Commission on Civil Rights. 1969.

Nonwhite Personnel in Selected Police Departments

Name of department	Number[5] police officers	Number[5] Nonwhite police officers	Number sergeants[5]		Number lieutenants[5]		Number captains[5]		Number above captain[5]	
			Nonwhite	White	Nonwhite	White	Nonwhite	White	Nonwhite	White
Atlanta, Ga............	968	98	2	12	3	56	0	15	0	6
Baltimore, Md..........	3,046	208	7	389	3	105	1	17	1	21
Boston, Mass..........	2,508	49	1	228	0	80	0	20	0	12
Buffalo, N.Y..........	1,375	37	1	60	1	93	0	24	0	32
Chicago, Ill...........	11,091	1,842	87	1,067	2	266	1	73	6	66
Cincinnati, Ohio......	891	54	2	68	2	34	0	13	0	7
Cleveland, Ohio.......	2,216	165	6	155	0	78	0	26	0	17
Dayton, Ohio.........	417	16	1	58	0	13	0	6	0	4
Detroit, Mich..........	4,326	227	9	339	2	156	0	0	1	62
Hartford, Conn........	342	38	0	32	1	16	0	9	0	2
Kansas City, Mo.......	927	51	7	158	0	36	0	11	1	14
Louisville, Ky.........	562	35	1	42	1	29	0	10	1	7
Memphis, Tenn........	869	46	0	0	4	192	0	45	0	44
Michigan State Police..	1,502	1	0	135	0	24	0	19	0	3
New Haven, Conn......	446	31	0	20	0	16	0	12	0	6
New Orleans, La.......	1,308	54	7	107	1	51	0	27	0	10
New York, N.Y.........	27,610	1,485	65	1,785	20	925	2	273	3	157
New Jersey State Police	1,224	5	0	187	0	43	0	17	0	4
Newark, N.J...........	1,869	184	5	97	3	95	1	22	0	0
Oakland, Calif........	658	27	1	95	0	25	1	10	0	3
Oklahoma City, Okla....	438	16	0	32	1	19	0	11	0	6
Philadelphia, Pa.......	6,890	1,377	26	314	8	139	3	46	0	23
Phoenix, Ariz.........	707	7	0	88	1	22	0	4	1	6
Pittsburgh, Pa........	1,558	109	3	137	3	47	0	17	0	11
St. Louis, Mo.........	2,042	224	21	201	3	46	4	17	0	10
San Francisco, Calif....	1,754	102	0	217	0	66	0	15	0	10
Tampa, Fla............	511	17	0	50	0	12	0	13	0	8
Washington, D.C.......	2,721	559	19	216	3	107	3	37	0	31
Total............	80,621	7,046	271	6,289	62	2,791	16	802	14	576

Name of department	Percent nonwhite population	Percent nonwhite police officers	Ratio: Sergeants to officers		Ratio: Lieutenants to officers		Ratio: Captains to officers		Ratio: Above captain to officers	
			Nonwhite	White	Nonwhite	White	Nonwhite	White	Nonwhite	White
Atlanta, Ga............	[1]38	10	1:49	1:73	1:33	1:16	0:98	1:58	0:98	1:14
Baltimore, Md........	[1]41	7	1:30	1:7	1:69	1:27	1:208	1:167	1:208	1:135
Boston, Mass..........	[1]11	2	1:49	1:11	0:49	1:31	0:49	1:123	0:49	1:205
Buffalo, N.Y..........	[1]18	3	1:37	1:22	1:37	1:14	0:37	1:56	0:37	1:42
Chicago, Ill...........	[1]27	17	1:21	1:9	1:921	1:35	1:1842	1:127	1:307	1:140
Cincinnati, Ohio......	[1]28	6	1:27	1:12	1:27	1:25	0:54	1:64	0:54	1:120
Cleveland, Ohio.......	[1]34	7	1:28	1:13	0:165	1:26	0:165	1:79	0:165	1:121
Dayton, Ohio.........	[1]25	4	1:16	1:7	0:16	1:30	0:16	1:67	0:16	1:100
Detroit, Mich..........	[1]39	5	1:25	1:12	1:114	1:26	No such rank		1:227	1:66
Hartford, Conn........	[2]20	11	1:38	1:10	1:38	1:20	0:38	1:34	0:38	1:152
Kansas City, Mo.......	[1]20	6	1:7	1:6	0:51	1:24	0:51	1:80	1:51	1:63
Louisville, Ky.........	[1]21	6	1:35	1:13	1:35	1:18	0:35	1:53	1:35	1:75
Memphis, Tenn........	[1]38	5	No such rank		1:12	1:4	0:46	1:18	0:46	1:19
Michigan State Police..	[3]9	(4)	0:1	1:11	0:1	1:63	0:1	1:79	0:1	1:500
New Haven, Conn......	[2]19	7	0:31	1:21	0:31	1:26	0:31	1:35	0:31	1:69
New Orleans, La.......	[1]41	4	1:8	1:12	1:54	1:25	0:54	1:46	0:54	1:125
New York, N.Y.........	[1]16	6	1:23	1:15	1:74	1:28	1:743	1:96	1:495	1:166
New Jersey State Police	[3]9	(4)	0:5	1:7	0:5	1:28	0:5	1:72	0:5	1:305
Newark, N.J...........	[1]40	10	1:37	1:17	1:61	1:18	1:184	1:77	None listed	
Oakland, Calif........	[1]31	4	1:27	1:7	0:27	1:25	1:27	1:63	0:27	1:210
Oklahoma City, Okla....	[1]15	4	0:16	1:13	1:16	1:22	0:16	1:38	0:16	1:70
Philadelphia, Pa.......	[1]29	20	1:53	1:18	1:172	1:40	1:459	1:120	0:1377	1:240
Phoenix, Ariz.........	[1]8	1	0:7	1:8	1:7	1:32	0:7	1:70	0:7	1:175
Pittsburgh, Pa........	[1]19	7	1:36	1:11	1:36	1:31	0:109	1:362	1:109	1:242
St. Louis, Mo.........	[1]37	11	1:11	1:9	1:75	1:40	1:56	1:107	0:224	1:165
San Francisco, Calif....	[1]14	6	0:102	1:8	0:102	1:25	0:102	1:110	0:102	1:165
Tampa, Fla............	[1]14	3	0:17	1:10	0:17	1:41	0:17	1:38	0:17	1:62
Washington, D.C.......	[1]63	21	1:29	1:10	1:186	1:20	1:186	1:58	0:559	1:70

[1]Percent black population figures, 1965 estimates by the Center for Research in Marketing, Cong. Quarterly, Weekly Report, No. 36, Sept. 8, 1967.
[2]Percent black population figures, 1966 estimates, office of Economic Opportunity.
[3]Percent black population figures for States of Michigan and New Jersey, 1960 Census figures.
[4]Less than ½ of 1 percent.
[5]All police data from a survey conducted for the Commission by the International Association of Chiefs of Police in October 1967.

Section VIII

ECONOMICS AND BUSINESS

OUTLOOK FOR BLACKS IN BUSINESS

When the existing patterns and structure of black-owned businesses are unraveled, a graphic—and disturbing—picture comes into sharp focus. Traditionally black businessmen have concentrated primarily on small-scale retail trade and the provision of personal services. Because racial discrimination restricted the access of blacks to housing and public accommodations, black businessmen came forward to meet most of the black demand for trade and services.

Now, unfortunately, blacks are still concentrated in these fields which are declining relative to the economy as a whole. Unless a major diversification occurs in the range and focus of black-owned businesses, blacks will be getting an even smaller share of the nation's business receipts in 1980 than they are receiving now. In order to increase the size and efficiency of black-owned firms, blacks will have to become much more willing to adopt the corporation as a form of business organization, relying far less on individual and personal ownerships. Blacks must also be more willing to tap the stream of risk-taking capital through joint-ventures with businessmen of other races. Finally, they must be prepared to undertake the hard task of acquiring the technical and managerial skills increasingly required to survive and prosper in the sophisticated business world unfolding before us.

In 1969, there were 163 thousand black-owned businesses in the United States. These firms represented about 1.4 percent of the 12 million firms in the country at large. These black-owned enterprises had gross receipts of $4.5 billion, accounting for 0.24 percent of the total. Thus, by either measure, it is obvious that blacks control only a meager share of the nation's business activity.

To put the business situation in perspective, it will be recalled that blacks represent 11.3 percent of the total population in the United States, and in 1970 they received 6.5 percent of the total money income. However, with respect to income sources, only 0.7 percent of the income for blacks was derived from property ownership (i.e., rents, interest, dividends, royalties, and inheritances) compared with 4.6 percent of the income of whites. So, while blacks got 6.5 percent of total income in 1970, they received less than 1.0 percent of investment and property income in that year.

Of the 163 thousand black-owned firms reporting in 1969 only 38 thousand had paid employees. The typical black firm with paid employees had about four workers on its payroll. In manufacturing and wholesale trade, the typical black firm had 8 employees; in retail trade, the average was 3 paid workers. In contrast, in the economy as a whole, the corresponding figures per firm were: manufacturing, 72 employees; wholesale trade, 15 employees, and retail trade, 6 employees. Collectively black firms had 152 thousand workers on their payrolls. Thus, it seems that black firms, which provide jobs for only 1.9 percent of all black workers in the country, are over-managed with few employees.

An alternative way to measure the size of black firms is in terms of business receipts. In 1969 the average black-owned firm with paid employees had gross receipts of $95 thousand. In manufacturing, the figure was $187 thousand, and in wholesale and retail trade it was $497 thousand and $96 thousand, respectively. The parallel figures for the typical firm in those industries in the country as a whole were: manufacturing, $2,068,000; wholesale trade, $1,974,000; and retail trade $197 thousand. In the factory sector, by this measure, the average black-owned firm was about one-tenth the size of its nation-wide counterpart. But in the case of wholesale trade, the average black-owned business was one-quarter that in the nation, and in retail trade it was in the neighborhood of one-half as large.

For the most part, black businesses have developed in response to the special needs of the black population. The historic discrimination against blacks in terms of access to public accommodations is traceable in the relative positions of black-owned eating and drinking places, amusement and recreation outlets, hotels, motels and other lodging places. Nearly one-tenth of all black businesses are restaurants, and similar establishments, however, these type establishments account for only 3 percent of the businesses at large. This segment of black industry—retail trade—accounted for over two-fifths of the gross receipts.

The legacy of racial discrimination against blacks in the provision of life insurance coverage is also still evident. Until well into the mid-20th century, white-owned insurance companies, concluding that the relatively short-life expectancy of blacks made it too risky to insure them using the same standards applied to whites, developed different standards for blacks which carried considerably higher insurance premiums. Thus, there was a real need for the establishment of black-owned insurance agencies to provide fair service to the black population. It is for this reason that the relative positions of black-owned and white-owned insurance companies were quite similar in 1969.

Of course, there were areas of business where racial segregation and discrimination were not so apparent, and it is in these areas that black participation remains modest. For example, the proportion of blacks operating factories was only one-half that for American industry as a whole. And, as with black-owned cosmetics companies, the black representation in manufacturing is related to the blacks' historical situation in this country. Their presence in printing and publishing, of course, is primarily a mirror of black-oriented newspapers, although a few magazine and book publishers have also made considerable headway in recent years.

In the case of wholesale trade, one has to look hard to find black-owned firms outside of food distribution. It will be recalled that the operation of retail trade outlets is the most important form of activity among black businessmen. So, the meager participation of blacks in wholesale trade means that blacks are essentially missing in one segment of the distribution network in this country.

The annual average rate of growth for the U.S. economy is estimated at 4.3 percent over the projected growth rate period 1968-80. Only four of the twenty-five industries which are so important to black firms have projected growth rates above that average, whereas half of the twenty-five have projected rates below the average. This seems convincing evidence that black business is heading downhill, and that even if blacks succeed in maintaining their share of those industries in which they are presently active, their share of total business will shrink somewhat by 1980.

The task for blacks now would seem to be to improve the quality of managerial talent available to the black community, as well as to expand their representation into those industries for which growth prospects are especially bright.

In the case of managerial talents and technical skills, one ought to distinguish among at least three situations: (1) the case of a person considering entering business for the first time; (2) the case of a person already owning his own business who needs to improve his own capabilities; and (3) the case of a person who is currently employed in a technical or managerial capacity by a major white firm. As far as the first category is concerned, the counsel to be given is straightforward: such an embryonic businessman ought to study the principles of business administration in college or technical school—or he should get a job and accumulate the skills required while serving an apprenticeship in someone else's business. For those in the second category, a number of private and publicly-supported options already exist, and these need not be catalogued here. They include counseling by numerous locally-based small business development centers and offices of the Federal Government's Small Business Administration.

The person in the third category might be of particular interest. To date—after nearly a decade of effort by large corporations to attract black college graduates to their organizations—a substantial number of blacks have developed considerable know-how in the field of business management. Undoubtedly, quite a few of these recruits have found life in the modern, large-scale corporation less than hospitable and have left for more personally promising opportunities. Yet, many have remained —and some have even made progress on the corporate ladder. Under the appropriate conditions, some members of these corporate cadres could provide the managerial and technical talents required if black-owned businesses are to be diversified. This is happening already in a modest way and a fair number of other blacks are looking for a chance to follow the same course.

The task of increasing the size of black-owned firms is far more difficult. Size is measured in three ways: by the number of employees per firm; the value of receipts per firm; and the value of receipts per employee.

Most of the high-growth manufacturing industries are those based on sophisticated technical processes in which major technological advances and substantial increase in productivity can be anticipated. At the same time, measured by employment, the average black-owned firm in the industries with the highest projected growth rates are typically less than one-tenth as large as its counterpart in the economy as a whole. Measured by value of shipments, the same kind of short-fall on the part of black-owned firms is evident. When value of

shipments per employee is used as a standard, the divergence is less sharp, but the relatively small scale of the existing black-owned firms still shows through.

Unfortunately, the typical black-owned firm is ill-equipped to raise capital. The propensity of blacks to rely on personal ownership as a form of business organization is the same as that for all firms. Blacks, however, tend to make more use of partnerships. But the dependence of blacks on the corporate form of organization is only three-fifths that among all firms in the country.

In 1968 black proprietorships accounted for 48 percent of the total vs. only 12 percent for all firms. This points clearly to the fact that blacks have, for the most part, avoided the corporate organization for their business.

The relative importance of the corporation as a form of business organization in the country at large has been increasing since the end of World War II. The reasons for this trend are quite evident. Corporations include limited liability and income tax advantages for the stockholders, but more important is that the corporate form allows the business to raise from outside sources far more capital than it could get if it had to rely wholly on the personal resources of a single owner or a few partners. This is a lesson which some black businessmen have already learned and it is imperative that others learn it as well—that is, if they are to move into the mainstream of American business.

Several other points with respect to business organization and capital requirements can be made at this juncture. These relate to the question of equity capital—meaning the amount of funds invested in a firm which belong to the owners, and thus available as a cushion to absorb losses or otherwise sustain a business during difficult times. Little is known with any precision about the relative amount of equity capital invested in black businesses. However, the general impression one gets from fragmentary data and discussions with businessmen is that capital, in general—and risk capital, in particular—is distressingly scarce.

In general, stockholders have a sizable stake in their firms compared with the amount of debt outstanding. Even in the credit agencies and hotel sectors (which have the lowest ratios), those who own the businesses have themselves supplied a sizable proportion of the capital employed in the enterprise.

With respect to manufacturing corporations, it will be noted that in 1972 stockholders had invested $2.30 for each $1.00 of borrowed money. The ratio increased somewhat with respect to size of firm—but only up to a point. Thus, it rose from 1.93 for those in the $5-$10 million class. The ratio then declined steadily as size increased to reach 2.00 in the $100-$250 million size group. Above this category, it again turned upward to reach 2.47 for corporations with assets of $1 billion and over.

From these statistics a conclusion emerges which is of vital importance for those interested in the future of black-owned businesses. If they are to prosper—even if they expect to concentrate in trade and moderate-scale manufacturing activities—they will need to raise a substantial amount of equity capital. They cannot expect to run their businesses by relying primarily on debt supplied by banks and other lenders. After all, banks are lending depositors money, and they cannot be expected to take the risk which properly belongs to those who supply equity capital.

Blacks will have to look beyond their own community if they wish to expand their participation in business ownership in a meaningful way. This is true with respect to both technical and managerial assistance and equity capital.

In the case of equity capital, blacks have displayed little eagerness to invest their resources in risk-taking ventures. This reluctance is understandable: given the low-level income of the typical black fami-ly—and the wide-spread inability to make long-range plans for family security—it is not surprising that blacks have not rushed into the purchase of common stocks. On the other hand, blacks have accumulated a modest amount of wealth, and some of the latter has been invested in equity issues.

For example, in 1966 (the only date for which statistics are available), black families had total asset holdings of $18.2 billion, of which $2.3 billion were financial assets. So blacks' holdings of the latter were 0.7 percent of the $337.1 billion aggregate amount of financial assets for the nation as a whole. In the same year, all American families had accumulated assets of $970.1 billion—including money in banks, government bonds, stocks in corporations, and equity investment in farms, businesses, and homes. So blacks had 1.9 percent of the accumulated wealth in 1966.

In the same year, blacks had about $200 million of stocks in corporations. This represented about 8.7 percent of their financial assets and 1.1 percent of their total wealth. This amount was equal to about $38 per family. In contrast, all families in the country had stockholdings of about $145.4 billion. This represented around 15.0 percent of their aggregate wealth and 43.1 percent of their total financial assets. This amount was equal to about $2,603 of stockholdings per family.

So, while blacks received about 6.3 percent of the nation's personal income in 1966, they owned less than 2 percent of the accumulated wealth. Their share of total financial assets was 0.7 percent, and they held 0.14 percent of the stocks owned by all families.

Thus, black businessmen would be unwise to look to the black community as the exclusive source of the equity capital they will need in the future. Instead, it seems that they will have to rely on joint ventures with businessmen and investors in the economy at large to meet their requirements. The exact form these joint participations may take cannot be anticipated;

however, one suggestion comes to mind. Large commercial banks might form subsidiaries through which they could acquire reasonable amounts of equity securities issued by predominantly black-owned firms. The model for this type of institution are the Edge Corporations owned by U.S. banks through which they do much of their business abroad. Under the 1970 amendments to the Bank Holding Company Act, it is now possible for U.S. banks —through holding company subsidiaries —to form similar corporations to finance community improvement projects in this country. Under certain circumstances, such corporations would be able to take equity participations in black-owned businesses.

Whatever approach one may prefer, the need for blacks to diversify their business activity—and the need for a vehicle to raise equity capital—cannot be disputed. If they fail in this effort, the outlook is bleak indeed.

Condensed with permission from: *The Road Ahead: Outlook for Blacks in Business*, Dr. Andrew F. Brimmer, Member Board of Governors of the Federal Reserve System; delivered in Cincinnati, Ohio, October 19, 1972.

Selected Characteristics for Black-Owned Firms: 1969

Subject	Total	With paid employees	Without paid employees
Firms: Number (thousands)..	163	38	125
Percent..	100	23	77
Gross Receipts: Amount (millions).....................................	$4,474	$3,653	$821
Percent..	100	82	18
Average receipts per firm (millions)...................................	$27.4	$95.4	$6.6
Employees:			
Number..	(X)	152	(X)
Average employees per firm..	(X)	25	(X)
PERCENT DISTRIBUTION			
Legal form of organization:			
Total firms..	100	100	100
Sole proprietorship..	91	79	95
Partnership..	7	13	5
Corporations..	2	8	—
Region of location:			
Total firms[1]..	100	100	100
Northeast..	15	15	15
North Central...	22	25	22
South...	51	49	52
West..	11	10	11

— Rounds to zero.   (X) Not applicable.
[1]Includes firms not specified by region.
Source: U.S. Department of Commerce, Social and Economic Statistics Administration, Bureau of the Census.

Ten Most Important Industry Groups of Black-Owned Firms
Ranked by Receipts: 1969

Rank	Industry	Firms (thousands)	Gross receipts (millions)
	ALL INDUSTRY GROUPS..	163	$4,474
	Ten most important industry groups...	97	3,072
	Percent of all industry groups..	60	69
	Percent...	100	100
1	Automotive dealers and gasoline filling stations............................	7	21
2	Food stores..	12	14
3	Wholesale trade..	2	13
4	Eating and drinking places..	15	12
5	Personal services..	35	9
6	Special trade contractors...	14	9
7	Miscellaneous retail stores..	7	9
8	General building contractors...	2	5
9	Trucking and warehousing...	7	4
10	Insurance carrier...	—	4

— Rounds to zero.
Source: U.S. Department of Commerce, Social and Economic Statistics Administration, Bureau of the Census.

Number and Gross Receipts for All and Black-Owned Firms,
by Industry Division: 1969

(Numbers in thousands. Receipts in millions of dollars)

INDUSTRY DIVISION	FIRMS			GROSS RECEIPTS		
	All firms[1] (number)	Black-owned firms (number)	Percent black of all firms	All firms[1]	Black-owned firms	Percent black of all firms
All industries..........................	7,489	163	2.2	$1,497,969	$4,474	0.3
Contract construction.........................	856	16	1.9	92,291	464	0.5
Manufactures..............................	401	3	0.8	588,682	303	0.1
Transportation and other public utilities.........	359	17	4.7	106,040	211	0.2
Wholesale trade.............................	434	1	0.2	213,196	385	0.2
Retail trade................................	2,046	45	2.2	320,751	1,932	0.6
Finance, insurance, and real estate.............	1,223	8	0.6	86,670	288	0.3
Selected services...........................	1,803	56	3.1	61,858	663	1.1
Other industries and not classified..............	367	17	4.5	28,481	228	0.8

[1]Based on data from IRS statistics of income for 1967.
Source: U.S. Department of Commerce, Social and Economic Statistics Administration, Bureau of the Census.

Selected Statistics for Black-Owned Firms by Selected Standard Metropolitan Statistical Areas: 1969

Standard Metropolitan Statistical Areas (SMSA)	ALL FIRMS		WITH PAID EMPLOYEES					WITHOUT PAID EMPLOYEES		
	Firms (number)	Gross receipts ($1,000)	Firms (number)	Employees (number)	Gross receipts ($1,000)	Average employees per firm (number)	Average receipts per firm ($1,000)	Firms (number)	Gross receipts ($1,000)	Average receipts per firm ($1,000)
Albuquerque, N. Mex.	72	$ 2,123	21	119	$ 1,892	6	$90	51	$ 231	$5
Atlanta, Ga.	2,137	74,591	514	2,473	63,626	5	124	1,623	10,965	7
Bakersfield, Calif.	188	4,938	43	167	4,097	4	95	145	841	6
Baltimore, Md.	3,522	72,643	692	2,428	55,317	4	80	2,830	17,326	6
Birmingham, Ala.	988	31,770	265	1,638	27,146	6	102	723	4,624	6
Boston, Mass.	582	33,451	165	712	30,684	4	186	417	2,767	7
Brownsville-Harlingen-San Benito, Tex.	16	662	6	30	581	5	97	10	81	8
Chicago, Ill.	8,747	332,197	2,390	10,193	283,567	4	119	6,357	48,630	8
Cincinnati, Ohio-Ky.-Ind.	1,360	28,019	296	1,105	21,982	4	74	1,064	6,037	6
Cleveland, Ohio	3,208	90,410	851	2,737	74,352	3	87	2,357	16,058	7
Corpus Christi, Tex.	134	6,123	43	254	5,641	6	131	91	482	5
Dallas, Tex.	2,080	55,175	465	1,807	44,800	4	96	1,615	10,375	6
Denver, Colo.	648	17,690	102	831	14,614	8	143	546	3,076	6
Detroit, Mich.	5,442	227,494	1,708	7,240	199,436	4	117	3,734	28,058	8
El Paso, Tex.	88	1,667	20	53	1,010	3	51	68	657	10
Fresno, Calif.	187	4,991	39	196	3,972	5	102	148	1,019	7
Houston, Tex.	4,326	83,530	890	3,219	61,193	4	69	3,436	22,337	7
Jacksonville, Fla.	984	26,408	218	1,111	22,069	5	101	766	4,339	6
Kansas City, Mo.-Kans.	1,411	28,701	287	1,037	22,359	4	78	1,124	6,342	6
Laredo, Tex.	4	550	4	70	550	18	138			0
Los Angeles-Long Beach, Calif.	8,318	210,950	1,675	6,855	167,961	4	100	6,643	42,989	6
Memphis, Tenn.-Ark.	1,464	50,336	392	2,257	43,292	6	110	1,072	7,044	7
Miami, Fla.	1,166	28,696	310	1,129	22,338	4	72	856	6,358	7
Minneapolis-St. Paul, Minn.	391	14,138	96	553	12,166	6	127	295	1,972	7
Mobile, Ala.	588	17,409	163	780	14,629	5	90	425	2,780	7
New Orleans, La.	2,723	86,594	644	2,789	71,463	4	111	2,079	15,131	7
New York, N.Y.	7,753	200,153	1,592	5,978	159,988	4	100	6,161	40,165	7
Newark, N.J.	2,432	76,962	614	2,091	62,358	3	102	1,818	14,604	8
Norfolk-Portsmouth, Va.	958	15,906	179	539	11,914	3	67	779	3,992	5
Philadelphia, Pa.-N.J.	6,246	151,866	1,342	4,663	115,524	3	86	4,904	36,342	7
Phoenix, Ariz.	290	6,788	57	223	5,309	4	93	233	1,479	6
Pittsburgh, Pa.	1,368	37,327	336	1,163	30,576	3	91	1,032	6,751	7
Richmond, Va.	840	21,298	171	680	17,161	4	100	669	4,137	6
Sacramento, Calif.	334	8,062	74	237	6,624	3	90	260	1,438	6
St. Louis, Mo.-Ill.	2,986	87,815	724	3,085	70,267	4	97	2,262	17,548	8
San Antonio, Tex.	584	14,643	147	636	12,142	4	83	437	2,501	6
San Bernardino-Riverside-Ontario, Calif.	441	13,588	102	425	11,405	4	112	339	2,183	6
San Diego, Calif.	504	13,229	129	578	11,029	4	85	375	2,200	6
San Francisco-Oakland, Calif.	3,358	90,791	770	3,033	73,079	4	95	2,588	17,712	7
San Jose, Calif.	366	11,948	89	555	9,897	6	111	277	2,051	7
Tucson, Ariz.	76	1,500	25	80	1,237	3	49	51	263	5
Washington, D.C.-Md.-Va.	7,768	123,184	1,039	4,048	93,276	4	90	6,729	29,908	4

BLACK ADVERTISING AGENCIES

AGENCY	PRESIDENT	FOUNDED
Burrell McBain, Inc. 360 N. Michigan Avenue Chicago, Ill. 60601 (312) 266-0880	Thomas J. Burrell	1971
Tom Cleveland & Associates 3119 Fenkl Detroit, Mich. (313) 345-6655	Tom Cleveland, Sr.	1954
Communicon, Inc. 333 N. Michigan Avenue Chicago, Ill. 60601 (312) 641-6468	William Fonvielle	1970
Vince Cullers Advertising, Inc. 520 N. Michigan Avenue Chicago, Ill. 60611 (312) 321-9296	Vince Cullers	1953
Eden Advertising & Communications, Inc. 327 E. 65th St. New York, N. Y. 10021 (212) 472-0091	Barbara Simmons	1971
Junius Edwards, Inc. 1370 Avenue of the Americas New York, N. Y. 10019 (212) 245-9030	Junius Edwards	1965
Few, Hunter & Wilson 44 11th, N.E. Atlanta, Ga. (404) 892-0634	Michael Wilson	1969
Phat Advertising Consultants 8 W. 40th St. New York, N. Y. (212) 868-3633	Walter Long	1967
Proctor & Gardner Advertising 111 E. Wacker Drive Chicago, Ill. 60601 (312) 644-7950	Barbara Gardner Proctor	1970
Howard Sanders Advertising 114 E. 55th St. New York, N. Y. 10022 (212) 759-2230	Howard Sanders	1966
John F. Small, Inc. 477 Madison Avenue New York, N. Y. 10022 (212) 935-9810	John F. Small	1970
Uniworld Group, Inc. 62 West 45th St. New York, N. Y. 10036 (212) 867-5700	Byron Lewis	1969
Vanguard Associates, Inc. 1111 Nic Avenue Minneapolis, Minn. (612) 335-8879	Thomas Tipton	1969
Wright Edelen Advertising, Inc. 6300 Wilshire Blvd. Los Angeles, Calif. 90048 (213) 651-1161	Norman E. Edelen	1971
Zebra Associates, Inc. 18 E. 50th St. New York, N. Y. 10022 (212) 353-6303	Joan Murray	1969

BLACK-OWNED BANKING INSTITUTIONS

NAME

	1972 Assets	1973 Assets*
Freedom National Bank New York City, N. Y.	$ 47,163,797	$ 54,079,601
Independence Bank Chicago, Ill. ....:......................	46,632,922	50,846,208
Seaway National Bank Chicago, Ill.	48,797,915	49,514,541
Industrial Bank Washington, D. C.	37,200,000	40,671,000
Citizens Trust Bank Atlanta, Ga.	40,744,588	38,953,195
Mechanics and Farmers Bank Durham, N. C.	37,694,158	37,115,659
First Independence National Bank Detroit, Mich.	27,304,651	34,841,052
Bank of Finance Los Angeles, Calif.	28,177,332	29,321,194
Consolidated Bank & Trust Richmond, Va.	19,566,200	23,154,772
Tri-State Bank Memphis, Tenn.	19,627,356	22,172,106
United Community National Bank Washington, D. C.	21,039,155	21,137,094
Gateway National Bank St. Louis, Mo.	16,700,513	20,482,757
Douglass State Bank Kansas City, Kan.	18,805,610	19,318,090
Unity Bank & Trust Roxbury, Mass.	14,218,000	14,821,000
National Industrial Bank Miami, Fla.	17,419,360	14,077,495
Highland Community Bank Chicago, Ill.	12,156,314	13,912,559
First Plymouth National Bank Minneapolis, Minn.	12,363,725	12,741,452
Gateway National Bank Chicago, Ill.	10,200,000	12,300,000
Swope Parkway National Bank Kansas City, Mo.	13,000,000	12,285,000
Riverside National Bank Houston, Tex.	10,787,823	12,230,000

NAME

	1972 Assets	1973 Assets*
Vanguard National Bank Hempstead, N. Y.	$ 10,922,686	$ 11,888,196
North Milwaukee State Bank Milwaukee, Wis.	9,023,000	10,349,000
First Enterprise Bank Oakland, Cal.	10,716,907	9,566,109
Citizens Savings Bank & Trust Nashville, Tenn.	8,423,238	9,351,021
Unity State Bank Dayton, Ohio	7,429,523	9,100,326
Carver State Bank Savannah, Ga.	7,371,000	8,665,598
Liberty Bank of Seattle Seattle, Wash.	6,414,679	7,940,238
First State Bank Danville, Va.	7,793,472	7,903,000
Midwest National Bank Indianapolis, Ind.	4,400,000	7,155,000
Atlantic National Bank Norfolk, Va.	8,870,252	6,767,726
Liberty Bank & Trust New Orleans, La.	6,089,718	6,624,379
Guaranty Bank & Trust Chicago, Ill.	5,300,000	6,200,000
Peoples National Bank Springfield, Ill.	5,300,000	5,631,000
Freedom Bank of Finance Portland, Oreg.	4,413,065	5,453,429
Victory Savings Bank Columbia, S. C.	5,044,069	5,511,807
American State Bank Tulsa, Okla.	4,127,458	5,200,838
Greensboro National Bank Greensboro, N. C.	3,578,496	4,982,556

Total Banks: 37   Total Assets: $614,816,982 $662,264,998

*(6-30-73)

TOP TEN BLACK LEGAL RESERVE LIFE INSURANCE COMPANIES

NAME	1971 ASSETS	1972 ASSETS
North Carolina Mutual Durham, N. C.	$123,000,000	$129,233,894
Atlanta Life Atlanta, Ga.	$ 78,161,000	$ 80,803,984
Golden State Mutual Los Angeles, Calif.	$ 39,433,000	$ 44,018,698
Universal Life Memphis, Tenn.	$ 38,392,000	$ 40,890,996
Supreme Life Chicago, Ill.	$ 37,872,000	$ 39,277,244
Chicago Metropolitan Mutual Chicago, Ill.	$ 26,985,000	$ 28,376,844
Mammoth Life Louisville, Ky.	$ 20,423,000	$ 20,997,420
Pilgrim Health and Life Augusta, Ga.	$ 14,132,000	$ 14,331,938
Afro-American Life Jacksonville, Fla.	$ 11,199,000	$ 11,275,598
Booker T. Washington Birmingham, Ala.	$ 11,169,000	$ 11,245,498
Total Assets:	$400,766,000	$420,452,114

BLACK LEGAL RESERVE LIFE INSURANCE COMPANIES

NAME	1971 ASSETS
American Woodmen's Life Denver, Colo.	$10,549,000
Benevolent Life Shreveport, La.	$ 568,000
Bradford's Industrial Birmingham, Ala.	$ 811,000
Central Life Tampa, Fla.	$ 6,407,000
Christian Benevolent Shreveport, La.	$ 902,000
Gertrude Geddes Willis Life New Orleans, La.	$ 1,208,000
Golden Circle Life Brownsville, Tenn.	$ 2,125,000
Good Citizens Life New Orleans, La.	$ 2,251,000
Guaranty Life Savannah, Ga.	$ 1,713,000
Keystone Life New Orleans, La.	$ 892,000
Lighthouse Life Shreveport, La.	$ 359,000
Lovett's Life Mobile, Ala.	$ 277,000

NAME	1971 ASSETS
Majestic Life New Orleans, La.	$ 366,000
National Service Industrial New Orleans, La.	$ 695,000
Peoples Life New Orleans, La.	$ 3,797,000
Peoples Progressive Burial Rayville, La.	$ 175,000
Progressive Industrial Life New Orleans, La.	$ 180,000
Protective Industrial Birmingham, Ala.	$ 3,100,000
Provident Home Industrial Philadelphia, Pa.	$ 2,380,000
Purple Shield Life Baton Rouge, La.	$ 570,000
Reliable Life Monroe, La.	$ 609,000
Security Life Jackson, Miss.	$ 905,000
Southern Aid Life Richmond, Va.	$ 3,913,000
Southern Life Baltimore, Md.	$ 949,000
Union Protective Life Memphis, Tenn.	$ 2,707,000
United Mutual Life New York, N.Y.	$ 8,489,000
Unity Burial Mobile, Ala.	$ 1,208,000
Virginia Mutual Richmond, Va.	$ 3,713,000
Winston Mutual Life Winston-Salem, N.C.	$ 4,827,000
Wright Mutual Detroit, Mich.	$ 2,105,000

Total Assets: $68,750,000

SAVINGS AND LOAN ASSOCIATIONS

NAME	ASSETS*—1972
Advance Federal Savings & Loan Association Baltimore, Maryland	$ 10,012,285
American Federal Savings & Loan Association Greensboro, North Carolina	$ 6,995,842
Berean Savings Association Philadelphia, Pennsylvania	$ 7,500,000
Berkley Citizens Mutual Savings & Loan Association Norfolk, Virginia	$ 4,243,059
Broadway Federal Savings & Loan Association Los Angeles, California	$ 60,451,990
Carver Federal Savings & Loan Association New York, New York	$ 60,000,000
Citizens Federal Savings & Loan Association Birmingham, Alabama	$ 15,000,000
Columbia Savings & Loan Association Milwaukee, Wisconsin	$ 4,653,771
Community Federal Savings & Loan Association Nashville, Tennessee	$ 4,200,000
Community Federal Savings & Loan Association Tampa, Florida	$ 2,478,713
Community Savings & Loan Association Newport News, Virginia	$ 552,613
Connecticut Savings & Loan Association Hartford, Connecticut	$ 7,500,000
Dwelling House Savings & Loan Association Pittsburgh, Pennsylvania	$ 3,550,280
Enterprise Savings & Loan Association Compton, California	$ 9,600,000
Equity Savings & Loan Association Denver, Colorado	$ 1,569,307
Family Savings & Loan Association Los Angeles, California	$ 30,196,000
First Federal Savings & Loan Association of Scotlandville Baton Rouge, Louisiana	$ 7,142,628
Gulf Federal Savings & Loan Association Mobile, Alabama	$ 3,240,000
Home Federal Savings & Loan Association of Detroit Detroit, Michigan	$ 15,966,000
Ideal Building & Loan Association Baltimore, Maryland	$ 918,272
Illinois Federal Savings & Loan Association Chicago, Illinois	$ 34,500,000

NAME	ASSETS*—1972
Imperial Savings & Loan Association .... Martinsville, Virginia	$ 900,000
Independence Federal Savings & Loan Association .... Washington, D.C.	$ 21,000,000
Magic City Building & Loan Association .... Roanoke, Virginia	$ 255,800
Major Industrial Federal Savings & Loan Association .... Cincinnati, Ohio	$ 4,800,000
Morgan Park Savings & Loan Association .... Chicago, Illinois	$ 1,356,648
Mutual Federal Savings & Loan Association .... Atlanta, Georgia	$ 12,500,000
Mutual Federal Savings & Loan Association .... Memphis, Tennessee	$ 3,900,000
Mutual Savings & Loan Association .... Durham, North Carolina	$ 13,194,647
New Age Federal Savings & Loan Association .... St. Louis, Missouri	$ 10,000,567
North Tulsa Savings & Loan Association .... Tulsa, Oklahoma	$ 230,000
Peoples Building & Loan Association .... Hampton, Virginia	$ 7,320,827
Quincy Savings & Loan Company .... Cleveland, Ohio	$ 9,145,094
Security Federal Savings & Loan Association .... Chattanooga, Tennessee	$ 1,528,863
Service Federal Savings & Loan Association .... Chicago, Illinois	$ 11,857,343
Standard Savings Association .... Houston, Texas	$ 6,355,000
State Mutual Federal Savings & Loan Association .... Jackson, Mississippi	$ 4,200,000
Tuskegee Federal Savings & Loan Association .... Tuskegee, Alabama	$ 5,500,000
United Federal Savings & Loan Association .... New Orleans, Louisiana	$ 9,601,189
Union Mutual Savings & Loan Association .... Richmond, Virginia	$ 2,707,646
Washington Shores Federal Savings & Loan Association .... Orlando, Florida	$ 3,500,000

TOTAL COMPANIES: 41   TOTAL ASSETS: $410,124,384

*All verified by interview, June, 1973

BLACK BOARD MEMBERS

Aiken, William
Certified public accountant, is president of the National Association of Black Accountants, Inc. and a partner of Aiken, Wilson & Brown, a black certified public accountant firm in New York, N.Y.
Board of Directors Member, Ethical-Fieldston Fund

Alexander, Clifford, Jr.
Attorney, Arnold & Porter; Washington, D.C.
Directorships: Dreyfus Third Century Fund, Octagon Industries, Inc., Pennsylvania Power & Light Co.

Allen, Aris T., M.D.
Physician and legislator, is in private practice of medicine in Annapolis, Md. and has been a member (Republican, Annapolis) of the Maryland Legislature since 1966.
Board of Directors and Executive Committee Member, Colonial Bank and Trust Co., Annapolis, Maryland

Allen, George Louis
City official, is a member of the Dallas, Tex., city council and is president of Tecog Service Industries, a building maintenance firm.
Board Member, Dallas County United Fund

Arlene, Herbert
Legislator, is a Democratic member of the Pennsylvania Senate.
Board of Directors Member, Greater Philadelphia Development Corp.

Atkins, Thomas I.
Administrator and state official, is secretary of communities and development for the state of Massachusetts.
Member, Harvard Board of Overseers

Bacon, Warren H.
Administrator, is assistant director manpower administration for Inland Steel Co. of Chicago.
Trustee, Russell Sage Foundation; Director, Hyde Park Federal Savings & Loan Association of Chicago

Banks, Ernest (Ernie)
Baseball coach, is the first base coach and former player with the Chicago Cubs.
Board Member, Chicago Transit Authority

Berry, Edwin C.
Corporate executive, is special assistant to the president of Johnson Products Co. and is director of the George E. Johnson Foundation. Board of Directors Member, Community Fund of Metropolitan Chicago

Booth, The Reverend L. Venchael
Clergyman, is the pastor of the Zion Baptist Church in Cincinnati, Ohio and the president of the Progressive National Baptist Convention.
Board of Trustees Member, University of Cincinnati

Branch, The Reverend Dorothy Sutton
Clergywoman, is pastor of the Commonwealth Community Church in Chicago, Ill.
Board Member, City Colleges of Chicago

Brown, George L.
Legislator, in 1956 became the first black man to be elected as a member of the Colorado State Senate.
Board of Directors Member, C.F. Kettering Foundation

Brown, James
Entertainer, is chairman of the board of James Brown Productions, James Brown Enterprises and Man's World, headquartered in Augusta, Ga.
Board Member, Wyandatte Hotel Corp. and Kansas City Board of Public Utilities

Browne, James H.
Insurance executive, president of American Woodmen's Life Insurance Co., Denver, Colo.

Brown, Tyrone
Vice President, Legal Affairs, Post-Newsweek Stations, Inc., Washington, D.C.
Directorship: Post-Newsweek Stations, Inc.

Cheek, James E.
President, Howard University, Washington, D.C.
Directorship: First National Bank of Washington

Clark, Kenneth B.
Professor of Psychology, College of the City of New York, New York, N.Y.
Directorship: Lincoln Savings Bank

Clark, Mamie Phipps
Executive Director, Northside Center for Child Development, New York, N.Y.
Directorship: American Broadcasting Co.

Coleman, William T., Jr.
Attorney, Dilworth, Paxon, Kalish, Levy & Coleman, Philadelphia, Pa.
Directorships: American Stock Exchange, First Pennsylvania Banking & Trust Co., First Pennsylvania Corp., Pan American World Airways, Inc., Penn Mutual Life Insurance Co., Philadelphia Electric Co., Western Savings Bank

Collins, Dr. Daniel A.
Publishing executive, Harcourt, Brace & Jovanovich, Inc., San Francisco, Cal.
Directorship: Harcourt, Brace & Jovanovich, Inc.

Colston, James A.
President, Bronx Community College; Bronx, N.Y.
Directorship: Dollar Savings Bank

Crawford, Dr. Esque
Physician, Cleveland, Ohio.
Directorship: Hamilton International Corp.

Crosby, Fred M.
Businessman, president and owner of Crosby Furniture Co., Inc. in Cleveland, Ohio.
Board of Directors Member, Ohio Council of Retail Merchants Association and Greater Cleveland Growth Association

Davis, Willie D.
President, Willie Davis Distributing Co., Los Angeles, Cal.
Directorship: J. Schlitz Brewing Co.

Dennard, Cleveland L.
President, Washington Technical Institute; Washington, D.C.
Directorship: Chesapeake & Potomac Telephone Co.

Duncan, Charles T.
Attorney, Epstein, Friedman & Duncan; Washington, D.C.
Directorship: National Bank of Washington

Edwards, Nelson Jack
Labor union official, is an international vice president of United Auto Workers in Detroit, Mich.
Executive Board Member, United Auto Workers, International

Elam, Lloyd C.
President, Meharry Medical College; Nashville, Tenn.
Directorship: Kraftco Corp.

Eskridge, Chauncey
Attorney, McCoy, Ming & Black; Chicago, Ill.
Directorship: Amalgamated Trust & Savings Bank

Evans, Robert
Personnel Director, Philadelphia National Bank, Philadelphia, Pa.
Directorship: Gino's, Inc.

Eversley, Frederick W.
Contractor, Frederick W. Eversley Co., Inc., New York, N.Y.
Directorship: Empire Savings Bank

Foster, Luther H.
President, Tuskegee Institute; Tuskegee, Ala.
Directorship; Teachers Insurance & Annuity Assn.

Franklin, John Hope
Professor of History, University of Chicago, Chicago, Ill.
Directorship: Illinois Bell Telephone Co.

Gibson, Paul
Vice President—Urban and Environmental Affairs, American Airlines, Inc.; New York, N.Y.
Directorship: Flagship International, Inc.

Graves, Earl G.
Publisher, Earl G. Graves Publishing Co., Inc., New York, N.Y.
Directorship: Liggett & Myers Cigarette & Tobacco Co.

Griffin, Gilroye A., Jr.
Vice President—Corporate Administration and Associate General Counsel, Kenyon & Eckhardt Advertising Co., New York, N.Y.
Directorship: Kenyon & Eckhardt Advertising Co.

Guscott, Kenneth I.
Contractor, Ken Guscott Associates, Boston, Mass.
Directorship: Boston Edison Co.

Hagans, Theodore R., Jr.
President, Hagans Management Co., Washington, D.C.
Directorship: Potomac Electric Power Co.

Harps, William S.
First Vice President—John R. Pinkett, Inc., Washington, D.C.
Directorships: National Bank of Washington, Perpetual Building Savings & Loan Assn.

Harris, Patricia R.
Former U.S. Ambassador to Luxembourg; Attorney, Fried, Frank, Harris, Shriver & Kampelman, Washington, D.C.
Directorships: Chase Manhattan Bank, International Business Machines Corp., National Bank of Washington, Scott Paper Co.

Haynes, Ulric St. Clair, Jr.
Vice President—Management Development, Cummins Engine Co., Columbus, Ind.
Directorships: Marine Midland Bank, Union Mutual Stock Life Insurance Co.

Haysbert, Raymond V., Sr.
Executive Vice President, H.G. Parks, Inc., Baltimore, Md.

Directorships: Equitable Bancorporation, Equitable Trust Co.

Henderson, Vivian W.
President, Clark College, Atlanta, Ga.
Directorship: Teachers Insurance & Annuity Assn.

Henry, Ragan A.
Attorney, Goodis, Greenfield, Henry, Shaiman & Levin, Philadelphia, Pa.
Directorship: Continental Bank.

Hill, Jesse, Jr.
President, Atlanta Life Insurance Co., Atlanta, Ga.
Directorship: Rich's, Inc.

Holland, Jerome
Former U.S. Ambassador to Sweden; New York, N.Y.
Directorships: American Telephone & Telegraph Co., Chrysler Corp., Continental Corp., Federated Department Stores, Inc., General Cigars Co., Inc., General Foods Corp., Manufacturers Hanover Trust Co., New York Stock Exchange, Union Carbide Corp.

Hubert, Frank
President, Hubert Enterprises, Inc., Newark, N.J.
Directorship: Barton Savings & Loan Assn.

Hudson, Roy D.
President, Hampton Institute, Hampton, Va.
Directorship: Chesapeake & Potomac Telephone Co.

Hughes, Joyce
Associate Professor of Law, University of Minnesota Law School, Minneapolis, Minn.
Directorship: First Plymouth National Bank

Hutcherson, Carl B.,
President, Carl B. Hutcherson Funeral Home, Lynchburg, Va.
Directorship: Fidelity National Bank

Johnson, George E.
President, Johnson Products, Inc., Chicago, Ill.
Directorships: Commonwealth Edison Co., Metropolitan Life Insurance Co.

Johnson, John H.
Publisher, Johnson Publishing Co., Chicago, Ill.
Directorships: Marina City Bank, Twentieth Century-Fox Film Corp. Arthur D. Little, Inc.

Jordan, Vernon E., Jr.
Executive Director, National Urban League, New York, N.Y.

Directorships: Bankers Trust Co., Bankers Trust New York Corp., Celanese Corp.

Kennedy, William J., III
President, North Carolina Mutual Life Insurance Co., Durham, N.C.
Directorships: National Broadcasting Co., RCA Corp.

Lawson, Belford, Jr.
Attorney, Lawson, Lawson, Nesbit, Taylor & Phillipps, Washington, D.C.
Directorship: Chesapeake & Potomac Telephone Co.

Lucy, William
International Secretary-Treasurer, American Federation of State, County and Municipal Employees, Washington, D.C.
Directorship: National Bank of Washington

Martin, Louis E.
Vice President and Editorial Director, Chicago Daily Defender; Chicago, Ill.
Directorships: Amalgamated Trust & Savings Bank, Chicago City Bank & Trust Co.

McDougald, Cornelius C.
Attorney; New York, N.Y.
Directorship: New York Bank of Savings

McLin, C.J., Jr.
Legislator, is a state representative in Ohio (Democratic, Dayton).
Board Member, Unity State Bank in Dayton, Ohio

Mitchell, Benson Doyle
Bank executive, is president and chairman of the board of directors of the Industrial Bank of Washington, D.C.
Secretary and Board Member, Northwest Securities Investors, Inc.

Morsell, John A.
Administrator, is assistant executive director of the NAACP
Member, New York City Board of Higher Education

Newman, Cecil
Publisher and Editor, Minneapolis Spokesman, Minneapolis, Minn.
Directorship: Midwest Federal Savings & Loan Assn.

Norford, George
Vice President, Westinghouse Broadcasting Co., New York, N.Y.
Directorship: Westinghouse Broadcasting Co.

Officer, Marion E.
Mortician, Officer Funeral Home, East St. Louis, Ill.

Directorship: Union National Bank

Owens, Sebastian C.
Executive Director, Urban League of Colorado, Denver, Colo.
Directorship: Mountain States Bell Telephone Co.

Parks, Henry G.
President and Chairman of the Board, H.G. Park, Inc., Baltimore, Md.
Directorships: First Pennsylvania Corp., Macrodyne-Chatillon Corp., Magnavox Co.

Patrick, William T., Jr.
Director, Community Relations, American Telephone & Telegraph Co., New York, N.Y.
Directorship: Manufacturers National Bank of Detroit

Pelham, Alfred M.
Insurance executive (ret.); Detroit, Mich.
Directorship: Michigan Consolidated Gas Co.

Peterson, Gerard M.
Assistant Dean for Placement, Graduate School of Business, Stanford University, Palo Alto, Cal.
Directorship: Hubbard & Co.

Phillips, Ralph L.
International Public Affairs Advisor, Mobil Oil Corp., New York, N.Y.
Directorship: DPF, Inc.

Pierce, Samuel R., Jr.
Attorney, Battle, Fowler, Lidstone, Jaffin, Pierce & Kheel, New York, N.Y.
Directorships: International Basic Economy Corp., International Paper Co., Prudential Insurance Co., U.S. Industries, Inc.

Poole, Cecil F.
Attorney, Jacobs, Sills & Coblentz, San Francisco, Cal.
Directorships: Dukor Modular Systems, Levi Strauss & Co.

Price, Albert H.
Vice President—Service, Ronson Co.; Woodbridge, N.J.
Directorship: First National Bank

Price, Judith
Business executive
Vice president and director of James B. Beam Import, Corp., a subsidiary of James B. Beam Distilling Co. in New York, N.Y.

Robbins, Millard D., Jr.
President , Robbins Mortgage Co., Chicago, Ill.
Directorship: Peoples Gas Co.

Robertson, Mary Ella
Professor of Social Service, Indiana University, Indianapolis, Ind.
Directorship: John Hancock Mutual Life Insurance Co.

Shaw, Leslie N.
President and Chairman of the Board, First City Savings & Loan Assn., Los Angeles, Cal.
Directorships: First City Savings & Loan Assn., Lockheed Aircraft Corp.

Shropshire, Thomas B.
Vice President—Marketing and Planning, Miller Brewing Co., Milwaukee, Wis.
Directorship: Miller Brewing Co.

Spaulding, Asa T.
Insurance executive (ret.), Durham, N.C.
Directorship: W. T. Grant Co.

Storey, Robert D.
Attorney, Burke, Haber & Berick, Cleveland, Ohio
Directorship: Capital National Bank

Sullivan, Rev. Leon H.
Zion Baptist Church, Philadelphia, Pa.
Directorships: General Motors Co., Girard Co., Philadelphia Saving Fund Society

Taylor, Hobart, Jr.
Attorney, Dawson, Quinn, Riddell, Taylor & Davis, Washington, D.C.
Directorships: Aetna Life & Casualty, Great Atlantic & Pacific Tea Co., Standard Oil Co., Westinghouse Electric Corp.

Thomas, Franklin A.
President, Bedford-Stuyvesant Restoration Corp., Brooklyn, N.Y.
Directorships: Columbia Broadcasting System, Inc., Cummins Engine Co., First National City Corp., New York Life Insurance Co.

Thomas, James S.
Bishop, United Methodist Church, Des Moines, Iowa.
Directorship: Equitable Life Insurance Co. of Iowa

Walker, The Rt. Reverend John Thomas
Clergyman, in 1971 became suffragan bishop of the Episcopal Diocese of Washington, D.C.
Chairman of the Boards of Trustees, St. Paul's School in New Hampshire and National Cathedral School for Girls in Washington, D.C.

Watson, Barbara
Federal official, is administrator of the Bureau

of Security and Consular Affairs of the U.S. State Department in Washington, D.C.
Board of Directors Member, United Mutual Life Insurance Co.

Weaver, Robert C.
Distinguished Professor of Urban Affairs, Hunter College, New York, N.Y.
Directorships: Bowery Savings Bank, Metropolitan Life Insurance Co.

Wharton, Clifton R., Jr.
President, Michigan State University, East Lansing, Mich.
Directorships: Burroughs Corp., Equitable Life Assurance Society, Ford Motor Co.

Williams, Franklin H.
President, Phelps-Stokes Fund, New York, N.Y.
Directorship: Consolidated Edison Co.

Wilson, Charles Z.
Vice Chancellor of Academic Programs, University of California, Los Angeles, Cal.
Directorship: Teachers Insurance & Annuity Assn.

Wood, Thomas A.
President, TAW International Leasing, Inc., New York, N.Y.
Directorship: Chase Manhattan Corp.

Yerby, Dr. Alonzo S.
Head, Dept. of Health Services Administration, Harvard University, Boston, Mass.
Directorship: Arthur D. Little, Inc.

Young, Mrs. Whitney M., Jr.
New Rochelle, N.Y.
Directorship: Philip Morris, Inc.

Source: *The Ebony Success Library,* Vol. 1, 1,000 Successful Blacks.

BLACK CONSUMER MARKET

The black consumer market comprised in 1971 approximately 23 million potential customers for a variety of goods and services. For these goods and services, this segmented market had in 1971 dollars $38.6 billion a year disposable income. Over 75 percent of the black population lives in the urban communities of the nation. Over one quarter of the consumers in the top 100 U.S. cities are black.

Big volume central city retailers insist on quick turnover and profits from national brands displayed on their shelves. Otherwise, valuable shelf space is made available to faster moving brands of competitors. Often these are the chain's own private labels which rival national brands in their sales impact. A brand cannot remain number one in sales in most of the nation's top 100 central city markets without black consumer support. These consumers constitute 40% to 95% of the retailer's customers.

As a result of action on the part of groups such as Rev. Jesse Jackson's Operation PUSH, The National Welfare Rights Organization, and other consumer-oriented groups such as those led by Florynce Kennedy, Ralph Nader and Betty Furness, consumer legislation geared toward "Truth in Lending," "Truth in Packaging," etc., has served to heighten the awareness factor of all consumers, and made him more aware of his rights. Class actions against purveyors of shoddy merchandise and "quick turnover" merchants have been undertaken, whether the items sold are on used car lots or by fast-talking door-to-door huckstering of other merchandise.

The result of the abuse of the consumer over the past several decades is stronger protective legislation at both national and local levels.

Usurious interest rates, contract buying and other pitfalls of "on-time" purchasing have received the attention of legal aid groups oriented to the low-income resident of ghetto areas, whether black, Spanish-speaking or white. It has not been uncommon for the big city ghetto dweller to pay as much as 100% over the list price for an item, such as a washing machine, television, stereo or freezer, while his counterpart shopping in the suburbs, or at the major retail outlet with standard interest and credit rates, paid the suggested retail price. The consumer with need to buy, and limited access to good credit sources, such as credit unions or banks, is still vulnerable. For in spite of the continuing exploitation of the black consumer, he is still the most sought after in the marketplace because he is willing to try new products and to consistently seek to upgrade his lifestyle with the acquisition of furniture, cars and appliances, travel, clothing and personal care items.

*Source: An Insight into the Black Community

THE TOP 100 BLACK BUSINESSES

The 100 leading black-owned or managed businesses represented on the charts that appear on the following pages are the result of intensive research by the staff of *Black Enterprise Magazine* to identify firms whose sales volume for the calendar year 1972 was in excess of one million dollars.

In compiling this comprehensive list of the top 100 black manufacturing and service companies in the country, *Black Enterprise* enlisted the assistance of every major minority economic development organization in the country, as well as such national organizations as the National Business League, the National Urban League, and the Interracial Council for Business Opportunity. Governmental agencies such as the Department of Commerce, the Department of Treasury and the Federal Reserve Board System have also been of invaluable assistance.

For the most part, these businesses are substantially different from businesses usually found on such national listings. With two exceptions, they are privately, not publicly owned. As such, their gross income—and particularly their net profits—is a private matter. In developing this list, that privacy has been respected.

Name of Company	Location	Chief Executive Officer	Type of Business	Year Started	Number of Em-ployees	Sales 1972*
MOTOWN INDUSTRIES	Los Angeles, California	Berry Gordy	Manufactures master recordings, disc and tape recordings	1949	325	$40.0
JOHNSON PUBLISHING CO., INC.	Chicago, Illinois	John H. Johnson	Publisher of "Ebony," "Jet," "Black World," "Black Stars," "Ebony Jr."	1942	245	23.1
FEDCO FOODS CORP.	New York, New York	J. Bruce Llewellyn	Supermarket chain	1969	450	23.0
F. W. EVERSLEY & CO. INC.	New York, New York	Frederick W. Eversley	General contractor and developer	1964	85	20.6
BOWERS REALTY & INVESTMENT CO.	Detroit, Michigan	France Bowers	Real estate	1968	30	18.0
JOHNSON PRODUCTS CO., INC.	Chicago, Illinois	George E. Johnson	Manufactures hair care products and facial cosmetics	1954	300	17.5
AL JOHNSON CADILLAC, INC.	Chicago, Illinois	Albert W. Johnson, Sr.	Retail sale and service of new and used Cadillacs	1967	104	14.5
H. G. PARKS, INC.	Baltimore, Maryland	Henry G. Parks	Processes sausage and pork products	1951	265	13.8
CAPITOL CITY LIQUOR CO., INC.	Washington, D.C.	Chester Carter	Wholesale distributor of wines and liquors	1970	60	12.5
GARLAND FOODS, INC.	Dallas, Texas	Mildren M. Montgomery	Meat processor	1969	180	12.0
TAW INTERNATIONAL LEASING, INC.	New York, New York	Thomas A. Wood	International leasor of capital equipment	1968	38	10.6
WRIGHT FORD SALES, INC.	Marina Del Rey, California	A. Gordon Wright	Automobile dealership and service	1967	89	10.3
STAX RECORD CO., INC.	Memphis, Tennessee	Al Bell	Manufactures records	1959	150	10.0
MYERS CENTURY CHEVROLET, INC.	Upper Darby, Pennsylvania	Robert Myers	Automobile dealership	1971	60	8.0
E. G. BOWMAN CO., INC.	New York, New York	Ernesta Procope	Insurance brokerage agency	1953	18	7.5
CONYERS FORD, INC.	Detroit, Michigan	Nathan Conyers	Automobile and truck dealership	1970	74	7.1
VIP LINCOLN-MERCURY, INC.	New Rochelle, New York	Daniel E. Brown Ronald Wayne	Automobile dealership	1965	30	7.0
WILSON-MC INTOSH BUICK, INC.	Washington, D.C.	Maurice McIntosh Joseph Wilson	Automobile dealership	1970	75	7.0
DRUMMOND DISTRIBUTING CO., INC.	Compton, California	Lancelot Drummond	Wholesale liquor distributor	1969	33	6.0
BILL NELSON CHEVROLET, INC.	Richmond, California	Bill Nelson	Automobile dealership	1969	60	6.0
P. B. DEVELOPMENT CO., INC.	Tucson, Arizona	Nathaniel Russell Peggy Brown	General contractor and project developer	1970	20	6.0
H. J. RUSSELL & CO.	Atlanta, Georgia	H. J. Russell	General contractor and project developer	1959	500	6.0
TRANS-BAY ENGINEERS AND BUILDERS, INC.	Oakland, California	Ray Dones	General contractor	1969	70	6.0
SUSSEX RECORDS, INC./ INTERIOR MUSIC CORP.	Los Angeles, California	Clarence Avant	Manufactures records, publishes music	1970	14	5.3

*In Millions

Name of Company	Location	Chief Executive Officer	Type of Business	Year Started	Number of Employees	Sales 1972*
PORTERFIELD WILSON PONTIAC, INC.	Detroit, Michigan	Porterfield Wilson	Automobile dealership	1972	52	5.3
A. L. NELLUM & ASSOCIATES, INC.	Washington, D.C.	Albert Nellum	Management and urban consultants	1964	100	5.0
W. T. SYPHAX ENGINEERING & CONSTRUCTION CO.	Arlington, Virginia	William T. Syphax	General contractor and developer	1953	12	5.0
TUESDAY PUBLICATIONS, INC.	New York, New York	W. Leonard Evans, Jr.	Publisher of "Tuesday" and "Tuesday at Home" magazines	1965	41	5.0
WATTS MANUFACTURING CORP.	Lynwood, California	Mark E. Rivers	Manufactures fabrics and metal products	1966	325	4.9
ALL-PRO ENTERPRISES, INC.	Pittsburgh, Pennsylvania	Brady Keys	Hamburger and chicken franchise	1967	675	4.5
CLARENCE S. CARTER CHEVROLET, INC.	Detroit, Michigan	Clarence S. Carter	Automobile dealership	1970	43	4.5
WILLIE DAVIS DISTRIBUTING CO.	Los Angeles, California	Willie Davis	Wholesale beer distributor	1970	35	4.5
JOE LOUIS MILK CO., INC.	Chicago, Illinois	Mr. and Mrs. George Jones	Wholesale dairy distributor	1935	35	4.2
FRIENDLY CHRYSLER PLYMOUTH, INC.	Los Angeles, California	Herbert Stephenson	Automobile dealership	1970	52	4.0
FIESTA LINCOLN-MERCURY, INC.	New York, New York	William Phillips	Automobile dealership	1971	29	3.5
TRAVIS REALTY CO., INC.	Chicago, Illinois	Dempsey Travis	Real estate	1949	40	3.5
T.W.O./HILLMAN'S, INC.	Chicago, Illinois	Lawrence W. Carroll	Supermarket	1970	50	3.3
TINSLEY BUICK, INC.	Redwood City, California	Bill and Donald Tinsley	Automobile dealership	1971	38	3.1
AFRO-AMERICAN NEWSPAPER COMPANY OF BALTIMORE	Baltimore, Maryland	Frances L. Murphy, II	Publisher of "The Afro-American" newspapers	1892	200	3.0
CALIFORNIA GOLDEN OAK PRODUCTS, INC.	Los Angeles, California	William M. Alexander, Jr.	Manufactures wooden office furniture	1968	130	3.0
ROBERTS MOTELS, INC.	Chicago, Illinois	Herman Roberts	Owns and operates motel chain	1960	450	3.0
RENMUTH, INC.	Detroit, Michigan	Robert Renfroe	Manufactures metal stampings and fabrication	1969	110	2.8
ALLIANCE FOOD CORP.	Los Angeles, California	Robert E. Bell	Drive-in restaurants	1970	200	2.5
BARRETT GROUP CORP.	New York, New York	Frederick E. Barrett	Manufactures military and commercial electrical equipment	1968	87	2.5
BERTIE INDUSTRIES, INC.	Windsor, North Carolina	Melvin Gillian	Manufactures garments	1966	90	2.5
CLIPPER INTERNATIONAL CORP.	Detroit, Michigan	Samuel Gorman	Manufactures mechanical and electrical components	1962	75	2.5
THE VANGUARD BOND & MORTGAGE CO.	St. Louis, Missouri	James Hurt	Manages multi-family housing for federal programs	1968	8	2.5
AMNEWS, INC.	New York, New York	Clarence B. Jones	Publisher of "The New York Amsterdam News"	1909	125	2.4
FUTON CORP.	Columbus, Ohio	Howard Spiller	Machine shop operation and drafting service	1970	44	2.4
LOWERY DISTRIBUTING CO., INC.	Chicago, Illinois	Mannie Lowery	Wholesale beer distributor	1969	16	2.4
AVI MANUFACTURING, INC.	Gardena, California	E. E. Barrington	Manufactures aircraft, electrical and mechanical sub-assemblies	1971	125	2.3
EBONY OIL CORP.	New York, New York	Lawrence J. Cormier	Retail fuel and oil	1954	47	2.3
ELECTORQUE ASSOCIATES, INC.	New York, New York	David Blaine	Electrical contractor	1968	72	2.3
LAWNDALE PACKAGING CORP.	Chicago, Illinois	William Franklin	Manufactures corrugated boxes	1970	55	2.3
HORACE NOBLE LINCOLN-MERCURY, INC.	Chicago, Illinois	Horace Noble	Automobile dealership	1971	33	2.3
PROGRESS AEROSPACE ENTERPRISES, INC.	Philadelphia, Pennsylvania	Fred Miller	Manufactures electronic and mechanical assemblies and cable design	1968	150	2.3

*In Millions

Name of Company	Location	Chief Executive Officer	Type of Business	Year Started	Number of Employees	Sales 1972*
ROBERT S. ABBOTT PUBLISHING CO., INC.	Chicago, Illinois	John H. Sengstacke	Publisher of "The Chicago Daily Defender"	1905	65	2.0
R. A. BANKS CONSTRUCTION CO., INC.	Atlanta, Georgia	Rubin A. Banks	General contractor	1965	18	2.0
CAMPBELL & MACSAI ARCHITECTS, INC.	Chicago, Illinois	Wendell J. Campbell	Architectural firm	1970	35	2.0
CENTRAL NEWS— WAVE PUBLICATIONS	Los Angeles, California	Chester L. Washington	Publisher of "The Southwest Wave" and seven other newspapers	1971	80	2.0
GLOPAK CORP.	Passaic, New Jersey	Harold Martin	Manufactures plastic bags	1966	50	2.0
HENDERSON TRAVEL SERVICE, INC.	Atlanta, Georgia	Jacob R. Henderson	Travel agency	1955	18	2.0
HOLLINGSWORTH GROUP, INC.	New York, New York	Edward Lewis	Publisher of "Essence" Magazine	1970	28	2.0
INTER-CITY CONTRACTORS SERVICE, INC.	Gary, Indiana	Larry Webb	General contractor	1969	12	2.0
LANCE INVESTIGATION SERVICE, INC.	New York, New York	Ralph Johnson	Security service	1962	300	2.0
MAGNIFICENT PRODUCTS, INC.	Los Angeles, California	Wilbur Jackson Dennis Taylor	Manufactures cosmetics	1965	42	2.0
SUMMIT LABORATORIES, INC.	Indianapolis, Indiana	Melvin Carroll	Manufactures cosmetics	1957	86	2.0
SUPERIOR TOOL, INC.	Fort Worth, Texas	Otis J. Martin	Machine shop	1970	30	2.0
W. T. SYPHAX MANAGEMENT CO.	Arlington, Virginia	William Syphax	Apartment management	1950	20	2.0
TRUE TRANSPORT, INC.	Newark, New Jersey	Leamon McCoy	Interstate trucking	1968	55	2.0
VASSALL MOTORS, INC.	Philadelphia, Pennsylvania	Ivan Vassall	Automobile dealership	1969	47	2.0
ONE AMERICA, INC.	Washington, D.C.	Elaine B. Jenkins	Management and urban consultants	1970	22	1.9
ALL-STAINLESS, INC.	Boston, Massachusetts	Mr. and Mrs. Albert Livingston E. V. Roundtree	Distributor of stainless steel products	1952	30	1.8
CLEAN-RITE MAINTENANCE CO., INC.	Washington, D.C.	Nathaniel D. Williams	Janitorial maintenance service	1969	155	1.8
AULT, INC.	Minneapolis, Minnesota	Luther Prince	Manufactures electrical components and custom systems	1960	125	1.7
EARL G. GRAVES PUBLISHING CO., INC.	New York, New York	Earl G. Graves	Publisher of "Black Enterprise" Magazine	1970	30	1.7
VANGUARD VOLKSWAGEN	St. Louis, Missouri	James Hurt	Automobile dealership	1970	23	1.7
ENTERPLASTICS INDUSTRIES, INC.	San Francisco, California	Dr. Henry Lucas	Manufactures industrial plastic moldings	1969	25	1.6
FIGHTON, INC.	Rochester, New York	William M. McGhee, Jr.	Manufactures electronic equipment, metal stampings and special orders	1968	85	1.6
OZANNE CONSTRUCTION CO., INC.	Cleveland, Ohio	Leroy Ozanne	General Contractor	1956	8	1.6
COMPETITION MOTORS, LTD., INC.	Chicago, Illinois	Robert P. Neal	Automobile dealership	1967	17	1.5
J. W. M. CORP.	Philadelphia, Pennsylvania	J. J. Williams	Manufactures microcircuit components and custom systems	1969	135	1.5
PASCHAL BROTHERS ENTERPRISES	Atlanta, Georgia	James and Robert Paschal	Hotel, restaurant and lounge	1947	110	1.5
SUPER PRIDE MARKET	Baltimore, Maryland	Charles Burns	Supermarket	1970	58	1.5
YEATMAN CENTRAL CITY FOODS, INC.	St. Louis, Missouri	James Hurt	Retail food	1969	25	1.5
COMPONENT CONCEPTS CORP.	Omaha, Nebraska	Joseph W. Saunders	Manufactures electronic components	1968	47	1.4
GROVE FRESH DISTRIBUTORS, INC.	Chicago, Illinois	Cecil Troy	Fruit juice, salad and dessert distributor	1961	23	1.3

*In Millions

Reprinted by permission from Earl G. Graves Publishing Co., Inc.

BUSINESS CHRONOLOGY: 1969–1973

1969

JULY

11   Philip Pruitt, black head of the Administrations Minority Business Program announced his resignation and charged that it was due to President Nixon's failure to make good on campaign promises to advance black capitalism programs. He said, "There's been lots of rhetoric in government about helping blacks, but no money has been forthcoming." Pruitt, who took office March 21, complained that action on a Treasury Department proposal to expand loans to minority businesses to about $370 million in fiscal 1969 had been delayed and that the "credibility gap is growing wider as far as blacks are concerned."

22   The House Select Committee on Small Business began an inquiry into the policies and activities of the Small Business Administration (SBA). The hearings, which concentrated on the impact of SBA programs to aid minority businessmen, were called following the resignation of Philip Pruitt, head of the SBA minority entrepreneur program. The agency had come under attack earlier in the Nixon Administration when SBA loans to a Mafia-linked leasing company had been disclosed and when a top SBA official had been dismissed following charges that he had engaged in "shakedowns of SBA loan recipients."

AUGUST

17   The SBA announced that the agency had made 4,331 loans totaling $100.7 million to members of minority groups since its program to aid minority businessmen began Aug. 13, 1968. Hilary J. Sandoval, the SBA administrator, predicted that the number of loans under the program, Operation Business Mainstream, would double during the next 12 months.

1970

FEBRUARY

13   Joseph L. Searles, III, a former New York director for local business development and other urban problems in New York City government began training as a floor partner in the firm of Newburger, Loeb and Co., thus becoming the first black member of the New York Stock Exchange.

MARCH

20   In a special message submitted to congress, President Richard Nixon proposed that special assistance be given to American small businesses, and he requested that permission be granted to banks to act as sole sponsors of a minority business enterprise under the MESBIC program of the Office of Minority Business Enterprise. Other requests which had relevance for minority entrepreneurs:

•   Authorization for the Small Business Administration to make direct grants to borrowers to avoid high interest rates during the first three years of the loan;

•   Extension of the SBA loan-guarantee program to foundations, pension funds, trusts and community groups;

•   A more liberal provision for small businesses to be treated like partnerships for tax purposes;

•   Permission for business losses to be carried forward for a ten year instead of five year period;

•   A management training program for entrepreneurs;

•   Federal assistance to offset "extraordinary cost of training employees until they become fully productive.

MAY

30   General Motors announced that its minority hiring was up 184% since 1965 and that minority workers made up 62% of the 5,333 employees hired since 1965.

DECEMBER

17   Maurice H. Stans, Secretary of Commerce, announced that the economic slump was primarily responsible for the slow progress of a major feature of the Nixon Administration's program to finance minority businesses. Stans indicated that the progress of MESBIC (Minority Enterprise Small Business Investment Companies) had been disappointing, but that as of June 30, 1970, a total of 25 small companies instead of 100 had been established under the program, nationwide. He indicated, however, that more than 100 committments had been made to black entrepreneurs for participation under the program.

1971

JANUARY

26   President Nixon submitted a proposal to Congress requesting "seed" capital for minority business.

SEPTEMBER

17   Acting Urban League executive director

Harold R. Sims, testifying before the Joint Economic Committee charged the economic program of the Nixon administration with doing "little to help the blacks and the poor." And he warned that "any more dramatic domestic policies which favor the rich over the poor will not be tolerated by the general public, which has to support the program if it is to work."

SEPT. 29-OCT. 3

The Third Black Economic and Business Exposition of Reverend Jesse Jacksons' Chicago based SCLC Operation Breadbasket was held in Chicago.

OCTOBER

13 Nixon announced new plans to aid black and minority business and that *39* MESBICS were operating, up 14 since the Stans report of December, 1970.

1972

FEBRUARY

15 The Administration announced that aid to minority business rose from 200 million in 1969 to 360 million in 1971, while federally aided low and middle-income starts rose from 156,000 in 1969 to an anticipated 566,000 in 1973.

MARCH

10-12 One proposal on the agenda of the National Black Political Convention which met in Gary, Ind., dealt with a proposal to ask for a presidential commission to explore procedures for "an appropriate reparations payment in terms of land, capital and cash," for the black community. Another proposal requested a $5 billion national black development agency (such as AID) to foster black ownership of business, media housing, schools and health facilities, and called for an urban homestead act to distribute land and housing.

SEPTEMBER

21-31 The Fourth annual Black Expo held under the auspices of Operation Push, drew over 700,000 visitors and grossed about $500,000. Rev. Jesse L. Jackson, President of PUSH, said that the boycott and picketing tactics of PUSH had obtained over $100 million in commitments from major corporations and banks in the form of hiring and promotion, deposits in black banks and contracts with black suppliers.* Some 500 companies, black and white, exhibited. Among the major corporations signing covenants with Operation Push were Joseph Schlitz Brewing Company of

Milwaukee, Wisconsin and the General Foods Corporation.

OCTOBER

James H. Gary, Sr., Washington, D.C., businessman, became the first black to own a Firestone Tire and Rubber franchise in Washington. He started his business with an $8,000 investment of his own and $110,000 SBA guaranteed loan. He employes six people in a building that accommodates showroom and service area.

NOVEMBER

29 Two major cable television franchisers and a coalition of 16 minority group organizations announced an agreement in San Francisco that would give to the groups control of several cable channels and permit the training of blacks and other minorities in broadcast skills. Cox Communications and the American Television Communication, Inc. said the plan would be effective upon completion of pending merger plans. The 16 minority groups involved in the agreement included the Black Panther Party, the western office of the NAACP and the Mexican-American Political Alliance. The new company would provide over a five-year period, up to three full-time channels in each of their eight California franchise areas at token fees of $1.00 each per year to non-profit minority organizations, provide all necessary video equipment in four of the areas, and begin training individuals in technical and program skills.

DECEMBER

30 PUSH opened a drive in Miami Beach Hotels to hire blacks to fill 15% of their jobs and to give 15% of their banking, laundry and other service business to black-owned businesses.

1973

JANUARY

29 In the Administration budget submitted to Congress for fiscal 1974, President Nixon asked for a modification of planned expansion in the area of the minority business enterprise program due to recent rapid growth in program and need to evaluate effectiveness. Major antipoverty efforts and landmark education-aid legislation was eliminated or reduced in the Nixon budget.

MARCH

2 Andrew F. Brimmer, a member of the Federal Reserve Board, said in a lecture at the University of California at Los Angeles that while black income contin-

ued to rise in 1972, unemployment remained a major problem, especially among youths. Blacks suffered disproportionately from the 1969–70 recession, with sharply increased joblessness among women and youths, so that "blacks suffered all of the recession-induced decline in jobs, while whites made further net job gains." According to Brimmer, unemployment among black youths had actually increased in the 1971–72 expansion, rising to 35.9% of the work force in the fourth quarter of 1972.

Among other points, Brimmer cited evidence that blacks earned as large a percentage of their income through jobs as whites, to refute charges of "excessive" dependence on welfare.

6   Black businessmen charged that proposed changes in requirements for certain federal aid to minority business enterprises would seriously damage one of the most successful of the minority business programs.

The Small Business Administration announced that day it proposed to require that businesses put under the "set-aside" program, under which federal contracts were reserved for minority businesses, would have to be both owned and controlled by minority group members. In the past, businesses could qualify, under an Executive order, if they were either minority owned or controlled.

The new rule would require that minority group members own 60% of the stock or partnerships of the company, and the company be financed by non-disadvantaged persons who held an interest. Theodore A. Adams Jr., executive director of the National Association of Black Manufacturers, said the rules would severely restrict white participation, and "would destroy the program."

Section IX

EMPLOYMENT AND LABOR

EMPLOYMENT AND LABOR

Since the mid 1960s, substantial gains have been made in narrowing the gap between the median income of black and white families. In 1971, the ratio of black to white family income was 60 percent, a noticeable increase over the 1964 ratio of 54 percent. No significant narrowing of the income differential was observed between families of black and other races and white families during the 13-year period preceding 1964.

Between 1970 and 1971, there was no significant change in the income ratio of black to white families.

Over the past 23 years, the median incomes of families of black and other races have increased proportionately more than those of whites in a vain effort to eliminate the 40 to 50% gap. The median income of blacks and other races increased by 132 percent compared with 87 percent for white families. With the rising median incomes for black and other races, there has been a shift in the income distribution as exhibited by the reduction in the proportion of families of blacks and other races with incomes under $3,000, and the corresponding increase in the percent with incomes $10,000 and over. In 1970, about one-fifth of the families were in the under $3,000 class, compared to 54 percent in 1947.

The dollar gap (adjusted for price changes) between black and other races and white families has widened—from $2,700, in 1947 to $3,700 in 1970.

The proportion of families of black and other races in the $10,000 and over income class has steadily increased since the early 1960s. In 1970, approximately 28 percent were at this income level, which was substantially greater than the 11 percent in 1960. About half of the white families had incomes of $10,000 or more in 1970.

In the North and West, about 38 percent of the families of black and other races were in the $10,000 and over income group in 1970. The comparable figure was about 18 percent for the South.

In both 1959 and 1971, the median income of black families was closer to that of white families in the North and West than was the case in the South. The ratio of black to white family income in 1971 was about 69 percent in the North and West, and 56 percent in the South.

Although the ratio of black to white income was lower in the South than in the North and West in 1959 and 1971, the ratio in the South had increased since 1959. On the other hand, there was no significant change in the ratio for the North and West during the same period.

In 1970, the relative disparity in incomes between black and white families was smaller for husband-wife families than for other types of families (most of which were headed by a woman). The same pattern was observed in the North and West, where the ratio of black to white income for husband-wife families was about 88 percent in 1970. There was no apparent difference in 1970 between the incomes of black and white husband-wife families outside the South, where the head was under 35 years old. In these young families, the ratio of black to white median income was approximately 96 percent in 1970, a significant increase over the 78 percent in 1959. However, these young black families in the North and West, whose incomes were about equal to those of whites, comprised a relatively small proportion, 10 percent, of the 4.9 million black families in the country in March, 1971.

An important part of the explanation of the narrowing gap between black and white family incomes is the working wife. The income parity observed for young black and white families in the North and West holds true only for families in which both the husband and wife worked. For these families, the ratio of black to white income was about 104 percent in 1970; the comparable figure was 85 percent in 1959. In contrast, no gains were made in closing the income gap by young black families in which only the husband worked in the North and West. In both 1970 and 1959, these black young families were making only about three-fourths as much money as comparable white families in the North and West.

In 1970 and 1959, black wives were more likely than white wives to have worked. In the North and West, the number of young black families in which both the husband and wife worked has increased by about 95 percent since 1959. By 1970, about 63 percent of young black wives in this area contributed to the family income by working, as contrasted to 54 percent for the young white wives.

In 1970, a higher proportion of these young working black wives than the comparable group of white wives held a job the year round. Of those working, approximately 52 percent of the black wives worked all year, compared to only about 36 percent of the white wives.

For the United States as a whole, black wives earned less, on the average, than white wives in 1970 ($3,300 and $3,500, respectively), but their earnings accounted for a greater share of the family income (31 percent and 26 percent, respectively). In contrast, young black wives in the North and West were earning approximately 30 percent more than their white counterparts, as well as making a larger contribution to the family income. The ratio of young wives' earnings to the family income was 35 percent for blacks and 27 percent for whites. In 1959, although young white and black wives earned about the same, there is some evidence that black wives contributed more to their family income than did white wives.

While black wives, overall, earned 95 percent as much as did white wives, the comparable ratio for husbands was only 71 percent. For those young black families in the North and West whose family incomes reached parity with whites and whose wives earned more than did comparable white wives, black husbands' earnings averaged 90 percent of the comparable white husbands' earnings. This represents a major improvement since 1959 when the ratio was 76 percent.

Regardless of race, men have higher incomes than women. However, the disparity in incomes between men and women tended to be less among blacks than among whites. Among year-round, full-time workers, the income of black women averaged about 70 percent that of the black men, while that of white women was about 59 percent of the white men.

While the proportion of both blacks and whites below the low-income level decreased between 1959 and 1971, the decline was greater for whites than for blacks. In 1971, approximately 10 percent of white persons and about 32 percent of black persons were below the low-income level. The comparable figures in 1959 were 18 and 55 percents, respectively. Since 1959, the number of whites below the low-income level dropped by about 37 percent as compared with a 25 percent reduction in the number of blacks.

Between 1970 and 1971, the number of low-income persons did not change. The apparent change between 1970 and 1971 in the number of low-income black persons (from 7.5 to 7.4 million) and the number of white persons below the low-income level (from 17.5 to 17.8 million) was not statistically significant. About 1.5 million black families and 3.8 million white families were below the low-income level in 1971—about 29 percent of all black families and 8 percent of all white families. For low-income families headed by a man, there was no statistically significant difference in the decline since 1959 of 49 percent for whites and 54 percent for blacks. In contrast, the number of low-income white and black families headed by women increased between 1959 and 1971. In 1971, about 54 percent of black families and 27 percent of white families with a female head were below the low-income level.

There was no change between 1970 and 1971 in the number of white and black families below the low-income level.

Blacks comprised about three-tenths of the population below the low-income level in 1971. About one-half of all black persons in 1971 were children under 18 years old. They represented about 37 percent of all low-income children. Aged family heads and unrelated individuals accounted for about 17 percent of whites below the low-income level, whereas the comparable proportion for blacks was about 7 percent.

Between 1959 and 1971, the proportion of persons below the low-income level who were living alone or with nonrelatives increased for both whites and blacks. In 1971, about 12 percent of blacks and 24 percent of whites below the low-income level were unrelated individuals. The comparable figures in 1959 were 8 percent and 18 percent, respectively.

Since 1959, the numbers of persons with income slightly above the low-income level has decreased by three-tenths—from 15.5 million in 1959 to 10.9 million in 1971. Between 1959 and 1971, white persons with incomes between 100 and 125 percent of the low-income level declined by 37 percent, while those of black and other races increased by 20 percent. Accordingly, black and other races as a percent of all persons with incomes slightly above the low-income level increased from 14 percent in 1959 to 23 percent in 1971. The proportion of all children in families with incomes between 100 and 125 percent who were black and other races increased greatly, from about 14 percent in 1959 to 27 percent in 1971.

In 1970 a greater proportion of low-income black families than of all black families were living in the South. About two-thirds of the low-income families resided in the South, but only about half of all black families lived in that region.

In the South, approximately 6 out of every 10 low-income families were living outside metropolitan areas, while in the North and West, the overwhelming majority—9 out of every 10 poor black families—were residents of metropolitan areas.

About 23 percent of all black families in metropolitan areas were below the low-income level in 1970. This rate did not vary significantly by region from the national figure. The low-income rate in the nonmetropolitan areas of the South was 50 percent as compared to 17 percent in the North and West.

Family heads with low educational attainment are more likely to be below the low-income level. This is true regardless of race or sex of head. About one-third of the black male heads and one-fifth of the white male heads with less than 8 years of schooling were below the low-income level in 1970, as compared to about 2 percent for male family heads with 4 years of college or more. The low-income rates for female family heads showed the same type of relationship, but were substantially higher than those for male heads.

The average number of persons per family was larger for black than for white families, both above and below the low-income level. Black families in metropolitan areas were smaller than those outside metropolitan areas, while the size of the average white family did not vary by residence.

Per capita income data permit a relationship to be shown between the incomes of blacks and whites by roughly reducing the effect of differences in average family size for these groups. In 1970, the average income per family member for black families was lower than that for white families, both above and below the low-income level. For low-income families, the average income per family member was $540 for blacks, $40 below the $580 for whites. The corresponding figures for families above the low-income level were $2,330 and $3,500, respectively, a difference of $1,170. The ratio of black to white income per family member was much higher for those families below the low-income level—93 percent, compared to 67 percent for families above the low-income level. The income per family member for blacks came closer to that of whites in metropolitan areas than in nonmetropolitan areas.

About 55 percent of black men and 30 percent of black women, who were heads of low-income families, were employed in 1971. The majority of both black and white men who were heads of low-income families worked at some time during 1970. However, the proportion (67 percent) of black male heads who worked was higher than for the comparable group of whites (61 percent). For both blacks and whites, year-round full-time workers represented about one-fourth of the low-income male family heads.

In March, 1971, about 25 percent of all persons of black and other races and 4 percent of all whites received public assistance or welfare income.

The proportion of all persons of black and

other races receiving Social Security payments (11 percent) was slightly less than that for whites (13 percent).

In 1970, about one-half of the low-income black families and one-third of the black unrelated individuals below the low-income level received public assistance income. The comparable figures for whites were 23 percent and 15 percent, respectively.

In contrast, a greater proportion of low-income whites than blacks received income from Social Security. About one-third of the white families below the low-income level in 1970 received Social Security benefits as compared to approximately one-fourth for black families. Of the 4 million white unrelated individuals below the low-income level, over one-half received Social Security payments. The comparable figure for blacks was 35 percent.

Regardless of race, a higher proportion of low-income families headed by women than headed by men received income from public assistance. Among the low-income families headed by women, about six out of every ten black families and about four out of every ten white families received income from this source.

In 1971 the number of unemployed persons of black and other races rose to .9 million. White unemployment also increased in 1971 to 4.1 million, surpassing the peak year (1961) of the last decade. Proportionately, the increase between 1970 and 1971 in the number of unemployed persons of black and other races was not statistically different from that for whites.

The unemployment rate for both black and other races and for whites declined continually in the 1960s after a sharp rise during the 1961 recession. The jobless rate of persons of black and other races averaged 9.9 in 1971, approximating the 1964 rate, whereas that for whites reached 5.4 percent, the highest level since 1961.

Proportionately, the increase from 1970 to 1971 in unemployment rates for blacks and other races was not statistically different from that for whites. Thus, the ratio of the jobless rate for black and other races to that for whites was unchanged from a 1970 differential of 1.8:1. During the 1960s, this ratio averaged 2.1:1.

Unemployment rates for teenagers were substantially higher than those for adults from 1960 through 1970. In 1971, this pattern continued. The rate in 1971 was highest for teenagers of black and other races, 31.7 percent, which was about double that for white teenagers, 15.1 percent.

Unemployment rates for adult men and

women of both races were up substantially from the 1970 levels.

As with the overall unemployment rates, the rates for married men of black and other races and married white men rose substantially between 1970 and 1971, after a declining trend from 1962 to 1969. The ratio of the unemployment rate for married men of black and other races to that for white married men remained at the 1970 differential of 1.6 to 1.

In 1971, the jobless rate for married men of black and other races, 4.9 percent, was still below the 1962 level. For white married men, the 1971 rate was about the same as the 1962 rate.

In October, 1971, approximately 24 percent of the 1.3 million black teenagers enrolled in school were in the labor force—14 percent were holding a job, and about 9 percent were seeking employment. Of those not enrolled in school, 18 percent were jobless, and the overwhelming majority of these unemployed black teenagers were looking for full-time work. Approximately 38 percent of the teenagers out of school were not in the labor force.

In 1971, the unemployment rate for men of black and other races 20 to 29 years old was 12.9 percent. The unemployment rate for Vietnam era veterans of black and other races appears to be higher than that for nonveterans. Among whites, the unemployment rate in 1971 for the white Vietnam era veteran was higher than that for the nonveteran—8.3 percent for veterans, compared to 6.6 percent for nonveterans.

Workers of black and other races are more likely than white workers to experience long periods of joblessness. In 1971, 2.4 percent of the labor force of black and other races, compared to 1.3 percent of the white labor force, had been jobless for 15 or more weeks. For each of these population groups, long-term unemployment represented about 24 percent of the total unemployment in 1971.

Loss of job as a result of layoff or discharge by employer was still the major reason for unemployment in 1971 for everyone. The largest proportions of unemployed women of black and other races had either lost their last job or were returning to the labor force.

The jobless rate for black and other races in the experienced labor force increased from 8.3 percent in 1970 to 10.0 percent in 1971. Among the workers, a rise in the unemployment rate was noted for black and other races in the professional, technical, craftsmen, operatives, and service occupations.

In both 1970 and 1971, black and other races employed in professional, technical and managerial occupations had the lowest jobless rates. Men of black and other races experienced the highest unemployment rates in nonfarm labor occupations.

Teenagers in the central cities experienced high unemployment rates. Among all metropolitan areas, the unemployment rate in 1971 for teenagers of black and other races was higher in the central cities (36 percent) than in the suburbs (29 percent). The jobless rate for adults living in the central cities was not statistically different from that in the suburbs.

In the 20 largest metropolitan areas, the unemployment rate for men of black and other races in the central cities was similar to that in the suburbs.

In the age groups 25 to 64 years, men of black and other races were less likely than white men to be in the labor force. On the other hand, for these same age groups, the labor force participation of women of black and other races was higher than that of white women.

For both teenage boys and girls, the labor force participation rates were lower for black and other races; for both women and men 20 to 24 years old the rates for black and other races and whites were about the same.

The proportion of men of black and other races in the labor force working year round, full time in 1970 was somewhat less than for white men. About three-fifths of men of black and other races, compared with two-thirds of white men, worked year round, full time.

About the same proportion of women of black and other races and white women worked year round, full time.

In the age groups 25 to 64 years, a larger proportion of men of black and other races than white men were not working because they were physically and mentally unable to work. For both groups (black and other races and whites) similar proportions (about 8 out of 10) of the teenagers not in the labor force were attending school.

About half of both black and white women who were heads of families were in the civilian labor force in March, 1971. About 10 percent of black women who were heads .of families and in the labor force were unemployed. The jobless rate for the comparable group of white women was 6 percent.

During the last 11 years, the number of workers of black and other races employed in the better paying white-collar, craftsmen and operatives occupations increased by 69 percent—from about 3 million in 1960 to about 5 million in 1971. For the white population employed in these jobs, the percentage increase was less, 23 percent between 1960 and 1971.

In 1971, black and other races constituted about 8 percent of employees in the higher skilled, better paying jobs compared to about 6 percent in 1960.

Despite the upgrading of employment for black and other races, marked differences still existed between black and other races and whites in the distribution of employment in 1971. About 13 percent of all employed workers of black and other races held professional, technical and managerial positions, compared with 27 percent for whites. Similarly, among craftsmen and foremen, the proportions were 8 percent for black and other races and 13 percent for whites. About 41 percent of employed persons of black and other races were engaged in service, private household, farm and laboring jobs—about double the 20 percent for whites.

About the same proportion, 13 percent, of men and women of black and other races were in professional, technical and managerial occupations. Higher proportions of white men than white women were in these occupations.

About 33 percent of employed men and about 44 percent of employed women of black and other races were in service, private household, and laborer occupations. Comparable proportions for white men and women were 14 and 20 percents, respectively.

Historically, blacks have been overrepresented in most lower-paying, less-skilled jobs and underrepresented in the better paying, high-skilled jobs. While this is still true, the 1970 census data show that blacks made some advances and are becoming more equally represented in the major occupation groups. In 1970, black workers constituted 10 percent of the employed population, but only 5 percent of the professional workers, 3 percent of managers and administrators, and 6 percent of the craftsmen, as contrasted to 17 percent of service workers (excluding private household), about 20 percent of laborers, and about 50 percent of all private household workers. With the exception of the categories service workers and private household workers, these 1970 figures represent an improvement over corresponding 1960 percentages.

The proportion of black workers of the total employment in the 9 industries with relatively high hourly earnings ranged from 6 to 13 percent in 1970. In spite of this, blacks held no more than 2 percent of the higher paying jobs (professional, technical or managerial) in any of the 9 industries. In all of the 9 industries, blacks were overrepresented in the lower-paying jobs, but their share of the middle-level jobs was more comparable to the proportion that blacks are of all employees.

In each of the 9 industries with high hourly earnings, the proportion of blacks in the highest paid jobs as professional, technical and managerial workers was far below the comparable proportion of all workers.

A higher proportion of blacks than of all workers held middle pay level jobs in all of the industries. In all of the industries, smaller percentages of the black employment were in the craftsmen jobs, the relatively well-paid middle-level jobs.

In the 9 industries with the largest proportion of black workers, blacks held 18 percent of all jobs, but only .5 percent of the higher paid occupations (professional, technical and managerial) in 1970. Blacks were employed in 12 percent of the craftsmen jobs, which tend to be well paying, 18 percent of the other middle level jobs, and 27 percent of the lower-paying jobs.

The proportion of black workers in the higher- and middle-level jobs was greater in the 9 industries than in all industries.

In higher paying jobs, the local passenger transit industry has the largest percentage (11) of black employees. The proportion of black workers in these jobs was 8 percent for medical and other health services, and 6 percent for eating and drinking places. For the remaining 6 industries, the percentage of blacks in these jobs was strikingly low—4 percent or less.

Blacks in the 9 selected industries are more likely than blacks in all industries to be in the lower paid occupations.

Black employees held 15.1 percent of all full-time federal jobs in May, 1971, compared with 13.5 percent in June, 1965. In 1971, blacks represented 11 percent of all federal employees paid under the Federal Classification Act; 21 percent under Wage System; 18 percent under Postal Field Service rates; and 6 percent under all other pay systems.

Blacks held about 3 percent of the GS–12 to 15 jobs and 2 percent of those in the highest grades (GS–16 to 18) under the Federal Classification Act.

Nearly all, 91 percent, of the black firms operated as sole proprietorships. Only a minority, about one-fourth, of the 163,000 black-owned firms had paid employees; however, they accounted for the major portion, 82 percent, of the gross receipts of black-owned businesses in 1969.

Over 50 percent of black-owned businesses were located in the South with less than half as many accounted for in the North Central region, the second region of concentration.

Labor force by sex, age, and color

Sex, age, and color	Total labor force				Civilian labor force			
	Thousands of persons		Participation rate		Thousands of persons		Participation rate	
	Jan. 1973	Jan. 1972	Jan. 1973	Jan. 1972	Jan. 1973	Jan. 1972	Jan. 1973	Jan. 1972
TOTAL MALE								
16 years and over............	54,905	54,473	77.9	78.5	52,548	51,918	77.1	77.7
16 to 19 years................	4,308	4,195	53.2	52.9	3,919	3,879	50.9	51.0
16 and 17 years...............	1,611	1,635	39.0	40.3	1,563	1,603	38.3	39.8
18 and 19 years...............	2,698	2,560	68.0	66.2	2,357	2,276	65.0	63.5
20 to 24 years................	7,701	7,582	84.1	83.8	6,705	6,321	82.2	81.2
25 to 54 years................	34,070	33,563	94.7	95.1	33,100	32,589	94.6	94.9
25 to 34 years................	13,080	12,471	95.4	95.8	12,474	11,887	95.1	95.6
35 to 44 years................	10,573	10,634	96.1	96.1	10,256	10,299	96.0	95.9
45 to 54 years................	10,416	10,459	92.6	93.3	10,371	10,403	92.6	93.3
55 to 64 years................	7,012	7,132	78.7	80.7	7,009	7,128	78.7	80.7
55 to 59 years................	4,146	4,175	86.6	87.7	4,144	4,172	86.6	87.6
60 to 64 years................	2,866	2,956	69.5	72.6	2,865	2,956	69.5	72.6
65 years and over.............	1,815	2,001	21.7	24.2	1,815	2,001	21.7	24.2
BLACK AND OTHER RACES								
16 years and over............	5,446	5,327	71.3	71.6	5,136	5,030	70.1	70.4
16 to 19 years................	453	411	40.3	37.9	396	373	37.0	35.7
16 and 17 years...............	130	130	22.3	23.0	124	127	21.4	22.5
18 and 19 years...............	323	280	59.7	54.4	272	246	55.4	51.1
20 to 24 years................	904	868	78.9	79.7	777	732	76.2	76.8
25 to 54 years................	3,372	3,288	88.9	88.6	3,247	3,165	88.5	88.2
25 to 34 years................	1,342	1,292	90.5	91.5	1,262	1,219	90.0	91.0
35 to 44 years................	1,103	1,066	91.5	88.6	1,062	1,021	91.2	88.1
45 to 54 years................	927	929	83.9	84.9	923	925	83.9	84.9
55 to 64 years................	560	592	69.8	73.8	560	592	69.8	73.8
55 to 59 years................	340	345	80.4	81.2	340	345	80.4	81.2
60 to 64 years................	220	247	58.0	65.5	220	247	58.0	65.5
65 years and over.............	156	168	20.1	22.1	156	168	20.1	22.1
TOTAL FEMALE								
16 years and over............	33,216	32,675	43.3	43.4	33,170	32,635	43.3	43.3
16 to 19 years................	3,227	3,176	41.0	41.2	3,218	3,167	40.9	41.1
16 and 17 years...............	1,216	1,245	30.3	31.6	1,215	1,244	30.3	31.6
18 and 19 years...............	2,012	1,931	52.0	57.1	2,003	1,923	51.9	51.0
20 to 24 years................	5,411	5,172	59.5	57.4	5,387	5,153	59.4	57.3
25 to 54 years................	19,377	18,989	51.3	51.1	19,364	18,976	51.2	51.1
25 to 34 years................	6,908	6,279	49.2	47.0	6,899	6,272	49.1	46.9
35 to 44 years................	6,087	6,100	52.7	52.4	6,084	6,097	52.7	52.4
45 to 54 years................	6,383	6,609	52.4	54.5	6,382	6,607	52.4	54.5
55 to 64 years................	4,192	4,294	41.5	43.1	4,192	4,294	41.5	43.1
55 to 59 years................	2,501	2,591	47.1	49.2	2,501	2,591	47.1	49.2
60 to 64 years................	1,691	1,703	35.4	36.3	1,691	1,703	35.4	36.3
65 years and over.............	1,008	1,046	8.6	9.1	1,008	1,046	8.6	9.1
BLACK AND OTHER RACES								
16 years and over............	4,218	4,161	47.6	48.2	4,212	4,156	47.5	48.2
16 to 19 years................	308	322	26.9	29.3	307	321	26.9	29.2
16 and 17 years...............	81	100	13.8	17.5	81	100	13.8	17.5
18 and 19 years...............	227	222	41.0	42.2	226	221	40.9	42.0
20 to 24 years................	696	642	56.5	54.2	692	639	56.4	54.1
25 to 54 years................	2,688	2,681	59.1	60.3	2,687	2,680	59.1	60.3
25 to 34 years................	1,081	1,028	61.3	60.9	1,080	1,027	61.2	60.9
35 to 44 years................	897	911	60.7	61.7	897	911	60.7	61.7
45 to 54 years................	710	742	54.3	57.9	710	742	54.3	57.9
55 to 64 years................	417	389	44.2	41.9	417	389	44.2	41.9
55 to 59 years................	247	241	49.8	48.8	247	241	49.8	48.8
60 to 64 years................	169	149	38.0	34.0	169	149	38.0	34.0
65 years and over.............	110	126	11.0	12.9	110	126	11.0	12.9

BLACKS AND THE LABOR MOVEMENT

In 1973, reliable observers of the Labor movement estimate that no more than 3 million of the estimated 20 million union members in the United States are black. This represents less than a third of the total black work force. The U.S. Census pays the total of all workers in labor unions at 31 percent and black workers at 35 percent.

At least half of all unionized black workers are to be found in the nation's three largest unions: the Teamsters, the United Auto Workers, and the United Steel Workers. The Teamsters, through a series of mergers and expansion into non-trucking areas, now account for an estimated 200,000 black unionists. The United Automobile Workers has the largest black membership, with an estimated 500,000 members. The United Steel Workers have another 200,000 black dues payers. The balance of black union membership is spread among the fast-growing and increasingly important American Federation of State, County, and Municipal Employees, the various teachers unions, and others, such as the Building Service, Garment Workers, Drug and Hospital Workers, Laborers, Hod Carriers, The Amalgamated Meat Cutters, etc.

Among the organizations identified with the black worker there are: The recently organized Coalition of Black Trade Unionists, a politically oriented group, which is open to all rank-and-file union members throughout the country; the A. Philip Randolph Institute; and The Negro American Labor Council, the oldest of the organizations, which was formed in 1960, specifically to address the particular needs of black trade unionists, and through its office which was to act as a clearing house for problems common to the black trade unionists, a coordinated effort to better the conditions of all could be mounted. From its founding until 1966, the Council was headed by A. Philip Randolph. It is now under the direction of its president, Cleveland Robinson, president of the National Council of Distributive Workers.

The A. Philip Randolph Institute, under the direction of Bayard Rusten, was founded in 1964 to develop and promote programs which will deal with the problems of an increasingly technological society, that has not made provision for the training or retraining of a vast segment of the labor force, willing but unable to make a transition from unskilled and semi-skilled jobs to positions that would provide living wages with the new economy.

RACISM AND ORGANIZED LABOR
By Herbert Hill*

Beginning with President Roosevelt's Executive Order 8802 issued in 1941, the declared policy of the United States Government has been to prohibit racial discrimination in employment. During the past thirty years, an imposing array of federal statutes, together with state and municipal laws have been enacted and seven executive orders have been issued by five presidents. A new body of decisional and administrative law has evolved interpreting these statutes and providing for the elimination of discriminatory employment practices through the orderly procedures of the law.

Discrimination and FEPC

An evaluation of the racial practices of organized labor during the past 30 years, that is, in the period between the creation of the first FEPC in 1941 and the establishment of the Equal Employment Opportunity Commission as a result of the passage of Title VII of the Civil Rights Act of 1964, provides a realistic basis to judge repeated claims about "great progress" in eliminating racist practices within organized labor.

Prior to the passage of Title VII labor unions used their extensive powers to eliminate or limit black workers as a group from competition in the labor market by a variety of methods. Among these were: exclusion from membership by racial provisions in union constitutions or ritual by-laws, exclusion of blacks by tacit agreement in the absence of written declarations, segregated locals, separate racial seniority and promotional provisions in union contracts limiting black workers to menial or unskilled jobs; refusal to admit blacks into union-controlled apprenticeship training programs; and denial of access to union hiring halls and other job referral operations especially where such systems of job control are the exclusive source of employment.

Although some isolated progress has occurred, patterns of discriminatory employment practices have not been eliminated. Thus, the broad patterns of racial discrimination remain intact. But two new phenomena have emerged: where once they were openly racist and acknowledged to be such, these practices have now become covert and subtle. New testing devices and non-job related qualifications, although non-discriminatory on their face, exclude black workers just as effectively as did the "white only" clauses in the past. Separate racial seniority provisions in union contracts which once were clearly designated as "white" and "colored" lines of promotion now continue to operate through a series of euphemisms which mean exactly the same thing. The nomenclature has changed, but the consequences for black workers remain the same.

Tokenism

The second new development is to be found in the way many labor unions have responded to the requirements of the new body of law prohibiting discriminatory racial practices, in the use of what has become known as "tokenism;" that is a device to preserve old patterns and as a tactic to evade genuine compliance with the law. Thus, at best, there has been a minimal strategic accommodation by labor organizations to the entire body of federal and state anti-discrimination laws and executive orders.

A detailed examination of the records of the FEPC in the 1940s involving labor unions, with the trade union cases that have come before the Equal Employment Opportunity Commission in the 1960s and 1970s, reveals that many major labor unions are substantially continuing their discriminatory racial practices. In some instances, such as in cases involving the machinists, the railway clerks, the building trades craft unions, the operating railroad unions, the longshoremen and other labor oragnizations, the practices are virtually identical to those of 25 years ago. In many instances, the Equal Employment Opportunity Commission has investigated and found "reasonable cause" involving the exact same discriminatory practices of the exact same labor unions cited by the FEPC more than a quarter of a century ago.

This is especially true on the fundamental problem of separate racial seniority lines and other discriminatory provisions regarding job assignment in collective bargaining agreements, and on the issue of membership practices of craft unions, where such unions control the right of black workers to a job through the operation of union-controlled hiring halls and other referral systems.

In the early 1940s, the Fair Employment Practice Committee received complaints against the International Longshoremen's Association, an affiliate of the American Federation of Labor, charging a pattern of segregated locals and discriminatory job assignments in many cities along the Atlantic Coast and in the Gulf District. Twenty-five years later, the Equal Employment Opportunity Commission

received many complaints against the International Longshoremen's Association involving the exact same issues. In Philadelphia, for instance, the Commission found "reasonable cause" to believe that ILA locals systematically deny black workers opportunities to enter into the more desirable higher-paying job classifications such as checkers and clerks. The EEOC found "reasonable cause" in charges brought by members of all-black segregated ILA locals that the all-white local 1242, which operates the hiring hall for checkers and clerks, refused to refer black workers to these jobs. The EEOC also found "reasonable cause" in charges brought by segregated black locals against white locals of the International Longshoremen's Association, Gulf Coast District in Galveston, and Port Arthur, Texas as well as other cities on the Atlantic Coast. The racial practices of the International Longshoreman's Association have changed little over the past quarter of a century, segregated locals with whites obtaining preferential treatment are a characteristic of the ILA. The Union has consistently refused to comply with fair employment practice laws and recently the U. S. Department of Justice filed suits against the ILA Gulf Coast District and 36 locals in ten Texas cities. Other court cases are pending in Baltimore and elsewhere and early in 1970 the New York State Commission for Human Rights received complaints from black workers in New York City against the ILA.

Transfer Rights Denied

In 1945, the Fair Employment Practice Committee received complaints against the Oil Workers International Union, now the Oil, Chemical and Atomic Workers International Union, charging discriminatory practices throughout the southwest. The Equal Employment Opportunity Commission in 1966 received charges filed by black workers against the same union on very much the same issues. For example, the Monsanto Chemical Company in El Dorado, Arkansas has collective bargaining agreements with a "lily-white" local of the International Association of Machinists, Local Lodge 224, and the Oil Workers Union, Local 5-434. This ostensibly integrated local of the Oil Workers Union is divided into two departments: the labor department, which is all-black and the operating department, which is all-white. Provisions in the union contract provide that a worker loses all seniority when transferring from one department to another.

In finding "reasonable cause" to believe that Local 5-434 has violated Title VII, the Commission found that jobs have been traditionally classified on the basis of race. The highest-paid black man earns less per hour than the lowest-paid white employee. Black workers have been denied access to training programs; and recently imposed qualifications, that is, new standards, now require all new members of the Operating Department to have a high school education and to pass a test which was not previously required of whites.

In another similar case, the Department of Justice initiated litigation against the Union and the Sinclair Refining Company of Houston. The suit alleges discrimination in job assignment and testing procedures. Thus, the racial practices of the Oil, Chemical and Atomic Workers International Union operating in the Southwest remain virtually unchanged after a quarter of a century.

The experience of the black workers in the Oil, Chemical and Atomic Workers Union is duplicated in many other sectors of the economy where industrial unions hold collective bargaining agreements, such as in steel, tobacco, and paper manufacturing. Before Title VII went into effect, black workers in the all-black labor classifications were absolutely prohibited from transferring into the all-white operating department by clauses in union contracts. Now the black worker has the theoretical right to transfer into higher-paying jobs in the all-white operating department, but only after passing a qualifying test which did not exist before 1965, and also losing all accumulated seniority. Progress here consists of a theoretical abstraction which serves to maintain the traditional pattern.

In many industries employing tens of thousands of black workers, powerful labor unions insist upon maintaining the old racist practices. More than two decades ago, black steelworkers began a campaign within the United Steelworkers of America to eliminate the discriminatory job provisions contained in that union's collective bargaining agreements with the United States Steel Corporation and other steel manufacturers. After more than twenty years of protest by black steelworkers against separate racial seniority lines together with the filing of complaints with the National Labor Relations Board, and futile confrontations with the union leadership, the United Steelworkers of America still persists in maintaining the discriminatory seniority provisions in its collective bargaining agreements. Today this union is vigorously defending their practices in a series of lawsuits pending in Federal district courts in Alabama, Ohio and Virginia. Last December the Justice Department finally initiated litigation against the Steelworkers Union after three years of conciliation failed.

Maintenance of Status quo through Litigation

Even though the Federal courts are now providing clear legal definitions of racial discrimination in employment, administrative remedies still are blocked, as many labor unions continue their defiance of the law and attempt to defend their traditional racist practices in complex court challenges. The legal departments of many labor unions are now busily engaged in introducing a tangle of procedural legal questions in an attempt to prevent change by conducting a rear-guard holding action in the courts. This must be regarded as a basic measure of the Federation's practices, more significant than the often repeated ritualistic pledges of "non-discrimination" by the leadership of the AFL and its affiliated unions.

Among the first hearings held by the Fair Employment Practice Committee in 1945 were those that involved the Plumbers and Steamfitters Union, the International Brotherhood of Electrical Workers and other major building trades unions in the Midwest. One cannot but be fascinated by the current findings of the Equal Employment Opportunity Commission and the recent decisions of the Federal courts in cases involving unions across the country, in the light of the historical record. If one reads the complaints of the 1960's and the 1970's one is forced to conclude, in the perspective of time, that the only change is in the names of the plaintiffs.

On September 13, 1968, in the U. S. District Court in Cincinnati, Ohio, Judge Timothy S. Hogan ruled that Anderson L. Dobbins, a black electrician, must be admitted to Local 212, a "lily-white" local of the International Brotherhood of Electrical Workers. Local 212 has jurisdiction in Cincinnati and in 13 surrounding counties in Ohio, Kentucky, and Indiana. Mr. Dobbins, a veteran of the United States Army, who holds a Bachelor of Science degree from Hampton Institute and who is a fully-certified journeyman electrician, had been attempting to gain admission into Local 212 of the IBEW since 1956. Because he had been repeatedly denied membership in the Union, which maintains an exclusive hiring hall system in the greater Cincinnati area, Mr. Dobbins has nòt been permitted to work in the vast new public and private construction projects in and around Cincinnati.

In a ninety-page opinion rendered by Judge Hogan in *Dobbins Vs. Local 212, International Brotherhood of Electrical Workers, AFL-CIO,* the Federal Court ordered, that because of Mr. Dobbins' extensive training and experience in the electrical field, he must be admitted into the union's membership immediately; that he must *not* be required to pass a union-qualifying journeyman's admission examination and that he must be placed on the union's referral list as of the time he last applied for union membership which was in September, 1965.

It should also be noted that in this significant ruling, the Court found that the Union had committed eleven separate acts of racial discrimination, that there was a clear pattern of racial discrimination under the terms of the Civil Rights Act of 1964 and a violation of an 1866 Civil Rights Statute which prohibits private, as well as, public discrimination. The Federal Court noted that Local 212 had limited its membership to white persons only and that it "effectively controls who will work for union contractors within its jurisdiction" through the referral system and hiring hall agreements it had established. Of great significance is the fact that the Court challenged the Union's control of employment through its hiring hall and suspended the union referral system.

But our story does not end here. Local 212 of the IBEW, as a result of the Court order, admitted Dobbins and one other black electrician into membership. All other black workers, who are potential litigants against the Union are given temporary working permits, but denied union membership and its various benefits. Furthermore, in February of last year, the IBEW asked for "relief" from the judicially imposed restraints upon the Union's racist practices. The Civil Rights Division of the U. S. Department of Justice, of course, opposed the Union's request. Thus, after twenty-six years, exactly two black men have been admitted into membership in Local 212 in Cincinnati and we are again back in court on the same issue that was first presented to a government agency in 1945. This case symbolizes the so-called "progress" that has been made by the AFL-CIO during the past quarter of a century in eliminating racist practices.

There now exists a significant body of decisional law, where the Courts did not merely redress the grievances of the individual plaintiffs, but acted on behalf of all blacks and Mexican-Americans, that is on behalf of an entire class of citizens. This holds true for cases involving the industrial unions where the courts have repeatedly held that race cannot be a factor in job assignment and promotion, as well as the craft unions. This emerging body of law directly affects the racial practices of virtually every labor union in the United States.

Organized Labor Resistance

There are real, but nonetheless, self-generated reasons for the adamant resistance of organized labor to the requirements of contemporary civil rights laws. Organized labor created patterns in the past that are institutionalized in the collective bargaining structure. But these are now challenged, although deeply imbedded in the entire labor management relationship.

By the turn of the century—1900—the labor movement had settled into a policy of racial exclusion expressed in the refusal to organize black workers in many occupations, or to establish segregated locals, or to exclude blacks from certain job classifications, or to create separate racial seniority lines in union contracts. All these and other practices had the effect of driving black workers out of competition with the white unionized labor force and to use the greater exploitation of the black worker as a means of subsidizing the higher wages of the white worker. To the extent that employers got union agreements to exclude or segregate black workers, it became economically advantageous to the employer to promote such practices.

This policy lowered total labor costs because the employer could trade off higher wages for white workers at the expense of low-paid more highly-exploited blacks. From the employer's point of view, this policy also diminished the power of organized labor, a point which the AFL leadership never understood.

This pattern continues today and is the legacy of the tradition established in the early years of AFL. For example, in many steelmills, the millright is white and the millright's helper is black. They do substantially the same work—in fact, the black helper usually teaches the white millright who receives higher pay and has a higher job classification. Many examples of this pattern can be cited in other industries; such as, in the paper industry, in tobacco manufacturing, in petro-chemicals, among others. Apart from its consequences to organized labor, employers derive substantial benefits from this labor policy as it results in lower total average labor costs.

A major current example of this is to be found in the trucking industry. Inter-city, or as they are known, "over the road" truck drivers who are white and organized by the Teamsters Union get paid an hourly-wage rate, plus a substantial mileage bonus. Thus, their annual earnings are much greater than that of black drivers limited to intra-city trucking where no mileage rate is paid. This greatly benefits the trucking industry, which can afford to pay the high wages of the white "over the road" driver subsidized by the low-wage exploitation of the black workers.

The clearest example of this policy is provided by the highly unionized railroad industry. There has existed for generations, the racial pattern of white brakemen versus the black train porter. This discriminatory pattern has been demonstrated in many legal suits. They do identical work, but black train porters receive less pay and segregated status. Employers and white workers benefit from the deprivation of blacks, which subsidizes higher wages and working conditions for whites—individually, and as a class. Organized labor and employers have jointly created a highly-exploited class of cheap black labor, rigidly blocked from advancing into the all-white occupations.

By the beginning of the 1970s, as a result of past practices, organized labor was confronted by serious problems of its own creation and engaged in vigorous resistance to civil rights law. But now, black labor challenges the historical pattern and tries to break through as the new body of law sustains these new demands.

The Nation's construction industry is of unique importance to black workers for many 'reasons:

1. It is a huge industry with vast growth potential.

2. Wages in the construction industry are among the highest in the Nation. The building trades represents a major area of the economy which could provide new job opportunities at high wages for large numbers of unemployed or underemployed black workers.

3. Jobs in the buildings trades are for men. In the highly important symbolic sense, as well as for practical consideration, construction jobs are "manly" jobs.

4. Jobs in the buiding trades are highly visible and much of new construction, including urban renewal, model cities, highway and roadbuilding and public housing is in or very near large black communities.

5. The construction industry in comparison with other large industries is highly dependent on public funds.

The basis of the so-called Philadelphia Plan in the construction industry was the concept of the manning tables developed in a landmark case sponsored by the NAACP, *Ethridge V. Rhodes*, decided on May 17, 1967 in the District Court in Columbus, Ohio, The NAACP originally proposed the idea of manning tables which established the legal principle that government agencies must require a contractual

commitment from building contractors to employ a specific minimum number of black workers in each craft at every stage of construction. Whatever its procedural limitations and escape clauses, the concept of the Philadelphia Plan was potentially the most effective means to enforce the Federal Executive Order.

The NAACP welcomed the Philadelphia Plan as it established the principle of manning tables on federal construction projects although we were critical of the low percentages given for the employment of black workers in the skilled craft occupations. But whatever its limitations, the guidelines incorporated within the Philadelphia Plan represented the most important step forward in attempting to secure compliance with the Federal Executive Order which, for all practical purposes, has now become a dead letter.

It should be noted that the manning table requirements indicated the minimum number, not the maximum number, of black workers to be hired, in contrast to the unofficial quota system which rigidly enforced the exclusion or limitation of black workers from jobs in federally-financed construction.

The record of thirty years of FEPC laws makes it absolutely clear that the concept of passive non-discrimination is totally inadequate and obsolete. A ritualistic policy of "nondiscrimination" or of "equal opportunity" in practice usually means perpetuation of the traditional discriminatory pattern. Now it is necessary to move on to the next stage where we establish on federal construction projects and elsewhere, concrete responsibility for the employment of a specified number of black workers in all job classifications at a given time. This is an absolutely essential tactic requiring a new concept of social responsibility by employers and labor unions, in which performance can be measured by tangible results, not by the proliferation of empty self-serving policy statements pledging "non-discrimination." It is within this context that the Philadelphia Plan, given all of its limitations, assumes its significance.

The law is clear on the many prohibitions against discrimination in employment, especially in the public sector of the economy. It has been defined again and again in court decisions. It has been enacted into a statute by the Congress. It has been declared a matter of public policy in Federal executive orders; but, no organized group in American society has more vigorously resisted these laws than the building trades unions affiliated with the AFL-CIO.

The essential point is that federal contract

compliance is the most potent instrument available to end job discrimination in American life and the federal guidelines enunciated in the Philadelphia Plan, if enforced, could do this is the nation's construction industry. I refer to the heart of the Plan which is the principle of the manning tables.

The Nixon Administration has again and again demonstrated that it clearly has no intention of fulfilling its legal obligations in this matter. In fact, it is a party to the continued violation of the law. This leaves us no choice but to seek enforcement of the law and the realization of the constitutional rights of black workers through a combination of litigation and social action.

But instead of enforcing the law, instead of obtaining compliance with federal guidelines in the construction industry, the U. S. Department of Labor, at the insistence of the politically powerful building trades unions, is promoting and funding so-called "home-town" solutions. These local plans, substituted for the Philadelphia Plan, are a meaningless exercise in deception. They do not establish contractual duties and obligations, they do not state time limitations, they do not contain legal sanctions, there are no guarantees of anything, nothing is spelled out. In short, the "home-town" solutions are a fraud.

The basic issue is that these "home-town" solutions perpetuate control of entry into construction industry jobs by the building trades unions and employers who have a vested interest in maintaining the racial *status quo*. Continued control of job opportunities by the racist building trades unions is the heart of the matter. Outreach Programs, which are supposed to prepare minority youth for admission into union-controlled apprenticeship training, are in fact another device to perpetuate the racial *status quo* in the building trades.

Apprenticeship

Spokesmen for organized labor tell us that the ratio of non-whites among registered apprentices increased between 1960 and 1970 from 2 percent to 7.2 percent. But, the significant ratio is the number of blacks and other non-whites in the skilled trades measured against their total number in the community at large. In relation to this ratio, the Outreach Programs have only succeeded in maintaining the appallingly low levels of non-white participation reached in the early 1960s.

In 1950, black workers constituted 1.5 percent of the apprentices and 13 percent of the population of New York City. In 1960, blacks constituted 2 percent of the apprentices and 22 percent of the population of New York City.

The 1970 census revealed that non-white constitute about 53 percent of the population of New York City. The same pattern is repeated in many urban centers throughout the country. The rapidly changing population characteristics of the black community provide the only meaningful context in which to measure the rate of progress of black workers in organized labor and in all other institutions.

Given the very significant increase in the non-white labor force, it is clear that the percentage of non-whites in the craft occupations has not changed in any significant way during the past decade. It is estimated by the Bureau of Labor Statistics that by 1980 the total non-white labor force will have risen by 41 percent compared with only a 28 percent increase among white workers. The percentage of blacks in apprenticeship in relation to population has either declined or in some trades, at best, remained the same—less than 2 percent.

Given the fact that government officials are aware that the system of apprenticeship training, especially in the construction trades, is obsolete, it is all the more scandalous that millions of dollars of public funds are spent annually to subsidize these programs. During the fiscal year of 1970, the Federal Government funded Outreach Programs in the amount of $4,785,290. Between 1967 and 1970, the United States Government spent $8,666,422 to directly subsidize the Outreach Programs. (On November 4, 1970, The Joint Apprenticeship Program of the Workers Defense League—A. Philip Randolph Institute received an additional $1,385,825 in federal funds as its Outreach contract was renewed by the Department of Labor.)

Has anything changed as a consequence of the expenditure of almost nine million dollars during a period of three years? What are the concrete results of the Outreach Programs? The Manpower Administration of the U. S. Dept. of Labor on October 31, 1970, revealed that over a period of three years, 7,813 workers have been initially admitted into Outreach Programs in the building trades. But let us take a close look at the figures. At least 2 percent of these are white persons. The official dropout figure is 1,319 which leaves a total of 6,494. However, as everyone in the Manpower Administration knows, the real dropout rate is much closer to 50 percent, which is the national dropout rate for both white and black workers in apprenticeship training. The official dropout rate of 1,319 is that reported to Washington by the local sponsors of Outreach Programs, and is not accurate. A large proportion of those remaining are in job categories where there has long been a concentration of non-whites, as in the trowel trades.

However, the fundamental problem is not apprenticeship. It is the issue of admitting black workers, many of whom have been certified by state licensing boards as fully-qualified journeymen, directly into union membership and into union-controlled jobs. On this crucial issue, the craft unions are bitterly resisting change in their traditional racial practices. The Equal Employment Opportunity Commission reported that black membership in the building trades unions had actually declined in 1969.

Although the myth of apprenticeship is repeatedly peddled by spokesmen for organized labor, the basic fallacy in the Outreach approach is that even if full racial integration of all union-controlled apprenticeship programs were achieved, no substantial integration of the craft unions would result because the overwhelming majority of white construction workers do not become journeymen through apprenticeship training. Data from the Manpower Administration of the U. S. Department of Labor reveals that well over 70 percent of the white journeymen in the craft unions do not advance through a formal apprenticeship program. About three-fourths of all the skilled construction workers in the United States are normally trained directly on the job. They do not have to be prepared or primed or tutored. They learn by doing. It is only blacks and members of other minority groups who must climb the slow apprenticeship ladder.

Apprenticeship is an exceedingly prolonged, inefficient, and socially undesirable system and in many cases it is unnecessary as there is little if any relation between training and the actual work to be performed. The entire system of apprenticeship training is obsolete, it should be reorganized on a completely new basis, independent of control by restrictive labor unions. Since all the available evidence indicates that the building trades unions do not get more than 30 percent, at the utmost, of their journeymen members from apprenticeship programs, it is discriminatory to make 100 percent of all black workers seek entry through dubious apprenticeship training programs.

Unemployment

Representatives of organized labor have frequently stated that unemployment among unionized white workers prevents the immediate integration of the labor force and that black workers must wait for some far distant future when there is full employment in order to have desirable jobs. The assumption that all white union members must be fully employed before blacks can be permitted to work, the notion that white workers have a prior right to a job is clearly an expression of the racist mentality within the craft unions. Unfortunately, it is also shared by too many public officials. These assumptions have no basis in law and certainly not in any concept of morality. For too many long hard years, black workers have disproportionately shared only unemployment. The time has now come for black workers to share fully in whatever employment opportunities there are at present and will be in the future. In response to the bitter intransigence of organized labor in refusing to make the fundamental changes that are required in their racial practices, black workers will continue to develop new labor and civil rights laws, and creatively use these laws to eliminate the racist practices that exist as the result of the historic collusion between employers and labor unions in major sectors of the American economy.

Law and Employment Discrimination

Racial discrimination in employment does not occur as individual random acts of bigotry; rather, it is the result of systemic patterns of practices which keep black workers as a class in a permanent state of economic and social depression. However, complaints of job discrimination have traditionally been regarded as isolated phenomena, and limited judicial remedies have been granted accordingly. After the law dealing with employment discrimination was included in the doctrine of fair representation of the National Labor Relations Act of 1935, successful plaintiffs were awarded individual relief. But the broad patterns of discrimination remained untouched by the courts. Thus, the major problem has been both the inadequacy of law in recognizing the social nature of employment discrimination and the limitations of judicial remedy. These deficiencies have been compounded by the general lack of enforcement of whatever law was available.

It has been demonstrated over and over again that complaints of employment discrimination by aggrieved workers are not the expression of occasional acts of private prejudice. Job discrimination does not occur—as spokesmen for employers and labor unions would have it—"in isolated pockets." Rather these "pockets" reflect the operation of a racist employment system: they constitute an extensive pattern of employment practices which can be broken only by sweeping measures. Specific instances of discrimination are the product of long-established employer and labor union practices involving the basic institutions of the workplace, the very structure of labor-management relations, including the collective bargaining process.

The General Condition

Administrative civil rights agencies do not perceive the essential nature of the problem—that is, that complaints of job discrimination are not expressions of an aberration, but are manifestations of the general condition. All too often, these agencies function as mediators rather than as law enforcement agencies, regarding themselves simply as conciliators between adversaries. A further reason for the dismal failure of agencies such as state civil rights commissions is that instead of enforcing the law to effect social change, administrative agencies usually become vehicles of social control, and their leaders act primarily to advance their own bureaucratic interests. In the crucial matter of jobs, federal and state governments have failed to attack patterns of employment discrimination through enforcement of the comprehensive body of civil rights laws and regulations. The burden of doing so has therefore fallen upon the courts.

Courts and administrative agencies have been involved in the contentious issue of racial discrimination in employment for over a quarter of a century. The 1944 case of *Steele v. Louisville & Nashville Railroad* marked the Supreme Courts entrance into the field of employment discrimination in the twentieth century. The first state fair employment practice agency was the New York State Commission Against Discrimination, which began operation in 1945. Prior to these beginnings, there had developed a body of law under the National Labor Relations Act—the doctrine of fair representation—which prohibited unions from exercising their collective bargaining powers to the detriment of blacks employed under their jurisdiction. A series of federal executive orders issued by five presidents have required nondiscrimination in government contracting, and administrative agencies from the World War II Fair Employment Practice Committee to the Office of Federal Contract Compliance were established to implement the executive orders. By July 1965, the effective date of Title VII of the Civil Rights Act of 1964, thirty-four states had enforceable fair employment practice statutes, with a variety of administrative agencies as provided for in state civil rights laws.

Thus, prior to Title VII, the public policy regarding discrimination in employment was clearly established. A large number of state laws, executive orders, and court decisions had prohibited employment discrimination. But although the law was relatively clear, it was never effectively enforced. The historical patterns of racial discrimination in employment continued unabated: agencies charged with enforcing the laws failed to recognize that discrimination in employment is the expression of long-established institutionalized systems based upon racist patterns.

Power to bring about change

Most state fair employment practice agencies have never lacked the power to function as instruments of broad social change. Professor Vern Countryman has written that "The chief shortcoming of the states as a source of protection against discrimination in employment, then, does not lie in their want of power to act. It lies, rather, in the unwillingness of some of them to do." By comparison, Title VII of the 1964 Civil Rights Act is among the weakest of the existing fair employment practice statutes. Many state agencies are empowered to initiate proceedings themselves, to issue some form of cease-and-desist order, and to have their orders enforced in state courts. The Equal Employment Opportunity Commission lacks these important powers. The state fair employment practice agencies, however, with rare exceptions, have refrained from using their extensive powers. These administrative agencies fail to understand that complaints of employment discrimination are not isolated occurrences but are evidence and manifestations of broad underlying patterns of discrimination. Civil rights agencies treat discriminatory practices as acts of random malevolence by individual bigoted whites. Since, in the most fundamental sense, they falsely approach the problem, they are unable and unwilling to eliminate racist practices.

N.Y. State Against Discrimination

The New York anti-discrimination law was the first such state statute, and it remains potentially the strongest fair employment practices legislation of all the states. In many respects, the New York State law is much stronger than Title VII of the Civil Rights Act of 1964, and the state agency possesses far broader enforcement powers than the EEOC. However, these powers have rarely been invoked, and the state agency has deteriorated into a passive, complaint-taking bureau. Two classic examples of the failure of a state civil rights agency to effectively enforce the law are to be found in the response of the New York State Commission for Human Rights to complaints filed by black workers against labor unions holding collective bargaining agreements in two major sectors of the economy of New York City—construction and garment manufacturing.

In 1948 the New York State Commission Against Discrimination ordered the New York Sheet Metal Workers Union, Local 28, to desist from "executing and/or maintaining constitution or by-law provisions which exclude Negroes." Yet fifteen years later no progress had been made, and not a single black worker had been admitted into membership. Obviously, the "Caucasian only" clause was removed from the union's constitution for public-relations purposes only.

"Automatic Exclusion"

In 1963, James Ballard, a twenty-two-year-old black air force veteran, initiated a complaint against Local 28 of the Sheet Metal Workers Union before the New York State Commission for Human Rights, with the assistance of the Civil Rights Bureau of the State Attorney General's Office. On March 4, 1964, after an extensive investigation and public hearings, the commission ruled that Local 28 of the Sheet Metal Workers Union had "automatically excluded" blacks over the entire seventy-eight years of the union's existence. This was held to be a violation of New York State Law Against Discrimination. The commission announced that it would order the union to cease and desist from such discriminatory practices and would demand affirmative action to guarantee an end to discrimination.

Local 28 refused to comply with the order of the state commission, and sixteen years after the original finding against the Sheet Metal Workers Union, the commission was forced to go to court to get the new order enforced. On October 14, 1964, Justice Jacob Markowitz of the state supreme court sustained the action of the state commission and ordered the adoption of a new set of admissions standards. The union publicly announced that it would begin to admit blacks into membership as both journeymen and apprentices.

Soon thereafter, Local 28 initiated a testing program ostensibly designed to provide equal treatment; in fact, the new testing procedures were used to screen out black applicants. On December 29, 1966, the New York State Supreme Court issued a restraining order against Local 28 at the request of the State Commission for Human Rights. The commission was forced to return to court, with the NAACP filing a brief, *amicus curiae*, when the union scrapped the results of a test for admission into the apprenticeship training program because the black applicants received "phenomenally" high scores.

"Qualified" Black Unionists

For years it was held that blacks were not qualified for union membership, but in 1966 it appeared that they were too well qualified for union membership. However, as a result of public protests and pressure from state and municipal civil rights agencies, together with the possibility of further lawsuits, Local 28 again announced that "qualified" blacks would be admitted. But two years later, on November 23, 1968, the city of New York —which at long last had begun to enforce the municipal contract compliance law—announced that twenty-six city contracts valued at more than $6 million were held up by the city's Contract Compliance Division and the City Housing Authority because Local 28 was unable to supply municipal contractors with a single black worker. The *New York Times* of November 24, 1968, in a news report headed "Bias Issue Delays 26 City Contracts," stated that "Local 28 of the Sheet Metal Workers International Association has not reported any Negroes qualified as journeymen mechanics among its more than 3,000 members."

Union Testing

On November 28, 1968, under the headline "City moves to Subpoena Union's Test," the *New York Times* reported that the city's Contract Compliance Division was forced to issue a subpoena to obtain a copy of the test used by Local 28. The *New York Times* reported: "James D. Norton, director of the compliance division, said that Local 28 of Sheet Metal Workers International Association had refused to supply a copy of the examination on his request. He said the Commission on Human Rights had been asked to initiate legal action to obtain a copy."

Twenty years after the New York State Commission originally ordered Local 28 to eliminate their "Caucasian only" clause and to admit non-white workers—after two decades of interminable conferences, negotiations, administrative procedures, lawsuits in the state supreme court, investigations, and repeated anti-bias pledges by the union—the racist pattern in this and other construction unions in New York State had not changed. (Data released by the EEOC in 1970 revealed that non-white membership in New York City building trades unions controlling jobs in the high-paying mechanical crafts is 2 percent.)

Nationality Locals

In 1946, a formal complaint was filed with the New York State Commission by a black worker against the International Ladies Garment Workers Union because Local 89, the

Italian Dressmakers Local, had barred her from membership. After the commission had notified the ILGWU that nationality locals violated state law, the commission sought to conciliate the case. Rather than utilize the specific complaint to eliminate the traditional pattern that excluded nonwhites from jobs in the high-paying skilled classifications, the state commission entered into a conciliation agreement with the union which provided that black and Spanish-speaking persons would not be barred from membership in the two Italian locals. The commission failed to perceive that the worker's complaint—as subsequent investigation revealed—was symptomatic of a policy and a practice which had serious discriminatory consequences for black and Puerto Rican workers. Twenty years later, not a single black or Spanish-speaking person holds membership in the two Italian locals, and the ILGWU has taken no action to comply with the state law.

Holmes Case

In 1961, Ernest Holmes, a young black worker, filed a complaint against Local 10 of the ILGWU with the New York State Commission, charging that he had been denied membership in the local because of his race. After attempting to conciliate the case for over a year, the commission made a formal finding of "probable cause" and ordered the union to accept Holmes into membership.

The *New York Times* reported: "A garment cutters' union has been ordered by the State Commission for Human Rights to arrange for employment of a Negro at union rates commensurate with his skill and to admit the Negro into union membership if his work is satisfactory."

The *Times'* story also stated: "With regard to the union, the decision found that 'the evidence raises serious doubt as to its good faith to comply with the State Law Against Discrimination in the matter of this complaint; and that there was "probable cause" to credit the allegations of the complaint."

It is clear that the commission would not even have issued a "probable cause" finding had the union made a token effort to conciliate. After the commission had made its finding, the investigating commissioner wrote to the union's attorney that the commission had "repeatedly requested, and for a period of eight months tried to obtain, data pertinent to a resolution of the charges of discrimination against Amalgamated Ladies Garment Cutters Union, Local 10. These efforts were unsuccessful. The failure of representatives of that local to cooperate in the investigation, despite their promises to do so, left me no alternative

but to find 'probable cause' to credit the allegations of the complaint." Finally, twenty-five months after the complaint had been filed in the case of *Holmes v. Falikman,* the ILGWU entered into a stipulation agreement, upon which the complaint was withdrawn. In the settlement obtained by the commission, the union agreed to admit Holmes into the Cutters local and to assist him in seeking employment and training. This was precisely what the commission had ordered the union to do one year earlier.

The *Holmes* case is typical of the approach of F.E.P. agencies. The commission sought to conciliate the case for over two years, even after it had issued a "probable cause" order over. Conciliation took precedence over enforcement of the law, and although the commission had been presented with overwhelming evidence of a broad pattern of discrimination by the local which controlled access to jobs in its jurisdiction, it centered its efforts on resolving the single pending case, ignoring the context of years of discriminatory practices which limited blacks and Puerto Ricans to the lowest-paying unskilled and semiskilled jobs in the largest manufacturing industry in New York City.

"Hard Hat Reactionaries"

A final comment on the significance of the hard-hat demonstrations. What has become known as the hard-hat movement is not merely a manifestation of narrow craft unionism as it goes far beyond this in its public support of the war and its support of the Nixon Administration and its repressive measures. The hard-hat labor unionists, and they are by no means limited to the building trades, have joined with the military elite and their political spokesmen. This suggests the great danger of the rise of a protofacist workers movement in the United States. Whatever social and cultural forces may be invoked to explain this development, it is already manifesting itself in a variety of ways. The street violence provoked by the craft unionists in many cities has occurred with the support of local police, the national government, and the head of the AFL-CIO. It is a movement against the aspirations of black workers, against the youth, against the antiwar movement, and against all dissenters. The hard-hat unionists in their embrace of "Law and Order" have become the working-class allies of American reaction.

*Herbert Hill is National Labor Director of the National Association for the Advancement of Colored People and teaches at the New School for Social Research. This article is based on a paper he gave at a labor relations meeting sponsored by the New School for Social Research and the League for Industrial Democracy and printed in the New School Bulletin.

LABOR AND "QUOTAS"

It is now nineteen years since the NAACP's victory in the school segregation cases known as *Brown* v. *Board of Education,* and it is nine years since Congress enacted the historic Civil Rights Act of 1964. But, instead of realizing the full potential of these great possibilities, our country is experiencing not merely a "backlash," but is in the grip of a dangerous counter-revolution against the cause of racial integration.

It is within this context that one must understand the significance of the attack upon job quotas. The antiquota movement has become a complacent cover for retreat in the civil rights battle, and the attack upon job quotas has become a major rallying cry in the counter-revolution against the struggle for civil rights.

Judging by the vast outcry, it might be assumed that job quotas in employment had become as widespread and destructive as racial discrimination itself. As with the much distorted subject of bussing, the defenders of the racial *status quo* have once again succeeded in confusing the remedy with the original evil. The word "quota," like "bussing" and "open housing," has become another code word for resistance to black demands for the elimination of widespread patterns of racial discrimination.

Much of the current controversy involves federal civil rights enforcement efforts in the construction industry and in educational institutions which do billions of dollars worth of research and provide other services for government agencies. Common to most attacks upon preferential hiring systems is the assumption that such approaches are both a "new form of discrimination" and that the quality of performance and work standards will be severely diminished as a result of the employment of nonwhites and women. The *a priori* assumption that no "qualified" blacks or women exist is implicit in the argument. Also implicit is the assumption that if blacks and women were to be employed, the alleged current high standards would be diminished. In reality, the so-called merit system in education operates to give preference to mediocre or incompetent whites at the expense of highly-talented blacks, as well as at the expense of mediocre and incompetent blacks.

In *Chance* v. *Board of Examiners* (in which the United Federation of Teachers filed a brief *amicus curiae* against the black and Puerto Rican plaintiffs and against what they described as "infamous quota systems"), Federal Judge Walter R. Mansfield, in his opinion of July 14, 1971, ruled that New York City must stop using its traditional examinations for selecting school principals because the tests had the "effect of discriminating significantly and substantially against qualified black and Puerto Rican applicants." The court concluded that the procedures of the Board of Examiners, allegedly based upon the merit system, could not be justified as being reasonably related to job performance.

To argue that there is a merit system in the building trades, as spokesmen for organized labor frequently do, is to depart from all reason and reality. As has been demonstrated in many lawsuits throughout the country, the worst forms of nepotism and favoritism prevail.

It should be evident that what is really involved in the debate over hiring quotas is not that blacks and other minorities will be given preference over whites, but, rather, that a substantial body of law now requires that discriminatory systems which operate to favor whites at the expense of blacks must be eliminated.

During the past quarter-of-a-century, the federal courts have increasingly recognized the validity of numerical quotas to eliminate traditional forms of discrimination. The courts had used quotas as a remedy to eliminate systematic discrimination in the selection of juries, in legislative reapportionment litigation, and in school segregation cases.

Although the courts have repeatedly spoken on this issue, the extensive public discussion of preferential hiring has ignored the major legal interpretations of the validity of quotas in civil rights enforcement efforts. Typical of current judicial opinion is the decision of the United States Court of Appeals for the Third Circuit in the Philadelphia Plan case. In response to the arguments of contractors and labor unions that the Plan contains illegal racial quotas, Judge Gibbons, in a unanimous opinion upholding the Plan stated, "clearly the Philadelphia Plan is color-conscious. . . . In other contexts color-consciousness has been deemed to be an appropriate remedial posture."

The court further held that:

> The Philadelphia Plan is valid executive action designed to remedy the perceived evil that minority tradesmen have not been included in the labor pool in which the Federal Government has a cost and preference interest. The Fifth Amendment does not prohibit such action.

In this important case, the Circuit Court decisively rejected the argument that government imposed goals and timetables for the employment of blacks was unconstitutional. On the contrary, the Court specifically validated the legality of this approach where necessary and the Supreme Court let stand by refusing to review. In a similar case involving a state government, *Builders Association* v. *Ogilvie,* the Seventh Circuit Court of Appeals in December 1972, *affirmed* the use of racial quotas and held that: "Numerical objectives may be the only feasible mechanism for defining with any clarity the obligation of federal contractors to move employment practices in the direction of true neutrality."

In the past decade, there has emerged a new judicial perception of racial discrimination in employment. There now exists an extensive body of case law in which federal courts recognize that racial discrimination in employment does not occur as individual random acts of bigotry; but, rather, it is the result of systemic patterns which keep black workers as a class in a permanent state of economic and social depression.

The most important consequence of the new judicial perception of employment discrimination is to be found in the nature of the sweeping relief and remedies ordered by the federal courts. In practical terms, this has taken two specific forms. First, the awarding of large sums of money as backpay to an entire effected class of minority workers who have been found to be the victims of discriminatory practices. These substantial backpay awards are certain to have an important deterrent effect upon the discriminatory practices of both employers and labor unions. Secondly, there are many decisions where the courts have required new preferential hiring remedies.

Increasingly, the courts are recognizing that race-conscious injuries require race-conscious remedies. In *Norwalk CORE* v. *Norwalk Redevelopment Agency,* the court stated:

> What we have said may require classification by race. That is something which the Constitution usually forbids, not because it is inevitably an impermissible classification, but because it is one which usually to our national shame, has been drawn for the purpose of maintaining racial inequality. Where it is drawn for the purpose of achieving equality, it will be allowed, and to the extent that it is necessary to avoid unequal treatment by race, it will be required.

In *United States* v. *Local 38, IBEW,* it was held that the "anti-preferential treatment" section of Title VII does not limit power of a court to order affirmative relief to correct the effects of past unlawful practices.

In *NAACP* v. *Allen,* the court found that the state of Alabama had engaged in blatant discrimination in its hiring practices. In its thirty-five-year history, there had never been a black state trooper and the only nonwhites ever employed in the department had been common laborers. The court enjoined the defendants and ordered:

> . . . One Negro trooper for each white trooper hired until approximately twenty-five (25) percent of the Alabama state trooper force is comprised of Negroes. . . . It shall be the responsibility of the Department . . . to find and hire the necessary qualified Black troopers.

The court further ordered that: ". . . Eligible and promotional registers heretofore used for the purpose of hiring troopers be . . . abrogated . . . to comply with this decree."

In *Carter* v. *Gallagher,* a case involving the fire department of Minneapolis, brought under Sections 1981 and 1983 of the Civil Rights Act of 1866, the trial court decreed: "That the defendants . . . give absolute preference in certification of fire fighters with the Minneapolis Fire Department to twenty (20) black, American Indian, or Spanish sur-named American applicants who qualify for such a position. . . ." Similar relief has been ordered by the federal courts in numerous other cases.

It is now clear that the validity of quotas and timetables as a remedy to eliminate job discrimination has been firmly established by the federal courts. The decision of the Third Circuit Court of Appeals in the Philadelphia Plan case and the decision of the Seventh Circuit Court of Appeals in *Builders Association* v. *Ogilvie,* as well as other decisions of the courts, have decisively established the legality of quotas as a necessary means to eliminate racist employment patterns.

Source: Excerpt from Address by Herbert Hill, National Labor Director, NAACP, Indianapolis, Ind. July 5, 1973

FAIR EMPLOYMENT PRACTICE
ACTS AND EQUAL EMPLOYMENT OPPORTUNITY

On June 25, 1941, President Franklin D. Roosevelt issued the historic Executive Order 8803, creating the President's Fair Employment Practice Committee, with a view to eliminating discrimination in employment because of race, color, creed, or national origin. The order was an act of emergency by the President in view of the menace of approaching war and pressure from the black community.

The Committee on Fair Employment Practices was the first administrative agency established in the United States to protect and enforce the rights of all Americans to equality of opportunity in employment.

Duties of the FEPC, as the committee was commonly called, were "to receive and investigate complaints of discrimination" in defense industries, and later in war industries and allied work and in federal government service, and "to take appropriate steps to redress the grievances it found to be valid."

The creation of the committee followed a threat by the March on Washington movement, initiated by A. Philip Randolph, president of the Brotherhood of Sleeping Car Porters, to bring 50,000 blacks to Washington to demonstrate against discrimination in employment, especially in defense and war industries.

The committee members appointed by the President were Milton P. Webster, Sr., vice president of the Brotherhood of Sleeping Car Porters; Earl B. Dickerson, Chicago attorney and city councilman; Mark Ethridge, publisher of the Louisville *Courier-Journal;* Phillip Murray, president of the Congress of Industrial Organizations; William Green, president of the American Federation of Labor; and David Sarnoff, president of the Radio Corporation of America. They served without pay, and were responsible to the Chief Executive. On July 30, 1942, the committee was transferred from the executive department of the War Manpower Commission headed by Paul V. McNutt.

During 1941 and early 1942 it was generally conceded that the order had accomplished a great deal in the matter of advancing employment for blacks. As time wore on, however, its effectiveness gradually decreased, until by 1943 FEPC had become almost completely ineffective. This was due, primarily, to the committee's lack of enforcement powers and inability to penalize violators.

Efforts toward saving and strengthening the FEPC were stepped up, but the committee, faced with many internal crises, was in serious trouble. On January 11, 1943, a decisive blow was struck at the committee by McNutt, when, without prior consultation with its other members, he summarily postponed the scheduled hearings on complaints against twenty-three railroads, mainly in the South, which had been accused of discriminating in the employment of black engineers and firemen. Within a few days, Dr. Malcolm S. McLean, committee chairman and former president of Hampton Institute, resigned to enter the Navy. Mark Ethridge and David Sarnoff resigned also, as did committee attorneys, Harold A. Stevens and Charles H. Houston.

On February 4, President Roosevelt announced a conference with committee members that would strengthen the committee's scope and powers. The conference was held on February 28 and a program for restoration of the agency to its original independent status in the President's Executive Office was adopted. Monsignor Frank J. Haas, president of Catholic University in Washington was appointed chairman.

On May 27 of the same year, President Roosevelt issued a new executive order (No. 9346) setting up a new committee, with somewhat expanded powers, under the Office of Emergency Management. Among the provisions added in the new order was one making it obligatory upon private industries signing contracts with the government for war work and other public works not to discriminate on account of race or color in the employment of labor.

Despite this new order, the FEPC continued to meet with difficulties. The 78th Congress was bent on killing the effectiveness of the order. Meanwhile, realizing that there would be no peace with the FEPC as long as it was an emergency or war measure, blacks began to fight for a "permanent FEPC."

On March 6, 1944, President Truman appointed Charles H. Houston to the President's Committee on Fair Employment Practices to succeed P.B. Young, Norfolk newspaper publisher, who had been one of its two black members. The committee had under scrutiny at the time the employment practices of the Capital Transit Company; and in November, 1945, following two work stoppages, the streetcar company was seized by the government. On November 23rd the committee unanimously voted to direct the company to "cease discriminatory policies in the employment of Negroes," but on the following day, the President ordered the directive withheld because "under the conditions imposed by the Congress on Government Seizure, existing conditions of employment were to prevail." Houston resigned and charged the administration "with a persistent course of conduct to give lip-service to matters of eliminating racial discrimination in employment . . . while doing nothing to make this policy substantial.

During 1944 and 1945 several bills (thirteen in 1945) were introduced in the Congress calling for the creation of a permanent fair employment body, but the sponsors were defeated in their attempts to have any of them brought to the floor for a vote. Repeated attempts were made in 1946, and a bill was brought on the Senate floor for discussion and vote. There it was killed by a filibuster led by southern Senators.

On February 20, 1946, President Truman signed the Compromise Employment Bill of 1946 which provided for three advisers to prepare economic reports to Congress. FEPC was dead.

Liquidation of the temporary FEPC began in April 1946 after the Congress refused to appropriate funds for its functioning, and at midnight, June 30, it expired. In the final report of the commission, Chairman Malcolm Ross and the five membes stated that only the force of law could stop job discrimination against minorities.

Meanwhile, agitation continued for the adoption of a permanent FEPC, and in March 1947 a bill, acceptable to blacks and other minority groups and their supporters, was introduced in the Senate by Senators Irving Ives (Republican, New York) and Dennis Chavez (Democrat, New Mexico). A similar measure was introduced in the House of Representatives by James G. Fulton (R., Pennsylvania) and Mary Norton (D., New Jersey). Black Congressmen William L. Dawson (D., Illinois) and Adam C. Powell (D., New York) co-sponsored the measure.

Public hearings were conducted on the Senate bill in June, and in July the Senate Subcommittee on Labor approved the measure by a vote of 4 to 1. In February, 1948, the full Senate Committee approved it by 7 to 5, but it was not brought to the floor for a vote during that session.

Late in 1947, A. Philip Randolph and New York State Commissioner of Corrections, Grant Reynolds, organized "The League of Non-Violent Civil Disobedience Against Military Segregation." On March 22, 1948, Randolph and a delegation of black leaders conferred with President Truman at the White House. Mr. Randolph declared that he was convinced "Negroes are sick and tired of being asked to shoulder guns in defense of democracy abroad until they get some at home. They are prepared to resort to civil disobedience and refusal to register for the draft if it means serving in a Jim Crow Army." The President was obviously angered by Randolph's outspoken statement. The following week, March 31, Randolph testified before the Senate Armed Services Committee: "I personally pledge myself to openly counsel, aid and abet youth, both white and Negro, in an organized refusal to register and be drafted." Leaving the Senate Committee room, Randolph set up a soapbox where he urged draft-age youths not to register and to refuse draft induction. Later he sold buttons in front of the White House on Pennsylvania Avenue, which said, "Don't Join a Jim Crow Army." These harassing tactics were continued at the two political conventions which were held that summer. A NAACP poll showed that 71 percent of the draft-age black students polled were sympathetic to the Randolph-Reynolds campaign.

On July 26, President Truman issued Executive Orders 9980 and 9981, creating a Fair Employment Board to eliminate racial discrimination in Federal employment, and a President's Committee on Equality of Treatment and Opportunity in the Armed Services. When the watered-down and amended bill finally passed the House and got to the Senate it was ultimately defeated after two attempts at cloture failed.

Following is a chronology of executive orders and other regulations dealing with equal employment which were issued during the 1950s and 60s.

February 2, 1951—President Truman issued Executive Order 10201 forbidding discrimination by government contractors.

December 3, 1951—Executive Order 10308 created Truman's Committee on Government Contract Compliance.

August 13, 1953—President Eisenhower's Executive Order 10479₀ placed the Government Contract Compliance agency under the chairmanship of the Vice President.

January 18, 1955—President Eisenhower's Executive Order 10590 established the President's Committee on Government Policy to enforce non-discriminatory policies in federal employment; and in replacing the Fair Employment Board, made heads of government departments responsible for preventing job discrimination in their agencies.

February 1957—The U.S. Civil Service Commission eliminated racial designation of employees from personnel forms.

August 1960—The U.S. Department of Labor upheld the right of United Auto Workers to enforce non-discrimination at the local union level in Memphis, Tennessee.

March 1961—President Kennedy's Executive Order 10925 created the Committee on Equal Employment Opportunity to combat. job discrimination in government employment and in private employment stemming from government contracts.

July 1961—The President's Committee on Equal Employment Opportunity issued new rules to enforce non-discrimination clause in federal contracts; regulations called for reports on compliance and authorized cancellation of contracts in cases of violation.

July 1961—The U.S. Labor Department's Bureau of Apprenticeship and Training announced that non-discrimination statements would be required in connection with all apprenticeship training programs in firms handling government contracts.

Summer of 1961—nine major defense contractors,* came forward with long range "plans for progress" in signing agreements with the President's Committee on Equal Employment Opportunity, designed to give black workers fair access to jobs and promotion.

September 1961—The President's task force on employee-management relations ruled that "dual locals" in unions of government employees represent de facto segregation, and could not deal with federal officials unless they took steps to merge memberships.

October 1961—The Federal Civil Rights Commission urged that Congress take action to bar racial discrimination in labor unions and to expand the powers of the President's Committee on Equal Employment Opportunity.

March 15, 1961—The Manpower Development and Training Act of 1962 was passed by Congress and signed by President Kennedy, providing for the retraining of jobless workers and those whose skills had become obsolete. The Secretary of Labor stated that this program and the apprenticeship program would be administered without discrimination.

June 24, 1962—President Kennedy established a President's Committee on Equal Opportunity in the Armed Forces to report on remaining problems of discrimination in the Armed Forces, including the National Guard, and make recommendations for corrective action.

On June 22, 1963, the committee reported to the President that conditions of discrimination on off-base facilities continued to impair the morale of black servicemen. The President directed the Secretary of Defense to investigate and report back on the situation within 30 days. The Department of Defense later issued regulations designed to eliminate discrimination in off-base facilities.

June 22, 1963—President Kennedy issued Executive Order 11114, requiring non-discrimination provisions in federally assisted construction contracts and providing for the termination of such federal participation when compliance is not achieved.

On July 2, 1964, the Civil Rights Act of 1964 (effective July 2, 1965) was signed by President Lyndon Baines Johnson in a White House ceremony. Title VII of the bill, entitled, "Equal Employment Opportunity," provided for the establishment, by July 2, 1965, of an Equal Employment Opportunity Commission—an independent, bipartisan agency, comprising five members appointed by the President and approved by the Senate.

The act prohibited discrimination because of race, color, religion, sex, or national origin, in hiring, upgrading, and all other conditions of employment.

The commission was originally concerned with discrimination by four major groups —employers, public and private employment agencies, labor organizations, and joint labor-management apprenticeship programs. Title VII applied to: (1) employers of 25 or more persons; (2) labor unions with 25 or more members, or which refer persons for employment, or which represent employees of employers covered by the Act; (3) employment agencies dealing with employees of 25 or more persons; and (4) joint labor-management apprenticeship programs of covered employers and unions.

The Commission is empowered to receive and investigate charges of employment discrimination. Individual commissioners may initiate charges if they receive information suggesting that the law has been violated. If the Commission decides, after investigation, that reasonable cause exists to believe that a violation of Title VII has occurred, remedy is sought through the process of conciliation.

Effective March 24, 1972, the Commission was empowered to file suit in a Federal District Court to achieve compliance with Title

*Boeing Airplane, Douglas Aircraft, General Electric, Lockheed Aircraft, the Martin Company North American Aviation, Radio Corporation of America, United Aircraft, and Western Electric.

VII. (This provision will not apply to charges filed by State and local government employees.) Cases pending with the commission at the time the EEOC Act was passed will be subject to the same enforcement provisions.

In addition, the commission promotes programs of affirmative action by employers, labor organizations, and employment agencies to put the principle of equal employment opportunity into practice.

On March 24, 1972, the President signed into law the Equal Employment Opportunity Act of 1972 (P.L. 92-261) to be effective immediately. This act extended coverage to include employees of State and local governments. Charges filed with EEOC are to be investigated and processed through conciliation and if that fails, EEOC will then refer the cases to the Attorney General for court action. Coverage was also extended to include employees of educational institutions, but does not include elected or appointed officials of State and local governments.

Effective March 24, 1973 (one year after passage of the EEO Act), coverage was extended to 15, or more, employees or members.

MINORITY GROUP EMPLOYMENT IN THE FEDERAL GOVERNMENT

Data from the November 1971 minority employment survey showed that the number of minority group federal employees in better paying jobs increased significantly from November 1970. In the General Schedule (i.e., white collar jobs) minorities increased by 10,520, comprising 33.4 percent of the total increase of 31,485 in this schedule. The total federal work force remained relatively stable during the period, increasing by 2,300 jobs.

As a group, blacks, Spanish-surnamed employees, American Indians, and Oriental Americans working full-time for the federal government numbered 502,752, or 19.5 percent of the work force. This is a net decrease of 2,300 from November 1970, when minorities comprised 19.6 percent of the federal work force.

The decrease of 2,283 in overall minority employment in the federal service was attributed by the commission to substantial work force cutbacks in the Postal Field Service, where minority employment declined by 9,600 jobs during the one-year period. The total decline in Postal Field Service employment during the period was 18,170. This decline in Post Office employment was not due to layoffs, but rather through not filling vacancies as they occurred.

At all but the lowest grade levels (GS–1 thru GS–4), minorities paid under the General Schedule (GS), or similar pay plans, showed gains. At the top GS–16 thru GS–18 levels, minority employment increased by 23.8 percent, from 130 to 161. Corresponding increases for minorities at other GS grade groupings are: 549 (up 20.4%) at the 14–15 levels: 1,337 (up 12.7%) at the 12–13 levels: 2,204 (up 8.4%) at the 9–11 levels: and 7,181 (up 10.8%) at the 5–8 levels. Additionally, an increase of 67 was reported in the number of minorities holding positions paying $26,000 per year or more under "Other Pay Plans."

Although black employment increased by 6,491 under General Schedule and similar pay plans, there was a net decrease of 4,361 in total jobs for this minority, reflecting declines in black employment at the lower grade levels of the Postal Field Service, and in blue-collar jobs in other agencies. Blacks showed gains in all Postal Field Service grade groupings above PFS–5, and in all white-collar grade groupings above GS–4. The percentage of total federal jobs held by black employees decreased from 15.2 percent (391,173) in November 1970 to 15.0 percent (386,812) in November 1971.

As of November 30, 1971, minority group employees working full-time for the federal government totaled 502,752, or 19.5 percent, of the 2,573,770 total. Minorities represented 15.2 percent of all federal employees paid under the General Schedule and similar pay plans; 28.4 percent of those paid under wage system; 22.1 percent of those paid Postal Field Service rates; and 8.8 percent of those under all other pay plans. Except in the Postal Field Service and wage systems, these percentages are higher than in November 1970.

During the period November 1970–71, minority employment decreased by 2,283, or 0.5 percent. In this same period, total federal employment increased by 2,266, or 0.1 percent.

The net decrease in minority employment since November 1970 reflects the following changes in minority employment by pay category: General Schedule or similar (plus 10,-520); wage systems (− 3,193); Postal Field Service (− 9,600); and all other pay systems (− 10). when compared with the government-wide changes by pay category, minorities comprised 33.4 percent of the net increase in General Schedule and similar employment; 31.9 percent of the net decrease in wage systems employment; 52.8 percent of the net decrease in Postal Field Service employment; and 1.0 percent of the net decrease under all other pay systems.

Except in the lowest grades (GS 1–4) of the General Schedule and similar pay plans, minorities continue to show a consistent upward trend. They decreased by 782 in GS 1–4, accounting for 29.8 percent of the government-wide net decreases for this grade grouping.

For grade groupings involving GS–5 and above, gains for minorities and their percent of government-wide increases were as follows: GS 5–8 (7,181 or 39.9 percent); GS 9–11 (2,204 or 78.9 percent); GS 12–13 (1,337 or 14.0 percent); GS 14–15 (549 or 15.2 percent); and GS 16–18 (31 or 18.3 percent). These increases brought minority representation under the General Schedule and similar pay plans to 15.2 percent—up from 14.7 percent in November 1970.

As of November 30, 1971, black employees held 148,957, or 11.3 percent of all full-time federal jobs paid under the General Schedule and similar pay plans; 20.4 percent of those under wage systems; 18.7 percent of those paid under Postal Field Service rates; and 6.4 percent of those under "all other" pay plans. Except under wage systems, and in the Postal Field Service, these percentages are higher than in November 1970. Blacks paid under those two pay systems accounted for 24.0 and 46.2 percent respectively of the year's losses under each pay system. Data for black employees show an average annual rate of loss of 0.3 percent since November 1969. The average annual rates of change by pay plan during the past two years for black employees are: General Schedule and similar (+ 4.0 percent); wage systems (− 2.3 percent); Postal Field Service (− 2.2 percent); and "all other" pay plans (− 20.9 percent).

The 148,957 black employees paid General Schedule and similar rates include 6,491 more than in 1970—an increase of 4.6 percent. Also, at each grade grouping except GS 1–4, black employees account for a larger percentage than in 1970. Specifically, black employees comprise 21.8 percent of employment in GS grades 1–4 (down from 22.3 percent in 1970); 14.8 percent of GS 5–8 (up from 14.0); 5.7 percent of GS 9–11 (up from 5.3); 3.1 percent of GS 12–13 (up from 2.8); 2.2 percent of GS 14–15 (up from 1.9); and 2.0 percent of GS 16–18 (up from 1.6). There are 1,883 fewer black employees in GS grades 1–4; 5,767 more in grades 5–8; 1,413 more in grades 9–11; 854 more in grades 12–13; 319 more in grades 14–15; and 21 more in grades 16–18.

In November 1971, the median grade for black employees under the General Schedule and similar pay plans was 4.9 as compared to a median grade of 7.6 for total employment. Since November 1969, minority group employment in the federal government has increased 2,216, for an average of 0.2 percent yearly. Black employees number 2,439 fewer than in 1969, for an average annual rate of change of minus 0.3 percent. Spanish-surnamed employment has increased by 2,098 since 1969, for an average annual growth rate of 1.4 percent. American Indian employees increased by 2,780, or 8.4 percent annually. Oriental American employees show an average annual rate of change of minus 0.5 percent, based on a net decrease of 223.

Source: U.S. Civil Service Commission SM 70-71B

Full- and part-time status of the civilian labor force by color, sex, and age
January 1973
(Numbers in thousands)

Age and sex	Full-time labor force					Part-time labor force			
	Total	Employed		Unemployed (looking for full-time work)		Total	Employed on voluntary part time[1]	Unemployed (looking for part-time work)	
		Full-time schedules[1]	Part-time for economic reasons	Number	Percent of full-time labor force			Number	Percent of part-time labor force
TOTAL									
Total, 16 years and over......	73,096	67,394	2,052	3,650	5.0	12,622	11,597	1,025	8.1
16 to 21 years.................	7,150	5,784	423	943	13.2	4,594	4,009	585	12.7
16 to 19 years.................	3,447	2,663	237	547	15.9	3,690	3,187	502	13.6
16 to 17 years.................	476	312	44	120	25.2	2,302	1,947	355	15.4
18 to 19 years.................	2,971	2,351	193	427	14.4	1,388	1,240	147	10.6
20 years and over.............	69,649	64,731	1,815	3,103	4.5	8,932	8,409	522	5.8
20 to 24 years.................	10,428	9,085	410	933	9.0	1,664	1,508	156	9.4
25 years and over.............	59,221	55,646	1,406	2,170	3.7	7,268	6,900	367	5.0
25 to 54 years.................	47,606	44,757	1,030	1,820	3.8	4,858	4,598	260	5.4
55 years and over.............	11,615	10,890	376	349	3.0	2,410	2,302	108	4.5
Males, 16 years and over....	48,186	45,042	990	2,156	4.5	4,360	3,913	447	10.2
16 to 21 years.................	3,976	3,259	202	521	13.1	2,383	2,045	338	14.2
16 to 19 years.................	1,972	1,550	110	313	15.8	1,947	1,655	292	15.0
20 years and over.............	46,216	43,492	880	1,844	4.0	2,413	2,258	155	6.4
20 to 24 years.................	5,935	5,202	196	537	9.1	770	699	71	9.2
25 years and over.............	40,281	38,290	684	1,307	3.2	1,644	1,558	84	5.1
25 to 54 years.................	32,465	30,895	487	1,084	3.3	635	598	36	5.7
55 years and over.............	7,816	7,395	197	223	2.9	1,009	961	48	4.8
Females, 16 years and over...	24,908	22,352	1,062	1,494	6.0	8,262	7,684	578	7.0
16 to 21 years.................	3,174	2,532	220	423	13.3	2,211	1,964	247	11.2
16 to 19 years.................	1,475	1,114	127	235	15.9	1,743	1,533	210	12.1
20 years and over.............	23,433	21,238	936	1,259	5.4	6,519	6,151	367	5.6
20 to 24 years.................	4,493	3,883	214	396	8.8	894	809	85	9.5
25 years and over.............	18,940	17,356	722	863	4.6	5,624	5,342	282	5.0
25 to 54 years.................	15,141	13,861	543	737	4.9	4,223	4,001	223	5.3
55 years and over.............	3,799	3,495	178	126	3.3	1,401	1,342	60	4.3
BLACK AND OTHER RACES									
Males, 16 years and over.....	4,746	4,283	143	320	6.7	390	313	77	19.7
16 to 21 years.................	509	398	21	90	17.6	177	120	57	32.1
16 to 19 years.................	245	181	8	56	22.7	151	100	51	33.9
20 years and over.............	4,501	4,102	135	264	5.9	239	213	26	10.8
20 to 24 years.................	716	602	29	85	11.8	61	56	6	9.3
25 years and over.............	3,786	3,501	105	179	4.7	178	158	20	11.2
25 to 54 years.................	3,157	2,933	73	150	4.8	90	82	7	7.8
55 years and over.............	628	567	33	29	4.6	88	76	12	13.6
Females, 16 years and over...	3,433	2,914	178	341	9.9	779	677	102	13.1
16 to 21 years.................	418	272	34	112	26.8	170	114	55	32.7
16 to 19 years.................	172	101	17	55	31.7	135	85	50	37.0
20 years and over.............	3,261	2,813	162	286	8.8	644	592	52	8.1
20 to 24 years.................	624	486	27	112	17.9	68	51	17	25.6
25 years and over.............	2,637	2,327	135	175	6.6	576	542	35	6.1
25 to 54 years.................	2,289	2,016	110	163	7.1	398	369	28	7.0
55 years and over.............	348	312	25	12	3.4	178	172	6	3.4

[1]Employed persons with a job but not at work are distributed among the full- and part-time employed categories.

Employment status of 14-15 year-olds by sex and color
January 1973
(In thousands)

Employment status	Total			Black and other races		
	Both sexes	Male	Female	Both sexes	Male	Female
Civilian noninstitutional population...............	8,297	4,218	4,079	1,205	602	603
Civilian labor force................................	1,120	625	495	61	51	10
Employed..	1,030	563	468	39	33	6
Agriculture.....................................	80	68	11	—	—	—
Nonagricultural industries.........................	951	494	457	40	33	6
Unemployed.......................................	90	62	27	22	18	4
Not in labor force................................	7,177	3,593	3,584	1,144	551	594
Keeping house....................................	72	15	57	14	—	15
Going to school..................................	6,840	3,450	3,390	1,081	526	555
Unable to work...................................	12	7	5	2	—	2
All other reasons.................................	252	121	131	48	26	22

Employment status of persons 16-21 years of age in the noninstitutional population by color and sex
January 1973
(In thousands)

Employment status	Total			Black and other races		
	Both sexes	Male	Female	Both sexes	Male	Female
Total noninstitutional population	23,471	11,869	11,602	3,271	1,614	1,657
Total labor force	12,656	7,248	5,408	1,404	813	591
Percent of population	53.9	61.1	46.6	42.9	50.4	35.6
Civilian labor force	11,744	6,359	5,386	1,274	686	587
Employed...	10,216	5,500	4,716	960	540	420
Agriculture..	343	284	59	23	20	3
Nonagricultural industries.............................	9,872	5,216	4,656	937	519	417
Unemployed...	1,529	858	670	314	147	167
Percent of labor force.................................	13.0	13.5	12.4	24.7	21.4	28.5
Looking for full-time work.............................	943	521	423	202	90	112
Looking for part-time work.............................	585	338	247	112	57	55
Not in labor force.....................................	10,815	4,621	6,194	1,867	801	1,066
Major activity: going to school						
Civilian labor force....................................	3,236	1,781	1,454	230	125	106
Employed...	2,706	1,453	1,253	136	70	67
Agriculture..	110	88	22	2	2	—
Nonagricultural industries.............................	2,597	1,365	1,231	134	67	67
Unemployed...	529	328	201	94	55	39
Percent of labor force.................................	16.4	18.4	13.8	40.8	44.1	36.9
Looking for full-time work.............................	36	22	13	3	2	1
Looking for part-time work.............................	494	306	188	91	53	38
Not in labor force.....................................	8,097	4,013	4,084	1,361	666	695
Major activity: other						
Civilian labor force....................................	8,509	4,577	3,931	1,043	562	482
Employed...	7,509	4,047	3,462	823	470	353
Agriculture..	233	196	37	21	18	3
Nonagricultural industries.............................	7,276	3,851	3,425	803	452	351
Unemployed...	999	530	469	220	92	128
Percent of labor force.................................	11.7	11.6	11.9	21.1	16.3	26.7
Looking for full-time work.............................	908	498	409	199	88	111
Looking for part-time work.............................	92	32	60	21	4	17
Not in labor force.....................................	2,718	608	2,110	506	135	372

Employment status of the noninstitutional population
16 years and over by sex, age, and color
(In thousands)

Employment status and color	Total		Men, 20 years and over		Women, 20 years and over		Both sexes, 16-19 years	
	Jan. 1973	Jan. 1972	Jan. 1973	Jan. 1972	Jan. 1973	Jan. 1972	Jan. 1973	Jan. 1972
TOTAL								
Total noninstitutional population	147,129	144,697	62,398	61,444	68,762	67,615	15,969	15,638
Total labor force	88,122	87,147	50,597	50,277	29,989	29,499	7,536	7,371
Percent of population	59.9	60.2	81.1	81.8	43.6	43.6	47.2	47.1
Civilian labor force..........................	85,718	84,553	48,629	48,039	29,952	29,468	7,137	7,046
Employed..................................	81,043	79,106	46,630	45,554	28,325	27,774	6,088	5,779
Agriculture................................	2,955	2,869	2,319	2,230	388	408	248	230
Nonagricultural industries...................	78,088	76,237	44,311	43,323	27,937	27,366	5,840	5,548
Unemployed................................	4,675	5,447	1,999	2,485	1,627	1,695	1,050	1,267
Percent of labor force......................	5.5	6.4	4.1	5.2	5.4	5.8	14.7	18.0
Not in labor force...........................	59,008	57,550	11,800	11,166	38,774	38,116	8,434	8,267
BLACK AND OTHER RACES								
Total noninstitutional population...........	16,506	16,077	6,516	6,361	7,721	7,532	2,269	2,183
Total labor force...........................	9,663	9,487	4,992	4,916	3,910	3,838	761	733
Percent of population.......................	58.5	59.0	76.6	77.3	50.6	51.0	33.5	33.6
Civilian labor force..........................	9,347	9,186	4,740	4,657	3,905	3,835	702	694
Employed..................................	8,508	8,161	4,450	4,258	3,566	3,460	491	443
Agriculture................................	211	233	180	195	17	22	15	16
Nonagricultural industries...................	8,297	7,928	4,271	4,063	3,550	3,438	476	427
Unemployed................................	840	1,025	290	398	339	375	211	251
Percent of labor force......................	9.0	11.2	6.1	8.6	8.7	9.8	30.1	36.2
Not in labor force...........................	6,843	6,589	1,523	1,445	3,811	3,694	1,508	1,450

Number of Employed and Unemployed Persons: 1960 to 1971
(Numbers in millions. Annual averages)

Year	Employed		Unemployed	
	Black and other races	White	Black and other races	White
1960..	6.9	58.9	0.8	3.1
1961..	6.8	58.9	1.0	3.7
1962..	7.0	59.7	0.9	3.1
1963..	7.1	60.6	0.9	3.2
1964..	7.4	61.9	0.8	3.0
1965..	7.6	63.4	0.7	2.7
1966..	7.9	65.0	0.6	2.3
1967..	8.0	66.4	0.6	2.3
1968..	8.2	67.8	0.6	2.2
1969..	8.4	69.5	0.6	2.3
1970..	8.4	70.2	0.8	3.3
1971..	8.4	70.7	0.9	4.1

Note: The information on employment and unemployment is obtained from a monthly sample survey of households. All persons 16 years of age and over are classified as employed, unemployed, or not in the labor force for the calendar week containing the 12th of the month. The unemployed are persons who did not work or have a job during the survey week, and who had looked for work within the past 4 weeks, and were currently available for work. Also included are those waiting to be called back to a job from which they had been laid off or waiting to report to a new job. The sum of the employed and the unemployed constitutes the civilian labor force.

Source: U.S. Department of Labor, Bureau of Labor Statistics.

Employed persons by major occupational group, sex, and color
(Percent distribution)

Occupational group and color	Total		Male		Female	
	Jan. 1973	Jan. 1972	Jan. 1973	Jan. 1972	Jan. 1973	Jan. 1972
TOTAL						
Total employed (thousands)............................	81,043	79,106	49,945	48,678	31,098	30,428
Percent..	100.0	100.0	100.0	100.0	100.0	100.0
White-collar workers...............................	49.1	48.7	41.4	40.9	61.5	61.3
Professional and technical..........................	14.7	14.3	14.3	14.0	15.3	14.7
Managers and administrators, except farm..............	10.2	10.0	13.5	13.5	4.7	4.4
Sales workers.......................................	6.7	6.5	6.7	6.3	6.8	6.9
Clerical workers....................................	17.5	17.9	6.8	7.1	34.6	35.3
Blue-collar workers................................	34.5	34.5	46.0	46.6	16.1	15.1
Craftsmen and kindred workers.......................	13.1	13.4	20.3	20.9	1.5	1.4
Operatives, except transport.......................	12.8	12.6	12.6	12.6	13.2	12.6
Transport equipment operatives......................	3.9	4.0	6.0	6.3	.5	.5
Nonfarm laborers....................................	4.7	4.5	7.1	6.9	.8	.6
Service workers....................................	13.2	13.6	8.1	8.1	21.4	22.4
Private household workers...........................	1.7	1.9	.1	.1	4.3	4.9
Other service workers...............................	11.5	11.7	8.0	8.0	17.1	17.6
Farm workers......................................	3.2	3.2	4.5	4.5	1.1	1.2
Farmers and farm managers...........................	2.0	2.0	3.0	3.1	.3	.2
Farm laborers and foremen...........................	1.2	1.2	1.5	1.4	.8	1.0
BLACK AND OTHER RACES						
Total employed (thousands)...........................	8,508	8,161	4,739	4,502	3,769	3,658
Percent...	100.0	100.0	100.0	100.0	100.0	100.0
White-collar workers...............................	32.1	29.6	23.1	22.3	43.5	38.5
Professional and technical..........................	10.9	9.7	9.2	8.5	13.0	11.2
Managers and administrators, except farm..............	3.6	3.5	4.6	4.7	2.5	2.1
Sale workers..	2.4	2.4	2.0	1.9	2.9	2.9
Clerical workers....................................	15.2	14.0	7.3	7.3	25.2	22.3
Blue-collar workers................................	40.0	39.3	57.8	58.1	17.7	16.2
Craftsmen and kindred workers.......................	8.6	8.6	14.7	14.5	.9	1.3
Operatives, except transport.......................	16.6	15.8	17.4	17.4	15.5	13.9
Transport equipment operatives......................	5.3	5.7	9.1	10.3	.4	.1
Nonfarm laborers....................................	9.6	9.2	16.5	15.8	.9	1.0
Service workers....................................	25.7	28.8	15.7	15.9	38.3	44.7
Private household workers...........................	6.1	7.8	.3	.1	13.5	17.2
Other service workers...............................	19.6	21.0	15.4	15.8	24.8	27.5
Farm workers......................................	2.1	2.3	3.4	3.7	.4	.7
Farmers and farm managers...........................	.6	.6	.9	1.0	.1	—
Farm laborers and foremen...........................	1.5	1.8	2.5	2.7	.3	.6

Employment by Broad Occupational Groups: 1960 and 1966 to 1971
(Numbers in millions. Annual averages)

Year	Total		White-collar workers, craftsmen, and operatives		All other workers[1]	
	Black and other races	White	Black and other races	White	Black and other races	White
1960............................	6.9	58.9	2.9	46.1	4.0	12.8
1966............................	7.9	65.0	4.0	52.5	3.9	12.6
1967............................	8.0	66.4	4.3	53.6	3.7	12.7
1968............................	8.2	67.8	4.6	54.9	3.6	12.8
1969............................	8.4	69.5	4.9	56.4	3.5	13.1
1970............................	8.4	70.2	5.1	57.0	3.4	13.2
1971............................	8.4	70.7	4.9	56.5	3.5	14.2
Percent change: 1960 to 1971..................	+22	+20	+69	+23	−13	+11

Note: Comparisons with data prior to January, 1971 are affected by the reclassification of census occupations that was introduced in that month. For an explanation of the changes see **Bureau of Census Technical Paper No. 26,** "1970 Occupation and Industry Classification Systems in Terms of Their 1960 Occupation and Industry Elements."

[1] Includes private household and other service workers, laborers and farm workers. Median usual weekly earnings were about $40 to $120 a week for these workers, compared with $120 to about $200 a week for white-collar workers, craftsmen, and operatives in May 1971.

Source: U.S. Department of Labor, Bureau of Labor Statistics.

Percent Distribution of Total and Black Persons Employed in High Hourly Earnings Industries in 1970, by Occupational Pay Level

Industry	Total employed (thousands)	Percent of total employment					
		Total	Higher paid[1]	Total	Middle pay level[2] Craftsmen	Other	Lower paid[3]
All industries:							
Total.....................	28,883	100	25	68	14	55	7
Black.....................	2,965	100	7	75	7	68	18
Nine industries:[4]							
Total.....................	9,368	100	20	78	18	60	2
Black.....................	840	100	3	92	10	82	5
Printing and publishing:							
Total.....................	579	100	23	75	25	49	2
Black.....................	37	100	6	82	10	72	12
Chemicals:							
Total.....................	933	100	27	71	15	55	3
Black.....................	80	100	4	89	9	80	7
Primary metal industry:							
Total.....................	1,139	100	13	86	20	65	2
Black.....................	151	100	2	96	10	85	3
Fabricated metal:							
Total.....................	913	100	13	86	20	65	1
Black.....................	92	100	1	96	12	84	3
Nonelectrical machinery:							
Total.....................	1,560	100	19	79	21	58	2
Black.....................	101	100	3	92	13	80	5
Electrical machines:							
Total.....................	1,822	100	20	79	12	67	2
Black.....................	148	100	3	93	7	87	4
Transportation equipment:							
Total.....................	1,767	100	19	79	21	58	2
Black.....................	194	100	2	93	13	80	5
Air transportation:							
Total.....................	282	100	38	51	20	31	12
Black.....................	16	100	15	63	12	52	22
Instruments:							
Total.....................	373	100	22	76	14	62	2
Black.....................	21	100	4	89	8	81	7

[1]Professional, managerial and sales workers.
[2]Technical, clerical, craftsmen, operatives and labor workers.
[3]Service workers.
[4]Nine high earnings industries.
Source: U.S. Equal Employment Opportunity Commission.

Black Persons Employed in Industries With a Large Proportion of Blacks by Occupational Pay Level: 1970

Industry	All occupations	Higher paid[1]	Middle pay level[2]			Lower paid[3]
			Total	Craftsmen and foremen	Other	
BLACK EMPLOYED						
All industries..............thousands......	2,965	206	2,227	222	2,005	531
Total, nine industries[4]........thousands......	465	31	183	13	171	251
PERCENT BLACK OF TOTAL EMPLOYMENT						
All industries............................	10	3	11	6	13	·27
Total, nine industries[4]......................	18	5	17	12	18	27
Tobacco...............................	23	4	25	7	27	49
Medical and other health services...............	16	4	13	11	14	28
Local passenger transit.......................	20	18	20	11	22	31
Water transportation........................	18	2	21	13	22	21
Eating and drinking places....................	18	8	19	23	18	20
Real estate...............................	13	2	12	7	14	26
Hotel and other lodging places..................	23	7	18	12	19	28
Personal services..........................	30	6	36	25	37	34
Miscellaneous repair services..................	10	2	12	11	13	26

[1]Professional, managerial and sales workers.
[2]Technical, craftsmen, operatives and labor workers.
[3]Service workers.
[4]Nine industries with a large proportion of blacks.
Source: U.S. Equal Employment Opportunity Commission.

Occupation of the Total and Black Employed Population: 1970

(Numbers in thousands)

Occupation	Total	Black	Percent Black of total
Total employed...............................	76,554	7,361	10
Professional, technical, and kindred workers.............	11,349	611	5
Engineers...........................	1,208	14	1
Physicians, dentists, and related practitioners.........	539	11	2
Health workers, except practitioners....................	1,205	101	8
Teachers, elementary and secondary schools..........	2,540	215	8
Other professional workers......................	5,857	270	5
Managers and administrators, except farm...............	6,371	170	3
Self-employed...........................	1,164	36	3
Sales workers............................	5,443	167	3
Clerical and kindred workers......................	13,745	1,011	7
Craftsmen, foremen, and kindred workers...............	10,608	665	6
Mechanics and repairmen......................	2,444	142	6
Metal craftsmen, except mechanics and machinists.....	720	36	5
Construction craftsmen........................	1,940	150	8
Other craftsmen............................	5,505	337	6
Operatives, except transport......................	10,496	1,327	13
Transport equipment operatives......................	2,958	417	14
Truck drivers............................	1,380	185	13
Other transport equipment operatives.................	1,578	232	15
Laborers, except farm............................	3,427	688	20
Construction laborers......................	600	133	22
Freight, stock, and material handlers.................	1,347	219	16
Other laborers, except farm.........................	1,479	336	23
Farmers and farm managers........................	1,426	43	3
Farm laborers and farm foremen....................	954	177	19
Service workers, except private household..............	8,625	1,475	17
Cleaning service workers........................	1,862	507	27
Food service workers........................	2,774	341	12
Health service workers........................	1,181	259	22
Personal service workers........................	1,154	125	11
Protective service workers........................	952	69	7
Private household workers...........................	1,152	610	53

Source: U.S. Department of Commerce, Social and Economic Statistics Administration, Bureau of the Census.

Black Persons Employed in Industries With High Average Hourly Earnings, by Occupational Pay Level: 1970

(Numbers in thousands)

Industry	All occupa-tions	Higher paid[1]	Middle pay level[2]			Lower paid[3]	Average hourly earnings of all workers[4] 1970
			Total	Crafts-men	Other		
BLACKS EMPLOYED							
All industries.........................	2,965	206	2,227	222	2,005	531	$3.22
Total, nine industries[5].....................	840	24	774	88	686	42	3.71
PERCENT BLACK OF TOTAL EMPLOYMENT							
All industries..........................	10	3	11	6	13	27	(X)
Total, nine industires[5]....................	9	1	11	5	12	20	(X)
Printing and publishing.......................	6	2	7	3	9	33	3.92
Chemicals............................	9	1	11	5	12	24	3.69
Primary metal............................	13	2	15	7	17	19	3.93
Fabricated metal..........................	10	1	11	6	13	19	3.53
Nonelectrical machinery......................	6	1	8	4	9	16	3.77
Electrical machinery.........................	8	1	10	4	11	19	3.28
Transportation equipment....................	11	1	13	7	15	24	4.06
Air transportation........................	6	2	7	3	9	11	[6]3.85
Instruments..............................	6	1	7	3	7	20	3.35

Note: Data for this and the following three tables are based upon reports filed with the Equal Employment Opportunity Commission by companies with 100 or more employees.
X Not applicable.
[1]Professional, managerial and sales workers.
[2]Technical, clerical, craftsmen, operatives and labor workers.
[3]Service workers.
[4]Data from Bureau of Labor Statistics Monthly Report on Employment, Payroll and Hours, 1970.
[5]Nine high earnings industries.
[6]Average hourly earnings includes "all transportation and public utilities."
Source: U.S. Equal Employment Opportunity Commission and Department of Labor, Bureau of Labor Statistics.

Distribution of Total and Black Persons Employed, by Occupational Pay Level, in Industries With a Large Proportion of Black Employment: 1970

Industry	Total employed (thousands)	Percent of total employed					
		Total	Higher paid[1]	Middle pay level[2]			Lower paid[3]
				Total	Craftsmen	Other	
All industries:							
Total..................	28,883	100	25	68	14	55	7
Black..............	2,965	100	7	75	7	68	18
Nine industries:[4]...............							
Total......................	2,625	100	24	40	4	36	36
Black.....................	465	100	7	39	3	37	54
Tobacco:							
Total........................	69	100	12	85	9	76	3
Black........................	16	100	2	91	3	89	7
Medical and other health services:							
Total........................	1,634	100	30	36	2	34	34
Black........................	259	100	8	30	1	29	61
Local passenger transit:							
Total........................	135	100	13	79	17	62	8
Black........................	28	100	11	77	9	68	12
Water transportation							
Total........................	82	100	16	81	13	67	4
Black........................	15	100	2	94	10	84	4
Eating and drinking places:							
Total........................	291	100	13	18	3	15	69
Black........................	53	100	6	18	3	15	76
Real estate:							
Total........................	47	100	26	48	9	39	26
Black........................	6	100	4	45	4	40	51
Hotel and other lodging places:							
Total........................	234	100	9	29	5	24	61
Black........................	54	100	3	22	3	20	75
Personal services:							
Total........................	105	100	18	73	4	69	9
Black........................	32	100	4	87	3	83	10
Miscellaneous repair services:							
Total........................	27	100	19	80	35	45	1
Black........................	3	100	4	93	36	58	3.

[1]Professional, managerial and sales workers.
[2]Technical, clerical, craftsmen, operatives and labor workers.
[3]Service workers.
[4]Nine industries with a large proportion of Negroes.
Source: U.S. Equal Employment Opportunity Commission.

Men Not in the Labor Force by Age: 1971

(Annual averages)

Age and race	Total not in labor force (thousands)	Reason not in labor force (percent)			
		Total	Going to school	Unable to work[1]	Others[2]
16 to 19 years:					
Black and other races................	554	100	81	1	18
White............................	2,696	100	83	1	16
20 to 24 years:					
Black and other races................	175	100	62	10	27
White............................	1,095	100	76	5	20
25 to 54 years:					
Black and other races................	327	100	9	57	33
White............................	1,215	100	17	47	36
55 to 64 years:					
Black and other races................	173	100	—	62	38
White............................	1,378	100	—	44	56
65 years and over:					
Black and other races................	525	100	—	27	73
White............................	5,578	100	—	12	88

— Represents zero or rounds to zero.
[1]Includes only those who have serious, long-term physical or mental illness.
[2]Includes retired workers and unpaid family workers working less than 15 hours per week, and those awaiting military service.
Source: U.S. Department of Labor, Bureau of Labor Statistics.

Unemployed persons by duration, sex, age, color, and marital status
January 1973

Sex, age, color, and marital status	Thousands of persons					Average (mean) duration, in weeks	Less than 5 weeks as a percent of unemployed in group		15 weeks and over as a percent of unemployed in group	
	Total	Less than 5 weeks	5 to 14 weeks	15 to 26 weeks	27 weeks and over		Jan. 1973	Jan. 1972	Jan. 1973	Jan. 1972
Total	**4,675**	**2,231**	**1,501**	**557**	**386**	**10.4**	**47.7**	**46.5**	**20.2**	**23.2**
16 to 21 years	1,529	836	429	189	75	8.2	54.7	52.4	17.2	20.0
16 to 19 years	1,050	569	295	138	49	8.1	54.2	52.8	17.8	20.2
20 to 24 years	1,089	570	334	113	72	8.9	52.3	48.3	17.0	21.2
25 to 34 years	996	480	321	107	88	10.7	48.2	46.3	19.6	22.0
35 to 44 years	555	228	207	63	58	11.7	41.0	40.3	21.7	25.8
45 to 54 years	528	217	196	66	49	12.1	41.2	44.6	21.7	23.7
55 to 64 years	356	130	128	51	47	14.7	36.6	39.6	27.6	30.3
65 years and over	100	37	21	19	24	15.8	36.5	27.9	42.6	48.9
Male	**2,603**	**1,144**	**896**	**322**	**241**	**11.4**	**44.0**	**42.6**	**21.6**	**24.6**
16 to 21 years	858	462	250	106	41	8.2	53.8	50.1	17.1	20.5
16 to 19 years	605	326	173	79	27	8.0	53.9	50.7	17.5	18.7
20 to 24 years	608	286	216	61	45	9.5	47.0	44.9	17.4	23.6
25 to 34 years	535	230	176	69	60	12.8	43.0	41.5	24.2	23.9
35 to 44 years	282	108	110	37	26	12.4	38.4	35.9	22.5	30.1
45 to 54 years	303	115	116	37	35	14.0	37.9	38.1	23.8	24.6
55 to 64 years	211	58	89	31	34	17.3	27.5	37.3	30.4	29.7
65 years and over	60	21	16	8	14	15.6	(1)	(1)	(1)	(1)
Female	**2,072**	**1,086**	**606**	**234**	**145**	**9.1**	**52.4**	**52.1**	**18.3**	**21.3**
16 to 21 years	670	375	179	83	34	8.2	55.9	55.7	17.4	19.2
16 to 19 years	445	242	122	59	22	8.3	54.5	55.8	18.1	22.3
20 to 24 years	481	284	118	52	27	8.1	59.0	53.5	16.4	17.4
25 to 34 years	461	250	145	38	28	8.3	54.3	53.2	14.2	19.3
35 to 44 years	274	120	97	26	31	11.1	43.7	46.5	20.8	19.8
45 to 54 years	225	103	80	29	14	9.5	45.6	52.4	19.0	22.7
55 to 64 years	145	72	38	21	13	11.1	49.9	44.1	23.5	31.5
65 years and over	41	15	5	11	9	16.1	(1)	(1)	(1)	(1)
Black and other races: Total	840	355	265	139	81	11.6	42.2	45.7	26.1	24.1
Male	397	177	113	67	39	11.7	44.6	41.7	26.8	26.0
Female	443	178	152	71	42	11.5	40.1	49.9	25.5	22.1
Male: Married, wife present	1,235	498	454	157	125	12.4	40.4	39.1	22.9	25.7
Widowed, divorced, or separated	187	70	69	25	23	14.0	37.4	39.8	25.8	31.5
Single (never married)	1,181	576	373	140	93	10.0	48.8	46.7	19.7	22.4
Female: Married, husband present	1,035	557	318	92	68	8.7	53.8	55.2	15.4	18.0
Widowed, divorced, or separated	389	196	122	46	25	8.6	50.5	44.6	18.1	25.9
Single (never married)	648	333	165	96	53	10.1	51.5	51.6	23.0	23.7

[1]Percent not shown where base is less than 75,000.

Unemployed Men, by Age, Veterans Status, and Race: 1969 to 1971
In thousands, except as indicated. Averages for periods indicated

ITEM	TOTAL			WHITE			BLACK AND OTHER		
	1969	1970	1971	1969	1970	1971	1969	1970	1971
Unemployed men, number:									
16 years old and over, total	1,403	2,235	2,776	1,137	1,856	2,302	266	379	474
20–29 years old, total	399	721	950	317	583	768	82	138	182
Percent of total, 16 and over	28.4	32.3	34.2	27.9	31.4	33.4	30.8	36.4	38.4
War veterans	114	219	326	98	185	277	16	34	49
Post-Korean peacetime veterans	22	35	30	19	29	25	3	6	5
Nonveterans	264	467	594	202	368	465	62	99	129
Unemployment rate, men:[1]									
16 years old and over, total	2.8	4.4	5.3	2.5	4.0	4.9	5.3	7.3	9.1
20–29 years old, total	3.6	6.1	7.6	3.2	5.6	7.0	6.3	9.9	12.4
War veterans	4.5	6.9	8.8	4.3	6.4	8.3	7.5	11.6	13.7
Post-Korean peacetime veterans	1.8	3.9	4.6	1.7	3.5	4.1	3.4	10.5	(B)
Nonveterans	3.6	6.0	7.3	3.2	5.5	6.6	6.2	9.5	12.0

B Not computed; base less than 75,000. [1] Unemployment as percent of the male civilian labor force.
Source: U.S. Bureau of Labor Statistics, unpublished data.

Unemployed persons by marital status, sex, age, and color

Marital status, age, and color	Male				Female			
	Thousands of persons		Unemployment rates		Thousands of persons		Unemployment rates	
	Jan. 1973	Jan. 1972	Jan. 1973	Jan. 1972	Jan. 1973	Jan. 1972	Jan. 1973	Jan. 1972
Total, 16 years and over............	2,603	3,240	5.0	6.2	2,072	2,270	6.2	6.8
Married, spouse present.............	1,235	1,518	3.1	3.9	1,035	1,107	5.3	5.7
Widowed, divorced, or separated.....	187	233	6.2	7.9	389	412	6.3	6.7
Single (never married).............	1,181	1,489	11.8	15.3	648	688	8.8	9.5
Total, 20 to 64 years of age........	1,939	2,413	4.1	5.2	1,586	1,659	5.5	5.8
Married, spouse present.............	1,149	1,433	3.0	3.8	946	1,021	5.0	5.5
Widowed, divorced, or separated.....	182	218	6.6	8.2	350	373	6.4	6.9
Single (never married).............	608	763	9.7	12.6	289	265	6.4	6.0
Black and other races, 16 years and over..........	397	527	7.7	10.5	443	498	10.5	12.0
Married, spouse present.............	146	198	4.4	6.0	145	178	7.1	8.6
Widowed, divorced, or separated.....	50	55	8.4	9.2	98	140	8.1	11.7
Single (never married).............	200	274	16.9	24.0	200	180	21.0	19.9
Black and other races, 20 to 64 years of age.......	279	383	6.1	8.5	335	372	8.8	10.0
Married, spouse present.............	131	192	4.1	6.1	129	163	6.5	8.3
Widowed, divorced, or separated.....	49	49	8.6	8.8	95	134	8.4	12.2
Single (never married).............	98	142	12.1	18.3	112	75	16.4	11.8

Unemployed persons by reason for unemployment, sex, age, and color

Reason for unemployment	Total unemployed		Male, 20 years and over		Female, 20 years and over		Both sexes 16 to 19 years		Black and other races	
	Jan. 1973	Jan. 1972	Jan. 1973	Jan. 1972	Jan. 1973	Jan. 1972	Jan. 1973	Jan. 1972	Jan. 1973	Jan. 1972
Unemployment level										
Total unemployed, in thousands........	4,675	5,447	1,999	2,485	1,627	1,695	1,050	1,267	840	1,025
Lost last job..........................	2,228	2,809	1,314	1,696	667	775	248	337	334	480
Left last job..........................	590	598	241	255	236	232	113	111	105	106
Reentered labor force..................	1,365	1,531	381	471	646	616	339	443	276	331
Never worked before....................	491	509	64	63	78	71	350	376	124	108
Total unemployed, percent distribution..	100.0	100.0	100.0	100.0	100.0	100.0	100.0	100.0	100.0	100.0
Lost last job..........................	47.7	51.6	65.7	68.2	41.0	45.7	23.6	26.6	39.8	46.8
Left last job..........................	12.6	11.0	12.1	10.3	14.5	13.7	10.8	8.8	12.5	10.3
Reentered labor force..................	29.2	28.1	19.1	19.0	39.7	36.4	32.3	35.0	32.9	32.2
Never worked before....................	10.5	9.3	3.2	2.5	4.8	4.2	33.3	29.7	14.8	10.5
Unemployment rate										
Total unemployment rate...............	5.5	6.4	4.1	5.2	5.4	5.8	14.7	18.0	9.0	11.2
Job-loser rate[1]......................	2.6	3.3	2.7	3.5	2.3	2.6	3.5	4.8	3.6	5.2
Job-leaver rate[1].....................	.7	.7	.5	.5	.8	.8	1.6	1.6	1.1	1.2
Reentrant rate[1]......................	1.6	1.8	.8	1.0	2.2	2.1	4.7	6.3	3.0	3.6
New entrant rate[1]....................	.6	.6	.1	.1	.3	.2	4.9	5.3	1.3	1.2

[1]Unemployment rates are calculated as a percent of the civilian labor force.

Distribution of Persons Below the Low-Income Level, by Family Status:
1959, 1966, and 1971

Family status and year	All races	Black	White	Black as a percent of all races
1959				
Total.....................millions..	38.8	9.9	28.3	26
Percent.........................	100	100	100	(X)
In families...........................	85	92	82	28
Head.......	21	19	21	23
65 years and over..................	5	3	5	16
Children under 18 years...............	41	51	37	32
Other family members................	23	22	24	25
Unrelated individuals..................	15	8	18	14
65 years and over..................	6	2	7	10
1966				
Total.....................millions..	28.5	8.9	19.3	31
Percent.........................	100	100	100	(X)
In families...........................	84	91	80	34
Head..............................	20	18	21	28
65 years and over..................	5	3	7	18
Children under 18 years...............	43	54	37	39
Other family members................	21	19	21	29
Unrelated individuals..................	16	90	20	17
65 years and over..................	9	3	12	11
1971				
Total.....................millions..	25.6	7.4	17.8	29
Percent.........................	100	100	100	(X)
In families...........................	80	88	76	32
Head..............................	21	20	21	28
65 years and over..................	4	3	5	20
Children under 18 years...............	40	52	36	37
Other family members................	19	16	20	25
Unrelated individuals..................	20	12	24	17
65 years and over..................	10	4	12	12

(X) Not applicable.

Source: U.S. Department of Commerce, Social and Economic Statistics Administration, Bureau of the Census.

Families Below the Low-Income Level, by Sex of Head:
1959 and 1966 to 1971

Subject	All families		Families with male head		Families with female head	
	Black	White	Black	White	Black	White
	Number (millions)					
1959..................	1.9	6.0	1.3	5.0	0.6	1.0
1966..................	1.6	4.1	0.9	3.1	0.7	1.0
1967..................	1.6	4.1	0.8	3.0	0.7	1.0
1968..................	1.4	3.6	0.7	2.6	0.7	1.0
1969..................	1.3	3.6	0.6	2.5	0.7	1.1
1970..................	1.4	3.7	0.6	2.6	0.8	1.1
1970r1.................	1.5	3.7	0.6	2.6	0.8	1.1
1970[1].................	1.5	3.8	0.6	2.6	0.9	1.2
	Percent below the low-income level					
1959..................	48	15	43	13	65	30
1966..................	36	9	28	8	59	26
1967..................	34	9	25	7	56	26
1968..................	29	8	20	6	53	25
1969..................	28	8	18	6	53	25
1970..................	29	8	18	6	54	25
1970r1.................	29	8	19	6	54	25
1971[1].................	29	8	17	6	54	27

rRevised using 1970 Census-based population controls.

[1]The low-income data for 1971 and 1970 (r) are tied in with figures using 1970 census-based population controls and are, therefore, not strictly comparable to the data for earlier years which are based on 1960 census population controls. For a more detailed explanation, see "Revisions in Current Population Survey," **Employment and Earnings**, Vol. 18, No. 8, and forthcoming **Current Population Report**, Series P-60, report on 1971 Low-Income.

Source: U.S. Department of Commerce, Social and Economic Statistics Administration, Bureau of the Census.

Earnings of Husband and of Wife for Families in Which Both the Husband and Wife Worked, by Region: 1959 and 1970

(In current dollars)

Earnings of husband and wife	Total			Husband under 35 years		
	United States	North and West	South	United States	North and West	South
1970						
Black						
Mean family income.................	$10,581	$12,403	$9,032	$9,905	$11,309	$8,516
Mean earnings of husband............	6,209	7,247	5,326	6,225	6,978	5,481
Mean earnings of wife................	3,327	4,015	2,742	3,307	3,903	2,719
Earnings as a percent of family income.....................	31	32	30	33	35	32
White						
Mean family income.................	$13,563	$14,022	$12,467	$10,969	$11,215	$10,439
Mean earnings of husband............	8,786	9,100	8,037	7,607	7,777	7,243
Mean earnings of wife................	3,490	3,537	3,376	2,973	3,008	2,898
Earnings as a percent of family income.....................	26	25	27	27	27	28
Black as a Percent of White						
Mean family income.................	78	88	72	90	101	82
Mean earnings of husband............	71	80	66	82	90	76
Mean earnings of wife................	95	114	81	111	130	94
1959						
Black						
Mean family income.................	$4,769	$6,237	$3,776	$4,560	$5,863	$3,603
Mean earnings of husband............	2,887	3,764	2,293	2,883	3,510	2,422
Mean earnings of wife................	1,323	1,804	998	1,340	1,881	942
Earnings as a percent of family income.....................	28	29	26	29	32	26
White						
Mean family income.................	$7,814	$8,112	$6,986	$6,407	$6,662	$5,809
Mean earnings of husband............	5,006	5,212	4,432	4,370	4,589	3,855
Mean earnings of wife................	2,097	2,144	1,967	1,749	1,777	1,683
Earnings as a percent of family income.....................	27	26	28	27	27	29
Black as a Percent of White						
Mean family income.................	61	77	54	71	88	62
Mean earnings of husband............	58	72	52	66	76	63
Mean earnings of wife................	63	84	51	77	106	56

Source: U.S. Department of Commerce, Social and Economic Statistics Administration, Bureau of the Census.

Median Income of Husband-Wife Families with Head Under 35 Years, by Work Experience of Husband and Wife, by Region: 1959 and 1970

(In current dollars)

Work Experience of Husband and Wife	1959			1970		
	United States	North and West	South	United States	North and West	South
Black, total[1]................................	$3,534	$4,594	$2,735	$8,032	$9,560	$6,788
Only husband worked......................	3,025	4,080	2,311	5,965	7,104	5,196
Husband and wife worked..................	3,845	5,320	3,060	9,267	11,045	7,464
White, total[1]................................	5,658	5,897	4,987	9,796	10,002	9,229
Only husband worked......................	5,233	5,467	4,436	9,065	9,373	8,210
Husband and wife worked..................	6,013	6,246	5,420	10,396	10,578	9,948
Black as a percent of White, total[1]..............	62	78	55	82	96	74
Only husband worked......................	58	75	52	66	76	63
Husband and wife worked..................	64	85	56	89	104	75

[1] Includes other combinations not shown separately.

Source: U.S. Department of Commerce, Social and Economic Statistics Administration, Bureau of the Census.

Black Male and Female Workers, by Median Income in 1970, by Region
(Numbers in thousands)

Subject	Number of Black workers, 1971		Median income of Black workers, 1970		Ratio: Female to male median income	
	Male	Female	Male	Female	Black	White
All wage and salary workers[1]	3,859	3,066	$5,370	$3,200	60	47
Year-round full-time workers[2]	2,878	1,786	6,435	4,536	70	59
Northeast	570	411	7,430	5,519	74	60
North Central	600	396	7,859	4,859	62	57
South	1,488	835	5,241	3,723	71	57
West	219	144	8,751	5,495	63	61

[1]With wage and salary income, including full- and part-time workers.
[2]Refers to total with income.
Source: U.S. Department of Commerce, Social and Economic Statistics Administration, Bureau of the Census.

Families and Unrelated Individuals Below the Low-Income Level in 1970 Receiving Public Assistance and Social Security Income, by Sex of Head
(Numbers in thousands)

Subject	All families		Male head[1]		Female head[1]	
	Black	White	Black	White	Black	White
FAMILIES						
Total	1,445	3,701	625	2,604	820	1,097
Receiving public assistance income	690	839	177	370	513	469
Percent	48	23	28	14	63	43
Receiving Social Security income	341	1,192	188	928	153	264
Percent	24	32	30	36	19	24
UNRELATED INDIVIDUALS						
Total	840	4,121	301	1,088	539	3,033
Receiving public assistance income	295	633	73	185	222	448
Percent	35	15	24	17	41	15
Receiving Social Security income	297	2,284	85	434	212	1,850
Percent	35	55	28	40	39	61

[1]For unrelated individuals, sex of individual.
Source: U.S. Department of Commerce, Social and Economic Statistics Administration, Bureau of the Census.

Persons Receiving Public Assistance and Social Security Income in March 1971
(Numbers in millions)

Subject	Black and other races	White
Total population	25.6	179.6
Receiving public assistance income	6.4	6.9
Percent of total	25	4
Receiving Social Security income	2.7	23.8
Percent of total	11	13

Percent of Families with Income of $10,000 or More, 1947 to 1970, and by Regions: 1966 to 1970

(Adjusted for price changes, in 1970 dollars. A $10,000 income in 1970 was equivalent in purchasing power to about $5,800 in 1947)

Area and year	Black and other races	White	Area and year	Black and other races	White
UNITED STATES			**UNITED STATES—(continued)**		
1947	4	15	1966	20	45
1948	2	13	1967	23	47
1949	2	13	1968	26	50
1950	3	14	1969	27	53
1951	2	14	1970	28	52
1952	3	16			
1953	6	19	**SOUTH**		
1954	4	19	1966	10	36
1955	4	22	1967	12	40
1956	6	25	1968	15	42
			1969	17	45
1957	7	24	1970	18	45
1958	7	25			
1959	9	29	**NORTH AND WEST**		
1960	11	31			
1961	12	32	1966	29	48
1962	11	34	1967	33	50
1963	12	37	1968	36	53
1964	15	39	1969	37	56
1965	16	41	1970	38	54

Source: U.S. Department of Commerce, Social and Economic Statistics Administration, Bureau of the Census.

Families by Median Income in 1971, and Black Family Income as a Percent of White, by Region: 1959, 1966, 1970 and 1971

Area	Number of families, 1972 (millions)		Median family income, 1971		Black income as a percent of white			
	Black	White	Black	White	1959	1966	1970	1971
United States	5,157	47,641	$6,440	$10,672	51	58	61	60
North and West	2,581	33,544	7,596	11,057	71	71	74	69
Northeast	1,068	11,447	7,601	11,291	69	67	71	67
North Central	1,057	13,582	7,603	11,019	74	74	73	69
West	456	8,515	7,623	10,803	67	72	77	71
South	2,576	14,097	5,414	9,706	46	51	57	56

Source: U.S. Department of Commerce, Social and Economic Statistics Administration, Bureau of the Census.

Median Income of Families of Black and Other Races as a Percent of White Median Family Income: 1964 to 1971

Year	Black and Other Races	Black
1964	56	54
1965	55	54
1966	60	58
1967	62	59
1968	63	60
1969	63	61
1970	64	61
1971[1]	63	60

Note: Most of the tables in this section show income data for the year 1970. Income figures for 1971 are from the Current Population Survey conducted in March 1972. Median family income in 1971 of black families was $6,440, not significantly different from the median of $6,279 in 1970.

[1] The 1971 income data from the March 1972 Current Population Survey are tied in with figures using 1970 census-based population controls. For a more complete explanation of changes, see "Revisions in Current Population Survey," **Employment and Earnings**, Vol. 18, No. 8, and forthcoming **Current Population Reports**, Series p-60 report on 1971 Income.

Source: U.S. Department of Commerce, Social and Economic Statistics Administration, Bureau of the Census.

TEN BEST CITIES FOR BLACKS*

Instead of wanting to abandon the cities, increasing numbers of blacks see them as suitable arenas for their economic, political and cultural development. While labor union discrimination is still a major problem and while the weakened job market of the early 1970s adversely affected the employment situation of many recent college graduates, job opportunities in the cities are available for the skilled and semi-skilled. Troubled by an increase in their school-age populations and the attendant problems of dropouts, drug addicts and functional illiterates, the cities, nevertheless, still command the best resources for educational development. Housing discrimination is still prevalent but blacks can live where they can afford the price in most cities. In short, almost any city in the United States is better today in the overall quality of life available to blacks than it was six years ago at the height of the urban rebellions. Some are better than others although the differences are not always easy to measure. This is especially so when the differences involve such subjective criteria as the choice of climate, recreational preferences and the general "soul affinity" of a city with personal life style. EBONY has selected ten of the best cities which, because of such objective factors as opportunities for self support, self betterment and self empowerment, seem to offer their black citizens the best overall quality of life. Alphabetically, the ten are: Atlanta, Chicago, Cleveland, Denver, Detroit, Houston, Los Angeles, Memphis, New York and Washington, D.C.

*Based on Ebony Magazine article, same title, November, 1973

Atlanta, Georgia

Black Median Income**
males: $4,254
females: $2,094

As the financial, manufacturing and communications center of the Southeast, Atlanta offers to blacks, who are 51.3 percent of its population, an opportunity for advancement on many fronts. The Atlanta metropolitan area has about 1,650 manufacturers who employ a fifth of the area's workers in the production of aircraft, automobiles, chemicals, furniture, iron and steel products, soft drinks, and textiles. In addition, the more than 3,000 wholesale firms in the city sell about $8.5 billion worth of goods yearly. Presently, about 15.7 percent of Atlanta's black wage earners have been defined by the U. S. Labor Department as high salaried as against 52.9 percent for whites. This disparity arises partially be-

cause many blacks do not have marketable skills in such booming occupational areas as accounting, engineering, marketing, retail selling and the skilled crafts. On the other hand, some blacks are still working below their ability because of job discrimination. The Atlanta Urban League is among those agencies waging a continuing battle to reduce the ranks, both of the underemployed and the unemployed.

Inevitably, the economics of black Atlanta will improve as blacks continue to make inroads into the city's politics. Blacks elected to public office during the 1960s included a congressman, a vice-mayor, five city council members and four school board members. And Atlanta will probably elect a black mayor in the near future—that is, providing the black electorate becomes fully registered and fully organized to vote in their own self-interests. Those interests were served recently when Atlanta blacks succeeded in gaining control of half of the administrative posts in Atlanta's 80-percent-black school system, including the superintendent's job. If blacks make similar gains in such other agencies as the police, housing and finance departments, this should have a profound effect on the city's overall quality of life.

**Detailed Characteristics, U.S. Census of Population, 1970 PC(1)-D

Chicago, Illinois

Black Median Income
males: $6,157
females: $3,272

In 1970, Chicago's blacks had annual incomes totaling an estimated $2.5 billion, or enough money to run the public schools, the transit system and the entire city government for a year and still have enough left over to buy every black household in town a brand new Buick Riviera or Grand Prix, according to the Chicago Urban League. This affluence reflects the city's prominence as the business and industrial center of the Midwest, the transportation center of the United States and one of the world's leading seaports. Thousands of factories in the Chicago metropolitan area make products worth more than $15.5 billion annually, and more than 12,000 wholesalers sell goods worth more than $20 billion.

In the midst of all of this wealth, however, blacks have been disproportionately represented among the unemployed. While making up 27 percent of the civilian labor force, they contribute 43 percent to the ranks of the unemployed. Comparatively, however, Chicago unemployment was consistently less than unemployment for the country in 1970. Unemployment for the entire country was 4.9 percent compared to Chicago's unemployment rate of 4.4 percent and it was 8.2 percent for blacks and other minorities in the country as against 6.9 percent for Chicago blacks. Despite the Chicago Urban League's ten-year experience with affirmative action, equal opportunity employment, training programs and other such efforts to promote increased black representation in the better-paying, white-collar occupations, the League reports no substantial improvement has been accomplished. As elsewhere in the country, black workers in Chicago are still over-represented in the lower-paying, blue-collar occupations and under-represented in the higher-paying, white-collar jobs.

Although Chicago offers a wide variety of educational opportunities, including 47 institutions of higher learning in the city and 93 in the metropolitan area, every index presented on the status of high school education appears to support the notion that the quality of education received by black children in the city has declined to a low level. Again, as in the case of Atlanta, the increasing politicalization of Chicago's extraordinarily large black population (1,102,620) could boost blacks in other areas of the city's life.

Cleveland, Ohio

Black Median Income
males: $6,142
females: $2,604

While some blacks will question whether Cleveland can still lay claim to its title of "The Best Location in the Nation," it certainly still qualifies as a city where aggressive blacks can successfully assert themselves. The 38.3-percent-black city boasts six black judges, 13 blacks on its 33-man City Council, a black school board president, five blacks on special boards and commissions, and blacks in the school administration. The black voter population holds the balance of power in every election and will determine the next mayor.

But high unemployment among blacks is a major problem in Cleveland, as elsewhere, even though the city is blessed with an extraordinary amount of industry—a center of steel manufacturing and fabrication, numerous auto assembly plants, and a wide range of other heavy and light industries. Thus job opportunities for the semi-skilled and skilled are present; the major problems are with the unskilled. In 1966, a riot in the all-black Hough ghetto increased racial tension. Race relations improved in 1967 after Carl B. Stokes, a black state legislator, was elected mayor. In 1968, a

series of gun battles between blacks and police in the Glenville area again increased racial tension. Since then, city programs have done much to ease the tension.

Meanwhile housing in Cleveland for middle-class blacks is better than in most cities because traditionally the city has allowed mobility in its eastern suburbs. Black home ownership hovers around the 41 percent mark —a relatively high figure. But good low-cost housing for the poor is a major problem. So also is education for the poor as is the case in most of the nation's big cities.

Denver, Colorado

Black Median Income
males: $5,137
females: $2,629

Perched exactly one mile above sea level at the far western edge of the Great Plains near the Rocky Mountain foothills, Denver, the capital of Colorado, is called the "Mile High City." It is a center for "smokeless industries" with 1,550 manufacturing companies, a tourist mecca and a gateway to vast recreational areas, including more than 20 major winter sports resorts. The city also has the largest number of U. S. Government national and regional headquarters of any city outside of Washington, D. C., and is the site of the Atomic Energy Commission's Rocky Flats and a U. S. Mint. All of these industries generated 22,000 new jobs this year for skilled tradesmen and technicians, clerks and keypunch operators. "Young people can come and get involved without waiting for somebody to die," says Sebastian C. Owens, executive director of the Urban League of Colorado. He also reports that the building trades unions, unlike elsewhere, have been placing on jobs those blacks who successfully pass the required tests.

Although blacks are only 9.1 percent of Denver's population they were once the victims of widespread racial discrimination by landlords and realtors. In 1965, a group of citizens formed the Metro Denver Fair Housing Center to help families of all races and nationalities rent or buy homes in areas where they had not traditionally lived. Today, blacks can live any place in Denver that they can afford. Nevertheless, the city is suffering a shortage of low- and middle-income housing. Despite this and problems with busing in the public schools, Denver qualifies as one of the communities where blacks have opportunities.

Detroit, Michigan

Black Median Income
males: $6,774
females: $2,714

Detroit, "The Motor City," is so named because its plants employ 215,000 workers who produce 25 percent of the nation's cars and trucks—more than any other city in the world. Yet, only 13 percent of the city's labor force is in the auto industry. Non-automotive manufacturing employs 343,000, and 1,054,000 are in non-manufacturing employment. Detroit's other leading products are machine tools, gray iron products, metal stampings, hardware, industrial chemicals, drugs, paints, wire products and office machinery. All of this suggests the variety of jobs available to blacks in Detroit who are skilled.

But racial tension has been a major problem in the city since the 1940s. Competition between the city's blacks and whites for jobs and housing led to a race riot in 1943. During the 1960s, blacks began to push harder for equal rights, and racial tension increased. In 1967, a riot broke out in a largely black section of Detroit. Afterward, many civic organizations were formed to ease the tension between the races and to help improve education, and job opportunities for blacks. Black political leverage in Detroit has been increased by its substantial number of black elected officials and the 43.7-percent-black city can be expected to be headed by a black mayor within a few years.

Houston, Texas

Black Median Income
males: $4,422
females: $1,809

Houston is nicknamed "Space City, U.S.A." because of its $250 million Manned Spacecraft Center which runs the nation's space program. In addition, the city is first in the nation as a refining center, converting 1.4 billion barrels of crude oil daily, first in the manufacture and distribution of petroleum equipment and in the pipeline transmission of natural gas. Nearly 60 percent of total U.S. sulphur is produced in the metropolitan Houston area. The city is also the nation's third largest seaport because of a 50-mile ship canal which connects it to the Gulf of Mexico. All of this makes for wide occupational diversity in Houston, and indeed blacks have been making job advances in such areas as accounting and engineering. Nevertheless, a number of blacks are unemployed and under-employed in this 25.7-percent-black city. Houston's 316,-551 blacks not only make it the South's blackest city but also constitute a potential political clout to address these problems as well as those of inadequate low-income housing, a failing school desegregation plan and a police department which reportedly mistreats racial minorities.

Los Angeles, California

Black Median Income
males: $5,683
females: $2,877

ABOUT half of the people of Los Angeles moved there from other parts of the country. Many were attracted by the city's scenic location, pleasant climate and outdoor way of life. But the city is also the business, financial and trade center of the Western United States and the "entertainment capital" of the world. It leads the nation in the production of aircraft and equipment for space exploration and generates thousands of jobs for accountants, engineers, architects, draftsmen, banking and insurance workers. In addition, Los Angeles County, with its 80,000 payrollers, is a major employer for the area.

Like any booming city, Los Angeles is not without its problems. Because of the rapid increase in its population the city has little open land left and housing—especially low-cost housing—is in short supply. The city's overall unemployment is 4.6 percent (9.1 percent for blacks). And because the Los Angeles area lacks a good public transportation system, its people depend almost entirely on nearly four million automobiles which clog the city's expressways and create a grave air pollution problem. In addition, such natural disasters as brush fires, earthquakes, and floods continually threaten the Los Angeles area.

Despite all these problems, many people consider Los Angeles the best place to live in the United States. That sentiment is shared by many of the 503,606 blacks who form the city's largest racial group and who recently helped elect its first black mayor. Many of them live in integrated parts of the city and its suburbs. In fact, more blacks live in suburban areas of Los Angeles than in those of any other U. S. city.

Memphis, Tennessee

Black Median Income
males: $3,363
females: $2,113

Memphis will perhaps always be remembered as the city where the Rev. Martin Luther King Jr., was assassinated. He had gone to Memphis in 1968 to support a strike by city sanitation workers, most of whom were blacks. After his death, the city made efforts to improve living conditions in the black community, worked with federal agencies to train blacks for jobs and to help them establish businesses. The Memphis Housing Authority rebuilt many old dwellings and constructed some new low-rental dwellings. In addition, the Memphis Area Chamber of Commerce sponsored a project called the Greater Memphis Program to create jobs for the unemployed. But some 4,200 families await public housing and employment above minimum salary levels in this major trade center is still a problem.

In spite of these problems, Memphis boosters say it has more potential than any other Southern city for orderly growth and development which gives due regard to the 40 percent of its citizens who are black. The black presence manifests itself politically with three blacks on the 13-member City Council, four blacks among the 11 County Court judges, three blacks on the nine-member school board and the potential for electing a black mayor.

New York, New York

Black Median Income
males: $5,623
females: $3,411

With a population of nearly eight million, New York is the largest city in the United States and the second largest in the world. Only Tokyo is larger. One of the world's most important centers of business, culture and trade, New York is also the home of the United Nations (UN), the "capital" of the world. Either the headquarters or branch offices of numerous national and international corporations are located in New York and its seaport makes it a terminus for many of the world's trade routes. These circumstances alone account for why New York is the finance center of the United States and the home base for the advertising industry. The city's preeminence in commerce is paralleled in the world of culture, insofar as it is a major hothouse for writers, musicians, dramatists and other artists. In short, much of what happens in New York City affects what happens throughout the United States and around the world.

The sheer breadth and depth of New York's activities makes it a city ripe with opportunity —even for criminals. About half the drug addicts in the United States live in the city and they commit many of its burglaries and attacks on individuals to get money for drugs. Also, because of its large population, 21.2 percent (1.6 million) of which is black, New York City has more crime than any other U.S. city. But the crime rate—the number of crimes committed for every 100,000 residents —is actually lower there than in many other cities. A concerted attack on the drug problem in Harlem has been mounted by community groups with the cooperation of city officials. Similar community concern has been directed

at the city's overcrowded and understaffed school system which, despite its multiple shortcomings, boasts specialized high schools in such activities as the performing arts and the maritime profession, and one of the nation's most extensive groups of city colleges. Politically, New York is a challenging city precisely because so much organizing work remains to be done. The increasing number of black politicians have not only sought to strengthen their political bases in the city's black communities but also establish coalitions with such other non-white groups as the Puerto Ricans and the Cubans.

Washington, D.C.

Black Median Income
males: $5,611
females: $3,684

Both the capital and the ninth largest city of the United States, Washington, D. C., influences the daily lives not only of Americans, but also of peoples in other parts of the world. The great majority of the people in Washington, D. C., either work for the federal government or serve the needs of government workers. Of every 100 employed persons in the city, about 53 work in the federal and local governments, 12 in wholesale and retail trade, 20 in professional services, and 3 in manufacturing. According to the 1970 census, the city ranked highest in the proportion (15 percent) of blacks employed in professional, technical and managerial occupations, followed closely by Los Angeles, Boston, Columbus and New York.

The 537,712 blacks who live in Washington, D. C., constitute 71.1 percent of its population or the largest black percentage for any American city. Yet they do not wield a political influence proportionate to their numbers because of their substantial nonparticipation in the city's political process. This is probably because Washington, D. C., does not have home rule. A step in that direction came in 1970 when Rev. Walter E. Fauntroy was elected as the city's first non-voting delegate in the House of Representatives. Receiving a full Congressional salary of $42,500 a year, he has a vote in committee, but not on the floor. But it will take much more than token black political representation to correct many of the problems besetting Washington's blacks. One particular sore spot is the school system which recently hired a black superintendent to save it from collapse. Another problem is street crime. Still another is extensive, substandard housing. Much of the leadership for the solution of these problems rests with Washington's relatively large black middle class.

EMPLOYMENT AND LABOR CHRONOLOGY

1969

JANUARY

13   Attorney General Ramsey Clark warned that "nothing could be better calculated to irreconcilably divide the country than the failure to enforce the civil rights of all our citizens." He reported that in an effort to end racial discrimination in employment, the Justice Department in 1968 initiated 25 cases under the equal employment section of the 1964 Civil Rights Act; only 10 such cases had been filed in previous years. More than half of the 1968 suits were brought in the North and West. The defendants included private employers, local unions and one state and one private employment agency. The state agency was the Ohio Bureau of Employment Service. Efforts to obtain voluntary compliance from defendants were often successful. By the end of the year, nearly 100 employment-bias investigations were under way.

14   The Supreme Court, in a unanimous ruling, held that blacks might take suits alleging job and union discrimination directly to federal courts without exhausting procedures prescribed by union and collective bargaining rules. The case was brought against the Brotherhood of Railway Carmen of America and the St. Louis-San Francisco Railway Co. of Birmingham, Ala. by a group of 13 black and white union members. The 13 members had charged that the company and union had conspired to bar blacks from promotions and better paying jobs. The court's decision overturned a lower court ruling that the plaintiffs had not exhausted all grievance procedures specified in their contract and through the National Railroad Adustment Board. The case was sent back to district court for trial.

17   The Justice Department filed suit in Columbia, S.C. on a charge that the Owens-Corning Fiberglass Corp. practiced job discrimination at its Anderson, S.C. plant.

30   A consent decree signed in Detroit ended a Justice Department suit charging the Parke, Davis & Co. pharmaceutical firm with job discrimination in its Detroit and Ann Arbor, Mich. plants.

FEBRUARY

4   Simeon Golar, a member of the New York City Housing Authority was named to the chairmanship of the City Human Rights Commission replacing William H. Booth, who had been labeled "insensitive to black anti-Semitism," by spokesmen for New York Jewish groups. Booth, whose term expired December, 1968, was appointed a judge in the New York Criminal Court by Mayor John Lindsay.

26   The Nixon Administration revealed an improvement project for the Watts section of Los Angeles, that it hoped would be a model for other ghetto areas. The project featured (a) self-help—a group of black and white businessmen had formed an Economic Resources Corp. in Watts and bought 45 acres of junkyard land for an industrial park; (b) initiative and help from the private sector—the Lockheed Aircraft Co. leased a $2 million plant for manufacturing aircraft parts in the park; (c) federal assistance—the Economic Development Administration provided $3.8 million in loans and grants for the project, and the Office of Economic Opportunity provided $3.8 million in grants. There also were plans for other federal assistance in Watts—Small Business Administration loans to businessmen, Labor Department training programs and a Housing and Urban Development model-cities project. The Lockheed plant was expected to employ 300 persons by 1972. The entire industrial park was designed to provide jobs for 2,400 poverty-area residents. The project had been initiated under the L. B. Johnson administration.

MARCH

27   Sen. Walter F. Mondale (D., Minn.), in Senate Judiciary Subcommittee hearings on equal employment opportunity under federal contracts charged that David Packard, Deputy Defense Secretary, had "totally bypassed the OFCC" and "personally accepted oral, nonspecific assurances despite the regulations' requirements for written, specific assurances," when he approved the award of $9.4 million in Defense Department contracts to three textile companies that had been found in violation of federal regulations against job discrimination. Packard said he had approved the contracts after receiving oral "assurances of affirmative action" by three firms to

eliminate discrimination. The Office of Federal Contract Compliance (OFCC) had recommended in January that the companies be barred from federal contracts because of noncompliance with equal employment policy. The three firms were Dan River Mills, J.P. Stevens Co. and Burlington Industries. Packard told the subcommittee that he had intervened personally because compliance negotiations with the companies had been "virtually deadlocked." Sen. Edward M. Kennedy (D., Mass.), chairman of the subcommittee, described Packard's oral agreement as an "unfortunate precedent."

28 The subcommittee of the Senate Judiciary on Equal Employment Opportunity under federal contracts was told of an order by Transportation Secretary John A. Volpe that contractors would not have to meet equal employment requirements before bidding on highway contracts as previously required. Volpe said that the Transportation Department would include non-discrimination clauses in its contracts. In testimony, Volpe said that the old policy had "undermined the competitive bidding system" and had not been applied evenly.

APRIL

8 The NAACP Legal Defense Fund filed suit against top Nixon Administration officials charging that a 1965 Executive Order requiring government contractors to adopt equal employment policies had been violated. Defendants in the suit were Deputy Defense Secretary David Packard, Defense Secretary Melvin R. Laird, Labor Secretary George P. Schultz and Ward McCreedy, OFCC acting director. The suit was filed on behalf of 20 blacks who were employees or job applicants at Dan River Mills, Burlington Industries and J. P. Stevens Co., the three textile firms involved in federal contract EEOC violations.

8 The Justice Department, in a suit filed in U.S. District Court in Greensboro, N.C., charged the Cannon Mills Co. of Kannapolic, N.C. with racial discrimination in employment and the rental of housing to employees, alleging that blacks were given "menial and low-paying" jobs and inferior housing as compared with white employees. It was the first anti-discrimination suit against a major Southern textile company.

14 President Nixon included in his domestic program message to Congress the need for a program to "increase the effectiveness of our national drive for equal employment opportunity."

16 New York's District 65 of the AFL-CIO Retail, Wholesale and Department Store Union disaffiliated from its parent union, AFL-CIO, accusing the groups of failure to provide "aggressive and progressive leadership" in organizing low-paid black and Puerto Rican workers. District 65, whose membership is about 30% black and 25% Puerto Rican, planned to work with the Alliance for Labor Action formed in 1968 by Walter P. Reuther's United Auto Workers and the Teamsters union.

22 The Justice Department filed suit against the International Longshoremen's Association (ILA) and two of its Baltimore, Md. locals, charging that the locals were operating on a segregated basis. The suit, filed in U.S. District Court in Baltimore, alleged that Local 829 was 99% white and Local 858 was 99% black although members of both did substantially the same work. The department said that the black workers got fewer and less desirable jobs than the white workers as a result of the alleged discrimination. A similar suit had been filed against Texas ILA locals earlier.

24 The Justice Department filed suit in U.S. District Court in Kansas City, Kan. to end alleged discrimination by a Kansas insulating material manufacturer and Teamsters Union Local 41 in Kansas City. The suit charged that the Gustin-Bacon Division of Certain-Teed Products Corp. discriminated against blacks and other nonwhites in hiring, job assignment and promotion. It also charged that the collective bargaining agreement between the company and Local 41 perpetuated the effects of the firm's alleged discrimination.

25 The Justice Department filed suit in U.S. District Court in Newark, N.J. to end alleged discriminate practices by Local 10 of the Sheet Metal Workers International Association in Newark and a labor-management apprentice training committee for Essex and Passaic counties in New Jersey. The suit charged that the union did not give equal employment opportunity to blacks and Puerto Ricans and that the committee applied more stringent requirements to non-white apprentice applicants.

JUNE

9 Earl Madison, 24, a black cellist with the Pittsburgh Symphony, and J. Arthur Davis, 34, a double-bass player with the Symphony of the New World, accused the New York Philharmonic of refusing to hire them because of their race. The musicians documented their charges by citing several auditions in which they had been given shorter and more perfunctory hearings than other applicants. C. Mosely, Philharmonic managing director, denied the charges by saying that the orchestra had a "standard auditioning procedure" by which the two musicians had been heard "in the same manner as other applicants but failed to qualify."

13 The Justice Department filed a consent order barring discrimination against blacks and Spanish-Americans and ending a March, 1968 suit against Sinclair Refining Division of Atlantic Richfield Co. and the Oil, Chemical, and Atomic Workers Union. Under the order, entered in the U.S. District Court in Houston, Tex., Sinclair, the union and its Local 4-227 agreed to halt discriminatory practices at the company's Houston refinery. Sinclair had merged with Atlantic Richfield after the suit was filed.

17 The AFL-CIO United Brotherhood of Carpenters & Joiners signed a contract with Stirling Homex Corp. of Avon, N.Y. authorizing its members to do on-site assembly of factory-built housing. Under the contract, the builders would use only union labor at the job sites. The contract also contained an agreement with the National Urban League for establishment of training centers to teach local residents skills for use in Stirling's factories.

23 The Justice Department asked that the NAACP Legal Defense Fund suit against three textile firms, Burlington Industries, Dan River Mills, and J.P. Stevens Co., be dismissed on grounds that the three mills had complied with regulations. The Justice Department claimed that the three companies involved had reached written agreements with the government.

24 The Justice Department filed suit in U. S. District Court against a San Francisco iron workers local and two joint committees that administered an apprenticeship training program, charging employment discrimination. The suit alleged that Local 377 of the International Association of Bridge, Structural and Ornamental Iron Workers and the two committees discriminated against blacks in recruiting and work referrals.

JULY

17 Labor Secretary George P. Schultz announced that as a result of agreements between the Labor Department and 325 building and construction contractors in 26 cities, more than 3,000 of the nation's hard core unemployed would be trained in construction and building skills under the Job Opportunities in the Business Sector (JOBS) program. The program was initiated in May, 1968 by the Department of Labor and the National Alliance of Businessmen to find employment for the hard-core jobless in the nation's 125 largest cities. The government had allotted $10 million to enable the jobless to learn any of 18 separate construction trades.

18 The 113-day strike at Charleston (S.C.) County Hospital ended when black non-professional workers agreed to return to work. The settlement was reached three weeks after a large strike at the South Carolina Medical University Hospital was settled.

20 William H. Brown III, chairman of the EEOC, explained that limited funds had caused an 18-month delay in the commission's task of processing complaints of alleged job discrimination. He said that by the time the commission delivered a decision, many of those who had lodged the complaint "have lost interest; many have moved away." The shortage of funds limited the effectiveness of the commission to do the job as it was mandated to do under a section of the 1964 Civil Rights Act barring discrimination in employment because of age, sex, religion, national origin, race or color, according to Brown, who also cited the need for a larger budget than the previous year's $8.9 million and greater authority to issue cease-and-desist orders in support of its findings.

21 Black employees of the General Services Administration (GSA) charged in a report that the agency practiced racial discrimination in its staffing and promotion procedures. Russell Gaskins, chairman of a task force formed by 100 black employees, said the group would submit a petition demanding changes to GSA Administrator Robert L. Kunzig, who earlier had acknowledged that patterns of racial discrimination in employment existed in the GSA.

AUGUST

12 The Justice Department filed an employment discrimination suit against a North Carolina trucking company and three locals of the International Brotherhood of Teamsters. The suit, filed in U.S. District Court in Asheville, N.C., charged that Central Motor Lines, Inc., of Charlotte, N.C. and union Locals 71, 391 and 701 had discriminated against blacks in employment practices. The suit said the trucking firm employed no blacks among its 300 interstate drivers and only two drivers among its 76 local drivers.

25-29 A coalition of black civil rights groups joined several hundred black construction workers and their white supporters to shut down $200 million worth of construction projects at 5 different sites in Pittsburgh, Pa., after trade unions refused to increase black employment on construction jobs. The Black Construction Coalition (BCC), a loosely organized alliance of several black groups, called for a work stoppage in protest against what it called discriminatory hiring practices for construction jobs. The BCC said black workers had been denied the jobs because they were not admitted to white-controlled labor unions. The BCC pledged to continue the shutdown at 10 construction sites unless the pace of job integration was "substantially increased." Five of the sites were shut down after more than 1,000 demonstrators surged into downtown Pittsburgh, snarled traffic and caused massive tie-ups throughout the city. The project sites were closed on the recommendation of Pittsburgh police, who sought to avert violence between the demonstrators and white construction workers. Work was halted at the other five sites by the presence of a five-block line of protesters, about half of them white. Police and demonstrators clashed the following day near the $31.9 million Three Rivers Stadium. One hundred and eighty persons were arrested during the skirmish. Forty-five, including 12 policemen, were injured. The stadium had been the focal point of BCC demands. A study by the Pittsburgh Mayor's Commission on Human Relations showed that of the 30,000 members of building and trade unions in Pittsburgh, only 2 percent were blacks. Police Superintendent James W. Slusser said the stadium scuffle began after some of the demonstrators disrupted traffic. The police moved in with riot clubs, and the demonstrators retreated into downtown Pittsburgh, tying up traffic. The police then cordoned off the marchers and moved in to make the arrests. Byrd Brown, chairman of the Pittsburgh chapter of the NAACP, told the demonstrators to disperse but asked them to return to the stadium site August 27. About 700 black and white protesters gathered August 27 across the street from the site of the $100 million, 64-story building scheduled to become the headquarters of the U.S. Steel Co. to press their demands. White construction workers perched atop the steel structure dropped objects on the demonstrators, and the demonstrators hurled bottles at the workers. The police reported 45 arrests and five injuries, none serious. The protestors had gone to the construction site after meeting with U.S. Steel officials at the company's temporary headquarters in downtown Pittsburgh. Following the hour-long meeting, a spokesman for U.S. Steel announced that the company "sympathized completely with their position that all persons should have the same privilege of union membership." The company said, however, it would not comply with the demonstrators' demand that work on the building be halted until more jobs were made available to blacks.

Pittsburgh Mayor Joseph M. Barr announced that the owners of the 10 halted construction projects had agreed to stop further operations to permit negotiations. The demonstrators responded by announcing that they would suspend further demonstrations. The leaders of the demonstrators sought a black-controlled job-training program, for 500 unemployed, that would guarantee graduates journeyman status in Pittsburgh's trade unions. The Master Builders Association, which represented the contractors, had refused to accept a black-run program. Angry white construction workers staged demonstrations Aug. 28-29, denouncing the decision to suspend all major building projects in Pittsburgh. The workers marched to city hall Aug. 28 and formed a picket line of more than 400 persons. About

100 workers entered the mayor's fifth-floor city hall office Aug. 29 demanding pay lost during the shutdown. Some 4,500 workers and their supporters gathered at city hall and demanded a meeting with Mayor Barr. The protesters dispersed after co-workers talked to the mayor and reported that the workers would be paid for the two days. At a 10-hour negotiation session in Barr's office Aug. 29, blacks rejected an offer under which up to 100 blacks would be trained in the construction trades.

SEPTEMBER

4   The delegation of governors met with the President and Vice President on the Administration's request for a 75% cutback on federally-aided state construction projects. Gov. John A. Love (R., Colo.), who led the group, said his colleagues agreed "without exception" to support the President's action to combat inflationary prices in construction. Vice President Spiro Agnew, who attended the meeting, also indicated that the Administration had softened its threat of withdrawing the federal share of project costs if the states did not act to cut back on projects. Agnew said there were no longer any "enforcer roles" or "deadline" involved in the request. C. J. Haggerty, president of the AFL-CIO's Construction & Building Trades Department voiced a complaint that the 75% construction cutback on federally aided state construction projects would hinder efforts to get more blacks into building trades jobs. "If we don't have the work for them, we can't very well put them on and train them," he said.

15 More than 4,000 blacks and their white supporters marched through downtown Pittsburgh, Pa. in a continuing demand for more skilled jobs in the construction industry. The leaders of the march said it would be the first of many "black Mondays" unless more blacks were hired by construction firms and admitted into building and trade unions.

18 Negotiations between the Coalition for United Community Action and the Building Employers Association, which represented the construction trades, broke down after black leaders turned down the association's offer to train 1,000 qualified blacks and to seek positions for 3,000 apprentices. The Rev. Jesse Jackson, director of Operation Breadbasket, the economic branch of the Southern Christian Leadership Conference, said the Association's plan was "like no jobs at all."

24 U.S. District Court at Los Angeles, Cal., approved consent decrees forbidding discrimination against blacks in the seamfitting and pipefitting trades in the Los Angeles area. The Justice Department said the court-approved decrees were against Steamfitters Local Union 250 of the United Association, and the Joint Apprentice Committee, Steamfitters and Industrial Pipefitters. The court's ruling concluded a civil suit filed by the Justice Department in February, 1968, charging the union and the committee with discriminating against blacks in membership, apprenticeship training and work referral in violation of the 1964 Civil Rights Act. The suit had charged that only one black was a member of Local's 2,800-man union. The court's consent decree with the union required the union to process all membership applications on a non-discriminatory basis, forbade denial of black applicants for lack of union sponsorship and provided that for the next three years black journeymen with acceptable credentials would receive priority work referrals.

25 More than 2,000 angry whites swarmed through downtown Chicago, Ill., obviously protesting a proposed Labor Department plan to withhold funds from federally-sponsored projects in the Chicago area unless contractors agreed to establish a minimum quota for hiring black workers. It was the third straight day that white workers had staged demonstrations. Fighting between protesters and police erupted when the construction workers attempted to block black leaders from entering the U.S. Customs House, where the Labor Department hearings were being held on discrimination in the building trade unions. White construction workers packed the conference room where Asst. Secretary of Labor Arthur Fletcher was to conduct hearings on discrimination in building trade unions, and refused to permit the meeting to begin. He adjourned the meeting until the following day, when the whites jammed the streets around the Customs House preventing Fletcher and other black leaders from entering the building. Police escorted Fletcher into the building and two other blacks were whisked out of the area by police who reported at least nine arrests. Five

persons, including four policemen, were injured in a scuffle between workers and police.

29 In testimony before the New York City Commission on Human Rights laureat conductor Leonard Bernstein denied Philharmonic bias, while admitting that neither of three black musicians had passed the preliminaries primarily because of their race, and had subsequently been allowed to play in final auditions.

29 AFL-CIO President George Meany attacked the "new Republican Southern strategy" in a speech to the AFL-CIO's Maritime Trades Department. He said the Administration was "trying to make a whipping boy out of the building trades" on the discrimination issue. While "they proclaim this policy of nondiscrimination and try to press down on the building trades," he said, "they go ahead and . . . further delay the integration of the school systems in the South . . ."

OCTOBER

6 Frederick D. O'Neal (Actors Equity Association) was elected a vice-president of the AFL-CIO at the annual convention in Atlantic City, N.J. O'Neal became the second black federation vice president, joining A. Philip Randolph (Brotherhood of Sleeping Car Porters), who was re-elected to the post.

8 More than 2,000 white construction workers and their supporters marched through downtown Seattle, Wash. to protest work disruptions staged by blacks demanding more jobs in Seattle's construction industry. The march followed a walkout by white electrical workers protesting black-on-the-job apprentice training at a construction site at the University of Washington. The predominantly black Central Contractors Association had led demonstrations for more than a month that affected millions of dollars in construction projects in the Seattle area.

16 More than 4,000 white construction workers and their sympathizers massed in front of the State Capitol in Olympia, Washington to protest the hiring of black apprentice workers and a multimillion cutback in construction.

31 The Labor Department filed a suit in U.S. District Court in Seattle, Wash. charging five Seattle construction unions with discrimination against blacks. In a complaint endorsed by At-

torney General John N. Mitchell, the department asked the court to enjoin the unions "from failing and refusal to recruit, refer for employment and accept blacks for membership on the same basis as white persons." White construction workers in Seattle had protested against what they called the government's insistence on accelerating black membership in craft unions and more jobs for minority workers by demonstrating in Seattle. The Labor Department's complaint asked the court to issue an injunction forbidding the unions to engage in any work stoppage designed to interfere with contractors' obligations on federally-sponsored construction projects. The suit named as defendants the ironworkers, electrical workers, plumbers and pipefitters, sheet metal workers, and operating engineers union locals.

NOVEMBER

12 Burton C. Hallowell, president of Tufts University (Medford, Mass.), announced that the administration had reached agreement with protesting students in a dispute over the hiring of minority group workers at a university dormitory construction site. On November 5, black students, led by the campus Afro-American Society, had occupied the construction site and stopped work.

17 Renard Edwards, 25, violinist with the Symphony of the New World, was hired by the Philadelphia Orchestra as their first black musician.

DECEMBER

5 About 150 black students occupied Harvard's University Hall (Cambridge, Mass.) for several hours in protest against Harvard's hiring policy. The demonstrators, led by the Organization for Black Unity (OBU), left after the university agreed to submit their demands to committees. They had demanded that 20% of all workers on university construction sites be members of minority groups and that the university promote a predominantly black group of painter's helpers to journeymen and raise their pay.

5 The U.S. Labor Department reported that the nation's unemployment rate declined in November to 3.4% of the labor force from its 3.9% rate in October. The decline was attributed mainly to a decline in the number of persons seeking work, largely "secondary workers" such as teen-agers, adult women

and young men. There was a continued slowdown in the expansion of the civilian labor force. The jobless rate among white workers was 3.1%, among non-whites 6.2%.

11   About 75 black students were temporarily suspended from Harvard' University after the OBU led a second five-hour occupation of University Hall. They left the hall after they were served with a court order to end the demonstration.

Charleston Hospital Strike
March 20 - June 27, 1969

MARCH

20   A strike of largely black female hospital workers started in Charleston, S.C. More than 130 persons were arrested for defying court injunctions to limit picketing during the first five days of the strike.

The major issue in the strike, which affected two state-aided hospitals in the city, was the refusal of hospital officials to recognize the union, an organization of laundry workers, kitchen helpers, nurses' aides, practical nurses, maids and orderlies. With the help of the National Organizing Committee for Hospital & Nursing Home Workers, the Charleston hospital workers had formed Local 1199B of the AFL-CIO Retail, Wholesale & Department Store Union, a New York-based union of which the Hospital & Nursing Home Workers was an outgrowth.

The strike began when 12 members of Local 1199B were dismissed by the city's Medical College Hospital. Among those fired was Mrs. Mary Moultrie, 27, president of the local. Claiming that the members had been dismissed for union activity, 425 of the hospital's workers walked out and were joined by 100 workers from Charleston County Hospital. Those who had walked out were soon replaced in their jobs; hospital officials claimed that state laws prohibited the recognition of hospital workers' union and said that the 12 had been fired for neglect of duty.

31   When Rev. Abernathy appeared for a mass meeting in support of the strike, Gov. Robert E. McNair alerted a unit of the S.C. National Guard in anticipation of an SCLC campaign, such as was launched in support of striking sanitation workers in Memphis.

APRIL

20   Mrs. Coretta Scott King, widow of the assassinated Rev. Dr. Martin Luther King Jr., joined with Abernathy and 12 other national civil rights leaders in a statement in support of the strikers. The others who signed the statement were Roy Wilkins, NAACP executive secretary; A. Philip Randolph, president of the Negro American Labor Council; Whitney M. Young, Jr., National Urban League executive director; Roy Innis, national director of CORE; Bayard Rustin, executive director of A. Philip Randolph Institute; Dorothy I. Height, president of the National Council of Negro Women; George A. Wiley, executive director of the National Welfare Rights Organization; Rep. Shirley A. Chisholm (D., N.Y.); Rep. John M. Conyers (D., Mich.); Gary Mayor Richard G. Hatcher; Cleveland Mayor Carl B. Stokes; and Julian Bond, a member of the Georgia House of Representatives.

21   Rev. Ralph' Abernathy arrived in Charleston to lead daily marchers in support of the strike. There were 400 more arrests.

22   Beginning a series of marches, Abernathy said he was prepared for arrest, with "my toothbrush and my toothpaste in my pocket." However, the Charleston Police Force issued the marchers a parade permit even though none had been requested.

25   Abernathy and more than 100 demonstrators were jailed for violating a court injunction limiting the number of pickets allowed around the Medical College Hospital. Although many protesters were arrested daily thereafter and National Guardsmen joined with state and local police to control the demonstrators, the marches remained nonviolent.

28   Warning that the city was "being turned into a battleground," the Charleston Evening Post had called for "straight talks from our officials."

29   A group of 21 Democratic Congressmen led by Rep. Edward K. Koch (N.Y.) petitioned President Nixon to "send your most trusted representative" to intervene in the dispute. Local pressure for a settlement increased when Charleston Mayor J. Palmer Gaillard and the Charleston County Democratic Executive Committee, in separate statements, asked the state to begin serious negotiations with the strikers.

30   Mrs. King led 20,000 blacks in a protest march through the city. She said that she wanted to fulfill "my husband's dream" and that she believed that "Charleston, like Selma and Memphis, has now become a national test of purpose."

30   The S.C. House adopted a resolution supporting Gov. McNair's prohibition of negotiations between state institutions and unions.

MAY

1   Gov. McNair declared a state of emergency in the city and imposed a 9 p.m. to 5 a.m. curfew. He said that the strike had become "more serious as each hour and day has passed" and that these measures had been taken because of "the danger of fires, vandalism, break-ins and other harm which may come to persons or property."

2   Charging South Carolina was attempting to "destroy" the movement through legal delays, Rev. Abernathy posted bond and was freed from jail. In a letter released the same day, Abernathy called on President Nixon to end the "crisis which exists in South Carolina."

4   During a 2,000-person march, Abernathy warned that he would issue a "national call" for reinforcements unless the state agreed to recognize the union.

6   In reponse to a request by 21 Democratic congressmen, the President had said in a letter: "I have directed the attorney general (John N. Mitchell) to have observers on the scene." Mr. Nixon said that Mitchell "is keeping me informed on a regular basis," but the President rejected the request that he send a personal representative to Charleston.

11   From 7,000 to 12,000 strike supporters demonstrated in a "Mother's Day March" in Charleston led by Abernathy and Walter Reuther, president of the United Automobile Workers. The marchers included five Democratic congressmen: William F. Ryan, Edwin I. Koch and Allard K. Lowenstein of New York; and John Conyers Jr. and Charles C. Diggs Jr. of Michigan. Reuther presented a UAW check for $10,000 to Mary Moultrie, president of the local union representing the hospital workers. Reuther also pledged $500 a week to SCLC to help defray the costs of the campaign.

15   A bipartisan group of 17 senators organized by Walter F. Mondale (D.,

Minn.) and Jacob K. Javits (R., N.Y.) asked President Nixon to send a federal mediator to help settle the strike.

JUNE

2   A curfew imposed early in the strike was lifted.

9   The Medical College Hospital offered to rehire the 12 discharged workers. The offer had been made in compliance with a June 5 directive by a U.S. Health, Education and Welfare Dept. regional office in Atlanta.

12   The hospital withdrew its offer. SCLC leaders charged that political interference by Sen. Strom Thurmond (R., S.C.) and Rep. L. Mendel Rivers (D., S.C.) had broken the agreement. Thurmond and Rivers had met separately with HEW Secretary Robert H. Finch. Thurmond said he had been assured that HEW would take no action against the hospital pending a full investigation of charges made by the HEW office in Atlanta.

21   The Rev. Ralph D. Abernathy, president of the Southern Leadership Conference, and the Rev. Hosea Williams, a top SCLC official, were arrested again. They were charged with inciting to riot after they led demonstrators in support of the strikers. They remained in jail after bond was set at $50,000 each.

21   Gov. McNair reimposed a dusk-to-dawn curfew after police, National Guardsmen and newsmen were struck by bricks and boards following the arrests of Abernathy and Williams.

25   William Kircher, AFL-CIO director of organization, said that the International Longshoremen's Association (ILA) and other maritime unions would close down the port of Charleston if the hospitals did not meet strike demands. The ILA had voted two weeks before to support the hospital workers. A shutdown of the city's port, fifth largest on the Atlantic seaboard, would be a serious threat to the state's textile industry.

27   A partial settlement was announced in the 15-week Charleston hospital workers' strike when the city's Medical College Hospital agreed to rehire all employees on the payroll as of March 15, including 12 workers whose discharge had precipitated the strike. However, the agreement did not extend to the Charleston County Hospital where workers rejected an offer by the hospital to reemploy half the strikers and find jobs for the rest in other Charles-

ton hospitals.

According to the agreement at the Medical College Hospital, the workers would be paid a minimum wage of $1.60 an hour. The higher wage, raised from $1.30 an hour, was authorized by South Carolina's new pay scale for state employees announced June 9. The agreement included new grievance procedures, which union officials considered a form of de facto recognition. Hospital officials and South Carolina Gov. Robert E. McNair had insisted that state laws prohibited bargaining with hospital employees.

27   Dr. Abernathy refused to leave jail after the Medical College Hospital settlement was reached although his bail had been reduced to $5,000. He said he would remain in jail pending settlement at the County Hospital.

JULY

18   The 113-day strike at Charleston (S.C.) County Hospital ended when black non-professional workers agreed to return to work. The settlement was reached three weeks after a large strike at the South Carolina Medical University Hospital was settled.

DECEMBER

22   The controversy over the job rights plan—the Administration's "Philadelphia plan" setting goals for the number of nonwhite employees to be hired on federal construction projects—involved a fiscal 1970 supplemental appropriations bill (HR 15209) to which the Senate December 18 added an amendment to kill the Philadelphia plan. The amendment granted the comptroller general authority to withhold funds for any program he deemed unlawful. Comptroller General, Elmer B. Staats had ruled August 5 that the plan was unlawful in its requirement for racial quotas in federal employment.

Prior to the House's consideration December 22 of the conference version of the bill, which retained the Senate amendment to kill the plan, President Nixon issued a statement urging removal of the amendment by a 208-156 vote and, by voice vote, signaled its intention to insist on the deletion.

1970

JANUARY

12   The U.S. Supreme Court declined to review an Ohio state court ruling that declared valid an equal employment plan

similar to the Nixon Administration's "Philadelphia Plan" setting goals for the number of nonwhite employes on a federal construction project. The court rejected an appeal from an Ohio contractor who had been denied a contract for a federally-subsidized college building even though he had been low bidder. The contractor had refused to give assurances, required by the federal government, that he would attempt to employ a specified number of black workers.

12   An agreement was reached in Chicago by black community leaders, labor and city officials which called for 4,000 blacks to be trained as skilled construction workers and admitted to the Chicago unions. Earlier negotiations had broken down after construction officials had refused to accept black demands for 9,000 on-the-job training positions. The unions offered instead to train 1,000 blacks and to seek apprenticeship positions for 3,000 others. Under the agreement, 1,000 blacks who could qualify as apprentices or journeymen would be put to work immediately.

A second 1,000 would start on-the-job training as soon as possible, and another 1,000 would be slated to begin journeyman training leading to full status as skilled workers. The other 1,000 would be given a specialized pre-apprentice training program for rudimentary construction skills.

30   The Black Construction Coalition, an umbrella organization of civil rights groups, announced that an agreement had been reached to employ 1,250 blacks as workers with journeyman status in Allegheny County, Pa., during the next four years. The accord was reached by the coalition, representatives of 15 contractor associations and the Pittsburgh Trades and Construction Council, who represented Pittsburgh's craft unions.

FEBRUARY

9   Harvard University announced that an agreement had been signed with a construction company obligating the builder to hire 19-23% nonwhite workers on campus construction projects.

28   The White House denied reports that the Administration had decided to relax its pressure on federal agencies to step up employment of minority group members.

MARCH

10   In a *New York Times* report, it was revealed that two weeks before President Nixon's inauguration, Daniel P. Moynihan sent to the President-elect a private memorandum in which he said that "the Negro lower class must be dissolved" by transforming it "into a stable working class population."

14   A federal district court judge in Philadelphia upheld the constitutionality of the Labor Department's controversial "Philadelphia Plan" to increase minority employment in the construction industry. Judge Charles R. Weiner rejected a suit filed January 6 by Contractors Association of Eastern Pennsylvania requesting an injunction against the plan and a declaration that it was unconstitutional.

Weiner said in his 22-page decision that the pilot job program did not in any way violate the Civil Rights Act of 1964 which forbade racial quotas in employment procedures. Weiner said "it is fundamental that civil rights without economic rights are mere shadows." He said it did not violate the civil rights act because it "does not require the contractor to hire a definite percentage of a minority group."

(The Philadelphia Plan required all contractors working on federally-funded projects to make good-faith efforts to hire specified percentages of blacks in those projects costing $500,000 or more.)

17   Nixon stressed action to help develop new programs to train returning servicemen in skilled construction jobs, to expand training and apprenticeship programs and to increase minority employment in the skilled building trades.

30   A black citizens' group, the Community Coalition on Broadcasting, in Atlanta, announced that it had successfully negotiated agreements with 22 of the city's 28 TV and radio stations, calling for increased black involvement in programming and employment. Details of the agreements varied with the size of the 22 stations.

The accord was reached after the Federal Communications Commission (FCC) had granted the bargainers for both sides an additional 30 days to settle their disputes over minority hiring and increased programming aimed at Atlanta's black community. The group had asked the FCC to grant the 30-day extension in February after protracted negotiations had been stalemated.

31   Seventy-two movie studios and television companies announced that they had agreed to implement immediately an equal employment plan for their industries that included hiring, training and upgrading of minorities and setting racial quotas. The agreement was worked out with the aid of lawyers from the Justice Department who entered the negotiations after the movie and television industry had been criticized during hearings in 1969 for practices of racial discrimination in hiring. Among the major companies signing the agreement were Columbia Pictures Industries, the Columbia Broadcasting System, Warner Brothers, Metro-Goldwyn Mayer, Bing Crosby Productions, Paramount Pictures Corp., Lucille Ball Productions, Walt Disney Productions and 20th Century Fox Film Corp.

APRIL

9   A spokesman for the Maritime Administration announced that the Newport News, Va. shipyard (largest in the U.S.) had agreed to end racial discrimination, opening up more skilled jobs among its 5,600 (28%) black workers. Maritime Administrator Andrew E. Gibson, the chief negotiator for the government during talks between the yard's officials and black workers, called the plan "a milestone" and "one of the most forward looking of any major industry."

The agreement removed the yard, the Newport News Shipbuilding and Dry Dock Co., from the government's black list, which had prohibited the company from signing contracts with federal agencies. (The yard had been placed on the black list March 12 when the Maritime Administration ordered the company to "produce an affirmative action plan" to meet the equal job opportunities provision of the 1964 Civil Rights Act.)

13   The Department of Transportation ordered a freeze on new roadway and airport construction contracts in the Washington, D.C. metropolitan area as part of a drive to bring more high salaried jobs to black and other minority group workers.

The director of the department's civil rights division, Richard F. Lally, reported that the suspension of funds had been ordered after three days of hearings during which contractors had been warned that if they did not implement their own job plan, the Labor Department "would be ready to impose" a mandatory job plan on the contractors.

14   The director of the Defense Department's Equal Employment Opportunities office announced that the U.S. Navy would require all contractors who were planning to bid for $2 million worth of new construction projects to comply with the minority-hiring provisions of the Labor Department's Philadelphia Plan.

15   Washington, D.C.'s Public Service Commission ordered the Potomac Electric Power Co., which provided electricity to the D.C. area, to hire more black workers and other minority group members on a preferential basis. Under the order, the utilities concern must specifically request "all minority group persons contact the company . . . to file an application for employment regardless of whether vacancies exist."

The order also provided that the firm maintain a file of applications from the minority applicants and "before consulting other sources for applicants . . . give every consideration to the hiring of applicants from this file."

30   Five black members and eight New York Democrats in the House of Representatives endorsed in separate statements the Campaign's proposal to add three public members to the GM board, including the Rev. Channing E. Phillips, a black minister. The black congressmen accused GM of being "unresponsive to the needs of black Americans." GM later countered with the disclosure that its minority hiring was up 184% since 1965 and that minority workers made up 62% of the 5,333 employes hired since 1965.

MAY

2   The Nixon Administration's Philadelphia Plan, designed by the Department of Labor to increase minority employment in the construction trades, was said to have fallen short of the expected minority hiring goals, according to initial progress reports. Citizen organizations in Philadelphia, where the plan was first set into motion, had reported

to the department's Office of Federal Contract Compliance that contractors were abusing and disregarding the plan by not taking on additional minority group employees.

JUNE

1   Secretary of Labor George P. Shultz imposed a department-devised arrangement, known as the "Washington Plan," that would require all contractors with federal jobs of $500,000 or more in Washington, D.C. to make "good faith" attempts to increase minority hiring on all their projects. Under the plan, as reported by the Washington Post, which was to go into effect immediately, 3,500 minority group workers had to be hired in 11 skilled construction trades on such federal jobs as construction of the metropolitan subway system, highway buildings, and federally subsidized housing projects.

4   William H. Brown 3d, chairman of the Equal Employment Opportunity Commission (EEOC), announced that he had filed charges of racial and sex discrimination against four companies and 15 labor unions in Houston on behalf of two EEOC Houston staffers. Brown accused the companies and the unions of discriminating in recruiting, hiring and upgrading of blacks, Mexican-Americans and women, in violation of the 1964 Civil Rights Act.

4   The Washington Area Construction Industry Task Force, a coalition of 25 black organizations, denounced the Washington Plan of June 1 as "devoid of promise" and "wholly unacceptable." The group sent a letter to Secretary of Labor, George P. Shultz demanding that 70%–80% of jobs in all crafts go to minority group workers. The federal plan called for unions to have from 25% to 43% black membership, depending on the trade, by May 31, 1974 for the Washington, D.C. metropolitan area.

8   New York Gov. Nelson A. Rockefeller met in Buffalo, N.Y. with members of the Minority Coalition, an organization that represented 60 loose-knit associations of Buffalo's black community. However, after four hours of discussion, the two sides were no nearer an agreement that had eluded them for two years and stalemated a massive New York state building program.

23   The Navy announced that Litton Industries had been awarded a $2.1 billion

contract to build 30 destroyers during the next eight years. When the cost of government-furnished radar and weaponry was included, the total price for the 30-ship fleet would be $2.55 billion, representing a cost of $85 million for each ship. A Litton official said the contract would provide 4,000 new jobs in the Pascagouls yards until 1974 with about half of them going to blacks.

29   The chairman of the board of directors of the National Association for the Advancement of Colored People (NAACP) labeled the Nixon Administration anti-Negro and accused it of a "calculated policy to work against the needs and aspirations of the largest minority of its citizens." The assessment of the Administration's policy towards blacks was made by Bishop Stephen G. Spottswood during his keynote address before the 61st annual convention of the NAACP, which opened in Cincinnati.

Spottswood detailed his contention that the Administration "can rightly be characterized as anti-Negro." He cited the "signing of defense contracts with textile companies long in violation of contract requirements," instead of canceling them as the NAACP had suggested. He cited what he termed the Administration's "pullback on school desegregation," emphasizing its efforts to obtain delays in districts where desegregation had already been ordered by the federal courts.

He cited the nominations of Judges Clement F. Haynsworth Jr. and G. Harrold Carswell to the Supreme Court as evidence that the Administration was anti-Negro. He also pointed to what he called the Administration's efforts to water down the voting rights act in the House.

As his final point, Spottswood cited President Nixon's description of the ideal federal judge: "someone who believes in the strict construction of the Constitution—a judge who will not use the power of the court to seek social change by freely interpreting the law or constitutional clauses." Spottswood called this "the Administration's expressed opposition to the equal protection clauses of the 14th Amendment."

30   The White House's response was in the form of a long telegram to Spottswood by Leonard Garment, Nixon's chief liaison with civil rights groups. Garment said Spottswood's charges painted a false picture, rallied every fear, reinforced every anxiety and made a just society more difficult to achieve.

30   Herbert Hill, key NAACP official at the close of its convention, denounced the Nixon Administration as being anti-Negro. Hill accused the Administration of "destroying the Philadelphia Plan," a pilot Labor Department-sponsored plan designed to increase minority employment in the construction trades.

Hill contended that, if enforced, the plan would have "broken the lily-white union monopoly in the building trades." Hill alleged that the Nixon Administration had abandoned any "pretense of enforcing the federal guidelines" to implement the orders of the Philadelphia Plan.

JULY
3   Daniel P. Moynihan, domestic adviser to President Nixon, suggested in a magazine article that black-white relations were "getting better." Moynihan's observations were in the summer issue of the quarterly, *The Public Interest*, and involved attitude samplings by the University of Michigan Survey Research Center in Ann Arbor.

The attitude samplings indicated that the number of whites favoring desegregation increased from 1964 to 1968, while the number of blacks favoring separatism fell from 6% to 3% in the same period. The attitude sampling indicated that integration had widened in housing, employment, and high schools.

4   One hundred and sixty-five persons were injured, many by police bullets, and more than 100 persons were arrested during a wave of looting, street violence and firebombings in the New Jersey beach resort community of Asbury Park, New Jersey.

9   Gov. William T. Cahill said that he would ask President Nixon to declare the seaside community "a major disaster area."

9   Labor Secretary James D. Hodgson warned that unless the construction industry opened up more jobs for black workers during the summer the government might begin to enforce federal hiring quotas in 73 cities. The labor secretary said "there has been too much of a lag in this work and the big push is on."

Hodgson said the 73 cities would be given an opportunity to develop voluntary plans to increase black employment in the construction trades, but unless it was done soon the Labor Department would impose quotas as it had already done in Philadelphia and Washington, D.C.

12 Asbury Park, New Jersey officials estimated that more than $4 million worth of damage was done during the four days and nights of disorders.

The violence erupted when crowds of youths, angered over what they said was the city's refusal to consider the housing and unemployment situation in the ghettos, roamed the streets of the West Side section smashing storefront windows, setting fires and looting.

26 New Orleans city officials joined local representatives of the construction industry, craft unions, and a coalition of area chapters of the National Association for the Advancement of Colored People (NAACP) and the Urban League to announce that they had agreed to a proposal to increase minority hiring and open the unions' rank-and-file membership to blacks. The "New Orleans Plan" was designed to place more members of minority groups, mainly blacks, in the construction industry labor pool in the New Orleans area. One official said, however, that the plan was put together to prevent the federal government from implementing more stringent racial hiring guidelines in the New Orleans area.

29 A federal judge in Montgomery, Ala. ordered seven Alabama state agencies to stop discriminating against blacks in their hiring practices and to give immediate job consideration to 62 black applicants turned away earlier.

District Court Judge Frank M. Johnson Jr. directed state authorities to take steps to eliminate all future racial discrimination in hiring practices. He ordered them to submit a report to the court within 30 days on what had been done to comply with his order.

AUGUST

16 The Labor Department reported that the June-July unemployment rate for youths 16-21 was 15.7%, the highest level in six years and a sharp advance above the 12.8% level in the summer of 1969.

The rate for black youths surged to 30.2% above 24.8% a year earlier. The total labor force for the entire youth group rose during the year to 13.3 mil-

lion from 13.1 million in 1969, but the number of those employed dropped for the first time in nine years. The Labor Department said the job squeeze for younger persons had been caused by the general economic slowdown and sharp cutback in manufacturing jobs.

19 The Nixon Administration announced that it would soon terminate a contract with a Pennsylvania contracting concern for its failure to comply with the government's Philadelphia Plan designed to train and employ blacks and other minority workers on construction jobs. It was the government's first enforcement action against a contractor charged with violating the job agreement. Secretary of Health, Education and Welfare (HEW) Elliot L. Richardson said that Edgely Air Products, Inc., of Levittown, Pa., had been notified by HEW's Office for Civil Rights that the office intended to cancel a contract and bar the concern from future federal contracts on the ground of noncompliance with the job accord ordered into effect by President Nixon.

31 AFL-CIO President George Meany viewed the younger generation with suspicion, the Democratic party as having "disintegrated" and the federation's relationship with the Nixon Administration as "fairly good." Meany expanded on these and other views in a pre-Labor Day (Sept. 7) interview with labor reporters.

Meany said the federation supported the Nixon Administration's Southeast Asia war policy and was "completely opposed to the idea of bugging out" or "setting a cutoff date for American participation."

SEPTEMBER

1 The Justice Department announced that a U.S. judge in Cleveland had entered a consent decree requiring the nation's third largest trucking concern to implement an equal employment program. The order brought to a close the department's first suit seeking to enjoin job discrimination throughout a company's nationwide operation.

The court order entered by Judge Thomas D. Lambros against Roadway Express Inc., of Akron, Ohio, enjoined the firm from engaging in any act or practice that had the purpose of denying blacks equal employment opportunities in hiring, upgrading and promotions.

OCTOBER

1   Civil rights legislation granting the Equal Employment Opportunity Commission enforcement powers was passed by a 47-24 vote of the Senate. The measure was sent to the House, where similar bills had been approved twice in the last several years only to be stymied by Southern opposition in the Senate. The enforcement power would be in the form of judicially enforceable cease-and-desist orders against employers. The power was denounced by Sen. Sam J. Ervin Jr. (D., N.C.) but an amendment by Sen. Peter H. Dominick (R., Colo.) to kill it was rejected 41-26 September 30.

12   The U.S. Commission on Civil Rights reported that there had been a "major breakdown" in the enforcement of the nation's legal mandates forbidding racial discrimination.

The commission urged President Nixon to exercise "courageous moral leadership" and to establish within the White House machinery committees to oversee enforcement of court decrees, executive orders and legislation relating to civil rights.

The commission's findings were announced by the Rev. Theodore M. Hesburgh, the panel's chairman and president of the University of Notre Dame. Hesburgh said the findings, based on a six-month study of the executive departments and agencies charged with enforcing the nation's civil rights laws, showed that "the credibility of the government's total civil rights effort has been seriously undermined." He added that "unless we get serious about this, the country is on a collision course."

20   The Labor Department reported that swelling unemployment in the third quarter of 1970 had hurt most severely black teen-agers in urban slums whose jobless rate grew to 34.9% from 29.3% a year earlier. Total national unemployment reached 4.34 million (5.2% of the civilian labor force), compared with three million (3.7%) in 1960's third quarter. In poverty neighborhoods, joblessness climbed to 8.3%, compared with 6.8% a year ago.

21   Three postal unions filed a suit in U.S. District Court in Washington to compel the government to bargain with them or stop the bargaining with seven other postal unions given exclusive bargaining

rights with the new postal corporation. The three unions—the National Postal Union, the National Alliance of Postal and Federal Employees and the Manhattan-Bronx Postal Union—also contended that the seven other unions—all AFL-CIO craft unions— discriminated against black workers.

24   A job plan to increase the number of black workers on construction projects in the Pittsburgh area was approved by the federal government, nearly 10 months after it was first introduced. The pact, which came out of negotiations between civil rights groups, Labor Department officials, construction union representatives and city labor leaders, was first made public January 30.

The government's decision to accept the plan marked the end of its freeze on $100,000 for federally assisted projects in the Pittsburgh area. The government had frozen the funds to force unions to comply with minority hiring guidelines.

The agreement called for 1,250 blacks to be employed as workers with journeyman status in the Pittsburgh area during the next four years.

NOVEMBER

10   The Supreme Court let stand a lower court ruling in Chicago that a job discrimination suit could be brought against employers and labor unions under the Civil Rights Act of 1866 rather than the more limited employment provisions of the 1964 Civil Rights Act.

DECEMBER

2   The federal government filed a suit accusing the Virginia Electric & Power Co. (Vepco), a utility which served a 32,000 square mile tri-state area, with racial discrimination in almost every phase of its employment operations.

Also named as defendants in the suit, filed in the U.S. District Court in Richmond, were the International Brotherhood of Electrical Workers and eight of its union locals. The suit asked the court for corrective orders and to grant back pay for black employes whom the government charged were restricted to menial jobs because of racial bias.

10   The Washington Post Co. announced that it was turning over its FM radio station valued at $750,000 to Howard University. The gift of WTOP-FM was aimed at improving employment opportunities of minority groups in all phases of broadcasting.

10 New York Gov. Nelson A. Rockefeller and New York City Mayor John Lindsay joined representatives of the construction industry and its unions in signing a job accord to help minority group members become skilled construction workers. The pact, known as the New York Plan, was announced in March.

Under the terms of the plan, whose cost had not yet been determined, an on-the-job training program would be started with 800 trainees. It would include periods of instruction, counseling and remedial education at a central educational facility.

11 The Equal Employment Opportunity Commission (EEOC) recommended that a request by the American Telephone and Telegraph Company (AT&T) for a telephone rate increase be rejected because of the company's gross discrimination against women, blacks and Spanish-Americans.

14 The chairman of the United States Steel Corp. accused the Justice Department of using the threat of a law suit to force the company to hire more black office and clerical personnel at its plant in Fairfield, Ala.

According to E.H. Gott, the chairman, when the corporation refused to accept the government's racial job quota, the Justice Department filed suit against U.S. Steel, charging it with discrimination. (The Justice Department had filed a suit in federal district court in Birmingham Dec. 11, charging the steel firm with discriminating against blacks at its Fairfield plant. The suit also accused the United States Steelworkers of America, the AFL-CIO and 12 Alabama steelworker locals with violating the 1964 Civil Rights Act and being parties to the alleged discriminating practices.)

18 The Justice Department warned a group of hotels, casinos and union locals in Las Vegas, Nev. that they had a month to present a plan to rectify what the government charged was discrimination against blacks by the businesses and unions in hiring and promotion practices.

Seventeen hotels and casinos and four union locals were involved.

The warning was in a letter by Jerris Leonard, chief of the department's Civil Rights Division, to the Nevada Resort Association, which represented 16 of the resort establishments. A separate letter was sent to the Riviera Hotel,

which was not a member of the association, charging it with violation of the 1964 Civil Rights Act.

1971

JANUARY

5 The Bethlehem Steel Corp., the second largest steel producer in America, was accused by a three-member federal labor panel of discriminating against blacks through its seniority system. In a statement accompanying the report, Bethlehem denied the charge but agreed to set new hiring, promotion and training quotas for black employes.

The action against Bethlehem was the second taken against one of the nation's steel corporations. An earlier Suit had been filed against the United States Steel Corp. by the Justice Department.

31 Caroline Hunter and Kenneth Williams, black employes of Polaroid Corp. testified before a United Nation Committee on apartheid that Polaroid's announced plan to increase the wages of black South African employes 13-30% before July, 1971, were camouflage to prevent Polaroid to continue doing business in South Africa. Miss Hunter, a chemist, was later suspended for "persistent activities in fomenting public disapproval" of Polaroid's sales to South Africa.

FEBRUARY

4 Eight black employes of the Department of Housing and Urban Development's (HUD) Chicago Regional Office, alleged that the Federal Service Entrance examination violated the equal opportunity guarantees of the Fifth Amendment. They said it also violated the 1964 Civil Rights Act, several executive orders and the regulations of HUD and the Civil Service Commission.

The class action suit filed in Federal district court in Washington, named George Romney, HUD secretary, and three Civil Service commissioners, as defendants.

The plaintiffs charged that the exam "has served systematically to exclude qualified blacks and members of other minority groups from obtaining managerial and professional level positions in the federal service, and has by other means denied plaintiffs and their class equal employment opportunities."

The suit asked the court to bar the use of the examination until its alleged discriminatory aspects were eliminated, and that the use of other testing procedures be stopped until a determination could be made of their relation to specific job requirements. According to the HUD employees, about 49% of the 100,000 persons who took the test in 1969 finished with scores above 70, with "a disproportionately low percentage" of blacks and other minority group members passing.

10   The Building and Construction Trades Department of the AFL-CIO said the group rejected "quotas under any name," and denounced allegations that they practiced racial discrimination as "reckless rhetorical and political pandering."

The government's proposed quota rules were published in the Federal Register January 2. According to the apprenticeship rules, which could be altered or withdrawn within 30 days after they first appeared in the register, unions with federally registered trainee programs would be required to adopt "affirmative action plans" to bring more nonwhites into the program.

In rejecting the proposed job quotas the unions maintained that "the goal of equal employment opportunity in apprenticeship has generally been achieved under existing regulations."

Although the proposed rules would give the craft unions some flexibility in drawing up programs to carry out "affirmative action," basically they required the unions to place a specified quota of nonwhites in the apprenticeship programs.

The federal quotas were reportedly designed to do on a national scale what various job programs had accomplished in local areas—bringing more blacks into the building and construction trades. The pilot plan for federal job quotas was known as the Philadelphia Plan.

15   The AFL-CIO Executive Council meeting in Bal Harbour, Florida, stated its opposition to President Nixon's proposal for general revenue sharing. The council, suggested that critical needs could be neglected if no strings were attached to the funds for specific programs. "Moreover," it said, "without specified and enforceable federal performance standards, there is no assurance that federal civil rights guarantees and fair labor practices will be applied to projects supported by 'no strings' federal grants." They approved an in-crease in federal funding to the states and local governments, and recommended full funding of existing federal grant programs federal assumption of the costs of public welfare, tax reform at all levels of government, a federal tax credit for state income tax payments instead of a deduction method, and establishment of a federal urban bank to offer state and local agencies long-term, low-interest loans for public housing, transit and other community facilities.

MARCH

3   The National Alliance of Postal and Federal Employes, a predominantly black union, remained outside a proposed merger of five postal unions on the grounds its championing of the black workers' problems would lose identity and focus, should it join the others. It joined the National Postal Union, with its 27,000-member Local in a suit to block negotiations between the new postal service and the AFL-CIO unions. They challenged the right of Congress to assign exclusive bargaining rights to the AFL-CIO unions.

This plan to merger included the independent group, the National Postal Union, and four AFL-CIO unions: the United Federation of Postal Clerks, the National Association of Post Office General Services and Maintenance Employes, the National Federation of Post Office of Motor Vehicle Employes, and the National Association of Special Delivery Messengers. It would be an industrial, rather than a crafts union.

The 210,000 member AFL-CIO National Association of Letter Carriers, and the National Association of Post Office Mail Handlers (AFL-CIO), also resisted merger.

8   The Supreme Court ruled 8-0 that employers could not use job tests that had the effect of screening out blacks if the tests were not related to ability to do the work. The court held that the employment bias section of the 1964 Civil Rights Act involved the consequences of employment practices, not simply whether the practices were motivated by racial bias.

The case grew out of applications for promotion by 13 black laborers at the Duke Power Co. generating plant at Dan River in Draper, N.C. Jack Greenberg of the NAACP Legal Defense Fund Inc. contended that the plaintiffs could challenge employment practices on the basis of discriminatory impact and need not prove bad motive on the part of the employer. The Justice Department and the Equal Employment Opportunity Commission also sought the ruling.

18   The National Education Association (NEA) reported that as Southern communities dismantled their dual school systems the number of black teachers and principals dropped while the number of white faculty and administrative personnel increased. The NEA made the figures public in an Amicus-Curial brief supporting the Justice Department in a desegregation suit against the state of Georgia filed with the U.S. Court of Appeals, in New Orleans. The NEA presented analyzed computer data showing, district by district, how black educators had been dropped from their posts as Southern school systems desegregated. Most of the figures dealt with school systems in Alabama, Florida, Georgia, Louisiana and Mississippi. Incomplete statistics from Texas were also presented.

School districts in those six states that received federal funds were required by law to report the racial compositions of their faculty and administrative staffs to the Department of Health, Education and Welfare (HEW). Of the districts that reported, 69% said the ratio of black to white faculty members had declined the last two years. During the same period, the number of black principals in those districts decreased by 20%.

In the districts that submitted figures, 1,040 black teachers were dropped while the number of white teachers rose by 4,192. The data on administration personnel in Alabama was not complete, but in the other four states 232 black principals lost their jobs while 127 white principals were added to school staffs.

The NEA said the figures "show that black educators, particularly black principals, have borne burdens incident to desegregation in measures greatly disproportionate to any burdens borne by white educators."

The case to which the NEA brief was attached involved the Justice Department's contention that the federal circuit court did not set strict enough standards for desegregating facilities in its December, 1969, order requiring 81

Georgia school districts to integrate.

APRIL
12   William L. Tutman, black Peace Corps' first director of minority affairs, resigned his post charging the agency with discriminating against women and minorities.

He filed a formal complaint with the Civil Service Commission documenting cases of discrimination against women and blacks. Tutman had been a staff member of the Peace Corps for five years, the last six months as minority affairs director.

In his complaint, Tutman included documents that showed that three blacks, one a woman, had been denied staff positions because of what he described as subjective comments by federal interviewers.

He also complainted that openings within the corps' top ranks were not made known until senior "white males" had been able to "anticipate" the vacancies and make recommendations for filling them.

23   The U.S. Court of Appeals for the 3rd Circuit upheld the legality of the "Philadelphia Plan" when it upheld a lower court's ruling that the plan did not violate the 1964 rights act because the contractors were not required to hire a "definite percentage" of a minority group.

The court had been asked by the Contractors Association of Eastern Pennsylvania to declare the plan illegal because it denied the group equal protection of the laws. The contracting group, in the suit it filed in January 1970, also charged that the plan violated the 1964 Civil Rights Act because it required racial "quotas."

MAY
5   The U.S. Labor Department announced that it would soon impose mandatory racial hiring quotas on federally-sponsored construction projects under way in San Francisco, St. Louis and Atlanta. In general, the quotas required contractors bidding on federal or federally-sponsored projects to agree to hire a fixed goal of minority group members by a certain date.

Negotiations to set up a similar job plan for federal construction in Chicago were also being held by Labor Department aides, Chicago officials, civil rights leaders and union and industry representatives.

JUNE

3   The Labor Department announced that
     it was imposing a mandatory racial hir-
     ing plan for federally-assisted construc-
     tion projects in San Francisco. San
     Francisco's minority job program was
     the third such plan set for the construc-
     tion industry. The others were imposed
     in Philadelphia and Washington, and
     affect federal construction costing over
     $500,000.

4   Arthur A. Fletcher, assistant secretary
     of labor for wages and labor standards,
     announced that the U.S. Labor Depart-
     ment was withdrawing its support of
     Chicago's voluntary equal hiring plan
     for federal construction projects and
     would impose mandatory racial quotas
     on federally-assisted projects through-
     out the city. Fletcher said the govern-
     ment's hiring program would be similar
     to the Philadelphia Plan which
     stipulated that a certain number of mi-
     nority group members be employed on
     federal projects exceeding $500,000.

     Chicago's voluntary plan, The Chicago
     Plan for Equal Opportunity, collapsed
     after 18 months.

     The program called for training and
     hiring 4,000 minority group members.
     By June 4, however, only 885 blacks
     and Spanish-Americans had been taken
     on for apprentice training and only a
     few had obtained membership in Chica-
     go's construction unions.

     The federal move was sparred by the
     disappearance of Alderman Fred D.
     Hubbard, program director, and the dis-
     covery that $94,500 of its funds were
     missing. A federal arrest warrant was
     issued for Hubbard, charging him with
     forging a $20,000 check drawn on the
     plan's account.

     More than $824,000 had been provided
     by the federal government to finance
     the Chicago job plan.

17   The Labor Department ordered federal
     minority-group hiring quotas for U.S.-
     assisted construction work in Seattle
     after rejecting the city's plan as ineffec-
     tive. The Seattle plan would affect all
     construction crafts except four—iron
     workers, sheet metal workers, plumbers
     and pipefitters and electricians—that
     were covered by a minority-hiring plan
     ordered by federal courts.

18   The Labor Department announced im-
     mediate implementations of a plan to
     bring more black workers into the high-

er-paying construction trades in Atlanta, Ga.

It became the fifth U.S. city to get a
federal job plan.

The terms of the Atlanta plan were announced by Arthur A. Fletcher, assistant secretary of labor. Fletcher said he
expected that "compliance would come
even easier" in Atlanta than it had in
other cities. He said his investigation of
labor practices in metropolitan Atlanta
had indicated that leaders of the higher
paid craft unions would turn to the
heavily black laborers unions where
men had worked as skilled laborers for
many years and invite them into their
unions. It was estimated that the plan
would probably add some 1,500 black
workers in 10 trades over the next four
years.

21   The 2nd Circuit U.S. Court of Appeals,
     in a unanimous ruling, ordered the
     United Steelworkers of America and
     Bethlehem Steel Co. to permit black
     workers to transfer from "hotter and
     dirtier" jobs at Bethlehem's plant in
     Lackawanna, N.Y. to higher paying and
     cleaner jobs with no loss in seniority or
     pay. The court held that "in hiring, jobs
     were made available to whites rather
     than to blacks in a number of ways.
     There were no fixed or reasonably ob-
     jective standards and procedures for
     hiring." The court also said that over
     80% of the black workers at the Lacka-
     wanna plant were placed in departments
     "which contained the hotter and dirtier
     jobs in the plant." Blacks, the court
     held, were excluded from "higher-
     paying and cleaner jobs."

     The case was brought to the appeals
     court by the federal government. The
     government had succeeded in getting a
     lower court to rule that the company
     and union did discriminate, but could
     not obtain a lower court order that
     "would have made the exercise (of
     transfer rights) more attractive."

     The decision was believed to be the first
     time a federal court had outlawed trans-
     fer and seniority provisions that violat-
     ed Title VII of the Civil Rights Act of
     1964. Such violations were interpreted
     as penalizing black employes who
     sought to shift their jobs within a plant.

AUGUST

2   The Rev. Jesse Jackson, leader of the
     Operation Breadbasket arm of the
     Southern Christian Leadership Confer-
     ence, charged that the U.S. Postal Ser-

vice was discriminating against blacks as it reorganized.

The reorganization of the Postal Service, as it was going, had placed thousands of black employes a step closer to welfare rolls. He explained that since the majority of black postal workers were in lower job categories, they were the first to be let go in any reorganization plans that included layoffs. Jackson also criticized the Postal Service decision to place most new district offices in the suburbs. He said that in Chicago, the new district office was being placed in Cicero, "where it is not even safe for blacks to pass through—let alone live."

He added that when the new offices were opened in suburban areas, "local residents get priority" for the new postal jobs.

Jackson said the alleged discrimination was attributable to a newfound interest in Postal Service jobs by whites.

OCTOBER

12 The Supreme Court rejected, without comment, a challenge by the Contractors Association of Eastern Pennsylvania to the Nixon Administrations Philadelphia Plan, which required percentage goals in the hiring of minority workers in federally financed building jobs. The action seemed to validate the approach to ending employment discrimination that had originated in Philadelphia in 1969 and was being extended to 21 other cities.

The contractors had argued that the plan violated 1964 Civil Rights Act equal employment provisions by setting up racial "quotas." Lower courts had ruled that the plan established "goals" stated in percentage ranges rather than absolute quotas.

Similar plans had been instituted in Washington, D.C., San Francisco, St. Louis and Atlanta. Other programs were scheduled for New York, Buffalo, Cincinnati, Detroit, Houston, Indianapolis, Kansas City, Mo., Miami, Milwaukee, Newark, N.J., New Orleans, Denver, Boston, Los Angeles and Seattle.

21 Julia P. Cooper, a federal hearing examiner ruled that the Housing and Urban Development Department (HUD) and its predecessor agencies had been guilty of systematic discrimination against blacks in hiring and promotion, at least until late 1970.

Miss Cooper, an Equal Employment

Opportunity Commission lawyer appointed examiner by the Civil Service Commission, recommended that HUD repay 106 employes who had lost a day's pay after an October 13, 1970, protest during work hours against alleged discrimination. She found that HUD supervisory personnel had frequently kept blacks in low grade levels while whites advanced, hired blacks at grade levels beneath their qualifications, limited or denied training opportunities to blacks, and penalized those who complained of these practices.

HUD officials, who had asked the Civil Service Commission to investigate the charges, admitted that discrimination had existed in the past, but denied that the problem remained. Secretary George Romney cited a rise in minority employment at the agency to 40.5%, including 19.6% of those in grades 7 and above.

NOVEMBER

8 The Commonwealth of Pennsylvania charged Local 542, International Union of Operating Engineers, and three contractor associations with bias against blacks. The suit, filed in U.S. district court in Philadelphia, said the union had failed to provide sufficient memberships or jobs for blacks despite spending almost $1 million provided by the state for job training of blacks. The court was asked to supervise the union's apprenticeship and referral practices until discrimination ceased.

11 The National Labor Relations Board (NLRB) ruled by a 3-1 vote that The Farmers' Cooperative Compress, a Lubbock, Texas employer, had not discriminated against black and Chicano employes. The board majority in the latest decision said that "in a plant where 85%-90% of the employees belong to minority groups," any actions by the employer "are likely to be subject to claims of discrimination." The lone dissenter, Howard Jenkins, Jr., a black, noted that whites held 85% of the higher-paid jobs, and said "such statistics, in themselves, sufficiently demonstrate the existence of racial discrimination."

The 1968 decision found the Farmers' Cooperative Compress guilty of unfair labor practices in opposing organization by the United Packinghouse Workers, since merged into the Amalgamated Meat Cutters. The board at that time ruled that discrimination against workers could be considered an unfair practice under NLRB jurisdiction, and ordered the firm to bargain with the union on the issue.

The U.S. Court of Appeals for the District of Columbia upheld the 1968 ruling, but ordered the NLRB to make a specific finding on whether discrimination had occurred. An NLRB trial examiner then found that the firm was in fact discriminating, present decision overturned that finding.

DECEMBER

3   The Equal Employment Opportunity Commission (EEOC) asked the Interstate Commerce Commission (ICC) to ban hiring bias among 15,000 interstate trucking firms employing over 1 million workers, charging the trucking industry with discriminating against women, blacks and Spanish-Americans by giving them only the lowest-paying jobs. The EEOC said the ICC's "life and death power to license truckers" could be used to end bias, but the American Trucking Association claimed "no lawful basis" for such ICC action.

1972

JANUARY

3   New York City Steamfitters Union Local 638 was ordered by a federal judge to upgrade 169 black and Puerto Rican apprentices to journeyman status. The ruling involved the largest number of reclassifications ordered in a suit brought by the federal government. The court reserved the right to rule on individual cases if the union tried to downgrade any of the 169 workers on grounds of incompetence.

MARCH

8   The Congressional Black Caucus called on President Nixon to nominate a black to the upcoming vacancy on the Federal Communications Commission (FCC) and planned a national task force of black political leaders and journalists to fight discrimination in employment and coverage of blacks in the news media.

The plans emerged after two days of hearings March 6-7 by the Caucus, at which blacks in the media charged employment bias, insensitivity by white-owned and edited newspapers, magazines and broadcast stations, and inadequate attention to the needs of black readers and viewers.

Charging that the FCC ignored "service to the community" when renewing broadcast licenses, the Caucus called for local "media watchdog committees" to study hiring, promotion and coverage, and to file bias lawsuits and challenge license renewals.

APRIL

22   The Labor Department reported that its 10-month investigation of the Rural Manpower Service (RMS) had disclosed widespread evidence of discrimination against blacks, Chicanos and women, and cooperation by the RMS in exploitation of migrant workers.

The probe was begun after 16 civil rights and farm labor groups filed a complaint against the RMS, formerly the Farm Labor Service, asking migrant worker takeover of RMS functions.

The probe uncovered a pattern of discrimination in the industry, frequently abetted by the Employment Service and the RMS, in job referrals, housing and transportation. Violations of minimum wage and child labor laws were also found, as well as substandard living facilities.

The probe found that the RMS consistently erred "in favor of the employer to the detriment of the worker."

Secretary of Labor James D. Hodgson said that the RMS would be consolidated at the local level with the Department's nonagricultural Employment Service, and that efforts would be made to allow non-college graduates to obtain posts in the new offices. He pledged immediate action to enforce the laws, admitting that past reforms had been ineffective.

MAY

11   In its first use of newly enacted powers, the Equal Employment Opportunity Commission (EEOC) filed suit in U.S. district court in Jacksonville, Fla. against the Container Corp. of America, four international unions and six union locals, charging job discrimination against women and blacks.

The suit alleged that women were confined to low-paying clerical positions, while blacks were denied training for better jobs, victimized by "unvalidated tests" for advancement, and confined to "more arduous and lower-paying jobs, than whites."

The court was asked to order a revision of seniority practices, special training programs, elimination of the tests, payment of back wages, hiring of blacks and women in specified ratios and revision of union by-laws.

The unions involved were the International Association of Machinists, the International Brotherhood of Electrical Workers, the Brotherhood of Painters, and the Pulp, Sulphite and Paper Mill Workers Union.

19 A National Education Association (NEA) survey found that over 30,000 teaching jobs for blacks had been eliminated in 17 Southern and border states through desegregation and discrimination since 1954.

According to Samuel B. Ethridge, NEA teacher rights director, "as early as 1968 one state department of education identified 25 counties which employed one or more black teachers in 1954, and employed none in 1968."

The proportion of teachers who were black declined in the region in 1954-70 from 21% to 19%, although the proportion of black students increased slightly. The percentage of existing or projected black teaching jobs displaced was lowest in Alabama, which the report attributed to court orders and continued segregation, and highest in Kentucky, Missouri and Delaware.

26 Federal Judge John P. Fullam in Philadelphia ordered the city's police department to hire at least one black policeman for every two whites added to the force during the next five weeks.

The order by Judge Fullam applied until July 1, pending further orders in a suit charging the city with racial bias in hiring and promoting black policemen. The suit before Fullam's court was filed in December 1970 by the state of Pennsylvania and several individual blacks as a class action against the city, the mayor, the police chief and other officials.

In his pretrial directive, Fullam instructed Philadelphia police officials to fill only police vacancies that existed before March 1, 1972.

JUNE

1 George Holland, director of the Office of Federal Contract Compliance (OFCC) since February, submitted his resignation effective July 1, charging that a recent reorganization if the agency had diminished its effectiveness in enforcing equal job opportunities in firms doing business with the federal government.

In his letter of resignation, Holland charged that the reorganization, which decentralized the agency and merged its field offices with other Labor Department units, "diminishes program impact, diffuses program authority and denies program uniformity."

JULY

1 The U.S. Civil Service Commission reported that the number of blacks, Spanish-Americans and other minority group members had increased in all grade levels of federal service above the lowest in the year ending November 1971. Overall federal minority employment excluding the Postal Service rose by 2.1% in the period, although the proportion of minorities in federal service dropped from 19.6% to 19.5% in the year, taking into account extensive postal job cutbacks. The gains in high-paying jobs resulted from a one-third minority share of the 31,485 increase in U.S. white-collar jobs.

6 The National Association for the Advancement of Colored People (NAACP), at its 63rd annual convention in Detroit July 3-7, passed a series of resolutions attacking the Nixon Administration's record on issues of interest to blacks. The 2,632 delegates also heard an appeal for unity and for a summit conference of black leaders by Rev. Jesse Jackson, head of People United to Save Humanity (PUSH).

Herbert Hill, the NAACP national labor director, told Delegates at the National Convention in Detroit that the Labor Department had wasted tens of millions of dollars in ineffective and deceptive programs for training black construction workers. Then, he cited training programs by the 527-member National Afro-American Builders Association, who collectively employed 3,200 black journeymen at wages averaging $10,000 a year.

11 The Federal Power Commission (FPC) issued a ruling that it did not have power under federal law or the "public interest" concept to enforce fair employment practices by utilities.

The ruling came after 12 civil rights groups petitioned the FPC to take such action, charging "rampant discrimination against blacks, women and Spanish-surnamed Americans" by gas and electric utilities. They cited a September 1971 letter to the FPC from David L. Norman, assistant attorney general for the Justice Department's Civil Rights Division, who said the agency could exercise such powers.

But the Commission said Congress had

relegated fair employment powers to the Equal Employment Opportunities Commission, and said its "public interest" regulatory functions no more' covered employment practices than it covered securities, taxes, wages or advertising, all of which were regulated by other agencies.

The 12 groups said they would appeal the ruling in federal courts.

AUGUST

7   The Justice Department, citing provisions of the 1972 Equal Employment Opportunity Act, filed civil suits against local government agencies in Los Angeles, California and Montgomery, Ala., charging them with racial discrimination in hiring for public jobs.

The Los Angeles Fire Department was accused of pursuing "policies and practices that discriminate against black, Mexican-American and Oriental applicants for employment." In its suit, the department asked the U.S. district court in Los Angeles for a permanent injunction to end the alleged job bias.

In the Montgomery suit, filed in U.S. district court in Montgomery, the Justice Department accused the city, its water department, sanitary sewer board and the city-county personnel board of giving some black workers lower-paying job classifications even though they performed the same work as higher-paid whites. The suit asked the court for a permanent injunction to halt the alleged discrimination.

24 President Nixon banned minority employment hiring quotas in the federal government.

The order, transmitted by Civil Service Commission (CSC) chairman Robert Hampton, was in response to a letter sent August 11 by the American Jewish Committee (AJC) to President Nixon and Democratic presidential nominee George McGovern expressing concern over the use of job quotas.

Hyman Bookbinder of the AJC said that quotas had become "particularly serious in our government education programs." Bookbinder said the AJC's position was not intended to "mean we should reduce efforts to increase the number of blacks, women and Chicanos. But we mustn't do it on a quota basis."

In his reply to the AJC, McGovern also opposed the use of quotas; however, he had also often promised jobs to blacks

in his administration in proportion to their number in the population, the Post said.

Nixon had included criticism of quota systems in his acceptance speech August 23 at the Republican nominating convention.

In an attempt to woo labor, particularly the construction trades, from the Democratic Party, the Nixon Administration decides to scuttle the Philadelphia Plan, and other similar programs which required building contractors to set percentage goals for minority employment. The first indication came in an August 18 letter from President Nixon to all executive departments which ordered them not to interpret minority job goals as quotas.

SEPTEMBER

3   In a Labor Day statement, President Nixon attacked quotas by saying, "Quotas are intended to be a short cut to equal opportunity, but in reality they are a dangerous detour away from the traditional value of measuring a person on the basis of ability." He said, "We are faced this year, with the choice between the 'work ethic' and the 'new welfare ethic.'" The former taught that "everything valuable in life requires some striving and some sacrifice, while the latter says that the good life can be made available to everyone right now and that this can be done by the government."

4   The Labor Department announced that while no decision had been made to drop the Philadelphia Plan, the controversial program begun in 1969, which required building contractors in the Philadelphia area to set percentage goals for minority employment, ranging up to 26% by 1973, all programs might involve quotas, "were being reviewed."

25 A memorandum from Secretary of Labor James D. Hodgson to "all heads of agencies" in the federal government effectively nullified minority hiring plans, according to the NAACP and other civil rights groups. The memo dated September 15 stated that the OFCC (Office of Federal Contract Compliance) did not require "quotas or proportional representation" of minorities, although the "goals required of government contractors" may have been misinterpreted or misapplied." Hodgson said the goals were "merely targets" and failure to reach them, "is

not to be regarded as a violation.' Herbert Hill, NAACP labor director, said the memo implied that the Philadelphia Plan, and all of the others had been abandoned, since it removed the "major standard for measuring good faith efforts in all previous minority hiring plans."

Hill criticized the Administration, contractors and building trades unions for hindering enforcement of the Philadelphia Plan, the first federal minority hiring agreement, and pointed out that more blacks were employed in the Philadelphia building trades than when the plan was begun in 1969. He said it should be retained, and charged that the Nixon Administration "retreat" on the issue was "in large part, part of a political payoff to the AFL-CIO" for its neutrality in the presidential election.

8   The Imperial Irrigation District was ordered by a U.S. district court judge in San Diego to hire blacks or Mexican-Americans to fill two-thirds of all new vacancies until the minority proportion of the district work force, then 15.2% rose to the minority percentage of the Imperial county population, 49.5. According to California Rural Legal Assistance, which had filed the suit, the two-thirds hiring ratios were the highest ever ordered by a federal judge.

OCTOBER

6   Lawrence J. Sherman, executive director of Migrant Legal Action Program, Inc., representing seventeen farm workers and civil rights groups filed suit in Washington district court to prevent Secretary of Labor James D. Hodgson from financing state rural manpower programs that practiced racial and sex discrimination and condoned illegal exploitation of migrant workers. The suit charged that the state migrant worker referral offices, financed by the federal Rural Manpower Service, favored white, Anglo and male applicants in recruitment, counseling, training and job referral, to the detriment of blacks and Spanish-surnamed workers. It further stated that workers were regularly referred to employers who violated minimum wage and child labor laws, who frequently failed to make Social Security payments to workers' accounts and who maintained worker housing that was racially segregated and below legal health standards. Workers who complained about conditions were ignored or blacklisted.

6   The U.S. Labor Department reported that $15.7 million, of 20 million) had been spent in a program to improve working and living conditions for migrant workers, and to train 6,000 of them for better jobs. Only 1,200 workers had completed training. The program was funded at $10 million for the current fiscal year.

Florida Rural Legal Services, Inc. had filed suit against Florida state agencies in September, charging that a $3.5 million grant to the Florida Department of Commerce under the program had not alleviated any of the abuses.

14   U.S. District Court Judge Frank M. Johnson, Jr. ruled in Montgomery, Ala. that the federal government could not be sued in a job discrimination case because of the doctrine of sovereign immunity.

But Johnson refused to apply the doctrine to government officials in a suit by two blacks who charged they had been denied promotions despite years of service in Air Force jobs. He left as defendants all Cabinet officers except the secretary of state, and criticized the government for invoking the doctrine, after "having so vigorously brought and prosecuted actions against various Alabama agencies to insure equal education and employment for blacks." The suit asked for promotions and back pay for the men, and for a general injunction against racial discrimination by federal employers, charging that only 2.6% of general schedule federal civil servants in Alabama were blacks, although blacks constituted 36% of the state's population.

NOVEMBER

29   New York construction union leader Peter J. Brennan was nominated to be labor secretary replacing James D. Hodgson.

Herbert Hill, national labor director of the National Association for the Advancement of Colored People, described the appointment as "one more in a long series of political payoffs to the enemies of the black population." Brennan had "zealously protected and defended the racist practices of the building trades unions" for more than a quarter of a century, according to the NAACP spokesman.

29   Cox Communications, Inc. and Ameri-

can Television Communications, Inc., two major cable television franchisers and a coalition of 16 minority group organizations announced agreement in San Francisco that would give the groups control of several cable channels and train minority group members in broadcast skills. They said the plan would be effective upon completion of pending merger plans. The new company would provide, over a five-year period, up to three full-time channels in each of their eight California franchise areas at a token fee of $1 a year to nonprofit minority organizations, provide all necessary video equipment in four of the areas, and begin training minority individuals in technical and program skills.

The 16 minority groups in the agreement included the Black Panther Party, the western regional office of the National Association for the Advancement of Colored People and the Mexican-American Political Alliance.

1973

JANUARY

16   The Labor Department ordered into effect a series of changes in seniority practices at Bethlehem Steel's Sparrows Point, Md. plant, to wipe out the continuing effects of past discrimination in job placement of blacks. The order was issued under the Executive Order enforcing job rights in federal contracts. Labor Secretary James D. Hodgson rejected a request by the Office of Contract Compliance that sanctions be imposed, "in light," he said, "of the company's spirit of cooperation." The order was the first to concern seniority rights.

A federally appointed panel had reported at the beginning of 1971 that as of November, 1967, 81% of the 7,864 black workers at the plant had been employed in all-black or predominantly black departments with lower pay and less sought-after jobs, including refuse disposal and coke oven maintenance, while most of the 12,602 white employees worked as time-keepers and sheet metal workers. Changes in hiring practices since March 31, 1968 eliminated discrimination against new workers, the government ruled, but limited transfer rights perpetuated the effects of previous policy.

The order provided that all employees hired before March 31, 1968 who had never transferred out of a black department be given written transfer offers, provided they could perform the new job "with minimal training." Bethlehem was ordered to see that "reasonable requirements" be set for jobs, and training be provided.

Employees asking for transfer to a predominantly white department would be hired for the first "available permanent vacancy" on the basis of total years of "plant service" in any department. Blacks transferring to a white department would retain their accrued seniority and their pay, if higher than the new job would otherwise provide. Bethlehem, along with the United Steelworkers of America, had agreed to comply with a federal court order imposing a similar program at a Lackawanna, N.Y. plant in 1971.

18   At a confirmation hearing before the Senate Labor Committee, Labor Secretary-designate Peter J. Brennan declared his opposition to Administration policies on minimum wages, compulsory arbitration, manpower and federal housing programs. He defended his record on minority employment and pledged to enforce federal laws against job discrimination.

Brennan opposed a special minimum wage for youth lower than the regular minimum wage such as sought in 1972 by the Administration; compulsory arbitration in any form; which would include the form of compulsory arbitration in the Administration's 1972 request for an emergency bill on transportation strikes; and a freeze on low and middle income housing funds because of the unemployment factor.

His nomination was opposed at the Jan. 18 hearing by Roy Wilkins, executive director of the National Association for the Advancement of Colored People, on the ground he had been "a major administrative obstacle" to minority employment in the construction industry, and by Clinton DeVeaux, vice chairman of Americans for Democratic Action, who objected on the minority employment issue and on the ground that Brennan had "stayed neutral in the face of acknowledged corruption" in New York construction unions.

Brennan said, "I'm proud of my record" and "I will do my damndest, my hardest," as labor secretary to work for equal opportunity.

24   The Justice Department filed a civil suit in U.S. District Court in Boston charging that the city of Boston Fire Commissioner James H. Kelly and the members of the Massachusetts Civil Service Commission had discriminated against blacks and Spanish-surnamed people in hiring new firemen.

Out of 2,100 firemen, only 16 were black and three had Spanish surnames, though these groups constituted 16% and 4% of the city's population, respectively. The department said the city had failed or refused to hire minority people on an equal basis with whites, and had used tests and qualifications that discriminated against minorities although they had "not been shown to be required by the needs of the fire department or predictive of successful job performance."

The Justice Department asked the court to order the defendants to begin an active recruiting program, hire enough minority group members to compensate for past discrimination and compensate individuals who had taken fire department examinations but had been unfairly denied jobs.

24   The Justice Department announced that its job rights suit against Montgomery, Ala. had been resolved by a consent decree filed Oct. 3, 1972, which "substantially expanded employment opportunities for blacks in the city government."

29   U.S. District Court Judge Jon O. Newman ordered Bridgeport, Conn. to hire blacks and Puerto Ricans to fill half the vacancies in the police force until they constituted 15% of the force. Newman said the city's Civil Service Examination denied equal protection of the law to minority groups. Only 14 blacks and three Puerto Ricans were on the 485-member force, though the groups constituted 25% of the city's population. All future job tests would be submitted to the court for approval. Newman also set minority hiring quotas for detective, sergeant, lieutenant and captain positions over the next two years. Bridgeport Mayor Nicholas A. Panuzio said the city would appeal the ruling, which was also opposed by the local unit of the American Federation of State, County and Municipal Employees.

31   The Equal Employment Opportunity Commission found that WRC-TV and WRC AM-FM, the National Broadcasting Company (NBC)-owned broadcast stations in Washington, had discriminated against women in hiring and promotion. EEOC upheld 27 women employees in their charge that before 1971, NBC's "word of mouth method of recruiting and/or announcing vacancies was inadequate" in informing all potential employees about new jobs as required by the 1964 Civil Rights Act. In addition, the commission ruled, the company's maternity leave and training policies discriminated against women. EEOC said it also found reasonable cause to believe the stations discriminated against blacks. The ruling left the way open for a court enforcement suit by the EEOC or by the plaintiffs. NBC claimed it employed larger proportions of women and blacks in important positions than most broadcast stations in the country. The company said the EEOC had held no hearings, heard no witnesses and allowed no cross-examination.

MARCH

7   Chrysler Corp. was ordered by a Michigan state hearing referee to pay workmen's compensation benefits, including psychiatric care expenses, to a black employee whose nondisabling psychotic tendencies had been aggravated by plant racism and unfair work conditions, causing him to kill three supervisors after he was fired in 1970.

James Johnson had been found legally insane at his trial and placed in a state mental hospital. In the latest ruling, a state examiner said Johnson had developed paranoic feelings toward whites during his childhood on a Mississippi plantation. He had then been unfairly assigned to undesirable jobs at the Chrysler plant, denied advancement opportunities, called "nigger" and "boy" by a foreman, denied medical benefits, suspended unfairly and fired after refusing what he considered a dangerous job. The National Association for the Advancement of Colored People, the League of United Latin-American Citizens, the American GI Forum and the Mexican-American Political Association filed a complaint with California's Fair Employment Practices Commission against the state's 28 largest cities, charging job bias against blacks and Spanish-surnamed people in police and fire departments. The organization said the two groups constituted 27% of the cities' population, but only 9% of the police and 5% of the firemen. They asked the commission to order population parity in the positions by 1977, to open up about 8,000 jobs.

The Justice Department filed a civil suit in U.S. district court in Chicago charging that the city had discriminated against blacks and Spanish-surnamed persons in hiring and promoting firemen. The Department noted that only 4% of Chicago's 5,000 firemen were black and only .5% Puerto Rican or Mexican-American, although 32% of the city's people were black and 11% had Spanish surnames. The suit sought a change in hiring practices, including elimination of allegedly unnecessary and discriminatory hiring and promotion tests, a recruitment program and compensation for past discrimination.

The suit was the third brought against a municipal fire department by the Justice Department, and the fourth filed against a municipal agency under the Equal Employment Act of 1972, which authorized such suits by the attorney general.

APRIL 6 Nassau and Suffolk Counties, N.Y. construction employers, unions and minority group representatives signed a three-year agreement to make a "good faith effort" to achieve 6% black membership in each local construction union.

It was the first "hometown plan" to be approved by the Office of Federal Contract Compliance of the U.S. Department of Labor since President Nixon emphatically rejected the "quota" concept of minority job advancement in 1972.

The plan had been delayed for nine months because of Administration insistence that the phrase "good faith effort" be inserted before mention of the 6% goal. The agreement could be canceled after each year, 60 to 90 days after written notification by any of the participant groups.

MAY 2 Federal district court judge Sam C. Pointer Jr., in Birmingham, Ala., ordered the U.S. Steel Corp. and the United Steelworkers Union to change discriminatory hiring and seniority systems at the company's Fairfield Works, where 3,800 of 12,000 workers were black.

The ruling on suits filed in 1970 created a uniform seniority system to replace 10 separate systems and established the right of workers to transfer from one line of promotion to another without losing seniority rights, opening previously closed jobs to blacks. Back pay was ordered for employees who had been held in menial jobs.

Timetables were set under which one black apprentice would be chosen for each white apprentice until 25% of all journeymen positions were held by blacks, and one black supervisor would be hired for every two white supervisors until 20% of all management positions were held by blacks. Blacks who had been laid off were given special rehiring rights. The ruling was to take effect Aug. 1 after an "intense education program" at the Fairfield Works and other company plants in Alabama, all of which were affected.

Section X

FARMS AND FARMING

The Black Farmer

Tables

THE BLACK FARMER

The position of the black farmer in America has been dictated to a large extent by the economic and social history of the South, and particularly by the problems of Southern agriculture and a developing technology which displaced the traditional farm worker. The lingering legacy of the plantation system, which was based on the dominance of cotton, was one of the prime factors responsible for this tragic story with the resultant system of usury, poverty, discontent, and virtual bondage. The tenant system and the credit system which accompanied it made it almost impossible for small black farmers to face adequately the results of one-crop planting, eroded land, along with the increased mechanization and industrialization of farming methods.

In 1910 black farm ownership was at its peak. At that time, blacks owned 219,000 farms encompassing more than 15 million acres, with an additional 550,000 farm operators acting as tenants or sharecroppers. According to the 1959 Agriculture Census, the number of black farm owners had dropped to 90,995 and the farms owned a total of less than 7 million acres of land. Thus in a period of time when almost all segments of the population were being assisted by economic advances in the national economy, the black in the rural South seemed to have benefited least.

Historically, more than 80 percent of all black farmers grew cotton. In 1903, when the boll weevil invaded the United States from Mexico, the black farmer in the Cotton Belt was particularly hard hit. The United States Department of Agriculture named Thomas M. Campbell of Tuskegee and John B. Pierce of Hampton as field demonstration agents to work with black farmers in Alabama and Virginia, respectively. This was a beginning of what might have been a successful effort to raise the level of black farming and the condition of the black tenant farmer and the sharecropper in the rural South.

The Smith-Lever Act which was passed in 1914 set the ground rules for a system of farm and home demonstration agents operating throughout the country. The Act which came to be known as Cooperative Extension Service allowed those State legislatures which had established segregated land-grant colleges under the Second Morrill Act of 1890 to designate either the white or the black college to administer the program of agricultural work. An attempt to include a specific requirement that extension work among blacks be carried out at the black land-grant colleges was defeated on the ground, among others, that "divided responsibility for the use of extension funds in a State might lead to dissimilar instruction being given to white and black farmers." In the 17 States which had segregated institutions the white land-grant college was chosen to administer the total program. In ensuing years, as the Southern extension services hired black workers, they were generally placed in the black land-grant college. Federally-supported State extension services in the South have been operated at both the State and county levels, on a segregated structural basis until recent years. This inevitably led to limited and deficient services with a bad situation being compounded as time went on. The needs of poor black farmers are the same as those of poor white farmers, and a progressive black farmer needs the same advice and information that a successful white farmer needs.

An average of 9,425,000 persons lived on farms in rural areas of the United States in the 12-month period centered on April, 1971. Since 1960 the farm population has declined by about two-fifths for an average annual decline of 4.6 per cent. During this 1960-71 period, the relative loss in the number of farm residents was significantly greater among blacks and other races than among whites. The average annual rate of decline for blacks and other races on farms was 9.7 percent, compared with 3.9 percent for whites.

In 1971, blacks and other races in the farm population numbered 884,000, or 9 percent, of the national total. Young children comprised a greater proportion of the blacks and other races farm population than they did of the white farm population. Of all blacks and other races on farms in 1971, 35 percent were under 14 years of age; the comparable proportion for whites was 24 percent. In contrast to the white farm population, where males outnumber females, there was no significant difference in the number of farm males compared to farm females among blacks and other races.

Labor force participation was higher among white farm residents than among blacks and other races on farms, with participation rates of 61 and 56 percent, respectively. This racial difference resulted from the disparity in the labor force participation of males, as there was no significant difference by race in the likelihood of females being in the labor force. On the other hand, in the male farm population 14 years old and over, 81 percent of the whites were in the labor force; the comparable proportion for blacks and other races was 74 percent. Blacks and other races had higher un-employment rates than whites regardless of whether they had a farm or nonfarm resi-dence. In the farm resident labor force, the 1971 unemployment rate was 7.2 percent for blacks and other races; and 2.2 percent among whites. In the noninstitutional civilian popula-tion living off farms, the comparable rates were 10.4 and 5.7 percent, respectively.

For the two major racial groups, the class of worker distribution differed greatly. Self-employment was the predominant class of work for 61 percent of white farm persons in agriculture, whereas among blacks and other races, about 27 percent were self-employed and 62 percent worked for wages or salary. The higher incidence of wage and salary em-ployment among blacks and other races can be attributed, at least in part, to the higher proportion of nonoperator population (per-sons living in other dwelling units on farms, such as households of hired farm workers) in the blacks and other races farm population, compared to whites.

According to a report of the Southern Rural Research Project (SRRP) in 1968, the Southern black farmer faced virtual extinc-tion. Two-thirds of the black farmers surveyed ended the 1967 farm year in debt, the report says. Nearly 25 percent of the farm families ate no fresh meat, and only 2.6 percent had ever had a tooth filled.

The report points out that federal programs, which are designed to help American farmers, rarely reach the black farmer of Alabama. Of the black farmers surveyed, 97 percent said they have never received any help from their Agricultural Stabilization and Conservation Service (ASCS, or more commonly called "the cotton office") community committee, and 95 percent said they have never received any help from their ASCS county committee. Some 85 percent said they have never even heard of any meetings held by the Farmers Home Administration (FHA).

The two-part SRRP report is the result of research work done by college students during the summer of 1967 in Autauga, Crenshaw, Dallas, Greene, Hale, Marengo, Perry, and Wilcox counties in Alabama. Using a 23-page questionnaire, the students interviewed 898 black families, representing the more than 5,000 people in these areas, and specifically questioned 243 black farmers on their experi-ences with federal farm programs.

The Division of Behavioral Science Re-search of Tuskegee Institute was asked to ana-lyze the responses to the questionaire. After determination that the data were sound, the division undertook the task of tabulating the frequency and percent distribution of the re-sponses.

Part II of the report ("The Extinction of the Black Farmer in Alabama") showed that almost half the families worked an average of nine to ten hours per day on their farms, and another 17 percent averaged from 11 to 15 hours of work per day.

But these long working hours still resulted in desperate poverty and hunger, the SRRP found. One-quarter of the households covered in Part I of the report ("Black Farm Famil-ies—Hunger and Malnutrition in Alabama") ate no fresh meat, and another 25 percent ate meat only once a week. Fresh milk was not used at all by 30 percent of the families, and 18.5 percent never ate eggs. In 14.2 percent of the farm households visited, the SRRP inter-viewers noted one or more children with very noticeably distended stomachs—a clear indica-tion of malnutrition.

In 93.2 percent of the homes, there was no indoor water supply, and 92.7 percent had no indoor toilets. Almost two-thirds of the house-holds did not have enough sheets and pillow-cases for the entire family, and 39.6 percent lacked enough dishes, glasses, and silverware.

Part I of the report considers the effect of the two federal food programs administered by local representatives of the U.S. Depart-ment of Agriculture. Half of those participat-ing in the food stamp program, the SRRP found, had to borrow money to pay for the stamps. "One of the expressed purposes of the program—to break the dependency chain of credit/debt that binds so many rural black farmers to their landlords and local grocers, who are frequently one and the same person —is defeated by the fact that the food stamps cost more than the average black fami-ly can afford to spend on food each month," the report states.

Half of those interviewed complained that it is extremely difficult to get to the food stamp office since there is usually just one of-fice in a county, located in the largest town. The median distance to the food stamp office for program participants—who often do not have cars—is 17.6 miles, the SRRP found.

Half of the people participating in the free commodity food program said the free food by itself is not enough to feed a family. The commodities—typically, grits, rice, flour, rolled wheat, red beans, corn meal, split peas, peanut butter, etc.—are essentially starch or "filler" foods. But of 135 free food recipients questioned, only 12 said they were able to supplement the commodities by raising meat on the farm. Fifteen were able to supplement the family diet by buying meat, and four by buying or raising eggs.

Part II of the report studies the impact of three other federal farm programs—the Agricultural Stabilization and Conservation Service (ASCS), the Farmers Home Administration (FHA), and the federal Extension Service. Explanations of the functions of these agencies are found in the report.

Of those responding in Part II, more than 92 percent of the black farmers said they are called by their first name in the ASCS and FHA offices, and more than half said this is also the case in the extension service office. "Frequently," the reports comments, "after spending a full day at the office, away from his work at the farm, a black farmer will be told to come back the next day."

As a result of being mistreated and ignored by those agencies, the black farmer is "isolated and appallingly uninformed about federal farm programs—and therefore, does not participate in or benefit from them," the SRRP found.

Obviously, blacks are not made aware of the very programs which seemingly were to have benefitted them. Nearly two-thirds of the farmers covered in Part II of the report did not know about ASCS programs to help with soil and water problems; two-thirds did not know that they could appeal the amount of their cotton allotments; and 41 percent did not know about ASCS programs for corn, sorghum, and harley. Almost three-quarters of

the black farmers had no knowledge of FHA loans for improvement of soil and water conditions, and more than two-thirds did not know about FHA loans for family or farming costs.

The SRRP's report notes remarks by high government officials to the effect that the American farmer—especially the small rural farmer—cannot hope to survive without the aid of these federal programs. It quotes President Johnson's instructions to Orville Freeman, U.S. Secretary of Agriculture: "The programs so essential to our continued welfare and economic growth must reach all in our rural areas if they are to be effective in lifting those areas to full economic self-sufficiency."

Yet, the report says, 70 to 90 percent of the rural black farmers are cut off from these essential programs, and many are left with no alternative but migration to the Northern ghettos.

"The responsibility for change lies with the federal government," says the SRRP. "The President of the United States, who appoints the Secretary of Agriculture, and the Secretary of Agriculture himself, who, at best, has shut his eyes or, at worst, has sanctioned the extinction of the black farmer in Alabama and in the South."

The farm labor union movement, spearheaded by Caesar Chavez, United Farm Workers Organizing Committee, and the identification of black civil rights organizations with the plight of farm workers and the migrant laborers throughout the United States, seems to indicate a long-range commitment to goals which will ultimately better the socioeconomic conditions of this class, whether black, white, or Spanish-speaking.

Farm population by operator status and race, South and United States, June 1970 and 1966

Operator status, race, and region	Population		Percentage change, 1966-70	Percentage distribution	
	1970	1966		1970	1966
	Thousands	Thousands	Percent	Percent	Percent
Total					
White	9,307	10,616	−12.3	100.0	100.0
Operator population	8,685	9,863	−11.9	93.3	92.9
Nonoperator population	622	753	−17.4	6.7	7.1
Black and other races	724	1,120	−35.4	100.0	100.0
Operator population	473	768	−38.4	65.4	68.6
Nonoperator population	250	352	−29.0	34.6	31.4
South					
White	3,415	3,993	−14.5	100.0	100.0
Operator population	3,120	3,609	−13.5	91.4	90.4
Nonoperator population	295	384	−23.2	8.6	9.6
Black and other races	671	1,072	−37.4	100.0	100.0
Operator population	434	730	−40.5	64.7	68.1
Nonoperator population	237	342	−30.7	35.3	31.9

Farm Population, by Race and Sex, for Broad Age Groups: April 1971 and 1960

(Numbers in thousands. Figures for April 1971 are April-centered annual averages; those for 1960 are for month of April)

Age and Race	Both Sexes		Male		Female	
	1971	1960	1971	1960	1971	1960
Total..............................	9,425	15,669	4,870	8,184	4,556	7,485
White.................................	8,542	13,092	4,422	6,871	4,120	6,221
Black and other races......................	884	2,577	448	1,313	436	1,264
Under 14 years..........................	2,395	4,995	1,227	2,586	1,168	2,409
White.................................	2,082	3,851	1,074	1,995	1,008	1,856
Black and other races......................	313	1,144	153	591	160	553
14 years and over........................	7,030	10,674	3,643	5,598	3,388	5,076
White.................................	6,460	9,241	3,348	4,876	3,112	4,365
Black and other races......................	571	1,433	295	722	276	711

Age and Race	PERCENT DISTRIBUTION					
	Both Sexes		Male		Female	
	1971	1960	1971	1960	1971	1960
Total..............................	100.0	100.0	100.0	100.0	100.0	100.0
White.................................	90.6	83.6	90.8	84.0	90.4	83.1
Black and other races......................	9.4	16.4	9.2	16.0	9.6	16.9
Under 14 years..........................	100.0	100.0	100.0	100.0	100.0	100.0
White.................................	86.9	77.1	87.5	77.1	86.3	77.0
Black and other races......................	13.1	22.9	12.5	22.9	13.7	23.0
14 years and over........................	100.0	100.0	100.0	100.0	100.0	100.0
White.................................	91.9	86.6	91.9	87.1	91.9	86.0
Black and other races......................	8.1	13.4	8.1	12.9	8.1	14.0

–Farm population by tenure of operator and race, June 1970 and 1966

Tenure of operator and race	Population		Percentage change, 1966-70	Percentage distribution	
	1970[1]	1966		1970	1966
	Thousands	Thousands	Percent	Percent	Percent
All races..............................	10,017	11,736	−14.6	100.0	100.0
Full and part owners................	8,962	10,078	−11.1	89.5	85.9
Tenants and managers...............	1,056	1,659	−36.3	10.5	14.1
White...............................	9,307	10,616	−12.3	100.0	100.0
Full and part owners................	8,407	9,268	−9.3	90.3	87.3
Tenants and managers...............	900	1,348	−33.2	9.7	12.7
Black and other races.................	711	1,120	−36.5	100.0	100.0
Full and part owners................	555	810	−31.5	78.1	72.3
Tenants and managers...............	156	311	−49.8	21.9	27.7

Excludes an estimated 13,000 Indians living in farm residences on reservations.

Population in farm operator households by race and tenure of operator, June 1970 and 1966

Race and tenure of operator	Population		Percentage change, 1966-70	Percentage distribution	
	1970[1]	1966		1970	1966
	Thousands	Thousands	Percent	Percent	Percent
All races............................	9,145	10,632	—14.0	100.0	100.0
Full and part owners................	8,187	9,096	—10.0	89.5	85.6
Tenants and managers..............	958	1,536	—37.6	10.5	14.4
White................................	8,685	9,863	—11.9	100.0	100.0
Full and part owners................	7,847	8,592	—8.7	90.4	87.1
Tenants and managers..............	838	1,272	—34.1	9.6	12.9
Black and other races................	460	768	—40.1	100.0	100.0
Full and part owners................	340	504	—32.5	73.9	65.6
Tenants and managers..............	120	264	—54.5	26.1	34.3

[1] Excludes an estimated 13,000 Indians living in farm residences on reservations.

Farm population in nonoperator households by race of head and tenure of operator, June 1970 and 1966

Race of head and tenure of operator	Population		Percentage change, 1966-70	Percentage distribution	
	1970	1966		1970	1966
	Thousands	Thousands	Percent	Percent	Percent
All races............................	873	1,105	—21.0	100.0	100.0
Full and part owners................	775	982	—21.1	88.8	88.9
Tenants and managers..............	98	123	—20.3	11.2	11.1
White................................	622	753	—17.4	100.0	100.0
Full and part owners................	560	676	—17.2	90.0	89.8
Tenants and managers..............	62	76	—18.4	10.0	10.1
Black and other races................	250	352	—29.0	100.0	100.0
Full and part owners................	215	305	—29.5	85.7	86.6
Tenants and managers..............	36	47	—23.4	14.3	13.3

·Farm population by tenure of operator and race, for regions, June 1970 and 1966

Region, tenure of operator, and race	Population		Percentage change, 1966-70	Percentage distribution	
	1970[1]	1966		1970	1966
	Thousands	Thousands	Percent	Percent	Percent
North and West......................	5,932	6,671	—11.1	100.0	100.0
Full and part owners................	5,326	5,810	—8.3	89.8	87.1
Tenants and managers..............	606	860	—29.5	10.2	12.9
South................................	4,086	5,065	—19.3	100.0	100.0
Full and part owners................	3,636	4,267	—14.8	89.0	84.2
Tenants and managers..............	450	799	—43.7	11.0	15.8
South by race:					
White............................	3,415	3,993	—14.5	100.0	100.0
Full and part owners.............	3,115	3,502	—11.1	91.2	87.7
Tenants and managers..........	300	491	—38.9	8.8	12.3
Black and other races.............	671	1,072	—37.4	100.0	100.0
Full and part owners.............	521	764	—31.8	77.6	71.3
Tenants and managers..........	150	307	—51.1	22.4	28.7

[1] Excludes an estimated 13,000 Indians living in farm residences on reservations.

Population in farm operator households by tenure of operator and race, for regions, June 1970 and 1966

Region, race, and tenure of operator	Population		Percentage change, 1966-70	Percentage distribution	
	1970[1]	1966		1970	1966
	Thousands	Thousands	Percent	Percent	Percent
North and West.....................	5,590	6,292	−11.2	100.0	100.0
Full and part owners...............	5,013	5,465	−8.3	89.7	86.9
Tenants and managers..............	577	827	−30.2	10.3	13.1
South.............................	3,555	4,340	−18.1	100.0	100.0
Full and part owners...............	3,174	3,631	−12.6	89.3	83.7
Tenants and managers..............	381	709	−46.3	10.7	16.3
South by race:					
White............................	3,120	3,609	−13.5	100.0	100.0
Full and part owners.............	2,857	3,162	−9.6	91.6	87.6
Tenants and managers...........	264	448	−41.1	8.4	12.4
Black and other races..............	435	730	−40.4	100.0	100.0
Full and part owners.............	317	469	−32.4	73.0	64.2
Tenants and managers...........	117	261	−55.2	27.0	35.8

[1]Excludes an estimated 13,000 Indians living in farm residences on reservations.

Farm population in nonoperator households by race of head and tenure of operator, for regions, June 1970 and 1966

Region, race of head, and tenure of operator	Population		Percentage change, 1966-70	Percentage distribution	
	1970	1966		1970	1966
	Thousands	Thousands	Percent	Percent	Percent
North and West.....................	342	379	−9.8	100.0	100.0
Full and part owners...............	313	345	−9.3	91.5	91.3
Tenants and managers..............	29	33	−12.1	8.5	8.7
South.............................	531	726	−26.9	100.0	100.0
Full and part owners...............	462	636	−27.4	87.0	87.6
Tenants and managers..............	69	90	−23.3	13.0	12.4
South by race:					
White............................	295	384	−23.2	100.0	100.0
Full and part owners.............	258	341	−24.3	87.7	88.6
Tenants and managers...........	36	44	−18.2	12.3	11.4
Black and other races..............	237	342	−30.7	100.0	100.0
Full and part owners.............	204	295	−30.8	86.1	86.5
Tenants and managers...........	33	46	−28.3	13.9	13.5

Farm Residents 14 Years Old and Over Employed in Agriculture by Class of Worker, Race, and Sex, April 1971 and 1960, and by Regions, April 1971

(Numbers in thousands. Figures for April 1971 are April-centered annual averages; those for 1960 are for month of April)

Class of Worker, Race, and Sex	TOTAL		North and West — 1971	South — 1971	PERCENT DISTRIBUTION				
					Total		North and West — 1971	South — 1971	
	1971	1960			1971	1960	1971	1971	
Total Agricultural Workers									
Both sexes......................	2,291	4,025	1,567	724	100.0	100.0	100.0	100.0	
Self-employed workers................	1,346	2,405	932	414	58.8	59.8	59.5	57.2	
Wage and salary workers..............	425	782	224	201	18.6	19.4	14.3	27.8	
Unpaid family workers................	521	838	411	110	22.7	20.8	26.2	15.2	
Male...........................	1,864	3,388	1,250	614	100.0	100.0	100.0	100.0	
Self-employed workers................	1,281	2,313	889	392	68.7	68.3	71.1	63.8	
Wage and salary workers..............	373	691	198	175	20.0	20.4	15.8	28.5	
Unpaid family workers................	209	384	162	47	11.2	11.3	13.0	7.7	
Female..........................	428	637	318	110	100.0	100.0	100.0	100.0	
Self-employed workers................	65	92	43	22	15.2	14.4	13.5	20.0	
Wage and salary workers..............	52	91	26	26	12.1	14.3	8.2	23.6	
Unpaid family workers................	311	454	249	62	72.7	71.3	78.3	56.4	
Black and Other Races									
Both sexes......................	160	599	16	144	100.0	100.0	(B)	100.0	
Self-employed workers................	43	220	5	38	26.9	36.7	(B)	26.4	
Wage and salary workers..............	100	246	7	93	62.5	41.1	(B)	64.6	
Unpaid family workers................	16	133	1	15	10.0	22.2	(B)	10.4	
Male...........................	134	477	14	120	100.0	100.0	(B)	100.0	
Self-employed workers................	40	202	5	35	29.9	42.4	(B)	29.2	
Wage and salary workers..............	84	200	7	77	62.7	41.9	(B)	64.2	
Unpaid family workers................	9	75	—	9	6.7	15.7	(B)	7.5	
Female..........................	27	122	3	24	(B)	100.0	(B)	(B)	
Self-employed workers................	3	18	—	3	(B)	14.8	(B)	(B)	
Wage and salary workers..............	16	46	—	16	(B)	37.7	(B)	(B)	
Unpaid family workers................	7	58	1	6	(B)	47.5	(B)	(B)	

— Represents zero or rounds to zero.

(B) Base less than 75,000.

Farm Residents 14 Years Old and Over Employed in Nonagricultural Industries, by Class of Worker, Race, and Sex, for Regions: April 1971

(Numbers in thousands. Figures are April-centered annual averages)

Class of Worker, Race, and Sex	TOTAL	North and West	South	PERCENT DISTRIBUTION		
				Total	North and West	South
Total Nonagricultural Workers						
Both sexes......................	1,864	1,066	798	100.0	100.0	100.0
Self-employed workers.................	172	89	83	9.2	8.3	10.4
Wages and salary workers..............	1,668	966	702	89.5	90.6	88.0
Unpaid family workers.................	24	11	13	1.3	1.0	1.6
Male............................	1,017	571	446	100.0	100.0	100.0
Self-employed workers.................	119	65	54	11.7	11.4	12.1
Wage and salary workers..............	893	503	390	87.8	88.1	87.4
Unpaid family workers.................	6	4	2	0.6	0.7	0.4
Female..........................	847	495	352	100.0	100.0	100.0
Self-employed workers.................	53	23	30	6.3	4.6	8.5
Wage and salary workers..............	775	462	313	91.5	93.3	88.9
Unpaid family workers.................	18	8	10	2.1	1.6	2.8
White						
Both sexes......................	1,726	1,052	674	100.0	100.0	100.0
Self-employed workers.................	166	87	79	9.6	8.3	11.7
Wage and salary workers..............	1,538	955	583	89.1	90.8	86.5
Unpaid family workers.................	22	10	12	1.3	1.0	1.8
Male............................	947	564	383	100.0	100.0	100.0
Self-employed workers.................	114	64	50	12.0	11.3	13.1
Wage and salary workers..............	827	497	330	87.3	88.1	86.2
Unpaid family workers.................	5	3	2	0.5	0.5	0.5
Female..........................	780	489	291	100.0	100.0	100.0
Self-employed workers.................	52	23	29	6.7	4.7	10.0
Wage and salary workers..............	711	458	253	91.2	93.7	86.9
Unpaid family workers.................	17	7	10	2.2	1.4	3.4
Black and Other Races						
Both sexes......................	137	13	124	100.0	(B)	100.0
Self-employed workers.................	7	3	4	5.1	(B)	3.2
Wage and salary workers..............	130	10	120	94.9	(B)	96.8
Unpaid family workers.................	1	1	—	0.7	(B)	—
Male............................	70	7	63	(B)	(B)	(B)
Self-employed workers.................	5	2	3	(B)	(B)	(B)
Wage and salary workers..............	65	5	60	(B)	(B)	(B)
Unpaid family workers.................	1	1	—	(B)	(B)	(B)
Female..........................	67	6	61	(B)	(B)	(B)
Self-employed workers.................	2	1	1	(B)	(B)	(B)
Wage and salary workers..............	65	5	60	(B)	(B)	(B)
Unpaid family workers.................	—	—	—	(B)	(B)	(B)

— Represents zero or rounds to zero.
(B) Base less than 75,000.

Employment Status of the Farm Population 14 Years Old and Over, by Race and Sex, for Regions: April 1971

(Numbers in thousands. Figures in April-centered annual averages)

Labor Force Status, Race, and Sex	TOTAL	North and West	South	PERCENT DISTRIBUTION		
				Total	North and West	South
White						
Both sexes..................	6,460	4,198	2,261	100.0	100.0	100.0
Labor force.................	3,942	2,655	1,287	61.0	63.2	56.9
Not in labor force..........	2,517	1,543	974	39.0	36.8	43.1
Labor force.................	3,942	2,655	1,287	100.0	100.0	100.0
Employed.................	3,858	2,604	1,254	97.9	98.1	97.4
Agriculture...........	2,131	1,551	580	54.1	58.4	45.1
Nonagricultural industries...........	1,726	1,052	674	43.8	39.6	52.4
Unemployed...............	85	52	33	2.2	2.0	2.6
Male......................	3,348	2,200	1,148	100.0	100.0	100.0
Labor force.................	2,720	1,826	894	81.2	83.0	77.9
Not in labor force..........	629	375	254	18.8	17.0	22.1
Labor force.................	2,720	1,826	894	100.0	100.0	100.0
Employed.................	2,677	1,800	877	98.4	98.6	98.1
Agriculture...........	1,730	1,236	494	63.6	67.7	55.3
Nonagricultural industries...........	947	564	383	34.8	30.9	42.8
Unemployed...............	43	26	17	1.6	1.4	1.9
Female....................	3,112	1,999	1,113	100.0	100.0	100.0
Labor force.................	1,223	830	393	39.3	41.5	35.3
Not in labor force..........	1,889	1,170	719	60.7	58.5	64.6
Labor force.................	1,223	830	393	100.0	100.0	100.0
Employed.................	1,181	804	377	96.6	96.9	95.9
Agriculture...........	401	315	86	32.8	38.0	21.9
Nonagricultural industries...........	780	489	291	63.8	58.9	74.0
Unemployed...............	42	26	16	3.4	3.1	4.1
Black and Other Races						
Both sexes..................	571	56	515	100.0	(B)	100.0
Labor force.................	320	31	289	56.0	(B)	56.1
Not in labor force..........	249	24	225	43.6	(B)	43.7
Labor force.................	320	31	289	100.0	(B)	100.0
Employed.................	298	30	268	93.1	(B)	92.7
Agriculture...........	160	16	144	50.0	(B)	49.8
Nonagricultural industries...........	137	13	124	42.8	(B)	42.9
Unemployed...............	23	2	21	7.2	(B)	7.3
Male......................	295	30	265	100.0	(B)	100.0
Labor force.................	217	23	194	73.6	(B)	73.2
Not in labor force..........	78	8	70	26.4	(B)	26.4
Labor force.................	217	23	194	100.0	(B)	100.0
Employed.................	204	21	183	94.0	(B)	94.3
Agriculture...........	134	14	120	61.8	(B)	61.9
Nonagricultural industries...........	70	7	63	32.3	(B)	32.5
Unemployed...............	13	2	11	6.0	(B)	5.7
Female....................	276	26	250	100.0	(B)	100.0
Labor force.................	105	10	95	38.0	(B)	38.0
Not in labor force..........	171	16	155	62.0	(B)	62.0
Labor force.................	105	10	95	100.0	(B)	100.0
Employed.................	94	9	85	89.5	(B)	89.5
Agriculture...........	27	3	24	25.7	(B)	25.3
Nonagricultural industries...........	67	6	61	63.8	(B)	64.2
Unemployed...............	11	1	10	10.5	(B)	10.5

— Represents zero or rounds to zero.

(B) Base less than 75,000.

Southern farm population by value of products sold and race, June 1970 and 1966

Value of products sold and race	Economic class	Population		Percentage Change, 1966-70	Percentage distribution	
		1970	1966		1970	1966
		Thousands	Thousands	Percent	Percent	Percent
South..........................		4,086	5,065	−19.3	100.0	100.0
$40,000 and over................	I	392	336	16.7	9.6	6.6
$20,000–39,999.................	II	263	279	−5.7	6.4	5.5
$10,000–19,999.................	III	358	432	−17.1	8.8	8.5
$5,000–9,999..................	IV	450	567	−20.6	11.0	11.2
$2,500–4,999..................	V	598	763	−21.6	14.6	15.1
$50–2,499.....................	VI	2,026	2,689	−24.7	49.5	53.1
$250–2,499...................		1,767	NA	—	43.2	—
$50–249......................		259	NA	—	6.3	—
White..........................		3,415	3,993	−14.5	100.0	100.0
$40,000 and over................	I	298	215	38.6	8.7	5.4
$20,000–39,999.................	II	213	234	−9.0	6.2	5.9
$10,000–19,999.................	III	308	348	−11.5	9.0	8.7
$5,000–9,999..................	IV	386	466	−17.2	11.3	11.7
$2,500–4,999..................	V	520	624	−16.7	15.2	15.6
$50–2,499.....................	VI	1,691	2,107	−19.7	49.5	52.8
$250–2,499...................		1,481	NA	—	43.4	—
$50–249......................		210	NA	—	6.1	—
Black and other races..............		671	1,072	−37.4	100.0	100.0
$40,000 and over................	I	94	121	−22.3	14.0	11.3
$20,000–39,999.................	II	50	45	11.1	7.5	4.2
$10,000–19,999.................	III	50	85	−41.2	7.5	7.9
$5,000–9,999..................	IV	64	101	−36.6	9.5	9.4
$2,500–4,999..................	V	78	139	−43.9	11.6	13.0
$50–2,499.....................	VI	335	582	−42.4	49.9	54.3
$250–2,499...................		286	NA	—	42.6	—
$50–249......................		49	NA	—	7.3	—

Population in farm operator households by value of products sold and race, June 1970 and 1966

Value of products sold and race	Economic class	Population		Percentage change, 1966-70	Percentage distribution	
		1970[1]	1966		1970	1966
		Thousands	Thousands	Percent	Percent	Percent
All races.........................		9,145	10,632	−14.0	100.0	100.0
$40,000 and over................	I	821	555	47.9	9.0	5.2
$20,000–39,999.................	II	1,145	976	17.3	12.5	9.2
$10,000–19,999.................	III	1,407	1,779	−20.9	15.4	16.7
$5,000–9,999..................	IV	1,116	1,583	−29.5	12.2	14.9
$2,500–4,999..................	V	1,155	1,443	−20.0	12.6	13.6
$50–2,499.....................	VI	3,501	4,295	−18.5	38.3	40.4
$250–2,499...................		3,026	NA	—	33.1	—
$50–249......................		474	NA	—	5.2	—
White..........................		8,685	9,863	−11.9	100.0	100.0
$40,000 and over................	I	816	548	48.9	9.4	5.6
$20,000–39,999.................	II	1,138	971	17.2	13.1	9.8
$10,000–19,999.................	III	1,386	1,751	−20.8	16.0	17.7
$5,000–9,999..................	IV	1,070	1,516	−29.4	12.3	15.4
$2,500–4,999..................	V	1,091	1,329	−17.9	12.6	13.5
$50–2,499.....................	VI	3,183	3,748	−15.1	36.6	38.0
$250–2,499...................		2,756	NA	—	31.7	—
$50–249......................		427	NA	—	4.9	—
Black and other races..............		460	768	−40.1	100.0	100.0
$40,000 and over................	I	5	8	−37.5	1.1	1.0
$20,000–39,999.................	II	7	6	16.7	1.5	.7
$10,000–19,999.................	III	21	28	−25.0	4.6	3.7
$5,000–9,999..................	IV	46	66	−30.3	10.0	8.6
$2,500–4,999..................	V	64	114	−43.9	13.9	14.8
$50–2,499.....................	VI	317	547	−42.0	68.9	71.2
$250–2,499...................		270	NA	—	58.7	—
$50–249......................		47	NA	—	10.2	—

NA = not available
[1]Excludes an estimated 13,000 Indians living in farm residences on reservations.

Section XI

HOUSING

Housing

Tables

HOUSING

The passage of the National Housing Act in 1934 signaled a new Federal commitment to provide housing for the nation's citizens. Congress made the commitment explicit 15 years later in the Housing Act of 1949, establishing as a national goal, the realization of "a decent home and suitable environment for every American family."

Today, after more than three decades of fragmented and grossly under-funded federal housing programs, decent housing remains a chronic problem for the disadvantaged urban household. Fifty-six percent of the country's nonwhite families live in central cities today, and of these, nearly two-thirds live in neighborhoods marked by substandard* housing and general urban blight. For these citizens, condemned by segregation and poverty to live in the decaying slums of our central cities, the goal of a decent home and suitable environment is as far distant as ever.

During the decade of the 1950s, when vast numbers of blacks were migrating to the cities, only 4 million of the 16.8 million new housing units constructed throughout the nation were built in the central cities. These additions were counterbalanced by the loss of 1.5 million central-city units through demolition and other means. The result was that the number of nonwhites living in substandard housing increased from 1.4 to 1.8 million, even though the number of substandard units declined.

Statistics available for the period since 1960 indicate that the trend is continuing. There has been virtually no decline in the number of occupied dilapidated units in metropolitan areas, and surveys in New York City and Watts actually show an increase in the number of such units. These statistics have led the Department of Housing and Urban Development to conclude that while the trend in the country as a whole is toward less substandard housing, "There are individual neighborhoods and areas within many cities where the housing situation continues to deteriorate."

In the black ghettoes [of the nation's cities], grossly inadequate housing continues to be a critical problem.

Nationwide, 25 percent of all nonwhites living in central cities occupied substandard units in 1960, compared to 8 percent of all whites. Census Bureau data indicated that by 1966, the figures had dropped to 16 and 5 percent,

respectively. However, if "deteriorating" units and units with serious housing code violations were added, the percentage of nonwhites living in inadequate housing in 1966 becomes much greater.

The Commission* carried out a special analyses of 1960 housing conditions in three cities [Detroit, Washington, D.C., and Memphis] concentrating on all Census Tracts with 1960 median incomes of under $3,000 for both families and individuals. It also analyzed housing conditions in Watts. The results showed that the vast majority of people living in the poorest areas of these cities were blacks, and that a high proportion lived in inadequate housing.

Blacks, on the average, occupy much older housing than whites. In each of 10 metropolitan areas analyzed by the Commission, substantially higher percentages of nonwhites than whites occupied units built prior to 1939.

Finally, black housing units are far more likely to be overcrowded than those occupied by whites. In U.S. metropolitan areas in 1960, 25 percent of all nonwhite units were overcrowded by the standard measure (that is, they contained 1.01 or more persons per room). Only 8 percent of all white-occupied units were in this category. Moreover, 11 percent of all non-white-occupied units were seriously overcrowded (1.51 or more persons per room), compared with 2 percent for white-occupied units.

Blacks in large cities are often forced to pay the same rents as whites and receive less for their money, or pay higher rents for the same accommodations.

In certain Chicago census tracts (1960), both whites and nonwhites paid median rents of $88, and the proportions paying various specific rents below that median were almost identical. But the units rented by nonwhites were typically:

—Smaller (the median number of rooms was 3.35 for nonwhites versus 3.95 for whites).

—In worse condition (30.7 percent of all nonwhite units were deteriorated or dilapidated units versus 11.6 percent for whites).

—Occupied by more people (the median household size was 3.53 for nonwhites versus 2.88 for whites).

—More likely to be overcrowded (27.4 percent of nonwhite units had 1.01 or more persons per room versus 7.9 percent for whites).

*The Department of Housing and Urban Development classifies substandard housing as that housing reported by the U.S. Census Bureau as (1) sound but lacking full plumbing, (2) deteriorating and lacking full plumbing, or (3) dilapidated.

*The National Advisory Commission on Civil Disorders

In Detroit, whites paid a median rental of $77 as compared to $76 among nonwhites. Yet 27.0 percent of nonwhite units were deteriorating or dilapidated, as compared to only 10.3 percent of all white units.

The second type of discriminatory effect—paying more for similar housing—is illustrated by data from a study of housing conditions in disadvantaged neighborhoods in Newark, N.J. In four areas of that city (including the three areas cited previously), nonwhites with housing essentially similar to that of whites paid rents that were from 8.1 percent to 16.8 percent higher. Though the typically larger size of nonwhite households, with consequent harder wear and tear, may partially justify the differences in rental, the study found that nonwhites were paying a definite "color tax" of apparently well over 10 percent on housing. This condition prevails in most racial ghettoes.

The combination of high rents and low incomes forces many blacks to pay an excessively high proportion of their income for housing. The high proportion of income that must go for rent leaves less money in such households for other expenses. Undoubtedly, this hardship is a major reason many black households regard housing as one of their worst problems.

Thousands of landlords in disadvantaged neighborhoods openly violate building codes with impunity, thereby providing a constant demonstration of flagrant discrimination by legal authorities. A high proportion of residential and other structures contain numerous violations of building and housing codes. Refusal to remedy these violations is a criminal offense, one which can have serious effects upon the victims living in these structures. Yet in most cities, few building code violations in these areas are ever corrected even when tenants complain directly to municipal building departments.

There are economic reasons why these codes are not rigorously enforced. Bringing many old structures up to code standards and maintaining them at that level often would require owners to raise rents far above the ability of local residents to pay. In New York City, rigorous code enforcement caused owners to board up and abandon over 2,500 buildings rather than incur the expense of repairing them. Nevertheless, open violation of codes is a constant source of distress to low-income tenants and creates serious hazards to health and safety in disadvantaged neighborhoods.

Housing conditions in the disorder cities surveyed by the Commission paralleled those for ghetto blacks generally.

Many homes were physically inadequate.

Forty-seven percent of the units occupied by nonwhites in the disturbance areas were substandard.

Overcrowding was common. In the metropolitan areas in which disorders occurred, 24 percent of all units occupied by nonwhites were overcrowded, against only 8.8 percent of the white-occupied units.

Blacks paid higher percentages of their income for rent than whites. In both the disturbance areas and the greater metropolitan area of which they were a part, the median rent as a proportion of median income was over 25 percent higher for nonwhites than for whites.

The result has been widespread discontent with housing conditions and costs. In nearly every disorder city surveyed, grievances related to housing were important factors in the structure of the black communities' discontent.

The reason most blacks live in decaying slums is not difficult to discover. First, and foremost, is poverty. Most ghetto residents cannot pay the rent necessary to support decent housing. This prevents private builders from constructing new units in the ghettoes or from rehabilitating old ones, for either action involves an investment that would require substantially higher rents than most ghetto dwellers can pay. It also deters landlords from maintaining units that are presently structurally sound. Maintenance, too, requires additional investment, and at the minimal rents that inner-city blacks can pay, landlords have little incentive to provide it, according to Commission findings.

The implications of widespread poor maintenance are serious. Most of the gains in black housing have occurred through the turnover which occurs as part of the "filtering down" process—as the white middle class moves out, the units it leaves are occupied by blacks. Many of these units are very old. Without proper maintenance, they soon become dilapidated, so that the improvement in housing resulting from the filtering-down process is only temporary. The 1965 New York City survey points up the danger. During the period that the number of substandard units was decreasing, the number of deteriorating units increased by 95,000.

The second major factor condemning vast numbers of black Americans to urban slums is racial discrimination in the housing market. Discrimination prevents access to many nonslum areas, particularly the suburbs, and has a detrimental effect on ghetto housing itself. By restricting the area open to a growing population, housing discrimination makes it profitable for landlords to break up ghetto apartments for denser occupancy, hastening housing deterioration. Further, by creating a "back pressure" in the racial ghettos, discrimination keeps prices and rents of older, more deteriorated housing in the ghetto higher than they would be in a truly free and open market.

To date, Federal building programs have done comparatively little to provide housing for the disadvantaged. In the 31-year history of subsidized federal housing, only about 800,000 units have been constructed, with recent production averaging about 50,000 units a year. By comparison, over a period only 3 years longer, FHA insurance guarantees have made possible the construction of over 10 million middle- and upper-income units.

It is only within the last few years that a range of programs has been created that appears to have the potential for substantially relieving the urban housing problem. Direct federal expenditures for housing and community development have increased from $600 million in fiscal 1964 to nearly $3 billion in fiscal 1969. To produce significant results, however, these programs must be employed on a much larger scale than they have been so far. In some cases the constraints and limitations imposed upon the programs must be reduced. In a few instances supplementary programs should be created. In all cases, incentives must be provided to induce maximum participation by private enterprise in supplying energy, imagination, capital and production capabilities.

Federal housing programs must also be given a new thrust aimed at overcoming the prevailing patterns of racial segregation. If this is not done, those programs will continue to concentrate the most impoverished and dependent segments of the population into the central-city ghettoes where there is already a critical gap between the needs of the population and the public resources to deal with them. This can only continue to compound the conditions of failure and hopelessness which lead to crime, civil disorder and social disorganization.**

Charges by blacks leveled against urban renewal and slum clearance programs have been raised since the late forties when black residents of deteriorated housing located in desirable areas of inner cities charged that "urban renewal was, in fact, black renewal." The facts, as evidenced by the character of the building that has generally replaced the deteriorated housing, lead credence to the charge.

In Chicago vast areas of the new "loop" and lake-shore areas on the south side have been systematically vacated as a result of fires, vandalism, or failure by owners to provide

basic services to tenants. Once vacated, the buildings, often substantially salvageable, are bulldozed and the area "renewed" with high-rent, high-rise dwelling units, appealing to a small fraction of the black community and almost none of the area's previous residents.

The same practice is repeated in city after city, as areas populated by black residents are permitted to deteriorate until elimination and razing is the only solution.

In Hamtramck, Michigan, U.S. District Court Judge Damon J. Keith April 3, 1973, ordered the City of Hamtramck to undertake a program of public housing construction and active fair housing promotion to assure that 4,000 black residents displaced by urban renewal could find new homes within the city. Keith ordered construction of 530 units of mostly low- and moderate-income housing, with some units reserved for the elderly, on acreage from which the former residents had been displaced. Relocated tenants would have first priority. In order to open an additional 530 units, Keith ordered city officials to accompany displaced residents seeking to buy houses and encourage owners to sell, and ordered anyone seeking to sell or lease housing to register the unit with a city agency. It was the first such ruling issued by a federal judge to compensate for past discrimination, and Hamtramck Mayor Raymond Wojtowicz countered that the city would appeal the ruling.

In other municipalities, such as Newark, N.J., black-sponsored building projects have run into organized resistance on the part of the white community. Kawaida Towers, Inc. promoted by Imamu Amiri Baraka, Temple Kawaida, and the Committee for a Unified New Ark, in Newark, has encountered almost insurmountable difficulties in building the projected 210 unit apartment building. The project, financed by a 6.4 million dollar mortgage on a site already cleared in Newark's North Ward, which has a substantial black population, as well as Puerto Rican and Italian, has been opposed by the Italian-American residents of the ward, and the construction unions, which have declared the site "unsafe", because of the white pickets. The white police commissioner resigned Baraka's claims because "he found it impossible to enforce the law against other whites." The new black police chief considers that he is "caught in the middle between two extremes." The entire situation points up the underlying dilemma which faces the black population in the U.S. in every area of life—racism.

**Report of *The National Advisory Commission on Civil Disorders*, March 1, 1968, pp. 257–260.

Percentage of Blacks Living in Substandard
Housing in Four Study Areas

Item	Detroit	Washington, D.C.	Memphis	Watts area of Los Angeles
Total population of study area..............	162,375	97,084	150,827	49,074
Percentage of study area, nonwhite............	67.5%	74.5%	74.0%	87.3%
Percentage of housing units in study area:				
Substandard by HUD definition..............	32.7	23.9	35.0	10.5
Dilapidated, deteriorating or sound but lacking full plumbing................	53.1	37.3	46.5	29.1

Source: U.S. Department of Commerce, Bureau of Census.

Percentage of White and Nonwhite Occupied Housing Units Built Prior to
1939 in Selected Metropolitan Areas

Metropolitan area	White occupied units	Nonwhite occupied units
Cleveland...	33.2	90.6
Dallas...	31.9	52.7
Detroit..	46.2	86.1
Kansas City..	54.4	89.9
Los Angeles-Long Beach................................	36.6	62.4
New Orleans...	52.9	62.2
Philadelphia..	62.0	90.8
Saint Louis...	57.9	84.7
San Francisco-Oakland.................................	51.3	67.6
Washington, D.C.......................................	31.9	64.9

Percentage of White and Nonwhite Occupied Units with 1.01 or More Persons
Per Room in Selected Metropolitan Areas

Metropolitan area	White occupied units	Nonwhite occupied units
Cleveland...	6.9	19.3
Dallas...	9.3	28.8
Detroit..	8.6	17.5
Kansas City..	8.7	18.0
Los Angeles-Long Beach................................	8.0	17.4
New Orleans...	12.0	36.1
Philadelphia..	4.9	16.3
Saint Louis...	11.8	28.0
San Francisco-Oakland.................................	6.0	19.7
Washington, D.C.......................................	6.2	22.6

Source: U.S. Department of Commerce, Bureau of Census.

Percentages of White and Nonwhite Occupied Units with Households Paying
35 Percent or More of Their Income for Rent in Selected Metropolitan Areas

Metropolitan area	White occupied units	Nonwhite occupied units
Cleveland...	8.6	33.8
Dallas...	19.2	33.8
Detroit..	21.2	40.5
Kansas City..	20.2	40.0
Los Angeles-Long Beach................................	23.4	28.4
New Orleans...	16.6	30.5
Philadelphia..	19.3	32.1
St. Louis...	18.5	36.7
San Francisco-Oakland.................................	21.2	25.1
Washington, D.C.......................................	18.5	28.3

Source: U.S. Department of Commerce, Bureau of Census.

Occupied Housing Units—Tenure, and Population Per Occupied Unit, by Race of Household Head and by Residence: 1900 to 1970

In thousands, except percent. Prior to 1960, excludes Alaska and Hawaii. Tenure allocated for housing units which did not report. Minus sign (—) denotes decrease.

YEAR, RACE, AND RESIDENCE	OCCUPIED UNITS[1]					PERCENT INCREASE OVER PRECEDING CENSUS		Population per occupied unit[2]
	Total	Owner occupied		Renter occupied		Total occupied units	Total population	
		Number	Percent	Number	Percent			
TOTAL								
1900	15,964	7,455	46.7	8,509	53.3	25.8	20.7	4.8
1910	20,256	9,301	45.9	10,954	54.1	26.9	21.0	4.5
1920	24,352	11,114	45.6	13,238	54.4	20.2	14.9	4.3
1930	29,905	14,280	47.8	15,624	52.2	22.8	16.1	4.1
1940	34,855	15,196	43.6	19,659	56.4	16.6	7.2	3.8
1950	42,826	23,560	55.0	19,266	45.0	22.9	14.5	3.4
1960	53,024	32,797	61.9	20,227	38.1	23.4	18.5	3.3
1970	63,450	39,885	62.9	23,565	37.1	19.7	13.3	3.1
RACE								
White:								
1900	14,064	7,007	49.8	7,057	50.2	25.0	21.2	4.8
1910	(NA)	(NA)	(NA)	(NA)	(NA)	(NA)	22.3	(NA)
1920	21,826	10,511	48.2	11,315	51.8	(NA)	16.0	4.3
1930	26,983	13,544	50.2	13,439	49.8	23.6	16.3	4.1
1940	31,561	14,418	45.7	17,143	54.3	17.0	7.2	3.7
1950	39,044	22,241	57.0	16,803	43.0	23.7	14.1	3.3
1960	47,880	30,823	64.4	17,057	35.6	22.5	17.5	(NA)
1970	56,529	36,979	65.4	19,551	34.6	18.1	11.9	(NA)
Black and other:								
1900	1,900	448	23.6	1,452	76.4	32.4	17.1	4.8
1910	(NA)	(NA)	(NA)	(NA)	(NA)	(NA)	11.5	(NA)
1920	2,526	603	23.9	1,923	76.1	(NA)	6.3	4.3
1930	2,922	737	25.2	2,185	74.8	15.7	14.7	4.3
1940	3,293	778	23.6	2,516	76.4	12.7	7.7	4.1
1950	3,783	1,319	34.9	2,464	65.1	14.9	17.1	3.9
1960	5,144	1,974	38.4	3,171	61.6	33.0	26.7	(NA)
1970	6,920	2,907	42.0	4,014	58.0	34.5	24.3	(NA)
RESIDENCE								
Nonfarm:								
1900	10,274	3,790	36.9	6,484	63.1	29.7	(NA)	(NA)
1910	14,132	5,454	38.6	8,678	61.4	37.5	(NA)	(NA)
1920	17,600	7,189	40.8	10,411	59.2	24.5	(NA)	4.2
1930	23,300	10,721	46.0	12,579	54.0	32.4	25.0	4.0
1940	27,748	11,413	41.1	16,335	58.9	19.1	9.5	3.7
1950	37,105	19,802	53.4	17,304	46.6	33.7	25.8	3.3
1960[3]	49,458	30,164	61.0	19,249	39.1	33.3	30.0	3.3
1970[3]	60,351	37,393	62.0	22,957	38.0	22.0	16.1	3.1
Farm:[4]								
1900	5,690	3,665	64.4	2,025	35.6	19.4	(NA)	(NA)
1910	6,124	3,847	62.8	2,276	37.2	7.6	(NA)	(NA)
1920	6,751	3,925	58.1	2,827	41.9	10.2	(NA)	4.7
1930	6,605	3,560	53.9	3,045	46.1	—2.2	—4.6	4.6
1940	7,107	3,783	53.2	3,324	46.8	7.6	0.2	4.3
1950	5,721	3,758	65.7	1,963	34.3	—19.5	—23.7	4.0
1960[3]	3,566	2,633	73.8	933	26.2	—37.7	—41.7	3.8
1970[3]	3,095	2,492	80.5	603	19.5	—13.2	—21.2	3.4

NA   Not available.
[1] Statistics on the number of occupied units are essentially comparable although identified by various terms—the term "family" applies to figures for 1930 and earlier; "occupied dwelling unit," 1940 and 1950; and "occupied housing unit," 1960 and 1970. For 1910 and 1920, includes the small number of quasi-families; 1900 and 1930 represent private families only.
[2] From 1950 to 1970, population in occupied housing units was determined by dividing population in housing units by number of occupied housing units.
[3] Not comparable with data for earlier censuses because of a basic change in definition of farm residence. For definitions used in 1960 and 1970, see text, p. 2.
[4] For 1900 to 1920, includes a small proportion of urban-farm families in addition to rural-farm.

Source: U.S. Bureau of the Census, "U.S. Census of Population and Housing: 1960" and "1970."

Occupancy, Plumbing and Financial Characteristics Of Housing Units with Black* Head of Household, for the United States, 1970

	United States
Total Black population	22,580,289
All occupied housing units	6,180,260
POPULATION	
Population in housing units	21,883,659
Per occupied unit	3.5
Owner	3.8
Renter	3.4
TENURE	
Owner occupied	2,567,920
Renter occupied	3,612,340
PLUMBING FACILITIES	
With all plumbing facilities	5,138,921
Lacking some or all plumbing facilities	1,041,339
Lacking only hot water	128,345
Lacking other plumbing facilities	912,994
PIPED WATER IN STRUCTURE	
Hot and cold	5,324,551
Cold only	361,135
None	494,574
FLUSH TOILET	
For exclusive use of household	5,428,754
Also used by another household	96,983
None	654,523
BATHTUB OR SHOWER	
For exclusive use of household	5,292,867
Also used by another household	94,181
None	793,212
COMPLETE KITCHEN FACILITIES	
For exclusive use of household	5,453,476
Also used by another household	33,982
No complete kitchen facilities	692,802
ACCESS	
With direct access	6,168,551
Lacking direct access	11,709

	United States
VALUE	
Specified owner occupied[1]	2,081,301
Less than $5,000	350,106
$5,000 to $7,499	320,383
$7,500 to $9,999	306,856
$10,000 to $12,499	285,427
$12,500 to $14,999	204,360
$15,000 to $17,499	189,052
$17,500 to $19,999	146,379
$20,000 to $24,999	147,772
$25,000 to $34,999	94,582
$35,000 to $49,999	28,161
$50,000 or more	8,223
Median	$10,600
With all plumbing facilities	1,794,617
Less than $5,000	176,078
$5,000 to $9,999	542,903
$10,000 to $14,999	472,462
$15,000 to $19,999	329,593
$20,000 to $24,999	145,447
$25,000 or more	128,134
Median	$11,600
CONTRACT RENT	
Specified renter occupied[2]	3,417,819
Less than $30	328,611
$30 to $39	221,635
$40 to $59	611,803
$60 to $79	801,061
$80 to $99	556,767
$100 to $119	328,324
$120 to $149	283,096
$150 to $199	108,341
$200 to $249	14,540
$250 or more	6,928
No cash rent	156,713
Median	$71
With all plumbing facilities	2,896,927
Less than $40	262,900
$40 to $59	533,856
$60 to $79	757,870
$80 to $99	539,432
$100 to $149	599,541
$150 or more	127,691
No cash rent	75,637
Median	$76

[1] Limited to one family homes on less than 10 acres and no business on property. [2] Excludes one-family homes on 10 acres or more.
* Denoted as Negro in Census.

Source: U.S. Summary, 1970 Census of Housing, General Housing Characteristics, U.S. Department of Commerce, December, 1971.

Utilization Characteristics of Housing Units With Black Head of Household, for the United States: 1970

	United States
All occupied housing units	6,180,260
UNITS IN STRUCTURE	
1	3,652,453
2 or more	2,482,228
Mobile home or trailer	45,579
ROOMS	
Owner occupied	2,567,920
1 room	6,730
2 rooms	27,968
3 rooms	124,256
4 rooms	431,006
5 rooms	744,972
6 rooms	723,229
7 rooms	290,418
8 rooms	135,359
9 rooms or more	83,982
Median	5.4
Renter occupied	3,612,340
1 room	123,816
2 rooms	266,507
3 rooms	873,413
4 rooms	1,146,885
5 rooms	709,266
6 rooms	350,522
7 rooms	90,204
8 rooms	34,377
9 rooms or more	17,350
Median	4.0
PERSONS	
Owner occupied	2,567,920
1 person	329,943
2 persons	617,787
3 persons	430,118
4 persons	366,391
5 persons	274,154
6 persons	197,138
7 persons	145,113
8 persons	115,845
9 persons or more	91,431
Median	3.3

	United States
Renter occupied	3,512,340
1 person	852,743
2 persons	804,751
3 persons	576,884
4 persons	451,902
5 persons	313,618
6 persons	217,472
7 persons	160,745
8 persons	131,877
9 persons or more	102,348
Median	2.8
PERSONS PER ROOM	
Owner occupied	2,567,920
0.50 or less	1,151,712
0.51 to 0.75	495,555
0.76 to 1.00	502,385
1.01 to 1.50	285,074
1.51 or more	133,194
Renter occupied	3,512,340
0.50 or less	1,297,613
0.51 to 0.75	596,928
0.76 to 1.00	804,072
1.01 to 1.50	484,135
1.51 or more	329,592
With all plumbing facilities	5,138,921
Owner occupied	2,182,204
1.00 or less	1,861,835
1.01 to 1.50	232,402
1.51 or more	87,967
Renter occupied	2,956,717
1.00 or less	2,363,705
1.01 to 1.50	393,991
1.51 or more	199,021
TELEPHONE	
Available	4,292,495
None	1,887,765

Source: U.S. Summary, 1970 Census of Housing, General Housing Characteristics, U.S. Department of Commerce, December, 1971.

Occupancy, Plumbing, and Structural Characteristics for the United States, by Inside and Outside Standard Metropolitan Statistical Areas and Urban and Rural: 1970

Inside and Outside Standard Metropolitan Statistical Areas Urban and Rural	United States — Total	United States — Inside SMSA's Total	United States — In central cities	United States — Not in central cities	United States — Outside SMSA's	United States — Urban	United States — Rural	Percent — Total	Percent — Inside SMSA's Total	Percent — In central cities	Percent — Not in central cities	Percent — Outside SMSA's	Percent — Urban	Percent — Rural
Total population	203,211,926	139,418,811	63,796,943	75,621,868	63,793,115	149,324,930	53,886,996	…	…	…	…	…	…	…
All housing units	68,679,030	46,295,423	22,593,884	23,701,539	22,383,607	50,142,601	18,536,429	100.0	100.0	100.0	100.0	100.0	100.0	100.0
Vacant—seasonal and migratory	1,022,464	219,557	24,700	194,857	802,907	151,949	870,515	1.5	0.5	0.1	0.8	3.6	0.3	4.7
All year-round housing units	67,656,566	46,075,866	22,569,184	23,506,682	21,580,700	49,990,652	17,665,914	100.0	100.0	100.0	100.0	100.0	100.0	100.0
POPULATION														
Population in housing units, 1970	197,399,913	135,691,091	61,929,073	73,762,018	61,708,822	144,609,589	52,790,324	…	…	…	…	…	…	…
Per occupied unit	3.1	3.1	2.9	3.3	3.2	3.0	3.3							
Owner	3.3	3.2	3.2	3.5	3.2	3.3	3.3							
Renter	2.8	2.6	2.6	2.8	3.1	2.6	3.4							
Population in housing units, 1960	174,373,302	116,243,448	58,383,878	57,859,791	58,129,854	129,952,660	52,420,642	…	…	…	…	…	…	…
Per occupied unit	3.3	3.2	3.1	3.5	3.4	3.2	3.6							
TENURE, RACE, AND VACANCY STATUS														
All occupied units	63,449,747	43,862,993	21,382,260	22,480,733	19,586,754	47,562,681	15,887,066	93.8	95.2	94.7	95.6	90.8	95.1	89.9
Owner occupied	39,885,015	26,089,015	10,290,044	15,798,971	13,796,165	27,778,090	12,107,090	59.0	56.6	45.6	67.2	63.9	55.6	68.5
Percent of all occupied	62.9	59.5	48.1	70.3	70.4	58.4	76.2							
Cooperative or condominium	370,493	348,156	213,166	134,990	22,337	353,388	17,105	0.5	0.8	0.9	0.6	0.1	0.7	0.1
White	36,978,651	24,023,340	8,831,017	15,192,323	12,955,311	25,505,971	11,472,680	54.7	52.1	39.1	64.6	60.0	51.0	64.9
Black	2,567,920	1,825,915	1,335,965	489,950	742,005	2,023,119	544,801	3.8	4.0	5.9	2.1	3.4	4.0	3.1
Renter occupied	23,564,567	17,773,978	11,092,216	6,681,762	5,790,589	19,784,591	3,779,976	34.8	38.6	49.1	28.4	26.8	39.6	21.4
White	19,550,723	14,534,704	8,356,795	6,177,909	5,016,019	16,249,377	3,301,346	28.9	31.5	37.0	26.3	23.2	32.5	18.7
Black	3,612,340	2,918,906	2,501,875	417,031	693,434	3,193,807	418,533	5.3	6.3	11.1	1.8	3.2	6.4	2.4
Vacant year-round units	4,206,819	2,212,873	1,186,924	1,025,949	1,993,946	2,427,971	1,778,848	6.2	4.8	5.3	4.4	9.2	4.9	10.1
For sale only	477,371	287,042	124,914	162,128	190,329	325,592	151,779	0.7	0.6	0.6	0.7	0.9	0.7	0.9
Homeowner vacancy rate	1.2	1.1	1.2	1.0	1.4	1.2	1.2							
For rent	1,655,390	1,134,628	741,340	393,288	520,762	1,327,178	328,212	2.4	2.5	3.3	1.7	2.4	2.7	1.9
Rental vacancy rate	6.6	6.0	6.3	5.6	8.3	6.3	8.0							
With all plumbing facilities	1,419,856	1,039,691	676,543	363,148	380,165	1,208,576	211,280	2.1	2.3	3.0	1.5	1.8	2.4	1.2
Rented or sold, awaiting occupancy	334,295	191,114	88,060	103,054	143,181	209,647	124,648	0.5	0.4	0.4	0.7	0.7	0.4	0.7
Held for occasional use	760,237	251,129	59,707	191,422	509,108	194,708	565,529	1.1	0.5	0.3	0.8	2.4	0.4	3.2
Other vacant	979,526	348,960	172,903	176,057	630,566	370,846	608,680	1.4	0.8	0.8	0.7	2.9	0.7	3.4
All year-round housing units	67,656,566	46,075,866	22,569,184	23,506,682	21,580,700	49,990,652	17,665,914	100.0	100.0	100.0	100.0	100.0	100.0	100.0
PLUMBING FACILITIES														
With all plumbing facilities	62,984,221	44,456,498	21,782,889	22,673,609	18,527,723	48,300,769	14,683,452	93.1	96.5	96.5	96.5	85.9	96.6	83.1
Lacking some or all plumbing facilities	4,672,345	1,619,368	786,295	833,073	3,052,977	1,689,883	2,982,462	6.9	3.5	3.5	3.5	14.1	3.4	16.9
Lacking only hot water	557,571	251,228	116,611	134,617	306,343	295,693	261,878	0.8	0.5	0.5	0.6	1.4	0.6	1.5
Lacking other plumbing facilities	4,114,774	1,368,140	669,684	698,456	2,746,634	1,394,190	2,720,584	6.1	3.0	3.0	3.0	12.7	2.8	15.4

PIPED WATER IN STRUCTURE

Hot and cold	64,436,305	45,307,637	22,348,324	22,959,313	19,128,668	49,250,668	15,185,637	95.2	98.3	99.0	97.7	88.6	98.5	86.0
Cold only	1,550,954	507,043	195,805	311,238	1,043,911	601,117	949,837	2.3	1.1	0.9	1.3	4.8	1.2	5.4
None	1,669,307	261,186	25,055	236,131	1,408,121	138,867	1,530,440	2.5	0.6	0.1	1.0	6.5	0.3	8.7

FLUSH TOILET

For exclusive use of household	64,304,275	45,063,038	22,086,809	22,976,229	19,241,237	49,075,969	15,228,306	95.0	97.8	97.9	97.7	89.2	98.2	86.2
Also used by another household	650,039	506,781	410,467	96,314	143,258	608,118	41,921	1.0	1.1	1.8	0.4	0.7	1.2	0.2
None	2,702,252	506,047	71,908	434,139	2,196,205	306,565	2,395,687	4.0	1.1	0.3	1.8	10.2	0.6	13.6

BATHTUB OR SHOWER

For exclusive use of household	63,741,678	44,788,797	21,933,974	22,854,823	18,952,881	48,663,633	15,078,045	94.2	97.2	97.2	97.2	87.8	97.3	85.4
Also used by another household	659,789	513,124	415,124	98,004	146,661	615,456	44,333	1.0	1.1	1.8	0.4	0.7	1.2	0.3
None	3,255,099	773,941	220,086	553,855	2,481,158	711,563	2,543,536	4.8	1.7	1.0	2.4	11.5	1.4	14.4

COMPLETE KITCHEN FACILITIES

All year-round units	67,656,566	46,075,866	22,569,184	23,506,682	21,580,700	49,990,652	17,665,914	100.0	100.0	100.0	100.0	100.0	100.0	100.0
For exclusive use of household	64,520,975	44,990,361	21,984,155	23,006,206	19,530,614	48,856,228	15,664,747	95.4	97.6	97.4	97.9	90.5	97.7	88.7
Also used by another household	130,021	107,575	85,611	21,964	22,446	121,309	8,712	0.2	0.2	0.4	0.1	0.1	0.2	
No complete kitchen facilities	3,005,570	977,930	499,418	478,512	2,027,640	1,013,115	1,992,455	4.4	2.1	2.2	2.0	9.4	2.0	11.3
Renter occupied	23,564,567	17,773,978	11,092,216	6,681,762	5,790,589	19,784,591	3,779,976	100.0	100.0	100.0	100.0	100.0	100.0	100.0
For exclusive use of household	22,253,099	17,166,617	10,694,281	6,472,336	5,086,482	19,105,086	3,148,013	94.4	96.6	96.4	96.9	87.8	96.6	83.3
Also used by another household	98,516	83,108	67,476	15,632	15,408	93,553	4,963	0.4	0.5	0.6	0.2	0.3	0.5	0.1
No complete kitchen facilities	1,212,952	524,253	330,459	193,794	688,699	585,952	627,000	5.1	2.9	3.0	2.9	11.9	3.0	16.6

ACCESS

With direct access	67,593,964	46,025,099	22,533,315	23,491,784	21,568,865	49,933,944	17,660,020	99.9	99.9	99.8	99.9	99.9	99.9	100.0
Lacking direct access	62,602	50,767	35,869	14,898	11,835	56,708	5,894	0.1	0.1	0.2	0.1	0.1	0.1	...

UNITS IN STRUCTURE

All year-round units	67,656,566	46,075,866	22,569,184	23,506,682	21,580,700	49,990,652	17,665,914	100.0	100.0	100.0	100.0	100.0	100.0	100.0
1	46,941,653	29,120,633	11,460,545	17,660,088	17,821,020	31,434,639	15,507,014	69.4	63.2	50.8	75.1	82.6	62.9	87.8
2 or more	18,864,501	16,107,920	10,935,143	5,172,777	2,756,581	17,800,373	1,064,128	27.9	35.0	48.5	22.0	12.8	35.6	6.0
Mobile home or trailer	1,850,412	847,313	173,496	673,817	1,003,099	755,640	1,094,772	2.7	1.8	0.8	2.9	4.6	1.5	6.2
Owner occupied	39,885,180	26,089,015	10,290,044	15,798,971	13,796,165	27,778,090	12,107,090	100.0	100.0	100.0	100.0	100.0	100.0	100.0
1	35,659,159	23,204,679	8,744,851	14,459,828	12,454,480	24,777,336	10,881,823	89.4	88.9	85.0	91.5	90.3	89.2	89.9
2 or more	2,681,148	2,178,443	1,412,893	765,550	502,705	2,385,702	295,446	6.7	8.4	13.7	4.8	3.6	8.6	2.4
Mobile home or trailer	1,544,873	705,893	132,300	573,593	838,980	615,052	929,821	3.9	2.7	1.3	3.6	6.1	2.2	7.7
Renter occupied	23,564,567	17,773,978	11,092,216	6,681,762	5,790,589	19,784,591	3,779,976	100.0	100.0	100.0	100.0	100.0	100.0	100.0
1	8,566,120	4,887,391	2,333,183	2,554,208	3,678,729	5,585,194	2,980,926	36.4	27.5	21.0	38.2	63.5	28.2	78.9
2 or more	14,692,908	12,745,167	8,717,837	4,027,330	1,947,741	14,058,809	634,099	62.4	71.7	78.6	60.3	33.6	71.1	16.8
Mobile home or trailer	305,539	141,420	41,196	100,224	164,119	140,588	164,951	1.3	0.8	0.4	1.5	2.8	0.7	4.4

TELEPHONE

All occupied units	63,449,747	43,862,993	21,382,260	22,480,733	19,586,754	47,562,681	15,887,066	100.0	100.0	100.0	100.0	100.0	100.0	100.0
Available	55,176,700	39,073,638	18,419,461	20,654,177	16,103,062	42,210,791	12,965,909	87.0	89.1	86.1	91.9	82.2	88.7	81.6
None	8,273,047	4,789,355	2,962,799	1,826,556	3,483,692	5,351,890	2,921,157	13.0	10.9	13.9	8.1	17.8	11.3	18.4

Source: U.S. Summary, 1970 Census of Housing, General Housing Characteristics, U.S. Department of Commerce, December, 1971.

Section XII

RELIGION

RELIGION

More than any other institution in black life, the church has been the most viable throughout the centuries since the black man was brought as chattel to the shores of the Americas. It has provided an outlet for the multiple pressures which have been placed on blacks in this nation, and it has influenced the growth and development of black business and economic development since its inception. The black church was in the forefront of the black revolution, and it was in a church that the Montgomery Bus Boycott evolved and the Rev. Martin Luther King was sent upon his historic mission. More than any other institution, the church has been responsive to the changing needs of its constituents, and in the present decade, the black church has seen its role as helping to provide for the needs of the present, while preparing for the hereafter through the process of prayer and self-help.

While the great majority of black Americans still worship in all-black congregations, a substantial number of blacks are members of the large national church organizations. In these organizations, over the past decade, black groups have developed within the white body seeking to focus on the aspect of church responsibility to the black constituency and for the black condition.

Economic development and jobs are seen as primary needs in the black community, and to this end, black ministers have organized programs outside the church walls to answer these crucial demands for food and jobs and housing. Notable among these programs are those of Reverend Leon H. Sullivan of Philadelphia, founder of Opportunities Industrialization Centers of America (OIC, 1964), and Dr. Martin Luther King, who established an economic arm of the Southern Christian Leadership Conference in 1966. Under the direction of Reverend Jesse L. Jackson, the organization known as Operation Breadbasket, became the most viable aspect of the SCLC program in Chicago and following Dr. King's assassination and a subsequent disagreement between Jackson and the SCLC Board of Directors, Reverend Jackson resigned and organized People United to Save Humanity (PUSH). The primary purpose of Operation PUSH, as was Breadbasket's, is to get jobs, retain capital in the black communities, and educate black consumers to get their money's worth. The primary purpose of OIC is to provide entry level job training, ranging across the employment spectrum, for black youth and those rendered jobless by increased industrial mechanization. Prior to the 1973 cutbacks in federal job training contracts, near-

ly 100,000 persons have completed training at OIC job centers and have entered the labor market in more than 100 cities. The primary funding for these training programs has come from the federal government under U.S. Labor Department and other federal agencies manpower training grants. The smaller share of funding has come from private and local government sources. These programs and training centers are threatened with closing and being forced out of business as a result of Nixon administration vetoes on manpower training and Office of Economic Opportunity programs.

The approach of Operation PUSH is through direct negotiations with major American corporations for a proportionate share of jobs, profits, investment capital and other tools for black economic development: advertising in black media; hiring black workers, all along the employment lines; hiring black contractors and sub-contractors for building projects, both in and out of the black community; giving a proportionate share of employee insurance premiums to black-owned companies; and placing a proportionate share of corporate funds in black-owned banks. Under two agreements negotiated by the Jackson forces in 1972, an estimated $100,000,000 in new money would come into the black community in the form of jobs and business.

Increasing numbers of black religious leaders, regardless of denominational affiliation, are entering into non-religious coalitions to bring about change for their worshippers, in terms of living conditions, job and educational opportunities, by working with community, civic and political groups, to bring about the desired ends.

A new sense of aggressive militancy was evidenced during the late 60s and saw its culmination in the attacks upon racism within the church by members of the ministry itself. In Chicago, in 1969, Roman Catholic Archbishop John Cody was denounced by the Rev. Rollins Lambert, a black priest, who saw his appointment to the pastorate of St. Dorothy's Church, with an all-black congregation, as a "political move." St. Dorothy's had been pastored by a white minister, and upon his "retirement" it was anticipated that the church would be assigned to the popular black assistant pastor, the Reverend George H. Clements. Rev. Clements, who enjoyed a wide following among Catholic and non-Catholic militants, intellectuals and youth, was transferred from the parish, and the ostensibly "moderate" Rev. Lambert named to the pastorate. Following community pressure and great publicity, Reverend Clements was assigned as pastor of Holy Angels, a ghetto Catholic church, whose once-prosperous white congregation had abandoned it with the influx of black communicants and students into the once fashionable neighborhood.

Black clergymen also made known their dissatisfaction with the response of their denominations to the problems of the poor and uneducated. In July, 1969, Rev. Albert Cleague of Detroit, whose Black Messiah movement has been one of the most militantly nationalistic, challenged the United Church of Christ Biennial General Synod meeting in Boston.

A special committee had submitted a proposal to authorize the raising of $10 million to aid in work with ghetto residents and to set up an all-black advisory group of ministers and laymen to participate in the decision-making use of the funds. In responding to this proposal, Rev. Cleague and three other black ministers, identified it as "tokenism," and reiterated that their minimal demand was a financially-supported "power base" in the church. Said Cleague: "If you don't want us to separate, you will have to rearrange the institutional pattern."

Earlier, James Forman, former head of the Student Non-Violent Committee (SNCC) had interrupted services at New York's fashionable Riverside Church to read a manifesto which demanded "$500 million in reparations owed black people by White America." Forman, as director of the National Black Economic Development Conference, demanded that churches and synagogues throughout the United States pay this sum to NBEDC as reparations. The manifesto called religious institutions "another form of government in this country," and held that "the exploitation of colored people around the world is aided and abetted by the white churches and synagogues." While many white and black churchmen and women agreed that the denominational white church was racist and that the amount of $500 million was not unreasonable, they disagreed with the method and the tone of the demands. The five points in the manifesto were that the church: (1) give 60% of its annual income from securities and real estate to the NBEDC by January 3 of each year; (2) give a proportion of its income from retirement, pension and investment funds to NBEDC; (3) must give NBEDC free office space and phone use; (4) give unrestricted use of its radio station (WRVR) for 12 hours a day and on weekends with the director and staff to be selected by the NBEDC; and (5) must give free use of its classrooms for Harlem residents. The demands were repeated in the national

headquarters of the Lutheran Church, the Roman Catholic Archdiocese, Episcopal Church, Baptists, Presbyterians, and Jewish groups. On May 5, 1969, the Rev. Jon L. Regier of the National Council of Churches said, "If we agree there is guilt on the part of whites, then we must agree that efforts at restitution are valid. The only question is how to do it."

Subsequently, the American Jewish Committee withdrew from the Interreligious Foundation for Community Organization, sponsors of the National Black Economic Development Conference, on the basis that the Foundation was unable to "take a clear-cut position on the revolutionary ideology and racist rhetoric" of the Black Manifesto.

Criticism of the black economic demands did not come alone from whites. Rev. Joseph H. Jackson, president of the all-black 6.3 million member National Baptist Convention U. S. A., Inc. "said that his church would 'not spend a dime' for reparations and accused the National Council of Churches of invading the spheres of economics and politics, when they voted to raise funds for a black-led development corporation that would dispense loans and grants to 'disadvantaged groups'."

Other events of religious interest were:

1969

MARCH

13   The Rev. Charles A. Spivey (of the Christian Methodist Episcopal Church) and George Mason Miller (of the African Methodist Episcopal Zion Church), were elected vice chairman and secretary, respectively, of the Disciples of Christ General Assembly.

MAY

17   Rev. Thomas Kilgore, Jr., Los Angeles minister civic leader, was unanimously elected first black president of the predominantly white American Baptist Convention at the annual convention in Boston.

AUGUST

8   The 80,000 member National Christian Missionary Convention, the black branch of the Christian Church (Disciples of Christ), voted to dissolve itself and join the church's predominantly white General Assembly. The vote culminated a 10-year merger process, which was approved by the church.

DECEMBER

15   The First Presidency (the president and his immediate advisers) of the 2.8 million-member Church of Jesus Christ of Latter-day Saints (Mormon) reaffirmed

church policy barring black members (about 200) from the priesthood. The policy statement was prompted by events which had caused the cancellation of athletic competition with the church-financed Brigham Young University in November because of alleged Mormon discrimination against blacks.

1970

JANUARY

17 Right Rev. John M. Burgess was installed as the 12th bishop of the Massachusetts Episcopal Diocese and the first black man to head an Episcopal diocese in the U.S. The installation service was in St. Paul's Cathedral, Boston. Bishop Burgess succeeded the Right Rev. Anson Phelps Stokes in the position.

APRIL

22 The general conference of the 11 million-member, United Methodist Church was held in St. Louis April 20–24. The church's 100 bishops opened the convention with a "state of the church" message which covered a wide range of social issues. The message, which cited racism, pollution and intergroup tensions, also issued a scathing denunciation of the war in Vietnam as a "fiasco impossible to justify" and called for the immediate step-up of troop withdrawals and accelerated peace talks in Paris.

The 1,000 delegates of the United Methodist Church meeting in St. Louis received a report which described those being served by the church's health and welfare agencies as more than 90% white and mostly middle class.

Among the findings, compiled by the church's Commission on Religion and Race and its General Board of Health and Welfare Ministries: (1) the resident population in 113 homes for the aged was 98.4% white; (2) agencies for children and youth were 94% white; (3) membership on the church's hospital boards was 99% white (15 blacks among 1,463 board members); 1.7% of the hospital's registered nurses were black; 5% of the professional staffs of the boards and agencies were black. The report concluded: "The major fact is that United Methodism has a history of discrimination against minority persons, and health and welfare agencies have not changed appreciably in practice, whatever their policies. The fact is that the agencies by and large, are reflecting the racism which is a part of United

Methodism." The United Methodist Church has 11 million members.

24 A caucus of black laymen, the Black Methodists for Church Renewal, presented requests for a total of $21 million to help fund secular and church-sponsored projects, economic development in poverty areas and 12 black Methodist colleges. Not less than $10 million a year was sought for higher education and not less than $5.5 million annually for "self-determination" projects. In response to the requests, the conference voted to cut regularly budgeted items to make $4 million available in 1971–72 for aid to minorities. Another $4 million was to be raised to help strengthen the 12 black colleges supported by the church.

JUNE

19 The two million-member Seventh-day Adventist Church held its 51st World Conference in Atlantic City, N.J. and adopted a basic policy statement which declared that racial discrimination was sinful and contrary to the mandates of God as revealed in the Bible. A "Declaration on Human Relations" urged Adventists to promote understanding "that differences among races serve to enhance unique cultural contributions and are in no way construed as indicators of inherent superiority or inferiority." Twenty percent of the membership is black.

Dr. Robert H. Pierson, world conference president, said his church would allocate an additional $300,000 in 1970 to aid inner-city areas. In the preceding four years, the church had spent $59 million on welfare and charity projects.

JULY

2 Delegates to the ninth general assembly of the Unitarian Universalist Association (UUA) held in Seattle voted against renewing funds to its Black Affairs Council (BAC). A resolution adopted at the week-long convention said, "The highest priority is the financial integrity of the association."

By a narrow margin of 426–399 the vote reflected a division of opinion by the general assembly for the decision of its board of trustees in the fall of 1969 to trim annual payments to the council from $250,000 to $200,000. At the time of its creation in 1968, the black group had received from the church a pledge of $1 million to span a four-year period in annual installments. Following the altered commitment from the trustees, the BAC had disaffiliated from the association in February. The action thus terminated the groups eligibility for money from the UUA's general fund.

The BAC announced establishment of a $550,000 fund to be called the May 26 Fund—the name corresponding with the 1968 date of the UUA's earlier pledge. Money for the fund would be solicited directly from individual congregations and would finance programs, including investment in black-owned businesses.

SEPTEMBER

10   The Rev. Dr. Joseph H. Jackson was re-elected president of the National Baptist Convention, U.S.A. Inc. at the body's annual meeting in New Orleans. Addressing the 15,000 delegates of the nation's largest black organization (6 million members), Rev. Jackson called for separatism on the basis of character, not color, and urged members to "work with white Americans who have given us black mayors and a black senator."

OCTOBER

11   The 3.5 million-member Protestant Episcopal Church, in Houston, met for its 63rd triennial general convention. President Bishop John E. Hines acknowledged the deep divisions within the church on the funding of minority group activities. Several parishes had refused to pay their annual quota to the national church for fear the funds would be channeled to militant black groups. Bishop Hines commented that the church's deepest problem did not concern questions of authority or administration, but the church's catapult into an era of radical change without a solution to "such great questions as the meaning of mission in Christ's name, or the nature of the church through which, in part, that mission is to be discharged, or the costs we are willing to pay in response to God's call."

15   The 700-member Episcopal House of Deputies voted to continue and expand the church's controversial special program to help minority groups and the poor finance their own self-determined programs. The 150 bishops, making up the House of Bishops, gave their concurring approval Oct. 16 to extension of the program for three years. The approval of the two houses signified that compromise revisions inserted in the program had met objections that certain recipients of the program's funds had

practiced or advocated violence in violation of the program's criteria established in 1967. According to one revision, no grant would be made to any organization if "any officer or agent" of the body had been "finally convicted of a crime" involving physical violence in carrying out the organization's program.

1971

MAY

26   The general assemblies of the United Presbyterian Church and the Presbyterian Church in the U.S. (Southern) agreed separately to study a proposed plan of union that would reunite the two churches after their division from the Civil War period.

26   The United Presbyterians at their Rochester, N.Y. meeting defeated an attempt by a black caucus to shelve the draft plan until 1975 so that four largely black denominations—the African Methodist Episcopal Church, the African Methodist Episcopal Zion Church, the Christian Methodist Episcopal Church and the Second Cumberland—could be included in the plan. A timetable for receiving recommendations and revisions from both bodies was set for January 15, 1973.

JUNE

29   The biennial general synod of the 2 million-member United Church of Christ was held in Grand Rapids, Mich. Among the major actions of the synod was authorization for $500,000 to be spent each year over the next biennium for the "empowerment" of black congregations in the denomination.

OCTOBER

8   Six black U.S. Roman Catholics met in Rome with Archbishop Giovanni Benelli, the Vatican's deputy secretary of state, to seek a black successor to Washington's Archbishop Patrick Cardinal O'Boyle. The group also presented requests for a separate black Catholic rite in the U.S. and black American representation in the Vatican's administrative branches.

Joseph Dulin, the group's spokesman and president of the National Black Catholic Lay Caucus, accused the U.S. hierarchy of "lying" to the Vatican about the well-being of black Catholics, whom he said were "leaving the church in droves." The delegation included Charles Hammock and Joseph Davis, chairman and executive, respectively, of the board of the National Office of Black Catholics;

Sister Martin de Porres Grey, chairman of the National Conference of Black Sisters; Estelle Collins of the Baltimore Black Caucus; and the Rev. Lawrence E. Lucas, president of the National Black Catholic Clergy Caucus.

NOVEMBER

18 The U.S. National Conference of Catholic Bishops adopted a proposed $9.8 million budget for 1972 that omitted funding for the National Office of Black Catholics.

1972

JANUARY

27 The white and black Methodist conferences in South Carolina, segregated since the Civil War period, voted separately in Columbia to accept a plan of union. The white conference voted 573–247 in favor of the merger and the black conference voted 135–44 in favor.

Under the plan, the present church structure of 11 geographical districts of the white conference and the four districts of the black conference would be reorganized into 12 districts with nine white and three black district superintendents.

A major change from a plan rejected in 1971 by the white conference was the removal of racial quotas for chairmen of committees, boards and commissions.

MAY

31 Union Theological Seminary's board voted to require that all students, faculty, staff and directors be one-third black and representatives of other minority groups and that one-half be women.

AUGUST

16 The Rev. Philip A. Potter, a Methodist from the West Indian island of Dominica, was named general secretary of the organization succeeding Rev. Eugene Carson Blake, a Presbyterian.

Potter, 50, had been director of the council's Commission on World Mission and Evangelism and had been chairman of the council's Section for Faith and Testimony.

The central committee's unanimous choice of Potter, a black, was viewed as a council commitment to the underdeveloped countries of the world.

22 The World Council of Churches' policy-making committee voted to liquidate its $3.5 million holdings in all corporations doing business with Rhodesia, Angola, Mozambique, South Africa and Portuguese Guinea, the white-ruled countries of Africa.

The decision taken by the council's central committee, which met in Utrecht, the Netherlands, would affect 22 U.S. corporations.

The action was followed by an announcement that no council funds would be deposited in banks that "maintain direct banking operations" in the proscribed African countries.

The council, representing 261 member churches, took the action despite the opposition of the central committee's finance unit, which questioned the effectiveness of the strategy. The finance committee suggested instead that the council take action as stockholders to bring pressure on corporations.

The Rev. Dr. Eugene Carson Blake, retiring as general secretary of the council after six years, backed the stock liquidation measure.

NOVEMBER

27 The United Methodist Church's all white North Mississippi Conference overwhelmingly approved a merger with the all black Upper Mississippi Conference, which had earlier supported the move, thus removing the last barrier to a plan ordered by the church general conference to end segregation.

DECEMBER

7 The Rev. W. Sterling Cary of New York City was unanimously elected president of the National Council of Churches (NCC) Dec. 7 at the group's triennial convention.

Cary, 45, the first black to hold that office, was an administrator of the United Church of Christ. At the 1969 council conference, Cary had supported demands for reparations voiced by black militant James Forman.

Previously, the General Assembly voted to abolish itself in approving a reorganization of the NCC. A 350-member central board, selected on a quota basis, was delegated responsibility for budgetary and program matters under the new plan.

1973

JANUARY

28 The Most Rev. Joseph Lawson Howze, 49, became auxiliary bishop of Mississippi in ceremonies in Jackson. Howze is the third black bishop in the contemporary Catholic church.

MAJOR BLACK DENOMINATIONS

There are 27 predominantly black religious congregations in the United States. The number of churches for the various denominations varies from 6 (The United Wesleyan Methodist Church of America) to 26,000 (National Baptist Convention, U.S.A., Inc.). Inclusive membership of the largest, National Baptist Convention, U.S.A., Inc., is 5,500,000, the fifth largest religious congregation in the United States.

Ten largest black denominations:

RELIGIOUS BODY	YEAR REPORTED	NO. OF CHURCHES	INCLUSIVE MEMBERSHIP	NO. OF PASTORS
National Baptist Convention, U.S.A., Inc.	1958	26,000	5,500,000	26,000
National Baptist Convention of America	1956	11,398	2,668,799	7,598
National Primitive Baptist Convention, Inc.	1971	2,198	1,645,000	601
African Methodist Episcopal Church	1951	5,878	1,166,301	5,878
African Methodist Zion Episcopal Church	1970	4,500	940,000	5,000
Progressive National Baptist Convention, Inc.	1967	655	521,692	863 (Clergy)
Church of God in Christ, International	1971	1,041	501,000	1,502 (Clergy)
Christian Methodist Episcopal Church	1965	2,598	466,718	2,214
The Church of God in Christ	1965	4,500	425,000	4,000
United Free Will Baptist Church	1952	836	100,000	915

THE NATION OF ISLAM

The Nation of Islam is a multi-million dollar religion with businesses established all over the country, a weekly newspaper (*Muhammad Speaks*) with an estimated circulation of over 500,000, some 50 mosques in cities across the nation (as well as rental halls in some smaller areas with sizeable black populations), and a growing number of Universities of Islam, their elementary-secondary schools, usually accredited.

Membership estimates between 100,000 and 150,000.

Founded in 1930: W.D. Fard.

Head: The Honorable Elijah Muhammad (Elijah Poole).

Precursors: Moorish Science Temple: founded 1913, Timothy Drew Ali.

Universal Negro Improvement Association: founded 1920, Marcus Garvey.

OFFICERS OF THE 10 LARGEST BLACK DENOMINATIONS

National Baptist Convention, U.S.A., Inc.
Pres., Rev. J. H. Jackson, 405 E. 31st St., Chicago, IL 60616
Vice-Pres.-at-large, Rev. E. D. Billoups, 904 N. 33rd St., Baton Rouge, LA 70802

National Baptist Convention of America
Pres., Dr. James C. Sams, 1724 Jefferson St., Jacksonville, FL 32209
Corr. Sec., Rev. Billy H. Wilson 2620 S. Marsallis Ave., Dallas TX 75216

National Primitive Baptist Convention, Inc.
Pres., Rev. Percy D. Brantley, 1795 N.W. 58th St., Miami, FL 33142
Rec. Sec., Rev. F. L. Livingston, 1334 Carson, Dallas, TX 75216

African Methodist Episcopal Church
Senior Bishop, Decatur Ward Nichols, 2522 Barhamvilly Rd., Columbia, SC 29204
New York Office: 2295 Seventh Ave., New York, NY 10030
Pres. of Bishops' Council, H. I. Bearden

African Methodist Episcopal Zion Church
Pres., Board of Bishops, Bishop William M. Smith, 3753 Spring Hill Ave., Mobile, AL 36608
Sec., Board of Bishops, Bishop Charles H. Foggie, 1200 Windermere Dr., Pittsburgh, PA 15218

Progressive National Baptist Convention, Inc.
Pres., Dr. L. Venchael Booth, 630 Glenwood Ave., Cincinnati, OH 45229
1st Vice-Pres., Rev. Nelson H. Smith, 903 6th Ave., S., Birmingham, AL 35233

The Church of God in Christ, International
Bishop Illie L. Jefferson, Senior Bishop, 15 Colonial Dr., Windson, CT 06095
Bishop Singleton R. Chambers, Asst. Senior Bishop, 1331 Quintero Blvd., Kansas City, KS 66104

Christian Methodist Episcopal Church
Sec., Rev. N. Charles Thomas, 664 Vance Ave., Memphis, TN 38126

The Church of God in Christ
Presiding Bishop, Bishop J. O. Patterson, 1774 So. Parkway, E., Memphis, TN 38114
1st Asst. Presiding Bishop, Bishop H. S. Bailey, 3230 Cambridge Rd., Detroit, MI 48221

The United Free Will Baptist Church
Vice-Mod., Rev. O. L. Williams, 1052 N. Missouri Ave., Lakeland, FL 33801
Chmn., Exec. Board, Rev. W. F. Cox, 1106 Holt St., Durham, NC 27701

*Source: Yearbook of American and Canadian Churches 1973, Constant H. Jacquet, Editor

A.M.E. BISHOPS

First District:
E. L. Hickman
336 Pelham Rd., Philadelphia, PA 19119

Second District:
Henry W. Murph
1239 Vermont Ave., Washington, DC 20005

Third District:
H. I. Bearden
11009 Wade Park Ave., Cleveland, OH 44106

Fourth District:
H. Thomas Primm
2820 Monaco Parkway, Denver, CO 80207

Fifth District:
Harrison J. Bryant
2804 Sewell St., Kansas City, KS 66104

Sixth District:
R. A. Hildebrand
171 Ashby St., S.W., Atlanta, GA 30314

A.M.E. ZION BISHOPS

First Episcopal Area:
Bishop Herbert Bell Shaw
520 Red Cross St., Wilmington, NC 28401

Second Episcopal Area:
Bishop William Milton Smith
3753 Springhill Ave., Mobile, AL 36608

Third Episcopal Area:
Bishop William Alexander Hilliard
690 Chicago Blvd., Detroit, MI 48202

Fourth Episcopal Area:
Bishop Alfred Gilbert Dunston, Jr.
P.O. Box 19788, Philadelphia, PA 19143

Fifth Episcopal Area:
Bishop Charles Herbert Foggie
1200 Windermere Dr., Pittsburgh, PA 15218

Sixth Episcopal Area:
Bishop James Clinton Hoggard
6401 Sunset La., Indianapolis, IN 46208

Seventh District:
D. Ward Nichols
2295 7th Ave., New York, NY 10030

Eighth District:
I. H. Bonner
1937 Peniston St., New Orleans, LA 70115

Ninth District:
V. R. Anderson
870 W. 6th St., Birmingham, AL 35204

Tenth District:
J. H. Adams
225 Garrison St., Waco, TX 76704

Eleventh District:
H. N. Robinson
1658 Kings Rd., Jacksonville, FL 32209

Twelfth District:
S. S. Morris, Jr.
2118 Cross St., Little Rock, AR 72206

Thirteenth District:
W. R. Wilkes
1002 Kirkwood Ave., Nashville, TN 37203

Special Assignment:
Frederick D. Jordan
Urban and Ecumenical Affairs,
5151 Franklin Ave., Hollywood, CA 90027

Location (Sick Leave):
G. Wayman Blakely
314 E. Montana St., Philadelphia, PA 19119

Retired:
Joseph Gomez
11116 Wade Park Ave., Cleveland, OH 44106
O. L. Sherman
2525 Chester, Little Rock, AR 72206

Seventh Episcopal Area:
Bishop James W. Wactor
709 Edgehill Rd., Fayetteville, NC 28302

Eighth Episcopal Area:
Bishop Clinton R. Coleman
3513 Ellamont Rd., Baltimore, MD 21215

Ninth Episcopal Area:
Bishop Arthur Marshall, Jr.
P.O. Box 41138, Ben Hill Sta., Atlanta, GA 30331

Tenth Episcopal Area:
Bishop John H. Miller
4588 W. Klest Blvd., Apt. 1100, Dallas, TX 75211

Eleventh Episcopal Area:
Bishop George J. Leake.
508 Grandin Rd., Charlotte, NC 28208

Twelfth Episcopal Area:
Bishop Ruben L. Speaks
305 Brookside Ave., Roosevelt, NY 11575

Retired:
Bishop William Jacob Walls
38 Aqueduct Pl., Yonkers, NY 10701
Bishop Stephen Gill Spottswood
1931 16th St., N.W., Washington, DC 20009
Bishop William Andrew Stewart
2314 20th St., N.W., Washington, DC 20009
Bishop Charles Ewbank Tucker
1715 Ormsby Ave., Louisville, KY 40210
Bishop Joseph Dixon Cauthen
2843 Princess Ann Rd., Norfolk, VA 23504
Bishop Felix Sylvester Anderson
741 S. 44th St., Louisville, KY 40211

PROTESTANT EPISCOPAL BISHOPS

DIOCESAN

John M. Burgess—Massachusetts

SUFFRAGAN

Richard Martin—New York
Quintin E. Primo, Jr. Chicago
John T. Walker—Washington, D.C.

ROMAN CATHOLIC BISHOPS

Joseph L. Howze—Mississippi
Harold Perry—Louisiana

Section XIII

THE PROFESSIONS

BLACK PROFESSIONALS

According to the 1970 Census of Population, the proportion of black and other races employed in white-collar jobs has increased from 23 percent in 1967 to 30 percent in 1972.

Despite a greater degree of occupational upgrading among blacks and other races than white workers, which has resulted in a more equitable distribution of employment, marked contrasts in blacks and other races to white job patterns persist. In 1972, blacks and other races still comprised a disproportionately small share of employed persons holding high-paying, high-status jobs. Blacks constitute about 11 percent of the total employed population. About 4 percent of blacks and other races, compared to 11 percent of whites, were employed as managers and administrators, and about 10 percent of blacks and other races, versus 15 percent of whites, were employed as professional and technical workers, (7% professional) and about 7 percent technical.

The black- and other races-to-white differences in occupational distribution were evident for men and women alike. The greatest disparities generally occurred among the highest and lowest level job categories. For example, nearly twice the proportion of white than blacks and other races men were employed in professional and technical, managerial and administrative jobs. Similarly, for women, whites were more likely than blacks and other races to be employed as professional and technical workers, managers and administrators. A large percentage increase in a professional category may not represent a large numerical increase.

For both the younger and older men who worked year round in 1969, the earning level of whites was substantially above that of blacks. Generally, blacks and whites are concentrated in different occupations within the major occupation categories and the level of earnings may vary with the specific occupation; these factors may account for some of the earning differences. The earnings of young black men 25 to 34 years old who worked year round were about equal (ratio of 0.90 or more) to those of young white men for a few specific occupations—engineers, teachers (except college and university), engineering and science technicians, bus drivers, taxicab drivers and chauffeurs, protective workers, and policemen and detectives.

For most occupations, the earnings of black women who worked year round in 1969, regardless of age, were closer to that of white women than those of black men to white men.

THE PROFESSIONS

Accountants: 15,814
Architects: 1,160
Clergymen: 12,458
College & University (teachers): 16,504
Dentists: 1,894
Engineers: 12,479
Engineering & Science Technicians: 26,414
Lawyers: 2,993
Librarians: 6,615
Nurses: 57,882
Pharmacists: 1,799
Physicians: 4,829
Social Scientists: 2,964
Social & Welfare Workers: 39,940
Elementary Schools (teachers): 144,571
Secondary Schools (teachers): 65,715
Health Workers: 23,182

Computer Specialists: 8,186
Mathematical Specialists: 673
Life & Physical Scientists: 6,007
Dietitians: 7,234
Chemists: 3,016
Other Related Practitioners: 594
Other Teachers: 5,222
Draftsmen & Surveyors: 7,766
Electrical Engineering: 4,864
Technicians, except health: 3,932
Airplane Pilots: 152
Writers, Artists, & Entertainers: 25,979
Actors & Dancers: 768
Authors, Editors, & Reporters: 1,571
Other Professional, technical & kindred workers: 98,747
TOTAL 611,924

Source: 1970 U.S. Census of Population-Detailed Characteristics-PC (1) D

BLACKS IN MEDICINE

The earliest known dark-skinned physician was Imhotep, who established schools of medicine and defined therapeutic principles in Egypt, about 3,000 B.C., and was deified 500 years after his death. The first known black American doctor was Lucas Santomee of New York, who studied medicine in Holland, and practiced under both the Dutch and the English. He received a grant of land for his services to the colony in 1667. James Derham, who was born into slavery in Philadelphia and acquired his medical knowledge from three doctors who were his successive owners, was freed in recognition of his ability, and in the 1780s built up a practice in New Orleans, where his reputation was high. The first black M.D. to practice in New York, Dr. James McCune Smith, received his degree at the University of Glasgow in Scotland in 1837, but it was not until 1847, when David J. Peck received his degree from Rush Medical College in Chicago that an M.D. was conferred on a black in the United States.

Blacks were first encouraged to enter the medical profession in some numbers by the American Colonization Society, which supported the training of doctors for service in Liberia, although some who were educated for this purpose refused to go. In 1849 Bowdoin College conferred M.D. degrees on John V. DeGrasse and Thomas J. White, and it was said that they were expected to go to Liberia, but did not do so. DeGrasse was admitted to the Boston Medical Society in 1854, and during the 1850s black physicians began to be accepted in some northern medical schools, and to practice in both the North and South. The first black woman physician, Dr. Susan McKinney, began practice in New York City in 1892.

The two oldest black medical schools, Howard and Meharry Medical Schools, which were founded just after the Civil War, are the only ones which still survive. Howard Medical School was opened in 1868 with eight students, with the facilities of Freedmen's Hospital as its teaching institution.

In 1876 Meharry Medical College was added to the Central Tennessee College in Nashville, with an initial endowment of $500 given by Samuel Meharry. A total of $12,000 was given to the school by the five Meharry brothers. There was only one in the first graduating class of 1877, and there were no hospital facilities, although later the students were able to use the Mercy Hospital for clinical experience. Meharry's first medical building was erected in 1880, followed in 1898 by the

dental building. The Meharry auditorium was built in 1904 and, finally, in 1910 the much needed W. Hubbard Hospital. Meharry was granted a separate new charter by the state of Tennessee in 1915, and it gradually took over and converted all of the buildings of Walden University, formerly the Central Tennessee College, which had declined and died over the years.

The facilities of the Howard Medical School had been much improved by the building of the new Freedmen's Hospital in 1909.

Both Meharry and Howard have continued to expand, with 80 in the 1973 graduating class of Meharry, and 94 in the 1973 graduating class of Howard. In its 97-year existence Meharry has graduated 197 women; Howard Medical College, since its opening 105 years ago, has graduated 374 women.

Blacks graduating from either Meharry or Howard found it almost impossible to obtain intern or residency appointments, or to be admitted to hospital staffs other than predominantly black institutions such as Freedmen's Hospital, or the Provident Hospital in Chicago, founded in 1891 by Daniel Hale Williams. In addition to providing staff appointments, internships, and residencies for black doctors in the new hospital, Dr. Williams founded a training school for black nurses at Provident, and later established another at Freedmen's. He was the first surgeon to perform a successful operation on the human heart and was, for many years, the only black member of the American College of Surgeons. His appointments, after he left Provident, included five years as surgeon-in-chief at Freedmen's Hospital, professor of clinical surgery at Meharry, attending surgeon at Chicago's Cook County Hospital, and a staff appointment at St. Luke's Hospital in Chicago. He died in 1931.

In 1895, black members of the medical profession, barred from membership in the American Medical Association, founded their own organization, the National Medical Association. Earlier associations were: the Medico-Chirurgical Society of the District of Columbia (1884); the Lone Star State Medical, Dental and Pharmaceutical Society in Galveston, Texas (1884); the Old North State Medical Society of North Carolina (1887); the Georgia State Medical Association of Physicians and Pharmacists; and the Arkansas Medical, Dental, and Pharmaceutical Association, both formed in 1893. In all, there were over a hundred separate black medical associations. In 1909, the National Medical Association began to publish its journal, in which black physicians found a medium of communication for publication of medical articles and research papers.

The high cost of medical education has meant that few black students could afford to qualify as doctors without financial assistance. In the twenties and thirties various philanthropic foundations became interested in helping black education, and funds for medical training were administered by the General Education Board and by the Rosenwald Foundation for hospital programs. During this period no attempt was made to allocate funds in a way that would combat discrimination and dubious "separate but equal" policies in the Southern states. After World War II, however, fellowships became available to black students, and one of the greatest contributors to the furtherance of black medical education has been National Medical Fellowships Inc., which was founded in 1946 by a group of Chicago physicians as Provident Medical Associates, changing its name in 1952 when the number of board members was increased to 15 to include black and white leaders in the field of medical organization, and the organization had become national, rather than local, in scope.

In 1972–73, grants of $1,730,438 were made by National Medical Fellowships to 1,288 black students who will study at U.S. medical schools. The N.M.F. offers other scholarships to undergraduate medical students, and loans to physicians who wish to continue training in a medical or surgical specialized field. Loan recipients who decide to go into academic medicine, rather than private practice, may apply for cancellation of their loans. The policy of advancing loans to postgraduate medical students and reserving scholarships and grants for undergraduates was adopted in 1954 since it was felt that the greatest need was to encourage gifted students to enroll in medical school.

Since its founding in 1946, National Medical Fellowships, Inc. reported having awarded $6,500,000 in fellowship help; it pays no fees to its directors, has no expenses other than office administration, and its program, having no endowment, is made possible only through the generosity of private contributors.

Every year the need for black doctors is greater and the opportunities for training increases, but the number of applications for scholarships and of enrollments has remained steady. It is reported by the National Medical Association that the number of places available for interns and residents now exceeds the supply, but that the wider range of professions now open to black graduates makes the practice of medicine less attractive than a career in science, where the initial training is shorter and less expensive. Blacks now represent more than 11 percent of the population, but only 5.5 percent of medical students are black. In 1972–73, 7.1 percent of medical students in their freshman year were black, and only about 2 percent of the physicians are black. The growing need for qualified doctors should be met in appropriate numbers by blacks with the necessary ability and devotion.

Discrimination in medical associations, hospital appointments and research projects has been gradually yielding under pressure from the National Medical Association, the NAACP and other black community oriented organizations. The 1964 Congress, in extending the 1946 Hospital Survey and Construction (Hill-Burton) Act providing federal aid for the construction of hospitals and nursing homes for a further five years, removed the section which allowed segregated hospital facilities "in cases where separate hospital facilities are provided for separate population groups, if the plan makes equitable provision on the basis of need for facilities and service of like quality for each group." This followed a 1963 Supreme Court decision which struck down this "separate but equal" section as unconstitutional, and which had caused a good deal of concern in Southern hospitals which were receiving federal aid. The U.S. Civil Rights Commission had reported to the President in 1963 urging the repeal of the offending clause. The Commission's survey showed that even in hospitals which had received federal aid on the basis of nondiscrimination, facilities were by no means equally available to white and black patients. In many cases, hospitals were refusing to assign white and black patients to share rooms, and this meant, in effect, that black patients were required to obtain private rooms; in some hospitals, it was reported that private rooms were charged at the semi-private rate to black patients who could not afford the private-room rate, and that the county welfare department was paying for private rooms for indigent black patients. Even in hospitals where rooms are assigned on a nondiscriminatory basis, black patients often could not be attended by their own doctors, since visiting privileges were not extended to black physicians.

In effect, the desegregation of hospital staffs and facilities has progressed through three stages. First, federal policy outlawed discrimination in government institutions, which meant that black physicians were accepted on the staffs of the hospitals of the Armed Forces, the Public Health Service and the Veterans Administration; second, federal funds available under the Hill-Burton Act, after the 1964 re-enactment, were restricted to hospitals not guilty of discriminatory practices; and third, following the 1964 Civil Rights Act, the Office of Equal Health Opportunity is checking hospitals for compliance with Title VI of the Act which says that "No person in the United States shall, on the ground of race, color, or national origin be excluded from participation in, be denied the benefits of, or be subjected to discrimination under any program or activity receiving federal financial assistance."

Although exact data is difficult to compile, preliminary data from a survey conducted by the National Medical Association Foundation shows approximately 6,000 black physicians distributed predominantly in urban areas, a third of whom are in the cities of Los Angeles, San Francisco, Chicago, New York City, Detroit and the District of Columbia (Washington, D.C.).

The majority of black physicians in the United States are general practitioners, but there is already a tradition of distinguished medical, surgical and research specialization.

In June, 1965, the National Dental Association's Committee to End Discrimination in the Dental Profession issued a statement saying that: "With significant exceptions, qualified black dentists practicing in the eleven Southern states have not been able to join the American Dental Association. They have been excluded from membership by 'Caucasian only' clauses in the constitutions and bylaws of these state societies, as well as by the unwritten law of segregation."

Since 1961, when the American Dental Association directed all constituent and component societies to insure that their bylaws contained no provision which discriminated against candidates for membership on the basis of race, creed, or color, the A.D.A. has attempted to enforce this policy. Its Board of Trustees reported in 1962 that "provisions not expressed in constituent or component society bylaws are being enforced to complete discrimination on the basis of race, creed, or color," and that "these unconstitutional procedures of constituent and component societies not sanctioned by their bylaws have not yet been challenged." The Association has established the legal and moral right to punish those state societies that discriminate, either by depriving them of their voting rights in the House of Delegates, or by revocation of their charter, but they have not so far exercised that power. The National Dental Association, the largest and oldest black dental association in the United States, was founded in 1913, at Buckroe, Virginia. In 1971, it had a membership of about 1,200 black dentists.

The Association, since the 1960s, has taken a much more active role in seeking to recruit more students into the field, and to politicize their membership to the importance of legislation and the importance of various provisions of federal programs, such as Medicaid to their profession. They have become aware of the lack of black dental input at policy-making levels in planning health care delivery services, and they are also seeking to recruit personnel for training in dental paraprofessional fields, such as X-ray technicians and dental hygienists.

BLACK MEDICAL STUDENTS

Spurred by the National Medical Association's Project 75, which was launched in July, 1970 as a five year intensive effort to recruit and retain black college students interested in medicine, the program seeks to raise the number of blacks in medicine to approximate their percentage in the general population. NMA's Project 75 is under the direction of Dr. Andrew Thomas, Chicago physician and trustee of the National Medical Association.

The effort to increase minority enrollment in all medical schools is beginning to show results. In 1969–1970 minority students were 5% of the total enrollment. In 1971–1972, minority students comprised 9% of the total medical student body. This represents a numerical increase of more than 2,000 minority students in three years.

The percentage of black students in the total enrollment of medical schools has more than doubled since 1968–1969. The number of blacks enrolled in U.S. medical schools in 1971–1972 was 2,090, or 4.8% of the enrollment. For the first time there is an increase in the percentage of graduates who are black.

In the past, the majority of black medical students were enrolled in two medical schools. In 1968–1969, Howard and Meharry together enrolled about 63% of all black medical students in the United States. In 1971–1972, however, these two schools enrolled only 27% of all black medical students. Three years ago (1968–1969), Howard and Meharry graduated 87% of all blacks receiving the MD degree. In 1971–1972, only 57% of graduating blacks received their degrees from Howard or Meharry. Three years ago, enrolled blacks numbered 817, or 2.3% of the total enrollment. If Howard and Meharry are excluded from the count, the black percentage of the total enrollment in 1971–1972 was four times greater than it was in 1968–1969.

In 1968–1969, the largest black enrollment was found to be in the schools of three regions:

East North Central, South Atlantic (excluding Howard and Meharry), and Pacific. In 1971–1972, New England schools had a 5.25% black student body. The Pacific schools were close behind, with a 4.92% black enrollment. The Middle Atlantic and East North Central schools had a 4.53% and 4.48% black enrollment, respectively.

This increase in minority enrollment is seen in both public and private schools. In the past four years, both types of schools have quadrupled their black enrollment. In the same period the private schools (not including

Howard and Meharry) have more than doubled the percentage of black graduates.

The percentage of black students enrolled in the first-year class has almost tripled in the past four years. Excluding Howard and Meharry, the percentage of first-year black students is more than four times greater than it was in 1968–1969. In August 1972, a group of schools was surveyed by telephone to ascertain the retention rate for minority students. There is evidence that a number of black students were enrolled in the first-year class for more than one year.

Percentage Black Enrollment in US Medical Schools, 1968-1969 to 1971-1972

	Total		First Year		Graduates	
	No.	%	No.	%	No.	%
1968-69	817	2.3	264	2.7	142	1.8
	325*	0.9*	130*	1.3*	48*	0.6*
1969-70	1,038	2.8	449	4.3	165	2.0
	555*	1.5*	326*	3.2*	60*	0.7*
1970-71	1,525	3.8	708	6.2	180	2.0
	1,026*	2.7*	580*	5.2*	62*	0.7*
1971-72	2,090	4.8	890	7.2	229	2.4
	1,521*	3.6*	717*	6.0*	98*	1.1*

*Excluding Howard, Meharry, and Puerto Rico.

Enrollment of Black Students by Type of School 1968-1969 to 1971-1972

	School Enrollment			First-Year Enrollment			All Graduates		
	School Total	No.	Black %	School Total	No.	Black %	School Total	No.	Black %
Public Schools									
1968-69	19,226	167	0.88%	5,332	66	1.24%	4,289	34	0.79%
1969-70	20,344	280	1.38%	5,812	156	2.68%	4,446	33	0.74%
1970-71	21,266	526	2.47%	6,269	301	4.80%	4,493	34	0.76%
1971-72	23,971	791	3.30%	6,920	386	5.58%	5,166	56	1.08%
Private Schools									
1968-69	16,607	650	3.91%	4,531	198	4.37%	3,770	108	2.87%
1969-70	17,325	758	4.37%	4,589	293	6.39%	3,921	132	3.37%
1970-71	18,568	999	5.38%	5,079	407	8.01%	4,344	146	3.36%
1971-72	19,679	1,299	6.60%	5,441	504	8.26%	4,385	173	3.95%
Private—Except Howard & Meharry									
1968-69	15,936	159	1.00%	4,340	64	1.47%	3,642	14	0.38%
1969-70	16,651	275	1.65%	4,421	170	3.85%	3,763	27	0.72%
1970-71	16,097	500	3.11%	4,872	279	5.73%	4,182	28	0.67%
1971-72	18,894	730	3.86%	5,214	277	5.31%	4,213	42	1.00%

*Percentages for 1968-1969 are based on enrollment in 96 schools; percentages for 1971-1972 are based on 108 schools.
†Howard and/or Meharry are excluded.

Source: *Journal of American Medical Association*, Nov. 20, 1972

Distribution of Black Dentists and Black Population
in 1970-1971 by Regions and States and Population
Per Black Dentist in the United States

Region and State	No. Black Dentists 1970-71	Black Population 1970	Population Per Dentist
New England	63		
Connecticut	33	181,177	5,490
Maine	0	2,800	2,800
Massachusetts	28	175,817	6,279
New Hampshire	0	2,505	2,505
Rhode Island	2	25,338	12,669
Vermont	0	761	761
Middle East	790		
Delaware	5	78,276	15,655
District of Columbia	152	537,712	3,537
Maryland	103	699,479	6,991
New Jersey	101	770,292	7,620
New York	250	2,166,933	8,667
Pennsylvania	165	1,016,514	6,161
West Virginia	14	73,931	529
South East	506		
Arkansas	15	357,225	23,815
Alabama	39	908,247	23,901
Florida	60	1,049,578	17,375
Georgia	52	1,190,779	22,900
Kentucky	15	241,292	16,086
Louisiana	37	1,088,734	29,453
South Carolina	41	788,772	19,238
Mississippi	26	815,770	31,376
North Carolina	86	1,137,664	13,229
Tennessee	40	631,696	15,792
Virginia	95	865,388	9,109
South West	128		
Arizona	6	53,344	8,891
New Mexico	0	19,555	19,555
Oklahoma	18	177,907	9,883
Texas	104	1,399,055	13,451
Central	432		
Illinois	141	1,425,674	13,451
Indiana	52	357,464	6,874
Iowa	6	32,596	5,432
Minnesota	4	34,868	8,717
Missouri	43	480,172	11,167
Ohio	58	970,477	16,732
Michigan	122	991,066	9,123
Wisconsin	6	128,224	21,370
North West	21		
Colorado	6	66,411	16,068
Idaho	0	2,130	2,130
Kansas	13	106,977	8,229
Montana	0	1,995	1,995
Nebraska	2	39,911	19,955
North Dakota	0	2,494	2,494
South Dakota	0	1,627	1,627
Utah	0	6,617	6,617
Wyoming	0	2,568	2,568
Far West	192		
California	175	1,400,143	8,000
Nevada	4	27,762	6,840
Oregon	4	26,308	6,577
Washington	7	71,308	10,184
Alaska	1	8,911	8,911
Hawaii	1	7,573	7,573
TOTAL	2,132	22,580,289	10,591

Source: U.S. Bureau of Census, General Population Characteristics, 1970 Final Report PC (1), United States Summary.
Rhodes Directory of Black Dentists Registered in the United States, 1972–1973 by Lord Cecil Rhodes, B.S., D.D.S., F.I.B.A.

BLACK LAW STUDENTS AND PRACTITIONERS

As of 1968 there were 325,000 lawyers in the United States with less than one per cent of those black. That meant there was one black lawyer for every 7,000 blacks, as compared with one white lawyer for every 637 white Americans. There was an even greater disparity in the South with only 17% (or approximately 506) of all black attorneys practicing there.

Since the years of law school desegregation there has been a tremendous increase in the number of black lawyers. In 1966 a Howard University study reported that the number of black lawyers and judges in the United States increased 107% between 1940 and 1960, and the ratio of the black population to black lawyers and judges improved by 35% in the same period. One avenue for increasing black law school enrollment was to strengthen and expand the existing predominately black law schools. The Ford Foundation gave Howard University a grant in 1964 for $1.8 million, $900,000 of which would be used for scholarship aid. Since then, Howard has tripled the size of its graduating classes. White law schools are also making gains to recruit black law students with the help of the Council on Legal Education Opportunity (CLEO) which was organized to raise funds for recruitment and scholarship aid for black law students.

But unfortunately, the law schools and foundations cannot supply enough money to meet the total need. The federal government, with its massive assistance programs in such areas as education and science has never set up a scholarship program for disadvantaged law students. But this assistance from the federal government as well as from white law schools will have to come before complete parity is realized. The black practitioner, it seems, has not fared as well as the law student. A National Bar Association-Howard University study in 1966 reported the median net income of full-time black lawyers and judges in the U.S. was $11,300. Only 6.5% earned over $25,000. For lawyers generally, the corresponding median in New Jersey, for example, was $14,000 in 1962, and in Florida it was $16,000 in 1965. This disparity can, in part, be attributed to the propensity of black lawyers to practice alone, even though the facts show partnerships to be more lucrative. In 1970 the average salary of a sole practitioner was $18,000, while the average partner in a firm earned $28,000. However, in 1966 73% of black lawyers practiced alone, whereas only 56% of all private practitioners were sole practitioners. It seems apparent that there is a need for blacks to obtain loans or other financial assistance in order to establish law firms making them more attractive for business with large corporate clients, and thus more profitable.

Source: Excerpted from an article by Christopher F. Edley in the "Harvard Law School Bulletin", February, 1971.

BLACK AMERICAN JUDGES AND LAWYERS, 1844–1973

1844
The first black American lawyer, Macon B. Allen, admitted to the Maine bar, July 3, 1844, and during Reconstruction admitted to Charleston, S.C. bar. In February 1873, elected judge of the inferior court of Charleston by the South Carolina General Assembly.

1852
Robert Morris, Boston, Mass., first black American magistrate, appointed by Massachusetts Governor George N. Briggs.

1855
John Mercer Langston, first black lawyer to win elective office as clerk of Brownhelm Township, Lorain County, Ohio.

1856
Aaron A. Bradley, admitted to Massachusetts Bar, February 2, 1856; later elected to Georgia Legislature.

1861
Edwin Garrison Walker, admitted to Massachusetts Bar, May 1861, first black American

legislator; elected to Massachusetts Legislature.

1865
John S. Rock, physician, dentist, and lawyer, first black admitted to practice before U.S. Supreme Court.

1870
Jonathan Jasper Wright, first black State Supreme Court Justice, elected to full 6-year term as Associate Justice, South Carolina Supreme Court.

1872
George Lee, elected by South Carolina Legislature judge of the inferior court of Charleston, March 13, 1872.
Charlotte Ray, first black woman lawyer, a graduate of Howard University Law School.

1873
First black law firm established—Whipper, Elliott & Allen (Judge Macon B. Allen). Whipper and Elliott, both members of South Carolina Legislature, and Robert Brown

Elliott later Representative in U.S. Congress.

1883–90

George L. Ruffin, one of the first black graduates of Harvard Law School (1869), served in Massachusetts Legislature and Boston Common Council, appointed municipal judge of Charleston, Mass., November 7, 1883. Other black judges—Judge Mifflin Gibbs, elected as city judge in Little Rock, Ark.; first black to hold this position; Judge John H. Ballou, Florida (1888), and Judge Joseph E. Lee, Florida (1890).

1869–1901

In Congress, 1869–1901, 6 of the blacks elected (2 Senators and 20 Representatives) were lawyers. They were: James Edward O'Hara, Robert Brown Elliott, James Thomas Rapier, Thomas Ezekiel Miller, George Henry White, John Mercer Langston.

1901

Robert H. Terrell, first black judicial appointment of President Theodore Roosevelt, judge of the District of Columbia Municipal Court, December 17.

1911

William H. Lewis, Boston, first black Assistant U.S. Attorney General, appointed by President William H. Taft.

1924

Albert B. George, elected municipal judge, Chicago, 1924, first black elected judge in the North since Reconstruction.

1926

Judge James A. Cobb appointed to Municipal Court for the District of Columbia by President Calvin Coolidge; reappointed by President Hoover, 1930.

1935

Judge Armond W. Scott appointed to Municipal Court for the District of Columbia by President Franklin D. Roosevelt; reappointed 1939 and 1943.

1936

Charles Anderson, former president of the National Bar Association, elected to Kentucky Legislature (later appointed United Nations Delegate by President Eisenhower).

1937

William H. Hastie appointed judge of the U.S. District Court for the Virgin Islands by President Franklin D. Roosevelt; succeeded by judges Herman Moore (appointed by Presidents Roosevelt and Truman) and Walter Gordon (appointed by President Eisenhower).

1939

Jane Matilda Bolin, first black woman judge, appointed by Mayor LaGuardia to the court of domestic relations in New York City.

1940–63

First elected black women judges—Chicago's Edith S. Sampson, former United Nations Delegate; and Juanita Kidd Stout in Philadelphia. First black woman judge appointed by President John F. Kennedy—Marjorie McKenzie Lawson, to the District of Columbia Juvenile Court. First black woman appointed judge in Los Angeles, Calif.—Vaino Spencer.

1945

Judge Irvin C. Mollison, first black lifetime federal judge, appointed by President Truman to the U.S. Customs Court.

1949

William L. Dawson, Member of Congress, first black chairman of a Congressional Standing Committee, House Committee on Government Operations.

William H. Hastie, first black judge, U.S. Circuit Court of Appeals, appointed by President Harry S. Truman.

1950

Judge Emory Smith and Judge Andrew Howard appointed to Municipal Court for the District of Columbia by President Truman.

1954

J. Ernest Wilkins, Chicago, first black Assistant Secretary of the U.S. Department of Labor, appointed by President Eisenhower.

1955

E. Frederic Morrow, first black Special Assistant to President Eisenhower.

1956

Archibald J. Carey, Chicago, first black chairman of President Eisenhower's Committee on Government Employment Policy; United Nations Delegate.

1957

George Johnson, former Howard Law School professor, appointed to U.S. Civil Rights Commission by President Eisenhower.

Scovel Richardson, appointed Judge, U.S. Customs Court, by President Eisenhower.

1958

Richard A. Harewood, now Judge of the Superior Court, Cook County (Ill.), first black to win statewide public office since Reconstruction, when elected Trustee of the University of Illinois.

Otis Smith, first black elected to statewide public office. Auditor of Public Accounts, Michigan.

1960

Frank Reeves, first black Special Assistant to President Kennedy.

1961

Thurgood Marshall, former Chief Counsel NAACP Legal Defense and Educational

Fund, appointed Judge, U.S. Circuit Court of Appeals, by President Kennedy.

Andrew Howard, reappointed by President Kennedy, judge of the District of Columbia Municipal Court.

1961–62

Hobart Taylor, executive vice chairman, President's Committee on Equal Employment Opportunity.

Otis Smith, first black associate justice of Supreme Court of Michigan since Reconstruction, in a statewide election.

Leroy Johnson, first black senator elected to Georgia's Legislature since Reconstruction, in a statewide election.

Gerald Lamb, first black elected State treasurer in Connecticut, in a statewide election.

Edward W. Brooke, first black elected attorney general in the United States (Massachusetts).

Spottswood Robinson III, appointed U.S. Civil Rights Commission; Clarence Ferguson, counsel; appointed by President Kennedy.

1961–63

James B. Parsons, Chicago, Ill., Wade McCree, Detroit, Mich., Spottswood Robinson III, Washington, D.C., appointed judges of the U.S. District Court.

Cecil Poole, San Francisco, Calif., and Merle McCurdy, Cleveland, Ohio, first U.S. attorneys.

Judge Joseph Waddy appointed to the Municipal Court for the District of Columbia for 10-year term.

A. Leon Higginbotham, member, Federal Trade Commission and appointed to U.S. District Court (Pa.).

Howard Jenkins, Jr., member, National Labor Relations Board.

John B. Duncan, member, District of Columbia Commission.

Luke Moore, marshal, District of Columbia (first black marshal was Frederick Douglass, appointed by President Hayes. Douglass was not a lawyer).

1964

Chester C. Carter, former deputy assistant state secretary for Congressional Affairs, was named Deputy Chief of Protocol, Department of State, first black to receive top post in the protocol division, May 1.

Frankie Muse Freeman, former assistant attorney general of Missouri, was appointed first woman member of the U.S. Civil Rights Commission February 29.

A. Leon Higginbotham Jr., first black member of the Federal Trade Commission from September 26, 1962, was appointed to the U.S. District Court for Eastern Pennsylvania January 7. (He had been appointed by the

late President John F. Kennedy, but not confirmed at the time of the President's assassination. He was reappointed by President Lyndon B. Johnson.)

Spottswood W. Robinson III, former Dean of Howard University Law School and member of the U.S. Civil Rights Commission, was appointed U.S. District Judge for the District of Columbia. (Again, this appointment was made by President Kennedy and a reappointment made by President Johnson, January 7.)

1965

Clifford L. Alexander Jr., former deputy special Presidential assistant for personnel and administration, was named associate special counsel to President Johnson, August 25.

William Benson Bryant, former Assistant U.S. Attorney for the District of Columbia and onetime professor of law at Howard University, was appointed by President Lyndon B. Johnson to the U.S. District Court in the District of Columbia, July 11, and became the second black appointed to that bench. He is famous for his work in the Mallory case which brought about a landmark decision by the U.S. Supreme Court in 1957.

Thurgood Marshall, Judge of the 2nd Circuit Court of Appeals was named Solicitor General of the United States by President Johnson, July 13.

Patricia Roberts Harris, assistant professor of law at Howard University, and member of the Commission to Study Puerto Rican Statehood, Commonwealth and Independence, was named Ambassador to Luxembourg, May 19, the first black woman ambassador.

Hobart Taylor Jr., former executive vice chairman of the President's Equal Employment Opportunities Committee and associate special counsel on the President's staff, became the first black member of the Export-Import Bank, September 7.

Franklin H. Williams, former African Regional Director of the Peace Corps and U.S. Representative on UNESCO, was named Ambassador to Ghanna, October 10.

1966

Lisle C. Carter Jr., Assistant Director of the Office of Economic Opportunity, was named Assistant Health, Education and Welfare Secretary for individual and family services, January 15.

Marjorie Lawson, former District of Columbia Juvenile Judge, was appointed U.S. representative to the Social Commission of UNESCO.

James Madison Nabrit Jr., former President of Howard University and U.S. Representative to the United Nations Security Council, was named chief deputy to Ambassador Goldberg on April 26. The ambassadorial post ranks second in the United Nations mission.

James L. Watson, former New York State Senator and Civil Court Judge, was appointed to the U.S. Customs Court, March 7.

Robert Weaver, Director of the Housing and Home Finance Agency, was named Secretary of the new Department of Housing and Urban Development, and became the first black member of a presidential cabinet.

Roger Wilkins, former Assistant Community Relations Service Director and acting head of the department, was named Director of CRS, January 14.

Constance Baker Motley, first black woman appointed Federal Court judge, in September. U.S. District Court in southern New York State. Former New York State Senator.

1967

Clifford L. Alexander Jr. named chairman of the Equal Opportunity Commission, June 27. He was formerly associate special council under President Lyndon B. Johnson.

Thurgood Marshall named by President Johnson as first black associate judge on the Supreme Court, September 13.

Attorneys Carl B. Stokes and Richard G. Hatcher on November 7, elected mayors of Cleveland, Ohio and Gary, Indiana, respectively. They were the first black mayors elected in major U.S. cities.

1968

Clarence M. Mitchell Jr., named as chairman of the National Leadership Conference

on Civil Rights, April 11. He was instrumental in the passage of landmark civil rights acts—including the 1968 Civil Rights Bill.

1969

David W. Williams, a Los Angeles County Superior Court judge, was named as a U.S. District Judge for Central California, May 8. He is the first black jurist to hold a federal judgeship west of the Mississippi.

1971

William T. Coleman, Jr., a black attorney and a partner in a Philadelphia law firm, was named by President Nixon to the Pay Board and Price Commission, October 22.

1972

Benjamin L. Hooks, a black Memphis lawyer, was nominated by President Nixon to a seven-year term on the Federal Communications Commission (FCC), April 11.

Yvonne Braithwaite Burke, California attorney and Assemblywoman, was approved as nominee for co-chairman of the Democratic National Convention by the Rules Committee, June 24.

Patricia Roberts Harris was named permanent chairperson of the Credentials Committee of the 1972 National Democratic Convention, June 27.

Basil A. Paterson, former New York State Senator, selected as the new national vice-chairman of the Democratic National Committee, July 14.

1973

Thomas Bradley, a California attorney, was elected mayor of Los Angeles in a nonpartisan election over incumbent Sam Yorty, May 29.

BLACK SCIENTISTS

The contributions of black Americans to the natural sciences and mathematics is a matter of historical record, but it is often overlooked, since it is not highly publicized or glamorized. In the past century, probably no black scientist has been as widely known as Dr. George Washington Carver (1864–1943). Dr. Carver's experiments with the lowly sweet potato and the peanut were the basis for the development of over 400 different products, from those two common plants. Carver is credited with having promoted a theory of crop rotation to aid in soil productivity. Dr. Charles R. Drew (1904–1950), the developer of a successful technique for blood plasma transport, was the director of the first Plasma Division Blood Transfusion and the first director of the American Red Cross Blood Bank. At the time he was serving the ARC Blood Bank, the segregationist prin-

ciples under which the organization operated would not permit even Dr. Drew's blood to be mixed with that of white donors. Dr. Ernest E. Just (1883–1941) did outstanding work at Howard University in the biological sciences. He specialized in studies on fertilization, parthenogenesis and animal cytology. He received the first Spingarn Medal in 1914 for his research.

Charles H. Turner (1867–1923), a University of Chicago Ph.D., was secretary of the Animal Behavior Section of the International Congress of Zoology in 1907. He was an authority on behavioral patterns of ants.

Dr. Percy Julian, unparalleled in organic chemical research, has had a long and distinguished career. Born in 1899, Dr. Julian served for several years as research director of the soya products and vegetable oil and food divisions of the Glidden Company of Chicago. In 1954, he founded Julian Laboratories, Inc., and in 1961, he sold the firm for $2,338,000. He founded U. Julian Associates, and is director of Julian Research Institute in Franklin Park, Ill. Among his many discoveries are the successful synthesis of physostigmine, used in the treatment of glaucoma; a synthesis of the female sex hormone progesterone and testosterone (male sex hormone), and a synthesis of soybean sterols permitting low-cost availability of cortisone.

Dr. Lloyd A. Hall (1894–1971), before his retirement as Director of Research for Griffith Laboratories, is reputed to have developed the most effective curing salt for meat in America. Dr. Hall was a pioneer in the method of sterilizing spices and other food materials, by the use of ethylene oxide.

Emmett W. Chappelle, an astrochemist at the Goddard Space Flight Center, received a patent for his method of detecting cancer through a mechanism similar to that by which a firefly gives off light.

The range of opportunities for black scientists and technologists in the decades ahead is unparalleled. (See also article, Black Inventors.)

THE BLACK INVENTOR

Perhaps the earliest invention was Benjamin Banneker's striking clock which he made in 1761. Between 1834 and 1900, at least 700 patents were granted to black patentees, according to information compiled by Henry E. Baker, an Assistant Patent Examiner in the U.S. Patent Office during the early 1900's. The four bound volumes containing these patents are to be found in the Moorland Foundation Room of the Howard University Founders Library in Washington, D.C.

It is believed that Henry Blair was the first black person to have been granted a U.S. patent for a seed planter, issued October 14, 1834. Blair was granted a second patent on a corn harvester in 1836. In both cases he was designated in the official records as "a colored man." Subsequently this practice was discontinued and no further racial description given for patentees.

The ban on issuing patents did not apply to free blacks, and so James Forten (1776–1842) had no difficulty in obtaining a patent for his sailhandling device; nor did Norbert Rillieux, who in 1846 invented and patented a vacuum pan, which in its day revolutionized methods of refining sugar, and aided very materially in developing the sugar industry of Louisiana.

However, as late as 1858, Jeremiah S. Black, Attorney General of the United States, confirmed a decision of the Secretary of the Interior, on appeal from the Commissioner of Patents, refusing to grant a patent on an invention by a slave, either to the slave as the inventor, or to his master, on the ground that, not being a citizen, the slave could neither contract with the government nor assign his invention to his master. Thus, it has been impossible to document the contributions made by innumerable unnamed slaves whose creative skill has added to the industrial might of the United States. Jo Anderson, slave on the plantation of Cyrus McCormick, is reputed to have made a major contribution to the McCormick Grain Harvester but is credited in the official records as being merely a handyman or helper.

Perhaps the best known black inventor is Jan E. Matzeliger, who was born in 1852. He was the son of a Dutch engineer and a native Guinean woman. As a young man, he came to the United States, became a naturalized citizen, and served as an apprentice cobbler, first in Philadelphia, and later in Lynn, Massachusetts. He invented a machine for lasting shoes. It was the first appliance of its kind that could peform all the steps required to hold a shoe on its last, grip and pull the leather down around the heel, guide and drive the nails into place, and then discharge the completed shoe from the machine. His machine was patented March 20, 1883, and later patents for refinements were issued in the same year and the year following his untimely death in 1889. This patent was purchased by Sidney W. Winslow and provided the foundation for the United Shoe Machinery Company, a multi-million-dollar corporation. Matzeliger never benefited from the tremendous economic potential of his invention.

The largest number of patents ever issued to a black inventor went to Elijah McCoy of Detroit, who received his first patent in 1872 and his last one, the fifty-seventh, in 1920. Most of McCoy's inventions were for machinery lubricating devices, and he is considered a pioneer in the method of steadily supplying oil to machines drop-by-drop from special cups. The method boosted production because it made unnecessary the practice of shutting down machines while they were being lubricated.

Granville T. Woods, who died in New York City in 1910, patented nearly fifty inventions between 1884 and 1910, primarily related to electrical equipment, such as telephone and telegraph instruments, electrical railways, and general systems of electrical control. Several of his inventions were for transmitting messages between moving trains. According to Patent Office Records, a number of his patents were bought by such companies as General Electric and American Bell Telephone and Westinghouse.

William B. Purvis of Philadelphia designed his first machine for making paper bags in 1884; and is credited with one of the first designs for cutters similar to those used on wax paper and aluminum foil boxes. Subsequently, he patented several variations on his original design.

In November, 1897, Andrew J. Beard of Alabama was granted a patent on an automatic car-coupling device which reputedly was sold to a railroad car company for fifty thousand dollars.

A.P. Albert of Louisiana, a creole, invented a machine for picking cotton.

Some inventions of black persons are so commonplace as to be a part of the everyday life of every American, and yet there is little awareness that the creativity of a black person is responsible. The potato chip, which was created by Hyram S. Thomas, a chef in the wealthy resort of Saratoga Springs, N.Y., was originally known as the "Saratoga chip." Augustus Jackson, the "man who invented ice cream" was a Philadelphia candymaker and confectioner (1832). George F. Grant invented the little pin which has made wives weekend widows from early spring to late fall—the golf tee. J. H. Dickinson and S. L. Dickinson invented the player piano machinery and Thomas W. Stewart, the conventional mopholder.

In contemporary times, the late Frederick M. Jones of Detroit, developed the first practical refrigerator system for trucks and railroad freightcars. Thomas J. Carter of the U.S. Bureau of Standards has developed a machine for testing the durability of various leathers. B. V. Montez of Chester, Pennsylvania, has developed numerous electronic devices in tape and wire recorders, listening aids and other instruments, including sending and receiving sets for helmets of professional football players. Emmanuel M. Moore of Pine Bluff, Arkansas,

designed an earth-moving machine with a capacity for scooping and side delivering of an average of 600 cubic yards of dirt per hour, twice as fast as most dragline machines used by excavators. Tony Helm of Chicago has perfected an all-angle wrench attachment that has proved so popular that he now has a factory to manufacture them. Sgt. Adolphus Samms, at the U.S. Army Weapons Test Station in Yuma, Arizona, has completed development of an "air frame center support"—using an engineering concept which eliminates the second and third stage engines from multistage rockets, thus stripping the vehicle of dead weight and making greater payloads possible. Samms to date has four patents on various rocket designs and his work has received the attention of the National Aeronautics and Space Administration as well as the President's Office of Science and Technology.

The list of contributions made by black inventors in almost every field is nearly endless but the examples cited are indicative of the range of creative ability which has been channeled into scientific and technical areas.

Among the significant twentieth century inventors and scientists are the following:

George W. Carver—producer of products of the peanut, sweet potato, and soy bean.

Dr. Lloyd A. Hall—Over 80 patents issued to Dr. Hall for his meat curing salt formulas which revolutionized the meat curing industry.

Dr. Percy L. Julian—Regarded as the world's foremost producer of synthetic steroid drugs from the soybean; holder of more than 80 patents; synthesization of the progesterone, estrone and testosterone hormones from plants.

Dr. Charles R. Drew—Apparatus for preserving blood (1942), considered one of the major advances in the history of blood preservation.

Dr. William A. Hinton—Test to determine syphilis.

Solomon Harper—Thermostatic controlled air implements.

W. Wiggins, Jr.—Submarine designs, marine and tug-boat designs.

Joseph Logan—Jet engine.

BLACK COLLEGE AND UNIVERSITY PRESIDENTS

Emmett W. Bashful
  Southern University
  New Orleans, Louisiana

Waldo W. E. Blanchet
  Ft. Valley State College
  Ft. Valley, Georgia

James C. Bond
  California State University
  Sacramento, California

Ernest A. Boykins
  Mississippi Valley State College
  Itta Bena, Mississippi

Herman R. Branson
  Lincoln University
  Lincoln, Pennsylvania

Edward J. Brantley
  Knoxville College
  Knoxville, Tennessee

Oswald P. Bronson
  Interdenominational Theological Center
  Atlanta, Georgia

Lyman B. Brooks
  Norfolk State College
  Norfolk, Virginia

Archie L. Buffkins
  University of Maryland
  Eastern Shore, Maryland

Calvin W. Burnett
  Coppin State College
  Baltimore, Maryland

Broadus N. Butler
  Dillard University
  New Orleans, Louisiana

James E. Cheek
  Howard University
  District of Columbia

King V. Cheek, Jr.
  Morgan State College
  Baltimore, Maryland

James A. Colston
  Bronx Community College
  Bronx, New York

Paul P. Cooke
  District of Columbia Teacher's College
  District of Columbia

Milton K. Curry, Jr.
  Bishop College
  Dallas, Texas

Walter C. Daniel
  Lincoln University
  Jefferson City, Missouri

Lawrence A. Davis
  University of Arkansas
  Pine Bluff, Arkansas

Lewis C. Dowdy
  North Carolina A & T State University
  Greensboro, North Carolina

Lloyd C. Elam
  Meharry Medical College
  Nashville, Tennessee

Luther H. Foster
  Tuskegee Institute
  Tuskegee, Alabama

Norman C. Francis
  Xavier University
  New Orleans, Louisiana

Hugh M. Gloster
  Morehouse College
  Atlanta, Georgia

Harry P. Graham
  Voorhees College
  Denmark, South Carolina

Wilbert Greenfield
  Johnson C. Smith University
  Charlotte, North Carolina

Jerome L. 'Gresham
  Barber-Scotia College
  Concord, North Carolina

J. W. Hairston
  Allen University
  Columbia, South Carolina

Allen C. Hancock
  Texas College
  Tyler, Texas

Henry E. Hardin
  Morris College
  Sumter, South Carolina

Wendell G. Hardway
  Bluefield State College
  Bluefield, West Virginia

James A. Hargraves
Shaw University
Raleigh, North Carolina

Charles L. Hayes
Albany State College
Albany, Georgia

Robert E. Hayes
Wiley College
Marshall, Texas

Walter Hazzard
Philander Smith College
Little Rock, Arkansas

Vivian W. Henderson
Clark College
Atlanta, Georgia

Carl M. Hill
Kentucky State College
Frankfort, Kentucky

Odell Horton
Le Moyne-Owen College
Memphis, Tennessee

Roy D. Hudson
Hampton Institute
Hampton, Virginia

Prince A. Jackson, Jr.
Savannah State College
Savannah, Georgia

Allix B. James
Virginia Union University
Richmond, Virginia

Thomas D. Jarrett
Atlanta University
Atlanta, Georgia

Elgy S. Johnson
Federal City College
District of Columbia

John Paul Jones
Jarvis Christian College
Hawkins, Texas

Ralph W. E. Jones
Grambling College
Grambling, Louisiana

John T. King
Huston-Tillotson College
Austin, Texas

James R. Lawson
Fisk University
Nashville, Tennessee

Herman H. Long
Talladega College
Talladega, Alabama

Charles A. Lyons, Jr.
Fayetteville State University
Fayetteville, North Carolina

Albert E. Manley
Spelman College
Atlanta, Georgia

Hubert V. Manning
Claflin College
Orangeburg, South Carolina

William A. McMillan
Rust College
Holy Springs, Mississippi

John A. Middleton
Morris Brown College
Atlanta, Georgia

Isaac H. Miller, Jr.
Bennett College
Greensboro, North Carolina

Luna I. Mishoe
Delaware State College
Dover, Delaware

Richard V. Moore
Bethune-Cookman College
Daytona Beach, Florida

Richard D. Morrison
Alabama A & M University
Normal, Alabama

John B. Murphy
St. Phillips College
San Antonio, Texas

Samuel L. Myers
Bowie State College
Bowie, Maryland

M. Maceo Nance, Jr.
South Carolina State
Orangeburg, South Carolina

G. Leon Netterville, Jr.
Southern University
Baton Rouge, Louisiana

Lionel H. Newsome
  Central State University
  Wilberforce, Ohio

J. C. Oliver
  Arkansas Baptist College
  Little Rock, Arkansas

George A. Owens
  Tougaloo College
  Tougaloo, Mississippi

John A. Peoples, Jr.
  Jackson State College
  Jackson, Mississippi

Benjamin L. Perry, Jr.
  Florida A & M University
  Tallahassee, Florida

Lucius H. Pitts
  Paine College
  Augusta, Georgia

Royal W. Puryear
  Florida Memorial College
  Miami, Florida

Robert Randolph
  Westfield State College
  Westfield, Massachusetts

Edgar E. Rankin, Jr.
  Mississippi Industrial College
  Holy Springs, Mississippi

Luns Richardson
  Benedict College
  Columbia, South Carolina

Prezell R. Robinson
  St. Augustine's College
  Raleigh, North Carolina

Calvin B. Rock
  Oakwood College
  Huntsville, Alabama

James A. Russell, Jr.
  St. Paul's College
  Lawrenceville, Virginia

Wendell P. Russell
  Virginia State College
  Petersburg. Virginia

Stanley E. Rutland
  Paul Quinn College
  Waco, Texas

Granville M. Sawyer
  Texas Southern University
  Houston, Texas

F. George Shipman
  Livingstone College
  Salisbury, North Carolina

William E. Sims
  Langston University
  Langston, Oklahoma

M. C. Southerland
  Virginia College
  Lynchburg, Virginia

William B. Stewart
  Edward Waters College
  Jacksonville, Florida

Harold N. Stinson
  Stillman College
  Tuscaloosa, Alabama

Rembert E. Stokes
  Wilberforce University
  Wilberforce, Ohio

Herman Stone, Jr.
  Lane College
  Jackson, Tennessee

Alvin I. Thomas
  Prairie View A & M College
  Prairie View, Texas

Marion D. Thorpe
  Elizabeth City State University
  Elizabeth City, North Carolina

Andrew P. Torrence
  Tennessee State University
  Nashville, Tennessee

William J. L. Wallace
  West Virginia State College
  Institute, West Virginia

Walter Washington
  Alcorn A & M College
  Lorman, Mississippi

Levi Watkins
  Alabama State University
  Montgomery, Alabama

Clifton Wharton
  Michigan State University
  Lansing, Michigan

Raymon E. White
  Morristown Normal & Ind. College
  Morristown, Tennessee

Albert N. Whiting
  North Carolina Central University
  Durham, North Carolina

Kenneth R. Williams
  Winston-Salem State University
  Winston-Salem, North Carolina

W. C. Williams
  Miles College
  Birmingham, Alabama

Wade Wilson
  Cheyney State College
  Cheyney, Pennsylvania

Section XIV

POLITICS AND GOVERNMENT

BLACKS IN THE UNITED STATES CONGRESS
1869-1973

41st Congress, 1869–71
Joseph Hayne Rainey, South Carolina
b. Georgetown, S.C., June 21, 1832
d. Georgetown, S.C., Aug. 2, 1887
Jefferson F. Long, Georgia
b. Knoxville, Ga., March 3, 1836
d. Macon, Ga., Feb. 5, 1900
*Hiram Rhodes Revels, Mississippi
b. Fayetteville, N.C., Sept. 27, 1827
d. Aberdeen, Miss., Jan. 16, 1901
42nd Congress, 1871–73
Josiah Thomas Walls, Florida
b. Winchester, Va., Dec. 30, 1842
d. Tallahassee, Fla., May 5, 1905
Benjamin Sterling Turner, Alabama
b. Weldon, Halifax Co., N.C.,
      March 17, 1825
d. Selma, Alabama, March 21, 1894
Joseph Hayne Rainey, South Carolina
Robert Carlos DeLarge, South Carolina
b. Aiken, S.C., March 15, 1842
d. Charleston, S.C., Feb. 14, 1874
Robert Brown Elliott, South Carolina
b. Boston, Mass., August 11, 1842
d. New Orleans, La., August 9, 1884
43rd Congress 1873–75
Robert Brown Elliott, South Carolina
Richard Harvey Cain, South Carolina
b. Greenbrier County, Va., April 12, 1825
d. Washington, D.C., Jan. 18, 1887
Alonzo Jacob Ransier, South Carolina
b. Charleston, S.C., Jan. 3, 1834
d. Charleston, S.C., Aug. 17, 1882
Joseph Hayne Rainey, South Carolina
James Thomas Rapier, Alabama
b. Florence, Ala., Nov. 13, 1837
d. Montgomery, Ala., May 31, 1883
Josiah Thomas Walls, Florida
John R. Lynch, Mississippi
b. Vidalis, La., September 10, 1847
d. Chicago, Ill., November 2, 1939
44th Congress, 1875-77
John R. Lynch, Mississippi
*Blanche K. Bruce, Mississippi
b. Farmville, Va., March 1, 1841
d. Washington, D.C., March 17, 1898
Josiah Thomas Walls, Florida
Jeremiah Haralson, Alabama
b. Columbus, Ga., April 1, 1846
d. Denver, Colo., *ca.* 1916
John Adams Hyman, North Carolina
b. Warrenton, N.C., July 23, 1840

d. Washington, D.C., Sept. 14, 1891
Charles Edmund Nash, Louisiana
b. Opelousas, La., May 23, 1844
d. New Orleans, La., June 21, 1913
Robert Smalls, South Carolina
b. Beaufort, S.C., April 5, 1839
d. Beaufort, S.C., Feb. 22, 1915
45th Congress, 1877–79
Richard Harvey Cain, South Carolina
Joseph Hayne Rainey, South Carolina
Robert Smalls, South Carolina
*Blanche K. Bruce, Mississippi
46th Congress, 1879–81
*Blanche K. Bruce, Mississippi
47th Congress, 1881–83
Robert Smalls, South Carolina
48th Congress, 1883–85
Robert Smalls, South Carolina
James E. O'Hara, North Carolina
b. New York, N.Y., Feb. 26, 1844
d. New Bern, N.C., Sept. 15, 1905
49th Congress, 1885–87
Robert Smalls, South Carolina
James E. O'Hara, North Carolina
51st Congress, 1889–91
Henry Plummer Cheatham, North Carolina
b. Henderson, N.C., Dec. 27, 1857
d. Oxford, N.C., Nov. 29, 1935
Thomas Ezekiel Miller, South Carolina
b. Ferrebeville, S.C., June 17, 1849
d. Charleston, S.C., April 8, 1938
John Mercer Langston, Virginia
b. Louisa, Va., Dec. 14, 1829
d. Washington, D.C., Nov. 15, 1897
52nd Congress, 1891–93
Henry P. Cheatham, North Carolina
53rd Congress, 1893–95
George Washington Murray, South Carolina
b. Rembert, S.C., Sept. 22, 1853
d. Chicago, Ill., April 21, 1926
54th Congress, 1895–97
George Washington Murray, South Carolina
55th Congress, 1897–99
George H. White, North Carolina
b. Rosindale, N.C., Dec. 18, 1852
d. Philadelphia, Pa., Dec. 28, 1918
56th Congress, 1899–01
George H. White, North Carolina
71st Congress, 1929-31
Oscar DePriest, Illinois
b. Florence, Ala., March 9, 1871

d. Chicago, Ill., May 12, 1951
72nd Congress, 1931–33
Oscar DePriest, Illinois
73rd Congress, 1933–35
Oscar DePriest, Illinois
74th Congress, 1935–37
Arthur W. Mitchell, Illinois
b. Lafayette, Ala., Dec. 22, 1883
d. Petersburg, Va., May 7, 1968
75th Congress, 1937–39
Arthur W. Mitchell, Illinois
76th Congress, 1939–41
Arthur W. Mitchell, Illinois
77th Congress, 1941–43
Arthur W. Mitchell, Illinois
78th Congress, 1943–45
William L. Dawson, Illinois
b. Albany, Georgia, April 26, 1886
d. Chicago, Ill., Nov. 9, 1970
79th Congress, 1945–47
William L. Dawson, Illinois
Adam Clayton Powell, Jr., New York
b. New Haven, Conn., Nov. 29, 1908
d. Miami, Fla., April 4, 1972
80th Congress, 1947–49
William L. Dawson, Illinois
Adam Clayton Powell, Jr., New York
81st Congress, 1949–51
William L. Dawson, Illinois
Adam Clayton Powell, Jr., New York
82nd Congress, 1951–53
William L. Dawson, Illinois
Adam Clayton Powell, Jr., New York
83rd Congress, 1953–55
William L. Dawson, Illinois
Adam Clayton Powell, Jr., New York
84th Congress, 1955–57
William L. Dawson, Illinois
Adam Clayton Powell, Jr., New York
Charles C. Diggs, Michigan
b. Detroit, Mich., Dec. 2, 1922
85th Congress, 1957–59
William L. Dawson, Illinois
Adam Clayton Powell, Jr., New York
Charles C. Diggs, Michigan
86th Congress, 1959–61
William L. Dawson, Illinois
Adam Clayton Powell, Jr., New York
Charles C. Diggs, Michigan
Robert N. C. Nix, Pennsylvania
b. Orangeburg, S.C., August 9, 1905

87th Congress, 1961–63
William L. Dawson, Illinois
Adam Clayton Powell, Jr., New York
Charles C. Diggs, Michigan
Robert N. C. Nix, Pennsylvania
88th Congress, 1963–65
William L. Dawson, Illinois
Adam Clayton Powell, Jr., New York
Charles C. Diggs, Jr., Michigan
Robert N. C. Nix, Pennsylvania
Augustus Hawkins, California
b. Shreveport, La., Aug. 31, 1907
89th Congress, 1965–67
William L. Dawson, Illinois
Adam Clayton Powell, Jr., New York
Charles C. Diggs, Jr., Michigan
Robert N. C. Nix, Pennsylvania
Augustus Hawkins, California
John Conyers, Jr., Michigan
b. Detroit, Mich., May 16, 1929
90th Congress, 1967–69
*Edward W. Brooke, Massachusetts
b. Washington, D.C., Oct. 26, 1919
Augustus F. Hawkins, California
William L. Dawson, Illinois
Charles C. Diggs, Jr., Michigan
John Conyers, Jr., Michigan
Robert N. C. Nix, Pennsylvania
Adam Clayton Powell, Jr., New York
91st Congress, 1969–71
Augustus F. Hawkins, California
William L. Dawson, Illinois
Charles C. Diggs, Jr., Michigan
John Conyers, Jr., Michigan
Shirley Chisholm, New York
b. Brooklyn, N.Y., Nov. 30, 1924
Adam Clayton Powell, Jr., New York
Robert N. C. Nix, Pennsylvania
William L. Clay, Missouri
b. St. Louis, Mo., April 30, 1931
92nd Congress, 1971–73
Augustus F. Hawkins, California
Ronald V. Dellums, California
b. Oakland, Cal., Nov. 24, 1935
Ralph H. Metcalfe, Illinois
b. Atlanta, Ga., May 29, 1910
George W. Collins, Illinois
b. Chicago, Ill., March 25, 1925
d. Chicago, Ill., Dec. 8, 1972
Parren J. Mitchell, Maryland
b. Baltimore, Md., April 29, 1922
Charles C. Diggs, Jr., Michigan
John Conyers, Jr., Michigan

William L. Clay, Missouri
Shirley Chisholm, New York
Charles B. Rangel, New York
b. New York, N.Y., June 11, 1930
Louis Stokes, Ohio
b. Cleveland, Ohio, Feb. 25, 1925
Robert N. C. Nix, Pennsylvania
Walter E. Fauntroy, D.C. Delegate
b. Washington, D.C., Feb. 6, 1933
93rd Congress, 1973–75
Augustus F. Hawkins, California
Ronald V. Dellums, California
Yvonne Brathwaite Burke, California
b. Los Angeles, Calif., Oct. 5, 1932
Andrew J. Young, Georgia
b. New Orleans, La., March 12, 1932
Ralph H. Metcalfe, Illinois
George W. Collins, Illinois
(Elected but killed in airplane crash prior to induction of 93rd Congress).

Cardiss Collins, Special Election, June 5, 1973. (Won election to fill vacancy created by death of husband).
b. St. Louis, Mo., Sept. 24, 1931
Parren J. Mitchell, Maryland
*Edward W. Brooke, Massachusetts
Charles C. Diggs, Jr., Michigan
John Conyers, Jr., Michigan
William L. Clay, Missouri
Shirley Chisholm, New York
Charles B. Rangel, New York
Louis Stokes, Ohio
Robert N. C. Nix, Pennsylvania
Barbara Jordan, Texas
b. Houston, Tex., Feb. 21, 1936
Walter E. Fauntroy, D.C. Delegate

*-Served in U.S. Senate; all others House of Representatives.

BLACK MEMBERS OF CONGRESS

BROOKE, EDWARD B.W.

U.S. Senator from Massachusetts, (Republican), elected in 1966 and reelected in 1972. He is a graduate of Howard University (B.S., 1941) and Boston University Law School (LL.B., 1948: LL.M., 1950). He has received 21 honorary degrees. A U.S. Army captain in World War II, he served with the Partisans in Italy and was awarded the Bronze Star and the Combat Infantryman's Badge. He was elected attorney general of Massachusetts in 1962 and reelected in 1964 with a majority of almost 800,000 votes. He is a member of the Senate Banking, Housing and Urban Affairs committee, the Committee on Appropriations, the Select Committee on Equal Educational Opportunity and the Special Committee on Aging. His honors include the Charles Evans Hughes Award of the National Conference of Christians and Jews, the AMVETS Distinguished Service Award and the Spingarn Medal of the NAACP. He is a fellow of the American Academy of Arts and Sciences and of the American Bar Association.

BURKE, YVONNE BRATHWAITE

Congresswoman, was elected Nov. 7, 1972 as a member of the U.S. House of Representatives from California (Democrat, 37th District, Los Angeles). She was the first black woman ever elected to Congress from California and the first woman in 20 years elected to the House from the State. Previously, she was a member of the Cali-

fornia State Legislature (1966–72). Born Oct. 5, 1932 in Los Angeles, she is a graduate of UCLA (B.A., political science, 1953) and the University of Southern California School of Law (J.D., 1956). She began practicing law in Los Angeles in 1956, and was an attorney on the staff of the McCone Commission which investigated the Watts rebellions. She was a Fellow of the Institute of Politics at Harvard University.

CHISHOLM, SHIRLEY A.

Congresswoman, is a U.S. representative from New York's 12th district. A Democrat, she was first elected in 1969. In 1972, she conducted a vigorous national campaign for the Democratic presidential nomination. Born Nov. 30, 1924 in Brooklyn, N.Y., she is a graduate of Brooklyn College (B.A. cum laude) and Columbia University (M.A.). She also has honorary degrees from Talladega College (LL.D.), Hampton Institute (LL.D.), North Carolina Central College (L.H.D.) and Wilmington College (L.H.D.). Prior to her election to Congress, she was a teacher and director of Bureau of Child Welfare and a member of the New York State Assembly (1964–68).

CLAY, WILLIAM LACY

Congressman, is a Democratic member of the U.S. House of Representatives from the First District of Missouri (St. Louis). Born April 30, 1931 in St. Louis, he is a graduate of St. Louis University (B.S., history and political science, 1953). A former executive board member of the St. Louis Branch NAACP and a member of CORE, he organized hundreds of sit-ins and civil rights demonstrations and served 112 days in jail for contempt of court in one civil rights case. His credentials as a black activist for many years helped elect him to the St. Louis board of aldermen in 1959 and again in 1963. He was elected to Congress in 1968 and reelected in 1972. He is a member of the House Committee on Education and Labor, the Ad Hoc Task Force on Poverty, and the House Democratic Steering Committee on Interest Rates. He is vice president of the Democratic Study Group and is a member of that organization's civil rights task force.

COLLINS, CARDISS

Congresswoman from Illinois' 7th Congressional District (Democrat). She was born in 1931 in St. Louis and is a graduate of Northwestern University (B.A. business, 1967). She worked successively as secretary, accountant and revenue auditor with the Illinois Department of Revenue; she resigned in January, 1973, after announcing her candidacy for the congressional seat vacated upon the death of her husband, the late Congressman George W. Collins. She was elected to Congress in June, 1973.

CONYERS, JOHN

Congressman, a Democrat, is a U.S. representative from Michigan's first Congressional District. He was born May 16, 1929 in Detroit, Mich. He received his B.A. and LL.B. degrees from Wayne State University and spent his political apprenticeship as legislative assistant for three years to Congressman John Dingell. In addition to his duties as a senior partner in the firm of Conyers, Bell and Townsend, he served as referee for the Michigan Workmen's Compensation Department, general counsel for the Trade Union Leadership Council, and a President John F. Kennedy appointee to the National Lawyers Committee for Civil Rights Under Law. Elected to Congress in 1964, he was reelected to his fifth consecutive term in 1972. Rep. Conyers is the first black to serve on the House Judiciary Committee, was co-sponsor of the Johnson Administration's Medicare program, and is an organizer of the Congressional Black Caucus.

DELLUMS, RONALD V.

Congressman, is the U.S. representative from California (7th District). He was born Nov. 24, 1935 in Oakland, Calif. He received degrees from Oakland City College (associate of arts, 1958), San Francisco State College (B.A., 1960) and the University of California at Berkeley (M.A., social work, 1962). He has served in various local and state social agencies, and lectured part-time at San Francisco State and the University of California School of Social Work. Instead of obtaining a Ph.D. at Brandeis in social policy, as he had planned, Rep. Dellums was persuaded to enter politics and was elected to the Berkeley City Council in 1967. His coalition of minority groups and students, as well as Americans for Democratic Action, the AFL-CIO Committee on Political Education, and a number of prominent liberal Democrats backed his successful 1970 campaign for U.S. congressman. In the House, he sits on the Foreign Affairs Committee and the District of Columbia Committee, and, by 1972, had co-sponsored nearly 200 pieces of legislation. Racism in the military, increased minimum-wage levels, national health care, and child-care centers are among his priorities for congressional action.

DIGGS, CHARLES C., JR.

Congressman, is a member of the United States House of Representatives from Detroit, Mich. (Democrat, 13th District). He was born Dec. 2, 1922 in Detroit and is a graduate of Wayne State University (B.S.). He has honorary degrees from Central State College and Wilberforce University. Mr. Diggs was elected in 1954 as Michigan's first black member of Congress. Previously, he was a two-term member of the Michigan State Senate. He is president of the House of Diggs, Inc., a mortuary establishment in Detroit. He is chairman (1973) of the House District of Columbia Committee and the House Foreign Affairs Subcommittee on Africa. He is dean of the Michigan Democratic delegation, founder and former chairman of the Congressional Black Caucus, president of the National Black Political Assembly and a former vice-chairman of the Democratic National Committee.

FAUNTROY, WALTER E.

Congressman, a Democrat, is the U.S. Congressional Delegate (non-voting) from the District of Columbia. He was born Feb. 6, 1933 in Washington, D.C. and is a graduate of Virginia Union University (A.B., history, 1955) and Yale University Divinity School (B.D., 1968). He has honorary degrees from

Virginia Union University (D.D., 1968), Yale University (D.D., 1969) and Muskingum College (LL.D., 1971). Rep. Fauntroy was elected to Congress on March 23, 1971 and was reelected to a second term on November 7, 1972. He is also pastor of New Bethel Baptist Church in Washington, D.C. Mr. Fauntroy was director of the Washington Bureau of SCLC from 1960 to 1971. He was chairman of the Congressional Black Caucus Task Force for the 1972 Democratic National Convention and chairman of the Platform Committee of the board of directors of the Martin Luther King Jr. Center for Social Change, and is a member of the board of directors of SCLC. He is a member of the Yale University Council and of the board of trustees of Virginia Union University.

HAWKINS, AUGUSTUS F.

Congressman, a Democrat, has been a member of the U.S. House of Representatives of the 21st District of California since 1962. He was elected to his fifth term in 1972 with 94.5 percent of the vote, the highest percentage in the election. He was elected to the California State Assembly in 1934 and authored or co-authored more than 300 laws, including one establishing California's low-cost housing program and one which removed racial designations from all state documents. Born Aug. 31, 1907 in Shreveport, La., he graduated from the University of California (A.B., economics) and attended graduate classes at the University of Southern California Institute of Government. In Congress he is chairman of the House Sub-committee on Equal Opportunity, and serves on the Education and Labor Committee and the Committee on House Administration. Representing a district with one of the highest unemployment rates in the country, he has taken an especially keen interest in various proposals to provide jobs. He sponsored the Economic Opportunity Act, the Vocational Education Act and the Equal Employment Opportunity section of the 1964 Civil Rights Act. He has sponsored legislation to make reparations to survivors and families of the Brownsville (1906) incident.

JORDAN, BARBARA

Congresswoman, a Democrat, is U.S. representative from the 18th District of Texas (Houston). Born Feb. 21, 1936 in Houston, she is a graduate of Texas Southern University (B.A., magna cum laude, political science and history, 1956) and Boston University School of Law (LL.B., 1959; LL.D., 1969). Before her election to Congress in 1972, she had practiced law since 1959 and was elected a Texas state senator in 1966. She was the first black to serve in the Texas senate since 1883. Unanimously elected president pro tempore of the Texas legislature on March 28, 1972, she became the first black woman ever elected to preside over a legislative body in the United States. As a state senator, she drew praise from former president Lyndon B. Johnson as being "the epitome of the new politics in Texas." She was instrumental in defeating a highly restrictive voter registration act, in giving Texas its first minimum wage law ($1.25 per hour), in bringing the first raise in workmen's compensation in 12 years, and in setting up the state's department of community affairs. She is the first black person to be elected to Congress from Texas.

METCALFE, RALPH H.

Congressman, a Democrat, was elected in 1970 as a member of the U.S. House of Representatives from Illinois (1st District, Chicago). Previously, he was a member and President pro-tem of the Chicago City Council (1955–71). Born May 29, 1910 in Atlanta, Ga., he is a graduate of Marquette University (B.Ph., 1936) and the University of Southern California (M.A., physical education, 1939). A former world famous athlete, he was a member of the U.S. track teams in the 1932 and 1936 Olympics. He was track coach and political science instructor at Xavier University in New Orleans, La. (1936–42). He was also director of the department of civil rights for the Chicago Commission on Human Relations (1945–49), and commissioner for the Illinois Athletic Commission (1949–52). He is founder of the Ralph H. Metcalfe Foundation in Chicago and director of the Illinois Federal Savings & Loan Association.

MITCHELL, PARREN J.

Congressman, a Democrat, is a member of the U.S. House of Representatives. He was elected in 1970 from the 7th Congressional District in Baltimore, Md. Previously, he was professor of sociology and assistant director of the Urban Studies Institute at Morgan State College (1968–70); executive secretary of the Maryland Committee on interracial Problems and Relations (1963–65); and supervisor of a program for Post Sentence Case Work for the Domestic

Relations Division of the Supreme Bench of Baltimore (1956–63). He also has served as sociology instructor at Morgan State College and as a probation officer. Born April 29, 1922 in Baltimore, Md., he is a graduate of the University of Maryland (M.A., sociology, 1952), and Morgan State College (A.B., sociology, 1950), and has taken courses at the doctoral level in sociology at the University of Connecticut. Awarded the Purple Heart in World War II, he was a leader of anti-war protests sponsored by the Moratorium Committee and John Hopkins University in 1970.

NIX, ROBERT N. C.

Congressman, a Democrat, has been a member of the U.S. House of Representatives since 1958. He represents the 2nd District of Pennsylvania (Philadelphia). He is a member of the House committees on Foreign Affairs, and Post Office and Civil Service. Born Aug. 9, 1905 in Orangeburg, S.C., he is a graduate of Lincoln University (A.B., 1921) and the University of Pennsylvania Law School (LL.B., 1924), and has been a practicing attorney since 1925. He is a member of numerous professional and civic organizations, including the Philadelphia Bar Association, the NAACP, the YMCA, and Omega Psi Phi fraternity. He was elected as 44th Ward executive committeeman, 9th division, in 1923 and has been consistently reelected.

RANGEL, CHARLES B.

Congressman, a Democrat, is a U.S. representative from New York City. Born June 11, 1930 in New York City, he is a graduate of New York University School of Commerce (B.S., 1957) and St. John's University School of Law (1960). In 1961, he was appointed assistant U.S. attorney for the Southern District of New York, and served as associate counsel to the speaker of the New York State Assembly, as well as the general counsel to the National Advisory Commission on Selective Service. In 1966–70, he served two terms in the New York State Assembly, the 72nd Assembly District (Central Harlem), and in 1969 he was a candidate for president of the New York City Council in the Democratic primaries.

STOKES, LOUIS

Congressman, a Democrat, is a member of the U.S. House of Representatives from the twenty-first Congressional District in Cleveland, Ohio. Congressman Stokes, a brother of former Cleveland Mayor Carl Stokes, is the first black to serve on the House Appropriations Committee. On Feb. 8, 1972, he was elected chairman of the congressional Black Caucus, consisting of the fifteen black members of the House of Representatives. Born Feb. 25, 1925 in Cleveland, he has degrees from Western Reserve University (B.A.) and Cleveland Marshall Law School (J.D.). In addition, he holds honorary degrees from Wilberforce University and Shaw University. Prior to being elected to his first term in office in November, 1968, Congressman Stokes was a practicing attorney in Cleveland. Active in civil rights and legal groups, he is currently on the executive board of the Cleveland branch of the NAACP and a member of the American Civil Liberties Union. He serves on the board of the Cleveland Bar Association and Cleveland State University.

YOUNG, ANDREW J.

Congressman, was elected in 1972 as a Democratic member of the U.S. House of Representatives from Georgia. Born March 12, 1932 in New Orleans, La., he attended Dillard University (1947–48) and is a graduate of Howard University (B.S., 1951) and Hartford Theological Seminary B.D., 1955). He is an ordained minister in the United Church of Christ and was pastor of various churches from 1952 to 1957. He was associate director of SCLC (1964–68) and executive vice president of SCLC (1968–71). He has won numerous awards for his civil rights work. He is chairman of the board of the Delta Ministry of Mississippi and is a board member of a number of organizations. He is the first black to be elected to Congress from Georgia since 1870.

BLACK STATE SENATORS AND REPRESENTATIVES

ALABAMA

Representatives
Gray, Fred D. (Dem.)
Reed, Thomas J. (Dem.)

ALASKA

Representatives
Bowman, Willard
Carroll, Selwyn

ARIZONA

Representatives
Hamilton, Art (Dem.)
Thompson, Leon (Dem.)

ARKANSAS

Senators
Jewell, Dr. Jerry D. (Dem.)

Representatives
Mays, Richard Leon (Dem.)
Townsend, Dr. William H. (Dem.)
Wilkins, Henry III (Dem.)

CALIFORNIA

Senators
Dymally, Mervyn M. (Dem.)

Representatives
Brown, Willie L., Jr. (Dem.)
Dixon, Julian C. (Dem.)
Greene, Bill (Dem.)
Holoman, Frank (Dem.)
Miller, John J. (Dem.)
Ralph, Leon D. (Dem.)

COLORADO

Senators
Brown, George L. (Dem.)

Representatives
Pettie, Floyd W. (Rep.)
Taylor, Arie (Dem.)
Webb, Wellington (Dem.)

CONNECTICUT

Senators
Smith, Wilber G. (Dem.)

Representatives
Billington, Clyde (Dem.)
Branner, James H., III
Brown, Otha N., Jr.
Frazier, Leonard G.
Giles, Abraham
Morris, Bruce L.
Morton, Margaret E.

DELAWARE

Senators
Holloway, Herman M., Sr. (Dem.)

Representatives
Johnson, Henrietta
McCluney, Amos B.

FLORIDA

Representatives
Cherry, Gwen Sawyer (Dem.)
Kershaw, Joe Lang
Singleton, Mary L. (Dem.)

GEORGIA

Senators
Johnson, Leroy R. (Dem.)
Ward, Horace T. (Dem.)

Representatives
Alexander, William H.
Blackshear, Rev. Jessie
Bond, Julian (Dem.)
Brown, Benjamin D. (Dem.)
Clark, Betty J.
Daugherty, J.C.
Dean, James E.
Dent, R. A.
Ezzard, Clarence G., Sr.
Hamilton, Grace T.
Hill, Bobby L.
McKinney, James E.
Sheperd, E. J.
Thompson, Albert W. (Dem.)

ILLINOIS

Senators
Chew, Charles, Jr. (Dem.)
Hall, Kenneth (Dem.)
Newhouse, Richard A. (Dem.)
Partee, Cecil A. (Dem.)
Smith, Fred J. (Dem.)

Representatives
Barnes, Eugene M.
Caldwell, Lewis A. H.
Carter, Richard A.
Davis, Corneal A. (Dem.)
Ewell, Raymond W. (Dem.)
Holloway, Robert H.
Jones, Emil, Jr.
Martin, Peggy Smith (Dem.)
McLendon, James A.
Patrick, Langdon
Sims, Isaac R.
Taylor, James C.
Thompson, Robert L.
Washington, Harold

INDIANA

Senators
Clay, Rudolph (Dem.)

Representatives
Alexander, William L.
Carson, Julia
Crawford, William
Crowe, Ray P.
Freeland, Robert
Harris, Jewell G.

IOWA

Representatives
Hargrave, William J., Jr. (Dem.)

KANSAS

Senators
McCray, Billy Q. (Dem.)

Representatives
Anderson, Eugene
Cribbs, Theo
Justice, Norman E.
Love, Clarence C.

KENTUCKY

Senators
Davis, Georgia M. (Dem.)

Representatives
Kidd, Mae Street
McGill, Charlotte S.

LOUISIANA

Representatives
Charbonnet, Louis, III
Connor, George C., Jr.
Jackson, Alphonse, Jr.
Jackson, Johnny, Jr.
Jones, Johnnie A.
Marchand, Theodore J.
Taylor, Dorothy Mae
Turnley, Richard, Jr.

MAINE

Representatives
Talbot, Gerald Edgarton

MARYLAND

Senators
Blount, Clarence W. (Dem.)
Dalton, Robert L.
Mitchell, Clarence, III (Dem.)
Welcome, Verda F.

Representatives
Allen, Dr. Aris T. (Rep.)
Boswell, Hildagardeis
Brailey, Troy
Chester, Joseph A., Sr. (Dem.)
Conaway, Frank M.
Dean, Walter Raleigh, Jr. (Dem.)
Dixon, Isaiah, Jr.
Douglass, Calvin A.
Douglass, John W.
King, Arthur A.
Lee, Lena K. (Dem.)
Randolph, Lloyal
Scott, James A., Jr.
Webster, Kenneth L. (Dem.)

MASSACHUSETTS

Representatives
Bolling, Royal, Sr.
Bunte, Doris
King, Melvin H.
Owens, William

MICHIGAN

Senators
Brown, Basil W. (Dem.)
Cartwright, Arthur
Young, Coleman A.

Representatives
Bradley, James
Edwards, George H.
Elliott, Daisy
Ferguson, Rosetta
Harrison, Charles, Jr.
Holmes, David S., Jr.
Hood, Morris, Jr.
Hood, Raymond W.
McNeeley, Matthew
Nelson, Earl
Saunders, Nelis J.
Stallworth, Alma G.
Vaughn, Jackie, III

MINNESOTA

Senators
Lewis, Dr. B. Robert (Dem.)

Representatives
Pleasant, Ray O.

MISSISSIPPI

Representatives
Clark, Robert G.

MISSOURI

Senators
Howard, Raymond (Dem.)
Payne, Franklin

Representatives
Aiken, Johnnie S.
Banks, J.B.
Calloway, DeVerne Lee
Carrington, James M.
Curls, Philip B.
Goward, Russell
Holliday, Harold, Sr.
Jordan, Orchid I.
Martin, Harold J., Sr.
McKamey, Leo
Quarles, Raymond
Rivers, Nathaniel J.
Williams, Fred

NEBRASKA

Senators
Chambers, Ernest W.

NEVADA

Senators
Neal, Joe (Dem.)

Representatives
Bennett, The Reverend Marion D. (Dem.)
Crawford, Cranford L., Jr.

NEW JERSEY

Senators
Lipman, Wynona M. (Dem.)

Representatives
Hawkins, Eldridge
Hicks, William H.
Owens, Ronald
Richardson, George C.
Wilkerson, Dr. William G.
Woodson, The Reverend S. Howard, Jr. (Dem.)

NEW MEXICO

Representatives
Malry, Lenton

NEW YORK

Senators
Beatty, Vander L. (Dem.)
Galiber, Joseph L.
Garcia, Robert
Van Luther, Sidney A. (Dem.)

Representatives
Brewer, Guy
Diggs, Estelle B.
Eve, Arthur O.
Fortune, Thomas R.
Gray, Jesse
Griffith, Edward
Lewis, Woodrow
Miller, George W.
Southall, Mark T.
Williams, Calvin
Wright, Samuel D.

NORTH CAROLINA

Representatives
Frye, Henry E.
Johnson, The Reverend Joy Joseph
Micheaux, Henry McKinley, Jr.

OHIO

Senators
Bowen, William F. (Dem.)
Jackson, M. Morris (Dem.)

Representatives
Bell, Thomas M.
Hale, The Reverend Phale D.
James, Troy Lee
Jones, Casey
Mallory, William L.
McLin, C. J., Jr.
Rankin, James W.
Thompson, Ike
Thompson, John D., Jr.

OKLAHOMA

Senators
Porter, E. Melvin (Dem.)

Representatives
Atkins, Hannah Diggs
Johnson, A. Visanio
McIntyre, Bernard J.

OREGON

Representatives
McCoy, William

PENNSYLVANIA

Senators
Arlene, Herbert (Dem.)
Hankins, Freeman (Dem.)

Representatives
Barber, James D.
Blackwell, Lucien E.
Hammock, Charles P.
Irvis, K. Leroy
Johnson, Joel J.
Melton, Mitchell W.
Rhodes, Joseph, Jr.
Richardson, David P.
Shelton, Ulysses
Vann, Earl
Williams, Hardy

RHODE ISLAND

Representatives
Coelho, Peter, J.

SOUTH CAROLINA

Representatives
Fielding, Herbert Ulysses
Finney, Ernest Adolphus, Jr.
Gordan, Rev. Benjamin
Johnson, I. S. Leevy
Woods, Robert, Jr.

TENNESSEE

Senators
Patterson, J. O., Jr. (Dem.)
Williams, Avon N., Jr.

Representatives
Brewer, Harper, Jr.
DeBerry, Lois
Ford, Harold
King, Alvin
Love, Harold M.
Murphy, I. H.
Pruitt, Charles W.

TEXAS

Representatives
Hall, Anthony
Hudson, Samuel W., III
Johnson, Eddie Bernice
Leland, George M.
Ragsdale, Paul
Sutton, G.J.
Thompson, Sefronia
Washington, Craig A., Sr.

VIRGINIA

Senators
Wilder, Lawrence Douglas
Representatives
Reid, William Ferguson
Robinson, Dr. William P., Sr.

WASHINGTON

Senators
Fleming, George
Representatives
Maxie, Peggie Joan

WEST VIRGINIA

Representatives
Moore, Ernest C.

WISCONSIN

Senators
Swan, Monroe (Dem.)

Representatives
Barbee, Lloyd A.
Ward, Walter, Jr.

BLACKS IN U.S. FOREIGN SERVICE

Ambassadors

Adams, Dr. Samuel, Assistant Administrator for African Agency for International Development

Carter, W. Beverly, Ambassador to Tanzania

Ferguson, Clyde C., Ambassador to U.N. Economic and Social Council

Fox, Richard, Deputy Assistant Secretary of State for Cultural Affairs

Haley, George, Assistant Director of U.S. Information Agency (USIA)

Nelson, Charles, Ambassador to Botswana, Lesotho, Swaziland

Reinhardt, Dr. John A., Ambassador to Nigeria

Todman, Terence A., Ambassador to Guinea

Watson, Barbara, Assistant Secretary of State for Consular Affairs

Black Legislators and Blacks Elected to Other Public Office: 1964, 1968, 1970, and 1972

SUBJECT	1964	1968	1970	1972
Total.................................	103	1,125	1,860	2,625
United States Senate:				
United States..........................	0	1	1	1
South................................	0	0	0	0
House of Representatives:				
United States..........................	5	9	13	15
South................................	0	0	2	4
State Legislatures:				
United States:.........................	94	172	198	238
South................................	16	53	70	90
Mayors:				
United States..........................	(NA)	29	81	83
South................................	(NA)	17	47	49
Other:[1]				
United States..........................	(NA)	914	1,567	2,288
South................................	(NA)	468	763	1,242

Note: Figures for the years 1964 and 1968 represent the total number of elected blacks holding office at that time, not just those elected in those years. The 1970 and 1972 figures represent the number of elected blacks holding office as of March 1971 and March 1973, respectively. NA Not available.
[1] Includes all black elected officials not included in first four categories.
Source: Potomac Institute and Joint Center for Political Studies.

BLACK FEDERAL JUDGES

PRESIDENT FRANKLIN D. ROOSEVELT 1933-1945
Judge William H. Hastie
  Virgin Islands   1937
Judge Herman E. Moore
  Virgin Islands   1939
PRESIDENT HARRY S. TRUMAN 1945-1953
*Judge Irvin C. Mollison
  Customs Court   1945
Judge Herman E. Moore (a)
  Virgin Islands   1949
Judge William H. Hastie
  3rd Circuit Court of Appeals   1949
PRESIDENT DWIGHT D. EISENHOWER 1953-1961
Judge Scovel Richardson
  Customs Court   1957
Judge Walter Gordon
  Virgin Islands   1958
PRESIDENT JOHN F. KENNEDY 1961-1963
Judge James B. Parsons
  Illinois   1961
Judge Wade H. McCree
  Michigan   1961
Judge Thurgood Marshall
  2nd Circuit Court of Appeals   1961
PRESIDENT LYNDON B. JOHNSON 1963-1969
Judge A. Leon Higginbotham
  Pennsylvania   1964
Judge Spottswood Robinson
  D.C.   1964
Judge William B. Bryant
  D.C.   1965
Judge Aubrey Robinson
  D.C.   1966
Judge Spottswood Robinson
  D.C. Circuit Court of Appeals   1966
Judge Constance B. Motley
  New York   1966
Judge Wade H. McCree
  6th Circuit Court of Appeals   1966
Judge James L. Watson
  Customs Court   1966
Judge Thurgood Marshall
  U.S. Supreme Court   1967
Judge Joseph C. Waddy
  D.C.   1967
Judge Damon Keith
  Michigan   1967
PRESIDENT RICHARD M. NIXON 1969-
Judge Almeric Christian
  Virgin Islands   1969
Judge Barrington Parker
  D.C.   1969
Judge David Williams
  California   1969
Judge Clifford Scott Green
  Pennsylvania   1971
Judge Lawrence W. Pierce
  New York   1971

Judge Robert L. Carter
  New York   1972
Judge Robert Duncan
  Military Court of Appeals   1972

D.C. COURTS

PRESIDENT THEODORE ROOSEVELT 1901-1909
Judge Robert H. Terrell   1901
Judge Robert H. Terrell (a)   1905
PRESIDENT WILLIAM H. TAFT 1909-1913
Judge Robert H. Terrell (a)   1910
PRESIDENT WOODROW WILSON 1913-1921
Judge Robert H. Terrell (a)   1914
Judge Robert H. Terrell (a)   1918
PRESIDENT WARREN G. HARDING 1921-1923
*Judge Robert H. Terrell (a)   1922
PRESIDENT CALVIN COOLIDGE 1923-1929
Judge James A. Cobb   1926
PRESIDENT HERBERT C. HOOVER 1929-1933
*Judge James A. Cobb (a)   1930
PRESIDENT FRANKLIN D. ROOSEVELT 1933-1945
Judge Armond W. Scott   1935
Judge Armond W. Scott (a)   1939
*Judge Armond W. Scott (a)   1943
PRESIDENT HARRY S. TRUMAN 1945-1953
*Judge Emory Smith   1950
*Judge Andrew Howard   1950
PRESIDENT DWIGHT D. EISENHOWER 1953-1961
Judge Austin Fickling   1956
PRESIDENT JOHN F. KENNEDY 1961-1963
Judge Joseph C. Waddy   1962
Judge Marjorie M. Lawson   1962
Judge Andrew Howard (a)   1962
PRESIDENT LYNDON B. JOHNSON 1963-1969
Judge Aubrey Robinson   1965
Judge Austin Fickling (a)   1966
Judge Harry T. Alexander   1967
Judge Richard Atkinson   1967
Judge John D. Fauntleroy   1967
*Judge Arthur Christopher   1967
Judge William C. Pryor   1968
Judge Austin Fickling
  (D.C. Court of Appeals)   1968
PRESIDENT RICHARD M. NIXON 1969-
Judge William S. Thompson   1969
Judge Normalie Johnson   1970
Judge Eugene Hamilton   1970
Judge Theodore Newman   1970
Judge John G. Penn   1970
Judge James A. Washington   1970
Judge Hubert Pair
  (D.C. Court of Appeals)   1970
Judge George Draper   1972
Judge Margaret Haywood   1972
Judge Robert Campbell   1972
Judge Luke C. Moore   1972
Judge H. Carl Moultrie   1972

*Deceased   (a) Reappointment

NATIONAL ROSTER OF BLACK JUDGES

FEDERAL JUDGES

SUPREME COURT OF U.S.
Hon. Thurgood Marshall
Associate Justice, Supreme Court
of the United States
Washington, D.C.

U.S. COURT OF APPEALS
Hon. Spottswood W. Robinson
U.S. Court of Appeals for District
of Columbia, Washington, D.C.
Hon. William Henry Hastie
Senior Judge, U.S. Court of
Appeals, Third Circuit, Phila. Pa.
Hon. Robert M. Duncan
U.S. Court of Military Appeals
450 E. Street, N.W.
Washington, D.C. 20442
Hon. Wade H. McCree, Jr.
U.S. Court of Appeals, Sixth
Circuit, Federal Bldg., Detroit

U.S. CUSTOMS COURT
Hon. Scovel Richardson, N.Y. City
Hon. James L. Watson, N.Y. City

U.S. DISTRICT COURT
District of Columbia
Hon. William B. Bryant
Hon. Aubrey E. Robinson
Hon. Joseph C. Waddy
Hon. Barrington D. Parker
New York City
Hon. Constance B. Motley
Hon. Lawrence W. Pierce
Hon. Robert Carter
Philadelphia
Hon. Clifford Scott Green
Hon. A. Leon Higginbotham, Jr.
Chicago
Hon. James B. Parsons
Hon. Damon J. Keith, Detroit
Hon. David W. Williams,
Los Angeles
Hon. Almeric Christian,
Virgin Islands

U.S. Magistrates
Hon. Arthur L. Burnett
Washington, D.C.
Hon. Willie J. Davis
Boston, Mass.
Hon. Joseph W. Hatchett
Jacksonville, Fla.
Hon. Calvin T. Pryor
Montgomery, Ala.

Referees in Bankruptcy
Hon. Harry Hackett, Detroit
Hon. Edward B. Toles, Chicago
ALABAMA
Hon. Orzell Billingsley, Jr.
Roosevelt City, Ala.
Hon. Peter A. Hall, Birmingham
Hon. Demetrius C. Newton
Brighton
Hon. Charles S. Connally
Tuskegee
Hon. William McKinley Branch
Greene County
ARIZONA
Hon. H. B. Daniels
Phoenix
CALIFORNIA
Los Angeles
Hon. Edwin L. Jefferson,
California Court of Appeals
Hon. Sherman W. Smith
Los Angeles
Hon. Bernard Jefferson
Hon. Thomas L. Griffith, Jr.
Hon. Vaino Spencer
Hon. Gilbert Alston
Hon. Harold Sinclair
Hon. Zenophan Lang
Hon. Everett Porter
Compton
Hon. Huey Shepard
Hon. Albert Matthew
Hon. Everett Ricks
Hon. Lionel Wilson, Oakland
Hon. Joseph Kennedy, San Francisco
Hon. William A. Ross, Norwalk
Hon. Earl C. Broady, Torrance
Hon. Raymond J. Reynolds,
San Francisco
Hon. Allen Broussard, Oakland
Hon. George Carroll, Richmond
Hon. Earl B. Gilliam, San Diego
Commissioners
Los Angeles
Hon. James N. Reese
Hon. William R. Clay
Hon. Consuelo B. Marshall
Hon. Donald Pitts
Hon. Homer Garrott
Norwalk
Hon. Giles Jackson
Hon. H. Randolph Moore
COLORADO
Denver
Hon. Gilbert Alexander
Hon. James Flanigan
Hon. Morris E. Cole

CONNECTICUT
Hon. Arthur G. Williams, Madison
Hon. Robert L. Levister, Stamford
Hon. Robert D. Glass, Torrington
DELAWARE
Hon. Leonard Williams, Wilmington
DISTRICT OF COLUMBIA
Court of Appeals of the
District of Columbia
Hon. Hubert Pair
Hon. Austin L. Fickling
Superior Court of the
District of Columbia
Hon. Harry T. Alexander
Hon. Eugene N. Hamilton
Hon. Norma Holloway Johnson
Hon. Theodore R. Newman, Jr.
Hon. John Garrett Penn
Hon. James A. Washington, Jr.
Hon. William S. Thompson
Hon. Margaret Haywood
Hon. Luke C. Moore
Hon. Robert Campbell
Hon. John D. Fauntleroy
Hon. Richard R. Atkinson
Hon. H. Carl Moultrie
FLORIDA
Hon. Thomas J. Reddick,
  Ft. Lauderdale
Hon. Harold R. Braynon, Miami
Hon. James Wesley Matthews,
  City of Opalocka
GEORGIA
Hon. R. Pruden Herndon, Atlanta
Hon. Romae Turner Powell, Atlanta
Hon. Edith Jacqueline Ingram, Sparta
Hon. Redwin Thomas, Atlanta
Hon. J. L. Jordan, Atlanta
ILLINOIS
Illinois Appellate Court
Chicago
Hon. George N. Leighton
Hon. Glenn T. Johnson
Full Circuit Court Judges, Chicago
Hon. Archibald J. Carey
Hon. James D. Crosson
Hon. Russell D. Debow
Hon. Richard A. Harewood
Hon. Mark E. Jones
Hon. Sidney A. Jones, Jr.
Hon. Maurice Pompey
Hon. Albert S. Porter
Hon. Edith S. Sampson
Hon. Earl Strayhorn
Hon. William S. White
Hon. Kenneth Wilson
Associate Circuit Court Judges, Chicago
Hon. Edwin C. Hatfield
Hon. E. C. Johnson

Hon. Earl J. Neal
Hon. Alvin Turner
Hon. James M. Walton
Hon. Willie Whiting
Hon. Richard Cooper
Hon. Charles Durham
Hon. Arthur Hamilton
Hon. William E. Peterson
Downstate
Hon. Billy Jones, East St. Louis
Hon. Ora Polk, East St. Louis
Hon. Louis K. Fontenot, Kankakee
INDIANA
Indianapolis
Hon. Rufus C. Kuykendall
Hon. Wilbur H. Grant
Hon. Clarence D. Bolden
Hon. Frederick T. Work, Gary
IOWA
Hon. Luther Glanton, Des Moines
KANSAS
Hon. Cordell Meeks, Kansas City
Hon. Myles C. Stevens, Kansas City
KENTUCKY
Louisville
Hon. Neville M. Tucker
Hon. D. Edward Turner
Hon. Charles H. Anderson
Hon. Darryl T. Owens
Hon. Benjamin F. Shobe
Hon. Prather Walker, Lexington
LOUISIANA
New Orleans
Hon. Israel Augustine
Hon. Ernest N. Morial,
  Court of Appeals
Hon. Robert F. Collins
MARYLAND
Supreme Bench of Baltimore City
Hon. Joseph C. Howard
Hon. Harry A. Cole
Hon. Robert B. Watts
Municipal Court of Baltimore City
Hon. John R. Hargrove
Hon. William H. Murphy
Hon. Solomon Baylor
Probate Court—Baltimore
Hon. Benjamin Forman
Hon. James H. Taylor,
  Upper Marlboro
Hon. Henry P. Johnson,
  Upper Marlboro
MASSACHUSETTS
Boston
Hon. Joseph Mitchell
Hon. David Nelson
Hon. G. Bruce Robinson
Hon. Harry J. Elam
Hon. Elwood S. McKenny

Hon. Richard Banks
Hon. James W. Bailey,
East Cambridge
MICHIGAN
Circuit Courts
Hon. Charles S. Farmer, Detroit
Hon. Ollie B. Bivins, Jr., Flint
Hon. John T. Letts, Grand Rapids
Recorder's Court—Detroit
Hon. Geo. W. Crockett, Jr.
Hon. Elvin L. Davenport
Hon. James Del Rio
Hon. Robert L. Evans
Hon. Geraldine B. Ford
Hon. Samuel C. Gardner
Hon. William C. Hague
Hon. Henry L. Heading, Recorder
Hon. Clarence Laster, Jr.
Probate Court
Hon. Willis F. Ward, Detroit
Common Pleas Court—Detroit
Hon. Frederick E. Byrd
Hon. Donald L. Hobson
Hon. Harold Hood
Hon. Julian P. Rodgers, Jr.
District Court
Hon. Charles A. Pratt, Kalamazoo
Hon. William S. Price, III, Flint
Hon. Christopher Brown, Pontiac
MINNESOTA
Hon. Stephen L. Maxwell, St. Paul
MISSOURI
St. Louis
Hon. Theodore McMilliam
Hon. Daniel T. Tillman
Hon. William S. Diguid
Hon. John W. Harvey
Hon. Frank S. Bledsoe
Kansas City
Hon. Lewis Clymer
Hon. Clifford Spotsville
Hon. Robert Smith, Kinloch
NEBRASKA
Hon. Elizabeth Pittman, Omaha
NEVADA
Hon. Robert E. Mullen, Las Vegas
NEW HAMPSHIRE
Hon. Ivorey Cobb, Colebrook
NEW JERSEY
Workmen's Compensation Court
Hon. James H. Coleman, Jr.,
Newark
Superior Court
Camden
Hon. Robert B. Johnson
Hon. Van Y. Clinton
County Court
Hon. William Fillmore Wood,
Elizabeth

Juvenile & Domestic Relations Court
Hon. Herbert H. Tate, Newark
Municipal Court of Newark
Hon. Harvey Hazelwood, Jr.
Hon. Irving B. Booker
Hon. Chester A. Morrison
Hon. Milton A. Buck
Municipal Courts
Hon. John J. Teare, East Orange
Hon. Samuel C. Scott, Jersey City
Hon. Anne E. Thompson, Trenton
NEW YORK
New York City
Hon. Harold A. Stevens
Appellate Division
First Judicial Department
Supreme Court, First District
Hon. Amos Bowman
Hon. Thomas Dickens
Hon. Edward R. Dudley
Hon. Jawn A. Sandifer
Hon. Ivan Warner
Hon. Manuel C. Gomez
Hon. Oliver C. Sutton
Hon. Herbert B. Evans
Supreme Court, Second District
Hon. Oliver D. Williams
Hon. Franklin W. Morton, Jr.
Hon. Thomas R. Jones
Criminal Court of New York
Hon. Julius Archibald (Retired)
Hon. William H. Booth
Hon. Dennis Edwards, Jr.
Hon. Walter Gladwin
Hon. Maurice Grey
Hon. William H. Loguen
Hon. Claudius S. Matthews
Hon. Albert R. Murray
Hon. Thomas G. Weaver
Hon. James M. Yeargin
Hon. Bruce Wright
Hon. John Carro (Puerto Rican)
Hon. Antonio S. Figueroa (Puerto Rican)
Hon. Mary Johnson Lowe
Hon. Eugene Sharpe
Family Court of New York
Hon. Jane M. Bolin
Hon. Joseph E. Dyer
Hon. Phillip D. Roache
Hon. Harold Wood
Hon. Reginald S. Matthews
Hon. Edith Miller
Hon. Emanuel G. Guerreiro (Puerto Rican)
Hon. Gilbert Ramirez (Puerto Rican)
Hon. Cesar H. Quinones (Puerto Rican)
Civil Court of New York
Hon. Howard E. Bell
Hon. Henry Bramwell
Hon. Kenneth Browns

Hon. Jose Ramos Lopez (Puerto Rican)
Hon. Charles B. Lawrence
Hon. George M. Fleary
Hon. Clifford A. Scott
Hon. James H. Shaw, Jr.
Hon. Samuel A. Welcome
Hon. Albert P. Williams
Hon. Fritz M. Alexander III
Hon. David Edwards
Hon. Robert J. Mangum
Hon. Harding, Buffalo
Hon. Marquette Floyd, Babylon
Hon. Richard L. Baltimore, Jr.,
  New Rochelle
Hon. Harold Woods, New Rochelle

NORTH CAROLINA
Hon. Samuel Chess, High Point
Hon. Elreta Alexander, Greensboro
Hon. Clifton E. Johnson, Charlotte

OHIO
Court of Appeals
Hon. Leo A. Jackson, Cleveland

Court of Common Pleas
Cleveland
Hon. Perry B. Jackson
Hon. George W. White
Hon. Lloyd O. Brown
Hon. Arthur Fisher, Dayton
Hon. Ira Turpin, Canton
Hon. Robert L. Franklin, Toledo

Municipal Court, Cleveland
Hon. Lillian W. Burke
Hon. Theodore M. Williams
Hon. Clarence Gaines
Hon. Sara J. Harper
Hon. Lloyd Haynes, Youngstown
Hon. Bush P. Mitchell, Dayton
Hon. James A. Pearson, Columbus
Hon. Joseph Rhoulac, Akron
Hon. Jack Franklin, Ottawa Hills

OKLAHOMA
Hon. Charles L. Owens,
  Oklahoma City
Hon. Cecil Robertson, Muscogee

OREGON
Hon. Mercedes F. Deiz, Portland
Hon. Aaron Brown, Jr., Portland

PENNSYLVANIA
Hon. Robert N. C. Nix, Jr.
  Supreme Court of Pennsylvania
  Philadelphia
  Superior Court of Pennsylvania
  Philadelphia

Common Pleas, Philadelphia
Hon. Thomas Reed
Hon. Robert Williams
Hon. Raymond Pace Alexander
Hon. Herbert R. Cain

Hon. Juanita Kidd Stout
Hon. Charles Wright
Hon. Julian F. King
Hon. Calvin T. Wilson
Hon. Curtis C. Carson
Hon. Harvey Schmidt
Hon. Doris M. Harris
Hon. Norman A. Jenkins
Hon. Matthew W. Bullock, Jr.

Common Pleas (Delaware County)
Hon. Robert A. Wright

Common Pleas (Pittsburgh)
Hon. Homer S. Brown
Hon. Henry R. Smith, Jr.
Hon. Warren Watson
Hon. Thomas A. Harper
Hon. Livingston M. Johnson

Municipal Court (Philadelphia)
Hon. Harry Melton
Hon. Edward S. Cox
Hon. Paul Dandridge

District Magistrates—Pittsburgh
Hon. Jacob Williams
Hon. Walter Wilson
Hon. John Chandler
Hon. Joseph W. Givens

SOUTH CAROLINA
Hon. Richard E. Fields, Charleston
Hon. Thelma Cook, Winnsboro
Hon. Eddie Kline, Seabrook
Hon. Earnest Yarborough, Pineland

TENNESSEE
Hon. W. Otis Higgs, Jr., Memphis
Hon. Adolpho A. Birch, Nashville

TEXAS
Hon. Louis Bedford, Jr., Dallas
Hon. Andrew L. Jefferson, Jr.,
  Houston
Hon. Harrel G. Tillman, Houston
Hon. Berlaind L. Brashear, Dallas

VIRGINIA
Hon. Thomas Monroe, Arlington
Hon. James A. Overton, Portsmouth
Hon. Hilary H. Jones, Jr., Norfolk
Hon. William Stone, Williamsburg
Hon. Philip Walker, Hampton

WEST VIRGINIA
Hon. Leon P. Miller, Welch

WASHNGTON
Hon. J. Jerome Farris
  Washington State Court of Appeals
Hon. Charles Z. Smith, Seattle
Hon. Charles M. Stokes, Seattle
Hon. Charles V. Johnson, Seattle

VIRGIN ISLANDS
Hon. Eileen Petersen, St. Thomas
Hon. Cyril Micheal, Presiding Judge
Hon. Wm. Moorehead
Hon. Antoine Joseph

Source: National Bar Association Judicial Council Newsletter, Vol. 2, No. 1 ———
supplied by Hon. Edward B. Toles, Judge of U.S. District Court

BLACK MAYORS, VICE MAYORS, MAYORS PRO TEM, ASSISTANT MAYORS, AND DEPUTY MAYORS

ALABAMA

Mayors

Cooper, Algernon J., Jr.
Prichard

Ford, John
Tuskegee

Foster, Clyde
Madison

Gibbs, Willie Louis
Ridgeville

Hayden, A. M.
Uniontown

Lewis, Richard L.
Brighton

Rogers, Freddie C.
Roosevelt City

Stringer, Rev. Judge L.
Hobson City

Mayors Pro Tem

Whitehead, Willie R.
Tuskegee

ARKANSAS

Mayors

Battle, Rev. W. E.
Sunset

Bowens, Arthur
Dumas

Brooks, Dave
England

Conley, Emmitt Jerome
Cotton Plant

Johnson, Moses W.
Tillar

Minis, Clifford
Edmondson

Smith, Frank W.
Menifee

Whitaker, Willard
Madison

Assistant Mayor

Bussey, Charles
Little Rock

CALIFORNIA

Mayors

Bates, Nathaniel
Richmond

Bradley, Thomas
Los Angeles

Davis, Doris
Compton

Jackson, Clarence, Jr.
East Palo Alto

White, Herbert
Pittsburg

Widener, Warren
Berkeley

Vice Mayors

Anderson, Booker T.
Richmond

Gross, Ben
Milpitas

White, Ralph Lee
Stockton

FLORIDA

Mayors

Barkley, Earnest, Jr.
Gretna

Jackson, John S., M.D.
Lakeland

Vereen, Nathaniel
Eatonville

Vice Mayors

Cox, Vernita
South Bay

Gibson, Leroy (Spike)
Miami

Saunders, John T.
Hallandale

Mayors Pro Tem

Caynon, Jackie
Fort Pierce

Ford, James Richard
Tallahassee

GEORGIA

Mayor

Jackson, Maynard H.
Atlanta

Mayors Pro Tem

Hooks, Cheeves
Sandersville

McClung, Arthur J.
Columbus

ILLINOIS

Mayors

Listenbee, Luvert
East Chicago Heights

Miller, Curtis
Alorton

Smith, Ernest
Centerville

Smith, Marion L.
Robbins

Thomas, George
Brooklyn

Watkins, L. K.
Harvey

Williams, James E., Sr.
East St. Louis

INDIANA

Mayors

Hatcher, Richard G.
Gary

KANSAS

Mayors

Day, Benjamin H.
Leavenworth

Patterson, Roy
Coffeyville

KENTUCKY

Mayors

Dullin, Will
Earlington

Twyman, Luska J.
Glasgow

Mayors Pro Tem

Harvey, Rev. Wardelle G.
Paducah

LOUISIANA

Mayors

Bobb, John, Jr.
Grand Coteau

Mims, Harry
Hodge

Woodard, B. T.
Grambling

Mayors Pro Tem

Hollins, Joseph Edward
Maringouin

MARYLAND

Mayors

Arrington, Henry
Seat Pleasant

Davis, Charles C.
Fairmont Heights

Trotter, Decatur, Jr.
Glenarden

MICHIGAN

Mayors

Bivens, Edward, Jr.
Inkster

Blackwell, Robert B.
Highland Park

Bradley, Gilbert H.
Kalamazoo

Joseph, Charles F.
Benton Harbor

Parker, Lyman S.
Grand Rapids

Mayors Pro Tem
Little, Edward E.
Flint
Poston, Carl C., Jr.
Saginaw
Tucker, Charles M.
Pontiac

Vice Mayors
May, Virgil
Benton Harbor

MISSISSIPPI
Mayors
Brooks, N. B.
Falcon
Evers, James Charles
Fayette
Lewis, Moses
Winstonville
Lucas, Earl S.
Mound Bayou

Vice Mayors
Johnson, Herman
Mound Bayou

MISSOURI
Mayors
Howard, Travis B.
Howardville
Metcalf, Robert
Kinloch

NEW JERSEY
Mayors
Gibson, Kenneth A.
Newark
Hart, William S., Sr.
East Orange
Moore, Hilliard T., Sr.
Lawnside
Phillips, George J.
Chesilhurst
Taylor, Rev. Walter S.
Englewood

Deputy Mayors
Howard, William
Somerset
McNatt, Isaac
Teaneck

NEW YORK
Deputy Mayors
Evans, Joseph
New Rochelle

NORTH CAROLINA
Mayors
Boone, James
Cofield

Brown, Alex
Rose Hill
Jennette, Elward
Bayboro
Lee, Howard N.
Chapel Hill
Matthewson, W. Ray
Tarboro

Mayors Pro Tem
Alexander, Frederick D.
Charlotte
Beatty, Ozell K.
Salisbury

Mayors Pro Tem
George, Marion C., Jr.
Fayetteville
Horton, Rev. W. C.
Morehead City
Jeffers, Thebaud
Gastonia
Lightner, Clarence E.
Raleigh
Morgan, Leander R.
New Bern
Russell, Carl H.
Winston-Salem
Smith, Reginald D.
Chapel Hill
Stewart, John S.
Durham

OHIO
Mayors
Berry, Theodore
Cincinnati
Burton, Robert L., Jr.
Springfield
Fox, Jesse C.
New Miami
Henry, James T., Sr.
Xenia
Keels, James
Woodlawn
Lowry, James
Lincoln Heights
McGee, James H.
Dayton
Perry, Samuel S.
Cleveland

OKLAHOMA
Mayors
Austin, Leslie R.
Langston
Foley, Lelia
Taft
Matlock, J. H.
Tullahassee

McClendon, R. E.
Rentiesville
McConmick, T. R.
Boley
Oliver, Lee
Tecumseh

SOUTH CAROLINA
Mayors
Ross, Charles
Summerville
Rucker, Millard
Atlantic Beach
Scott, Louis N.
Eastover
Seabrook, Silas N.
Santee
Wilson, Charlie Bell
Sellers

TENNESSEE
Vice Mayors
Davis, Fred L.
Memphis
Malone, James Deotha
Gallatin

TEXAS
Mayors
Robinson, David K.
Easton
Rundles, Dennis D.
Detroit
Sams, Eristus
Prairie View

VIRGINIA
Mayors
Fauntleroy, Hermanze E., Jr.
Petersburg

Vice Mayors
Barbour, Charles Lee
Charlottesville
Davis, Robert G., Jr.
Clifton Forge
Jordan, Joseph A., Jr.
Norfolk
Marsh, Henry L., III
Richmond
Owens, Hugo Armstrong
Chesapeake
Riddick, Moses
Suffolk
Seay, Clarence W.
Lynchburg

WEST VIRGINIA
Vice Mayors
Connolly, Allan
Bluefield

THE BLACK VOTE

Blacks have proven in past presidential elections, that in a close race, they could hold the balance of power.

Almost every victorious presidential candidate since 1936 has carried the black vote in Northern central cities. In at least nine major states—California, New York, Illinois, Indiana, Michigan, New Jersey, Missouri, Ohio, and Pennsylvania—the black vote has had an important influence on large blocs of electoral votes. In the South, blacks make up an even larger proportion of the population, and with the Voting Rights Act of 1965, they have become a sizeable part of the electorate. Blacks have provided the margin of victory in a close national race, and, with sophisticated voter education, may again. The failure of the black vote to register a significant impact in the 1972 presidential campaign indicates the necessity for a close study of the realignment of other voting blocs within the electorate.

Analysis of the six presidential elections preceding 1972 shows the importance of the black vote. In 1948, for example, Truman could not have defeated Dewey without the black vote. California, Illinois, and Ohio were key electoral states in Truman's election, and he carried them by only 17,000, 33,000, and 7,000 votes respectively. Blacks in those states voted overwhelmingly for Truman; of 100,000 block votes in California, 70,000 were cast for Truman; of 119,000 black votes in three wards in Chicago, 85,000 were cast for Truman; and 130,000 of 20,000 blacks voted for Truman in Ohio. Truman's commitment to civil rights and the Fair Employment Practices Commission in particular, is thought to have been responsible for the large black vote which provided him with the margin of victory in these crucial states.

According to a Gallup Poll, black support of Eisenhower increased from 21 percent in 1952 to 39 percent in 1956. Despite the greater black support of the Republican incumbent, the black vote was not decisive either in 1956 or in 1952 because of Eisenhower's widespread popularity.

John F. Kennedy's victory in 1960 owed much to black voters. According to various estimates, his narrow winning margin included 70-80 percent of the black vote. In the large cities, the black vote was firmly in the Democratic column. Kennedy received 77.7 percent of the black vote in Chicago; in Cleveland, he received 77.5 percent; in Detroit, 89.9 percent; in Gary, 81.9 percent; in Los Angeles, 86.6 percent; in New York, 76.3 percent; and in Philadelphia, 77.1 percent. A small shift of the

black vote in Illinois, Michigan, and South Carolina would have lost the election for the Democrats. The black vote exceeded the overall Democratic majority in four other states that year—Mississippi, New Jersey, Pennsylvania, and Texas.

Because of the Johnson landslide in 1964, the black vote was less important in the outcome of the election, even though it has been estimated that 94 percent of all blacks voted for President Johnson. The black vote did, however, provide the margin of the Democratic victory in Arkansas, Florida, Tennessee, and Virginia.

The black vote did not affect the 1972 presidential election, unless considered from the point of view that black voters overwhelmingly denied Richard Nixon their vote, giving him only 21 percent to Senator McGovern's 79 percent. However, anti-black forces overwhelmingly supported Nixon's candidacy. The black turnout in Northern states was lower in 1968 than in 1960; ninety-five percent of Chicago's black votes went to the Democrats, but 25 percent fewer blacks voted in 1968 than had voted in 1960. In New Jersey, Humphrey won 89 percent of the black vote, but turnout in heavily black precincts declined by 30 percent. Turnout in black precincts in St. Louis and Kansas City, Mo., was also down 30 percent, even though 96 percent of voters in these areas voted Democratic. One quarter fewer blacks voted in Philadelphia in 1968 than in 1960, and in Detroit, the black vote was down 35 percent.

The U.S. Census Bureau estimates that 57.6 percent of voting age blacks actually voted in 1968 as against 69.1 percent of eligible whites. In the North and West, 64.8 percent of potential black voters actually voted, while in the South the figure was 51.6 percent.

In Texas, for instance, in 1972 there were 918,744 blacks of voting age. In 1968 the Democrats carried the state by 38,960 votes. Thus, if groups other than blacks were to have voted the same way in 1972 as they had in 1968, only four percent of potential black voters would have needed to stay home to give Texas to the Republicans. Only two percent black shift from the Democrats to the Republicans is necessary to produce the same result. Actually, the 1972 Republican vote in Texas was 2,098,087 opposed to 1,063,125 for the Democrats.

Conversely, the Republicans carried Ohio by 90,428 votes in 1968. There were 617,225 potential black voters in Ohio in 1972. If an additional 14 percent of the potential black vote had gone to the Democrats, or if seven percent had switched from Republican to Democrat, Ohio might have gone to the Democrats, other things being equal.

A sophisticated and enlarged black electorate could well prove as decisive in some of these states as it has in the past. In considering the black population of major U.S. cities, statistics indicate that the black vote in Northern central cities, which is crucial in the major elections, is not only the swing vote, but represents a large proportion of all potential votes in these cities.

According to a 1972 study conducted by the Voter Education Project in Atlanta, black support accounted for over 50 percent of the entire Democratic vote in six Southern states and over 30 percent in the other five Southern states. Over 90 percent of the votes for the Democratic presidential candidate in Mississippi is estimated to have been cast by blacks. A two-party race, rather than a three-party race, can make the black vote even more important in any close contest.

The ranks of the black electorate of 1972 have grown as a result of the increase in voter registration following the Voting Rights Act of 1965. Black interest and participation in politics have increased over the past decade, with marked moves away from adherence to party organizations.

The possibility that black voters may determine the margin for victory in future years means that major candidates will be taking a realistic view of the black electorate, with an eye to viable coalitions. Black Republicans and Democrats alike are determined to win, and black voters are a factor, in either positive or negative connotations.

STATES

The potential black vote in the U.S. is 14,219,777. The largest number of potential black voters are concentrated in 26 states and the District of Columbia. Over half of these (14) are industrial states outside of the South.

Thirteen states each have a black voting age population in excess of one-half million. However, Mississippi is the only state in which potential black voters comprise over 30 percent of the total voting age population. In Alabama, Georgia, Louisiana, and South Carolina, the black voting age population is 20 to 29 percent of the total population.

Young blacks represent 12.8 percent of the total number of potential voters between the ages of 18 and 20 years. They comprise 10 percent of the total black voting age population.

In the District of Columbia, new black voters make up 79.4 percent of the total number of 18- to 20-year-old voters. In six states and the District of Columbia, young black voters represent 30 percent or more of the total youth vote. These states are Alabama, Georgia, Louisiana, Mississippi, South Carolina, and Virginia.

Young black voters comprise between 20 and 30 percent of the total youth vote in Arkansas, Maryland, and North Carolina.

CITIES

There are 89 cities with total populations of 50,000 or more which have at least a 20 percent black population. On the average, the total black population is 31.6 percent of the population of these cities. The average black voting age population in these 89 cities is 28.3 percent. Eleven of the cities have a black voting age population exceeding 40 percent.

In East St. Louis, Ill., Washington, D.C., and Compton, Calif., the black voting age population exceeds 50 percent. Three other major cities—Gary, Ind., Newark, N.J., and Atlanta, Ga.—have black voting age populations between 47 and 49 percent.

CONGRESSIONAL DISTRICTS

Based on the 1970 census, there are 50 congressional districts with 30 percent or more black populations. Thirty-three of these districts are in Southern states.

Ten congressional districts have a black population which exceeds 50 percent, and another 10 congressional districts have 40 to 49 percent black populations. Voting age population by congressional districts is not available.

All majority-black congressional districts have black congressmen. The district from which the late George Collins of Illinois was originally elected (6th.), had less than 50 percent black voters. The seat, now held by his widow, Mrs. Cardiss Collins, contains approximately 55 percent black voters (7th District, Illinois). Congressman Ronald Dellums is the only black member elected from a district with less than a 30 percent black population. Congressman Ralph Metcalf of Illinois' 1st District (Chicago), has the highest percentage black population, 89.0 percent.

Georgia and Texas both elected black representatives to Congress in 1972. Rev. Andrew Young's Georgia seat is in a predominantly white district (62%), 37% black voters, (5th Congressional District, Georgia). Barbara Jordan (Texas senator) represents the 18th District of Texas (Houston). Also, the 37th district in California (Los Angeles) elected a black congresswoman, Yvonne Brathwaite Burke, former California assemblywoman.

Reported Voter Participation and Registration of the Population of Voting Age, by Region: 1964, 1968, and 1972

(Numbers in thousands)

SUBJECT	BLACK			WHITE		
	1964	1968	1972	1964	1968	1972
Number who reported that they voted:						
United States..............................	6,048	6,300	7,033	70,204	72,213	78,167
South.............................	1 2,576	3,094	3,324	15,813	17,853	20,201
North and West........................	1 3,891	3,206	3,707	54,392	54,362	57,966
Percent of voting age population who reported that they voted:						
United States..........................	58	58	52	71	69	64
South.............................	1 44	52	48	59	62	57
North and West........................	1 72	65	57	75	72	68
Percent of registered population who reported they voted:						
United States..........................	(NA)	87	80	(NA)	92	88
South.............................	(NA)	84	75	(NA)	87	82
North and West........................	(NA)	90	85	(NA)	93	90

NA Not available.
1 Includes persons of "other races."
Source: U.S. Department of Commerce, Social and Economic Statistics Administration, Bureau of the Census.

Reported Voter Participation for the Black Population of Voting Age in the 1972 Election, by Region and Age

(Number in thousands)

AGE	United States	South	North and West
Number who reported that they voted:			
18 years and over...	7,033	3,324	3,707
18 to 24 years...	1,040	469	569
25 to 44 years...	2,851	1,327	1,524
45 to 64 years...	2,326	1,108	1,218
65 years and over..	816	420	396
Percent in each age group who reported that they voted:			
18 years and over...	52	48	57
18 to 24 years...	35	31	38
25 to 44 years...	56	53	58
45 to 64 years...	62	56	68
65 years and over..	51	43	62

Source: U.S. Department of Commerce, Social and Economic Statistics Administration, Bureau of the Census.

Reported Voter Registration for Persons of Voting Age, by Region: 1968 and 1972

(Numbers in thousands)

Subject	Presidential elections			
	Black		White	
	1968	1972	1968	1972
All persons of voting age:				
United States............................	10,935	13,494	104,521	121,241
South.............................	5,991	6,950	28,834	35,415
North and West......................	4,944	6,544	75,687	85,830
Number who reported they registered:				
United States............................	7,238	8,836	78,835	88,986
South.............................	3,690	4,449	20,416	24,707
North and West......................	3,548	4,386	58,419	64,278
Percent of voting-age population:				
United States............................	66	65	75	73
South.............................	62	64	71	70
North and West......................	72	67	77	75

Source: U.S. Department of Commerce, Social and Economic Statistics Administration, Bureau of the Census.

GOVERNMENT/POLITICS CHRONOLOGY 1969–1973

1969

JANUARY

3   Rep. Adam Clayton Powell, Jr. (D., N.Y.) was seated in the House after a five-hour debate and following a 251–160 vote approving a proposal to seat him but to deprive him of his 22 years of Congressional seniority and to fine him $25,000 for alleged misuse of payroll and travel funds while committee chairman. The fine was to be taken ($1,150 a month until paid) from his $30,000-a-year salary. Powell had been excluded from the 90th Congress in 1967 on charges of misuse of $40,000 in Congressional funds while he was chairman of the House Education & Labor Committee. Powell had also been involved in a libel action initiated in New York in 1960. The U.S. Supreme Court Nov. 18, 1968, had announced its acceptance for review of a suit contending that Powell's exclusion from Congress was unconstitutional. After his exclusion, Powell had won re-election to the House both in a special election and in Congressional elections of Nov. 5, 1968. His 18th Congressional District in Harlem had been unrepresented in the House since his exclusion.

Mrs. Shirley Chisholm (D., N.Y.), the first black woman ever elected to Congress, took her seat in the House of Representatives. Ten blacks were serving in Congress, including the only black senator, Edward W. Brooke, (R., Mass.).

APRIL

1   Los Angeles City Councilman Thomas Bradley, 51-year-old black lawyer and former police lieutenant, won 42% of the vote and incumbent Sam Yorty only 26% in a nonpartisan, Los Angeles mayoral election. Since neither won a majority, the two primary candidates were to compete in a runoff election May 27.

MAY

6   Howard Lee, 34, black director of employee relations at Duke University in nearby Durham, was elected as the first black mayor of Chapel Hill, N.C., an 80% white town. Chapel Hill (12,400 residents) is run by a town manager under the guidance of the mayor and aldermen. Lee said his race was not a major factor in the campaign, which was "settled on the issues, and a lot of credit is due to my opponent." The mayoral job was a part-time one (salary $100 a month).

8   David W. Williams, 59, a Los Angeles County Superior Court judge, was named as a U.S. District Judge for Central California. He is the first black jurist to hold a federal judgeship west of the Mississippi.

13   Charles Evers, 48, NAACP field director in Mississippi, won the Democratic nomination for mayor of Fayette, Miss. (pop. 2,000; 1,200 black). Evers' victory was tantamount to election since he was unopposed in the June election. The Evers' slate of five black aldermen also won in Fayette. Three blacks won seats on Jonestown's five-member city council, three won in Bolton, one each in Hollandale, Moorehead, and Arcola, and 12 more won the right to runoff elections.

27   Los Angeles Mayor Sam W. Yorty, 59, was elected to his third term of office in a runoff vote May 27. He defeated City Councilman Thomas Bradley, 51 who was seeking to become the city's first black mayor. The vote totals: Yorty 447,030 (53%); Bradley 392,379 (47%). Both were Democrats; Los Angeles elections were legally nonpartisan. The racial issue was raised by Yorty in the runoff campaign. He warned that the city was "one big campus" that would be taken over by "black militants and left-wing extremists" if Bradley won. He asked the electorate to "imagine what would happen here with a Negro mayor." Yorty had charged that Bradley was "anti-police" and hundreds of policemen would quit the force if he won.

JUNE

4   City Councilman Douglas F. Dollarhide became the first black mayor of Compton, Calif. by winning a run-off election against Dr. Walter Tucker, also black. The town's population of 78,000 was about 65% black and 10% Mexican-American.

JULY

8   J(ames) Charles Evers was installed as

mayor of Fayette, Miss., the first black to become mayor of a biracial Mississippi City since Reconstruction.

29 Six black members of the National Democratic Party of Alabama won special elections in Greene County giving blacks control of the county commission and school board. The special election had been ordered by the U.S. Supreme Court after the six black candidates had been denied a place on the November 1968 general election ballot by order of Probate Judge James Dennis Herndon, the political boss of Greene County.

Elected to the five-member county commission were Vassie B. Knott, Harry C. Means, Levi Morrow, Sr. and Frenchie Burton. Two seats on the five-man school board were won by Robert Hines and J. A. Posey, Sr.

SEPTEMBER

9 The Detroit mayoral primary was won by Richard H. Austin, a black, and Roman S. Gribbs, white sheriff of Wayne County. Austin, Wayne County auditor, polled 124,941 votes out of 339,000 cast for a field of 28 candidates. Gribbs received 105,640 votes. Both were Democrats (the primary was nonpartisan) and were considered moderates, 40% of the city's 1.6 million residents were black.

11-14 Black elected officials gathered in Washington, D.C. to inaugurate the Institute of Black Elected Officials, the first national attempt to organize the 1,200 black men and women in elective office. The conference was sponsored by the Metropolitan Applied Research Center, Inc. of Washington and New York.

OCTOBER

7 Black Atlanta (Ga.) attorney Maynard Jackson, 31, defeated a white candidate to become the first black vice mayor in Atlanta's history.

NOVEMBER

4 In Cleveland, Ohio, Mayor Carl B. Stokes (D.), who became the first black to be elected mayor of a major American city in 1967, won re-election in a close race with Cuyahoga County Auditor Ralph J. Perk (R.). Mayor Stokes retained his post with a 3,700-vote plurality out of some 240,000 votes cast.

William S. Hart (D.) became the first black mayor of a major New Jersey municipality, East Orange.

An Episcopal minister and lawyer, the Rev. S. Lester Ralph, was elected mayor in Somerville, Mass.

Kentucky's first black mayor, Luska J. Twyman (R.) won a 4-year term in Glasgow. (He had attained the office by appointment after a resignation.)

Thomas I. Atkins won a seat on the Boston City Council, making him the only black member.

A black candidate for mayor, County Auditor Richard H. Austin, lost by a 7,000-vote margin out of 509,000 votes cast. The victor was County Sheriff Roman S. Gribbs, white. Both were Democrats. The election was nonpartisan. The major issues were crime and race.

1970

JANUARY

17 Cleveland Mayor Carl B. Stokes named Lt. Gen. Benjamin Oliver Davis, Jr., 57, deputy commander of the U.S. Strike Command and the highest-ranking black in the U.S. military as Cleveland's public safety director. Davis, the son of the General Benjamin Oliver Davis, Sr., was the first black to attain the rank of general in the armed forces.

MARCH

11 Sen. Edward W. Brooke (R., Mass.), the Senate's only black member, charged in Washington that the Nixon Administration had made a "cold, calculated political decision" to shun the needs of blacks in America in favor of pursuing a Southern strategy to win re-election in 1972.

JUNE

9 Blacks won city council seats for the first time since Reconstruction in Roanoke, Charlottesville, Lynchburg and Emporia.

16 Kenneth A. Gibson, 37, a civil engineer, was elected mayor of Newark, N.J. to become the first black mayor of a major Eastern city. Gibson's margin was decisive—54,892-43,339 votes, the largest turnout (73% of those registered) in a mayoral runoff election in the city's history—over two-term incumbent Hugh J. Addonizio, whose campaign was based on the racial theme

that Gibson was a "puppet" of black extremists, led by Immanu Amiri Baraka, who sought to take over the city.

In a Newark, N.J. mayoral election May 12, Kenneth A. Gibson, 37, a civil engineer, won more than twice as many votes as incumbent Mayor Hugh J. Addonizio, his nearest competitor in a seven-candidate field, but Gibson's 42% of the total was short of the majority needed for election. A runoff election was set for two weeks after Addonizio, who was under federal indictment for extortion and income-tax evasion, was scheduled to stand trial in Trenton on the charges.

Gibson, a black, had been nominated in November, 1969 by a black and Puerto Rican convention in Newark, whose population of 402,000 was more than 50% black. Addonizio called upon Gibson May 13 to repudiate the convention's support and an Addonizio spokesman said "race is going to be the issue." Gibson accused the Addonizio forces of trying "to create fear." Two losing candidates, John P. Caufield, who received 13% of the vote, and State Senator Alexander Matturri, who received 5%, endorsed Gibson May 13. Another candidate, Harry Wheeler, a black, had withdrawn prior to the election and backed Gibson. Another black in the field, State Assemblyman George C. Richardson, had drawn 2% of the vote. Anthony Imperiale, a white militant, polled 15% of the vote.

JULY
15   James H. McGee, 51, lawyer, was sworn in as Dayton, Ohio's first black mayor. Dayton, with a population of 250,000, including 70,000 blacks, was the fourth largest city in the U.S.—behind Cleveland, Washington, D.C. and Newark, N.J.—to have a black mayor.
24   William L. Clay (Mo.), Louis Stokes (Ohio), and Augustus F. Hawkins (Calif.), all Democrats, made public a letter to President Nixon that said "the patience of many black Americans is exhausted." The letter charged that Nixon's course on civil rights during the past 18 months "is destined to destroy all possibilities of unity and brotherhood." Clay, Stokes, and Hawkins joined six other black representatives in requesting a meeting with President Nixon to convey their views to him on social problems. Stokes said that the

group "didn't get an answer for two months." He added that the answer came from "a staff assistant nobody ever heard of," and said "don't call the President, he'll call you." The new letter accused the President of traveling "to all corners of the earth" but not coming "to black America." The three congressmen also noted that the President had greeted "30,600 personal guests at the White House . . ." but that black officials representing America's black citizens had not been granted an audience with the President.

27   Benjamin O. Davis, Jr., 57, Cleveland safety director in charge of the police and fire departments, resigned after six months in his post, charging that the administration of Mayor Carl B. Stokes was providing "support and comfort" to enemies of the police. He said "the enemies" were not "holdup men or narcotics pushers." Davis added that "the mayor and his administration continue not to give me support for programs that I require, and continue to provide support and comfort to the enemies of law enforcement."

SEPTEMBER
29   Mrs. Gwen Cherry, 47, a black attorney was elected to the Florida House of Representatives. Mrs. Cherry was a member of the board of directors of the National Organization of Women.

NOVEMBER
3   Ronald V. Dellums (D., Calif.) 34, a black city councilman from Berkeley, liberal, who won in a predominantly white district against six-time incumbent Jeffrey Cohelon. Dellums was an antiwar candidate.
3   Wilson Riles, black, defeated Max Rafferty for the non-partisan office of state superintendent of public instruction.

Richard Austin, a black Democrat who ran unsuccessfully for mayor of Detroit in 1969, was elected Michigan secretary of state over Emil Lockwood, a Republican state senator.

Twelve black Democrats were elected to Congress. Seven were incumbents: Mrs. Shirley Chisholm (N.Y.), William Clay (Mo.), John Conyers (Mich.), Charles C. Diggs, Jr. (Mich.), Augustus F. Hawkins (Calif.), Robert N.C. Nix (Pa.) and Louis Stokes (Ohio). The five newcomers were: George Collins (Ill.), Ronald V. Dellums (Calif.),

Ralph Metcalfe (Ill.), Parren J. Mitchell (Md.), and Charles B. Rangel (N.Y.). There were 10 blacks in the 91st Congress, including, as in the 92nd, one Republican senator, Edward W. Brooke (Mass.), who was not up for re-election Nov. 3. Rangel replaced Rep. Adam C. Powell (D., N.Y.), who lost in the primary. Metcalfe replaced veteran William L. Dawson (D., Ill.) who retired after 14 terms in the House.

9   William L. Dawson, 84, first black congressman to chair a major Congressional committee (House Committee on Government Operations), and who, since 1942 had been re-elected from predominantly black 1st Congressional District in Chicago, vice chairman of Democratic party; died in Chicago.

17   Dr. Melvin H. Evans, 56, won a runoff election against Cyril E. King, to become the first elected governor of the U.S. Virgin Islands. Evans, a Republican, had been appointed by President Nixon in June 1969 to serve as governor until legislation to allow the islanders to elect their governor was implemented. After his inauguration, Evans would become the first popularly elected black governor on American soil.

DECEMBER

7   James Farmer, the Nixon Administration's most prominent black official, resigned as assistant secretary for administration of the Department of Health, Education, and Welfare, effective Dec. 21. Farmer, 50, founder of the Congress of Racial Equality, said he had been blocked in his efforts to halt discrimination and improve health delivery systems.

Frederick M. Porter, 44, a black police lieutenant in Princeton, N.J., was named chief of police.

1971

JANUARY

1   Princeton Township, N.J., named James A. Floyd, 48, a Democrat, its first black mayor. Floyd was selected unanimously by the five-member Township Committee, Princeton's governing body.

4   Dr. Melvin H. Evans was installed as the first elected governor of the Virgin Islands with the oath administered by Thurgood Marshall, the first black U.S. Supreme Court Justice.

12   The Rev. Walter E. Fauntroy, 37, a Baptist minister, and a key aide to the late Rev. Dr. Martin Luther King, Jr., won the Democratic nomination for non-voting delegate to the House of Representatives from Washington, D.C. in a primary election. Fauntroy won 44% of the total vote in a seven-man field. His closest competitors were Joseph P. Yeldell (31%) and the Rev. Channing E. Phillips (22%). John A. Nevius, 50, white, a former city councilman, was unopposed for the Republican nomination.

14   The Supreme Court ruled that Southern communities must obtain federal approval before making changes that might affect the rights of black voters, as provided by the 1965 Voting Rights Act. The ruling came in a case brought by two black voters and six defeated black candidates in 1969 municipal elections in Canton, Miss.

A federal district court had rejected the plaintiffs' contention that the city—in shifting polling places, annexing neighborhoods with white majorities and changing to at-large elections of aldermen—had discouraged and diluted the black vote. The Supreme Court sent the case back to the district court to decide if the election should be re-run. Justice Hugo L. Black dissented, and Justice John M. Harlan, in a partial dissent, said he was "somewhat mystified" that the court took no further action. Chief Justice Warren E. Burger and Justice Harry A. Blackmun, in an opinion concurring with the majority said the decision followed from a 1969 Supreme Court ruling that upheld the Voting Rights Act provisions.

21   The 12 black members of the House informed the President they were boycotting his address of the State of the Union message because of his "consistent refusal to hear the pleas and concerns of black Americans." The protesters said they had been trying, without success, since 1970 to meet with the President.

FEBRUARY

22   The U.S. Supreme Court refused an emergency plea by the Rev. Jesse L. Jackson, a civil rights leader, to order Illinois to place his name on the ballot for the Feb. 23 mayoral primary in Chicago. Justice Douglas wrote that Jackson's challenge to the petition system was too complicated for the court to handle quickly and "responsibly."

MARCH

23 Membership of the Black Caucus increased to 13 with the election of the Rev. Walter E. Fauntroy (D.), 37, a Baptist clergyman, as the District of Columbia's first non-voting Congressional delegate in a century. Fauntroy would receive a full Congressional salary, $42,500 a year, and would be allowed to vote in committee, but not on the floor and to have a seat on the House District Committee.

25 President Nixon conferred with the black members of the House of Representatives, all Democrats, and appointed a White House staff panel to study a list of recommendations made by the Congressional Black Caucus. The request for the meeting by the group, to discuss the problems of blacks and other minorities, had been made a year earlier. Rep. Charles C. Diggs, Jr. (D., Mich.), Black Caucus leader, described the tone of the meeting as good and the President's attitude as sympathetic.

APRIL

6 Warren Widener, 33, black, was elected mayor of Berkeley, Calif. and two black candidates won seats on the City Council. They were lawyers, D'Army Bailey, 29, and Ira T. Simmons, 28. James E. Williams, Sr. was elected the first black mayor of East St. Louis, Illinois.

13 John Franklin, an educator and businessman, was elected the first black city commissioner in the history of Chattanooga, Tennessee.

16 Cleveland Mayor Carl B. Stokes announced he would not seek re-election after his current term of office. He said that he would seek development of a "people's lobby" to bring pressure on the two major political parties toward "responsive" presidential candidates in 1972 and toward a reordering of the nation's priorities.

18 The Mississippi Democratic party unanimously nominated James Charles Evers, 48, as its candidate for governor of Mississippi, the first black candidate for governor in the state's history. Evers, in his election as mayor of Fayette, Miss. in 1969, had become the first black mayor of an integrated community in the South.

27 A three-judge federal panel in Biloxi, Miss., ruled that the new open-primary law was inoperable unless it was approved, under the· 1965 Voting Rights Act, by U.S. attorney general John N. Mitchell, or the federal district court in Washington. Its unanimous opinion referred to Mitchell's "Pilate-like" pose on the matter and the "obtuse, patronizing failure by federal government officials to discharge the duties" imposed by the 1965 law.

30 Hosea Williams was rearrested along with some 370 mainly black demonstrators who were blocking the entrances to the Justice Department. Outside the building SCLC President Ralph Abernathy read a "poor people's bill of particulars" against the Justice Department, accusing the agency of undermining voting rights, failing to act against police repression and "intimidating the people with illegal searches."

MAY

7 Attorney General John Mitchell, using his authority under the Voting Rights Act, rejected reapportionment plans for Virginia's legislative districts on the ground that the plan discriminated against blacks. Mitchell's actions were based on his authority to block enactment of any new voting laws in any of seven Southern states if he found the changes discriminatory. His application of the Voting Rights Act to prevent a change in election laws was the first since the Supreme Court held that reapportionment plans were covered by the requirements of the voting act.

11 Vice President Spiro Agnew was boycotted by about half of the 20 black members of the Illinois legislature, when he addressed the Illinois General Assembly in Springfield. Democratic Assemblyman Harold Washington, leader of the boycott, said Agnew was "anti-black, anti-student, anti-peace, and anti-poor. He's like the Ku Klux Klan, he's anti-everything."

24 The Black Caucus detailed their criticism of the Nixon Administration response to their requests and indicated the caucus might work outside both major political parties, if necessary, to solve a "crisis that approaches the intolerable" in black problems. The Caucus stressed the "political implications" of the 1970 census report showing that half of the nation's 25 million blacks were concentrated in 50 cities and that 30 cities had populations that were more than one-third black.

Tough enforcement programs against job discrimination were lacking in both the private and government sectors. It noted that the welfare income floor of $2,400 supported by the Administration was less than currently provided in 45 states for welfare.

The Caucus contrasted the $315 million federal programs of loans and grants for minority businesses with $250 million proposed for helping the Lockheed Aircraft Corp. and aid to the ailing Penn Central Railroad. It noted the increase from $10.4 million to $22 million in federal contract work for black contractors while more than $100 billion in federal contracts was let annually.

25 The Justice Department reported that it would now prevent the enactment of all new voting laws in the South unless the states could show that the new measures were not racially discriminatory.

Attorney General John Mitchell was responsible for the decision to adopt a more stringent interpretation of the Voting Rights Act. Under the Voting Act, enacted in 1965, all changes in state and local election laws in seven Southern states had to be cleared by the attorney general or a special U.S. court to make certain they did not dilute black voting strength. The guidelines would put the burden of proving that new election laws did not discriminate on the Southern states. According to the new policy, the attorney general would not allow changes in the existing laws to go into effect when he could not decide whether or not they had "a racially discriminatory purpose or effect."

26 John Conyers, Jr. (Mich.), Democratic member of the House Judiciary Subcommittee on Civil Rights, charged that the Nixon Administration provided inadequate enforcement of the Voting Rights Act and looked aside while Southern states sought to diminish the political power of black voters.

JUNE
1 President Nixon disagreed with the section of the May 10 Civil Rights Commission report which said "that this nation and the American people do not have a commitment to the cause of civil rights." "I believe that's an unfair charge. . . . I do not think they should question the sincerity of the great majority of the American people on this issue, particularly in view of the great progress

that has been made," said Mr. Nixon.
1 The U.S. Supreme Court held unanimously that persons had a right to sue in federal court against private individuals who conspired to deprive them of civil rights. The court discarded a 1951 precedent that said the 1871 civil rights law applied only to public officials acting under color of law. The ruling overturned lower court decisions dismissing a suit brought by four black Mississippians who were beaten in 1966 by two white men who thought they were civil rights workers.

9 The House of Representatives passed a three-year extension to the Sugar Act which set allotments for domestic production and provided quotas on foreign imports. The action came after defeat of an attempt, spearheaded by members of the Congressional Black Caucus, to delete a 60,000 ton annual quota for South Africa in response to that country's apartheid policy.

The Black Caucus adopted a statement accusing the U.S. of "complicity with apartheid" through subsidization of south African sugar. Rep. Charles Diggs (D., Mich.), chairman of the Caucus and leader of the attempt to open the bill to amendment, called South Africa "the most racist country in the world."

JULY
3 The U.S. Supreme Court, in an unsigned 6–3 decision held that reapportionment plans for state legislatures imposed by federal courts could be implemented without approval by the U.S. attorney general or a special federal court in Washington.

The majority held that a federal district court was "not within the reach" of a provision of the 1965 Voting Rights Act requiring submission of voting rights changes in states to review in Washington. The provision was designed to prevent local impairment of voting rights newly won by blacks.

29 Robert Lee Grant, a black official in the Department of Housing and Urban Development (HUD), was dismissed six days after he renewed his criticism of the Nixon Administration's commitment to civil rights.

SEPTEMBER
8 Sen. Edmund S. Muskie (Maine), a leading contender for the Democratic

presidential nomination, ruled out a black running mate on the grounds "such a ticket was not electable" and therefore "would not serve the purposes" of either the ticket or the cause of equal rights. Muskie stated that the observation had occurred "in the context" of a discussion about how to deal effectively with the problem facing the blacks in America, and that the question of a black vice-presidential running mate "was put to me in a way that seemed to call for an honest and direct and frank political judgment."

"There are only three answers." "Yes, no, or maybe. I chose what I thought was the honest answer." He said it was an attempt to convince blacks who might support his candidacy that "what we needed to do was to elect a ticket that would be committed to dealing effectively with questions of racial inequality."

8   Charles Evers, the black mayor of Fayette, Miss., who was running for governor of Mississippi, reported that Muskie "told the truth" Sept. 8 when he said that a black could not be elected vice president in 1972. Evers said "I don't think a black man in the country wouldn't admit that Muskie told the truth."

16   President Nixon said with regard to "the general proposition" of prejudice in the U.S. "as it affects politics," he believed "that it is frankly a libel on the American people to suggest that the American people, who do have prejudices, just like all people . . . would vote against a man because of his religion, or his race, or his color." "It is very important for those of us in positions of leadership not to tell a large number of people in America, whoever they are, that because of the accident of their birth they don't have a chance to go to the top."

25   The bill repealing the Emergency Detention Act (Title 2 of the 1950 Internal Security Act) was approved by 356–49 House vote Sept. 14 and Senate voice vote Sept. 16. The act had provided for detention of persons suspected of possible espionage or sabotage in periods of invasion or insurrection. It, and six camps established under it, had never been used for detention. There was concern among minority groups, especially blacks that the law could be

used against them. Japanese-Americans also were wary of the legislation in light of the detention after Pearl Harbor in 1941 of more than 110,000 American citizens of Japanese origin in relocation centers.

President Nixon signed the repeal and noted the "concern among many Americans that the act might someday be used to apprehend and detain citizens who hold unpopular views." His signature was "to put an end to such suspicions."

26   Rep. Shirley A. Chisholm (D., N.Y.) announced that she would enter the 1972 presidential primaries in Florida, Wisconsin, California and North Carolina. Rep. Chisholm, the only black woman in Congress, said she would not, however, lead a third-party movement at the Democratic national convention in Miami Beach if she failed to get her party's nomination

Mrs. Chisholm said her decision to enter the primaries was to assure that the selection of the party's presidential nominee "will not be a white, male decision."

OCTOBER
19   Mrs. Chisholm's candidacy loomed as a possible stumbling block for a group of black leaders who wanted to line up behind one candidate at the Democratic national convention. Julian Bond, a Georgia state representative and a spokesman for a group of black strategists, said that black leaders favored lining up behind Mayor Carl B. Stokes of Cleveland. Bond's group included most top black political and civil rights leaders. Bond said they intended to present a unified bargaining position to win more government jobs for blacks. The group felt that such a deal could be tied to a quota based on black percentages and the appointment of blacks to a number of his positions. Bond said the group would withhold support of the nominee in the hope of inducing him to endorse the groups' demands.

22   William T. Coleman, Jr., a black attorney and a partner in a Philadelphia law firm, was named by President Nixon to the Pay Board and Price Commission.

NOVEMBER
2   Richard G. Hatcher, a black Democrat. won re-election to a second term as mayor of Gary, Indiana.

4   William H. Rehnquist, in response to

opposition to civil rights leaders, recanted his opposition to a public accommo-. dations ordinance adopted in Phoenix in 1964 by saying that "I would not have the same feeling now." He added that he had "come to realize the strong concern of minorities for the recognition" of their civil rights.

8   The nominations of Lewis F. Powell, Jr. and William H. Rehnquist to the Supreme Court met with opposition by civil rights leaders who charged that Rehnquist was insensitive to the rights of blacks.

9   U.S. Supreme Court sustained a lower court ruling against Julian Bond and Andrew Young, both of Atlanta, who had challenged the constitutionality of a new Georgia law that required a majority vote in general elections for the U.S. Senate and House of Representatives.

Clarence Mitchell, director of the National Association for the Advancement of Colored People (NAACP) bureau in Washington, read into the record Rehnquist's opposition to a 1964 open accommodations law in Phoenix and his opposition to end de facto school segregation in Phoenix's public schools in 1967. Mitchell said that with the nomination of Rehnquist, "the foot of racism is placed in the door of the temple of justice."

Mr. Mitchell also asked the committee to further investigate reports that Rehnquist had used his position as a Republican "challenger" of Democratic votes to obstruct blacks from voting in Phoenix. Rehnquist had denied the reports earlier, but Mitchell disputed Rehnquist's explanation.

19   About 150 black-elected officials convened in Washington by the Congressional Black Caucus Nov. 19, named a committee to study the "feasibility" and mechanics of calling a national black political convention in 1972 to develop a unified bargaining position toward the Democratic party.

DECEMBER

7   Walter E. Fauntroy, the District of Columbia's delegate in Congress, announced his plans to run in the District's Democratic presidential primary May 2, 1972 as a favorite-son candidate and, if successful, to head a delegation to the Democratic National Convention to press for District home rule and for national economic opportunities for blacks.

1972

JANUARY

3   A three-judge U.S. court in Montgomery, Ala. ordered the adoption of a new reapportionment plan that would divide the Alabama legislature into single-member districts. The order was seen as a major victory for black political forces in the state. Supporters of the court plan claimed that it could put as many as 20 more blacks in the legislature. Republicans also stood to gain additional representation from the order.

9   More than 150 black-elected-and-appointed officials from Maryland, Pennsylvania, New Jersey, New York, Connecticut and the District of Columbia met in New York to elect delegates and plan for a national black political convention. Leaders said the main goal of the regional and national meetings was to insure proportionate representation of blacks and other minority groups at the major party nominating conventions, and to persuade the parties to develop programs to meet the needs of blacks.

11   The formal presidential campaign of Roy Wilkins, executive director of the National Association for the Advancement of Colored People, said that Senator Edmund S. Muskie was "probably right" when he said that voters would not support a national ticket with a black vice-presidential candidate. Wilkins said that Muskie met the question "head on" when asked about the likelihood of having a black nominee for vice president.

17   A House Judiciary subcommittee charged in a report that the Justice Department had failed to adequately enforce provisions of the 1965 Voting Rights Act when it approved re-registration of voters in 26 Mississippi counties in 1971.

The panel said the department allowed the counties to continue implementing their re-registration plans although they had not obtained prior approval from the attorney general or the federal district court in Washington, as required by the 1965 Act. The subcommittee added that the department, in accepting local government claims that no discrim-

minatory purpose was intended, had
shifted the burden of proof of discrimination to the local citizen in violation
of the law.

In fact, the re-registration could have
had a racially discriminatory effect,
since many black voters lived in rural
areas, or may have had difficulty getting time off from work.

24   The U.S. Supreme Court unanimously
rejected appeals by black voters in Mississippi to invalidate the state's 1971
legislature elections on grounds of malapportionment and racial discrimination.

25   Rep. Shirley Chisholm (N.Y.), the first
black woman to serve in Congress, for-
mally announced in Brooklyn, N.Y.
that she would seek the Democratic
presidential nomination. Her entry
marked the first time that a black
woman had sought a major-party presidential nomination.

FEBRUARY
8   Rep. Louis Stokes (D., Ohio) was elected chairman of the Congressional Black
Caucus, replacing Rep. Charles C.
Diggs, Jr. (D., Mich.) who resigned. The
caucus was made up of the 13 black
members of the House, all of whom
were Democrats.

26   John Mitchell, on his last day as attorney general March 1, before assuming
direction of President Nixon's re-election campaign, said he would advise
Nixon to eschew a constitutional amendment, favoring instead a legislative approach, which he said could be effected
more quickly and would be legally
sounder.

Mitchell, who had been appointed to a
Cabinet-level committee to recommend
an Administration integration policy suggested a law delaying court busing orders
pending Supreme Court appeals or further Congressional action.

The Black Council, a group of 40 black
senior civil service and appointed officials, told a Nixon Cabinet committee it
opposed either legislative or constitutional busing curbs, according to Council
chairman Samuel C. Jackson, assistant
secretary of housing and urban development. The Council offered to present its
own proposals "to limit excessive busing" in a private memorandum to Nixon
and the Cabinet committee.

MARCH
8   The Congressional Black Caucus called

on President Nixon to nominate a black
to the upcoming vacancy on the Federal
Communications Commission (FCC)
and planned a national task force of
black political leaders and journalists to
fight discrimination in employment and
coverage of blacks in the news media.

10-12 Some 3,300 voting delegates and 5,000
observers met in Gary, Ind. at the first
National Black Political Convention
and voted to set up a permanent representative body to set the direction for
black political and social actions. Convention co-chairmen were Rep. Charles
C. Diggs (D., Mich.), Mayor Richard
G. Hatcher of Gary, Ind. and Imamu
Amiri Baraka. The proposed National
Black Assembly would have 427 delegates chosen from the District of Columbia and the 43 states represented at
the Gary convention. The assembly
would choose a council of 43 members,
with guaranteed representation for all
regions, viewpoints, organizations, youth,
and women. While the functions of
the assembly, which was authorized
by a 2,404–405 vote March 12, were
left largely undefined, Imamu Amiri
Baraka, one of the three convention co-
chairmen, said it "could endorse candidates, support candidates, run national
voter education and registration drives,
lobby for black issues, assess black
progress, make recommendations to the
national convention" (which itself would
be convened every four years) and "be
a chief brokerage operation for dealing
with the white power political institutions."

15   The 13 Black Caucus members issued a
statement on the administrations plans
to limit busing saying: "we strongly
reaffirm our support of busing as one
of the many ways to implement the
constitutional requirement of equal opportunities in education," although
"massive busing" would usually not be
required. They criticized "those who
would exploit this issue for personal,
political, or monetary gain."

Mayor Richard G. Hatcher, of Gary,
Indiana, who had helped chair the National Black Political Convention reported that the convention, after passing a
resolution against busing that was widely reported in the press, passed a up-
plementary resolution supporting the
practice "in cases where it serves the
end of providing quality education for

black people."

20   The Council of Black Appointees of the
      Nixon Administration said it was study-
      ing ways to amend Nixon's legislative
      proposals "to safeguard the rights of
      black Americans," since the bills posed
      "grave constitutional questions" which
      "unintentionally may adversely affect"
      blacks.

27   The Justice Department filed suit to bar
      elections in 1972 for the Georgia House
      of Representatives, contending that a
      scheduled redistricting plan "would oc-
      casion a serious potential abridgement of
      minority voting rights." They asked the
      court to order the state to come up with
      a plan in conformity with the 14th and
      15th Amendments and federal voting
      rights laws.

28   Clarence Mitchell, Washington director
      of the National Association for the Ad-
      vancement of Colored People, said the
      NAACP would challenge Nixon's pro-
      posals in the courts "before the ink is
      dry," if passed by Congress. He called
      the bills "the most blatant products of
      racism that I have seen in the federal
      government."

APRIL

11   President Nixon announced that Benja-
      min L. Hooks, 47, a black Memphis
      lawyer and Baptist minister, would be
      his nominee to a seven-year term on the
      Federal Communications Commission
      (FCC). Hooks, a political independent
      had been associated as a co-producer
      and participant on several Memphis tel-
      evision programs. He is a board mem-
      ber of the Southern Christian Leader-
      ship Conference and a member of the
      National Association for the Advance-
      ment of Colored People. He would re-
      place retiring commissioner Robert T.
      Bartley July 1. The position requires
      senate confirmation.

12   A three-judge federal court in Newark,
      by a 2–1 vote, ordered into effect a
      New Jersey Congressional district plan
      that would add one seat for the state's
      growing suburbs and create a predomi-
      nantly black district centering on New-
      ark. The state . legislature had been
      given until April 12 to correct the old
      system's violation of the one-man-one-
      vote rule, but the court mandated its
      own plan when the legislature failed to
      act. The plan was similar to one backed
      by state Republicans. Under the plan a

normally Democratic Hudson County
district would be eliminated.

MAY

19   The National Black Political Conven-
      tion released the "black agenda" May
      19 that had been approved by the
      March founding meeting in Gary, Ind.
      Provisions on school busing and on Is-
      rael, although modified by the steering
      committee, continued to provoke con-
      troversy, and the National Association
      for the Advancement of Colored People
      (NAACP) withdrew from the group.

JUNE

1   The Congressional Black Caucus issued
      a list of "nonnegotiable" demands that
      it planned to present for adoption by
      the Democratic Platform Committee as
      a prerequisite for its support of the
      Democratic presidential candidate. The
      demands included: full employment and
      a guaranteed family income plan with a
      $6,500 floor for a family of four; im-
      mediate withdrawal from Indochina; an
      increase in aid to black Africa; with-
      drawal of support to Portugal; and
      closing of the U.S. embassy in South
      Africa. The demands also included: in-
      creased aid to more black control of
      education and compliance with Su-
      preme Court busing decisions; massive
      aid to cities; national health insurance
      and free care for those with low in-
      come; a proportionate black share of
      Cabinet, judicial and other federal ap-
      pointments; and home rule for the Dis-
      trict of Columbia.

2   U.S. Supreme Court Justice William J.
      Brennan denied a petition by a black
      coalition asking the court to reverse the
      panel's ruling in the decision of the 3
      judge federal panel which permits New
      Jersey voters to cast their ballots in
      either the Democratic or Republican
      primary. The National Association for
      the Advancement of Colored People's
      Newark branch had said the ruling
      would allow Republicans to "raid" the
      Democratic primary and thus dilute the
      party's nonwhite vote.

8   The House approved and sent to Presi-
      dent Nixon June 8 a combined higher
      education-integration aid bill with three
      moderate antibusing provisions. The
      vote was 218–180. Voting against the
      measure were foes of busing who
      thought the compromise gave only an
      "illusion of relief," in the words of Rep.

Edith Green (D., Ore.), as well as liberals, including members of the Congressional black Caucus, who questioned the constitutionally and segregationist implications of the provision limiting court desegregation powers.

10 A reported 2,500 blacks met at a Washington conference and $100-a-plate dinner, sponsored by the Black Vote Division of the Committee to Re-Elect President Nixon, to devise strategy to obtain a goal of 25% of the black vote for the re-election of President Nixon. Stanley S. Scott, assistant director of communications at the White House, said many participants were "beneficiaries of government contracts and should show the Administration they care about where their money came from."

11 U.S. District Court Judge Dan M. Russell, Jr. deferred decision in Biloxi, Mississippi, in a delegate-selection case involving rival factions of the state party and urged an out-of-court settlement. The regular party group, headed by Gov. William L. Waller, was being challenged by a predominantly black "loyalist" group, recognized by the national party.

19 District Court Judge George L. Hart, Jr. ruled in Washington that delegate slates could not be excluded from the Democratic convention solely because of the race, age or sex of individual delegates or groups of delegates. The case involved the challenged Chicago slate of Mayor Richard J. Daley. New party reform rules required reasonable proportional representation at the convention for blacks, women, and young people.

20 The U.S. Court of Appeals for the District of Columbia overturned a district court's decision that slates of delegates to the Democratic National Convention could not be barred for lacking an adequate number of blacks, women, and young people. The three-judge appeals court found insufficient likelihood of injury to the constitutional rights of Chicago delegates to warrant action by the court without recourse first to the party's credentials committee. The credentials committee had 54 different challenges on its docket, involving 43% of the delegates selected thus far. More than three-quarters of the challenges involved the requirements for reasonable balances in race, sex and age.

24 The Democratic National Convention Rules Committee approved the nomination of California Assemblywoman and Congressional nominee Yvonne Braithwaite as cochairman of the convention. Democratic National Chairman Lawrence F. O'Brien, who was slated to become chairman, had pledged to the committee June 23 that a woman vice chairman would have "a full and equitable role in sharing of the platform of the convention."

Rep. Patsy T. Mink (Hawaii) had been expected to be recommended for the post but withdrew from consideration after the black caucus within the committee insisted on a black for the position.

One of the reforms approved by the committee was a recommendation that a woman be named chairman of the 1976 national convention and every alternative convention thereafter.

26 A bloc of black delegates led by Walter E. Fauntroy, the District of Columbia's nonvoting delegate to Congress, endorsed Senator McGovern for president, and committed 57.75 delegate votes. This, with other revisions in the complex delegate allotments, was 61.85 votes short of the total needed for nomination.

26 In return, McGovern had endorsed much of the program of the black group, which consisted of the Black Political Caucus, the 13 blacks in the House of Representatives, and the Black National Convention, a coalition group that had met in March in Gary, Ind. He also pledged to name blacks to the Supreme Court, the Cabinet, the sub-cabinet and other posts in proportion to their percentage in the general population.

27 Patricia Roberts Harris was elected permanent chairman of the Democratic National Convention. Her subcommittee was given 80 credentials challenges to dispose of before the business of nominating the candidates for President and Vice President of the United States could be handled. The Credentials Committee voted 71–61 to oust Mayor Richard J. Daley and his group of elected Chicago delegates and to seat the challengers that were led by the Jesse Jackson-Bill Singer faction. The recommendation went to the floor of the convention where the body voted to seat

the California delegation won by McGovern in the winner-take-all primary, and to seat the Illinois challengers. Prominent in the California McGovern delegation was State Rep. Willie L. Brown, Jr.

28 An alliance of McGovern forces and black leaders won a 72–59 vote to reconstitute the Georgia delegation by replacing two white delegates with blacks and enlarging it with half-votes for more delegates, and other minor concessions.

30 The Lawyers Committee for Civil Rights under law, a Washington group, sued the Justice Department for failing to oppose changes in election procedures in Canton, Miss. that the plaintiffs said discriminated against blacks. Canton had changed its district election of aldermen to an at-large basis and had annexed areas in 1968 that increased the proportion of whites in the town of 11,000. The suit charged that no black had ever held municipal office in Canton, and that the town had a record of racial discrimination and violence. The Justice Department had reported May 19 that it would not oppose the changes. Federal law required the department to screen proposed voting rule changes for possible bias.

JULY

9 A Poor Peoples Coalition, formed by members of the Southern Christian Leadership Conference, the National Tenants Organization and the National Welfare Rights Organization (NWRO), established a "tent city" at the campsite for all non-delegates attending the Democratic National Convention and the NWRO's five-day conference in Miami Beach which concluded July 9.

14 The Democratic National Committee selected as its new national vice-chairman former New York State Sen. Basil A. Paterson. McGovern's choice, campaign aide Pierre Salinger, withdrew. The late Congressman William L. Dawson had served as Vice Chairman of the Democratic National Committee from 1948 to his death.

AUGUST

3 The Federal Communications Commission (FCC) upheld the right of a candidate to broadcast paid political appeals that contained racist remarks if no danger of violence or incitement to violence were involved.

Atlanta, Ga. lawyer J. B. Stoner had used radio and television ads in his Senate primary campaign asking the people to "vote white" and to back "white racist J. B. Stoner." He said in the ads "the main reason why niggers want integration is because the niggers want our white women," and "you cannot have law and order and niggers, too." The FCC held there was no "clear and present danger of imminent violence which might warrant interfering with speech which does not contain any direct incitement to violence." Federal law prohibited a broadcaster from censoring political ads of legally qualified candidates. The ad protest was put before the FCC by the Atlanta chapter of the National Association for the Advancement of Colored People (NAACP), the Anti-Defamation League and a civic coalition.

4 Samuel J. Simmons resigned as Assistant Secretary of Housing and Urban Development to become the president of the new National Center for Housing Management. The Center was created by executive order to investigate the high rate of failures in federally subsidized housing, according to a Washington Post report. Simmons had been the highest ranking black in the Administration.

14 Edward C. Sylvester, Jr., was named as a national campaign coordinator for Sen. McGovern. A former Assistant Secretary of Health, Education and Welfare, Sylvester was the highest ranking black in the campaign structure. His role would involve him in all levels of the campaign and go beyond the "traditional concept of a minority adviser set apart in a separate office," according to McGovern spokesmen.

21 The Republican National Convention in Miami Beach had 1,348 delegates in attendance. There were 29.8% women (compared with 17% in 1968); 8.4% were over 65 years of age; 8.1% were under 30 years; 4.1% were blacks (1.9% in 1968); and 70.5% were participating in a convention for the first time. The delegates included three-quarters of the Republican governors, more than half of the Republican senators and a quarter of the Republican members of the House.

22 The Republican National Convention approved an amendment to the Rules Committee's report, calling upon the

party chairman to appoint a representative of "a black Republican organization" to the party's executive committee. The Rules Committee's report, adopted by voice vote, called upon the Republican National Committee and state committees to take "positive action to achieve broadest possible participation by everyone in party affairs, including such participation by women, young people, minority and heritage groups and senior citizens in the delegate selection process."

Another provision said "each state shall endeavor to have equal representation of men and women" in its delegation to the 1976 convention.

The Rules Committee had killed by a 70–27 vote a proposal to add 10 more members to the national committee to "better reflect the representation of young people, senior citizens and racial and ethnic minorities." The prevailing argument warned against setting quotas for particular groups.

OCTOBER

6   McGovern appealed to black ministers meeting with him in Chicago to get out the vote and counteract the "immoral" effort by Republicans to discourage blacks from voting.

19   Presidential candidate George McGovern told a black audience in Brooklyn, N.Y., where he was campaigning with Rep. Shirley Chisholm, "it's not my neck that's on the line—it's yours" and "it's the life and the freedom and the dignity of the ordinary citizen of this country that's at stake in this election."

NOVEMBER

7   In Richard M. Nixon's land-slide victory for re-election, surveys indicate that he lacked support only among black voters and the very poor. McGovern won only in Massachusetts, which gave him a 55% majority, and in the District of Columbia, with its black majority, where he pulled 79% of the vote.

1973

JANUARY

2   John Conyers, Jr. (D., Mich.) received 25 votes in his bid to become Speaker of the House. Carl Albert received 202 votes for his second term in the position.

3   Only 52% of black voters eligible participated in the 1972 presidential election, according to a Census Bureau Report. Sixty-five percent of eligible white

voters participated. Fewer than one-half of the newly enfranchised 18–20 year old voters participated in the 1972 presidential election, constituting 6% of the total vote.

20   James Farmer, most prominent black official before his resignation, who had served the Nixon Administration in 1970 as HEW assistant secretary accused the President of being isolated from contact with blacks.

Farmer had steadfastly refused to criticize the Administration publicly, but said he had had "great difficulty" maintaining a non-critical position, in the face of Nixon's nominations of G. Harrold Carswell and Clement F. Haynsworth, Jr. to the Supreme Court. Farmer said Nixon's chief adviser on matters concerning blacks was Leonard Garment, a white lawyer in the civil rights division of the Justice Department.

24   The Congressional Black Caucus January 24 re-elected Reps. Louis Stokes (D., Ohio), chairman; Parren J. Mitchell (D., Md.), vice chairman; Charles B. Rangel (D., N.Y.), secretary; and William Clay (D., Mo.), treasurer. Augustus A. Adair, professor of political science at Morgan State College, Baltimore, was named executive director.

FEBRUARY

3   John Lewis, head of the Atlanta Voter Education Project (VEP) reported that the number of black elected officials in 11 Southern states had reached 1,144 in 1972, with a net increase of 241 as a result of the November elections. The total was more than ten times the number of black officeholders in 1965, before passage of the federal Voting Rights Act.

Mississippi, with 145 officials, was followed by Alabama with 144, an increase of 61 during the year. Arkansas gained 49 black officeholders, including a state senator and two state representatives, who integrated the last all-white Southern legislature and brought the state's total to 140.

Louisiana had 127 black officials (including a state appeals court judge, the highest elected black judge in the region); North Carolina, 108; Georgia, 104; Texas and South Carolina, 98 each; Tennessee, 69; Virginia, 60; and Florida, 51.

The officials included two Congressmen, six state senators, 55 state representatives, 126 county officials, 38 mayors,

14 vice mayors, 441 other municipal officials, 198 law enforcement officials (nine of them judges), and 268 education officials.

VEP had reported Feb. 3 that 598 blacks had won election to office in the 11 states during 1972 out of 1,276 black candidates, both record figures.

5 Stanley S. Scott, 39, was named as the President's liaison with minority groups, making him the highest-ranking black in the Administration. He had been a press officer with the National NAACP, before joining the Nixon Administration.

8 The FCC ruled 5–2 that the Congressional Black Caucus had no inherent right to free television time to respond to a Presidential address.

Benjamin L. Hooks, one of the dissenters and the first black to sit on the commission, said the caucus, "as the major elected voice of the black community is the obvious entity to proffer positions on important racial issues and their proper resolution in contradistinction to those views and solutions held by the executive," just as one political party had the right of response to another under the fairness doctrine. Hooks said the networks had effectively deprived the public of minority viewpoints.

Regarding the caucus' contention that its First Amendment rights had been violated, the FCC noted that its earlier ruling, that a broadcaster could adequately give the public access to a group's views without granting the group air time, was before the Supreme Court after being overturned by a federal appeals court. The FCC said it was currently studying another plea raised by the caucus, that the network's policy of excluding broadcasts on controversial issues by nonmedia people be overturned. The commission said its policy was to "consistently reject the claims of groups and individuals requesting a specific right of access to broadcast facilities," since Supreme Court rulings had "stressed the right of the public to be informed" rather than a broadcaster's or individual's right to be heard over the air.

The cases arose from President Nixon's January, 1973, State of the Union message.

MARCH

2 President Nixon said in a Press Conference that he did not believe he had mistreated blacks in the matter of civil rights. "This nation owes something to all of its people and it owes something particularly to those who have been disadvantaged," he said. "We, I believe, have done a very effective job in that respect, in terms of what we have done, maybe in terms of what we have said . . . and we are going to continue to do well and we hope eventually that our citizens will recognize that we have done so."

5 The Supreme Court allowed to stand a lower-court decision denying relief to a group of black Mississippi taxpayers who claimed their assessments were raised by local officials in retaliation for a boycott of white merchants. The lower court said the plaintiffs had not exhausted their right of appeal in the state courts.

14 H. R. Crawford, 34, manager of subsidized housing project in Washington, D.C. and a public housing critic was named assistant secretary of housing and urban development.

23 The Democratic National Committee endorsed a slate of 25 new members selected by its new chairman, Robert S. Strauss. The additional at-large members raised the committee's total membership to 303.

The action was considered a test of party unity since the new posts were sought by various factions, most notably a Black Caucus effort to gain black appointments and AFL-CIO effort to gain eight designated labor seats for unionists who had followed AFL-CIO President George Meany's policy of neutrality in the 1972 presidential election. There were 8 black at-large members: Mayor Richard G. Hatcher, Sen. George Brown, Mrs. Mattlyn Rochester, Percy Sutton, Mrs. Orchid Jordan, Patricia Harris, Matthew Perry, Mrs. Mary Widener.

APRIL

3 Los Angeles City Councilman Thomas Bradley and Mayor Sam Yorty entered a two-man runoff by being the two leading vote-getters in a nonpartisan mayoral primary. Bradley, 55, a former Los Angeles police lieutenant and attorney had lost to Yorty in a similar runoff in 1969, Bradley polled 233,789 votes to 190,649 for Yorty by preliminary count. The issues of race did not surface in the primary campaign, and Bradley termed it "an irrelevant factor" in the election. Approximately 18% of the city's population was black.

John F. Bass (D.), 46, former St. Louis

welfare director, was elected controller, the first black to hold the city's second highest office.

10   Philip J. Rutledge, highest ranking black in the Department of Health, Education and Welfare, resigned to join the National League of Cities and U.S. Conference of Mayors.

James A. Scott, a Democrat appointed to the Maryland state legislature in December, 1972, to fill an unexpired term, was indicted by a federal grand jury in Baltimore on charges of allegedly distributing 40 pounds of heroin.

Clarence M. Mitchell, III, a Maryland state senator was indicted on four counts of evasion of federal income taxes.

17   Bobby Seale, one of the founders of the Black Panther Party, won 19% of the vote to finish second in a field of nine candidates running for mayor of Oakland, Calif. The Republican incumbent, John Reading, fell 168 votes short of a majoriy (wining 55,342 votes) and faced a runoff fight with Seale May 15.

The contest resulted from Seale's efforts to abandon revolutionary rhetoric for political and social assistance programs. Elaine Brown, another Panther candidate, outpolled Seale but failed to win a seat on the city council.

In Berkeley, Calif., a moderate-liberal coalition, the Berkeley Four, won three of four city council seats and blocked a bid by the April Coalition, the radical slate which had won three seats in 1971, to establish a majority position on the council.

MAY

2   Samuel R. Pierce, Jr., one of the highest ranking blacks in the Nixon Administration, resigned as general counsel of the Treasury Department.

5   A national survey conducted by the University of Michigan, found a 16 point decline in the percentage of blacks who identify with the Democratic Party. The dissident Democrats did not necessarily become Republicans, the survey showed, but did increase the number who considered themselves to be independents, unaffiliated with either party.

29   Thomas Bradley was elected mayor of Los Angeles in a non-partisan election over incumbent Sam Yorty, who was seeking a fourth four-year term. Bradley, a city councilman for 10 years and before that a police lieutenant, would take office July 1 as the city's first black mayor. The city's total black population

was approximately 18%.

Bradley polled about 56% of the vote. In the preliminary count Bradley had 431,222, Yorty 334,297. Bradley said it proved "that people will listen to a candidate and make their judgment on merit, instead of race or creed."

A last minute campaign effort attempting to link Bradley to left-wing radicals was unsuccessful.

JUNE

1   Gloria E. A. Toote, 41, was confirmed as assistant secretary for equal opportunity in the Department of Housing and Urban Development, succeeding Samuel J. Simmons.

5   Mrs. Cardiss Robertson Collins (D.), 41, was elected to Congress June 5 from the 7th Congressional District in Illinois, the seat left vacant when her husband George was killed in an airplane crash in December, 1972. Mrs. Collins would be Illinois' first black congresswoman.

JULY

23   Southern black Democrats testifying before the Democratic Party's Commission on Delegate Selection went on record as being opposed to any proposals which would drop the "quota" system in selecting delegates to National Presidential Conventions.

Thomas Reed, president of the Alabama NAACP, said: "Unless there are built-in safe guards and mandates, people will not fall in line and let minorities have their share."

AUGUST

11   Rep. Parren Mitchell told the Democratic Commission on Delegate Selection that any attempt to repeal or cut-back the 1972 guidelines would be "an attempt to turn back the clock. Until the time when we [blacks] achieve economic and political parity, I'm going to insist on quotas for blacks."

22   D'Army Bailey, militant Berkeley city councilman, was unseated in a recall election by a simple majority vote. Originally elected in a coalition of radicals, Bailey was replaced by William B. Rumford Jr., 39, a black moderate.

SEPTEMBER

17   Gov. Daniel Walker (D., Ill.) signed a bill legalizing January 15, Dr. Martin Luther King Jr.'s birthday, as a state holiday. The chief sponsor of the legislation was Rep. Harold Washington (D.), of Chicago. Illinois is the first state to take this action.

Section XV

PRESS

THE BLACK PRESS

One of the oldest black business institutions and one of the most potent weapons in the long struggle for freedom is the black press. In its 136-year existence, it has been no less vigilant than the white press of America in affecting social issues and influencing their outcome.

Though modest in scope and small in circulation in its early days black-owned and -edited newspapers contributed to the anti-slavery struggle in the pre-Civil War years, and, in the century that had passed since Emancipation was proclaimed, have been unflagging in the cause of the civil rights for black Americans.

Freedom's Journal, founded in 1827 by John B. Russwurm and Rev. Samuel E. Cornish, was born out of the need for both a banner to carry the blacks' cause and an answering cannon to the attacks made upon the race by an anti-black New York paper. Russwurm had been an honor graduate of Bowdoin College, and the first black U.S. college graduate, while Rev. Cornish was a man described by historians as "of wonderful intellectual parts, having keen perception . . . probably the most thoughtful and reliable, certainly the most popular and conversant, editor of his time."

The third issue of *Freedom's Journal,* published in New York on March 30, 1827, carried on its front page three articles indicative of the intent of the publication. One concerned the "Memoirs of Capt. Paul Cuffee," a successful free black fisherman; another, entitled "People of Colour," addressed itself to the examination of slavery as a legal institution; the third dealt with a "Cure for Drunkenness." From this it appears that the *Journal* aimed to report the accomplishments of blacks; bring about, by reason and persuasion, the abolition of slavery, and uplift the black community.

But the road of *Freedom's Journal,* like the road to freedom itself, was rocky. In the opinion of journalistic historian I. Garland Penn, "this publication . . . met with more and greater obstacles than did any other paper ever published upon the continent. Besides having to fight for a cause which then had but few advocates, it could see in the popular mind no indication of support. The Afro-Americans in the North that would patronize the journal were few, while the Abolitionists numbered no great throng at that time." Within three years, *Freedom's Journal,* by then renamed *Rights of All,* was dead. Like some men of his time, Editor Russwurm had fa-

vored a back-to-Africa solution, while most others placed faith in their future in a free America.

Since the first black journalistic experiment of 1827, some 2,800 black newspapers have appeared in America, of which 153 survive today. These publications, though bedeviled by mounting operational costs and increasing competition for readers from the white press and TV continue to voice the aspirations, articulate the demands and protests, and mirror the progress and problems of 22 million black Americans.

While *Freedom's Journal,* which fought for the abolition of chattel slavery in the South and citizenship rights for free blacks in the North, came into being as "an organ of protest against the inhumanity of man to man" 147 years ago, significantly, the contemporary black press finds itself waging the same war against racism and injustice. The first black newspapers urged a crusade to destroy slavery; in 1963 black publishers issued a call for support of the Kennedy Administrations civil rights legislation by "all friends of freedom."

A continuity of concern for human rights has characterized the black press throughout its history. It has provided the black masses with an effective voice for freedom, a forum for racial grievances and a reflector of discontent. In doing so, its total function has not been wholly negative, despite assertions of detractors. Black publications were recording black achievement and publishing enlightening and inspiring facts about the black history long before the Emancipation, the black press, including weekly papers, popular magazines and academic journals, has generally been the chief means of disseminating the truth about black history and rebutting the slanders of the black's enemies.

Before the Civil War, some 24 black-owned periodicals had joined the national chorus of demand for abolition of slavery and civil rights for the black Americans. Though chiefly read by freed black men and women, about 500,000, who formed the literate section of the population, they spoke for all black Americans. Abolitionist-minded whites read these black organs as well, and to the same degree that liberals and pro-civil rights whites read black newspapers today.

The earliest black papers appeared in such Northern cities as New York, Boston, Philadelphia and Pittsburgh. Among them was the *North Star,* founded by Frederick Douglass in 1847 and published in Rochester, N.Y. Douglass sensed the value of "a well-conducted press" to the black freedom movement and the upward battle of the black American. Richard T. Greener, a Harvard graduate, published *The New National Era* during this period. Greener's publication was probably the first black paper to send a foreign correspondent abroad, dispatching a man to Paris in 1871 to report the First International Workingmen's Conference, presided over by Karl Marx. Since then, a long line of correspondents have been assigned by black papers and magazines to cover wars, revolutions and other news of world interest all over the globe.

One of the most astonishing publications in the early history of black journalism was the *New Orleans Tribune*, the first black daily paper to appear in the United States and published in both English and French. It was owned by Dr. Louis Charles Roudanez and edited by Paul Trévigne. New Orleans-reared Roudanez was a Paris-trained physician and a vigorous champion of the interests of his people. Trévigne, who spoke several languages was a teacher and during the Civil War had, at the risk of his life, been editor-in-chief of a militant journal named *L'Union*.

The *New Orleans Tribune* started as a tri-weekly in July, 1864, but after October of that year was published daily except Mondays. It was an official organ of the Republican Party of Louisiana, selling for five cents a copy. Its platform included: "For every citizen his rights, universal suffrage; equality before the law; to every laborer his due, an equitable salary; eight hours a legal day's work." Its influence was considered to be immense, with copies being sent to every member of Congress. The *Tribune* demanded the payment of weekly wages to ex-slaves, declaring the yearly contracts recommended by the Freedman's Bureau to be virtually another form of slavery. The paper also insisted upon rejection or dismissal of Southern representatives in Washington, asserted that freedmen could never be safe without the ballot, and prophesied that persecution of blacks would attend the withdrawal of federal troops from Louisiana. To round out its coverage, the *Tribune* carried local intelligence, literary prose and verse, legal items and notices to mariners. But despite its brilliant journalistic success, the *Tribune* was a financial failure. After spending some $35,000—no inconsiderable sum in those days—from his personal fortune, Dr. Roudanez was forced to suspend publication in 1868, but resumed it the following year. Roudanez died in 1890.

In less than two decades after the disastrous defeat of Reconstruction in the South, black newspapers multiplied from 31 to 154 in 1890. Most had small circulations and did not often survive for long, however.

During the first half-century following Emancipation, the black press expanded swiftly, precisely because the need for it was even greater than before 1863. The withholding of civil rights to blacks proved that Emancipation did not create a millennium. The return to political power of the black's worst enemies in the Southern states, and the abandonment of the black masses by Northern white interests which had previously fought slavery, forced the black American to rely on himself and his own institutions of protest and struggle. The black press was thus vitally needed to give hope to the embattled millions forced back onto the defensive by an increasing wave of anti-black feeling throughout the country. The last 25 years of the nineteenth century saw a worsening of the status of the American black, and Professor Rayford Logan has written: "At the beginning of the twentieth century, what is now called secondclass citizenship for blacks was accepted by Presidents, the Supreme Court, Congress, organized labor, the General Federation of Women's Clubs—indeed, by the vast majority of Americans, North and South, and by the 'leader' of the black race."

Grievances and desires had to be expressed somehow, and the black press became the chief vocal agency of this expression, as well as the chronicler of contemporary life and activities in the black communities. Against immense odds, the black press began to remake the popular image of the American Black which had already been distorted by the stereotyped or selective reporting of the white press. Except for a few successful black entertainers and artists, the white press described the race only in derisive terms, emphasizing its crime and inadequacies.

Even during this struggle black papers were evolving commercially into more business-like organizations, devoting more time and money to improving coverage and distribution. Staffs were enlarged, printing facilities came under black ownership and ties were established with political parties. From the turn of the century to the beginning of World War I, black newspaper publishing matured, and the first black newspapers of modern times, such as *Baltimore Afro-American*, *Philadelphia Tribune*, *Pittsburgh Courier* and *Norfolk Journal and Guide* were launched.

Just as fine newspapers emerged, so did the giants of black journalism: T. Thomas Fortune of *New York Age*, William Monroe Trotter of *Guardian,* the *Courier*'s Robert L. Vann and Robert S. Abbott of *Chicago Defender.* For 75 years of the first century of its exisence, the U.S. black press appealed primarily to a small but influential group, the educated and informed, the so-called "talented tenth." The papers possessed little potential for mass circulation. Abbott, who founded *Chicago Defender* in 1905, changed this approach and sought a mass audience by emulating the succesul yellow journalism of the day. It was a new kind of journalism for the black press, featuring sensational banner headlines, yet based on militant protest and racial uplift. Abbott's *Defender* grew prosperous on this style, and by encouraging Southern blacks to migrate to the North in search of manhood and opportunity.

The great Northward migration of blacks, starting with and following World War I, stimulated to some extent by aggressive appeals by such publications as *Chicago Defender,* resulted in a new expansion of the black press field and a burgeoning of its circulation. The post-World War I black newspaper was eagerly and widely read in black communities by the highly literate members of the race, and increasingly by those less educationally favored. Its influence was powerful and rising. By 1940, around two hundred black publications served a consolidated audience of close to 1.5 million. World War II stimulated sales generally, and a survey of 144 papers in the 1942–44 period reported a combined net circulation of 1,613,255. Syndicated columnists came into being, many of them, such as the NAACP's Walter White, having attained status outside the journalistic field. And the Associated Negro Press, a service regularly supplying weeklies with news and features, was developed by Claude Barnett into a stable, alert and competently functioning institution. In 1940, the Negro Newspaper Publishers' Association, now re-named the National Newspaper Publishers Association, was formed to coordinate thinking and interest.

While World War I accelerated the development of the black press and demonstrated its power to influence black thinking on national issues, World War II confronted the press with a challenge and crisis from which it emerged with heightened prestige and stimulated circulation. During these two great conflicts, the U.S. government recognized that the black press could be both a dangerous irritant and a critical ally. In World War I, black papers supported the nation's war aims but generally denounced segregation and mistreatment of black troops. (In 1918 the War Department

summoned a number of black leaders, including 31 newspaper editors and publishers, to Washington to discuss the black role in the national emergency. The leaders called for an end to anti-black mob violence and wider participation in the war effort.) During World War II, the black press became an outlet for black resentment, humiliation and discontent. Its editorials affirmed support of the country's war aims, but demanded integration into the military and industrial machinery created to win the war.

Discrimination against black members of the U.S. armed forces was attacked and exposed so aggressively by the black press in World War II that high government officials, including at least two members of President Franklin D. Roosevelt's cabinet, recommended either severe censorship or outright suppression of black papers. Government officials began to read black papers regularly; the Federal Government was displeased and discomforted by their accounts of discrimination against black soldiers in the South, and by editorials complaining about the failure to integrate blacks into the war economy. The FBI took an active interest in the black press, sending agents to confer with a number of its ediors about their policies, which continued unchanged after the interviews ended.

In 1941, A. Philip Randolph's March on Washington movement was dramatized almost exclusively by the black press, and resulted in the issuance by President Roosevelt of an executive order setting forth the first Federal Fair Employment Practices declaration.

Today, the black press remains a unique institution in our society—owned, managed and staffed by blacks and serving a predominantly black readership. During a century of recurrent unrest and movement for improvement, editors and publishers have been projected as key opinion-makers in the black community, political leaders, and movers and shakers in time of crisis. Those who control the press interpret black needs as they see them, and formulate demands.

The developing crisis of race relations caused by the dramatic surge of the black masses has made the black press even more important, and its informational function has been modified in that black publications concern themselves more with relations between the races than with publishing purely black news. Surveys of stories appearing on the front pages of the nation's top 28 newspapers show that over two-thirds are about race relations, less than a third exclusively racial. This reflects the black accelerated thrust toward equality and integration, as well as the slowly changing fabric of American society.

Whereas the black press formerly enjoyed a near monopoly of strictly black news and comment on the dreams and drives of black America, since the black revolt began the white press has devoted increasing attention to what blacks resent and desire, how they live and why they demonstrate. The superior resources and facilities of the white press give it a big edge in its capacity for coverage of the present racial upheaval. Stories which blacks once had to wait a full week to read are now being flashed to millions within hours via the TV screen, or are reported within the day by the general press. Even the function of the protest, once sole province of black periodicals, is being assumed by more and more white publications. The role of the black press is changing fast in the face of history.

The black press has traditionally been a special pleader, an advocate of black rights and a ventilator of grievances. But it is essentially a commercial press, subject to all the vagaries of business trends and responsive to the ebb and flow of the economy. Viewed in business terms, black publishers face the same problems of spiralling costs and sharpening competition for advertising and readership from outside media as do their white counterparts in the weekly newspaper field.

For most of its history, the black press was forced to depend wholly upon circulation revenue and as a consequence its papers had to price themselves higher than the general papers. This tended to limit their potential mass audience and to weaken their financial position. Advertising from the white business world at first came in trickles. Since World War II, however, the advertising picture has changed with a new knowledge and appreciation of the financial strength of the black consumer market. This awareness of the buying power of blacks has resulted in added revenue sources on the black press.

Black publishers and editors are critically re-examining the role of the advocacy press in the current rights revolution in an effort to find out how they can more adequately meet the challenge of the present crisis and serve the changing needs of their readers. The black press must give the kind of dynamic leadership that our very first paper, *Freedom's Journal*, and the other crusading black papers, gave a century and more ago.

EDITORS, PUBLISHERS AND JOURNALISTS

Robert S. Abbott, founder and editor of the *Chicago Defender*, was born on St. Simms Island, November 24, 1870, off the Georgia Coast. He attended Hampton Institute, Virginia, and in May, 1899, earned a Bachelor of Law Degree from Kent College of Law in Chicago. He was told by Attorney Edward H. Morris that he was "a little too dark to make any impression on the courts in Chicago." He was never admitted to the Illinois bar. After a few years, during which time he tried to get established in Gary, Indiana, and Topeka, Kansas, Abbott returned to Chicago, where he got a job in a loop printing house setting type for railroad time tables.

On May 5, 1905, Abbott brought out the first issue of the *Chicago Defender* with borrowed funds and contributions. He was editor, publisher, writer and newsboy selling papers from door to door in barber shops, pool rooms, drug stores, and churches. His strong editorials encouraging Southern blacks to come North where the social and economic conditions were more favorable soon gained the *Chicago Defender* a national reputation. He died February 29, 1940.

Abbott was succeeded by his nephew, **John Herman Sengstacke,** who controls, in addition to the Robert S. Abbott Publishing Company, Sengstacke Enterprises and the Amalgamated Publishers, Incorporated, which include *The Michigan Chronicle, The Tri-State Defender* and the *Pittsburgh Courier* chain.

Claude A. Barnett, the founder of the *Associated Negro Press*, was born in Sanford, Florida in 1889. He received his educational training in Tuskegee just where he came in contact with Booker T. Washington and T. Thomas Fortune.

Following World War I, Barnett started the *Associated Negro Press*—an earlier effort funded by Washington which had failed.

The *A.N.P.*, using stringers as sources from across the country, compiled a weekly news packet which could be utilized by small newspapers and other media for a modest subscription fee.

Barnett, because of his drive and contacts, made *A.N.P.* a national force, and in World War II was influential with other black publishers in gaining accreditation for black war correspondents. Barnett was early a believer in Pan Africanism and published *A.N.P.* releases on African, Caribbean and South American. Chatwood Hall (Homer Smith) sent his dispatches from Moscow over the *Associated Negro Press* dateline for over ten years during the First and Second Five Years Plans and World War II.

Claude Barnett died in Chicago on August 2, 1967.

Thomas Morris Chester (1834–92) was born in Harrisburg, Pa., the son of a free black father, George Chester, and a mulatto mother who had run away from her slave master. Young Chester's home was a station on the Underground Railroad and he grew up in an atmosphere of intellectual excitement. He was sent to high school in Monrovia, Liberia, and remained there for a year. On his return, his parents sent him to prep school at Thetford Academy in Vermont, where he entered in the junior class. He finished in 1856 with second highest honors. In 1857 he returned to Liberia where he was appointed superintendent of an organization formed to teach civilized customs to Africans liberated from American slave vessels. He became the editor and publisher of *The Star of Liberia* and served as a correspondent for the *New York Herald*.

The outbreak of hostilities between the states brought Chester back to the U.S., and he served with Frederick Douglass and others on a recruiting committee for Massachusetts which was looking for volunteers to fill a black regiment. He refused to join the service himself because of the discriminatory treatment meted out to blacks and the fact that a black, at that time, could not receive a commission.

While attending a meeting of the African Methodist Episcopal Church in Philadelphia, Chester was offered a job at the front as a general correspondent for the *Philadelphia Press*. For three years he covered the progress of the war, writing under the name of "Rollin," and under the general head "Affairs Among the Colored Troops." He was at Petersburg, Virginia, in August, 1864 and at the attack on Fort Fisher, near Wilmington, N. C. in December, 1864. He was one of the first reporters to enter the Confederate capital when Richmond fell to the Union troops.

Following the war, Chester went to England where he entered the Middle Temple, and became the first black barrister admitted to practice before English courts. Years later he was admitted to practice before the Pennsylvania Supreme Court, another first for this pioneer war correspondent. He died of a heart attack in Harrisburg in 1892 at age 58.

Samul E. Cornish, born of free black parents about 1795 in Delaware and raised in the relatively free environment of Philadelphia and New York City. After graduating from the Free African School, he was ordained a minister and organized the first black Presbyterian Church in the United States. A group of New York City blacks backed the publication of a newspaper that would answer the need for a "full-bodied articulation of their ideals and aspirations." Samuel Cornish and John Russwurm were assigned the task of starting the paper. As a result the first black newspaper was published in New York on March 16, 1827, under the name of *Freedom's Journal.* In September, 1827, Cornish resigned as senior editor and became an agent for the Free African Schools, retaining his financial interest in the paper. In February, 1829, when Russwurm became convinced of the wisdom of colonization, Cornish returned as senior editor of *Freedom's Journal,* whose name was later changed to *The Rights of All.* From that point on he was associated with a number of newspapers, chief among them the *Weekly Advocate,* which later became the *Colored American.* Cornish was responsible in part for the black press becoming identified with the role of protest. He called for a fight to the finish in America: "Let there be no compromise," he said, "but as though born free and equal, let us contend for all the rights guaranteed by the constitution of our native country."

Frederick Douglass, born a slave in Maryland in 1817, acquired an education, escaped to freedom, and gained renown as an abolitionist, spokesman for the "free" black, and fighter for human rights and peace. Douglass founded and edited his paper, the *North Star* (first published on November 1, 1847 in Rochester, New York) after returning to the United States from England, where he had fled to escape re-enslavement. Douglass was so well known that his paper was readily accepted as one of the most outspoken foes of slavery, and from the outset it received a great deal of assistance from abolitionist forces. Douglass was not only a good speaker, he was an effective and forceful writer. The *North Star* was published for sixteen years, first under that title, and later as *Frederick Douglass' Paper.* It ceased publication following the Emancipation Proclamation.

Douglass died in 1895 at his home in Washington, D.C.

Roscoe Dunjee was born June 21, 1883, at Harper's Ferry, West Virginia.

He was educated in the public schools and attended Langston University. He prepared himself for his newspaper career by writing whenever he had an opportunity.

For years, he worked in various capacities for any newspaper published in Oklahoma City. He wrote news copy and later editorials, preparing himself for the first publication of the *Black Dispatch* in November, 1915. Aside from his newspaper activities, he interested himself in all aspects of community life. He was a militant and vigorous fighter for black people, but he believed that inter-racial cooperation was necessary.

T. (Timothy) Thomas Fortune gained the greatest fame as the editor of the *New York Age.* He was born of slave parents in Mariana, Florida, October 3, 1856, and attended Stanton School at Jacksonville and later Howard University in Washington, D.C. After the Civil War, his father became active in the politics of Reconstruction Florida. Fortune went to New York City in 1879, and worked in the composing room of the *Weekly Witness.* In 1880 he became editor of the *Rumor* (the title was soon changed to the *New York Globe*), a weekly newspaper published by George Parker and William Walter Sampson. The *Globe* rapidly attained an influential position as an opinion-maker, but due to differences between the partners, it was suspended in November, 1884. During the period that he had worked as editor of the *Globe,* Fortune had formulated a policy position for effective journalism: to be a power for good among the people a paper must be fearless in tone; its editor should not fail to speak his just convictions; he should hold himself aloof from parties, and maintain his position untrammelled by parties and party bosses. A week after the *Globe* suspended publication, Fortune returned as the editor and publisher of the *New York Freeman,* which began publication November 22, 1884. In typographical make-up it was an excellent paper, and it contained the important news relating to blacks, contributed by a string of able correspondents. In this respect, it surpassed any other black-owned-and-operated journal. As a bold and aggressive writer, Mr. Fortune jumped to the forefront of black journalists, and was one of the first blacks to hold a position on the editorial staff of a white daily, the *New York Evening Sun.* He continued as publisher of the *New York Age* with Jerome Peterson of Brooklyn, New York, as his partner, until he sold his interest in the paper to Fred R. Moore in 1905. At that time, Fortune joined the staff of Booker T. Washington and the National Negro Business League. His relationship with Washington caused considerable controversy, and his power and prestige went into an eclipse from which they never emerged. Though Booker T. Washington freely acknowledged his indebtedness to Fortune in conversation, he never mentioned him in his books. It was said by researchers that Fortune wrote or edited all of Washington's books and speeches. He and Washington ultimately broke off relations, but Fortune was never again the power that he had been. Up to the time of his death in Philadelphia on June 2, 1928, articles under his byline appeared from time to time in the *New York Amsterdam News*, the *Norfolk Journal and Guide* and the *Philadelphia Tribune*.

Chester Arthur Franklin was born June 7, 1880, in Denison, Texas, and educated in the Omaha, Nebraska public schools. He attended the University of Nebraska for two years. Starting his first paper, the *Denver Star* in 1899, he continued its operation until 1913 when he moved to Kansas City, where he brought out the *Kansas City Call* in 1919. The *Kansas City Call*, under his leadership, was considered one of the most fearless papers published in the cause of black people. *The Call* editorialized on behalf of better housing, safety from police brutality, and participation of blacks on juries. In June, 1931, Franklin established a corporation of $100,000, full paid, with no stock held by outsiders. These shares were donated to some of the older employees for their faithful service to the paper—a revolutionary step in black business. Roy Wilkins was among the early editors on the *Kansas City Call*. Franklin died on May 7, 1955.

John Henry Murphy (1840–1922), founder of the *Baltimore Afro-American* newspaper which is presently in the third generation of dynamic leaderships under the guiding head of his descendants.

John Murphy was born a slave in Baltimore, Maryland, with emancipation. In 1863, he joined the Union Forces to fight for the freedom of those still enslaved and in 1892, he founded the *Baltimore Afro-American Newspaper*, setting his own type and delivering the finished paper to his customers.

Upon his death in 1922, his son **Carl Murphy** became the publisher. In 1967, **John H. Murphy III,** became president of the Afro-American Company and **Frances Murphy,** Carl's daughter, its publisher.

The paper presently prints a national edition and local editions for Baltimore, Washington, Richmond, Virginia and Newark, New Jersey. It has had a consistently high quality of reportage and maintains a reputation for credibility among its black readership.

Plummer Bernard Young, Sr. was born July 27, 1884, in Littleton, North Carolina (two sons, Bernard Jr. and Thomas W.). He was educated at Littleton, North Carolina High School and St. Augustine's academy.

In 1911, he founded the Guide Publishing Company and maintained it until his death, when he was succeeded by his son, Plummer Bernard, Jr. *The Guide*, at the height of its influence, was known as the black "*New York Times*."

John B. Russwurm, editor, politician, and salesman, the first black college graduate in the United States (Bowdoin, 1826) was born in Jamaica on October 1, 1799, of a white father and a Jamaican mother. His father sent him to Canada under an assumed name to be educated, but after his father's death, his mother financed his college education and gave him the right to use his father's name.

With Samuel E. Cornish, Russwurm was assigned to the task of starting a black newspaper. *Freedom's Journal* was the result (*see* Cornish and "The Black Press,") and as molders and reflectors of black opinion and sentiment, the editors played an important role in the shaping of the abolitionist position. By 1829, however, Russwurm had decided that the American Colonization Society had the right solution. In February, 1829, he announced his support of "the return to Africa movement." The black leadership in New York City under Boston Crummell which had selected him for the job of editor was enraged and forced his resignation. Russwurm now took an even stronger position. Stating that "The man of color would never find a place in the Western hemisphere to lay his head," he called for a return to Africa and a review of the great empires of the middle age. After receiving a master's degree from Bowdoin College in 1829, Russwurm accepted a liberal offer from the conservative Maryland Colonization Society and went to Liberia, where he founded the *Liberia Herald* and served as superintendent of schools. He later became governor of the Maryland colony at Cape Palmas, where he died on June 17, 1851. Contemporary black leaders never forgave Russwurm for what they considered "selling out."

William Monroe Trotter, publisher and editor of the *Boston Guardian*, was born April 17, 1872, in Springfield Township, Ohio. He was the son of James Monroe Trotter and Virginia Isaacs Trotter (reputed to be the granddaughter of Thomas Jefferson). He was educated in Boston and received his A.B.

(magna cum laude) from Harvard in 1895, and his M.A. in 1896. He was the first black elected to the Phi Beta Kappa at Harvard. Following his graduation, he worked in real estate and insurance, but his consuming passion for truth caused him to found, in 1901, the *Boston Guardian*, a weekly newspaper devoted to securing absolute equality for the black people. Trotter was a leader with W. E. B. DuBois in the Niagara Movement, and later became the National Secretary of the National Equal Rights League, a militant civil-rights organization. As spokesman for this group, he took the case of the blacks to the League of Nations, and later went to Paris where he placed several petitions on the black problem in the U.S. before the World Peace Conference. Unable to secure a passport, Trotter went abroad as a ship's waiter. He confronted Woodrow Wilson and later presidents on the issue of black rights and discrimination. He was articulate, fearless and idealistic, and under his editorship, the *Guardian* played an important role in re-establishing the black press as a dominant force in the fight for black rights. Disillusioned and broken in health, Trotter jumped, or fell, to his death from the roof of his Boston home on April 7, 1934, at the age of 62.

Ida B. Wells was born at Holly Springs, Mississippi, on July 16, 1862. Her parents were both slaves, though her father, who had lived on his white owner-father's plantation since birth, was highly literate, and skilled as a carpenter. She attended Rust College (a Freedmen school) of which her father was a trustee and later took some courses at Fisk Univerity. Her parents died in a yellow fever epidemic when she was fourteen and she became the principal support of her orphaned brothers and sisters. She soon started teaching in country schools, first in rural Mississippi, then in Shelby County, Tennessee. It was at this time that she started writing for a black newspaper, *The Living War*, under the name, "Iola." Shortly after this she went to Memphis and started teaching at the Memphis Schools. Her outspoken opposition to injustices in the educational system caused her to lose her

teaching post, and she became part-owner and editor of the *Memphis Free Speech*. Under her editorship, it became an increasingly effective voice against racial injustice.

In May, 1892, three black businessmen were horribly lynched in Memphis and Ida Wells charged in the columns of her paper that the murders had been instigated and planned by the white business community. She hammered away at the fact that blacks must not support the white business establishments that had been the root cause of the lynchings, and she urged blacks to migrate to the new Oklahoma territory. Business suffered, and blacks migrated by the scores. Fortunately, she had gone to Philadelphia to attend a religious convention, and her male business associate was forewarned of the impending mob action the night the presses and equipment in her office were destroyed and the building burned. Rumor was that she was to be shot on sight. Her last column had implied that not all blacks accused of raping white women were guilty; sometimes the women were willing partners. Unable to return to Memphis she went on to New York, where she became associated with T. Thomas Fortune on the *New York Age*, to which she had been a frequent contributor from Memphis. Her moving, but factual, accounts of the lynching of blacks in the South focussed international attention on this crime against humanity, and she published in the pages of the *New York Age* and later in *Red Book* the first authentic evidence of lynching in the United States. As a result, she was given a testimonial dinner by a group of women in Brooklyn and Manhattan, from which sprang the first of the black women's clubs and an invitation for her to lecture in England on lynching.

Ever militant, she became active, with William Monroe Trotter, in the National Equal Rights League and a friend of Frederick Douglass and his wife, Helen. She was married in 1895 to Ferdinand L. Barnett, a brilliant Chicago lawyer, and her career as a civic and political leader continued until her death in Chicago on March 25, 1931. Her contribution to the black press was a major one.

BLACK PUBLICATIONS

ALABAMA—Birmingham: *Baptist Leader,* est. 1912, weekly, Baptist; *Mirror,* est. 1948, weekly, independent; *Times,* est. 1964, weekly; *World,* est. 1932, weekly, independent. Huntsville: *Weekly News, The,* est. 1969, bi-weekly. Mobile: *Alabama Citizen,* est. 1954, weekly, Democratic; *Beacon,* est. 1954, weekly, Democratic. Montgomery: *Mirror,* est. 1955, weekly. Selma: *Mirror,* est. 1965, weekly; *Sun-Post,* est. 1972, weekly.

ARIZONA—Phoenix: *Arizona Informant,* est. 1971, weekly; *Arizona Tribune,* est. 1958, weekly.

ARKANSAS—Little Rock: *Southern Mediator Journal,* est. 1938, weekly, independent.

CALIFORNIA—Albany: *Black Times,* weekly, independent. Altadena Pasadena: *Eagle,* est. 1968, weekly. Bakersfield: *Observer,* est. 1955, weekly. Berkeley: *Post,* weekly, independent; *Richmond Post,* weekly, independent; *San Francisco Post,* weekly, independent; *Seaside Post,* weekly, independent. Compton: *Metropolitan Gazette,* est. 1966, weekly, Republican. East Palo Alto: *Peninsula Bulletin,* est. 1966, weekly, Independent Democratic. Hayward: *New Lady Magazine,* monthly, black women's service. Fresno: *California Advocate,* est. 1967, weekly. Los Angeles: *Central News-Wave Publications,* est. 1938, weekly, independent; *Citizens' Voice* (only information available); *Firestone Park News & Southeast News Press,* est. 1916, weekly; *Herald-Dispatch,* est. 1952, semi-weekly, independent; *News,* est. 1959, weekly; *News Press,* est. 1962, weekly; *Sentinel,* est. 1934, weekly, Democratic; *Soul Illustrated,* bi-monthly, entertainment; *United Pictorial Review,* weekly, independent; *Watts Star Review,* est. 1929, weekly. Menlo Park Ravenswood: *Post,* est. 1953, weekly. Oakland: *The Black Panther,* est. 1965; *California Voice,* est. 1919, weekly, independent; *Post,* est. 1963, semi-weekly. Palo Alto: *Black Times,* est. 1971, monthly, Pomona: *Clarion,* est. 1970, weekly. Sacramento: *Observer,* est. 1962, weekly, independent. San Bernardino: *Precinct Reporter,* est. 1965, weekly. San Diego: *Voice and Viewpoint News,* est. 1959, weekly. San Francisco: *Metro,* monthly. *Sun Reporter,* est. 1944, weekly, independent. Santa Ana: *Orange County Star Review,* est. 1971 weekly.

COLORADO—Denver: *Drum,* est. 1971, weekly; *Weekly News,* est. 1971, weekly.

CONNECTICUT—Bridgeport: *Harambee,* est. 1968, monthly. Hartford: *Star,* est. 1969, weekly. New Haven: *Star,* est. 1971, weekly.

DELAWARE—Wilmington: *Delaware Defender,* est. 1962, weekly, independent.

DISTRICT OF COLUMBIA—Washington: *Afro-American,* est. 1933, semi-weekly, independent; *Capitol Spotlight,* est. 1953, weekly; *Informer,* est. 1964, weekly; *Journal of Negro Education, The,* est. 1932, quarterly, black research and education; *Negro History Bulletin,* est. 1937, monthly, history and education; *New Observer,* est. 1960, weekly; *Tribune,* est. 1933, semi-weekly, independent.

FLORIDA—Ft. Myers: *Star-News,* est. 1971, weekly. Ft. Lauderdale: *Westside Gazette,* est. 1971, weekly. Ft. Pierce: *Chronicle,* est. 1957 weekly. Jacksonville: *Florida Star-News,* est. 1951, weekly, independent. Miami: *Florida Courier,* weekly; *Times,* est, 1923, weekly, independent. Orlando: *Florida Sun,* est. 1932, weekly; *Mirror* est. 1932, weekly. Pensacola: *Exposure,* weekly; *Times,* est. 1968, weekly. St. Petersburg: *Weekly Challenger,* est. 1967, weekly. Sarasota: *Weekly Bulletin,* est. 1959, weekly. Tampa: *Florida Sentinel-Bulletin,* est. 1945, semi-weekly independent; *News Reporter,* est. 1958, weekly. West Palm Beach: *Photo Illustrated News,* est. 1955, weekly, independent.

GEORGIA—Albany: *Times,* est. 1964, weekly; *Southwest Georgian,* est. 1940, weekly. Atlanta: *Face the Nation* (only information available); *Foundation, The,* quarterly, religious; *Inquirer,* est. 1960, weekly, independent; *Atlanta Magazine,* monthly, business and chamber of commerce; *Voice,* est. 1966, weekly; *Daily World,* est. 1928, (4 days a wk.), independent. Augusta: *Voice,* est. 1970, weekly; *News Review,* est. 1971, weekly. Columbus: *Times,* est. 1958, (Mon., Thu., Sat.). Macon: *Times,* est. 1966, weekly. Savannah: *Herald,* est. 1945, weekly independent. Thomasville-Tallahassee; *News,* est. 1967, weekly.

ILLINOIS—Chicago: *Black Stars,* monthly; *Bulletin,* weekly, independent; *Citizen,* est. 1965, weekly; *Courier,* est. 1959, weekly, independent; *Daily Defender,* est. 1905, daily, independent; *Defender,* weekly, independent; *Ebony,* monthly, black news and pictures; *Gazette,* est. 1950, weekly, independent; *Indepen-*

dent Bulletin, est. 1958, weekly; *Jet,* weekly, black interest; *Metro News,* est. 1972, weekly; *Muhammad Speaks,* est. 1961, weekly; *Negro Traveler,* monthly, black transportation and hotel world; *New Crusader,* est. 1940, weekly, Democratic; *Woodlawn Booster,* weekly, independent; *Woodlawn Observer,* weekly. East St. Louis: *Crusader,* est. 1941, weekly; *Monitor,* est. 1962, weekly. Evanston: *North Shore Examiner,* est. 1968, bi-weekly. Maywood: *Suburban Echo-Reporter,* est. 1964, weekly. Rockford: *Crusader,* est. 1950, weekly, independent.

INDIANA—Gary: *American,* est. 1927, weekly, Democratic; *New Crusader,* est. 1961, weekly, Democratic; *Info,* est. 1961, weekly. Indianapolis: *Indiana Herald,* est. 1959, weekly; *Recorder,* est. 1895, weekly, independent. South Bend: *Reformer,* est. 1967, weekly.

IOWA—Des Moines: *New Iowa Bystander,* est. 1894, weekly, Republican. Waterloo: *Defender,* est. 1963, bi-weekly.

KANSAS—Wichita: *Times,* est. 1970 weekly.

KENTUCKY—Louisville: *American Baptist, The,* est. 1880, weekly, Baptist; *Defender,* est. 1933, weekly, independent.

LOUISIANA—Alexandria: *News Leader,* est. 1962, weekly. Baton Rouge: *News Leader,* est. 1952, weekly. LaFayette: *News Leader,* est. 1970, weekly. Lake Charles: *News Leader,* est. 1965, weekly. Monroe: *News Leader,* est. 1962, weekly. New Orleans: *Louisiana Weekly,* est. 1926, weekly, independent. Shreveport: *Sun,* est. 1920, weekly, independent.

MARYLAND—Baltimore: *Afro-American,* est. 1892, semi-weekly, independent.

MASSACHUSETTS—Boston: *Bay State Banner,* est. 1970, weekly.

MICHIGAN—Detroit: *Michigan Chronicle,* est. 1936, weekly, independent; *Pyramid, The,* est. 1942, quarterly, Masonic. Ecorse: *Telegram,* est. 1945, weekly. Grand Rapids: *Times,* est. 1957, weekly. Jackson: *Blazer,* est. 1962, weekly. Saginaw: *Valley Star, The,* est. 1970, weekly.

MINNESOTA—Minneapolis: *Spokesman,* est. 1934, weekly, independent; *Twin Cities Courier,* est. 1966, weekly, independent; *Twin Cities Observer,* est. 1941, weekly, independent. St. Paul: *Recorder,* est. 1934, weekly, independent; *Sun,* est. 1941, weekly, independent.

MISSISSIPPI—Greenville: *Negro Leader,* est. 1962, monthly. Jackson: *Advocate,* est. 1940, weekly, black interest; *Mississippi Enterprise,* est. 1939, weekly, Democratic. Meridian: *Memo Digest,* est. 1966, weekly. Natchez: *News Leader,* est. 1971, weekly. New Albany: *Community Citizen,* est. 1948, semi-monthly, Democratic.

MISSOURI—Kansas City: *Black Progress Shopper News,* est. 1968, weekly; *Call, The,* est. 1919, weekly, independent; *UNIQUE,* monthly, black interest. St. Louis: *American,* est. 1928, weekly, Democratic; *Argus,* est. 1912, weekly, Democratic; *Crusader,* est. 1963, monthly; *Evening World,* monthly; *Metro Sentinel,* est. 1971, weekly; *Sentinel,* est. 1968, weekly.

NEBRASKA—Omaha: *Everybody,* monthly, black interest; *Star,* est. 1938, weekly.

NEVADA—North Las Vegas: *Voice,* est. 1968, weekly.

NEW JERSEY—Camden: *Jersey Beat,* est. 1955, weekly. Newark: *Afro-American,* est. 1892 weekly; *Nite Life,* est. 1958, weekly. Plainfield: *Voice,* est. 1968, weekly.

NEW YORK—Brooklyn: *New York Daily Challenge,* est. 1972, semi-weekly; *New York Recorder,* est. 1953, weekly, independent. Buffalo: *Challenger,* est. 1962, weekly; *Criterion,* est. 1925, weekly, independent; *Fine Print,* 1971, weekly. Hastings-on-Hudson: *Westchester County Press,* est. 1910, weekly, independent. Jamaica: *New York Voice,* est. 1958, weekly. Mount-Vernon: *Westchester Observer,* est. 1947, weekly. New York: *African Progress,* monthly, African-American relations and life in Africa; *Amsterdam News,* est. 1909, weekly, independent; *Contact,* monthly, equal employment; *Crisis,* est. 1910, monthly, black advancement; *Journal of the National Medical Association,* bi-monthly, black medical; *Manhattan Tribune,* est. 1968, weekly; *National Scene,* black American interest; *Our Colored Missions,* monthly, Catholic black education; *Say,* est. 1954, bi-weekly, black interest; *Voice of Missions,* est. 1892, monthly, African-Methodist. Rochester: *Communicade,* est. 1972, weekly.

NORTH CAROLINA—Asheville: *Southern News,* est. 1936, bi-weekly. Charlotte: *Metrolinian News,* est. 1971, weekly; *Post,* est. 1940, weekly; *Quarterly Review of Higher Education Among Negroes,* est. 1933, quarterly, black education; *Star of Zion*, est. 1976, weekly, A.M.E. Zion. Durham: *Carolina Times*, est. 1927, weekly independent. Gastonia: *Gaston Times*, est. 1972. Greensboro: *Carolina Peacemaker*, est. 1965, weekly, independent. Raleigh: *Carolinian, The*, est. 1940, weekly, independent. Wilmington: *Journal*, est. 1945, weekly.

OHIO—Bedford Heights Cleveland: *Metro*, est. 1955 monthly. Cincinnati: *Call and Post*, est. 1950, weekly; *Herald*, est. 1956, weekly, independent. Cleveland: *Call and Post*, est. 1920, weekly. Columbus: *Call and Post*, est. 1960, weekly, independent. Toledo: *Bronze Raven*, est. 1946, weekly, independent. Youngstown: *Buckeye Review, The*, est. 1937, weekly, black interest; *Mahoning Valley Challenger*, est. 1967, weekly, independent.

OKLAHOMA—Lawton: *Community Guide*, est. 1971, weekly. Oklahoma City: *Black Dispatch*, est. 1909, weekly, independent. Tulsa: *Oklahoma Eagle*, est. 1921, weekly, Democratic.

OREGON—Portland: *Observer*, est. 1970, weekly.

PENNSYLVANIA—Philadelphia: *Afro-American Newspaper*, est. 1893, weekly; *Black Beauty*, semi-annually, beauty culture; *Black Careers*, bi-monthly, jr. & sr. high school & college career development; *National Beverage Leader*, monthly, black beverage market; *Nite Life*, est. 1953, weekly; *Nite Owl*, est. 1957, weekly; *Nite Scene*, est. 1967, weekly; *Pride Magazine*, bi-monthly, black interest; *Scoop*, est. 1959, weekly; *Tribune*, est. 1885, semi-weekly. Pittsburgh: *New Courier*, est. 1910, weekly, independent.

SOUTH CAROLINA—Charleston: *Chronicle*, est. 1971, weekly. Orangeburg: *Vue South*, est. 1964, monthly, black progress in South Carolina.

TENNESSEE—Memphis: *Tri State Defender*, est. 1951, weekly, independent; *Whole Truth,*

The, est. 1935, monthly, religious. Nashville: *A.M.E. Christian Record*, est. 1846, weekly, religious; *A.M.E. Church Review*, quarterly, religious; *Broadcaster, The*, est. 1923, quarterly, educational.

TEXAS—Austin: *Capital City Argus*, est. 1962, weekly; *Inter-racial Review*, est. 1970, monthly. Dallas: *Elite News, The*, est. 1966, weekly; *Key News*, est. 1960, weekly; *Post Tribune*, est. 1949, weekly, independent; *Weekly*, est. 1953, weekly. Fort Worth: *Bronze Thrills*, est. 1951, monthly, black interest; *Como*, est. 1940, bi-weekly, independent; *Hep*, monthly, black interest; *Jive*, est. 1951, monthly, black interest; *La Vida*, est. 1958, weekly; *Mind*, est. 1932, weekly; *Sepia*, est. 1954, monthly, black interest. Houston: *Defender*, est. 1934, weekly; *Forward Times*, est. 1960, weekly, independent; *Globe Advocate*, est. 1965, weekly; *Informer*, est. 1892, weekly, independent; *Tempo* (only information available); *Texas Freeman*, est. 1892, weekly, independent; *Voice of Hope*, est. 1967, weekly. Lubbock: *West Texas Times*, est. 1962, weekly. San Antonio: *New Generation*, est. 1972, weekly; *Register*, est. 1930, weekly, independent. Tyler: *Leader*, est. 1951, bi-weekly; Waco: *Messenger*, est. 1927, weekly, independent.

VIRGINIA—Charlottesville: *Albermarle Tribune*, est. 1954, weekly. Norfolk: *Journal and Guide*, est. 1909, weekly, independent. Richmond: *Afro-American*, est. 1939, weekly, independent; *Planet*, est. 1939, weekly, independent; Roanoke: *Tribune*, est. 1940, weekly, independent.

WASHINGTON—Seattle: *Facts News*, est. 1961, weekly; *Medium*, est. 1970, weekly. Tacoma: *Facts News*, est. 1969, weekly.

WISCONSIN—Milwaukee: *Courier*, est. 1963, weekly, independent; *Star-Times*, est. 1971, weekly. Racine: *Star News*, est. 1972, weekly.

BLACK PERIODICAL PRESS

The black periodical press, which had begun during the 19th century with church-oriented magazines and scholarly journals such as *Journal of Negro Education, Journal of Negro History, Negro History Bulletin, Phylon,* and *Crisis,* took on new life during World War II. The great upsurge in the quest for knowledge by and about blacks led to the founding of the first Johnson publication, *Negro Digest* (1942). *Negro Digest* was the brainchild of John H. Johnson, a 24 year old migrant from Arkansas to Chicago. *Negro Digest,* a compendium of reprint articles from other magazines and newspapers with enough original thought-provoking material to give it focus and personality, within three years became the cornerstone of what had never existed before—a commercially successful black slick magazine. *Ebony* magazine was founded November, 1945, and where *Negro Digest* was frankly patterned after the eminently successful *Reader's Digest,* *Ebony* was an over-size format entry into the field of photo-journalism à la *Life* magazine. In order to sell advertising in the infant magazine, Johnson began training and developing a staff of space salesmen, particularly knowledgeable about "The Negro Market." Johnson used facts and figures and his intuitive sense of "why" the black consumer market differed from the general or white market for goods and services, and he stressed the point that an ad in a general magazine did not address itself to the black reader, while an ad in *Ebony* magazine was a personal invitation to buy. He paid for and developed market analyses showing the larger share of the black consumer's spendable dollar that went into various goods and services. He published brochures telling "How to Sell the Negro Market," and his staff pioneered in the use of film strips and motion pictures to tell the "Ebony" story. Johnson's singleminded approach to magazine publishing sought to reflect itself through identifying with the black communities' goals and aspirations. In the three decades since Johnson entered the publishing field, *Ebony* has achieved the highest monthly paid circulation of any black publication in history—one and a quarter million copies. Other publications followed: *Tan,* a women's service magazine, in 1950; *Jet,* a compact size weekly news magazine, in 1951; *Negro Digest,* which was not published for several years, was revived in 1961, and in 1970 changed its focus and name to *Black World.* *Black Stars* incorporated *Tan* in 1971 and *Ebony, Jr.,* a magazine for young black readers, made its debut in May, 1973.

The success of Johnson Publications provided incentive for other publications and by 1973, *Black Enterprise,* a controlled circulation magazine devoted to black business, labor, employment and economic viability, was being published regularly. *Essence* is devoted to fashion, fiction, feature articles and the young liberated black woman. *Encore, Black Sports, Black Scholar,* etc. all reflect facets of black life and interest. *Tuesday,* a newspaper magazine supplement, published by J. Leonard Evans, has also carved a niche for itself in an otherwise hostile environment.

The black periodical press, catering to the special needs and consciousness of its black readers, has exhibited more viability than its counterparts in the general periodical field.

SELECTED BLACK BOOK PUBLISHERS

Afro-Am Publishing Company
1727 South Indiana Avenue
Chicago, IL 60616

Black Academy Press
135 University Avenue
Buffalo, NY 14214

Broadside Press
12651 Old Mill Place
Detroit, MI 48238

Drum and Spear Press
1802 Belmont Road, N.W.
Washington, D.C. 20009

Emerson Hall Publishers
62 W. 85th St.
New York, NY 10024

Jihad Publishing Co.
Box 663
Newark, NJ 07102

Johnson Publishing Company, Inc.
820 South Michigan Avenue
Chicago, IL 60605

Third Press
444 Central Park West
New York, NY 10025

Third World Press
7850 South Ellis Avenue
Chicago, IL 60619

DISCRIMINATION IN THE MASS MEDIA

The Congressional Black Caucus held hearings on the mass media, March 6 and 7, 1972. The hearings, chaired by Rep. William L. Clay, marked the first major, national attempt by black people to interpret their own relationship with the powerful field of communications. Representative Clay said, the hearings found:

• "widespread, long-standing and deeply entrenched racism throughout its massive communications network.

• the black community, the black media worker and the black movement grossly excluded, distorted, mishandled and exploited by the white-controlled news media.

• conscious or unconscious conspiracy to prevent the public from learning of the massive exploitation of black and poor people by the major corporations which advertise on radio, television and in the newspapers."

Clay showed that the mass media:

• "failed to report accurately and honestly day-by-day news emanating from black communities.

• one of the major American industries is directly responsible for the inability of blacks and other disadvantaged persons to improve their standards of living, to enjoy equal protection of the law, and to develop their full potential as individuals.

• has consistently failed to point up the hypocrises of its own existence in dealing with blacks and the minorities, by failing to investigate its own bad practices with the 'same zeal with which it has run into investigations of every other human endeavor'."

The following testimonies were presented at the hearings:

• Tony Brown, dean of Howard University School of Communications, stated, "40% of black children watch television an average of 6½ hours daily, and believe it is true to life. Black people watch TV 25 hours a week, as compared to 16 hours for whites.

• Ernest Dunbar, former editor with *Look* magazine, stressed the need for federal laws to protect the privileges of newspaper writers and their right to refuse to appear in closed courts or grand jury hearings. Pointing to the fact that black reporters working for white newspapers are on a more limited ground than their white counterparts is the case of *New York Times* reporter, Earl Caldwell, who was ordered to testify in a closed door grand jury session about the Black Panther Party. He refused, on the grounds that it would jeopardize his news-gathering sources, and was given little support from the *Times* in fighting his case.

Recommendations made at the hearings included:

- Appointments of black persons to the FCC.
- Immediate promotion of more blacks into decision-making positions to help offset the "distortion, mutilation and censorship of the true black experience."
- Possible legislation to protect the newsman's right to refuse to appear in closed courts or grand jury hearings.
- Possible legislation to protect defendants from "excessive adverse publicity," such as in the case of Angela Davis.
- Investigate the appointment of a black group to conduct an independent study of the long and short term effects of television on black children.
- Encourage black students to enter journalism and to seek employment in all aspects of the media.
- Formation of a media watchdog committee by local black organizations to monitor fairness of the media, challenge licenses and file lawsuits. Black lawyers are urged to work with such committees.
- Establishment of a national task force of black-elected officials and black media specialists to work for the elimination of discriminatory practices in the media.

Statistics revealed the following facts concerning the black media:

- Amount of black exclusion: 4.2 percent of all newspaper employees are black. In the professional class that includes reporters, only 1.5 percent are black; of 7800 news-editorial jobs available at 196 daily newspapers, blacks held only 157, or 2 percent; of 1,219 news-executive positions available, blacks held only five.*
- Electronic media: Minority employment on public television stations dropped from 12 percent in 1970 to 8 percent in 1971. Blacks own none.[1]
- There are 13 bills currently pending in the U.S. House of Representatives that would make it virtually impossible to challenge stations seeking license renewals. The Federal Communications Commission (FCC), which is legally responsible for overseeing the broadcasting industry, favors such legislation. There is no black member on the FCC.[2]

*Source: EEOC Research Study, 1970.

[1]In 1973 Dr. William Banks gained ownership of TV station 62, UHF, in Detroit, Michigan.
[2]One black member has since been appointed to the FCC—Benjamin Hooks.

BLACK-OWNED RADIO STATIONS, 1973

At the beginning of 1973 only 28 of the more than 7,000 commercial broadcast stations in the United States were owned by blacks. No commercial TV station was black owned, though one—WLBT, in Jackson, Mississippi—has interracial ownership and a black general manager, William H. Dilday. Black control of the radio waves which program the minds of black citizens through "soul-stations," is less than one-tenth of 1 percent. Yet, black programming on a full-time basis accounts for at least one and, in many cases, several stations' output in major metropolitan areas. The programming of these stations is designed to reach the black consumer audience and to influence their purchases of products advertised on the station.

The Congressional Black Caucus charged: "Most of the white giants in the radio industry are southerners who not only control radio communications in the South, but also hold a death grip on black radio communications in northern metropolitan areas. These stations produce programs of the lowest calibre, reaching for the lowest common denominator in the black community and offering material devoid of any social concern for real public service and the well being of the black community."

They further charged that pending legislation, which would make it virtually impossible to challenge the licenses of broadcasters, would inevitably slow the employment of blacks in broadcasting and would bring to a halt the almost imperceptible toehold that blacks have gained in ownership of radio stations. The legislation under question is known as the Broyhill Bill (Congressman James T. Broyhill, N. C.), and would permit renewal of licenses if "broadcast service during the preceding license period has reflected a good faith effort to serve the interests and needs of its area," and "has not demonstrated a callous disregard for law." H. Carl McCall, President of WLIB in New York and chairman of the Association of Minority Broadcasters, said, "The legislation virtually frees the broadcaster of any defineable or enforceable responsibility to serve his community."

The minority owners and the Black Caucus back legislation, introduced by Congressman Charles B. Rangel (D., N. Y.), which provides that an applicant's license shall be renewed only if the renewal applicant "is legally, financially and technically qualified and if his service during the last license period has been substantially attuned to meeting his community's needs and interests and if the operation of the station has not otherwise been charac-

terized by deficiency." This type of legislation was viewed by the groups as the only process by which blacks can challenge the licenses of broadcasters who have not been responsive to the community.

Black owners include James Brown, the singer, whose radio stations are a division of James Brown Enterprises. He owns WJBE in Knoxville, Tenn., WRDW in Augusta, Ga., and WEBB in Baltimore, Md. Bell Broadcasting in Detriot is the pioneer black owner in the radio field. They own WCHB and WCHD (fm) in Detroit and KWK in St. Louis. Bell is owned by Dr. Wendell Cox, Dr. Robert Bass, and heirs of the late Dr. Haley Bell, the founder and the principal owner of the stations.

WAUC Atlanta University station, Atlanta, Georgia
  Lorenzo Jelks, owner
WRDW Augusta, Georgia
  James Brown Enterprises, owner
WEBB Baltimore, Maryland
  James Brown Enterprises, owner
WILD Boston, Massachusetts
  owned by Sheridan Broadcasting Corporation in Pittsburgh, Pa.
  Arthur Edmonds and Ronald R. Davenport, chief owners
WUFO Buffalo, New York
  owned by Sheridan Broadcasting Corporation in Pittsburgh, Pa.
  Arthur Edmonds and Ronald R. Davenport, chief owners
WVOE Chadbourn, North Carolina
  owned by Ebony Enterprises
  Ralph Vaught, Jr., station manager and principal owner
WGRT Chicago, Illinois
  Johnson Publishing Company Inc., owner
WMPP Chicago Heights, Illinois
  Charles Pinkard, owner
KJLH (fm) Compton, California
  John Lamar Hill, owner
WCHB Detroit, Michigan
  Bell Broadcasting Company, owner
WCHD (fm) Detroit, Michigan
  Bell Broadcasting Company, owner
WGPR (fm) Detroit, Michigan
  owned by WGPR, Inc.
  Dr. William V. Banks, president and chief owner
  also owned by Detroit Masonic Lodge
WORV Hattiesburg, Mississippi
  Vernon Floyd, owner
WEUP Huntsville, Alabama
  Leroy Garrett, president and general manager
WTLC (fm) Indianapolis, Indiana
  owned by Frank Lloyd and Calojay Enterprises

KTYM (fm) Inglewood, California
Avant Garde Broadcasting, Inc.
Clarence Avant, president and chairman of the board

KPRS (fm) Kansas City, Missouri
owned by KPRS Broadcasting
Andrew (Skip) Carter, president and general manager
Mildred Carter, program director and part owner
Jay Carter, station manager

WJBE Knoxville, Tenn.
James Brown Enterprises, owner

WNOV Milwaukee, Wisconsin
Jerrel W. Jones, owner

WLIB New York, New York
H. Carl McCall, president of Inner City Broadcasting Corp.
also owned by Percy Sutton, Pierre Sutton, Dr. M. S. Woolfolk, Clarence B. Jones

KOWH (fm) Omaha, Nebraska
Reconciliation, Inc.
Rodney S. Wead, spokesman

KOZN Omaha, Nebraska
Reconciliation, Inc.
Rodney S. Wead, spokesman

WAMO (fm) Pittsburgh, Pennsylvania
owned by Sheridan Broadcasting Corporation in Pittsburgh, Pa.
Arthur Edmonds and Ronald R. Davenport, chief owners

WSHA (fm) Raleigh, North Carolina
Elizabeth Czech, supervisor

WWWS (fm) Saginaw, Michigan
owned by Earl Clark and Clark Broadcasting in Detroit

WSOK Savannah, Georgia
Billy Taylor, Benjamin Tucker, G. Douglas Pugh, owners

KWK St. Louis, Missouri
Bell Broadcasting Company, owner

WHUR (fm) Howard University station, Washington, D.C.

WGPR Radio, Detroit, was granted a permit to construct WGPR-TV (channel 62) on June 1, 1973. The television station is owned by the International Masons, a black fraternal organization, and Dr. William Banks, Supreme Grand Master of the Organization, is president of the all-news UHF station.

Section XVI

ARTS AND LETTERS

AGENDA FOR ACTION: BLACK ART AND LETTERS, 1972

Dr. Margaret Walker Alexander

Black America stands today at the crossroads of destiny for the future of all our people in the world. This is not a time of joyous freedom, but a crucial time of unmitigated tyranny. An age of technological tyranny. Not a time of tranquility, but a stormy time of senseless war and killing. Militarism is the weapon of politicians and the lives of men have become a political football. There is no lull of mercy in the oppressor's brutality. The 1970's threatens to be more intense decade than the 1950's of repression in a police state. Starvation and suffering exist in the midst of affluence and waste. Spiraling inflation ticks off the hours of economic instability. Death and destruction control all the nations while we fight against evils of injustice. Most people recognize the assassin's bullet and the racist's rhetoric as belchings of a sick society. We are threatened with annihilation of an entire planet because of the greed and short-sightedness of one race in the family of man. A cancerous sore of white racism eats at the heart of all American life. Five major issues daily headline the news! First, racial enmity and hatred generating violence; second, a perpetual foreign war dating from the beginning of the century; third, industrial contamination of all nature, earth, water and air; fourth, the extreme dilemma of urban life with the new controlling economy of crime and drugs; fifth, political chaos and economic collapse, for the two go hand-in-hand. Witness the three ring circus of political primaries in White America, while the faltering, fluctuating stock market is sick enough to die and prove it. The twilight of the western world has come. This is the state of our society. What is the state of Black Art and Letters in the year of 1972? Alive and well, doing fine and improving everyday, struggling to thrive and survive in a hostile society. It is as if we were some kind of paradox, a strange anachronism, the handicapped horse that wins the race. For Black Art seizes on this time of oppression and repression and makes us use our art functionally for the people. Not art for art sake. Art cannot exist in a vacuum. What is the hope for black people? How can we talk about life tomorrow for our children unless we dare do something today to shape that life? There is no question but that world wide societal revolution is a fact of our times. It is not a question of whether we want revolution, as one of our young black poets says, "there is nothing we can do to stop it . . ." What then can we do?

In this death struggle for freedom, for peace, and for human dignity the black artist and the black scholar must see and understand their role as scholars and as artists. We must first see the state of our world which our art and actions must reflect, and we must understand our role as thinkers in the struggle. We must begin to use the black mind as a tool for black liberation, not as yoga to liberate a single individual but to liberate an entire people. Then we can accept the challenge of a thinking black world whirling into action. We must understand that the masses of our people expect and need, no, more than that, demand, from the black mind a new paradigm, for the shape of our borning society. That society is not waiting for the first day of the 21st century to be born—it is converging upon us now.

It becomes the awesome duty and destiny of the black man to bring about complete societal change because he is the slave that must throw off the yoke of oppression. He cannot expect the oppressor to condemn the chains of his slave. We black people can—and must—accept the challenge and the task because we have the creative minds, and the spiritual strength to do what must be done. We are the mythmakers, and the timeless dreamers with a vision for the world. We are the priests, and the prophets with the cultic magic to bring the creative fire and energy of imagination to the inanimate and transform the dust of things and ideas into living action and spirits of power. We must put on our thinking caps and decide the shifting shape of our Utopian World that is already emerging. There are only two pillars left under this toppling house, political and economic, and every day we are watching them crumble into decay. Lawd, if I had my way, I'd tear this building down.

Recently I read what seems to me to be serious tactical mistake. One of our black brothers said, "the problem of rebuilding society is Whitey's bag, not ours." I think that is going back through the same revolving door we used to come outside. Why should we expect Whitey to do better for us, when we consider the mess his industry and technology have already wrought for him? We do not wish to rebuild this society as Stokley said, but we wish to create a better one.

Man should be the master of money and machines and not their slaves. The white man has used the black man's mathematics and the black man's labor to build his technological universe, but it is against us and destructive to all life, rather than for us and constructive of life. How do we turn these cybernic automotons into vehicles for man's good. Where are our black engineers? Human relations cannot become positive when the moral values are subject to the power of money and machines. Black people have the creative and spiritual power that is not depleted nor wasted by the Western Diaspora, because it is rooted in the earthy, natural, realistic and humanistic welter of our African and Oriental heritage. The black scholar and artist is challenged as never before to tap the roots of this creative and spiritual power and name the paradigm for our past revolutionary society. Before all the concrete action and change that is necessary takes place, there must be a bonafide paradigm. What kind of paradigm do we want to create for our new and borning society? What is the nature of the world we want for our children?

You may answer: First, a different economy and a new political system. Does anyone doubt that the old paradigm has failed, is collapsing and chaos exists in it's place? Before there can be a new paradigm there must be a malfunctioning of the old, a crisis of purpose or philosophy and a crisis of function. The social scientists, namely the economist and the political scientist know that such a crisis now exists. The mass problems of unemployment in a war economy are clear evidences of malfunction of the system. We need a new paradigm. Is Socialism the answer? Of one thing we are sure, black people must remember that whatever form the new economy and political system may take they must be fashioned by us, for our own particular problems in this dying western world! Hence, we know that neither Russian, nor Cuban, nor Chinese, nor Algerian Communism will work for Black America. Black America needs its own special brand and system of its own making. That is why we—must name the paradigm.

In every age of mankind's history and recorded progress, the scholar, whether scientific inventor, philosopher or political scientist, has come forth with a new paradigm when a scientific revolution has changed the concept of the universe. Such a time is now. The Einstein revolution has changed man's concept of the universe. We live in an illimitable universe where everything is relative, where there must be unity in diversity, and where the space-time continuum challenges man to the outer depths or limits of space. And yet, this is only evident in physics and mathematics, not in the social sciences and the humanities. The family of man has not yet learned to live with the beneficial and peaceful uses of atomic energy, and

with the social, moral and spiritual implications of this nearly century-old scientific revolution. We need a new socio-economic, and political paradigm. Black mankind is no less creative and inventive than those in other ages have been. We are a charismatic numinous people of the black experience caught in a vortex of this time of crisis. Destiny declares that the responsibility is ours.

We sorely need and surely want a new religious belief for our new universe. Institutionalized religion in White America has broken down under the challenge of racial integration while the black Church has been revitalized during the civil rights movement as a revolutionary instrument for social change. Today as a separatist institution, because it's always been segregated, the black church looms large in prophetic power with it's cultic strength from blood and fire serving the needs for emotional catharsis within the oppressed black community as seen in the fervor of the gospel music and shout songs that flow directly out of the streams of our folk life and direction. What this welter of black emotion needs is channeling and direction. Most local black churches are lacking in harnessing these dynamics. A new religious belief will challenge the highest sense of Deity and divinity in human personality, while at the same time more than encouraging religious tolerance for all world religions, as it is respectful of all world cultures, languages and spiritual entities of all human beings. Such a spiritual philosophy of humanism is destined to prevail.

We expect black people to continue to conceive of new uses for education, so that old curricula such as the liberal arts college, long since outdated and obsolete, will disappear and more relevant, productive and creative schools will develop. There will be less emphasis for the young child on the cognitive and more on the affective aspect of learning. Our black institutions will relate more closely to the black communities that inspire and support them. Sociological studies of the black family, the black community, and all other black institutions will focus themselves largely on our folk history, life and culture rather than watered down theories of outmoded white racists. The black scholar must provide more than the white rhetoric that he has learned from his white education. We must stop apeing the very racism that oppresses us. Change is the name of the game and dedication to the struggle for black people's complete emancipation into a new world of thought and action is what the black artist must be about.

The masses of our people are pleading,

therefore, for the word. They want to know the name of that new paradigm. They have handed down a mandate for freedom. We have heard a new declaration for independence. Oddly enough it is not the black intellectuals who have come out of white universities with our monstrous degrees who are filling this need for intellectual leadership that the black masses demand. There is a new young black intelligentsia. They are truly a prophetic generation. They have the dreams of a man and the words of a God, and they have been spawned largely from the horrible oppression of the prisons. Whether it is poetry, painting or pure intellectual constructs . . . they are coming from the prisons. They are not only vocal and articulate, they are terrible in their majesty and splendor. It behooves all black artists and scholars to listen to what they have to say, for these young men and women are like the veterans of a foreign and unholy war. They have lost all fear of death. They are desperate people who have had much time to think and are not afraid of action. They do not feel that they have anything to lose in action. Violent, though it may be. They have had a baptism of fire, and they preach a vision to rebirth to the entire world.

I'm not here to reiterate what a famous young black writer said 35 years ago in his "Blueprint for Black Writers." For the state of Black Art and Letters is not in such a bad way today. I believe we are on our way to a greater height than ever—despite oppression and despite repression, for we have just come through a cultural revolution designed to blackenize our mind. And as Dr. W.E.B. DuBois said, "the blacker the mantle, the mightier the man!" In 1933 at the Rosenwald Economics Conference held in Washington, D.C., Dr. W.E.B. DuBois spoke on the subject "Where Do We Go From Here?" He said then that we are facing revolution. I quote this, "The other matter, and the matter of greatest import is instead of our facing today a stable world moving at a uniform rate of progress toward well defined goals we are facing revolution. I'm not discussing a coming revolution, I'm trying to impress the fact upon you, that you are already in the midst of war. That there has been no war of modern times that has taken so great a sacrifice of human life and human spirit as the extraordinary period through which we are passing today. Some people envision revolution cheaply as a matter of blood and guns, and the more visible methods of force, but that after all is merely the temporary and outward manifestation. Real revolution is within. That comes before or after the explosions. Is a matter of long suffer-

ing and deprivation. The death of courage and a bit of triumph of despair. This is the inevitable prelude to decisive and enormous change and that is the thing that is on us now. We are not called upon, then, to discuss whether we want revolution or not, we have got it. Our problem is how we are coming out of it." and he continues by—in the next section—saying "this matter of world depression and revolutionary changes in social life and industry is not primarily the problem of the American Negro," this is what he's saying in 33, "and just because it is not our problem we have plan proof of the thing that I have said before. Namely that we are not, in reality, a part of this nation. We stand even in its greatest crisis at one side . . . only partly connected with its remedies, but dumb victims of its difficulties and by just that token because we are outside the main current of the country we have got most carefully to ask ourselves what we are going to do to protect our past and to insure our future." And that's the end of his quotation. Now, when we have experienced all the revolutions brought on by the electronic revolution, all except political and economic, and we are facing more political and economic upheaval despite repression and facist totalitarianism, military and financial imperialism. Now, again, we should ask ourselves, where do we go from here? Let us stop and take stock, where are we now? Where do we wish to go? How can we get there?

We can be eternally grateful for the revolutionary decade of the 60's for a cultural reawakening to the worth of our heritage, and the great potential of our peoples' destiny. What we inherit from the civil rights movement and the black revolution of racial consciousness are gems of inestimable worth. What have these social events done for us? They have given us renewed pride and dignity and a greater sense of manhood and womanhood. They have moved us one step closer toward emancipation of mind and spirit. For we no longer possess a mass slave mentality.

Culturally we have watched a renaissance of the arts mushrooming across the length and breadth of this land. We have been inspired by all our martyred men. Medgar, Malcolm and Martin—and all our poetry, music, drama, painting and sculpture powerfully attest to this fact. When this century is over some of the greatest literature, painting and music America has ever known will prove to be a product of black genius. Looking back across the centuries we reaffirm the humanistic tradition Afro-American literature and art, the search for freedom, peace and dignity, for social justice and for truth. This pervades all our cultural achievement. The world will recognize this great black genius despite White America's racist rejection. Because the world will recognize and identify the universality of human experience in the products of this black genius. We have constantly hewn to the line of the spiritual and manifold destiny of man and it is manifest in our art.

And now about this renaissance across the land. From New York to Texas, from California to the Carolinas, our cultural art centers dot the entire nation. Our young poets, painters, musicians, actors and playwrights are legion. It is time we made a record of this. It is time we pledge our support to them. In this city today—in Chicago we see black art forms of every description—Film; *Buck and the Preacher,* theatre; *Wedding Band,* poetry, poets, groups of poets. Painting; we have an exhibit upstairs from the prisons. But they need support. The black community must sustain them as well as generate them. The white man is not about to support us. The black community must support and sustain the great—black—renaissance and explosion of the arts. The organization of the Black Academy means more than a list of distinguished names. It should mean a bulwark of strength, to nourish both the old and the new—the established as well as the young black artists who are coming on. One of the items on the Agenda for Action at this conference is to do just this thing, to consider the support, the substance, of black art in the black community. To prepare a directory of cultural centers and move toward building a Resource Bank of our cultural assets. Moreover, we need to compile a directory of all cultural activities in the black community, and I think it's past time that we get a synchronized calendar of events, listing these conferences, conventions and all national meetings concerning black art, artists and scholars in order that there will be no further conflicts. The Black Academy can serve as a clearing house for this. Already to my knowledge there are black art centers in Chicago, in New York, in Boston and San Francisco, in Atlanta, in Houston, in Miami, in Newark, Philadelphia and Detroit. But these are only a handful in less than a dozen cities. Other cities with the potential for art centers where our young people are clamoring for artistic activity are Washington, D.C., Nashville, Memphis, Durham, New Orleans, Jackson, Birmingham, Los Angeles, San Diego, and Milwaukee, to mention only a few.

One of the goals of the Black Academy should be to identify such centers and establish others so that we build a network of these centers across the United States where the cul-

tural activities include painting, sculpture, poetry reading and writing, theatre, jazz institutes, film festivals, etc. This conference is therefore called to find out the facts of our black art and artists; locate and establish these art centers in order to compile a directory of cultural activity in the black community, and prepare calendars of these cultural events. The business of these centers shall be the total development of these young artists. To teach craft to our young people, so that they may learn the difference between craft and art . . . between technique and artistry. We must continue to encourage them and to provide new outlets and avenues for their talent. Of what value is this? This seems to me of immeasurable worth to our black struggle and our black communities where the new concepts of education are just beginning to sprout. We are seeding the future of our children. Another generation will reap the harvest. There is a real intellectual ferment in the black community today, and this ferment touches all black life on all fronts. Political, economic, social, educational, and above all aesthetic or artistic. The black scholar must seize on this black ferment which is a natural raw material of his artistic and scholarly productivity and we must direct the tide on which we ride, until we come to the overwhelming flood of success to the highest of all our endeavors.

The Black Academy must promote and support this rising tide of black art and letters. Black unity is the watch word and the rallying cry of our struggle today. The black artist must remember what our brother Floyd McKissick has written in his article "The Way to A Black Ideology."

"It is the task of black intellectuals to provide the cohesive philosophy which will propel the black-led revolution, which must happen if justice is to be achieved in America." We must not wait for others to lead the attack. Ideas are the key to organized action. And the intellectual must not be guilty of the proverbial indecision and reluctance to act." I like very much the definition of the Black Scholar which appears on the inside cover of that illusrious publication.

"A black scholar is a man of both thought and action. A whole man who thinks for his people and acts with them. A man who honors the whole community of black experience. A man who sees the Ph.D., the janitor, the businessman, the maid, the clerk, the militant, as all sharing the same experience of blackness, with all of its complexities and rewards."

If we are to meet the challenge of our crucial times, if we are in truth to define the paradigm for our children's tomorrow we cannot afford the pussyfooting in-fighting and petty jealousy that ape the white world and divide us between town and gown. If we are to take seriously the mandate of all black people for freedom in our time we must solemnly go about our business of creativity, expressing the highest essence of black art and intellect, that which is most authentic and germane to the black experience, for in doing most what we do best we serve with our greatest devotion our peoples' most glorious cause.

I do not stop writing to join the activist in the struggle, I am in the struggle when I am writing. . . .

*Keynote address by Dr. Margaret Walker Alexander at the Conference to Assess the State of Black Arts and Letters in the U.S., 1972, Chicago, Illinois.

THE BLACK ARTS

While black painters and sculptors of earlier eras had sought acceptance by white critics, the emphasis of the first years of the seventies was on black-supported community art centers and black-originated art conferences. Some of the nation's leading artists converged on Pittsburgh in early 1972 for a multi-media exposition at Carnegie-Mellon Institute, under the direction of Dr. J. Brooks Dendy. The Black Academy of Arts and Letters, under a grant from the National Endowment for the Humanities and Johnson Publishing Company, sponsored a three-day conference in May, 1972, to assess the state of Black Arts and Letters. The City of Chicago donated property in Washington Park to the DuSable Museum of African-American History, which artist Margaret Burroughs and her husband, Charles, had kept going in their South Side home for many years. In that same city, the South Side Community Art Center presented outstanding exhibits of works by artists such as sculptor Frank Hayden, while exhibits of this sort were the usual fare at the Museum of the National Center of Afro-American Artists in Dorchester, Massachusetts. The Studio Museum of Harlem made history when it staged an exhibit, in late 1971, of works by Elizabeth Catlett Mora, her first major show in the United States since she took up residence in Mexico. Moneta Sleet, *Ebony* photographer, won the Pulitzer Prize for feature photography in 1969. Sleet was the first black to be recognized outside the field of letters. Gwendolyn Brooks had won in poetry (1950) and Charles Gordone was a recipient in 1970 for his play, *No Place to Be Somebody*. Major museums such as the Museum of Modern Art (N.Y.) exhibited such towering black artists as sculptor Richard Hunt and Romare Bearden. Hunt also had a one-man show at Chicago's Art Institute. Sculpture by Hunt and Geraldine McCullough were commissioned for the new Johnson Publishing Company Chicago building, a magnificent structure at 820 S. Michigan Avenue, Chicago. The architectural firm of Dubin, Dubin, Black and Moutoussamy were responsible for the design. John W. Moutoussamy, a black architect, was in charge of the project. Throughout the building's eleven floors, the work of black American and African artists and sculptors is in evidence. The following names are representative of the artists whose work will be found in collections across the country.

BLACK ARTISTS

(Code: P—Painter, S—Sculptor)

Billie L. Alexander—P
Charles Alston—P
Eileen Anderson—P
Ralph Arnold—P
William E. Artis—S
Richmond Barthé—S
Romare Bearden—P
Sherman Beck—P
Wilson Bégaud—P
Ben Bey—P
Michelle C. Bey—P
John Biggers—P, S
Gloria Bohanon—P
Lorraine Bolten—P
Shirley Bolton—P
Elmer Brown—P
Samuel Brown—P
Herbert Bruce—P
Joan Bryant—P
Selma Burke—S
Calvin Burnett—P
Margaret Burroughs—P, S
Nathaniel Bustion—P
William Carter—P
Elizabeth Catlett—P
Barbara Chase—P
Benjamin Clark—P
Irene Clark—P
Floyd Coleman—P
Eldzier Cortor—P
Samuel Countee—P
G. Caliman Coxe—P
Ernest Crichlow—P
Allan R. Crite—P
Alonzo J. Davis—P
Charles Dawson—P
Richard Dempsey—P
Jeff Donaldson—P
Harold S. Dorsey—S, P
Aaron Douglass—P
Annette Ensley—S
Marion Epting—P
Helen B. Evans—S
P. Fernand—P
Fred Flemister—P
Ausbra Ford—S
LeRoy Foster—P

Rex Gorleigh—P
Joseph Grey—P
Eugene Grigsby—P
John W. Hardrick—P
Robin Harper—P
Frank Hayden—S
Palmer Hayden—P
Vertis Hayes—P
Eselean Henderson—S
Alvin C. Hollingsworth—P
Humbert Howard—P
Kenneth Howard—P
Richard Hughes—P
Richard Hunt—S
J. D. Jackson—P
Wilmer Jennings—P
Lester Johnson—P
Malvin Johnson—P
Sargent Johnson—P
William Johnson—P
Ben Jones—P, S
Lawrence A. Jones—P
Mark Jones—P
Charles Keck—S
James Kennedy—P, S
Joseph Kersey—S, P
Henri King—P
Omar Lama—P
Jacob Lawrence—P
Clifford Lee—P
Leon Lank Leonard, Sr.—P, S
Hughie Lee-Smith—P
Edward Leper—S
Norman Lewis—P
Anderson Macklin—P
William Majors—P
Stephen Mayo—P
Dindga McCannon—P
Geraldine McCullough—S
Eva Hamlin Miller—P
Rosetta Dotson Minner—P
Corinne Mitchell—P
J. Marcus Mitchell—P
Norma Morgan—P
Jimmie Mosely—P
Archibald Motley—P
Lois Jones Pierre Noel—P

David Normand—S
Hayward L. Oubre—P
Sandra Peck—S
Alvin Turtel Phillips—P
Deliah Pierce—P
Georgette Powell—P
Leslie Price—P
William C. Pryor—S
Junius Redwood—P
John Rhodes—S
John Robinson—P
Arthur Roland—P
Arthur Rose—S
Walter Sanford—P
John T. Scott—P
Charles Sebree—P
Thomas Sills—P
Merton Simpson—P
Zenobia Smith—P
Frances Allen Sprout—P
Thelma J. Streat—P
Freddie L. Styles—P
Ann Tanksley—P
Herbert Temple—P
Mildred Thompson—P
Willie Tucker—P
Leo Twiggs—P
Al Tyler—P
Anna Tyler—P
Steve Walker—P
James E. Washington, Jr.—S
Mary Parks Washington—P
James L. Wells—P
Charles White—P
Garrett Whyte—P
Ceola Williams—P
Douglas Williams—S
Gerald Williams—P
Walter Williams—P
Walter J. Williams, Jr.—P
Ellis Wilson—P
George Wilson—P
John Wilson—P
Roger Wilson—P
Hale Woodruff—P
Kenneth Young—P
Barbara Zuber—P

THE BLACK WRITER

The major efforts of the 70s by black writers represented a shift away from the earlier need simply to "tell it like it is" and "tell off the white man." It was deemed far more important to analyze why things were the way they were, what could be done about them, and how black intellectuals might build institutions that could serve as incubators for fresh lines of thought.

One of the immediate results of this thrust was the establishment of countless new journals and literary magazines. Many were spawned by the black studies programs that had gained a firm foothold in colleges and universities throughout the nation. Others were developed independently, but were designed to serve the needs of these programs and the expanding body of inquisitive young blacks. The pace had been set by Dr. Nathan Hare in 1969 when he began publication of the *Black Scholar* which, along with the older, well-established *Black World* and *Freedomways*, provided a forum for scholarship presented in a suitably black context. Among the notable new periodicals were *Black Books Bulletin*, edited by Sterling D. Plumpp, and *NOMMO* from the OBAC Writers Workshop, both published in Chicago; *Renaissance II*, a quarterly journal produced by the Afro-American Studies Program and Afro-American Cultural Center at Yale University; *Nkombo, a* New Orleans-based journal published by Black Arts/South, a cultural organization that had grown out of the Free Southern Theater Writing Workshop; the *Cricket*, a black music journal from Jihad Productions in Newark, New Jersey; *Imani*, produced by black students at New York University, and *Black Creation*, a product of the Institute of Afro-American Affairs at New York University. Significant new magazines of a highly specialized nature included the *Review of Black Political Economy*, published by the Black Economic Research Center in New York City, and *African Progress*, issued by the Africa Investors and Placement Services of New York. With the establishment of these new outlets for opinion, the stage was set for the development of a group of black critics who could evaluate black works independent of the white cultural "mainstream."

This movement toward autonomy was underscored by black-owned publishing houses* such as Dudley Randall's Broadside Press of

*Johnson Publishing Company, Inc. Book Division since 1961 published over 50 titles—adult, juvenile, reference—dealing with various aspects of the black experience.

Detroit, which was given no small boost when the noted Pulitzer Prize-winning poet Gwendolyn Brooks broke her contract with a leading white company and chose Broadside to publish her long-awaited autobiography, *Report From Part One*. When the book was reviewed on the front page of the *New York Times Book Review*, it seemed an indication that black publishing houses had, at last, forced the white literary establishment to take cognizance of them. When Howard University founded the first black university press in the nation in 1972, under the direction of veteran editor Charles Harris, the trend seemed to bode well for the future.

The black intellectual's deepening awareness of a broader role within the society was epitomized at a meeting that took place in Chicago, Illinois, in May, 1972. At that time, the Black Academy of Arts and Letters, an organization composed of leading scholars and artists, called together 175 black artists to assess the state of black arts and letters in the United States. The eminent poet and teacher, Dr. Margaret Walker Alexander, addressed herself to the fundamental issue when she said:

"We need a new socio-economic and political paradigm. Black mankind is no less creative and inventive than those in other ages have been. We are a charismatic numinous people of the black experience caught in a vortex of this time of crisis. Destiny declares that the responsibility is ours."

This note was reflected in the first annual awards presented by the Black Academy in 1971 to recognize artistic and scholarly excellence in relationship to black needs. Significantly, the first award for nonfiction in literature went to the late George Jackson for his book, *Soledad Brother: The Prison Letters of George Jackson*. The author, who had arrived at his painful vision from behind bars where he also was slain, was, indeed, the symbol of the new black intelligentsia Dr. Alexander had acknowledged as having been spawned "largely from the horrible oppression of the prisons." Other awards presented by the academy that year went to poet Mari Evans for her book, *I Am A Black Woman*; William Melvin Kelley for his novel, *Dunfords Travels Everywheres*; Franklin W. Knight for the scholarly work, *Slave Society in Cuba During the 19th Century*; poet Gwendolyn Brooks for "outstanding achievement in letters"; dancer-anthropologist Katherine Dunham for "outstanding achievement in the arts," and Edward Kennedy "Duke" Ellington, who received the group's Medal of Merit. Those inducted into the group's Hall of Fame were Frederick Douglass, author and abolitionist; Ira Aldridge, the nineteenth-century actor, and the pioneering historian, George Washington Williams.

The awards presented by the academy in 1972 also reflected this tone. Cited for his achievement in nonfiction was journalist Samuel Yette for his book, *The Choice: The Issue of Black Survival in America*, a chilling exploration of the possibility of genocide as it might apply to "obsolete" blacks in today's white America. Other awards went to novelist Ernest Gaines for *The Autobiography of Miss Jane Pittman*, an extraordinary account of the day-to-day life of a slave who lived for one hundred years after the Civil War; Michael Harper for his book of poetry, *History Is Your Own Heartbeat*; Chancellor Williams, a Howard University professor, for *The Destruction of Black Civilization*, a study of the African past.

Though the conservative shift in the national temper tended to cool the enthusiasm of white publishers for black subjects, several other notable works did manage to reach print by the end of 1972. Novelist Chester Himes, a published author since 1945, who was rediscovered by the American public when his *Cotton Comes to Harlem* found its way into film, published the first part of his autobiography, *The Quality of Hurt*, an event that was hailed by many black critics who felt that he had been overlooked in favor of lesser talents for far too long.

Addison Gayle Jr. published *The Black Situation*, a book of autobiographical and sociopolitical essays, and *The Black Aesthetic*, an impressive anthology in which several artists and thinkers examined the philosophy underlying contemporary black culture. The personal essay was the form chosen by James Baldwin, master of this literary genre, for *No Name in the Street*, a sort of retrospective view of his involvements during the turbulent sixties. Another book of essays was Lerone Bennett's *The Challenge of Blackness*, published by Johnson Publishing Company. This form also was used to advantage by Orde Coombs in his book, *Do You See My Love For You Growing?* During this period, Coombs compiled two excellent anthologies, *We Speak As Young Black Liberators*, based on the writings of new generation poets, and *What We Must See: Young Black Storytellers*.

In the area of literary criticism, Broadside Press inaugurated a series of volumes by black critics on black writers, the first of these being *Dynamite Voices* by Don L. Lee, dealing with the works of young poets who emerged during the sixties. Darwin T. Turner analyzed the works of Jean Toomer, Countee Cullen, and Zora Neale Hurston, all products of the Harlem Renaissance, in his book *In A Minor Chord: Three Afro-American Writers and Their Search for Identity*. The College Language Association published *Langston Hughes, Black Genius: A Critical Evaluation*, edited by Therman B. O'Daniel, an English professor at Morgan State College. Sherley Anne Williams, a young college teacher, undertook a thematic study of neo-black literature in *Give Birth to Brightness*, which examined fully the works of James Baldwin, Imamu Hughes (LeRoi Jones), and Ernest Gaines. Mel Watkins served as editor of *Black Review*, a two-volume work featuring essays by prominent black writers and illustrations by Ellsworth Ausby.

Dr. Joyce A. Ladner tackled the provocative subject of the black woman in her book *Tomorrow's Tomorrow*, basing many of her observations on interviews with young black women attempting to survive in an inner-city mire. The racial implications of religion were scrutinized by Rev. Albert Cleage in *Black Christian Nationalism*, while Earl Ofari was critical of some governmental proposals for progress in *The Myth of Black Capitalism*. A quite notable scholarly effort came from Dr. Eileen Southern, chairman of the music department at York College of the City University of New York, who wrote *The Music of Black Americans*, an authoritative textbook which contained much previously neglected information on black musical activities before the twentieth century and also provided a broad view of the evolution of modern popular forms of music.

In the field of fiction, black writers combined artistic and technical excellence with social consciousness. John O. Killens published *Cotillion*, a searingly satirical novel exposing the foibles of the black middle class, while John A. Williams authored *Captain Blackman*, which was hailed critically for its innovative interpolation of history in fiction. Frank Yerby, long considered the most commercially successful of black writers, though not the most relevant, departed from previous themes to produce *The Dahomean*, the story of a nineteenth-century African chieftain who was sold into slavery after being betrayed by relatives. Some black critics, who had been waiting for a hint of racial awareness in Yerby's work, considered it his finest book. Many new voices also made an impact. Toni Morrison wrote poetically of a black girl's plight in *The Bluest Eye*, while George Cain escorted readers into the nether world of a promising col-

lege athlete who had become a junkie in
Blueschild Baby. The gifted poet and composer Gil Scott-Heron produced his second novel,
The Nigger Factory, depicting the conflicts
centering about a black college. The West
Coast writer Ishmael Reed, who is equally
adept in poetry and literary criticism, displayed a dazzling technique in his surrealistic
novel, *Mumbo Jumbo*. Cyrus Colter, the winner of a University of Iowa Letters Award on
his volume of short stories, the *Beach
Umbrella* (1970), followed with novels, *Rivers of Eros* (1972) and *The Hippodrome*
(1973), which received critical praise in scholarly quarters for its style and perception.

In poetry, volumes upon volumes of works
were published, often privately. Attention
most commonly was focused on works by established writers. Most of the published works
of Gwendolyn Brooks, including many long
out-of-print, were issued in a volume titled
The World of Gwendolyn Brooks. The multi-
talented Maya Angelou, who directed the film,
Georgia, Georgia based on her book, was represented by a book of poems, *Just Give Me A
Cool Drink of Water 'Fore I Die*. Imamu
Baraka effectively combined the photographs
of Fundi (Billy Abernathy) with a poetic col-
lage of black urban directives in *In Our Terribleness*. Meanwhile, one of the most prevalent
personages of this period was Nikki Giovanni,
who emerged as a sort of cultural heroine
among young black people, due to frequent
television appearances. She authored a book
of poems for children called *Spin a Soft Dark
Song*, with illustrations by Charles Bible, and
a somewhat autobiographical book of essays,
Gemini. Also active during this period was
poet-critic Carolyn Rodgers.

BLACKS IN TELEVISION

Television in the late sixties and early
seventies reflected the national attitude toward
the black community: "benign neglect." This
most powerful and pervasive communications
medium ever devised by man offered little of
relevance to black people. "Black Journal,"
the only nationally televised black show dealing with public affairs, was aired over public
television for one-half hour a week. And even
this minimum exposure was threatened by
funding problems. "Soul," hosted by Ellis Haiz-
lip, and "Soul Train," hosted by disk jockey
Don Cornelius, by 1972 were threatened with
cancellation.

The usual commercial television fare presented plastic pictures of contemporary American life, and one of the surprise hero-villains
to emerge from the montage of misrepresen-
tation was a white bigot called Archie Bunker,
whose attitudes were applauded by the multi-
tudes when he was portrayed as the central
figure in a spectacularly successful situation
comedy, "All in the Family." When Diahann
Carroll was chosen to star in the family situation series "Julia," launched in 1968, she became the first black to have her own regular
dramatic show and quickly attracted a large
following. Though, again, many considered the
character of Julia to be little more than a white
woman with a black face, the approach worked
and she was able to hold her own where others
had failed, although this series did not last past
the second season.

Several black professionals held onto fea-
tured roles in long-running series, among them
Clarence Williams III in "Mod Squad," Denise
Nicholas and Lloyd Haynes in "Room 222,"
Greg Morris in "Mission Impossible," and
Don Mitchell in "Ironside." Others with series
roles were: Tracy Reed and James Watson, Jr.
in "Love American Style;" Georg Stanford
Brown, in "The Rookies;" Janet MacLachlan
and Harrison Page in the "suburban series"
"Love Thy Neighbor;" and Ester Rolle in
"Maude." Flip Wilson continued to ride high
in the ratings with his own show on which he
portrayed the stereotyped black character,
"Geraldine." However, the greatest success
was scored by veteran comedian Redd Foxx
who swept blacks and whites alike off their
collective feet as the star of "Sanford and
Son," the story of a whimsical junkman and
his quarrelsome son, portrayed by Demond
Wilson. No one since Flip Wilson had scored
such a hit with the television public, and
blacks, who were familiar with Redd Foxx's
off-color humor when he was a nightclub star,
were able to tune into his portrayal of a lova-
ble but crotchety character. One of the reasons for this empathy was that the show frequently utilized the talents of black writers,
though they were not always listed in the credit
lines. Though black reporters were to be seen on
local newscasts throughout the nation, and in
some larger cities—New York, Boston, Washington, Philadelphia, Atlanta, Chicago, and
Los Angeles—black "talk" shows were presented as local public service, by and large the
black man in America was the "invisible man"
on national network television.

THE THEATRE: PROBLEMS AND PROSPECTS

By Frederick O'Neal

For a number of years, black Americans were not allowed to perform on the legitimate stage in America. Black characters were played by white actors in blackface. Down through the years, casting patterns in the various entertainment media have changed to some extent, but not a great deal.

During the period roughly between 1910 and 1930, black stars such as Bert Williams and others were spotted in white shows as if they were so "super special" that they had to be shown in almost wholly unrelated roles and mostly alone. They were just the darlingest, quaintest, oddest, most interesting, sexiest, most exotic or, in other words, just about the best thing in the show, but not really a part of it. The most common method of handling the black actor in the straight play was to cast him exclusively in so-called "Negro roles," which inevitably meant in some servile capacity, such as the maid, butler, cook, etc. Until recently, the characterization, presentation and interpretation of these parts took the form of lazy, shuffling characters speaking a dialect that even black folks had never heard. The *types* of roles played by blacks are more of a barometer than the number of these roles.

It would seem that blacks and Orientals are the only groups whose roles are circumscribed by race. The Irish actor can play a Japanese character; the Jewish actor can play the Indian; German actors play Italian characters and vice versa, but the black actor only has a chance of being cast if the part specifically indicates "Negro."

Earle Hyman, a Black American Actor, has been playing periodically with the Norwegian State Theatre since 1965 in all types of roles. He won the Award (Order of the Purple Nose) for the Best Artist of the Season a few years ago. The only other actor to win this Award was Charles Chaplin. A bust of Mr. Hyman was placed in the lobby of the Norwegian State Theatre in Oslo. But here in the land of his birth the imagination of the agent, casting director, play director, playwright or manager, preoccupied with time-worn casting patterns, does not generally extend beyond the racially designated description in the manuscript. But these same individuals have no difficulty whatsoever with their imaginations when it comes to the selection of, for instance,

David Wayne for the part of the Japanese character Sakini in *Teahouse of the August Moon*, or of Jeff Chandler as an American Indian.

Now all of this sounds paradoxical when we realize that by and large, people of the theatre have been opposed to discrimination, segregation and other forms of bigotry and hypocrisy. Actors' Equity Association is the union that represents those actors, dancers and singers who work in the legitimate theatre, musical theatres, summer, winter, and year 'round stock theatres, repertory theatres, children's theatres, dinner theatres, puppet shows, some industrial shows, and book shows in night clubs and other spots, etc. The Council of Actors Equity (its governing body) includes six blacks among the seventy-five members. For almost thirty years, Equity and the League of New York Theatres (the organization of theatrical producers) have worked in cooperation with other elements inside as well as outside the theatre community to make this area of entertainment free and healthy. The League, Equity, the Dramatists' Guild and other organizations and individuals have, on more than one occasion, joined together to defeat the threat of official censorship. During the dark days of McCarthyism, the Anti-Blacklist Committee in Actors' Equity, working with the League, managed to keep the theatre relatively free from political persecution and the principle of guilt by association. As a result of this kind of cooperative effort, the theatre has remained the most free of all entertainment media. More recently, motion pictures have enjoyed a certain amount of freedom from censorship, particularly in respect to racially and sexually mixed scenes.

In the mid-1940s, Washington, D.C. was one of the most lucrative stops on the touring theatre circuit, but the management of the National Theatre in that city maintained a policy of racial discrimination. The League and Equity pleaded with the management to drop this vicious and immoral policy and when their request was refused, these two organizations, together with members of the Dramatists' Guild, decided to refuse bookings in this or any other theatre in Washington until such time as the management could see fit to change its policy. This was in 1948. The National Theatre remained closed for the next five years while touring shows played the Gayety Theatre, a former vaudeville house that had dropped this discriminatory policy. The National was finally remodeled and redecorated under a new management and reopened in 1952, with a welcome to all races and nationalities on a non-discriminatory basis.

Inasmuch as Washington was just about the most segregated city in the United States at that time, perhaps it was this collective action that broke the dam of prejudice and bigotry, releasing the first wave of the changes that have taken place in that city since 1952. It was a healthy action that could only terminate in a wholesome result.

Since 1962, by contractual agreement, Equity does not permit its members to work in any theatre where segregation and discrimination are practiced. Inquiries are often made of the union as to the number of blacks there are among its 18,000 members. Due to the fact that the racial background of members is not indicated in the union's records, no one actually knows. Some say a thousand or more; others maintain that the figure is much lower. Equity's Ethnic Minorities Committee has made an unofficial effort to determine the number of black members in the union by asking members, both black and white, what black actors are known to them as members of Equity. After examining a number of lists submitted, we found a great deal of duplication. But, from this somewhat unorthodox method, we learned that the figure is around six hundred. There may be black artists who are members of other performing unions, such as: American Guild of Musical Artists, American Federation of Television and Radio Artists, American Guild of Variety Artists and Screen Extras Guild.

American blacks as a whole have plumbed more levels of society, economic, religious, political, etc., than any other comparable group. Such experiences are of particular value to the black actor, especially in contemporary drama. Where more restrained portrayals are demanded, however, as in the classics, the black has not fared too well. Such style demands dedicated study and effort. Far too many members of the profession (black and white) have aligned themselves with the generally accepted lay opinion that one does not have to study in order to become an actor or actress. Within the last few years, that segment of the profession has dwindled considerably and we now have a fairly large group of competent young actors and actresses who are ready for almost any assignment.

The prospects for the black actor in search of a career in the theatre are lessened by the black fact that many producers feel the so-called "Black Show" is not a good financial risk (as theatrical investments go) compared to investments in white shows. They seem to forget about the many successful black shows over the years. One could include among them such plays as *Green Pastures, Shuffle Along, Porgy and Bess, Carmen Jones, Emperor Jones,* and others. *Anna Lucasta* still remains among the all-time record holders for Broadway runs of straight plays. Paul Robeson's *Othello* holds the all-time record for the Broadway run of a Shakespeare play. Even with the bad judgement exercised by some producers in their selection of black plays, it is quite possible that an objective survey would indicate that there is a greater proportion of success among these black shows, based on the total number produced, than among white shows under similar circumstances.

The availability of stars also plays a great part in the producers' decisions. The legitimate stage has not, peculiarly enough, developed many black stars. Few of the current crop of luminaries was developed by the theatre and yet plays have been shelved for lack of a competent available black star of sufficient magnitude to head such productions. This does not mean that black actors are not available who could do just as well or possibly better than the desired stars, but the precarious economic position of the commercial theatre does not allow for such experimentation.

In some lay circles, the term "star" has been used rather loosely and it has lost a great deal of its former meaning except to those producers, theatrical investors and others who still know and respect the true meaning of the term. Opportunities for black actors in the legitimate theatre, however, are so few it is seldom that they can grow steadily to the point where they can reach the star category.

The legitimate theatre has been forced to borrow black personalities that have been developed in other media. Many a star has found his original medium more lucrative though, and cannot afford the luxury of doing an occasional play or musical. Top box-office attractions such as Lena Horne, Sammy Davis, etc., are not always available and quite often the roles to be filled are not suited to the particular talents and personalities of this small group. Since the employment of black stars usually means the employment of black supporting players, it follows that whenever a play is shelved or abandoned a number of black actors have been denied a chance to develop toward the star circle. The box-office draw of such stars as Miss Horne and Mr. Davis was demonstrated in their appearances on Broadway. Both appeared in plays that did not receive very favorable critical comment, yet Miss Horne's vehicle, *Jamaica,* and Mr. Davis' *Mr. Wonderful,* had runs of more than a year. Mr. Davis' musical, *Golden Boy,* ran over a year on Broadway and continued on the London stage. Without a doubt, such plays would have closed long since with lesser names. This would be equally true of shows with white stars.

The figures on the employment of blacks during the season, 1964–65, as compared to previous seasons, are interesting. During this period, the total employment of black actors on and off Broadway dropped considerably from that of the previous season (1963–64). Figures on total employment of black actors during the seasons 1960–61 to 1964–65 (5 years), as noted in the figures below, are quite interesting:

	1964–65	1963–64	1962–63	1961–62	1960–61
Employed					
Bdwy.	74	168	51	123	126
Off-Bdwy.	32	116	26	50	29
Shows employing blacks					
Bdwy.	22	24	21	14	18
Off-Bdwy.	20	27	12	20	9
Shows with integrated casts					
Bdwy.	15	16	13	10	8
Off-Bdwy.	11	11	7	11	4

The drop in the total number of jobs available to black actors during the season 1964–65, as in certain other past periods, is mainly due to the number of shows produced with entirely or predominantly black casts. For example, during the 1963–64 season, three shows: *Porgy and Bess* (46), *Tambourines to Glory* (29), *Sponono* (24) accounted for 99 of the total of 168 employed that year. That same season Off-Broadway, three shows, *Jericho Jim Crow* (20), *Ballad for Bimshire* (26) and *Cabin in the Sky* (18) accounted for all but 52 of the total employed in that area.

The most important figures are those under the heading "Shows with integrated casts." These figures indicate parts played by blacks that are not designated by the author as so-called "black parts," where race is not thematically necessary to the story and not so directed as to imply racial identification. It will be noted that these figures have held up pretty well and, in fact, increased somewhat. Figures for the past season, 1972–73, as nearly as are available, are as follows: Of the 86 shows produced under the Equity Production Contract, 32 included blacks and other minorities in their casts, totaling 118. The breakdown is not available at this writing.

In addition to the increasing number of black artists being used in non-racially designated roles, another encouraging factor is the number of black playwrights whose works have been produced in recent years. Not all of them are necessarily new playwrights, but with the possible exception of the late Langston Hughes, they are new to Broadway and off Broadway. Such writers as James Baldwin, LeRoi Jones, Lorraine Hansberry (deceased), Louis Peterson, Ann Flagg, Adrienne Kennedy, Errol John, Ossie Davis, William Hairston, Loften Mitchell, Alice Childress, Irving Burgie, Abram Hill, William Branch, Douglas Turner Ward, Wole Soyinka, Micki Grant, Melvin Van Peebles, Joseph A. Walker, Langston Hughes (deceased), Phillip Hayes Dean, J. E. Franklin, Lonnie Elder, Charles Gordone, and others. Most of these writers have been produced during the past five years.

Dr. Alain Locke wrote in 1927 as follows: "Propaganda, pro-Negro and anti-Negro, has scotched the dramatic potentialities of the subject [Negro drama]. Especially with the few black playwrights has the propaganda motive worked havoc. They have had the dramatic motive deflected at its source. Race drama has appeared to them a matter of race vindication, and pathetically, they have pushed forward their moralistic allegories or melodramatic protests as dramatic correctives and antidotes for race prejudice." Today, however, the black playwright, having become aware of his potential strength in the battle for full citizenship, has been able to some extent to overcome this emotional preoccupation.

In addition to the established and promising black playwrights there is further reason for optimism occasioned by some degree of progress in other areas.

George McClain has worked in several management capacities and is now assistant manager of the St. James Theatre. He has served as company manager for several large productions on pre-Broadway tours. Dick Campbell was company manager for the Langston Hughes show, *Tambourines to Glory* and for *Ballad for Bimshire*. Blacks have emerged as producers of plays (as well as motion pictures) and this development is significant in that now these producers are employers of talent and are in the position to determine what is to be done and how. Several blacks have also directed Broadway and Off-Broadway production. These include Lloyd Richards (currently President of the Society of Stage Directors and Choreographers), Vinette Carrol, Frank Silvera (deceased), Osceola Archer, Edward Cambridge, Melvin Van Peebles, Alice Childress, Ossie Davis, Woodie King, Shauneille Perry, Charles Gordone, and Michael Schultz. Several black choreographers have also done a few shows Off an On Broadway. Among these are Louis Johnson, Donald MacKayle, Alvin Ailey, Albert Popwell, Walter Nicks, and Talley Beatty.

One of the more successful talent agents is Ernestine McClendon, who holds franchises from all of the major performer unions. Her clients include almost as many white artists as blacks.

There is a growing use of black musicians in the pit orchestras of Broadway shows and since the desegregation of the New York locals of the State Hands Union black craftsmen are working the broadway theatres. Margaret R. Harris conducted the pit band for "Two Gentlemen of Verona" (1971–73).

Civil rights organizations are beginning to realize that the black creative artist, and particularly the playwright and actor, exert a great influence in the establishment of the black image. Conferences have been held with the NAACP in the hope of establishing an NAACP National Performing Artists Advisory Committee as a permanent department within the national office, with a staff person on both the east and west coasts to pursue the ultimate objective of complete desegregation of the performing arts.

THE THEATRE: USE BY BLACKS
AS LIBERATION MEDIUM

Where black America was concerned, the theatre of the seventies was, in many respects, far different from the theatre in which blacks, such as the late Bert Williams and George Walker had to black their faces and do subtle minstrel routines in order to become stars at the turn of the century. However, the awards and brand new black names emblazoned on the Great all-too-White Way are only part of the story of what happened during the fifties and sixties. Playwrights came to use their craft as a means of transmitting important messages—sometimes directed exclusively toward their own people. This is the idea central to what came to be known as black theater—theater directed to the black community and its needs while being controlled by blacks in all facets. Due to this development, theatrical events in the fifties and sixties separate themselves into three categories: (1) legitimate "white" theater; (2) plays by or prominently featuring black performers presented off-Broadway; (3) black theater.

It is in the first two categories that one finds most of the major award winners and those whose names have become known to the public. Though militant blacks decry these achievements, they were important in opening the doors more widely to those who went on to attain recognition in the theater.

Many tend to place the beginning of a new era in the theater as March 11, 1959, when a play entitled *Raisin in the Sun*, by a young Chicago-born playwright named Lorraine Hansberry, opened on Broadway.

Hansberry's play was the first written by a

black to win the New York Drama Critics Award as Best Play of that season.

Before *Raisin in the Sun*, few blacks had been able to penetrate the neon curtain as writers or purveyors of ideas. Actors had fared a little better, though the shows in which they had appeared were often limited to such strange creations as *Carmen Jones*, a black version of Bizet's opera which captivated New York audiences when it opened on Broadway in 1943. In a similar vein was a play of this period, *Anna Lucasta*, written by a white playwright, originally about a Polish family. It was notable only for the talented blacks who moved in and out of its cast, among them Hilda Sims, Frederick O'Neal, Alice Childress, Earle Hyman, Canada Lee, Ossie Davis, Ruby Dee, Isabelle Cooley, Sidney Poitier and Frank Silvera.

During the early forties, Paul Robeson, the versatile actor-singer-lawyer-scholar-athlete and early Phi Beta Kappa from Rutgers had appeared like a reincarnation of Ira Aldridge when he re-created the role of Othello for a record-breaking Theater Guild presentation.

Other roles given black actors either emphasized their "exotic" qualities or exploited their value as song or dance specialists. In 1949, singer-actress Juanita Hall had become nationally famous for her portrayal of "Bloody Mary," a "Tonkinese" woman in the highly successful Broadway musical *South Pacific* which won for Miss Hall the Tony, Donaldson, Box Office, and Bill Bojangles Awards. In 1954, Pearl Bailey and Diahann Carroll had starred in Truman Capote's *House of Flowers* while Eartha Kitt was featured in the revue *New Faces*. Sammy Davis Jr. enjoyed considerable success as star of *Mr. Wonderful* in 1956, and Lena Horne starred in the musical *Jamaica* the following year. But none of these were really black plays and they did not deal with black ideas.

By 1959, the year of *Raisin in the Sun*, less than a dozen plays written by blacks had reached Broadway or even off-Broadway in the whole post-World War II period and none had been a real hit. Among them had been Richard Wright's *Native Son* of 1941 on which the author had collaborated with Paul Green; Theodore Ward's *Our Lan'* in 1947; Louis Peterson's *Take a Giant Step* in 1953; William Branch's *In Splendid Error*, presented off-Broadway in 1954 and Loften Mitchell's *The Land Beyond the River*, also off-Broadway, in 1957. Langston Hughes was represented by five efforts. His *Simply Heavenly*, based on his popular character, Jesse B. Semple, reached Broadway in 1957. A play named *Mulatto*, which he had written in 1934, was adapted into the opera *The Barrier* in 1950.

Hughes supplied libretto and lyrics for *Troubled Land* in 1949 and collaborated with two other blacks, Charles Sebree and Greer Johnson, on *Mrs. Patterson*, in 1954.

Raisin in the Sun was a landmark, a highly successful play in both critical and financial terms, which had been written by a black for an almost totally black cast and dealt with some of the problems peculiar to black life. It was notable for the stars-to-be in its cast: Sidney Poitier in the leading role as Walter Younger (followed by Ossie Davis), Ruby Dee, Claudia McNeil, Diana Sands, Ivan Dixon, Louis Gossett, Lonne Elder III and Douglas Turner Ward. It also brought recognition to its black director, Lloyd Richards.

Though some blacks looked askance at this play for some of the stereotypes it relied upon—the strong matriarchal mother dominating a weak son as the black male figure—and did not believe it black enough in the resolution of its conflicts, it established its author as a major figure, though she was represented by only one other play during her brief lifetime. This was *The Sign In Sidney Brustein's Window* which was about the quandary of a white liberal. It opened on Broadway on October 15, 1964, and closed after 101 performances on January 12, 1965, the day of the author's death at the age of 34. Posthumously she was represented on Broadway by *To Be Young, Gifted and Black*, a dramatization of her selected writings, in 1968, and *Les Blancs*, in 1970.

There was another burst of theatrical activity in 1961. Ossie Davis starred in his own satirical play *Purlie Victorious* which made its points through the exaggeration of both black and white racial stereotypes. This play, which co-starred Davis's wife, Ruby Dee, established its actor-author as an important figure in contemporary theater. Meanwhile in the reaches of Off-Broadway, *The Blacks*, a play written by the Frenchman Jean Genet, took a phantasmagorical look into the minds of an oppressed people in a state of revolt and presented blacks in white-face. It ran for two years and was one of the main factors in establishing Off-Broadway theater as a valid cultural force. The comedian Godfrey Cambridge won an Obie award for his performance. Other distinguished members of that cast were, at various times, Roscoe Lee Browne, James Earl Jones, Cicely Tyson, Maya Angelou, Raymond St. Jacques, Vinie Burrows, Louis Gossett, and Charles Gordone. This year also saw the emergence of a versatile young composer-singer-actor from Chicago, Oscar Brown Jr., who took to salons, clubs and even television to raise $400,000 to produce his musical play

Kicks & Co. The play, unfortunately, was a failure, though many of its songs were popularized by Brown in his nightclub act.

During the remaining years of the sixties, blacks appeared both on and off-Broadway with greater frequency and there were some high points. In 1962, Diahann Carroll starred in *No Strings*, a musical written especially for her by Richard Rogers and dealing with a black woman who becomes a successful high fashion model in Paris. Nineteen sixty-three brought Langston Hughes' *Tambourines to Glory* under the direction of Vinette Carroll, and Adrienne Kennedy's *Funny House of a Negro*. In 1964, LeRoi Jones made his debut as playwright with the production of his one-act play *Dutchman*; Baldwin's *Blues For Mr. Charley* gained recognition for Diana Sands and Al Freeman Jr., while Miss Sands also starred opposite Alan Alda in the nonracial comedy *The Owl and the Pussycat*; Sammy Davis Jr. starred in *Golden Boy*, a black musical version of a white play, and Gloria Foster received an Obie Award for a shattering performance in *In White America*. Meanwhile, Frederick O'Neal became the first black president of Actor's Equity. Baldwin's *Amen Corner* was produced in 1965 and starred veteran actress Beah Richards. During the 1965–66 season, new black playwrights began appearing, including Douglas Turner Ward, who introduced a duo of plays, *Day of Absence* and *Happy Ending* which won the Drama Disk-Vernon Rice Award in 1966, and Lonne Elder III with his critically applauded *Ceremonies In Dark Old Men*. Pearl Bailey and Cab Calloway romped through a black version of the long-running musical *Hello, Dolly!* in 1967 while Leslie Uggams starred in *Hallelujah Baby*.

The 1968–69 season brought a personal triumph for James Earl Jones who received a Tony award for his stellar performance in *The Great White Hope* which was based on the life of Jack Johnson, the first black heavy-weight boxing champion. Though the play was written by a white man, Howard Sackler, it brought stardom for Jones who earlier had received critical praise for his *Othello*, among a great variety of roles, and had won an award in 1962 for his performance in *Moon On a Rainbow Shawl*. The following year he starred in a film version of *The Great White Hope*, reaping more praise.

The year 1970 brought a bonanza of black talent to the boards, but two productions were of particular significance. A new musical version of Ossie Davis' *Purlie Victorious* was offered on Broadway as *Purlie*. Though many blacks found the material out-dated and one critic called the show "an anachronism," its stars were well rewarded. Cleavon Little, who played the title role, became the second consecutive black man to win a Tony Award—for best performance by an actor in a musical—following James Earl Jones's award for best performance in a dramatic play. Furthermore, his co-star Melba Moore, a petite former school-teacher with a big voice, won a Tony as best supporting actress in a musical. This year also saw Charles Gordone become the first black playwright to win a Pulitzer Prize. (The only other blacks ever awarded the Pulitzer Prize in any field were Gwendolyn Brooks for poetry in 1950 and *Ebony* photographer Moneta Sleet Jr. for feature photography in 1969). Gordone's prize came for his play *No Place To Be Somebody*, a brawling, barroom drama soaked in profanity and weird symbolism. Off-Broadway offerings of special note included the South African writer Athol Fugard's *Boesman and Lena*, with Ruby Dee giving what most critics considered to be the finest dramatic performance of many a season; LeRoi Jones's *Slave Ship*, a message drama reliving the bitter black past with startling musical support; William Wellington Mackey's *Billy Noname*, a promising musical drama dealing with a young man's personal development during the Civil Rights movement, which closed after mixed notices; a *Black Quartet*, produced by Woodie King and featuring plays by Ronald Milner, Ed Bullins, LeRoi Jones and Bea Caldwell. Meanwhile, the leading producer of plays in New York was a black woman, Ellen Stewart, who operated through her Off-Broadway Cafe LaMama. During a six-year period, she produced more than two hundred plays by more than one hundred playwrights, though few of these dealt with black situations or were by blacks.

As most of the events mentioned above took place on Broadway or within the limits of Off-Broadway associated with the theatrical "mainstream," other events of great import centered about attempts to establish black theaters that would present works related to the needs of the black community. The most highly publicized of these was the Negro Ensemble Company of New York City which in late 1967 received a $434,000 Ford Foundation grant which was to be used to establish a black theater. It was under the direction of playwright Douglas Turner Ward and actor Robert Hooks.

Another move in this direction came with the founding of the New Lafayette Theater in 1968. It was supported by grants from the Ford and Rockefeller Foundations, plus state and private contributions. One advantage the

New Lafayette claimed was location in the heart of the black metropolis of Harlem. Furthermore, it benefited from having Ed Bullins as writer-in-residence. This young playwright had been associated with the shortlived Black House in San Francisco. He won the Vernon Rice Award in 1968 for his trilogy of plays *Clara's Old Man, The Electronic Nigger* and *A Son Come Home*, which had been presented in New York at the American Place Theatre. Thus several of his plays, dealing with black people at the unidealized nittygritty level were premiered at the New Lafayette, among them *In the Wine Time*. This theater also did Ronald Milner's *Who's Got His Own*.

A further experimental thrust came through Barbara Ann Teer, who had won the Vernon Rice Award as best actress for 1965 in the Off-Broadway production *Home Movies*. As director of the National Black Theater Workshop in Harlem, she aimed her efforts exclusively at the black community, looked to it, instead of white foundations, for financing and took a total approach to her subject. Miss Teer maintained that black theater should draw on such sources as the ritualism and release to be found in black churches and black music in order to accomplish this end.

It was the contention of Ernie McClintock, director of the Harlem-based Afro-American Studio for Acting and Speech, that a black theater functioning in its total sense should also provide training for blacks and thereby help to shape their course away from conventional Broadway success and closer to a reflection of black life.

Though New York remained the capital of the theatrical world even for blacks engaged in community pursuits, similar efforts were undertaken in other cities. Outstanding among these were Ernie McClintock's Afro-American Studio for Acting and Speech, Roger Furman's New Heritage Theatre, Hazel Bryant's Afro-American Total Theatre, Woodie King's New Federal Theatre, and Barbara Ann Teer's National Black Theater, which specialized in the development of ritual theater as a form of emotional release. Al Fann's Theatrical Ensemble indicated new directions the others might well seek when it produced *King Heroin*, a cooperatively conceived drama that pointed up the horrors of drug addiction and attempted to show why black communities should mobilize to combat this menace. Meanwhile, black theater was alive and well in places other than New York, where the emphasis was on community involvement and development of social awareness. This was the task taken by such groups as Imamu Baraka's

Spirit House Movers of Newark, New Jersey, Val Gray Ward's Kuumba Workshop of Chicago, Black Arts/West of Seattle, Black Arts South of New Orleans, and the Free Southern Theater, founded in 1963 by John O'Neal and Gilbert Moses, two black college graduates who had been active in the Mississippi Freedom project of 1964.

In surveying black theatrical activities, a distinction must be made between these which were designed for the public as a whole and community-related black theater projects. Considering the former, black talent was much in evidence on Broadway and its close relative Off-Broadway. One of the most omnipresent figures on the entire entertainment scene was Melvin Van Peebles, whose freeform musical *Ain't Supposed to Die a Natural Death* was a long-run hit on Manhattan's neon strip, highlighted by brilliant staging and the direction of Gilbert Moses. Producer Van Peebles wrote lyrics, music, and dialogue for the show. While it was still on the boards in 1972, he performed the same multiple feats for another musical effort, *Don't Play Us Cheap*, built around the theme of a Harlem house party, which was far less successful.

White critics and audiences as a whole heaped laurels on *Don't Bother Me, I Can't Cope*, a gospel-tinged musical that grew out of Vinnette Carroll's Urban Arts Corps. After making the rounds as community theater, it was taken to Broadway in 1972, where it won Drama Desk, Obie, and Outer Critics Circle awards. Micki Grant was cited for her music and lyrics as well as her performance as an actress and singer; Vinnette Carroll for direction; gospel singer Alex Bradford for performance, while the show as a whole was voted best musical.

Several shows with other than racial themes brought recognition to black actors and actresses. A little-known singer named Linda Hopkins won a Tony Award as best supporting actress in a musical for her moving performance in *Inner City*, a short-lived show based on Eve Merriam's *The Inner City Mother Goose*. Jonelle Allen and Clifton Davis were propelled to instant stardom for their performances in *Two Gentlemen of Verona*, a mod version of Shakespeare. Several black and Puerto Rican youngsters captivated the public in *The Me Nobody Knows*, a tune-fest partly based on the writings of schoolchildren, while *Purlie*, which had won Tony awards for Melba Moore and Cleavon Little in 1970, returned to Broadway with new names in the cast. In 1972 Ruby Dee gave a superb performance in black playwright Alice Childress's *Wedding Band*, which played in Greenwich

Village at Joseph Papp's Public Theater. Earlier, James Earl Jones had appeared on Broadway in *Les Blancs,* the last play by the late Lorraine Hansberry as adapted by Robert Nemiroff, which was granted a less than lukewarm reception. One of the most heartwarming and realistic portrayals of black life came in 1971 with J.E. Franklin's *Black Girl,* which was directed by another young black woman, Shauneille Perry, and later was made into a film. It was produced by Woodie King Jr., who gave a helping hand to many other black plays. Other notable dramatic presentations were Imamu Baraka's *Slaveship,* with music by Archie Shepp, Vinie Burrows's one-woman historical show *Walk Together Children,* Richard Wesley's *The Black Terror,* Ed Bullins's *The Fabulous Miss Marie,* and Aishah Rahman's *Lady Day: A Musical Tragedy.*

BLACK EMPLOYMENT IN THE FILM INDUSTRY

The black performer has been dealt with in the following article on black film. The battle for the use of blacks in areas away from the camera and in attempts to pry a wedge into the Hollywood trade unions took a new thrust at the end of the sixties and the beginning of the seventies.

A 1965 survey taken by the Beverly Hills-Hollywood NAACP covering 15 motion picture and television production firms showed that in 11 movies and 45 television series, black actors were being starred or featured in a total of 36 roles. In other areas of employment after 1965, blacks became more visible in the industry in positions ranging from "grips," janitors and lamp operators, to secretaries, researchers, staff attorneys and publicists.

Of nine studios responding to the NAACP survey on employment of blacks in non-performing jobs, figures show only 10 so employed prior to 1963. Since 1965, the total number of non-artist employees at the studios has increased from 81 in 1963 to 215 in 1966.

Wendell Franklin, the first black member of the Directors' Guild of America in 1968, moved from assistant director to director at Universal, and in 1972 became a producer with K-Calb Productions in *The Bus is Coming*. Walter Burrell, a publicist, and Louise Meriweather, a story analyst, are also at Universal. Other blacks were, by 1972, to be found in the art departments, film center, and wardrobe.

One of the early breakthroughs came in the hiring of Vincent Tubbs, the first full-time publicist hired by a major studio to work outside the black consumer market. Tubbs, a war correspondent and journalist for the Afro-American newspapers and later for Johnson Publications, joined Warner Brothers, as a publicist. After a stint at American-International and a period of working with individual stars such as Steve McQueen, Tubbs returned to Warner Communications, Inc. as assistant to the director of publicity where he is currently press director of community relations. He was the first black member of The Hollywood Publicists Guild and later served that group as vice-president and president.

In 1969, under the direction of Clifford Alexander, chairman of the EEOC, an investigation of "pattern and practice of discrimination as outlined in Section 707 of the Civil Rights Act of 1964" was conducted.

The reports compiled by the EEOC revealed that at that time there were no blacks among the 288 officials and managers of Walt Disney Productions. There were 9 blacks among the firm's 900 white-collar employees.

At Warner Brothers-Seven Arts there were 184 union technicians, one black; of 250 office and clerical workers only 7 were black.

At Universal studios there were 3 blacks among the 361 managers and officials. At 20th Century Fox, there were no blacks among 174 technicians and unionized craftsmen.

Of 400 members of the International Alliance of Theatrical and Stage Employees, only 8 were black, while there were no blacks among the 40 illustrators and artists.

The pattern of exclusion of blacks from the film industry was clearly documented by the EEOC bearings.

Following Melvin Van Peebles, who showed the way when he handled production, direction, filming, and the starring role of *Sweet Sweetback's Bad-Ass Song* (1971), increasing numbers of blacks are becoming the independent entrepreneurs for black films. Sam Greenlee's best-selling novel, *The Spook Who Sat by the Door* was brought to the screen by Greenlee and Ivan Dixon. Hugh Robertson, who began by editing *Shaft* and *Midnight Cowboy* for which he received an Oscar nomination, directed *Honey, Baby* the last film completed by Diana Sands before her untimely death in September, 1973, and the successful *Melinda*.

Gordon Parks directed *The Learning Tree* in 1969 and Ossie Davis, *Cotton Comes to Harlem*. Mark Warren directed *Come Back Charleston Blue* with background and experience gained in television. Robert L. Goodwin has formed an independent motion picture production company whose first production is *Black Charlot*. Maya Angelou, whose screenplay of *Georgia, Georgia*, moves into direction on the film treatment of her autobiography, *I Know Why the Caged Bird Sings*.

Bill Greaves, the documentary film maker whose work on educational T.V.'s "Black Journal" gained him a national reputation has also moved into production of films.

Ossie Davis, playwright-actor-director has been in the forefront of activity to get blacks into film distribution, without which and until which he feels "racism" would continue to be prevalent. One black distribution company has been started—"T.A.M." Communications.

BLACKS IN FILM

An overview of the history of blacks in cinema is, with few exceptions, a chronicle of stereotypes and distortions. From the beginning, white film-makers pictured blacks as happy slaves, savage cannibals, and brainless phalli.

In 1902, *Off to Bloomingdale Asylum,* by George Melies, marked the debut of racism on the screen, stereotyping blacks as superstitious halfwits and presented slaveowners as gentle paladins.

In 1905, *The Wooing and Wedding of a Coon,* and in 1907, *The Masher* still showed whites in blackface. In fact, it wasn't until 1914 that white producers permitted a black, Sam Lucas, to portray Tom in *Uncle Tom's Cabin,* making Lucas the first black actor to be used in a film about blacks. Although the racist nature of films did not change, at least blacks were given an opportunity to display their acting talents.

In 1918 D. W. Griffith directed his infamous *Birth of a Nation,* based on Thomas Dixon's novel, *The Clansman.* Unfortunately the film classic painted blacks as rapists, murderers, shrews, and ninnies—brutes to be hated, humiliated, avoided, and condemned; to be kept at bay if possible, or thrown into concentration camps if necessary. Then in a series of shrewd, maliciously distorted characterizations, he hammered at the concept of freedom. The NAACP mounted a nation-wide protest and in some cities succeeded in having the film withdrawn.

E. J. Scott and Oscar Micheaux emerged from the protest as the first black filmmakers. Scott, Booker T. Washington's secretary at Tuskegee Institute, was angered by *Birth of a Nation.* He hired a writer to script a cinematic reply to Griffith's distortions, then sold stock in the black community to produce it; but without sufficient capital the project failed.

Oscar Micheaux fared better by touring the nation with his scripts under his arm and persuading theater managers to give him an advance against booking. Consequently he promoted such films as *The Spider's Web, The Broken Violin, Dark Princess,* and *A Daughter of the Congo.* In fact he is credited with having made the first full-length, all-black film, *Birthright,* as early as 1918. For the next twenty years, Micheaux shot and sold a film a year without bureaucratic support or studio censure. And although some of his movies left much to be desired, Micheaux is to be lauded for his courage, his sincerity, and his success in opening screen doors for black actors.

Nobel Johnson also became a producer and director around 1919. He was sponsored by white-owned companies.

Hal Roach's *Our Gang* comedy series featured a black named Farina, who was the butt of jokes organized by a gang of mischievous white toddlers.

In early 1927 Universal Studios produced another version of *Uncle Tom's Cabin,* with James B. Lowe selected over Charles Gilpin, who was rejected for· the part of Tom after balking at the screen translation of the character.

Al Jolson ushered in the first talkie in 1927 by starring in *The Jazz Singer,* entertaining former silent film addicts with his singing ability since recorded dialogue had not yet been perfected. Although white audiences enjoyed his debut, blacks deplored the fact that Jolson made his appearance in blackface.

Hollywood promptly capitalized on this technological achievement by importing a multitude of black singers, dancers, and musicians from New York to appear in an epidemic of "all-colored" movies. The first all-black Hollywood film was Twentieth Century Fox's *Hearts in Dixie* (1929). Clarence Muse starred as an aging black man who makes a sacrifice for his son, while Stepin Fetchit provided comic relief.

During the same year, MGM produced *Hallelujah,* a farce which poked fun at the black man's church services. The situation improved a bit in 1932 when Warner Brothers selected Mervyn LeRoy to direct *I Am a Fugitive from a Chain Gang,* a socially conscious drama about unjust labor camp practices in the South. Black convict Everett Brown appeared in time to aid Paul Muni's prison break and was remembered as a warm, courageous man for his efforts.

In terms of stardom, the year 1933 belonged to Paul Robeson, black law school graduate, Phi Beta Kappa, actor, singer, and orator. Robeson starred in the film version of Eugene O'Neill's *Emperor Jones,* portraying a black fugitive whose delusions of grandeur established him as a monarch in a jungle. Robeson's splendid performance earned him critical acclaim from laymen and artists alike.

Two black actresses played key roles in the 1934 film production of Fannie Hurst's book, *Imitation of Life,* with Louise Beavers and Fredi Washington playing the mother and daughter roles.

Stepin Fetchit and Bill ("Bojangles") Robinson were growing in popularity. Fetchit mastered his lazy-acting style in such films as *Stand Up and Cheer* and *David Harum.* Robinson polished his dancing technique in a trio of Shirley Temple films: *The Littlest Rebel, The Little Colonel,* and *Rebecca of Sunnybrook Farm.*

The Green Pastures, produced by Warner Brothers in 1936, utilized the talents of Rex Ingram as De Lawd and Eddie ("Rochester") Anderson as Noah—and reinforced an earlier myth: blacks are hooked on a heaven filled with fish fries and baptisms in long white robes.

But in 1937 *They Won't Forget,* by Mervyn LeRoy, marked the indictment of lynch-mob mentalities by featuring Clinton Rosemond as a black porter who is hounded by white vigilantes for a crime he didn't commit.

For her role in *Gone with the Wind,* written by Margaret Mitchell, and produced by David O. Selznick, in 1939, Hattie McDaniel won an Oscar as Best Supporting Actress. It was the first time in the history of motion pictures that a black person was so honored—even though many civil rights groups considered the role derogatory. And few can forget Butterfly McQueen's secondary characterization of a scatterbrained black servant girl.

With World War II patriotic dramas, musical comedies, and war stories were ground out by the dozens. It was not until Dorie Miller had won a chestful of medals as the first black war hero that Hollywood began the practice of including one black actor in each film it produced—usually as part of a crowd scene.

Lena Horne, Ethel Waters, Bill ("Bojangles") Robinson, Katherine Dunham, Louis Armstrong, Duke Ellington, Count Basie, Fats Waller, Dorothy Dandridge, Josephine Baker, Lillian Randolph, and Hazel Scott sang and danced in movies such as *Stormy Weather, Cabin in the Sky,* and *Star Spangled Rhythm.* Meanwhile, Langston Hughes and Clarence Muse collaborated on the script for *Way Down South.*

Between 1940 and 1945, there were several nonwar, nonmusical films available to blacks. Canada Lee, for example, appeared in *Lifeboat,* a 1944 vehicle from Fox Studios, playing the underdeveloped character of the sole black in a motley crew of shipwrecked survivors sharing a lifeboat. Leigh Whipper fared better in the *Ox-Bow Incident,* portraying a fearless preacher who risked his own neck to stop a lynching. As a serious young black clerk in a Bette Davis film, *In This Our Life,* Ernest Anderson manages to avoid the usual stereotypes. Black servants, however, were regularly featured in films during the forties.

Paul Robeson and Ethel Waters were featured in *Tales of Manhattan,* and Walt Disney's *Song of the South* featured black actor James Baskett as Uncle Remus singing "Zippity Doo Dah." The stereotyped role earned Baskett a special award from the Academy of Motion Picture Arts and Sciences.

After the war, Hollywood directed its efforts toward racial problems. The first movie to deal with the subject in depth was *Home of the Brave,* a 1949 vehicle that introduced James Edwards as a black soldier, a victim of military bigotry, who is wounded in action in the Pacific.

In *Pinky,* white actress Jeanne Crain played a nurse passing for white. Problems crop up when her charwoman-grandmother, Ethel Waters, expects her to live black. Pinky ends up repenting for her evil ways and lives happily ever after. Again, Ethel Waters came under critical fire for playing another "mammy" role, although the part was flecked with dignity.

The reels of progress turned faster in 1950, the year Juano Hernandez refused to a "good Negro" in his portrayal of a Southerner in MGM's *Intruder in the Dust.* Accused of killing a bigot, Hernandez gave a gripping performance that not only affected the characters in the film, but evoked sympathy from audiences as well.

Hernandez was also featured as an aging black jazz musician in *Young Man with a Horn,* which starred Kirk Douglas as his protégé.

Another noteworthy film was produced during the same year—one that brought stage rookie Sidney Poitier to the big screen. As a medical intern in *No Way Out,* Poitier clashes with a psychopathic Richard Widmark, who charges him with professional malpractice. Poitier skirts a race riot, dodges an assassin's bullet and finally proves his innocence. Spiced with salty dialogue, the film showed Poitier in a favorable light and set the stage for future pictures.

The Jackie Robinson Story (1950), was a mild biographical treatment with Robinson playing himself and Ruby Dee portraying his wife. Richard Wright played the lead role in the screen version of his novel, *Native Son* (1951). Filmed on location in Argentina, the story dealt with the racial pressures which drove a young black man to murder a white woman.

Neither *The Joe Louis Story* (1953) nor *Bright Road* (based on Mary E. Vroman's story, "See How They Run") sparked as much interest as did *Carmen Jones* (1954). Dorothy Dandridge received a Best Actress nomination for her portrayal of a temptress in the film, while Harry Belafonte exercised his acting talents, to the delight of female audiences.

Sidney Poitier bounced back in *Edge of the City* (1957) as a middle-class husband, father, and dock foreman involved in one of the first sensitive integration movies in the history of cinema. *Island in the Sun* (1957) explored interracial romance by pairing Dorothy Dandridge and Harry Belafonte with a white couple in the Carribbean. But neither film matched the taut drama of *The Defiant Ones* (1958), which literally linked fugitives Sidney Poitier and Tony Curtis in a tense flight from a chain gang.

Poitier and Dandridge, costarred in the musical drama, *Porgy and Bess* (1959). *Band of Angels* (1959) ranked among Poitier's lesser screen achievements.

Belafonte played in *The World, the Flesh, and the Devil* (1959), which examined the relationships of three survivors of an atomic holocaust, and in *Odds Against Tomorrow* (1959), a drama filmed by Belafonte's Harbel Productions and written by John O. Killens, Belafonte appeared as a night-club musician caught in a web of gambling debts and haunted by a rocky marriage.

Louis Peterson contributed *Take a Giant Step*, which gave Johnny Nash the opportunity to play a black adolescent who strides from carefree childhood through a confused adolescence to a vague but definite maturity.

Lorraine Hansberry brought her prize-winning drama, *A Raisin in the Sun*, to motion picture houses—with the omnipresent Sidney Poitier portraying Walter Lee, an over-thirty chauffeur with a persecution complex stemming from his inability to provide adequate support for his wife, mother, sister, and son. Audiences were now being given a look at black people, black reality, and the trauma of harsh black existence.

In *Anna Lucasta*, the story of a reformed prostitute, Eartha Kitt and Sammy Davis, Jr. costarred with Frederick O'Neal. *Paris Blues* (1961) featured Sidney Poitier and Paul Newman as jazz musicians in a Paris night spot. Louis Armstrong sat in on a jam session while Diahann Carroll doubled as a vacationing teacher-mistress.

Muscular Woody Strode brought 1962 in as John Wayne's unlikely sidekick in *The Man Who Shot Liberty Valance*.

In the same year, Maidie Norman was loyal to Joan Crawford but was bludgeoned to death by a demented Bette Davis in *Whatever Happened to Baby Jane?* and Juano Hernandez was devoted to Paul Newman in Hemingway's *Adventures of a Young Man.* Even the versatile Sammy Davis, Jr. played a minor role in *Sergeants 3,* although his stature as an entertainer won him star billing along with Frank Sinatra, Dean Martin, and Peter Lawford.

Stanley Kramer guided Sidney Poitier through *Pressure Point,* considered the leading black characterization of the year, despite the fact that Poitier's role was originally written with a white actor in mind. Poitier portrayed a prison psychiatrist and had Bobby Darin as his patient.

Ten motion pictures involved black characters in 1963. Diana Sands played a free-lance photographer in *An Affair of the Skin.* Ruby Dee masqueraded as a prostitute in *The Balcony;* and the skillful Frank Silvera etched the dual role of chauffeur and mulatto lover in *Toys in the Attic,* a drama about miscegenation. Still groping his way through undesirable scripts, Sammy Davis, Jr. embodied another negative ethnic myth as a dice addict in *Johnny Cool.* Eddie ("Rochester") Anderson played a doltish cabbie in *Its a Mad Mad Mad Mad World,* and Frederick O'Neal was accused of raping a blonde Swedish Freedom Rider in *Free, White and 21.* The rape theme was equally popular in *To Kill a Mockingbird,* which had Gregory Peck defending Brock Peters, who was falsely accused of assaulting a white Southern woman.

Ossie Davis played another Southern black, a priest, in *The Cardinal,* traveling to Rome to enlist the aid of the Pope in desegregating a Catholic school in Georgia. Davis and his wife, Ruby Dee, displayed their acting talents in *Gone Are the Days,* the screen version of Davis's play, *Purlie Victorious*—a satire on the racial customs of the old South. All the major characters in *Gone Are the Days* are deliberate stereotypes, a ploy used by Davis as a method of social criticism.

Sidney Poitier made history with his portrayal of a handyman in *Lillies of the Field.* Demonstrating a flair for comedy as well as drama, Poitier plays a maverick-of-all-trades who is persuaded, or inspired, to build a chapel for a group of impoverished nuns. Poitier's powerful performance garnered him an Oscar as the year's Best Actor, another "first" for blacks in cinema.

In 1964, football star-turned-actor Jim Brown was introduced to film audiences in *Rio Conchos,* a Western that had Brown playing a no-nonsense army sergeant, while an increasing number of black actors were used as extras.

Greg Morris showed up in *The New Interns.* Joel Fluellen made a brief appearance in a low-budget Western, *He Rides Tall. The Troublemaker* involved Godfrey Cambridge as a fire inspector and Al Freeman, Jr. as an intern in brief, satirical interludes, and *Shock Treatment* engaged Ossie Davis as a mental patient. James Earl Jones made appearances in *Dr. Strangelove, Or: How I Learned to Stop Worrying and Love the Bomb,* a satire on nuclear activity. And Sammy Davis, Jr. surfaced again in the movie *Robin and the 7 Hoods,* which was a slapstick musical comedy about Chicago gangsters.

Black Like Me surprised film audiences with a black militant character, played by Al Freeman, Jr. Based on John Howard Griffin's novel of the same name, the movie traces the path of a white man, James Whitmore, disguised as a black in the South. Freeman played a college-bred civil rights activist who challenged audience nonchalance on the race issue and noted the need for social change.

One Potato, Two Potato earned a well-deserved niche in motion picture history as the first film to wrestle with the theme of interracial marriage between a black man and a white woman. Starring Barbara Barrie as a sensitive divorcee and Bernie Hamilton as a kind factory worker, the movie unveiled the conflicts, anxieties, and hazards of mixed love. Tastefully done, the film showed Hamilton as a whole man, instead of the usual caricature.

Another important motion picture showed similar merits. It was an independent production called *Nothing But a Man,* featuring Ivan Dixon and Abbey Lincoln in the lead roles. The plot concerned Dixon's efforts to earn a decent salary so that he could support his family and walk with earnest pride. The black couple manage to overcome their hardships and emerge triumphant at the close of the film. Warm reviews followed strong public support, an indication that producer Robert Young was on the right track, with the right script and the right actors.

In 1966, Raymond St. Jacques, who would later become a star, was required to shoot craps in *Mr. Buddwing,* the story of a white amnesiac portrayed by James Garner. Ena Hartman swooned over James Coburn in *Our Man Flint.* Juanita Moore received no blessings as a sister in *The Singing Nun.* Woody Strode was a silent archer in the Burt Lancaster-Lee Marvin movie, *The Professionals.* Errol John, as an alcoholic criminal, helped Frank Sinatra commit a mid-ocean heist in *Assault on a Queen,* and Joel Fluellen resisted racial bigotry in *The Chase.*

Sidney Poitier buckled his gunbelt for *Duel at Diablo,* a fast-paced Western about a brash, black, cigar-chomping former cavalry sergeant who likes to gamble between verbal bouts with James Garner.

A Man Called Adam deserves special mention because blacks glittered both before and behind the cameras during its production. Ike Jones was a co-producer of the film and "Cannonball" Adderly provided most of the music. Sammy Davis, Jr. starred as Adam, a brilliant black trumpet player whose drinking habit causes the blindness of another musician, as well as the death of his own wife and child. Cicely Tyson provided the romantic interest, Ossie Davis portrayed Adam's friend, and Louis ("Satchmo") Armstrong played Tyson's musician-grandfather.

Black artists were involved in a more favorable assortment of films in 1967 than they were during the previous year, largely because urban rioting in major ghettos provided the motion picture industry with more relevant subject matter. The practice of making white-oriented films prevailed, however. The few exceptions were pictures which used dependable black favorites.

The Comedians depicted black discrimination against whites. Set in Haiti, the movie dealt with that country's political dictatorship and featured Raymond St. Jacques as a ruthless police officer; Gloria Foster as the widow of a government official; James Earl Jones as a rebel doctor; Cicely Tyson as a friendly prostitute; Roscoe Lee Browne as a gossip columinst; and George Stanford Brown as a young radical.

Jim Brown displayed his athletic prowess as one of twelve convict-saboteurs in *The Dirty Dozen,* eleven of whom constantly mocked his blackness. Godfrey Cambridge stabbed a man to death in *The President's Analyst,* then confessed the murder to his psychiatrist. Brock Peters and Ruby Dee were victims in *The Incident,* a drama about the occupants of a late-night subway car seized by white thugs.

Another subway drama unfolded in *Dutchman,* the film version of LeRoi Jones' (Imamu Amiri Baraka) play. Shirley Knight played a psychotic white girl who attempts to seduce black actor Al Freeman, Jr. while the train rolls through the city. Portraying a bourgeois black man, Freeman resists her advances until he loses his patience and flogs her with words of rage—implying that every black man is a potential revolutionary. Following this outburst, the girl kills Freeman and the movie ends with another black man boarding the train.

Black novelist John A. Williams's "Nigh Song" hit the screen as *Sweet Love, Bitter,* starring comedian Dick Gregory as a jazz saxophonist whose life is eaten away by sex, liquor, and drugs.

Hooks appeared again in *Hurry Sundown,* this time as a young farmer with a yearning for school teacher Diahann Carroll. Veterans Beah Richards and Rex Ingram figured as the younger couple's kin. Hooks emerged as a superhero in his confrontations with the film's white characters.

Sidney Poitier was accused of murder in *In the Heat of the Night,* another film placed in the South. Playing a police detective on a family visit in Mississippi, Poitier is ridiculed and despised by white police-chief Rod Steiger, who reluctantly turns to Poitier for help in finding the real killer.

In *To Sir With Love,* Sidney Poitier adopted a British accent for his role as a teacher in a London slum. Still the superhero, Poitier transforms a class of uncouth students into a group of model pupils.

Guess Who's Coming To Dinner was the screen surprise of the year. Poitier's engagement and intended marriage constituted the plot of the movie. The controversy arose because his fiancée was white, but the film came under fire from critics who described the portrayals as unreal.

There were four outstanding black-oriented films during 1968. The first, *If He Hollers, Let Him Go,* was important enough to make Raymond St. Jacques a star, although its plot left much to be desired. St. Jacques played a fugitive on the run from Georgia, where he had been wrongly convicted of assaulting a white girl. Barbara McNair was also featured. In *The Split,* the pattern was followed by costars Jim Brown and Diahann Carroll, calling for Brown to portray the leader of a gang of white criminals out to grab the gate receipts of a gridiron game. Superstar Sidney Poitier also made screen love to a black woman, Abbey Lincoln, in *For Love of Ivy*—a first for America's black film giant. Finally, *Up Tight,* was the first film to depict the Black Revolution. Set in a Cleveland slum shortly after the death of Dr. Martin Luther King, Jr., the plot illustrated the efforts of black militants to rob a munitions warehouse and dealt with the emotional problems of their leader, portrayed by Julian Mayfield. The supporting case included Ruby Dee, Raymond St. Jacques, Frank Silvera, Roscoe Lee Browne, and Janet McLachlan.

In 1969, Jim Brown made love to Racquel Welch in *100 Rifles,* and Gordon Parks, Sr. wrote, directed, and scored the autobiographical *Learning Tree,* making the former *Life* magazine photographer the first black director of a major Hollywood film. A short while later, black actor Rupert Crosse earned an Academy nomination for Best Supporting Actor in *The Reivers*—another first.

Films have seldom been made with every-one in mind, but rather have thrived by focusing on one segment of society. In the 1970s, that segment is black and Hollywood is cashing in.

Cotton Comes to Harlem, directed by Ossie Davis and costarring Raymond St. Jacques and Godfrey Cambridge, tapped the previously untested black market, grossed more than $90 million, and spawned a host of other films. *Shaft* (1971) starred Richard Roundtree as a cool, hard-hitting private eye and made some $15 million. Melvin Van Peebles' conversial independent movie, *Sweet Sweetback's Baadassss Song* (1971) earned Van Peebles at least $12 million and ushered in the "black superstud" vogue.

Between 1970 and 1971, at least fifty "black" movies flooded the market, including *Blacula* (black Dracula), *Buck and the Preacher* (black Western), *Georgia, Georgia* (black singer), *Halls of Anger* (black teacher), *The Legend of Nigger Charley* (radical slave), *The Liberation of L. B. Jones* (extramarital black-white sex), *Melinda* (black deejay), *Skin Game* (master-slave con artist), *Slaughter* (black thriller), *Top of the Heap* (black cop), *Hammer* (black boxer), *Sounder* (black sharecroppers), *Come Back Charleston Blue* (sequel to Cotton), *Shafts Big Score* (sequel to Shaft and Shaft in Africa), *Lady Sings the Blues* (Billie Holiday story), and *Super Fly* (black cocaine pusher), which made more than $1 million after only a week at two theaters in New York.

Such cinemas gave new impetus to the movie industry and created new job opportunities for black artists who had been denied the chance to practice their craft because of racial barriers. Directors Gordon Parks, Sr., Gordon Parks, Jr., Hugh Robertson, Maya Angelou, Mark Warren, Christopher St. John, Ivan Dixon, and Wendell Franklin were among the black artists moved into directorial positions on various properties.

There was still the suspicion, however, that white film-makers only used black craftsmen to lend authenticity to exploitation films and as "showcase" workers in the event that aware blacks protested. Excepted were Sidney Poitier, who was both rich and famous enough to finance *Buck and the Preacher,* and Melvin Van Peebles, who wrote, produced, directed, starred in, scored, and distributed his own film. And while it is true that *Super Fly* was created and financed by blacks, Warner Brothers brought distribution rights to it and offered its backers a percentage of the gate receipts. Other studios planned sequels to *The Legend of Nigger Charley, Slaughter, Blacula* and others, such as *Blackenstein, Black Bart,*

The Werewolf from Watts, Blackfather, Black Christ, The Nigger Lover, and *Sundown in Watts.*

It seemed that white producers were more interested in profits than in quality, since the majority of black films during this period were of the cheap rush-order caliber. But the low-budget quickie was popular, perhaps because the black market, starved to see itself on movie screens, cared less at the time whether a film cost one dollar or one million dollars to make, as long as its cool black hero somehow stuck it to "the man."

Quite a number of the new black films were criticized for portraying black women as sex symbols, such as the strong comments aired against the negative female images in *Sweet Sweetback.*

Other critics criticized the black movies for making a mockery of black oppression. In *Super Fly,* three civil rights organizers are portrayed as money-grubbing extortionists, and in *Sweet Sweetback* the black revolutionary is depicted as a bumbling incompetent. *Lost Man* showed black militants whose ability to conduct a revolution was as doubtful as their ability to plan the bank job they bungled. *Watermelon Man* starred Godfrey Cambridge as a horrified "white" insurance agent who wakes up one morning and finds himself black. And *Come Back Charleston Blue* poked fun at everything and had blacks laughing at themselves.

The credibility gap between realism and fantasy remained a source of concern in 1972. It appeared that every hero had to be a superhero so that the fearless, faultless black stars really amounted to little more than black John Waynes or James Bonds foisted off on black audiences. Both white and black producers responded to criticism of such treatment by claiming that they were "only giving audiences what they wanted."

Charging that the switch from the Stepin Fetchit stereotype to the super-black image was proof that black film portraits had come full circle, Junius Griffin, president of the Beverly Hills-Hollywood NAACP, described *Super Fly* as "an insidious film which portrays the black community at its worst." Jesse Jackson, head of Operation PUSH, cautioned that the movie came "very close to being an inadvertent advertising medium for drugs" and called for a change in Hollywood's presentation of blacks. Roy Innis, national director of CORE, demanded the right of censorship of such black films.

Source: Reprinted from a special report, "Blacks in Film," by B.J. Mason Vol. 4, Ebony Pictorial History of Black America, Johnson Publishing Co. Inc. 1973

BLACKS IN SELECTED FILMS

MOVIE	YEAR	FEATURED PERFORMERS	PRODUCERS	DIRECTORS
Uncle Tom's Cabin	1914	Sam Lucas[1]	World Studios	Wm. R. Daly
Dark Town Jubilee	1914	Bert Williams	Bert Williams Productions	
The Nigger	1915	William Farnum		
Birthright[2]	1918		Oscar Micheaux**	Oscar Micheaux*
The Birth of a Nation[3]	1918	George Seigmann	D. W. Griffith	D. W. Griffith
Uncle Tom's Cabin	1927	Margarita Fischer		
Hearts in Dixie[4]	1929	Clarence Muse, Stepin Fetchit	20th Century Fox	Paul Sloane
Hallelujah	1929	Daniel Hayes, Nina Mae McKinney	King Vidor	
St. Louis Blues	1929	Bessie Smith		
Borderline	1930	Paul Robeson		
The Black King	1932	Vivian Baber, Harry Gray		
Flying Down to Rio	1933	Etta Moten	RKO	
Gold Diggers of 1933	1933	Etta Moten	Warner Brothers	
Emperor Jones	1933	Paul Robeson	John Krimsky	Dudley Murphy
West of Singapore	1933	Hazel Jones	Monogram	
Imitation of Life[5]	1934	Louise Beavers, Fredi Washington	Carl Laemmie, Jr.	John M. Stahl
Sanders of the River	1935	Paul Robeson, Leslie Banks		
Symphony in Black	1935	Leslie Banks		
Green Pastures	1936	Rex Ingram	Warner Brothers	Marc Connolly, William Keighly
Siren of the Tropics	1937	Josephine Baker		
Song of Freedom	1937	Paul Robeson		
Spirit of Youth	1937	Joe Louis, Clarence Muse		
Harlem on the Prairie[6]	1938	Herb Jeffries	Jed Buell	Sam Newfield
Way Down South[7]	1939	Clarence Muse	Sol Lesser	Bernard Vorhaus
Gone With the Wind	1939	Hattie McDaniel†	David O. Selznick	Sam Wood
Keep Punching	1941	Henry Armstrong		
Casablanca	1942	Dooley Wilson	Warner Brothers	
Talk of the Town	1942	Rex Ingram	Columbia	
Panama Hattie	1942	Lena Horne	MGM	
Cabin in the Sky	1943	Lena Horne	20th Century Fox	Vincente Minnelli
Right About Face	1943	Lena Horne	MGM	
As Thousands Cheer	1943	Lena Horne	MGM	
Somewhere in the Sahara	1943	Rex Ingram (Humphrey Bogart)	Columbia	
Fired Wife	1943	Rex Ingram	Universal	
Crash Dive	1943	Ben Carter	20th Century Fox	
Ox-Bow Incident	194?	Leigh Whipper		
Sahara	1943	Rex Ingram	Columbia	
Mission to Moscow	194?	Leigh Whipper		
Dark Waters	1944	Rex Ingram		
Song of the South	1947	James Baskett†	Walt Disney	Harve Foster
No Way Out[8]	1950	Sidney Poitier	20th Century Fox	Joe Mankiewicz
Bright Road[9]	1953	Dorothy Dandridge	Sol Fielding	Gerald Mayer
Carmen Jones	1954	Dorothy Dandridge†	20th Century Fox	Otto Preminger
Anna Lucasta	1958	Eartha Kitt		
Odds Against Tomorrow[10]	1959	Harry Belafonte	Harbel Productions**	Robert Wise
A Raisin in the Sun[11]	1961	Sidney Poitier	Columbia Pictures	Daniel Petrie
Take a Giant Step[12]	1961	Johnny Nash	United Artists	Philip Leacock
Lilies of the Field	1963	Sidney Poitier†	United Artists	Ralph Nelson
One Potato, Two Potato	1964	Bernie Hamilton	Cinema V	Larry Peerce
Nothing But a Man	1964	Ivan Dixon	Mike Roemer	Mike Roemer
Rio Conchos	1964	Jim Brown	20th Century Fox	Gordon Douglas
A Man Called Adam	1966	Sammy Davis, Jr.	Ike Jones**	Leo Penn

MOVIE	YEAR	FEATURED PERFORMERS	PRODUCERS	DIRECTORS
Dutchman[13]	1967	Al Freeman, Jr.	Gene Persson	Anthony Harvey
If He Hollers, Let Him Go	1968	Raymond St. Jacques	Charles Martin	Charles Martin
Up Tight[14]	1968	Julian Mayfield	Jules Dassin	Jules Dassin
The Learning Tree[15]	1969	Kyle Johnson	Warner Brothers	Gordon Parks, Sr.*
100 Rifles	1969	Jim Brown	20th Century Fox	Tom Gries
The Reivers	1969	Rupert Crossett††	National General	Mary Rydell
Watermelon Man	1970	Godfrey Cambridge	Columbia Pictures	Melvin Van Peebles
Cotton Comes To Harlem[16]	1970	Godfrey Cambridge, R. St. Jacques	Warner Brothers	Ossie Davis*
The Great White Hope	1970	James Earl Jones††	20th Century Fox	Martin Ritt
Sweet Sweetback's Baadasssss Song[17]	1971	Melvin Van Peebles	Melvin Van Peebles	Melvin Van Peebles
Shaft[18]	1971	Richard Roundtree	Warner Brothers	Gordon Parks, Sr.*
The Legend of Nigger Charley	1971	Fred Williamson	Martin Goldman	Larry Spangler
Blacula[19]	1972	William Marshall	Amer. Int. Pictures	William Crain
Buck and the Preacher	1972	Sidney Poitier, Harry Belafonte	Columbia Pictures Sidney Poitier**	Sidney Poitier*
Georgia, Georgia[20]	1972	Diana Sands	Quentin Kelly	Maya Angelou*
Melinda	1972	Calvin Lockhart	MGM	Hugh Robertson*
Top of the Heap	1972	Chris St. John	Chris St. John**	Chris St. John*
Come Back Charleston Blue	1972	R. St. Jacques, Godfrey Cambridge	Warner Brothers	Mark Warren*
Lady Sings the Blues	1972	Diana Ross††	Berry Gordy, Jr.**	Sidney J. Furie
Super Fly	1972	Ron O'Neal	Sig Shore	Gordon Parks, Jr.*
Trouble Man	1972	Robert Hooks	MGM	Ivan Dixon*
Sounder[21]	1972	Cicely Tyson††, Paul Winfield††	20th Century Fox	Martin Ritt
Wattstax	1973	Watts (Cal. 1972) Film Festival— Documentary	Shaw-Stuart	Mel Stuart
Warm December	1973	Sidney Poitier		

NOTE: This table lists historically significant movies of the last seventy years.   *Black director.   **Black producer or coproducer.   †Academy Award.   ††Academy Award Nomination.

1. First black actor in an American movie.
2. First film directed by black.
3. First major racist film.
4. First sound film about blacks.
5. First film to use black actresses in key roles.
6. First black western.
7. Screenplay by Langston Hughes and Clarence Muse.
8. First Poitier film.
9. Based on story by Mary E. Vroman.
10. First major modern film written by black (John Killens).
11. Screenplay by Lorraine Hansberry.

12. Screenplay by Louis Peterson.
13. Screenplay by Imamu Amiri Baraka.
14. First film about the Black Revolution.
15. First film directed by a black in modern times.
16. Chiefly responsible for current pattern of black films.
17. Ushered in black "superstud" vogue.
18. Black composer Isaac Hayes won Academy Award for best musical score.
19. First black horror film.
20. First film directed by black woman.
21. Screenplay by Lonne Elder, III.††

BLACK MUSIC

As music always has been the black man's "thing," his activities in this field were so diverse during the fifties and sixties as to almost defy definition. Yet they might be roughly broken down into three categories: (1) jazz, (2) soul music, and (3) classical or formal music.

JAZZ

As blacks began to define their own terms of acceptance, some of the finest jazz musicians and composers were becoming determined to carry this art form back to its black roots, to free the music of the conventional Western techniques that it had acquired, and to incorporate into it some elements of non-Western music.

If there was any single factor that tended to keep jazz the vital and constantly changing music that it was in this period, it was that forces of the past mingled with forces of the present to chart new directions for future growth. Those who had helped to shape the music during its formative years were still around and active. Again, Duke Ellington was a key figure as a representative of the continuing past. With more than one thousand compositions to his credit by the mid-sixties, he produced new works, including a suite entitled *The Golden Broom and the Green Apple.* When it premiered in the summer of 1965 at Lincoln Center, he conducted the New York Philharmonic Orchestra. He also undertook a series of concerts of his sacred compositions. Following the first presentation of these concerts at San Francisco's Grace Cathedral and New York's Fifth Avenue Presbyterian Church, he carried his new concept to churches and other institutions throughout the country. He toured Europe and the Far East, as well as the United States and finally, in his golden years, became one of the most honored of men, continuing to win jazz poll after jazz poll, though he had been a working musician for fifty years. His course was marred by the death of his musical collaborator, Billy Strayhorn, on May 31, 1967, and alto saxophonist Johnny Hodges in early 1970.

Another perennial, Louis Armstrong, was still on the scene in 1970, when he celebrated his seventieth birthday, but illness prevented him from playing his instrument. However as a singer, he had made his first million-selling record at the age of 65 in 1965, an inimitable version of the show tune *Hello, Dolly!* Among other senior musicians continuing to perform were big band leader Count Basie, composer Eubie Blake, who recorded at 87,

pianist Earl Hines, and tenor saxophonists Ben Webster and Coleman Hawkins.

Overlapping these musical giants were those who had evolved from the bebop period of the late forties—Dizzy Gillespie and Thelonious Monk—the latter achieving white recognition in 1964 when he appeared on the cover of *Time* magazine. Another, trumpeter Miles Davis, who had played with Charlie Parker as a very young man, went on to become one of the major musical figures of the fifties and sixties. The records he made in 1949–50 were marked by a quiet introspection and ingenious understatement. His approach was to influence not only black musicians but many whites who played what came to be known as "cool jazz." Remaining essentially "cool," Davis stood as a major force playing upon white musicians throughout the late sixties when he helped move white "rock" toward jazz.

When whites copied black innovations, the blacks consistently developed new styles not so easily imitated. Charlie Parker had been the foremost of these, though his motives were more creative than racial. As Leonard Feather has written of Parker in his *Encyclopedia of Jazz:* "In bringing the art of improvisation to a new peak of maturity, Parker had an inestimable influence on jazz musicians, regardless of what instrument they played . . . his work set a new standard on every level: harmonic, tonal, rhythmic and melodic." But though many of the white musicians impressed by Parker acknowledged their debt, the cultural establishment as a whole denied him his due.

Black musicians who knew Parker or had worked with him tended, during the fifties, to seek different paths with a certain deliberateness based on their awareness of their position in society. The emergence of "hard bop," "funk" and "soul" jazz during the mid and late sixties was, quite often, a deliberate attempt on the part of these musicians to play music that was somehow "blacker" and more reliant on a certain fire to be found in African music and traditional black gospel and popular music. The drummers Art Blakey and Max Roach often referred to these origins in their works of the late fifties and sixties. Horace Silver and Bobby Timmons were known as "funky" pianists, which was a way of describing certain black musical elements distinguishing their styles.

This is not the place to attempt to give complete details of musical developments during this period but some features should be mentioned. The quest for respectability and new directions was represented on one hand by pianist-composer John Lewis's Modern Jazz Quartet: Milt Jackson on vibraphone; Percy Heath on bass, and Connie Kay on drums, replacing the initial drummer Kenny Clarke. The MJQ were among the "coolest of the cool," and sometimes took a "third stream" approach to their music, meaning that it was an amalgamation of jazz with classical music. Meanwhile, as jazz came to be dominated by the saxophone instead of the trumpet or piano, greater emphasis was placed on use of the instruments as counterparts of the human voice in all its harshness and free expressiveness. During the mid- and late-fifties, the tenor saxophonist Sonny Rollins placed hard and even harsh sounds against a churchlike background. Horace Silver often thumped out his chords like a transplanted gospel pianist; alto saxophonist Cannonball Adderley veered from his post-Parker style to join the "soul" school, and Jimmy Smith almost single-handedly made the organ, long a church instrument, into a "funky" jazz voice. As jazz became more readily accepted, some musicians made their music more consciously "popular" in a black sense, among them pianist Les McCann who was a leading exponent of the pop-soul-jazz school. Even such sophisticated creators as bassist-composer Charles Mingus referred to folksy black components in their works and tried to imbue them with the same feeling to be found at the black roots.

Above all, the major direction during the sixties was toward freeing the music of any inhibiting elements. In addition, there developed a desire to make the music reflect the philosophical or spiritual objectives of its prime movers. In this respect, it is significant that the late John Coltrane became a great cultural hero among blacks after his death in 1967 and was regarded as a sort of musical messiah. His personal evolution mirrored so much that was a part of the development of jazz during these years. He had started out playing with rhythm 'n' blues groups and was a member of Dizzy Gillespie's big band in the late-forties. His sense of musical freedom was enhanced by a stint with Thelonious Monk in 1957 while his recordings with Miles Davis during the mid-fifties brought his first public renown. When he later went on to lead his own groups, Coltrane amplified his style by the use of extended lines in which chords were played out note by note and with such rapidity that one critic referred to his technique as "sheets of sound." As Parker led, Coltrane also carried the music out toward new horizons. Fundamentally, his influence on the music itself was such that when he passed away, other musicians sought

to carry on his tradition, most notably the tenor saxophonists Archie Shepp and Pharoah Sanders, the vocalist Leon Thomas who, with Sanders, recorded one of the memorable albums of the late-sixties, *Karma,* which was shot through with a certain African-based joy and expressiveness.

Yet Coltrane was not the only one who moved in the direction of musical freedom. The classically trained and highly intellectual pianist Cecil Taylor must be counted among the significant innovators. Certainly, the boldest of these has been Ornette Coleman, the alto saxophonist and sometime trumpeter and violinist LeRoi Jones called, in 1963, ". . . the most exciting and influential innovator in jazz since Parker."

SOUL MUSIC

Though jazz reflected social change in some ways, the major change to be noted in this area was that black popular music was accepted as a valid form of expression by those who formerly had rejected it. Furthermore, the same emphasis on "soul" that found its way into jazz was manifest in an even more dramatic manner in the hits of two decades. At almost precisely the time when blacks were making their first big news on the civil rights front, a blind former gospel singer from Albany, Georgia, named Ray Charles was taking major steps toward popularization of black "soul" music through the sheer force of his genius. His flexibility was such that he bridged the gaps between jazz, in which he was an accomplished arranger, gospel music, of which he was an established exponent, and the blues, which had gone into the making of every ounce of his being.

Indeed, commercial aspects did have some influence on these developments, but the essence of black expressiveness to be found in the popular music of the day had a significance beyond the commercial. The early sixties brought the sound of Motown, a black-owned recording company in Detroit, top national popularity and this appeal was not to ebb throughout the following years that saw star status accorded such Motown artists as Smokey Robinson and the Miracles, Diana Ross, The Supremes (who were among the most glamorous young black women to grace any stage), Martha and the Vandellas, The Temptations, the Four Tops, Marvin Gaye, Tammi Terrell, the Jackson Five, and a host of dance-stimulating vocalists. While Motown seemed to reign supreme, a former shoeshine boy from Georgia named James Brown became known as "Soul Brother No. 1" as he implanted in the mind of his collective audience a most significant thought: "Say it Loud! I'm black and I'm proud!" By 1967, a true "Queen of Soul" came into being in the person of Aretha Franklin, a piano-playing, shouting Baptist minister's daughter from Detroit. When Aretha spelled out the title of the Otis Redding original R-E-S-P-E-C-T, she was a mistreated lover but the attitude of a whole people.

Protest became an even more apparent theme in black popular music of the sixties as Nina Simone, a popular nightclub chanteuse, injected heavy social messages into her original songs, among them *Mississippi Goddam!, Four Women,* and *To Be Young Gifted and Black,* inspired by her late friend, the playwright Lorraine Hansberry.

The infectious sounds of soul music, which had revolutionized popular music throughout the world, were openly acknowledged as an international cultural force when the West African nation of Ghana climaxed its fourteenth Independence Celebration in March, 1971, with a fifteen-hour, all-night concert featuring Amercan soul artists and popular Ghanaian musicians. An audience of more than 100,000 crowded into Accra's Black Star Square to witness uninhibited, funky performances by headliner Wilson Pickett, Ike and Tina Turner, the Staple Singers, the Latin-soul group, Santana, the Voices of East Harlem, jazz musicians Les McCann and Eddie Harris, Willie Bobo, and songstress Roberta Flack. Much of the concert and other cultural events planned for the occasion were documented in the film *Soul to Soul.*

Soul music also received unprecedented recognition from the film industry in the spring of 1972 when singer-composer Isaac Hayes won an Oscar at Hollywood's Academy Awards ceremonies for his theme from the film, *Shaft,* which was cited as "the best original song for a movie." His soundtrack for the film, which was scored by J. J. Johnson, became one of the most popular in the history of the recording industry, selling more than a million copies in the first three weeks after it was issued. As a result of this success, several other leading soul music composers were invited to create scores for films, among them Curtis Mayfield (*Super Fly*), Marvin Gaye (*Trouble Man*), and Donny Hathaway (*Come Back Charleston Blue*). Meanwhile, jazz arranger Quincy Jones remained one of the most prolific of all Hollywood composers, creating background music for both films and television.

Aretha Franklin, still the undisputed queen of soul, reached back into her past as a gospel artist to produce her first gospel album since becoming a superstar. A two-record set called *Amazing Grace,* released on the Atlantic label, featured her with Rev. James Cleveland, the nation's leading male singer of black religious music, and the Southern California Community Choir. Another outstanding recording of this period was Marvin Gaye's *What's Going On,* an extended musical commentary based on related social themes, which was considered by many critics to be the most innovative and significant recording yet to come from the famous Motown Studios. Elsewhere on the Motown front, the Jackson Five reigned supreme as top exponents of "bubble-gum soul" and were featured in a television cartoon series. Blind pianist-singer Stevie Wonder ceased to be regarded merely as a producer of hit tunes and began to be acknowledged as a highly original composer and arranger. Diana Ross, who had made the Supremes into a top pop act, went out on her own as a single artist and began a new career as an actress by starring in the film, *Lady Sings the Blues,* based on the life of the late great jazz singer Billie Holiday.

One of the most notable new talents to emerge in the early seventies was singer-pianist Roberta Flack, a former schoolteacher from Washington, D.C., who employed a subtly soulful style that also found favor among followers of jazz and "easy-listening" music. Her star ascended in 1971 when she created a stir in the music world by being voted top female vocalist in the *Downbeat* magazine jazz poll, toppling the veteran Ella Fitzgerald from a spot she had held for twenty years. Another new talent of note was singer Al Green, who had become the top-selling soul singer by the end of 1972. Meanwhile, a former baseball aspirant named Charlie Pride made forays into an unusual musical territory for blacks by becoming the nation's leading country music artist.

Beyond all this, black popular music was copied by young whites to such an extent that it was one of the main founding factors in the development of "rock," a music derived from black sources but played by young whites and reflecting their rebellious attitudes toward their society. As young whites came to probe the origins of the sounds they liked, they discovered black blues and thus many black blues musicians who had been working hard for years without recognition for the quality of their artistry, or financial remuneration for their efforts, became heroes to whites, as well as to their own people. Foremost among these was the blues singer-guitarist B.B. King who had been a professional musician for more than twenty years when he made his first big hit with a record in 1969, the scathing social commentary *Why I Sing the Blues.*

CLASSICAL OR FORMAL MUSIC

Dramatic gains were made over the years since the 50s in the field of classical or formal music, though here they were primarily interpreters instead of creators. Rebelling against the old idea that all blacks could sing and dance out of some innate gift, but could not excel in forms where extensive special training was required, dark-hued singers, instrumentalists and composers became some of the leading figures in this field of expression.

In 1955, the celebrated contralto Marian Anderson had become the first black to sing a major operatic role with the Metropolitan Opera. This was long after she had passed her peak and the honor was a token one. Other blacks to follow her at the Met were Mattiwilda Dobbs, Gloria Davy and Robert McFerrin, one of the few black men to break through the velvet operatic curtain excluding blacks. Several years after Marian Anderson's debut, Leontyne Price, the gifted operatic soprano from Laurel, Mississippi, was to make history in many ways, ushering in a new era for the black artist in the classical music field. She was accorded a 35-minute ovation when she made her Metropolitan Opera debut in *Il Trovatore* in 1961. In 1962 she was chosen to open the Met season by playing the romantic lead in Puccini's *The Girl of the Golden West.* She sang in such traditionally white roles as *Turandot, Eugene Onegin, Tosca* and Donna Anna in *Don Giovanni.* In 1965 she was awarded the Order of Merit by the Italian Republic, the Medal of Freedom from President Lyndon Johnson, and was the fiftieth Spingarn Medalist of the NAACP. However the most signal honor came in 1966 when she was chosen to open the Metropolitan Opera's new house in Lincoln Center, singing the lead in Samuel Barber's *Antony and Cleopatra,* which had been written for her.

Though Leontyne Price made history by becoming the first black *prima donna assoluta,* she was followed by many other blacks at the Met, among them Grace Bumbry, Felicia Weathers, Shirley Verrett, Reri Grist, and Martina Arroyo, while George Shirley, a fine tenor, became the sole black male in the regular company.

In the ranks of instrumentalists, Andre Watts became the first top-rated black concert pianist of modern times when he made his debut with the New York Philharmonic in 1963.

Blacks also made their mark as conductors of symphony orchestras though they contin-

ued to be shut out of the ensemble ranks in most cases. Leading these new black classical conductors was Dean Dixon, who had become an expatriate because he could find no permanent position with an orchestra in the United States. Dixon served as resident conductor of orchestras in Sidney, Australia, and Frankfurt, Germany, before returning to the U.S.A. in the summer of 1970 to lead the New York Philharmonic in a special concert in Central Park. Henry Lewis, a classical bassist who had become the youngest member of the Los Angeles Philharmonic in 1946 at the age of sixteen, became resident conductor of the New Jersey Symphony Orchestra in 1970, the first black to hold such a major position.

Black classical composers were finding a long-denied audience as the seventies opened. Among the leading figures were Howard Swanson, Julia Perry, Arthur Cunningham, Olly Wilson, and Ulysses Kay, while William Grant Still endured as the dean of black composers.

Though operatic prima donna Leontyne Price was absent by choice from the Metropolitan and was seldom heard in the United States, there were a few minor breakthroughs for black classical composers, possibly the most neglected of all artistic groups. America's celebrated symphony orchestras continued to ignore their existence, but smaller, interracial groups, such as the Symphony of the New World and the Harlem Philharmonic, included their works in most of their performances. Pianist Natalie Hinderas single-handedly rescued many of their finest compositions from obscurity by recording a two-record set, *Music by Black Composers,* on the Desto label, featuring works ranging from R. Nathaniel Dett's folk-based "In the Bottoms" and William Grant Still's "Three Visions" to compositions by such modernists as George Walker, Arthur Cunningham, Stephen A. Chambers, Hale Smith, and Olly Wilson. Desto also released a group of orchestral works as performed by the Oakland Youth Orchestra on a recording, *The Black Composer In America.* A truly novel event took place in January, 1972, when the Atlanta Symphony Orchestra, under conductor Robert Shaw, premiered the opera, *Treemonisha,* which had been written by the great ragtime composer Scott Joplin in 1911, and had never been given a true performance since the composer attempted to present it in Harlem in 1915. This time it got the full treatment with new orchestration by T.J. Anderson and staging by Katherine Dunham. In the related field of the dance, black troupes, led by Arthur Mitchell and Eleo Pomare, were ranked among the best in the country, while Alvin

Ailey's Dance Company produced a superstar of ballet. Judith Jamison, a lithe, beautiful dancer, gained international acclaim for her sensitive portrayals of black women in such ballets as *Cry!* and *Revelations.* Ailey also brought jazz veteran Mary Lou Williams into new prominence by featuring her sacred work *Mary Lou's Mass,* with the composer at the piano.

Source: Articles on Music, Theatre, Television, based on Vol. 4, *Ebony Pictorial History of America,* "The Black Arts," by Phyl Garland, 1973.

Section XVII

SPORTS

SPORTS

To a great extent, sports has had a significant effect in providing the pathway to economic freedom for the American black. The displaced African was noted for speed and strength from slavery days, and he was without the education and training necessary for many of the more desirable occupations. So it was that the black man found that by becoming proficient at "play" he could attain substantial economic rewards as well as social mobility.

Before the 1954 Supreme Court ruling removed legal segregation as a barrier to public education, the mass of black youth could only aspire to success in those areas where a robust, versatile body could be trained to produce for an appreciative and paying audience.

Boxing was one of the first sports whose doors were opened to the black athlete, insuring him financial remuneration for the energy expended. Therefore, the young athlete could identify more with boxers like Jack Johnson and Joe Louis than with scientists or educators like Percy Julian or Ralph Bunche. As an individual activity, it did not require a capital investment greater than many young blacks who came off the streets and up through the ranks of A.A.U. and Golden Gloves had to offer.

While white reaction to black champions in boxing had been exhibited early when the hue and cry for a "white hope" was raised during Jack Johnson's reign, black boxers continued to win most titles within their reach, ranging from the Olympic heavyweight crowns lifted by Joe Frazier, through A.A.U. and Golden Gloves titles to the world's heavyweight championship where Muhammed Ali (Cassius Clay), Joe Frazier, and George Foreman have done much to put excitement back into the game.

Today, the black man is in the forefront of most of the mass appeal team sports as a "player" with the exception of hockey. Before 1964 he was accepted only in token numbers in such sports as baseball, football and basketball. Greater awareness of the athletic potential has brought better and more competent coaching for black athletes, who have developed both physically and mentally to a higher degree than ever before. Today's black athletes are almost super-sportsmen. In a quarter of a century, major league baseball alone has grown from one black player to more than three hundred, or over 30 percent of the playing personnel. However, coaching, managerial and front office posts are still marginal at best. The late Jackie Robinson's last public pronouncement was: "I am extremely proud and pleased to be here . . . but must admit that I am going to be tremendously more pleased and more proud if I look at that third base coaching line one day and see a black face managing in baseball." These words were spoken upon the occasion of his being awarded a plaque at the completion of the 1972 World's Series commemorating the twenty-fifth anniversary of his entry into major league baseball.

The top black baseball player in the United States in 1972 was Dick Allen of the Chicago White Sox, who was voted most valuable player in the American League. He led the American League with homeruns, batting in 37 for the season. Allen also led the league with runs batted in, 113 for the season. Hank Aaron was steadily pushing in on the all-time run record set by Babe Ruth. By September 1973 with 713, Aaron had only one run to go before overtaking the Babe Ruth record of 714 homeruns. The closer Aaron came, the more hate mail and threats he received from racist fans of the All-American sport.

BASEBALL

Twenty-five years after Jackie Robinson endured the trauma of becoming the first black in organized baseball, he stood before an audience that had come to honor the anniversary and told them that he could not truly be happy until there was a black manager in baseball. A few days later, on October 24, 1972, Jack Roosevelt Robinson was dead and, mourned though he was, in September, 1973, there is still no black manager in organized baseball.

In the quarter-century since Jackie Robinson and Branch Rickey combined to break the color-bar in major league baseball, there have been so many black stars, it seems almost impossible to recall a time when there were none. Yet, the front office, where all of the important decisions are made is still lily-white.

Among those who broke into the major leagues around the same time as Jackie Robinson, are Sam Jethro of the Boston Braves; Luke Easter and Harry "Suitcase" Simpson of the Cleveland Indians; Roy Campanella, Joe Black and Dan Bankhead, who joined Robinson on the Dodgers; Monte Irvin and Hank Thompson of the New York Giants; Don Newcombe, Brooklyn Dodgers; Larry Doby, Cleveland Indians; and Elston Howard, New York Yankees.

Later there was Maury Wills, of the Los Angeles Dodgers; Ernie Banks of the Chicago Cubs; Frank Robinson and Hank Aaron of the Milwaukee (later Atlanta) Braves; Willie Mays and Orlando Cepeda of the San Francisco Giants; Chicago's Billy Williams; and Pittsburgh's Roberto Clemente.

In 1971 baseball's World Series crown went to the National League's Pittsburgh Pirates, who were paced by Roberto Clemente. Clemente hit .414, collecting a hit in each of the seven games and becoming the second player in history to hit safely in every Series game on two occasions. (The first time he did it was in the 1950 Series against the New York Yankees.) He also won the Most Valuable Player (MVP) Award in the best-of-seven contest against the American League's Baltimore Orioles.

Willie Mays and Hank Aaron were still super-stars. Aaron, thirty-seven, hit 47 home runs in 1971 and became the third player in baseball history to hit 600 home runs. As the 1973 baseball season drew to a close, Aaron was only t w o runs short of surpassing Babe Ruth's home run record of 714. Aaron also set his own personal first in the 1972 All-Star game, belting a home run into left field as the National League won in a 4-3 squeaker. This was Aaron's first extra-base hit in an All-Star game.

Mays, forty, who yielded his No. 2 spot on the all-time homers list to Aaron, became the National League's all-time scoring champion, crossing the plate with 1,950 runs. The San Francisco Giants traded Willie Mays to the New York Mets for a young pitcher and a reported $100,000 in cash. (Mays, in twenty-two years, had never played professional baseball for anyone except the Giants—first in New York, and later in San Francisco.) In his first game with the Mets, Mays slammed a home run giving the Mets a 5-4 victory over his former teammates and bringing his career four-bag total to 647.

Veteran St. Louis Cardinals' pitcher, Bob Gibson, chalked up his first no-hitter on August 8, 1971, and Ferguson Jenkins of the Chicago Cubs posted his fifth and sixth straight seasons of winning twenty or more ball games. His fifth consecutive twenty-game season brought him the Cy Young Award for being the league's top hurling ace and a $125,000 contract for 1972. Pitcher Vida Blue won twenty-four games in his first full season with the Oakland Athletics to become, at age twenty-two, the youngest pitcher to win the Cy Young Award in the American League.

Blue, who had played too many innings the year before to qualify as a rookie, and Dock Ellis of the Pittsburgh Pirates became the first two black starters in All-Star game history. In that game, Reggie Jackson hit the water tower at Detroit's Tiger Stadium with a home run, but Frank Robinson of the Baltimore Orioles won the game's Most Valuable Player Award by batting the American League to victory.

Billy Williams of the Chicago Cubs took the 1972 National League batting title but was edged out by Johnny Bench of the Cincinnati Reds for the National League's MVP honors. Dick Allen, traded to the Chicago White Sox from the Los Angeles Dodgers, won the home run title with 37, the RBI crown with 113, and was named the league's Most Valuable Player.

In 1973 black baseball headlines were:

- Bobby Bonds, San Francisco Giants, 38 Home Runs, More Than 30 Stolen Bases
- Willie Stargell, Pittsburgh Pirates, 39 Home Runs, 112 Runs Batted In
- Hank Aaron, Atlanta Braves, 41 Home Runs, 1 Short of Breaking Ruth's Mark
- Rod Carew, Minnesota Twins, Batting .344
- Reggie Jackson, Oakland A's, 31 Home Runs, 112 Runs Batted In
- Vida Blue, Oakland A's, 17 Wins 9 Losses
- John Mayberry, Kansas City Royals, 93 Runs Batted In
- Ken Singleton, Montreal Expos, .305 Average, 94 Runs Batted In
- Cesar Cedeno, Houston Astros, .317 Average, 44 Stolen Bases
- Lou Brock, St. Louis Cardinals, .293 Average, 52 Stolen Bases

On September 20, 1973, Willie Mays announced his retirement from baseball.

BASEBALL HALL OF FAME

Jackie Robinson	1962
Roy Campanella	1969
Satchel Paige	1971
Josh Gibson	1972
Buck Leonard	1972
Monte Irvin	1973
Roberto Clemente	1973

BLACK BATTING CHAMPIONS (NATIONAL LEAGUE)

	Year	Games	Hits	Average
Jackie Robinson, Brooklyn Dodgers	1949	156	203	.342
Willie Mays, New York Giants	1954	151	195	.345
Hank Aaron, Milwaukee Braves	1956	153	200	.328
Hank Aaron, Milwaukee Braves	1959	154	223	.355
Roberto Clemente, Pittsburgh Pirates	1961	146	201	.351
Tommy Davis, Los Angeles Dodgers	1962	163	230	.346
Tommy Davis, Los Angeles Dodgers	1963	146	181	.326
Roberto Clemente, Pittsburgh Pirates	1964	155	211	.339
Roberto Clemente, Pittsburgh Pirates	1965	152	194	.329
Matty Alou, Pittsburgh Pirates	1966	141	183	.342
Roberto Clemente, Pittsburgh Pirates	1967	147	209	.357
Rico Carty, Atlanta Braves	1970	136	175	.366
Billy Williams, Chicago Cubs	1972	150	191	.333

BLACK BATTING CHAMPIONS (AMERICAN LEAGUE)

	Year	Games	Hits	Average
Tony Oliva, Minnesota Twins	1964	161	217	.323
Tony Oliva, Minnesota Twins	1965	149	185	.321
Frank Robinson, Baltimore Orioles	1966	155	182	.316
Rod Carew, Minnesota Twins	1969	123	152	.332
Alex Johnson, California Angels	1970	156	202	.328
Tony Oliva, Minnesota Twins	1971	126	164	.337
Rod Carew, Minnesota Twins	1972	142	170	.318
Rod Carew, Minnesota Twins	1973	149	203	.350

OLYMPICS

The 1972 Summer Olympic Games in Munich, Germany got under way with eighteen African-American athletes joining black stars from Kenya, Trinidad, Jamaica, Senegal, Venezuela, the Bahamas, and Barbados in a boycott of a preliminary track and field meet to protest the presence of representatives of the illegal white regime in Zimbabwe (Rhodesia). When it became apparent that the boycott threatened the very existence of the Games, the International Olympic Committee (IOC) voted to ban white Rhodesia.

There was disappointment when U.S. light-middleweight boxer Reginald Jones was declared the loser of a bout against Russia's Valery Tregubov. Many observers felt that Jones dominated the contest.

Because of a schedule mix-up, Stan Wright, assistant United States track coach, gave sprinters Eddie Hart and Reynaud Robinson the wrong time for their 100-yard-dash heats, causing them to miss the events. A third sprinter, Robert Taylor, was scheduled to run in a later heat and barely made it to the starting line, finishing second behind Russian Valery Borzov, without benefit of a warm-up. Robinson and Hart later won gold medals as members of the American 1600-m relay team.

Also winning gold medals were Rod Milburn, 110-meter hurdles; Randy Williams, long jump; Sugar Ray Seales, light welterweight boxing. Two other medalists, Vince Matthews and Wayne Collett, were banned from competition in future Olympiads as the IOC penalized them for what it called a "disgusting display" on the victory platform after the two won gold and silver medals, respectively, in the 400-meter run and casually received their awards during the playing of "The Star Spangled Banner."

The Olympics ended on a tragic note with the terrorist slaying of eleven Israeli athletes.

BASKETBALL

Basketball is the only major sport where black players constitute a 65 percent majority. Sixteen of the 23 basketball players with million dollar contracts in 1973 were black. Among those were Kareem Abdul Jabbar's 5 year contract with the Milwaukee Bucks of the NBA for a reputed 2 million, and the ABA Kentucky Colonels' $1.5 million contract with Artis Gilmore.

Of the 23 pro basketball players reported to have signed million dollar, multiyear contracts the 16 players with million dollar contracts are:

$2	—Kareem Abdul-Jabbar, Milwaukee Bucks
$1.6	—Charlie Scott, Phoenix Suns
$1.5	—Artis Gilmore, Kentucky Colonels
$1.5	—Spencer Haywood, Seattle Super Sonics
$1.3	—Bob Lanier, Detroit Pistons
$1.25	—Connie Hawkins, Phoenix Suns
$1.2	—Austin Carr, Cleveland Cavaliers
$1.2	—Elmore Smith, Buffalo Braves
$1.1	—Wilt Chamberlain, Los Angeles Lakers
$1.1	—Ralph Simpson, Denver Rockets
$1	—Jim Chones, New York Nets
$1	—Joe Caldwell, Carolina Cougars
$1	—Mel Daniels, Indiana Pacers
$1	—Walt Frazier, New York Knicks

Black players in pro basketball are relative newcomers. Chuck Cooper of the Boston Celtics was signed in 1950, thus becoming the first black professional in the game. This same year, Nat "Sweetwater" Clifton, whose prowess on the court had become legend when he starred with the Harlem Globetrotters, signed a contract with the New York Knickerbockers.

In rapid succession black stars were signed by the major teams. Minneapolis signed Elgin Baylor. Sam Jones, K.C. Jones, and Bill Russell were soon in the Boston Celtics lineup. Ray Felix and Willie Naulls joined the Knickerbockers. Wilt "The Stilt" Chamberlain signed on with Philadelphia and "The Big O," Oscar Robertson, with Cincinnati. Elvin Hayes was signed by San Diego, as was Connie Hawkins of the Phoenix Suns.

By 1970 black super-stars were dominating the game. Lew Alcindor, a three-time All American at the University of California, Los Angeles, lived up to his pre-pro billing in his first season by leading the Milwaukee Bucks to a second place in the Eastern Division semifinals of the NBA.

A few contemporary greats are Wes Unseld and Earl Monroe with Baltimore, Milwaukee's Kareem Abdul Jabbar (Lew Alcindor) and veteran Oscar Robertson, Bob Love of the Chicago Bulls, Willis Reed of the New York Knicks, and the legendary Wilt Chamberlain, who with the Los Angeles Lakers in his 13th year of professional play, set a mark as the NBA's all-time rebound leader in this 932nd NBA game with the 21,772 rebound of his career. The previous record was held by Bill Russell, the great star of the Boston Celtics. On February 16, 1972, in a game with the Phoenix Suns, Chamberlain also became the first player in NBA history to score 30,000 points.

In 1972, Bob Douglas, 87, owner and coach of the fabled New York Renaissance Five, was named to the Basketball Hall of Fame, the first black to be recognized for achievement and contribution to the game. In the 22 years that Douglas coached the "Rens," they had 2,318 victories and in 1933 held an 88 consecutive game winning streak. The New York Renaissance Five is one of four teams in the Naismith Basketball Hall of Fame.

On January 2, 1973, the National Basketball Association named Simon Gourdine Vice President of Administration. (He was former assistant to Commissioner Walter Kennedy.) He became the highest-ranking black in any administrative capacity in professional sports. A graduate of City College of New York and Fordham Law School, he was a former assistant United States attorney before joining the legal department of the Celanese Corporation. He joined the NBA June 1, 1970.

John McLendon, former coach at Tennessee State University, joined the Cleveland Pipers in the old American Basketball League in 1961 to become the first black coach of a major professional team;* Bill Russell became player-coach for the Boston Celtics in 1966; and in 1973 for the Seattle Supersonics.

Other blacks in front offices are:

Wayne Embry, General Manager and Vice President, Milwaukee Bucks,

Herman J. Russell, Board of Directors, Part owner, Atlanta Hawks,

Al Attles, Coach, Golden State Warriors,

Ray Scott, Coach, Detroit Pistons,

K. C. Jones, Coach, San Diego Conquistadores (ABA), 1973, Capital Bullets

Wilt Chamberlain jumped from the Los Angeles Lakers of the NBA to ABA for $600,000 per year for 3 years as player-coach for San Diego Conquistadors (ABA).

---

*McLendon became the first black coach in ABA May 14, 1969 when he signed a 2-year contract with the Denver Rockets.

BLACK SCORING LEADERS IN THE NBA

Year	Player and Team	Points Scored	Avg.
1959–60	Wilt Chamberlain, Philadelphia Warriors	2707	29.2
1960–61	Wilt Chamberlain, Philadelphia Warriors	3033	37.9
1961–62	Wilt Chamberlain, Philadelphia Warriors	4029	50.4
1962–63	Wilt Chamberlain, San Francisco Warriors	3586	50.4
1963–64	Wilt Chamberlain, San Francisco Warriors	2948	44.8
1964–65	Wilt Chamberlain, Philadelphia 76ers	2534	34.7
1965–66	Wilt Chamberlain, Philadelphia 76ers	2649	33.5
1967–68	Dave Bing, Detroit	2142	27.1
1968–69	Elvin Hayes, San Diego	2327	28.4
1969–70	Lew Alcindor, Milwaukee Bucks	2596	31.7
1970–71	Kareem Abdul Jabbar, Milwaukee Bucks	2822	34.8
1971–72	Kareem Abdul Jabbar, Milwaukee Bucks		
1972–73	Nate Archibald, Kansas City-Omaha		34.0

BLACK REBOUND LEADERS IN THE NBA

Year	Player and Team	Rebounds	Avg.
1956–57	Maurice Stokes, Rochester	1256	
1957–58	Bill Russell, Boston	1564	
1958–59	Bill Russell, Boston	1612	
1959–60	Wilt Chamberlain, Philadelphia	1941	
1960–61	Wilt Chamberlain, Philadelphia	2149	
1961–62	Wilt Chamberlain, Philadelphia	2052	
1962–63	Wilt Chamberlain, San Francisco	1946	
1963–64	Bill Russell, Boston	1930	
1964–65	Bill Russell, Boston	1878	
1965–66	Wilt Chamberlain, Philadelphia	1943	
1966–67	Wilt Chamberlain, Philadelphia	1957	
1967–68	Wilt Chamberlain, Philadelphia	1952	
1968–69	Wilt Chamberlain, Los Angeles	1712	21.1
1969–70	Wilt Chamberlain, Los Angeles		
1970–71	Wilt Chamberlain, Los Angeles	1493	18.2
1971–72	Wilt Chamberlain, Los Angeles	1572	19.2
1972–73	Wilt Chamberlain, Los Angeles		18.6

BLACK ASSIST LEADERS IN THE NBA

Year	Player and Team	Assists	Avg
1960–61	Oscar Robertson, Cincinnati	690	
1961–62	Oscar Robertson, Cincinnati	899	
1962–63	Guy Rodgers, San Francisco	825	
1963–64	Oscar Robertson, Cincinnati	868	
1964–65	Oscar Robertson, Cincinnati	861	
1965–66	Oscar Robertson, Cincinnati	847	
1966–67	Guy Rodgers, Chicago	908	
1967–68	Wilt Chamberlain, Philadelphia	702	
1968–69	Oscar Robertson, Cincinnati	772	
1969–70			
1970–71			
1971–72			
1972–73	Nate Archibald, Kansas City-Omaha		11.4

1972–73 NBA

Wilt Chamberlain—.727 field goal percentage for new record

MOST VALUABLE PLAYERS

1969	West Unseld, Baltimore
1970	Willis Reed, New York
1971	Lew Alcindor, Milwaukee
1972	Kareem Abdul-Jabbar (Lew Alcindor), Milwaukee

SCORING LEADERS

		Pts.	Avg.
1969	Elvin Hayes, San Diego	2327	28.4
1970	. . . .		
1971	Kareem Abdul-Jabbar (Lew Alcindor), Milwaukee	2822	34.8
1972	Nate Archibald, Kansas City-Omaha Kings	2719	34.0

REBOUNDING LEADERS

		G	No.	Avg.
1969	Wilt Chamberlain, Los Angeles	81	1712	21.1
1970	Elvin Hayes, San Diego	82	1386	16.9
1971	Wilt Chamberlain, Los Angeles	82	1572	19.2
1972	Wilt Chamberlain, Los Angeles	82	1526	18.6

ASSISTING LEADERS

		G	No.	Avg.
1969	Oscar Robertson, Cincinnati	79	772	9.8
1970	Lenny Wilkens, Seattle	75	683	9.1
1971	. . . .			
1972	Nate Archibald, Kansas City-Omaha Kings	80	910	11.4

MISCELLANEOUS INFORMATION FOR 1972–73 ABA SPORTS

Julius Erving, Virginia—31.4 points per game
Artis Gilmore, Kentucky—17.6 rebounds per game
Bill Melchronni, New York—7.5 assists per game
Bill Kell, Indiana—.870 free throw percentage

TRACK

Jesse Owens, winner of four gold medals in the epochal 1936 Olympics, was one of the greatest sprinters of all time, while Rafer Johnson, decathlon champ of the 1960 Olympics, is rated one of track's best all-around athletes. Among other track greats are Ralph Boston, John Carlos, Bob Hayes, Bob Beamon, John Thomas, Wilma Rudolph, Lee Evans, Charlie Greene, Ralph Metcalfe, Milt Campbell.

HORSE RACING

Blacks have been participants in the sport of kings since the early days of America, but not since the late 1800s have black jockeys had the opportunity to ride the winners. However, among great jockeys, no list is complete without the name of Isaac Murphy, the first jockey to ride three Kentucky Derby winners. Murphy won his first Kentucky Derby on Buchanan in 1884, his second on Riley in 1890 and his third on Kingman in 1891. His record was not equaled until 1930, when Earl Sand won his third Derby on Gallant Fox. The first Kentucky Derby winner was Aristedes and the black jockey riding him to victory was Oliver Lewis. Black jockey Bill Walker and trainer Ed Brown were responsible for the winner of the 1877 Kentucky Derby, Baden-Baden. Isaac Murphy is in the Hall of Fame in the National Museum of Racing at Saratoga Springs, N.Y. Jimmy Winkfield, another great black jockey, won two consecutive Derby victories with His Eminence in 1901 and Alan-a-Dale in 1902.

Black jockeys in the twentieth century have been few and far between. Hosea Lee Richardson rode at Hialeah in 1951 and, in 1971, Juan Arias, a black South American, became the first black trainer of a Derby winner in modern times by nursing Canonero II to a first-place finish at the 97th Kentucky Derby. Cheryl White, a scrappy seventeen-year-old Ohioan, became the first black female jockey, riding for the first time June 15, 1971, and making her first win September 2, 1971.

BOXING

In 1805, Bill Richmond, who had been born in Staten Island, N.Y. (August 5, 1763) and taken to England as a child (1777), became the first professional black boxer to earn a living as a boxer. Fighting with bare knuckles, Richmond lasted for an hour and thirty minutes against English boxer Tom Cribb, in 1805. Cribb, now champion, later fought Tom Molineaux, a black freed slave from Virginia, for the boxing title, and on December 10, 1810, after forty rounds, Molineaux collided with a post, fracturing his skull. The fight was ended in the 41st round with Cribb victorious and still the champion.

George Godfrey, born on Prince Edward Island, March 20, 1853, moved to Boston and became the first "colored heavyweight champion of America." He was once matched with John L. Sullivan, but Sullivan refused to fight a black boxer and the bout was cancelled. On August 24, 1888, Godfrey was beaten in 19 rounds by Peter Jackson at the California Athletic Club.

Peter Jackson was born July 3, 1861, in St. Croix, Danish West Indies. He has been admitted to the pioneer group in the Boxing Hall of Fame. A dockhand and sailor, he fought in Australia, where he became a champion in 1886. He fought Tom Lees 30 rounds on September 25, 1886. On May 21st, 1891, he fought Jim Corbett at the California Athletic Club for a $10,000 purse. They fought 60 rounds and, at the end of the 61st round, the referee called the fight a draw. Neither man had been able to defeat the other. On May 30, 1892, Jackson knocked out Frank Slavin in 10 rounds to win the British Empire Heavyweight Title. He was defeated by Jim Jeffries in the third round at San Francisco on March 22, 1898. He died July 13, 1901 at Roma, Queensland, New Zealand, where he was buried.

George Dixon was the first black to win the world bantamweight title and the first to win the world featherweight title as well. He was called Little Chocolate and, by some critics, "the greatest fighter of all time."

Joe Gans was born November 25, 1874, in Philadelphia, and was the first black to win the lightweight title. On July 15, 1901, he fought three men, winning one and the other two being no-decision bouts. On May 12, 1902, he won the world lightweight title from Frank Erne. On September 3, 1906, he defeated Battling Nelson in 42 rounds at Goldfield, Nevada. The purse for the winner was $34,000, but he had made a pre-fight agreement to give Erne all over $11,000, win-lose- or draw. He died August 16, 1910, in Baltimore, Md.

Joe Walcott, the last of the pre-Jack Johnson greats, was born on April 7, 1872 in Barbados, where he grew up, leaving home as a sailor in his teens. He left the sea in Boston, where he got jobs as a handyman in a restaurant. Later he took boxing lessons, winning his first professional fight on a two-round knock out from Tom Powers on February 29, 1890. On December 18, 1901, he won the welterweight championship by knocking out Jim Ferns in five rounds at Lake Erie. He lost the title to Dixie Kid, on a foul, after 20 rounds at San Francisco. He was killed in an automobile accident, October of 1935, but fought for the last time November 13, 1911.

The first black boxer under modern conditions was Jack Johnson. Johnson, born March 31, 1878 in Galveston, Texas, started fighting in 1894, when he was sixteen years old. He won the title by knocking out Tommy Burns in Australia, in the 14th round on December 26, 1908. He lost the title, in a controversial fight with Jess Willard, in the 26th round at Havana, on April 5, 1915. He had the title longer than any other heavyweight up to that time. Of 97 fights, he lost only five. He died following an automobile accident at Raleigh, N.C., June 10, 1946. He was elected to the Boxing Hall of Fame in 1954.

Following Jack Johnson's defeat by Willard in 1915, boxing became a "white" sport, until June 22, 1937, when the 23-year-old Joe Louis knocked out James J. Braddock in the 8th round at Chicago, to win the world heavyweight title. Louis was born May 13, 1914, in Lexington, Alabama. He started boxing in Detroit as a Golden Glove amateur and began fighting professionally in 1934. The 12-round knockout of Louis by Max Schmeling on June 19, 1936, was his major defeat during the prime part of his career. Joe retired following World War II, following a fight with Billy Conn, June 19, 1946, at which a hundred dollars was charged for a ringside seat. Louis knocked out Conn in the 8th round.

On June 22, 1949, Ezzard Charles won a decision over Jersey Joe Walcott on points in a fifteen-round bout in Chicago. Responding to the clamor of fight fans and promoters, Joe Louis came out of retirement, fought Ezzard Charles at Yankee Stadium in New York, September 27, 1950, and lost to Charles in a 15-round decision.

Charles was defeated, July 18, 1951, by Jersey Joe Walcott in 7 rounds at Pittsburgh. Walcott (Arnold Cream, born January 31, 1914) was the oldest fighter to ever become heavyweight champion. Walcott was defeated by Rocky Marciano, September 23, 1952. Marciano held the title until April, 1956, when he retired.

On November 30, 1956, Floyd Patterson won the vacant world title by knocking out Archie Moore in the fifth round at Chicago. Patterson held the title until Ingemar Johannson of Sweden knocked him out in the third round of a New York bout. On June 20, 1960, Patterson regained the heavyweight title by knocking out Johannson in 1:51 of the fifth round at the Polo Grounds, N.Y. He became the first man to regain his heavyweight title by knocking out his opponent.

On September 25, 1962 at Comiskey Park in Chicago, Charles "Sonny" Liston knocked out Floyd Patterson in 2:06 minutes of the first round to win the heavyweight title. In a return bout, July 22, 1963, Liston again knocked out Patterson in the first round at Las Vegas, Nevada.

Sonny Liston failed to come out for the 7th round in a title bout with Cassius Clay (Muhammad Ali), at Miami Beach, Florida, February 25, 1964, and on May 25, 1965, Clay knocked out Liston in the first minute of the first round, in Lewiston, Maine.

Cassius Clay was born in Louisville, Kentucky, January 18, 1942. Following his 1964 victory over Liston, Clay announced that he had adopted the Islamic faith and had changed his name to Muhammad Ali. As a follower of the Honorable Elijah Muhammad, the boxer was not the favorite of sports writers and journalists that he had been as the fast-talking versemaker, who had won an Olympic gold-medal in the light heavyweight division in 1960.

In 1967 after defending his title eight times, the New York State Athletic Commission and the World Boxing Association declared the title vacant, because Muhammad Ali refused to step forward and take the oath inducting him into the armed services. He claimed that he should have been exempt from the draft on the basis of his being a minister of the Islamic faith. Ali's first defeat came at the hands of Joe Frazier, March 8, 1971, after 31 pro victories.

Joe Frazier was born in Beaufort, S.C., January 17, 1944. He won the title, March 8, 1971, and defended it twice successfully, until his defeat by George Foreman, January 22, 1973. Frazier fought Muhammad Ali, March 8, 1971, and won a decision on points in a unanimous 15 round decision.

George Foreman won the world's heavyweight championship from Joe Frazier on January 22, 1973. Born January 22, 1948, in Marshall, Texas, Foreman started boxing while in a Job Corps' camp recreational program. He won a place on the U.S. Olympic squad and won a Gold Medal at the 1968 Mexico City Olympics, by a 2nd-round knock out of Russia's Ionas Chepulis. He started fighting professionally, July 1969. After winning 21 fights, he knocked out George Chuvalo in the 3rd round of a bout in 1970, and completed a string of 37 straight wins (34 by knock outs) at the time of his bout with Frazier in Kingston, Jamaica. The championship changed hands at 1:35 of the 2nd round on a technical knock out.

TITLE BOUTS OF BLACK BOXING CHAMPIONS

GEORGE FOREMAN

May 10, 1971—Won North American Heavyweight Title by knocking out Gregory Peralta, in Oakland, California. Tenth round.

January 22, 1973—Knocked out Joe Frazier to win World Heavyweight Championship, in Kingston, Jamaica. Secondth round.

August 31, 1973—Defended World Heavyweight Title by defeating Joe (King) Roman, in Tokyo, Japan. First round.

JOE FRAZIER

March 4, 1968—Won portion of title, by knocking out (technical) Manuel Ramos, in New York. Second round.

December 1, 1968—Retained title, by defeating Oscar Bonavena, in Philadelphia. Fifteenth round.

June 23, 1969—Retained title, by knocking out (technical) Jerry Quarry, in New York. Seventh round.

February 16, 1970—Won undisputed official title, by knocking out (technical) Jimmy Ellis, in New York. Fifth round.

March 8, 1971—Retained title, by decision over Muhammad Ali, in New York. Fifteenth round.

January 15, 1972—Retained title, by knocking out Terry Daniels, in New Orleans, Fourth round.

May 25, 1972—Retained title, by knocking out Ron Stander, in Omaha. Fifth round.

January 22, 1973—Knocked out (technical) by George Foreman, in Kingston, Jamaica.

MUHAMMAD ALI

February 25, 1964—Knocked out Sonny Liston, in Miami Beach. Seventh round.

May 25, 1965—Knocked out Sonny Liston, in Lewiston, Maine. First round.

November 22, 1965—Knocked out Floyd Patterson, in Las Vegas. Twelfth round.

March 29, 1966—Defeated George Chuvalo, in Toronto. Fifteenth round.

May 21, 1966—Knocked out Henry Cooper, in London. Sixth round.

August 6, 1966—Knocked out Brian London, in London. Third round.

September 10, 1966—Knocked out Karl Mildenberger, in Frankfurt. Twelfth round.

November 14, 1966—Knocked out Cleveland Williams, in Houston. Third round.

March 8, 1971—Lost in Title Bid, being defeated by Joe Frazier, in New York. Fifteenth round.

November 17, 1971—Defeated Buster Mathis, in Houston. Twelfth round.

December 26, 1971—Knocked out Jurgen Blin, in Zurich, Switzerland. Seventh round.
April 1, 1972—Defeated Mac Foster, in Tokyo. Fifteenth round.
May 1, 1972—Defeated George Chuvalo, in Vancouver, Canada. Twelfth round.
June 27, 1972—Knocked out Jerry Quarry, in Las Vegas. Seventh round.
September 20, 1972—Knocked out Floyd Patterson, in New York. Seventh round.
March 31, 1973—Lost, by split decision to Ken Norton, in San Diego. Twelfth round (broken jaw in first).
September 10, 1973—Won, by split decision from Ken Norton, in Los Angeles. Twelfth round.

SONNY LISTON

September 25, 1962—Won World Heavyweight Championship, by knocking out Floyd Patterson, in Chicago. First round.
July 22, 1963—Retained World Heavyweight Title, by knocking out Floyd Patterson, in Las Vegas. First round.
February 25, 1964—Knocked out by Cassius Clay, in Miami Beach. Seventh round.
May 25, 1965—Knocked out by Cassius Clay, in Lewiston, Maine. First round.

FLOYD PATTERSON

November 30, 1956—Knocked out Archie Moore, in Chicago. Fifth round.
July 29, 1957—Knocked out Tommy Jackson, in New York. Tenth round.
August 22, 1957—Knocked out Pete Rademacher, in Seattle. Sixth round.
August 18, 1958—Knocked out Roy Harris, in Los Angeles. Twelfth round.
May 1, 1959—Knocked out Brian London, in Indianapolis. Eleventh round.
June 26, 1959—Knocked out by Ingemar Johansson, in New York. Third round.
June 20, 1960—Knocked out Ingemar Johansson, in New York. Fifth round.
March 13, 1961—Knocked out Ingemar Johansson, in Miami Beach. Sixth round.
December 4, 1961—Knocked out Tom McNeeley, in Toronto. Fourth round.
September 25, 1962—Lost World Heavyweight Title, being knocked out by Sonny Liston, in Chicago. First round.
July 22, 1963—Knocked out by Sonny Liston, in Las Vegas. First round.
November 22, 1965—Knocked out by Cassius Clay, Las Vegas. Twelfth round.
July 14, 1972—Knocked out Pedro Agosto, in New York. Sixth round.
September 20, 1972—Knocked out by Muhammad Ali, in New York. Seventh round.

JERSEY JOE WALCOTT
(ARNOLD CREAM)

December 5, 1947—Defeated by Joe Louis, in New York. Fifteenth round.
June 25, 1948—Knocked out by Joe Louis, in New York. Eleventh round.
June 22, 1949—Defeated by Ezzard Charles, in Chicago. Fifteenth round.
March 7, 1951—Defeated by Ezzard Charles, in Detroit. Fifteenth round.
July 18, 1951—Knocked out Ezzard Charles, in Pittsburgh. Seventh round.
June 5, 1952—Defeated Ezzard Charles, in Philadelphia. Fifteenth round.
September 23, 1952—Knocked out by Rocky Marciano, in Philadelphia. Thirteenth round.
May 15, 1953—Knocked out by Rocky Marciano, in Chicago. First round.
Retired to become a parole officer, a referee, and New Jersey public official.

EZZARD CHARLES

June 22, 1949—Defeated Joe Walcott, in Chicago. Fifteenth round.
August 10, 1949—Knocked out Gus Lesnevich, in New York. Seventh round.
October 14, 1949—Knocked out Pat Valentino, in San Francisco. Eighth round.
August 15, 1950—Knocked out Freddy Beshore, in Buffalo. Fourteenth round.
September 27, 1950—Defeated Joe Louis, in New York. Fifteenth round.
December 5, 1950—Knocked out Nick Barone, in Cincinnati. Eleventh round.
January 12, 1951—Knocked out Lee Oma, in New York. Tenth round.
March 7, 1951—Defeated Joe Walcott, in Detroit. Fifteenth round.
May 30, 1951—Defeated Joey Maxim, in Chicago. Fifteenth round.
July 18, 1951—Knocked out by Joe Walcott, in Pittsburgh. Seventh round.
June 5, 1951—Defeated by Joe Walcott, in Philadelphia. Fifteenth round.
June 17, 1954—Defeated by Rocky Marciano, in New York. Fifteenth round.
September 17, 1954—Knocked out by Rocky Marciano, in New York. Eighth round.

JOE LOUIS

June 22, 1937—Won the Heavyweight Championship of the World, by knocking out James J. Braddock, in Chicago. Eighth round.
August 30, 1937—Defeated Tommy Farr, in New York. Fifteenth round.
February 23, 1938—Knocked out Nathan Mann, in New York. Third round.
April 1, 1938—Knocked out Harry Thomas, in Chicago. Fifth round.
June 22, 1938—Knocked out Max Schmeling, in New York. First round.
January 25, 1939—Knocked out John Henry Lewis, in New York. First round.
April 17, 1939—Knocked out Jack Roper, in Los Angeles. First round.
June 28, 1939—Knocked out Tony Galento, in New York. Fourth round.
September 20, 1939—Knocked out Bob Pastor, in Detroit. Eleventh round.
February 9, 1940—Defeated Arturo Godoy, in New York. Fifteenth round.
March 29, 1940—Knocked out Johnny Paychek, in New York. Second round.
June 20, 1940—Knocked out Arturo Godoy, in New York. Eighth round.
December 16, 1940—Knocked out Al McCoy, in Boston. Sixth round.
January 31, 1941—Knocked out Red Burman, in New York. Fifth round.
February 17, 1941—Knocked out Gus Dorazio, in Philadelphia. Second round.
March 21, 1941—Knocked out Abe Simon, in Detroit. Thirteenth round.
April 8, 1941—Knocked out Tony Musto, in St. Louis. Ninth round.
May 23, 1941—Defeated Buddy Baer, by disqualification, in Washington, D.C. Seventh round.
June 18, 1941—Knocked out Billy Conn, in New York. Thirteenth round.
September 29, 1941—Knocked out Lou Nova, in New York. Sixth round.
January 9, 1942—Knocked out Buddy Baer, in New York. First round. (Donated Purse to Army Relief Fund)
March 27, 1942—Knocked out Abe Simon, in New York. Sixth round. (Donated Purse to Army Relief Fund)

June 19, 1946—Knocked out Billy Conn, in New York. Eighth round.

September 18, 1946—Knocked out Tami Mauriello, in New York. First round.

December 5, 1946—Defeated Jersey Joe Walcott, in New York. Fifteenth round.

June 25, 1948—Knocked out Jersey Joe Walcott, in New York. Fifteenth round.

March 1, 1949—Louis announced his retirement as undefeated world heavyweight champion.

September 27, 1950—Defeated by Ezzard Charles, in New York. Fifteenth round.

RAY ROBINSON

Won Golden Gloves featherweight title in 1939 and lightweight title in 1940 in New York and in inter-city competition.

Engaged in 85 amateur bouts. Had 69 KO's (40 first round). Boxed as Walker Smith.

December 20, 1946—Won Vacant World Welterweight Title, by defeating Tommy Bell, in New York. Fifteenth round.

June 24, 1947—Knocked out Jimmy Doyle, in Cleveland. Eighth round.

December 19, 1947—Knocked out Chuck Taylor, in Detroit. Sixth round.

June 28, 1948—Defeated Bernard Docusen, in Chicago. Fifteenth round.

July 11, 1949—Defeated Kid Gavilan, in Philadelphia. Fifteenth round.

June 5, 1950—Defeated Robert Villemain, in Philadelphia. Fifteenth round.

August 9, 1950—Defeated Charley Fusari, in Jersey City. Fifteenth round.

August 25, 1950—Knocked out Jose Basora, in Scranton. First round.

October 26, 1950—Knocked out Carl Olson, in Philadelphia. Twelfth round.

February 14, 1951—Knocked out Jake LaMotta, in Chicago. Thirteenth round.

July 10, 1951—Defeated by Randy Turpin, in London. Fifteenth round.

September 12, 1951—Knocked out Randy Turpin, in New York. Tenth round.

March 13, 1952—Defeated Carl (Bobo) Olson, in San Francisco. Fifteenth round.

April 16, 1952—Knocked out Rocky Graziano, in Chicago. Third round.

June 25, 1952—Knocked out by Joey Maxim, in New York. Fourteenth round.

December 9, 1955—Knocked out Carl (Bobo) Olson, in Chicago. Second round.

May 18, 1956—Knocked out Carl (Bobo) Olson, in Los Angeles. Fourth round.

January 2, 1957—Defeated by Gene Fullmer, in New York. Fifteenth round.

May 1, 1957—Knocked out Gene Fullmer, in Chicago. Fifth round.

September 23, 1957—Defeated by Carmen Basilio, in New York. Fifteenth round.

March 25, 1958—Defeated Carmen Basilio, in Chicago. Fifteenth round.

January 22, 1960—Defeated by Paul Pender, in Boston. Fifteenth round.

June 10, 1960—Defeated by Paul Pender, in Boston. Fifteenth round.

December 3, 1960—Defeated Gene Fullmer, by decision, in Los Angeles. Fifteenth round.

March 4, 1961—Defeated by Gene Fullmer, in Las Vegas. Fifteenth round.

HENRY ARMSTRONG

Fought early in career as Melody Jackson. Won 58 out of 62 amateur bouts.

October 29, 1937—Knocked out Petey Sarron, in New York. Sixth round.

May 31, 1938—Defeated Barney Ross, in Long Island City. Fifteenth round.

August 17, 1938—Defeated Lou Ambers, in New York. Fifteenth round.

November 25, 1938—Won Welterweight Title Bout, by defeating Ceferino Garcia, in New York. Fifteenth round.

December 5, 1938—Retained title, by knocking out Al Manfredo, in Cleveland. Third round. (Armstrong relinquished Featherweight Championship)

August 22, 1939—Defeated by Lou Ambers, in New York. Fifteenth round.

December 11, 1939—Knocked out Jimmy Garrison, in Cleveland. Seventh round.

October 4, 1940—Defeated by Fritzie Zivic, in New York. Fifteenth round.

January 17, 1941—Knocked out by Fritzie Zivic, in New York. Twelfth round.

JACK JOHNSON

December 26, 1908—Defeated Tommy Burns, in Sydney. Fourteenth round.

May 19, 1909—Defeated P. Jack O'Brien, by "no decision," in Philadelphia. Sixth round.

June 30, 1909—Defeated Tony Ross, by "no decision," in Pittsburgh. Sixth round.

September 9, 1909—Defeated Al Kaufman, by "no decision," in San Francisco. Tenth round.

October 16, 1909—Knocked out Stanley Ketchel, in Colma, California. Twelfth round.

July 4, 1910—Knocked out James J. Jeffries, in Reno, Nevada. Fifteenth round.

July 4, 1912—Defeated Jim Flynn, in Las Vegas. Ninth round.

November 28, 1913—Knocked out Andre Spoul, in Paris. Second round.

June 27, 1914—Defeated Frank Moran, in Paris. Twentieth round.

April 5, 1915—Knocked out by Jess Willard, in Havana, Cuba. Twenty-sixth round.

BOXING HALL OF FAME

Henry Armstrong, Feather, Light, Welter
Ezzard Charles, Heavy
Kid Chocolate, Feather
George Dixon, Bantam, Feather
Tiger Flowers, Middle
Joe Gans, Light
Kid Gavilan, Welter
Beau Jack, Light
Peter Jackson, Heavy
Joe Jeannette, Heavy
Jack Johnson, Heavy
Sam Langford, Middle
Joe Louis, Heavy
Tom Molineaux, Heavy
Archie Moore, Light
Bill Richmond, Heavy
Ray Robinson, Middle
Sandy Saddler, Feather
Jersey Joe Walcott, Heavy
Joe Walcott, Welter
Harry Wills, Heavy

Source: *Ring Record Book*

BLACK BOXING CHAMPIONS
(ALL DIVISIONS)

HEAVYWEIGHT

Name	Years Held
Jack Johnson	1908-1915
Joe Louis	1937-1949
Ezzard Charles	1949-1951
Jersey Joe Walcott	1951-1952
Floyd Patterson	1956-1959
	1960-1962
Sonny Liston	1962-1964
Cassius Clay (Muhammad Ali)	1964-1967*
Joe Frazier	1970-1973
George Foreman	1973-

LIGHT HEAVYWEIGHT

Name	Years Held
Battling Siki	1922-1923
John Henry Lewis	1935-1939
Archie Moore	1952-1961
Harold Johnson	1961-1963
Jose Torres	1965-1966
Dick Tiger	1966-1968
Bob Foster	1968-

MIDDLEWEIGHT

Name	Years Held
Tiger Flowers	1926
Gorilla Jones	1931-1932
Sugar Ray Robinson	1951; 1951-1952 1955-1957; 1957; 1958-1960
Randy Turpin	1951
Dick Tiger	1962-1963; 1965-1966
Emile Griffith	1966-1968

WELTERWEIGHT

Name	Years Held
Joe Walcott	1901-1904; 1904-1906
Young Jack Thompson	1931
Henry Armstrong	1938-1940
Sugar Ray Robinson	1946-1951
Johnny Bratton	1951
Kid Gavilan	1951-1954

Johnny Saxton	1954-1955; 1956
Virgil Akins	1958
Benny Kid Paret	1960-1961
Emile Griffith	1963-1966
Curtis Cokes	1966-1969

*Title declared vacant by World Boxing Association when Ali refused induction into military.

LIGHTWEIGHT

Name	Years Held
Joe Gans	1901-1908
Henry Armstrong	1938-1939
Beau Jack	1942-1944 (New York)
Bob Montgomery	1944-1947 (New York)
Ike Williams	1945-1947 (NBA) 1947-1951
Jimmy Carter	1951-1952 1952-1954; 1954-1955
Wallace Bud Smith	1955-1956
Joe Brown	1956-1962

FEATHERWEIGHT

Name	Years Held
George Dixon	1890-1899
Kid Chocolate	1932-1934 (New York)
Henry Armstrong	1937-1938
Chalky Wright	1941-1942
Sandy Saddler	1948-1949; 1950-1957
Hogan Kid Bassey	1957-1959
Davey Moore	1959-1963

BANTAMWEIGHT

Name	Years Held
George Dixon	1890-1892
Panama Al Brown	1929-1935
George Pace	1940
Harold Dade	1947
Jimmy Carruthers (abandoned title)	1953-1954

FOOTBALL

Blacks made their entrance into professional football at its very beginning. Fritz Pollard of Brown University joined the Akron (Ohio) Indians as player and coach in 1919. He coached for seasons 1919, 1920, 1921, and 1922. The Indians won the world's professional football championship in 1920 and were guests at the Rose Bowl where they played. Later, they played at Chicago against George Halas and the Staley's, a team that was the forerunner of the Chicago Bears. Pollard was responsible for bringing Paul Robeson to the Akron Indians in 1921. Other blacks in pro football during that era were Mayo (Ink) Williams and Dick Hudson, who played with the Hammond, Indiana team in 1921, and Fred (Duke) Slater of Iowa, who played with Rock Island, Illinois in 1922, and later with the American Football League and the Chicago Cardinals. Joe Lillard also played with the Chicago Cardinals as late as 1933. From 1933 to 1946 there were no black professional football stars. On March 21, 1946, the Los Angeles Rams signed Kenny Washington, and on May 7, 1946, Woody Strode. The Cleveland Browns of the All-America Conference signed Bill Willis on August 6, 1946, and Marion Motley, August 9, 1946.

Motley's record as a professional football star places him among the all-time great fullbacks in the sport. Other great black stars of this period are Claude "Buddy" Young (New York Yankees), Joe Perry (San Francisco 49ers), and "Tank" Younger (Los Angeles Rams). During the 50s and 60s the game was dominated by Jim Brown of the Cleveland Browns, who was perhaps the first superstar of the period. Others were Lenny Moore and Jim Parker of the Baltimore Colts, Emlen Tunnell of the N.Y. Giants, Jim "Big Daddy" Lipscomb of the Baltimore Colts and Pittsburgh Steelers, Dick "Night Train" Lane of Detroit, Ollie Matson of the Chicago Cards and Roosevelt Grier of the New York Giants. The Chicago Bears' Gale Sayers won six NFL records and 20 with the Chicago Bears, earned as star-running half-back. He retired at age 29 because of knee injuries received in 1972.

In football, John Brockington of the Green Bay Packers rushed for 1,027 yards and won the Rookie of the Year Award in the National Football Conference (NFC). Two other blacks were among the 1,000-yard gainers in 1971. Floyd Little of the Denver Broncos compiled 1,133 yards and Willie Ellison of the Los Angeles Rams reached 1,000 yards even. En route to his 1,000-yard season, Ellison picked up a record 247 yards against the New Orleans Saints in Los Angeles.

Even though criticism against the increased usage of synthetic turfs mounted and defensive linemen and linebackers were coming in bigger sizes and faster speeds, ten rushers (eight of them black) ran for 1,000 yards or more in 1972. Ron Johnson netted 1,182 yards for the New York Giants. Calvin Hill of the Dallas Cowboys gained 1,050 yards. Mike Garrett saved an otherwise disappointing season for the San Diego Chargers, netting 1,027 yards. Mercury Morris earned a regular running-back spot in the Miami Dolphins' backfield and churned out 1,000 yards. Franco Harris, the sensational Pittsburgh Steelers' back, gained 1,055 yards and tied Jim Brown's mark of six straight 100-yard games. And although Larry Brown of the Washington Redskins missed the last two games of the regular season due to an injury, he finished the year with 1,216 yards to win the NFC's rushing title. O. J. Simpson, former Heisman Trophy winner, won the American Football Conference's rushing title and topped all runners with a 1,250-yard season for the hapless Buffalo Bills.

The defense made its case over the two-year period as Willie Lanier (Kansas City Chiefs), Alan Page (Minnesota Vikings), Bubba Smith (Baltimore Colts), and Joe Greene (Pittsburgh Steelers), won top defensive awards. Packer cornerback Willie Buchanon snared Rookie of the Year honors in the NFC in 1972, but offensive players Franco Harris (AFC Rookie of the Year) and Larry Brown (Player of the Year) won the major awards in 1972.

On September 16, O.J. Simpson of the Buffalo Bills rushed on 250 yards and a new National Football League record.

COLLEGE FOOTBALL

In the college football ranks, Grambling football coach Eddie Robinson's Tigers defeated California State College, 59–26, for Robinson's 204th win over a thirty-year period, making him the second black coach in history to win 200 or more grid games. (Retired Florida A&M coach Jake Gaither won 203 games.)

Another 1972 leader was Chuck Ealey, a University of Toledo quarterback, who led his Rockets to thirty-four straight wins. Racism seemed apparent as players were bid for and, although Ealey was eligible for the 1972 draft, he was passed over by NFL teams. He later signed a $100,000 contract to play quarterback for the Hamilton Tiger Cats in the Canadian League. Ealey proved his worth in the league by winning the Rookie of the Year Award.

Jimmy Jones, University of Southern California quarterback, set thirteen school records and was also passed over by the professional teams. There was no demand for his services as a quarterback and he finally settled for a business career in Los Angeles.

Georgia Tech's first black quarterback, Eddie McAshan, who also set thirteen records for his team, was suspended from the last regular-season game of his career and the subsequent Liberty Bowl game for missing two practice sessions.

The outstanding college back of 1972 was Nebraska's Johnny Rodgers, who won the Heisman Trophy and ended his collegiate career with a dazzling Orange Bowl performance against Notre Dame. He established Big Eight Conference records for most pass receptions, 150; total career yardage, 2,703; most touchdowns in a season, 11; total punt return yardage, 1,654; and most punt return yardage in a single game, 170. Oklahoma's Greg Pruitt, who finished second in the Heisman balloting, set a rushing record for the Sooners in 1971, running for 1,665 yards. He also shattered the single-game rushing record, formerly held by Gale Sayers and Charlie Davis, by going 294 yards against Kansas State.

GOLF

Lee Elder, one of the few blacks on the pro golf circuit, has consistently been in contention, but has yet to win a major tournament. He is, however, in the league of top money winners on the PGA 1973 golf tour, winning $41,774 for the year up to May 23, 1973. In 1972 he earned over $70,000 in official earnings. He has been in the top 60 for all but one of the last 5 years. He ranks 29th among the top 60 money winners; however he has yet to reach his ambition to become the first black to play the Master's Invitational Golf Tournament in Atlanta.

The current rules under which a golfer is invited to participate limit the event to tournament winners, amateur champions and foreign players. An earlier black golf pro, Pete Brown, was the winner of a major American tournament, but he was not invited because under the rules they were using at that time, the Master's was open only to the top 60 money winners, leading observers to charge the Master's with changing the rules every time a black golfer qualifies.

Charles Sifford, the pioneer who broke the color line in pro golf, also won two regular tour titles, but failed to be invited to participate in the Master's which is ranked with the U.S. and British Opens and the American PGA National Championship as the "Big Four" of pro golf.

Other black pro golfers are George Johnson and Charles Owen, both of whom have won satellite events, but no major tournaments.

TENNIS

Althea Gibson, who was the first black to win the U.S. and Wimbledon tennis championships, was named to the National Lawn Tennis Hall of Fame in 1972. She retired from professional tennis in 1958.

Arthur Ashe in the 1960s came to the forefront as an international champion in this predominately white sport, winning intercollegiate championships, as well as the U.S. Men's Hard Court, the U.S. Amateur, the Australian Open and the U.S. Men's Clay Court championships.

In 1972 Ashe was defeated by Rod Laver 6–2, 3–6, in the World Cup tournament at Hartford, Conn. (March 12, 1972) giving Australia a 6–1 decision over the U.S. However Ashe won $10,000 as the first place prize July 31, in the First National Tennis Classic at Louisville, Ky., defeating Mark Cox of Great Britain 6–4, 6–4.

He was defeated by Ilie Natase of Rumania, 3–6, 6–3, 6–7, 6–4 and 6–3 for the Men's U.S. Open Tennis Championship in N.Y., September 10. Ashe, as the loser, earned $12,000.

November 26, Arthur Ashe won the World Championship Tennis Winter tournament and $25,000 first place money in Rome by defeating Bob Lutz, an American, 6–2, 3–6, 3–6, 7–6.

In 1973 Arthur Ashe won $10,000 in a final round of play on March 4, in the World Championship Tennis (WCT) final match. The U.S. Tennis Team, of which Ashe was a part, lost the Aetna World Cup in Hartford, Connecticut, to the Australian team, March 11, as he split $10,000 with three other team players and the captain.

Section XVIII

MONUMENTS

Monuments of Interest to the Black American

MONUMENTS OF INTEREST TO THE BLACK AMERICAN

Monuments commemorating contributions of black Americans whose suffering and achievements have become an indelible part of the historical record are located across the length and breadth of the nation. A selected list of many of these follow, arranged by states.

Alabama

On the Tuskegee Institute campus can be seen the marker commemorating the site of Washington's original cabin; the Oaks, Washington's home, in which the den is still maintained as it was in his lifetime; the Booker T. Washington Monument, and the George Washington Carver Museum with Carver's plant, mineral, and bird collections, exhibits of his products and paintings as well as many of his papers.
The Handy Heights Housing Development & Museum in Florence, the birthplace of W. C. Handy, composer and "father of the blues."

Arizona

A series of murals in the State House in Phoenix includes a representation of Estevan (or Estevanico), the black explorer who made his way alone and discovered much of the Arizona and New Mexico territory, in search of the legendary "Seven Golden Cities of Cibola." He was murdered at the gates of "the golden city" by Hawikuh Indians, and the expedition that followed him found it to be no more than a village of cliff-dwellers, glorified by the suns rays on the natural cliff formations into the appearance of a fabulous city.

California

Beckwourth Pass (5,220 alt.), the lowest crossing of the Sierra Nevada in central and southern California, was discovered by James P. Beckwourth, son of a Revolutionary War Officer and a slave mother.
Liedesdorff Street, a short street in the center of the San Francisco financial district, named for William Alexander Liedesdorff, pioneer San Francisco entrepreneur and first black millionaire.
Golden State Mutual Life Insurance Company Murals, Los Angeles, retell a part of the little known story of the blacks' contribution to California history. Artists Hale Woodruff and Charles Alston were commissioned to do the paintings.

Colorado

The settlement and naming of Pueblo are credited to James P. Beckwourth (see Beckwourth Pass, California), a trader and one-time war chief of the Crow Indians.

Georgia

Atlanta, site of Martin Luther King, Jr. Center and grave site of assassinated leader.
Statue of Booker T. Washington in front of Atlanta high school which is named in his honor.
The Bragg Smith Marker in the Columbus Colored Cemetery marks Atlanta's marble memorial at the grave of a black hero who lost his life trying to rescue the city engineer from a caved-in excavation in 1903.
Rev. George Lisle Monument at First Bryan Baptist Church in Savannah is dedicated to the first black Baptist missionary, 1782.

Illinois

Chicago's first building, the home of Jean Baptiste Pointe du Sable, a black fur trader and trapper, was located at a site just east of the Michigan Avenue Bridge on the north bank of the Chicago River. The site is marked by a plaque. The site is also marked by a tablet in Pioneer Court at the site. Another plaque commemorating Du Sable is in the lobby of the Du Sable High School, and a portrait of him hangs in the school's library. A sculptured bust of Du Sable by artist Marion Perkins is on view at the Du Sable Museum of African-American History.
The Provident Hospital, founded by Dr. Daniel Hale Williams as the first training school for black nurses in 1891, is at 51st and Vincennes Avenue. In 1893 Dr. Williams performed one of the first successful operations on the human heart at the Provident Hospital.
An Underground Railway marker can be found at 9955 South Beverly Avenue.
Black soldiers who served in World War I are memorialized in the Victory Monument, by Leonard Candle, which stands at 35th Street and Dr. Martin Luther King, Jr. Drive.
A statue of Dr. Martin Luther King, Jr. by Geraldine McCullough stands at the West Side Development Company in Chicago.

Iowa

John Brown's headquarters at Todd House (1854-56) are located in Tabor.

Kansas

The site of George Washington Carver's homestead in Beeler is indicated by a marker.
The ghost town of Nicodemus remains as a reminder of the black freedmen who fought to start a new life.
John Brown's cabin still stands in the Memorial Park at Osawatomie.

Maryland

Frederick Douglass statue on Morgan State College campus, Baltimore.

Frederick Douglass' birthplace memorial at Tuckahoe.

Plaque commemorating Matthew Henson, member of Admiral Peary's expedition to the North Pole, at Annapolis.

Massachusetts

Crispus Attucks Monument on Boston Common. Dedicated 1888 in honor of the victims of the Boston Massacre.

Shaw Monument on Beacon Street, Boston, facing the State House: a group statue by Augustus Saint-Gaudens of Colonel Robert Gould Shaw and the 54th Massachusetts Volunteers, a black regiment in the Union army which distinguished itself in the battle for Fort Wagner, South Carolina in 1863.

Prince Hall's grave, in Boston, in memory of the Revolutionary War soldier and founder of the Prince Hall Masonic Society.

Bunker Hill monument on Breed's Hill, Boston, marks the site of the battle in which a number of blacks fought with Revolutionary troops.

Workshop-cabin of James Weldon Johnson, diplomat, poet, and first NAACP Field Secretary, in Great Barrington.

Great Barrington is also the site of the birthplace of W.E.B. DuBois.

Michigan

Sojourner Truth's grave in Oak Hill cemetery, the Soldiers and Sailors monument in Detroit's Cadillac Square, and her home in Battle Creek, commemorate the freed slave who fought the battle for emancipation in lecture tours and in the law courts.

An Underground Railroad marker lies 2½ miles east of Cassopolis on M60.

The Douglass-Brown Marker on East Congress Street in Detroit marks the site of the William Webb House, where John Brown and Frederick Douglass met in March, 1859 to plan abolitionist strategy.

The Crosswhite Boulder in Triangle Park, Marshall, marks the site of a pitched battle in defense of a fugitive slave named Adam Crosswhite in 1946.

Missouri

The Carver National Monument in Diamond, a park containing a statue of the famous scientist, George Washington Carver, the site of the cabin where he was born, trails leading to points of interest, as well as a visitors' center and a museum, was the first national monument created in honor of a black.

Borromeo Cemetery, St. Charles, contains the grave of Jean Baptiste Pointe du Sable (*see* Chicago, Illinois).

In St. Louis, the Old Courthouse was the scene of the Dred Scott case. In 1847 a slave named Dred Scott first brought suit to win his freedom. The U.S. Supreme Court ruled against Scott, although his owners freed him as soon as the case was settled, but the controversy did not die down until the passage of the Fourteenth Amendment at the close of the Civil War.

New York

The original draft in Lincoln's hand of the preliminary proclamation issued in September, 1862 is in the New York State Library at Albany.

Harriet Tubman's home in Auburn was restored in 1953. She was credited with leading 300 slaves to freedom on the Underground Railroad, and her home was often used as a way-station. During the Civil War Miss Tubman served as a scout for the Union Army.

There is a memorial to Frederick Douglass at Staten Island, and a plaque dedicated to Booker T. Washington in the New York University Hall of Fame, New York City.

John Brown's grave is situated at North Elba, six miles south of Lake Placid on NY 86A.

New York City's Mayor John Lindsay renamed the Singer Bowl to Louis Armstrong Stadium.

Fraunces's Tavern, a major black-owned-and-operated business in the pioneer period, located in New York City's financial district, is the site of George Washington's farewell to his troops.

Ohio

John Brown's house in Akron has been preserved as a museum; there is also a monument to John Brown in Perkins Park.

Harriet Beecher Stowe's home can be seen in Cincinnati.

In Dayton, the home of the poet Paul Laurence Dunbar, on 219 North Summit Street, has been maintained as he left it, furnished with his personal belongings and manuscripts.

In Ripley, the John Rankin House Museum was once an Underground Railway station and is believed to be the refuge of the original fugitive slave on whom Harriet Beecher Stowe based Eliza of *Uncle Tom's Cabin*.

Pennsylvania

The grave of James A. Bland, composer of "Carry Me Back to Old Virginny" and other songs, is in Lower Marion Township.

The Mother Bethel AME Church, 419 South

Sixth Street, Philadelphia, is the fourth built on the site where Richard Allen and Absalom Jones founded the Free African Society in 1877, which developed into the African Methodist Episcopal Church, one of the largest and most powerful black denominations in the country.

Philadelpha has one of the nation's two monuments to black soldiers.

South Carolina

In Beaufort, a statue commemorates Robert Smalls, the first black captain in the American Navy, who, while a slave, stole the Confederate ship, *Planter,* out of Charleston harbor and delivered it to Union officials. He was later a Reconstruction Congressman.

Tennessee

The W. C. Handy Park in Memphis contains a bronze statue by Leone Tomassi of William Christopher Handy.

Virginia

A national monument to Booker T. Washington is found at his birthplace at Rocky Mount; also in Virginia is the Hampton Institute, where he studied and taught before going to Tuskegee.

Richmond's first monument to a black man, Bill (Bojangles) Robinson, the "King of Tap Dancers" during the 30's and 40's, stands at the site of a traffic light donated by Robinson years ago. The nine-foot aluminum statue was presented to the city by the Astoria Beneficial Club.

Washington, D. C.

Frederick Douglass' 20-room, colonial style home, at 1411 W. Street, S. E., is a national monument. There is also a Douglass memorial in Anacostia.

The Emancipation statue in Lincoln Park is the oldest memorial to Lincoln in the Washington area. The memorial was erected and paid for by former slaves.

West Virginia

Harper's Ferry National Monument, at the junction of the Potomac and Shenandoah Rivers, was a headquarters of Stonewall Jackson and it changed hands nine times during the Civil War. John Brown's famous plan to make it a fortress and place of refuge for fugitive slaves led to the disastrous seizure of the U. S. arsenal and capture of the village. The village turned against Brown and he was defeated by Colonel Robert E. Lee in the battle that followed and subsequently he was hung for treason.

Crossing the Bluestone River is the 1,334-foot Sgt. Cornelius Charlton Bridge, named for the second black Congressional Medal of Honor winner.

Wisconsin

At Milton, the Milton House Museum is the oldest cement building in the United States; it was a station used by slaves escaping on the Underground Railway.

Section XIX

OBITUARIES

OBITUARIES: 1969 - 1973

ABNER, WILLOUGHBY B.
(1920 - Dec. 2, 1972)
Director of the National Center for Dispute Settlements of the American Arbitration Association.

ABRAMS, JAMES E.
(1911 - June 21, 1969)
First black to be elected surrogate in New Jersey's Essex County. Elected to a 5-year term in 1964.

ABULLAH, ZAKARIYA (Leslie Scott)
(1921 - Aug. 20, 1969)
Actor and singer during the 1940's and 1950's who played on Broadway in "Shuffle Along."

ARMSTRONG, DANIEL LOUIS ("Satchmo")
(1900 - July 6, 1971)
Singer and trumpet player who was widely regarded as one of the central figures in the history of jazz.

ARMSTRONG, LILIAN HARDIN
(1902 - Aug. 27, 1971)
Pianist, composer, and second wife of Louis Armstrong.

AUSTIN, CORA ("Lovie")
(1887 - July 8, 1972)
Show business star of the twenties and thirties.

AUSTIN, ROBERTA
(1913 - Jan. 13, 1969)
Founder and director of the Roberta Martin Singers, a gospel singing group.

BANKS, EDWARD
(1922 - Oct. 28, 1969)
Publisher of The Arizona Tribune, one of the outstanding black publishers in the United States.

BARNETT, HERMAN A.
(1926 - May 27, 1973)
Physician and surgeon, president of the Houston School Board, the first black elected to that position.

BELL, HALEY
(1896 - March 12, 1972)
Detroit dentist and civic leader; first black radio station owner in Michigan.

BIGGS, ROBERT A.
(1903 - July 8, 1972)
Mortician and alderman of Chicago's Twenty-ninth Ward.

BOLDEN, BLANCHE
(1924 - Jan. 15, 1969)
Director of Cleveland's refuse and garbage collectors, appointed by Cleveland Mayor Stokes.

BOND, HORACE MANN
(1904 - Dec. 19, 1972)
Former president of Fort Valley (Ga.) State College and Lincoln (Pa.) University.

BONDS, MARGARET ALLISON
(1913 - May 18, 1972)
Pianist, conductor, and composer ("Georgia," "Peachtree Street," and "Ballad of the Brown King").

BONTEMPS, ARNA
(1903 - June 4, 1973)
Nationally known author and poet; he received national poetry prizes in 1926 and 1927.

BOUSFIELD, MAUDELLE
(1885 - Oct. 14, 1971)
The first black woman to serve as a high school principal in Chicago, Illinois.

BRIGHT, JOHN D. SR.
(1916 - July 2, 1972)
Presiding bishop of the First Episcopal District of the African Methodist Episcopal Church.

BROWN, LAWRENCE
(1894 -   1973)
Composer, vocalist and pianist. One of the foremost arrangers of Negro spirituals and for many years was accompanist for Paul Robeson.

BROWN, WILLIAM O.
(1900 - Feb. 1, 1969)
Founder of African Studies Center at Boston University, considered to be one of the persons most responsible for the development of African Studies in the United States.

BULLOCK, HENRY
(1907 - Feb. 8, 1973)
Educator and writer, considered an authority

on the life of blacks in America. One of his books, "A History of Negro Education in the South," received the Bancroft Award for the best history book in 1968.

BUNCHE, RALPH J.
(1904 - Dec. 9, 1971)
Undersecretary-general of the United Nations, from 1955 to his retirement in October, 1971.

BUSSEY, JOHN W.
(1904 - Oct. 5, 1969)
First black to serve on San Francisco's Municipal and Superior Courts.

BYAS, CARLOS WESLEY ("Don")
(1913 - Aug. 24, 1971)
Tenor saxophonist who played with Dizzy Gillespie, Count Basie, and Duke Ellington.

BYNUM, MARSHALL F.
(1912 - Nov. 2, 1969)
Member of the Chicago Park District Board, the first black to hold the position, businessman and civic leader.

CAMPBELL, E. SIMMS
(1906 - Jan. 27, 1971)
Cartoonist and illustrator for Esquire Magazine and King Features Syndicate.

CARTER, EUNICE HUNTON
(1901 - Jan. 25, 1970)
Social worker, lawyer, the first black woman assistant district attorney in New York City (1935-45) under Thomas E. Dewey, former member (1962) of the U. S. National Committee for the U. N. Educational, Scientific and Cultural Organization.

CAYTON, HORACE
(1903 - Jan. 22, 1970)
Ran largest black community house in the world, located on Chicago's South Side.

CLARK, CORTELIA
(1902 - Dec. 24, 1969)
Hard-luck blues singer whose only record album, "Blues in the Street," won a Grammy Award in 1967. The album did not sell, and he went back to street singing.

CLARK, FELTON G.
(1904 - July 5, 1970)
Black educator, former president of Southern University in Baton Rouge, La. for more than 30 years.

CLARK, MICHELE
(1941 - Dec. 8, 1972)
First black woman correspondent for CBS-TV.

CLARKE, JOSEPH A.
(1902 - Jan. 1969)
Special assistant to Postmaster General Arthur Summerfield during the Eisenhower Administration; served as Executive of the New Jersey Urban Commission.

CLEMENTE, ROBERTO
(1934 - Dec. 31, 1972)
Pittsburgh Pirates star who was considered by many as one of the greatest baseball players of all times. He was named to the National League All-Star team four times and won the National League batting title four times.

COLE, BENNIE JAMES
(1922 - May 11, 1969)
Assistant to the President for Community Relations at Texas Southern University.

COLLINS, GEORGE W.
(1925 - Dec. 8, 1972)
U. S. Congressman from Chicago's West Side. He was elected to a second term in November, 1972.

CORNISH, CHARLES E.
(1897 - March 27, 1969)
Maryland's first black City Council President (Cambridge).

CROMWELL, JOHN WESLEY JR.
(1884 - Dec. 16, 1971)
First black certified public accountant in the U. S. and former comptroller of Howard University.

CURTIS, KING (Curtis Ousley)
(1935 - Aug. 14, 1971)
Saxophone player and recording star.

DAVIS, BENJAMIN O., SR.
(1877 - Nov. 26, 1970)
First black to reach the rank of general in U. S. armed forces (1940), 50-year career began in the Spanish American War.

DAWSON, WILLIAM L.
(1886 - Nov. 9, 1970)
First black congressman to chair a major Congressional committee (House Committee on Government Operations). Since 1942 he had been re-elected from a predominantly black South Side Chicago ward and was vice chairman for the Democratic National Committee.

DELAHOUSSAYE, ROBERT B.
(1913 - Nov. 18, 1969)
First black since Reconstruction to run as an independent candidate for the Louisiana House of Representatives.

DePARIS, WILBUR
(1901 - Jan. 3, 1973)
Bandleader and trombonist, played New Orleans jazz more than 50 years. He played in orchestras with Louis Armstrong, Ella Fitzgerald, and Duke Ellington.

DOBBS, IRENE THOMPSON
(1885 - July 22, 1972)
An Atlanta civic leader and the mother of opera singer Mattiwilda Dobbs.

DORHAM, McKINLEY HOWARD ("Kenny")
(1911 - Nov. 23, 1972)
A pioneer modern jazz trumpet star.

DUNBAR, PAUL LAURENCE
(1936 - Jan. 1969)
Jazz bassist with Miles Davis, Wynton Kelly, Kenny Burrell, John Coltrane and Cannonball Adderley.

DYETT, THOMAS B.
(1886 - Nov. 2, 1971)
New York City attorney who was the first black to serve on the city's Civil Service Commission (1952-54), held numerous posts in city government and law associations; cofounder of black-owned Carver Federal Savings and Loan Association and Allied Federal Savings and Loan Association.

EDWARDS, JAMES
(1918 - Jan. 4, 1970)
Black actor best known for his performance in the 1949 film "Home of the Brave."

ENGLISH, MAURICE ("Lou")
(1907 - Apr. 29, 1969)
Internationally known dramatic actor and concert singer, most noted role being in the play "Glory Road."

FERGUSON, HENRY C.
(1890 - Feb. 20, 1973)
Retired Municipal Court judge in Chicago, past president of the Cook County (Ill.) Bar Association.

FERGUSON, LLOYD ALLEN
(1933 - Jan. 1, 1973)
Associate professor in the department of medicine at the University of Chicago Pritzker School of Medicine. During his career he served on the medical staffs of Massachusetts General Hospital, Mount Sinai Hospital (Chicago), and Michael Reese Hospital (Chicago).

FORBES, FRANKLIN L.
(1904 - Aug. 22, 1972)
Chairman of the Physical Education Department of Morehouse College for thirty-nine years.

GARDNER, J. HORACE
(1900 - Jan. 20, 1972)
A Republican member of the Illinois Assembly.

GIBBS, EDWARD A.
(1919 - Jan. 1, 1973)
Assistant commissioner for the Federal Code Enforcement Program in New York's Department of Rent and Housing Maintenance; aviator who founded the Negro Airmen International, Inc. in 1967.

GIBSON, TRUMAN K.
(1882 - Aug. 29, 1972)
Civic leader and chairman-emeritus of Supreme Life Insurance Company of America. In 1929, he received the Harmon Award for his work in bringing about a merger of Supreme Life and Casualty Company of Illinois and the Northeastern Life Insurance Company of New Jersey. This merger resulted in the Supreme Life Insurance Company of America, the largest black-owned company in the North.

GILES, J. W.
(1922 - Apr. 20, 1969)
Director of the Veterans Administration Hospital in Tuskegee, Alabama.

GLENN, ROY
(1915 - Mar. 12, 1971)
An actor who appeared on stage and in motion pictures.

GOLLIDAY, JIM
(1932 - Apr. 10, 1971)

Called "the world's fastest human" during the fifties when he ran track for Northwestern University, Chicago.

GRANT, EARL
(1931 - June 10, 1970)
Organist, recording star.

GRAY, WILLIAM H. JR.
(1911 - Jan. 26, 1972)
Former president of Florida A&M College.

HALL, LLOYD
(1894 - Jan. 2, 1971)
Chief chemist and technical director of Griffith Laboratories for more than thirty years. Hall was a specialist on food preservatives and held many patents in his field.

HAMILTON, ROY
(1929 - Aug. 3, 1969)
Popular singer with such hits as "Ebb Tide," "Let There Be Love," and "You'll Never Walk Alone."

HAMPTON, GLADYS NEAL
(1918 - Apr. 30, 1971)
Wife and business manager of Lionel Hampton.

HARRELD, KEMPER
(1885 - Feb. 24, 1971)
Retired chairman of the Department of Music at Morehouse College.

HARRISON, HAROLD J.
(1910 - June 5, 1973)
An assistant superintendent of the Detroit school system.

HARVEY, BURWELL T.
(1892 - Nov. 11, 1971)
Coach and businessman.

HAWKINS, COLEMAN
(1905 - May 19, 1969)
Tenor saxophonist who influenced the development of jazz by creating the first recognized jazz style for the tenor sax. (His 1939 recording of "Body and Soul" is considered a classic jazz ballad.)

HENDERSON, SYLVESTER CLARENCE
(Brother Henderson)
(1925 - Apr. 9, 1973)
Promoter of gospel music and gospel singing groups including "The Mighty Clouds of "Joy" and the "Inspirational Souls." He was producer and executive director of Kent Gospel records and organizer of the Watts' Choir.

HENDRIX, JIMI
(1942 - Sep. 18, 1970)
Rock guitarist and singer.

HERNANDEZ, JUAN G.
(1896 - July 17, 1970)
Hollywood actor, college professor in the School of Dramatic and Liberal Arts at the University of Puerto Rico.

HIGGINBOTHAM, JAY CEE
(1906 - May 26, 1973)
Jazz trombonist featured in such bands as Louis Armstrong's and Fletcher Henderson's during the 1930's and 1940's.

HOLMAN, CLAUDE
(1904 - June 1, 1973)
One of the most powerful black politicians in Chicago; mayor pro tem of the City Council, the second black to hold this position.

HOLMES, TALLEY R.
(1889 - March 1969)
Hotel owner, banker, teacher, attorney, and founder of the American Tennis Association. He was ATA singles champion in 1917-18, 1921 and 1924 and doubles champ eight times.

HOPKINS, CHARLES A.
(1931 - Dec. 27, 1972)
Neurosurgeon, on the staffs of three Chicago hospitals, the first black neurosurgeon in Chicago.

HOWARD, CHARLES P.
(1895 - Jan. 25, 1969)
United Nations correspondent, writer of UN Report.

HUTCHINSON, LESLIE ("Hutch")
(1900 - Aug. 18, 1969)
Pianist and singer who often performed for members of the Royal Family in England.

HUTTON, MERVIN
(1930 - Apr. 21, 1971)
First black American conductor of the Vienna Symphony.

JACKSON, GEORGE
(1942 - Aug. 21, 1971)
Author, revolutionary prisoner, and field marshal of the Black Panther party. Sentenced to prison for robbery, he wrote two books, *Soledad Brother* and *Blood in My Eye*, and was considered by many to be one of the finest writers of his generation.

JACKSON, INMAN ("Big Jack")
(1907 - Apr. 6, 1973)
Former Harlem Globetrotter, credited with introducing showmanstyle into the team.

JACKSON, MAHALIA
(1911 - Jan. 27, 1972)
World famous gospel singer.

JAMES, NEHEMIAH ("Skip")
(1902 - Oct. 3, 1969)
Jazz performer; recorded 26 songs in 1930 and 1931 and disappeared from public view until 1964.

JOHNSON, HALL
(1888 - Apr. 30, 1970)
Pianist, composer, choral director and most prolific arranger of Afro-American spirituals.

JOHNSON, LONNIE
(1897 - June 7, 1970)
Blues singer-guitarist and composer.

JONES, E. PAUL
(1904 - June 22, 1969)
Administrative consultant for the Jefferson County (Alabama) school system.

JONES, JAMES FRANCIS ("Prophet")
(1908 - Aug. 13, 1971)
Flamboyant leader of a Detroit religious cult, the Universal Triumph, the Dominion of God, Inc.

JONES, SAM ("Sad")
(1933 - Nov. 6, 1971)
Former basketball star who played for twelve years with the Boston Celtics.

JOYNER, ROBERT
(1894 - Apr. 16, 1973)
Pioneer among black chiropodists who practiced for 40 years in Chicago.

KELLY, WYNTON
(1931 - Apr. 12, 1971)
Pianist and composer, who was a featured performer with Dizzy Gillespie, Miles Davis, and Wes Montgomery.

KING, A. D. WILLIAMS
(1931 - July 21, 1969)
Civil rights leader, board member of Southern Christian Leadership Conference (younger brother of the late Rev. Dr. Martin Luther King Jr.) who had led racial integration movements in Birmingham, Ala. and Louisville, Ky. and had assumed the co-pastorate of Ebenezer Baptist Church (Atlanta) in 1968 after his brother's death.

KIRKPATRICK, JOHN M. SR.
(1915 - Feb. 24, 1972)
Publisher of the *East St. Louis Crusader*.

LAMPKINS, DANIEL
(1882 - July 10, 1969)
First black to run for the city commission of Grand Rapids, Michigan and founder of the city's first black newspaper.

LAWLESS, THEODORE K.
(1892 - May 3, 1971)
Dermatologist and philanthropist. He received the Harmon Award for outstanding achievement in the field of medicine in 1929 and was awarded the Springarn Medal in 1954.

LAWSON, WARNER
(1904 - June 3, 1971)
Retired dean of the Howard University College of Fine Arts.

LISTON, CHARLES ("Sonny")
(1932 - Jan. 5, 1971)
Former heavyweight boxing champion (1962-64).

LOMAX, LOUIS E.
(1923 - July 30, 1970)
Author, television commentator and director, professor of humanities at Hofstra University, Hempstead, N. Y.

LONG, FREDERICK ("Shorty")
(1940 - June 29, 1969)
Recording artist, writer and producer. Wrote "Devil With The Blue Dress On," "Function At The Junction," and "Here Come The Judge."

LOOBY, Z. ALEXANDER
(1899 - Mar. 25, 1972)
Attorney and leader of Civil Rights movement. He was counsel in many of the landmark civil rights cases and was one of the first blacks elected to the Nashville (Tenn.) City Council.

MACHEN, EDDIE
(1932 - Aug. 7, 1972)
A ranking heavyweight boxer.

MacKAY, CLIFF WESLEY
(1908 - Mar. 22, 1971)
Executive editor of the *Afro-American* newspapers.

MacKAY, LULA JONES
(1905 - Sep. 22, 1972)
Woman's editor of the *Afro-American* newspapers.

MAGHETT, SAM ("Magic Sam")
(1934 - Dec. 1, 1969)
Chicago blues singer and guitarist who toured folk and blues festivals in the Midwest and Europe.

MARTIN, EUGENE MARCUS
(1888 - Oct. 28, 1969)
Vice president-secretary of the Atlanta Life Insurance Co.

MARTIN, J. B.
(1923 - Dec. 27, 1969)
Past president of the Negro American Baseball League (1940–61) and first black trustee of the Chicago Metropolitan Sanitary District.

MARTIN, WILLIAM
(1923 - Dec. 27, 1969)
Head basketball coach at Virginia State College, Richmond; former football coach at Dillard University, New Orleans.

McLAURIN, DUNBAR S.
(1920 - July 10, 1973)
A former member of the organizing committee of Freedom National Bank in New York and operator of the Universal National Bank.

McPHATTER, CLYDE
(1931 - June 13, 1972)
Singer and nightclub star.

MILLER, FLOURNOY
(1887 - June 7, 1971)
Composer and entertainer of the famous show business team of Miller and Lyles, which made history with *Shuffle Along, Runnin' Wild,* and other shows.

MING, WILLIAM ROBERT
(1911 - June 30, 1973)
NAACP lawyer, former assistant attorney for the Illinois Commerce Commission and he also served as a professor of law at Howard University.

MITCHELL, FRANK W., SR.
(1905 - June 12, 1970)
Publisher of the *St. Louis Argus.*

MORGAN, LEE
(1939 - June 7, 1971)
Composer and trumpet virtuoso who was a featured performer with Dizzy Gillespie and Art Blakey.

MORON, ALONZO G.
(1909 - Oct. 31, 1971)
First black president of Virginia's Hampton Institute (1949–59), commissioner of education of the Virgin Islands, deputy regional director of the Department of Housing and Urban Development in Puerto Rico.

MUHAMMAD, CLARA
(1900 - Aug. 12, 1972)
Wife of Elijah Muhammad, leader of the Nation of Islam.

MULZAC, HUGH N.
(1886 - Jan. 30, 1971)
First black captain (1942) of a U.S. merchant ship, the *Booker T. Washington.*

MURRAY, PETER MARSHALL
(1889 - Dec. 19, 1971)
Pioneer in cancer research and the use of radioactive gold; first black member of the AMA House of Delegates.

ORY, EDWARD ("Kid")
(1886 - Jan. 23, 1973)
Dixieland jazz trombonist who wrote "Muskrat Ramble." One of Louis Armstrong's first jobs was with Ory's band.

PANKEY, AUBREY
(1906 - May 8, 1971)
Concert singer who moved to Europe in post-World War II period.

PARKER, JUNIOR
(1902 - Nov. 11, 1971)
Blues singer and harmonica player.

PETERS, ART
(1929 - Apr. 11, 1973)
Nationally syndicated columnist for the Philadelphia Inquirer, and lawyer who was considered to be one of the most influential columnists in Philadelphia.

PETERSON, DAVID
(1851 - May 31, 1973)
Former slave, believed to be the oldest living American.

PHINNIE, LUCILLE
(1918 - Jan. 2, 1973)
Chief librarian at the Johnson Publishing Company (Chicago) for 10 years.

PITTMAN, BOOKER
(1909 - Oct. 3, 1969)
Jazz clarinetist and grandson of Booker T. Washington who played with the bands of Louis Armstrong, Duke Ellington, and Count Basie.

POWELL, ADAM CLAYTON, JR.
(1908 - Apr. 4, 1972)
Minister, protest leader, and former congressman from Harlem.

PURVIS, TOMMY
(1938 - Aug. 16, 1969)
Jazz musician.

RAZAF, ANDY
(1895 - Feb. 4, 1973)
Composer and lyricist who wrote the words for "Honeysuckle Rose," "Ain't Misbehavin' " and "Stompin' at the Savoy." Inducted into Songwriters Hall of Fame in 1972.

REEVES, FRANK D.
(1916 - April. 8, 1973)
Civil rights lawyer, politician, educator, former NAACP counsel under Thurgood Marshall; first black Democratic National Committeeman from the District of Columbia.

ROBINSON, BERNARD W.
(1918 - Aug. 23, 1972)
First black to be appointed ensign in the U.S. Navy.

ROBINSON, DANIEL T.
(1888 - Apr. 11, 1973)
First professional black printer in Atlanta.

ROBINSON, JACK ROOSEVELT ("Jackie")
(1919 - Oct. 24, 1972)
The first black to play in major league baseball with the Brooklyn Dodgers in contemporary U.S. He was also a businessman and civic leader.

ROBINSON, JAMES H.
(1907 - Nov. 6, 1972)
Founder and executive director of Operation Crossroads Africa, which was a model for the Peace Corps. He was founder and pastor (1938 - 1962) of the Church of the Master in New York City.

ROBINSON, WILLIAM H.
(1910 - March 23, 1973)
First black appointed to be director of the Cook County (Ill.) Public Aid Department, former Illinois representative (1955–65).

ROGERS, T. Y., JR.
(1936 - March 25, 1971)
Director of affiliates and chapters of the Southern Christian Leadership Conference.

RUSHING, JAMES ANDREW ("Jimmy")
(1904 - June 8, 1972)

Singer who was known as "Mr. Five by Five." He won fame with the Count Basie orchestra during the thirties and forties.

SAMUEL, HERBERT
(1917 - Feb. 3, 1972)
Vice president of a New York restaurant chain.

SANDS, DIANA
(1934 -Sept. 22, 1973)
Stage and screen actress, was the recipient of several awards—one of which was for her outstanding performance in *Raisin in the Sun.*

SCOTT, E. T.
(1884 - Dec. 4, 1969)
Physician who was medical director of Mercy Hospital (Philadelphia), and chief of its outpatient department for 25 years.

SHAVERS, CHARLES
(1918 - July 9, 1971)
Composer and trumpet player.

SILVERA, FRANK
(1914 - June 11, 1970)
Character actor.

SKYLES, CHARLES
(1905 - Apr. 6, 1970)
Supervisor of Cook County (Ill.) Probation Department; former state legislator, a member of the Illinois General Assembly in 1960.

SMITH, HOMER
(1907 - Aug. 15, 1972)
Journalist and foreign correspondent. He was the author of *Black Man in Red Russia,* which detailed his experiences in Russia in the thirties and forties.

SMITH, MAYBELLE ("Big Maybelle")
(1925 - Jan. 23, 1972)
Singer and recording star.

SMITH, SYLVESTER B.
(1900 - Oct. 10, 1969)
American Tennis Association national men's singles champion in 1919

SMITH, WENDELL
(1914 - Nov. 26, 1972)
Sports writer and TV commentator who played a key role in the signing of Jackie Robinson by the Brooklyn Dodgers.

SMITH, WILLIE ("The Lion")
(1894 - Apr. 18, 1973)
Jazz pianist and composer.

STAMPS, JAMES E.
(1890 - Oct. 29, 1972)
Retired senior administrative officer of the Social Security Administration.

STRATTON, SAMUEL BEARD
(1897 - Oct. 4, 1972)
Historian and educator.

STRICKLAND, JOSEPH
(1928 - Sept. 23, 1972)
Journalist and assistant to the dean of the Graduate School of Arts and Sciences at Harvard University.

TAYLOR, CLAUDE RANDOLPH
(1904 - May 27, 1972)
Professor of microbiology at the Howard University Medical School.

TAYLOR, HOBART, SR.
(1896 - Dec. 5, 1972)
Businessman and civic leader.

TERRELL, TAMI
(1946 - March 16, 1970)
Blues singer, performed with Marvin Gaye.

THIGPEN, BENJAMIN
(1909 - Oct. 18, 1971)
Drummer who played with Andy Kirk.

THOMAS, JESSE O.
(1885 - Feb. 18, 1972)
Founder of the Atlanta Urban League and the Atlanta University School of Social Work.

THOMAS, JULIUS A.
(1897 - May 20, 1973)
Director of Industrial Relations of the National Urban League from 1943–61.

THOMPSON, HENRY ("Hammerin' Hank")
(1926 - Sept. 30, 1969)
Former New York Giants third baseman, played on two World Series teams. He and Monte Irvin were the first blacks on the Giants.

TINDAL, ROBERT R.
(1930 - July 30, 1971)
One of three blacks on the Detroit City Council.

TURNER, HERBERT
(1885 - March 20, 1973)
Physician and civil rights leader, founder of the Cook County (Ill.) Medical Assn. and first black president of the Chicago chapter of the NAACP and founder of the Chicago chapter of the Urban League.

TURNER, LORENZO DOW
(1895 - Feb. 10, 1972)
Professor-emeritus of English at Roosevelt University, Chicago, and an authority on African culture. He was the author of several monographs and books, including *Africanisms in the Gullah Dialect.*

WALL, FREDERICK P.
(1915 - June 18, 1973)
Publisher of the *Chicago Courier,* the largest black weekly newspaper in that city; former secretary to the late U.S. Rep. William Dawson (D., Ill.). He was the first black in Illinois to serve as vice-chairman of the State Democratic Central Committee.

WALKER, NATHANIEL
(1886 - May 15, 1971)
Physician in Selma, Ala. for 54 years.

WALKER, ODELL BASCOMB ("Dud")
(1916 - Dec. 25, 1972)
Played trumpet with Erskine Hawkins and Duke Ellington.

WARD, CLARA
(1925 - Jan. 16, 1973)
World famous gospel singer, leader of Clara Ward Singers, who began her singing career at age nine.

WASHINGTON, GENOA
(1895 - Oct. 14, 1972)
Republican representative in the Illinois Assembly and a former delegate to the United Nations.

WASHINGTON, KENNY
(1918 - June 24, 1971)
UCLA football star who became the first black signed by a professional football team, the Los Angeles Rams (1946). He later played character roles in Hollywood movies.

WASHINGTON, DEON D.
(1910 - Feb. 18, 1973)
Noted jazz saxophonist, music arranger, and union official; co-composer of "Hambone." In 1966 he successfully completed a merger in Chicago of two locals in the musicians union, one all white, the other all black.

WASHINGTON, SYLVESTER
(1906 - Oct. 2, 1971)
Legendary Chicago policeman who earned the nickname "Two Gun Pete" during the thirties and forties when he wore two pearl-handled revolvers on his beat in Chicago's "Death Valley."

WHITE, WILLIAM S., SR.
(1885 - July 24, 1972)
Retired pharmacist and former senior chemist with the Chicago Health Department.

WILKINS, ALONZO
(1939 - Feb. 29, 1972)
Disabled Korean War veteran and first member of the Wheelchair Hall of Fame.

WILLIAMS, BILLY
(1910 - Oct. 12, 1972)
Composer and singer who won fame as lead singer of the Billy Williams Quartet.

WILLIAMS, DONALD
(1943 - May 16, 1973)
Founder of United Sickle Cell Anemia Association in 1969.

WILLIAMS, POINDEXTER, SR.
(1898 - March 17, 1969)
Retired Negro American League Baseball umpire, a member of the original Birmingham Black Barons.

WILSON, LILLIAN BROWN
(1886 - June 8, 1969)
Vaudevillian male impersonator in the 1920's

and 30's who appeared on Broadway in the 30's and 40's.

WOOD, EUGENE W.
(1909 - Jan. 30, 1973)
Real estate executive, former president of the St. Louis Real Estate Association, and was a management broker for the Federal Housing Authority and Urban Development.

WOOD, GREEN T.
(1921 - Dec. 17, 1972)
Assistant deputy director for the southeast area of the Department of Housing and Urban Development.

WOODWARD, PRICE
(1920 - Jan. 13, 1972)
First black mayor of Wichita, Kansas from 1970-71.

YOUNG, JOHN H., III
(1916 - Nov. 25, 1971)
Director of the Harlem anti-poverty program.

YOUNG, WHITNEY M., JR.
(1921 - Mar. 11, 1971)
Civil rights leader and executive director of the National Urban League since 1961.

Section XX

ORGANIZATIONS

ORGANIZATIONS

Alpha Kappa Alpha Sorority, Inc.
5211 South Greenwood Avenue
Chicago, Illinois 60615
(312) 684-1282

Mrs. Mattelia B. Grays, President,
Chairman of the Board
Mrs. Jessie M. Rattley, Treasurer
Mrs. Carey B. Preston, Executive Secretary

Main Purpose and Emphasis—
To cultivate and encourage high scholastic and
ethical standards, to promote unity and friendship among college women, to study and help
alleviate problems concerning girls and women
in order to improve the social stature, to maintain a progressive interest in college life, and
to be of service to all mankind.

Founded: 1908

For further information contact:
Mrs. Carey B. Preston

Alpha Phi Alpha Fraternity, Inc.
4432 Martin Luther King Drive
Chicago, Illinois 60653
(312) 373-1819

Laurence T. Young, Sr., Director,
Executive Secretary
Dr. Walter Washington, President,
Chairman of the Board
Leven C. Weiss, Treasurer
J. Herbert King, Assistant Director

Main Purpose and Emphasis—
Service Organization. To stimulate the ambition
of its members; to prepare them for the greatest
usefulness in the causes of humanity, freedom,
and dignity of the individual; to encourage the
highest and noblest form of manhood and to aid
down-trodden humanity in its efforts to achieve
higher social, economic, and intellectual status.

Founded: 1906

For further information contact:
Laurence T. Young, Executive Secretary

American Civil Liberties Union
22 E. 40th Street
New York, New York 10016
(212) 725-1222

Aryeh Neier, Director
Edward Ennis, President, Chairman of the Board
Winthrop Wadleigh, Treasurer
Alan Reitman, Assistant Director

Main Purpose and Emphasis—
Litigation, legislative action, research and education for civil liberties.

Founded: 1920

For further information contact: Alan Reitman

**American Federation of Labor and
Congress of Industrial Organization**
815 16th Street, N. W.
Washington, D.C. 20006
(202) 293-5270

Don Slaiman, Director
George Meany, President
Lane Kirkland, Secretary-Treasurer
Robert McGlotten, William E. Pollard,
Elmer T. Kehrer, Assistants

Main Purpose and Emphasis—
To encourage all workers without regard to race,
creed, color, national origin or ancestry to share
equally in the full benefits of union organization.

Founded: 1955

Black Academy of Arts and Letters
475 Riverside Drive
New York, New York 10027
(212) 663-4740

Dr. C. Eric Lincoln, President Emeritus
John O. Killens, President
Doris E. Saunders, Vice President and Secretary
Alvin F. Poussaint, M.D., Treasurer

Main Purpose and Emphasis—
To promote, cultivate, and motivate black arts
and letters.

Founded: 1969

For further information contact:
Mrs. Yolanda Wilson

Congress of Racial Equality (CORE)
200 W. 135th Street
New York, New York 10030
(212) 281-9650

Roy Innis, Director
Victor Solomon, Associate Director

Main Purpose and Emphasis—
Developing and implementing programs for the
betterment and liberation of black people.

Founded: 1942

For further information contact: Mrs. Doris Innis

Congressional Black Caucus
House of Representatives
415 2nd Street, N.E.
Washington, D.C. 20002
(202) 546-3425

Louis Stokes (Ohio), Chairman
Augustus F. Hawkins (California), Vice Chairman
Charles B. Rangel (New York), Secretary

Main Purpose and Emphasis—
To review, monitor, and affect legislation; to
make known to Congress, the administration, and
the public the intense hardship, denial of basic
rights, and harm of current national policies; to
articulate the problems of their constituents and
to work for prompt and effective solutions to
them.

Founded: 1971 (91st Congress)

Delta Sigma Theta Sorority, Inc.
1707 New Hampshire Avenue, N.W.
Washington, D.C. 20009
(202) 483-5460

Mrs. Lynnette Taylor, Director, Exec. Secretary
Mrs. Lillian P. Benbow, President, Chairman of
the Board
Mrs. Betty Williams, Treasurer

Main Purpose and Emphasis—
Public Service—Five-Point Program Thrusts:
Educational Development, Economic Development, Community and International Development, Housing and Urban Development, Mental
Health, as well as scholarship and Social Action
Programs. Delta's major program activity takes
place at the chapter level where 440 chapters use
their membership, training, resources, and wo-
manpower to meet community needs.

Founded: 1913

For further information contact:
Miss Clara M. Allen, Information Officer

The Drifters, Inc.
Mrs. Betty Johnson: National President
444 East 82nd Street
New York, New York
(212) 861-4303

Federation of Masons of the World, Inc.
1017 East 11 Street
Austin, Texas 78702
(512) 477-5380
M. J. Anderson, President
Dr. Wm. J. Fitzpatrick, Chairman of the Board
Joe Johnson, Treasurer
Obie Ellison, 2nd Vice President
O. H. Elliott, Executive Secretary
Main Purpose and Emphasis—
Unification of Masonic bodies
Founded: 1958
For further information contact:
M. J. Anderson
1017 East 11 Street
Austin, Texas 78702

Frontiers International
1901 W. Girard Avenue
Philadelphia, Pennsylvania 19130
(215) CE-5-5959
Clyde D. Mitchell, President
Willie Climmons, Treasurer
Dr. Charles Moore, 1st VP
N.B. Allen, President Emeritus
Harold L. Pilgrim, Exec. Secretary
Main Purpose and Emphasis—
The Frontier's purpose and basic concept is service—not for itself, nor for its members, but for others. However, it is almost impossible to help others without being helped oneself, even if the rewards are not immediately recognizable, and are more of spiritual and intellectual value than of material. A club which does many kinds of good services for the needy and it also uncovers, develops, and puts to work leadership which operates through supporting other organizations in their programs and direct community activities when no other group or organization is functioning adequately in a given area. It does not endorse political candidates.
Founded: 1936
For further information contact:
Mr. Harold L. Pilgrim

Girl Friends, Inc.
c/o Mrs. Jacqueline Robinson
4503½ Crest Lane
McLean, Virginia 22101
Mrs. Jacqueline Robinson, President
Alyce Moore, Chairman of the Board
Patricia Higgins, Treasurer
Chrystine Shack, Executive Secretary
Main Purpose and Emphasis—Friendship
Founded: 1927
For further information contact:
Mrs. Jacqueline Robinson

Improved, Benevolent, Protective Order of Elks of the World
1522 North 15 Street
Philadelphia, Pennsylvania 19121
(215) GE-2-0150
Hobson Reynolds, Grand Exalted Ruler
Carl O. Dickerson, Grand Secretary

Judge Perry B. Jackson, Treasurer
Main Purpose and Emphasis—
A fraternal organization which provides for the welfare of its members. It emphasizes the principles of charity, justice, brotherly love, and fidelity.
Founded: 1929
For further information contact:
Mrs. Bessie Coston

Institute of the Black World
87 Chestnut Street, S.W.
Atlanta, Georgia 30314
(404) 523-7805
Main Purpose and Emphasis—
As an independent Research Center, they are involved in publishing, speaking, writing and research activities geared to a definition of the black experience.
Founded: 1969
For further information contact: The Institute

Interracial Council for Business Opportunity
470 Park Avenue South
New York, New York 10016
(212) 889-0880
Dr. Clifford C. Davis, President
Rodman C. Rockefeller
William R. Hudgins
John J. McSadden, Secretary, Treasurer
Albert C. Lasker
Nelson Bengston
Robert L. Wechsler
Main Purpose and Emphasis—
To assist minority businessmen in the development and management of their own enterprises.
Founded: 1963
For further information contact:
Vaughn Thomas

Iota Phi Lambda Sorority, Inc.
1940 McClure Avenue (Always address of current National President)
Youngston, Ohio 44505
Mrs. Bessie Coston, President (Term expires August, 1973)
Mrs. Mildred S. Keeys, Treasurer (Term expires August, 1973)
Mrs. Alva S. Williams, Secretary (Term expires August, 1973)
Main Purpose and Emphasis—
To promote interest in business education among high school and college girls through planned programs and scholarships; and to encourage development of personalities for all areas of leadership and further intellectual development of our members through higher education.
Founded: 1929
For further information contact:
National President

Kappa Alpha Psi Fraternity, Inc.
2320 North Broad Street
Philadelphia, Pennsylvania 19132
(215) 228-7184
Ernest H. Davenport, Chairman of the Board and President
Earl A. Morris, Executive Secretary
H. H. Holloway, Treasurer

Main Purpose and Emphasis—
To unite college men of culture, patriotism, and honor in a bond of fraternity. To encourage honorable achievement in every field of human endeavor. To promote the spiritual, social, intellectual, and moral welfare of members. To assist the aims and purposes of colleges and universities. To inspire service in the public interest.

Jack and Jill of America, Inc.
Mrs. Eleanor C. DeLoache, National President
991 Sunbury Road
Columbus, Ohio 43219
Main Purpose and Emphasis—
To cultivate the educational, cultural, philosophical, and social needs of our children.

Lambda Kappa Mu Sorority, Inc.
Marie G. Leatherman, Grand Basileus
503 Trowbridge Street
Detroit, Michigan 48202
Main Purpose and Emphasis—
Organized in 1937 to encourage higher education among high school graduates, the 1500-member group provides scholarship aid to deserving girls, it emphasizes scholarship, achievement, and community service among youth.

Leadership Conference on Civil Rights
2027 Massachusetts Avenue, N.W.
Washington, D.C. 20036
(202) 667-1780
New York Office
55 West 42 Street
New York, New York 10036
(212) 563-3450
Roy Wilkins, Chairman
Joseph L. Tauh, Jr., Counsel
Arnold Aronson, Secretary
Bayard Ruston, Chairman, Executive Committee
Clarence Mitchell, Legislative Chairman
James Hamilton, Chairman, Compliance and Enforcement Committee
Main Purpose. and Emphasis—
To bring about federal legislative and executive action to assure full equality for all Americans; and to facilitate the planning, speaking, and cooperative actions of a coalition of more than 120 national civil rights, religious, labor, civic, professional, and fraternal organizations for this purpose.
Founded: 1949
For further information contact:
Marvin Caplan
Yvonne Price

National Alliance of Postal and Federal Employees
1644 11th Street., N.W.
Washington, D.C. 20001
(202) 332-4313
Mr. Robert L. White, President and Chairman of the Board
Mr. Enormel Clark, Treasurer
Mr. Votie D. Dixon, Executive Secretary
*Main Purpose and Emphasis—*Labor Union
Founded: 1925
For further information contact:
Mr. Votie D. Dixon

National Association for the Advancement of Colored. People
1790 Broadway
New York, New York 10019
(212) 245-2100
Kivie Kaplan, President
Bishop S. G. Spottswood, Chairman of the Board of Directors
Roy Wilkins, Secretary
Alfred Baker Lewis, Treasurer
Main Purpose and Emphasis—
To end all barriers to racial justice and guarantee full equality of opportunity and achievement in the United States.
Founded: 1909
For further information contact:
Henry Lee Moon

National Association of Black Accountants
P. O. Box 726 F.D.R. Station
New York, New York 10022
Frank Ross, President
William Aiken, Vice President
Donald Bristow, Vice President
Kenneth Drummond, Vice President
Arlene Robinson, Secretary
Bertram Gibson, Treasurer
Main Purpose and Emphasis—
To assist and encourage members of minority groups to enter the profession of accounting; stimulate acquaintance and fellowship among members of minority groups; provide opportunities for members to increase their knowledge of accounting practices and individual capabilities; unite through membership in the association, persons interested in enhancing opportunities for minority groups in accounting.
Founded: 1970
For further information contact:
Frank Ross

National Association of Black Social Workers, Inc.
2008 Madison Avenue
New York, New York 10035
(212) 348-0035
Cenie Williams, National President
Nwab Shah, 1st Vice President
James Madry, Secretary
Chester Wright, Treasurer
Main Purpose and Emphasis—
To support, develop and/or sponsor community welfare projects and programs which will serve the interest of the black community and move it toward control over its social institutions.
Founded: 1968
For further information contact:
Cenie Williams, National President

National Association of College Deans, Registrars & Admissions Officers (Nacdrao)
Albany State College
Albany, Georgia
(912) 555-1212
Mrs. Helen M. Mayes, Secretary
Main Purpose and Emphasis—
To exchange ideas and practices that are pertinent to each of these offices in the various schools holding membership; keep abreast of new trends in admissions and record keeping; determine transcript adequacy, i.e., what should and should not appear on a student's transcript.
Founded: In the early 1920s.

For further information contact:
  G. H. Taylor

National Association of Colored Women's Clubs, Inc.
  1601 R Street, N.W.
  Washington, D.C. 20009
  (202) DE-2-8160
Mrs. Myrtle Ollison, President
Mrs. Carole A. Early, Headquarters Secretary

Main Purpose and Emphasis—
  To raise the standard of the home and extend service to help make better communities.

Founded: 1896

National Association for Health Services Executives
  2600 Liberty Heights Avenue
  Baltimore, Maryland 21215
  (301) 523-4005

Henry J. Whyte, President
Joseph Mann, President-Elect
Herman J. Glass, 1st Vice President
William Andrews, 2nd Vice President
Charles Tildon, Corresponding Secretary
Haynes Rice, Secretary
Waverly B. Johnson, Treasurer
Claude Reynolds, Parliamentarian

Main Purpose and Emphasis—
  To elevate the quality of health-care services rendered to poor people and members of minority races in the United States, improve the quality of care in inner-city health institutions and encourage capable members of minority groups to enter health care administration.

Founded: 1968

For further information contact:
Charles Tildon, Corresponding Secretary

National Association of Market Developers, Inc.
  201 Ashby Street, N.W.—Suite 306
  Atlanta, Georgia 30314
Mr. Charles J. Smith, President
Mr. Paul E. X. Brown, Executive Director

Main Purpose and Emphasis—
  To exchange knowledge, information, experience and know-how about the marketplace, and in particular the black market; to foster creativity and excellence at all levels in these areas of the association; to inspire students to carve out new careers in the field; to support, extend, and interpret the functions of the professions in a democracy; to demonstrate the power of competence; to stimulate, conduct, and utilize research in the development and expansion of the black market; to accept responsibility for the evaluation and improvement of the profession; to contribute to the solution of educational, social, and cultural problems of local, regional, and national concern; and to promote professional fellowship and cooperation as a means to positive action.

Founded: 1953

For further information contact:
Paul E. X. Brown

National Association of Media Women, Inc.
  157 W. 126th Street
  New York, New York 10027
  (212) 666-1320

Lois Alexander Lane, President
Xerona Clayton, 1st Vice President
Ella Kay Mays, 2nd Vice President
Vivian Robinson, Corresponding Secretary
Louise Meadows, Treasurer

Main Purpose and Emphasis:
  A national association of women in communications whose primary purpose is to develop professional relationships and to upgrade the status of black women in the field of media.

Founded: 1965.

For further information contact:
  Vivian Robinson

National Association of Negro Business and Professional Women's Clubs, Inc.
  2861 Urban Avenue
  Columbus, Georgia 31907

Mrs. Margaret L. Belcher, President
Mrs. Rosalie McGuire, 1st Vice President
Miss Florence V. Lucas, 2nd Vice President
Mrs. Edythe Harris, Treasurer
Mrs. V. Alyce Foster, Secretary
Mrs. Dorothy Boswell, National Editor

Main Purpose and Emphasis—
  To promote and protect the interest of business and professional women; to create good fellowship among them; to direct the interest of business and professional women toward united action for improved social and civic conditions; to encourage the organization of subsidiary associations throughout the United States and the world and to create and develop opportunities for Negro women in business and the professions; to develop youth through scholarships, affording them formal training through leadership and through the creation of job opportunities; to recognize achievements for use in school organizations and elsewhere that all people may be informed and that young black people know their heritage and help promote world peace and universal brotherhood.

Founded: 1935

For further information contact:
  Mrs. Margaret L. Belcher

National Association of Real Estate Brokers
  1025 Vermont Avenue, N.W.—Suite 1111
  Washington, D.C. 20005
  (202) 638-1280

William Hamilton, National President
Willis Carson, President-Elect
Otis Thorpe, 1st Vice President

Main Purpose and Emphasis—
  To advocate legislation in housing reform for blacks; create and develop seminars for real-estate brokers in management, appraisal, and development.

Founded: 1947

For further information contact:
  Mrs. Ann Toliver

National Bankers Association
  1325 Massachusetts Avenue, N.W.
  Washington, D.C. 20005
  (202) 628-8188

William R. Hudgins, President
I. Owen Funderburg, First Vice President
Donald E. Sneed, Jr., Second Vice President
Sharnia Buford, Secretary
Walter S. Tucker, Treasurer

Executive Committee (officers plus): Carl M. Carroll, Jr.; Paul R. Hernandez, B. Doyle Mitchell, L.C. Squires, Edward E. Trillmon.

Main Purpose and Emphasis—
To strengthen existing member banks; to increase their numbers and ultimately to increase the economic impact of minority-owned banks in their communities.

Founded: 1927

For further information contact:
Charlotte P. Hall

National Baptist Convention, USA., Inc.
405 E. 31st Street
Chicago, Illinois 60616
(312) 842-1081

Dr. J. H. Jackson, President
Dr. L. G. Carr, Treasurer
Dr. T. J. Jemison, Executive Secretary

Main Purpose and Emphasis—
Uniting Baptist churches and other Baptist organizations to promote home and foreign missions, and to encouraged and support Christian education.

Founded: 1880

For further information contact:
Dr. J. H. Jackson

National Bar Association
1314 North 5th Street
Kansas City, Kansas 66101

Judge Edward F. Bell, President
Elmer C. Jackson, Jr., Membership Secretary

Main Purpose and Emphasis—
To advance the science of jurisprudence; to help preserve the independence of the judiciary; to work for a more equitable representation of all racial groups in the judiciary of our cities, states, and nation; to promote legislation that will improve the economic condition of all the citizens of the United States; to aid all citizens, regardless of race or creed in their effort to secure a free and untrammeled use of the franchise guaranteed by the constitution of the United States; to promote social intercourse among the members of the American Bar; to uphold the honor of the legal profession; to protect the civil and political rights of the citizens and residents of the several states of the United States; to work for the integration of the American Bar; and also seeks to improve the caliber and the techniques of the practitioner by sponsoring practicing law institution.

Founded: 1925

For further information contact:
Mrs. C. Clayton Powell, Referee
Fulton County Juvenile Court
Atlanta, Georgia 30315

National Beauty Culturists League, Inc.
25 Logan Circle, N.W.
Washington, D.C. 20005
(202) 332-2695 or 232-4509

Mr. Henry R. Davenporte, Director
Dr. Katie E. Whickam, President
Mrs. Serena B. Ross, Chairman of the Board
Mrs. Josephine R. Thompson, Treasurer and Executive Secretary

Main Purpose and Emphasis—
To raise the standards of the profession in order to maintain the confidence of the public and distribute informative educational material among its members.

Founded: 1919

For further information contact:
Mrs. Gladys W. Davis

National Business League
4324 Georgia Avenue, N.W.
Washington, D.C. 20010
(202) 726-6200

Berkeley Burrell, President
Charles T. Williams, Chairman of the Board
Theodore R. Hagans, Senior Vice President
Wendell C. Croft, Vice Chairman
Edward L. Feggans, Secretary
B. Doyle Mitchell, Treasurer

Main Purpose and Emphasis—
To assist prospective and existing minority businessmen through management training and technical assistance. To aid in capital and contract procurement.

National Committee of Black Churchmen, Inc.
110 East 125 Street—Suite 503
New York, New York 10035
(212) 862-9628

Bishop H. B. Shan, Chairman of Board of Directors
Bishop John D. Bright, President
H.A.L. Clements, Secretary
Gilbert Caldwell, Treasurer

Main Purpose and Emphasis—
To unite black churchmen (lay and clergy) throughout the nation to develop strategies related to the empowerment of the black community.

Founded: 1967

For further information contact:
J. Metz Rollins or Leon Watts, II

National Council of Negro Women, Inc.
1346 Connecticut Avenue, N.W.—Suite 832
Washington, D.C. 20036
(202) 223-2363
    Field Office
    884 Third Avenue
    New York, New York 10022
    (212) 371-8520

Dorothy I. Height, National President
Ruth A. Sykes, Special Assistant
Sylvia H. Williams, Director of Development

Main Purpose and Emphasis—
To represent the concerns of women on matters affecting the general welfare of the black community. It is a charitable, educational organization with objectives of achieving equal opportunity for all.

Founded: 1935

For further information contact: Dorothy Height

National Dental Association
P. O. Box 197
Charlottesville, Virginia 22902
(703) 293-8253 or 293-6991

Ellard N. Jackson, D.D.S., Director and Executive Secretary
Eddie G. Smith, Jr., D.D.S., President
George F. Jackson, D.D.S., Assistant Director

Main Purpose and Emphasis—
To promote the art and science of dentistry; to raise the standards of the dental profession and of dental education; to stimulate favorable relations and good fellowship among dentists and also between dentists and the other health

professions; to nurture the growth and diffusion of dental knowledge; to sponsor and work for the enactment of just dental laws; to promote the elimination of religious and racial discrimination and segregation.

Founded: 1913

For further information contact:
Ellard N. Jackson, D.D.S.

National Funeral Directors and Morticians Association

802 Madison Avenue
Baltimore, Maryland 21202

Charles R. Law, President

Main Purpose and Emphasis—
Organization of black morticians who seek to promote the mortuary profession and to interpret local and national legislation affecting funeral directors and morticians.

National Insurance Association

2400 S. Michigan Avenue
Chicago, Illinois 60616
(312) 842-5125

C. O. Hollis, President
I. H. Burney II, Chairman of the Board
Charles A. Davis, Executive Director
Byron Beverly, Treasurer

Main Purpose and Emphasis—
Economic security and well being of the insuring public and interests of its members.

Founded: 1921

For further information contact:
Charles A. Davis

National Links, Incorporated

118 Nelson Street
Durham, North Carolina 27707
(919) 682-4772

Dr. Helen G. Edmonds, President
Mrs. Veatrice Butler, Treasurer
Mrs. Ruth McCants, Financial Secretary
Main Purpose and Emphasis—
To promote civic, cultural, and educational undertakings in the towns and cities where chapters are located. The specific program vehicles are: services to youth, the fine arts, and national and international trends and services.

Founded: 1946

For further information contact:
Dr. Helen G. Edmonds

The National Medical Association

1717 Massachusetts Avenue
Washington, D.C. 20036

Dr. Wiley Thurber Armstrong, President

Main Purpose and Emphasis—
The bonding together for mutual cooperation and helpfulness the men and women of African descent who are legally and honorably engaged in the practice of cognate professions of medicine, surgery, pharmacy, and denistry.

Founded: 1895

For further information contact:
Dr. Wiley Thurber Armstrong, President

National Newspaper Publishers Association

3636 16th Street
Washington, D.C. 20010
(202) 332-7174

Carlton B. Goodlet, President
Howard B. Woods, Vice President
Mrs. Lenora Carter, Secretary
Howard H. Murphy, Treasurer
Main Purpose and Emphasis—
To promote the interest of the black press by securing unity of action in all matters relative to the profession of journalism and the business of publishing newspapers.

Founded: 1940

For further information contact:
Mr. Sherman Briscoe

National Pharmaceutical Association

Howard University College of Pharmacy
Washington, D.C. 20001
(202) 797-1341

Thomas E. Allen, President
Joan K. Strong, Secretary
Howard L. Burly, Treasurer
Main Purpose and Emphasis—
To promote the practice of professional pharmacy and contribute to the health and welfare of all people.

Founded: 1947

For further information contact:
Chauncey I. Cooper

National Scholarship Service and Fund for Negro Students (NSSFNS)

1776 Broadway
New York, New York 10019
(212) 757-8100
  Southern Regional Office:
  93112 Hunter Street, N.W.
  Atlanta, Georgia 30314
  (404) 577-3990

John Mortimer, Chairman
Charles Duncan, Vice Chairman
D. John Heyman, Vice Chairman
Frank Simpson, Secretary
Thomas R. Horton, Treasurer
Main Purpose and Emphasis—
NSSFNS is a college advisory and referral agency operating specifically for black students at no fee to the student.

Founded: 1947

For further information contact:
Kitty Ellison, Director of Public Information

National Urban League, Inc.

55 East 52nd Street
New York, New York 10022
(212) 751-0300

Vernon E. Jordan, Jr., Director
Donald H. McGannon, President
William J. Trent, Jr., Treasurer
Helen Mervis, Secretary
Main Purpose and Emphasis—
Securing equality of opportunity for blacks and other economically and socially disadvantaged groups through the use of social work. It is a professional, non-profit community service agency.

Founded: 1910

For further information contact:
James D. Williams, Director of Communications

N.A.A.C.P. Legal Defense and Education Fund, Inc.
10 Columbus Circle-Suite 2030
New York, New York 10019
(212) 586-8397
William T. Coleman, Jr., President
Louis H. Pollack, Vice President
Dr. George D. Cannon, Secretary
Mrs. Thornburg Cowles, Treasurer
James M. Nabrit, Ill., Assoc. Counsel
Main Purpose and Emphasis—
To render legal aid to blacks and other minorities who suffer legal injustices due to race; seek and promote educational opportunities denied blacks and other minorities because of race; conduct and publish information on educational opportunities for blacks and other minorities.
Founded: 1939 by N.A.A.C.P.
For further information contact:
Mrs. Sandy O'Gorman

Omega Psi Phi Fraternity, Inc.
2714 Georgia Avenue, N.W.
Washington, D.C. 20001
(202) 667-7158
James S. Avery, President and Chairman of the Board
Harold J. Cook, National Executive Secretary
John H. Moore, Treasurer
Main Purpose and Emphasis—
The support of the fraternal concept of social action, scholarship activity and community uplift undertaken through various programs and projects.
Founded: 1911
For further information contact:
Harold J. Cook

Opportunities Industrialization Center
1225 North Broad Street
Philadelphia, Pennsylvania
(215) 849-3010
    Western Region:
    100 McAllister Street
    San Francisco, California
Rev. Leon H. Sullivan, Founder and Chairman of the Board
Main Purpose and Emphasis—
Educational and training program for developing technical skills of community people regardless of race, creed, sex, or color within the broad field of industry.
For further information contact:
Frederick E. Miller

Phi Beta Sigma Fraternity, Inc.
1006 Carroll Street
Brooklyn, New York 11225
(212) 493-5425
Dr. Parlett L. Moore, National President and Chairman of the Board
William E. Doar, Jr., Executive Secretary
Charles W. Moore, Treasurer
Main Purpose and Emphasis— Founded: 1914
National programs of bigger and better business, education, and social action—"Sigma Against Drugs and Defects."

Source: Questionaire, June, 1973.

For further information contact:
William E. Doar, Jr.

A. Philip Randolph Institute
260 Park Avenue South
New York, New York 10010
(212) 533-8000
Bayard Rustin, Director
A. Philip Randolph, President
Frederick O'Neal, Vice Chairman of the Board
Robert W. Gilmore, Treasurer
Main Purpose and Emphasis—
To further civil rights and to build an alliance between blacks and other groups.
Founded: 1964

Sigma Gamma Rho Sorority, Inc.
1254 25th Street
Indianapolis, Indiana 46205
Dr. Lorraine A. Williams, President
Mrs. Evelyn H. Hood, Chairman of the Board of Directors
Main Purpose and Emphasis—
To provide community service; to develop leadership abilities and individual talents; to emphasize an awareness and appreciation for Afro-American heritage and contributions.
Founded: 1922

Southern Christian Leadership Conference
334 Auburn Avenue, N.E.
Atlanta Georgia 30303
(404) 522-1420
Dr. Ralph D. Abernathy, President
Rev. Bernard Scott Lee, Special Asst. to the President
Main Purpose and Emphasis—
SCLC is a movement organization, working throughout the nation in the struggle for human rights and justice.
Founded: 1957
For further information contact:
President's Office

Unitarian Universalist Caucus, Inc.
18 West Chelten Avenue
Philadelphia, Pennsylvania 19144
(215) 438-7878
Chairman (revolving)
Richard L. Traylor, Administrative Secretary
Benjamin Scott, Treasurer
Main Purpose and Emphasis—
To support and fund those programs within the black Community which lead to empowerment, unification, and self-determination.
Founded: 1967
For further information contact:
Richard L. Traylor, Administrative Secretary
Lew Gothard, Program Director

United Mortgage Bankers of America, Inc.
840 East 87th Street
Chicago, Illinois 60619
(312) 994-7200
Dempsey Travis, President
Main Purpose and Emphasis— Founded: 1962
A mortgage banking association established to unite black persons interested in mortgage banking, to exchange information and establish educational programs for recruiting blacks into banking.

APPENDIX

Spingarn Medalists
"Lift Every Voice and Sing"

SPINGARN MEDALISTS

The Spingarn Medal awards were instituted by the late Joel E. Spingarn, chairman of the board of directors of the National Association for the Advancement of Colored People, in 1914. The awards are in the form of gold medals and are given each year to the Black American, who, according to the board, shall have reached the highest achievement in his field of activity.

The winners of the awards follow:

1915—Ernest E. Just, head of the department of biology, Howard University, for research in biology.

1916—Major Charles Young, U.S. Army, for organizing the Liberian constabulary and developing roads in Liberia.

1917—Harry T. Burleigh, composer and singer, for work in creative music.

1918—William Stanley Braithwaite, poet, literary critic, for distinction in literature.

1919—Archibald H. Grimke, president, American Negro Academy and former U.S. Consul at Santo Domingo, for achievement in politics and literature.

1920—William E. Burghardt DuBois, author, editor of *The Crisis*, for the founding of the Pan-African Congress.

1921—Charles S. Gilpin, actor, for his outstanding role in Eugene O'Neill's play, "Emperor Jones."

1922—Mary B. Talbert, former president of the National Association of Colored Women, for leadership in restoring the home of Frederick Douglass in Washington, D.C. as a shrine.

1923—George Washington Carver, head of the department of chemical research at Tuskegee Institute for his outstanding work in agricultural chemistry.

1924—Roland Hayes, tenor singer, for his international reputation in the music world.

1925—James Weldon Johnson, secretary of the NAACP, former U.S. Consul in Venezuela and Nicaragua, for achievement in literature.

1926—Carter G. Woodson, historian and educator, for collecting and publishing the records of the black in America.

1927—Anthony Overton, businessman, for his achievement in securing the admission of the Victory Life Insurance Company into New York State.

1928—Charles W. Chestnutt, novelist and short story writer, for his pioneer work in the field of literature, depicting the life of blacks in story form.

1929—Mordecai Wyatt Johnson, president of Howard University, for his success in administering the affairs of the University as its first black president.

1930—Henry A. Hunt, principal, Fort Valley High and Industrial School, Georgia, for his 25 years of work in the field of education in the South.

1931—Richard B. Harrison, actor, for his portrayal of the "Lawd" in Marc Connelly's play, "The Green Pastures."

1932—Robert Russa Moton, president of Tuskegee Institute, for his "thoughtful leadership in conservative opinion and action," his stand on education in Haiti, and his support of equal opportunity for the black in public schools.

1933—Max Yergan, a secretary of the YMCA, for his work among the natives of South Africa where he spent ten years, and his work in forstering inter-racial amity between white and black students.

1934—William Taylor Burwell Williams, field agent of the Jeanes and Slater Funds and dean of the college of Tuskegee Institute, for his work in education.

1935—Mary McLeod Bethune, president of Bethune-Cookman College, Florida, for her founding and building up of the school against great difficulties.

1936—John Hope, postumously, president of Atlanta University, for his successes in the field of education.

1937—Walter White, secretary of the NAACP, for his outstanding work in leading the fight for the passage of a federal anti-lynching bill and for civil rights for black Americans.

1938—No award was given.

1939—Marian Anderson, contralto singer, for international fame in the field of music.

1940—Dr. Louis T. Wright, physician and surgeon, for outstanding work in surgery and civic affairs.

1941—Richard Wright, novelist, for writing one of the bestselling novels of the year, *Native Son*.

1942—A. Philip Randolph, president, Brotherhood of Sleeping Car Porters, for initiating the March-on-Washington demonstration.

1943—Judge William H. Hastie, for his distinguished career as a jurist and an uncompromising champion of equal justice, who resigned from his position as civilian aide to the Secretary of War in protest against discriminatory treatment of blacks in the armed forces.

1944—Dr. Charles R. Drew, professor of surgery, Howard University, for his work in blood plasma banks, which served as a model for the system of blood banks used throughout the country and in England.

1945—Paul Robeson, athlete, actor, singer, and scholar, for his achievement in theater and on the concert stage.

1946—Thurgood Marshall, attorney for the NAACP, for his contributions as a lawyer before the Supreme Court.

1947—Percy L. Julian, scientist, educator, and chemist, for his outstanding contribution to research in chemistry.

1948—Channing H. Tobias, minister, educator, civic leader, for his role in defending fundamental American liberties.

1949—Ralph J. Bunche, diplomat, for his distinguished scholarship in Myrdal study, *The American Dilemma.*

1950—Charles H. Houston, lawyer involved with fair employment practices, for his outstanding leadership in the legal profession.

1951—Mabel K. Staupers, nurse, for her contribution of the betterment of blacks in the field of nursing.

1952—Harry T. Moore, Florida coordinator for NAACP, posthumously, for his courageous fight for greater black political participation.

1953—Paul R. Williams, architect, for contribution to design and architecture.

1954—Dr. Theodore K. Lawless, dermatologist, for his outstanding work in research of skin and skin-related diseases.

1955—Carl Murphy, publisher, for his leadership role in employment, education, and recreation.

1956—Jack R. Robinson, athlete, for his leadership role in baseball.

1957—Martin Luther King, Jr., minister, civil rights leader, for his leadership in the Montgomery bus boycott.

1958—Mrs. Daisy Bates, civil rights leader, and publisher, and the Little Rock Nine, a group of students, for their struggle to effect school integration in Arkansas.

1959—Edward Kennedy (Duke) Ellington, musician, bandleader, composer, for his outstanding musical achievement.

1960—Langston Hughes, poet, lyricist, newspaper columnist, for his disinction as "black poet laureate."

1961—Kenneth B. Clark, educator, sociologist and psychologist, for his research in the field of psychology.

1962—Robert C. Weaver, economist, for his development of a doctrine of "open occupancy" in housing.

1963—Medger W. Evers, civil rights leader, posthumously, for his dedication to the "fight for freedom."

1964—Roy Wilkins, civil rights leader, for his contribution to "the advancement of the American people and the national purpose."

1965—Leontyne Price, lyric soprano, for her outstanding accomplishments in music.

1966—John H. Johnson, publisher, businessman, for his preeminence in black publishing.

1967—Edward W. Brooke, attorney, politician, for his distinguished career as a public servant and first black senator in the 20th century.

1968—Sammy Davis, Jr., entertainer, for his "superb and many-faceted talent."

1969—Clarence Mitchell, Jr., NAACP executive, for his meaningful contribution to the cause of civil rights.

1970—Jacob Lawrence, painter, for his eminence as an artist portraying black life and history on the American scene.

1971—Rev. Leon H. Sullivan, clergyman and organization head, for his inspirational guidance of his church to the social and economic needs of the black people.

1972—Gordon Parks, photographer, writer, filmmaker, and composer, for his multi-faceted creative achievements.

1973—Wilson C. Riles, superintendent of public instruction in the State of California for his outstanding contributions in the field of education.

LIFT EVERY VOICE AND SING

Lift ev'ry voice and sing
Till earth and heaven ring,
    Ring with the harmonies of Liberty
Let our rejoicing rise
High as the list'ning skies
Let it resound loud as the rolling seas;
Sing a song full of the faith that the dark past has taught us,
Sing a song full of the hope that the present has brought us;
Facing the rising sun
Of our new day begun,
Let us march on till victory is won.

Stony the road we trod,
Bitter the chast'ning rod
Felt in the days when hope had died;
Yet, with a steady beat,
Have not our weary feet
    Come to the place for which our fathers sighed,
We have come over a way that with tears has been watered,
We have come, treading our path thro' the blood of the slaughtered,
Out from the gloomy past,
Till now we stand at last
Where the white gleam of our bright star is cast.

God of our weary years,
God of our silent tears,
    Thou who hast brought us thus far on the way;
Led us into the light,
Keep us forever in the path, we pray,
Lest our feet stray from the places, our God, where we met Thee,
Lest, our hearts drunk with the wine of the world, we forget Thee,
Shadowed beneath Thy hand,
May we forever stand,
True to our God, true to our Native Land.

Lead us into the light,

James Weldon Johnson

ADDITIONAL INFORMATION

ARMED FORCES

July 16, 1973

Gen. Thomas E. Clifford was appointed the third black Air Force General on active duty. He is Vice-Commander of the 17th Air Force —Europe.

November 12, 1973

Frederic E. Davison, the highest-ranking black in the U.S. Army and the first black general to command a division in the history of the U.S. Army (see p. 204), was appointed commander of all army troops in Washington, D.C.

DEATHS

Staples, Cynthia (1952-Oct. 29, 1973), youngest family member of the world-famous Staple Singers.

Tharpe, Rosetta (1916-Oct. 9, 1973), first black gospel singer to do a Carnegie Hall concert.

Wiley, (Dr.) George A. (1931-Aug. 8, 1973), National Welfare Rights Organization head, an organizer of major reform in the welfare system, accidentally drowned in Chesapeake Bay.

EDUCATION

October 18, 1973

Dr. Thomas Jarrett, president of Atlanta University was appointed chairman of the Georgia Selection committee for the Rhodes Scholarships for 1973.

EMPLOYMENT AND LABOR

October 26, 1973

Ruth Harris, NASA's highest-ranking black female, was fired following her charges of the agency's discriminatory hiring practices of minorities and women.

POLITICS

September 29, 1973

Sen. Edward Brooke, only black member of the U.S. Senate announced his affiliation with the Black Caucus at the 3rd annual fund raising dinner in Washington, D.C. The principal speaker at the dinner, Brooke characterized himself as the Senate arm of the Black Caucus.

November 6, 1973

Clarence Lightner, 52, black businessman and member of the City Council of Raleigh, North Carolina, was elected first black mayor of that city. Raleigh is 70 percent white. Lightner served 6 and one half years as a member of the City Council; 2 years as Mayor Pro Tem. He serves on the Board of Directors of the North Carolina League of Municipalities.

Coleman A. Young, 55, active Detroit union politician and member of the Michigan State Senate since 1964, where he served as minority floor leader, was elected the first black mayor of that city.

November 18, 1973

Alabama Governor George C. Wallace was given a rousing welcome at Tuskegee, Alabama where he addressed the Southern Conference of Black Mayors. The day before, he crowned Terry Points the queen of homecoming at the University of Alabama at Tuscaloosa, the scene of his 1963 "schoolhouse door" confrontation.

RELIGION

November 17, 1973

Rev. Harold Louis Wright was elected Suffragan Bishop in the Episcopal Diocese of New York City, making him the first black to hold that rank in 188 years in that city. The election of Rev. Wright brings the number of black bishops in the Episcopal Church to five.

INDEX

I N D E X

DATE DUE

FEB 25 '78			
FE 5 '80			
AP 29 '81			
FE 12 '83			
MR 31 '83			
AP 14 '83			
GAYLORD			PRINTED IN U.S.A